SHAKESPEARE
for Students
B O O K III

National Advisory Board

SHAKESPEARE

for Students

BOOK III

Critical Interpretations of:

All's Well That Ends Well
Antony and Cleopatra
The Comedy of Errors
Coriolanus
Measure for Measure
Richard II
The Sonnets
The Winter's Tale

Kathy D. Darrow & Ira Mark Milne, editors

GALE GROUP

Detroit
New York
San Francisco
London
Boston
Woodbridge, CT

STAFF

Kathy D. Darrow, Ira Mark Milne, *Editors*

Elizabeth Bellalouna, Elizabeth Bodenmiller, Angela Y. Jones, Michael L. LaBlanc, Polly Rapp, *Contributing Editors*

Dwayne D. Hayes, *Managing Editor*

Victoria B. Cariappa, *Research Team Manager*

Cheryl Warnock, *Research Specialist*

Corrine A. Boland, Tamara Nott, Tracie A. Richardson, *Research Associates*

Timothy Lehnerer, Patricia Love, *Research Assistants*

Maria Franklin, *Permissions Manager*

Margaret A. Chamberlain, Edna Hedblad, *Permissions Specialists*

Erin Bealmear, *Permissions Associate*

Sandra K. Gore, *Permissions Assistant*

Mary Beth Trimper, *Production Director*

Evi Seoud, *Assistant Production Manager*

Stacy Melson, *Production Assistant*

Randy Bassett, *Image Database Supervisor*

Robert Duncan, *Imaging Specialist*

Michael Logusz, *Graphic Artist*

Pamela A. Reed, *Imaging Coordinator*

Dean Dauphinais, *Robyn V. Young, Senior Image Editors*

Kelly A. Quin, *Image Editor*

Cynthia Baldwin, *Product Design Manager*

Pamela A. E. Galbreath, *Senior Art Director*

Gary Leach, *Graphic Artist*

This book is printed on acid-free paper that meets the minimum requirements of American National Standard for Information Sciences—

Permanence Paper for Printed Library Materials, ANSI Z39.48-1984.

Library of Congress Catalog Card Number 86-645085
ISBN 0-7876-4362-9
ISSN 1529-2150

Printed in the United States of America
Published simultaneously in the United Kingdom
by Gale Research International Limited
(An affiliated company of Gale Research)
10 9 8 7 6 5 4 3 2

The Gale Group

Contents

How to Get the Most out of *Shakespeare for Students, Book III*

Purpose of the Book

Shakespeare for Students is intended to present the beginning student of Shakespeare and other interested readers with information on Shakespeare's most popular and frequently taught plays. A further purpose of SFS is to acquaint the reader with the use and function of literary criticism itself. Selected from the immense and often bewildering body of Shakespearean commentary, the essays and excerpts in this series offer insights into Shakespeare's plays from a wide range of commentators representing many different critical -- Readers do not need a wide background in literary studies to use this book. Students can benefit from using SFS as a basis for class discussion and written assignments, new perspectives on the plays, and noteworthy analyses of Shakespeare's artistry.

How an Entry is Organized

Each play entry consists of the following elements: an **introduction** to the play, **essays and excerpts** of critical commentary on the play, and an annotated bibliography of sources for further study.

The **introduction** places each play in relation to Shakespeare's body of work, presents a descriptive list of the play's major characters, summarized the plot, and outlines the principal thematic issues and character studies found in the criticism.

The **criticism** is arranged by important topics and themes that have emerged in published commentary.

Annotations precede and introduce each piece of criticism.

A complete **bibliographic citation** follows each piece of criticism. This enables the interested reader to locate the original book or article from which the reprint is taken.

The **sources for further study** list at the end of each entry includes suggested sources for further study of the play and informs the reader of motion picture, television, and radio adaptations of the play (many available on videocassette).

Other Features

Throughout the book, various **illustrations**—including artist's renditions of certain scenes and performance photographs—add a visual dimension, enhancing the reader's understanding of the critical discussion of each play.

An alphabetical **index to major themes and characters** at the end of each volume identifies the principal topics and characters from each play.

A Note to the Reader

When writing papers, students who quote from <u>Shakespeare for Students</u> may use the following general formats to cite reprinted criticism. The first example pertains to material from periodicals, the second to material reprinted from books.

[1]Ribner, Irving. "Macbeth: the Pattern of Idea and Action," *Shakespeare Quarterly* X, No. 2 (Spring 1959), 147-59; excerpted and reprinted in *Shakespeare for Students,* Vol. 1, ed. Mark W. Scott (Detroit: Gale Research, 1992), pp. 245-51.

[2]Wilson, John Dover. *"The Merchant of Venice* in 1937," in *Shakespeare's Happy Comedies* (Northwestern University Press, 1962); excerpted and reprinted in *Shakespeare for Students,* Vol. 1, ed. Mark W. Scott (Detroit: Gale Research, 1992), pp. 326-34.

Acknowledgments

The editors wish to thank the copyright holders of the excerpted criticism included in this volume and the permissions managers of many book and magazine publishing companies for assisting us in securing reproduction rights. We are also grateful to the staffs of the Detroit Public Library, the Library of Congress, the University of Detroit Mercy Library, Wayne State University Purdy/Kresge Library Complex, and the University of Michigan Libraries for making their resources available to us. Following is a list of the copyright holders who have granted us permission to reproduce material in this volume of SFS. Every effort has been made to trace copyright, but if omissions have been made, please let us know.

COPYRIGHTED EXCERPTS IN *SFS*, VOLUME 3, WERE REPRODUCED FROM THE FOLLOWING PERIODICALS:

American Imago, v. 25, 1968. Copyright 1968 by The Johns Hopkins University Press. Reproduced by permission of The Johns Hopkins University Press.--*Ball State University Forum,* v. XXII, Winter, 1981. Copyright 1981 by Ball State University. Reproduced by permission.--*CLA Journal,* v. XXVI, March, 1983. Copyright, 1983 by The College Language Association. Used by permission of The College Language Association.--*College Literature,* v. 1, Winter, 1974. Copyright (c) 1974 by West Chester University. Reproduced by permission.--*Critical Survey,* v. 5, 1993. (c) C.Q. & S. 1993. Reproduced by permission.-- *The Dalhousie Review,* v. 63, Spring, 1983 for "Taking the Measure of Manliness" by Ronald Huebert. Reproduced by permission of the publisher and the author.--*ELH,* v. 49, Summer, 1982. (c) 1982 by The Johns Hopkins University Press. Reproduced by permission.--*English Literary Renaissance,* v. 10, Autumn, 1980. Copyright (c) 1980 by English Literary Renaissance. Reproduced by permission.--*English Studies,* v. 43, October, 1962; v. 61, February, 1980. (c) 1962, 1980 Swets & Zeitlinger. Both reproduced by permission.--*Essays in Criticism,* v. XVII, October, 1967 for "Who Deposed Richard the Second?" by A. L. French./ v. XXXIX, October, 1989 for "Finding a Part for Parolles" by David Ellis. Both reproduced by permission of the Editors of Essays in Criticism and the author./ v. II, January, 1952 for "Formal Elements in Shakespeare's Sonnets: Sonnets I-VI" by Winifred M. T. Nowottny. Reproduced by permission of the Editors of Essays in Criticism.--*Essays in Literature,* v. XIV, Spring, 1987. Copyright 1987, Western Illinois University. Reproduced by permission.--*Essays in Theatre/ Études Théâtrales,* v. 3, November, 1984 for "Hermione's Trial in 'The Winter's Tale'" by David Bergeron. Reproduced by permission of the author.--*Iowa State Journal of Research,* v. 58, February, 1984. Reproduced by permission.--*JEGP: Journal of English and Germanic Philology,* v. LX, 1961. Copyright 1961 by the Board of Trustees of the University of Illinois. Used with the permission of the University of Illinois Press.--*Literature and History,* 3rd series, v. 5, Spring, 1996. Reproduced by permission of Manchester University Press.--*Modern Language Quarterly,* v. 33, March, 1972. (c) 1972 University of Washington. Reproduced by permission of Duke University Press.--*New Literary History,* v. 9, Spring, 1978. Copyright (c) 1978 by New Literary History. Reproduced by permission of The Johns Hopkins University Press.--*Philological Quarterly,* v. 65, Spring, 1986 for "Imperial Love and the Dark House: All's Well That Ends Well" by Eileen Z. Cohen. Copyright (c) 1986 by The University of Iowa. Reproduced by permission of the author.--*PMLA,* v. 97, October, 1982. Copyright (c) 1982 by the Modern Language Association of America. Reproduced by permission of the Modern Language Association of America.--*The Psychiatric Quarterly,* v. 39, July, 1965 for "Shattered Personality in Shakespeare's Antony" by John W. Draper. Copyright 1965 by The Psychiatric Quarterly/ v. 31, July, 1962 for "Coriolanus and His Mother" by Rufus Putney. Copyright (c) 1962 by The Psychoanalytic Quarterly, Inc. Renewed 1976 by Psychoanalytic Quarterly. Both reproduced by permission of Plenum Publishing Corporation.--*Rocky Mountain Review of Language and Literature,* v. 41, 1987. Reproduced by permission.--*Shakespeare Quarterly,* v. 32, Autumn, 1981; v. 32, Spring, 1981; v. 33, Autumn, 1982; v. 34, Spring, 1983; v. 45, Winter, 1994. (c) The Folger Shakespeare Library, 1981, 1982, 1983, 1994. All reproduced by permission of Shakespeare Quarterly.--*Shakespeare Studies: An Annual Gathering of Research, Criticism, and Reviews,* v. XV, 1982 for "Innocence in The Winter's Tale" by Naomi Conn Liebler. Copyright (c) 1981 The Council for Research in the Renaissance. Reproduced by permission of the author.--*Shakespeare Survey: An Annual Survey of Shakespearian Study and Production,* v. 27, 1974 for "The Antic Disposition of Richard II" by Lois Potter/ v. 34, 1981 for "Characterizing Coriolanus" by Michael Goldman. (c) Cambridge University Press 1974, 1981. Both reproduced by permission of Cambridge University Press and the authors.--*Studies in English Literature, 1500-1900,* v. 23, 1983; v. 31, Spring, 1991. (c) William Marsh Rice University 1983, 1991. Both reproduced by permission of The Johns Hopkins University Press.--*Studies in Philology,* v. LXXX, Summer, 1983. Copyright (c) 1983 The University of North Carolina Press. Used by permission of the publisher.--*Tennessee Studies in Literature,* v. IX, 1964. Copyright (c) 1964 by The University of Tennessee Press. Reproduced by permission of The University of Tennessee Press.--*Texas Studies in Literature and Language,* v. XVIII, Winter, 1977. Copyright (c) 1977 by the University of Texas Press. Reproduced by permission of the publisher.--*Women's Studies,* v. 9, 1981. (c) Gordon and Breach Science Publishers, Inc. 1981. Reproduced by permission.

PHOTOGRAPHS AND ILLUSTRATIONS APPEARING IN *SFS,* VOLUME 3, WERE RECEIVED FROM THE FOLLOWING SOURCES:

Chronology of Shakespeare's Life and Works

1564   William Shakespeare is born in Stratford-upon-Avon. His notice of baptism is entered in the parish register at Holy Trinity Church on April 26. While the actual date of his birth is not known, it is traditionally celebrated on April 23.

1571   Shakespeare probably enters grammar school, seven years being the usual age for admission.

1575   Queen Elizabeth visits Kenilworth Castle, near Stratford. Popular legend holds that the eleven-year-old William Shakespeare witnessed the pageantry attendant on the royal progress and later recreated it in his dramatic works.

1582   Shakespeare marries Anne Hathaway of Shottery. The eighteen-year-old Shakespeare and twenty-six-year-old Hathaway are married on November 27 at Temple Grafton, a village about five miles from Stratford.

1583   Susanna, the first child of William and Anne Shakespeare, is born. Susanna's birth occurs five months after Shakespeare and Hathaway wed. Susanna dies in 1649.

1585(?)   Shakespeare leaves Stratford sometime between 1585 and 1592 and joins a company of actors as a performer and playwright.

1585   Twins Hamnet and Judith Shakespeare are born. Hamnet dies in 1596. Judith dies in 1662.

1589-90   Shakespeare probably writes *Henry VI, Part One*. The dates given for the composition of Shakespeare's plays, though based in scholarship, are somewhat conjectural.

1590-91   Shakespeare probably writes *Henry VI, Part Two* and *Henry VI, Part Three*.

1592   Shakespeare was known in London as an actor and a playwright by this time as evidenced by his being mentioned in Robert Greene's pamphlet *A Groats-worth of Wit*. In this pamphlet (published this year), Greene chides Shakespeare as an "upstart crow" on the theater scene. Greene charges that Shakespeare is an unschooled player and writer who "borrows" material from his well-educated betters for his own productions.

London theaters are closed due to plague.

1592-93 Shakespeare probably writes *Venus and Adonis, Richard III,* and *The Two Gentlemen of Verona.*

1592-94 Shakespeare probably writes *The Comedy of Errors.*

1593 Shakespeare probably begins composing his sonnets. He will eventually write 154 sonnets.

Shakespeare's narrative poem *Venus and Adonis* is published.

1593-94 Shakespeare probably writes *The Rape of Lucrece, Titus Andronicus,* and *The Taming of the Shrew.*

1594 Shakespeare performs with the theater troupe the Lord Chamberlain's Men. The group includes leading actor Richard Burbage and noted comic performer Will Kempe.

1594-95 Shakespeare probably writes *Love's Labour's Lost.*

1594-96 Shakespeare probably writes *King John.*

1595 Shakespeare probably writes *Richard II.* The play is first performed the same year.

Shakespeare probably writes *A Midsummer Night's Dream.* The play is probably composed for performance at a wedding.

Shakespeare probably writes *Romeo and Juliet.*

1596 Henry Carey, Lord Hunsdon, Lord Chamberlain, and patrons of the Lord Chamberlain's Men, dies.

Shakespeare's company comes under the patronage of George Carey, second Lord Hunsdon.

Shakespeare probably writes *The Merry Wives of Windsor.* The play was performed before the Queen during the Christmas revels.

1596-97 Shakespeare probably writes *The Merchant of Venice* and *Henry IV, Part One.*

1597 Shakespeare purchases New Place and the grounds surrounding the spacious Stratford home.

1598 Shakespeare appears in a performance of Ben Johnson's *Every Man in His Humour,* and is listed as a principal actor in the London performance.

Shakespeare probably writes *Henry IV, Part Two.*

1598-99 Shakespeare probably writes *Much Ado About Nothing.*

1599 Shakespeare probably writes *Julius Caesar, Henry V,* and *As You Like It.*

The Lord Chamberlain's Men lease land for the Globe Theatre. Nicholas Brend leases the land to leading shareholders in the Lord Chamberlain's Men, including Shakespeare. Later this year, the Globe Theatre opens.

Earliest known performance of *Julius Caesar.* Thomas Platter, a German traveler, mentions the production at the Globe Theatre on September 21 in his diary.

John Weever publishes the poem "Ad Guglielmum Shakespeare," in which he praises Shakespeare's *Venus and Adonis, The Rape of Lucrece, Romeo and Juliet,* and other works.

1600-01 Shakespeare probably writes *Hamlet.*

1601 Shakespeare probably writes the narrative poem *The Phoenix and Turtle.*

1601-02 Shakespeare probably writes *Twelfth Night; or, What You Will* and *Troilus and Cressida.*

Shakespeare probably writes *All's Well That Ends Well.*

1603 *A Midsummer Night's Dream* is performed before the Queen at Hampton Court.

Queen Elizabeth dies. The new king, James I (James VI of Scotland), arrives in London a month later, and proves to be a generous patron of the theater and of acting troupes.

King James grants a patent, or license, to Shakespeare's acting troupe, the Lord Chamberlain's Men. The patent is required for the troupe to perform. They take the name the King's Men to honor the new king.

The King's Men enact a play, probably *As You Like It*, before King James at Wilton.

Shakespeare appears in a performance of Ben Johnson's *Sejanus.* This is the last recorded occasion of Shakespeare appearing in a theatrical production.

An epidemic of the Black Death kills at least 33,000 in London. This is the worst outbreak of disease in London until the plague recurs in 1608.

1604 Shakespeare probably writes *Measure for Measure.* The play is staged at court before King James.

Shakespeare probably writes *Othello.* The play is first performed at Whitehall on November 1.

1605 Shakespeare probably writes *King Lear.*

The Merchant of Venice is performed at court. The play is performed twice and is commended by the king.

Shakespeare probably writes *Macbeth.* This play's Scottish background was almost certainly intended to celebrate the new king's ancestry.

1606 Shakespeare probably writes *Antony and Cleopatra.*

1607 *Hamlet* and *Richard III* are performed. The plays are acted aboard the English ship *Dragon* at Sierra Leone.

1607-08 Shakespeare probably writes *Coriolanus, Timon of Athens,* and *Pericles.*

1608 The King's Men lease the Blackfriars Theatre. The Blackfriars was the first permanent enclosed theater in London. Shakespeare, Richard Burbage, Cuthbert Burbage, Thomas Evans, John Hemminges, Henry Condell, and William Sly lease the theatre for a period of twenty-one years. Stage directions indicate that Shakespeare wrote *The Tempest* with specific features of the new playhouse in mind.

London theaters are closed due to plague. This is one of the longest periods of theater closure due to plague: the playhouses are shut from spring 1608 throughout 1609.

1609 Shakespeare's sonnets are published. This publication of Shakespeare's sonnets is unauthorized.

1609-10 Shakespeare probably writes *Cymbeline.*

1610 The King's Men perform *Othello* at Oxford College during the summer touring season. An Oxford don records his impressions of the play in Latin, finding the spectacle of Desdemona's death, in particular, deeply moving.

1610-11 Shakespeare probably writes *The Winter's Tale.*

1611 Shakespeare probably writes *The Tempest.*

1612-13 Frederick V, the elector platine and future king of Bohemia, arrives in England to marry Elizabeth, King James's daughter. The King's Men perform several plays, including *Othello* and *Julius Caesar*.

Shakespeare probably writes *Henry VIII*, most likely collaborating with John Fletcher, another highly reputed dramatist, on this history play.

Shakespeare probably writes *Cardenio,* the only play of Shakespeare's that has been completely lost.

1613 Shakespeare probably writes *The Two Noble Kinsmen*. An entry in the Stationer's Register for 1634 indicates that this play was jointly written by Shakespeare and John Fletcher.

The Globe Theatre burns down.

1614 The Globe Theatre reopens on the opposite bank of the Thames.

1616 Shakespeare dies on April 23. His burial is recorded in the register of Stratford's Holy Trinity Church on April 25.

1619 *Hamlet* and several other of Shakespeare's plays are performed at court as part of the Christmas festivities.

1623 Anne Hathaway Shakespeare dies.

Shakespeare's fellow actors, John Hemminges and Henry Condell, compile and publish thirty-six of the dramatist's works. This collection is known as the First Folio.

To the Student: An Introduction to *Shakespeare for Students, Book III*

by Cynthia Burnstein, Plymouth-Salem High School, Canton, Michigan

This may be a scene from your experience: You have been assigned to read a play by William Shakespeare in your literature class. The students look a little skeptical as the books are distributed. That evening at home you do your best to understand as you read the play alone, fiercely studying the footnotes and employing a dictionary, but you still have serious doubts that you are correctly grasping the plot. Although the next day's class discussion helps enormously, you are now positive that you will never get all the characters' names straight. Then one day in class a couple of students disagree about the motivation of the main character and press each other to back up their interpretations with evidence from the text. The rest of the class sits forward in their seats. The debate is intense. For some reason, your teacher is smiling. Hours later you find yourself thinking about the play. Finally, you watch a film version of the play, or, if you are really lucky, you see it performed live. Now everyone in the class has a question as well as an opinion, and the discussions that ensue take a tone of authority that is new and exhilarating.

Someone has said that books are like having the smartest, wittiest, most profound and poetic friends in the world, friends who are there to speak to you anytime you wish. Literary criticism, which is what the book you are holding in your hands is primarily concerned with, is valuable for just the same reason. It is a way of having a thought-provoking conversation about a piece of literature with an intelligent friend. As sometimes happens between friends, you may not always agree with or fully grasp his or her point. Other times, a particular interpretation may seem so preposterous that you stomp off, sputtering. But then there are times you listen and say, "I never thought of it *that* way. . ." or better yet, "Wow!"

The purpose of this book, then, is to enable you to continue those discussions. The heart of *Shakespeare jor Students, Book III* is a collection of essays by Shakespeare scholars which have been carefully selected to be of interest to students at the high school or undergraduate college level. Some essays appear as excerpts for your convenience. For efficiency's sake, you may want to read the general introductions to the essays on certain characters or topics to determine whether that subject is what you're interested in. If it is, you can then turn to the specific introduction for each separate essay. This will help you determine which essays are the most promising. If you are still hungry for more discussion, you will find the Sources for Further Study section to be very helpful. This section lists not only more titles of essays about the plays, but can also aid you in locating other valuable resources such as Shakespeare on video.

Sbakespeare for Students, Book III contains a number of other features that will help you as you **study** Shakespeare's plays. For each of the seven plays and the entry on Shakespeare's sonnets, there is:

1. an **introduction,** which provides basic background information about the play
2. a character list, which briefly describes the role and personality of each character in the play
3. a plot synopsis, which summarizes the action by act
4. an overview of the principal topics, which are the most commonly discussed issues the play explores
5. character studies, which provide a closer look at the play's major characters, and
6. a conclusion, which is a summary of what some of the critics have had to say about the play through the years.

Here is a scene I am imagining about your future: Scholars from the past and students from the present are speaking to each other intensely. They are discussing the plays of William Shakespeare. Ideas are everywhere-in the air, careening off of walls, bouncing through space. As I look around the room at the faces that glow with energy, I see one that looks very familiar. It is yours.

ALL'S WELL THAT ENDS WELL

INTRODUCTION

Scholars generally agree that *All's Well That Ends Well* was written between 1600 and 1605, although some believe that the play is the lost Shakespearean drama titled *Love's Labour Won,* which was written before 1598. Most critics believe that Shakespeare's primary influence in constructing the main plot of the play was William Painter's English translation of Giovanni Boccaccio's story of Giletta of Narbonne in his *Decameron* (1353), titled *The Palace of Pleasures* (1575). Shakespeare added the characters of Parolles (and the subplot in which Parolles is the main character), the Countess of Rousillon, Lavache, Lafeu, and the second ring at the end of the play. Some commentators have remarked that the uneven nature of the play suggests that it was written at two different times in Shakespeare's life.

All's Well That Ends Well has often been called one of Shakespeare's "problem plays" or "problem comedies," a category of his work that usually includes *Measure for Measure* and *Troilus and Cressida,* because these works often seem more similar in tone and theme to the tragedies Shakespeare was writing during the same time period than they do to the romantic comedies he wrote in the 1590s. Most critics acknowledge the folktale elements in the play. Some critics condemn the play outright, considering it a comedic failure. Others take into account how the play would have been received by Elizabethan audiences and find it successful, despite what might seem to be its oddities to twentieth-century readers. Rarely does a critic praise the play without reservation.

Early critics of the play focused on the incongruous plot elements and the thematic concerns of merit and rank, virtue and honor, and male versus female. More recent critics address these issues, but they focus more attention now on topics such as gender and desire. Helena's sexuality and the reversal of gender roles has generated much discussion, especially as they intertwine with other main conflicts in the play, such as social class, the bed-trick, and marriage. The ending of the play (whether the play does end well, as the title suggests it does) has historically been much-debated and continues to be so in recent criticism.

The three main characters—Helena, Bertram, and Parolles—have generated a great deal of literary criticism and comment as well. Some critics brand Helena as conniving and obsessive in her love for Bertram, while others find her wholly virtuous and noble. In general, critics are united in their displeasure with the character of Bertram, though some judge him more harshly than others. Some critics find Bertram thoroughly unrepentant and unredeemable at the end of the play, making the ending implausible. Others are more sympathetic toward him, finding him merely immature at the beginning of the play and in need of life experience in order for him to "grow up." Parolles has generated less controversy in terms of the nature of his character (even Parolles himself recognizes his deficiencies and is not ashamed of them), and some critics find the subplot involving Parolles the only thing that saves the play from utter failure.

PRINCIPAL CHARACTERS

King of France: Represents a dying breed of nobility, one in which honor and virtue are tantamount. He is suffering from a debilitating illness and is nostalgic for the past. He is persuaded by Helena to let her try to cure him, she succeeds, and in return the King makes good on his promise that she may marry any of his noblemen.

Bertram: Young Count of Rousillon, son of the Countess of Rousillon and the recently deceased Count of Rousillon. Finding himself trapped in a marriage to Helena, whom he does not love, he flees to Italy to join the wars. While there, he attempts to seduce the virgin Diana but instead beds his wife Helena, unbeknownst to him. After the wars are over, he returns home and discovers his wife is pregnant with his child and possesses his family ring. *(See* **Bertram** *in the* **CHARACTER STUDIES** *section.)*

Lafeu: An old lord, friend of the Countess. Perceives the true character of Parolles and warns Bertram against him, although he saves Parolles at the end of the play by offering him a position. Lafeu is one of Helena's defenders.

Parolles: Mentor and confidant to Bertram, social climber and would-be gentleman. Accompanies Bertram to the wars in Italy, where his boasting and deceit finally bring about his unmasking, at last enlightening Bertram as to Parolles's true character. *(See* **Parolles** *in the* **CHARACTER STUDIES** *section.)*

Lavache: A clown and servant of the Countess of

Rousillon. Provides some comic relief in the play.

Countess of Rousillon: Mother of Bertram and guardian of Helena. Kind and generous, she exemplifies the best of the noble tradition and encourages Helena's love for Bertram, the Countess's son. She rates honesty and virtue higher than valor in battle or nobility of rank, even when this means that she must side against Bertram.

Helena: Daughter of the famous physician, Gerard de Narbon, from whom she has inherited healing powers. She is the ward of the Countess of Rousillon and is admired by nearly everyone except Bertram. Helena falls in love with Bertram, which sets her on a quest first to become his wife and then to have him accept her as his wife. *(See* **Helena** *in the* **CHARACTER STUDIES** *section.)*

Old Widow of Florence: Helena's landlady in Florence and Diana's mother. She tells Helena that Bertram has been trying to seduce Diana. She accompanies Diana and Helena back to Rousillon at the end of the play when Bertram's lies and deceit are exposed.

Diana: Daughter of the Old Widow of Florence, courted by the Count of Rousillon after he leaves Helena. Diana agrees to help Helena deceive Bertram so that Helena can fulfill the demands of Bertram's letter concerning their marriage.

Two French Lords: Serve with Bertram in the wars in Italy. They succeed in exposing Parolles as a liar and coward.

PLOT SYNOPSIS

Act I: The Countess of Rousillon's son, Bertram, prepares to leave for the court of the King of France. The Countess and her friend Lafeu discuss the King's poor health, and the Countess laments the fact that the father of Helena, her ward, has died, as he was a great physician and would likely have been able to cure the King. After Bertram departs, the Countess learns that Helena is in love with her son and encourages her to follow him. Helena devises a plan to cure the King using a prescription of her father's and the Countess agrees to assist her in traveling to Paris to see the King.

Act II: Helena arrives in Paris and is presented to the King by Lafeu. Helena persuades the King to try her medicine, and wagers her life that the remedy will work within twenty-four hours. In return, she is to be allowed to choose a husband from among all the noblemen of his court. The King recovers from his illness and fulfills his promise to Helena. She selects Bertram for her husband, who promptly refuses to marry Hel-

ena because of her low social rank. The King orders him to marry Helena, which he does. Immediately following the marriage, Bertram sends Helena back to the Countess before the marriage is consummated and he runs away with Parolles to the wars in Italy under the Duke of Florence.

Act III: Helena, bearing a letter to the Countess from Bertram, arrives back in Rousillon. The Countess reads aloud the portion of the letter in which Bertram proclaims that he will not acknowledge Helena as his wife until she wears his ring and bears him a child. Helena decides to leave France and become a wanderer so that her husband will be not be tied down by an unwanted wife. She dresses as a pilgrim and travels to Saint Jacques le Grand, later allowing a letter to reach the Countess with the news that she is dead. In the meantime, Bertram has become a distinguished general in the army and returns to Florence at the same time that Helena enters the city dressed as a pilgrim. She secures lodging from the Widow, from whom she learns that Bertram has been trying to seduce her daughter Diana. Helena sees an opportunity to fulfill the conditions of Bertram's letter to the Countess. Helena convinces Diana's mother to allow her to take Diana's place in her tryst with Bertram, unbeknownst to him, promising a substantial dowry for Diana if she agrees to the deception.

Also in this act, two of the King of France's lords decide to prove to Bertram that Parolles is a liar and a coward. They devise a plan whereby they will kidnap Parolles and make him believe he has been captured by the enemy. They are certain that, in fear, he will betray his fellow men, and the lords will arrange for Bertram to overhear Parolles's interrogation. Parolles brags to the lords and Bertram that he will retrieve a captured regimental drum, a prized emblem. He leaves, and the first lord follows him to prepare to carry out the plan. The second lord accompanies Bertram to visit Diana.

Act IV: The first lord's men pose as foreign mercenaries, and when Parolles meets up with them, he has to figure out how he can return without the promised item. He is captured by these "foreigners" and promises to divulge military secrets in exchange for his life.

Meanwhile, Bertram attempts to convince Diana to sleep with him, and she demands (in accordance with Helena's plan) that he give her his ring, that he not speak to her when they meet later that evening, and that he promise to marry her when his wife is dead. Bertram agrees to these conditions, and Helena's plan succeeds. She takes Diana's place that night and puts on Bertram's finger a ring the King of France had given her. Soon afterward, Bertram receives a letter from his mother with the news that Helena is dead and that she would like him to return home.

Bertram does return home, but not before Parolles's treason is exposed by the two lords. Blindfolded, Parolles is brought in to be interrogated. He reveals military secrets to his "captors" and makes disparaging remarks about both Bertram and the lords. The blindfold is then removed, and Parolles finds that his lies have been exposed. Proven to be a fool by his own admission, he is dismissed.

Back in Rousillon, before Bertram arrives, the Countess, Lafeu, and Lavache lament Helena's death. Lafeu proposes to the Countess that Bertram marry his daughter, and she agrees to the match. They await the arrival of the King, who has been reported as on his way from Marseilles to Rousillon, and Bertram's return from the wars.

Act V: Everyone is now in Rousillon, including Helena, the Widow, and Diana. Parolles is now in rags and begs help from Lafeu, who offers him a position in his household. The King pardons Bertram for his role in Helena's death and is about to give the hand of Lafeu's daughter to Bertram when he notices the ring on Bertram's finger. The King recognizes it as the one he gave to Helena, but Bertram tells him it was a gift given to him in Florence. The King does not believe him, and, thinking Bertram has had a more serious role in Helena's death, orders that he be arrested. As Bertram attempts to explain further how he acquired the ring, without giving the exact nature of his relationship with the giver of the ring, Diana arrives on the scene with her mother. Diana produces Bertram's family ring as further proof of their relationship (indicating as well that Parolles can be called upon to attest to the nature of their relationship) and demands that Bertram keep his promise to marry her. Parolles confirms Diana's assertions. Helena now appears, claiming Bertram as her husband because his conditions have now been fulfilled— she is wearing his ring and bearing his child. She reveals that it was she in Diana's bed. Bertram and Helena are thus reconciled.

PRINCIPAL TOPICS

Gender Issues/Desire

Commentary on the issues of gender and desire necessarily centers on the character of Helena, although some mention of Bertram is warranted as he is directly involved in what some critics call the reversal of gender roles in the play. More recent critics focus less on whether Helena was justified in her actions— bartering with the King to gain Bertram as a husband, following Bertram to Italy, engaging Diana in the bed-trick to fulfill Bertram's otherwise impossible conditions and thus tricking him— and instead confront such issues as Helena as subject rather than object, as desiring rather than desired, as pursuer rather than pursued, and she embodies both activity and her passivity.

Several critics note the similarity between the masculine quest-romance or the theme of the knight-errant and the plot of *All's Well That Ends Well,* only in the latter the initiator of action, the savior, the hero, is a woman. Helena possesses the knowledge and skill to influence events and other characters and thus is able to secure Bertram as a husband. However, she cannot force him to love her, and his repudiation of her necessitates her pursuing an alternate plan of action. Some critics note that Helena's active role, her ability to go out and get what she wants (Bertram), is motivated only by physical, sexual desire. Others excuse her perhaps unorthodox means of fulfilling Bertram's conditions because they were created with the intent of being impossible to fulfill and because she had no other recourse after having been publicly humiliated by Bertram.

Some commentary takes note of the dual nature of Helena's character— she has elements of both the "traditional," passive female character and the more "masculine" active character. Helena, as desiring subject, sets out to gain Bertram for a husband by curing the King. Yet when it comes time for her to select a husband as payment for curing the King, she emphasizes her low social status and how unworthy she is. When Bertram rejects her and humiliates her in front of the entire court, she retracts her choice. When Bertram leaves her to go the wars in Italy, for a time she passively sits at home and then wanders off as a pilgrim so that Bertram can remain unfettered. Even when Bertram sends the letter with the conditions of his acceptance of her as his wife, conditions that he believes she could never fulfill, Helena is not angered but takes pity on him instead, noting how she "stole" rank by marrying him. Finally, once Helena has completed the tasks Bertram required of her and he takes her as his wife, she is satisfied with the role of wife and mother.

Bed-trick/Marriage

The issue of the bed-trick in *All's Well That Ends Well* pervades much of the commentary on the play and necessarily intersects with any discussion of marriage. Commentators tend to focus on whether Helena's use of the bed-trick is justified and lawful and whether it provides a means for a satisfactory ending to the play. Critics who believe Helena's switching places with Diana is justified and warranted argue that as Bertram's wife, Helena had every right to take Diana's place and consummate their marriage, thus saving both Diana and Bertram from dishonor. Helena saves a virgin maiden from what would have been a grave mistake, and she keeps Bertram from committing what would have been an unlawful act of adultery. By thus "saving" Bertram, and, as a result, securing his ring and carrying his child, Helena is an agent in restoring the dying kingdom. Those who find Helena's actions unlawful note that Helena is in actuality encouraging Bertram to engage in an act of adultery (even though Helena knows that what she is doing is technically lawful). They note that although Helena satisfactorily fulfills Bertram's requirements in his letter, this does not necessarily dictate a happy ending, since their sexual union was based on deception.

Social Class

Commentators on the element of social class in *All's Well That Ends Well* generally remark on this issue within the context of the relationship between Helena and Bertram. Helena, we are told early on in the play, possesses "true" nobility and honor, which cannot be obtained by birth. Bertram, though born with wealth and status, has no nobility or honor to speak of. The noble and honorable "older generation," represented by the King, the Countess, and Lafeu, recognize Helena's virtues and Bertram's lack of them. Thus the King orders Bertram to marry Helena when he initially refuses to do so.

A few commentators have noted that wealth and rank actually mean little to either Helena or Bertram. Helena wants Bertram, not his money, and Bertram wants his freedom, not a marriage to a woman everyone considers noble and virtuous, the daughter of an esteemed physician. If Bertram were truly in pursuit of great rank, he would have accepted Helena, whom the King has endowed with wealth to make her Bertram's equal (although a few critics note that this is actually unnecessary, for Helena's fine qualities erase the social gap between her and Bertram). Bertram also would not engage in a friendship with Parolles, a man of notably low birth and, worse, base and vile qualities.

Endings

Commentary regarding the ending of *All's Well That Ends Well* usually centers on whether all really does "end well." Most modern critics conclude that the ending is unsatisfactory and unconvincing, even though it provides the required comedic resolution whereby the hero and heroine are joined at last. Early commentators, however, tended to have less trouble accepting the abrupt ending and argued that Elizabethan audiences would not have found the ending lacking.

Of those critics who find the ending poorly done, one has argued that Shakespeare's interest in the character of Helena waned when she had succeeded in securing Bertram, and he proceeded to a hasty closing scene. Several critics find it difficult to believe that only hap-

piness lies ahead for Helena and Bertram, especially when there is no apparent change of heart or character in Bertram and his acknowledgment of her as his wife takes place in half a line.

CHARACTER STUDIES

Helena

Helena is usually considered the central figure in the play, and all of the topics discussed above (gender issues/desire, bed-trick/marriage, social class, and endings; see these sections above an below for more extended commentary) have direct bearing on her character. As the heroine of *All's Well That Ends Well*, Helena is often described by her admiring commentators as noble, virtuous, honorable, and regenerative, and by her detractors as obsessive, degraded, or narrow-minded. Her single-minded quest to wed Bertram and her actions thereafter inspire and inform these assessments of her. Most critics fall in between strict admiration or abhorrence of her, finding her a complex character.

Those commentators who unequivocally admire her find her guiltless in plotting to wed Bertram and in fulfilling the terms of his letter through the bed-trick. One critic even refers to her as a "genius." Scholars who are decidedly critical of her character find her obsessed by sexual passion and an example of noble womanhood degraded, using her abilities as a "huntress" to realize her plans for a union with Bertram with no thought of their consequences to others (primarily Diana).

Most critics, however, see Helena as a many-sided character. Several critics have noted her regenerative and restorative powers. She is the key to restoring a kingdom whose noble elders are dying with no honorable replacements. Helena heals the king, restoring the kingdom at least for a time, and saves Bertram (and Diana) from making what would have been a mistake of lifelong regret. She is pregnant at the end of the play, symbolically the provider of a restorative new generation of nobility. Other critics have noted her embodiment of both "feminine" passivity and "masculine" activity. She is the desiring subject (the pursuer of Bertram), yet she longs to be the desired object (pursued by Bertram).

Bertram

Commentators are similarly divided regarding the character of Bertram as they are with Helena. Most agree that he is decidedly immature and full of shortcomings, but while some critics find him thoroughly sincere and repentant by the end of the play and thus worthy of the honorable Helena, others find this turnaround in his character implausible and false. (See "Endings" above and below.)

Critics who argue that Bertram has truly repented by the end of the play suggest that it is his immaturity and desire for "life experience" that cause him to reject Helena. Elizabethan audiences, they argue, would find his wanting to go to war and earn his honor on the battlefield entirely normal and, in fact, laudable. His inability to see through Parolles and recognize him for what he is until Parolles's true nature is shown to him is thus attributed to Bertram's inexperience. Those scholars who find him entirely despicable and without merit conclude that his acceptance of Helena in the final scene of the play is one calculated to save his neck, as he finds himself backed into a corner with all the evidence (Helena, Diana, and Parolles all "testify" against him) stacked against him. A few critics abstain from roundly praising or condemning Bertram, offering other ways to interpret his character.

Parolles

Most critics tend to roundly praise Shakespeare for his creation of Parolles, a character not included in Boccaccio's version of the tale, whether they like him or not. He appears in thirteen of the play's twenty-three scenes, and some critics consider the scene of his unmasking (the longest scene in the play) as the structural center of the play (since the critical scene of the bed-trick occurs offstage). Parolles is responsible for most of the laughter (albeit scant) in the play, and although he is generally regarded as a liar, a coward, crude, foppish, and lacking in honor and principle, he is essential to understanding the play. Critics agree that Parolles is aware of his baseness— he possesses self-knowledge, unlike Bertram— and never has any intention of changing, even after he is exposed as a liar and traitor. He is actually grateful for his exposure— he is released from his life of pretending.

CONCLUSION

There is no definitive answer as to whether *All's Well That Ends Well* truly does end well, and the question will likely continue to be debated as new interpretations of the characters of Helena and Bertram appear, as they are integral in any interpretation of the ending. The play ends "properly," as a comedy should, with the hero and heroine reunited, but most modern critics tend to view their future beyond this momentary reunion as uncertain. Central to this debate is whether the gender role reversal experienced by Helena and Bertram is ultimately resolved as Helena assumes her proper "feminine," passive role, and Bertram his "masculine" active one, and whether the desires of the two

main characters will be realized in their union, which has been achieved through the deception of the bed-trick.

OVERVIEW

Anne Barton

SOURCE: "All's Well That Ends Well," in *The Riverside Shakespeare*, edited by J. J. M. Tobin, Herschel Baker, and G. Blakemore Evans, Houghton Mifflin Company, 1997, pp. 499-503.

[*In this brief essay, Barton postulates that the plot of* All's Well That Ends Well *was nothing out of the ordinary in its day— similar folk motifs and story elements could be found in the literature of other languages and in literature of the past. Barton demonstrates how Shakespeare's* All's Well That Ends Well *was strongly influenced by an English translation of Boccaccio's story of Giletta of Narbona in his* Decameron, *noting the similarities and especially the differences between Helena and Giletta, and Bertram and Beltramo. Barton also discusses the play's nostalgia for the past and the notion of honor as they pertain to the play's main characters.*]

The plot of *All's Well That Ends Well* is a tissue of traditional folk motifs. The story of the abandoned wife who performs a seemingly impossible series of tasks in order to regain her husband is at least as old as the myth of Eros and Psyche. It has analogues in many of the literatures of the world. The hero or heroine who achieves great good fortune by knowing how to cure the sickness of the king when everyone else has failed, the bed-trick, the exchange of rings, and the association of virginity with magical power are all story elements with reverberations originating far back in the past. In shaping them into a dramatic plot, Shakespeare was strongly influenced by the story of Giletta of Narbona, told as the ninth story of the third day in Boccaccio's *Decameron*. It is possible that he read the Italian original, but his chief source was probably the English translation, in William Painter's collection *The Palace of Pleasure* (1566-67, 1575).

Giletta of Narbona is the daughter of a wealthy and celebrated physician. She falls in love with Beltramo, the only son of the noble count by whom her father is employed. The count dies and Beltramo goes to Paris as a ward of the French king, who is suffering from an apparently incurable disease. When Giletta's own father also dies, she follows Beltramo to Paris, heals the king with the help of a remedy she has inherited, and then claims Beltramo as her reward. Beltramo himself is horrified by the idea, and even the king is reluctant to agree to a marriage so unequal. He keeps his word to Giletta, however, and Beltramo is forced to yield. Immediately after the wedding, Beltramo flees to Italy and enters the service of the Florentines against the Sienese. Giletta, an unhappy virgin wife, remains for a time in Rossiglione, where she wins the love and respect of all her husband's subjects. Hearing, however, of Beltramo's bitter jest, that he would consent to live with his wife when she possessed herself of a ring from which he was never parted and came to him with their son in her arms, conditions impossible (as he thought) to fulfill, she disguises herself as a pilgrim and journeys to Florence. There, discovering that Beltramo is paying court to the daughter of an impoverished gentlewoman of the city, she persuades the two women to help her. The daughter exacts Beltramo's ring as the price of her surrender, and Giletta then, for some time, secretly supplies her place in Beltramo's bed. When she is sure she is pregnant, she puts an end to these nocturnal meetings, rewards the gentlewoman and her daughter, and sends them out of Florence. Beltramo returns to Rossiglione where, some time later, Giletta suddenly appears to confront him with the ring and twin sons so like their father that Beltramo cannot help but recognize them as his own. All the courtiers and ladies of Rossiglione plead that Giletta should be accepted, and Beltramo, "perceiving her constant mind and good wit, and the two fair young boys," gladly agrees: he sets up a great feast and "from that time forth he loved and honored her as his dear spouse and wife."

As told by Boccaccio and Painter, this story has a simple shape and a clarity which are satisfying and wholly unproblematic. Everyone, even the king, is agreed at the beginning that Giletta, though wealthy, is too low-born to be Countess of Rossiglione. In her first attempt, made as the physician's daughter, she fails to win anything more than the outward appearance of rank. Subsequently, while administering Beltramo's estates, and then in Florence, she demonstrates an innate aristocracy of wit and enterprise so compelling that it annihilates the class barrier. She wins over Beltramo's household and subjects, then Beltramo himself, through sheer intellect and resourcefulness. No one in the story blames Beltramo for his initial repudiation. The king forced him into a demeaning marriage, and it rests entirely with Giletta to prove by her "diligence" that there might be something to recommend such a misalliance after all. It is true that the reader wants Giletta to succeed, but no blame attaches itself to Beltramo for being hard to persuade. Only through sheer intelligence, and by demonstrating that she can give her husband sons who inherit his face as well as his name, can Giletta make herself Beltramo's equal, his wife in fact and not in law only.

As usual, Shakespeare greatly compressed the time-span of Boccaccio's story, reducing it to a more manageably dramatic compass. He also made some significant changes in the situation and characters of the two protagonists. Helena, unlike Giletta, is poor as well as low-born, and she lacks the total self-sufficiency and some of the cunning of her prototype. Bertram, her reluctant husband, stands convicted of faults considerably more damning than Beltramo's aristocratic pride. He is callow and insensitive, a lecher, an oath-breaker, and a liar, who not only misprizes Helena but makes other serious mistakes of judgment as well. Shakespeare also added four major characters for whom there were no equivalents in his source; the old Countess of Rossillion, Lafew, Parolles, and the fool Lavatch. All four have one thing in common: they operate in their different ways, throughout the comedy, to raise Helena in our estimation and to degrade Bertram. The play that results has sacrificed the simplicity and clear emotional emphasis of the folk-tale from which it derives. Indeed it seems positively to stress the incompatibility between characters who are sophisticated and complex and a plot which is neither of these things. Like its successor *Measure for Measure*, *All's Well That Ends Well* often seems to be questioning its own story material and, particularly in the final scene, to look ironically at its own title and at the very nature of comedy.

It is virtually axiomatic in comedy since the time of Menander that when a young man or woman wishes to marry purely for love, overleaping disparities of birth, wealth, and position, the older generation represented by fathers, mothers, uncles, and guardians will strenuously oppose such an attempted infringement of the laws of established society. *All's Well That Ends Well*, with no help whatever from its source, insists upon inverting this pattern. Boccaccio's king, though grateful for his cure, did not relish bestowing Beltramo upon a rich physician's daughter. Shakespeare's King, by contrast, is warmly approving of the match, even though Helena, unlike Giletta, is not only a commoner but poor. The old lord Lafew, the most eminent of the King's courtiers, also adopts the attitude that nothing can be too good for her. Most surprising of all, the old Countess of Rossillion, Bertram's mother, greets the news that her only son has been married to her waiting-gentlewoman with unfeigned delight. In this play it is the old who are generous and flexible in their social attitudes while the young— Bertram, Parolles, and (according to one view) the young lords whose constraint and inner fear at the prospect of being chosen by Helena are mocked by Lafew— tend to be class-conscious snobs.

All's Well That Ends Well is a play filled with nostalgia for the past, concerned to evoke the remembrance of better times. Rossillion, where the action begins and ends, is an almost Chekhovian backwater, elegiac and autumnal, a world preserved in amber. It derives its character chiefly from the old Countess, from the shrewd and "unhappy" fool favored by her late husband, and from memories of the dead: Bertram's father, or that wonder-working physician Gerard de Narbon whose skill, ultimately, was not proof against his own mortality. It is understandable, to some extent, that young Bertram should be impatient to leave this place, even as it is understandable that he should experience an initial psychological shock when told he must marry a girl he has known there all his life as a dependent, a kind of inferior sister. Yet neither Paris nor Florence, the two places to which he tries to escape, functions for him as that heightened, more extraordinary world familiar in so many of Shakespeare's comedies. In neither is he transformed.

In Paris as at Rossillion, the Golden Age lies in the past. The King is old and fretful, a man who has outlived his health, his friends, and his pleasure in living. The court which surrounds him is hard-headed and rational and Lafew summarizes its ordinary way of thinking when he complains, from the standpoint of an older generation, that

> They say miracles are past, and we have our philosophical persons, to make modern and familiar, things supernatural and causeless. Hence is it that we make trifles of terrors, ensconcing ourselves into seeming knowledge, when we should submit ourselves to an unknown fear.
>
> (II.iii.1-6)

Into this sceptical, hard-headed world comes Helena, offering something quite alien to it, in the form of a miraculous cure, and demanding a fairy-tale marriage as her reward. The cure, achieved by way of a secret transmitted to her from the past, is unexpectedly successful. The marriage is not. Bertram refuses to accommodate himself to the archetypal story pattern, to recognize any return of the Golden Age. A struggle develops between the demands of romance, or comic form, and the stubborn resistance set up by a realistic, everyday world in which merit is not always rewarded, or even recognized for what it is. In this world, unicorns do not exist to testify to the mystic power of virginity, and Prince Charming is likely to prefer the fashionably dressed elder sisters to beauty in rags. Love itself is not simply the servant of a fantastic plot, but a matter of complex adjustments within the personality.

From Paris, Bertram flees to Florence, a place to which his thoughts inclined him even before Helena's arrival. Like the other young lords, he is susceptible for all his rationalism to the glamour of war, and the Florentines and the Sienese are, as the King puts it, "by th' ears" (I.ii.1). The phrase suggests a dogfight more than it does an epic combat out of the pages of chivalry, but the noble youth of France are still eager to go and fight on either side of this dispute, purely for the sake of personal honor. Honor is an important word in *All's Well That Ends Well* generally, but it is also one that takes some hard, Falstaffian knocks. The King of France will have nothing to do himself with the Italian imbroglio, for hard-headed political reasons, nor does he care

An engraving of Helena and Bertram The University of Michigan Special Collections Library.

if his courtiers join the Florentines or the Sienese. The First Lord tells the Duke of Florence at the beginning of Act III, after he has heard (but the theatre audience has not) "the fundamental reasons of this war," that "Holy seems the quarrel / Upon your Grace's part; black and fearful / On the opposer," and the words are recognizably a parody of what anyone involved in any war, for whatever reason, always says. Basically, Italy is a kind of gymnasium where the youth of France may exercise idle limbs and minds and indulge the only romanticism in which they still believe. The conflict itself ends in a peace treaty of an unspecified kind, after the usual quantity of bloodshed and embarrassing accidents: "There was excellent command— to charge in with our horse upon our own wings, and to rend our own soldiers!" (III.vi.48-50). Helena comes close to echoing Falstaff's words at Shrewsbury, although the emotion which prompts them is very different, when she laments that "honor but of danger wins a scar, / As oft it loses all" (III.ii.121-22). Moreover, as Lavatch points out (IV.v.94-101), even honor's scar may be ambiguous. The velvet patch on the face of the returning warrior may conceal wounds inflicted by syphilis rather than the sword.

Although Lafew, the King, and the old Countess fondly remember an age in which martial honor was something tangible and significant, it seems to have declined now into a matter of game-playing and mere words. Honor is not the only quality to be trivialized in this way. Shakespeare is concerned throughout to contrast a vanished world of the past in which words were subordinate to facts with a debased, present-day society in which language has become an empty and often a lying substitute for deeds. The King remembers and praises Bertram's father, his dead friend, as a man whose "tongue obey'd his hand" (I.ii.41). This proper subservience of speech to behavior tends now to be reversed or else, even more disturbingly, there is simply no connection at all between what people say and what they think and do. The King, Lafew, and the Countess constantly stress the rightful primacy of facts and intrinsic qualities over misleading verbal descriptions. All these members of an older generation know what the King later tries to tell Bertram, that

> Good alone
> Is good, without a name; vileness is so:
> The property by what it is should go,
> Not by the title.
>
> (II.iii.128-31)

"The mere word's a slave," he goes on, trying to make Bertram see that the fact that Helena is young, wise, and fair matters far more than the superficial social description of her as "a poor physician's daughter." He wastes his breath, however, on a young man whose best friend and greatest influence is called, entirely accurately, Parolles.

Parolles is an embodiment of that discrepancy between words and deed which plays so important a part in the play as a whole. The glorious, swashbuckling past upon which he lives, dines out at ordinaries, and attracts rich young patrons like Bertram is nothing but a verbal construct. He is really a parasite and a coward, sheltering behind a facade of language and fine clothes. He talks constantly of honor but has none, of guns and drums and wounds but in fact is timorous as a mouse. Parolles descends from a venerable line of braggart warriors, talkers and not doers, who originate with Aristophanes and then swagger their way through Menander, Plautus, and Terence into Elizabethan comedy. Shakespeare had already experimented with the *miles gloriosus* type in Don Armado, Ancient Pistol, and (with a difference) Falstaff. Parolles, however, is the most severely criticized of them all. He bears a heavy weight of moral blame for encouraging Bertram to corrupt "a well-derived nature" (III.ii.88), for upholding snobbery and vice. Lafew is entirely accurate when he declares that "there can be no kernel in this light nut; the soul of this man is his clothes" (II.v.43-44). Here, as elsewhere in the comedy, an extravagance of dress concealing emptiness or corruption within is used as a variant on the theme of fine words cloaking innate baseness. It is the way of the world that, for a time, the

deception should pass, that Parolles should convince Bertram with words and clothes, while "virtue's steely bones / Looks bleak i' th' cold wind" (I.i.103-4). Lafew, Helena, Lavatch, and the Countess are never deceived by him, however, and ultimately he is subjected to a public exposure and humiliation that is crushing in a manner more usually associated with the "comical satires" of Ben Jonson than with Shakespeare. At the end, this "manifold linguist" is forced ignominiously into the position that Helena has maintained gracefully all along: "Simply the thing I am / Shall make me live" (IV.iii.333-34).

Helena herself is prized by the older generation not only because they recognize her intrinsic worth, but because she is a living example of the attitudes of the past. Certainly she makes her distrust of disembodied words plain from the start. In her imagination, the court to which Bertram has been despatched is a place of verbal conceits, "Of pretty, fond, adoptious christendoms" (I.i.174) which dress love up in fashionable disguises, losing the substance in the show. Left behind at Rossillion, she worries with some cause about what may happen to Bertram there and laments, characteristically, that "wishing well had not a body in't, / Which might be felt" (I.i.181-82). In Paris, she achieves the man she loves through an action, the healing of the King, and then discovers that her victory is hollow, a matter of words alone. She is only "the shadow of a wife . . . The name, and not the thing" (V.iii.307-8). Defeated and self-accusing, she attires herself as a pilgrim and makes her way towards Saint Jaques le Grand. Unlike Giletta, who intended quite specifically to find her husband and accomplish the task set, Helena seems to arrive in Florence more by accident than purpose. Once there, however, she proceeds to make the same use of Diana and her mother that Giletta had done, and with the same success. It is at this point that problems of a kind nonexistent in Boccaccio's story rear themselves in Shakespeare's play.

Although some scholars have tried to identify *All's Well That Ends Well* with the mysterious *Love's Labor's Won*, a play mentioned by Meres in 1598 among the other early comedies of Shakespeare, its whole quality and verbal character really argue for a date around 1602-3, after *Hamlet* and *Troilus and Cressida* and just before *Measure for Measure*. The verse of *All's Well That Ends Well*— compressed, elliptical, abstract, often tortuous and obscure— is very different from the fluid, concrete, and playful language of the early comedies but, in some respects, like that of *Troilus and Cressida* and *Measure for Measure*. Even more important, the comedy ends by using the folk-motif of the bed-trick to force a clash between those opposing elements of fairy-tale and realism, of romance motivation and psychological probability, which have existed in so uneasy a harmony throughout. In the final scene of *All's Well That Ends Well*, romance wins a kind of pyrrhic victory, even as it does, again through the bed-trick, in a blatantly fictional last act of *Measure for Measure* a year later. Both victories are disturbing, because they raise in a particularly acute and deliberate fashion doubts as to the validity of comedy as an image of truth.

Bertram pays adulterous court to Diana with vows and false promises which she recognizes as such: "therefore your oaths / Are words and poor conditions, but unseal'd" (IV.ii.29-30). Back in France, he will deny that he ever made them. Helena, by contrast, takes words which Bertram originally intended only as a formula, a heightened way of declaring that he would never accept her as his wife, and interprets them literally. She forces language to become fact and confronts Bertram at the end not with words but with two talismanic things: the ring and the child she has conceived. Thematically, in terms of the debate between words and deeds which has been sustained throughout the play, this resolution is entirely right and proper. Psychologically, and in dramatic terms, it is difficult in ways that Shakespeare seems to have wanted to emphasize rather than to conceal.

In Boccaccio's story, Giletta is never believed to be dead. She reappears at Rossiglione after a long absence but not, as Helena seems to do, from the grave. Helena's supposed death is credited by other characters in the play on the best evidence: letters received from her at Saint Jaques le Grand describing her grief and illness and finally, confirmation of her decease from "the rector of the place" (IV.iii.58-59). Critics who do not like Helena often point out that she has apparently not only concocted a monstrous lie in these letters but, apparently, has bribed the rector to forge a death certificate. Helena's "death," however, will not bear investigation in such literal terms, any more than will Hermione's in *The Winter's Tale*, and for much the same reasons. Helena dies so that Diana in the final scene can expound her riddle, "one that's dead is quick" (V.iii.303), and so that the transformation of Helena herself from a condition of nothingness— a "ghost," a "shadow," a wife in name alone— into a condition replete with life and joy may be as striking as possible. There is a powerful emotionalism in the last scene of this play. It derives, however, from an accord which, unlike the wholly consistent ending of *The Winter's Tale*, seems to ignore and leave unresolved the major issues of the play.

By introducing Helena's mock-death and resurrection, Shakespeare debased Bertram in a way for which there was no precedent in his source. In Boccaccio, the poor gentlewoman and her daughter remained in Florence after helping Giletta. Diana and her mother, on the other hand, appear in Rossillion to remind Bertram that he has sworn to marry Diana after his wife's death, and to claim fulfillment now of that promise. Bertram's behavior in these straits is very like that of Angelo when faced with Isabella and Mariana at the end of *Measure for Measure*: he turns and twists, lies and calumniates, providing an entirely realistic demonstration of just how

far he can go in prevarication and meanness. The revelation of Helena, her fairy-tale task accomplished, clears him of a murder charge, but it does not elicit from him anything but the most perfunctory indication of acceptance and apology. Shakespeare might easily have made Bertram eloquent here, but he did not choose to. He was perhaps too conscious of the fact that the second winning of Bertram, although more arduous, nonetheless belongs to exactly the same world of fairy-tale and romance as the first. In terms of psychological truth, there is no more reason for Bertram to accept Helena because of the bed-trick than because of the miraculous healing of the King. This second clash between realism and fable, the old world and the new, is suggested but comes to no issue. Instead, the entire scene gradually fades away and becomes dim, retreating visibly into the realm of romance.

The character of the verse of *All's Well That Ends Well* alters markedly in the last fifty lines of the play. It becomes simple, direct, and archaic: the transparent language of riddle-games and fables. Most of it is further distanced by being cast in the form of rhyming couplets whose inevitability of sound and rhythm help to characterize the larger inevitability of the archetypal happy ending. Diana plays with the situation like a good fairy about to restore a princess who vanished long ago, teasing the baffled King, enjoying mystification for its own sake. By the time Helena appears with her two talismans, the ring and the unborn child, the comedy has loosed its moorings and floated off into a poignant, but attenuated, world of unbelief. Blithely, the King turns to Diana and enjoins her to select any husband she fancies from among the nobles of his court. One might think that the misfortunes of Helena would make him wary of this particular matrimonial method, but no one moves to break the spell. Only in the odd conditional introduced into the King's final couplet, the unexpectedly tentative "seems" and "if," is a shadow of doubt allowed to return:

> All yet seems well, and if it end so meet,
> The bitter past, more welcome is the sweet.

The title of the comedy itself, referred to now by the King as it was previously, but more confidently, by Helena herself (IV.iv.33-36, V.i.25), was proverbial. Like the proverbs continually employed in a perverse and contradictory fashion by the bitter fool Lavatch— traditional bits of lore existing uneasily in a world grown too complex for such simplifications— it serves as a gentle reminder that fairy-tales, ultimately, are not true.

GENDER ISSUES/DESIRES

Alice Shalvi, Katharine Eisaman Maus, Susan Snyder, **David McCandless**, and Lisa Jardine all comment on the reversal of gender roles in the play. Alice Shalvi notes that the play can be considered a variation on the theme of the knight-errant, who cures the king, restores the kingdom, and wins the beautiful girl, only in this play the knight is a woman and a man is wooed instead. However, Shalvi notes, Helena occasionally lapses into a more sub-servient, "feminine" role in the midst of her acts of cour-age and assertiveness. Snyder notes this dichotomy in Helena's character— how she occasionally suppresses the active, desiring side of herself and reveals the passive side— and finds Bertram's running off to war an assertion of his "proper" role as active male. Maus finds some similarities in the play with the masculine quest-romance pattern, but in this case the quest is for a man and the quester is female.

McCandless argues that Helena, while being the desiring subject, at the same time wants to be the desired object. She wants to consummate her love for Bertram, but takes a passive stance and says she wants to be "mated." She appropriates the usually male gaze in adoring Bertram, but does so without any return affection from him. Fur-ther, McCandless notes, Bertram's situation is problematic in that he is attempting to enter the traditional male "space" through military and sexual prowess, yet he finds himself submitting to a marriage with a woman he does not want. Jardine notes how Helena's knowledge of medicine, typi-cally a "male" skill, is unusual, but such skill is "reassur-ingly temporary" for the sexually active, desiring Helena, who becomes the virtuous, ideal wife at the end of the play when Bertram finally accepts her as his wife.

Although, as Julia Briggs notes, Helena's desire drives the story forward (Robert Ornstein comments that Helena's physical desire for Bertram causes Helena to accept "any humiliation for the sake of love"), Snyder also offers the theory that God's desire might come into play. For ex-ample, Helena miraculously cures the king, her trip to Saint Jacques gets rerouted to Florence, where Bertram is, and the money she promises to Diana for her role in the bed-trick helps create a dowry for Diana that will ensure that she can marry well. Barbara Hodgdon and McCandless comment on the desire-laden language Helena uses, and Quentin Skinner argues that it is the absence of male desire that forces Helena to use the bed-trick to solve a problem that began with gender asymmetry (Helena's selecting of Bertram as a husband).

David McCandless

SOURCE: "Helena's Bed-trick: Gender and Performance in *All's Well That Ends Well*," in *Shakespeare Quarterly*, Vol. 45, No. 4, Winter, 1995, pp. 449-68.

[*In the following essay, McCandless examines Helena as a desiring subject with the masculine gaze and the "masculine privilege of choice" in selecting Bertram for her husband— she is the "chooser" instead of the chosen. McCandless rejects the characterization of* Helena as a "two-faced manipulative manhunter," and instead emphasizes the fact that Helena's "feminine" responses to certain events (Bertram's rejection of her, for example) are a result of her internalization of a "culturally imposed image of Woman." McCandless also explores Bertram as "Other" and as a desired object and then incorporates these evaluations into a discussion of the bed-trick.*]

The starting point for this essay is Susan Snyder's recent characterization of *All's Well* as a "deconstructed fairy tale": lurking beneath the folkloric narrative of the poor physician's daughter who deploys magic and cunning in order to overcome a dashing count's disdainful resistance are the unrepresentable specters of female sexual desire and male sexual dread. Indeed, the play invests the fairy-tale motifs that W. W. Lawrence believes undergird *All's Well*— "The Healing of the King" and "The Fulfillment of the Tasks"— with potent erotic subtexts. In adapting "The Healing of the King," Shakespeare, like his model Boccaccio, departs from tradition in making the King's healer a woman. Lawrence barely mentions this innova-tion, but it seems to me highly significant, especially since Shakespeare, unlike Boccaccio, makes Helena's gender— more particularly her sexual ardor and allure— indispens-able to the cure.

Integral to the narrative of "The Fulfillment of the Tasks" is the bed-trick, an explicitly sexual event in which a disprized wife wins back her husband by making love to him incognito, taking the place of another woman, in some versions the wife herself in disguise, whom he has wooed. *All's Well* deconstructs this folkloric device by wedding it to genuine sexual perturbation. The bed-trick is not simply the consummation of a marriage, in which Helena cleverly satisfies Bertram's seemingly impossible conditions, but an act of prostitution, in which Helena services Bertram's lust and submits to humiliating anony-mous "use," and a type of rape, in which Helena coerces Bertram into having sex with her against his will.

Yet, as many critics have noted, the play seems to sup-press its own erotic subdrama. Certainly Shakespeare ide-alizes and mystifies the sexual arousal that empowers Helena's cure of the King. He lends Helena magical and hieratic powers, giving her the capacity to effect a super-natural cure. He similarly desexualizes her erotic agency in the bed-trick, allowing Diana to serve as Helena's sexual-ized double. Diana suffers Bertram's degrading slander in the final scene, thus allowing Helena to reenter the play as a saintly resurrected figure whose visible pregnancy sanctifies her sexuality and who elicits an instantaneous reformation from Bertram. The bed-trick becomes a tran-scendent event, vastly removed from bodies groping in the dark, from the kind of event imaged as "defil[ing] the pitchy night" (4.4.24).

In performance the bed-trick is further removed from sexual experience precisely because it is undramatized, not part of the play's visceral theatrical life, a plot mechanism scarcely capable of disconcerting audiences as it has critics. I want to examine how staging the bed-trick can assist in dramatizing the "deconstructed fairy tale" that lies at the heart of *All's Well*, thus bringing to the surface the erotic subdrama that the play represses, and, in so doing, extend the play's provocative interrogation of gender roles.

I

Helena has been a puzzle and provocation to critics because she occupies the masculine position of desiring subject, even as she apologizes fulsomely for her unfeminine forwardness and works desperately to situate herself within the feminine position of desired object. Bertram, too, poses problems because he occupies the feminine space of the Other, even as he struggles to define himself as a man by becoming a military and sexual conqueror. He is the desired object, the end of the hero's— or in this case heroine's— gendered journey of self-fulfillment.
Helena's opening soliloquy conveys the plight of a woman trapped between active ("masculine") and passive ("feminine") modes of desire. She clearly expresses her desire to consummate a sexual love, calling herself a "hind" who wishes to be "mated by the lion" (1.1.85-92). At the same time, she adopts a "feminine" posture: she cannot mate but can only be "mated." Furthermore, as a hind desiring a lion, she cannot mate at all. Helena thus naturalizes the culturally established distinctions of gender and class that make Bertram a forbidden object. In addition, Helena appropriates the masculine privilege of the gaze, submitting her "curled darling" to rapturous objectification, only to affirm a "feminine" helplessness, lamenting the impossibility of eliciting her beloved's look. Her gaze becomes masochistic: it is pleasurable torment— "pretty, though a plague"— to survey his beauteous, unattainable form every hour" (ll. 92-93).

Once galvanized by Parolles's bracing antivirginity jape, however, Helena resolves to "feed" her desirous gaze, to make the object of worship an object of consumption:

> What power is it which mounts my love so
>   high,
> That makes me see, and cannot feed mine
>   eye?
> The mightiest space in fortune nature
>   brings
> To join like likes, and kiss like native
>   things.
>
> (ll. 220-23)

That Helena imagines a sexual feeding here seems plausible, given the imagery of "joining" and "kiss-

ing," not to mention the suggestive phraseology of "mount[ing] my love." The "space" separating her and Bertram she portrays as a product not of nature, which favors their "join[ing]," but of "fortune," which seems here to mean "standing in life" and thus to represent culture.

The language Helena employs is characteristically elliptical, stemming from her guarded, coded, sexually charged dialogue with Parolles. The obscurity of her discourse perhaps reflects the unspeakability of her desire. Her exchange with Parolles begins as a theatrical turn, with Helena playing straight man for the swaggering poseur. As straight man Helena channels her unspeakable desire into the discourse of male bawdry, seeking a kind of release through the sublimated pleasures of naughty talk, even if her lines serve principally as cues for Parolles's ribaldry.
At a certain point, however, Helena seems to take seriously Parolles's aspersion of virginity— or, more specifically, his vision of the naturalness and regenerativeness of sexuality; she steps outside the scene's theatrical frame and trades the role of straight man for that of surprised pupil: "how might one do, sir," she asks, "to lose it [her virginity] to her own liking?" (ll. 150-51). She disregards his censure of her wish to choose rather than be chosen ("Off with't while 'tis vendible; answer the time of request" [ll. 154-55]) and answers his challenge— "Will you anything with it?"— decisively if obscurely:

> Not my virginity yet:
> There shall your master have a thousand
>   loves,
> A mother, and a mistress, and a friend,
> A phoenix, captain, and an enemy,
> A guide, a goddess, and a sovereign,
> A counsellor, a traitress, and a dear;
> His humble ambition, proud humility;
> His jarring concord, and his discord dulcet;
> His faith, his sweet disaster; with a world
> Of pretty, fond, adoptious christendoms
> That blinking Cupid gossips.
>
> (ll. 163-75)

Modern editors have been inclined to assume a missing line between Helena's terse defense of virginity and her expansive list of lovers' endearments. "There" is usually taken to mean "at the court," and the speech is explained as Helena's anxious contemplation of courtly rivals whose enchantments may well stir Bertram's desire. The speech may perhaps be better understood, however, as a coded disclosure of Helena's own erotic stirrings. That she speaks cryptically and elliptically may simply reflect the difficulty of articulating female desire. If one gives up the idea of a missing line, the sense of Helena's response is captured in G. Wilson Knight's paraphrase: "'I shall not part with my virginity to anyone yet, because therein your master has an infinite love.'" Knight, however, backs away from the aggressively sexual connotations of this decoding and asserts, "I do not think that, at this early stage in her story, it can mean 'In giving your master my virginity I shall give him a thousand loves', since she has no good reason at this stage to expect such an event." Helena's lacking any reason to expect "such an event" is surely beside the point; she clearly desires to "mate" with Bertram, and, stoked by Parolles's libidinous exhortations, she presumably builds on the tantalizing possibility of losing her virginity to her own liking, that is, to Bertram. The speech thus becomes the link between this heretofore unthinkable idea and the conception of her bold plan for winning him. Perhaps "at the court" has seemed the best candidate for Helena's imagined "there" because virginity— or rather the unpenetrated female territory it predicates— has been perceived, within a phallocentric register of meaning, not as a "there" but as a "nowhere," a "nothing-to-be-seen," in Luce Irigaray's striking phrase.

Thus the key to the speech may lie not in a missing line but in a missing language— one that embodies a woman's "thereness" and enables the articulation of a distinct female desire. From a Lacanian perspective, female desire is literally unspeakable, inconceivable within a phallocentric linguistic system that makes woman a signifier of man, reducing her difference to opposition, reconfiguring her desire as the desire for his desire. The unspeakability of Helena's passion perhaps compels her to express it evasively and mystically. She thus characterizes her "virginity" as a kind of philosopher's stone, a "tinct and multiplying medicine" (5.3.102) that blesses Bertram with a supernally expansive love and allows her, for his sake, to assume all the guises of the courtier's beloved, to become a kind of shape-shifting superwoman. Helena, however, continues to believe that she must be "mated": she cannot unleash this mystical female power— cannot become Bertram's idealized courtly lover— until Bertram "has" her maidenhead, discovers her wonders "there." Once more the play seems to dramatize the contradiction of female subjectivity: Helena expresses an active (masculine) longing to consummate her passion in terms that betray a "feminine" urge to empower and sustain Bertram, to fit herself to his fantasies— or at least to his received images of femininity. Helena's (feminine) hope that Bertram might find her desirable after "having" her sexually eventually impels her (masculine) orchestration of the bed-trick.

Helena continues to feminize her desire throughout her campaign to win Bertram, offering compensatory performances of exemplary chastity to atone for the unchaste boldness of her plan. Forced by the Countess to confess her love for Bertram, Helena disclaims the desire to win him that we know she harbors, reviving the self-abasing hopelessness of her first soliloquy, once more portraying Bertram as an unattainable heavenly

body that she worships (1.3.204-7). In conversation with the King she betrays a similar compulsion to appear normatively chaste, instantly withdrawing her suit when he taints her proffered cure with imputations of prostitution, "Humbly entreating" a "modest" thought— requesting the King's belief in her chastity— as she prepares to take her leave (2.1.127-28). Her willingness to suffer a prostitute's punishment if her cure fails seems designed to dispel any lingering suspicions of unchastity, to distance her holy magic from wanton witchery (ll. 170-73).

In 2.3, the scene in which Helena is to choose a husband, Helena's status as desiring subject becomes public. The King, parading a contingent of eligible wards, formally confers on her the power of the gaze: "Fair maid, send forth thine eye. . . . Peruse them well" (ll. 52, 61); he also lends her the masculine privilege of choice: "Thou hast power to choose, and they none to forsake" (l. 56). Her public position as dominant woman is so unprecedented that Lafew mistakenly believes the young lords have rejected her rather than vice versa: as a woman she cannot be the chooser but only the object of choice. Helena's singular ascent requires another compensatory performance of "femininity." Though she has, in fact, "command[ed]" the King to grant the fulfillment of her desire (2.1.194), she protests her chastity to the assembled suitors and blushingly retires before the King ratifies her authority and compels her to continue. In Susan Snyder's words, "when [Helena] finally addresses Bertram, she does her best to deny her role as aggressive, desiring subject and to recast herself properly as object." ("I dare not say I take you, but I give / Me and my service, ever whilst I live, / Into your guiding power" [2.3.102-4]). Bertram, however, discerns and resists this implicit emasculation, dismissing her protestations of vassalage and demanding the return of masculine looking power: "I shall beseech your Highness, / In such a business, give me leave to use / The help of mine own eyes" (ll. 106-8).

To call attention to Helena's "performative" femininity is not to accuse her of hypocrisy or willful deception. To point out that her self-effacements are self-serving is not to rehearse the tired, limited characterization of her as a two-faced, manipulative manhunter. It seems to me more helpful to understand Helena's hyperfemininity as a kind of Lacanian misrecognition that she persistently reenacts. Helena performs femininity so convincingly because she has successfully internalized a culturally imposed image of Woman. When Helena seems to affect femininity for the sake of covering her unfeminine, predatory tracks, she may not be crudely dissembling but rather, like a good method actress who loses herself in the role, truthfully simulating, thereby authenticating the role demanded of her. "The action of gender," Judith Butler suggests, "requires a performance that is repeated. This repetition is at once a reenactment and reexperiencing of a set of meanings already socially established." Butler is not alone in contending that subjectivity entails a subjection to cultural norms, predicating a process by which socialization is mistaken for individuation. Helena challenges a restrictive standard of feminine chastity, but, while doing so, she must answer to the chaste self-image shaped by patriarchal society. As John Berger puts it, a woman is "almost continually accompanied by her own image of herself." One reason, no doubt, that critics have so often discerned two Helenas— saintly maiden and cunning vixen— is that Helena so vividly embodies the contradiction that Teresa de Lauretis identifies as essential to female subjectivity: self and cultural mirror, woman and Woman.

In performance one way to call attention to that contradiction would be to assign two actors to the role of Helena: a woman and a man in drag who would step in whenever Helena "acts feminine." These two Helenas would then take turns, sometimes within the same scene (Helena's interview with the King in 2.1, for instance) or even the same speech (for example, the first soliloquy), while at other times a single Helena would dominate (the female for Helena's combative exchanges with Parolles, the crossdressed male for her doleful evasions of the Countess). In a modern-dress production of *All's Well*, costuming could accentuate this duality, with the crossdressed male (as cultural mirror) far more unerringly "feminine" in appearance than the female, whose attire could be freer and more individualized, even androgynous. The prettified, feminine (male) Helena then becomes kin to the lavishly festooned Parolles, a culturally constructed gender image compelling imitation. Such a choice dramatizes the process of misrecognition, participating in a postmodern fragmenting of subjectivity. A less ostentatious approach might, however, prove even more theatrically potent. Since Helena's essential provocation lies in her capacity for forcing masculine and feminine modes of desire to collide, the director might prefer to capture her doubleness not through double casting but through the concentration of its contradictory effects in a single actor, making her as self-possessed and unself-consciously sensual in her "masculine" moments as she is self-effacing and studiously chaste in her "feminine" ones.

Helena's "masculine" desire is no less subject to cultural construction than her "feminine" chastity. As Foucault has argued, sexual desire is derived as much from culture as from nature. Accordingly, Helena's desire is directed toward the culturally approved goal of marriage, an institution that, at least according to the "Protestant doctrine" of Shakespeare's time, confirms a woman in femininity by delivering her to permanent chastity— and subservience. In 2.5, her only scene with Bertram prior to the play's final moments, Helena seems to savor "feminine" subservience as the reward for her "masculine" boldness. She embraces wifely subjugation with a fervor that mortifies Bertram. "Come, come, no

more of that," he protests when she pronounces herself his "most obedient servant" (ll. 72-73). From a Freudian perspective, she accepts— even flaunts— a neutered passivity for the sake of eliciting male love. When Bertram annuls the marriage she has taken such pains to effect, she takes the desexualization one step further, embracing a monastical chastity by reconfiguring herself as a penitent whore getting herself to a nunnery, disavowing her desire and receding into iconicity, inspiring the Countess to compare her, I would argue, to the Virgin Mary (3.4.25-29).

The sexual renunciation ends when Helena locates another mirror of misrecognition: Diana, the young Italian woman who defines femininity for Helena by virtue of her attractiveness to Bertram. As Catherine MacKinnon asserts, "socially, femaleness means femininity, which means attractiveness to men, which means sexual attractiveness, which means sexual availability on male terms." In order to win Bertram, Helena the devoted would-be wife must refashion herself as sexual object. Her goal shifts from the fulfillment of desire to the achievement of desirability. Her desire is no longer simply the desire to wed but the desire to be desired. She thus identifies with, and acts through, the woman whom Bertram covets. In a Lacanian context, Helena says not "I wish to become a woman" but rather "I wish to be like her whom I recognize as a woman." Her deputization of Diana offers an extreme instance of Helena's need to conceal her desire. Only when she secures the services of a surrogate who agrees to embody that desire and risk the "tax of impudence" that Helena herself carefully dodges does Helena manage to secure Bertram.

II

Perhaps the best demonstration of the distance between Helena and Bertram comes when Parolles, urging Bertram to "steal away" to the wars in order to avoid the emasculation of marriage, characterizes Helena's "virginity" in terms radically different from her own:

> He wears his honor in a box unseen,
> That hugs his kicky-wicky here at home,
> Spending his manly marrow in her arms,
> Which should sustain the bound and high curvet
> Of Mars's fiery steed.

(2.3.279-83)

The site of Helena's miraculously generative sexual love becomes a "box unseen," a lack that threatens to contain and consume Bertram's manly essence, an effeminizing, contemptible "kicky-wicky" that would preclude his purchase of masculine honor. The opportunity to mount Mars's fiery steed in manly combat rescues Bertram from an emasculating stint as

Act I, scene iii. Helena and the Countess of Rossillion. By Francis Wheatley.

"forehorse to a smock" (2.1.30)— that is, a woman's beast of burden— a humiliating reversal of the roles of man/woman, rider/horse, master/slave that had become homologous in Shakespeare's England.

Parolles embodies a fiction of masculine grandeur that Bertram attempts to actualize, a mirror of misrecognition in which Bertram insists on seeing himself, a narcissistic reflection of an idealized self that confers an illusion of wholeness. In particular, the supposedly battle-tested, sumptuously plumed Parolles offers Bertram an image of military glamor and promotes participation in the Italian war as a rite of passage into manhood. Thus he praises Bertram's determination to fight as evidence of potency: "Why, these balls bound, there's noise in it. 'Tis hard!" (2.3.297).

Yet the Countess and the King both define manhood for Bertram as the imitation of his father, the true "perfect courtier" (1.1.61-62 and 207; 1.2.19-22 and 36-48). Parolles becomes a rival father-figure whom Bertram's own father, speaking through the King, indirectly disparages with his criticism of meretricious fashionmongers who beget nothing but clothes ("whose judgments are/Mere fathers of their garments" [1.2.61-62]). Later, Lafew implies that Parolles was begot *as* clothes, that he was not born but made— by a tailor (2.5.16-19). These images impute to Parolles and his

like both sterility and unmanliness and— through the emphasis on costume— imposture and barren theatricality. Parolles functions as a symptom of the tailoredness of gender, performing a masculinity that seems as much a caricature of the cultural norm as does the performed femininity of Helena. In following this counterfeit soldier-courtier, Bertram appears to be doing what Helena has already done: internalizing and authenticating a culturally inscribed myth of gender, saying not "I'm a man" but rather "I'm like him whom I recognize to be a man."

Despite exhorting Bertram to emulate his father, the King denies him the opportunity to do so by forbidding his soldiership, rendering him unable to prove himself the son of a worthy Frenchman (2.1.11-12). Rather than being allowed to "woo" and "wed" honor (to use the King's language to his departing soldiers), Bertram becomes an object of a woman's wooing and wedding. The King, at Helena's behest, subjects Bertram to the very calamity he urged his soldiers to avoid— bondage to female sexuality:

> Those girls of Italy, take heed of them.
> They say our French lack language to deny
> If they demand. Beware of being captives
> Before you serve.
>
> (2.1.19-22)

Bertram is captive before he serves, in thrall not to one of those "girls of Italy" whom the King stigmatizes but to the girl from Rossillion, the girl next door. While he is primed to resent any imposed responsibility that keeps him from going a-soldiering, marriage to Helena is the very worst of fates, taking him even further back into boyhood by returning him to the maternal domination he presumably escaped by ending his constrictive "marriage" to the Countess. ("In delivering my son from me, I bury a second husband" [1.1.1-2], she asserts as the play begins.)

Bertram protests that he "cannot" love Helena. She cannot be an object of his sexual desire, cannot be a "real girl," in Havelock Ellis's terms. This fact is striking, since she so easily achieves that status with the other men in the play, sexually provoking Parolles, Lafew, and the King alike. Lafew considers Helena so much a "real girl" that he would like to consign those seemingly standoffish suitors to the fate of castration (2.3.86-88). From Lafew's perspective, anyone who would not consider Helena a "real girl" is not a real man.

From a psychoanalytic perspective, Bertram cannot love Helena because she is a forbidden object. The Count's responsibility for "breeding" Helena (2.3.114) reinforces her status as a sister-figure. The Countess's sponsorship of Helena's matrimonial campaign makes Helena a kind of mother-surrogate as well. The Countess sees in the passionate Helena an image of her younger self (1.3.128-31). By colluding in Helena's plot, the Countess aims to help Helena secure her son as husband and thus to revive by proxy the relationship she herself has lost. Helena may also be considered a maternal figure by virtue of her status as partner to Bertram's surrogate father, the King. In a reversal of a Freudian plot, in which the son sacrifices the mother as the price of masculine autonomy, the King blocks Bertram's achievement of manhood by forcing on him the woman whom Bertram sees as the object of the King's own sexual interest: "follows it, my lord," Bertram protests, "to bring me down / Must answer for your raising?" (2.3.112-13).

In addition, the first of the identities Helena hopes to derive from marriage to Bertram is the one conspicuously removed from the realm of courtly love that engenders them: "mother" ("There shall your master have a thousand loves, / A mother, a mistress, and a friend"). On one level, of course, Helena simply invokes a biological fact: she may become pregnant as a consequence of intercourse with Bertram. On another, she explicitly identifies with the very maternal image that repels Bertram and, by raising the specter of castration, drives him to the wars. In one sense, then, Bertram's military campaign represents a retreat: like Parolles, he runs away for advantage when fear— in this case fear of Helena's sexuality— proposes the safety (1.1.201-3). Lavatch later characterizes Bertram's campaign in precisely the same terms: Bertram will not be "killed"— his manhood will not be lost— because he runs away from Helena: "The danger is in standing to't; that's the loss of men, though it be the getting of children" (3.2.37-42, esp. 41-42).

III

In appointing Helena her impossible tasks, Bertram sets up a fairy-tale framework only for the sake of demolishing it. While the tasks themselves present a fairy-tale challenge— do these things and "then call me husband"— his decoding of them precludes a fairy-tale solution: "but in such a 'then' I write a 'never'" (3.2.57-60). Helena, however, insists on the fairy-tale framework, reading his metaphor of rejection as a scenario of acceptance and orchestrating the bed-trick, a folkloric convention, in order to secure him as husband. Helena, however, describes the actual event in anything but fantastical terms:

> . . . O, strange
> men,
> That can such sweet use make of what they
> hate,
> When saucy trusting of the cozen'd
> thoughts
> Defiles the pitchy night; so lust doth play
> With what it loathes for that which is away.
> (4.4.21-25)

Helena here configures Bertram as male Other, as personification of difference, as a creature from whom she is estranged. In addition to the folkloric narratives that Lawrence identifies, *All's Well* also discloses affinities with other "old tales" that more directly address this problem of difference. I am thinking, in particular, of "The Loathly Lady," which deals with male fear of female sexuality, and "Beauty and the Beast," which dramatizes the female's struggle with male sexuality. In each tale, the protagonist's love— acceptance of the loathliness or beastliness (that is, sexual difference) of their opposite— converts ugliness into beauty. "Beauty and the Beast" depicts a young woman's transference of love from father to Beast, the sexually menacing male Other. According to Bruno Bettelheim, "only after Beauty decides to leave her father's house to be reunited with the Beast— that is, after she has resolved her oedipal ties to her father— does sex, which before was repugnant, become beautiful." At the start of the play, Helena has already made this transference. "What was . . . [my father] like?" Helena muses. "I have forgot him. My imagination/Carries no favor in't but Bertram's" (1.1.81-83). Moreover, far from fearing male sexuality, Helena embraces Bertram's beastliness as the play begins, portraying him as a lion with whom she wishes to mate. Indeed, by portraying herself as a hind, Helena both affirms her own sexuality and evokes a fundamental difference in "kind" that divides them. The bed-trick forces Helena to confront the un-kind Beast within Bertram and to undertake his taming. bertram, by contrast, recoils from Helena's loathliness, her menacing sexual difference ("what [he] hate[s]"), seeing in her an image of the old crone or castrating mother.

Helena's story— and by implication *All's Well* itself— also contains intriguing parallels to what Jane Yolen identifies as the common features of the traditional "Cinderella" tale: "an ill-treated though rich and worthy heroine in Cinders-disguise; the aid of a magical gift or advice by a beast/bird/mother; the dance/festival/church scene where the heroine comes in radiant display; recognition through a token." Helena fits this profile to a significant degree: a worthy yet socially undesirable young woman who finds herself, thanks to a magical gift, miraculously conveyed to and radiantly displayed at a royal public ceremony (*"Mort du vinaigre!"* exclaims Parolles, apparently stunned by her glamorous appearance, "is not this Helen?" [2.3.44]). Indeed, it is surely no accident that both Tyrone Guthrie and Trevor Nunn, directors of two celebrated modern productions of *All's Well*, staged this scene as a lavish ball and costumed the poor physician's daughter in an elegant gown, effectively portraying her as Cinderella-turned-Princess. And, while she fails to enchant the Prince at first, she does become the object of his desire at another clandestine encounter, which she later proves publicly by means of a token that seals their marriage. The token in this instance is a ring, as it is in several versions of the traditional tale.

In a psychoanalytic context, the Cinderella tale presents a heroine coming to terms with her own sexuality. Her cinders-guise externalizes her dread of the dirtiness of her own sexual drives. Her awareness of the underlying dirtiness impels her to exit the dance prematurely three times, unable to yield to her sexual longing for the reciprocally desirous prince. (The midnight deadline that prompts her departure is not part of the traditional tale but rather the invention of Charles Perrault, whose seventeenth-century version provides the source for the well-known Disney movie.) In the climatic scene she affirms her sexuality by meeting the Prince in her cinders-guise and, in an overtly phallic gesture, triumphantly inserting her foot into the slipper. In *All's Well*, by contrast, the Prince runs from the heroine, whose active sexuality begrimes her chaste feminine persona. She wins the Prince by catching him and taking him into the cinders with her.

Traces of "Beauty and the Beast" and "Cinderella" may be found in the twentieth-century romance novel, a kind of fairy tale that also sports parallels to *All's Well*. The "new heroine" of those novels

> is no longer split between two archetypal female characters: the plain-naive-domestic-selfless-passive-chaste heroine and the beautiful-sophisticated-worldly-selfish-assertive-sexually active Other Woman. Instead, the New Heroine is both good and sexual.

Helena holds in unresolved tension the roles of good girl and sexual adventuress that the new heroine has apparently successfully assimilated. A motif of "taming the beast" figures prominently in these modern tales: a seemingly beastly—that is, hard and unyielding—man loses his heart to the worthy heroine and becomes a sensitive lover. As though ruled by this fantasy, Helena endeavors, through the power of her love, to transform the beastly Bertram into the Prince Charming of her fantasy. Helena's own narrative of self-fulfillment—and a narrative pressure of the play itself—resembles a romance novel in which the cruel hero's callous disregard of the desirous heroine masks a depth of adoration he ultimately avows. The romance novel—and possibly *All's Well*—predicates a retributive fantasy of benign dominance-and-submission. As Tania Modleski puts it:

> A great deal of our satisfaction in reading these novels comes, I am convinced, from the elements of a revenge fantasy, from our conviction that the woman is bringing the man to his knees and that all the while he is being so hateful, he is internally groveling, groveling, groveling.

It may be said that Helena seeks to transform Bertram's fantasy by enabling it, replacing the pornographic narrative of violating an idealized virgin with the romance-novel plot of eliciting a redemptive kindness from an unyielding male.

Indeed, if the bed-trick were dramatized, it would literally dislocate the narrative of Bertram's debauchery: "I will tell you a thing," the Second Lord confides to his brother, "but you shall let it dwell darkly with you" (4.3.10-11). This report of female victimization would then give way to the dramatization of female desire. "The place and time of feminine desire," says de Lauretis, are "nowhere" and "now," which are representable only from an "elsewhere of vision" and within "a different narrative temporality." In virtually all performances of *All's Well*, the place of the bed-trick is precisely "nowhere" or "elsewhere." Its narrative temporality is other than the play's—parallel but not precisely coincident with that of the French captains' gossip. Indeed, the literal death they ascribe to Helena (4.3.47-59) becomes the only means of registering the metaphorical death she experiences during the bed-trick, the only means of invoking her sexual pleasure. Through the bed-trick Helena deflects Bertram's teleological quest for manhood into the timeless "now" of her desire, replacing the march of "masculine" time with the occupation of "feminine" space. The site of the bed-trick emblematizes female difference, expresses the "unseen wonders" of the woman's own enclosed space and thus is not only unrepresented but unrepresentable within a phallocentric framework that associates that site with a "nothing-to-be-seen." In that sense Helena's reported death—signifying her ultimate absence—becomes symbolic of the "lack" culturally inscribed on her body. How then does one stage an event whose place is unseen and unseeable ("nowhere") and whose subject—female sexuality—is unrepresentable? Can one theatrically embody or evoke the "there" to which Helena cryptically alludes?

As Jeanie Forte notes, contemporary feminist performance artists have instinctively searched for the theatrical equivalent of the distinctive female language imagined by Luce Irigaray and Hélène Cixous, a mode of representation that would liberate women from a phallocentric signifying economy. These artists aim to "perform the body" in much the same spirit that Cixous exhorts feminists to "write the body," achieving what Forte calls "erotic agency," either by dramatizing a bodily "pleasurability" or enacting a resistance to bodily oppression, in the first instance asserting subjectivity, in the second defying objectification. As an example of the former, Forte cites the work of Marianne Goldberg, whose dance texts celebrate "her subjective pleasure in her own body and its possibilities for movement"; for instance, in "Hudson Rover" (1987) "she rolls on the floor, slowly wrapping and then unwrapping her (clothed) body in blue fabric, seemingly oblivious to anything other than the feel of hard and soft surfaces." As an example of the latter, Forte points to Karen Finley, whose penchant for smearing her body with food, candy, and ashes evokes "both self-abuse and self-pleasuring" and confounds an objectifying gaze that equates looking with consuming.

While the tactics and techniques of feminist performance art offer fascinating possibilities for deconstructive stagings of Shakespeare, they are not especially well suited to Helena's bed-trick, which unfolds within the very realm of desire that these artists reject and thus precludes exclusive focus on a pansexual, performed female body. By maintaining rather than abandoning the phallocentric system of representation, however, one may stress the singularity of Helena's ascent to the position of desiring subject in order to accentuate her contradictory status within the play's narrative and, in doing so, underline the contradictory position of women within patriarchy's limited signifying economy. This effect seems in accord with de Lauretis's notion that feminism must

> redirect identification toward the two positionalities of desire that define the female's oedipal situation; and if the alternation between them is protracted enough . . . the viewer may come to suspect that such duplicity, such contradiction cannot and perhaps even need not be resolved. . . . The most exciting work in cinema and in feminism today is not anti-narrative and anti-oedipal. It is narrative and oedipal with a vengeance for it seeks to stress the duplicity of that scenario and the specific contradiction of the female subject in it.

In staging the bed-trick, one might actually make explicit Helena's dominance, a dominance that the text only hints at. Helena effectively inscribes a condition of lack onto Bertram's body. The restrictions that she imposes— darkness and silence— deprive him of the two patriarchal capacities that define him as (masculine) subject: the gaze and speech. She positions Bertram so that he lacks the language to deny what she commands. The language of bodies now prevails, and Helena, like Diana in 4.2, secures control of Bertram partly through manipulation of the lust she elicits.

An often overlooked marker of Helena's control is her curious postcoital detention of Bertram. "When you have conquer'd my yet maiden bed," Diana says on Helena's behalf, "Remain there but an hour, nor speak to me" (4.2.57-58). What, one must ask, is the point of this detention? What takes place during that hour? Does the dilation of the trick create a space for the operations of a less propulsively phallic, consumptive sexuality? Does it summon the freer, more resourceful and expansive processes of female desire? Certainly it seems that Bertram is being set up for something— but that something is never explicitly revealed. This ellipsis perhaps offers yet another register of unrepresentable female desire which a staged bed-trick could represent.

The staged bed-trick could, for example, begin with Diana's placing a blindfold on Bertram and yielding her place to Helena. The blindfold would not only provide a realistic explanation for Bertram's inability to distinguish her from Diana but also visually link him with his double, Parolles, who is likewise blindfolded and tricked in the very next scene. The blindfold would both deprive Bertram of the gaze and signify his blindness to the threat of castration that originally drove him away from Helena.

The principal strategy in staging the bed-trick would be to present a kind of suspended foreplay, Helena deflecting Bertram's propulsive, lust-driven energies into more dilatory, sensual rhythms, with Helena positioned as gazing subject and Bertram as gazed-upon object. Helena's masculine gaze, initially frustrated by her feminine powerlessness, would here operate freely and powerfully.

The play provides other possibilities for reinforcing such a gaze. Just as Diana, her mother, and Mariana all positioned themselves as spectators to the triumphal procession of soldiers in 3.5, with Diana sending forth her eye over the glistening combatants, one could turn Bertram's attempted seduction of Diana into a spectacle by positioning Helena, the Widow, and Mariana as spectators, concretizing the female frame of reference that contains the scene. Within this play-within-a-play, Diana acts the part of sexual tease, defamiliarizing the role of "the-girl-who-says-no-but-means-yes" by exposing it as performative, presenting herself instead as "the-girl-who-says-yes-but-means-no." The concealed female audience also marks Bertram's incipient masculinity as performative: "My mother told me just how he would woo," exclaims Diana, "As if she sate in 's heart. She says all men / Have the like oaths" (4.2.69-71). Like Helena in her hyperfeminine mode, Bertram enacts a culturally inscribed script without knowing it, affirming his kinship with "all men" by venting unctuous oaths and fulsome endearments in order to arrange a one-night stand. Since the play's audience not only watches Bertram's performance but also watches women watching it, the scene parallels that of Parolles's capture, in which concealed pranksters also watch their victim walk into a trap.

Even if the voyeurism and fetishism of this gaze reverse rather than overturn masculine-feminine polarities, the powerful position of gazing subject afforded Helena by the staged bed-trick would not only empower her desire but perhaps also momentarily free her from a process of representation that enables her consumption as sexual object. There are at least two scenes, in particular, that position Helena, the desiring subject, as desired object: her early skirmish with Parolles and her interview with the King. Performance could make clear the extent to which Parolles not only jests with Helena but also cheekily flirts with her, launching, behind the cover of licentious badinage, an assault on her own virginity. In the latter scene, performance could also emphasize the erotic arousal enveloped by magical incantation and miraculous faith healing. Some productions have, in fact, attempted to bring the scene's erotic undercurrents to the surface. In John Barton's 1967 production Helena was "a tease of a girl," titillating the King by sitting on his bed and fluffing up his pillows, and in Elijah Moshinsky's BBC version she was a very proper young woman whose provocation of the King—culminating in a lingering, erotic kiss—seemed utterly unintentional. Barry Kyle, in his 1989 RSC production, apparently attempted both to accent the scene's eroticism and to preserve its mysticism: his Helena "kick[ed] off her shoes to perform a circling, energetic, sexually assertive, slightly fey dance," exuding an aura of "white witchery."

In both scenes Helena claims the only kind of female power available in a phallocentric economy by activating and frustrating male desire, "blow[ing] up" both Parolles and the King, making them swell with desire (1.1.118-26, esp. 118-19). Helena's active sexuality is discernible throughout the play but, beyond the space of the bed-trick, is constricted not only by internalized notions of normative femininity but also by the external operations of an objectifying gaze.

As befits Helena's status as desiring subject, the ultimate goal of her bed-trick seems to be that of "taming difference." In the immediate aftermath of the trick, she recoils from male lust and affirms Bertram's strangeness ("O, strange men, / That can such sweet use make of what they hate"). In the play's final scene, however, she emphasizes his kindness, a word that connotes kindredness as well as gentleness or generosity: "O my good lord, when I was like this maid, / I found you wondrous kind" (5.3.309-10). Helena needs to claim Bertram as one of her kind, needs to create him in her own image—the same image she has sought doggedly to impose despite all his obstinate assertions of alienness. In the final scene, Helena tries to confirm Bertram in kind-ness by "crush[ing]" him "with a plot."

Helena avenges her earlier humiliation at Bertram's hands by orchestrating his utter ruin: he is censured, disgraced, and threatened with execution. She enacts a version of the romance-novel retributive fantasy, bringing Bertram to his knees—a posture he has, in fact, assumed in more than one production—abusing him in order to please him, positioning him to savor the bondage he initially abhorred. It appears that Helena schemes to rescue Bertram from the calamity she has herself created in order to elicit feelings of indebtedness conducive to capitulation. She depends on his feeling like the rescued sinner of the medieval morality plays to ensure her reception as savior and wife. Her strategy, which recalls Duke Vincentio's determination to make Isabella "heavenly comforts of despair" (*Measure for Measure*, 4.3.110), appears to work: in penitently promising

love and accepting her as wife, Bertram accepts transformation from beast to Prince Charming, at long last consenting to actualize her fantasy (5.3.315-16 and 308).

The success of Helena's plot does not, however, guarantee a successful marriage with Bertram, for it validates neither the sincerity of his conversion nor the seemliness of their union. Critics have lamented the paltriness of Bertram's conversion speech, but the problems with the play's final scene run much deeper. Since Bertram has twice before falsely professed admiration for Helena (2.3.167-73, 5.3.52-58), no words of his, no matter how eloquently or torrentially penitential, could ever suffice to confirm his sincerity. Nor, for that matter, could his actions. Even the most extravagant self-abasing gestures may simply be symptoms of feverish gratitude rather than of genuine conversion. Helena may be able to work up feelings in Bertram that simulate and even enable love but do not actually generate it. And of course Bertram may simply cunningly simulate a penitential swoon. In either case, Helena manipulates Bertram into affecting a kind-ness that he may quickly discontinue upon assuming his male prerogatives in marriage. Perhaps Bertram functions here as a male Kate—a seemingly tamed lout who performs the submissive role his dominant spouse has taught him, but who may, after all, only be performing. Since, in the play's second half, Helena's aim seems to shift from wedding Bertram to eliciting his desire, it may be that, for the second time in the play, her goal eludes her even as she appears to achieve it.

Moreover, Helena's success seems mitigated by not only the dubiousness of Bertram's conversion but also the dubiousness of her own objectives, her willingness to deliver herself unequivocally to normative femininity. Her dominance of Bertram ultimately enables her to submit to him in marriage. Ever in thrall to Bertram, she wins him only by putting him temporarily in her thrall so that she may put herself permanently in his. Although Helena's narrative dominates Bertram's and allows her to construct him as the Other out of whom she creates herself, at the same time her fundamental, culturally prescribed desire is to become the object of his desire, the Other out of whom he creates himself:

> The end of the little girl's journey, if successful, will bring her to the place where the boy will find her, like Sleeping Beauty, awaiting him, Prince Charming. For the boy has been promised, by the social contract he has entered into at his Oedipal phase, that he will find woman waiting at the end of his journey.

Indeed, while Bertram may or may not gratify Helena's fantasy, Helena seems prepared to embrace Bertram's. His "impossible conditions" essentially ask for assurance that Helena can conceive a child without sexually contaminating herself or surrendering maternal purity.

Bertram's apparent acceptance of Helena's success in meeting his conditions subjects them to a final reinterpretation: "I'll be your husband if you can have sex with me without shaming or emasculating me." Through the bed-trick Helena allows Bertram to fulfill his forbidden desire for her involuntarily, assimilating for his sake the seemingly unassimilable roles of wife and lover, mother and "real girl."

The finale of All's Well could be said to dramatize the amelioration of castration anxiety. Helena steps forward as the eroticized mother-figure of Bertram's dreams. Her resurrection at the play's end represents the final mystification of her own sexuality, an unthreatening eroticizing of the saintly guise she assumed for the pilgrimage. She replaces her own degraded double, rescuing and retiring the wayward desiring self that the beleaguered Diana personifies. Her pregnancy— that is, her status as mother— purifies the sexuality it affirms. It also ratifies Bertram's manhood, signaling his conquest of her, his success in "blowing her up." Moreover, given the belief circulating in Shakespeare's day that a woman could conceive only if she experienced an orgasm, Helena's pregnancy serves as the proof not only of his potency but also of her pleasure, of her satisfaction by him. The bed-trick thus becomes Bertram's initiation into manhood, with Helena serving as his initiator. This fact may simply mean that, in this world of absent fathers, no viable model of manhood exists for Bertram. His father's masculinity, as Bertram confronts it in 1.2, may be no more authentic than that of Parolles, for it is also derived from a performance, from the King's dramatic, deathbed celebration of the Count. The King constructs an exceptional figure, a hero/courtier of fabulous proportions who seems partly a product of the King's intense nostalgia for a lost youth. Bertram is thus left with a choice between two equally fantastical images of manhood: the inaccessibly legendary and the insidiously fashionable. In marrying Helena, Bertram finds his manhood affirmed through a reassuring maternal presence and gets what he may have wanted all along: a wife/lover/mother who allows him to become a man by remaining a boy.

The play's refusal to dissipate its tensions or substantiate its tentative resolutions leaves its drama of sexual difference suspended, arrested in an unresolved but provocative, even poignant tension. Helena's attempt to tame difference meets with uncertain success, and Bertram seems to reaffirm difference in the play's final moments, confronting a female strangeness that mystifies rather than repels. When he declares, "if she, my liege, can make me know this clearly" (5.3.315), the "this" he wishes to know surely encompasses a good deal more than the details of Helena's fulfillment of his conditions: it must include the mystery of female otherness. The body Bertram used and discarded returns in the person of a would-be wife, a once and future lover, to claim him like an avenging spirit. Helena brings him, however obscurely, new knowledge of female sexuality, offering tantalizing allusions to their time in bed and visible proof of their mutual gratification. Bertram may wish to know more, to see the unseen wonders to which he was previously blind. Bertram's "this" becomes homologous with Helena's "there," suggesting that the performance of sex has possibly solved his problem with sexuality. Yet this solution and the knowledge it assumes are simply intriguing possibilities. As the play ends, Helena and her body remain unknown and perhaps unknowable to Bertram— objects of fascination, further knowledge, perhaps even desire.

Helena remains a mystery to be solved by the reader and spectator— and director and actor— as well. So too does Bertram. Both characters aim to ground themselves in genders that the play suggests are groundless— or at least unstable, fluid, performative. Neither manages to forge a stable identity or secure a clear destiny. Modern performance could underline Helena's and Bertram's status as subjects-in-process, active agents inextricably engaged with subjugating myths of gender. And a staged bed-trick, by fetishizing the male body and empowering a female gaze, could underline the instability of the genders that Helena and Bertram seek to stabilize, taking the play's provocative dramatization of difference to startling and invigorating lengths.

BED-TRICK/MARRIAGE

Alice Shalvi and J. A. Bryant argue that since Helena is legally Bertram's wife, her use of the bed-trick is lawful. Bertram set before her impossible demands, and the bed-trick proves a useful and legal way of meeting those demands. **Eileen Z. Cohen** notes that the disguise of the bed-trick solidifies the marriage between Helena and Bertram, and Helena saves Bertram in the process. Shalvi adds Diana to the people whom Helena saves— she saves Diana's virtue as a virgin as well as Bertram from the shame of adultery.

Michael Shapiro, Maurice Charney, Julia Briggs, and **Janet Adelman** take a different approach toward the bed-trick, doubting its efficacy. Shapiro argues that although the bed-trick surely allows Helena to meet Bertram's demands, she is not convinced herself that her actions are entirely legal. Charney finds the substitution of one woman for another, as if all women are alike, unsavory. (According to Kenneth Muir, Helena is well aware of this.) Briggs argues that the "happy" ending is based on deception precipitated by the bed-trick, leaving the reader uncertain as to whether it is truly a "happy" one, although Helena's use of the bed-trick effects marriage by consummating it and allows Bertram to be redeemed. Adelman argues that, at its core, a bed-trick is a trick after all, and clearly Bertram is desirous of Diana not Helena. Thus Adelman concludes that the ending of the play is tenuous at best.

Margaret Loftus Ranald and Katharine Eisaman Maus provide commentary on the institution of marriage in Elizabethan England. Ranald notes that although the marriage between Helena and Bertram is consummated by the bed-trick, this ensures the marriage's solubility. Had the trick not occurred, Bertram would have had recourse to annul the marriage, since it had not been consummated. If it had been Diana and not Helena in that bed, under Elizabethan law Bertram would have been bound to Diana, not Helena, because of his promises to Diana and his sexual union with her. Maus comments on the institutions of wardship and the bawdy courts and their influence in regulating marriage. The King's ability to dictate to Bertram that he must marry Helena was entirely in keeping with Elizabethan practice, according to Ranald and Hazelton Spencer. **Mary Free** argues that what makes the marriage between Bertram and Helena unique among Shakespearean comedies is Bertram's wholehearted rejection of Helena, and the trickery involved in mending the "broken nuptial" creates an unsatisfying resolution to the play.

J. Dennis Huston finds an example of a verbal bed-trick early on in the play, in Helena's discussion of virginity with Parolles. Instead of dismissing Parolles, who is roundly despised by everyone except Bertram, Helena instead engages in banter and double-entendres with Parolles. In this way she can get "closer" to Bertram and enter his world. Later, instead of merely talking about virginity, she will use her own virginity in her own bed-trick.

Eileen Z. Cohen

SOURCE: "'Virtue Is Bold': The Bed-trick and Characterization in *All's Well That Ends Well* and *Measure for Measure*," in *Philological Quarterly*, Vol. 65, No. 2, Spring, 1986, pp. 171-86.

[*In the following excerpt, Cohen examines how Helena and Isabella in, respectively,* All's Well That Ends Well *and* Measure for Measure, *use the bed-trick as a disguise, and in doing so, these characters "reverse traditional female behavior, invent stereotypes, and turn apparent lechery into the service of marriage."*]

Western literature abounds in characters who have arranged bed-tricks— from Lot's daughters to Iseult, and by the seventeenth century the bed-substitution was a commonplace convention of English drama. Yet it is Shakespeare's use of the device in *All's Well That Ends Well* and *Measure for Measure* that disturbs us, doubt-less because of the women who perpetrate it, Helena, a virgin-bride, and Isabella, a would-be nun. We seem unwilling to accept that Shakespeare deliberately intends to disrupt our sensibilities. Scholars have told us that we must accommodate ourselves to conventions or fairy tale traditions that are outmoded, or they call these heroines sluts, or saints and tell us to forget about the bed substitutions.

Shakespeare, however, does none of these. Instead, he requires us to believe that virtuous maidens can initiate and participate in the bed-trick. He insists that it saves lives and nurtures marriage, that it leads the duped men out of ignorance and toward understanding, and that the women who orchestrate it end with a clearer image of themselves. Thus, we have a simple theatrical device that effects complex response in the characters and in us, the audience. The convention "deconventionalizes" and makes the world of each play and the characters therein more real. Paradoxically, a device associated with lust abets love and marriage; it utilizes illusion and deception to bring perception and understanding. In so doing, it strips away stock responses to the women who design the deception. Shakespeare apparently does not associate virtue in women with blindness or passivity— or even predictability. He will not allow the audience to generalize about female virtue. Given popular sixteenth-century attitudes towards women, Helena and Isabella must have been as disturbing to their original audience as they have been to subsequent ones, and the bed-trick, because of its ultimate affirmation of the complexity of virtue, just as jarring.

In the sixteenth and seventeenth centuries, the controversy concerning women was part of the literary and social experience of the middle and upper classes of society. It surfaced in the 1540s and again at the beginning of James I's reign, with reprintings of various pieces throughout these decades. What emerges from the debate, whether the writer was a critic or a defender of women, is that he or she rarely considers women except in the most general ways. Devil or angel, she is a stereotype. A flurry of popular pamphlets was precipitated by the publication of *Schole House of Women*, which went through four editions between 1541-1570, and is alluded to in several other pamphlets. Here, women are "loud and sour" (Aiii), gossipy (Aiv), adulterous (Bii), frail, crooked, crabbed, lewd (Cii), and weak and feeble in body (Cii). A female's function, because she is made of man's rib, "in every nede / Shulde be helpe to the man, in word and dede" (Biii). There is a remedy for each of man's afflictions, except gout and marriage ([London: John Kyng, 1560], Biii).

Responses to this attack abound. Readers were assured that woman was not created out of dog bones, but from man— the crown of creation. There have been many good women, a fact to which the Bible, the classics, and their very own Queen attest. Anthony Gibson, in addition to cataloguing great women, ebulliently lists their virtues: Women are beautiful and their voices are soft (20). Since they are by nature inclined to sadness, they are wiser than men (21), and more charitable (30). Philip Stubbes, too, had a good word to say for virtuous women— or rather, a virtuous woman, in a eulogy to his dead wife, *A Christal Glasse for Christian Women* (London: R. Ihones, 1592). He describes her as a perfect pattern for virtue: modest, courteous, gentle, and zealous for truth. (A2). "If she saw her husband merry, then she was merry: if he were sad, she was sad: if he were heavy or passionate, she would endeavor to make him glad: if he were angry, she would quickly please him so wifely she demeaned herselfe towards him" (A3). In both Stubbes and Gibson, the burden of virtue is as heavy as that of vice.

Very few of the writers in this controversy approach women as other than very good or very bad. Perhaps the most aggressive of those who do blur the stereotypic perceptions of both men and women is the author of *Jane Anger Her Protection for Women* (London: Richard Jones, 1589). "She" is less rigid than most of her contemporaries with regard to male and female characteristics. "Jane Anger" lowers the barriers between the sexes in that she does not say that women are necessarily more or less virtuous than men. Rather, she equalizes the sexes by suggesting that women pay men in just coin. "Deceitful men with guile must be repaid . . ." (B2). Woman's greatest fault is that she is too credulous (B2). Though "Jane Anger" still deals in stereotypes, she perceives the weaknesses and strengths of men and women in different ways from most of her contemporaries. She condemns men for failing to see women in terms of these strengths, "We being wel formed, are by them fouly deformed" (B3).
Even though many of these pieces are satiric and were probably written because there was a ready market for them, rather than out of sincere beliefs, their popularity indicates an interest in the nature of women and an insistence that their virtues were different from those of men. From these pages and more, there emerges an ideal woman in whom the virtues were chastity, patience, piety, humility, obedience, constancy, temperance, kindness, and fortitude— all passive characteristics. Even her supporters urged her to suppress assertiveness. The ideal male virtues were justice, courtesy, liberality, and courage. For a man the ideal was self-expansion and realization of self; for a woman, self-abnegation and passivity. For a man chastity was unimportant; for a woman it was everything. Her honor and reputation were defined in terms of it. The educator Vives frankly states, "As for a woman [she] hath no charge to se to, but her honestie and chastitie."

Helena and Isabella offer a marked contrast to many of the prevailing presumptions about women that the popular literature manifests, and in some ways a sharp difference from the portrayals of Rosalind and Viola, both in earlier plays. If art does hold a mirror up to nature, then Shakespeare's drama reflects, refracts, and re-focuses the ideas of his time. In *Twelfth Night* and *As You Like It*, the remover of affectation from the other characters is a woman, who for much of the play is disguised as a man. Necessarily, disguise was inherent in the role even before the play began since the woman was played by a male actor. But now the deception is double because we have a male actor, dressed as a woman, disguised as a man, and in the case of Rosalind, sometimes pretending to be a woman. Disguise, instead of conveying ambiguity, gives the audience distance from the characters, whose dialogue is now ironic and conveys double meanings. Our response thus becomes intellectual rather than emotional, as perhaps it had been when we were faced with Rosalind's exile and Viola's grief— before they donned male clothing. In these comedies disguise thus clarifies and helps to confirm the point of view of the play.

However, in *All's Well* and *Measure for Measure* Shakespeare alters this presentation of illusion. Rather than wearing male clothing, Helena and Isabella assume another form of disguise, the bed-trick. Isabella perpetuates the disguise because she believes in the legality of Marianna's plight-troth and Helena because she is a married woman. Among Shakespeare's most interesting and courageous characters, they reverse traditional female behavior, invert stereotypes, and turn apparent lechery into the service of marriage. The ultimate irony, or secret hidden behind illusion, is that resourceful, autonomous women shore up marriage. Helena and Isabella show why they force us to redefine virtue, rather than simply lowering our opinion of them. They encourage the audience to reevaluate virtue, chastity, honesty, and honor in the context of character development. Stock responses to these characters, merely to like or dislike them, will not do because their subtlety demands that the audience respond with subtlety as well.
The bed-trick can be thought of as a kind of disguise since the female lover is disguised by darkness and silence from the male lover. In that sense it is no more or less deceptive than disguise. Like Rosalind and Viola, Helena and Isabella know who they are— a wife and novice, respectively; the characters whom they trick do not see them as they see themselves. One might here use the defense of "Jane Anger" that deceitful men should be repaid in kind, that to men for whom all women are the same in the dark, deception is exactly what they deserve. The bed-trick is, however, far more significant and more "theatrical" than that. Disguise is obviously conventional, but the bed-trick is even more unrealistic if we concede that disguise— that is, role playing and putting on uncharacteristic clothing— is the reality of actors and plays. The bed-trick serves, in addition to its obvious plot function, as the inherent

Act II, scene iii. Helena, the King, lords, and attendants at the King's palace in Paris. Painted by Francis Wheatley, R.A. The University of Michigan Special Collections Library.

symbol of the play, comparable to Hermione's statue coming to life. Life, death, fertility, and renewal cannot easily be portrayed realistically on the stage. Bertram and Angelo do not get what they deserve. In fact, they get far better, and the bed-trick provides the opportunity to effect their union with feeling and harmony. Lust may have driven them to their ignorance of the women with them, but these women in their love both demand recognition.

Ironically, as the disguise device that is embodied in the bed-trick becomes more theatrical, the plays in which the bed-trick appears are more realistic than the earlier comedies in which the disguise is of a more conventional nature. Here, we have sickbeds, barracks, courtrooms, and cities instead of pastoral forests and imaginary seacoasts. The heroines, themselves, are less mannered and witty; instead they have the drive and zeal of conviction. Perhaps Shakespeare is suggesting in these later comedies that the male protagonists, who are also not typical and indeed are very unlikely heroes, make obvious disguise impossible. Their corruption ought to be confronted directly. Male disguise establishes Viola and Rosalind as the friends of Orsino and Orlando, and it momentarily submerges their feminine identity. Bertram and Angelo cannot be treated in the same way. For Isabella and Helena to put on

male clothing is to create a visual similarity between them and their antagonists. Such disguise would imply amicable relationships. Perhaps, too, Shakespeare is suggesting that in ethical confrontations such as these, one cannot stare down ruthlessness in someone else's clothes. One must take a stand in one's own person. Isabella and Helena must simultaneously be themselves and more daringly theatrical in order to reinforce the differences between them and the men they confront. The bed-trick affirms the feminine sexuality of these women and, in part, their identities. Helena must be recognized as wife and consummate her marriage, and Isabella must be recognized as virgin and not consummate the relationship with Angelo. They will also ensure that the men will honor their vows as a result.

With this peculiar merging of the realistic and the theatrical, Shakespeare redefines societal expectations of female virtues. Role playing, identity, and integrity of self are examined through the characters involved in this obviously sexual disguise, in plays that are about life and death, marriage, fertility, and renewal— all of which are tied together by the image of the bed.

Both Helena and Isabella are associated with and ultimately effect recovery and generosity in their respective plays. The outcome of their machination is marriage. Thus the stereotypic female roles— nurturing and insuring generation— are at the heart of the plays. However, the rare, unstereotypic personalities of these women and the use of the bed-trick— a seemingly adulterous theatrical device, establishes them as unconventional. The bed-trick, with its secrecy, silence, and deceit, is the device that strips away illusion and ignorance, and confirms truth and understanding. It uses carnal knowledge to effect compassion and knowledge of the spirit. Thus, the use of the bed-trick to beget marriage and the miracle of loving confirms what is unique in these women.

Both the stereotype of nurturer and the more complex and realistic portrait of a passionate-virtuous woman are established very early in *All's Well*. A litany of family designations begins this plays as the Countess says, "delivering my son from me, I bury a second husband" (1.1.1-2), thus initiating the rhythm of family, generation and death— in short, all of life. In the ensuing exchange between her and Lefew, family designations recur, *father, child, husband*, as they will in act 1, scene 2, when the King greets Bertram, and again in act 1, scene 3, when the Countess and Helena have their exchange between *mother* and *daughter*. Also in act 1, scene 1, Helena and Parolles discuss virginity. Though chaste, Helena does indicate that virgins do fall in love and do passionately feel desire.

The stereotyping and unstereotyping of Helena is further established in her two "miracles." She takes her legacy from her father to the court to heal the King and her love to Bertram's bed to give him the blessings of life. She does not perform a miracle in either case unless the human capacities to cure and to love are miracles. If the healing and loving are wondrous, then the bed-*trick* is a misnomer and is the bed-*miracle*, instead, just as the King's recovery apparently is. Miracle or not, loving sets people apart from the rest of the natural world, and both the King and Bertram benefit from Helena's precipitation of event. Indeed, Helena anticipates the similarities between her two *miracles*, both occurring in bed as they do. She acknowledges her daring in her venture to heal the King and tells him that should she fail she will feel the "Tax of impudence, / A strumpet's boldness, a devulged shame, / Traduc'd by odious ballads; my maiden's name / Sear'd otherwise" (2.1.169-172). In short, her reputation will be destroyed. Like her discussion about virginity with Parolles and her asking for a husband in payment for curing the King, this speech reveals Helena's many facets, not the least of them being her vulnerabilty. She acknowledges the sexuality of love and marriage; indeed, she welcomes it. She also acknowledges that there are risks of failure, suffering, and public disgrace in acts of daring. There are hazards in shaping destiny.

Helena later decides to make her pilgrimage to save her husband from the dangers of war by encouraging him with her absence to come home. This decision, made from love, will lead to resolution of events by the bed-trick. Helena's motive for leaving Rousillion is quite different from Giletta's in *The Palace of Pleasure*, where the latter planned to seek and bed her husband from the outset of her journey. In *All's Well*, as in the variation from the source in *Measure for Measure*, Shakespeare gives greater complexity to his character. Indeed, fate seems to approve of Helena's love and generosity for it introduces her to the Widow and Diana, the means to love Bertram. Had ambition been her motive for marriage, she would not have denied herself the comforts of her new station in life. At Rousillion she has the name of wife without the excess baggage of a petulant boy-husband.

However, she cares about Bertram's well-being and off she goes. She ruefully describes herself to Diana and the Widow as being "too mean / To have her name repeated; all her deserving / Is a reserved honesty, and that / I have not heard examin'd" (3.5.60-63). As with Parolles in act 1, scene 1, her virginity is the topic of discussion, but now the stakes are quite different. Then the question was how a modest maid might pursue the man she loved; now virginity should no longer be the normal condition of her life. As before when she declined modesty in favor of Bertram, she is aware of the ambiguities of what she is about to do. She acknowledges that her plan may be misunderstood and must be defended, "which, if it speed, / Is wicked meaning in a lawful deed, / And lawful meaning in a lawful act / Where both not sin, and yet a sinful fact" (3.7.44-47).

With it all, she will save Bertram from adultery and give him love. . . .

The men whom Helena and Isabella confront expect stereotypic replies from them; Bertram and Angelo judge by appearances and are taken in by the bed-trick while it asserts complexity and reality over superficiality and mere appearances. George Bernard Shaw described Bertram as a very ordinary young man with "unimaginative prejudices and selfish conventionality." Bertram certainly seems to embody some of the attitudes toward women that the sixteenth century expressed. He expects that Helena will passively accept the role of virgin-wife which he assigns to her and that his superior intelligence will defeat her. For him women are wives to be rejected, or wenches to be seduced. When Diana defends her honor and equates her chastity with his aristocratic legacy, he is so enmeshed in his lust that he gives away the symbol of that legacy. Want of feeling marks his behavior throughout, culminating in his description of his night's work. He has "buried a wife, mourn'd for her, writ to my lady mother I am returning, entertain'd my convoy, and between these main parcels of dispatch effected many nicer needs; the last was the greatest, but that I have not ended yet" (4.3.85-89). The last is the liaison with Diana-Helena.

Bertram will not accept his good fortune, either in marrying Helena or in the contingent good will of the king. He sees her not as herself, but as his "father's charge / A poor physician's daughter" (2.3.114-115). The King, recognizing her virtues, in gratitude defines honor in terms of deeds, not heritage. "Honours thrive / When rather from our acts we them derive / Than our foregoers" (2.3.135-37). He makes a distinction that the myopic Bertram cannot see, "Virtue and she / Is her own dower; honour and wealth from me" (2.3.143-44). Bertram rejects her and goes off to be a soldier, to be brave, and to wench. Thus, he even makes a stereotype of himself. Parolles delivers his lord's message in conventional courtly love language— serious business has called Bertram away from his "rite of love" (2.4.39). Bertram later smugly declares, "I have wedded her, not bedded her, and sworn to make the 'not' eternal" (3.2.20-1). He is too arrogant to realize that his decision may not be Helena's, and he anticipates that she will do as she is told. Lavatch had sung, "marriage comes by destiny" (1.3.60). Surely the action of this play denies that platitude. It comes to Helena in name and in actuality through her own actions. Bertram will not bed her; so she will bed him.

As the bed-trick is being planned, so is the drum-trick. Both Parolles and Bertram will be in the dark, literally and metaphorically. Neither will know that his "friends" are beside him. One will speak and hear nothing and the other will be blindfolded and hear foreign sounds. By agreeing to the strictures of darkness and silence, Bertram acknowledges his lust. Love seeks and knows the differences between people; lust makes them all the same. Ultimately, each will reveal his worst when caught. It is Parolles who says, "Yet who would have suspected an ambush where I was taken?" (4.3.291-92). Bertram could as well have said the same thing.

When Bertram makes his assignation with Diana, his language is once again that of the highly conventional, literary, courtly tradition. He will do "all rights of service" (4,2.17); Diana is "holy-cruel" (4.2.33); and he suffers from "sick desires" which only her acquiescence will cure (4.2.35-36) He vows "for ever" (4.2.16). The darkness then disguises Helena from Bertram, but he also does not know himself, so caught up is he in the roles of lover and warrior. The bed-trick will open him up to feeling and an understanding of his own vulnerability.

Helena, through her active assertion of first, her role as physician, and then her role as wife, acts as restorative for Bertram and will perhaps enable him to cultivate the kinds of feelings that do heal and comfort, that do express humanity and the complexity of the human experience, "a mingled yarn, good and ill together" (4.3.68). Helena brings intelligence, compassion, and fertility to the world of Bertram and Parolles. Theirs is the world of battle and of superficial friendship based on flattery and self-seeking. . . .

Like the bed-trick, the endings of *All's Well* and *Measure for Measure* are at once conventional and unconventional. They both end with marriage, but "happily ever after" may not rule the day. Equally, the heroines who have effected these endings and revealed the subtleties of a world in which the illusions of the characters who have expected stereotypic behavior have been removed elude arbitrary classifications.

In *All's Well*, when morning comes, after the bed-trick, Helena anticipates better times, "When briars shall have leaves as sweet as thorns / And be as sweet as sharp" (4.4.32-33). Thus she expresses hope but is also mindful of the "mingled yarns of life" (4.3.74). Even in the final scene when it is full daylight and many voices of propriety and family are heard, the bed-trick seems re-enacted as it had been anticipated by the King's illness, with the exchange of rings, the substituted women, the oaths, the lies— all until the light comes and the truth is revealed. Once more the ambiguities of life are defined. In an ideal world, all would be well. Here all is well only *if* Helena can make the riddle clear to Bertram (5.3.310). *If* she cannot, divorce will follow (5.3.311). The play is a success *if* the suit for applause is won (epilogue, 1-2). Of course, she will prove the consummation, there will be no divorce, and we will applaud when the player asks us to. With the introduction of the *ifs*, however, comes the confirmation that people behave in individual ways. There are

mitigating circumstances, and not to recognize them condemns us to a life based on appearances and assumptions. Bertram thought he got an evening's fling; what he got instead was blessing and love. The *ifs* tell us that life can go sour; it can also rise and bake sweet.

Women like Helena are more risky to love than passive, conformable women. They ask for more— that their husbands be as chaste as they for one thing— and give more. They are reckless and dare to assert themselves with the means available in order to give their gifts. The convention of the bed-trick confirms and enriches their specialness. Further, it ties together the past and present, dying and fertility, role playing and disguise, all of it, to deny the ordinary and unimaginative.

The final discovery in *Measure for Measure*, like that in *All's Well*, exposes a man who has misjudged the subtleties and complexities of the personality of the woman who confronts him. Isabella, to expose Angelo's misuse of power, allows her good name and reputation to be tarnished. She publicly denounces him but must say that he has seduced her in order to do so. For her, reputation of chastity is not the same as chastity itself. And virtue means much more than chastity as she risks public disgrace to expose evil. Throughout, however, Angelo remains alienated. He is given love and marriage, neither of which he wants. Because he cannot tolerate public shame, he requests death, which is denied him. Finally, Isabella makes her grandest assertion for life, and once more her sincerity and directness surface. Angelo's death will not revive Claudio; therefore she pleads for his life. As she had participated in the bed-trick to save her brother's life, so she now pleads for Angelo's out of compassion for Marianna.

As in *All's Well*, the ending of *Measure for Measure* is precarious. None of the marriages seems ideal. We do not believe that distress is over and happiness necessarily follows. Instead, there is sense of a beginning, of new opportunities and second chances, rather like life. We have arrived at this realization in part by having had our sensibilities shocked. Chastity typically demands reticence and passivity, but Shakespeare says *no* in these plays. The bed-trick is unseemly to the unimaginative, indecorous to the conventional and undemanding. These plays ask of their heroines that they be virtuous and assertive, chaste and outspoken; that they search for the harmonies of life. These characters and their participation in the bed-trick shock, disorient and ultimately extend a reality— that part of virtue which actively reaches for the elusive commitment to life. In creating plays in which the stereotypes are distorted, Shakespeare via an old and much used convention seeks to define honor, chastity, virtue— not as abstractions but as realities.

Janet Adelman

SOURCE: "Bed Tricks: On Marriage as the End of Comedy in *All's Well That Ends Well* and *Measure for Measure*," in *Shakespeare's Personality*, edited by Norman N. Holland, Sidney Homan, and Bernard J. Paris, University of California Press, 1989, pp. 151-74.

[In the following excerpt, Adelman explores the male desire to sexually contaminate a pure woman (as played out in the characters of Bertram in All's Well That Ends Well *and Angelo in* Measure for Measure, *and how this is integral to the bed trick and the unsustainability of marriage based on trickery. She also examines the "incestuous potential of sexuality" and how these two male characters are drawn to sexual relations outside the context of marriage (and, for Bertram, outside the context of "family," as he regards Helena almost as a sister).]*

In the midst of Hamlet's attack on deceptive female sexuality, he cries out to Ophelia, "I say we will have no moe marriage" (3.1.147). *Hamlet* begins with the disrupted marriage of Hamlet's mother and father; by the end of the play both the potential marriage of Hamlet and Ophelia and the actual marriage of Claudius and Gertrude have been destroyed. This disruption of marriage is enacted again in the tragedies that follow immediately after *Hamlet;* the author of *Troilus and Cressida* and *Othello* seems to proclaim with Hamlet, "we will have no moe marriage." But the comedies written during this period—*All's Well That Ends Well* and *Measure for Measure*—end conventionally in marriage; in them Shakespeare was, I think, experimenting to discover by what means he might make marriage possible again.

Marriage rests on the legitimization of sexual desire within society; insofar as sexuality is felt to be illicit, marriage itself will be equivocal at best. As Hamlet proclaims the abolition of marriage, he repeatedly orders Ophelia to a nunnery (3.1.120-49). Here the double sense of nunnery as religious institution and bawdyhouse explicates perfectly the sexual alternatives left when marriage is abolished; or rather, it explicates the sexual alternatives—absolute chastity or absolute sexual degradation—that make the middle ground of marriage impossible. These are the sexual alternatives for the male protagonists of both problem comedies, where the middle is absent and sexual desire is felt only for the illicit. Bertram and Angelo are both presented as psychological virgins about to undergo their first sexual experience. In the course of their plays, we find that both can desire only when they imagine their sexuality as an illegitimate contamination of a pure woman, the conversion in effect of one kind of nun into the other. Both plays exploit this fantasy of contamination. The drama of the last scene in each play depends heavily on the sexual shaming of the supposedly violated virgins. The public naming of Diana as a "common gamester

to the camp" (*All's Well That Ends Well,* 5.3.188); Lucio's comment that Mariana, who is "neither maid, widow, nor wife," may be a punk (*Measure for Measure,* 5.1.179-80) and his extended joke about who has handled, or could handle, Isabella privately (5.1.72-77); even Escalus's claim that he will "go darkly to work" with Isabella, a claim that Lucio promptly and predictably sexualizes (5.1.278-80)— all assume the instantaneous transformation of the virgin into the whore, the transformation implicit in Hamlet's double use of "nunnery." Though the contamination is apparently undone in these scenes insofar as the continuing status of Diana and Isabella as virgins is eventually revealed, these revelations do not undo the deeper fantasies of sexual contamination on which the plots rest; at the end, as at the beginning, male sexual desire is understood as desire for the illicit, desire to contaminate.

Since the impediment to the conventional festive ending in marriage in both comedies is thus the construction of male sexual desire itself, the ending turns on the attempt to legitimize sexual desire in marriage— an attempt epitomized in both plays by the bed trick, in which the illicit desires of men are coercively directed back toward their socially sanctioned mates. (See Neely 1985, Kirsch 1981, and Wheeler 1981 for very similar accounts of the problem and the solution in both plays; of these, Neely and Kirsch tend to be more sanguine than I am about the effectiveness of the cure.) In the bed tricks in both plays the act imagined to have been deeply illicit is magically revealed as having been licit all along— but only at the expense of the male protagonists' sexual autonomy. Through a kind of homeopathic cure both Bertram and Angelo are allowed to enact fantasies of the sexual soiling of a virgin and are appropriately shamed for these fantasies, only to find out that their sexual acts have in fact been legitimate and that the soiling has taken place only in fantasy. Bertram and Angelo are thus saved from their own imaginations; presented with legitimate sexuality as a fait accompli, they can— or so we might hope— go on to accept the possibility that they have been tricked into: the possibility of sexuality within marriage. But given the status of the bed tricks as tricks and the characters' failure to provide much evidence that they have been transformed by them, our hope seems frail indeed and the marriages at the end of both plays remain equivocal. Moreover, because they so clearly betray the desires of the male protagonists, the bed tricks in both plays tend to become, not a vehicle for the working out of sexual impediments, but a forced and conspicuous metaphor for what needs working out.

Comparison with Shakespeare's source for *All's Well*— there is no bed trick in the sources for *Measure for Measure*— can help us to gauge the tonality of the bed trick in both plays. In *The Palace of Pleasure*, William Painter's translation of Boccaccio's *Decameron* (day 3, story 9), the bed trick is a rather well-mannered and genial affair, repeated often and with affection. We are specifically told that the count (equivalent to Bertram) "at his uprising in the morning . . . used many courteous and amiable words and gave divers fair and precious jewels" (Bullough 1958, 2:395). In both *All's Well* and *Measure for Measure* the bed tricks are portrayed as one-night stands that the male protagonists have no desire to repeat—and not only, I think, for reasons of dramatic economy and credibility. Both Bertram and Angelo lose desire for their virgins as soon as they have ravished them; for both, apparently, the imagined act of spoiling virginity is the only source of sexual desire. In both plays the prohibition against speaking (*AWW*, 4.2.58; *MM*, 3.1.247) and the male recoil from the object of desire utterly transform the encounter reported in Painter, so that it becomes the epitome not only of the dark waywardness of desire but also of its depersonalization, the interchangeability of the bodies with which lust plays (*AWW*, 4.4.24-25). The potentially curative affectionate mutuality of the source is utterly absent: these bed tricks demonstrate the extent to which sexuality is a matter of deception on the one side and hit-and-run contamination on the other. They do not bode well as cures.

Insofar as the bed tricks represent sexuality in these plays, it is portrayed as deeply incompatible with the continuing relationship of marriage; the very trick that imports sexuality back into marriage reveals the incompatibility. In "Upon Some Verses of Virgil," an essay that some have found a source both for *Othello* and for *All's Well*, Montaigne registers a similar sense of incompatibility. (See Cavell 1979, 474, for *Othello* and Kirsch 1981, 122-27, for *All's Well*; I am particularly indebted to Kirsch's account.) Montaigne says, "Nor is it other then a kinde of incest, in this reverent alliance and sacred bond, to employ the effects and extravagant humor of an amorous licentiousness" (1928, 72). Here Montaigne seems to me to come very close to the psychological core of the "problem" that I find definitive of the problem comedies. When Montaigne registers his sense of the incompatibility between the sexual and the sacred by calling that incompatibility incest, he associates the soiling potentiality of sexuality with the prohibitions surrounding the male child's first fantasies of soiling a sacred space; insofar as marriage is felt as sacred, sexuality within it will replay those ancient fantasies and their attendant anxieties. Angelo's anguished self-questioning upon the discovery of his own desire reiterates powerfully the core of Montaigne's concern: "Having waste ground enough, / Shall we desire to raze the sanctuary / And pitch our evils there?" (*MM*, 2.2.169-71). For the male sexual imagination represented in both Bertram and Angelo, sexuality within marriage is, I think, an ultimately incestuous pollution of a sanctuary; they can desire only when they can imagine themselves safely enacting this pollution outside the familial context of marriage. In both plays, however, the very fact of sexuality binds one incestuously to family, so that all sexuality is ultimately felt as incestuous. I want

to look at this incestuous potential within both plays and then to suggest the ways in which they finally seem to me to undercut the accommodations to sexuality apparently achieved by their bed tricks.

The recoil from a sexuality felt as the soiling of a sacred space is split in two in *All's Well* and analyzed in two separate movements. Bertram's flight from, and slander of, Diana analyze his recoil from the woman felt as whore once his own sexuality has soiled her; even at the end of the play the deep shaming that Diana undergoes makes her the repository for his sense of taint. But the flight from Diana curiously echoes Bertram's earlier flight from helena. This initial flight analyzes his aversion toward sexual union with a woman who is terrifying to him partly insofar as she is identified with a maternal figure and thus with the incestuous potential of sexuality. In the end, I shall argue, the splitting of the sexual object into the legitimate but abhorred Helena and the illegitimate but desired Diana will be undone as Helena and Diana begin to fuse; their fusion will serve the deepest of the play's sexual paradoxes. But before the end Diana seems the solution to the problem created by Helena: the problem of sexuality within a familial context.

Bertram's initial flight from Helena is phrased in terms that suggest a flight from this familial context. Here, too, Shakespeare's management of his source emphasizes issues central to the play: the figure of the Countess and the crucial association of her with Helena are his additions to Boccaccio/Painter. *All's Well* begins with the image of a son separating from his mother, seeking a new father (1.1.5-7) and new possibilities for manhood elsewhere. The formation of a new sexual relationship in marriage is ideally the emblem of this separation from the family of origin and hence of independent manhood. But marriage with helena cannot serve this function, both because of the association of her with Bertram's mother—an association so close that Bertram's only words to her before their enforced marriage are a parenthesis within his farewell to his mother ("Be comfortable to my mother, your mistress, / And make much of her" [1.1.77-78])—and because she becomes the choice of his surrogate father. Marriage to her would thus be a sign of his bondage to the older generation rather than of his growing independence. In Richard Wheeler's brilliant account of the play—an account to which this discussion is much indebted—Bertram's flight from Helena and his attraction to a woman decidedly outside the family structure become intelligible as attempts to escape the dominion of the infantile family (Wheeler 1981, especially 40-45; see also Kirsch 1981, 141, and Neely 1985, 70-71).

Bertram's exchange with the king suggests the extent to which marriage with helena threatens to obliterate necessary distinctions between father and son, mother and wife:

KING: Thou know'st she has rais'd me
  from my sickly bed.
BERTRAM: But follows it, my lord, to
  bring me down

Must answer for your raising? I know her
  well;

She had her breeding at my father's charge—
A poor physician's daughter my wife! Disdain
Rather corrupt me ever!

(2.3.111-16)

Bred by his father, Helena is virtually his sister. More-over, she becomes in the king's words virtually a surrogate mother. Lafew's reference to himself as a pander ("I am Cressid's uncle, / That dare leave two together" [2.1.97-98]) and the earlier sexualization of "araise" (2.1.76) combine to make the sexualization of the king's "she has raised me from my sickly bed" almost inevitable here (see Wheeler 1981, 75-76, and Kirsch 1981, 135). Bertram imagines himself sexu-ally brought down by the woman who has raised up his surrogate father (see Neely 1985, 70). Beneath his social snobbery, I think we can hear a hint of the ruin threatened should Bertram become sexually al-lied with his surrogate father's imagined sexual part-ner. The escape from the parents' choice thus be-comes in part an escape from the incestuous poten-tial involved in marriage to a woman who is allied to his mother not only by their loving association but also by her position as fantasied sexual partner of his surrogate father. Bertram's response to the king suggests his terror at losing the social and familial distinctions that guarantee identity, distinctions pro-tected by the incest taboo. His terror is unlikely to be assuaged when the king answers him by denying the distinction between Helena's blood and his: "Strange is it that our bloods, / Of color, weight, and heat, pour'd all together, / Would quite con-found distinction" (2.3.118-20). Bertram's fear is, I think, exactly that the mingling of bloods (see *The Winter's Tale*, 1.2.109) in his sexual union with Hel-ena would confound distinction.

Bertram faces an impossible dilemma: he must leave his family to become a man, and yet he can take his full place as a man in this society only insofar as he can be reconciled with his mother and the king, hence with the woman they have chosen for him. Moreover, the play insists on the full impossibility of the task facing Bertram by emphasizing at once the distance between him and his father and the social expectation that he will turn out to be like his father. From the first, Bertram's manhood is the subject of anxious specula-tion on the part of his mother and the king, speculation expressed in the desire that he be like his father in moral parts as well as in shape (1.1.61-62; 1.2.21-22). For them— hence for the ruling society of the play— manhood is defined as living up to one's father, in effect becoming him. Bertram himself unwittingly plays

Act II, scene ii. Parolles, Bertram, and Helena. The University of Michigan Special Collections Library.

into this definition: he will accept the validity of the marriage only when Helena can show him "a child begotten of thy body that I am father to" (3.2.58-59). This stipulation in effect makes his own achievement of paternity the condition of his resumption of adult status in France: he can become a man only by becom-ing his father, and he becomes his father only by as-suming his role *as father*— by becoming a father himself. But if paternity is imagined as becoming one's own father, then one's sexual partner again takes on the resonance of one's mother. The social world of the play and his own fantasy of himself as father finally allow Bertram his place as a man only insofar as he can form a sexual alliance with the woman he and the play identify with his mother. The route toward manhood takes Bertram simultaneously away from the mother and toward her; hence the incestuous double bind in which Bertram finds himself.

Given Bertram's association of Helena both with his mother and with his surrogate father's sexuality, we can begin to make sense of both the impossible conditions Bertram sets for Helena: the act by which Helena si-multaneously makes Bertram a father and gets his father's ring is, I think, a fantasized replication of the act of parental intercourse by which Bertram himself was bred. Hence the complex logic governing the exchange of rings in the dark: Bertram's father's ring is given unawares to Helena, the mother's choice, and the ring taken from Helena turns out to have been the father king's. Even here, when poor Bertram thinks that he has escaped his family, the exchange of rings is in effect between father and mother; in the last scene the ring play turns out to have been a symbolic sexual exchange between surrogate parental figures. (On the sexualization of the rings see Adams 1961, 268-69.) In attempting to define his manhood by locating it elsewhere, Bertram thus finds himself returned to his mother's choice; flee as he might, there is no escaping Helena. Indeed, in its portrayal of Helena the play seems to me to embody a deep ambivalence of response toward the mother who simultaneously looks after us and threatens our independence. Astonishing both for her willfulness and her self-abnegation, simultaneously far below Bertram's sphere and far above it, apparently all-powerful in her weakness, present even when Bertram thinks most that he has escaped her, triumphantly proclaiming her maternity at the end, Helena becomes the epitome of the invisible maternal power that binds the child, especially the male child, who here discovers that she is always the woman in his bed.

Insofar as *All's Well* splits the sexually desired woman from the maternally taboo one, the project it sets for itself in reinstituting marriage is to legitimize desire, to import it back into the sacred family bonds. The bed trick is, as I have suggested, an attempt at such importation. But the bed trick as Shakespeare presents it here fails to detoxify or legitimize sexuality; instead it tends to make even legitimate sexuality illicit in fantasy, a "wicked meaning in a lawful deed" (3.7.45-47). Despite Shakespeare's apparent attempt to rescue sexuality here, he seems incapable in this play of imagining any sexual consummation— legitimate or illegitimate— that is not mutually defiling. Musing on the bed trick that technically legitimizes sexuality, Helena makes this sense of mutual defilement nearly explicit:

> But, O, strange men,
> That can such sweet use make of what they
>   hate,
> When saucy trusting of the cozen'd thoughts
> Defiles the pitchy night.
>
> (4.4.21-24)

It's very hard to say just what is defiling what here. The sexual interchange itself is replaced in Helena's words by a defiling interchange between "saucy trusting" and "pitchy night," in which "saucy trusting" seems to stand in for Bertram's part and "pitchy night" for Helena's. We might imagine that the defilement here is the consequence of Bertram's belief that he is committing an illicit act; but in fact Helena suggests that the very trusting to deception that legitimizes the sexual act is the agent of defilement. The defilement thus seems to be the consequence of the act itself, not of its status as legitimate or illegitimate. Moreover, in her odd condensation of night, the bed, and her own apparently defiled body, Helena seems to assume the mutual defilement attendant on this act. In the interchange, Bertram/trust defiles Helena/night. But the night itself is "pitchy"; and as Shakespeare's frequent use reminds us, pitch defiles (see, for example, *Much Ado About Nothing*, 3.3.57, *Love's Labor's Lost*, 4.3.3, and *I Henry IV*, 2.4.413). Bertram thus defiles that which is already defiled and that which defiles him in turn; that is, in the process of trying to sort out legitimacy and defilement, the play here reveals its sense of the marriage bed as both defiled and defiling. The bed trick thus works against itself by locating the toxic ingredient in sexuality and then replicating rather than removing its toxicity.

It is, moreover, revealing that both the sexual act and the bed tend to disappear in Helena's account, the one replaced by the mental process of trusting to deception, the other by the pitchy night. The sexual act at the center of *All's Well* is absent; its place in our imagination is taken by the process of working out the deception. One consequence of this exchange is the suggestion that mistrust and deception are at the very root of the sexual act, as though the man is always tricked, defiled, and shamed there, as though to engage in sexual union is always to put oneself into the manipulative power of women. At the same time, the disappearance of the sexual act in Helena's musing on the bed trick points toward the larger disappearance of the sexual act enabled by the bed trick. Ultimately, that is, the bed trick in *All's Well* seems to me as much a part of a deep fantasy of escape from sexuality as it is an attempt to bring the married couple together; as its consequences are unraveled in the last scene, it allows for a renewed fantasy of the flight from sexuality even while it seems to be a means of enabling and legitimizing sexual union.

Just before Helena appears in the last scene, Diana says, "He knows himself my bed he hath defil'd, / And at that time he got his wife with child" (5.3.300-301). In effect she separates the mental from the physical components of the sexual act, Bertram's intentions from his actual deed, ascribing the shame and soil to herself and the pregnancy to Helena. This split in part explains the insistence on Diana's shame in the last scene; her words here identify her role as substitute strumpet, the figure onto whom Bertram and the play can displace the sense of sexuality as defilement, thus protecting Helena from taint. The structure of the last scene is calculated to replicate the magical legitimization of sexuality in the bed trick insofar as it substitutes the pure Helena for the shamed Diana in our imaginations; we are put through the process of imagining a defiling sexual contact with Diana and then released from that image by the magical reappearance of Helena. (Hence, I think, the lengthy insistence on the mutual shame of Diana and Bertram, which is not strictly necessary for the plot.) But in the process of repudiating the taint attaching to sexuality, the last scene enables a fantasy repudiating sexuality itself. As Diana begins the process of repudiating her shame, the sexual act is done and then undone in our imaginations as the ring— emblematic of the sexual encounter— is given ("this was it I gave him, being a-bed" [5.3.228]) and ungiven ("I never gave it him" [5.3.276]). The business of the ring makes this portion of the last scene into a ritual of doing and undoing, from which the soiled Diana emerges purified, not a "strumpet" but a "maid" (5.3.290-93). Diana's last words— the riddle to which the appearance of Helena is the solution— again hint at this ritual of doing and undoing: in substituting the pregnant wife for the defiled bed— "he knows himself my bed he hath defil'd, / And at that time he got his wife with child"— Diana comes close to making the bed itself disappear, as though the act of impregnating did not take place in that bed at all. Her words suggest the almost magical quality of the act by which Bertram impregnates Helena: defiling one woman, he impregnates another. The pregnancy is thus presented as the result of Bertram's copulation with Diana, as though the child were Helena's by a magical transference through which Diana gets the taint and Helena gets the child.

Diana's riddle reinterprets the bed trick in effect as an act split into a defiling contact and a miraculous conception. As the defiled bed disappears, the sexual act itself seems to vanish, to become as imaginary as Bertram's knowledge of defilement. The stress throughout the scene has been on the undoing of the sexual act rather than on conception. In the logic of fantasy here, I think that the sexual act has not happened at all, not with Diana and not with Helena. The prestidigitation expressed in Diana's riddle brings the promised birth of Helena's child as close to a virgin birth as the facts of the case will allow. The sense of miracle that greets Helena's return is not wholly a consequence of her apparent return from the dead; it also derives partly from the apparently miraculous conception that Diana's riddle points toward. At the end Helena can thus assume her new status as wife and mother without giving up her status as miraculous virgin; she can simultaneously cure through her sexuality and remain absolutely pure. This simultaneity should seem familiar to us: it in fact rules the presentation of Helena's cure of the king, where her miraculous power depends equally on her status as heavenly maid and on the sexuality that could "araise King Pippen" (2.1.76). (See Neely's fine discussion of Helena's various roles, 1985, especially 65-70.) The play asks us nearly from the beginning to see Helena both as a miraculous virgin and as a deeply sexual woman seeking her will: thus the early dialogue with Parolles, in which we see her meditating both on how to defend her virginity and on how to lose it to her liking (1.1.110-51). Helena's two roles are ultimately the reflection of the impossible desire for a woman who can have the powers simultaneously of Venus and of Diana— who can in effect be both Venus and Diana,

both generative sexual partner and sacred virgin. (Adams [1961, 262-64] finds the desire possible insofar as procreation legitimizes sexuality.) This is the fantasy articulated in Helena's re-creation of the Countess's youth, when "your Dian / Was both herself and Love" (1.3.212-13). The role of the character Diana should ultimately be understood in this context. As Helena chooses Bertram at court, she imagines herself shifting allegiance from Diana to Venus (2.3.74-76). The emergence of the character Diana shortly after Helena renounces her allegiance to the goddess Diana suggests the complexity of the role that Diana plays: if Bertram can vest his sense of sexuality as soiling in her, Helena can also vest her virginity in her. Both as the repository of soil and as the preserver of virginity, she functions as a split-off portion of Helena herself: hence, I think, the ease with which her status as both maid and no maid transfers to Helena in the end. Both in the bed trick and in the larger psychic structures that it serves, Helena can thus become Venus and reincorporate Diana into herself.

The buried fantasy of Helena as Venus/Diana, as secular virgin mother, is the play's pyrrhic solution to the problem of legitimizing sexuality, relocating it within a sacred familial context. The solution is pyrrhic insofar as it legitimizes sexuality partly by wishing it away; it enables the creation of familial bonds without the fully imagined experience of sexuality. But this is exactly what Bertram has told us he wants. The impossible condition that Helena must meet stipulates that she can be his wife only when she can prove herself a virgin mother, that is, prove that she is with child by him without his participation in the sexual act. This condition suggests that she can be safely his only when she can remove sexuality from the establishment of the family and hence sanctify and purify the family itself. The slippery riddle of the bed trick satisfies this condition both for Bertram and for the audience: he knows he has not had sexual relations with Helena; and we have watched the sexual act be defined out of existence in the last scene. Here sexuality can be allowed back into the family only through a fantasy that enables its denial: the potentially incestuous contact with Helena is muted not by denying her association with his mother but by denying the sexual nature of the contact. The fantasy of Helena as virgin mother thus allows Bertram to return to his mother and surrogate father; he can now accept his mother's choice and achieve paternity safely, in effect becoming his father without having had to be husband to his wife/mother.

In the multiple fantasies of All's Well the marriage can be consummated only insofar as Bertram can imagine himself as defiling a virgin or insofar as the act itself is nearly defined out of existence, so that it becomes a fact without act as it becomes a sin without sin, a "wicked meaning in a lawful deed, / And lawful meaning in a lawful act, / Where both not sin and yet a sinful fact" (3.7.45-47). Despite the overt attempt to make sexuality curative, suspicion of sexuality remains the dominant emotional fact of the play. Even here, where Shakespeare attempts Pandarus-like to bring two together, we are left with a sense of failure about the sexual act itself and with a final queasiness about the getting of children. . . .

If we take the bed tricks of *All's Well* and *Measure for Measure* as diagnostic of the two plays, then the shift in their management can point to the ways in which *Measure for Measure* is an undoing of *All's Well.* (Both Neely 1985, 92-95, and Wheeler 1981, 12-13, 116, compare these bed tricks in terms very similar to mine.) In *All's Well* marriage is a cure, even if an enforced cure; in *Measure for Measure* it is a punishment. Despite its final muted fantasy of Helena as virgin mother, *All's Well* had seemed to promise that legitimate sexuality could be redemptive; in *Measure for Measure* the relationship between legitimate and illegitimate sexuality itself becomes vexed and all sexuality seems corrupting. Characteristically, then, the bed trick in *All's Well* functions dramatically to enforce marriage, while the bed trick in *Measure for Measure* functions to protect virginity. The direction of these differences is summarized in the shift in the agent through whom the bed tricks are realized. The bed trick in *All's Well* is under the management of Helena, a powerfully sexual woman. But exactly this management seems to be the central image that calls forth male fears in the play—fears of being drained or spent (see, for example, 2.3.281 and 3.2.41-42), ultimately fears of being absorbed into a female figure imagined as larger and more powerful than oneself, fears that Lavatch localizes in his "That man should be at woman's command, and yet no hurt done!" (1.3.92-93). *Measure for Measure* responds to the fears released in *All's Well* by redoing the bed trick so that it is under the management of a powerful and asexual man, in whose hands the women are merely cooperative pawns (see Riefer's discussion of the diminution of Isabella's power, 1984). That is, the play takes power back from the hands of the women and consolidates it in the Duke; and it allows him special power insofar as it represents him as a ghostly father, divorced from the bonds of natural family. In effect, then, *Measure for Measure* redoes the sexual act under the aegis of the protectively asexual father rather than of the sexually intrusive mother; in the end it is the pure father rather than the sexual mother who proves to have been everywhere unseen. That the doing and undoing in this pair of plays so closely anticipates that of *The Winter's Tale* and *The Tempest* suggests the centrality of these issues in Shakespeare's imagination.

Mary Free

SOURCE: "*All's Well That Ends Well* as Noncomic Comedy," in *Acting Funny: Comic Theory and Practice in Shakespeare's Plays,* edited by Frances Teague, Fairleigh Dickinson University Press, 1994, pp. 41-45.

[*In this brief excerpt, Free examines how* All's Well That Ends Well *is unlike Shakespeare's other comedies through its central coupling (marriage) of Helena and Bertram. The play has only this one pairing, whereas Shakespeare's other comedies have many couples. Helena and Bertram share only five scenes together, during which they do not always engage each other in dialogue. There is no battle of wit and will between them. Helena's role "outside" her social sphere further increases the comic distance, and there is scant "lightness" or "playfulness" in the play.*]

. . . Marriage is a central element in the construct of Renaissance comedy. In the Shakespearean canon, a number of the comedies include marriages, placing them (or implying that they impend) close to or at the plays' ends as a reaffirmation, restoration and promise for the continuation of society. Other comedies deal with married women as in *The Comedy of Errors* and *The Merry Wives of Windsor;* or they move the marriage forward, thus foregrounding it and making it precipitate further action in the main plot as in *The Taming of the Shrew* and *Much Ado about Nothing.* What makes *All's Well That Ends Well's* foregrounded marriage unique is the undeniable fact that Bertram does not want Helena regardless of how much she wants him or how much the members of the nobility—most notably the King, the Countess, and Lafew—want him to want her. Further, in its institution, its mixing of high personages with low, and the alliances between social groups, the foregrounded marriage in *All's Well That Ends Well* subverts the comic by creating discomfiting inversions in the play's social spheres. While the concept of marriage as regenerative force via Helena's pregnancy obtains in principle at the end, when the "broken nuptial" comes together, no wonder we, along with the King in the epilogue, feel little if any delight: things but "seem" well; we have no guarantees. We cannot be certain even there that Bertram truly wants her.

A distinction that contributes to my thesis is that *All's Well That Ends Well* stands apart from the Shakespearean comedic mainstream in that Helena and Bertram, however estranged their relationship, remain the single couple in the play. Elsewhere Shakespeare provides us with sets of couples: twins who marry and woo in *The Comedy of Errors* and *Twelfth Night,* two men in pursuit of one woman in *The Two Gentlemen of Verona* and *A Midsummer Night's Dream,* two married women who plot to outwit one man and teach another a lesson in *The Merry Wives of Windsor,* Rosalind and Celia with their loves in *As You Like It,* and a triad of lovers in *The Merchant of Venice.* Even *Measure for Measure,* the play most often closely linked to *All's Well That Ends Well,* provides us pairings. *All's Well That Ends Well* gives us two windows, a virgin, and a wife in name only. While all these pairings deal with power in relationships, they do not constitute the exact marked hierarchies of power that *All's Well That Ends Well* presents to us.

The foregrounded marriage in *All's Well That Ends Well* differs from those in *The Taming of the Shrew* and *Much Ado about Nothing* in origination and ordination. While Kate in *The Taming of the Shrew* has no more choice than does Bertram about whom each marries (Baptista and Petruchio merely strike a bargain as do the King and Helena), Petruchio and Kate as a pair remain this play's focal point. We observe the battle of wit and will between them, and the entire fourth act centers on them. Whether we grant or disallow the concept of mutuality of consent, whether the production relies on Zefferellian horseplay or a more restrained production concept, *The Taming of the Shrew* provokes laughter— the *sine qua non* of the comic— because of the physical and verbal interaction between the principal characters. The same holds true for *Much Ado about Nothing*. Like Kate and Petruchio, Beatrice and Benedick command our attention, their wit and wordplay amuse and distract us, and they are more interesting to us than the play's other couple Claudio and Hero. Even in that relationship, the comedy of *Much Ado about Nothing* remains more comic than does *All's Well That Ends Well*. Claudio and Hero agree to marry, an important distinction between their relationship and that of Helena and Bertram. The distasteful circumstances of the broken nuptial notwithstanding, the separation between Claudio and Hero fails to disrupt wholly the play's overall comic spirit for two reasons: first, we know Dogberry and the Watch hold the key to reconciliation; second, as well as more important, the comic Beatrice and Benedick remain our primary focal point.

Helena and Bertram appear on stage together in but five scenes. Their exchanges generally indicate the dynamic of power in their relationship as Helena oozes subservience to her lord and master, while Bertram, until the final scene, plays his superiority, both of class and gender, for all its worth. In three scenes where they appear together, they speak to or about one another but engage in no dialogue. In 1.1 Bertram in one and a half lines commands that Helena, "Be comfortable to my mother, your mistress, / And make much of her" (76-77). In 2.3 she subserviently offers herself to him in two and a half lines:

> I dare not say I take you, but I give
> Me and my service, ever whilst I live,
> Into your guiding power

(2.3.102-104)

The remainder of this scene has them each talking to the King, but not to one another. In a third scene (3.5), Helena merely views Bertram from a distance as the army passes and asks about him. Only two scenes have them exchanging dialogue. In 2.5, comprising thirty-five lines, Bertram, without having consummated the marriage and refusing Helena's modest request for a departing kiss, dismisses his bride by sending her back to Rossillion. His language is primarily in the command

form, hers acquiescent. She comes "as [she] was commanded from [him]" (2.5.54). She declares herself Bertram's "most obedient servant" in a scene that allows for no possible irony (2.5.72). Even when she musters the courage to hint at a parting kiss, she hesitates and stumbles as a young woman very much in love and unsure of herself. In 5.3, the reconciliation, they exchange two lines each, and arguably Bertram's "If she, my liege, can make me know this clearly / I'll love her dearly, ever, ever dearly" is addressed more to the King than to Helena. These two encounters comprise but thirty-nine lines all told.

All's Well That Ends Well remains a comedy in structure, yet Helena's agency in the enforced marriage, as well as the subsequent separation and ploys, distances us from the comic. Other elements distance us as well. When the Countess learns that Helena loves Bertram, we have the perfect occasion for a traditional blocking figure, but no. The Countess not only enjoys, but also encourages Helena in her aspirations. No witty bantering about sex, love, fidelity in wedlock— that which might create the comic within the matrix of comedy— takes place between Helena and Bertram, the play's only couple. Certainly some comic playfulness occurs within the play. No one will deny its presence in the virginity dialogue between Helena and Parolles, nor in the choosing scene as Helena walks from budding youth to budding youth before "giving" herself to Bertram, nor in Parolles's humiliation. Nevertheless, what lightness exists remains apart from the focal couple. Of added significance is how little of the playfulness associated with earlier comedies takes place among the women. Beyond the Countess' hope for Helena's love, her brief acknowledgement of her own past, and her teasing in the "I say I am your mother" dialogue (1.3), women's dialogue as they assess man's fecklessness has a more brittle edge than do similar assessments given in the earlier comedies.

Helena's actions set her apart from her Shakespearean sisters. Other independently-acting heroines— Viola, Rosalind, Portia— play at their love-games and are, in some cases, willing to leave Time to fadge things out. They also employ masculine disguise to effect the amount of control or empowerment they enjoy. Helena does what she does without disguise. In some respects Helena and Portia are the most closely akin. Portia is willing to comply with her father's will; Helena is willing to submit herself to Bertram's. Both work purposefully to achieve their goals. However close that kinship, differences obtain. Allies from the play's outset, Portia and Nerissa plot to test true love's faith; Helena, who must create her allies, has yet to gain mere acceptance as wife. To achieve her goals, she acts with what Western culture sees as male prerogatives. As A. P. Riemer has said, she acts with a "male purposefulness" (Riemer 1975-76, 54). In order for her to succeed undisguised, she must perform these actions in a way that the empowering male structure (i.e., the King and Lafew as members of the *ancien régime*) fails to recognize as violating sex or class differences.

In *All's Well That Ends Well* Helena follows Bertram to Paris. There she originates the marriage by striking a bargain with the King and curing him. Unlike the other pairings and marriages in the comedies, however, no tacit nor overt mutuality exists between this nuptial pair. Here the King must ordain an enforced marriage of his ward Bertram to comply with the terms of the bargain. Such ordination violates the usual circumstances that we find in the festive comedies. In those comedies, ordination, directed against a woman, may initiate the flight from authority into the saturnalian world of comic license.

Bertram's response to the King's command is like that of Silvia or Hermia: forced into marriage ordained against his will, a marriage that is originated by a spouse who is not loved, he runs away, as do the heroines. Bertram's running away to Florence offers a different kind of escape from that of the heroines. Not only is his escape to a city but to one associated with sexual licentiousness. The King himself warns his courtiers against "Those girls of Italy." When Helena discovers Bertram in Florence, she entraps him by means of the bed trick, which inverts predicated male-female sex roles just as "girl gets boy" inverts what we would recognize as the clichéd phrasing. Her action substitutes the legal for the licentious. Helena entraps Bertram a second time as well in 5.3 by her further employment of Diana before the King. Even the King becomes confused as Helena employs her skills. What allows everyone to escape prison is Helena's ability to use the language of empowerment without disturbing the status quo. . . .

SOCIAL CLASS

Robert Ornstein and **John M. Love** have provided the most comprehensive commentary on the barrier of social class in *All's Well That Ends Well*. Ornstein argues that Bertram would likely have opposed any marriage forced on him at that particular stage in his life. What makes it worse for him is that Helena is a dependent in his household. Although the differences in their social station is his voiced objection to the union, he cares little about rank and wealth at this point in his life. If they were concerns, he would have likely embraced a union with a royal favorite whom the King has promised to grace with honor and wealth to make up for the disparity in their rank. Love calls the barrier of social class the play's "source of darkness" and its "alien, ineradicable element." He argues that social rank determines the fate of the three main characters— Helena, Bertram, and Parolles— despite their virtues and vices.

W. W. Lawrence notes that by the time Shakespeare wrote this play, social conventions had changed and there would not have been a huge difference in rank between Helena and Bertram. By bestowing Helena with so much honor and virtue, Shakespeare constructs Bertram's rejection of her as one precipitated by his own arrogance and inability to see Helena's superior qualities. Katharine Eisaman Maus notes that Helena's marriage to Bertram would help shore up a "lapse in the proper social order," with her excellence making up for his lack of it.

Alice Shalvi and Kenneth Muir both argue that in the play Shakespeare provides a running commentary on nobility and gentility— true versus false nobility and whether gentility is inherited by birth, based on wealth, or attained through one's virtue.

John M. Love

SOURCE: "Dark Comedy and Social Class in *All's Well*," in *Texas Studies in Literature and Language*, Vol. XVIII, No. 4, Winter, 1977, pp. 520-26.

[*In this excerpt, Love examines how social rank "debases" Helena and Bertram and determines their fate as well as that of Parolles. He argues that the issue of social rank is pervasive throughout all of the action of the play. Love also points out the differences between* All's Well That Ends Well *and Boccaccio's story of Giletta of Narbonne, particularly in terms of the difference between Helena's and Giletta's stations and how this is directly related to their actions.*]

. . . The alien, ineradicable element of *All's Well that Ends Well* and the source of its darkness is the barrier of class. Class debases the characters of Bertram and Helena throughout the play, and in the final scene it determines their fates and that of Parolles, despite the measure of virtue and vice each character possesses. At that point Helena, "a maid too virtuous / For the contempt of empire" (II.ii.30-31), must plead with a pampered husband, Bertram's fellow-prodigal Parolles appears beaten into due submission, and Bertram is, in Johnson's words, "dismissed to happiness." The difference between *All's Well* and the comedies that preceded it lies in its greater darkness, for class pervades the action and influences all the main characters.

Shakespeare's Helena hardly resembles the heroine of William Painter's tale of "Giletta of Narbona," the likeliest source of the play. In the first place, she has been deprived of the wealth and independence that made Giletta her spouse's equal in all respects save those of blood. Giletta, "diligently loked unto by her kinsfolke (because she was riche and fatherlesse)," clearly managed her own affairs. Having "refused manye husbandes, with whom her kinsfolke would have matched her," she journeyed to Paris alone and unaided, and there sealed her bargain with the King. Once married, she "went to Rossiglione, where she was received of all his subjects for their Lady. And perceyving that through the Countes absence, all things were spoiled and out of order: she like a sage Ladye, with great diligence and care, disposed his thinges in order againe, whereof the subjects rejoysed very much, bearing to her their harty love & affection." By contrast, from the moment the Countess presents Helena to Lafew as Gerard de Narbon's "sole child . . . bequeath'd to my overlooking" (I.i.35-36), Helena's dependence upon her mistress and adopted mother is apparent. As much "unseason'd" as Bertram, she presumes to travel to Paris only with the Countess's knowledge and approval, "my leave and love, / Means and attendants, and my loving greetings / To those of mine at court" (I.iii.246-48). There, with the aid of Lafew, Helena gains a timid entrance to the King. But she does not in any sense come into her own upon her return to Rossillion as the wife of Bertram.

In those scenes which Painter's narrative suggested, Helena's application to the King in act 2 and her encounters with Diana and the Widow, Helena displays a heroic confidence in the heavenly source of her healing power and in her eventual success. Elsewhere in the play, in keeping with the dependent status that Shakespeare bestowed upon her, she remains mistrustful of others, fearful of earning their contempt by her slightest gesture of self-assertion, and self-effacing before her wayward husband.

Fearfulness leads her first of all to deceive the Countess, ironically her staunchest ally. After the soliloquy she utters upon Bertram's farewell, Parolles's meditation on virginity, and his farewell, "Get thee a good husband, and use him as he uses thee" (I.i.210-11), the soliloquy with which Helena concludes the first scene clearly outlines a plan to win Bertram by means of the king's disease:

> Our remedies oft in ourselves doe lie,
> Which we ascribe to heaven; the fated sky
> Gives us free scope; only doth backward pull
> Our slow designs when we ourselves are dull.
> . . . . .
> The king's disease— my project may deceive me,
> But my intents are fix'd, and will not leave
>   me.
>
> (I.i.212-25)

Under persistent questioning by the Countess, Helena admits her love, but equivocates, and finally denies any intention of pursuing Bertram, notwithstanding the audience's knowledge to the contrary:

> . . . I follow him
>   not
> By any token of presumptuous suit,

> Nor would I have him till I do deserve him;
> Yet never know how that desert should
>   be. . .
>   . . . O then give
> pity
> To her whose state is such that cannot
>   choose
> But lend and give where she is sure to lose;
> That seeks not to find that her search implies
> But riddle-like lives sweetly where she dies!
>
> (I.iii.192-212)

Helena admits only that Bertram's journey reminded her of the king's illness, and when in the scene immediately following her interview with the Countess she demands of the King, "What husband in thy power I will command" (II.i.93), the deception becomes unmistakable. Helena's guardedness in the first scene and her frequent reiteration of courtesy titles and deferential gestures in the presence of the Countess suggest the acute consciousness of an inferior place that might lie behind this unwarranted secrecy.

Helena remains uneasy even after her miraculous cure of the King. In act 2, scene 3, she balks at the mere prospect of choosing a husband from among the assembled courtiers, anticipating a rebuke even though the King has expressly forbidden one:

> Please it your majesty, I have done already.
> The blushes on my cheeks thus whisper me:
> "We blush that thou should'st choose, but,
>   be refused,
> Let the white death sit on thy cheek for ever,
> We'll ne'er come there again."
>
> (II.iii.68-72)

The terms of her address to individual lords indicate that Helena fears contempt for her class, not her person or unmaidenly forwardness:

> The honour, sir, that flames in your fair eyes
> Before I speak, too threat'ningly replies.
> Love make your fortune twenty times above
> Her that so wishes, and her humble love!
> . . . . .
> Be not afraid that I your hand should take;
> I'll never do you wrong, for your own sake.
> . . . . .
> You are too young, too happy, and too good,
> To make yourself a son out of my blood.
>
> (II.iii.80-97)

Like the unswerving support of the Countess, the young lords' protestations at being passed over underscore the extent of Helena's misapprehension.

Thereafter, the most poignant moments of the play grow out of Helena's self-effacement in the presence of her renegade husband: her choosing of him, "I dare not say I take you, but I give / Me and my service, ever whilst I live" (II.iii.102-03); their farewell, in which Bertram denies her the courtesy of the kiss that she can barely bring herself to ask; her self-accusing letter to the Countess; her bittersweet recollection of the rendezvous with Bertram, "But, O, strange men! / That can such sweet use make of what they hate" (IV.iv.21-22); and finally, her dramatic reappearance at Rossillion:

> *King.*   Is there no
>   exorcist
>   Beguiles the truer office of mine eyes?
>   Is't real that I see?
> *Hel.*   No, my good
>   lord;
>   'Tis but the shadow of a wife you see;
>   The name and not the thing.
>
>   (V.iii.298-302)

Though Shakespeare gave Helena a far greater advantage over Bertram than Giletta held over Beltramo, Painter's heroine confronted her husband far more conscious of her power: "knowing that they were all assembled. . . . shee passed through the people, without chaunge of apparell, with her twoo sonnes in her arms. . . . 'My Lorde, . . . I nowe beseche thee, for the honoure of God, that thou wilt observe the conditions, which the twoo (knightes that I sent unto thee) did commaunde me to doe: for beholde, here in myne armes, not onely one sonne begotten by thee, but twayne, and likewyse thy Ryng. It is nowe time then (if thou kepe promise) that I should be received as thy wyfe.'"

Unlike her mistrust, Helena's humility is a virtue, yet the circumstances under which it appears make her at least potentially a pathetic heroine. Her nature and her circumstances ally her more nearly to the heroines of the later romances than to her predecessors in the festive comedies, but the pathos she evokes finds its closest counterpart in Desdemona. Even though it leads to a reconciliation with Bertram, her manner during the final scene cannot but recall her character and status throughout, as well as the somber emotions she has frequently stirred.

That the unworthy husband presumes upon the class barrier that works against his virtuous wife is one of the pervasive ironies of *All's Well*, and in that sense Bertram's nobility of blood corrupts him by licensing his misdeeds. But Shakespeare's juxtaposition of each stage of Bertram's career and its counterpart in Parolles's creates a second irony, for the two finally emerge as wayward youths, possessed of the same degree and kind of vice, but distinguished by class and thus by fate.

The parallel courses that Bertram and Parolles run begin with their farewells to Helena in the opening scene. The Count, characteristically attentive to the niceties of rank, departs with the charge, "Be comfortable to my mother, your mistress, and make much of her" (I.i.73-74). The farewell between Helena and Parolles that follows parodies Bertram's patronizing air, from the opening gambit:

> *Par.* Save you, fair queen!
> *Hel.* And you, monarch!
> *Par.* No.
> *Hel.* And no.
>
>   (I.i.104-07)

to the valedictory:

> *Par.* Little Helen, farewell. If I can remember thee, I will think of thee at court.
> *Hel.* Monsieur Parolles, you were born under a charitable star.
>
>   (I.i.184-87)

That in the presence of the despised Parolles Helena relaxes the guard she had earlier maintained, and that his absurd meditation on virginity proves more fruitful advice than the elders' precepts, only increases the apparent distance between Helena and the nobles, a distance that her earlier silence and tears had suggested.

Parolles's fall from grace likewise mirrors Bertram's. In the same scene in which Bertram's presumption earns the King's rebuke, the Captain runs afoul of Lafew for forgetting his proper place:

> *Laf.* Your lord and master did well to make his recantation.
> *Par.* Recantation! My lord! My master!
> *Laf.* Ay. Is it not a language I speak?
> *Par.* A most harsh one, and not to be understood without bloody succeeding. My master!
> *Laf.* Are you companion to the Count Rossillion?
> *Par.* To any Count; to all Counts; to what is man.
> *Laf.* To what is Count's man.
>
>   (II.iii.186-94)

Lafew objects less to Parolles's outlandish garb and manner than to the pretensions to equality with his social superiors which the manner and garb signify: "Why dost thou garter up thy arms a' this fashion? Dost make hose of thy sleeves? Do other servants so? . . . You are more saucy with lords and honourable personages than the commission of your birth gives you heraldry" (II.iii.245-58). In this sauciness Parolles copies Bertram, yet reverses the attitude of his fellow-commoner, Helena. In his own humiliation Parolles seconds Bertram's resolve to flee "to those Italian fields / Where noble fellows strike" (II.iii.286-87), strengthening the parallel.

Throughout the third and fourth acts, each step of the French lord's plot against Parolles immediately precedes the corresponding step in Helena's winning of Bertram. In the final two scenes of act 3, the lords unfold their scheme to Bertram and enlist his aid, and Helena does the same with Diana and the Widow. Act 4 begins with the ambush of Parolles, and his vow to reveal "all the secrets of their camp" (IV.i.84), a promise that seals his fate as surely as Bertram's gift of his family ring and promise of a rendezvous seals his in the scene following. In act 4, scene 3, the parallel lines converge. Not only does Bertram report his nocturnal meeting, which the audience knows to be the last stage of Helena's plan, but Parolles's exposure becomes the exposure of both wayward youths. Although they would have Bertram believe that they aim at Parolles only "for the love of laughter" (III.ii.32), among themselves the French lords "would gladly see his company anatomiz'd, that he might take the measure of his own judgements" (IV.iii.30-32). Their disapproval of Bertram's conduct with Helena and Diana, his concern over the Captain's confession, "Nothing of me, has a'?" (IV.iii.109), the pointed warning that "If your lordship be in't, as I believe you are, you must have the patience to hear it" (IV.iii.111-12), the aptness of Parolles's slanderous portrait of the Count as "a foolish idle boy, but for all that very ruttish" (IV.iii.207), and the contrast between Bertram's rage and his companions' amusement at the slanders, all serve to unite the two youths in folly.

Once the time comes for Parolles and Bertram to answer for these equivalent offenses, the parallel abruptly breaks off. In the soliloquy that follows his exposure, Parolles seems beyond chastisement:

> Yet am I thankful. If my heart were great
> 'Twould burst at this. Captain I'll be no more,
> But I will eat and drink and sleep as soft
> As captain shall. Simply the thing I am
> Shall make me live. Who knows himself a
>   braggart,
> Let him fear this; for it shall come to pass
> That every braggart shall be found an ass.
> Rust, sword; cool, blushes; and Parolles live
> Safest in shame; being fool'd, by fool'ry thrive.
> There's place and means for every man alive.
> I'll after them.
>
> (IV.iii.319-29)

Nevertheless, his offenses earn him the lowest place and the poorest means. When he reappears in the fifth act, he shows respect even to the Clown, whom he had earlier patronized: "Good Master Lavatch, give my Lord Lafew this letter; I have ere now, sir, been better known to you, when I have held familiarity with fresher clothes; but I am now, sir, muddied in Fortune's mood, and smell somewhat strong of her strong displeasure" (V.ii.1-5). In the same scene, he abjectly confesses to Lafew, "O, my good Lord, you were the first that found me"

(V.ii.41). He acknowledges Bertram as his master in the trial scene, and that Lafew will see to it that atonement follows conviction of sin and repentance is apparent from the charge he gives his newest servant as they observe the lovers reunited: "Good Tom Drum, lend me a handkercher. So, I thank thee. Wait on me at home, I will make sport with thee. Let thy curtsies alone, they are scurvy ones" (V.iii.315-18).

Bertram sins more than this and suffers less. He arrives at Rossillion unmuddied, spared the "exceeding posting day and night" (V.i.1) that Helena endured, needing no letter to the King, and in the height of fashionable attire. In the trial scene, Parolles suffers the contempt of Diana, Lafew, the King, and even Bertram, while Bertram lies, contemns, slanders, but finally embraces Helena. In the absence of Parolles, one might call the treatment that Bertram receives mercy; the Captain's presence makes it something less attractive than that. . . .

ENDINGS

Robert Grams Hunter, W. W. Lawrence, Hazelton Spencer, and Robert H. Hethmon concur that the ending of the play is perfectly acceptable. Hunter, Lawrence, and Spencer argue that Shakespeare's audience would have been satisfied with the ending. Hethmon argues that Bertram endures enough suffering to effect a change in his character and thus makes his union with Helena at the end plausible. Michael Shapiro argues that although Helena has succeeded in fulfilling the terms of Bertram's letter, she has failed to secure his love after all until he forgives her and they serve as each other's mutual redeemer. **Gerard J. Gross** argues that the ending is plausible, but the future happiness of Helena and Bertram will likely be a more subdued one than usually dictated by a romantic comedy.

Susan Snyder, Kenneth Muir, and Katharine Eisaman Maus disagree. Snyder and Muir find the lack of a significant speech of endorsement by Bertram of Helena one of the main elements contributing to the unsatisfactory ending. Maus finds the ending of the play considerably arbitrary and without resolution. Throughout the play, Maus argues, our narrative expectations are consistently dashed, and just when a promised ending seems to emerge, especially for Helena, she must regroup and expend more energy and effort to get the desired result. Gerard J. Gross argues that just when we are ready to accept a changed and redeemed Bertram at the end of the play (the King has forgiven him, he has agreed to marry Lafeu's daughter), Diana enters and we see once again the more base nature of his character.

Act IV, scene i. Parolles, Lord, and soldiers. The University of Michigan Special Collections Library.

Although Muir and Robert Hapgood agree that the ending, as it was written by Shakespeare, is lacking, a good performance on stage might help remedy that deficiency. Gross notes that the casting of Bertram is central to how the audience reacts to the ending of the play.

Gerard J. Gross

SOURCE: "The Conclusion to *All's Well That Ends Well*," in *Studies in English Literature*, Vol. 23, No. 2, Spring, 1983, pp. 257-76.

[*In this essay, Gross traces the events of the play leading up to its conclusion, especially emphasizing how we must have some sense of progress in the love between Helena and Bertram if we are to understand the end of the play. He argues that there is indeed evidence that Bertram has come to love Helena, making the ending more plausible despite its brevity and continued lack of physical expression of affection between the two. He also examines the subplot of Parolles in its effect on the ending of the play, arguing that it injects some much-needed optimism.*]

The web of our life is a mingled yarn, good and ill together: Our virtues would be proud if our faults

whipt them not, and our crimes would despair, if they were not cherish'd by our virtues.

First Lord

The title of *All's Well That Ends Well*, a title which epitomizes comic or romantic endings, invites us to pay special attention to the ending of *this* play, to examine it against the norm of comic ending. Some critics take the sense of the title at face value, and believe with Hazelton Spencer that all does indeed end well, that "the play's title clinches the argument against its detractors." Others would see the meaning as wholly ironic, or would agree with the reviewer of a 1959 Tyrone Guthrie production that the play "raises a dozen issues, only to drop them all with a cynical, indifferent 'all's well that ends well'." The intent of this study will be to examine not simply whether all ends well, for our reactions at the end of any play are often complex, but rather what factors in the play and its ending contribute to our total response to the ending. I hope in my analysis to emphasize effects which were intended by Shakespeare, and to be comprehensive enough to avoid the criticism Richard Levin raises against an ironic approach which "operates at such a high level of abstraction that it can easily pass over such concrete details as the dramatic rhythm and its emotional effect." I will be very much concerned with "dramatic" aspects of the play, not only with what is said, but with how it is said, with action, with characterization, and with rhythm or pacing in the ending.

Previous studies of the ending of *All's Well* have concentrated on some limited aspect of the ending. Roger Warren's analysis in 1969 emphasized the light which the sonnets shed on the characteristic of Helena's love and Bertram's reaction to it. More recently, Ian Donaldson has found throughout the play a concentration on endings and beginnings, on ends and the means to those ends. His article, though intimately concerned with the problem of "ending well," does not devote extensive detail to the final scene itself. I would look on my attempt to analyze the entire context of the ending of *All's Well* as a means of complementing and extending these previous analyses.

A close look at the title can help identify two separate, though related, aspects of comic ending which will play an important role in the discussion to follow, for the cliché, "all's well that ends well," can be taken in two distinct senses. First, comedies and romances usually entail a great many complications, reversals, and perils before a resolution and happy conclusion are reached. Where the pure spirit of comedy reigns, the ending generates a feeling that all that went before can be reckoned at naught as long as the story has ended happily. The trials and tribulations are worth it. It is the end that counts—the sense of Helena's statement midway through the play:

All's well that ends well! still the fine's the
   crown;
What e'er the course, the end is the renown.
                                   (IV.iv.35-36)

An emphasis on the "all" of "all's well that ends well"
yields a second sense of the phrase, one close to the
notion "they all lived happily ever after." In romances and
fairy tales, and in comedies derived from these types,
audiences are invited to believe that the marriage or reunion at the end is the panacea to all problems raised in
the story, and that thereby future happiness is assured.
Because the story ends well— in marriage or betrothal—
all *will be* well. Beyond the end of the story lies a prospect
of nothing but bliss. These two aspects of the title are
related: the stronger the feeling that the final happiness
has conquered any sadness or anxiety encountered during
the story, the stronger will be our conviction that the
happiness will endure. Conversely, if we are somehow led
to suspect that the goal for which the hero or heroine has
travailed so arduously has not been worth the effort— as
E. K. Chambers reacts to Helena's conquest, "but after all
it is a poor prize for which she has trailed her honour in
the dust"— we would also be inclined to have some doubts
about the future happiness of that hero or heroine.

A question that may legitimately be raised is whether we
are ever justified in speculating on the future happiness of
the hero and heroine in a story such as *All's Well*. thomas
Marc Parrott voices a stricture against peering beyond the
end of the play:

> We may be fairly sure that Shakespeare's audience
> accepted the performance as an entertaining example
> of the old saying: 'all's well that ends well'. To ask
> whether the marriage of such an ill-matched pair was
> likely to be a happy one is to confuse drama with
> contemporary life, much in the fashion of a small boy
> at a performance of *Hamlet* who asked his father why
> Mr. Evans didn't marry Ophelia.

Yet, though it is undoubtedly over-naive to confuse drama
and real life, it would also seem overly simplistic to rule
out from drama or fiction any concern whatever for what
happens beyond the end of a story. The writer of romance is generally not concerned about the psychological
plausibility of events or of their consequences. If he tells
us that the villain was suddenly converted, we believe him.
And if he tells us that the couple lived happily ever after,
we have no reason to doubt his word. But in a story
where psychological plausibility has a legitimate place, where
the motivation of characters is a clear concern of the
author, and where the characters themselves examine or
question their beliefs, feelings, or reasons for action, we
have every reason to question the plausibility of the ending. This is not to say that we should speculate about
some specific action of a character well beyond the conclusion of the plot. But if an author tries to tell us, "The
marriage was a happy one," while the characters them-

selves, by their behavior or by what they tell us of themselves, preclude the possibility of that ever being so, we
can well question the artistic integrity of the ending. As
Barbara Smith points out in her study of poetic closure,
marriage may not be an effective theme of closure when
all that follows after marriage is not felt by the reader to
be predictable.

These distinctions suggest that our response to the ending
of *All's Well* depends to a large extent on what kind of
play it is. For the most part, critics who see no real
problems with the ending are those who are satisfied with
a limited interpretation of the play, usually with an emphasis on romantic fable, or those who would emphasize the
difference between the expectations of Elizabethan audiences and of modern audiences.

Thus, for Hazelton Spencer, "it was in a later age, when
the old romances were no longer human nature's daily
food, that it occurred to anyone to question whether the
ending is really a happy one." There is a danger, however,
of underestimating both the sophistication of Elizabethan
audiences and of Shakespeare's intentions in the drama.
Joseph Price, in his thorough review of critical reaction to
All's Well, has identified six categories of interpretations of
the play: "farcical comedy, sentimental romance, romantic
fable, serious drama, cynical satire, and a thematic dramatization." After presenting capsule summaries of the play
as it might be acted with each of the six major interpretations dominant, Price concludes as follows:

> Such constricted interpretations of *All's Well* have
> achieved at times a unity of form, but only at the
> expense of Shakespeare's intention, only by distortion
> of his play. For, the very recurrence of six major ap-
> proaches throughout its history suggests a complexity
> which cannot legitimately be reduced to a single focus.
> . . . . Criticism generally has insisted that these ele-
> ments jar, that only by the elimination of several can
> an artistic unity be imposed. But the very essence of
> Shakespearean comedy is variety, a blending of seem-
> ingly jarring worlds.

I would agree, with Price, on the valid existence in *All's
Well* of all the elements identified here. There may even
be a certain unity or artistic coherence in the very juxtaposition of romance and realism in the play, in the tension
between these aspects. G. B. Harrison has stated of *All's
Well* that Shakespeare "has asked himself the question: if
this story had really happened, what sort of people would
these characters have been?" As I hope to show, not only
in character portrayal, but in other aspects of romance,
particularly that of the typical happy ending, Shakespeare
seems to be holding the conventions up to the scrutiny of
realism.

In examining the aspects of romance and realism, it is
particularly important to recognize the difference between the play itself and the romance narrative from
which the plot is drawn. If we look specifically at the

ending of *All's Well,* in terms of simple plot line we recognize the conclusion of a traditional "fulfillment of the tasks" episode, of which Boccaccio's tale of "Giletta of Narbona" is the nearest source. A nobleman, forced to marry a woman beneath him in rank, imposes on her what he thinks are impossible conditions before he will accept her love. The woman cleverly and resourcefully fulfills the conditions, and the nobleman, faced with her presentation of the *fait accompli,* is moved to a change of heart, agrees to love her, and they live happily ever after. At the level of Boccaccio's tale we are not inclined to inquire about the motivation of either person in loving or not loving, about the worthiness or unworthiness of either person for the other's love, or about whether we have a right to suppose that they really did live happily ever after. If the ending of the story, including the hero's change of heart, occurs abruptly, our attention is not attracted to it in the fable because of the pace of the entire fable. But if we attend with some degree of sensitivity to the play *All's Well,* I would maintain that on all the accounts mentioned above we have, at least potentially, some cause to pause and wonder. Because the characters have come alive for us, have involved us in their motivations throughout the play, and because the play seriously addresses such themes as the problem of birth versus merit, the role of the woman as pursuer, and the differing male and female perspectives on honor, we find ourselves, with justification, concerned at the end of the play with how believable Bertram's conversion is, how believable Helena's and Bertram's love for each other is, and whether we are meant to feel that their lives *will* be happy ever after. And if events seem to conclude abruptly, we are warranted in asking why, or to what effect, since the rest of the play has been developed at a comparatively sophisticated level of psychological and motivational detail.

The potential problems with the ending, then, cluster around the two distinct, yet closely related aspects of the conclusion: the effect of the actions of both Bertram and Helena near the end on their relationship with one another, and the brevity or abruptness of the conclusion, especially the thirty lines after Helena's final entry. Since Bertram, but not Helena, is on stage in the last scene before the final thirty lines, it is natural to start with his part in the scene.

Bertram has been castigated by numerous critics, beginning with Samuel Johnson, and has been defended by others as an acceptable romantic hero, even as "almost a model youth." One way of getting close to Shakespeare's intentions in establishing Bertram as a romantic hero is by comparing his treatment of Bertram with that of Beltramo in the source story by Boccaccio, retold by William Painter. The final episode of "Giletta of Narbona" is the aspect of the tale most modified by Shakespeare. In the original tale, after Giletta has obtained the ring and conceived twin sons, Beltramo hears

that she has left Rossiglione, and he returns there, taking his place as rightful lord, and presumably ruling in prosperity for several years. Giletta, after having borne twin sons, returns to Rossiglione, arriving at an All Saints Day feast, at which are present many ladies and knights. Falling prostrate at the count's feet, Giletta begs to be received as his wife, and tells the whole story of how she fulfilled the conditions. (Though her dialogue is not repeated in the tale, we can imagine this retelling taking a long time, and the count gradually responding with greater and greater admiration.) Beltramo reacts in a way that in no way diminishes his stature, but rather raises him in our esteem at the end:

> For which cause the Counte knowing the thinges she had spoken, to be true (and perceiving her constant minde, and good witte, and the twoo faire young boyes to kepe his promise made, and to please his subjectes, & the Ladies that made sute unto him, to accept her from that tyme foorth, as his lawefull wife, and to honour her) abjected his obstinate rigour: causing her to rise up, and imbraced and kissed her, acknowledging her againe for his lawefull wyfe. And after he had apparelled her, according to her estate, to the great pleasure and contentation of those that were there, & of al his other frendes not onely that daye, but many others, he kept great chere, and from that time forth, hee loved and honoured her, as his dere spouse and wyfe.

Shakespeare, however, instead of allowing Helena simply to appear before Bertram and beg to be received by him, as in the original tale, devises the entire episode where Diana confronts Bertram with the evidence of their supposed affair. By so doing, Shakespeare, instead of heightening Bertram's stature as "romantic hero," permits him to sink lower and lower in our estimation and in that of the characters of the play who are present. Even more significant, Bertram's exposure occurs just at that point in the play where he is *beginning* to rise in esteem. At the opening of Act V, the King is ready to allow Bertram a new start:

> My honor'd lady,
> I have forgiven and forgotten all,
> Though my revenges were high bent upon
>   him,
> And watch'd the time to shoot.
>
> (V.iii.8-11)

The Countess and Lafew argue that Bertram's deeds were "done i' th' blade of youth" (V.iii.6) and are ready to give him the chance to prove himself wiser and more virtuous. We are at that stage in the plot where a typical romance might show the hero reformed, reconciled to the heroine, and where we would, with reason, expect him from that time forth to love and honor her as his dear spouse and wife. If Helena entered at this moment, we would have a typical happy ending with little to complain about other than its being somewhat expected and lacking in suspense.

But Shakespeare consciously (since it required considerable change from the original plot) chose *not* to end the play at this point. First Lafew, then the King, then the Countess notice that Bertram has Helena's ring, and Bertram tells a half-truth to explain his way out. Then Diana enters, and Bertram lies, then lies again in futile attempts to defend himself. His stature diminishes perilously from the promise shown at the beginning of the scene. It is obvious that Bertram has lost his composure and is thoroughly rattled: "*Countess.* He blushes, and 'tis hit" (V.iii.195). "*King.* You boggle shrewdly, every feather starts you" (V.iii.232). What sort of candidate is this lying, shaken creature for the "happily ever after" romantic ending? Bertram bears little resemblance to Beltramo, and seems to have gone far beyond the "few mistakes before he straightens out and settles down" posited for the romantic hero by Spencer.

We might sense in Bertram's degradation a degree of burlesque of romantic heroes and plots, a deliberate inversion of the expected progress of a romantic hero. Viewed against the ideal image of a romantic hero, Bertram's actions have a comic cast. One can imagine a performance in which the actor, taking a cue from the King's "You boggle shrewdly," stutters and overplays his responses in an obvious, desperate attempt to fabricate a story. Yet the comic aspect can be carried too far. The more we laugh at Bertram, the less believable he is as a beloved of Helena. A totally comic, over-acted Bertram would destroy any sense of romantic reconciliation between Helena and Bertram in their final reunion.

The question of how Bertram can be what he is, and still be attractive to Helena is, indeed, one of the knottiest in the play, and it is a problem demanding the utmost sense of balance in the actor playing the part of Bertram. Bertram has so many faults that it would be easy to play him at the opposite extreme, not as a comic figure, but as a totally unsympathetic character— an arrogant, conceited, headstrong, lecherous, deceitful, shallow cad. Such a characterization would likewise make Helena's love for Bertram look absurd. There are, however, clear indications in the text that Bertram possesses attractive qualities. A key scene is Helena's arrival in Florence. We learn immediately from Diana that Bertram has indeed shown the bravery, won the "honor," which he had dreamed of. Perhaps most significant is Diana's spontaneous exclamation at Bertram's appearance as the French soldiers march by (even though she has been warned of his dishonest solicitations):

> 'tis a most gallant
> fellow.
> I would he lov'd his wife. If he were

> honester
> He were much goodlier. Is't not a handsome
> gentleman?
>
> (III.v.78-80)

This is in one sense a variation upon the statement of the First Lord, "The web of our life is of a mingled yarn, good and ill together" (IV.iii.71-72). But its principal effect is to emphasize the credibility of Bertram as an object of Helena's love. Throughout the play, despite Bertram's dishonorable acts, there must be that flair, that presence— and it must show through in the acting of the part— that elicits the response, "'tis a most gallant fellow."

If Bertram is, at least to some degree, credible as a person whom Helena might love, what can be said of the course of that love throughout the play? It is crucial for an understanding of the conclusion of the play to have some sense of the progress of the love between Bertram and Helena. I would like to turn, therefore, to a closer look at Helena, first at her love for Bertram, and then at her as a possible object of Bertram's love.

In Helena's meditation on Bertram in the first scene she appears the typical young romantic heroine, perhaps slightly self-consciously so, and concerned perhaps too much with appearance:

> 'Twas pretty, though a plague
> To see him every hour, to sit and draw
> His arched brows, his hawking eye, his curls.
>
> (I.i.92-94)

She is at once idealistic and adolescent in her adoration, and also aware of her excesses. If Bertram is unseasoned, Helena is also, in matters of love. Both will mature; their romantic ideals will be tempered in the course of the play.

After Bertram's shameful treatment of Helena following the marriage, we may have difficulty understanding her unswerving adulation for him, expressed immediately after reading his disdainful letter to her at Rossilion:

> Poor Lord, is't I
> That chase thee from thy country, and expose
> Those tender limbs of thine to the event
> Of the none-sparing war?
>
> (III.ii.102-105)

Helena here lapses into romantic sentiment similar to that expressed in the first scene, and we may find that the dichotomy between what we know of Bertram and how Helena responds to him makes this one of the most difficult moments of the play. However, this soliloquy again reinforces the feeling that Bertram possesses some quality which inspires such devotion.

In the bed-trick episode, Bertram reaches a low in honor, which contrasts with his "honorable service" on the battle-field, when he parts with the family ring in exchange for an expected night with Diana. We do not, of course, witness the bed scene with Helena, but we are allowed as close an approach as possible to the event, one which pushes Elizabethan decorum to the limit, in Helena's re-flections after lying with Bertram. Her comments in IV.iv are significant in two ways. They serve to emphasize the distance of this play from pure romantic fable, a story told for story's sake. The play is at this point perhaps farthest removed in spirit from its source tale. Can we imagine any heroine in a romance reflecting and express-ing her thoughts in terms such as these?

> But O, strange men,
> That can such sweet use make of what they
>   hate,
> When saucy trusting of the cozen'd thoughts
> Defiles the pitchy night; so lust doth play
> With what it loathes for that which is away—
> But more of this hereafter.
>
> (IV.iv.21-26)

Here Helena, aware that Bertram's sexual advances were made to one he thought to be Diana, most vividly reveals herself capable of feelings, reflections, and changes of mood. It is this change of mood that is the second important aspect of this speech. There is present an unmistakable sense of disillusion which contrasts sharply with Helena's earlier idolatry of Bertram. She has heard talk, from the women of Florence, of Bertram's lust; now she has experienced it herself. What a contrast this first union of Helena and Bertram is to the typical romantic meeting of lovers, and what a contrast to the union she would have idealized in her daydreams at Rossilion. It has been a union from which their child will be born, but on Bertram's part there has been no love in it, only lust. Helena, it is true, takes up the pursuit with her customary zeal— "All's well that ends well yet" (V.i.25)— but I would claim that from this point on some doubt has been cast, in Helena's mind, on whether the prize will, in fine, be worth the effort of the chase.

The words "prize" and "chase" underscore the fact that in this play it is definitely the woman who takes the initiative in seeking a mate. This active role of Helena has, however, been overplayed by some ana-lysts. One strain of criticism sees her as relentlessly pursuing Bertram by a plan carefully thought out and consciously executed at every point in the play. Thus, for E. K. Chambers, Shakespeare has turned "man's tender helpmate, like Mr. Bernard Shaw's Anne Whitefield, into the keen and unswerving huntress of man." Bertrand Evans has espoused this view of Hel-ena (though her pursuit is seen as ultimately for the good of Bertram), and a recent article by Richard A. Levin carries the interpretation of Helena as deceptive schemer to even greater extremes. Such an interpreta-tion, however, though supportable at certain points in the play, strains for credibility at other points, and even posits a kind of perversion of theatrical conventions. Moreover, this view of Helena as huntress does little to make her a plausible object of Bertram's love at the end of the play.

Granted that Helena is the initiator of the "romance" with Bertram, her dominant qualities appear to be vi-tality (we have seen the like in Bertram), shown both in her actions and her speech, and a remarkable re-sourcefulness— an ability to spot and take advantage of circumstances to further her ends. An important ex-ample of this is the scene of Helena's first arrival in Florence. After some discussion of a countryman of Helena's, it is the widow, and not Helena, who first suggests the possibility of Diana's aiding Bertram's wife to regain her husband: "This young maid might do her / A shrewd turn, if she pleas'd" (III.v.67-68). The story of what unfolds after Helena's meeting with the women of Florence is much more plausible, as well as more fascinating and appealing, if seen as an instance of Helena's exceptional ability to seize the occasion and respond to opportunities as they arise, rather than as a plot preplanned in every detail. Up to at least this point in the play the evidence suggests that Shakespeare in-tended Helena as an engaging, sympathetic character, whose love includes a strong concern for the good and happiness of Bertram.

With the information from the widow that Bertram is soliciting Diana's favors, Helena's ready wit conceives the plan of having Diana agree to a meeting, and then substituting herself for Diana in the dark. At this point there is no doubt that the sudden prospect of fulfilling Bertram's seemingly impossible conditions is a strong motive for Helena. The conditions were stated as a cruel, cynical jest by Bertram; but since they were set down in writing, she will hold him to them, if she can. Yet even here, motives of Bertram's better welfare are not entirely absent. Bertram is, after all, bent on com-mitting adultery. Conveniently, Helena can save Bertram from sin in deed, if not in intent, while at the same time fulfilling his conditions. By this time she is clearly bent on helping herself to win a husband. However, the progress of her pursuit has not manifested the stealthy, predatory quality that many commentators find so unlikeable.

The final scene of the play, when Bertram is con-fronted with his misdeeds, contains the instance where Helena's scheming is the most deliberate and calculat-ing. We can ask, now, what effect the actions of this final scene have on Helena's character and on the possibility of Bertram's loving her. Whatever her mo-tivation, Helena has placed Bertram in an extremely tight spot in the moments before the conclusion of the play. It has been observed that Helena's absence from the stage till the final moments, with Diana managing the exposure of Bertram (after the careful instructions of Helena, of course), keeps our sympathies from being turned too strongly from Helena. This piece of plotting is theatrically effective in keeping our attention from Helena; yet she *is* the person directly responsible for planning Bertram's confrontation with his own misdeeds.

Helena's actions are explained by some critics on the basis that Bertram must reach some extreme limit of psychological or moral shock before he can be "converted" by the virtuous or providential Helena. Her motives are mainly a redemption of Bertram. As Harold Wilson says,

> Helena in *All's Well* is not seeking justice of the King but Bertram's love. In Boccaccio's tale, the heroine's fulfillment of the tasks is enough to win her happy union with the hero. In Shakespeare, Helena's efforts would go for nothing did not Bertram experience a change of heart. In the climax, everything is directed toward this end; and this is the abundant psychological justification of the means used, for Bertram is still far from penitent as we see him in the opening of the last scene.

Yet there is evidence that Bertram has come to love Helena, evidence that occurs well before Bertram is faced with Helena's reappearance. At the beginning of the last scene, when Bertram first meets the King, under no prompting or pressure, in the course of explaining a previous affection for Lafew's daughter, he refers to Helena:

> Thence it came
> That she whom all men prais'd, and whom myself,
> Since I have lost, have lov'd.
>
> (V.iii.52-54)

Though the reference is made obliquely, Shakespeare seems to have intended the audience to advert to it, for he has the King repeat the reference to Bertram's love for Helena, and so reinforce the impression:

> Well excus'd.
> That thou didst love her, strikes some scores away
> From the great compt.
>
> (V.iii.55-57)

Shakespeare, then, seems to have fashioned the latter part of the play as it relates to Bertram's love for Helena with the following effects. The audience is told that Bertram has finally come to love Helena— and this in conditions in which they would have no strong reasons to suspect the statement. Then Bertram undergoes the unexpected reversals, some schemed by Helena, that lead up to her sudden appearance. At this point,

Bertram has lied himself into a position from which he cannot escape without help. He is, independent of what Helena's intentions are, trapped. There is nothing *in what immediately preceded*, or in what Helena has contrived, to motivate Bertram's love or to support our belief that he means his later claim to love her "ever dearly." Yet we know from his previous statement that he did profess to love her. He is at one and the same time in a state of having previously inclined towards love of Helena, yet forced to submit by actions which have not served to reinforce that love, but if anything, to undermine it. Bertram could not be blamed if he went back on his statement at the beginning of this scene and turned a cold heart towards Helena.

Furthermore, Bertram has lied so much that he is in danger of being in the position where no one will believe *anything* he says thereafter, much like the shepherd in the fable who cried "Wolf! Wolf!" On Helena's part, though Bertram had shown qualities that made her love for him believable, most recently he has behaved so despicably that we are entitled to serious doubts about how Helena or anyone could now accept and cherish such a creature. She has already expressed signs of disillusionment after her midnight tryst with Bertram. The possibility of a "happily ever after" ending may still be within reach, but considerable dialogue and action would seem to be needed to present such a happy ending convincingly to an audience. Yet, as presented by Shakespeare, what do we have? Thirty lines of compressed dialogue, much of it stated in negative or conditional language. A close analysis of the final section of the dialogue will help identify some of the effects it produces.

First, I have noted an apparent change in Helena's attitude towards Bertram with her earlier words, "But O, strange men." I would maintain that this same bitter-sweet mood, tinged with melancholy, is manifested in the final scene. Helena's entry is not triumphant, jubilant. Her opening words, spoken to the King, are

> No, my good lord,
> 'Tis but the shadow of a wife you see,
> The name, and not the thing.
>
> (V.iii.306-308)

Though the sense refers directly to the fact that her marriage (in Bertram's and the world's eyes) was never consummated, is there not some connotation that she will never now quite attain "the thing" of wife-hood, the ideal of love she had sought so earnestly? The words imply that her love is now but a shadow of what it once was. Her words to Bertram,

> O my good lord, when I was like this maid,
> I found you wondrous kind,
>
> (V.iii.309-10)

do not overtly claim that he is *not* "wondrous kind" now, but the implication is there. Helena has fulfilled the conditions, reached her goal—

> There is your ring,
> And look you, here's your letter. This it says:
> "When from my finger you can get this ring,
> And are by me with child, etc." This is done.
> (V.iii.310-13)

But missing is the sense of victory we may have earlier been led to expect from her words, "the fine's the crown . . . the end is the renown." One senses a hint of weariness at so long and arduous a chase after an object of ever diminishing brightness and value.

As for Bertram, we might ask what effects in his final words lend credibility to his professions of repentance and love. One way in which a character caught in falsehood might convince his hearers that what he now says should be believed is by lengthy explanations, giving reasons for his past conduct and emphatic assurance of reform in the future. But the very opposite strikes us in the concluding lines of the play. The extreme brevity of both Bertram's and Helena's speeches contrasts with the duration of dialogue we might expect, given the seriousness of the complications to be resolved. Some critics have seen this brevity as a defect on Shakespeare's part. For example, Kenneth Muir would have preferred more explanation by Bertram— "If the clown were given better jokes and Bertram a better speech at the end, the play would leave us with feelings of greater satisfaction." On the positive side, it must be conceded that seeing and hearing the actor express repentance can make the scene more effective on the stage than in reading. Also on the side of believability for Bertram, his speech patterns, despite the brevity, have a ring of sincerity. The repetitions— "Both, both. O, pardon!" and "I'll love her dearly, ever, ever dearly"— seem intended by Shakespeare as an earnest mode of speech. A similar example might be Cordelia's "No cause, no cause" (*Lear*, IV.vii.74).

Yet, in spite of these positive aspects, there is still a sense of something missing from Bertram's protestations. They lack weight: three lines in all to accomplish repentance, reconciliation, and assurance of love. Also countering the earnestness given the lines by the repetition of words is the curious fact that Bertram's expression of love is stated as a condition:

> If she, my liege, can make me know this clearly,
> I'll love her dearly, ever, ever dearly.

> (V.iii.315-16)

Even more curious, these words are spoken not to Helena, the one he is professing to love, but to the King. Bertram's *only* statement directly to Helena is the brief "Both, both. O, pardon!" Despite the desirability of not allowing the audience to dwell too much on Bertram's faults, it would have been easy for Shakespeare, if he had wanted, to have given Bertram more words, if not of explanation, at least of positive profession of his love.

If Bertram's dialogue is brief, Helena's is somewhat fuller. There exists, however, the same shortage of direct address to Bertram, and the same conditional tone. Her first words, on entering, are addressed not to Bertram, but to the King, which may be natural enough, since the King raises the question, "Is't real that I see?" (V.iii.306). But then, in response to Bertram's conditional statement of love, her reply is phrased not only as a condition, but also in strongly negative words:

> If it appear not plain and prove untrue,
> Deadly divorce step between me and you!
> (V.iii.317-18)

The conditional phrasing may be meant, in part, with the rhyming couplets, to balance Bertram's statement. But if the balance and repetition have any effect of emphasis, what they call attention to is the very conditional nature of the statements. Then, after Helena's statement, "Deadly divorce step between me and you," almost in the same breath it would seem, Helena turns to the Countess and exclaims, "O my dear mother, do I see you living?" (V.iii.319). The Countess's love for Helena must, of course, be acknowledged; but the quickness with which Helena turns from Bertram to the Countess says little for the capability of Bertram to hold her attention.

Finally, Helena's attention to the Countess raises the interesting question of when, if at all, Helena and Bertram might be expected to embrace. If the words of the conclusion are abrupt, but the playwright intended a fully genuine feeling that all is well, we could expect this to be shown by a kiss and embrace between Bertram and Helena. But if one reads the final lines beginning from Helena's "No, my good lord, / 'Tis but the shadow of a wife you see," to the end, and tries to imagine plausible stage action, there is no moment when Helena and Bertram might reasonably embrace without doing violence to the dialogue or interrupting it awkwardly with stage action. Bertram might fall on his knees with "Both, both. O, pardon!" but it is difficult to imagine them kissing at this point. The last plausible moment when they might embrace is at Helena's final words to Bertram, "Deadly divorce step between me and you!" Fine words on which to hug and kiss. We can imagine Helena falling on the Countess's neck at the words, "O my dear mother, do I see you living?," but not upon Bertram's neck.

The inescapable impression from the final thirty lines is one of a deliberate holding back of effects which could easily have produced a much more convincing, resounding ring of all being well than we now have in the play. One feels that Shakespeare has taken the standard romantic happy ending, and if not stood it on its head, has at least abbreviated it and diluted its impact so much that we are forced to question whether the simple fact that hero and heroine are united at the end is any guarantee of their achievement of happiness. If such is the effect of the ending, is it to be seen as entirely skeptical on Shakespeare's part? An example of Northrop Frye's category of irony; a cynical demonstration of the impossibility of all ending well? Thus far in this analysis I have discussed solely the main plot, and have said nothing of the subplot of Parolles. I believe, however, that this subplot has an important role in the play, not only thematically, but also in determining how the ending works.

Though Parolles is undoubtedly a secondary character, he is in some ways the most memorable in *All's Well*. Whatever else may be said of Parolles, he is not lacking in faults. He is boastful, vain, ostentatious, untruthful, lecherous, and under all that, cowardly. Do we like him? Well, yes. Our sympathies turn more towards him after his exposure; but even at his worst he has a quality that attracts us to him. As Helena remarks early in the play,

> Yet these fix'd evils sit so fit in him
> That they take place when virtue's steely
>   bones
> Looks bleak i' th' cold wind.
>
> (I.i.102-104)

But what primarily maintains our liking for Parolles is his vitality of spirit. Parolles is enthusiastic; he lives. He may be eager about the wrong things— the latest clothes; the latest words; the esteem of the court; the esteem of his fellow soldiers— but he is constantly eager. His vitality virtually bursts its bonds when he senses the chance of accompanying Bertram to the Tuscan wars: "To th' wars, my boy, to th' wars!" (II.iii.278). Perhaps Parolles's vitality shows forth most prominently in his language. Though he is an aspirer after the status of courtier, and though being fashionable is of highest concern, he is no Witwoud, no *mere* imitator of the fashionable wit of others. Even when being held blindfolded at the hands of his supposed captors, the inventiveness of his language is irrepressible. Descriptions such as his claim of the first Captain Dumaine's corruptibility— "Sir, for a cardecue he will sell the fee-simple of his salvation, the inheritance of it, and cut th' entail from all remainders, and a perpetual succession for it perpetually" (IV.iii.278-81)— elicit the admiration of his captors: "He hath outvillain'd villainy so far, that the rarity redeems him" (IV.iii.273-74). Finally, and most important, when Parolles has been beaten as low as anyone can be, it is his supreme vitality that sparks his recovery.

Up to the beginning of Act IV we had seen much of Parolles the braggart. Now, in the first scene of Act IV, with Parolles on his solitary foray at night near enemy lines, we are allowed to peer a little into his soul. We find out that Parolles *realizes* he is a braggart and a coward: "I find my tongue is too foolhardy, but my heart hath the fear of Mars before it, and of his creatures, not daring the reports of my tongue. . . . What the devil should move me to undertake the recovery of this drum, being not ignorant of the impossibility, and knowing I had no such purpose?" (IV.i.28-36). With his overhearers we respond in amazement, "Is it possible he should know what he is, and be that he is?" (IV.i.44-45), and we may begin to have some compassion for Parolles.

The double-talk scenes are some of the funniest in Shakespeare, not only because of Parolles's wit in his responses, but because of the ironies and the asides of his captors. But when Parolles shows his abject cowardice, and when his blindfold is removed and he is completely humiliated by the revelation that his captors are his friends, the humor changes. We have an instance, common in Shakespeare, of a baiting where the edge is allowed to become too sharp. The departure first of Bertram and the Lords, and then of the Interpreter and Soldiers, becomes cruel. Parolles, left alone on stage to face his humiliation, is a pathetic sight. It would not be surprising if he were to remain crushed, completely undone. But there are still remnants of his irrepressible *esprit*. In his touching speech of self-knowledge and acceptance, he resolves to make the best of what he has:

> Yet am I thankful. If my heart were great,
> 'Twould burst at this. Captain I'll be no more.
> But I will eat and drink, and sleep as soft
> As captain shall. Simply the thing I am
> Shall make me live.
>   . . . . .
> Rust sword, cool blushes, and, Parolles, live
> Safest in shame! Being fool'd, by fool'ry thrive!
> There's place and means for every man alive.
> I'll after them.
>
> (IV.iii.330-40)

Parolles not only achieves self-acceptance; he is also accepted by Lafew, previously his sharpest critic. Though Lafew still teases Parolles, he concludes their meeting after Parolles's return affectionately and encouragingly: "Sirrah, inquire further after me. I had talk of you last night; though you are a fool and a knave you shall eat. Go to; follow" (V.ii.52-54). As E. M. Blistein observes of Parolles, "from artificial captain he has become a nobleman's genuine fool, and he does not mind. He is, in fact, grateful. The audience has laughed at him for pretending to be something he was not. Lafew henceforth will laugh with him for being what he is."

The parallel between Parolles's exposure and humiliation at the hands of his comrades and Bertram's later exposure at the hands of Diana has often been commented upon. Both are liars, and both are confronted directly with the evidence of their lies. There is stark irony in Bertram's disavowal of Parolles's testimony at the very moment when Bertram is speaking lies of much more serious consequences:

> He's quoted for a most perfidious slave,
> With all the spots a' th' world tax'd and
>   debosh'd.
> Whose nature sickens but to speak a truth.
> Am I that or this for what he'll utter,
> That will speak any thing?

> (V.iii.205-209)

The fact that Bertram has been blind enough to be "misled with a snipt-taffeta fellow" (IV.v.1-2) may lessen his stature in our eyes; yet it contributes to making his blindness to Helena's worth more believable. One might expect that being made aware of the possibility of deception by Parolles might open Bertram's eyes to his lack of perception elsewhere, specifically to the meanness of his behavior towards Helena. In fact, the failure of Bertram to profit from the lesson of Parolles has been seen by some critics as a flaw in the play. G. K. Hunter, for example, states that Parolles, as well as Helena, the Countess, the King, and Diana, all have to face an "acceptance of death leading to fuller life," a point of reconciliation "reached only by self-sacrifice, by an acceptance of oneself as outcast and despised." Hunter concludes, "that the pattern is not fully achieved by Bertram is the major thematic failure of the play." Shakespeare, however, chose not to complete the parallel in such a neat fashion as this.

Though a relationship between the lesson learned by Parolles in the sub-plot and the concluding action of the main plot is not made explicit by Shakespeare, the episode of Parolles is intended to affect the way the ending works for us. What the unmasking of Parolles and his conversion to foolery adds is a badly needed note of optimism. We have seen that Bertram and Helena have achieved, at the conclusion of the play, a state of outward, but not entirely convincing, reconciliation. The conclusion lacks the weight and positiveness required to assure us that all indeed will be well, given the obstacles that seem to exist to a happy union between Bertram and Helena. But this uncertainty is relieved by Parolles—by his presence and by the memory of his previous scenes.

Parolles does not have a part in the dialogue at the very conclusion of the play, the last thirty lines. Yet he is not only present, but definitely a part of the concluding action of the play. Shakespeare's technique here, though used with less emphasis, is reminiscent of his ending *Much Ado* with the conclusion of the Benedick-Beatrice story. He turns the audience's attention from potential problems to a more satisfying emotional resolution. Parolles, accepting himself as he is, had earlier been received into the graces of Lafew. Now our attention is again directed toward this part of the plot, though it is a sub-plot.

Lafew's final speech aids the conclusion in several ways. His emotional reaction, "Mine eyes smell onions, I shall weep anon" (V.iii.320), though comic, convinces us, as neither Bertrams's nor Helena's words have, that there *is* something genuine in this reunion. His request of a handkerchief from Parolles (rather than from someone else) is not without purpose: "Good Tom Drum, lend me a handkercher. So, I thank thee; wait on me home, I'll make sport with thee. Let thy curtsies alone, they are scurvy ones" (V.iii.321-24). The reference to "Good Tom Drum" is a brief reminder of the scenes where Parolles was humiliated because he offered to recapture his drum. The sight of Parolles dressed in smelly, muddy clothes is an additional reminder of his disgrace, and also of his self-acceptance. In the simple gesture of asking for a handkerchief, Lafew indicates his complete acceptance of Parolles. His scorn at the end is entirely good-humored, and his invitation to "make sport" is an invitation to laugh with him and not at him.

Parolles's "conversion" has helped establish the spirit of this comedy, and his presence in the last scene, a symbol of self-knowledge and self-acceptance, cannot but help influencing the audience's reaction to the scene. Even though Helena and Bertram do not make explicit application of Parolles's dictum, "There's place and means for every man alive," the audience should be in such a frame of mind. Bertram may have proved that Parolles's earlier description of him, "a foolish idle boy, but for all that very ruttish" (IV.iii.215-16), was all too true, and he may now, in Helena's eyes, be far from the romantic hero she had doted on. Helena, for all the fine qualities the Countess had admired in her, may have become too persistent in her pursuit in the end. "The web of our life is of a mingled yarn, good and ill together." But, if there's place and means for such as Parolles, there can well be place and means for such as Bertram and Helena to find happiness, in spite of their shortcomings.

In the ending of *All's Well*, Shakespeare seems to have directly confronted the traditional romantic ending, where the marriage or reunion of hero and heroine is assumed to guarantee that all problems are resolved and that bliss will ensue for ever after. The ending of *All's Well* is constructed so that we cannot possibly project for Bertram and Helena the ecstatic happiness of the traditional romance—the happiness that was perhaps naively expected by Helena at the start of the play. But neither is the play entirely cynical about any possibility of happiness. Helena has matured, and Bertram may at least be at the threshold of maturity. We may expect happiness, but a much more subdued happiness than posited by romance—neither mate will be a perfect person. The happiness foreshadowed for Bertram and Helena may be similar to that expected by Parolles. He has not now the esteem he'd had; his goals and expectations are greatly reduced. But he has also not the constant pressure to *seem* a courtier nor the fear of being found out. He can live at peace with himself. "Though you are a fool and a knave, you shall eat." So with Bertram and Helena, their goals and expectations may be modified. But within these limitations, why not expect that they will be happy? All may be well at the end of the play, but on very different terms from what was projected earlier in the play and from what romantic convention would tell us.

HELENA

W. W. Lawrence and Robert Hapgood evaluate Helena in glowing terms; everything she says and does is noble, heroic, and fully justified. They find her ability to fulfill the terms of Bertram's letter clever and courageous. E. K. Chambers and Clifford Leech conclude otherwise. Chambers describes her as a woman driven by sex alone and a degraded example of womanhood. Leech finds her devious in her ambition and the planning of her ultimate victory—her final union with Bertram—unsavory.

Other critics argue that her character is more multidimensional than the critics above suggest. Robert Grams Hunter and Sharon R. Yang, for example, find in her regenerative qualities, whereby she restores the kingdom and redeems Bertram. Michael Shapiro argues that Helena and Bertram are mutual redeemers, whereby each character "regains through submission and humility what has been lost through self-assertion."

Susan Snyder describes the odd mix in Helena of initiative and passivity, a combination that is unusual for Shakespeare's heroines. All of Shakespeare's heroines (except, oddly enough, Helena in *A Midsummer Night's Dream*) wait to be courted; Helena overtly chases the man she wants. **Robert Ornstein** also finds Helena to be a complex character. She is single-minded in her determination to form a romantic attachment with Bertram, yet her temperament is decidedly unromantic. He notes that she is calculated (not calculating) and intelligent in her planning and pursuit of Bertram.

Robert Ornstein

SOURCE: "*All's Well That Ends Well*," in *Shakespeare's Comedies: From Roman Farce to Romantic Mystery*, University of Delaware Press, 1986, pp. 173-94.

[*In the following excerpt, Ornstein examines the characters of Helena and Bertram throughout the play, focusing primarily on Helena. He finds her more complex than Bertram, though she, like he, is somewhat self-absorbed in her own desires (hers is to become Bertram's wife). Ornstein also notes that the play is lacking in romantic idealism because of the characterizations of Helena and Bertram.*]

It is not easy to say why Shakespeare wanted to write a play about characters as limited and uninspiring as Helena and Bertram. A relatively straightforward dramatization of Boccaccio's tale of Giletta and Beltramo, *All's Well* is the only comedy that centers on a single love—or rather, a single love-hate—relationship. No Hero, Nerissa, or Celia stands by Helena's side; for most of the play she is a solitary figure who keeps her own counsel and pursues her ends without confiding them to any other person. For a time Bertram has Parolles as a companion, but he is nearly incapable of intimacy or emotional attachment. The minor characters of *All's Well* are, by and large, more attractive than its romantic protagonists, but none are as fully realized or as important to the plot as Leonato is in *Much Ado*. Nevertheless the warmheartedness of the Countess, Lafew, the King, and Bertram's fellow officers is important to the emotional resolution of the play precisely because it is a quality somewhat lacking in Helena and completely absent in Bertram.

Compared to the comedies I have discussed already, *All's Well* seems gray if not bleak, not because its viewpoint is jaded or disillusioned but because its chief characters do not delight us by their verve or humor or expansiveness of thought. Bertram is the least philosophical and perhaps the least intelligent of the heroes of the comedies. He does not reflect on his experiences, much less on life, and he seems incapable of introspection and selfknowledge. He never wrestles with alternatives even though he finds himself repeatedly in difficult predicaments. Although his conduct appalls those who love him, he is never burdened by shame or guilt, and he can be dishonest as well as callous. Because his inner life (if he has one) is hidden from an audience, it knows and judges him by his acts, which are thoroughly unlovely. Helena is a more complex character who is revealed as much through soliloquy as through dialogue. Unlike Bertram she is thoughtful and reflective by nature, yet her speeches lack choric amplitude and range because she is as self-absorbed as he is, forever occupied with her quest to become his wife. More than any other heroine, Helena is single-minded in her romantic dedication, and yet she is the least romantic in temperament of any Shakespearean heroine. As serious as her namesake, Helena of *A Dream*, she is incapable of light-heartedness or gaiety. Love does not inspire her to flights of whimsical or ecstatic poetry, and she seems nearly incapable of spontaneity. Thus while Helena will dare all for love, the Countess's remembrance of her youthful passion is the most poignant expression of romantic yearning in the play; and the only love scene, ironically enough, is the one in which Bertram attempts to seduce Diana. The hero and heroine are alone together only once and that is when Bertram takes his leave, never expecting to see Helena again. He seems almost incapable of tenderness, and she is almost indifferent to what he desires in her determination to become his wife.

The absence of romantic idealism in *All's Well* is not an inevitable result of Shakespeare's choice of the Boccaccian tale, which ends with the loving embrace of husband and wife. Even as Petruchio is less attractive than his counterpart Ferando in *A Shrew,* Bertram is less attractive than Boccaccio's Beltramo, although he is not coarsely contemptuous of women, as Petruchio is. Immature and inexperienced, he is quite incapable of seeing through Parolles' preposterous affectations, which he takes for courtly graces. He is also incapable of seeing beyond his immediate desires, but his faults would seem pardonable enough if Helena's determined pursuit of him did not bring out the worst in his character. He wants what most young gentlemen want— to win honor on the field of battle and to sow a few wild oats before he settles down to marriage and adult obligations. His youthful male instinct for freedom and adventure is opposed by Helena's desire to turn the would-be hero into a husband and father. Having just escaped his mother's watchful eye, Bertram yearns to prove himself a man among men. The disclosure in act 5 of his earlier attraction to Lafew's daughter seems almost an afterthought by Shakespeare because one cannot imagine Bertram in love or desiring to share his life with a woman. He does not love Diana or seek to win her love; he wants only the spoil of her maidenhead, which is no less a trophy than the capture of an enemy's drum. After he has proved his gallantry, won the esteem of his fellow officers, and possessed the prize of Diana's virginity, he is ready to marry Maudlin, especially when it will redeem him in the eyes of the King, his mother, and Lafew.

Bertram does not pose any problems of interpretation; apart from his gallantry in war, he is incurably ordinary and lacking in scruple. Helena is less easily explained. As the play opens, her situation at Rossillion is comparable to Viola's situation in Orsino's household; both adore a great nobleman who is far above their station in life and who knows nothing of their love. Where Viola is resigned to her unhappy circumstances, Helena is determined to wed Bertram, and her single-minded quest of that goal inspires continuing critical debate. No critics have said of Olivia what distinguished Shakespeareans have said of Helena, that she is enthralled and degraded by sexual passion, even though Olivia's desire for Cesario is more obsessive and reckless than Helena's desire for Bertram. But then Olivia responds to what is beautiful in Viola's character while Helena's attraction to the callow Bertram must necessarily be merely physical, just as her pursuit of him must be calculated and covert. Like Olivia, Helena will

accept any humiliation for the sake of love, but she is never impulsive or reckless in seeking Bertram, and she does not, like Olivia, openly declare her love and beg to be loved in return. She has adored Bertram for some time, it seems, without once speaking or even hinting of her feeling for him and without trying to draw his attention to her. When she confesses her love in soliloquy, she does not speak rapturously of Bertram the way Olivia does of Cesario or Juliet does of Romeo. She does not dream of embraces and kisses; she dwells on, even fantasizes, the hopelessness of her love in lines that seem to belie any immediate physical longing:

> I have forgot him [her dead father]. My
>   imagination
> Carries no favor in't but Bertram's.
> I am undone, there is no living, none,
> If Bertram be away. 'Twere all one
> That I should love a bright particular star
> And think to wed it, he is so above me.
> In his bright radiance and collateral light
> Must I be comforted, not in his sphere.
> Th' ambition in my love thus plagues itself:
> The hind that would be mated by the lion
> Must die for love.
>
>   (1.1. 82-92)

The verse is clumsy in movement and the statements curiously flat and lacking in emotional intensity. Whenever Helena speaks of her desire she feels compelled to abstract it from anything resembling sensual longing. As a result, her poetic figures are stilted and even grotesque in their incongruities: She is a hind that would be mated by a lion, a violent consummation indeed.

It is conventional for poets to speak of a loved one as a star; so Astrophil speaks of Stella in Sidney's sonnets. But Sidney does not, like Helena, at once imagine Stella as a point of light in a distant heaven and speak of wedding this star as if he could yearn for physical union with a galactic sphere. The peculiarity of Helena's lines cannot be ascribed to a failure of Shakespeare's poetic imagination because he knows how to make the traditional conceit of "love's star" a vehicle for romantic ardor. Compare, for example, Helena's soliloquy with Juliet's soliloquy as she awaits her wedding night with Romeo:

> Come, gentle night, come, loving, black-brow'd
>   night,
> Give me my Romeo, and, when I shall die,
> Take him and cut him out in little stars,
> And he will make the face of heaven so fine
> That all the world will be in love with night,
> And pay no attention to the garish sun.
>
>   (3.2. 20-25)

Helena's statement that she cannot live without Bertram does not express a comparable immediacy of longing but rather a determination to be his wife. Even when she is alone her responses are guarded; instead of a spontaneous rush of feeling there is cautious appraisal of possibilities and practicalities. If her passion for Bertram were not all-consuming, it would seem jejune because she dwells on his features as an adolescent might linger over the publicity photo of a movie star. What she describes she reduces to conventional epithets, thereby robbing Bertram of any distinctiveness of face or form:

> 'Twas pretty, though a plague,
> To see him every hour, to sit and draw
> His arched brows, his hawking eye, his curls,
> In our heart's table— heart too capable
> Of every line and trick of his sweet favor.
>
> (1.1. 92-96)

Since she will not allow herself to imagine kissing, embracing, and joining bodies with Bertram, Helena's deepest longing for him is expressed not in soliloquy but in her teasing, riddling conversation with Parolles about losing her virginity to her liking. The more directly she thinks of sexual union with Bertram, the more blurred her lines become, until she recovers her self-control and remarks of the pity that "wishing well had not a body in't,"

> Which might be felt, that we, the poorer
>   born,
> Whose baser stars do shut us up in wishes,
> Might with effects of them follow our
>   friends,
> And show what we alone must think, which
>   never
> Returns us thanks.
>
> (1.1. 181-86)

She knows what Parolles is but can appreciate the flair with which he pretends to valor and courtesy. She gives him scope for his scurrilous argument against virginity and pretends to fear the loss of her maidenhead when in fact she is thinking of making love to Bertram; that is, wishing him well with a body that might be felt. She also manages with smiling, gentle mockery to suggest that Parolles is an absolute coward without seeming to insult him. When she is alone again, she represses all sensual longing and coolly assesses in soliloquy the difficulty of the task that lies before her:

> Our remedies oft in ourselves do lie,
> Which we ascribe to heaven. The fated sky
> Gives us free scope, only doth backward pull
> Our slow designs when we ourselves are dull.
> What power is it which mounts my love so high,
> That makes me see, and cannot feed mine eye?
> The mightiest space in fortune nature brings
> To join like likes, and kiss like native things.
>
> (1.1. 216-23)

Act IV, scene iii. Soldiers, Bertram, and Parolles. The University of Michigan Special Collections Library.

This kind of rhyming sententiousness is more customary in a choric speech than in a personal meditation, but the very stiltedness of Helena's images is an intimation of the emotional turmoil that lies beneath her seemingly measured and generalized statements. Since she can look up to her high love and feed her eye with Bertram's sight, the unsatisfied appetite that she is determined to "feed" is not for his sight but for his body, an appetite that is half-acknowledged in the murky lines about joining "like likes to kiss like native things."

Helena's incapacity to express her sensual longing for Bertram is analogous to Angelo's recoil from his sexual desire for Isabella in *Measure for Measure.* Convinced of his superiority to the common sensual herd of men, Angelo is shattered by his longing for a virginal novitiate, and yet an audience realizes that his desire, unlike Helena's, is not immediately physical in origin. He responds to the beauty of Isabella's spirit, her religious ardor and anger at his complacency, even as Olivia responds to Viola's liveliness of mind and depth of feeling. For though Isabella is fair, her physical beauty is in large part hidden by her novice's habit. Only a woman like Isabella, Angelo says, could have aroused his desire, and we believe him, for any calculated or sophisticated sensual appeal would have aroused his contempt and disgust. He hungers to possess Isabella's purity, and since that desire horrifies him, he must hate her for inspiring it. If he could freely accept his passion, he could ennoble it by his genuine admiration for her and turn desire to love. Unable to accept his passion, he is like Helena incapable of appealing for the love he desires. Just as Helena never hints to Bertram of her love, Angelo does not woo Isabella with tender vows or seductive praise. Revolted by his longings, he cannot voice them and would have Isabella catch the drift of his veiled suggestions and submit to his lust without his having to make it explicit. Her ignorance of his desire infuriates him because it forces him to speak frankly; and when he finally does it is with a desire to drag her innocence down into the mire of his lust, to prove that she is like him despite her show of purity. Like Bertram with Diana, he would have Isabella stop playing the modest virgin and put on the destined livery of all women—the soiled garment of a whore.

Like Helena's soliloquies, Angelo's soliloquies have a detached quality, even when he immediately confronts his passion, because he must seek to maintain control or lose his sense of self. His lawyerly assessment of his case is, like Helena's stilted conceits, an attempt to distance himself from sexual desire. When that attempt fails, he necessarily has to satisfy that desire in a way that degrades Isabella and himself. Because Helena can turn sexual longing into a quest to prove her worthiness, she can channel it into a goal that engages the best of her intelligence and daring. And because she can separate that goal from Bertram's nature, she can endure insult and humiliation from him without feeling degraded. We cannot speak then of Helena's love as demeaning her when it expresses what is essential in her nature. Apart from that love, she does not exist for us in the way that Portia, Beatrice, Rosalind, and Viola do. She lacks their warmth and imagination, their pleasure in others and responsiveness to their worlds. Except for the comedy of the denouement, which she invents and stage manages, and apart from her brief sparring match with Parolles, Helena is without humor. Of course, she is more burdened by circumstances than other heroines but one doubts that she would be playful even if her situation allowed it because she is too earnest and practical by nature.

In fairy tales Cinderellas live happily ever after with their princes because love and fairy godmothers annihilate barriers of money and class. In All's Well, as in Boccaccio's tale, these barriers are not easily waved away with a magic wand. Although Giletta is a wealthy heiress in Painter's version of Boccaccio's tale, she is not of noble blood. The King, therefore, "was very loath" to grant Beltramo to her and would not have allowed it had he not pledged to do so earlier. Beltramo is shocked by the command to marry Giletta and protests that she is not of "a stock convenable to his nobility." Shakespeare increases the disparity of rank between Helena and Bertram by turning Boccaccio's rich heiress into a ward in the Rossillion household whose only dowry is the medical cures left to her by her father. Yet the difference of rank matters only to Bertram in All's Well. The King does not hesitate at Helena's choice of Bertram as a husband, and he immediately condemns Bertram's snobbery in refusing Helena. Praising Helena's virtues, he promises to make her honor and estate at least as great as Bertram's. Lafew, who watches while Helena chooses a husband, thinks her worthy of the best in France, and the Countess, learning that Helena loves her son, welcomes her as a daughter. Only Bertram finds Helena too mean to be his wife, and his objection is prompted less by aristocratic hauteur than by distaste for a woman who was no better than a dependent in his household— "a poor physician's daughter," from whom he parted in scene 1 with the command one gives to a servant, "Be comfortable to my mother, your mistress."

Bertram's contemptuous attitude toward Helena is not supported by the choric commentary in the play on aristocratic values. The King's complaints of the decline of courtesy and chivalry invoke a standard of gentility that is the opposite of Bertram's disdain, one of gracious respect for inferiors. Indeed, the King's praise of Bertram's father in 1.2 measures Bertram's failing as a courtier, not Helena's lack of nobility. To be sure, Bertram is not by nature rude or arrogant; he does not demand a cringing obedience from servants and retainers. If he were infatuated with the idea of great rank, he would not reject Helena but rather rejoice in having a wife who is a royal favorite and will bring him great wealth and esteem. One suspects that Bertram would have turned as angrily on any marriage that was going to be forced upon him.

If Shakespeare wanted an audience to recognize Helena as a social climber he had only to give her some of Malvolio's hunger for money and status or allow her to lord it over others when she becomes the Countess of Rossillion. Nothing in her words or manner intimates that wealth and title mean much to her. She wants Bertram, not his estates; the goal she aggressively pursues is to submit to Bertram, to surrender her virginity— her body—to him and be accepted as his wife. Parolles, not Helena, is the upstart of the play, the dependent who affects aristocratic airs. Indeed, it is doubly ironic that Bertram, unable to appreciate Helena's virtues, despises her baseness but accepts Parolles, who is all sham and bluster, as his mentor in chivalry. It is doubtful, moreover, that Shakespeare's audiences were scandalized by Helena's desire to wed Bertram, for the vitality of their society depended on its relative openness, on the opportunity it offered men of talent and energy to rise above their birth and enter the ranks of a nobility that had not grown moribund. The New Men whom Elizabethans and Jacobeans despised and feared were the unworthy royal minions who gained power and wealth through a monarch's thoughtless largesse or granting of monopolies.

I have suggested elsewhere that if Hamlet did not keep accusing himself of failing to revenge his father, no reader would think that he hesitates or delays taking revenge against Claudius. Similarly, no reader would be inclined to label Helena a social climber if she did not persist in accusing herself of ambitious and overreaching love. It is she who keeps harping on her humble origin and on Bertram's great height above her and who feels a continuing need to apologize for her presumptuous desire when no one impugns her motives. Proclaiming that she is unworthy of Bertram, she stalks him relentlessly, without seeming to be hypocritical, and she resorts to a bed trick without seeming to degrade herself. If she were conniving by nature, she would rely on the King to make Bertram accept her as wife after their marriage. But she turns neither to him nor to the Countess and Lafew, who would willingly aid her if she asked. She never desires something for nothing; she offers good value to the King for the reward she seeks, and she is scrupulous in fulfilling the letter of the terms Bertram sets for accepting her as his wife. She would not have him, she says, without deserving him. Since he is a radiant star she will shine forth with her own glowing achievement. She will be a fairy tale heroine who wins her love by daring and skill as so many fairy tale heroes win a king's daughter. To succeed she must use guile and deception because his terms leave her no other alternative; or rather the only other choice she has is to be revolted by his mistreatment of her.

It never seems to occur to Helena that success in winning Bertram might depend on his feeling for her; assuming that she is nothing to him, she never attempts to gain his affection. Because she says nothing to him of her love before she publicly chooses him as her royal reward, he is utterly unprepared for and dumbfounded by her choice. Because she conceals her love from everyone it is only by accident that it is discovered and brought to the attention of the Countess; even then she will not readily admit it. Boccaccio's heroine is not, like Helena, a loner by nature as well as circumstance. She is surrounded by relatives before she marries and wins the love and loyalty of all her people after the Count rejects her and departs. From the beginning Shakespeare makes Helena a solitary figure, one who grew up alone on the periphery of a great household in which she had no assured place or station. Accustomed to this aloneness, she does not reach out to anyone except when an alliance with the King or with Diana and her mother will further her goal of obtaining Bertram. Her joyful greeting of the Countess in the final scene is the single occasion when she openly returns the affection of those who love her. At other times she hoards her emotion as if she must channel it all toward Bertram and the task of achieving him.

As soon as she learns of Helena's love for her son, the Countess makes clear her approval by inviting Helena's confidences. When she asks Helena to think of her as a mother, the response is that the Countess is her "honorable mistress." The Countess persists in speaking of her as her daughter, and Helena persists in denying the possibility of such a relationship. Although she has already concluded that she can deserve to become Bertram's wife, she speaks here as if she would never dare link her name with the Rossillions:

> The Count Rossillion cannot be my brother:
> I am from humble, he from honored name;
> No note upon my parents, his all noble.
> My master, my dear lord he is, and I
> His servant live, and will his vassal die.
> He must not be my brother.
>
> (1.3.155-160)

Helena's equivocations are transparent to the audience; she cannot allow Bertram to be her brother because she would be his wife, and she hints more directly at her yearning for him when she says that she wishes the Countess were her mother, "so that my lord, your son, were not my brother . . . So I were not his sister." The Countess, having offered her sympathy and love is annoyed by this evasiveness. She declares that Helena's looks, sighs, and tears express her love of Bertram, and "only sin / And hellish obstinacy tie thy tongue, / That truth should be suspected." Although the Countess charges her to speak truly, Helena continues her zigzag course, begging for pardon, refusing to say she loves Bertram until finally she slips to her knees and "confesses":

> Here on my knee, before high heaven and you,
> That before you, and next until high heaven,
> I love your son.
> My friends were poor, but honest, so's my
>   love.
> Be not offended, for it hurts not him
> That he is lov'd of me; I follow him not
> By any token of presumptuous suit,
> Nor would I have him till I do deserve him;
> Yet never know how that desert should be.
>
> (1.3.192-200)

Since she cannot believe by this point that the Countess will be offended by her love of Bertram, Helena's evasiveness must be prompted by her own emotional needs rather than a fear of rebuke. Her humility is genuine and yet equivocal because she kneels only to declare her intention to pursue Bertram— but not in "any token of presumptuous suit." That is, she will not "have him" till she deserves him. This is the humbleness of one who will not claim great merit as yet, but who is absolutely certain that one day she will deserve a place among the best. This kind of self-effacement is slyly glossed by Lavatch just before Helena enters:

> Though honesty be no puritan, yet it will
> do no hurt; it will wear the surplice of
> humility over the black gown of a big
> heart.
>
> (1.3.93-94)

Ordinarily humility and simplicity go hand in hand, but there are times when plainness becomes ostentatious and a sign of self-righteous superiority. Repelled by the rich panoply of Anglican worship, the puritan minister wears a simple black gown beneath the showier surplice church law required, thus making his disdain for episcopal finery a gesture of spiritual pride. To say there is a like pride in Helena's humbleness is not to accuse her of hypocritical earnestness, for she must be certain of what she can achieve to dare what she does, and she must also believe in her inferiority to Bertram to bow before his abuse and rejection. If she did not keep telling herself that she is unworthy of him, she could not accept the contemptuous conditions he sets for accepting her as his wife. At the same time, once she has proved her worthiness to be his wife, she is determined to enjoy the prize she has won. Sometimes Helena plays the poor little waif for herself and others, but she invariably slips from this self-image to that of a female knight-errant who will accomplish impossible tasks to win her curled darling.

Helena's proud humility and kneeling pride are vividly expressed in her audience with the King, who must be convinced that he can be cured when his learned doctors have given him up as lost. First she is all humbleness, ready to accept his denials; then she refuses to be denied because she is heaven's emissary, an agent of providence, an instrument of miracles as great as the parting of the Red Sea. Finally she is a high priestess of mysterious powers and incantatory prophesies who promises a cure in less than forty-eight hours. She will wager all on belief in her father's cure, aware, no doubt, that the melodramatic punishments she names as her forfeit would not be imposed should she fail. When she asks what reward she will obtain if she succeeds, she specifies nothing until the King has pledged his scepter and hopes of heaven on his good faith. Then she avoids any hint of guilty presumption by declaring that she would not think of joining her "low and humble name" to the royal blood of France but seeks as husband only a vassal whom the King is free to bestow.

The public ceremony in which Helena pretends to pick and choose among the young noblemen at court before settling on Bertram is not in Boccaccio. It is invented by Shakespeare— or, rather, it is invented by Helena as an ostentatious show of humility in her choice of a husband, and as such it wins the hearts of all save Bertram, who is ignorant of his role in the charade. It also allows him no time to digest the stunning news and no way to protest his fate without open defiance of the King. Since she cannot be sure of Bertram's response,

her timidity may be real. She acts as if she were so fearful of rejection that she prefers not to choose, yet she knows that she cannot be refused by any of the lords because the King informs them that Helena has power to choose any and they "none to forsake." When Helena hesitates, the King insists that she make a choice and turns a threatening eye on the assembly: "Make choice and see, / Who shuns thy love shuns all his love in me." So reluctantly, blushingly, shamefacedly, Helena is "forced" to do what she has set her mind on doing. She could choose Bertram outright, but that would be too obvious; she will settle on him only after considering various other young noblemen. One lord, she says, deserves a wife twenty times above herself. Another she would not wrong, for he deserves a fairer fortune in bed. A third she says is "too young, too happy, and too good" to be the father of her son. Only after these lords have protested their willingness to be her husband does she humbly turn to Bertram:

> I dare not say I take you, but I give
> Me and my service, ever whilst I live,
> Into your guiding power.— This is the man.
>
> (2.3.102-4)

What she says is heartfelt but it does not alter the fact that that though she dares not "take" Bertram, she does take him.

Bertram's outcry is understandable. Just before he was deprived of an opportunity to fight in the war by the King, who said he was too young. Now he is being deprived of his right to choose his own wife; although not old enough to be a soldier, he is old enough to be given away in marriage as a royal reward. This is especially bitter to one who complained to Parolles that he must remain at court in the service of women as "the forehorse to a smock." Bertram is probably the only lord foolish and heedless enough to refuse Helena, but his refusal is frank and prompted by the fact that he does not love her. Shall he be denied the right to choose his own wife because Helena is a worthy choice? Or can he not rebel against an enforced marriage with the same justification that Silvia, Hermia, and Juliet rebel? The abuse of wardships through enforced marriages was a scandal in Shakespeare's time, and the misery of enforced marriage was poignantly depicted by contemporary playwrights. The moral issue does not change because a man rather than a woman is thrust into a loveless marriage by a guardian's prerogative.

When Bertram asks leave "in such a business . . . to use / The help of mine own eyes," he is a sympathetic figure. When he speaks scornfully of Helena as one who would bring him down, his snobbery is nasty because he speaks of her as if she were a horse or a dog who "had her breeding at my father's charge." This arrogance merits the King's angry reply about the superiority of Helena's active virtue to a dropsied inherited honor. Nevertheless, *honor* and *dishonor* become slippery terms when they depend merely on the King's favor or disdain. Helena says she is glad of the King's cure and would let the rest go. That is not possible, however, because his honor is engaged on her behalf and he cannot allow himself to be publicly humiliated. "Obey our will," he commands Bertram,

> Or I will throw thee from my care for ever
> Into the staggers and the careless lapse
> Of youth and ignorance; both my revenge
>   and hate
> Loosing upon thee, in the name of justice,
> Without all terms of pity.
>
> (2.3. 162-66)

Threatened in this fashion, Bertram asks pardon, and with just a bit of insouciance declares that Helena, who just before seemed most base to him, is now with the King's praise as noble as if born so. It would be sensible for Bertram to marry Helena and learn to cherish her qualities, but it would also be sensible for Hermia to marry Demetrius rather than risk death by eloping with Lysander. It is not shameful of Bertram to state his feelings openly; what is shameful is the cowardly revenge he takes on Helena afterward.

Furious at Bertram's response to being chosen by Helena, Lafew takes out his rage on Parolles as if Parolles were responsible for Bertram's callowness. An audience knows, however, that Parolles' influence on Bertram is limited. When he sneers at Lafew as an idle lord, Bertram bluntly disagrees: "I think not so." His decision never to sleep with Helena or live with her is made without Parolles' assistance, and he shows his contempt for his wife by having Parolles inform her that there will be no wedding night before she returns to Rossillion. Enjoying his role as messenger, Parolles mockingly addresses Helena as "fortunate lady," and assures her that he prayed for her success. He probably also embroiders Bertram's message with a few rhetorical flourishes of his own, promising that the postponed pleasures of the wedding night will be sweeter still when enjoyed later. Helena shows immense composure in the face of Bertram's rejection of her. Wanting Parolles' good will she does not tease him, nor does she protest the fact that she learns her fate from him, not her husband. The quiet with which she accepts Bertram's will suggests a resilience and perhaps a heart already prepared for the blow. Her responses are simple and matter-of-fact: "What's his will else? . . . What more commands he? . . . In everything I wait upon his will." It is as if she continues to regard herself as Bertram's vassal even after she has become his wife. Her parting from Bertram is equally restrained; she shows no self-pity and makes no appeal. Bertram seems, if anything, more uncomfortable than she, and makes his lame excuses in lines that are sinuous, stilted, and patently insincere:

> You must not marvel, Helen, at my course,
> Which holds not color with the time, nor
>   does
> The ministration and required office
> On my particular. Prepar'd I was not
> For such a business; therefore am I found
> So much unsettled.
>
> (2.5. 58-63)

Here, as later in the play, Bertram proves to be a bad liar— one of the more hopeful signs of his nature. He is unable to be brutal to Helena face to face, and he is unable to withstand her long-suffering patient humility. When she replies to his threadbare excuses, "Sir, I can nothing say / But that I am your most obedient servant," he says, "Come, come; no more of that." But she has much more to offer; she swears that she shall ever,

> With true observance seek to eke out that
> Wherein toward me my homely stars have
>   fail'd
> To equal my great fortune,
>
> (2.5 74-76)

a statement that inspires in Bertram an overwhelming desire to cut short the interview.

Once again Helena's humility seems sanctimonious and manipulative, a denial of self calculated to make Bertram squirm. Yet the acceptance of her situation is real; she timidly begs for a parting kiss as if she recognizes that affection cannot be earned or "achieved," it can only be given or begged for. The Countess's response to the letter in which Bertram swears never to have Helena as his wife is unequivocal. She is angry and also fearful for this "rash and unbridled boy" who risks the King's wrath by "misprising of a maid too virtuous / For the contempt of empire." When Helena reads aloud her "passport" from Bertram, the Countess is ready to disown him: "He was my son." Helena will not permit herself any outcry; the most she will say is that Bertram's decision is a dreadful sentence and "bitter." Even when she rereads the letter alone on stage she cannot acknowledge its brutality. She must pity Bertram rather than pity herself; indeed, she must accuse herself of being the reason he fled his home and country for the Italian wars or else face the reality of his contempt. Her pity is like the pity Julia feels for Proteus when she discovers his faithlessness to her. Julia, however, can admit the ugliness of Proteus's behavior, whereas Helena must heap abuse upon herself so that she can blot out the callousness of Bertram's actions. Melodramatizing her guiltiness, she declares that it will be her fault if he dies in battle. For his sake she will renounce all claim to him and steal away like a "dark, poor thief" so that he can return to Rossillion; yet like the Countess she speaks of him as if he were a defiant child who has run away from home because she was too harsh, one whose "tender limbs" are being exposed "to the event / Of the none-sparing war." It would be more appropriate, she thinks, if she met a ravenous lion than he be a mark for smoky muskets. Helena's self-accusations become more unctuous still in the letter she leaves for the Countess when she departs Rossillion. Once again she speaks of the offense of her ambitious love that only a barefooted pilgrimage can expiate. Ignoring Bertram's mistreatment of her, she promises to sanctify his name "with zealous fervor," begs forgiveness for driving him to the war, and declares that she will go away because "he is too good and fair for death and me." Can Helena believe that such a letter will soften the Countess's anger at Bertram and bring him home from the war? The Countess notes the "sharp stings . . . in Helena's mildest words" and sends a letter to Bertram that is full of praise of his saintly wife.

No letter from the Countess will reform Bertram, who is now openly defiant of his wife and the King. If he is to be redeemed, it will have to be by Helena, who is willing to meet his mocking demands and win him twice. Her pretense of a holy pilgrimage is no more devious than Portia's pretense that she intends a religious retreat when she sets off with Nerissa for Venice. Her attitude of self-sacrifice is very different, however, from Portia's refusal to praise herself or be praised for her effort to rescue Antonio. But then one could not be like Portia and accept the humiliations that Bertram heaps on Helena. To undertake and accomplish Helena's venture, one must have immense self-confidence but not much pride, for one must believe that this "god" has the right to set whatever terms he pleases for his wife.

More alone in Florence than at the start of the play, Helena confides in no one. She will not admit to the Widow that she knows Bertram, much less that she is his wife. When she hears that Parolles has spoken coarsely of her, she agrees that Bertram's wife "is too mean / To have her name repeated." Boccaccio's heroine is more open and direct in managing the bed trick, but Shakespeare does not emphasize Helena's craftiness so much as he does the viciousness of Bertram's attempted seduction. Mariana warns Diana of the deceitfulness of men like Bertram, whose oaths and promises are merely "engines of lust" and who leave the maids they have despoiled to the misery of a ruined reputation. Her appraisal of Bertram's motives is painfully accurate because he is callous as well as unskilled at seduction. First he attempts some conventional Petrarchan flatteries and a bit of Parollesian casuistry about the value of losing one's virginity. When these fail, he swears that he will be her servant, and when she ridicules these vows, he discards the pose of courtly lover and bluntly demands her surrender:

> Stand no more off,
> But give thyself unto my sick desires,
> Who then recovers. Say thou art mine, and ever
> My love, as it begins, shall so persever.
>   (4.2. 34-37)

Later Bertram will boast of this night's work to his comrades, but it is he— not Diana— who surrenders. Instructed by Helena, she insists on having his ancestral ring— his honor— in exchange for her maidenhead— her honor. He holds out for only a moment and then barters for one night's lust the ring that was "bequeathed down from many ancestors"; such is the regard for name and lineage of one who disdained a poor physician's daughter. The mention of vows and holy oaths and the exchange of rings turn the supposed seduction into a mock nuptial in which Diana acts as Helena's proxy even as Helena will serve as Diana's substitute in bed with Bertram.

The ironies and moral ambiguities that surround the bed trick in *Measure for Measure* are absent in *All's Well.* There is no surrender to unlawful coercion, no bribery of justice, no soliciting of a woman for a stealthy assignation by a mock friar. The Widow and Diana will be rewarded by Helena for their part in the duping of Bertram, but they do not agree merely for the sake of reward. The Widow would not put her reputation "in any staining act" and must first be convinced that Helena's purpose is legitimate and will not harm her daughter. Then she and Diana join with Helena as women, as natural allies, against predatory men like Bertram. After listening to Bertram's lying protestations, Diana decides that it is "no sin / To cozen him that would unjustly win." More candid with herself and others than Duke Vincentio is about the bed trick, Helena does not attempt to invest it with high moral purpose. It is lawful, she says, and yet it involves on Bertram's part a "wicked meaning" (that is, vicious intention); she and Bertram will not sin in making love because they are married, and yet the act she knows is "a sinful fact." Diana risks very little and because of Helena's generosity will no longer be dowerless and prey to the enticements of men like Bertram; Helena will lose her virginity to her liking and gain Bertram in the bargain. She has no illusions anymore about her bright star; she knows him well enough now to wager that he will give his ancestral ring "to buy his will," but she does not recoil from that knowledge. Perhaps it is comforting to know the full extent of his shabbiness, because the shabbiness justifies the means she uses to gain him. . . .

Most of the comedy of the final scene derives from Helena's artful choreographing of Diana's accusations against Bertram and her provocative riddling about Helena's ring. Shakespeare aids Helena's cause by allowing Diana to enter just as a bewildered Bertram, suspected of wicked deeds, is being led away under guard. But Helena does not need much help from Shakespeare because she is able to contrive her own masterly version of the discovery scenes that close *Errors* and *Twelfth Night,* one in which the clamor of false accusations mounts until the entrance of a single character— Antipholus S. or Sebastian or Helena— resolves all difficulties. Except for Bertram's mistaken assumption that he made love to Diana, none of the supposes in this discovery scene is the result of mistaken identities. Moreover, the crucial issue is not the discovery that Helena is alive but the unmasking of Bertram's moral nature, which resembles the exposure of Parolles down to the extravagant lies each one tells when caught in the trap. Where Parolles rises to heights of comic calumny, Bertram descends to depths of falsehood and vicious slander, but the comic confusion that surrounds his possession of Helena's ring and Diana's saucy manner keep the revelation from becoming so nasty that a happy ending is impossible. The tone is as artfully balanced as in the analogous ring episode in *The Merchant,* although the dramatic circumstance and moral issue are far more serious.

Things go wrong from Bertram as soon as his love token for Maudlin is recognized by the King as a ring he gave Helena. Although the Countess and Lafew confirm the identity of the ring, Bertram is convinced that they are mistaken, because he knows that he got it from his Florentine dish. Too tactful to brag of his sexual conquests, he invents the facile lie that the ring was thrown to him from a window by a woman who desired him. Since Helena told the King she would not part with the ring except to her husband in bed, he is incensed by Bertram's falsehood and begins to have dark suspicions about how Bertram obtained the ring. After Diana enters to accuse Bertram of seducing her with false promises of marriage, the King wonders why Bertram wishes to marry Maudlin when he has apparently fled from two other "wives," and Lafew decides to "buy me a son-in-law in a fair." Bertram admits that he knows Diana but will not admit he attempted her seduction. Even granting his shock and panic, his lines suggest that his view of women has not changed:

My lord, this is a fond and desp'rate creature,
Whom sometime I have laugh'd with. Let
　　your Highness
Lay a more noble thought upon mine honor
Than for to think that I would sink it here.
　　　　　　　　　　　　　　(5.3. 178-81)

Sinking lower, Bertram describes Diana as "a common gamester to the camp," but she shows his ancestral ring, and that is enough to convince the Countess that Diana is his wife. Bertram reaches his nadir with the lie that Diana obtained his ring by angling for him, madding his desire with "infinite cunning" until he gave it

for that "which any inferior might / At market-price have bought." Since Parolles, who is called to testify, can expose this falsehood, Bertram must also vilify his former companion as

a most perfidious slave,
With all the spots a' th' world tax'd and
　　debosh'd,
Whose nature sickens but to speak a truth.
　　　　　　　　　　　　　　(5.8. 205-7)

Bertram seems all the more shabby when Parolles proves reluctant to condemn him and charitable in his assessment of Bertram's character: "My master hath been an honorable gentleman. Tricks he hath had in him, which gentlemen have." According to Parolles Bertram loved Diana "as a gentleman loves a woman . . . He lov'd her sir, and lov'd her not." This explanation is less equivocal than the King supposes, for Parolles implies that gentlemen marry ladies but make love to women of no birth without loving them and have no intention of marrying those who surrender to them. If Bertram had been more sophisticated he would not have pursued a virgin; he would have made love to a woman who had already lost her maidenhead and honor and who could not be further degraded by a gentleman.

Parolles' statement, like those which Diana, Helena, and Mariana make about men, make the battle of the sexes in *All's Well* more explicit than it is in earlier comedies, for here the aggressiveness and callousness of male appetite is opposed to the woman's need to lose her virginity to her liking or husband it as a priceless commodity. Like the cynical Lavatch, the ruttish Bertram travesties romantic ideals by reducing the "service" of love to that which a bull offers a cow. Portraits like Bertram and Lucio of *Measure for Measure* do not imply, however, that Shakespeare has lost faith in the romantic ideal that informs his earlier comedies; they simply confirm that the ideal of love depends on an ability to cherish others and a capacity for generosity that Bertram does not possess.

Since too much emphasis on Bertram's failings will make a shambles of the denouement, Shakespeare focuses attention on the mystery of Helena's ring after Parolles has spoken. Coached by Helena, Diana, who has already given false testimony about Bertram, responds to the King's questions with such riddling equivocations that Lafew and the King believe she is, as Bertram claimed, "some common customer," "an easy glove" that goes off and on at pleasure. Threatened with death, Diana grows more impudent; she is cheekily familiar with the King, and hinting that she is still a virgin, she suggests also that Bertram is "guilty and he is not guilty." Her impudence is a welcome note given Helena's willingness to abase herself before Bertram in earlier scenes, for at last the women in the play do not bow before the will of men. At the last moment Diana

Act V, scene iii. Rousillion, the count's palace, the King, Countess, Lafeu, Bertram, Helena, Diana, lords, attendants, and widow Painted by Francis Wheatley, R.A. The University of Michigan Special Collections Library.

plays her trump card: she produces a Helena whose pregnant state is the simple truth hinted at by her equivocations: "one that's dead is quick."

No one is more overjoyed at Helena's appearance than Bertram, for she alone can rescue him from ignominious disgrace. Like Hero in the last scene of *Much Ado*, Helena does not dwell on the wrongs that were done her. When the King asks, "Is't real that I see?" she answers:

> No, my good lord,
> 'Tis but the shadow of a wife you see,
> The name, and not the thing.
>
> (5.3. 306-8)

To which Bertram cries out, "Both, both. O, pardon!" Reminding Bertram that she found him "wondrous kind" when he thought he was making love to Diana, she also reads aloud the conditions he set down for accepting her as his wife and asks, "Will you be mine now you are doubly won?" This is not the Helena of earlier scenes who

bowed before Bertram's scorn; instead of timidly begging for affection, she asks Bertram to acknowledge publicly that she deserves him. In a last attempt at masculine pride Bertram makes his answer not to her but to the King:

> If she, my liege, can make me know this clearly,
> I'll love her dearly, ever, ever dearly.

Keeping her emotional distance from Bertram, Helena embraces the Countess, whom she can at last acknowledge as her "dear mother." Diana's future seems assured, for the King promises to provide a dowry when she marries. Wiser than before, he does not propose to enforce her choice of husband with his prerogative, and still wary of her glibness he makes his promise as conditional as Bertram's to Helena: if Diana is still a virgin, he will see that she marries well. Too ready before to jump to erroneous conclusions, now he is cautious about assessing the outcome of events:

> All yet seems well, and if it end so meet,
> The bitter past, more welcome is the sweet.

If all is well it is not because Bertram is more mature or more sensitive in the last scene than in the first, but because, after his narrow escapes, he is no doubt ready for a quiet life at Rossillion. He promises that he will love Helena dearly, and no doubt he will, insofar as "loving dearly" can be a matter of deliberate choice. Helena's progress is more certain and significant. She knows more about Bertram than any wife should know about a husband and yet she loves him still. She is not revolted by his desire for Diana because she knows how circumstance affects sexual longing and pleasure. He rejected her out of anger and spite but enjoyed her body in Florence, thinking she was a prize that had been won with difficulty. She can acknowledge the lure of stealthy illicit sex without feeling the need to justify Bertram's lust. Once too ready to proclaim her unworthiness, she now is fully assured of her selfworth. At the beginning, she imagined the attaining of Bertram as an achieving of the impossible, a striving for a star. After the bed trick, she no longer speaks of what she can achieve by a determined will. In a speech to Diana and the Widow, she puts her faith in the passing of time that brings life again to barren twigs and that will confirm the new life that exists in her womb:

> . . . the time will bring on summer,
> When briers shall have leaves as well as
>   thorns,
> And be as sweet as sharp. We must away:
> Our waggon is prepar'd, and time revives us.
> All's well that ends well! still the fine's the
>   crown;
> Whate'er the course, the end is the renown.
>   (4.4. 31-36)

Helena's alliance with Diana and the Widow is important to the denouement of *All's Well* because she is no longer apart from others, absorbed in her determination to have Bertram. When she embraces the Countess, the familial drama of the play reaches its happy conclusion: an orphaned child raised as a ward in a great household has found a mother as well as a husband at Rossillion. Despite the earlier melancholy sense of lost values, there is hope of better days to come. Bertram is in good hands and Helena carries the child that will assure the future of the noble lineage he very nearly compromised. . . .

BERTRAM

E. M. W. Tillyard, W. W. Lawrence, Hazelton Spencer, and Michael Shapiro all find Bertram a thoroughly reformed character at the end of the play. Tillyard and Lawrence find it completely plausible that Bertram has grown from an immature, inexperienced man at the beginning of the play into a sincere hero. Spencer argues that the "play's title clinches the argument against the play's detractors." Shapiro concludes that Bertram's reluctance to marry Helena is entirely credible. The King orders him to marry Helena when the last thing he wants is to be tied down in marriage. What he desires is the "masculine" form of honor earned on a battlefield.

Larry S. Champion's assessment of Bertram is generally a positive one. If Helena finds him worth pursuing, Champion argues, there must be something worthy in his character. (Gerard J. Gross agrees.) His association with Parolles, his treatment of Helena and Diana, and his disobedience of the King taint his character, but in the end, he is "apparently purged" and repents. Katharine Eisaman Maus similarly finds him capable of reform, not merely through the efforts of Helena but through the actions of his mother and the King as well. His dismissal of Parolles also reflects well on him, indicating that he can indeed discern the difference between honorable and dishonorable behavior. **Richard P. Wheeler**, acknowledging the discontent critics express in assessing Bertram's character, refrains from making an overall judgment of Bertram's character (though he is somewhat sympathetic toward him). He argues that it is useful instead to examine how the events of the play as experienced by Bertram define his role in the play and shape the play as a whole.

Robert Ornstein and Robert Hapgood are more dubious about Bertram's transformation. Ornstein finds him a simple, unintelligent character, one with an inability to reflect on his actions or consider their consequences and incapable of guilt or shame. Hapgood finds Bertram's quick repentance at the end of the play unconvincing and argues that his acceptance of Helena is merely his settling for her instead of Lafeu's daughter.

Richard P. Wheeler

SOURCE: "Imperial Love and the Dark House: *All's Well That Ends Well*," in *Shakespeare's Development and the Problem Comedies: Turn and Counter-Turn*, University of California Press, 1981, pp. 34-35.

[*In this excerpt, Wheeler argues that examining the character of Bertram can "help identify unresolved tensions" in the play. Wheeler acknowledges the critical discontent regarding the success of* All's Well That Ends Well *and suggests that analyzing Bertram's role can be useful in the context of these disagreements over the efficacy of the play. Wheeler argues that Bertram finds his situation at court intolerable and has to escape, especially when forced into a marriage by the King, a father-figure, with the approval of his mother (in essence, his parents are forcing him to do something against his will). Bertram wants to experience the world, physically and sexually. Through Bertram's actions, Shakespeare orchestrates his ultimate retrieval.*]

Shakespeare's decision to base a comedy on Boccaccio's story about a young man who flees rather than pursues his eventual wife, despises rather than adores her, creates for *All's Well That Ends Well* an altered set of comic conflicts. Instead of accommodating the marital aspirations of a Bassanio or an Orlando, the play's action must bring Bertram to accept Helena as his wife. Before this action is completed, the young count is identified at various moments as a nobleman of great promise, an object of adoration, a complete fool, a snob, an ungrateful son and subject, a whimpering adolescent, a warrior of heroic stature, a degenerate rake, a liar, a moral coward, a suspected murderer, and, perhaps, a regenerate husband. Few characters in Shakespeare's comedies are called upon to fit so many different images, certainly none of Bertram's more compliant comic predecessors. Partly because he has often been seen through responses he generates in other characters, who repudiate him as son, subject, and comrade, Bertram has long held a reputation among critics as a "thoroughly disagreeable, peevish and vicious person." Recent attempts to brighten Bertram's character have often accompanied attempts to salvage the play from a long tradition of critical discontent, to demonstrate "that *All's Well* is a good play," that in fact, "All does end well." I think instead that a close look at *All's Well* as it is experienced by Bertram can help identify unresolved tensions that not only define his position in the action but that shape the play as a whole and indicate the place it occupies in Shakespearean comedy.

Bertram, Marriage, and Manhood

KING   Youth, thou bear'st thy father's
     face.
Frank nature, rather curious than in haste,
Hath well composed thee. Thy father's moral
    parts
Mayst thou inherit too!

                   (I.ii.19-22)

Dr. Johnson's indictment of the young count can speak for many:

> I cannot reconcile my heart to Bertram; a man noble without generosity, and young without truth; who marries Helen as a coward, and leaves her as a profligate: when she is dead by his unkindness, sneaks home to a second marriage, is accused by a woman whom he has wronged, defends himself by falsehood, and is dismissed to happiness.

Johnson's denunciation seems to be exactly the response to Bertram that the moral context of the play demands. But Sir Arthur Quiller-Couch remarked, introducing his edition of *All's Well*, that Bertram "has something to say for himself against the moralizers":

> There is nothing in him, until we come to the final scene, that we cannot find it in our hearts to forgive, if only he will give us the right excuse. . . .

For, consciously or not, we have felt Helena's love pleading his cause with us all the while. The follies of youth—"lusty juventus"—come of nature and mettle, and arrogance of birth may be a fault well on this side of sin. There *must* be some attractiveness in Bertram to justify such devotion, and this will surely reveal itself, to satisfy us or nearly, before the curtain falls. But the final scene destroys our hope.

The contrast between Quiller-Couch's tolerant view of Bertram and Dr. Johnson's severe indictment is present in the play, without seeming to come under the control of dramatic irony. The tension between these two perspectives, and between each of them and Helena's adoration of the youthful count, can be used to clarify the problem that Bertram poses, not only for *All's Well,* but for the development of Shakespearean comedy.

The first scene reveals little of Bertram directly beyond the impatience of an "unseasoned courtier" (I.i.66) anxious to realize the promise of manhood in the service of aristocratic ideals. The initial image of Bertram is focused chiefly through Helena's extravagant praise as she celebrates the "bright particular star" (I.i.82) of her imagination. Again at the French court, there is a strong trend to assimilate Bertram to identities that others impose upon him. In his first encounter with the king, Bertram plays an entirely passive role as the king weaves into rambling speeches wistful recollections of the old Count Rossillion, sober thoughts on his own approaching death, and impatient reflections on his youthful courtiers. As the king moves toward a nostalgic identification with the dead count, Bertram, by his mere presence, comes to be invested with a double, partially contradictory role. Bertram becomes, in the eyes of the king, a son ("Welcome, count; / My son's no dearer" [I.ii.75-76]) who represents both the promise of vicarious fulfillment through identification with his youthful promise and the threat posed by a younger generation unworthy of the tradition it inherits. Both of these projected identities become actively important in Bertram's subsequent meetings with the king.

Bertram begins to appear defined by his own presentation of self through action and sentiment in II.i. The young count watches the king issue an official farewell to the lords bound for the wars in Italy, which "may well serve / A nursery to our gentry, who are sick / For breathing and exploit" (I.ii.15-17). The king's speech is rich in the idealized rhetoric of ennobling war:

              Farewell, young lords.
Whether I live or die, be you the sons
Of worthy Frenchmen. Let Higher Italy
(Those bated that inherit but the fall
Of the last monarchy) see that you come
Not to woo honor, but to wed it, when

The bravest questant shrinks: find what you
    seek,
That fame may cry you loud.

                                        (II.i.10-17)

The king pronounces an ideal of honorable combat
that promises self-fulfillment, liberation, and fame. These
young lords may prove themselves worthy sons, brave
men, and esteemed comrades. Opposed to the warlike
courtship of honor are the snares of Italian women:

Those girls of Italy, take heed of them.
They say our French lack language to deny
If they demand; beware of being captives
Before you serve.

                                        (II.i.19-22)

The king presents his lords with a world of masculine
activity familiar to our culture and our poetry. War
offers sexualized aggressive release, idealization through
the commitment to honor, and affectionate communion among men; heterosexual activity brings the threat
of emasculation and is to be shunned or carefully subordinated to the masculine ideal. "Our hearts receive
your warnings" (II.i.23), the lords reply, while Bertram
eagerly looks on.

But Bertram must remain at court: "I am commanded
here and kept a coil with / 'Too young,' and 'The next
year,' and ''Tis too early'" (II.i.27-28). Denied access to
heroic masculine endeavor by the king who has just
exalted it, Bertram's forced stay at court takes its shape
from his frustration:

I shall stay here the forehorse to a smock,
Creaking my shoes on the plain masonry,
Till honor be bought up, and no sword worn
But one to dance with. By heaven, I'll steal
    away!

                                        (II.i.30-33)

Encouraged by Parolles and the other lords, who join
for a moment in the masculine camaraderie from which
Bertram is about to be severed, Bertram bristles with
resentment toward the court life he now regards as
effeminate. Bertram, who went to court to realize himself as a man, as a seasoned courtier, is treated as a
boy, a condition Parolles uses to put salt into his barbed
advice: "An thy mind stand to't, boy, steal away bravely"
(II.i.29). Confined to the court he perceives as womanly, where the sword, the virile means to honor, merely
adorns ballroom apparel, Bertram makes his first, precocious, gesture toward rebellion.

Bertram's implicit son relationship to the king— who
tells him how to be a man and tells him also that he
cannot be one yet— and his festering resentment at
being "kept a coil" at court furnish essential background for the conflict shortly to develop when, after

the king's mysterious cure, Bertram is appointed husband to Helena. His confrontation with the king in II.iii
toughens and deepens the presentation of a Bertram
just beginning to emerge as a character whose youthful
ambitions seem destined for frustration. The scene
appears to be heading for a triumphant culmination in
Helena's selection of Bertram as husband. Helena's
almost coquettishly ritualistic rejection of the other
prospects lends comic momentum to her final decision.
"This is the man," Helena announces, and the king
sanctions the choice: "Why then, young Bertram, take
her; she's thy wife" (II.iii.104-5). Because Bertram is
caught off guard, and because he in turn catches the
king off guard, the intensity now injected into the scene
has a special emotional authority. Bertram's immediate
response is astonishment: "My wife, my liege?" But he
is quickly able to channel the logic of his position into
a plea for freedom of choice: "I shall beseech your
highness, / In such a business give me leave to use /
The help of mine own eyes." The king seems a bit
bewildered, but counters with a question that implicitly
develops the authoritarian logic of his own position:
"Knows't thou not, Bertram, / What she has done for
me?" Bertram in turn challenges this argument: "Yes,
my good lord, / But never hope to know why I should
marry her" (II.iii.105-9).

As this exchange becomes increasingly heated, Bertram
fights for his autonomy and the king insists on his own
absolute power in a struggle that pits demanding father
against rebellious son. The king identifies phallic mastery with honor and power: "My honor's at the stake,
which to defeat, / I must produce my power" (II.iii.
148-49). Either Bertram bends before the all-powerful
father or the king's restored virility is invalidated. Lafew
has already comically injected the castration theme into
the scene when, standing apart from the ritual elimination of all suitors but Bertram, he thinks that the courtiers Helena passes over have instead refused her: "Do
all they deny her? An they were sons of mine, I'd have
them whipped, or I would send them to th' Turk to
make eunuchs of" (II.iii.85-87). But in the struggle of
wills between Bertram and his king, this anxiety is
developed into irreconcilable conflict. When Helena
suggests that the marriage be waived, the king erupts in
rage at the threat reluctant Bertram poses to his own
restored manhood:

                        Here, take her hand,
Proud scornful boy, unworthy this good
    gift, . . .
                        Check thy contempt.
Obey our will, which travails in thy good.
Believe not thy disdain, but presently
Do thine own fortunes that obedient right
Which both thy duty owes and our power
    claims;
Or I will throw thee from my care forever,
Into the staggers and the careless lapse

Of youth and ignorance, both my revenge
  and hate
Loosing upon thee, in the name of justice,
Without all terms of pity. Speak! thine answer!
                  (II.iii.149-50; 156-65)

Under the shaming force of the king's violent anger, Bertram relents: "Pardon my gracious lord; for I submit / My fancy to your eyes" (II.ii.166-67). Bertram not only is the submissive son viewed from the lofty position of a towering king: he literally sees, for the moment of surrender, the situation through the king's eyes. He becomes, through a radical, forced suspension of self ("Believe not thy disdain"), an extension of the king's person. The validity of his own experience is defined by the king's imperative: "As thou lov'st her, / Thy love's to me religious; else, does err" (II.iii.181-82).

This submissive attitude toward the king must be abandoned, however, largely because the pressures that force Bertram to succumb to him are further complicated by conflict aroused by Helena herself. On the surface, Helena exacerbates Bertram's already expressed resentment at being confined to the effeminizing court. But this, too, builds on deeper dangers that Bertram has no means of understanding or adequately expressing:

> KING Thou know'st she has raised me
>   from my sickly bed.
> BERTRAM But follows it, my lord, to bring
>   me down
> Must answer for your raising? I know her
>   well;
> She had her breeding at my father's charge.
> A poor physician's daughter my wife? Disdain
> Rather corrupt me ever!
>   (II.iii.110-15)

Bertram interprets his abhorrence of Helena in social terms, but his snobbery covers deeper fears. Helena has raised the king from his sickbed, cured him, and, symbolically, restored his virility, made him erect. But, asks Bertram, must this woman therefore "bring me down" to the marriage bed?

The forced marriage to Helena deflects him from his quest for a masculine identity and toward a sexuality he fears. "Undone, and forfeited to cares forever!" (II.ii.263), he whines, sounding like a little boy because he has been made a little boy through submission to the king. He can reopen future potentialities of manhood only by fleeing the sexual union forced upon him: "Although before the solemn priest I have sworn, / I will not bed her" (II.iii.265-66). Parolles' defensive rhetoric in counseling flight brings to the surface the unsavory resonance of debasing sexual anxiety, and opposes to it the ideal of war. "France is a dog-hole," advises Parolles, speaking not only to Bertram but for him,

To th' wars, my boy, to th' wars!
He wears his honor in a box unseen
That hugs his kicky-wicky here at home,
Spending his manly marrow in her arms,
Which should sustain the bound and high
  curvet
Of Mars's fiery steed. To other regions!
France is a stable; we that dwell in't jades.
Therefore to th' war!
                  (II.iii.268; 272-79)

Marriage, from such a view, means dishonor and emasculation, a symbolic mode of castration ("A young man married is a man that's marred" [II.iii.292]); it drains off "manly marrow" better expended in the field of war than in "the dark house and the detested wife" (II.iii.286). Bertram's horror of marital sexuality, his fear of having his precarious masculinity overwhelmed by his wife, drives him to "those Italian fields / Where noble fellows strike" (II.iii.284-85).

The tensions provoked by this marriage are realized dramatically in Bertram's painfully dishonest parting from Helena, a scene brought to an anxious climax when his "clog" desires a farewell kiss. This is only the second time Bertram has spoken to Helena in the play, and the second time he says farewell; he is unable to speak to her at all in the scene in which the marriage is arranged. As he repeatedly bids a persistent Helena to go home without further ado, a squirming Bertram resorts for the first time to the lying that will characterize his behavior in relations to women henceforth. But within the lie he tells Helena, Bertram obliquely expresses a deeper truth about his situation:

> Prepared I was not
> For such a business; therefore am I found
> So much unsettled. This drives me to entreat
>   you
> That presently you take your way for home,
> And rather muse than ask why I entreat you;
> For my respects are better than they seem,
> And my appointments have in them a need
> Greater than shows itself at the first view
> To you that know them not.
>   (II.v.60-68)

Bertram's options are to lie to Helena or lie with her, and the latter is unacceptable to him for reasons he is powerless either to alter or to articulate fully, to Helena or to himself.

All's Well That Ends Well, through those relationships centered subjectively in Bertram, deals with a young man's inevitable problem of freeing mature sexuality from threats that originate in the mutual development of family ties and infantile sexuality. Bertram's exchanges with Parolles and Helena as he prepares to flee France demonstrate how far he falls short of having won that freedom midway through the play. The "need / Greater than shows itself at the first view" that makes the prospect of marital sexuality intolerable is the unconscious dimension of his association of Helena, who "had her breeding at my father's charge," with his own family.

In I.iii, just after Bertram has gone to the French court, Shakespeare suggests the incestuous context of this relationship when the countess teases Helena into acknowledging her love for Bertram: "You know, Helen, / I am a mother to you" (I.iii.130-31). For the two women, Helena's pained protest in this prolonged exchange gives way to a simple resolution:

> HELENA You are my mother, madam.
>   Would you were—
> So that my lord your son were not my
>   brother—
> Indeed my mother! or were you both our
>   mothers,
> I care no more for than I do for heaven,
> So I were not his sister. Can't no other,
> But I your daughter, he must be my brother?
> COUNTESS Yes, Helen, you might be my
>   daughter-in-law.
>
> (I.iii.154-60)

But the countess jests with the very association of Helena with the Rossillion family Bertram fears, and which he cannot so easily resolve.

Bertram mentions his mother nearly every time he talks to or about Helena, casually at first (I.i.71-72), but more compulsively in the press of emotionally intense occasions later on (II.iii.272; II.v.69: IV.iii.85-86). A son's affection for a mother is directed by Bertram toward the countess; a son's fears of female domination and of his own oedipal wishes are aroused in Bertram by Helena. The situation builds on but complicates childhood circumstances in which an incestuous object-choice must be abandoned, for Bertram is forced to accept a woman unconsciously associated with the object of repressed incestuous impulses. Instead of allowing Bertram to find a sexual love removed from infantile conflict, the forced marriage reopens and concentrates the hazards of an oedipal relationship that has undergone repression. The marriage to Helena means for Bertram accepting a sexual bond made repugnant by its incestuous associations and abandoning the possibility of achieving a masculine identity independent of infantile conflict. In the typical oedipal situation, the son protects his own developing autonomy by relinquishing, through repression, the incestuous object to the father; in Bertram's situation, the father's power both transgresses the son's effort to achieve manly autonomy ("It is in us to plant thine honor where / We please to have it grow" [II.iii.155-56]) and compels the son to act out incestuous impulses made intolerable by repression ("I cannot love her, nor will strive to do't" [II.iii.145]).

In the Italian war Bertram finds release from the paralyzing force of this situation:

>   This very day,
> Great Mars, I put myself into thy file.
> Make me but like my thoughts, and I shall
>   prove
> A lover of thy drum, hater of love.
>
> (III.iii.8-11)

He serves heroically, realizing in action the masculine ideal held up earlier by the French king to his restless courtiers. In place of the overpowering king, Bertram finds in the duke of Florence a family romance father whom he serves and saves, and who rewards him for conduct the king of France has forbidden. The comic exposure and renunciation of Parolles as a "counterfeit module" indicate further Bertram's escape from conflicts that beset him in France, for Parolles, however obviously bogus to others in the play, has been a necessary ally in bolstering the young count's courage at court. No longer in need of Parolles' assistance, Bertram can afford to recognize his duplicity. Among men and the affairs of war, Bertram in Italy becomes "the general of our horse," a "most gallant fellow" who has "done most honorable service," "taken their great'st commander," and who "with his own hand . . . slew the duke's brother" (III.v.).

In affairs of women and sexuality, Bertram also finds a strategy for evading conflict in Italy. Once he has located matters of honor, loyalty, and affection in a context independent of heterosexuality, he attempts to establish a sexual relationship with Diana that is independent of honor, loyalty, affection, and the conflicted impulses that have driven him away from Helena. Bertram attempts to escape infantile undercurrents of sexual inhibition by letting them rise to consciousness in a depersonalized context. He appeals to Diana: "And now you should be as your mother was / When your sweet self was got" (IV.ii.9-10). Here the maternal association emerges, not as a hidden inner block against marital sexuality, but as Diana's mother, a woman doing the universal, necessary— and therefore justified— act for begetting children. In Florence, Bertram can perform the act he has fled in disgust because he has— or, rather, he thinks he has— removed himself from conditions responsible for his fearful loathing. In his attempted seduction of Diana, however, Bertram is forced to use a symbol that binds his sexuality to his place in a family tradition, a ring that, as Helena explains to Diana, "downward hath succeeded in his house / From son to son some four or five descents / Since the first father wore it" (II.vii.23-25). Bertram relates to Diana his full awareness of the ring's significance, but he soon hands it over: "Here, take my ring! / My house, mine honor, yea, my life be thine, / And I'll be bid by thee" (IV.ii.51-53). In this impulsive gesture, Bertram completes the logic of his rebellion; he repudiates in an instant the inheritance leading back to "the first father" who wore this very ring. Bertram can win a measure of sexual freedom only by symbolically forfeiting his place among those familial bonds that have complicated his relation to Helena.

In Bertram Shakespeare invests in embryonic form the essential components of a romantic rebel who can only thrive by rejecting the society that has shaped him. Bertram has written this note to his mother on leaving France:

> I have sent you a daughter-in-law. She hath recovered the king, and undone me. I have wedded her, not bedded her, and sworn to make the 'not' eternal. You shall hear I am run away; know it before the report come. If there be breadth enough in the world, I will hold a long distance. My duty to you.
>
> Your unfortunate son,
>
> Bertram
> (III.ii.19-26)

Geographical distance here corresponds to the psychological distance Bertram must put between action and inner conflict if he is to pursue a desired identity. To preserve the purity of his deepest loyalty, that to his mother, Bertram must escape the marital claim of her surrogate Helena. He must find a new father, seek action in a land far removed from France, win a woman he can isolate from an unconscious dread of incest. Bertram's disillusionment at court; his flight from France and an unwanted marriage; his success among men at war in a foreign country; his cavalier attempt to seduce Diana; his symbolic repudiation of patriarchal loyalties in giving up the ring— these are gestures belonging to the Don Juan story, which Bertram brings into a comic art deeply committed to the family.

The problem Bertram puts to Shakespeare resides in the nature of the solution Bertram finds for his own intolerable situation at court. Bertram must be reinstated, for he threatens precisely those social and domestic values celebrated in the festive comedies. Although Shakespeare sketches out the logic of romantic flight in Bertram, the young count is released, ultimately, in order to be retrieved. Every step Bertram takes toward seducing Diana is a step toward the bed, and finally the household, of Helena, Shakespeare's chief agent for reclaiming him. But the effort to reassimilate Bertram further intensifies the pressures on comic form in this play. The nature of these pressures becomes clearer if *All's Well* is understood as a development out of earlier comedies.

PAROLLES

J. Dennis Huston calls Parolles "a curious mixture of the corrupt and the commendable." He acknowledges that Parolles is foolish and corrupt, but he also points out that Parolles injects a good deal of energy into the play. Gerard J. Gross finds his enthusiasm similarly engaging. When Parolles meets up with Helena as she is despairing, their discussion of sex and virginity cause Helena to be energized and desirous of taking action to fulfill her goals. Robert Hapgood draws a similar conclusion, arguing that Parolles's exuberance, even in his betrayal of Bertram and his fellow soldiers, is "disarming" in its "zest." Parolles also draws off criticism from Helena, Katharine Eisaman Maus argues, as they are both social climbers, but Parolles's character and actions seem much more reprehensible in the light of Helena's virtue and honor.

Harold C. Goddard praises Shakespeare for his "masterpiece" in Parolles. Goddard argues that Shakespeare poured all of his venom toward the "gentleman" in this one character and thus made him utterly vile and deserving of universal scorn from everyone except Bertram. Robert Grams Hunter absolves Parolles of any responsibility for Bertram's behavior, arguing that Parolles is a symptom of Bertram's misbehavior, not the cause of it. **David Ellis** agrees that although Parolles may be a tempter, he generally does not initiate wrongdoing but merely encourages it in Bertram. George Philip Krapp concludes that there must be something redeemable in Parolles's character if Helena endures his conversation.

Maurice Charney and Michael Shapiro find that Parolles shows a definite resiliency, even after he has been exposed. He is not surprised, nor ashamed, and finds himself able to "play the fool without hypocrisy or deceit" and is accepted back into the community at court.

David Ellis

SOURCE: "Finding a Part for Parolles," in *Essays in Criticism*, Vol. XXXIX, No. 4, October, 1989, pp. 289-303.

[*In the following essay, Ellis argues that Parolles is not a "corrupter of youth" and that Bertram is not under his spell. Parolles supports and encourages Bertram's misbehavior but is not the cause of it. Ellis also discusses how Lavache and Parolles both contain elements of the fool and the knave.*]

Shakespeare's plays often include characters ready to save us the bother of seeing for ourselves. Generally speaking, the higher their social status, the more chance they have of being listened to. Maria's character-sketch of Malvolio in Act II, Scene iii of *Twelfth Night* would not have enjoyed so much success if her mistress hadn't already pronounced him 'sick of self-love'. When in Act III, Scene ii of *All's Well That Ends Well* the two French lords deliver Bertram's unpleasant letters to Rossillion, the Countess asks who is with him in Florence and, on hearing that it is Parolles, complains, 'A very tainted fellow, and full of wickedness;/My son corrupts a well-derived nature/With his inducement'. This interpretation receives some support from the Florentine ladies watching the soldiers go by in Act III, Scene v. Diana remarks that it is a pity such a good-looking young man as Bertram is not honest and adds, 'Yound's that same knave/That leads him to these places. Were I his lady/I would poison that vile rascal'. The context makes clear that she is shifting to Parolles some of the blame for Bertram's 'dishonesty' in paying court to her when he is already married. But much weightier confirmation of the Countess's belief that Bertram has been led astray comes from Lafew. With the war in Tuscany over and Helena supposed dead, Act IV, Scene v opens in Rossillion as Lafew is saying,

> No, no, no, your son was misled with a snipp'd-taffeta fellow there, whose villainous saffron would have made all the unbak'd and doughy youth of a nation in his colour. Your daughter-in-law had been alive at this hour, and your son here at home, more advanc'd by the king than by that red-tail'd humblebee I speak of.

The notion of Parolles as a successful corrupter of youth has received wide critical approval despite the obvious vested interest of those figures in *All's Well* who propound it (Bertram's mother, a young girl physically attracted to him and an old friend of the family). One reason is that critics, unlike ordinary playgoers, have recognised in Parolles vestiges of the medieval Vice. A similar recognition, allied to a similar inclination to trust 'the quality', leads several of them to believe those at Henry IV's court who say that Hal has been corrupted by Falstaff. The interpretation is no more satisfactory in one case than it is in the other, but for different reasons. There is never a moment in the Henry IV plays when an audience feels that Hal is in any genuine danger from Falstaff. *All's Well* begins with a few half-hearted indications that we shall be shown a well-bred young man tempted from the straight and narrow by a flashy companion; but it quickly becomes the tale of a headstrong youth with all the natural gifts for going to the bad on his own.

Joseph Price claims that Parolles 'prompts the plan that leads to his young master's flight' and the editor of the Arden edition goes further when he says that Parolles 'ships (Bertram) off to the war'. They can only refer to the one occasion in the play on which Parolles appears to initiate rather than merely encourage wrong-doing. This is in Act II, Scene i when Bertram is complaining

of the King's refusal to allow him to go to the Tuscan wars and Parolles says, 'And thy mind stand to't, boy, steal away bravely'. Urging a fiery young man to defy authority is perhaps wrong but it is hardly criminal, and any discredit which attaches to the gesture is lessened by the support Parolles receives from the two French Lords. After Bertram has decided that he will indeed steal away, the first of the Lords says, 'There's honour in the theft'; and when Parolles interjects, 'Commit it, count', the second adds,\ 'I am your accessory'. If Parolles is a wicked corrupter, so too are they.

When the two Lords have left the stage, Parolles makes an absurdly affected speech in which he tells Bertram that he ought to have used 'a more spacious ceremony to the noble lords' and urges him to go after them to 'take a more dilated farewell' (II.i. 49-56). Bertram's 'And I will do so' is the last serious indication we have of his being under Parolles's influence. There is no suspicion that he is acting on any but his own head-strong authority when in Act II, Scene iii he responds with indignant, snobbish dismay to the idea of marrying Helena ('A poor physician's daughter my wife! Disdain/Rather corrupt me ever!'); and after the King has forced him to accept her, he takes no-one's advice before flatly announcing his intentions, 'I'll to the Tuscan wars and never bed her'. Parolles is enthusiastic in Bertram's support and clearly not averse to being the young Count's instrument in fobbing Helena off; but he is a means of bad behaviour not its cause. This remains true for the rest of the play and, as R. L. Smallwood has pointed out, that 'Parolles is not the wicked angel responsible for leading Bertram astray is vividly shown in the final scene where, long after he has been made to see his companion for what he is, Bertram goes on to show himself independently capable of his most objectionable behaviour, in that long demonstration of weakness, cowardice, and lying'. The demonstration Smallwood refers to also militates against efforts to represent the exposure of Parolles as a necessary stage in Bertram's moral regeneration. 'The two scenes which conclude Act III', writes Joseph Price, 'prepare for the expulsion of Parolles's influence and the cure of Bertram' and he goes on to claim that, 'when Bertram realizes the folly of his model he will begin to understand his own faults'. It is true that in Act IV, Scene iii the two French Lords succeed in convincing Bertram that Parolles is not the courageous captain he pretends to be; but the young Count is shown as far less disturbed by this discovery than by the realization (via the letter to Diana discovered in Parolles's pocket) that his messenger in his own double-dealings with women can't be trusted. His indignation reaches its height when he learns that Parolles has not only made a feeble effort to seduce Diana on his own behalf ('Men are to mell with, boys are not to kiss'), but also had the audacity to tell her that a man like Bertram tells lies and doesn't keep his promises.

The failure of Shakespeare's text to support the readings which the Countess, Diana and Lafew try to impose upon it has clearly led to strange goings-on in the theatre, some of which must be reflected in J. L. Styan's relatively recent commentary on Act II, Scene iv of *All's Well* in the 'Shakespeare in Performance' series. This is the scene in which Parolles comes to tell Helena that Bertram will be leaving Paris before consummating his marriage. According to Styan, Parolles 'takes his time before he breaks the news that Bertram is leaving (Helena), for us an intolerable delay'; he 'relishes his secret', 'teases Helena with the unaccustomed colourfulness of his notion that this obstacle in the way of her wedded love will make fulfilment all the sweeter when it comes', and ends the scene 'beside himself with triumph'. Although they purport to be a statement of the theme on which variations could be played, these comments on Act II, Scene iv sound much more like the description of a specific performance. But if Parolles does not immediately deliver his message to Helena it is because he makes the mistake on his entrance of acknowledging the Clown, who happens to be present, 'Oh, my knave! How does my old lady?' Lavatch is never complimentary to anyone, but he is particularly scathing with Parolles, calling him a nothing, a knave and a fool in rapid succession. Of the 150 or so words in their exchange, Parolles only has 27. He is too patently the unwilling recipient of a stream of witty insults to be relishing any secret, and would clearly be only too glad to say what he has to say to Helena, if he could only get rid of the Clown. When he is able to speak to her, his language is colourful; but it is difficult to make much of that in a figure who is continually shown priding himself on elaborate speech. There is no convincing evidence in the text that Parolles takes any *special* pleasure in doing dirty work which, as the following scene shows, Bertram is in any case always prepared to do for himself. Parolles has told Helena that her new husband wants her to take 'instant leave a' th' king' and in Act II, Scene v she comes to Bertram to report that she has done so. He assures her that his reasons for going away and not consummating the marriage are better than they seem, when they are in fact much worse (ll. 58-69); and after a series of painful exchanges meanly denies her a parting kiss. In productions from the 1950s which Styan describes, Parolles was made responsible for preventing a kiss which would otherwise have come about. It is in the spirit of these productions, or of others like them, that Styan writes his commentary on Act II, Scene iv. To present Parolles as more enterprisingly and, above all, effectively wicked than any lines he is given suggest he should be, makes it easier to turn him into a scapegoat; and if directors often share the same interest as the Countess, Diana and Lafew in achieving that result it is because it lessens the unattractiveness of a Bertram to whom, as Dr. Johnson memorably complained, it is difficult to reconcile one's heart.

Giving Parolles behaviour which exaggerates his effectiveness also has the advantages of making him seem more coherent. 'Character criticism' may be long out of fashion among academics but, in the theatre, actors and directors are still inclined to look for some centre around which they can organise the various manifestations of a Shakespearian role. To see Parolles as the corrupter of youth helps to impose order on what, in the first half of *All's Well*, is an unusually loose assemblage of comic types. As an addition to the faint indications of the corrupting Vice which he offers, Parolles is also—with varying but never complete conviction on his creator's part—the traditional boasting soldier, the parasite, the foppish would-be courtier, the traveller and, in the feature of his many-sidedness which arbitrarily determines his name, the man of many words. In other circumstances, this variety of constituents might have been a sign of satisfying complexity; but in *All's Well* it leaves an audience wondering what or who Parolles is supposed to be. Their puzzlement is only likely to be increased by the fact that no-one in *All's Well*, apart of course from Bertram, believes in any specific part he attempts to play. (So strikingly is this so that Bertram's failure to see through his companion comes to seem more and more of an obvious dramatic convenience.) Parolles moves forward via a series of mortifying encounters as first Helena, then Lavatch and Lafew successfully call his bluff and oblige him to fall back on lame expostulation or excuse. The ineffectuality of his efforts to impose upon the world, and his lack of success in trying to hold his own in any company other than Bertram's, make it impossible to credit him with the force to corrupt anybody, least of all a young nobleman capable of replying to his king as impudently as Bertram does in Act II, Scene iii (111 - 3).

Parolles has too many features for Helena's accusation of cowardice in Act I, Scene i (186-202) to fix him in the mind as the *miles gloriosus* and Lavatch's refusal to take him seriously as a gentleman (II.iv. 17-36) doesn't determine how he should be taken. In remarks which excite Parolles to unwise and untypical self-defence, Lafew casually assumes that Bertram must be his 'master' (II.iii. 84-230), but servant is too broad a category to be usefully defining. These bruising encounters are effective in demonstrating that Parolles is not what he pretends to be but they fail to make clear what he is. The illusion of what a Shakespearian character 'is' most frequently establishes itself through monologue or soliloquy. The various parts which Iago plays in *Othello*, for example, are put into perspective by the explanation of his intentions which he offers in private to the audience. It is not until Act IV, Scene i of *All's Well* that Parolles is found communing with himself and on that occasion the consequence is not the tardy discovery of some 'key' to his character but engaging confirmation of an audience's feeling that—*qua* Captain, in this instance—he is not much of an actor. 'They begin to smoke me, and disgraces have of late knock'd too often at my door' (27-8). With the First Lord and his associates listening in, Parolles curses his habit of talking himself into situations which he has no means of handling. Since Bertram's enterprise and his own general ineffectuality up to this point prevent Parolles from being perceived as a serious threat, it is hard not to feel some stirrings of sympathy for him in his dilemma: 'I must give myself some hurts, and say I got them in exploit; yet slight ones will not carry it. They will say, "Came you off with so little?" And great ones I dare not give' (37-40). This sympathy is important because of the fine balance Shakespeare achieves during the great scene (IV. iii) in which the blindfolded Parolles is interrogated in the presence of Bertram and the two Lords.

The comedy in Act IV, scene iii depends not only on the irrepressible fatuity of Parolles in a 'life-threatening' situation but also on the way the balance of power shifts towards him as the conditions of the joke oblige Bertram and the two Lords to stand by helpless whilst he insults them. As the scene progresses, a vital difference emerges, which is not merely comic, between the first Lord's amused tolerance of the outrageous lies Parolles tells about him and Bertram's anger at characterizations ('lascivious boy' etc.) which are broadly accurate. Like the great Boar's Head Tavern scene (II.iv) in *1 Henry IV*, Act IV, Scene iii of *All's Well* gets even better after the reader or spectator is persuaded it has reached its climax. The play is a long way from being Shakespeare's most successful work, but there are few *more* effective moments in his drama than when Parolles is 'unmuffled'. With a laughing audience on one side and the social superiors he has just been betraying and abusing on the other, no-one's situation could be more humiliating. His first reaction is to protest with some justice that anyone can be crushed with a plot. But after the officers have bid him their ironic farewells, and the interpreter has left him alone on the stage with the ominous, 'Fare ye well, sir. I am for France too; we shall speak of you there', what every reader or spectator of *All's Well* remembers is the first half of Parolles's full response to his plight,

> Yet am I thankful. If my heart were great
> 'Twould burst at this. Captain I'll be no more,
> But I will eat and drink and sleep as soft
> As captain shall. Simply the thing I am
> Shall make me live.
>
> (IV.iii. 319-323)

Every critic of the play refers to these famous lines, but there is considerable confusion and disagreement over what to make of them. This is partly because the most striking of them— 'Simply the thing I am/Shall make me live'— depend for their full effect on everything that has gone before. But a further difficulty for many has been that the lines have to be reconciled with the strong moral disapproval of Parolles which has

become part of the orthodox interpretation of this play, and which is usually sustained by adding to a sense of his egregious shortcomings much of the blame for Bertram's. How the reconciliation is effected can be traced back at least as far as H. B. Charlton who, in the tone of a superior officer criticising a disgraced subaltern for failing to blow his brains out, described Parolles's response to his final discomfiture as 'his ignominious acceptance of mere existence'. The critical climate which this remark suggests was evident in Michael Hordern's Parolles at the Old Vic in 1953, or at least in Richard David's account of that performance.

> When Parolles is finally unblindfolded, and discovers his captors to be his own comrades, Hordern managed an immediate and breathtaking transition from farce to deadly earnest. At the discovery he closed his eyes and fell straight backward into the arms of his attendants; then, as with taunts they prepare to leave him, he slithered to the ground, becoming wizened and sly on the instant, and with 'simply the thing I am shall make me live' revealed an essential meanness not only in Parolles but in human nature as a whole.

David's whole description is vivid enough for its essentials to have found their way into Robert Hapgood's 'The Life of Shame: Parolles and *All's Well*', a short piece, published in these pages in 1965, which usefully reminded its readers that Charlton had called Parolles, 'that shapeless lump of cloacine excrement'. (At the height of his anger in Act IV, Scene iii, even Bertram could only manage, 'I could endure anything before but a cat, but now he's a cat to me').

At the beginning of Act IV, Scene iii the first Lord shakes his head over Bertram's conduct and complains, 'As we are ourselves, what things we are!'. His 'things' here are human beings who are spiritually degraded because they ignore the teachings of religion. It is unlikely that Parolles ever paid much attention to these teachings either, but it is hard to see why so many commentators have found his celebration of being a 'thing' memorable if the intended sense is the same as the first Lord's. Harder still to understand is how a good proportion of these commentators could find something exhilarating in the celebration if all it revealed was, 'an essential meanness not only in Parolles but in *human nature as a whole*'. Robert Hapgood was justified in refusing to believe that 'Shakespeare intended an effect simply of revulsion'. He attributes the positive way in which many people respond to Parolles's soliloquy to the character's comic vitality, describing as 'his most redeeming trait' 'a love of life so strong that it can make him welcome (all too easily, it's true) even the prospect of living safest in shame'. Like Falstaff, Parolles turns his back on the precept 'Death rather than dishonour' and celebrates not the meanness of human nature but its resilience and powerful instinct for survival— its 'all-surviving tensile-strength', as Hapgood puts it.

His remarks are helpful but insufficiently specific— after all, many other comic figures, apart from Parolles, have a jack-in-the-box resistance to misfortune— and they don't do enough to counter Charlton's charge that Parolles's thankful acceptance of life, after being deprived of any respectable social identity, is 'ignominious'. The memorability of Parolles's soliloquy, and its exhilarating effect on some, cannot only be dependent on his delighted relief that all his desperate efforts to stay alive— 'Let me live, sir, in a dungeon, i'th' stocks, or anywhere, so I may live' (IV.iii. 235 - 6)— have been successful. What they depend on more is implied in his witty recognition that escaping death would not have done him much good had he in fact been the greathearted captain the joke was designed to prove he wasn't. 'If my heart were great/'Twould burst at this'. One certainly responds to the instinct for survival in his words, but even more to the feeling of relief in having to throw off a social role which had become a burden. Being a captain was especially burdensome to Parolles because, as the audience recognized and he himself acknowledged in his first soliloquy, he was such a poor performer in the part; but the oppressiveness of a defined social position is something which everyone occasionally feels from captains to authors with bad reviews ('Author I'll be no more,/But I will eat and drink . . . etc.'). Shakespeare has already instructed us in these matters earlier in *All's Well*. The King of France has consulted all the best doctors as only Kings can and is so convinced he is dying that his first instinct is to refuse Helena's offer of a cure.

> I say we must not
> So stain our judgement or corrupt our hope,
> To prostitute our past-cure malady
> To empirics, or to dissever so
> Our great self and our credit, to esteem
> A senseless help, when help past sense we
>   deem.
>
> (II.i. 118-123)

These lines are good enough to bring to mind the intolerable dilemma of someone in the last stages of a fatal illness who is trapped between 'What harm could it do?' on the one hand and 'Have I not the courage to face up to the truth?' on the other. The King believes that he owes it to himself as a rational creature to reject what would constitute— and what in fact turns out to be— 'a miracle cure'. Impossible to disentangle in his lines (especially as they move from the first person singular to the first person plural) is what he expects from himself as the individual who happens to be King, and his awareness of the general responsibilities of his position; but his sense of the latter is plain enough in his reference to the dangers of separating his 'great self' from his 'credit', or reputation. What he

might think of himself if he welcomed Helena's offer is inextricably bound up with his sense of what other people would think of a King who accepted 'A senseless help'. In his case, the oppressiveness of a defined social position comes near to having fatal effects and it is evident that, if he could have followed the example Parolles is later to give and said, 'King I'll be no more', his resistance to his good fortune would have disappeared more speedily.

Parolles offers a momentary glimpse of a world where people have to play, not Jaques's 'many parts', but no part at all. In the best Falstaffian tradition, he turns the tables on his recent captors, emerging triumphantly from his ordeal like a Brer Rabbit thrown into the briar patch of non-identity by those who failed to realise how far his previous experiences would incline him to welcome it as his natural habitat. He makes of necessity an exhilarating virtue as does also, one might reasonably say, the Shakespeare who, up until this point in *All's Well*, has given Parolles a number of different personae none of which has proved wholly satisfactory. Now he both explains and excuses the relative failure of Parolles as a 'character' by allowing the audience to share in a utopian escape from the necessity of having any character at all: 'Simply the thing I am/Shall make me live'. In general, Shakespeare is always inclined to be more interested in immediate dramatic effect than larger questions of consistency or coherence. It is as if he wrote his parts in the foreknowledge that there would one day be a Coleridge to lay the foundations of a method for filling in all gaps and explaining away all discrepancies. Here he can be taken as using Parolles to entertain very briefly the notion of a 'thingness' which would absolve the dramatist from the duty of giving his figures adequate social definition. There can of course be no such absolution just as, when 'dropping out' is always as firmly defining as social conformity, Parolles can have no realistic hope of living both off and free from society. Shakespeare is obliged to draw back from having a 'thing' on the stage and Parolles will have to re-integrate himself into social life. The two processes are simultaneous and have already begun in the second and less memorable half of Parolles's soliloquy.

> Who knows himself a braggart,
> Let him fear this; for it will come to pass
> That every braggart shall be found an ass.
> Rust, sword; cool, blushes; and Parolles live
> Safest in shame; being fool'd, by fool'ry thrive.
> There's place and means for every man alive.
> I'll after them.
>
> (IV.iii. 323 - 9)

The move here into a different and, for modern ears, more conventional idiom exemplifies the struggle between two different kinds of drama which goes on throughout *All's Well*. The conflict is easiest to locate in Helena and has given rise to much dispute as to whether the emphasis should fall on revelations of a delicately sensitive inner life (as in III.ii. 99 - 129, for example), or on the actions to which she is committed by Shakespeare's sources and which, when the point of view remains psychological, mark her out as a predatory schemer. In Parolles's soliloquy the change of manner is evident in the appearance of couplets, but also in his reminder of one of the several stock types ('braggart') with which he has been loosely associated. Now all of these are no longer serviceable, either for himself or Shakespeare, there is a hint of what will replace them ('being fool'd, by fool'ry thrive'), but as yet no clear or obvious indication. His decision to follow his recent tormentors into France ('I'll after them') is nevertheless a plain enough sign that the release from association of any kind, which he has just been celebrating, is imaginary.

'Simply the thing I am/Shall make me live' may be a defiant assertion of freedom from social definition, but by the end of his soliloquy Parolles is already referring to the 'place' which exists for every man alive. It is significant that in his quest for a new 'place', and in Shakespeare's final efforts to place or characterise him, the first person Parolles should meet is Lavatch. In a play in which many figures are problematic, Lavatch is not the least puzzling. This is not because, like Parolles, the impression he initially makes is indeterminate. On the contrary, the dominant features of his composition are immediately apparent on his first entrance and only become more so with each subsequent appearance. The difficulty lies rather in trying to follow the by now well-established custom of thinking of him along with the other domestic fools Robert Armin is assumed to have played; Touchstone, Feste and the Fool in *King Lear*. When the Countess excuses Lavatch to Lafew by saying, 'My lord that's gone made himself much sport out of him' (IV.v. 61 - 2), she is paying a very considerable tribute to the sturdiness of her late husband's sense of humour. To an even greater extent than the other three Fools, Lavatch has his order's earthy cynicism, especially on sexual matters; and his Fool status is confirmed by the memories and threats of whipping in Act II, Scene ii. Several important similarities between the four figures can be established, but Lavatch is unlike the others in that at no point in *All's Well* does he offer the slightest hint of mental unbalance. Touchstone and Feste can lay claim to being the cleverest people in their respective plays: they are much more clearly than the Fool in *King Lear* 'artificial'. But neither of them abandons completely a protective colouring of madness without which their manner of talking to social superiors would become unacceptable. Lavatch is different in that he never appears to feel he needs folly as a stalking-horse, and one consequence is that Lafew's question in Act IV, Scene v— 'Whether dost thou profess thyself— a knave or a fool?'— becomes a highly pertinent enquiry. The knave/boy collocation found in *King*

A scene from All's Well That Ends Well. *By Audibran. The University of Michigan Special Collections Library.*

Lear is obviously irrelevant and the dialogue which follows Lafew's question— the one in which Lavatch expounds the bawdy implications of his claim to be a fool at a woman's service and a knave at a man's— makes it clear that the issue is not whether Lavatch is a domestic fool or an ordinary servant or menial. 'So you were a knave at (a man's) service indeed', says Lafew, after Lavatch has explained that he would give the man's wife his bauble 'to do her service'; and he has then to admit, 'I will subscribe for thee; thou art both knave and fool'.

In the official designations of *All's Well*, Lavatch is more Fool than knave and Parolles the opposite. Their second encounter (V.ii) temporarily justifies the old adage that fools and knaves divide the world. Lavatch is even more scathing to the ragged and dischevelled Parolles than he had been on their first meeting and Parolles is only saved from his scorn by the entry of Lafew. After first of all failing to recognize the former dandy, Lafew offers Parolles a symbolic handshake. Earlier in the play, he had asked parolles to acknowledge that he had been detected as a fraud by shaking hands: 'So, my good window of lattice, fare thee well; thy casement I need not open, for I look through thee. Give me thy hand' (II.iii.

212 - 14). The offer had been indignantly rejected. There is now no reason for Parolles not to acknowledge openly that all his disguises have been stripped away, but despite Lafew's 'though you are a fool and knave you shall eat', what if anything they will be replaced by is not yet clear. The process of clarification is interrupted by the entry of the King and the final scene of reconciliation between Bertram and Helena. Parolles's minor role in this includes humbly accepting the King's reference to Bertram as his 'master', and then talking himself of the tricks 'which gentlemen have' in a way which makes it obvious that he no longer aspires to be one of them (V.iii. 233 - 9). But it is only after Helena and Bertram have been finally brought together that his own fate is decided. 'Mine eyes smell onions; I shall weep anon,' says Lafew, and then to Parolles, 'Good Tom Drum, lend me a handkercher. So, I thank thee. Wait on me home, I'll make sport with thee. Let thy curtsies alone, they are scurvy ones' (314 - 318). That the Countess's husband enjoyed making sport with Lavatch strengthens the impression that Parolles is here being adopted as Lafew's household fool and confirms the appropriateness of his advice to himself in his great soliloquy: 'being fool'd, by fool'ry thrive'. Looking back over *All's Well* in the light of this conclusion, it becomes evident that Parolles has already shown several attributes of the Fool or Clown, the most easily identifiable being his opening discussion with Helena on virginity (I.i. 104 - 160). When this dialogue is compared with the one in Act I, Scene iii in which the Countess plays the straight-man for Lavatch and when the topic is also sexual (7 - 93), it is hard not to feel that, in comparison with the Countess, Lafew has arranged for himself the better or at least more comfortable deal. Now that there are two Fools, it is also hard not to conclude that the official account of who is more knave than fool will have to be reversed.

From experimenting with various roles— none of which, either singly or in combination, he is much good at— Parolles moves to an exhilarating shedding of all social categorization, and is then finally accounted for as a domestic fool. Like the recovery of Bertram, his reintegration into society is a sign of that 'tolerance' so often stressed in thematic accounts of *All's Well*: 'There's place and means for every man alive'. Yet the ending to his career is no more unambiguously happy than the one which in the final scene unites the two protagonists. The lesson it provides as to what it means to be social— the stress on our inevitable dependence on the social group— is sobering. Interiorized social norms are always more likely to govern our behaviour than the promptings of some putative essential self.

The progress of Parolles is also illustrative of a problem of casting which Shakespeare appears to be struggling with, or at least working on, throughout *All's Well*. In the first part of the play the figure is too unfixed and ineffectual to be capable of the serious knavery of corrupting Bertram, a task for which Shakespeare does not give him the necessary character. As he moves from one humiliat-

ing encounter to another, his efforts to find himself a place in a world of gentlemen are too unsuccessful to be seriously threatening. The decisive contribution to the problem of how Parolles should be regarded is probably made in Act IV, Scene iii by the First Lord. When the blindfolded Parolles first begins to talk about the First Lord and suggests he was whipped from Paris 'for getting the shrieve's fool with child, a dumb innocent that could not say him nay' (181 - 2), Bertram has to restrain his fellow officer from violent retaliation. But after Parolles has slipped into his comically abusive stride and made a long speech on the First Lord's 'honesty', the latter's response is, 'I begin to love him for this' (253). A few lines later the First Lord says of Parolles, 'He hath out-villain'd villainy so far that the rarity redeems him' but the truth is rather than his insults are so outrageously and ineptly wide of the mark that they are laughable. It is this ability to provoke laughter which, after Shakespeare's brief euphoric toying with a drama of 'things', marks Parolles out as a Fool or Clown.

In *As You Like It*, Jaques is 'ambitious for a motley coat' (II.vii. 43) and in *Twelfth Night* Malvolio is reduced to the status of a 'poor fool' (V.i. 368); but only at the end of *All's Well* is there a genuine doubling of the number of Fools. In the traditional method for distinguishing one kind of fool from another, 'natural' refers to those who are mentally deranged and 'artificial' to those who only pretend to be. The distinction can also be extended to refer to Fools whose humour is either inadvertent or deliberate. Lavatch is very clearly 'artificial' in that he tells jokes and exercises full control over the comedy of the situations in which he is involved. Parolles has some control in his opening dialogue with Helena but, in general, he might well have said of his rival Lavatch's fooling what Sir Andrew Aguecheek says of Sir Toby's, 'Ay, he does well enough, if he be disposed, . . . but I do it more natural' (II.iii. 82-4). Perhaps the disapproves of Parolles, and latter-day Johnsonians anxious for Shakespeare to demonstrate more clearly his antipathy to vice, can be comforted with the thought that his likely role in Lafew's household would be less to make his new master laugh than to be laughed at by him.

SOURCES FOR FURTHER STUDY

Literary Commentary

Briggs, Julia. "Shakespeare's Bed-Tricks." In *Essays in Criticism* XLIV, No. 4 (October 1994): 293-314.
    Discusses the influences on Shakespeare in his use of the bed-trick and how Shakespeare used the bed-trick in his own work. Briggs focuses on *Arcadia*, a work preceding Shakespeare's plays, and Shakespeare's own *Measure for Measure* and *All's Well That Ends Well*.

Brown, John Russell. "Love's Ordeal and the Judgements of *All's Well That Ends Well, Measure for Measure,* and *Troilus and Cressida.*" In *Shakespeare and His Comedies,* pp. 183-200. London: Methuen & Co. Ltd., 1957.

Argues that these three comedies— *All's Well That Ends Well, Measure for Measure,* and *Troilus and Cressida*— are, like their Shakespearean predecessors, "informed by Shakespeare's ideals of love's wealth, love's truth, and love's order," even though they are often classified as "problem plays" and set apart from Shakespeare's other comedies. Brown argues that the three plays "refine and extend Shakespeare's comic vision" and that understanding them enhances one's appreciation of the earlier comedies.

Bryant, J. A., Jr. "*All's Well That Ends Well* and *Measure for Measure.*" In *Shakespeare and the Uses of Comedy,* pp. 203-20. Lexington: University Press of Kentucky, 1986.

Examines how the two plays, although "traditional" comedies, veer from the usual paths of such tales, arriving "at the prescribed destination with marks of the passage still showing."

Chambers, E. K. "*All's Well That Ends Well.*" In *Discussions of Shakespeare's Problem Comedies,* edited by Robert Ornstein, pp. 38-41. Boston: D. C. Heath and Company, 1961.

Briefly explores the "degradation" of Helena in *All's Well That Ends Well.*

Champion, Larry S. "The Problem Comedies." In *The Evolution of Shakespeare's Comedy: A Study in Dramatic Perspective,* pp. 96-128. Cambridge, MA: Harvard University Press, 1970.

Examines how *All's Well That Ends Well* centers on the character of Bertram and how Parolles, Lavache, Lafeu, and Helena contribute to the comic perspective of the play.

Charney, Maurice. "*All's Well That Ends Well.*" In *All of Shakespeare,* pp. 95-103. New York: Columbia University Press, 1993.

Provides an overview of *All's Well That Ends Well* intended for classroom use or for the general reader.

Dowden, Edward. "The Role of Helena." In *Discussions of Shakespeare's Problem Comedies,* edited by Robert Ornstein, pp. 35-37. Boston: D. C. Heath and Company, 1961.

Briefly explores the character of Helena in *All's Well That Ends Well,* finding her noble, active, and courageous.

Fraser, Russell, ed. Introduction to *All's Well That Ends Well,* pp. 1-37. Cambridge: Cambridge University Press, 1985.

Provides an overview of *All's Well That Ends Well,* including its genesis; how Shakespeare drew on historical figures and tales for his creation of characters (acknowledging Boccaccio's *Decameron*); the uniqueness of Bertram as a Shakespearean hero; and various other much-discussed elements of the play, such as its ending, the characters' sexuality, and the importance of Parolles. Fraser also puts this play in context with some of Shakespeare's other plays and provides a brief stage history. This introduction is followed by the actual text of the play.

Friedman, Michael D. "Male Bonds and Marriage in *All's Well* and *Much Ado.*" In *Studies in English Literature* 35, No. 2 (Spring 1995): 231-49.

Discusses male bonding in *All's Well That Ends Well* and *Much Ado about Nothing,* primarily the relationship between Bertram and Parolles, and Claudio and Benedick, and how it pertains to marriage in the plays.

Goddard, Harold C. "All's Well That Ends Well." In *The Meaning of Shakespeare,* pp. 424-35. Chicago: University of Chicago Press, 1951.

Explores the possibility of examining *All's Well That Ends Well* in two different ways— as a folktale and as a "less clandestinely ironical" *Two Gentlemen of Verona.* In the folktale interpretation, Helena is the "good angel" who rescues Bertram from Parolles, the "bad angel." If this was Shakespeare's intent, Goddard argues, he did a poor job of it, as Bertram's character is simply too "blackened" for the reader to think the ending plausible. In the second interpretation, Parolles and Bertram are the two "gentlemen," and Parolles, especially, takes center stage as a universally scorned and abhorred character.

Haley, David. "Bertram at Court." In *Shakespeare's Courtly Mirror: Reflexivity and Prudence in* All's Well That Ends Well, pp. 17-51. Newark: University of Delware Press, 1993.

Examines *All's Well That Ends Well* as a courtly play (and Shakespeare's approach to the courtier in general), with specific emphasis on Bertram as a courtier.

———. "Helena's Love." In *Shakespeare's Courtly Mirror: Reflexivity and Prudence in* All's Well That Ends Well, pp. 87-122. Newark: University of Delware Press, 1993.

Examines Helena's character, including her love melancholy, her "prophetic virtue" and "providential mission," and her "erotic motive" to be united with Bertram after he has rejected her (thus abandoning "providence for Eros").

Hapgood, Robert. "The Life of Shame: Parolles and *All's Well.*" In *Essays in Criticism* XV, No. 3 (July 1965): 269-78.

Discusses Parolles's vitality, how the King, Helena, Diana, Bertram, and Parolles are faced with an ordeal in which death is a real possibility, and the issue of telling the truth.

Hethmon, Robert H. "The Case for *All's Well:* What Is Wrong with the King?" In *Drama Critique* VII, No. 1 (Winter 1964): 26-31.

Provides a very brief overview of the main characters and scenes in *All's Well That Ends Well,* with some discussion of how certain scenes should be performed, especially the ending of the play.

Hodgdon, Barbara. "The Making of Virgins and Mothers: Sexual Signs, Substitute Scenes and Doubled Presences in *All's Well That Ends Well*." In *Philological Quarterly* 66, No. 1 (Winter 1987): 47-71.

> Approaches a reading of *All's Well That Ends Well* from Helena's point of view, examining in particular how Shakespeare based his play on Boccaccio's play and what he did differently; how "sexual signs are articulated in character and event"; and how substitute scenes are used, particularly the bed-trick.

Hunt, Maurice. "Words and Deeds in *All's Well That Ends Well*." In *Modern Language Quarterly* 48, No. 4 (December 1987): 320-38.

> Examines the "competition" between words and deeds in *All's Well That Ends Well* primarily through the King of France, who vacillates between valuing word and deed and thus the two cannot be brought into harmony; Helena, through whom Shakespeare implies that "not only that deeds can on occasion speak but also that they can prompt an eventual honesty in words"; and Bertram, who merges word and deed in the final scenes of the play when he embraces Helena.

Hunter, Robert Grams. "*All's Well That Ends Well*." In *Shakespeare and the Comedy of Forgiveness*, pp. 106-31. New York: Columbia University Press, 1965.

> Highlights the main scenes and dialogue in *All's Well That Ends Well*. Hunter describes how the play has a special significance in its oddities and in how our expectations are continually disappointed. He emphasizes the theme of a "dying world in need of regeneration," and classifies the play as a "comedy of forgiveness."

Huston, J. Dennis. "'Some Stain of Soldier': The Functions of Parolles in *All's Well That Ends Well*." In *Shakespeare Quarterly* XXI, No. 4 (Autumn 1970): 431-38.

> Argues that Parolles is not an entirely unworthy figure in *All's Well That Ends Well*. He does provide some energy amid the backdrop of solemnity and death at the opening of the play, and he does infuse Helena with energy when she is despairing over her love for Bertram. However, Huston also argues that Parolles represents the very worst of the younger generation, whose failings are facilitating social decay and "darkness," which the older generation, especially the King, laments.

Jardine, Lisa. "Cultural Confusion and Shakespeare's Learned Heroines: 'These Are Old Paradoxes.'" In *Shakespeare Quarterly* 38, No. 1 (Spring 1987): 1-18.

> Discusses how Helena and Portia, in, respectively, *All's Well That Ends Well* and *The Merchant of Venice*, possessed knowledge traditionally associated with the "male sphere." Helena, in particular possessed knowledge as a healer (the community's "wise woman"), in her upbringing (her "education"), and as the "woman who knows" in her deception of Bertram. Jardine discusses the tension between possessing knowledge as a part of female virtue and possessing it in the "male sphere."

Kastan, David Scott. "*All's Well That Ends Well* and the Limits of Comedy." In *ELH* 52, No. 3 (Autumn 1985): 575-89.

> Argues that although *All's Well That Ends Well* and Shakespeare's other "problem plays" are classified as comedies and not tragedies because "fictive aspirations have been gratified," the reader is not entirely satisfied with these "aspirations" and indeed has been "made suspicious of them," thus making the plays "generic mixtures" or "mutations."

Krapp, George Philip. "Parolles." In *Shaksperian Studies*, edited by Brander Matthews and Ashley Horace Thorndike, pp. 291-302. New York: Russell and Russell, Inc., 1962.

> Argues that it is erroneous to connect Parolles with the creation of the character of Falstaff, or to equate him with the "braggart soldier" of Renaissance comedy. Rather, the character of Parolles parallels that of the Elizabethan "young wits" of the last part of the sixteenth century—he was "a transcript from Elizabethan life."

Lawrence, William Witherle. "*All's Well That Ends Well*." In *Shakespeare's Problem Comedies*, pp. 32-77. New York: Macmillan, 1931.

> Focuses on the characters of Helena and Bertram using two well-known themes of popular story— The Fulfillment of the Tasks and The Healing of the King— and by looking at Parolles and Lavache. In general Lawrence concludes that Helena is wholly deserving of admiration, not scorn; the ending is unreservedly a happy one; and that the play must be examined in an Elizabethan context to interpret it properly.

Leech, Clifford. "The Theme of Ambition in *All's Well That Ends Well*." In *ELH* 21, No. 1 (March 1954): 17-29.

> Touches on the possible folktale elements in *All's Well That Ends Well;* the juxtaposition of older and younger characters; the unsatisfactory ending; and how the element of ambition is intertwined with Helena's love for Bertram. Leech paints a fairly negative portrait of Helena, finding her devious even in her modest language.

Leggatt, Alexander. "*All's Well That Ends Well:* The Testing of Romance." In *Modern Language Quarterly* 32, No. 1 (March 1971): 21-41.

> Suggests that instead of praising or condemning *All's Well That Ends Well*, it is much more instructive to investigate how this controversy arose. Leggatt attempts to do this by focusing on the characters as "creations springing from, and inextricably wedded to, the peculiar dramatic mode of the play," concentrating in particular on the concepts of romance and realism.

Magee, William H. "Helena, A Female Hamlet." In *English Miscellany* 22 (1971): 31-46.

> Explores the "similarities amid many differences" between Helena in *All's Well That Ends Well* and Hamlet. For example, they are similar in their capacity for affection and love, both are attractive characters, they face

comparable difficulties and they have an essential dignity and a "passion for friendship and love together with an awareness of love's nasty side." Spiritually, however, they are quite different. Hamlet is philosophical, a scholar, and muses on abstract ideas; Helena lives in the here and now, in the physical world, relying on divine providence. According to Magee, we can "observe in the comparison of Helena and Hamlet how Shakespeare's unique absorption with his unusually vapid young hero type can be related to his continual interest in the young heroines."

Makaryk, Irene Rima. "The Problem Plays." In her dissertation, *Comic Justice in Shakespeare's Comedies*, 1979.
Discusses *All's Well That Ends Well* within the context of the two other "problem plays" with which it is usually aligned—*Measure for Measure* and *Troilus and Cressida*.

Maus, Katharine Eisaman. "*All's Well That Ends Well*." In *The Norton Shakespeare*, edited by Stephen Greenblatt, pp. 2175-81. New York: W. W. Norton, 1997.
Provides an overview of *All's Well That Ends Well*, touching on such topics as the reversal of gender roles, the lack of "endings" in the play, desire, honor, and social class.

Muir, Kenneth. "*All's Well That Ends Well*." In *Shakespeare's Comic Sequence*, pp. 124-32. Liverpool: Liverpool University Press, 1979.
Provides a brief overview of *All's Well That Ends Well*, focusing on the actions and motivations of Helena and Bertram.

Ranald, Margaret Loftus. "The Betrothals of *All's Well That Ends Well*." In *The Huntington Library Quarterly* XXVI, No. 2 (February 1963): 179-92.
Examines the laws of marriage in Elizabethan England and how they can be used to analyze the marriage contracts between Helena and Bertram, and Diana and Bertram.

Richard, Jeremy. "'The Thing I am': Parolles, the Comedic Villain, and Tragic Consciousness." In *Shakespeare Studies*, Vol. XVIII, pp. 145-59. Burt Franklin & Co., Inc., 1986.
Demonstrates how the character of Parolles fits into Shakespeare's development of the metamorphosis of the comedic villain in his work: "Parolles and the manner in which he suggests that all is not well that ends well creates a new Shakespearean drama of the pitfalls of the mental world rather than the pratfalls of the physical."

Roark, Christopher. "Lavatch and Service in *All's Well That Ends Well*." In *Studies in English Literature, 1500-1900* 28, No. 2 (Spring 1988): 241-258.
Argues that examining the role of Lavatch, the clown, can add an important dimension to understanding the play, especially its more problematic elements, such as the unsatisfying ending.

Shalvi, Alice. "The Pursuit of Honor in *All's Well That Ends Well*." In *Studies in English Language and Literature*, Vol. XVII, pp. 9-34. Jerusalem: Magnes Press, Hebrew University, 1966.
Examines how Shakespeare represented various types of and attitudes toward honor through different characters and groups of characters in *All's Well That Ends Well*. The "older generation" of nobility, represented primarily by the King of France, the Countess of Rousillon, and Lafeu, values honor and virtue, regardless of social rank or birth. The "younger generation," represented primarily by Bertram (and excluding Parolles and Helena), "have inherited none of their elders' virtue and wisdom; they are noble in title, not character."

Shapiro, Michael. "'The Web of Our Life': Human Frailty and Mutual Redemption in *All's Well That Ends Well*." In *JEPG* LXXI, No. 4 (October 1972): 514-26.
Argues that Helena and Bertram in *All's Well That Ends Well* can be seen as symmetrical, parallel characters. At the beginning of the play, both characters need to prove themselves and attain distinction through achievement—Bertram goes off to war and Helena cures the King. However, both experience failure in the process— Bertram gains glory in battle but loses his honor with Diana, and Helena gains Bertram's hand but not his heart. In the end, these two characters redeem each other. It is often noted that Helena redeems Bertram, but he is also an agent of her redemption through his forgiveness of her deception and acceptance of her as his wife.

Simpson, Lynne M. "The Failure to Mourn in *All's Well That Ends Well*." In *Shakespeare Studies* XXII (1994): 172-88.
Examines the Oedipal anxieties in Helena and Bertram as they pertain to the failure of each to mourn the death of her/his father. Helena substitutes Bertram for her dead father, and Bertram substitutes the King of France for his. Simpson takes a psychoanalytic approach with regard to the concepts of guilt, death, forgetting, memory, and forgiveness in the play.

Snyder, Susan. "*All's Well That Ends Well* and Shakespeare's Helens: Text and Subtext, Subject and Object." In *English Literary Renaissance* 18, No. 1 (Winter 1988): 66-77.
Examines two aspects of *All's Well That Ends Well* as they relate to Helena. The first concerns the "gaps, disjunctions, and silences" in the play, "where we lack an expected connection or explanation in the speeches or actions" of Helena, primarily as they concern her character's mixture of initiative and passivity. In the second part of the essay, Snyder compares the Helena of *All's Well* with the Helena of *A Midsummer Night's Dream* and with Helen of Troy, demonstrating how *All's Well's* Helena, even at the end of the play, stands in marked contrast to the other two similarly named heroines as undesired subject rather than desired object.

Spencer, Hazelton. "*All's Well That Ends Well*." In *Discussions of Shakespeare's Problem Comedies*, edited by Robert

Ornstein, pp. 42-44. Boston: D. C. Heath and Company, 1961.

Argues that one must "accept the romantic plot" of *All's Well That Ends Well* as is if one is to enjoy the play and find it worthwhile. Spencer especially notes that the bed-trick should not be considered unnatural or unusual, "since the condition was imposed on Helena by her husband," and that the plot of the play necessitated the stupidity and viciousness of the character of Bertram, "if we are to be wholeheartedly for Helena."

Styan, J. L. "*All's Well That Ends Well.*" *Shakespeare in Performance Series.* Manchester: Manchester University Press, 1984.

Describes how *All's Well That Ends Well* has been performed primarily on stage but also on television in the twentieth century. The first part addresses issues of performance; the second part takes the play scene by scene; and the appendix contains listings of twentieth-century productions, major productions, and principal casts.

Tillyard, E. M. W. "*All's Well That Ends Well.*" In *Shakespeare's Problem Plays*, pp. 94-123. Toronto: University of Toronto Press, 1949.

Finds *All's Well That Ends Well* an overall failure due to its lack of execution, its lack of "steady warmth pervading the whole creation," and a "defective poetical style." However, he does find some merit in the plot and in Shakespeare's three main characters, Helena, Bertram, and Parolles.

Ure, Peter. "*The Problem Plays*" and "*All's Well That Ends Well.*" In *The Problem Plays*, pp. 7-18. London: Longmans Green & Co., 1961.

Provides a brief overview of the problematic nature of *All's Well That Ends Well*, focusing primarily on the ending of the play as it relates to the character development— or lack thereof— of Helena and Bertram. Ure finds that in the end, Bertram's character remains unchanged despite his tutelage from the King regarding honor, his "education" in the military, and his witnessing of Parolles's destruction. Bertram's inability to "grow up" and Helena's unflagging goodness provide an unsatisfactory reconciliation of the two in the final act of the play, and thus an unsatisfactory ending (albeit a "proper" comedic one).

Vaughn, Jack A. "*All's Well That Ends Well.*" In *Shakespeare's Comedies*, pp. 153-59. New York: Frederick Ungar Publishing Co., 1980.

Provides a very brief overview of *All's Well That Ends Well*, touching on the difficulty critics face in assessing the motives and actions of Helena, Bertram, and Parolles. Also provides a brief stage history.

Warren, Roger. "Why Does It End Well? Helena, Bertram, and the Sonnets." In *Shakespeare Survey: An Annual Survey of Shakespearean Study & Production*, edited by Kenneth Muir, pp. 79-92. London: Cambridge University Press, 1969..

Finds that Shakespeare's sonnets provide "illuminating commentary" to discussions of *All's Well That Ends Well*. Warren interweaves sonnets and excerpts from the play to explore Helena's "passionate love and the power of its expression," the "curiously unsympathetic portrait" of Bertram; the social gulf between Helena and Bertram; and the unlikely ending to the play.

Wells, Stanley. "Plays of Troy, Vienna, and Roussillon: *Troilus and Cressida, Measure for Measure,* and *All's Well That Ends Well.*" In *Shakespeare: A Life in Drama*, pp. 234-244. New York: W. W. Norton, 1995.

Follows the relationship of Helena and Bertram in *All's Well That Ends Well* to illuminate the play's "moral self-consciousness."

Yang, Sharon R. "Shakespeare's *All's Well That Ends Well.*" In *The Explicator* 50, No. 4 (Summer 1992): 199-203.

Briefly explores the parallels between the characters of Lavache and Bertram, particularly how Lavache's "words and experiences expose the absurdity of Bertram's perspective."

Media Adaptations

All's Well That Ends Well. BBC Time/Life Series, 1981.
Television production starring Ian Charleson, Angela Down and Celia Johnson. Distributed by Ambrose Video. 141 minutes.

ANTONY AND CLEOPATRA

INTRODUCTION

Antony and Cleopatra was first listed for publication in 1608, but evidence strongly suggests that the play was written and performed one or two years earlier. No evidence exists to indicate that *Antony and Cleopatra* appeared in print before its inclusion in the First Folio of 1623; therefore, the First Folio version of the play is considered by most critics to be authoritative.

Thomas North's "The Life of Antonius" in his *The Lives of the Noble Grecianes and Romans compared together* (1579)—an English translation of a work by Plutarch—is the principal source for *Antony and Cleopatra*. Scholars have remarked that Shakespeare followed North's translation of Plutarch closely for his play; they note in particular a close match between Shakespeare's poetic rendition of Enobarbus's description of Cleopatra on her barge and North's own prose translation of the episode. Critics, however, are divided on whether Shakespeare's characterizations of Antony and Cleopatra are more or less flattering than they are in North's translation of Plutarch.

Scholarly debate over *Antony and Cleopatra* has centered around Antony's "dotage" or decline and the relative nobleness of his character; Cleopatra's contradictory behavior and the significance of her death; the nature of the lovers' passion for one another; and the comparative wisdom or rashness of their actions. Commentators have also examined *Antony and Cleopatra*'s comparatively minor but nonetheless dramatically significant characters Octavius, Octavia, and Enobarbus. Some scholars have focused on the connections between Shakespeare's *Antony and Cleopatra* and John Dryden's sixteenth-century version of the play, *All for Love* (1678). Other issues of interest to critics include the play's language, imagery, structure, and political context, as well as its treatment of the mores and politics of a changing Rome versus those of Egypt. Thematic concerns include the relationship in the play between reason and imagination or passion, the nature of love, the choice between love and empire, and political or social disintegration. Recent scholarship has stressed the nature of the play's mythological and supernatural elements; the degree of sexism practiced by earlier critics with regard to Cleopatra's character; and the relative merit of *Antony and Cleopatra* as a tragedy when ranked against such works as *Hamlet*, *Othello*, *King Lear*, and *Macbeth*. The irony and paradox that pervade *Antony and Cleopatra* and that render much of the play's action and many of its themes problematic are of particular interest to critics today, and there appears to be a growing consensus that Shakespeare in fact intended that this drama of love, politics, aging, and death be both ambivalent and ambiguous.

PRINCIPAL CHARACTERS

(in order of appearance)

Philo: Friend and follower of Antony. As the play opens Philo tells of his disgust with Antony's "dotage" or infatuation with Cleopatra.

Cleopatra: Queen of Egypt and lover of Antony. Although she is aging, Cleopatra is celebrated in the play for her beauty and sexual magnetism. She is jealous of Antony's connections with Rome and of his apparent subservience to Octavius Caesar. She and Antony join forces to fight Octavius, but when they are ultimately defeated by him, Antony accuses Cleopatra of betrayal. She responds to Antony's anger by locking herself away in her monument and feigning suicide. Antony himself commits suicide as a result of her apparent death, and Octavius arrives claiming victory over Egypt. Mourning Antony and afraid of being led in captivity back to Rome, Cleopatra uses poisonous serpents, or asps, to kill herself in her monument. (*See* **Cleopatra** *in the* **CHARACTER STUDIES** *section.*)

Antony (Mark Antony): Roman triumvir, or co-leader, and lover of Cleopatra. He spends a great deal of his time in Alexandria with Cleopatra, much to the disgust of his younger, fellow triumvir, Octavius. After his first wife, Fulvia, dies while rebelling against Octavius, Antony marries Octavius's sister, Octavia, to achieve reconciliation with the Roman triumvirate. Antony, however, soon returns to Cleopatra, and Octavius angrily declares war against them both. After losing at Actium, Antony asks to be allowed to retire to Egypt with Cleopatra, but Octavius refuses to grant his request. Antony resumes his war with Octavius, winning one skirmish but badly losing another. In despair over his lost honor and the apparent death of Cleopatra, Antony mortally wounds himself. He dies in Cleopatra's arms. (*See* **Antony** *in the* **CHARACTER STUDIES** *section.*)

Charmian: Attendant or maid-in-waiting to Cleopatra. She and Iras are Cleopatra's closest servants. Charmian attends Cleopatra in the monument where the Queen commits suicide; after mournfully straightening Cleopatra's crown, Charmian follows her example by poisoning herself to death with the bite of a serpent, or asp.

Alexas: Attendant to Cleopatra. He jokes with Cleopatra's maids, Charmian and Iras, at the beginning of the play. Late in the play, Alexas is reported to have joined with and then been executed by Octavius Caesar.

Soothsayer: Egyptian fortune-teller. He predicts that Charmian and Iras will die with their queen, Cleopatra, in her monument. The Soothsayer travels to Rome with Antony where he warns Antony to beware of Octavius Caesar.

Enobarbus (Domitius Enobarbus): Friend and follower of Antony. He delivers the famous description of Cleopatra on her barge and accurately predicts that Antony will never be able to leave the Egyptian Queen for Octavia. After the sea battle of Actium, Enobarbus decides to desert Antony, whom he thinks is overly influenced by Cleopatra. When Antony learns of his betrayal and generously sends him his belongings, Enobarbus is stricken with guilt and dies of remorse.

Iras: Attendant or maid-in-waiting to Cleopatra. She and Charmian are the Egyptian Queen's closest servants. Along with Charmian, Iras waits upon Cleopatra in the monument. Iras helps to dress Cleopatra, then dies of grief shortly before the Queen commits suicide.

Octavius (Octavius Caesar): Roman leader and head of the triumvirate that includes himself, Antony, and Lepidus. Octavius is disgusted with Antony's love for Cleopatra and condemns Antony for luxuriating in Alexandria. Octavius and Antony are briefly reconciled through Antony's marriage to Octavius's sister, Octavia. Octavius imprisons Lepidus— the weakest member of the triumvirate— and declares war on Antony, claiming that he has betrayed Rome by deserting Octavia and returning to Cleopatra. Octavius ultimately defeats Antony and Cleopatra's forces, and becomes emperor of the known world, but is saddened by Antony's suicide and prevented by Cleopatra's suicide from parading her in triumph back to Rome. *(See **Octavius** in the **CHARACTER STUDIES** section.)*

Lepidus (M. Aemilius Lepidus): The third and weakest member of the Roman triumvirate. Lepidus tries to act as conciliator between the two rival members of the triumvirate— Antony and Octavius. He has a minor role in the peace negotiations with Pompey. Afterward, Lepidus becomes the most drunken participant in the celebration on Pompey's galley. In Act III we are told that Lepidus has been accused of treason and jailed by Octavius, who intends to have him executed.

Mardian: Eunuch in attendance at Cleopatra's court. Mardian entertains Cleopatra with sexually suggestive

jokes in Act I, and in Act IV, the Queen sends him to Antony with false news of her death, thus precipitating Antony's own suicide.

Pompey (Sextus Pompeius): A rebel against the triumvirate. Pompey feels secure in his battle as long as the strongest member of the triumvirate— Antony— is luxuriating in Egypt. Once Pompey hears of Antony's return to Rome, he decides to seek peace with the triumvirate, and the negotiated settlement is celebrated on board Pompey's galley. During the celebration Pompey rejects as dishonorable Menas's offer to assassinate the members of the triumvirate while they are drunk on board his galley. Pompey and the triumvirate are at war again later in the play, and in Act III, we hear that Pompey has been murdered.

Menas: Pirate and supporter of Pompey. Menas believes that Pompey is too cautious in his dealings with the triumvirate. After Pompey refuses to follow Menas's advice to assassinate the triumvirs, Menas deserts him.

Varrius: Friend and follower of Pompey. He informs Pompey of Antony's return to Rome, thus setting in motion the peace treaty between Pompey and the triumvirate.

Agrippa: Friend and follower of Octavius Caesar. It is Agrippa who suggests that differences between Antony and Octavius might be resolved through marriage between Antony and Caesar's sister, Octavia. Later, Agrippa leads Octavius Caesar's forces against Antony.

Octavia: Sister of Octavius Caesar. Octavia's marriage to Antony is meant to result in reconciliation between the two antagonistic triumvirs. Although devoted to her brother, Octavia is loyal to Antony once she becomes his wife, and thus she tries— unsuccessfully— to mediate between the two men and their disagreements.

Eros: Servant to Antony. In Act III, Eros announces the resumption of war between Octavius and Pompey as well as Octavius's imprisonment of Lepidus. In Act IV Antony (who is in despair over his losses to Caesar and the apparent suicide of Cleopatra) orders Eros to kill him. The devoted Eros responds to this command by killing himself instead.

Canidius: Lieutenant-general to Antony. Along with Enobarbus, Canidius advises Antony against engaging Octavius Caesar in a sea battle at Actium. After the defeat at Actium, Canidius decides to desert Antony and join Octavius.

Scarus: Friend and follower of Antony. In Act III, a distressed Scarus describes Antony's retreat at Actium, but unlike Enobarbus and Canidius, Scarus remains faithful to Antony throughout his defeats.

Dolabella: Follower of Octavius Caesar. In Act V, Dolabella warns Cleopatra that Octavius Caesar plans to humiliate her by parading her in disgrace back to Rome. Thus Dolabella precipitates Cleopatra's decision to commit suicide.

Thidias (also called Thyreus): Follower of Octavius Caesar. After Antony's defeat at Actium, Octavius sends Thidias to bribe Cleopatra to abandon Antony. When Antony hears of Thidias's mission, he orders that the man be whipped and returned to Octavius.

Diomedes: Attendant to Cleopatra. Diomedes is sent by a worried Cleopatra to tell Antony that she is not really dead. But her message comes too late, and the dying Antony asks Diomedes to deliver the final deathblow with his own sword. Diomedes refuses and instead helps deliver Antony to Cleopatra in her monument.

Proculeius: Friend and follower of Octavius Caesar. When Antony is dying, he tells Cleopatra that Proculeius is the only follower of Octavius whom she can trust. Proculeius in fact proves unreliable: on orders from Caesar, he lies to Cleopatra and prevents her from committing suicide so that she can be brought back to Rome in humiliation.

Seleucus: Treasurer to Cleopatra. In Act V, Seleucus contradicts Cleopatra, claiming that she has purposely lied to Caesar regarding the extent of her wealth. Cleopatra cites his betrayal as an example of her ebb in fortune.

Clown: A comical rustic character. At Cleopatra's command, the Clown brings her poisonous serpents, or asps, hidden in a basket of figs. Thus, the Clown delivers to Cleopatra her means of suicide in Act V.

PLOT SYNOPSIS

Act I: The Roman triumvir Mark Antony luxuriates in Alexandria with his lover, Cleopatra, while his men complain that their once great military leader has been ruined by his infatuation with this Queen of Egypt. Messages arrive from Rome, and Cleopatra teases Antony about his subservience to his wife, Fulvia, as well as to the younger triumvir, Octavius Caesar. In defiance, Antony sends the messengers away unheard.

Shortly afterward, Cleopatra's two maids-in-waiting, Charmian and Iras, ask a Soothsayer to tell them their fortunes. When he ominously suggests that they will not live long, the women misinterpret his warnings and instead joke about their good luck.

Meanwhile, Antony hears of separate battles being waged against Octavius Caesar— one of which has been started

by Antony's wife, Fulvia. After another messenger tells him of Fulvia's death, Antony berates himself for being enchanted by Cleopatra and decides to return to his duties in Rome. Cleopatra is hurt and angered by this news, but when he insists on going she relents and affectionately bids him farewell.

Back in Rome, Octavius Caesar tells his fellow triumvir, Lepidus, that he is disgusted with Antony's infatuation with Cleopatra and with his dissipation in Egypt. Word comes that Pompey is rebelling against the triumvirate, and Octavius once more laments that Antony is wasting his time and his reputation in Egypt.

Act II: Antony's return to Rome worries the rebel, Pompey, and pleases at least one member of the triumvirate— Lepidus. Antony wins back Octavius Caesar's confidence by demonstrating his loyalty to Rome through marriage with Octavius's sister, Octavia. Afterward, the followers of Antony and of Octavius chat among themselves, and Enobarbus predicts that despite his marriage to Octavia, Antony will never abandon Cleopatra. Meanwhile, members of the triumvirate make preparations for war against Pompey, and the Soothsayer warns Antony that Octavius will eclipse him in greatness as long as he stays with him in Rome. Back in Egypt, Cleopatra hears of Antony's marriage to Octavia and becomes furious, then depressed. She sends a messenger to Rome to find out whether Octavia is beautiful.

Pompey and the triumvirate settle on terms for peace. They celebrate their successful negotiations with a feast aboard Pompey's galley. When Pompey's ally, the pirate Menas, offers to assassinate the triumvirs while they are celebrating, Pompey rejects the idea. As the celebrants become increasingly drunk, Octavius Caesar suggests that it is time to go home.

Act III: Antony's subordinates wage successful battles abroad. As Antony and his new wife, Octavia, prepare to leave Rome, Octavius makes it clear to Antony that he still distrusts him. Back in Egypt, Cleopatra's messenger returns from Rome with the reassuring news that Octavia is unattractive. Meanwhile, now settled in Greece, Antony tells Octavia that her brother has resumed warring with Pompey and has also begun slandering Antony. Octavia offers to mediate between Antony and Octavius and returns to Rome to do so. Enobarbus reports that Octavius and Lepidus defeated Pompey and that thereafter, Octavius rid himself of Lepidus by accusing him of treason and throwing him in jail. Back in Rome, Octavius is outraged at news that Antony has abandoned Octavia and returned to Cleopatra. Octavia arrives to mediate between her brother and husband, only to be convinced by Octavius that Antony has been unfaithful. Octavius prepares for war against Antony.

In Egypt, Cleopatra rejects Enobarbus's protests that her presence on the battlefield will distract Antony rather than help him. Antony enters, announcing that Octavius Caesar has challenged him to a sea battle at Actium. He and Cleopatra agree— against the wishes of his men— to accept the dare. The warring fleets engage in battle, and Antony's side gains the upper hand until Cleopatra's ships retreat and Antony's follow hers. Cleopatra apologizes to a despairing, shame-filled Antony, and he forgives her. He sends word to Octavius requesting to be allowed to retire to Egypt or Athens, and Cleopatra requests that her sons be allowed to succeed her. Caesar rejects Antony's proposal and instead sends his ambassador, Thidias, to bribe Cleopatra so that she will betray Antony. When Antony sees Thidias kissing Cleopatra's hand, he becomes enraged; he berates Cleopatra and orders Thidias to be whipped. Eventually, however, Cleopatra cajoles Antony out of his anger, and the two of them go off to celebrate before resuming battle with Octavius Caesar. Meanwhile Enobarbus— a witness to what has happened— decides that Antony has lost his reason and thus makes plans to desert him.

Act IV: Octavius Caesar scoffs at a challenge sent by messenger from Antony to fight with him in a duel, remarking that Antony is desperate because many of his men have already deserted him and joined Caesar. He prepares for battle with enthusiasm; meanwhile, Antony's camp makes its own preparations with foreboding. The next day, Cleopatra affectionately helps Antony with his armor. Word comes that Enobarbus has deserted to Octavius, and Antony generously forgives his old friend and sends his belongings after him. When Enobarbus learns of his former leader's generosity, he dies of a broken heart. The fighting begins: Antony is at first victorious, but later, during another sea battle, Cleopatra's forces again retreat and Antony's forces are routed. Antony blames Cleopatra for the defeat and threatens to kill her. Cleopatra takes refuge in a monument and sends a message to Antony that she has killed herself. When Antony— who is already ashamed of his military dishonor— receives word of Cleopatra's apparent suicide, he resolves to end his own life and orders his servant Eros to stab him. The devoted Eros reacts by killing himself instead. More ashamed than before, Antony responds to Eros's death by attempting to commit suicide. When a messenger from Cleopatra appears with news that she is not dead, the dying Antony asks to be carried to her monument. Antony and Cleopatra are lovingly reunited. He warns her that out of all of Octavius Caesar's entourage, only Proculeius can be trusted; then he dies in her arms.

Act V: In Rome, Octavius Caesar hears that Antony has committed suicide, and he laments the destruction of a great warrior. Octavius sends Proculeius to Egypt to meet with Cleopatra; once there, Proculeius prevents the Queen from stabbing herself— a move that would

have foiled Caesar's plan to parade her in captivity through Rome. Octavius himself goes to Egypt to meet with Cleopatra, and he assures her that she will be well-treated. Shortly afterward, Caesar's follower Dolabella warns Cleopatra of his leader's actual plans for her. As a result, Cleopatra arranges for a Clown, or comical rustic, to supply her with poisonous serpents, or asps, hidden in a basket of figs. The Queen's maids attend to her in her monument. Just before Cleopatra kills herself, her maid, Iras, faints and dies. The Queen poisons herself to death with the asps, and dies calling out Antony's name. Charmian follows Cleopatra's example by poisoning herself with an asp bite. When Octavius Caesar finds Cleopatra dead, he orders that her body be buried with Antony's.

PRINCIPAL TOPICS

Language and Imagery

Antony and Cleopatra is distinguished among Shakespeare's plays for its lush, evocative language. Some critics have even suggested that it should be classified with Shakespeare's long poems rather than ranked alongside his plays. Scholarly discussion has focused on Enobarbus's vividly detailed depiction of Cleopatra on her barge and on the lovers' continual use of hyperbole, or exaggerated language, to describe each other as well as their affection for one another.

Some critics have argued that the hyperbolic language in *Antony and Cleopatra* makes it a highly problematical play to stage. What actor, for example, is so physically fit that he can portray a character like Antony, whose "legs bestrid the ocean" and whose "rear'd arm / Crested the world"? What actress is charismatic enough to play Cleopatra, who is described as more seductive than Venus, the goddess of love? Other critics have observed that Shakespeare was well aware of this conflict between language and reality and that he makes this clear in Act V when the defeated Cleopatra imagines that plays written in Rome about the former lovers will feature Antony as a drunk and herself as a "whore" played— as was the custom in Renaissance England— by a "squeaking . . . boy."

Scholars have in fact identified a variety of reasons for the existence of heightened language and vivid imagery in *Antony and Cleopatra*. Some have demonstrated its usefulness in highlighting the changing moods or fortunes of particular characters. Thus Antony's men effectively display their disappointment in their leader and his noticeable transformation when they complain that Antony has been reduced from acting like the god of war to behaving like the mere fawning servant of a lustful woman. Similarly, it has been pointed out that while Antony describes his love for Cleopatra in hyperbolic terms, he does not lose sight of his own importance in the world of politics. For instance, even as he asserts that his love for Cleopatra renders everything else in the world unimportant, he demands that the people of the world take note of his love or else face punishment from him. Thus we are introduced to the conflicting feelings— romantic love versus honorable renown— that plague Antony and that ultimately destroy him.

Several critics have suggested that *Antony and Cleopatra's* hyperbolic poetry mirrors the paradoxes at work in the play: love versus death and immortality versus aging, for example. In connection with this, several scholars have noted the frequent use of images that link death, love, and immortality. The preponderance of death imagery intensifies the tragic nature of Antony and Cleopatra's love. Death imagery also emphasizes the fact that both lovers are aging. Aging and death are things that the extraordinary Antony and Cleopatra have in common with ordinary people, all of whom must come to terms with their mortality; therefore, some critics conclude that the imagery and hyperbole in *Antony and Cleopatra* are intended to reinforce the fact that all human beings are by their very nature extraordinary.

Dualism

Much of the commentary on *Antony and Cleopatra* has been devoted to the play's numerous thematic pairings: Antony and Cleopatra; love and war; Antony and Octavius; self-restraint and luxury; reason and emotion. Scholars customarily argue that all or at least a large portion of this dualism flows from one essential pairing— Rome (under the guardianship of the strictly disciplined Octavius Caesar) versus Egypt (under the sway of the flamboyantly unpredictable Cleopatra). Antony is traditionally regarded as the go-between or victim of the Rome/Egypt dualism. As such, commentators have remarked, Antony must deal with his own set of internal conflicts: his Roman honor giving way to dishonor in Egypt; his youthful warrior's physique diminishing with age and dissipation; and his love for Cleopatra undermining his loyalty to Rome.

On the other hand, many critics have countered that the elements at work in *Antony and Cleopatra* cannot be neatly grouped into rigid pairs because just as the political alliances in the play shift, so do the groupings in the play's structure. For example, Antony's dilemma has been described as one involving a choice between love and war; between, that is, his life with Cleopatra in Egypt and his profession as a soldier in Rome. In contrast, critics have argued that Antony's dilemma is solved when love and death are paired through his and Cleopatra's suicides. Commentators have observed that when Octavius commands the burial of the lovers in the same grave, he acknowledges that death has immortalized the love of "a pair so famous" as Antony and Cleopatra.

In addition to thematic dualism, scholars have found linguistic forms of duality in the play. Irony, for example, occurs when the lovers use hyperbolic, or exaggerated, language to describe their devotion to one another even as the action of the play casts doubt on this devotion. Paradox occurs when death is used to solve the problems of the living. One critic has noted that, paradoxically, Octavius Caesar becomes emperor of the world at the close of the play, but his earthly power is eclipsed by the transcendent love achieved through Antony and Cleopatra's deaths.

Disagreements between critics concerning the play's meaning also underscore the dualism of *Antony and Cleopatra*. For example, commentators who assert that the play is about the transcendence of love are contradicted by critics who maintain that the play's real focus is on the moral transgressions of the two lovers and the deadly price they are obliged to pay for their sins. Critics who regard Cleopatra as selfish and whimsical are countered by those who argue that her actions in the play are misunderstood. Those who consider Antony a noble character are at odds with scholars who regard him as weak. Today, many critics conclude that the play's dualism or ambivalence is intentional, and that the insoluble conflicts which surface repeatedly in *Antony and Cleopatra* are meant to provoke audience members into thinking about the ambiguities present in their own lives.

Rome versus Egypt

Traditional scholarly assessments of Egypt and Rome as depicted in *Antony and Cleopatra* treat the nations as polar opposites. Thus Rome is a guardian of moral restraint, personal responsibility, social order, and military discipline. Further, Rome places a high value on honor and duty toward one's country. By contrast, Egypt is seen as a magnet for decadence, concupiscence, and indolence. Egypt, according to this view, places a high value on physical enjoyment and luxuriant fertility. Egypt is the place to have fun; Rome is the place to work. Egypt equals private life; Rome equals public life. By extension, traditional criticism asserts that Cleopatra symbolizes Egypt, Octavius Caesar represents Rome, and Antony is torn between the two worlds until he is finally destroyed.

More recent criticism, however, suggests that Rome and Egypt are alike to the degree that they are both in decline, and that the love of Antony and Cleopatra does not reflect the opposition between the two countries or the conflict endured by Antony, but the temporary triumph of imperialism. The love shared by Antony and Cleopatra, some critics argue, is as imperious and undemocratic as the new government in Rome. The lovers themselves describe their feelings in imperial terms; Antony, for instance, claims that his affection is capable of conquering whole worlds and of blotting out geographical formations.

Scholars have also remarked that the decline of Rome and Egypt is the result of changes in both nations: Republican Rome is now Imperial Rome; Egypt is ruled by an unpredictable and aging queen. Rome is prey to shifting alliances and political betrayal by Octavius, who bickers with one triumvir (Antony) and jails another (Lepidus); Egypt is subject to the flooding of the Nile and the unpredictable fortunes of Antony and Cleopatra's love. Both Egypt and Rome, one critic has observed, are pagan nations, which will soon give way to Christianity. Ultimately, commentators suggest that it is less constructive to view Rome and Egypt as "separate" entities than as shifting and intermingling locations of waxing and waning power that affect and are affected by the two lovers.

CHARACTER STUDIES

Antony

While there is critical consensus that Mark Antony functions as a tragic hero in the play, there is disagreement concerning exactly when he becomes tragic and what it is that transforms him. Those commentators who describe Antony as torn between his Roman values of duty and valor and his Egyptian obsession with sex and dissipation assert that he achieves tragic status when he reclaims his honor through the Roman death of suicide. Similarly, critics have suggested that as long as Antony allows himself to be treated in Egypt as "a strumpet's fool," he remains a ridiculous figure; after he is defeated at Actium, however, Antony's shame is so intense that his fate becomes tragic. Some critics regard Antony's own "weakness" as the source of his tragedy. In essence, these critics argue that Antony's tragedy is that he sacrifices everything— physical strength, honor, political power, respect— simply to indulge his senses in Egypt. Finally, some scholars assert that Antony stumbles tragically when he in fact tries to have it all— power and respect in Rome alongside ease and love in Egypt.

An alternative take on Antony's tragic status is that he operates according to a moral code different from the one followed by Octavius. According to this view, the public-oriented Octavius adheres to a standard, Roman code of honor that takes into account such issues as political expediency. Antony, on the other hand, defines honor in more personal terms. Loving Cleopatra and enjoying himself in Egypt at the expense of his duties in Rome do not impinge on his sense of honor. However, retreating from the sea battle at Actium is, according to Antony, an unchivalrous act and is therefore highly dishonorable. In light of this assessment, Antony's role in the play is a tragic one because he is unable to reconcile his private concept of honor with the general one exemplified by the activities of the triumvirs in Rome.

Antony's tragic status has also been discussed in tandem with Cleopatra's role. Commentators who view the lovers as equals argue that at the beginning of the play, both are self-absorbed despite their love for one another and thus they are in continual conflict with one another. These critics note that toward the close of the play, Antony and Cleopatra transcend their selfishness as a result of their suffering, and from there they learn to recognize each other's worth and together achieve status as tragic heroes.

Cleopatra

Critical reaction to Cleopatra has been strong and often negative. Early commentators in particular characterized the Egyptian Queen as self-indulgent, self-pitying, capricious, and treacherous. They considered the character Philo's description of her in Act I as a lustful "strumpet," or whore, to be appropriate. They found her taunting of Antony cruel and her apparent acceptance of Octavius Caesar's bribe in Act III untenable. They roundly blamed her for Antony's downfall. Today, scholarly evaluations of Cleopatra are more moderate. Increasingly, commentators have come to regard Antony and Cleopatra as "mutually" responsible for their fates. Several critics have described the earlier assessments of Cleopatra as extreme and sexist; they emphasize the importance of objectivity to any discussion of the Egyptian Queen; further, they observe that she deserves no more and no less sympathy than does, for example, a tragic hero like King Lear or Othello.

Those commentators who view Cleopatra in a negative light usually insist that she is too self-absorbed to qualify for tragic status. There are those, however, who regard her selfish ignorance as the very source of her tragedy. A more temperate version of this argument is that Cleopatra acts out of self-interest until she witnesses Antony's death. At that point, some critics assert, she recognizes too late Antony's worth and the extent of her love for him; as a result, she achieves tragic status. Cleopatra's tragedy has also been ranked as commensurate with Antony's. Scholars contend that both characters are initially self-interested and untrustworthy in love: Cleopatra is jealous of Antony's preoccupation with Rome; at the same time, Antony tries to satisfy political ambitions through marriage with Octavia. Neither, some commentators assert, achieves tragic status until both reach mutual understanding and love before their deaths at the close of the play.

Some commentators dispense with any discussion of Cleopatra's qualification as a tragic hero and concentrate instead on the lines accorded to her in the play. She is, they observe, the vehicle for some of Shakespeare's most eloquent poetry. Her remembrance in Act I, scene v, for example, of her youth as her "salad days, / When [she] was green in judgment, cold in blood," and her vision of Antony in Act V, scene ii, as someone so remarkable as to be "past the size of dreaming" are evocative and justifiably famous.

Octavius

While earlier critics regarded Octavius Caesar primarily as a representative of Imperial Rome, today most commentators look to the play for what it reveals about Octavius as a character. Significantly, it has been noted that this leader of the triumvirs delivers no soliloquies or personality-revealing asides. Octavius is so terse in his remarks that several commentators are in disagreement concerning such details as whether or not he becomes drunk along with the other triumvirs on Pompey's galley in Act II.

Most scholars agree that Caesar is cold and self-restrained. Some argue that he is thus meant to function as a foil to the extravagant lovers, Antony and Cleopatra. Others consider his prudish criticism of Antony as hypocritical in light of the fact that he cruelly betrays the weakest triumvir, Lepidus. There is a general consensus that Octavius carefully calculates each move he makes and that he is a manipulator. Thus he exploits Antony's sensitivity about his honor by challenging his competitor to a sea battle in Act III. Similarly, Octavius sends Thidias to Cleopatra in Act III, hoping to bribe and flatter her away from Antony.

An alternative perspective on Octavius Caesar is that he lacks imagination and empathy and is therefore vulnerable to faulty judgment. So, for example, he is unable to prevent either Antony or Cleopatra from committing suicide and as a result is robbed of the satisfaction of parading them—and their defeat—through Rome. According to this view, Octavius is less in control than he thinks he is or than he wishes to be.

CONCLUSION

Antony and Cleopatra stands as one of Shakespeare's most poetic plays. It is noted for its evocative word paintings and vivid hyperbole. It is also regarded by many as a problem play, presenting as it does the ambiguity and ambivalence of life without providing clear or comfortable answers. The two lovers presented in the play may be world leaders but they are also, after all, only human beings—flawed and aging ones at that. We as human beings share their mortality; many of us recognize their strong feelings of jealousy, love, shame, and insecurity. Despite their historical grandeur and thanks to Shakespeare's sensitive portrayal of them, Antony and Cleopatra are no more—and no less—extraordinary than we are.

OVERVIEW

Walter Cohen

SOURCE: "Antony and Cleopatra," in *The Norton Shakespeare*, edited by Stephen Greenblatt, W. W. Norton & Company, 1997, pp. 2619-27.

[*In this introduction, Cohen places* Antony and Cleopatra *within its literary context—with Shakespeare's own* Julius Caesar *as its prequel and the writings of Plutarch as its source. Cohen also remarks on the dualism and eroticism that pervade the play, and notes that Shakespeare is asking us to consider whether heroic acts can survive in the "post-heroic world" of Octavius Caesar's Rome or in the "private terrain" of Antony and Cleopatra's love. Finally, Cohen briefly examines Shakespeare's characterizations of Octavius, Antony, and Cleopatra.*]

Antony and Cleopatra (1606-07) picks up where *Julius Caesar* leaves off. It presupposes familiarity not only with events dramatized in that play but also with earlier Roman conflicts. During the first century B.C., Rome, the overwhelming military power throughout the Mediterranean and beyond, entered into a protracted civil war that culminated in its transition from a republic (rule by a senatorial aristocracy) to an empire (monarchical power). As *Julius Caesar* opens, Caesar has already defeated his archrival Pompey the Great and governs Rome as dictator. The play recounts the republican assassination of him, led by Brutus and Cassius, and the assassins' subsequent defeat and death at the hands of Mark Antony (Caesar's lieutenant) and Octavius (Caesar's young grandnephew and adoptive son, who took the name of "Caesar" upon Julius Caesar's death and turned it to political use). *Antony and Cleopatra*, which covers the period from 40 to 30 B.C., completes the narrative of Roman civil war and the final destruction of the republic. Rome and its vast holdings are now ruled by the triumvirate of Lepidus, Octavius Caesar, and Mark Antony, who govern, respectively, the Mediterranean portions of Africa, Europe, and Asia. Yet Shakespeare's tragedy shifts the focus from the struggle over Rome's internal political system to Rome's external imperial domination of the East (the present-day Middle East) and to affairs of the heart. Mark Antony and Octavius Caesar contend for political supremacy, but the love between Antony and Cleopatra occupies center stage.

Much of the play's fascination arises from this intertwining of empire and sexuality. The issue is already present in Thomas North's translation of *Plutarch's Lives of the Noble Grecians and Romanes*—Shakespeare's favorite source, with the exception of Raphael Holinshed's *Chronicles of England, Scotland, and Ireland*, and one that he follows closely here. Plutarch and other writers of

Greek and Latin antiquity were preoccupied with the opposition between the conquering West, often thought by them to stand for political and moral virtue, and the older civilizations it subjugated in the East, frequently supposed to represent luxury and decadent, feminized sexuality. This particular understanding of empire re-emerged in the Renaissance during a new era of Western expansion, as Europe entered the path to genuine global domination armed with an increasingly racialized and still sexualized view of the peoples it sought to subdue. *Antony and Cleopatra* is one response to European expansion, and the play's subsequent fortunes testify to its connection with the imperial enterprise of the West.

Long supplanted onstage by John Dryden's *All for Love* (1677), a rewriting of Shakespeare's story as a tragedy of private life, Shakespeare's version came into its own only after 1800, when England became the world's leading power. During the last two centuries, both Cleopatra and the East with which she is identified have seemed female, dark, colonized, available, animalistic, exotic, and excitingly dangerous. Comments on the text or on its performance have stressed the play's "strange pervasive influence of Oriental luxury and vice," its "effect of Oriental repose," Cleopatra's "corrupt and half-barbarous Oriental court." "Just as Antony's ruin results from his connection with Cleopatra," one critic argued, "so does the fall of the Roman Republic result from the contact of the simple hardihood of the West, with the luxury of the East." Actresses playing Cleopatra recall "an Indian dancer" and "Asiatic undulations of form." They bring to mind a "panther," a "sensuous tigress," "a wicked monkey," and a creature full of "feline cunning."

Not all of these responses chauvinistically assume Western superiority, and *Antony and Cleopatra* itself seems designed to elicit complicated judgments. Rome is contrasted to Egypt, West to East, the conquerors to the conquered; rapid shifts of scene across enormous distances accentuate this division. A sober, masculine military ethos opposes a comically frivolous, pleasure-loving, feminized, emasculated, and sexualized court. Antony must decide between Octavius Caesar and Cleopatra, Octavius's sister Octavia and Cleopatra, the world and the flesh. Political opportunism drives Antony's marriage to Octavia, love and sexual desire his relationship with Cleopatra; he chooses between fidelity to a chaste, white wife and adultery with a promiscuous, "tawny," "black" seductress (1.1.6, 1.5.28). Where Caesar employs a rational self-interest (he is the "universal landlord," 3.13.72), Antony revels in an impetuous, extravagant generosity and challenges Caesar to one-on-one combat. Young Caesar is a bureaucrat of the future, old Antony a warrior of the past. Caesar's concerns are public and political, Antony's private and personal. Whereas Antony's brother and his previous wife, Fulvia, attack Caesar, Caesar promises

that "the time of universal peace is near" (4.6.4). This assertion anticipates the *pax Romana* (Roman peace) instituted by Caesar throughout the empire. It also links the empire to Christianity by evoking the birth of Christ, which occurred in a Roman province during Caesar's long rule.

Through these conflicts, the play investigates the possibility of heroic action in a post-heroic world. It offers an epic view of the political arena, but deprives that arena of heroic significance. In this diminished environment, the protagonists' flaws are writ large. *Antony and Cleopatra* then asks whether heroic meaning can be transplanted to the private terrain of love. Throughout, Shakespeare maintains a studied ambivalence: critics disagree about whether the protagonists' concluding suicides are fruitless or redemptive. Following a series of tragedies—*Hamlet, Othello, King Lear*, and *Macbeth*—in which the protagonist's psychology is consistently probed, *Antony and Cleopatra* almost completely avoids soliloquy and thus inaugurates a final phase in Shakespeare's career, in which individual tragic intensity is sacrificed in favor of more broadly social representation. As a result, Antony's and Cleopatra's motives remain opaque to audiences and readers, to other characters in the play, to each other, and, arguably, even to themselves. Though we are invited to guess, we never definitively learn why Cleopatra flees at Actium, why she negotiates with Caesar in the last two acts, or why Antony thinks marriage to Octavia will solve his political problems. Instead of self-revelation, the play offers contradictory framing commentary by minor figures. These external perspectives help impart an epic feel, as do the geographical and scenic shifts, which also produce a loose, fragmentary, and capacious structure alien to classically inspired notions of proper dramatic form. Furthermore, like the other Roman plays based on Plutarch—*Julius Caesar* and *Coriolanus*—*Antony and Cleopatra* relies heavily on blank verse while almost entirely avoiding rhyme: Shakespeare may have been following the Earl of Surrey's sixteenth-century blank verse translation of part of the *Aeneid* (19 B.C.), Virgil's enormously influential epic of the founding of Rome. The Roman Empire would thus seem the obvious stage for heroic performance.

Yet this proves not to be the case, partly because the play's structuring dichotomies are unstable. It is as if *Antony and Cleopatra* created distinctions only to undermine them. For instance, the antitheses between Caesar and Antony and between Rome and Egypt lack political resonance. *Julius Caesar*'s struggle between republic and empire arises only peripherally in *Antony and Cleopatra*, where it is voiced by Pompey:

>   what
> Made the all-honoured, honest Roman Brutus,
> With the armed rest, courtiers of beauteous

Marilyn Lightstone as Iras, Eric Christmas as Soothsayer, Dawn Greenhalgh as Charmian, James Blendick as Mardian, and Brian Petchey as Alexas in the Stratford Festival's 1967 production of Antony and Cleopatra.

freedom,
To drench the Capitol but that they would
Have one man but a man?

                                                      (2.6.15-19)

Pompey's rebellion is bought off by Caesar, Antony, and Lepidus. Pompey is then attacked by Lepidus and by Caesar (who later disposes of Lepidus) and is subsequently murdered by one of Antony's men, who may or may not have been acting on his master's orders. Although Antony supposedly "wept / When at Philippi he found Brutus slain" (3.2.56-57), he asserts that "'twas I / That the mad Brutus ended" (3.11.37-38). The republic is thus already dead when *Antony and Cleopatra* opens. Caesar astutely conforms to the style of a republic, whereas Antony offends traditional Roman sensibilities by ostentatiously taking on the trappings of monarchy (3.6.1-19). Nonetheless, their political conflict concerns not rival systems of government but simply the desires of two ambitious men, each of whom wants absolute power. The independence of Egypt is at stake, although this occurs to no one except Cleopatra and then only belatedly and perhaps duplicitously. The end of civil war is also important, but it is hard either to celebrate the victory of the ruthless Caesar or to lament the defeat of the incompetent Antony.

Other apparent distinctions between the rivals also conceal basic similarities. Antony boasts of his valor at Philippi, while Caesar "alone / Dealt on lieutenantry" (battled exclusively through his officers; 3.11.38-39). Earlier, however, Antony's "officer" Ventidius, whom Plutarch calls "the only man that ever triumphed of the Parthians until this present day," remarks, "Caesar and Antony have ever won / More in their officer than person" (3.1.16-17). In addition, Caesar's promise of "universal peace" is anticipated in a version of Christ's Last Supper that Antony shares with his followers.

                                        Tend me tonight.
Maybe it is the period of your duty.
Haply you shall not see me more; or if,

A mangled shadow. Perchance tomorrow
You'll serve another master.

                                        (4.2.24-28)

Appropriately, Antony is criticized for moving his friends to tears by Enobarbus, a Judas-figure soon to betray Antony by defecting to Caesar and destined to die shortly thereafter, his heart broken by Antony's generosity.

Even the geographical contrast of the play partly dissolves into parallelisms and connections: Egyptian love is militarized, Roman war eroticized. Shakespeare does give Cleopatra a smaller political role than she has in Plutarch, to accentuate the basic conflict and perhaps also to reduce the threat of a powerful woman. But the external representation of the lovers' relationship, the absence of scenes of them alone, and their pride in exhibiting their affair intensify the feeling that love and war influence each other, that there is no distinction between public and private because nothing is private. Further, love is on both sides of the divide. Antony is preceded in suicide by his aptly named servant Eros (love), a figure from Plutarch. But the play opens with a criticism of "this dotage of our General's" by Philo (also "love"; l.l.l), a figure invented by Shakespeare.

Antony and Cleopatra also renders problematic the object of desire. Presumably that object is Cleopatra. Loved by Antony, she elicits powerful responses from Enobarbus and Dolabella and had been the lover of "great Pompey" and "broad-fronted Caesar" (1.5.31, 29). Though this list may indicate the power of the Eastern femme fatale, the roll call of Romans in love has no Egyptian equivalent. It is unclear what they literally see in Cleopatra. Enobarbus's description of her initial meeting with Antony at Cydnus (2.2.192-232) elicits enthusiastic responses from Agrippa— "Rare Egyptian!" and "Royal wench!" (224, 232). But when Enobarbus says that "her own person . . . beggared all description" (203-04), he draws the logical inference, almost renouncing "all description":

            She did lie
    In her pavilion— cloth of gold, of tissue—
    O'er-picturing that Venus where we see
    The fancy outwork nature.

                                        (2.2.204-07)

All we know of Cleopatra's appearance is that she was reclining.

This absence of the seductress points in the same direction as the list of Roman lovers— toward the feelings of Roman men and away from any inherent attractiveness of an Egyptian woman. Some of these feelings are directed toward Antony. The Pompey and Caesar of *Antony and Cleopatra* at times act almost as if they were the sons— rather than the younger brother (Pompey) and grandnephew and adopted son (Caesar)—

of Cleopatra's former lovers, whose paternal roles Antony has now assumed. In lines whose erotic charge goes beyond the intended objects (Antony and Cleopatra) to include the speaker himself, Pompey expresses pleasure that Antony takes him seriously (2.1.35-38). And Caesar is disgusted by Antony and Cleopatra's theatrical coronation:

            At the feet sat
    Caesarion, whom they call my father's son,
    And all the unlawful issue that their lust
    Since then hath made between them.

                                        (3.6.5-8)

Here, there is a possible confusion between Antony and the older Caesar and a definite one between Caesarion and the younger Caesar, both of whom are "my father's son." This is not the only intense familial feeling Caesar has for Antony. When he weeps at Antony's death, Maecenas sees a noble narcissism: "When such a spacious mirror's set before him / He needs must see himself" (5.1.34-35). Caesar himself recalls Antony movingly:

    thou, my brother, my competitor
    In top of all design, my mate in empire,
    Friend and companion in the front of war,
    The arm of mine own body, and the heart
    Where mine his thoughts did kindle.

                                        (5.1.42-46)

This outpouring of emotion, however calculated, leads in contradictory directions. By calling Antony his "mate" and invoking a meeting of "heart" and mind, Caesar on the one hand suggests an intimacy between the two men that recalls Renaissance celebrations of close male friendship but that also borders on the erotic. On the other hand, he neutralizes any filial anxiety he may feel by describing Antony as "my brother" and then as a subordinate, "the arm of mine own body."

Though Caesar betrays various kinds of emotional intensity, that is not what he consciously espouses. His ideal Antony is not the lover who "o'erflows the measure" (1.1.2) but the soldier who exercised heroic self-deprivation (1.4.58-61). He certainly does not emulate the older Caesar, whose sexual and military conquests were completely intertwined (3.13.82-85). Thus Octavius Caesar represents not the preservation but the diminution of traditional Roman values, a constriction of a heroic culture of which Antony is the last survivor. The jaundiced view of political power that emerges could be construed as an implicit critique of the centralizing monarchs of Shakespeare's own time. In any case, the play insists that one can no longer have it both ways, that politics and sex (or any kind of grandeur) are irrevocably sundered.

Antony and Cleopatra must exercise their peculiar brand

of paradoxical hyperbole in this new and smaller world. Antony's heart "is become the bellows and the fan / To cool a gipsy's lust": his heart is a fan that cools Cleopatra's lust by satisfying it, but in so doing he rekindles her passion, as if his heart were also a bellows (1.1.9-10). Similarly, when Cleopatra meets Antony, "pretty dimpled boys" (2.2.208) attend her

> With divers-coloured fans whose wind did
>   seem
> To glow the delicate cheeks which they did
>   cool,
> And what they undid did.
>
>   (2.2.209-11)

And when told that marriage to Octavia will force Antony to abandon Cleopatra, Enobarbus demurs in perhaps the play's most famous lines:

>   Never. He will not.
> Age cannot wither her, nor custom stale
> Her infinite variety. Other women cloy
> The appetites they feed, but she makes
>   hungry
> Where most she satisfies.
>
>   (2.2.239-43)

But the protagonists' inexhaustibility and their "infinite variety" do not fare well until the final scene. Though Shakespeare makes Antony and Cleopatra more sympathetic than they are in Plutarch, they remain maddeningly self-absorbed and self-destructive— ignoring urgent business, acting impulsively, bullying underlings, reveling in vulgarity, lying, apparently betraying each other.

Moreover, except for the first Battle of Alexandria, in which the couple briefly synthesize military and amorous arms, the fighting scenes testify to their belatedness, their irrelevance. Shakespeare's uncharacteristic decision to follow the practice of classical theater and keep all fighting offstage leaves only a feeling of being let down, as helpless observers report on the debacle. Thus, Enobarbus laments at Actium:

> Naught, naught, all naught! I can behold no
>   longer.
> Th'*Antoniad,* the Egyptian admiral,
> With all their sixty, fly and turn the rudder.
>
>   (3.10.1-3)

At the last battle of the play, it is Antony's turn:

>   All is lost.
> This foul Egyptian hath betrayèd me.
> My fleet hath yielded to the foe, and yonder
> They cast their caps up, and carouse together
> Like friends long lost.
>
>   (4.13.9-13)

Beginning with Act 4, however, the restlessness of the play diminishes as Antony and Cleopatra's sphere of activity is reduced to Alexandria. The manipulative report of her death that Cleopatra sends Antony, his botched suicide in response, and her refusal to leave her monument to attend him as he lies dying convert Antony's presumably climactic death into a mere false ending and shift the weight of significance to the final scene. Instead, Egypt and Cleopatra are what matter. Both have been associated throughout with the overflowing that Antony is faulted for at the outset. Antony declares his love for Cleopatra by rejecting the state he rules: "Let Rome in Tiber melt, and the wide arch / Of the ranged empire fall" (1.1.35-36). Upon hearing of Antony's marriage to Octavia, Cleopatra prays, "Melt Egypt into Nile, and kindly creatures / Turn all to serpents!" (2.5.78-79). This apocalyptic imagery, which dissolves all distinction, anticipates Antony's loss of self when he thinks Cleopatra has betrayed him. His body seems to him as "indistinct / As water is in water" (4.15.10-11).

The language of liquefaction is also connected to the confusion of gender identity. Antony

>   is not more manlike
> Than Cleopatra, nor the queen of Ptolemy
> More womanly than he.
>
>   (1.4.5-7)

And Cleopatra reports, "I . . . put my tires and mantles on him whilst / I wore his sword Philippan" (2.5.21-23). Depending on one's perspective, this behavior either dangerously confuses gender roles, thereby leading to Antony's ignominious flight at Actium, or overcomes a destructive opposition. Furthermore, the language of inundation recalls not only the rise of the Nile, which fertilizes the surrounding plain, but Cleopatra herself, who is identified with Egypt throughout the play. The conclusion seeks this regenerative property in her. Shakespeare's probable recourse to Plutarch's *Of Isis and Osiris* apparently inspires the repeated invocation of the goddess Isis, the sister-wife of Osiris, whom she restores after he is pursued to his death by his brother-rival. Typhon. When Caesar complains of Antony's monarchical behavior, he finds Cleopatra's divine impersonation "of the goddess Isis" even more galling (3.6.17).

Cleopatra's suicide makes good on these imagistic patterns, retrospectively justifying Antony's decision to die for her. Unlike the protagonists' deaths in Shakespeare's earlier tragedies, this outcome is desired by readers and audiences. The ending also evokes the synthesis precluded by the play's dichotomies but implied by its more subtle patterns. Cleopatra dies a death that might be associated with a Roman man:

> My resolution's placed, and I have nothing

Of woman in me. Now from head to foot
I am marble-constant. Now the fleeting
   moon
No planet is of mine.

                        (5.2.234-37)

But in rejecting the inconstancy of the moon, of which Isis was goddess, arguably she also dies the death of a faithful Roman wife.

                  methinks I
   hear
Antony call. I see him rouse himself
To praise my noble act. . . .
         . . . . .
             . . . Husband, I come.
Now to that name my courage prove my
   title.

                        (5.2.274-79)

And in taking the poisonous asp to her breast, she may become a Roman matron as well:

               Peace, peace.
Dost thou not see my baby at my breast,
That sucks the nurse asleep? . . .
As sweet as balm, as soft as air, as gentle.
O Antony!
    [*She puts another aspic to her arm*]
        Nay, I will take thee too.

                        (5.2.299-303)

Since the Folio lacks the stage direction included here, perhaps the final line can mean that she takes Antony to her breast, like a mother comforting her infant son.

But "O Antony" is also a cry of orgasm that looks back to Cleopatra's earlier sexual assertions, "I am again for Cydnus / To meet Mark Antony" and "Husband, I come," and forward to Charmian's orgasmic dying words, which Shakespeare added to his source: "Ah, soldier!" (5.2.224-25, 319). Furthermore, Cleopatra's manner of death is clearly Egyptian. The asp recalls Antony's description of her as "my serpent of old Nile" (1.5.25). Thus Rome and Egypt, Antony and Cleopatra, martial valor and sexual ecstasy, are united in death as they cannot be in life. "Dido and her Aeneas" (4.15.53), in Antony's vision soon to be eclipsed by himself and Cleopatra, wander together through the afterlife of the play. But the two legendary lovers remain bitterly unreconciled in the *Aeneid,* Shakespeare's source for the characters. With full awareness of the complexities and ironies at stake, Virgil narrates Aeneas's abandonment of Dido, who is associated with Eastern sensuality, in the name of a higher cause, Roman civic virtue. *Antony and Cleopatra* thus answers the *Aeneid,* ambivalently distancing itself from Roman and, by extension, Renais-

sance imperialism. It seems to be saying that you *can* have it both ways. East and West, conquered and conquerer are affirmed in a final synthesis.

Yet countercurrents trouble even the metaphorical validation of Cleopatra's "immortal longings" (5.2.272). She resolves on suicide not when she learns that Antony killed himself for her but when she becomes certain that Caesar plans to lead her in a humiliating triumph in Rome. This explains her pleasure in imagining that Antony will "mock / The luck of Caesar," that the asp will "call great Caesar ass / Unpolicied" (5.2.276-77, 298-99). The concluding triumphant rhetoric thus cleans up earlier dubious behavior and puts the best face on defeat. Heroic aristocratic individualism can act in the world only by leaving it. Moreover, the domestic Cleopatra of the conclusion can be seen as the reduction to a conventional gender role of a woman who challenged sexual hierarchy. At her death, Cleopatra "lies / A lass unparalleled" (5.2.305-06), or has the play instead presented "lies alas unparalleled"?

How *Antony and Cleopatra* should be interpreted depends on the relationship one sees between the ending and the partly incompatible material that has preceded it. Most, though not all, critics have found the conclusion affirmative on balance. But the work registers ambivalence to the last. This duality is captured in Cleopatra's account of the response she expects in Rome:

                 The quick comedians
Extemporally will stage us, and present
Our Alexandrian revels. Antony
Shall be brought drunken forth, and I shall
   see
Some squeaking Cleopatra boy my greatness
I'th' posture of a whore.

                        (5.2.212-17)

Cleopatra shudders at the absurdity of a boy actor badly impersonating her, yet the part of Cleopatra in *Antony and Cleopatra* was originally performed by a boy. This reminder punctures the dramatic illusion just when it would seem most essential. Arguably, we are being asked to recognize that a boy in the role of an extremely seductive woman can establish the same emotional intensity with the men in the audience that sometimes seems to exist between the male characters in that play. These lines certainly look back to Cleopatra's deliberate blurring of gender division. And they emphasize the artifice of Cleopatra herself, a veteran actress in her final performance. Shakespeare is here flaunting the power of his medium. But if it is impossible to "boy" Cleopatra's "greatness," to represent her adequately, perhaps that is merely an invitation to look beyond what can be shown, to take seriously her "immortal longings."

LANGUAGE AND IMAGERY

David Daiches focuses on the rich poetic language of *Antony and Cleopatra*, arguing that imagery is present in the play not simply as a source of visual pleasure but also as a means of defining the various characters. So, Daiches explains, Antony's men vividly depict their disgust with their general's attraction to Cleopatra when they compare their former opinion of Antony as "plated Mars" to their current image of him as a mere "fan / To cool a gipsy's lust." Similarly, Daiches points out that the evolving language employed by Octavius Caesar to describe the lovers' feelings for each other alters our own view of Antony and Cleopatra. Daiches focuses in particular on the words Caesar uses to describe the dead lovers at the close of Act V: "'Famous,' 'high,' 'glory,' 'solemn. . . .'" Daiches remarks that "these are the terms which Caesar now applies to a love story which earlier he had dismissed as 'lascivious wassails.'"

Both **Janet Adelman** and Madeleine Doran note that Shakespeare intensifies the effect of the play's imagery by relying on hyperbole— that is, grandiose or exaggerated language. Thus Antony hyperbolically declares that Rome can dissolve into the Tiber River and that the world is nothing but mere "clay" compared to the great love that he and Cleopatra have for one another. Paul A. Cantor agrees that this particular speech of Antony's displays his deep love for Cleopatra, but argues that in the next few lines, the Roman general makes use of hyperbole for a far different purpose— in other words, to indicate that despite his love, he still considers himself an important part of public life; this, Cantor explains, is made clear when Antony asserts his leadership role by grandly ordering the world, or "binding" it on "pain of punishment," to treat the love that he and Cleopatra share as incomparable. In either case, Adelman remarks that the lives of Antony and Cleopatra seldom fulfill the extravagant claims that each makes for the other. Doran asserts that such hyperbolic language is not meant to convince us of the lovers' grandeur, but to impress upon us the extraordinary nature of all human beings.

Katherine Vance MacMullan examines a particular image that frequently appears in *Antony and Cleopatra*: the figure of Death. Noting that the play's use of the image of Death as a bridegroom was commonplace to Renaissance audiences, MacMullan asserts that Shakespeare developed the image beyond this familiar cliché. In *Antony and Cleopatra*, MacMullan contends, death imagery is meant to symbolize Antony's overpowering passion for Cleopatra, his diminishing political powers, and "the weakening of his judgment in the command of practical affairs." MacMullan also demonstrates how Shakespeare connects the image of death with those of sleep, darkness, and light to emphasize

the inevitability of the lovers' tragic fate. For additional commentary on language and imagery in the play, see the excerpt by Janet Adelman in the DUALISM section.

David Daiches

SOURCE: "Imagery and Meaning in *Antony and Cleopatra*," in *English Studies*, Vol. 43, No. 5, October, 1962, pp. 343-58.

[Daiches demonstrates how Shakespeare uses vivid imagery and point of view to depict the various roles of both Antony and Cleopatra. In the language of his soldiers, for example, Antony is a great general who has been made foolish by love. By contrast, the metaphors exchanged between Antony and Cleopatra depict them as magnificent lovers whose affection for each other surpasses boundaries and inspires our admiration. Daiches remarks further that the contrasting imagery in the play coalesces as each lover commits suicide but that it also leaves us wondering whether the play is about "human frailty or human glory."]

Antony and Cleopatra is at once the most magnificent and the most puzzling of Shakespeare's tragedies. Its magnificence resides in the splendour and amplitude of its poetry, in the apparently effortless brilliance with which language is employed in order to search and illuminate the implications of the action; it puzzles because the action itself seems to be of no moral interest yet it compels a kind of wondering attention which would normally be given only to a play with a profoundly challenging moral pattern. Bradley sensed this paradox when he asked, 'Why is it that, although we close the book in a triumph which is more than reconciliation, this is mingled, as we look back on the story, with a sadness so peculiar, almost the sadness of disenchantment?' And he added: 'With all our admiration and sympathy for the lovers we do not wish them to gain the world. It is better for the world's sake, and not less for their own, that they should fail and die.' This is surely to simplify the problem to the point of distortion, for it is not that Anthony and Cleopatra arouse our admiration while doing wrong, so that we thrill to them yet cannot in conscience wish them success. It is rather that in this play Shakespeare seems to be building a moral universe out of non-moral materials. Yet I do not think that we can answer Bradley merely by making a spirited defence of the characters of the hero and heroine, as Dover Wilson does, convincingly enough, if not altogether relevantly.

Shakespeare's play is not, of course, as Dryden's was to be, about 'All for Love, or the World Well Lost', though this is one strand woven into the total fabric. It is— to summarize it crudely— about the different rôles that man can play on the various stages which human activity provides for him, and about the relation of these rôles to the player's true identity. Shortly before his suicide, when Antony sees events as having cheated him out of his rôle both of lover and of conqueror, he expresses his sense of the dissolution of identity:

> Sometime we see a cloud that's dragonish,
> A vapour sometime, like a bear, or lion,
> A tower'd citadel, a pendent rock,
> A forked mountain, or blue promontory
> With trees upon 't, that nod unto the world,
> And mock our eyes with air.

He goes on to say that he

> made these wars for Egypt, and the
>   queen,
> Whose heart I thought I had, for she had
>   mine,

and having, as he believes, lost Cleopatra's heart, he no longer has a real identity either as lover or as man or action. The melancholy music of the lines rises up to involve us in this sad sense of loss of self. When however, he is informed by Mardian that Cleopatra has killed herself for love of him, his identity as lover is immediately re-established and he assumes this rôle again with a new confidence:

> I will o'ertake thee, Cleopatra, and
> Weep for my pardon. So it must be, for now
> All length is torture: since the torch is out,
> Lie down and stray no farther. Now all
>   labour
> Mars what it does: yea, very force entangles
> Itself with strength: seal then, and all is done.
> Eros!— I come, my queen:— Eros!— Stay for
>   me,
> Where souls do couch on flowers, we'll hand
>   in hand,
> And with our sprightly port make the ghosts
>   gaze:
> Dido, and her Aeneas, shall want troops,
> And all the haunt be ours.

At first it seems that the re-establishment of his identity as lover means the abandonment of his identity as soldier— 'No more a soldier', he exclaims; but soon it becomes clear that in his resolution to follow Cleopatra to death he is at last adequately uniting both rôles. Cleopatra has now assumed the rôle of conqueror, and he will imitate her:

> I, that with my sword
> Quarter'd the world, and o'er green Neptune's
>   back
> With ships made cities, condemn myself, to lack
> The courage of a woman, less noble mind
> Than she which by her death our Caesar tells
> 'I am conqueror of myself.'

When he discovers that Cleopatra has not killed herself

after all, he does not fall back into his earlier state of disillusion with her; he remains the lover and the loved, ready to act out the last of love's gestures:

> I am dying, Egypt, dying; only
> I here importune death awhile, until
> Of many thousand kisses, the poor last
> I lay upon thy lips.

Finally, at the moment of death, he re-assumes the character of conqueror also:

> but please your thoughts
> In feeding them with those my former
>   fortunes
> Wherein I liv'd: the greatest prince o' the
>   world,
> The noblest; and do now not basely die,
> Not cowardly put off my helmet to
> My countryman: a Roman, by a Roman,
> Valiantly vanquish'd.

Cleopatra's great cry of grief at his death is the equivalent from her side of Antony's speech about the changing shapes of the clouds: no identities are now left in the world, no distinction between mighty and trivial; she is overwhelmed in a patternless and so meaningless world in which all rôles are interchangeable:

> O, wither'd is the garland of the war,
> The soldier's pole is fall'n: young boys and
>   girls
> Are level now with men: the odds is gone,
> And there is nothing left remarkable
> Beneath the visiting moon.

Her love for Antony, we now realise, had been what gave meaning to reality for her; it had been the top in a hierarchy of facts, and when Antony is gone there is no hierarchy, no order, and so no significance in reality. Her own position as queen equally becomes meaningless: she is

> No more but e'en a woman, and commanded
> By such poor passion as the maid that milks,
> And does the meanest chares.

At the end of the play Cleopatra re-establishes order by the culminating rôle-taking of her death.

There are many ways in which Shakespeare uses poetic imagery to establish his main patterns of meaning. The opening lines give us with startling immediacy the stern Roman view of Antony's love for Cleopatra, separating at once the Roman from the Egyptian world:

> Nay, but this dotage of our general's
> O'erflows the measure: those his goodly eyes,
> That o'er the files and musters of the war

Have glow'd like plated Mars, now bend, now
turn
The office and devotion of their view
Upon a tawny front: his captain's heart,
Which in the scuffles of great fights hath burst
The buckles on his breast, reneges all temper,
And is become the bellows and the fan
To cool a gipsy's lust.

The word 'dotage' strikes hard in the very first lines— a damning and degrading word. But note that it is 'this dotage of our general's'. Antony is still, to the Roman onlooker, 'our general': there is a shared pride in that word 'our' and a deliberate placing in the hierarchy of command in the word 'general'. The general is a general, but his observed behaviour is to be described by this viewer as dotage. This *viewer*, because when Philo says '*this* dotage' he is pointing at what he sees, drawing his companion's attention to the visible paradox, a general, yet in his dotage. Antony is seen by Philo as playing two contrary rôles at the same time— and this is not in accordance with the proper proportions of things, it 'o'erflows the measure'. It would be proportionate for a general to love, but not for him to *dote*. For a general to dote 'reneges all temper', that is, it renounces all decent self-restraint, it is disproportionate, an improper placing of a particular kind of behaviour in the hierarchy of human activities and emotions.

A general has his proper 'office and devotion', his appropriate service and loyalty. For a general's eyes— 'goodly eyes', it is emphasised, that have in the past appropriately and suitably 'glowed like plated Mars'— now to turn

The office and devotion of their view
Upon a tawny front

is again outrageous indecorum, wild disproportion. This disproportion is emphasized again and brought to a climax in the lines about 'a gipsy's lust'. What has military glory to do with such domestic objects as a bellows and a fan? The juxtaposition is deliberately outrageous. Similarly, the captain's heart put at the service of a gipsy's lust reiterates the disproportion, the total scrambling of that hierarchy which gives people and objects their proper virtue and the proper meaning. As the spectacle of the two lovers moves across to the middle of the stage to Philo's cry of 'Look, where they come'— the lovers are now before our eyes as well as his— Philo's sense of the disproportion involved becomes agonizing:

Take but good note, and you shall see in him
The triple pillar of the world transform'd
Into a strumpet's fool.

And he invites his companion, in biblical-sounding language, to 'behold and see'.

But it is we, the audience or the reader, who now both see and hear. And what is it that we hear?

Cleopatra: If it be love indeed, tell me how
much.
Antony: There's beggary in the love that can
be reckon'd.
Cleopatra: I'll set a bourn how far to be
belov'd.
Antony: Then must thou needs find out
new heaven, new earth.

We move at once from the Roman soldier's view of Antony's behaviour to the view of the lovers themselves. Here, too, is disproportion, but disproportion of a very different kind from that seen by Philo. Antony declares that there is no limit to his love, that to measure it would involve going beyond the confines of both heaven and earth. To part of the audience— Philo and Demetrius, the shocked Roman soldiers— the rôle represents a monstrous confounding of categories; to the actors themselves, it is a glorious extravagance and subsumes everything else; to us who read or watch the play— well, what is it to us? Whose side are we on? We are jolted from Philo's offensively debasing comments to the sight and sound of the two lovers protesting their love. 'All the world loves a lover', the proverbs goes, and one naturally takes the lovers' side. But with Philo's words ringing in our ears we remain watchful, eager, interested: what is the true identity of this pair?

No pause for speculation is allowed. At once an attendant enters, saying

News, my good lord, from Rome

—from that Rome whose representative has just so devastatingly described Antony's behaviour. The brisk official announcement crashes into the world of amorous extravagance that the lovers' dialogue has been building up. Antony's barked, annoyed response— 'Grates me, the sum'— shows him forced suddenly out of one rôle into another which he is most reluctant to play. At this Cleopatra suddenly changes too, quite unexpectedly yet wholly convincingly, into the playful, teasing mocker of her lover:

Nay, hear them, Antony:
Fulvia perchance is angry; or who knows
If the scarce-bearded Caesar have not sent
His powerful mandate to you, 'do this, or this;
Take in that kingdom, and enfranchise that;
Perform't, or else we damn thee.'

This shocks Antony out of his second rôle— the lover whose love-making is broken into by the claims of business— into yet a third, the surprised and puzzled lover:

A battle scene from the Stratford Festival's 1967 production of Antony and Cleopatra.

How, my love?

With what wonderful economy does Shakespeare capture this third movement of mind and feeling in Antony. He is surprised out of his annoyance with the interrupter, wondering what Cleopatra is up to. She soon shows him, as she goes on:

Perchance? nay, and most like:
You must not stay here longer, your dismission
Is come from Caesar, therefore hear it, Antony.
Where's Fulvia's process? Caesar's I would say. Both?
Call in the messengers. As I am Egypt's queen,
Thou blushest, Antony, and that blood of thine
Is Caesar's homager: else so thy cheek pays shame
When shrill-tongued Fulvia scolds. The messengers!

She ends, note, by brusquely telling him to attend to the messengers: but she has made sure that, for the time being at least, he won't. Her mocking references to Fulvia, Antony's deserted wife, sting Antony into rejection of all that Rome means. In his next speech he confirms Philo's view of the monstrous disproportion of his behaviour in a remarkable outburst which gains our sympathy not by any explicit or implicit justification but by its taking in all of human existence by the way and then including and surpassing it:

Let Rome in Tiber melt, and the wide arch
Of the rang'd empire fall! Here is my space,
Kingdoms are clay: our dungy earth alike
Feeds beast as man; the noblenesss of life
Is to do thus: when such a mutual pair,
And such a twain can do't, in which I bind,
On pain of punishment, the world to weet
We stand up peerless.

All nobility of action is subsumed in the embrace of 'such a noble pair'. If the two poles between which

Antony moves are Rome and Egypt, for the moment the Roman pole is annihilated. But Antony has a long way to go before he can find a rôle which combines his character of man of action and lover, which *justifies* him (not perhaps in a moral sense but in the sense that it accommodates his full *psyche*): the chain of events which finally drives him to suicide is made, in virtue of the poetic imagery in the play, to be the only way in which his various rôles can come together in the same act. At this stage, we see him changing parts, but every change is accompanied by some awareness of what is being given up by not participating in other kinds of human action. How compelling and inclusive is the phrase 'our dungy earth alike / Feeds beasts as man', taking as it does into its purview in one sweep of perception the very basis of human and animal life and their common dependence on the 'dungy earth'. And how that phrase 'dungy earth' stresses the coarse and common, yet rich and life-giving, elements that link the highest with the lowest in any hierachy. In a sense Antony is not here abandoning everything in the world by his and Cleopatra's mutual love: he is taking it all with him. But only in a sense: as the play moves on Shakespeare develops more and more ways of taking all life with him in presenting the adventures of this couple. Between this speech and the recurrence of the image in a different context in Cleopatra's speech in Act V, scene II, whole worlds of meaning have been established:

> My desolation does begin to make
> A better life: 'tis paltry to be Caesar:
> Not being Fortune, he's but Fortune's
>   knave,
> A minister of her will: and it is great
> To do that thing that ends all other deeds,
> Which shackles accidents, and bolts up
>   change;
> Which sleeps, and never palates more the
>   dung,
> The beggar's nurse, and Caesar's.

Here the search for a timeless identity, 'which shackles accidents, and bolts up change', is movingly linked to a profound sense of the common necessities of all human existence. And when the dying Cleopatra, with the aspic at her breast, exclaims

> Peace, peace!
> Dost thou not see my baby at my breast,
> That sucks the nurse asleep?

the imagery takes on yet another new dimension, so that not only does Cleopatra establish herself at the end as combining the roles of mistress and wife, of courtesan and queen, of Egyptian and Roman, of live-giver and life-taker, but this final unification of rôles is linked— in ways that go far beyond the actual

story— to a compassionate awareness of the sad yet satisfying realities of human needs and human experience.

But to return to the dialogue in Act I, scene I. Antony's moment of abandon to his vision of his and Cleopatra's mutual love cannot be sustained, for it cannot at this stage correspond to all the demands of his and Cleopatra's nature. He again repudiates his Roman business and then, by associating love with pleasure and pleasure with mere sport, modulates rapidly from the lover to the mere hedonist:

> There's not a minute of our lives should stretch
> Without some pleasure now. What sport
>   tonight?

Cleopatra with continuing provocativeness acts the part of his Roman conscience— 'Hear the ambassadors' is her only reply to the speech just quoted— but Antony, who has moved from passion to hedonism to joviality, insists on taking this as simply part of her attractive variety:

> Fie, wrangling queen!
> Whom everything becomes, to chide, to
>   laugh,
> To weep: how every passion fully strives
> To make itself, in thee, fair and admired!

This topic of Cleopatra's infinite variety is to sound again and again, in many different ways, throughout the play before the hero and the heroine come to rest in the final and fatal gesture that can make variety into true identity. At this stage in the play Shakespeare deftly moves the royal lovers off the stage to let us hear again the two tough Roman soldiers whose comments had opened the action.

> I am full sorry
> That he approves the common liar, who
> Thus speaks of him at Rome,

says Demetrius, giving another shake to the kaleidoscope so that we now see Antony neither as the debauched general nor as the passionate lover but simply as a nasty item in a gossip column.

We move straight from this splendid opening, with its shifting points of view and provocative contrasts between the former and the present Antony and between the Roman and the Egyptian view, to be given what Granville-Barker calls 'a taste of the chattering, shiftless, sensual, credulous Court, with its trulls and wizards and effeminates'. The queen enters, seeking Antony, aware that 'A Roman thought hath struck him', and worried. She prepares her tactics, bidding Enobarbus fetch Antony and then sweeping out as Antony enters. Antony, when he appears, is purely Roman: the blank verse he speaks is brisk and business-like, moving in short sentences. The news from Rome shames him. He is shaken into wishing to hear Cleopatra named 'as she is call'd in Rome' and to see himself through Fulvia's eyes. He has changed rôles very thoroughly, and the atmosphere of the Egyptian Court, to which we have just been exposed, helps to make us sympathize. When Cleopatra reappears she has already been diminished, not only by the Court atmosphere and by Antony's Roman speech, but— and most of all— by Enobarbus' sardonic commentary on her behaviour and motives. Her tricks are all in vain, and after trying out a variety of moods and responses she is firmly shut up by Antony's Roman 'Quarrel no more, but be prepared to know / The purposes I bear'. She then tries the pathetic—

> Sir, you and I must part, but that's not it:
> Sir, you and I have lov'd, but there's not
> it;—

and in the end, unable to deflect him from his 'Roman thought', she acts the goddess of Victory and leaves him with the memory of an impressive parting:

> Upon your sword
> Sit laurel victory, and smooth success
> Be strew'd before your feet!

But Antony has already come to see himself as Philo and Demetrius had seen him at the play's opening; we have heard him repeat Philo's very word, 'dotage'—

> These strong Egyptian fetters I must break,
> Or lose myself in dotage.

At this point it looks as though the play is to be a tug-of-war comedy, with Antony being pulled now by Egyptian sensuality, now by Roman duty. And indeed, there is an element of this in the play, and some critics have seen this element as its main theme. But any attempt to see the play as merely a balancing of opposites, geographical and psychological, impoverishes it intolerably and also results in the sharpening of the dilemma I described at the beginning. *Antony and Cleopatra* is a play about ways of confronting experience, about variety and identity.

In Act I scene IV we suddenly see Antony in yet another light, when Octavius Caesar refers to him as 'our great competitor', and this is followed by further images of disproportion applied to Antony— 'tumble on the bed of Ptolemy', 'give a kingdom for a mirth', and so on; yet with these words still in our ears we are brought back to Alexandria to hear Cleopatra, seeing Antony's meaning for her more clearly at a distance, describe him as

> The demi-Atlas of this earth, the arm

> And burgonet of men

— a first foretaste of the grand mythological description she gives of him after his death to Dolabella:

> His legs bestrid the ocean, his rear'd arm
> Crested the world: his voice was propertied
> As all the tuned speres, and that to friends:
> But when he meant to quail, and shake the
> orb,
> He was as rattling thunder. For his bounty,
> There was no winter in 't: an autumn 'twas
> That grew the more by reaping: his delights
> Were dolphin-like, they show'd his back
> above
> The element they lived in: in his livery
> Walk'd crowns and crownets: realms and
> islands were
> As plates dropp'd from his pocket.

These tremendous images of power, benevolence and sensuality— or of greatness, love and joy— sum up the different aspects of Antony's identity, which are seen together, as co-existing, at last after his death. In life they interfered with each other, and can only be described separately. Nevertheless, the introduction of the figure of 'the demi-Atlas of this earth' so soon after Octavius Caesar's complaints about what Antony has declined to, is deliberate and effective. We should note, too, that even Caesar shows himself fully aware of the heroic Antony, though he sees him as the Antony who was and who may be again, not as the present Antony:

> Antony,
> Leave thy lascivious wassails. When thou once
> Was beaten from Modena, where thou slew'st
> Hirtius and Pansa, consuls, at thy heel
> Did famine follow, whom thou fought'st
> against,
> Though daintily brought up, with patience
> more
> Than savages could suffer. Thou didst drink
> The stale of horses, and the gilded puddle
> Which beasts would cough at: thy palate then
> did deign
> The roughest berry, on the rudest hedge;
> Yea, like the stag, when snow the pasture
> sheets,
> The barks of trees thou browsed. On the
> Alps
> It is reported thou didst eat strange flesh,
> Which some did die to look on: and all
> this—
> It wounds thine honour that I speak it
> now—
> Was borne so like a soldier, that thy cheek
> So much as lank'd not.

This is not only imagery suggestive of almost superhuman heroism: it is also violently anti-sensual imagery.

The contrast between 'lascivious wassails' and 'thy palate then did deign' / 'The roughest berry' is absolute. Victory in Egypt is associated with riotous celebration; in Rome, with endurance. Cleopatra at the end of the play combines both these notions in her death, which is both a suffering and a ceremony.

When Caesar and Antony confront each other in Rome, Antony admits the most important charge— that in Egypt he had not sufficiently known himself:

> And then when poisoned hours had bound me
> up
> From mine own knowledge.

Caesar, cold and passionless, never has any doubt of his own identity; that is one of the advantages of having such a limited character. Lepidus' character consists in wanting to like and be liked by everybody; he has no real identity at all. Not that Shakespeare presents all this schematically. The presentation teems with life at every point, and some of the situations in which Lepidus is involved are richly comic.

Meanwhile, Antony acts out his re-acquired *persona* of the good Roman leader and dutiful family man. He marries Caesar's sister Octavia, and is all courtesy and affection. But Enobarbus has been with the back-room boys satisfying their eager curiosity about Egypt. In replying to their questions, this sardonic realist with no illusions tells the simple truth about Cleopatra's irresistible seductiveness. It is into his mouth that Shakespeare puts the magnificent and well-known description of Antony's first meeting with Cleopatra (from Plutarch, but how transmuted!), thus guaranteeing its truth; it is Enobarbus too who evokes her quintessential sex appeal with the brief but brilliant account of her captivating breathlessness after hopping 'forty paces through the public street', and above all it is Enobarbus who replies to Maecenas's 'Now Antony must leave her utterly' with

> Never; he will not:
> Age cannot wither her: nor custom stale
> Her infinite variety: other women cloy
> The appetites they feed, but she makes hungry,
> Where most she satisfies. For vilest things
> Become themselves in her, that the holy priests
> Bless her, when she is riggish.

This is not rôle-taking: it is the considered opinion of a hard-boiled campaigner, and in the light of it we know that Antony has a long way to go before his different *personae* can unite.

If *we* are never allowed to forget Cleopatra, how can Antony? It takes only a casual encounter with an Egyptian soothsayer to turn him to Egypt again:

> I will to Egypt;

> And though I make this marriage for my peace,
> I' the east my pleasure lies.

Mere sensuality is drawing him, it appears. Never up to this point has the love theme, as Antony reflects it, seemed so tawdry. It almost seems as though there is an obvious moral pattern emerging, with Rome on the good side and Egypt on the bad. This is further suggested by the following scene in Alexandria showing Cleopatra's reaction to the news of Antony's marriage to Octavia. Yet, after all her tantrums, with her

> Pity me, Charmian,
> But do not speak to me,

a new note of quiet genuineness emerges in Cleopatra's love for Antony. And if we have come to feel that the political world of Roman efficiency represents the moral good in this conflict between Rome and Egypt, we are soon brought to the scene in Pompey's galley in which power and politics are reduced to their lowest level. Antony fools the drunken Lepidus by talking meaningless nonsense in reply to Lepidus' questions about Egypt; Menas tries to persuade Pompey to slaughter his guests and so secure the sole rule of the world, and Pompey replies that Menas should have done it first and told him about it afterwards; the reluctant Caesar is persuaded to join in the heavy drinking. Lepidus has already been carried off drunk, the man who bears him away carrying, as Enobarbus points out, 'the third part of the world'. And finally Enobarbus persuades Caesar to join in a dance with Antony and Pompey while a boy sings a drinking song. The utter emptiness of this revelry is desolating, and it casts a bleak light on the whole Roman world.

In the light of this dreary and almost enforced celebration we think of Enobarbus' description of Cleopatra's first welcome to Antony or the later presentation (Act IV, scene VIII) of Antony's response to temporary victory and realise that there is another aspect to Egyptian revelry than the dissolute chatter of Act I, scene II. Egyptian celebration has a humanity and a fullness wholly lacking on Pompey's galley.

> Enter the city, clip your wives, your friends,
> Tell them your feats, whilst they with joyful
> tears
> Wash the congealment from your wounds, and
> kiss
> The honour'd gashes whole,

exclaims Antony in genial triumph to his men and, to Cleopatra when she enters:

> My nightingale,
> We have beat them to their beds. What, girl,
> though grey
> Do something mingle with our younger
> brown, yet ha' we

A brain that nourishes our nerves, and can
Get goal for goal of youth. Behold this man,
Commend unto his lips thy favouring hand:
Kiss it, my warrior: he hath fought to-day
As if a god in hate of mankind had
Destroy'd in such a shape.

And Antony goes on to proclaim a victory celebration:

Give me thy hand,
Through Alexandria make a jolly march,
Bear our hack'd targets like the men that owe
them.
Had our great palace the capacity
To camp this host, we all would sup to-
gether,
And drink carouses to the next day's fate,
Which promises royal peril. Trumpeters,
With brazen din blast you the city's ear,
Make mingle with our rattling tabourines,
That heaven and earth may strike their
sounds together,
Applauding our approach.

Kissing, touching and shaking of hands are frequent where Antony is the center of a celebratory scene; it is the human touch, the contact, the insistence on sharing feeling. So against 'I' the east my pleasure lies' we must set on the one hand Roman pleasure as symbolized by the scene in Pompey's galley and on the other the warm human responsiveness to environment which Antony evinces in so many of his Egyptian moods. The latter part of the play is not simply a psychological study of the decline of the sensual man in intellectual and emotional stability as his fortunes decline (as Granville-Barker, brilliant though his study of the play is, seems to imply). If it were that, it would be merely pathetic, and it would be hard to account for the note of triumph that rises more than once as the play moves to its conclusion. The play is in fact both triumph and tragedy; Antony, and more especially Cleopatra, achieve in death what they have been unable to achieve in life: the triumph lies in the achievement, the tragedy in that the price of the achievement is death. In the last analysis the play rises above morality to strike a blow in vindication of the human species. Queen or courtesan or lover or sensualist, or all of these, Cleopatra in her death does not let humankind down.

Antony's emotional vagaries in the long movement of his decline exhibit him as beyond the control of any stablishing self; it is almost as though Shakespeare is making the point that in order to gain one's identity one must lose it. Antony is seen by his friend Scarus, whose military advice he rejects as he rejects everybody's except Cleopatra's, as 'the noble ruin of her (i.e., Cleopatra's) magic', and Shakespeare makes it clear that this is one aspect of the truth. Antony's military judgment is overborne by Cleopatra's reckless desires

and intuitions. Even Enobarbus breaks out of his sardonic acquiescence in whatever goes on, to expostulate with Cleopatra herself in a tone of rising anxiety. Soldier and lover are here contradictory rôles, which must be acted separately. To attempt to act them out simultaneously is to risk ruining both. Shakespeare spares us nothing— the bickering, the infatuate action, the changes of mood, the melodramatic gesturing. Yet the poetic imagery works in another direction, not so much in its actual verbal suggestions as in its rising energy and human comprehensiveness. And at least Antony acts all his own parts. His chief reason for scorning Octavius Caesar is that he plays simply the rôle of cunning policy spinner and refuses to prove himself in any other capacity.

The richness of Antony's humanity increases with the instability of his attitudes. His rage with the presumptuous Thidias, who dares to kiss Cleopatra's hand, is of course partly the result of Thidias' being Caesar's messenger and of Cleopatra's looking kindly on him— he himself shortly afterwards gives Cleopatra Scarus's hand to kiss. But more than that, it is a release of something humanly real within him, and his expression of it has a ring of appeal about it, appeal to our understanding of his emotional predicament, of the human-ness of his situation:

Get thee back to Caesar,
Tell him thy entertainment: look thou say
He makes me angry with him. For he seems
Proud and disdainful, harping on what I am
Not what he knew I was. He makes me
angry,
And at this time most easy 'tis to do 't:
When my good stars, that were my former
guides,
Have empty left their orbs, and shot their fires
Into the abysm of hell.

The phrase 'harping on what I am / Not what he knew I was' has no equivalent in Plutarch. Antony's consciousness of his different selves represents an important part of Shakespeare's intention. At the same time Antony's almost genial acknowledgement of his own weakness has not only an engaging confessional aspect but also draws on its rhythm and movement to achieve a suggestion of human fallibility which increases rather than diminishes Antony's quality as a man:

He makes me angry,
And at this time most easy 'tis to do 't: . . .

When Cleopatra approaches him, hoping that his angry mood has passed, he is still talking to himself:

Alack, our terrene moon
Is now eclips'd, and it portends alone
The fall of Antony!

It is Cleopatra who is the moon— the changeable planet. (We recall Juliet's reproof to Romeo:

> O, swear not by the moon, th' inconstant
> moon,
> That monthly changes in her circled orb . . .)

But while he is lamenting Cleopatra's changeableness, she is awaiting the change in him that will bring him back to a full recognition of her love for him: 'I must stay his time'. He accuses her of flattering Caesar, and she replies simply: 'Not know me yet?' To which in turn he replies with another simple question: 'Cold-hearted toward me?' Her answer to this, beginning with the quietly moving 'Ah, dear, if I be so, . . .' brings him round at once. 'I am satisfied', is all he says to conclude the dispute, then proceeds at once to talk about his military plans. Having declared these, he suddenly realises just who Cleopatra is and where he stands in relation to her:

> Where hast thou been, my heart? Dost thou
> hear, lady?
> If from the field I shall return once more
> To kiss these lips, I will appear in blood,
> I, and my sword, will earn our chronicle:
> There's hope in't yet.

He is both warrior and lover now, and well may Cleopatra exclaim 'That's my brave lord!' This in turn encourages Antony to move to his third rôle, that of reveller:

> I will be treble-sinew'd, hearted, breath'd,
> And fight maliciously: for when mine hours
> Were nice and lucky, men did ransom lives
> Of me for jests: but now, I'll set my teeth,
> And send to darkness all that stop me.
>   Come,
> Let's have one other gaudy night: call to me
> All my sad captains, fill our bowls once more;
> Let's mock the midnight bell.

More rôle-taking now takes place on a very simple and moving plane. Cleopatra adjusts herself to Antony's recovered confidence:

> It is my birth-day,
> I had thought t' have held it poor. But since
> my lord
> Is Antony again, I will be Cleopatra.

Cleopatra's reference to her birthday is almost pathos, but it rises at once to grandeur with 'But since my lord / Is Antony again, I will be Cleopatra'. The question posed by the play is, What do these two characters finally add up to? When Antony is Antony again and Cleopatra Cleopatra who *are* they? One cannot give any answer less than the total meaning of the play.

Enobarbus, the 'realist', gives his comment on this dialogue. He knows his Antony; his shrewd and knowing mind give its ironic diagnosis:

> Now he'll outstare the lightning; to be
> furious
> Is to be frighted out of fear, and in that
> mood
> The dove will peck the estridge; and I see still,
> A diminution in our captain's brain
> Restores his heart; when valour preys on
> reason,
> It eats the sword it fights with: I will seek
> Some way to leave him.

But it is the realist who does not see the reality, and Enobarbus' death in an agony of remorse for having deserted Antony in the name of *Realpolitik* is Shakespeare's final comment on this interpretation.

The death of Antony leaves a whole act for Cleopatra's duel with Caesar before she finally outwits him and dies in her own way and in her own time. It is an act in which she plays continuously shifting rôles, and while these are obviously related to the exigencies of her conflict with Caesar and the fluctuations in her position, they also show her exhibiting varied facets of her character before deciding on the final pose she will adopt before the world and before history. She is not fooled by Caesar but plays a part designed to fool Caesar into thinking that she wants to live and make the best bargain possible for herself, exclaiming contemptuously to her ladies in waiting: 'He words me, girls, he words me'. Caesar is not an accomplished actor— he is not used to rôle-taking— and he gives himself away. 'Feed and sleep', he tells Cleopatra, thinking that the exhortation will disarm and soothe her. But the words suggest the treatment one gives to a caged beast and give away, what Dolabella is easily charmed by Cleopatra into confirming, that Caesar intends to lead Cleopatra and her children as captives in his triumphal procession. This rôle, for all her infinite variety, is one Cleopatra will never play. If she does not arrange her last act properly, the Romans will put her in *their* play:

> Nay, 'tis most certain, Iras: saucy lictors
> Will catch at us like strumpets, and scald
> rhymers
> Ballad us out o' tune. The quick comedians
> Extemporally will stage us, and present
> Our Alexandrian revels: Antony
> Shall be brought drunken forth, and I shall
> see
> Some squeaking Cleopatra boy my greatness
> I' the posture of a whore.

The pageant of her death which she arranges is a sufficient antidote to this. Preceded as it is by the characteristically enlarging dialogue with the clown who brings the figs— enlarging, that is, the human implications of the action— she goes through death to Antony whom at last she can call by the one name she was never able to call him in life— 'Husband, I come'. The splendour and dignity of the final ritual brings together in a great vindication the varied meanings of her histrionic career and temperament:

> Give me my robe, put on my crown, I have
> Immortal longings in me.

It is both a subsuming and a sublimating ritual. Love and loyalty and courage and queenliness are here together at last. And so is sexyness and sensuality, for this is a vindication through *wholeness* not through a choice of the proper and the respectable elements only. Iras dies first and Cleopatra exclaims:

> This proves me base:
> If she first meet the curled Antony,
> He'll make demand of her, and spend that kiss
> Which is my heaven to have.

This almost flippant sensuality has its place in the summing up, which transcends morality. Charmian, who dies last, lingers to set her dead mistress's crown straight:

> Your crown's awry,
> I'll mend it, and then play.

'Play' means play her part in the supreme pageant of ceremonial death and at the same time refers back, with controlled pathos, to Cleopatra's earlier

> And when thou hast done this chare, I'll give
> thee leave
> To play till doomsday: . . .

When Caesar arrives, the striking and moving spectacle of the dead queen in all her regal splendour flanked by her two dead handmaidens forces even this cold schemer to see her in the great inclusive rôle she has arranged for herself. Love, which in the Roman view of the matter has hitherto been opposed to history, the enemy of action and dignity and honour, is now at last, and by the very epitome of Roman authority and efficiency, pronounced to be part of history and of honour:

> Take up her bed,
> And bear her women from the monument:
> She shall be buried by her Antony.
> No grave upon the earth shall clip in it
> A pair so famous: high events as these
> Strike those that make them: and their story is
> No less in pity than his glory which
> Brought them to be lamented. Our army
> shall
> In solemn show attend this funeral,
> And then to Rome. Come, Dolabella, see

> High order, in this great solemnity.

'Famous', 'high', 'glory', 'solemn', 'order', 'solemnity'— these are the terms which Caesar now applies to a love story which earlier he had dismissed as 'lascivious wassails'. Is the play about human frailty or human glory? We are left with the feeling that one depends on the other, an insight too subtly generous for any known morality.

Katherine Vance MacMullan

SOURCE: "Death Imagery in *Antony and Cleopatra*," in *Shakespeare Quarterly*, Vol. 14, No. 4, Autumn, 1963, pp. 399-410.

[*MacMullan describes the artistic and literary image of Death that was familiar to Renaissance audiences— a grim but erotic bridegroom coming to claim his mate. MacMullan then explains that in* Antony and Cleopatra, *Shakespeare "individualized" this conventional image so that it focused less on the figure of Death and more on the characters of Antony and Cleopatra as they experienced the act of "dying tragically" in their own world filled with both love and violence.*]

Certain conventional methods of evoking the subject of death, either verbally or pictorially, were common to the Elizabethans, among them that of the *danse macabre*. That this convention was present virtually everywhere in sixteenth-century England is clear from its widespread employment as a decorative motif in art and as a theme in poetry, sermon, and the drama. The death imagery in Shakespeare's early plays seems largely to be drawn from the conventional antic figure of Death as he is personified and equipped in paintings, etchings, and emblemata. The images have a similar precise, decorative, grotesque quality and descriptive, moralistic emphasis and intent in both artistic mediums. Shakespeare employed an unusual variety of *memento mori* devices in his earlier dramatic compositions, in particular within and surrounding battle scenes, funerals, and executions, to emphasize widespread destruction and violence. The iconographical tradition provided a rich source of grim pictorial representations of devastation which may, in part, have inspired his verbal expression of the idea of death. Preparation for death in the drama provided Shakespeare with a natural justification for creating the proper atmosphere through the medium of language to foretell the action which his audience should anticipate. Death images skillfully introduced help to provide the context for deeds of violence and the sorrow and havoc which ensue. The Dance of Death, with its concentration on the deaths of kings, clergy, and noblemen, provides an apt analogy in the graphic arts to the course of destruction in an historical drama, for example, treating, as it often does, the rise and decline of royal fortunes.

Perhaps the most grotesque death images in the early histories are those of Constance in *King John*, picturing Death as the fatal bridegroom (III.iv.25 ff.). The idea of the marriage with Death is one of the most vivid and terrifying subjects of the iconographical tradition. Shakespeare has employed this figure, with all its attributes of sensual horror and grim fascination, as one of the predominating images of death in a number of his plays, notably in his tragedies of love, *Romeo and Juliet* and *Antony and Cleopatra*. The direct personification of Death in the earliest of the tragedies performs a unique function within the plot beyond that of the merely decorative or descriptive. Death appears as an active force within the context of events much as it does in the *danse macabre*, giving the play an intensity and quality of the grotesque. The notion that when a person dies he has a sort of physical union with Death is a macabre convention peculiarly suited to the nature of Shakespeare's *Romeo and Juliet*, in which the suicide of the lovers appears in the guise of a wedding or a final consummation in and with death. Subtle variations on this theme, in both its pictorial and dramatic aspects, are to be found in a number of Shakespeare's later dramatic compositions. The bedchamber scene from *Othello*, for example, incorporates many of the commonplace symbols of the union with death familiar to the Elizabethan audience— the snuffing of the candles, preparation of the spirit by prayer, the suggestion of damnation— and these elements combine to provide the atmosphere for the kiss of death which Othello bestows on the sleeping Desdemona. In addition Shakespeare's technique of employing imagery of love and death, light and darkness, heaven and hell in this scene serves to communicate an inescapable sense of the tension and tragic irony present in the final moment before death.

Death, not as an end, but as a part of the physical or natural cycle of life, is thematically present throughout the Shakespearian canon. The images of the earlier plays, individually considered, do not appear comprehensive or cosmic in scope, however, nor do they reverberate echo-like with meanings. It is only with Shakespeare's later explorations into the grotesque, the subtly complex, and the paradoxical that the death images begin to function as a part of the plot, viewed as a whole and taking into account the manifold relationships of all its parts. In turning once more to a consideration of the omens or emblems of death in a play such as *Antony and Cleopatra* it is valuable to take cognizance of the development of style and subject-matter of Shakespeare's imagery so that we may perceive a growing awareness through the characters in this drama of death as a part of life and experience. Death has become more individualized— that is, less conventional— as Shakespeare's dramatic emphasis concentrates less on death itself than on the process of dying tragically present in the life of his characters.

Antony and Cleopatra is the last Shakespearian play in which the theme of love and death is employed as an integral part of the dramatic situation. The images depict both plot and character in this most expansive of plays, and they serve in addition to relate it to *Romeo and Juliet* and *Othello*, the two earlier tragedies in which the images of love and death predominate. The quality of love and the deaths of the lovers may refer to a more cosmic scope of existence, but this is in keeping with the vast scale of the plot and the towering stature of the characters. The death images which foretell and attend their deaths, however, are significantly related to Shakespeare's earlier portrayal of passion culminating in death. The tragic protagonists Romeo, Othello, and Antony all "die with a kiss" and in their suicides attest to a kind of immortal union in death with Juliet, Desdemona, and Cleopatra. Thus, while concentrating on the significance of the death imagery as it enriches the portrayal of the tempestuous love of Antony and Cleopatra, I shall occasionally draw analogies with Shakespeare's use of imagery in previous dramatic situations.

Imagery of death accompanies Antony's tragic passion and decline, demonstrating with forceful irony the strengthening of his attachment to Cleopatra and the weakening of his judgment in the command of practical affairs. His defeat and fall are foreordained by omens derived in part from Plutarch's account, but it is in his relationship to the inexhaustible nature of Cleopatra that Shakespeare has most skillfully traced the stages of his decline in Fortune's favor. The sensuous imagery which originates in and surrounds Cleopatra herself, partaking as it does both of the passion and vitality of life and of the search for "easy ways to die", instills itself into the pattern of the lovers' destruction. The seductiveness which entices and which accompanies her own death is mentioned by the sullen Enobarbus at the beginning of the play:

> Cleopatra, catching but the least noise of this, dies instantly; I have seen her die twenty times upon far poorer moment: I do think there is some mettle in death, which commits some loving act upon her, she hath such a celerity in dying.

> (I.ii.145-149)

This quality in her entrances Caesar as he gazes on her silent form at the end of the play:

> . . . she looks like sleep,
> As she would catch another Antony
> In her strong toil of grace.

> (V.ii.349-351)

She is vital and enticing even in the sleep of death, and her nature is partially revealed to us by the sensual and extravagant images of sleep and death. Her "infinite variety" characterizes the death imagery as it is used by all those who come within the sphere of her influence, including the cynical Enobarbus and, finally, the all but "passionless" Octavius Caesar. It is natural that Antony should employ her imagery of love and death when he is within her ken. Following the report of Fulvia's death he says almost nothing:

> *Ant.* Fulvia is dead.
> *Eno.* Sir?
> *Ant.* Fulvia is dead.
> *Eno.* Fulvia!
> *Ant.* Dead. . . .
>
> (I.ii.162-166)

and in the presence of Octavia he speaks coldly, in an avowal devoid of vital images, of honor:

> . . . if I lose mine honour,
> I lose myself: better I were not yours
> Than yours so branchless.
>
> (III.iv.22-24)

But in the presence of the Egyptian queen he can rail thunderously of death with all the hate instilled in the nature of his passion:

> I have savage cause;
> And to proclaim it civilly, were like
> A halter'd neck which does the hangman thank
> For being yare about him.
>
> (III.xiii.128-131)

And in a moment, his hopes revived by her avowals of constancy, he can challenge Death himself with an even more brilliant image:

> Come on, my queen;
> There's sap in't yet. The next time I do fight,
> I'll make death love me; for I will contend
> Even with his pestilent scythe.
>
> (III.xiii.191-194)

Cleopatra has met fire with fire. Her own elaborate declaration of her love for him embraces the enduring of a hideous "graveless" death. If she proves faithless to him may her life "dissolve", and may she, she proclaims,

> Together with my brave Egyptians all,
> By the discandying of this pelleted storm,
> Lie graveless, till the files and gnats of Nile
> Have buried them for prey!
>
> (III.xiii.164-167)

Her impassioned avowal transforms his anger into the ironic figure of the pursuit of love even into the arms of Death. Death personified does not seem merely Antony's opponent, as he is Romeo's, but the symbol of his emotional subjugation to Cleopatra and the im-

age of his own destruction in the toils of passion. Antony's death images, rooted as they are in the extravagant nature and language of Cleopatra, ironically mock his weakness, as does his failure to kill himself when he falsely believes that Cleopatra has preceded him in death. Shakespeare employs death imagery skillfully to depict aspects of weakness, bravado, and destructiveness through character and action but culminating in a display of nobility in the presence of death infused with a sense of the immortal nature of passion.

Shakespeare uses the imagery of love and death to portray the character of Cleopatra and to foretell the decline of Antony early in the play (see I.ii.145 ff., III.x.8 ff.), but the individual images occur more frequently and contain greater variety and significance following Antony's first defeat at Actium. Act III, scene xiii marks an important turning-point in the plot and introduces the sequence of death images which culminates only in the deaths of the lovers. This scene opens with the suggestion of dying, as the disgraced Cleopatra asks Enobarbus:

> *Cleo.* What shall we do, Enobarbus?
> *Eno.* Think, and die.
>
> (III.xiii.1-2)

Later in the scene Enobarbus compares Antony to a sinking ship (l.63 ff.), a traditional omen of death, an image which echoes Antony's significant figure in the preceding encounter with Cleopatra:

> Egypt, thou knew'st too well
> My heart was to thy rudder tied by the strings,
> And thou shouldst tow me after: o'er my spirit
> Thy full supremacy thou knew'st, and that
> Thy back might from the bidding of the gods
> Command me.
>
> (III.xii.56-61)

The forerunners of this image occurred earlier in the play; Caesar termed the enamored Antony an "ebb'd man" (I.iv.43), and Cleopatra as the siren figure described her fatal attraction as the lover's port of death:

> . . . great Pompey
> Would stand and make his eyes grow in my brow;
> There would he anchor his aspect and die
> With looking on his life.
>
> (I. V. 31-34)

Then in a series of varied images Shakespeare weaves Cleopatra's charms into the omens of Antony's fall and death. As Act III, scene xii progresses, Enobarbus compares Antony to an old lion dying (l.95), Antony deplores the fall of his guiding stars "into the abysm of hell" (1.147), Cleopatra will be true to him or "lie graveless" (1.166, and see above), and Antony determines once more to "fight maliciously . . . / And send to darkness all that stop me" (ll.179, 182). The scene ends with Antony's rash challenge to Death, as quoted above. This latter image, combining the notions of love and death, dominates the following scenes, and its noble irony sets the tone for Antony's fall. A suggestion of this image occurs again in Antony's farewell to his followers on the night before the battle of Alexandria:

> Mine honest friends,
> I turn you not away; but, like a master
> Married to your good service, stay till death.
>
> (IV.ii.29-31)

The love-death omen reappears more forcefully, with all its mock-heroic and sensuous connotations, as Antony attempts to kill himself in the belief that his mistress is already dead:

> My queen and Eros
> Have by their brave instruction got upon me
> A nobleness in record: but I will be
> A bridegroom in my death, and run into 't
> As to a lover's bed.
>
> (IV.xiv.97-101)

This figure, derived from the notion of a marriage with death, mocks Antony's failure to die an heroic Roman death. Interestingly enough, Shakespeare has twice given Antony this figure before his strategical failures, as if to emphasize the cause and degree of his weakness. This striking image serves also to link the deaths of the lovers, separated as they are by the space of nearly an act; as such, it is one of a series of brilliant figures which unite the dying pair during the last five scenes of the play. As Antony had witnessed the death of Eros before uttering the lines on marriage with death, so Cleopatra as the faithful Iras falls at her feet comments on the impassioned pain of dying:

> Dost fall?
> If thou and nature can so gently part,
> The stroke of death is as a lover's pinch,
> Which hurts, and is desired.
>
> (V.ii.296-299)

These variations on the ancient notion of Death as the lover, as Shakespeare employed the figure in *Romeo and Juliet*, are peculiar to the sensual, bitter-sweet language of Cleopatra and Antony, who would seem to seek the pleasures of love even in the arms of death. The image, as we have seen, rose out of the nature of Cleopatra (Enobarbus, satirically, saw her death as the embrace of a lover, I.ii.147 ff., above); its mock-heroic cast has tinged the martial speeches of Antony (III.xiii. 192 and IV.ii.29 above); and, finally, it serves to characterize Cleopatra's own sense of a kind of honorable seduction

in the act of dying.

Another primary death image, which occurs with increasing frequency in the scenes following Act III, scene xiii, is that of sleep and death, an image which Shakespeare employed effectively in dramatizing the fall of Macbeth. Unlike the "murder of sleep" image in the latter play which serves to reveal Macbeth's engrossment in sin, the sleep of death now attaches itself to Cleopatra as a characteristic expression of her personality. Shakespeare employs all the languid, luxurious connotations of sleep to portray the dying queen in all her regal seductiveness. The sleep image reveals, in addition, Shakespeare's skillful technique in uniting the deaths of the lovers. In fact, it is Antony who first uses the expression. Antony's tirade against Cleopatra for her betrayal is suddenly transformed by Mardian's report that Cleopatra has killed herself. His life and his defeat by Caesar now seem meaningless, and he replies quietly:

> Unarm, Eros; the long day's task is done,
> And we must sleep.
>
> (IV.xiv.35-36)

He determines to "lie down, and stray no further" but rather to seek the realm "where souls do couch on flowers" (ll.47,51). He will face death as if running "to a lover's bed" (l.101). In the scene in the monument following Antony's actual death, Cleopatra echoes Antony's words in an image of sleep which seems a part of her decision to follow him in death:

> I dream'd there was an Emperor Antony:
> O, such another sleep, that I might see
> But such another man!
>
> (V.ii.74-76)

The dream, which she suggests as a symbol of her own desire for death, is evoked in her attempt to win over Dolabella, Caesar's emissary; but even here she does not deny her attachment to the notion of reuniting with Antony in death.

Her own death is leisurely and displays the cunning and "infinite variety" for which she is noted, ranging from her clever deception of Caesar to her humorous sallies with the Clown who brings her "the pretty worm of Nilus" (V.ii.243). "She is herself to the very end", as Granville-Barker has noted (p.447). Her consummate sensations are restful as sleep itself:

> Peace, peace!
> Dost thou not see my baby at my breast,
> That sucks the nurse asleep?
>
> As sweet as balm, as soft as air, as gentle,—
> O Antony!
>
> (V.ii.312-314, 315-316)

It remains only for Charmian to close the "downy win-

Doug Adler as an attendant, Antoni Cimolino as Alexas, Douglas Chamberlain as Mardian, Alison Sealy-Smith as Charmian, Yanna McIntosh as Iras, and Goldie Semple as Cleopatra in the Stratford Festival's 1993 production of Antony and Cleopatra.

dows" (l.319) of the queen, her youthful charm restored once more in death:

> Now boast thee, death, in thy possession lies
> A lass unparallel'd.
>
> (V.ii.318-319)

The impression Shakespeare has created for us through imagery of a Cleopatra most like sleep in her death is confirmed by Caesar, usually so business-like and confident in speech and manner:

> . . . she looks like sleep,
> As she would catch another Antony
> In her strong toil of grace.
>
> (V.2.349-351)

The conqueror too is transformed for a moment by the spectacle of the fallen Cleopatra, enchanting and seductive even in death. And, briefly, her influence colors his language with an image most befitting her vital nature. The qualities so often transmitted to

Antony's Egyptian tongue thus reappear as the final tribute to Cleopatra. Her death serves, in addition, to illustrate Shakespeare's technique of deriving imagery from the nature of character and action, using that imagery to link the fates of his central figures. Just as Othello's language displays Iago's influence when the tragic culmination is approaching, so Cleopatra's speech and character seem to communicate through those who surround her a quality of the exotic and passionate. The comprehensive range of the plot of *Antony and Cleopatra* challenged Shakespeare's resources of imagery in preserving the relationships between characters and their actions, and gave rise to the devices of technique which portray the fall of Antony and the deaths of the lovers.

Another series of images which attends the decline of Antony and Cleopatra and which illustrates how the lovers appear to each other is that of the opposition of light with darkness. Shakespeare used this paired association in *Romeo and Juliet* and *Othello* to depict love and tragic loss. As Caroline Spurgeon has noted, Romeo and Juliet see each other as beacons of light gleaming against a dark background (pp. 310-316). Even in the blackness of the tomb Juliet's presence illuminates her surroundings as she appears through the eyes of Romeo:

> . . . here lies Juliet, and her beauty makes
> This vault a feasting presence full of light.
>
> (V.iii.85-86)

She too is like sleep, beautiful in her supposed death.

Othello, transforming image into symbolic action, quenches the light over the sleeping form of Desdemona before stifling her, she who once had seemed a "radiant angel" to him. At the conclusion of his deed, Othello conveys his sense of loss as an image of darkness, an eclipse of sun and moon. These are only the last in a series of images of light and dark which display the alteration of Othello's love as he falls prey to Iago's devil-like influence. Othello's "put out the light" and Macbeth's "out, out, brief candle" are but two of Shakespeare's variations on the traditional literary and iconographical image depicting the approach or the actual moment of death. The image of the waning of the lamp or candle of life occurs frequently in the early histories to describe or poetize the act of dying. An example of Shakespeare's previous use of this figure, uncomplicated by symbolic meanings or thematic associations, is found in *I Henry VI*. The dying Mortimer says:

> These eyes, like lamps whose wasting oil is
> spent,
> Wax dim, as drawing to their exigent.
>
> (II.V.8-9)

and his image is echoed by Richard Plantagenet: "Here dies the dusky torch of Mortimer" (II. v. 122).

Death is described dispassionately in emblem-book figures, which often depict Death personified snuffing out the candle of life. Shakespeare consistently places darkness in opposition to light as the omen or symbol of death; but he also uses an analogous image to create atmosphere for the perpetration of dark deeds, for the decline of a character's fortunes, for the death of lovers, or for the destruction of love itself. The extinguishing of light attends destructive acts and impulses of every sort. But in *Antony and Cleopatra* an added dimension is supplied to this traditional concept. The quenching of the torch describes death as it did in *Henry VI*, but the image serves also to relate characters and actions within the context of the play as a whole. Mortimer's image serves a descriptive purpose only, but the analogous figure as it is used by both Antony and Cleopatra fulfills a multiple function in the plot.

In *Antony and Cleopatra* the lovers are consistently linked by association with the great cosmic forces of the universe, particularly the stars. The "Herculean" stature of Antony is portrayed in images of light from the very first scene of the play (see I.i.2), and omens of darkness presage his fall. In keeping with the sequence of light-and-dark images which attend Antony's eclipse, his death appears as the extinguishing of a brilliant light. In the final acts of the play, however, Antony's radiance seems a reflection of his "eastern star", and from this point on, darkness, or the quenching of light, becomes one of the primary symbols relating the deaths of the lovers. After his defeat in Act IV, when Antony thinks Cleopatra has betrayed him, he proclaims:

> O sun, thy uprise shall I see no more:
> Fortune and Antony part here; even here
> Do we shake hands.
>
> (IV.xi.18-20)

But when Mardian reports Cleopatra's death his anger turns to grief, "all length is torture: since the torch is out" (IV.xiv.46), and with the extinction of his source of light Antony determines to die. Gazing on the mortally wounded commander moments later, a guard proclaims "the star is fall'n" (l. 106); and, catching sight of him, Cleopatra expands this image of Antony as the destruction of the heavenly bodies:

> O sun,
> Burn the great sphere thou movest in!
> darkling stand
> The varying shore o' the world. O Antony.
>
> (IV.xv.9-11)

He dies in her arms and she cries to her attendants "our lamp is spent, it's out!" (l. 85). Her resolution to "do it after the high Roman fashion" (l. 87) recalls Antony's image of her as the torch and his attempt to follow her into darkness. In her praise of him to Dolabella, Antony appears as the source of light illuminating the vast regions of the earth:

> His face was as the heavens; and therein stuck
> A sun and moon, which kept their course,
> and lighted
> The little O, the earth.
>
> (V. ii. 79-81)

Cleopatra's hopes in Caesar dead, Iras sanctions her release to death in the image Cleopatra has adopted as the omen of her own fate, now linked with the death of Antony:

> Finish, good lady; the bright day is done,
> And we are for the dark.
>
> (V.ii.193-194)

In the consummation of her resolve to join Antony, Cleopatra becomes all "fire and air", but her light too is extinguished in death; such a pair of noble eyes will never gaze on "golden Phoebus" again. Thus the lovers, like the "starcross'd" Romeo and Juliet, appear to each other in images of light, and their deaths as the quenching of that radiance. Their brightness serves to illuminate each other as well as to brighten the sphere in which they move. *Antony and Cleopatra* illustrates, in addition, Shakespeare's mature technique of using a conventional emblematic death-image for the purposes of characterization and for establishing the important relationships of the play. Shakespeare has used the images of death and love, of sleep and death, and of light and darkness to display the natures of the central figures, their influences upon each other, the continuity of their fates, and the union of all these factors in the dramatization of their deaths. To a greater degree than in *Romeo and Juliet* or even in *Othello*, imagery of death has become organic to the structure of Shakespeare's plot in *Antony and Cleopatra*, and it functions to preserve a kind of unity within the tragedy's vast scope.

There are numerous peripheral death images in *Antony and Cleopatra*, a number of which suggest analogies to the iconographical tradition. For example, the Servants on Pompey's galley discuss the royal feast within and the ill-omened dissension among the participants, which inspires one of them to describe moving in a sphere of greatness with a figure that suggests the death's head:

> To be called a huge sphere, and not to be seen to move in't, are the holes where eyes should be, which pitifully disaster the cheeks.
>
> (II.vii.15-17)

A similar image is reiterated and expanded in the conversation between Eros and Enobarbus following the murder of Pompey:

> *Eros.* . . . so the poor third is up, till death
>   enlarge his confine.
> *Eno.* Then, world, thou hast a pair of chaps,
>   no more;
> And throw between them all the food thou
>   hast,
> They'll grind the one the other.
>
> (III.v.13-16)

The "chaps" or jaws which destroy by grinding again suggest the skull, but it is clearly the strife between rulers which enlarges the "confine" of death, as the rotten jaws of the tomb engulf Shakespeare's heroes and lovers. "Death" here approaches personification as the devouring skeleton which appears in Baldung Grien's etchings. The figure of Death, however, is invoked at least twice in the play, first upon the occasion of Enobarbus' death: "The hand of death hath raught him" (IV.ix.29). This conventional phrase suggesting the Dance of Death occurs again in the plea of Cleopatra as Proculeius wrenches the dagger from her hand:

> Where art thou, death?

> Come hither, come! come, come, and take a
>   queen
> Worth many babes and beggars!
>
> (V.ii.46-48)

In this brief cry to Death, Cleopatra manages to call to mind the whole progression of Death's victims of every age and condition. When Cleopatra contemplates the morality of suicide she speaks of rushing "into the secret house of death, / Ere death dare come to us" (IV.xv.81-82), again suggesting the personification of Death and creating an image which is pictorially realistic if not directly related to the *danse macabre* tradition. The feeding of the mortal worm is not specifically designed to suggest the gruesome funeral statuary familiar in the Renaissance, but the punning of Cleopatra and the rustic Clown should recall Hamlet's conceits on the medieval theme, "wormes fode thu schald beo", though the context and dimension of these scenes differ widely.

A number of the death images echo the natural associations with death as Shakespeare had employed them in earlier plays. Antony links death with the preservation of honor, a theme akin to that of death in battle found in the Histories. Likewise Cleopatra's imagery of a "graveless" death and of corpses lying prey to flies and vermin (III.xiii.164 ff.; V.ii.58 ff.) recalls the description of Shakespearian battle scenes. Scarus, Antony's general, describes the rout of Actium as "the token'd pestilence, / Where death is sure (III.x.9-10), echoing plague imagery associated with death in *Timon of Athens*, for example. Antony consumed by anger against Cleopatra uses the conventional curse, "die the death" (IV.xiv.26). A series of familiar omens of death portend Antony's fall— mysterious music, "black vesper's pageants", and Fortune's desertion.

Finally Shakespeare's tragedies of love, culminating in *Antony and Cleopatra*, are related to each other by their dying scenes. The lovers Romeo, Othello, and Antony, having suffered from various forms of delusion drawn from the nature of their passions, "die with a kiss"— Romeo in joining Juliet to save her from the lustful advances of Death, Othello in realizing the innocence of Desdemona, and Antony in snatching the last moment of life to proclaim once his love for Cleopatra. Othello's is a kiss of parting, Romeo's and Antony's of reunion with the beloved. Antony's death at Cleopatra's feet allays his ironic failure by evoking a tragic pathos from his devotion to his queen:

> I am dying, Egypt, dying; only
> I here importune death awhile, until
> Of many thousand kisses the poor last
> I lay upon thy lips.
>
> (IV.xv.18-21)

His tribute to their love inspires a similar image from Cleopatra:

... die where thou hast lived:
Quicken with kissing: had my lips that power,
Thus would I wear them out.

(IV.xv.38-40)

Tragic is the realization that all her powers of attraction cannot seduce death into releasing Antony to her. Kisses will not reclaim her lover, and her grief vents itself on "the false housewife Fortune" (l. 44), whom she has offended by her enchanting of Antony. Life is suddenly meaningless to her, as it was for Romeo and Othello, when Antony has breathed his last. Cleopatra's ranting is histrionic and impatient but the storm of her emotions is quickly over, giving way to the calm nobility of aspect in which we last see her. Her characteristic sensuality and emotion color her expression to the end, transforming the death scenes into final expressions of passion. Caesar's last tribute to her and his order for the burial of the lovers is appropriate to the character of the pair and the immortal reunion they sought in death:

Take up her bed;
And bear her women from the monument:
She shall be buried by her Antony:
No grave upon the earth shall clip in it
A pair so famous.

(V.ii.359-363)

The royal burial was derived from Plutarch, but the images relating character and circumstance which make the death scenes memorable are peculiarly Shakespeare's own. There is no greater tribute to his art than the consummate fascination evoked by the spectacle of the dying queen, garbed in all the verbal apparel of seductiveness and death.

DUALISM

Dualism in its various forms— contrast, paradox, irony— plays a significant role in *Antony and Cleopatra*. **Peter Berek** describes the play as one "in which mighty opposites meet, struggle, and embrace. Rome encounters Egypt, Reason feels emotion, Spirit wars with Flesh, Duty yields to Leisure." Richard C. Harrier contrasts Cleopatra— whom he sees as representative of Egypt, undisciplined fertility, and inconstancy— with Octavius Caesar— with whom he links Rome, order, and power. Cynthia Kolb Whitney focuses on the contrasts which exist between Rome and Egypt, asserting that the two have completely different value systems and that "behavior which is almost divine to one is repugnant and silly to the other." **Janet Adelman** observes that many of the paradoxes in the play are the result of the frequent use of hyperbole, or lavishly extravagant language. Adelman argues that while many of the characters use hyperbole for dramatic effect (as when Philo complains that Antony's heart has "become the bellows and the fan / To cool a gipsy's lust") Antony and

Cleopatra, by contrast, seem to be absolutely serious in their use of exaggerated language. Adelman asserts that the lovers' references to the gods and to powerful forces of nature to describe their love for one another have the paradoxical effect of sounding comical to an audience. Adelman concludes that the resulting conflict between what the audience feels and what the lovers believe is resolved in this intentionally complex play when Cleopatra acknowledges the existence of a very human foolishness behind everyone's dreams.

Commentators have suggested a variety of ways in which dualism directs the action and outcome of *Antony and Cleopatra*. Paul A. Cantor, for example, argues that the play does not in fact neatly establish an opposition between private and public life but that the love affair of Antony and Cleopatra is intended to mirror the antagonisms which occur in the public life of Rome. Thus according to Cantor, the distrust and jealously that Antony and Cleopatra feel regarding their love for one another is reflected in the suspicions that Antony and Octavius harbor toward each other with regard to their political alliance. Cynthia Kolb Whitney argues that of the principal characters, Antony is the one who is most profoundly affected by the play's dual worlds. Whitney asserts that the "external combat between Egypt and Rome" becomes a source for internal conflict for Antony— who must choose between his love for Cleopatra and his loyalty to his country. Sheila M. Smith also refers to Antony's inner struggle, but she sees it as a reflection of a more specific conflict between Cleopatra and Octavius Caesar. Further, Smith argues that such dualism can only be resolved in the play through death. Peter Berek views death in Antony and Cleopatra as the expression of duality as well as its resolution— for, paradoxically, it is through death that the two lovers make their love immortal.

Finally, Stephen A. Shapiro presents two conflicting views of *Antony and Cleopatra* once held by scholars: the "moral" view asserts that the play is critical of the two lovers; the "transcendental view" contends that the play "exalts romantic love." Shapiro rejects both views, arguing instead that in *Antony and Cleopatra* Shakespeare withholds all judgment and that the play's opposites— love versus war, Rome versus Egypt, and fertility versus death— are meant to underscore the ambivalent nature of life.

Janet Adelman

SOURCE: "'Nature's Piece 'gainst Fancy': Poetry and the Structure of Belief in *Antony and Cleopatra*," in *The Common Liar: An Essay on* Antony and Cleopatra, Yale University Press, 1973, pp. 102-68.

[Adelman evaluates the dualistic vision that pervades the play, remarking on such paradoxes as the fact that characters' actions often fall far short of their elaborately poetic descriptions

of one another, and that Antony and Cleopatra at last resort to death to keep their love alive. Adelman observes that this dualism is established not only through paradox but also through the poetic device known as "hyperbole"—descriptive language that is exaggerated to extremes in order to create a particular effect. Adelman concludes that this hyperbolic and paradoxical dualism causes us to wonder whether to take the action in the play seriously, but she suggests that the lovers themselves are very serious in their descriptions.]

Skepticism and Belief

From the first words of the play ("Nay, but"), our reactions have been at issue. We are given judgments that we must simultaneously accept and reject; we are shown the partiality of truth. But finally we are not permitted to stand aside and comment with impunity any more than Enobarbus is: we must choose either to accept or to reject the lovers' versions of themselves and of their death; and our choice will determine the meaning of the play for us. But the choice becomes increasingly impossible to make on the evidence of our reason or our senses. How can we believe in Enobarbus's description of Cleopatra as Venus when we see the boy actor before us? The Antony whom Cleopatra describes in her dream is not the Antony whom we have seen sitting on stage in dejection after Actium or bungling his suicide. Although the lovers die asserting their post-mortem reunion, all we see is the dead queen and her women, surrounded by Caesar and his soldiers. The stage action necessarily presents us with one version of the facts, the poetry with another. This is the dilemma inherent in much dramatic poetry; and the more hyperbolical the poetry, the more acute the dilemma. Critics are occasionally tempted to read *Antony and Cleopatra* as a very long poem; but it is essential that we be aware of it as drama at all times. For how can one stage hyperbole? Reading the play, we might imagine Antony a colossus; but what shall we do with the very human-sized Antony who has been before us for several hours? In a sonnet, for instance, an assertion contrary to fact will be true within the poem; standards must be imported from outside the work by which to find the assertions improbable. As Shakespeare points out, not every girl be-sonneted has breasts whiter than snow, despite the assertions of her sonneteer. But a play carries its own refutation within itself: even with the most advanced stage technology, the action and the human actors will undercut these assertions even as they are made. Precisely this tension is at the heart of *Antony and Cleopatra*: we can neither believe nor wholly disbelieve in the claims made by the poetry.

The poetry of the last two acts is generally acknowledged as the sleight-of-hand by which Shakespeare transforms our sympathies toward the lovers, in despite of the evidence of our reason and our senses. Although even Caesar speaks in blank verse, the language of most richness and power is in the service of the lovers:

it is the language in which Enobarbus creates Cleopatra as Venus and the lovers assert the value of their love and their death. In this play, the nay-sayers may have reason and justice on their side; but as Plato suspected when he banished poetry from his republic, reason and justice are no match for poetry. The appeal to mere reason will not always affect fallen man; according to Renaissance theorists, it was precisely the power of poetry to *move*, occasionally against the dictates of all reason, that made it at once most dangerous and most fruitful. And modern critics are as wary of the power of poetry as their predecessors: the poetry in *Antony and Cleopatra* is almost always praised, but the praise frequently coincides with the suspicion that it has somehow taken unfair advantage of us by befuddling our clear moral judgment. It is that doubtless delightful but nonetheless dubious means by which the lovers are rescued from our condemnation at the last moment, rather as Lancelot rescues Guinevere from her trial by fire. We are pleased but suspect that strictest justice has not been done. If it is true that Shakespeare uses the poetry to dazzle our moral sense and undo the structure of criticism in the play, then we may find *Antony and Cleopatra* satisfying as a rhetorical showcase, but we cannot admire the play as a whole. It is refreshing to find this charge made explicit by G. B. Shaw [in *Three Plays for Puritans*], who clearly enjoys expressing his contempt for a poet who finds it necessary to rescue his lovers from our moral judgment by means of a rhetorical trick.

> Shakespear's Antony and Cleopatra must needs be as intolerable to the true Puritan as it is vaguely distressing to the ordinary healthy citizen, because after giving a faithful picture of the soldier broken down by debauchery, & the typical wanton in whose arms such men perish, Shakespear finally strains all his huge command of rhetoric & stage pathos to give a theatrical sublimity to the wretched end of the business, & to persuade foolish spectators that the world was well lost by the twain. Such false-hood is not to be borne except by the real Cleopatras & Antonys (they are to be found in every public house) who would no doubt be glad enough to be transfigured by some poet as immortal lovers. Woe to the poet who stoops to such folly! . . . When your Shakespears & Thackerays huddle up the matter at the end by killing somebody & covering your eyes with the undertaker's handkerchief, duly onioned with some pathetic phrase . . . I have no respect for them at all: such maudlin tricks may impose on tea-house drunkards, not on me.

The final poetry, detached from character and situation, does indeed give us the glorified vision of love that Shaw mistrusted, a vision not wholly consistent with the merely human Antony and Cleopatra, though Antony is far more than a debauchee and Cleopatra anything but typical, no matter how wanton. But the poetry is not a rhetorical Lancelot. Its assertions and the problems they present to our skepticism have been inherent throughout: and if the poetry strains our credulity toward the end, the strain itself is a necessary part of our experience. Are the visions asserted by the poetry mere fancies, or are they "nature's piece 'gainst fancy"? Precisely this tension between belief and disbelief has been essential from the start. When the lovers first come on stage, very much in the context of an unfriendly Roman judgment, they announce the validity of their love in a hyperbolical poetry which contrasts sharply with Philo's equally hyperbolical condemnation. Here, at the very beginning, two attitudes are set in juxtaposition by the use of two equally impossible images which appeal to two very different modes of belief. Philo uses hyperbole as *metaphor*: "his captain's heart / . . . is become the bellows and the fan / To cool a gipsy's lust" (1.1.6-10). This is the deliberate exaggeration which moral indignation excites; it does not in any sense call for our literal belief. The hyperbolical metaphor is morally apt, and that is all. The Roman metaphor is carefully delineated as metaphor: it never pretends to a validity beyond the metaphoric. But what of the lovers? "Then must thou needs find out new heaven, new earth" (1.1.17); "Let Rome in Tiber melt" (1.1.33). Strictly speaking, these hyperboles are not metaphor at all. Antony's words assert his access to a hyperbolical world where such things actually happen, a world beyond the reach of metaphor. They claim, like Cleopatra's dream, to be in the realm of nature, not of fancy. His words do not give us the protection of regarding them merely as apt metaphors: they make their claim as literal action. We may choose to disbelieve their claim; but in doing so, we are rejecting a version of reality, not the validity of a metaphor. And precisely this kind of assertion will become more insistent— and more improbable— as the play progresses.

The poetry of the final acts should not take us unawares: if at the last moment it surfaces, like the dolphin who shows his back above the element he lives in, the whole of the play and a good deal of Shakespeare's career should have prepared us for its appearance. The validity of the imaginative vision as it is asserted in the poetry is a part of Shakespeare's subject in *Antony and Cleopatra*. But the play is not therefore "about" the vision of the poet: we are presented with lovers creating the image of their love, not with poets poetizing. For the association of love with imagination or fancy is one of Shakespeare's most persistent themes. Love in Shakespeare almost always creates its own imaginative versions of reality; and it is almost always forced to test its version against the realities acknowledged by the rest of the world. Theseus in *Midsummer Night's Dream* tells us that the lover, like the lunatic and the poet, is of imagination all compact (5.1.7-8): in that play, "fancy" is generally used as synonymous with "love." We remember Juliet, valiantly making day into night in despite of the lark that sings so out of tune. Imagination is essential to love; but if it is totally unmoored to

reality, it becomes love's greatest threat. Othello's love will turn to hate as Iago poisons his imagination. Spenser circumscribes his book of chaste love (*The Faerie Queene*, book 3) with just this kind of warning about the uses and misuses of imagination in love. Britomart falls in love with Artegall when she sees him in Merlin's magic mirror; she immediately assumes that the vision has no basis in reality and that she is doomed to "feed on shadowes" (*FQ* 3.2.44). But her vision is directed by Merlin's art: her Artegall exists, though she does not recognize him when she first meets him in the real world. The vision here is no shadow but an idealized version of reality; and in time Britomart will recognize the real Artegall whose ideal form she has seen. Her love depends initially on the idealizing vision, but it passes the test of reality. But at the end of book 3, we see the consequences of an abandonment to self-willed imagination. Amoret is subject to Busirane's tormented perversion of love: and the masque of Cupid which holds her captive is led by Fancy (*FQ* 3.12.7).

Love is an act of imagination, but it cannot be an act of *mere* imagination. In the plays that deal with lovers, Shakespeare continually emphasizes the need to circumscribe the tyranny of imagination in love. The arbitrary loves of *Midsummer Night's Dream* must be subjected to the chaos of unbridled fancy (stage-managed by Puck) before they can be sorted out. At the end of *As You Like It*, Orlando proclaims that he can live no longer by thinking (5.2.55). But in the Forest of Arden, thinking makes it so: Orlando's imagined Rosalind can reveal herself as the real Rosalind because her game has permitted her to test the realities of love. The matter is more complex in *Twelfth Night*, where mere imagination prevails in the self-willed loves of Olivia and Orsino. Here the emblem for the dangerous prevalence of the imagination in love is Malvolio, reading the supposed letter from Olivia and finding himself in every word. Malvolio here is exactly like any lover, searching reality for clues to confirm his own delusions; that the letter is constructed precisely so that he will find such confirmation simply emphasizes the process. Given all this imagination run rampant, it is no wonder that Viola insists on testing her imagination, even to the point of stubbornness: "Prove true, imagination, O, prove true" (*Twelfth Night* 3.4.409), she says, and then quizzes Sebastian extensively about his parentage and his early history before she will allow herself to believe that he is her brother.

If the theme of imagination in love is a concern in these plays, it is an obsession in *Troilus and Cressida*, where the consequences of mere imagination are delineated with chilling accuracy. Before Troilus meets with Cressida, "expectation" whirls him round; "th' imaginary relish is so sweet" (3.2.19-20) that it enchants his sense. But even Troilus knows that the imaginary relish will exceed the act; and his description of the physiology of sex is true of all enterprise in this world of frustration:

This is the monstruosity in love, lady, that the will
is infinite and the execution confin'd, that the desire is boundless and the act a slave to limit.

[*Troilus and Cressida* 3.2.87-90]

Troilus watching Cressida give herself to Diomed will
learn exactly how much desire or imaginary relish is
bound by the limits of reality. He has throughout the
play assumed that thinking makes it so: during the
council scene he asks, "What is aught, but as 'tis valu'd?"
(2.2.52). At the end, he will learn the hard facts of
value, the facts implicit in Hector's answer to his question:

But value dwells not in particular will;
It holds his estimate and dignity
As well wherein 'tis precious of itself
As in the prizer.

[*Troilus and Cressida* 2.2.53-56]

Troilus and Cressida is Shakespeare's most horrifying vision of untested imagination in love. In that sense, it is
a necessary counterpoise both to the earlier comedies
and to *Antony and Cleopatra*. For *Antony and Cleopatra* is
Troilus and Cressida revisited: if *Troilus and Cressida* portrays desire as a slave to limit, *Antony and Cleopatra*
asserts the power of desire to transcend limits; if Troilus's
subjection to mere imagination nearly destroys him,
Cleopatra's imagination of her Antony virtually redeems
them both. Later, in the romances, the desires of the
lovers will usually become their realities: the art itself is
nature, and imagination purely redemptive. *Troilus* and
the romances are in this sense at opposite ends of the
scale: in *Troilus and Cressida*, our credulity is at the mercy
of our skepticism, as Troilus himself will discover; in
the romances, our skepticism is banished by an act of
total poetic faith. But *Antony and Cleopatra* is poised in
a paradoxical middle region in which skepticism and
credulity must be balanced. In this sense, the perspectives of both *Troilus and Cressida* and the romances are
included within *Antony and Cleopatra;* and it is precisely
because of this inclusiveness that imagination can emerge
triumphant.

The process of testing the imagination is essential to
the assertion of its validity: for only through an exacting balance of skepticism and assent can it prove true.
And more than any other play, *Antony and Cleopatra*
insists on both our skepticism and our assent. For it is
simultaneously the most tough-minded and the most
triumphant of the tragedies, and it is necessarily both
at once. Throughout, Shakespeare disarms criticism by
allowing the skeptics their full say: the whole play is in
effect a test of the lovers' visions of themselves.
Cleopatra herself presents the most grotesquely skeptical view of her own play:

. . . The quick comedians
Extemporally will stage us, and present

Our Alexandrian revels: Antony
Shall be brought drunken forth, and I shall
    see
Some squeaking Cleopatra boy my greatness
I' the posture of a whore.

[5.2.215-20]

Once she has spoken, this Roman version of her greatness becomes untenable; we know that Shakespeare's
Antony and Cleopatra is not an item in Caesar's triumph.
It is only in the context of "Nay, but" that we can
answer "yes": if the imaginative affirmations were not
so persistently questioned, they could not emerge triumphant. The extreme of skepticism itself argues for
affirmation: and here the affirmations are no less extreme than the skepticism. Throughout the play, we are
not permitted to see Cleopatra merely as a fallen woman:
we are asked to see her in the posture of a whore. And
when the time has come for affirmation, we are asked
to believe not in the probable but in the palpably impossible: not that the lovers are worthy though misguided, but that they are semidivine creatures whose
love has somehow managed to escape the bonds of
time and space, and even of death. Whore or goddess,
strumpet's fool or colossus: the play allows us no mid-
point. After all the doubt which has been central to our
experience, we are asked to participate in a secular act
of faith. This is the final contrariety that the play demands of us: that the extreme of skepticism itself must
be balanced by an extreme of assent.

If we come to believe in the assertions of the poetry,
it is, I think, precisely because they are so unbelievable.
One of the tricks of the human imagination is that an
appeal to the rationally possible is not always the most
effective means of insuring belief: occasionally an appeal to the impossible, an appeal to doubt, works wonders. *Antony and Cleopatra* embodies in its structure the
paradox of faith: the exercise of faith is necessary only
when our reason dictates doubt; we believe only in the
things that we know are not true. The central strategy
of *Antony and Cleopatra* depends upon this process: we
achieve faith by deliberately invoking doubt. And in
fact this process dictates not only the broad structure
of the play but also its poetic texture. The imaginative
vision of the play is based firmly on the two rhetorical
figures that are themselves dependent on this strategy:
paradox and hyperbole.

The incidence of paradox and hyperbole in *Antony
and Cleopatra* is not merely an accident or
Shakespeare's sleight-of-hand: these figures inform
the shape and the substance of the play. For they
posit in their very structure the tension between
imaginative assertion and literal fact that is part of
the state of love. Even [Francis] Bacon [in "On Love"]
is willing to concede that love is appropriately expressed in hyperbole, precisely because its assertions
are palpably untrue.

It is a strange thing to note the excess of this passion, and how it braves the nature and value of things, by this: that the speaking in a perpetual hyperbole is comely in nothing but love. Neither is it merely in the phrase; for whereas it hath been well said that the arch-flatterer, with whom all the petty flatterers have intelligence, is a man's self; certainly the lover is more. For there was never proud man thought so absurdly well of himself as the lover doth of the person loved.

As Bacon points out, love infects the thought as well as the language of lovers with hyperbole. Biron and the other lovers fall hopelessly into paradox as they fall in love in *Love's Labour's Lost;* even Hamlet is subject to paradox and hyperbole in love, as his poem to Ophelia demonstrates. Only the contradictions of paradox are capable of expressing the contradictions of love: for paradox is a stylistic *discordia concors,* a knot intrinsicate like love itself. In his discussion of the Neoplatonic doctrine of Blind Love [in *Pagan mysteries in the Renaissances*], [Edgar] Wind says,

> In reducing the confusions of the senses to reason, the intellect clarifies but it also contracts: for it clarifies by setting limits; and to transcend these limits we require a new and more lasting confusion, which is supplied by the blindness of love. Intellect excludes contradictions; love embraces them.

In embracing contradictions, love transcends the limits of the intellect and of reality as the intellect normally perceives it: and no figure more vehemently asserts this transcendence than hyperbole, Puttenham's over-reacher. Shakespeare expresses his sense that love transcends the limits of reason and fact in the overreaching paradoxes of "The Phoenix and the Turtle": here the lovers can transcend number ("Two distincts, division none," line 27), space ("Distance, and no space was seen / 'Twixt this turtle and his queen," lines 30-31), and identity ("Property was thus appalled, / That the self was not the same," lines 37-38). Reason itself is confounded by these paradoxes and cries: "Love hath Reason, Reason none, / If what parts can so remain" (lines 47-48).

Antony and Cleopatra is the exploration of this *if:* it is the working out of these paradoxes in human terms, with all their human contradictions. The paradoxes so easily stated in "The Phoenix and the Turtle" are the hard-won conclusions of the lovers: that one must lose oneself to gain oneself; that the only life is in death, the only union in separation. To regard either paradox or hyperbole as merely rhetorical ornament is to overlook their enormous potency in the play: in a very literal way, they shape not only the language but also the presentation of character, the structure, and the themes. And if the tension between skepticism and belief is resolved for a moment at the end, it is resolved only insofar as we for a moment accept paradox and hyperbole as

literally true, despite their logical impossibilities. These are large claims; in order to substantiate them, I shall have to discuss the figures and some related concepts at length.

The structure of *Antony and Cleopatra* is the structure of paradox and hyperbole themselves: according to Renaissance figurists, both gain our credence by appealing to our doubt.

> *Paradoxon,* is a forme of speech by which the Orator affirmeth some thing to be true, by saying he would not have beleeved it, or that it is so straunge, so great, or so wonderfull, that it may appeare to be incredible.

Thus Henry Peacham defines paradox [in *The garden of Eloquence*]. The figure *paradoxon,* or as [George] Puttenham calls it [in *The Arte of English Poesie*], "the wonderer," affirms faith by appealing to doubt. Paradox was for the Renaissance a figure pliable to any use: if John Donne as a young man could use it as an occasion for the display of witty and cynical extravagance, he could also use it in his sermons to express the central tenets of Christianity. A seventeenth-century theologian cast these tenets into the form of paradox precisely because they impose such a strain on our logical categories and nonetheless are not to be questioned— that is to say, because they demand the operation of our faith, not our reason. All paradox demands an act of faith; but hyperbole is that species of paradox which poses the crisis in its most acute form. Hyperbole must, by definition, assert that which is literally untrue. George Puttenham in *The Arte of English Poesie* discusses hyperbole along with other figures which work by altering the meaning of words or phrases:

> As figures be the instruments of ornament in every language, so be they also in a sorte abuses or rather trespasses in speech, because they passe the ordinary limits of common utterance, and be occupied of purpose to deceive the eare and also the minde, drawing it from plainnesse and simplicitie to a certaine doublenesse, whereby our talke is the more guilefull & abusing, for what els is your *Metaphor* but an inversion of sense by transport; your *allegorie* by a duplicitie of meaning or dissimulation under covert and darke intendments: one while speaking obscurely and in riddle called *Aenigma:* another while by common proverbe or Adage called *Paremia:* then by merry skoffe called *Ironia:* . . . then by incredible comparison giving credit, as by your *Hyperbole.*

"By incredible comparison giving credit": this is the paradox of hyperbole. And if all these figures are in some sense deceivers, then the worst in this kind are the hyperboles. Puttenham later says,

> Ye have yet two or three other figures that smatch a spice of the same *false semblant* but in another sort

and maner of phrase, whereof one is when we speake in the superlative and beyond the limites of credit, that is by the figure which the Greeks called *Hiperbole*, the Latines *Dementiens* or the lying figure. I for his immoderate excesse cal him the over reacher right with his originall or [lowd lyar] & me thinks not amisse: now when I speake that which neither I my selfe thinke to be true, nor would have any other body beleeve, it must needs be a great dissimulation, because I mean nothing lesse than that I speake.

Precisely this great dissimulation gives credit, as Puttenham has told us earlier; and although the speaker does not believe himself and expects no one else to believe him, he means no less than what he says. This very illogical state of affairs reduces Puttenham to a similar illogic; but with this illogic he suggests the central force of hyperbole and its fascination for poets at the end of the sixteenth century. If we are to take it seriously, hyperbole must elicit some sort of belief or assent: that is to say that it demands of us the simultaneous perception of its literal falsehood and its imaginative relevance. It presents the spectacle of man making his own imaginative universe in despite of all reality, in despite of all human limitation: the struggle of Tamburlaine, or Richard II, or the lover in Donne's love poetry.

But can we take paradox and hyperbole seriously? If the two figures challenge our reason by their very structure, the play takes up that challenge: for paradox and hyperbole are to some extent embodied in the lovers; and the degree to which we can believe in these figures will determine our response to the play. Cleopatra herself seems to embrace contradictions; she is usually described in terms which confound all our logical categories. One need only look at Shakespeare's additions to Plutarch's description of Cleopatra at Cydnus for confirmation: by the use of paradox, Shakespeare transforms Plutarch's beautiful but entirely probable description into something rich and strange. The wind from the fans of her Cupids "did seem / To glow the delicate cheeks which they did cool" (2.2.203-4). Her barge burns on the water. She animates nature with love for her: the waters follow her barge, "As amorous of their strokes" (2.2.197), as Antony will follow her at Actium. "She did make defect perfection, / And, breathless, power breathe forth" (2.2.231-32). She embodies all the paradoxes of sexual appetite, which grows the more by reaping: she "makes hungry, / Where most she satisfies" (2.2.237-38). Like the woman in the sonnets, she is black with Phoebus's amorous pinches (1.5.28) and yet the day of the world (4.8.13): black and wholly fair. She is wrinkled deep in time (1.5.29), and yet age cannot wither her. And if Cleopatra is paradoxical in her nature, Antony is hyperbolical in all that he does: in his rage, his valor, his love, and his folly. From Philo's description of him as Mars to Cleopatra's description of him as her colossus, he is seen

in hyperbolic terms; and his own passionate use of hyperbole confirms its association with him.

The paradoxes surrounding Cleopatra are in a sense verified early in the play by Enobarbus's portrait of her at Cydnus. Enobarbus's speech is placed between Antony's resolution to marry Octavia and his decision to leave her; placed here, it serves to tell us why Antony will return to Cleopatra. In this sense, it functions as a substitute for a soliloquy in which Antony could announce his intentions to us. But a soliloquy would tell us about Cleopatra only as Antony perceives her: this description comes from Enobarbus, the most consistently skeptical voice in the play. That Enobarbus is the spokesman for Cleopatra's paradoxes establishes the portrait of her as one of the facts of the play. We are presented with her paradoxical nature as a fait accompli, as one of the premises from which the action of the play springs. In this sense, paradox itself is embodied in the person of Cleopatra, and we are forced to acknowledge its presence on stage. Her nature is fixed from that moment: and although she changes constantly, paradox can accommodate all the change; it is, after all, central to the paradox that everything becomes her and that she becomes everything. Cleopatra's definition by paradox comes early in the play and remains relatively static; Antony's definition by hyperbole is a continuing process, a continuing attempt to redefine him. And our education is at stake in his definition: for we are continually reeducated in the possibilities of hyperbole and in the kind of belief we can accord it. If Antony's hyperboles are verified, it is only at the end of the play, after a continual process of testing. The entire play leads us to Cleopatra's hyperbolical portrait of him; but it leads us there by subjecting hyperbole to skepticism as well as to assent.

Like the play itself, Antony's hyperboles can be verified only by surviving the test of the comic structure. Hyperbole can indicate either the similarity or the discrepancy between assertion and reality; or it can indicate both together. Whether the effect of the hyperbole is comic or tragic depends largely on the extent to which we are permitted to believe in the untruth it asserts. In purely comic hyperbole, the effect lies precisely in the discrepancy between the fact and the assertion. The hyperbolical claims about Antony are frequently subject to just such mockery. For Ventidius, who has just won a battle by his own harsh labor, Antony's name is "that magical word of war" (3.1.31). Agrippa and Enobarbus mock Lepidus's sycophantic love for his two masters by citing his hyperbolical praise of them:

> *Eno.* Caesar? Why he's the Jupiter of men.
> *Agr.* What's Antony? The god of Jupiter.
> *Eno.* Spake you of Caesar? How, the nonpareil?
> *Agr.* O Antony, O thou Arabian bird!
> [3.2.9-12]

Max Helpmann as Lepidus, Alan Scarfe as Octavius Caesar, Keith Baxter as Antony, Don Goodspeed as a soldier, Robert Benson as Sextus Pompeius, J. Kenyon as Maecenas, William Needles as Menas, Larry Lamb as Agrippa, and Daniel Buccos as Dolabella in the Stratford Festival's 1976 production of Antony and Cleopatra.

But not all the hyperboles in the play are comic: and as hyperbole becomes imaginatively relevant, it begins to invoke our belief, in despite of all reason. For *Antony and Cleopatra* is virtually an experiment in establishing the imaginative relevance of hyperbole and consequently the kind of belief we can accord it: and our final sense of Antony depends on this process.

Throughout the play, we are given a medley of hyperboles ranging from the purely comic to the purely tragic. Antony, as one of the three triumvirs, is "the triple pillar of the world," according to Philo (1.1.12); and even Antony seems to imagine that when he takes his support from the world, a significant portion of it will collapse ("Let Rome in Tiber melt, and the wide arch / Of the rang'd empire fall!" 1.1.33-34). Cleopatra later imagines Antony bearing up the heavens rather than the earth: her Antony is "the demi-Atlas of this earth" (1.5.23). But these very hyperboles are mocked when the drunken Lepidus is carried offstage:

Eno. There's a strong fellow, Menas.
Men. Why?
Eno. 'A bears the third part of the world, man;
see'st not?
Men. The third part, then, is drunk.

[2.7.88-91]

When Octavius hears of Antony's death, he comments, "The breaking of so great a thing should make / A greater crack" (5.1.14-15). In his words, the concept of universal order crumbles; but so does our hyperbolical vision of Antony upholding earth and heaven. At his death, there is no crack. But the effect of this sequence of hyperboles is balanced by another sequence. When the serving men on Pompey's barge compare the drunken Lepidus to a star, the poetical clothing is clearly too large for him, and the effect is comic:

To be called into a huge sphere, and not to be seen to move in't, are the holes where eyes should be, which pitifully disaster the cheeks.

[2.7.14-16]

The servant's shift from the cosmic and outsized to the human and minute in mid-metaphor is wholly appropriate: for poor Lepidus is in a sense a mere mortal caught in a world filled with hyperbolical figures. But when we find Antony dressed in the same poetical clothing, he wears it with grace. Lepidus compares his faults to the spots of heaven (1.4.12-13); and the comparison is not ludicrous. By the time the second guardsman responds to Antony's suicide by reiterating the hyperbolical association ("The star is fall'n" 4.14.106), we are, I think, quite prepared to believe him. And he in turn prepares us for Cleopatra's assertion that the crown of the earth doth melt and the soldier's pole is fallen.

If the hyperboles that describe Antony are subject to a continual process of testing, so are the hyperboles that Antony himself uses. In his education in the hyperbolical, Antony appeals to his ancestor Hercules as teacher:

> The shirt of Nessus is upon me, teach me,
> Alcides, thou mine ancestor, thy rage.
> Let me lodge Lichas on the horns o' the
>   moon,
> And with those hands that grasp'd the
>   heaviest club,
> Subdue my worthiest self.
>
> [4.12.43-47]

But Antony does not even manage to subdue his worthiest self. What is possible for the god inevitably remains impossible for the mortal—impossible and consequently slightly foolish. Cleopatra suggests by her mockery at the beginning of the play that this emulation is folly in a mere mortal: she notes to Charmian "how this Herculean Roman does become / The carriage of his chafe" (1.3.84-85). In imitating his ancestor's gigantic rage in act 1, Antony is merely playacting and is as foolish as Pistol or any other Herculean stage braggart whose language is clearly too big for his worth— he is a slightly larger version of Moth. The frequent reference to Herod, the conventional stage blusterer, would remind the audience of the dangers inherent in the use of hyperbole: it was the language of tyrants. For much of the play, Antony's hyperbolical passion is subject to this kind of comic testing. The long scene in which Antony rages in Hercules' vein and Enobarbus consistently undercuts him (act 3, scene 13) is fundamentally comic in structure; as I have noted elsewhere, it follows the classical pattern of *miles gloriosus* and servant. His rage here does not fully engage our sympathy; when he says, "O that I were / Upon the hill of Basan, to outroar / The horned herd, for I have savage cause" (3.13.126-28), we are disinclined to believe in the extent of his grievances or in his hyperbolical expression of an action appropriate to them. The hyperbole here dissuades us from belief and becomes mere rant. But the situation is more complex after the Egyptian fleet has joined with Caesar's. Antony in call-

ing on his ancestor for instruction seems to recognize that his own hyperbolical language is not altogether equal to the occasion. His language here is proportionate to the cause of his rage: it is not merely rant, and it is surely no longer comic. Moreover, Cleopatra immediately verifies the heroic extent of his rage: "O, he's more mad / Than Telamon for his shield, the boar of Thessaly / Was never so emboss'd" (4.13.1-3). Though we still cannot believe in Antony's hyperbolical actions as literal, at least we believe in his rage. The hyperbole becomes an appropriate expression for the gigantic rage and, in that sense, imaginatively relevant. And after Antony hears of Cleopatra's death, he echoes her reference to Ajax in an image which sounds hyperbolical but is in fact absolutely literal: "The sevenfold shield of Ajax cannot keep / The battery from my heart" (4.14.38-39).

If Cleopatra is the first to mock Antony's hyperboles, she is also the final advocate of their truth. Cleopatra asserts to Dolabella that her dream of Antony belongs to the realm of nature, not of fancy: "to imagine / An Antony were nature's piece, 'gainst fancy, / Condemning shadows quite" (5.2.98-100). But this assertion comes only after five acts of continual testing. Even while Antony is dying, Cleopatra can acknowledge the folly of hyperbole. As she struggles to lift him into her monument, she says,

> . . . Had I great Juno's power,
> The strong-wing'd Mercury should fetch thee
>   up,
> And set thee by Jove's side. Yet come a little,
> Wishers were ever fools.
>
> [4.15.34-37]

Yet side by side with this quiet resignation to the literal is her hyperbolical appeal to the sun ("Burn the great sphere thou mov'st in" 4.15.10): precisely the crack the absence of which Caesar notes. "Wishers were ever fools": "O, see, my women: / The crown o' the earth doth melt" (4.15.62-63). If we are finally able to believe Cleopatra's hyperbolical portrait of her Antony, it is only because she herself tells us that wishers are fools.

Peter Berek

SOURCE: "Doing and Undoing: The Value of Action in *Antony and Cleopatra*," in *Shakespeare Quarterly*, Vol. 32, No. 3, Autumn, 1981, pp. 295-304.

[Berek locates the source of the play's dualism in the verbs "to do" and "to undo." He notes the play's frequent focus on the paradox that "doing" or completing an action also ends it, or "undoes" action. Berek remarks further that in Antony and Cleopatra, the verb "to do" refers both to making love as well as to waging war. Finally, he observes duality at work in the

paradox that Antony and Cleopatra find the ultimate expression of their life and love together through suicide.]

Antony and Cleopatra is a Play in which mighty opposites meet, struggle, and embrace. Rome encounters Egypt, Reason feels Emotion, Spirit wars with Flesh, Duty yields to Leisure. These fatal conflicts corrupt Mark Antony (in the older view of the play) or (as more recent critics argue) translate the lovers into a realm of "pure nobility." In the latest book on the play [*The Common Liar: An Essay on Antony and Cleopatra*], Janet Adelman refuses to take sides in this lovers' quarrel. She argues that Shakespeare made it impossible to arrive at tidy, formulaic judgments of his characters and their deeds. Following Maynard Mack (who is quoting George Meredith), Professor Adelman directs those who are "hot for certainties in this our life" to some other play than this. In asserting the problematic nature of judgment and the encompassing vision of the play, she is nearer the mark than those who yield to the magnetism of one pole or another. Critical compasses which point resolutely in a single direction tell us as much about the polarities of their own needles as about the location of true North.

I don't propose to deny the existence of polarities in *Antony and Cleopatra*. But in this essay I focus on a perception shared by Antony, Cleopatra, and Octavius Caesar. These major characters, and minor characters as well, have a common understanding of the possibilities for action the world of the play makes available to them. Though there are great and obvious differences among their actual behaviors, characters in the play are in substantial agreement about what "doing" is worth. While they often disagree on how or when or even whether to act, they agree that there are grim limits to the joy one can take in earthly achievements.

I

My concern for visions of "doing" in *Antony and Cleopatra* arises from a wish to make sense of a recurring, and somewhat peculiar, use of forms of the verb "do" in the play. Early in the action, as Enobarbus describes Cleopatra's first appearance to Mark Antony on the river Cydnus, he tells how Cleopatra's attendants cope with the intemperate Egyptian climate:

> On each side of her
> Stood pretty dimpled boys, like smiling
>   Cupids,
> With divers-color'd fans, whose wind did
>   seem
> To [glow] the delicate cheeks which they did
>   cool,
> And what they undid did.

Shakespeare is following North's Plutarch closely here, but the paradoxical last two lines are entirely his own.

Later, when Antony hears the false news of Cleopatra's death, he says, "Now all labor / Mars what it does; yea, very force entangles / Itself with strength" (IV. xiv. 47-49). As Cleopatra herself prepares to die, she announces to her attendants,

> . . . it is great
> To do that thing that ends all other deeds,
> Which shackles accidents and bolts up change,
> Which sleeps, and never palates more the
>   dung,
> The beggar's nurse and Caesar's.
>
> (V. ii. 4-8)

Enobarbus describes a state of affairs in which the fans of Cleopatra's attendants cool her cheeks even as the wind from those fans seems to make the same cheeks glow ardently. "Undoing"— in this case, mitigating the effects of heat with the breeze of a fan— and "doing"— making cheeks glow more brightly— are the same action, despite their ostensible opposition. The lines are puzzling because they reverse the way we would expect to find the terms used: Johnson emended them to "what they did, undid." Not only does Enobarbus conflate an action and its opposite, but he celebrates the fact that this is so and makes it one measure of Cleopatra's infinite variety. However, when Antony thinks Cleopatra is dead, "doing" creates an "undoing": "labor / Mars what it does." The act of laboring to do something brings one's labors further from fruition. Finally, with Antony dead, for Cleopatra the greatest of "doings" is "that thing that ends all other deeds." Only one labor is worth performing, and that will be the last.

All three uses of forms of "do" emphasize the paradoxical qualities of action, Enobarbus' phrase most of all. Paradox, of course, is central to the play's presentation of Cleopatra (as Adelman points out, adding that hyperbole is the characteristic trope used in presenting Antony). Paradox characterizes not just Cleopatra herself but the whole relationship between Antony and Cleopatra. Just as it is hard for us, as members of the audience, to know how to judge this mutual pair, so it is also hard for them and for other characters in the play to assess the effects of any particular cause. It's hard to know what any "doing" will in fact do. Philo's opening speech in Act I, scene i, for example, roundly condemns Antony for dereliction of duty. "This dotage of our general's / O'erflows the measure" (I. i. 1-2). Antony's eyes, in a gesture which anticipates Cleopatra's maidens who "made their bends adornings" (II. ii. 208), "now bend, now turn / The office and devotion of their view / Upon a tawny front" (I. i. 4-6). Philo describes dereliction of duty in the vocabulary of secular and religious commitment, "office and devotion"; and a "tawny front" can be a forehead he adores or a battlefield where he opposes an enemy. Antony, like the cupids of the Cydnus speech, "is become the bellows and the fan / To cool a gipsy's lust" (I. i. 9-10).

But the phrase Philo uses is itself paradoxical in a way Philo surely doesn't intend. The winds of a fan cool, but the winds of a bellows are intended to make a fire burn hotter. Just as Cleopatra "makes hungry / Where most she satisfies" (II. ii. 236-37), so Antony in "dotage" heats the very lust he overtly tries to cool.

The vocabulary of doing and undoing, then, in part works to emphasize the paradoxes which are central to the relationship between the great lovers and which find their fullest expression in Enobarbus' Cydnus speech. But this vocabulary also renders more abstract than they would otherwise be the two basic actions of *Antony and Cleopatra*: making love and making war. Forms of the verb "do" serve as euphemisms or elliptical phrases for both sets of actions and thus stress the continuities as well as the conflicts between them. For example, Cleopatra jokes with the eunuch Mardian and asks if he has affections:

> *Mar.* Yes, gracious madam.
> *Cleo.* Indeed?
> *Mar.* Not in deed, madam, for I can do
>   nothing
> But what indeed is honest to be done;
> Yet have I fierce affections, and think
> What Venus did with Mars.
>
> (I. v. 13-18)

"Doing" is used as a sexual euphemism by a character who is limited in the here-and-now to perpetual dreams of possibility— as, one can argue metaphorically, Antony and Cleopatra are limited themselves. Cleopatra takes up Mardian's locution in lines charged with sexual energy as she thinks of Antony on his horse. "O happy horse, to bear the weight of Antony! / Do bravely, horse, for wot'st thou whom thou mov'st?" (I. v. 21-22). The word "do" helps bring together the world of warfare, where Roman Antony reigns supreme, and a sexual Egyptian kingdom where Cleopatra herself "does bravely" with her lover.

The verb that the queen and her eunuch use in the female world of Egypt recurs again in an aggressively masculine Roman setting. After the triumvirs make peace with Pompey, Menas and Enobarbus, two grizzled warriors, acknowledge the comradeship of fellow-craftsmen and a shared scorn for their opposed masters' politicking:

> *Men.*—You and I have known, sir.
> *Eno.* At sea, I think.
> *Men.* We have, sir.
> *Eno.* You have done well by water.
> *Men.* And you by land.
> *Eno.* I will praise any man that will praise
>   me,
> though it cannot be denied what I have done
>   by land.

> *Men.* Nor what I have done by water.
>
> (II. vi. 84-90)

Both speakers, free for a moment of diplomatic constraints, feel one another out and strut a bit in martial pride. Their euphemistic use of "do" for "fight" is partly good manners, because being forthright in acknowledging past quarrels might strain a potential drinking companionship. But their peculiar diction also implies that warfare, like sex, is the deed that dares not speak its name. Both realms are potentially so charged with emotion that one tiptoes about with periphrasis. At the same time, both realms are so important that one can count on being understood despite the obscurity of euphemisms. However, although euphemisms are a tribute to the emotional importance of the thing euphemized, they also to some degree trivialize the activity they refuse properly to name. They can be overly cute, as Mardian and Cleopatra are in their exchange. And employing the same euphemism for lovemaking and for battlefield heroism makes heroism seem as fleeting as love. Enobarbus acknowledges the fragility of heroic renown when he says, "I will praise any man that will praise me," and both Enobarbus and Menas, before their conversation ends, shift from the euphemism of "done well" to the reductive:

> *Eno.* You have been a great thief by sea.
> *Men.* And you by land.
>
> (II.vi.92-93)

Indeed, military victory in *Antony and Cleopatra* is an ambiguous prize. The relationship is vexed between the prize of victory and the means chosen to attain that prize. Menas, man of action that he is, offers his master Pompey dominion over the world if he will let him cut the cable and fall to the throats of the carousing triumvirs (II. vii). Giving the grim deed its proper name takes the gloss off it for Pompey: "Ah, this thou shouldst have done, / And not have spoke on't!" (II. vii. 73-74), he replies. We find it hard to judge between the shrewd treason of Menas' oathbreaking and the pompous and self-defeating honor with which Pompey refuses his own best advantage. Neither action seized nor action rejected can avoid a sour aftertaste.

Doing great deeds can sometimes lead to being undone. When Ventidius enters "as it were in triumph," he shrewdly rejects urgings to extend his victory over the fleeing Parthians (III. i). Once again Shakespeare follows North closely. North writes, "Howbeit Ventidius durst not undertake to follow [the Parthians] any further, fearing least he should have gotten Antonius displeasure by it" (Arden ed., p. 267). Taking up Plutarch's hint that Antony and Caesar "were alway more fortunate when they made warre by their Lieutenants, than by them selves" (Arden ed., p. 267), Shakespeare has Ventidius explain the motives for his actions more fully than in North:

I have done enough; a lower place, note well,
May make too great an act. For learn this,
    Silius:
Better to leave undone, than by our deed
Acquire too high a fame when him we serve's
    away.

. . . . .

Who does i' th' wars more than his captain can
Becomes his captain's captain; and ambition
(The soldier's virtue) rather makes choice of loss
Than gain which darkens him.

                    (III.i.12-15, 21-24)

A military victory can turn into a political defeat. There is nothing unambiguous about Ventidius' triumph.

Octavius Caesar is the paragon of worldly success in *Antony and Cleopatra*. He is accurate in his judgments of others, effective in his generalship, and accomplished in politics. Except for his frustrated plan to display Cleopatra in his Roman triumph, Caesar accomplishes what he sets out to accomplish. But Caesar's own expressed opinions on the worth of the successes he and others achieve are carefully measured and more than a bit rueful. In I. iv, the first scene in which we see Caesar, he tells Lepidus and his followers not to be surprised at the news that men are rallying to the rebellious Pompey:

                    I should have known no
    less:
It hath been taught us from the primal state
That he which is was wish'd, until he were;
And the ebb'd man, ne'er lov'd till ne'er
    worth love,
Comes [dear'd] by being lack'd.

                    (I.iv.40-44)

From the beginning of government, he who has power was wished to be in power until that power was attained. The "ebbed" man (in this case, Pompey), unloved until he loses the power which truly makes one worthy of love, becomes dear to the populace by his very lack of power. Caesar asserts that being successful costs one the very love of others which helped one win success; conversely, failure, even when due to one's own misdeeds, wins popular affection. Caesar's grim realism places strict limitations upon the satisfaction one can take in the success of one's deeds or the fulfillment of one's wishes. Accomplishing one's desires, at least in the public realm, costs the very acclaim which seemed the just reward of accomplishment. That the process is cyclical and natural to politics is implied by Caesar's simile in the succeeding lines:

                This common body,
Like to a vagabond flag upon the stream,
Goes to and back, [lackeying] the varying tide,
To rot itself with motion.

                    (I.iv.44-47)

The bloom of political success rides the tide of popular favor. That tide sometimes ebbs, sometimes flows, but never moves beyond its own bounds; the "vagabond flag" may give the illusion of motion, but its only sure change is decay.

That wishes accomplished, deeds achieved, bear within themselves the cause of the wisher's own disappointment is a perception Caesar shares with his great opposite, Mark Antony. In I. ii, Antony mediates upon the news of Fulvia's death, saying,

            Thus did I desire it.
What our contempts doth often hurl from
    us,
We wish it ours again. The present pleasure,
By revolution low'ring, does become
The opposite of itself. She's good, being
    gone;
The hand could pluck her back that shov'd
    her on.

                    (I. ii. 122-27)

Antony agrees with Caesar that our doings often make us wish themselves undone.

II

It is not surprising that Caesar and Antony should speak so similarly. Even after harshly criticizing Antony as "a man who is th' [abstract] of all faults / That all men follow" (I. iv. 9-10), Caesar praises his consummate soldiership. But the terms of praise raise questions about the costs of the heroism Antony once epitomized. Though Shakespeare follows North closely in Caesar's speech, he greatly intensifies the loathsomeness of the adversity Antony has endured and adds a reference to "the stale of horses" which echoes other excremental images in the play:

                Thou didst drink
The stale of horses and the gilded puddle
Which beasts would cough at; thy palate then
    did deign
The roughest berry on the rudest hedge;
Yea, like the stag, when snow the pasture
    sheets,
The barks of trees thou brows'd. On the
    Alps
It is reported thou didst eat strange flesh,
Which some did die to look on; and all this
(It wounds thine honor that I speak it now)
Was borne so like a soldier, that thy cheek
So much as lank'd not.

                    (I. iv. 61-71)

Before the great general entered his Egyptian dotage he was so like a soldier that he was tougher than a beast. Ordinary men, like animals, grow pale, cough, and die when called upon to ingest urine or "strange flesh," but he who would be master of heroic "doing" is capable of swallowing anything at all. But the taste, Antony and Caesar seem to agree, is unsavory indeed.

In defeat, Antony's rejecting success as dungy is psychologically plausible. But even his return to valor after the first defeat at Actium attends more to his own moods and taste for posturing than to strategic plausibility. "The next time I do fight, / I'll make death love me" (III. xiii. 191-92), says Antony, prompting that grizzled realist Enobarbus to seek some way to leave him, saying, "A diminution in our captain's brain / Restores his heart" (III. xiii. 197-98). Enobarbus soon discovers that there is no clear connection between his own brain and heart: Antony's magnanimity after his subordinate's betrayal makes Enobarbus conclude that death is better than Roman triumph purchased by brainy practicality. In victory after the second battle, Antony and Cleopatra continue to be absorbed in private rather than public feelings. Antony's heart, which Philo at the start of the play described as having burst the buckles on his breast in the "scuffles of great fights" (I. i. 7), is now the panting recipient of Cleopatra's ardor:

> O thou day o' th' world,
> Chain mine arm'd neck, leap thou, attire and all,
> Through proof of harness to my heart, and
>   there
> Ride on the pants trimphing!
>
> (IV. viii. 13-16)

The crucial triumph of the happy pair is within, not in the political and military world. With respect to that world, Cleopatra perceives Antony not so much as victor but as successful fugitive:

> Lord of lords!
> O infinite virtue, com'st thou smiling from
> The world's great snare uncaught?
>
> (IV. viii. 16-18)

The heroic Rome that Antony intermittently rejects and ultimately loses for love is, like Alpine valor, a world of excrement. Caesar wants to call Antony back to the same kingdom he rejected when he dismissed the first of the play's many messengers from Rome: "Let Rome in Tiber melt. . . . Kingdoms are clay; our dungy earth alike / Feeds beast as man" (I. i. 33, 35-36). The dungy earth isn't fructifying [as *D. A. Traversi argues in Shakespeare: The Roman plays*]; rather it is an ignoble arena in which those without vision to imagine a better are doomed to do their deeds. (Fertility in *Antony and Cleopatra* is associated not with dung, but with the simultaneously destroying and fertilizing "overflowing the measure" of the Nile.) Caesar, Antony, and Cleopatra agree on the appropriate language to describe the glories which Caesar achieves and the lovers eventually scorn; ruling the world requires the tasting of excre-

ment, and there is some matter that Antony and Cleopatra will not eat. Better, says Cleopatra, to seek doing in undoing and enter the sleep of death which "never palates more the dung, / The beggar's nurse and Caesar's" (V. ii. 7-8). There is no substantial difference between Cleopatra's claim that Caesar, like beast or beggar, palates the dung to do high deeds on earth, and Caesar's own praise of Antony's greatness. Caesar persists in his efforts, swallows whatever needs to be swallowed (incuding the scorn of his critics), and masters the real world. Antony and Cleopatra agree with Caesar about the nature and cost of earthly "doing," but decide its cost is too high. For them, the undoing of self is preferable to the doing of earthly glories.

III

Traversi speaks of a world of Alexandria in which the sensual imagination "loses itself in the gratifying imagination of boundless fulfillment" (p. 85). I have tried to show that in the political and military— perhaps one should say the "geographic"— world of the play, there are rigorous bounds to fulfillment by action. "Doing" is possible, but it carries within itself inevitable "undoing," as the "wish'd" man loses esteem by accomplishment and all achievements lackey the varying tides of historical change. But Antony asserts at the start of the play that "There's beggary in the love that can be reckon'd" (I. i. 15). The lovers' kind of doing seeks after private or emotional efficaciousness rather than the reckonable achievements of Caesar's world. In their eyes, the highest form of doing occurs in supremely dramatic gestures, gestures that give specificity to the speakers' euphemistic language. The first such moment comes at the start of the play when Antony says,

> the nobleness of life
> Is to do thus [*embracing*]— when such a
>   mutual pair
> And such a twain can do't.
>
> (I. i. 36-38)

"Doing" takes on meaning, not with idea, but with gesture— it is "doing *thus*" that matters, and such deeds can be done only in Cleopatra's presence. The gesture's grandeur lies in its imaginative sweep, not in its truth to any actual world beyond the lovers' consciousness: Cleopatra jeers in reply, "Excellent falsehood" (I. i. 40), but mere contradictoriness doesn't wither the gesture's wonder. As the play proceeds, Antony comes more and more to substitute the dramatic gesture for practicable deeds. After having Thidias whipped, Antony knows "our terrene moon / Is now eclips'd, and it portends alone / The fall of Antony!" (III. xiii. 153-55). But self-dramatizing reconciliation with Cleopatra restores his heart, and he assures her that he and his sword will earn their "chronicle" (III. xiii. 175) without troubling about the distinction between legend and victory. "One other gaudy night" (III. xiii. 182) is the grand "doing thus" of this scene, and by the theatrical gesture toward his sad captains Antony, reunited with Cleopatra, takes his stance firmly in the cloud-castle world of imagination.

Antony's imaginative apprehension of Cleopatra, and Cleopatra's apprehension of him, alone validates these dramatic gestures. When Antony thinks he is scorned by Cleopatra, death is simply the way to "end ourselves" (IV. xiv. 22). But when Mardian reports that Cleopatra has died with the name of Antony on her lips, Antony's tone takes on a new serenity: "Unarm, Eros, the long day's task is done, / And we must sleep" (IV. xiv. 35-36). So long as death reunites him with Cleopatra, death's undoing is the noblest of doings. He has no regret about leaving the vile world; without Cleopatra,

> All length is torture; since the torch is out,
> Lie down and stray no farther. Now all labor
> Mars what it does; yea, very force entangles
> Itself with strength.
>
> (IV. xiv. 46-49)

By echoing Cleopatra's death, Antony's suicide affirms their union and asserts that the true realm of action is neither Rome nor Egypt, but that private dramatic space in which Antony and Cleopatra perform their grandest gestures. The nobleness of life was to do "thus" as Antony and Cleopatra embraced in I. i. Now, after her death and Eros',

> My queen and Eros
> Have by their brave instruction got upon me
> A nobleness in record; but I will be
> A bridegroom in my death, and run into 't
> As to a lover's bed. Come then and, Eros,
> Thy master dies thy scholar: to do thus
> [Falling on his sword.]
> I learnt of thee.
>
> (IV. xiv. 97-103)

The only worthwhile "doing" is "to do thus"—an ultimate gesture in which sexual climax and the end of life are joined.

The gestures which accompany the phrase "do thus" give its vagueness specificity. But at the same time, the euphemistic formula obscures distinctions that we ordinarily think of as fundamental. Surely one reason death seems so available a deed to both Antony and Cleopatra is that they think of it in terms which minimize the distinctions among warring, loving, and dying. It is easier to die if you regard life as a chore and death as restful sleep. The similarity between dying and other human deeds implied by the lovers' euphemisms makes death seem a logical furthering of the nobleness of life. For the audience, euphemistic language and glamorous gesture join to create an imponderable moral dilemma. We

know before we enter the theatre that falling on one's sword or holding an asp to one's breast isn't the same as defeating Caesar and ruling the world. (Critics who roundly condemn the lovers know nothing else.) But the rhetoric and gestures of the actors exhort our assent to a condition superior to fact. How can we decide whether they are heroic or self-deluded?

"Doing thus" locates the lovers unequivocally in a world of imagination, and the imaginary nature of that world is underscored by two grim realities: Cleopatra isn't dead, and Antony botches his own suicide. But that real-world actions should fail to live up to the lovers' "gratifying imagination of boundless fulfillment" is by now hardly a surprise. Astonishingly, neither Antony nor Cleopatra even acknowledges the ironies surrounding Antony's death. Together for the last time in the ultimate space of their kingdom, Cleopatra's monument, they play their last scene as though wished affection transcended all the frailties of clay. Cleopatra yields none of her infinite variety; she can chide and laugh while weeping. But she accepts Antony as he wishes to be seen, and he does the same for her.

With Antony dead, Cleopatra knows the wonder has gone out of life: "the odds is gone, / And there is nothing left remarkable / Beneath the visiting moon" (IV. xv. 66-68). Antony's death dims Cleopatra's polymorphous splendor and makes her a mere woman whose "doings" have no more glamour than a milkmaid's "meanest chares" (IV. xv. 75). But only a few more "chares" remain to be done. Cleopatra sends Charmian and Iras to fetch her best attires and tells Charmian, "when thou hast done this chare, I'll give thee leave / To play till doomsday" (V. ii. 231-32). Reunion with Antony in death, for Cleopatra, is a translation from a world of toil to a world of freedom. She goes from "chares" to "play." Her doings are theatrical; she returns to the mode of "doing thus" as she tells her women to show her like a queen, garbed as she was on Cydnus when she met Mark Antony. She gives up the fruits of the dungy earth; her noble act turns her to fire and air. Dying as a "lass unparallel'd" (V. ii. 316), Cleopatra transfigures the asp's poison into a lover's pinch and a nursing babe. Cleopatra transforms death's undoing into a magical doing that replicates in a dying moment courtship, begetting, and childrearing. But such magical deeds exist only in the play-world of imagination. Shackling accidents and bolting up change costs not just kingdoms, but all doing hereafter. She has done the deed that ends all other deeds.

IV

Caesar, Antony, and Cleopatra all agree that there are grim limits to the joys one can take in earthly achievements. Antony and Cleopatra refuse to palate the dung. So long as they are united, they assert, performing deeds of love— "doing thus"—has intrinsic value without reference to its effects in the public world. Embracing paradox as they embrace one another, they choose life and die, though the realm in which they will forever play their parts is knowable only in imagination. For Caesar, the absence of pleasure is no reason for an absence of action. Unheroically, he presses on from success to success, knowing that the power he achieves assures neither permanence nor affection. If the world is not well lost, neither is it well won.

How does this shared perception of the limited joys rewarding worldly success affect our response to *Antony and Cleopatra*? I believe that it reinforces [A.C.] Bradley's conclusion [in "Shakespeare's *Antony and Cleopatra*"] that the tragic effect of the play is different from, and lesser than, that of *Hamlet, Othello, Lear,* or *Macbeth*. Bradley points out that the external magnitude of the play's public conflicts "fails to uplift or dilate the imagination." He attributes this failure to the selfishness of the contending politicians, whose narrow concerns make it difficult for us to care deeply about the outcome of their quarrels. But it seems to me that the "failure"—surely part of Shakespeare's conscious artistic intention—arises rather from the sharpness of the play's rendering of the limited joys of worldly success. By and large, the play's politicians and soldiers aren't bad men; it is not they who are flawed so much as it is the dungy element they work in. Bradley goes on to say that "we are saddened by the very fact that the catastrophe saddens us so little; it pains us that we should feel so much triumph and pleasure." Because the lovers have from the first been "tarnished," "it is better for the world's sake, and not less for their own, that they should fail and die." Though right in his basic response, Bradley is surely wrong in this last detail. The reason we aren't saddened, as we are at the end of other great tragedies, is that we cannot value highly the world the lovers have lost. Antony and Cleopatra haven't been defeated in their efforts to achieve and sustain success in the world; they have decided, for reasons even Caesar would have no trouble understanding, that beneath the wide arch of the ranged empire there are no successes worth having. Only deeds blessed by the paradoxical imaginations of the loving pair escape the decay of the varying tide. Contemplating dead Antony, dead Cleopatra, we may echo Cleopatra's words to Iras:

> Dost thou lie still?
> If thus thou vanishest, thou tell'st the world
> It is not worth leave-taking.
> (V. ii. 296-98)

ROME VERSUS EGYPT

Rome and Egypt function effectively as characters in *Antony and Cleopatra*, and the two are traditionally depicted as opposites. Rome, according to Sheila M. Smith,

represents "military glory, honor, and moral duty"; Egypt represents "instinctive passion, . . . extravagant love, fertility, and magnanimity." Rome, Cynthia Kolb Whitney suggests, values power and warfare; Egypt admires ease and sexuality. As William D. Wolf observes, Egypt has come to be regarded as "the place of love" and of private life, while Rome is the center of politics and public life. Smith, Whitney, and Wolf all share the view that Cleopatra personifies Egypt and Octavius Caesar embodies Rome; Antony, meanwhile, is caught between both worlds.

By the same token Wolf, along with **Michael Platt** and **Larry S. Champion**, argues that Rome and Egypt have several aspects in common. Platt, for instance, asserts that the two powers are on the wane and that Rome is losing its military integrity just as Egypt is losing its lushness. As pagan worlds, Platt concludes, both will soon be eclipsed by a new, Christian world. Wolf likewise describes Rome and Egypt as subject to change: Egypt is affected by Cleopatra's emotional fluctuations and by nature's cycles; Rome is prey to political intrigue, betrayal, and war. Wolf asserts that the change or "mutability" reflected by both worlds is what Antony and Cleopatra hope to escape from through death. Larry S. Champion condemns both Egypt and Rome as "tainted" and morally bankrupt thanks to their leaders. Champion observes that Cleopatra is self-absorbed and addicted to luxury, while Octavius Caesar is "cynical" in his arrangement of a political marriage between his sister and Antony, and Machiavellian in his dealings with Lepidus.

Michael Platt

SOURCE: "Antony and Cleopatra," in *Rome and Romans According to Shakespeare*, Jacobean Drama Studies, edited by Dr. James Hogg, No. 51, Institut für Englische Sprache und Literatur, 1976, pp. 246-64.

[*Platt begins by comparing the Republican Rome of Shakespeare's* Coriolanus *and* Julius Caesar *with the Roman Empire of* Antony and Cleopatra. *Republican Rome, he explains, was characterized by "equality and friendship"; in contrast, the Roman Empire is distinguished by "love" (or the adoration of one ruler) and "inequality." Republican Rome, Platt asserts, was based on public life, the Roman Empire, on private life. Platt argues that in the play, Rome borrows the attributes of love and private life from the part of its empire that includes Egypt. He concludes that in* Antony and Cleopatra, *both Rome and Egypt are in a state of decline—Rome has lost its valor and Egypt has lost its fertility—and that the world is on the verge of a new era that includes the birth of Christianity.*]

"She's good, being gone" (1.2.122) says Antony of his dead wife. He could just as well say the same of the Roman Republic as it fades in the hearts and deeds of his countrymen. The fall of so great a thing reverberates throughout *Antony and Cleopatra;* the men in this play either were molded by the Republic or judge their nobility by its resplendent memory. Pompey's son recalls the Republican sentiments and declares his allegiance to them. To the Triumvirs he is about to fight he says:

> What was't
> That moved pale Cassius to conspire? And what
> Made all-honored, honest, Roman Brutus,
> With the armed rest, courtiers of beauteous freedom,
> To drench the Capitol, but that they would
> Have one man but a man? And that is it
> Hath made me rig my navy, at whose burden
> The angered ocean foams; with which I meant
> To scourge th' ingratitude that despiteful Rome
> Cast on my noble father.
>
> (2.6.14-23)

These sentiments are given the lie by his subsequent deal with the Triumvirs. Menas observes that his father would not have agreed to such a deal (2.6.82-83). The sincerity of his Republican sentiments is further compromised by the subsequent banquet scene. Approached by Menas with the plot to cut the cable and the throats of his guests, he admits without shame to the desire to be "lord of all the world" (2.7.60). However, his desire is checked by his honor. While his virtue impedes his vice, let us note, it does not guide him. We even suspect that it is the weakness of his desire rather than the consideration of honor which prevents him from acting. The sensual momentum of the banquet and excess of wine sap his ambition. He laughs his fortune away, as his alert and abstaining lieutenant, Menas, observes.

In Pompey and throughout the play we see the fading of Roman virtue. It survives, but fitfully, in the intermittent courage of Antony; in his magnanimity it glows but ember-like; and in his sensuality it bows before a new god, both unRoman and uncivil, Eros. The manners and morals of the Empire appear on the horizon of the East where Antony's pleasure lies; in Egypt will reside the private life of the Romans. At the play's end one man, Octavius, will command the streets and public places of Rome; he will sum up in himself all the public things, sharing honor and power (the old aims of the ambitious sons of the Republic) with no equal; he alone will be the Republic, the *res publica,* the public things. Under his rule and beneath the canopy of his peace, the private and erotic life of his subjects (no longer citizens) will come into its own.

What will succeed the Republic was already indicated by Antony in his funeral oration for Caesar. He stressed love and gratitude, the love that Caesar showed Brutus and the assembled multitude and the gratitude owed to Caesar by Brutus and by the multitude. In other words, for relations of equality and friendship he substitutes inequality and love. With the disappearance of equality under post-Republican rule, friendship will languish but love will prosper.

The Roman friendships so important in *Julius Caesar* will be replaced by erotic relations; all the passions (to chide, to laugh, to weep according to Antony's view of Cleopatra [1.1.49-50]), will vie to make themselves fair and admired. Erotic relations will not be those characterized by equality, but by inequality; each lover will hang by chains of passion (golden chains and *therefore* all the more chains); each will be each other's slave, each, each other's master. The *thymetic* warrior will be replaced by the soft voluptuary. The lush flora and fauna of *eros,* under the beneficent rays of the world empire, will choke out the hardy stalks of *thymos.* Nowhere is this transvaluation of values more present than in Antony; in *Julius Caesar* he was unscrupulous, hard, cold but also grasping and ambitious. Only the comment of Caesar about his love of pleasure and music prepares our expectation to meet this new Antony. It is hard to believe this was the man who proscribed the hundred Senators (including Cicero), altered Caesar's will, and smirked behind Lepidus' back. These changes occur within a changing world, and are an index of that change itself; Rome changes around Antony and the change is most visible in Antony.

To appreciate these changes we turn to the impressions which hit our senses as the play opens. All of Shakespeare's plays set in Rome which we have treated so far have begun with a street scene in the capital city itself, for the condition of Rome is evident in her streets. The tumultuous pleb-filled streets of *Coriolanus* were natural to the early Republic and the decay of that Republic was evident in the street scenes which open *Julius Caesar.* The plebs who then filled the streets with tumult were corrupted by a certain servile adulation of one man, and a later Cassius measures this departure from republican ways by appealing to the accord between Rome's ancient streets and her ancient regime:

> When could they say (till now) that talked of Rome
> That her wide walks encompassed but one man?
>
> (1.2.154-155)

The first casualty of Antony's regime, Cinna, poet and friend to Caesar, is slain in the same wide walks.

Antony and Cleopatra opens indoors in the palace of an Eastern Queen. We are within the Roman Empire, but not in Rome. Gone are the civil streets of the Republic, replaced by a courtly interior. Still, elements of continuity are evident—a continuity which the republican eyes of Cassius would smart to look upon. "A triple-pillar of the world" (1.1.12) is Philo's image for Antony, an image which Cassius would not use unless he were persuading a friend to join him in tyrannicide. "Since when could they say ('til now) that Rome's wide streets held but *three* men?" Cassius would murmur. But Philo (his Alexandrian name is significant) feels no slight in his master's greatness; he is a courtier whose fortunes hang on his master; not for him the honors of a con-sulship, or a statue with his ancestors. He chides his master for failing to pursue fortune, for failing to share his own motives. Towards the close of this scene we glimpse the streets outside this indoor court. Antony dismisses the Ambassadors and turns to Cleopatra:

> Fie, wrangling queen!
> Whom every thing becomes—to chide, to
> laugh,
> To weep; whose every passion fully strives
> To make itself, in thee, fair and admired.
> No messenger but thine, *and all alone*
> *To-night we'll wander through the streets and note*
> *The qualities of people.* Come, my queen;
> Last night you did desire it.
>   (1.1.48-55, my italics)

The tumultuous and public streets of Rome, the scene of both struggle and of triumphs, the place of politics and the arena in which honor was pursued, here give way to the uses of pleasure, diversion, privacy. All alone, their attendants dismissed and (doubtless) in disguise, these lovers will wander to the neglect of public things. What a world of manners and morals Shakespeare manages to compress into this invitation of Antony's. True, these streets will be filled with people, but what will count to these exemplary public figures will be the light fair surface of things, the diverting look on a passing slave's face, the amusement of bargaining in the market; all the pleasant and passing impressions which occupy modern tourists will distract these lovers from the cares, the solitude, and the boredom of Imperial public life. It is impossible to imagine Coriolanus, Menenius, Volumnia, Brutus, Cassius, even Julius Caesar occupying themselves in this manner. Elsewhere Cleopatra, eager for diversion, calls for music, suggests billiards, and then fishing (2.5.1ff.). Later Antony pleads with Caesar to allow him to lead a private life in Athens. Octavius Caesar disdains it but he is about to create a world in which these will be the chief pleasures available. *Magna civitas, magna voluptas.*

So far we have examined the manners and morals of both Rome and Egypt from the perspective of an older, but not entirely extinguished Rome, the Rome of the Republic present on the lips of Pompey and evident by its alteration in the sensuous streets of Alexandria. We have been alerted to the fact, therefore, that when we speak of Rome in this play we must be careful to distinguish the Republic and the Empire, the Rome fought for by Brutus and Cassius, and the new Rome which arrives at the play's end when Augustus' victory over Antony leaves him absolute ruler of a peaceful Empire.

This distinction is of great importance. Often remarked by commentators of this play is the sense that two worlds of value divide the play, one Roman, one Egyptian; in the center between the world of Rome and the world of Egypt is Antony. The struggle between the two worlds focuses upon his fitful and compromising allegiance to the two worlds. This account of the play is founded in our first impressions of the action. At first glance we would say that the virtues to the Romans are the vices of the Egyptians and the vices of the Romans are Egyptian virtues. However it must be amended and modified in important respects; for each of these two worlds as they face each other are not characterized by unity; in each there is a disharmony between first impressions (often the product of the declared self-presentations of the characters) and subsequent realities. Rome is not what it appears to be; Octavius is not what he represents himself as. Nor, on the other hand do Egypt and Cleopatra live up to their first gorgeous and fertile image.

For example, there is the seductive duality which seems to face Antony. The frequent references to Antony as Hercules tempt one to see him as a Hercules who, when faced with the choice of Hercules (between Virtue pictured as a chaste woman and Vice pictured as a seductively unparalleled wench, see Xenophon's *Memorabilia*, 2.1.21ff.), chooses Vice. To see Antony in this mythological light is to succumb to the Roman view. The opposition between virtue and vice is not so clear as the Romans seek to represent it. Moreover, the play's chief Roman (in the sense of most exclusively Roman) is Octavius and he replaces the choice of virtue and vice with the struggle of *virtù* with Fortuna, a lady who, unlike Virtue, forgives the vices of the powerful and effective. And Egyptian "vice" possesses not only a certain charm for all the Romans in the play but it contains what neither Egyptian nor Roman are sensible of, the seed of new order whose new tablet of virtues and vices will transvalue ancient virtues and vices.

We will continue our treatment of Rome. Then we will treat Egypt.

In ascertaining the nature of Rome in this play the most often quoted passages are taken from the frequent condemnations of Antony. Certainly these give an impression of Roman values; but we must measure the reality of Rome by Roman deeds as well as by guilty, nostalgic speeches. A mark of the condition of Roman virtue is the conduct of Enobarbus. Brutus would never be a traitor to his cause; Coriolanus was choleric just to hear the word "traitor." Enobarbus calls his treason "reason."

> When valor preys on
> reason,
> It eats the sword it fights with: I will seek
> Some way to leave him.
>
> (3.13.199-201)

To Enobarbus' credit he comes to grieve his loss of integrity; however, the nature of his loyalty is personal and has no mixture of impersonality and principle in it. His integrity is hostage to Antony not to Rome. Like other Romans in the play, Enobarbus seems disposed to acknowledge something higher than himself, a disposition which would correct the immoderate Roman longing for immortality (in a Coriolanus) if it were not focused on a man much like himself.

Speaking of Antony's life in the East, Caesar censures his "lascivious wassails" (1.4.56), his drunkenness (1.4.20), and his familiarity with slaves. His own conduct belies his code. While Caesar is too cold to permit familiarity (having already begun to follow his namesake's habit of third-person self-reference) he is not above drunkenness at the banquet with Pompey (2.7); though he holds a prim silence through most of the wassails, he has to ask for Antony's hand in order to leave the ship. Nor are his censures of Antony moral in character; he only raises them in protest of the burdens placed upon him by Antony's absence (1.4.16ff.).

His praise of Antony's former self is in what Cleopatra calls the high Roman fashion:

> When thou once
> Was beaten from Modena, where thou slew'st
> Hirtius and Pansa, consuls, at thy heel
> Did famine follow, whom thou fought'st
> against
> (Though daintily brought up) with patience
> more
> Than savages could suffer. Thou didst drink
> The stale of horses and the gilded puddle
> Which beasts would cough at. Thy palate
> then did deign
> The roughest berry on the rudest hedge.
> Yea, like the stag when snow the pasture
> sheets,
> The barks of trees thou browsed. On the
> Alps
> It is reported thou didst eat strange flesh,
> Which some did die to look on. And all this
> (It wounds thine honor that I speak it now)
> Was borne so like a soldier that thy cheek
> So much as lanked not.
>
> (1.4.56-71)

This praise of the Roman martial virtues of courage

and fortitude stands in marked contrast to the conduct of the Romans in the play; Antony alone offers to test these qualities and it is the very utterer of these praises who refuses his challenge. Caesar's battles are all fought at sea and unlikely to test fortitude over a long engagement.

These discrepancies between the values by which Caesar measures Antony and Roman conduct in the play raise a pertinent question: is there any use for Roman courage, Roman valor? When the death of Antony gives the Empire to Augustus and peace to the Empire, of what value will be fortitude? What far-flung military engagements will require the kind of courage evinced by Antony? What scope will be provided for the exercise of ambition? What avenues will be open for the pursuit of honor? "None," is the answer provided by a scene apparently designed to answer these questions. On the edge of the Empire lies one force which might insure that Roman virtue will not languish, that Roman swords will not rust; this force lies in Parthia. At the end of *Julius Caesar* Cassius set free a Parthian and made him his executioner (5.3.37ff.). In *Antony and Cleopatra* the distant Parthians are often mentioned. Their significance, however, is concentrated into a single scene designed to reveal the moral and military condition of Rome. This scene (3.1) marks a simple contrast to its immediate predecessor (2.8). There the three pillars of the wide world (four if you count Pompey) shook, banqueted, sang, and danced to "Egyptian Bacchanals" (2.8.103) in a mutual pleasure which could not disguise their mutual distrust. The hollow drums and flourish which convey these limp pillars of the world to shore (in 2.8) ring in the mind's ear as a real warrior, Ventidius, enters in the scene immediately following (3.1).

The scene is Syria. Ventidius has just evened the death of Marcus Crassus with the death of Orodes' son Pacorus; he has just kept the Parthians from Judea, where Antony has installed Herod as King of Jewry (1.2.28). The trust and friendship his companion in arms, Silius, shows when he urges Ventidius to pursue the Parthians, contrasts with the unsteady contract which passes for friendship among the Triumvirs. Silius shows neither mistrust of his companion nor envy of his achievements; he attributes to Ventidius his own pursuit of honor and derives a frank pleasure from the honor due Ventidius. Were this the early Republic we would think these men consuls; moreover, we would expect immediate pursuit of the Parthians. Ventidius explains why he will not offer pursuit, and by explaining anatomises the present state of Rome:

> O Silius, Silius,
> I have done enough. A lower place, note well,
> May make too great an act. For learn this,
> Silius,
> Better to leave undone, than by our deed
> Acquire too high a fame when him we serve's
> away.
> Caesar and Antony have ever won

More in their officer than person. Sossius,
One of my place in Syria, his lieutenant,
For quick accumulation of renown,
Which he achieved by th' minute, lost his
    favor.
Who does i' th' wars more than his captain
    can
Becomes his captain's captain; and ambition
(The soldier's virtue) rather makes choice of loss
Than gain which darkens him.
I could do more to do Antonius good,
But 'twould offend him. And in his offense
Should my performance perish.

                                        (3.1.11-27)

Ambition is now checked and men must be wary of showing distinction; how long will it be before valor falls into desuetude?

Now that the borders of the Empire have been set, what's the use of valiantness? But the toll incurred by the approaching peace of Augustus is not alone in valiancy; it is in truth. "That truth should be silent I had almost forgot," observes Enobarbus (2.2.108). Indeed, a fitting comment upon the repeated episodes of men being struck and cursed for delivering true reports or speaking truth (e.g., 2.5.23ff.). In the new era a fussy taste for truth will earn the displeasure of one's master and an invitation to take poison as a chaser. Truth, the measure of human affairs, even as Antony, the odds, is the measure of men, truth too suffers that injury called the Empire.

Underlying the hurry of action in this play is the approaching stillness of the Augustan Peace. The security of the Empire will be accompanied by inactivity. You can feel the course of Rome coming to a halt as the civil war winds up. Up until this time Rome had *motion;* it was a mover and a sweater (though not a breather and a panter like the Queen of the Nile). This motion might have been tumult but that tumult kept the fortunes and territories of Rome on the increase. But when Ventidius, an able commander, halts his advance against the Parthians we are given to see something revealing about the course of the Empire; now her motion and her station are as one. These words describe Rome no less than Octavia, the sister of Octavius Caesar. The peace which the death of Antony brings to the world which is known as the Pax Augusta may make the Mediterranean world as stale and as motionless as a "gilded puddle."

Hence, whenever a Roman tries to measure Antony's conduct by pristine Roman virtues we receive an impression of a decay in Rome of which the speaker is not fully aware. Their eulogies are elegies to a disappearing world; when they praise they bury. When Cleopatra tries to describe the consequences of the disappearance of Antony from the world,

            The odds is gone,
And there is nothing left remarkable
Beneath the visiting moon . . .

                                        (4.15.66-68)

she portrays not only the disappearance of a man but of a whole order which reared him. The elegy she composes for Antony combines with the words of Caesar:

    The breaking of so great a thing should make
    A greater crack. The round world
    Should have shook lions into civil streets,
    And citizens to their dens. The death of
        Antony
    Is not a single doom, in the name lay
    A moiety of the world . . .

                                        (5.1.14-19)

to make us realize the remarkable stature of what is disappearing; to Cleopatra, Antony is the last man; she chooses death over Octavius. To Caesar Augustus, Antony is the last worthy antagonist. From the vantage point occupied by Shakespeare, though by neither Caesar nor Cleopatra, we can see that Antony is also the last Roman. When Rome is unable to produce even the flawed nobility of an Antony its order is senescent.

Something like the sense of the world about to fall apart, or held together in an order which stupefies, is presented in the Rome of *Antony and Cleopatra.* Shakespeare focuses upon Rome at times of grave constitutional crisis or innovation. In *The Rape of Lucrece* we have the transition from tyranny to an aristocratic Republic; in *Coriolanus* we have the innovation of Tribunate representation of the plebs whose bodies are now required for Rome's armies; in *Julius Caesar* we have the struggle of Republicans against the post-Republican rule of Caesar; in *Antony and Cleopatra* we see the funeral of the dead Republic and the elements which will thrive under Imperial peace. When the Roman world finally reaches a period of peace— the Augustan Peace which comes with the defeat of Antony— it is a peace of exhaustion; in *Antony and Cleopatra* the Roman order still rules, but posthumously; it is felt to be dead and incapable of producing more great men. It is dead at what seems its greatest victory.

If Rome has lost its motion and if its order is no longer youthful where can one find motion and a new order? Put in different words, where does all that's quick and lively go when it leaves politics and the city? Apparently it goes to the East and to Cleopatra; it follows Antony to the beds of the East. There in the person of Antony a warrior's integrity is replaced by the integrity of a lover. In the arms and charms of Cleopatra, Antony finds the motion which Rome now lacks; her motion and her station are not as one; in the play of passions in her breast Antony will discover whole early Republics of tumult. To the inconstancy of the passions, Antony dedicates his integrity. He seems to find a constancy in a life immersed in *eros* for there he finds the motion and quickness which characterized Rome.

The experience of *eros* in the play is focused upon Cleopatra. Unlike his source, Plutarch, Shakespeare has spent prodigally of his great poetic powers to make us feel her attraction. In her, *eros* is infinite in its variety; it fascinates the gazer, be he Enobarbus, Antony, or the many critics who have testified to her enchantment. There is no need to add to the appreciations of her charms which have been offered. What is needed is a unenchanted understanding, for Shakespeare has not made her attractions blinding. The very degree of *eros* which appears in her suggests her deficiency. She practices a sensual calculation designed to heighten pleasure, but not to provide satisfaction; she sauces every meal with something elusive; appetite swells with what it feeds on. Full satisfaction she will not or cannot provide, and so with her *eros* thrives on its own dissatisfaction. The passionate life of *eros* seems to point beyond itself to a place of where dissatisfaction is banished. The longing for Cleopatra fills the lover with longings which she cannot satisfy because they are immortal longings. The life of the lover shares with the life of the *thymetic* warrior (e.g., Coriolanus) a desire for immortality, an immortality which Antony and then Cleopatra reach for in their suicides. Both she and Antony seem to testify to the inadequacy of motion when they seek to shackle up change through suicide. Something lacks in their *eros*.

In a famous banquet marked by a sobriety which contrasts with the banquet of Pompey and the Triumvirs, Socrates and his friends give eulogies to *eros*. The most moving and hence erotic of the speeches is one a woman gave to the young Socrates. According to Diotima, love is a lack of something and ultimately this thing is immortality; in the variety of things which it pleases men to pursue there is always the desire to secure immortality. To adopt Cleopatra's phrase, all men have "immortal longings." Hence, the philosopher who seeks to dwell among the noble, fair and wise ideas lives the most satisfying life. He is most perfectly the lover and he most perfectly fulfills human nature.

For reasons which will emerge subsequently, I do not believe that Shakespeare means us to measure these lovers by the measure of wisdom praised by Diotima. Hence something which Diotima mentions on her ascent up the ladder of love is more pertinent. There are two modes of life, below the philosophic life, which secure a lesser portion of immortality; they are the mode of the warrior who loves honor and the mode of the parent who achieves immortality through the child. Of this mode Diotima says,

All men, Socrates, have a procreative impulse, both

Antony and Cleopatra. The University of Michigan Special Collections Library.

spiritual and physical, and when they come to maturity they feel a natural desire to beget children. . . . There is something divine about the whole matter; in procreation and bringing to birth the mortal creature is endowed with a touch of immortality.

It is this mode, the lowest rung on the classical ladder, which claims our attention in regard to *Antony and Cleopatra*. The fascination of Cleopatra begets nothing. Despite her association with fertile flooding of the Nile, Cleopatra lacks the substance of fertility. True, there is mention of her children, but we never see them. The fruits of her union(s) are nowhere vividly and forcefully presented. When Caesar threatens the destruction of her children (5.2.128-133), Cleopatra is unmoved (5.2.134ff.). Her "fertility" is of the eye not the womb. It dazzles the eye of the beholder, but it does not make him a father. The very manner of her suicide calls attention to her infertility; at her breast a viper sucks, not an infant. Eros in Egypt appears to be a eunuch, it begets nothing. (Indeed, the character Eros, Antony's companion, slays himself.) This effectual infertility is not limited to Egypt and Cleopatra. The men in the play are nowhere presented as fathers. Both Rome and Egypt are without children. Though most of the principal figures in the play are old, there seems to be no young generation on the horizon, no children inherit the earth. Octavius was the adopted son of Julius Caesar and adoption will be a common relation between one Caesar and the next.

This absence of children is all the more remarkable in the midst of so much talk of fertility and of the fascination of *eros*. This remarkable observation seems all the more deliberate in the light of an event alluded to in the play. The frequent references to Herod of Jewry speak in a tongue which no Roman or Egyptian can interpret. No Roman or Egyptian could interpret God's infinite book of secrecy sufficiently to understand allusions to a King of the Jews who was disturbed at the news of the birth of a King of kings and who slew the innocent babes in Bethlehem.

It is the end of an era though neither Romans nor Egyptians know it. The "valiant" Romans do not know that they are deedless; the "fertile" Egyptians do not know that they are seedless. The union of Antony and Cleopatra of Rome and Egypt is an old union unable to give birth to a new political and moral order. Yet unbeknownst to itself, this Empire cradles a new order in its womb. It will come from the East, but further East than Alexandria. In *Antony and Cleopatra* the new order provided by Christianity, whose focus upon the child is pronounced, seems just over the horizon, visible to Shakespeare and some of his audience, if not to his Romans. The birth of the Christ child which inaugurates the Christian era lies in pointed obscurity behind the foreground sterility of both Rome and Egypt. One sees a similiar pointed obscurity in the paintings of Breughel, in his Crucifixion and his Fall of Icarus.

Rome supplies a roughness, Egypt supplies a panting, to a beast which unconsciously slouches toward Bethlehem. With astonishing concentration Shakespeare has portrayed the demise of old Rome, the transfer of its *thymetic* motion to the erotic East; finally he has upstaged even the attractions of Cleopatra and pointed to a new order founded on *eros* and inaugurated with the birth of a Divine child. Yet he has done this with such a light hand that we cannot know whether the emphasis falls upon the divinity or the child, whether Christianity is the new order because it gives to each soul an afterlife which can shackle up mortal accidents (and hence really fulfills both Roman and Egyptian longings for immortality) or whether it is the new order because its canon against self-slaughter heralds a new loyalty to the living, changing, impermanent, and perishable things. From these frequent and sonorous reminders of the birth of Christ, we cannot tell whether Christianity is the new order because it fulfills Ancient (both Roman and Egyptian.' longings for immortality or whether it is a new order because it brings to mere living a new affection capable of sustaining weary inhabitants of the Empire without the heroic exit of suicide. The image of a child who is also divine would

seem to contain both these apparently contrary valuations. On the one hand, whoever hears of a child who so prefers life to death that she kills herself. On the other hand, the divinity of *this* child would suggest that the divine or eternal things are far superior to the mortal and momentary things. But to understand Shakespeare's account of Christianity is another task.

Shakespeare's *Antony and Cleopatra* makes us long for a better world, for world where the beauty we apprehend fitfully and uncertainly in these lovers will be strong, constant, and viable, where what is in passionate tension in them is knit whole. There we could submit wholly to wonder, unqualified as here by skepticism and uncertainty. Reading or beholding this play means struggling to judge these lovers aright, a task they struggle with too; it also means never denying either what skepticism sees or wonder divines in them. "Divines" is the precise word; we are not to think these lovers do deserve, except fitfully, our faith. Instead, we are by their imperfections meant to long for something better: by struggling to judge them we come to long for something better; by struggling to judge Rome and Egypt, we come to long for something beyond ancient politics and ancient pleasures.

Larry S. Champion

SOURCE: "The Social Dimensions of Tragedy: *Timon of Athens, Coriolanus, Antony and Cleopatra*," in *Shakespeare's Tragic Perspective*, The University of Georgia Press, 1976, pp. 201-65.

[*In this brief excerpt, Champion contends that the worlds of Rome and Egypt are "equally tainted." Cleopatra, he remarks, cares more about herself and her pleasure than about her subjects' needs; similarly, the supposedly disciplined Roman leaders are shown engaging in a drunken orgy on a barge.*]

In *Antony and Cleopatra*, whether actually his last tragedy or not, Shakespeare achieves his most powerful delineation of these secular values between which man struggles to make the choices for a successful life. Gone is a clear distinction between virtue and vice, between material and spiritual choice. The drama operates within the world of man, within the conflict created out of the struggle for power and influence between a Roman emperor and an Egyptian queen. And the values of these two worlds are equally tainted.

Cleopatra's world, for instance, is decadent and enervating. Nowhere do the spectators have even the slightest sense of the queen's concern for her kingdom and for the welfare of her subjects; nowhere are they convinced that her affairs with heads of the Roman state, past or present, are motivated by any sort of determination to protect her nation at any price. To the contrary, she utilizes her unlimited power and her limited beauty for the gratification of her own vanity. The first visual impression is almost cloying— Cleopatra in lavish array, the elaborate train of attendants, the eunuchs fanning her, her ladies catering to her smallest whim. Virtually every action through the first half of the play underscores this egocentric posturing. She tauntingly persuades Antony to refuse a message from Rome as a token of his doting affection. Rebuking him moments later, in total disregard for the news of his wife's death and of adverse political developments at home, she is apprehensive not because of his grief but because of the looming possibility that he might escape from her clutches. This same egocentric vanity is evidenced again later when she receives word of Antony's marriage to Octavia. At first striking the messenger and threatening to dispatch him forthwith, she finally resorts to the rather childish ploy of questioning him about Antony's wife feature by feature and then convincing herself that she is superior in every respect. Enobarbus, in mocking hyperbole, brands her passions as "pure love" (I, ii, 144), her sighs and tears as "greater storms and tempests than almanacs can report" (145-46). And she herself admits to the role she plays in maintaining a close rein on Antony by irritating and crossing him at every turn (I, iii).

The Egyptian world is also morally vitiated. For one thing, it reeks of sensuality. The bawdy wit of Iras and Charmian in the opening scene (over where best to have an additional inch of fortune in a husband and over how delightful it would be to see Alexas cuckolded) is prologue to Cleopatra's own banter with Mardian after Antony has departed for Rome. She takes "no pleasure / In aught an eunuch has" (I, v, 9-10); his affections cannot be shown "in deed" (15); one would do as well to play with a woman as "with an eunuch" (II, v, 5); his "good will" perforce will "come too short" (8). What Octavius terms her "lascivious wassails" (I, iv, 56), Enobarbus describes as occasions for sleeping "day out of countenance" and making "the night light with drinking" (II, ii, 178-79). She recalls with obvious pleasure how often she laughed Antony "into patience" at night:

> and next morn,
> Ere the ninth hour, I drunk him to his bed;
> Then put my tires and mantles on him,
>   whilst
> I wore his sword Philippan.
>
> (II, v, 20-23)

Such a moment, as Maurice Charney observes [in *Shakespeare's Roman Plays*], visually depicts Cleopatra in "control of her lover's sword, the symbol of his manliness and soldiership." She, in her own words, is one who "trade[s] in love" (II, v, 2), trained by Julius Caesar in her "salad days" (I, v, 73). For another thing, this queen is totally devoid of the fortitude essential to leadership. She finds it easy to articulate her role as

commander of her forces, insisting both that Antony fight by sea and that she accompany him as the "president" of her kingdom and fight by his side; with almost equal ease she later assumes she can erase with a word the onus of her retreat which proves so disastrous to Antony: "I little thought / You would have followed" (III, xi, 55-56).

If there is no moral fiber in Cleopatra and her court attendants, so also no such quality is to be found in Octavius and his associates. Robert Ornstein aptly remarks [in "The Ethic of the Imagination: Love and Art in *Antony and Cleopatra*"] that "the decay of Roman idealism is so advanced that it is difficult to say whether a Roman thought is of duty or disloyalty." In any event, Shakespeare methodically undermines the spectators' confidence in the Roman leaders through reflection of Lepidus' dissipation and Octavius' duplicity. Ironically, for example, despite all the references to the orgies of the East, the only such scene in the play involves the Western leaders on Pompey's barge. So drunk are Lepidus and Antony that "the least wind i' th' world will blow them down" (II, vii, 2-3); their sense "steeped" in "conquering wine" (106), they dance hand in hand, drowning their cares in a song to Bacchus. Although the "high-colored" (4) Lepidus is especially mocked by his servants, both he and Antony have turned themselves into hollow shells of the power they espouse; with an easy slit of the throat, as Menas observes, Pompey could be an "earthly Jove" (66) greater than those "world-sharers" and "competitors" (69).

Disconcerting also is the Roman marriage by which Octavius intends to insure "perpetual amity" (II, ii, 125) with Antony. Arranged lock— born not in love but in material convenience— is, of course, conventional practice both in Shakespeare's day and Caesar's. Even so, the context of heated words followed by historionic displays of affection results in a union which looks cynical indeed to the friends of the triumvirs, who have no illusions about the game they watch. Octavius bequeaths a sister to join their kingdoms and their hearts. Blest by the third triumvir, this business will be the cement with which to build and hold their love, "the ram to batter / The fortress of it" (III, ii, 30-31); Octavia will be a "blessed lottery" (II, ii, 244) to her husband. Again there is little to choose between; in trading in love Rome can better Egypt at her own game! Most degrading of all, Octavius forces truth to serve his convenience. While Antony is in Alexandria with Octavia, Caesar is quick to violate their agreement, engaging in a new war against Pompey and speaking "scantly" (III, iv, 6) of his brother-in-law to the public ear. Moreover, on his individual initiative he removes Lepidus from a position of command, denying him "rivality" and seizing him "upon his own appeal" after "having made use of him" in the wars against Pompey (v, 6-10). His claims that he is merely responding to Antony, who has returned to Egypt to dole out kingdoms to Cleopatra's brood, are clearly post facto; Antony's actions subsequent to this power play merely provide Octavius a convenient excuse and a ready response to Octavia's queries. This use of wit to distort the facts he finds useful again in his later pronouncement that only with great hesitation was he "drawn into this war" against Antony, that he ever proceeded with calmness and gentleness in all his writings. Such boasting of leniency and mercy is mocked by the spectators' memory of Antony's earlier plea that he be allowed to "breathe between the heavens and the earth" as a "private man in Athens" (III, xii, 14-15), to which Caesar coldly responded that he would not hear the request. In the same breath he offered audience to Cleopatra only if she drove Antony from Egypt or assassinated him. So, too, Proculeius' claim in Caesar's name that Cleopatra should "fear nothing" from his "princely hand" (V, ii, 22) is belied by the soldiers' stealthy attack upon her immediately thereafter and by Dolabella's later admission that Caesar plans to lead her in triumph.

ANTONY

J. Leeds Barroll describes Mark Antony as "one of Shakespeare's most complexly imagined tragic heroes," and indeed, scholarly response to Antony has been various. Barroll characterizes him as lacking in conventional ideas of "social responsibility"— Antony does not, for example, feel the duty toward Rome that characters such as Octavius Caesar and Enobarbus feel he should. Nor does he feel ashamed when he neglects Roman politics or when he indulges himself in Egypt. Barroll notes that Antony does, however, feel ashamed when he flees the fighting at Actium; thus Barroll concludes that Antony is not motivated by orthodox theories of politics as Caesar is, but by his own personal notion of chivalry and public honor.

Much of the critical discussion regarding Antony has focused on his conflicting ties to Rome and Egypt. Like Barroll, Paul A. Cantor observes that despite his extravagant claims to the contrary, Antony has not completely rejected the world for the sake of his love for Cleopatra but instead remains concerned about his role as a world leader. Unlike Barroll, Cynthia Kolb Whitney argues that Antony's conflict amounts to a sense of duty toward Rome rather than simply toward himself; specifically, she contends that Antony's "Roman honor is at war with his Egyptian sexuality." William D. Wolf describes Antony as someone who is "caught between [the] irreconcilable poles" of Egypt and Rome, love and military duties, Cleopatra and Octavius Caesar— and whose ultimate response to these two, fluctuating worlds is death.

Ruth Nevo and Sheila M. Smith assess Antony's role in

the context of his relationship to Cleopatra. Smith views Antony and Cleopatra as equals whose power over one another continually shifts. "Each," she observes, "is a shifty lover, guilty of treachery towards the other." Nevo describes the lovers as different personalities within a "mutual pair"— two people who approach their love for one another in conflicting ways until the closing, tragic acts of the play. Within this pairing, Nevo sees Antony as too much at home in both Rome and Egypt; further, she observes that Antony's tragedy lies in the fact that he is unwilling to choose between preeminence in Rome or devotion to Cleopatra.

Austin Wright also focuses on Antony as a tragic figure. After depicting him as "a natural athlete" with a great deal of "personal charm," Wright observes that Antony loses everything through "his own weakness": in other words, Wright contends, Antony foolishly sacrifices his former reputation for honor and military prowess to satisfy his needs as a lover.

E. A. J. Honigmann and **John W. Draper** approach Mark Antony from somewhat unconventional perspectives. Honigmann tackles Antony's generic role in the play. At first, Honigmann remarks, Antony appears to be almost comical as he repeatedly serves as the butt of Cleopatra's jokes and submits himself to her teasing. However Honigmann contends that after his defeat at Actium, Antony refuses to put up with Cleopatra's capriciousness; at this point, he becomes a tragic figure. Draper asserts that Antony's tragedy stems from a neurosis that is brought on by middle age and that is put under unbearable strain from the conflicting pressures of Cleopatra's love, Octavius Caesar's authority, and Enobarbus's insubordination. For additional commentary on the character of Antony, see the excerpt by Walter Cohen in the **OVERVIEW** section, the excerpts by David Daiches and Katherine Vance MacMullan in the **LANGUAGE AND IMAGERY** section, the excerpts by Janet Adelman and Peter Berek in the **DU-ALISM** section, the excerpt by Maurice Charney in the section on **CLEOPATRA**, and the excerpt by Gordon Ross Smith in the section on **OCTAVIUS**.

John W. Draper

SOURCE: "Shattered Personality in Shakespeare's Antony," in *The Psychiatric Quarterly*, Vol. 39, No. 3, July, 1965, pp. 448-56.

[Draper provides a psychological portrait of Antony, arguing that the Roman general becomes the victim of his own emotional struggle between his duty to Octavius Caesar and his fascination with the "wiles" of Cleopatra. Draper observes that, as Antony ages, he suffers from a type of psychological exhaustion that prevents him from pursuing his proper role as a Roman but that instead drives him to madness and thus to suicide when he pursues Cleopatra and the sybaritic life in Egypt.]

According to Aristotle, a tragic plot consists of a chain of episodes causally related in which, given the characters and the initial situation, the final catastrophe is as inevitable as the outcome of a chemical experiment. Hegel, however, from a hint in Aristotle devised a variant theory that the basic principle was not so much causality as conflict, in which one or both of the adverse forces at last meets inescapable disaster. These might be objective forces portrayed by opposing characters or groups, as for example, Lear against his daughters; or the forces might be subjective, a psychological struggle within a single person—a matter more easily expressed in the fuller exposition of the novel than in the brief compass of drama. The first type, objective conflict, is common in tragedy; the second is rarer; but in Shakespeare's middle plays, it occasionally appears: In Act I of *Julius Caesar*, the affection of Brutus for his friend briefly contends against the patriotic arguments of the conspirators; but soon his republican idealism makes him join them in the plot against Caesar; and so this inner conflict is a mere introduction to the tragedy. Lady Macbeth likewise must suppress her womanly compunction before she embarks upon the murder of her king and guest. These subjective conflicts are only incidental: The main action appears objectively in the conflict between individuals and/or groups, such as the republican conspirators versus Caesar and Antony.

Indeed, Shakespeare's only tragedy in which the dominant conflict is subjective seems to be *Antony and Cleopatra*, one of his latest plays. Here the hero's political rivalries in Rome and his wars in the Orient are little more than background; and the main contest, apparent in the very first lines, concerns his political and military ambition over against his infatuation for Cleopatra; and, throughout the episodes that follow, he vacillates between these two contending motives. By birth and rearing, Antony is a Roman with a Roman's ambition in the forum and the field; and his intelligence tells him that these are his rightful careers; but, more and more, his overmastering passion and his growing taste for exotic luxury draw him to the fleshpots of Egypt. Indeed, the soldier Enobarbus, whom Shakespeare developed from his source as a kind of chorus and as a contrast to the wavering Antony, repeatedly reminds us that his general, even in the welter of Roman politics, is bound to return to Cleopatra; for she had "pursed up his heart upon the river of Cydnus" so that "He will to his Egyptian dish again." Rome and Alexandria were poles apart: the former, the military and political mistress of the world with a tradition of plain, soldierly virtue; the latter, the commercial link with India and the emporium of Oriental luxury and splendor superimposed upon Hellenistic sophistication; and one can understand why the emperors so long forbade the public celebration in Rome of the orgiastic rites of Isis. Antony was torn between the conflicting ideals of soldier and sybarite.

The course of the tragedy shows this vacillation between Roman rigor and the relaxing indulgences of Egypt; and Cleopatra had at her command an "infinite variety" of allurements. Even in the first scene, Philo says that "his captain's heart . . . is become the bellows and the fan / To cool a gipsy's lust"; and Antony himself declares that love and pleasure are "the nobleness of life," and so "let Rome and Tiber melt, and the wide arch / Of the ranged empire fall," and he concludes, "What sport tonight?" But news of his wife's death and public affairs in Rome tear him away from the temptress: Despite her wiles, he still is more a Roman than a love-sick sensualist; and his intellect still governs his emotions. In Act II, he gives himself to politics in Italy, and even makes a marriage of convenience with Octavia; but Enobarbus tells us that he has not forgotten his Egyptian paramour and must return to her. In Act III, war breaks out between him and Caesar, who wins at Actium because, against the advice of Enobarbus and an unnamed "Soldier," Antony fights on the sea and not on land: His military judgment has deserted him. Indeed, as Caesar says,

> . . . Cleopatra
> Hath nodded him to her. He hath given his empire
> Up to a whore. . . .

In the midst of the carnage, the queen and her fleet suddenly sail away; and he, "doting" as ever, takes after them, and so ruins his career. This is the crisis of the play and hereafter both his fortunes and his mental powers rapidly decline. In Act IV, again in Egypt, he forgives her against his better judgment, desires one more "gaudy night" on the town, and fondly hopes against hope, now boasting, now despairing. His followers, even his divine protector, Hercules, and the faithful Enobarbus at last desert him; his martial spirit is burned out; he is no longer a soldier. When he hears that his beloved is making sly overtures to the enemy, he kills himself, true Roman at the last—or perhaps mere disillusioned sensualist.

Plutarch's *Life of Antony*, on which the play is based, concentrates on political and military matters, and hardly even implies its hero's psychology. It tells us merely that the sumptuous meeting with Cleopatra on the river Cydnus "ravished" Antony; it quotes Caesar's opinion that Cleopatra used charms to subdue him; and it states that just before the Battle of Actium Antony had become "subject" to her; but Plutarch shows no inward conflict between love and duty, and his Antony seems to take things quite nonchalantly just as they come—politics in Italy, fighting in the East, and luxurious sport in Egypt. Antony's instability on his return from Actium to Alexandria, his mad vacillations, his despairings and his hopes, are Shakespeare's additions, an essential motivation for the events barely set forth in Plutarch. A biography can concentrate objectively on mere fact; but a tragedy that would not sink to melodrama must show clearly in its dialogue motive and emotional detail. Therefore, one might inquire where Shakespeare got this motivation and detail that he supplied and whether it is psychologically right.

The humoral theory that was derived from Galen and accepted by Elizabethans usually gave Shakespeare motives for his characters, but Plutarch's facts forbid its use in Antony. In actual history, though Shakespeare, for dramatic compression, does not emphasize the point, some 12 years pass during the course of the tragedy: In Act I, Antony is already over 40; and, by the middle of the play, he is well beyond 50, which the Elizabethans, with their short life-expectancy, would consider old age. In Shakespeare also he is far from young: He refers to his "white" hairs among the brown and to his "grizzled head"; and soon after Caesar calls him "the old ruffian." In contrast to the freedom with which Shakespeare used Plutarch in *Julius Caesar,* this play follows the source closely; but Plutarch's narrative hardly allowed the dramatist to pattern his hero's psychology on Elizabethan medical theory: Generals and rulers, according to this theory, should be hot and dry in physique and in character choleric; and the heat in time burned out, with diminishing vital fluids, to the cold, decrepit melancholy of old age. It did not give place to Antony's infatuated ardor of the "amorous surfeiter," cold but wet and phlegmatic, under the astral influence of sensual Venus or the lunatic moon. According to the then current medical ideas, his enamored slavery fits neither his military status, which should be choleric, nor his "grizzled" hair, which should herald melancholic senility. He does not age like that old lecher Falstaff, who drinks strong wine to maintain the choler essential to his military caste, and who displays no inward struggles, no matter what he does, and no blunting of his wit; nor is Antony like Adam in *As You Like It* whose physical exhaustion does not impair his steadfast mind, nor like ancient Lear, whose royal choler, much prolonged, suddenly leaves him to senility and melancholy madness: All these in their several ways accord with the current theory; but Antony's advancing years, despite the exhaustion of "gaudy" nights in Alexandria, show a renewing of youthful ardor. Not melancholy debility but phlegmatic lust makes him desert the battle and steer his ship after the fleeing Cleopatra, and then forgive her for the unforgivable. He has changed from the choleric Roman of Act I, who left her at political behest, into a phlegmatic voluptuary, who has no thought of consequences, in fact, no thought at all; and Enobarbus notes with soldierly disgust a "diminution" in his general's intellect. In short, Plutarch has obligated the playright to set aside accepted medical theory, and depict advancing years as turning the soldier into the sybarite; and such a change implies a protracted tension in which native ideals and obvious good sense give way by degrees to overwhelming passion.

The younger Antony of *Julius Caesar,* sharp politician and successful general, properly looked forward to becoming a power in the state; but the older Antony, having achieved great power and a time of life that ought to have brought wisdom, looks forward more and more only to Cleopatra; and, as the tragedy unfolds, the inner conflict of this strange transition becomes close to psychosis, a conflict between past and present, between intellect and emotion, that reduces the sufferer to bad judgment at Actium and later in Egypt to instability and utter folly. In Act IV, Antony's oscillation between bravado and despair and his escapist fantasies might make some Elizabethans suppose that at the last he lapsed into a melancholy madness; but the lines of the play lack the terminology of the Galenic humors, except for Enobarbus' reference to the "damp of night" as "melancholy" when he is about to kill himself; and Antony's psychological evolution seems to follow no contemporary theory: He is not a younger Lear.

Modern psychiatry, however, attests to the substantial accuracy of Shakespeare's portraiture. Antony's type of severe disorder often "develops slowly and insidiously over a long period of years," and, as in Antony, may hardly be evident until "later life": furthermore, "toxic-exhaustion factors," which should be especially potent as bodily strength declines, would speed the progress of the disease; and Antony's dissolute life would grow increasingly exhausting. The consequence is a "disharmony between mood and thought"—a sort of shattered personality. By degrees, he shows "great instability," which often is a symptom of psychosis, and at the end extremes of ambivalence, which Scarus notes:

>   . . . Antony
> Is valiant, and dejected, and by starts
> His fretted fortunes give him hope and fear,
> Of what he has and has not.

Indeed, Cleopatra calls him "mad." The "genius type" was believed to be subject to such fits, and Antony was no ordinary man. By following his paramour in her flight after Actium, he shows "domination of thinking entirely by emotion." The sufferer "may shrink from facing the situation directly, and may temporize in the hope that something will turn up;" and so, on his return to Egypt Antony still hopes against hope. He takes refuge in "phantasy" and the illusion that he still can win; but outwardly, he has "coherent speech" that seems like sanity. Shakespeare, indeed, has filled out Plutarch's narrative with a true realism of psychological detail.

Today, with better hygiene and longer life-expectancy, men are not lacking who prolong their sexual urge beyond the threshold of old age; and, doubtless, some such existed in Elizabethan times, and in that boisterous day experienced conditions that tore their personalities apart. Shakespeare may well have noted their changing symptoms: Even obvious lunatics, if not actually violent, could be seen walking the streets of London without restraint; and Antony's disease, at least in its earlier stages, might pass for mere eccentricity. Personal observation was undoubtedly the basis for Shakespeare's vivid local color in the Falstaff plays; and, even when his characters were conceived in terms of current humoral and astrological theory, he doubtless supplemented this with his own eyes and ears, and, like all of us, subconsciously interpreted what he saw and heard in terms of the patterns that he and his audience accepted as true science. Late in his career, however, he used as his source a famous biographical classic that Galenic theory could not explain; and, perhaps because the strictures that Ben Jonson is thought to have made on *Julius Caesar* now caused him to follow Plutarch more carefully, or because the authority of traditional science was declining— as evidenced in Bacon— Shakespeare, rather than change Plutarch, apparently trusted his own observation in depicting the course of a mental disease. Antony's malady may originally have been precipitated by the shock of this new and startling Egyptian life, stage-managed so astutely by the queen; but, as this initial shock took place before the play began, Shakespeare leaves it as mere inference; but he correctly charts the case history of Antony's illness until at the last, Roman custom combines with loss of mental balance to bring on suicide.

Cleopatra is the perfect foil to Antony: She has the same two humors, choler of dominion and phlegm proper to womanhood; but she keeps her phlegm subordinate to the requirements of her choler; and so there is no conflict; and, when she is not playing a part, she shows an integrated, almost masculine, choler. Whereas Antony's intellect and strength of character are lapsing into irresolution; Cleopatra's shrewd intelligence is always in command; it calculates the wiles by which she holds her lover; it tells her when his star is setting so that she looks forward hopefully to Caesar and turns Actium into Caesar's victory; it finally shows her that his fair promises are false and her hope to rule him an illusion; and so, to avoid the degradation of gracing his Roman triumph, she kills herself, secretly, quickly, and as painlessly as she can, for she had provided even for this outcome. Antony had been a fine figure of a man and ruler of the East, even if "ruffian" and half-barbarous Roman; and she had ruled him; for, since her personal and her political interests ran concurrently, she had no inner struggle: Her problems were not of aim and purpose but only of the details for accomplishing these aims, a matter not of strategy but mere tactics.

For a whole generation, she had kept Egypt independent and herself its queen by enchanting her would-be conquerors; but the future Emperor Augustus was as cool and calculating and well integrated as herself, and so was not to be enchanted. Antony was her last conquest. Cleopatra's two contrasting humors apparently follow Galenic theory: In seeming, she is as supine, luxurious and amorous as the phlegmatic Antony; and, as this accorded with her sex, the appearance was all the more convincing. But in her this humor was subject to strong choler under the astral influence of the sun, astute but hidden like that of Iago and more extreme than that of Shakespeare's independent heroines. Like them, she gets what she wants by shrewd maneuvering under the guise of poor, weak womanhood: As a mere girl, she got Julius Caesar and so saved herself and Egypt; in middle life, she got Antony; and, when she saw that she could not get the future Augustus, she put an asp to her breast. Antony, still something of a Roman, falls on his sword; and she with crown and jewels dies in the panoply of the last Egyptian queen.

Most of Shakespeare's plays are based on old stories, often-times crude, that were well known and popular; but, as his art developed, he generally revised these stories to give them motive and characterization in terms of the accepted psychology of the day; but he did not so revise the Antony of Plutarch, for it could not be so explained: Plutarch's Antony is no youthful sanguine lover like Orlando or Ferdinand, nor a weakly mercurial Macbeth, who could hardly have committed regicide without his wife's support. In the Roman scheme of life, he had desired and achieved both military glory and high office, as Shakespeare shows in *Julius Caesar* and as the audience well knew. Not his weakness, therefore, but his very strength must be made to cause his downfall; and strength makes conflict all the more severe. Even as he aged, he was still very much a man, with a man's virile urges; and Cleopatra was very much a woman, with all the arts of the Orient at her command; and Antony succumbed. His ruin could come only by the ruin of his inner self; and so the tragedy had to show the conflict of shattered personality; and, since Elizabethan popular science had no pattern for such a conflict, Shakespeare had to depict and interpret life as he saw it, and hope that the audience would understand. Half a century later, Dryden's heroic plays likewise present the clash between love and honor, but not with Shakespeare's depth of understanding. *Coriolanus*, Shakespeare's final tragedy, again presents the ruin of a strong man; but the major conflict is objective, between the hero and the plebs; and not until Act V, Scene iii does an inner struggle appear: The malign effects of choleric pride were a commonplace of Elizabethan thought, and so the plot could proceed clearly to its catastrophe. *Antony and Cleopatra* presented a far more vexing problem; for Plutarch's depiction of Antony obliged the dramatist to depend for character-analysis on his own observation, and hope that the audience could follow; and the truth of his portrayal as attested by modern science shows that the master-playwright could see even beyond the problems of the normal human mind and express the progress of a psychiatric state uncharted in popular theory. Each of the major figures that surrounds Antony represents a force straining upon his personality: Enobarbus, whom Shakespeare developed from Plutarch to express the Roman military ideal; Caesar, the civic success expected of every Roman; and Cleopatra, whose entangling web enmeshed and overcame the other two forces in Antony's character, so that at last Antony, having negated his inborn Roman self, was also overcome.

J. Leeds Barroll

SOURCE: "Mark Antony and the Tournament of Life," in *Shakespearean Tragedy: Genre, Tradition, and Change in Antony and Cleopatra*, Associated University Presses, Inc., 1984, pp. 83-129.

[*In this excerpt from his chapter-length analysis of Mark Antony, Barroll argues that Antony refuses to be ruled by other characters' ideas of honor. Antony does not, Barroll suggests, think in terms of politics or strategy as Caesar does, nor does he feel ashamed that he has spent so much time luxuriating in Egypt. Instead, Barroll asserts, Mark Antony has a chivalric sense of honor that celebrates bravery and courage rather than military theory; linked to and perhaps more important than this chivalry is a strong reliance on Cleopatra's belief in their "mutual" love. Thus when Antony loses a battle he becomes depressed, but when he hears that Cleopatra has apparently killed herself, he becomes suicidal.*]

I

Mark Antony is one of Shakespeare's most complexly imagined tragic heroes. For this we thank, of course, Shakespeare's human empathy and genius. But the compelling quality of Antony's humanity owes as much to strategy as to genius. And if, in the end, these are perhaps the same thing, then the strategy by which genius brings Antony to life, makes him a tragic "character," is Shakespeare's emphasis on desire. For this in us is a complicated and deeply implicated phenomenon whose entangled state is much more specifically human than is grief, anger, or fear. These responses animals share with us. But our humanity is delineated by the kaleidoscopic focusings and terrible steadiness of our wishing.

That the strangeness of desire is Shakespeare's basic framework for "talking about" the character of Mark Antony is apparent at the outset. We are immediately confronted with a life being torn between "Egypt" and "Rome." But Rome and Egypt, in turn, are mere geographical or political expressions that, in the end, oversimplify everything. Indeed, if we allow the idea of Egypt and the concept of Rome to act as allegorical stations we lose the point. West tugging with East over

Antony's fallible but attractive Renaissance soul; psychomachia pitting Duty vs. Lust, Love vs. Greed, or Imagination vs. Reason—these are all attractive dualities. But Shakespeare's drama is a tragedy about an imagined human being, not an Essay on the Good Life in which Antony is to be significantly manipulated from pillar of Roman virtue to post of Egyptian inebriation. Ancient Rome and ancient Egypt in Shakespeare's drama are suggestions about confusion, not the panels of a medieval painting. Desire is not a simple duality: that is why it is complex.

Enobarbus, that careful (but often careless) observer of Antony, says about him, "Antony will use his affection where it is." And, in the long run, Enobarbus cannot help but mislead us too. For in Shakespeare's time, as today, "affection" was a multiplex word for a difficult envisioning, more complicated than what Enobarbus seems to intend by his words. After Antony follows Cleopatra's prematurely panicking battleship, thus fatally confusing his fleet and losing the empire of the world, the lamentations and shock are succeeded by a quiet scene in which Cleopatra reflects about what has happened.

Whose fault is all this? she asks Enobarbus and again he talks about "affection." The battle, he says, was lost by

> Antony only, that would make his will
> Lord of his reason. What though you fled
> From that great face of war, whose several
> ranges
> Frighted each other? Why should he follow?
> The itch of his affection should not then
> Have nick'd his captainship, at such a point,
> When half to half the world oppos'd, he
> being
> The meered question.
>
> (3.13.2-10)

"Affection," we are to understand, then, is that thing in Antony which draws him from his true Roman interests to Cleopatra and the Egyptian life.

Symmetrical enough—at least for Enobarbus—but for Antony himself the choices do not seem quite so cut and dried. "I'th'East my pleasure lies" was indeed the frank statement of one kind of allegiance, but other statements, other allegiances render and blend "affection" into something complexly hued beyond dualities. What happened at Actium denied any neatly distributed, defined, and scaled hierarchies of value in Antony. For there, fighting not simply against something, but for something—for his relationship with Cleopatra—and with everything to gain from victory, he nevertheless allowed himself to lose.

And having lost, why could he not have been content with Cleopatra, the world well lost for love? Indeed, his passion, his anger, his regrets force us to seek Antony somewhere within the complex of these contradictions, beyond the pale of Enobarbus's adages. Our quest begins at Actium in these Antonian writhings.

> Hark, the land bids me tread no more
> upon't,
> It is asham'd to bear me.
>
> (3.11.1-2)

And, to Cleopatra here.

> O, whither has thou led me, Egypt? See
> How I convey my shame out of thine eyes
> By looking back what I have left behind
> 'Stroy'd in dishonor.
>
> (3.11.51-54)

There is much in this play of Antony and shame. Very early on, Caesar talks about it. Antony's "shames" should from luxurious Egypt "quickly drive him to Rome." But in this case Antony is not so affected. Free from a sense of guilt despite the spate of moralisms which have surrounded him (and us) since the play began, Antony in Rome responds to the Caesarean lecture as if he came from another planet. Antony, we gather, cannot be held responsible for the activities of relatives or of wives fomenting civil wars. Nor, for that matter, can he be expected to inconvenience himself for messengers who come too early in the morning from Caesar, especially when one might have a hangover. Caesar urges that Antony broke his oath— but Antony will not stand for this either.

> as nearly as I may,
> I'll play the penitent to you; but mine
> honesty
> Shall not make poor my greatness, nor my
> power
> Work without it.
>
> (2.2.91-94)

And it is presumably with the same aplomb that Antony will later alternate infidelities. Barely speaking four lines, he will agree to marry Caesar's sister to establish stronger political ties with him. Barely speaking two lines, he will desert Octavia for Egypt, and for war with Caesar, whom he sought to reassure by marrying Octavia in the first place.

No, Antony is not ashamed to have been truant— in fact, so little is he affected on this Roman score that one wonders why he left Egypt at all. For indeed the play began with this awakening. But the drama began too by making it clear that Antony departs from the East for reasons which do not wholly embrace ideas of Roman imperium. Otherwise, why, on his way to Rome, did he send back a pearl to Cleopatra with the message that he would "piece her opulent throne with kingdoms?"

When it comes to shame, Antony will know his own personal cue.

> Since Cleopatra died
> I have liv'd in such dishonor that the gods
> Detest my baseness. I, that with my sword
> Quarter'd the world, and o'er green Neptune's
> back
> With ships made cities, condemn myself to
> lack
> The courage of a woman— less noble mind
> Than she which by her death our Caesar tells,
> "I am conqueror of myself."
>
> (4.14.55-62)

Honor and nobility— to Antony these mean one thing: bravery, physical courage. As when Eros, having put a sword through himself before his master did, elicits this:

> Thrice-nobler than myself!
> Thou teachest me, O valiant Eros, what
> I should, and thou couldst not. My queen
> and Eros
> Have by their brave instruction got upon me
> A nobleness in record.
>
> (4.14.95-99)

In the wreckage of Actium, that central point in tragedy, this, for Antony is the only, the real, issue. For the very notion of seeming to flee, of seeming to act the coward by following Cleopatra's retiring ship arouses in Antony a sense of self-destroying more profound than he ever experienced leaving Rome for revels in Egypt. At Actium, one has "instructed cowards" and thus one has left oneself. He has lost his way forever and he is most profoundly ashamed. "I follow'd that I blush to look upon." "For indeed," as he dismisses his friends, "I have lost command." Yet, in our sense, how could he have been a coward? He followed Cleopatra's ship when she herself fled. True. That following broke up the order of the fleet and of course brought disaster is true too. So Antony worried about the queen and became a tactical imbecile. Yet he thinks "*coward*," not "imbecile."

Contrast this with a future mood, the élan of the second, strategically futile battle before Alexandria. "You that will fight," he calls to his soldiers, "follow me close. I'll bring you to't." And from this fight— the only one we ever see him win— we watch him come and note his high celebration. But not as a general— he has won nothing. As a successful gladiator.

> Through Alexandria make a jolly march,
> Bear our hack'd targets like the men that owe
> them.
>
> (4.8.30-31)

Act III, scene xi. Alexandria, Cleopatra's palace. Antony, Cleopatra, Eros, Charmian, and Iras. Painted by Henry Tresham. The University of Michigan Special Collections Library.

Euphoria overwhelms as he paints his magnificent hyperbole.

> Had our great palace the capacity
> To camp this host, we all would sup to-
>   gether,
> And drink carouses to the next day's fate,
> Which promises royal peril. Trumpeters,
> With brazen din blast you the city's ear,
> Make mingle with our rattling tamborines
> That heaven and earth may strike their
>   sounds together,
> Applauding our approach.   *Exeunt.*
>   (4.8.32-39)

This is a tragedy about love, as critics all must tell us, but love is not a single, simple thing. In the dawn before his battle, when Antony meets a soldier armed and ready, he says:

> Thou look'st like him that knows a warlike
>   charge.
> To business that we love, we rise betime,
> And go to't with delight.
>   (4.4.19-21)

Antony, as his queen noted, is up early himself. Strange then that Actium should be such a terrible failure.

But what is not so strange by these lights is how the play itself begins; this soldier sense in Antony makes his "awakening" clear. Our earliest cue for him in this play has always seemed to be Cleopatra's when she tells us that Antony was inclined to mirth, but now "a Roman thought hath struck him." Yet the only "Roman" thoughts available up to now have been the opening remarks of those two shadowy figures, Demetrius and Philo. (But if these two had actually hailed each other by name, they would have struck their seventeenth-century auditors not as Roman, but as Greek.) It is they who tell us, anyhow, that Antony, the once-great leader, has now become "the bellows and the fan to cool a gypsy's lust." Sometimes, too, we gather, "when he is not Antony, he comes too short of that great property which still should go with Antony."

Thus emerges the first Antonian "self" molded from the sensitivities of Roman (?) soldiers (?). But when Antony himself comes to prove Cleopatra's accuracy about Roman thoughts— to show some second "self"— he has not become a Roman. Hearing that Labienus and his Parthian forces are on the move against him, Antony urges his faltering messenger:

> Speak to me home, mince not the general
>   tongue;
> Name Cleopatra as she is call'd in Rome.
> Rail thou in Fulvia's phrase, and taunt my
>   faults
> With such full license as both truth and malice
> Have power to utter. O then we bring forth weeds
> When our quick winds lie still, and our ills
>   told us
> Is as our earing.
>
>   (1.2.105-11)

"These strong Egyptian fetters I must break," he mutters, "or lose myself in dotage." Perhaps there is here some Roman "shame," but it is an oddly aphoristic and mannered guilt, contrasting with the passions to come at Actium. Here all this weed-growing seems small stimulus.

The news of his wife's death prompts proper regret and muted encomium— "there's a great spirit gone"— and even some properly moral words about Cleopatra:

> I must from this enchanting queen break off;
> Ten thousand harms, more than the ills I
>   know,
> My idleness doth hatch.
>
>   (1.2.128-30)

But, as the messengers succeed one another to inundate him with news to which he now responds— if not attends— it becomes quite clear that government affairs are not the issue. The challenge is Pompey.

Antony speaks to Enobarbus about him at length, and then to Cleopatra too. Caesar also speaks of Pompey, far away in Rome, but when Caesar talks about him and the danger he poses, the Roman leader tends to comment in Tudor words appropriate to Shakespeare's *Henry IV*: giddy rebelling Roman multitudes surging behind some Roman Jack Cade. Antony dutifully moves in the fringes of these ideas too, but the thrust of his meaning is elsewhere.

>   Sextus Pompeius
> [Hath] given the dare to Caesar, and com-
>   mands
> The empire of the sea. Our slippery people,
> Whose love is never link'd to the deserver

> Till his deserts are past, begin to throw
> Pompey the Great and all his dignities
> Upon his son, who, high in name and
>   power,
> Higher than both in blood and life, stands
>   up
> For the main soldier.
>
>   (1.2.183-91)

This is the concept that engages Antony. Some one else is acting the "main soldier." And Antony describes Sextus to Cleopatra— he speaks to her about him too— as "the condemn'd Pompey, rich in his father's honor." The "main soldier" is merely riding on the military reputation of Pompeius Magnus whom the tribunes lamented at the beginning of *Julius Caesar*.

In Rome, Antony turns to the subject with Caesar. His words here are not the quintessence of *realpolitik*. They are almost chivalric, redolent of tournament.

> I did not think to draw my sword 'gainst
>   Pompey,
> For he hath laid strange courtesies and great
> Of late upon me. I must thank him only,
> Lest my remembrance suffer ill report;
> At heel of that, defy him.
>
>   (2.2.153-57)

The news, however, is bad.

> *Ant.* What is his strength by land?
> *Caes.* Great and increasing; but by sea
>   He is an absolute master.
> *Ant.*   So is the fame.
>   Would we had spoke together!
>
>   (2.2.161-64)

"Speaking together" means "joining battle."

The triumvirate meet with Pompey, who begins the proceedings with a passionate speech of defiance. Caesar responds in his usual matter-of-fact, take-it-or-leave-it tone. What we hear from Antony is something else.

> Thou cans't not fear us, Pompey, with thy
>   sails;
> We'll speak with thee at sea. At land, thou
>   know'st
> How much we do o'er-count thee.
>
>   (2.6.24-26)

Caesar has already mentioned the hopelessness of trying to match the pirate-leader on the water, but Antony must, it seems, respond. And if there is more emotion than reason in Antony here, it produces that cautious compliment of a later exchange. Pompey (significantly) shakes hands with Antony before he does with the others, saying

                    Let me have your
hand.
     I did not think, sir, to have met you
here.
Ant. The beds i'th'East are soft, and thanks
     to you,
     That call'd me timelier than my purpose
hither;
For I have gain'd by't.

                              (2.6.48-52)

We must attend this Antony, for although it is not all
of him, it is part of his sense of himself, and that is all
of him. "O love," he says to Cleopatra before that
victorious, futile battle toward the end of the tragedy.

     That thou couldst see my wars to-day, and
          knew'st
     The royal occupation, thou shouldst see
     A workman in't.

                              (4.4.15-18)

"I'll leave thee now like a man of steel." And even
after the final disaster his language figures forth his
vision of the warrior supreme. "Bruis'd pieces go, you
have been nobly borne." Later, in rage, this supremacy
is of almost Herculean transcendence.

          Teach me,
     Alcides, thou mine ancestor, thy rage.
     Let me lodge Lichas on the horns o'th'moon,
     And with those hands, that grasp'd the
          heaviest club,
     Subdue my worthiest self.

                              (4.12.43-47)

Antony's private feeling of self lives away from all
those judging notions of his duties which others of the
play are always so ready to envisage for him. From
these judges we hear many versions of what Antony
"is" and what he should be—from Pompey, Lepidus,
Enobarbus, Caesar, and Cleopatra—but it is interesting
that, in the end, not one of these judging or supposedly
knowing characters can avoid being surprised, startled,
or disappointed. For in Antony's world, honor, baseness, duty, nobility achieve their definition not in conventional terms, but, perhaps, in a context illuminated
by Antony's own metaphor when he breaks in upon the
tearful farewell between his bride, Octavia, and her
brother to whom she clings for a moment. Antony
takes Caesar's hand in farewell.

          Come, sir, come,
     I'll wrastle with you in my strength of love.
     Look, here I have you, thus I let you go,
     And give you to the gods.

                              (3.2.61-64)

The wrestling is figurative, but Antony is the victor.

The moment, light and fleeting enough to die under the
hand of analysis, tells in the silent language of drama
of one of Antony's worlds, more real than Egypt or
Rome.

                              II

If Antony were wedded to physical courage—to some
naïve concept of "manliness"—he would have anticipated the Hemingway ideal by three hundred or so
years. But Shakespeare endowed his tragic hero more
complexly, beyond the dimensions of Ajax, whose solution to most problems, in *Troilus and Cressida,* was
"pashing" some one. Antony seems related to a general
pattern of behavior in what Shakespeare's contemporaries would have termed "pleasure," that conglomera-
tion of yearnings for sensual stimuli of all kinds, as well
as an attraction to physically induced and totally enjoyed euphoria to which the dramatist Thomas Lodge
and his contemporaries interestingly gave the name of
"sloth." Such moral terms need not overconcern us—
they concern Caesar and his fellow Romans too much
already, ever anxious as they all are to wrap up the
hero squirming into the amber of a morality drama in
which he can forever play sinner to Caesar's redeemed
man. But we must all the same—and without Caesar's
eager help—take note of Antony's propensities.

There is, for example, love—not a simple thing in Mark
Antony's universe.

     Now for the love of Love, and her soft
          hours,
     Let's not confound the time with conference
          harsh;
     There's not a minute of our lives should stretch
     Without some pleasure now. What sport to-
          night?

                              (1.1.44-47)

Here is Antony, the much-discussed voluptuary, fond
of physical beauty. At Cleopatra's first banquet he "for
his ordinary pays his heart for what his eyes eat only,"
as Enobarbus put it. And even to Octavia, Antony is
not totally indifferent. These are his words about his
new wife as she talks weepingly to her brother, Caesar,
the hero making his remarks beyond their hearing:

     Her tongue will not obey her heart, nor can
     Her heart inform her tongue—the swan's
          down feather,
     That stands upon the swell at the full of tide,
     And neither way inclines.

                              (3.2.47-50)

Enobarbus speaks of "our courteous Antony whom
ne'er the word of 'No' woman heard speak" and it is
obvious that women indeed do something for Antony.
It is as if they help his imagination. When he prepares

for the Battle of Actium he takes Cleopatra with him, much to Enobarbus's consternation as he argues this out with the queen. But "we'll to our ship," Antony announces in grand exit with the Egyptian queen:

Away, my Thetis!

This was the sea-nymph of the silver feet who danced on the dark waves with her sisters in the moonlight before the secret and astounded eyes of Peleus who bravely entwined with her Protean and savage forms to win her and engender in her Achilles.

But let us not rush to implicate Cleopatra as the only begetter of Antony's sensualities and thus to make his woes a tale of her fashioning. It is important that we allow the queen to stand apart. Voluptuousness is Antony's own leaning, as is emphasized by the Roman banquet which presents the only revels we observe in the drama. This celebration is a triumvirate affair and Caesar predictably complains of unseemly levity and of washing the brain with wine, which makes it dirtier. But it is our Antony who urges things on. "Be a child o'th'time," he tells Caesar, and Antony and Pompey, their host, respond with alacrity as Enobarbus celebrates:

> Ha, my brave emperor!
> Shall we dance now the Egyptian bacchanals
> And celebrate our drink?
> *Pom.*   Let's ha't, good
> soldier.
> *Ant.* Come, let's all take hands,
>   Till that the conquering wine hath
> steep'd our sense
>   In soft and delicate Lethe.
>
> (2.7.103-8)

So they dance, and shout the refrain: "Cup us till the world go round!" If we search for Cleopatra in this entertainment, we will find that she is far away, in Egypt. For we are now in Italy.

Where Shakespeare makes Antony especially interesting is in the fact that the hero is proud of this voluptuary mode in himself. In truth, the pleasures of the flesh and of combat and of the idea of women are his personal way to a sense of exaltation which he sees as the gates to a kind of transcendence. The ambition of his soul achieves its natural mode of expression in these domains. To be preeminent in existence is the core of ambition, and if "existence" resides especially in life's physical feelings and beauties, then preeminence must be there too— somehow.

Thus self-admiration is everywhere in his physical life. The queen quotes him.

> When you sued staying,
> Then was the time for words; no going then;

Eternity was in our lips and eyes,
Bliss in our brows' bent; none our parts so
  poor
But was a race of heaven.

(1.3.33-37)

It is a state that can even extend beyond death.

> Where souls do couch on flowers, we'll hand
>   in hand,
> And with our sprightly port make the ghosts
>   gaze.
> Dido and her Aeneas shall want troops,
> And all the haunt be ours.
>
> (4.14.51-54)

So Antony's opening statement is wholly appropriate to him.

> Let Rome in Tiber melt, and the wide arch
> Of the rang'd empire fall! Here is my space,
> Kingdoms are clay; our dungy earth alike
> Feeds beast as man; the nobleness of life
> Is to do thus . . . when such a mutual pair
> And such a twain can do't, in which I bind,
> [On] pain of punishment, the world to weet
> We stand up peerless.
>
> (1.1.33-40)

So, what of it? To love these things and to think this way— to live with feasting, battle, women— is not necessarily to court disaster. Indeed, Philo speaks of a "great property" in Antony. Pompey says of the hero's soldiership that it is indeed "twice the other twain." Antony is not deluding himself about his military reputation. For these opinions about him are reinforced further with the words of Eros. In Plutarch's *Life of Antonius*, Shakespeare's primary source for events in this play, Antonius lost badly to the Parthians, but in Shakespeare, when Eros refuses to help Antony kill himself, he mitigates this Parthian disaster:

> Shall I do that which all the Parthian darts,
> Though enemy, lost aim and could not?
>
> (4.14.70-71)

Antony's soldiership also receives the praise of the scarred soldier, Scarus, after the land-battle at Alexandria, when he corroborates Agrippa's surprise at the military reversal of Caesarian momentum.

> Oh my brave Emperor, this is fought indeed!
> Had we done so at first, we had droven
>   them home
> With clouts about their heads.
>
> (4.7.4-6)

Yet there is an irony in Scarus's words, just as it lurks in Caesar's magnificent description of that Antony to whom even he must yield respect.

> When thou once
> Was beaten from Modena, where thou slew'st
> Hirtius and Pansa, consuls, at thy heel
> Did famine follow, whom thou fought'st
>   against
> (Though daintily brought up) with patience
>   more
> Than savages could suffer. Thou didst drink
> The stale of horses and the gilded puddle
> Which beasts would cough at; thy palate then
>   did deign
> The roughest berry on the rudest hedge;
> Yea, like the stag, when snow the pasture
>   sheets,
> The barks of trees thou brows'd. On the
>   Alps
> It is reported thou didst eat strange flesh,
> Which some did die to look on; and all this
>
>   . . . . .
>
> Was borne so like a soldier, that thy cheek
> So much as lank'd not.
>
>   (1.4.56-71)

For despite all this, there are the facts. Antony lost at Modena, he lost in Parthia, he loses at Actium, and he will lose the last battle. When he triumphs in the fighting celebrated by Scarus, Antony gains little but the desertions which collapse the last battle around him. And when there is a victory in Parthia, it is won by Antony's general, Ventidius, who tells his lieutenant that

> Caesar and Antony have ever won
> More in their officer than person.
>
>   (3.1.16-17)

For Caesar this is not important— he has no personal military aspirations. For Antony, it is crucial. Is it true?

"Now Antonius was made so subject to a woman's will that though he was a great deal stronger by land, yet for Cleopatra's sake, he would needs have this battle tried by sea," writes Plutarch. Cleopatra again emerges as the destructive *femme fatale*. But in one of the most significant deviations from this source in the whole play, the line Shakespeare adopts is not this at all. The hero speaks to his general Canidius.

> *Ant.* Canidius, we
>   Will fight with him by sea.
> *Cleo.* By sea, what else?
> *Can.* Why will my lord do so?
> *Ant.* For that he dares us to't.
> *Enob.* So hath my lord dar'd him to single
>   fight.
> *Can.* Ay, and to wage this battle at Pharsalia,
>   Where Caesar fought with Pompey. But

> these offers,
>   Which serve not for his vantage, he
> shakes off,
>   And so should you.
>
>   (3.7.27-34)

It is of the utmost importance to note that Shakespeare's version of why Antony chose a naval battle has little to do with what Cleopatra does or does not want, no matter how much her subsequent flight may obscure this. The point is even reemphasized by the scene before the final battle wherein Caesar, having lost the land-battle at Alexandria, apparently has less concern for his own "honor."

> *Ant.* Their preparation is to-day by sea,
>   We please them not by land.
> *Scar.* For both, my lord.
> *Ant.* I would they'ld fight i'th'fire or i'th'air;
>   We'ld fight there too. But this it is: our
>   foot
>   Upon the hills adjoining to the city
>   Shall stay with us— order for sea is given,
>   They have put forth the haven.
>
>   (4.10.1-7)

Again this is not Plutarch; this is Shakespeare's Antony and his response to what he sees as a "dare."

It is not possible to restrain Antony in these things, any more than it is possible for the soothsayer to reveal the unpleasant fact of Caesar's dominance. "Speak this no more." Antony always rejects the idea that his subjectivity may not be all-sufficient, and this adamantine streak in his geniality is always there. Ventidius was afraid to follow up his victory against the Parthians.

> I could do more to do Antonius good,
> But, 'twould offend him; and in his offense
> Should my performance perish.
>
>   (3.1.25-27)

This is what must be done to avoid irritating Antony:

> I'll humbly signify what in his name,
> That magical word of war, we have effected;
> How with his banners, and his well-paid ranks,
> The ne'er-yet-beaten horse of Parthia
> We have jaded out o'th' field.
>
>   (3.1.30-34)

Before Actium, in his effort to persuade Antony to avoid that sea-battle, Enobarbus alters his own characteristically blunt way of speaking to adopt the same "magical-word-of-war" line. "By sea, by sea," Antony persists, and Enobarbus:

> Most worthy sir, you therein throw away
> The absolute soldiership you have by land,
> Distract your army, which doth most consist

Of war-mark'd footmen, leave unexecuted
Your own renowned knowledge.

(3.7.41-45)

The fact, however, is that Shakespeare's Mark Antony tends to view military problems with the moods of a swordsman rather than with the detachment of a general. And though his performance in the battle line itself is always formidable, in concepts of strategy his predispositions render him indifferent or inept. Before Actium, speaking of Caesar's deployment, he sounds naïve.

> Is it not strange, Canidius,
> That from Tarentum and Brundusium
> He could so quickly cut the Ionian Sea,
> And take in Toryne?

(3.7.20-23)

More news of Caesar. He has indeed taken Toryne.

> Can he be there in person? 'Tis impossible
> Strange that his power should be.

(3.7.56-57)

In all justice, Canidius, and the other soldiers too, share this wonder.

> *Can.* This speed of Caesar's
>   Carries beyond belief.
> *Sold.* While he was yet in Rome,
>   His power went out in such distractions
> as
>   Beguil'd all spies.

(3.7.74-77)

This justifies Antony's own amazement, but it does impose certain important limitations on Pompey's dictum about Antony's soldiership as "twice the other twain." Apparently, one of the "other twain" is an astounding master of the art of troop movement. Whether this counts for "soldiership" depends on the viewpoint, but it is clear that for Antony such matters do not induce the boredom of familiarity.

There are debates on the strategic issues before the battle of Actium. Shakespeare allows Enobarbus to expand on details which have little actual relevance to the battle we experience— we will only need to be told that the hero followed Cleopatra's flight. But Enobarbus's "details" are important for us simply because Shakespeare shows Antony ignoring them. Why should Antony not fight at sea? Well, Enobarbus says,

> Your ships are not well mann'd,
> Your mariners are [muleters], reapers, people
> Ingross'd by swift impress. In Caesar's fleet
> Are those that often have 'gainst Pompey
>   fought;
> Their ships are yare, yours heavy. No disgrace

> Shall fall you for refusing him at sea,
> Being prepar'd for land.

(3.7.34-40)

It would, in one way, be a relief if Cleopatra were at the bottom of all this, for then we could simply say that Antony acts as a man infatuated. But she is only agreeing with Antony and he, reacting to Caesar's dare, ignores all else, even though the soldier Scarus, showing his wounds, hints at the mood of an infantry nervous at the prospect of fighting on unstable ships against a fleet of experienced pirates. But Antony only remarks "Well, well. Away," and exits.

Antony's attitudes and needs are continually at odds with the reality he must comprehend to survive a war, and the time after Actium emphasizes this. Muttering to himself in his shame, reminiscing about Philippi, he says of Caesar that

> he alone
> Dealt on lieutenantry, and no practice had
> In the brave squares of war; yet now— No
>   matter.

(3.11.38-40)

Sharing with Iago that contempt for the theoreticians, for those who delegate authority, who ignore prowess as the crucial stuff of war, Antony's remark is no casual one, penned by Shakespeare unthinkingly. The motif has been developed through the play until its eloquent articulation in Antony's response, after Actium, to the messenger from Caesar. Caesar sends a refusal to grant Antony's highly interesting request to be allowed to live "a private man in Athens." "To him again!" says Antony.

> Tell him he wears the
>   rose
> Of youth upon him; from which the world
>   should note
> Something particular. His coin, ships, legions,
> May be a coward's, whose ministers would
>   prevail
> Under the service of a child as soon
> As i'th'command of Caesar. I dare him
>   therefore
> To lay his gay comparisons apart,
> And answer me declin'd, sword against
>   sword,
> Ourselves alone. I'll write it. Follow me.

(3.13.20-28).

"Coward," "child," "dare." The whole complicated mechanism of war which under Caesar's guidance has swept over Antony at such a speed as even to astound the generals is, here, relegated to the realm of the superficial. Toy baubles fit for a child, these forces are unreal, cloudlike wisps which trivially obscure that ultimate and profound moment, the determination of manhood: "sword against sword, ourselves alone."

It is not strange that Antony should look at war like this, for he cannot even look at life in any other way. This would be to deny himself. And often when he cannot deny himself, he harms himself the most. It is true that military daring can be decisive too, no matter the dictates of theory, and it is true that Antony was holding his own quite well at Actium before Cleopatra's flight—vantage like "a pair of twins" appeared. But Antony cannot put daring into a larger perspective. For in defeat, he responds with rage and rationalization. It is as if victory were not determined by victory, but by bravery. Perhaps Caesar "cheated" but he won and the answer he sends Antony's duel-challenge points the difference between them. For this answer precipitates a moment of stunning naïveté as Antony tries to comprehend a challenge that, unlike Sossius's generalship in Africa, the hero has no power to waive from existence.

> *Ant.* He will not fight with me, Domitius?
> *Eno.*   No.
> *Ant.* Why should he not?
>
> (4.2.1-2)

"Antonius being thus inclined," runs Shakespeare's source, "the last and extremest mischief of all other (to wit, the love of Cleopatra) lighted on him." Although Plutarch's slant is misleading for the play, his attribution of the love affair to other than strictly sexual penchants in Antony is suggestive. For in Shakespeare's play, Antony's relationship with Cleopatra simply reinforces and illustrates elements that we see in his personality when romance is not his immediate concern.

>   As for my wife,
> I would you had her spirit in such another;
> The third o' th'world is yours, which with a
>   snaffle
> You may pace easy, but not such a wife.
>
> (2.2.61-64)

"There's a great spirit gone," he said at the beginning of the play when he heard of her death, and it is clear—especially by contrast with his attitude toward the meek Octavia—that Antony admires Fulvia for the kind of qualities he finds in himself. Cleopatra has caught this to use it for her own purpose. She not only flatters Antony's self-portrait but replicates it when accusing him of infidelity early in the play. She recalls to him his words in this manner:

>   none our parts so
>   poor
>   But was a race of heaven. They are so still,
>   Or thou, the greatest soldier of the
>   world,

> Art turn'd the greatest liar.
> *Ant.* How now, lady?
> *Clea.* I would I had thy inches, thou shouldst
>   know
>   There were a heart in Egypt.
>
> (1.3.36-41)

She plays the "great spirit," acts masculine. She gives the astonished Antony the lie and wishes she were big enough to back up her insult (or big enough to compete with him in other suggestive ways).

And Antony does admire Cleopatra as a mirror of himself. When she taunts his surprise before Actium at Caesar's speed of maneuver, he is happy to be impressed.

>   A good rebuke,
> Which might have well becom'd the best of
>   men,
> To taunt at slackness.
>
> (3.7.25-27)

But she is something more than mirror. This is clear enough early in the play as he leaves Egypt. He says to her:

> Quarrel no more, but be prepar'd to know
> The purposes I bear; which are, or cease,
> As you shall give th'advice. By the fire
> That quickens Nilus' slime, I go from hence
> Thy soldier, servant, making peace or war
> As thou affects.
>
> (1.3.66-71)

This when leaving for Rome.

But perhaps what we see is merely his indifference to politics. War is what he treasures to himself. What then are we to make of an episode the queen relates to Charmian?

>   next morn,
> Ere the ninth hour, I drunk him to his bed;
> Then put my tires and mantles on him, whilst
> I wore his sword Philippan.
>
> (2.5.20-23)

What principles in Antony's life are most important? He leaves her, and Egypt, marries Octavia, yet he follows her in flight at Actium. And though Antony forgives Cleopatra after Actium when he considers himself unmanned, he will be ready to kill her when he thinks she has betrayed him. How does she fit in?

There is Antony's answer to her after Actium when she says she hadn't thought he would follow after her fleeing ship.

>   You did know

How much you were my conqueror, and that
My sword, made weak by my affection, would
Obey it on all cause.

(3.11.65-68)

It is Enobarbus's use of "affection." But if Antony here wishes to blame Cleopatra by constructing an allegory that reminds us of the revels described earlier by Cleopatra, what he said a moment before was naked of moral attitudinizing.

O'er my spirit
[Thy] full supremacy thou knew'st, and that
Thy beck might from the bidding of the gods
Command me.

(3.11.58-61)

This is not totally true. There are other tugs at him, else Antony would not be so disconsolate now. But he seems to be saying that she is almost as important to him as his soldier "self." As he leaves Egypt, the psychology of interchange, despite its manifest Platonism, is complex.

Let us go. Come;
Our separation so abides and flies,
That thou residing here, goes yet with me;
And I hence fleeting, here remain with thee.
Away!

(1.3.101-5)

It is as if in some important way, Cleopatra actually expressed the soldier principle for Antony. For if he were merely "her soldier" as protector, he would not necessarily react as he does when he hears of her death. At that time we see an impressive piece of behavior, accompanied by appropriate imagery and activity emphatically visible to the audience. Brooding about the betrayal of his fleet, he speaks dispiritedly and despairingly. But when he hears the queen is dead, he immediately begins to take off his armor.

All length is torture; since the torch is out,
Lie down and stray no farther. Now all
labour
Mars what it does; yea, very force entangles
Itself with strength.

(4.14.46-49)

Strength has lost its meaning, as if the queen had, in Antony's life, been the ideal in terms of which his existence was to be organized. A force usually exerted by a philosophy, a creed, or a god—this was the "grave charm"

Whose eye beck'd forth my wars and call'd
them home,
Whose bosom was my crownet, my chief end.

(4.12.26-27)

This is something more than drunken companionship

with the fleshpots of Egypt. At the same time, ideals are not essentially products of altruism. They tend to be defined in accordance with those traits loved in the self, and if Antony holds Cleopatra more important than politics, it is not only understandable but inevitable. "The nobleness of life is to do thus, when such a mutual pair and such a twain can do't," and "nobleness" is defined as that which Antony thinks good. He sees himself preeminently suited to enact this end, and Cleopatra is part of the enactment.

What would happen then, if the queen flouted this great Idea (whatever it is)? We see when she lets Caesar's messenger, Thidias, kiss her hand. Antony, on fire, rages:

what's her name,
Since she was Cleopatra?

Cleopatra is not "herself" anymore if she does not share Antony's opinion of the grandeur isolating him, with her, from the rest of the world. So instead of being grief-stricken and faithfully continuing to love Cleopatra as if he were her slave, Antony thrusts her from the crucial circle of his self-esteem into the "Roman" context, the Caesarean mode.

You were half blasted ere I knew you;
Ha?
Have I my pillow left unpress'd in
Rome,
Forborne the getting of a lawful race,
And by a gem of women, to be abus'd
By one that looks on feeders?
Cleo.   Good my Lord—
Ant. You have been a boggler ever,
But when we in our viciousness grow
hard
(O misery on't!), the wise gods seel our
eyes,
In our own filth drop our clear judg-
ments, make us
Adore our errors, laugh at's while we
strut
To our confusion.
Cleo.   O, is't come to this?
Ant. I found you as a morsel, cold upon
Dead Caesar's trencher, nay, you were a
fragment
Of Cneius Pompey's— besides what
hotter hours,
Unregist'red in vulgar fame, you have
Luxuriously pick'd out; for I am sure,
Though you can guess what temperance
should be,
You know not what it is.

(3.13.105-22)

We need not see this speech as any kind of orthodox repentance of the error of his ways: Antony, by "temperance," simply means that Cleopatra should only be intemperate with him. His true attitude emerges from another figure.

> Alack, our terrene
>   moon
> Is now eclips'd, and it portends alone
> The fall of Antony!
>
>   (3.13.153-55)

Cleopatra seems to be the "objective correlative" of his own being when she acts appropriately. But when she does not enhance his self-esteem she is no longer "himself." And when this living symbol of his own identity, as he sees it, is gone, what is to become of him? She is his conception of himself made flesh.

CLEOPATRA

There is much critical debate about the true nature of Shakespeare's Cleopatra. **Maurice Charney** calls her "the most puzzling figure in *Antony and Cleopatra*" and examines the ways in which other characters view her. Charney notes that Enobarbus refers to Cleopatra as no longer young even as he asserts that she is fascinating to men. Charney quotes Cleopatra's own instructions to her maid Charmian concerning Antony as an example of her "infinite variety": If you find him sad, / Say I am dancing; if in mirth, report / That I am sudden sick." Ultimately, Charney suggests that Cleopatra is a proud figure desiring both admiration and sympathy.

Richard C. Harrier describes her as the embodiment of Egypt, possessing "vitality and change, the fecund earth, the Nile's slime and ooze, and the inconstant moon-sea spirit." Harrier holds the more traditional view of Cleopatra as a negative force— arguing that her "selfish and capricious domination of Antony" ruins him. **L. J. Mills** and Austin Wright also regard Cleopatra from a negative perspective. Mills considers her manipulative, self-absorbed, and possibly treacherous. Austin Wright's views reflect the 1950s during which he wrote. He criticizes Cleopatra for her failure to be supportive of Antony during his time of trouble; he also condemns her lack of virtue and modesty and calls her opportunistic, lubricious, and common. At the same time, Wright concludes that Cleopatra is irresistible to men.

L. T. Fitz and Ruth Nevo provide more sympathetic portraits of Cleopatra. After asserting that the Egyptian queen is complex enough to elicit a variety of interpretations, Nevo suggests that Cleopatra behaves unpredictably toward Antony because she is afraid of losing him to Rome; to his first wife, Fulvia; and later to Octavia. Fitz argues that the misogynistic views of critics, and not Shakespeare's characterization, are the source of negative attitudes toward Cleopatra. Both Fitz and J.

Leeds Barroll remark that there are two traditional and opposing interpretations of Cleopatra: first, that she is a treacherous harlot; or second, that her love for Antony "transcends" all boundaries. Fitz also asserts that male critics are particularly virulent in their dislike of Cleopatra and that they find her behavior in the play incomprehensible. Fitz contends that Cleopatra's actions are no more confusing than those of an equally complex Shakespearean character such as Hamlet, and that in order to judge her fairly, scholars must dispense with their "sexist bias."

Another question that concerns critics is whether or not Cleopatra functions as a tragic figure. Robert E. Fitch calls Cleopatra a character who "does not touch our affections" because her love for Antony is "devious" and without "courage or honor or faith." Thus, he concludes that she does not qualify for tragic status. By contrast, L. J. Mills, J. Leeds Barroll, and Richard C. Harrier suggest that Cleopatra does achieve a tragic dimension to a greater or lesser degree. Mills asserts that Cleopatra is tragic simply because in the end she lacks the time or sensitivity to attain the self-awareness usually attributed to tragedy. Harrier argues that Cleopatra achieves tragic status when she chooses to follow Antony's example and end her life in suicide as a Roman would do. Barroll assert that Cleopatra's death is as tragic as King Lear's— both, he contends, die with the knowledge that they have been "destructive" to themselves and to someone they love. For additional commentary on the character of Cleopatra, see the excerpt by Walter Cohen in the **OVERVIEW** section, the excerpts by David Daiches and Katherine Vance MacMullan in the **LANGUAGE AND IMAGERY** section, the excerpts by Janet Adelman and Peter Berek in the **DUALISM** section, the excerpt by Larry S. Champion in the **ROME VERSUS EGYPT** section, the excerpts by J. Leeds Barroll and John W. Draper in the section on **ANTONY**, and the excerpt by Gordon Ross Smith in the section on Octavius.

L. J. Mills

SOURCE: "Cleopatra's Tragedy," in *Shakespeare Quarterly*, Vol. XI, No. 2, Spring, 1960, pp. 147-62.

[Mills argues against critics who regard Antony as the play's tragic figure to the exclusion of Cleopatra. Mills points out that after Antony's death, there is still one more entire act left in the play— with Cleopatra alive and the action unresolved. Mills then defines what makes Cleopatra tragic: she is a self-centered, "self-pitying," and manipulative character who is unable to admit her love for Antony or to recognize his worth or his love for her until it is too late.]

Interpretations of Shakespeare's *Antony and Cleopatra* have emphasized, with varying degrees of stress, one or another of the three principal themes in the play, which are, as summarized by John Munro [in *The London Shakespeare*]:

> . . . first, the East represented by Egypt and lands beyond versus the West represented by Rome; secondly, the strife in the Triumvirate who divided and governed the world, and the reduction of the three, Octavius, Lepidus and Antony, to one, Octavius; and thirdly, the love and tragedy of Antony and Cleopatra. Of all these the last is dramatically dominant.

But among the commentators who regard the third theme as dominant there is much difference of opinion. Some write as if the play were entitled "The Tragedy of Antony"; for example, J. Middleton Murry [in *Shakespeare*]:

> . . . up to the death of Antony it is from him that the life of the play has been derived. She [Cleopatra] is what she is to the imagination, rather in virtue of the effects we see in Antony, than by virtue of herself. He is magnificent; therefore she must be. But when he dies, her poetic function is to maintain and prolong, to reflect and reverberate, that achieved royalty of Antony's.

Others give Cleopatra more significance but yet make Antony central, as does Peter Alexander, who allots to Cleopatra a somewhat more distinct, more nearly self-contained personality than does Murry [in *Shakespeare's Life and Art*]:

> Antony dies while the play has still an act to run, but without this act his story would be incomplete. For Cleopatra has to vindicate her right to his devotion.

Any interpreter, however, who concentrates on the tragedy of Antony is confronted with the difficulty pointed out by Robert Speaight [in *Nature in Shakespearian Tragedy*]:

> . . . if you are thinking in terms of Antony's tragedy alone, and if you are trying to make his tragedy conform to a classical definition, then you may find it awkward to face a fifth act, in which only his heroic and fallen shadow is left to keep Cleopatra company.

Moreover, such an interpreter overlooks the title of the play as it appears in the Folio: "The Tragedie of Anthonie, and Cleopatra", with the significant comma after "Anthonie." The nature of the play *Antony and Cleopatra*, really in itself more than from the comma signal but given added emphasis by it, should be self-evident: the play presents the tragedy of Antony and then the tragedy of Cleopatra. Such recognition, however, does not obscure the fact that each tragedy gives significance to the other and increases its effect.

Judicially objective critics have granted Cleopatra more stature as a tragic figure in her own right than those who think of the play as Antony's tragedy. [In *Approach to Shakespeare*] J. W. Mackail, for instance, though he does not point out that Cleopatra's tragedy differs from Antony's, says:

> It is the tragedy not of the Roman world, but of Antony and Cleopatra: and of both of them equally. . . . Here, neither single name gives the central tone to the drama; Antony does not exist for the sake of Cleopatra (as one might put it), nor does Cleopatra exist for the sake of Antony: they are two immense and in a sense equivalent forces which never coalesce, and the interaction between them is the drama.

And Virgil K. Whitaker, though insisting [in *Shakespeare's Use of Learning: An Inquiry into the growth of His Mind and Art*] that "the tragic action of the play is centered upon Antony, who has so yielded himself to the passion of love that it has possessed his will and dethroned his judgment", gives Cleopatra stature as a tragic figure: "Cleopatra, although she is developed almost as fully as he is, remains the seductress, and only at the end does she become a participant in a tragedy of her own." "A tragedy of her own"—just what is it? "A question to be asked", and answered.

It is trite to remark that an audience's first impression of a character is very important; it is not commonplace to call particular attention to Cleopatra's first word in the play: "If". It is obvious—or should be—that in saying "If it be love indeed, tell me how much", she is following up a previous declaration, on Antony's part, of great love for her by teasing and bantering him. She is playful, but within her brief demand may be discerned one of her chief devices, contradiction. Immediately, by the entrance of the messenger from Rome, her tone changes; the contradictions become blunt, the taunts amazingly bold and affrontive. Antony's submitting to them proves that Philo's term "dotage" is not an exaggeration. That Cleopatra's contradictory behavior (as in I.ii.89-91; iii. 1-5) is calculated is obvious from her rejoinder to Charmian's warning: "Thou teachest like a fool. The way to lose him!" (I.iii.10). Simultaneously Cleopatra's constant fear is revealed: that Antony will leave her.

When Antony, having determined to break off with Cleopatra and return to Rome, goes to her to announce his departure, she perceives that he is in a serious mood and, surmising his intention, gives him no chance to talk. Six times she interrupts him when he starts to speak. In her tirades she taunts him (1) by references to his wife Fulvia, charging him with falsity to her; (2) by the accusation that he has treacherously betrayed her (Cleopatra); and (3) by recounting his compliments to her when he was wooing, practically calling him a

Charlton Heston and Garrick Hagan in the 1973 film of Antony and Cleopatra.

liar. And when eventually Antony commands her to listen to him and hear his reasons for leaving, ending with a reference to Fulvia's death, she then accuses him of lying, of expecting her, like a child, to believe fairy tales. When he offers proof, the letter he has received, she then charges him with insensibility for not weeping over his wife's death and predicts that he would be equally unmoved by her death. And as he protests his love for her she begins one of her fainting spells but changes her mind; she is, she says, "quickly ill, and well", as changeable as Antony is in his love. She mockingly urges him to produce some tears for Fulvia and pretend they are for her, ridicules him for not making a better show at weeping, and calls on Charmian to join her in laughing at Antony's rising anger.

Antony turns to walk away. Then Cleopatra brings him back by the one appeal that just then could do it, a quavering "Courteous lord". It is the first time in the play that she has spoken to him in anything like a complimentary fashion. Then she pretends to have something serious to say, or that she was going to say and has now forgot. Antony recognizes that she is playing for time, and she perceives his recognition. She has drawn on her coquette's kit for a variety of tools, and

they have failed her, even her appeal to pity (her most effective, much used tool); Antony is going despite all she can do. But perhaps, if she says something kind, for once, it may eventually bring him back:

> Your honour calls you hence;
> Therefore be deaf to my unpitied folly,
> And all the gods go with you! Upon your
>   sword
> Sit laurel victory, and smooth success
> Be strew'd before your feet!
>
>   (I.iii.97-101)

Or something that may seem kind! Her reference to his honor is much belated; she makes another appeal to pity; and the sequence of *s* sounds and the concatenation of *b*'s and *f*'s and *e*'s *t*'s in the last line may suggest, by the conceivable hissing and sneering, an unconscious extrusion of her essentially serpentine nature.

During Antony's absence Cleopatra's behavior is self-characterizing. She evinces no interest in the business he is engaged in; she is concerned as to what he may be thinking of her, is enveloped in thoughts physical and sensual, and reviews the list of her great lovers, "Broad-fronted Caesar", "great Pompey", "brave Mark Antony". She revels in memories of her behavior to Antony— trickery in fishing, laughing him out of and into patience, dressing him in tires and mantles while she "wore his sword Philippan", contrarieties all. She is aghast when the news comes that Antony has married Octavia and beats the messenger, but regains hope from the description he gives of her.

We do not see Antony and Cleopatra together again until just before the battle of Actium. Were it not for Enobarbus' description of her on the river Cydnus and his analysis of her charms (II.ii.195-245), there would be little about her in the first half of the play that to an objective reader is alluring. But even Enobarbus' account hints at Cleopatra's oppositeness, for he pictures Antony, "Enthron'd i' th' market place", waiting for Cleopatra to appear before him, which she does not do, and accepting her refusal to dine with him and her counter-invitation "to come and suppe with her". The description follows closely the reconciliation scene between Antony and Octavius in which Antony, then at his best, is shown as firm master of himself and thus provides the background to contrast with his sorry self when manipulated by Cleopatra. But there is no such admirable background for Cleopatra; it is apparent that her tragedy will have to be of a distinctly different sort from Antony's. It cannot be a "tragic fall", for there is nothing for her to fall from.

After Actium, where Antony at her urging has fought at sea, she offers as her reason for leaving the scene of the battle that she was afraid. But that reason does not satisfy everyone. [In *Shakespeare Studies*] E. E. Stoll, for instance, lists among various unanswered questions in Shakespeare's plays the query "Why does Cleopatra flee from the battle and Antony?" Later [in *Poets and Playwrights*] he wonders whether in examining such a question as that, and about her later dealings with Thyreus and her responsibility in the second sea-fight, we may not be "then considering too curiously". Certainly the question about her behavior at Actium exists and must be considered; but just as certainly it cannot be answered. Cleopatra's "I little thought / You would have followed" (III.xi.55-56), besides putting the blame on him, may reveal a more nearly true reason than her "fearful sails": Is her leaving the battle at the critical point a test of Antony, to see whether the political leader or the lover is stronger in him? Does she fear that military success and political mastery would be a dangerous rival to her charms? And when Antony reproaches her with

> You did know
> How much you were my conqueror, and that
> My sword, made weak by my affection, would
> Obey it on all cause
>
> (III.xi.65-68)

and she cries "Pardon, pardon!" is she really sorry? Her behavior to Thyreus soon after makes us wonder.

When Thyreus tells Cleopatra that

> He [Caesar] knows that you embrace not
>   Antony
> As you did love, but as you fear'd him
>
> (III.xiii.56-57)

she exclaims "O!" What does she mean by that? There are those who seem to know; e. g., G. L. Kittredge (note on 1. 57):

> Cleopatra's exclamation is meant to convey to Thyreus not only eager acceptance of Caesar's theory of her union with Antony, but also gratified surprise that Caesar should have shown so sympathetic an understanding of the case. All this she expresses in plain terms in her next speech: 'He is a god,' etc.

That interpretation implies that Cleopatra, suddenly perceiving a way out of the impasse, is deserting Antony and preparing to entangle Caesar in her "toils of grace", through the pity for her that she hopes to inspire. But conceivably the "O!" may merely imply painful shock at the idea that anyone could even think she feared Antony and did not love him. If so, the idea of appealing to Caesar's pity may not occur at the moment but be suggested by Thyreus'

> The scars upon your honour, therefore, he
> Does pity, as constrained blemishes,
> Not as deserv'd.
>
> (ll.58-60)

It is doubtful whether one is justified in saying that "All this she expresses in plain terms in her next speech", inasmuch as Thyreus' statement comes between her "O!" and "her next speech". Or, perhaps, the previous lines should be taken into consideration; Thyreus says,

> Caesar entreats
> Not to consider in what case thou stand'st
> Further than he is Caesar,
>
> (ll.53-55)

which seems to promise noble treatment, with possible emphasis on the good will of Caesar the man. If the idea of attempting to entangle Caesar has already occurred to her, her enthusiastic "Go on. Right royal!" is flattery intended to be relayed to Caesar. But then Thyreus'

> He knows that you embrace not Antony
> As you did love, but as you fear'd him

is definitely cooling, and her "O!" may involuntarily escape her, indicating sudden awareness of Caesar's realization that she "embraced" Antony because of his power more than for love of the man himself and thus is on guard against any designs she might have on him now that he has conquered Antony. If that is the situation, then Thyreus' speech suggesting Caesar's pity for the scars upon her honor "as constrained blemishes, / Not as deserv'd" arouses hope and prompts her flattering and pity-inviting

> He is a god, and knows
> What is most right. Mine honour was not
>   yielded
> But conquer'd merely,
>
> (ll.60-62)

a bare-faced lie, as Enobarbus recognizes.

Whatever the significance of the "O!" it is soon obvious that Cleopatra proceeds to cajole Thyreus, hoping thereby to make him a friend in court. But whether she is actually deserting Antony and staking all on a hope of ensnaring Caesar or is planning a deep deception of Caesar it is impossible to tell. Nor is her behavior to Antony clear when he enters unexpectedly and in fury orders punishment to Thyreus and condemns her. She attempts to defend herself with four questions: "O, is't come to this?" "Wherefore is this?" "Have you done yet?" and, after a parenthetical "I must stay his time", "Not know me yet?" What does she mean by the fourth question? She probably intends for Antony to understand that she was just temporizing, meeting Caesar's suspected treachery with pretended submission. When Antony, still pained by what he is sure is betrayal of him, asks, "Cold-hearted toward me?" she breaks out in impassioned speech:

> Ah, dear, if I be so,
> From my cold heart let heaven engender hail,
> And poison it in the source, and the first
>   stone
> Drop in my neck; as it determines, so
> Dissolve my life! The next Caesarion smite!
> Till by degrees the memory of my womb
> Together with my brave Egyptians all,
> By the discandying of this pelleted storm,
> Lie graveless, till the flies and gnats of Nile
> Have buried them for prey!
>
> (III.xiii.158-167)

Actually her plea that, if her heart is cold, from it hail, poisoned in its source (her heart), should be "engendered" only to fall in her neck, melt, and in melting dissolve her life, is basically nonsense. For if there were enough poison in the source, her heart, to kill her when, incorporated into hail, it was carried to her neck and then caused her life to dissolve, she would have been dead long ago. To say nothing of the amount of poison it would take to dispose of Caesarion and "my brave Egyptians all"! She has created a barrage of words that by the excess of emotion and the deficiency of sense seem to denote complete devotion to Antony but which by the very excesses reveal the opposite. "The lady doth protest too much, methinks." Her speech is not the bald lie that she tells Antony when later she sends him word that she has killed herself, but there is deception, masked by the barrage of words and the vehemence of her utterance.

What a narrow escape that was for her! She has convinced Antony ("I am satisfied") but not Enobarbus; for him it is the last straw. He knows that Antony is now lost, for "When valour preys on reason, / It eats the sword it fights with" (ll. 199-200). Though Enobarbus speaks only of Antony, he reveals his interpretation of Cleopatra's behavior in the crisis.

Antony declares that he will fight Caesar again, gains Cleopatra's "That's my brave lord", and joins with her in anticipation of her birthday festivities. The next morning she playfully helps Antony don his armor and kisses him as he departs for battle. She comments to Charmian, "He goes forth gallantly", and expresses a wish

>   That he and Caesar might
> Determine this great war in single fight!
> Then Antony— but now—
>
>   (IV.iv.36-38)

Since she apparently thinks Antony will be defeated, she is surprised at his victorious return:

> Lord of lords!
> O infinite virtue, com'st thou smiling from
> The world's great snare uncaught?
>
> (IV.viii.16-18)

Though she thus compliments Antony in exaggerated terms and rewards Scarus extravagantly ("An armour all of gold", l. 27), she hardly discloses her real thoughts. Nor is it certain that she did not betray Antony in the second sea-fight. Antony is sure: "This foul Egyptian hath betrayed me!" (IV.xii.10) and he is exceedingly bitter about the "triple-turn'd whore" that

> Like a right gypsy hath at fast and loose
> Beguil'd me to the very heart of loss!

He calls for Eros, but Cleopatra appears, having mistakenly thought, perhaps, that Antony was summoning her by calling on the deity of love (Eros), and is met by "Ah, thou spell! Avaunt!" In innocence or seeming innocence she asks, "Why is my lord enrag'd against his love?" Then at Antony's threats she leaves. Exclaiming that he is "more mad / Than Telamon for his shield" (xiii. 1-2), she sends Mardian to Antony:

> Mardian, go tell him I have slain myself.
> Say that the last I spoke was 'Antony'
> And word it, prithee, piteously. Hence, Mardian,
> And bring me how he takes my death.
>
> (IV.xiii.7-10)

The lie, with the appeals for pity— "I have slain myself" (for love of Antony), "piteously"— is her final deception of Antony. Knowledge about how he takes her death may be intended to provide her with a clue as to possible appeasement of his wrath, but the lie is the climax of all her tricks, and ironically causes his death. Though it be argued that she did not betray Antony, his thinking she did is understandable, in the light of her behavior throughout the play up to the time of the second sea-fight.

What would be— to return to Cleopatra's entrance and exit for a moment— the impression on an audience of Cleopatra's behavior? Antony's brief but vivid description of the fleet's surrender and his repeated charge that Cleopatra has betrayed him, plus remembrance of what happened at Actium, may well make an audience suspicious of her when she appears. And her exit, following immediately upon Antony's detailed picture of her as the captive of Caesar and the victim of Octavia's wrath, may well give the definite impression that her self-interest has been and is the force that motivates her action. She does not even think of fainting or of attempting to kill herself in disproof of Antony's accusation. And her question "Why is my lord enrag'd against his love?" is colored by her accustomed plea for pity. Altogether, whether or not she betrayed Antony to Caesar is left an unanswered question, like the motives for her behavior at Actium.

There are some obvious facts. Cleopatra, to satisfy her ego, must have as her lovers the world's greatest. The outcome of the war between Antony and Octavius, since it is for world mastery, will determine which will emerge as the greater. Suppose Antony should win: he will certainly be immersed in state affairs and neglect her. Suppose Octavius should win: then there is the question as to whether she can ensnare him. Her equivocal behavior to Antony and her flirting with Caesar through Thyreus may reflect her uncertainty.

Yet there can be no doubt that Cleopatra has love, of a sort, for Antony, and when he, dying, is brought to her in the monument it is the realization of his personality as a man, her lover, and her belated recognition of the stalwart Roman qualities he represents (emphasized by the pride in them shown in his dying speech) that for the moment overshadow everything else. Even though self-pity is not completely absent— "Noblest of men, woo't die? / Hast thou no care of me?" (IV.xv.59-60)— she is genuine in lamenting that "The crown o' th' earth doth melt", and she is quite humbled:

No more but e'en a woman, and commanded
By such poor passion as the maid that milks
And does the meanest chares."

(ll. 73-75)

Some appreciation of Antony's worth, now that he is no more, comes to her:

It were for me
To throw my sceptre at the injurious gods,
To tell them that this world did equal theirs
Till they had stol'n our jewel.

(ll. 75-78)

But there is no admitting, apparently no perception, of the fact that she is responsible for his defeat and death. Her self-pity, her concentration on self, makes it impossible for her to see the situation objectively. If she could see it objectively, she would not be Cleopatra. It is her very Cleopatra-ness that is the basis for her ultimate tragedy. If she were a Juliet she would kill herself immediately for love of Antony, not merely talk about suicide. The fact that she does not act but talks precludes any interpretation of her tragedy as a love tragedy, even though there is pathos in her

what's brave, what's noble,
Let's do it after the high Roman fashion
And make death proud to take us.

(ll. 86-88)

She has learned something; she has gained unconsciously some insight into what virtue, Roman virtue as embodied in Antony, is. There is no sneering now at "a Roman thought" (I.ii.87). But though she knows no "friend / But resolution and the briefest end", she is yet a long way from declaring "Husband, I come"; her tragedy is by no means yet manifest.

When we next see her (V.ii) some time has elapsed; she still talks of suicide, but not of "the briefest end": "My desolation does begin to make / A better life." Better than what? Since she immediately speaks of Caesar and his subjection to Fortune, she will show a "life" superior to his by doing that which ends all the influence of Fortune. Is it unconscious irony that she uses the word "life" in speaking of the ending of her life? Her whole speech (ll. 1-8) is of herself in relation to Caesar, and she does not attempt suicide until the Roman guardsmen make a move to capture her. Meanwhile she has parleyed with Proculeius and through him made a bid for pity from Caesar— "a queen his beggar"— and professes "A doctrine of obedience". But she adds, significantly, "and would gladly / Look him i' th' face" (ll. 31-32).

When she is prevented from killing herself (not for love of Antony but to forestall capture) she moans,

Where art thou, death?
Come hither, come! Come, come, and take a
queen
Worth many babes and beggars.

(ll. 46-48)

The real reason for her attempted suicide is made plain by her outburst after Proculeius' "O, temperance, lady!":

Sir, I will eat no meat; I'll not drink, sir;
If idle talk will once be necessary,
I'll not sleep neither. This mortal house I'll
ruin,
Do Caesar what he can. Know, sir, that I
Will not wait pinion'd at your master's court
Nor once be chastis'd with the sober eye
Of dull Octavia. Shall they hoist me up
And show me to the shouting varlotry
Of censuring Rome? Rather a ditch in Egypt
Be gentle grave unto me! Rather on Nilus'
mud
Lay me stark-nak'd and let the waterflies
Blow me into abhorring! Rather make
My country's high pyramides my gibbet
And hang me up in chains!

(V.ii.49-62)

Proculeius had been commended to her by Antony (IV.xv.47-48), but he has proved untrustworthy. When Dolabella follows and attempts to gain her confidence by "Most noble Empress, you have heard of me?" (V.ii.71), she tests him: "You laugh when boys or women tell their dreams; / Is't not your trick?" He does not understand what she means, and is puzzled as she pours out an elaborate eulogy of Antony (ll. 79 ff.). She glorifies Antony's power and bounty and wins Dolabella's sympathy to the degree that he answers truthfully her question as to what Caesar intends to do with her: lead her in triumph in Rome. She has told Dolabella that she "dreamt there was an Emperor Antony" and asked whether "there was or might be such a man / As this I dreamt of". It appears that she was giving him an opportunity to assure her that Caesar, now Emperor, is such a man; since he did not respond affirmatively, she puts her direct question. Immediately after his answer, Caesar enters.

It is through the glorified Antony of her dream that the audience is made aware of the fact that Cleopatra now has gained some conception of the worth of Antony. But that is in retrospect; she indicated no such recognition while Antony was alive. The idealization of Antony in the dream contrasts with the unideal realism of her treatment of him while he lived. (Dramatically, the idealized Antony comes between the deceitful Proculeius and the cold, unmalleable Caesar. Cleopatra's acquired recognition of Antony's excellence cannot be left to the very end of the play but must be made evident, for it is vital to the formation of her tragedy.) But she is in many ways still the former Cleopatra; she schemes, and uses a new device to arouse pity for herself. There is no admission of responsibility for what has happened, no hint of a sense of guilt. And she obviously has not given up hope of a future if one can be contrived that is not shameful to her. That future depends on what she can gain from Caesar.

Since she is still alive and has not become penitent nor admitted— even realized— any responsibility for the dire situation she is now in, it is inevitable that she should carry on. Indeed the force of momentum, not checked by a change in character, leads the audience to anticipate an attempt to captivate Caesar: Julius Caesar, Pompey, Antony; and now Octavius is Caesar, the world's greatest. And it is to be expected that she will use the old tools, or rather the most effective one, the appeal to pity. When Caesar enters, she kneels to him:

> Sir, the gods
> Will have it thus. My master and my lord
> I must obey;
>
> (V.ii.115-117)

then

> Sole sir o' th' world,
> I cannot project mine own cause so well
> To make it clear; but do confess I have
> Been laden with like frailties which before
> Have often sham'd our sex.

Caesar's response gives her little encouragement, ending as it does with a threat:

> If you apply yourself to our intents,
> Which towards you are most gentle, you shall find
> A benefit in this change; but, if you seek
> To lay on me a cruelty by taking

Antony's course, you shall bereave yourself
Of my good purposes, and put your children
To that destruction which I'll guard them
from
If thereon you rely.

There follows the Seleucus incident. Whether she is providing for herself if she should have a future or, as some think, tries to convince Caesar by the planned exposure of her concealing half her wealth that she has no intention of following "Antony's course", or has contrived the whole thing as a means of eliciting pity, she unquestionably utilizes it for the latter purpose:

> O Caesar, what a wounding shame is this,
> That thou vouchsafing here to visit me,
> Doing the honour of thy lordliness
> To one so meek, that mine own servant should
> Parcel the sum of my disgraces by
> Addition of his envy! Say, good Caesar,
> That I some lady trifles have reserv'd,
> Immoment toys, things of such dignity
> As we greet modern friends withal; and say
> Some nobler token I have kept apart
> For Livia and Octavia— must I be unfolded
> With one that I have bred? The gods! It smites me
> Beneath the fall I have. . . .
> Be it known that we, the greatest, are misthought
> For things that others do; and, when we fall,
> We answer others' merits in our name,
> Are therefore to be pitied.
>
> (V.ii.159-171;176-179)

But her flattery, her profession of complete subjection to him, and her tearful appeals for pity have no effect on the astute Caesar, who answers her by the royal "we" and to her final, more quaveringly piteous "My master and my lord", says bluntly, "Not so. Adieu." She has done her best, but her practised methods, particularly the previously much-used pleas for pity, do not touch Caesar. And when he leaves she is vehement in her outburst— "He words me, girls, he words me", and adds "that I should not / Be noble to myself!" There is nothing left for her but to fall back on her resolution. The confirmation by Dolabella of what he had already told her about Caesar's intentions and his specification of a time limit,

> Caesar through Syria
> Intends his journey, and within three days
> You with your children will he send before,
>
> (V.ii.200-202)

incites her to immediate action. She describes vividly to Iras the exhibition Caesar would make in Rome of Iras and herself (she would no doubt include Charmian if she were then present) and applauds Iras' determination to pluck out her eyes rather than see it—

> Why, that's the way
> To fool their preparation, and to conquer
> Their most absurd intents.

Caesar having proved to be untouched, she reverts to the scene of her conquest of Antony:

> Show me, my women, like a queen. Go fetch
> My best attires. I am again for Cydnus,
> To meet Mark Antony.
>
> (ll.227-229)

With an implied confession of dillydallying, she declares:

> My resolution's plac'd, and I have nothing
> Of woman in me. Now from head to foot
> I am marble-constant. Now the fleeting
>   moon
> No planet is of mine.
>
> (ll.238-241)

In her final moments, as she carries out her resolution, Cleopatra has "immortal longings", hears Antony call, gloats over outwitting Caesar, addresses Antony as "husband", shows jealousy in her fear that Iras may gain the first otherworld kiss from Antony, sneers at Caesar again, speaks lovingly to the asp at her breast, and dies with "Antony" on her lips and with a final fling of contempt for the world. But, it should be noted, she does not "do it after the high Roman fashion", nor with the singleness of motive that actuated Antony, whose tragedy gains ironical poignancy because he thought Cleopatra— really the lying Cleopatra— had anticipated him in nobility (IV.xiv.55-62).

Does she kill herself to be with Antony or to escape Caesar? It is the final question, to be placed along with others. Would she have killed herself if she could have added Caesar to her string of "greats"? Why did she leave the battle of Actium? Why did she urge Antony to fight at sea? Did she betray Antony in the second sea-fight? What was the meaning of her "O"? Why did she behave in such a way as to lose her country instead of preserve it? Did she ever really love Antony or did she love herself for having captivated him? Why did she tease, taunt, and cross Antony, very rarely saying anything kind to him? These questions, and others that could be asked, show that it was not accidental that the first word she speaks in the play is "If". The appropriate symbol for her is a big interrogation point. There is testimony, of course, by Antony and especially by Enobarbus, the clear-headed, cynical logician, as to her infinite variety. Somehow she has enchanted the world's greatest men, and she is beloved by her attendants, even to the death. But in her behavior through-

out the play, from the effrontery of her appearing on the Cydnus to her wily proceedings with Octavius Caesar, there are repeated evidences that she is unaccountable. It is certain that Antony never penetrates her real character; he may call her gypsy and witch, but that is begging the question. How, in the face of and through his presentation of Cleopatra's behavior to Antony, does Shakespeare make of her a force powerful enough to bring about the downfall of the great Antony? Does he not supply the answer, paradoxically, by depicting her as the world's great question mark, alluring and magnetic because of all the unanswerable questions about her? Does he not imply that the secret of her charm lies in the fact that neither Antony nor we (including Shakespeare himself) can identify the secret of her charm? Such an interpretation was suggested by Gamaliel Bradford many years ago [in "The Serpent of Old Nile"] but apparently disregarded by most commentators on the play:

> I have said that Cleopatra was mysterious. Perhaps it is an element of the art of Shakespeare to puzzle us a little, to make us feel that we cannot interpret him always conclusively. It detracts nothing from the truth of his characters that we cannot always determine what their motives are as we can with that poor little creature of Dryden. . . . I, at least, do not feel clear as to her good faith to Antony. That she loves him there is no doubt at all, loves him as she is capable of loving. But it is more than doubtful whether she kills herself for love of him or in sheer desperation to avoid the scorn and vengeance of Caesar. I greatly fear that if she had been confident of Caesar's favor, confident of reigning in Rome as she had reigned in Alexandria, Antony's poor dust might have tossed forgotten in the burning winds of Egypt. And yet, I do not know— who can know? That is precisely what gives the character its charm.

But whatever interpretation of Cleopatra's character may be given— and to survey all that has been said would demand a volume devoted to her— the final question remains: What is *her tragedy?* One can agree with Willard Farnham's statement (p. 174) that "It is part of her tragedy that with her subtlety she wins control of his [Antony's] force and by winning this control ruins him and herself", but that is hardly the whole story. Nor is it satisfactory to become rhapsodic, to glorify Cleopatra beyond warrant, as J. Middleton Murry does:

> Now [after Antony's death] in very deed, Cleopatra loves Antony: now she discerns his royalty, and loyalty surges up in her to meet it. Now we feel that her wrangling with Caesar and her Treasurer which follows is all external to her— as it were a part which she is still condemned to play 'in this vile world': a mere interruption, an alien interlude, while the travail of fusion between the order of imagination and love, and the order of existence and act is

being accomplished: till the flame of perfect purpose breaks forth [V.ii.226-229 quoted]. No, not *again* for Cydnus: but now for the first time, indeed. For that old Cydnus, where the wonder pageant was, was but a symbol and preparation of this. That was an event in time; this is an event in eternity. And those royal robes were then only lovely garments of the body, now they are the integument of a soul. They must show her like a queen, now, because she *is* a queen, as she never was before.

(Pp.375-376)

Much nearer to the text of the play and to all the evidence is E. E. Stoll [in *Poets and Playwrights*]:

> . . . in [an] . . . audacious, sensuous key, for all her exaltation, she expresses herself on her deathbed. She is tenderer with her women, and stronger and more constant, than she has ever been; but her thoughts of Antony, though now an inviolable shade, are not celestial or Platonic. They are steeped in amorousness, and she is waiting, coiled on her couch. She loves him more than at the beginning; but neither now nor at his death is she, as Professor Schücking declares, "all tenderness, all passionate devotion and unselfish love"; nor does she quit life because it is not worth the living. On life she really never loosens her greedy grip. Her beauty she clutches to her dying bosom as the miser does his gold. Her robe and jewels are, even in death, assumed to heighten the impression of it upon Caesar— though only to show him what he has missed. She hears Antony mock him now, from over the bitter wave; and at the beginning of the scene she cried,

> > go fetch
> > My best attires; I am again for Cydnus—

> as one who, to please both him and herself, and vex their rival, would fain die at her best, reviving all the glories of that triumph. To an ugly death she could scarcely have brought herself; . . . the death which . . . she is choosing and devising [is] . . . an event, a scene, well-nigh an amour . . . she thinks the stroke of death is as a lover's pinch, which hurts and is desired. . . . she is wrapped and folded up in sensuous imaginations to the end.

Indeed, to have Cleopatra glorified and transfigured is to forgive her treatment of Antony, to imply that it was well worth the destruction of the great Roman to bring about her regeneration. If the tragedy of Antony and the tragedy of Cleopatra are to interact to intensify each other, it is necessary *not* to have a transfiguration of Cleopatra; the poignancy of Antony's tragedy is intensified by Cleopatra's unregeneracy, and it increases the pathos and tragedy of Cleopatra that she is never penitent, not even conscious of the debacle she has wrought. That she does change somewhat, that she does attain some realization of what Antony was, is to be recog-

nized. That she did not realize it earlier, and to a much greater degree, is her tragedy: the too little and the too late. Thus the tragedy of Cleopatra is different in kind from that of Antony; the play contains the tragedy of Antony and then the tragedy of Cleopatra.

The "too little" involves a considerable pathetic element. Cleopatra, though appearing on the Cydnus as Venus, is really Isis in environment, interests, and obsessions. Of that the fertility connotations made obvious in the conversation of her companions Iras and Charmian with the Soothsayer (I.ii), the Nile imagery frequent in the play, and the trend of Cleopatra's own thoughts as revealed in her speeches give plentiful proof. Her basic interests show themselves in her imagination as she visualizes Antony in Rome (I.v.19 ff.). They permeate the glowing dream of Antony she describes to Dolabella, as she concentrates on Antony's power and his bounty (not on aspects of character and personal qualities). They suffuse her final speeches; "but even then what emerges is a state of trance, a vision of the divine lover Antony, filling Heaven and Earth, the kiss of the bridegroom, Love lifted to a higher plane among the Homeric gods, all an aspiration and a wild desire, the eagle and the dove." This last characterization of her vision is over-etherealized; a more moderate statement is Willard Farnham's:

> If we are to understand that the love of Cleopatra for Antony, like her character, continues to be deeply flawed to the end of her life, we are nevertheless to understand that, like her character, it has its measure of nobility. If Cleopatra never comes to have a love for Antony to match his love for her, she at least comes to have magnificent visions of what it would be like to achieve such a love, and her climactic vision leads her to call him husband as she dies.

(P.202)

To that extent we may credit Cleopatra with some ennobling; but it is just enough to intensify and illuminate her tragedy. "She's good, being gone; / The hand could pluck her back that shov'd her on", said Antony (I. ii. 130-131), on hearing of Fulvia's death. Cleopatra only after Antony's death comes to some realization of what he was; he's good, being gone. Only after he is wounded or dead does she call him "noble"; only in a sort of funeral hymn does she recognize his power and bounty. But she never feels any sense of guilt such as Antony confesses; there is no *peccavi;* there is no repentance, no consciousness even, of the need for remorse. She is no Othello; her tragedy can be only partial, not complete. The picture she imagines of rejoining Antony in another world could never become actual; she still would have considerable explaining to do.

Cleopatra's tragedy is inherent in her equivocality, in her utter self-interest, and in her complete ignorance of the existence of an unselfish love apart from the physical. She has had no comprehension of Roman virtues, no recognition of Antony's fundamental character, no appreciation of his courtesy and devotion to her. She gloried in his greatness as a soldier and as the most powerful of the triumvirs, not for his sake but for her own— and undermined both his military prowess and his power. She evinces, throughout the play, little concern about the country of which she is queen; she is woman, not queen, in her interests and behavior. She is as innocent of morality as Falstaff of honor. But she does learn something, through frustration and suffering, of what virtue— Roman virtue— means. It is pathetic and tragic that a beginning of anything other than sensual self-interest comes when there is neither the opportunity nor the time for growth to ensue. In that irony— in the too little and the too late— lies her tragedy. That is all the tragedy there is for her, but it is none the less profound, and gains poignancy through contrast to Antony's as his gains pathos through contrast to hers.

Maurice Charney

SOURCE: "Antony and Cleopatra," in *All of Shakespeare*, Columbia University Press, 1993, pp. 289-98.

[*Charney discusses Cleopatra from the point of view of other characters in the play. He asserts that Enobarbus, for example, sees her in "objective" but flamboyant terms, while Antony— who knows her personally— does not use exaggerated language to describe her. Charney also notes that Cleopatra is characterized via food metaphors and sensual images; her depiction can be contrasted with that of Antony's new Roman wife, Octavia, who is presented coldly via "building imagery."*]

The most puzzling figure in *Antony and Cleopatra* is Cleopatra herself, Shakespeare's most complex representation of a woman. As Enobarbus explains her charms (and the reason that Antony, though newly married to Octavia, will return to Egypt), "Age cannot wither her, nor custom stale / Her infinite variety" (2.2.241-42). Cleopatra is no young ingenue like Juliet, but an experienced and artful lover, "with Phoebus' amorous pinches black / And wrinkled deep in time" (1.5.28-29). How old is that? Certainly closer to Gertrude's age in *Hamlet* than to Ophelia's. Her "infinite variety" in the play is expressed in terms of artifice and erotic games, as she explains to Charmian: "If you find him sad, / Say I am dancing; if in mirth, report / That I am sudden sick" (1.3.3-5). She plays in contraries in a way that frightens Charmian, who follows conventional women's doctrine: "In each thing give him way, cross him in nothing," which Cleopatra is certain is wrong: "Thou teachest like a fool: the way to lose him!" (9-10).

As Enobarbus attests elsewhere, Cleopatra is "a wonderful piece of work" (1.2.155-56), and he celebrates her infinite variety in a specifically sexual sense:

> other women cloy
> The appetites they feed, but she makes hungry
> Where most she satisfies; for vilest things
> Become themselves in her, that the holy priests
> Bless her when she is riggish.
>
> (2.2.242-46)

Rig is a common word for strumpet, and *riggish* means wanton and licentious. In Enobarbus's account the imagery of appetites and feeding is sexual and there is a dark innuendo in "vilest things." Why should the holy priests bless Cleopatra's lasciviousness if it doesn't represent some apotheosis of sexuality? Enobarbus's paradoxes puzzle us, and his sense of wonder and admiration for Cleopatra is entirely different from Antony's, who is personally involved with her.

It is not surprising that Enobarbus should speak the heightened description of Cleopatra in her barge on the river Cydnus. He describes her mythologically as she first appeared when she went to meet Mark Antony. Unlike his commanding general, he is an objective observer of the marvels of Egypt, which he never hesitates to celebrate. In Shakespeare's play Antony could never possibly utter this hyperbolic oration because he is too aware of Cleopatra's dangers. He never speaks of her in hyperbole, or overwrought, exaggerated, even excessive rhetorical figuration. Actually, Enobarbus says almost nothing about Cleopatra herself except that, in the Marlovian fashion of invidious comparison, she is "O'erpicturing that Venus where we see / The fancy outwork nature" (2.2.206-7).

Enobarbus expends his effort in describing "The barge she sat in, like a burnished throne" (2.2.197), whose "poop was beaten gold" (198), and whose sails were purple (presumably the royal purple, or deep red). In a notable sadomasochistic image very relevant to the context, the silver oars of the barge "made / The water which they beat to follow faster, / As amorous of their strokes" (201-3). This is like the stroke of death, which, like a lover's pinch, "hurts, and is desired" (5.2.296). Cleopatra's costume and stage setting is opulent in the style of a Busby Berkeley musical. It is really overwrought, and the sense of stasis creates a feeling of puzzlement and wasted effort, as in the description of the pretty dimpled boys with divers-colored fans, "whose wind did seem / To glow the delicate cheeks which they did cool, / And what they undid did" (209-11). This sense of defeated motion may be part of a larger pattern of "discandying" in the play.

We see a very different Cleopatra in act 2, scene 5, while she is waiting for the absent Antony to return. A high degree of sexual innuendo, an impatient shifting of mood, an impetuous violence— all steeped in an impenetrable boredom— permeate this scene. Cleopatra begins by calling for music: "music, moody food / Of us that trade in love" (1-2), which recalls Duke Orsino's langourous lament at the beginning of *Twelfth Night:* "If music be the food of love, play on" (1.1.1). Cleopatra is histrionic, even faintly ridiculous, in speaking of music as "moody food" and of herself as a trader in love, like Pandarus in *Troilus and Cressida.*

But as soon as Mardian the Eunuch enters, she abandons music and wants to play billiards, a wildly anachronistic game for ancient Egypt. Charmian, her waiting woman, begs off: "My arm is sore (2.5.4), and sets up an obvious sexual pun: "best play with Mardian (4). Cleopatra cannot resist the unsubtle wordplay: "As well a woman with an eunuch played / As with a woman" (5-6), but she drives home the sexual point with a knowing smirk: "And when good will is showed, though't come too short, / The actor may plead pardon, (8-9). We already know from a previous encounter in act 1, scene 5, that Mardian the Eunuch has "fierce affections" and thinks "What Venus did with Mars" (17-18). So Cleopatra has already played the scene before with its set dialogue and prepared jokes.

But Cleopatra suddenly switches her interest to fishing, and her image of hooking "tawny-finned fishes" (2.5.12) is violently sexual:

> My bended hook shall
>   pierce
> Their slimy jaws; and as I draw them up,
> I'll think them every one an Antony,
> And say, "Ah, ha! y' are caught!"
>
>   (12-15)

Slimy jaws is not exactly attractive, but the image of Antony floats in a wide medium of instantaneous sexual attraction. Earlier, it was "O happy horse, to bear the weight of Antony" (1.5.21), and later Cleopatra commands the messenger with phallic impudence: "Ram thou thy fruitful tidings in mine ears, / That long time have been barren" (2.5.24-25).

Reporting the news of Antony's marriage to Octavia, the messenger is struck down, haled up and down, and threatened with a knife. This is the Cleopatra of the "vilest things" (2.2.244) that the holy priests bless when she is riggish. At the end of the scene, when the grieving Cleopatra has been fully informed about Antony's new wife, Octavia, she utters to Charmian a mysterious line that is one of her most characteristic flourishes: "Pity me, Charmian, / But do not speak to me" (2.5.118-19). She is infinitely above Charmian in social station and in complexity of feeling; she wants her pity but not her conversation. This teeters on the edge of magnificence and absurdity, like Mae West's "Beulah, peel me a grape."

Octavia, Caesar's sister, is set out as the opposite of Cleopatra, as hard and material Roman values are set against the luxurance of Egypt. Enobarbus, who is an insightful observer, says that Octavia is "of a holy, cold, and still conversation" (2.6.122-23)— *conversation* is used in the larger sense of personal behavior and manner. Menas asks naively: "Who would not have his wife so?" (124), meaning that this describes an ideal Roman wife, but Enobarbus answers definitively: "Not he that himself is not so; which is Mark Antony. He will to his Egyptian dish again" (125-26).

Cleopatra is irresistibly presented in terms of food and sensual attraction, while Octavia unfortunately shares in the coldness and impersonality of Rome, expressed in building imagery: she is the "piece of virtue" who is set between Caesar and Antony "as the cement of our love / To keep it builded" (3.2.29-30). Cement is not a very romantic image, nor is the alternative military siege instrument: "the ram to batter / The fortress of it" (30-31). Cleopatra could never be presented in such alternative images: either the positive "cement" or the negative "ram." Later on Octavia herself speaks of wars between Caesar and Antony in the metal-working image of solder: "As if the world should cleave, and that slain men / Should solder up the rift" (3.4.31-32). All these images separate the Roman world of Octavia from the Egyptian world of Cleopatra and focus the alternatives on which the play turns.

Antony is caught in this bifurcated system of values. The play opens with a choral scene between the Roman soldiers, Demetrius and Philo, who comment directly on Antony's degeneration in Egypt. All the heroic, military, manly values of Rome have been destroyed by Cleopatra, and the first words of the play are about Antony's "dotage," which "O'erflows the measure" (1.1.1-2). *Dotage* is an Elizabethan word specifically connected with foolishness in love, especially on the part of an old lover for his young mistress. The warlike Antony, whose eyes "glowed like plated Mars" (4)— Mars in his resplendent armor— "now bend, now turn / The office and devotion of their view / Upon a tawny front" (4-6). There is a pun on *front,* both battlefront and Cleopatra's dark and sensual forehead or face (or her own "front" in a more general sense). This is dotage, when the doter forgets his manliness and duty and is overwhelmed by the love object. Antony's "captain's heart" (6) now "reneges all temper" (8)— and the image is one of the hardness and resiliency of metal, especially the blade of a sword— "And is become the bellows and the fan / To cool a gypsy's lust" (9-10). Then, in a very Shakespearean move to connect words with gestures, Antony and Cleopatra enter with their train and *"with Eunuchs fanning her"* (10 s.d.). This specifically identifies Antony with the Eunuchs because he has been made effeminate in Egypt.

The representation of Antony in this play oscillates between Roman and Egyptian images, and there is a sense of dichotomy that cannot be bridged. Caesar praises

Antony for his fortitude and endurance (as Cassius praises himself in *Julius Caesar* for his physical superiority to Caesar). After the battle of Modena, a famine followed and Antony "didst drink / The stale of horses and the gilded puddle / Which beasts would cough at" (1.4.61-63). There are admirable qualities for a soldier but not for a lover, especially the ability to drink horse piss. One can see why Caesar admires this. He continues, with a hyperbolic enthusiasm rare for him in this play, to enumerate Antony's accomplishments: "The barks of trees thou browsed" (66), and, most climactic of all, on the Alps "It is reported thou didst eat strange flesh, / Which some did die to look on" (67-68). Caesar's admiration borders on the ridiculous. Antony is the ideal Roman soldier whom Caesar wants his sister Octavia to marry, and it is clear that Caesar understands nothing about love either for himself or for Antony.

But Antony thinks of his own tragic conflict in the dichotomized terms of Caesar and Philo and Demetrius. He always sees Cleopatra as perilous, even when he is most attracted to her—especially when he is most attracted to her. When he has lost the Battle of Actium through Cleopatra's machinations, he speaks of "My sword, made weak by my affection" (3.11.67), and there is a strongly erotic association of sword throughout the play. Cleopatra's simple apology immediately elicits the rapturous vaunting of love rhetoric: "Give me a kiss; / Even this repays me" (70-71). There is no way to reconcile Antony's contradictory impulses. He is rendered both effeminate and noble by Cleopatra, and the unresolvable paradox deepens the meaning of *Antony and Cleopatra*. Shakespeare doesn't work out the love / honor dichotomy, unlike Dryden in *All for Love, or The World Well Lost* (1678), his version of Shakespeare's play.

In the extraordinary death scenes that occupy our attention in act 4, scenes 14 and 15, and in act 5, scene 2, the play moves away from tragedy as we know it from earlier Shakespearean plays to a celebration of the lovers united finally in death. The moral formulas of Egypt versus Rome are forgotten, and we glory in the grand passions and poetic speeches of the protagonists. After his final defeat, everything becomes deliquescent for Antony, and Shakespeare has invented a *dis-* prefix set of words to carry this meaning: *disarming, dissolving, discandying, dislimning.* At the beginning of act 4, scene 14, Antony sees the masquelike cloud shapes (like those in *The Tempest*) that keep changing and that symbolize his present reality: "here I am Antony, / Yet cannot hold this visible shape" (13-14). Like Othello, Antony's "occupation's gone" (*Othello* 3.3.354); he is "No more a soldier" (4.14.42), and with his occupation his identity is gone, too. Therefore, like the cloud shapes he sees,

> That which is now a horse, even with a
> thought

The rack dislimns, and makes it indistinct
As water is in water.

(9-11)

This dislimning is in the languorous Egyptian style of the barge on Cydnus passage.

It is not surprising in this symbolic setting that Antony cannot successfully run on his sword and accomplish his Roman suicide. He has to beg Diomedes to "give me / Sufficing strokes for death" (4.14.116-17). He is heaved aloft, mortally wounded, to Cleopatra in her monument, and she puns on the erotic overtones of the dying Antony: "Here's sport indeed!" (4.15.32)—*sport* is a specifically sexual word—"How heavy weighs my lord! / Our strength is all gone into heaviness" (32-33). This echoes the earlier exclamation: "O happy horse, to bear the weight of Antony!" (1.5.21). There is no feeling of contradiction between these two different contexts. By the time we reach Cleopatra's dream of Antony, Antony has been mythologized: "It's past the size of dreaming; nature wants stuff / To vie strange forms with fancy" (5.2.94-95). The Roman issue of effeminacy and unmanliness has ceased to exist and there is only room to exercise the imagination, yet even to imagine an Antony as once having really existed is "nature's piece 'gainst fancy, / Condemning shadows quite" (99-100). Shakespeare was fond of debating the properties of nature and art, as in the talk of the gillyvors (or pinks) in *The Winter's Tale* (4.4.73ff.).

Roman history enters powerfully into *Antony and Cleopatra*, especially as Shakespeare encountered it, in biographical form, in Plutarch's *Lives*. Some things in the play are difficult to understand without reference to Plutarch. The role of Pompey, who also figured in *Julius Caesar*, is notably compressed in *Antony and Cleopatra* and depends upon some historical knowledge outside the play (or at least a diligent reading of the notes). The politics in this play are strongly presented, as they are in *Julius Caesar*, and there is a significantly chilling sense of amorality and brute force. Antony's oration, the death of Cinna the Poet, and the proscription scene right afterward in *Julius Caesar* all show us the frightening implications of revolution. In *Antony and Cleopatra*, two scenes that follow each other reveal how politics really works: the scene on board Pompey's galley (2,7) and the scene of Ventidius's victory over the Parthians (3,1).

The scene on board Pompey's galley is a wonderfully composed social unit, where the three world-sharers and their associates celebrate the peace that Pompey has made. Everyone is tipsy or well on the way, including Octavius Caesar, whose "own tongue / Splits what it speaks" (2.7.125-26), and there is also vigorous singing and dancing. Lepidus is the farthest gone of all, and Antony makes merciless fun of him, for example, in his truistic description of the crocodile: "It is shaped, sir, like itself, and it is as broad as it hath breadth" (43-44).

Beneath the joviality and good fellowship, Menas takes Pompey aside and offers him the whole world:

> These three world-sharers, these competitors,
> Are in thy vessel. Let me cut the cable,
> And when we are put off, fall to their
>   throats.
> All there is thine.
>
>   (2.7.72-75)

It is wonderfully simple, but Pompey reluctantly refuses: "Ah, this thou shouldst have done, / And not have spoke on't" (75-76). Pompey's refusal of the world is disturbingly political, since it is based not on moral realities but on appearances: "Being done unknown, / I should have found it afterwards well done, / But must condemn it now" (80-82). This is Machiavellian in the sense of the manipulation of political events that we find in the history plays, such as *Richard III*. Menas thinks Pompey merely a fool and will never follow his "palled fortunes more" (84). His desertion is like that of Enobarbus.

Act 3, scene 1 immediately following repeats the same political reality in a different form, it is a companion scene to act 2, scene 7. Antony's general, Ventidius, is having a great triumph over the Parthians in Syria, but he rejects Silius's sound advice to continue the war and pursue the "fugitive Parthians" (7), which Silius thinks will please Antony, who will "Put garlands on thy head" (11). Ventidius feels, however, that he should stop and that there is a political dimension to military triumph (this is quite unlike Coriolanus's personal victory over the Volscians). There is a certain wistful melancholy in Ventidius's speech to Silius:

>   O Silius, Silius,
> I have done enough: a lower place, note well,
> May make too great an act.
>
>   (11-13)

This kind of compromise seals the fate of Antony, which we understand that Ventidius is forecasting: "Who does i' th' wars more than his captain can / Becomes his captain's captain" (21-22), and in paraphrase: "I could do more to do Antonius good, / But 'twould offend him" (25-26). This is unusually explicit, and it explains why Antony may be full of bravado but he is not a heroic figure. Ventidius perceives him in all his vanity and political weakness.

There is a great deal that is theatrical in *Antony and Cleopatra*, or, more properly, metatheatrical, since it is the theater conscious of itself in Brecht's sense. Cleopatra doesn't want to be staged in Caesar's triumphal procession, and she goes into detail about the kinds of scenes she wants to avoid, like the mob scenes in *Julius Caesar* for Brutus and Antony's orations: "mechanic slaves / With greasy aprons, rules, and hammers shall / Uplift us to the view" (209-11). Not only will Cleopatra and

her girls be "shown" (208) in Rome in a public spectacle, but they will also be the subject of extempore plays like those put on by commedia dell'arte troupes: "The quick comedians / Extemporally will stage us, and present / Our Alexandrian revels" (16-18).

Cleopatra cannot bear the thought of the histrionic impersonation of scenes that were already quite histrionic when they took place in reality:

>   Antony
> Shall be brought drunken forth, and I shall
>   see
> Some squeaking Cleopatra boy my greatness
> I' th' posture of a whore.
>
>   (5.2.218-21)

This is alarmingly specific, since the role of Cleopatra on the Elizabethan stage was played by an adolescent boy actor, whose squeaking voice was just breaking. The reference is doubly histrionic since Cleopatra's "real" part is exceedingly stagy. The passage on Caesar's triumph leads directly into the ending, where Cleopatra wants to be staged appropriately: "Show me, my women, like a queen: go fetch / My best attires" (227-28). Costume and properties are emphasized in Cleopatra's final sequence: "Give me my robe, put on my crown, I have / Immortal longings in me" (280-81).

Another staged scene is the mysterious act 4, scene 3, where a company of soldiers enter—there are only three speaking parts—and then *place themselves in every corner of the stage* (7 s.d.). Presumably Shakespeare is remembering the medieval staging of the world and its four corners. There are also portentous sound effects: *Music of the hautboys is under the stage* (11 s.d.). This is like the music of hautboys, or oboes, in *Macbeth* when the Witches' caldron sinks (4.1.106 s.d.). The scene of the anonymous soldiers in *Antony and Cleopatra* signifies that "the god Hercules, whom Antony loved, / Now leaves him" (4.3. 15-16). The music in the air and under the earth, like the uncanny music of Ariel in *The Tempest*, indicates the defeat of Antony because his tutelary deity, Hercules, now departs.

This gives a mythological largeness to this strange scene. Incidentally, it is probable that this is the exact moment when Enobarbus also leaves Antony. The theatricality of act 4, scene 3 changes the dimension of the play, whose dramatic realities it translates onto another level of significance. I think Shakespeare wanted us to think that there is no way of separating the histrionic from the real: there is only a single reality in *Antony and Cleopatra* composed of many contradictory parts.

OCTAVIUS

J. Leeds Barroll observes that the character Octavius

Caesar has been described as "mysterious" and "remote," and notes that Octavius does not deliver a soliloquy in the play, nor does he speak in self-revealing asides or even utter more than a few lines at a time. He suggests that this taciturnity of Caesar's makes him seem a distant, unapproachable character. **Gordon Ross Smith** sees Octavius's brief comments as an intentional contrast to and puritanical criticism of the hyperbolic, flamboyant speeches of Antony and Cleopatra; further, Smith interprets such brevity in Octavius Caesar as a sign that he is "self-controlled"—witness his apparent sobriety during the orgy on Pompey's ship. Finally, Smith regards Octavius as cruel and Machiavellian in his arrest of the third and weakest member of the triumvirate, Lepidus. Richard C. Harrier describes Octavius as a "cool manipulator" who looks closely at the outcomes of events before he makes decisions.

By contrast, Barroll focuses more on the fact that, due to a lack of imagination, Octavius is prone to misjudgment. Caesar miscalculates events or people at least three times during the play: once when he is convinced Antony will lose a battle; later when he is unprepared for Antony's suicide; and lastly when he is foiled in his attempt to prevent Cleopatra's suicide. Thus, Barroll suggests, Octavius Caesar—who desires power—has less power over actions and people than he thinks he does. For additional commentary on the character of Octavius, see the excerpt by Walter Cohen in the **OVERVIEW** section and the excerpt by Larry S. Champion in the **ROME VERSUS EGYPT** section.

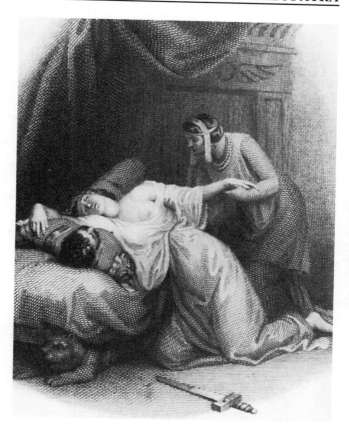

Act IV, scene iii. Antony, Cleopatra, and attendant. The University of Michigan Special Collections Library.

Gordon Ross Smith

SOURCE: "The Melting of Authority in *Antony and Cleopatra*," in *College Literature*, Vol. 1, No. 1, Winter, 1974, pp. 1-18.

[Smith evaluates five politicians in the play—Octavius, Antony, Lepidus, Cleopatra, and Pompey—and concludes that none of them can be regarded as ideal leaders according to the standards of Shakespeare's time. Smith characterizes Octavius as "restrained" but "somewhat puritanical" in his judgment of others—especially of Antony and Cleopatra. Smith further remarks that while Octavius is a "competent" ruler, he is also self-serving and untrustworthy—as his treatment of Lepidus makes clear.]

Since my principal concern in this instance is with the political behavior in this play, I shall examine how it appears in Octavius, Antony, and other Romans, and the ways in which they are manipulated by Shakespeare to set each other off. The flickering enticements of Cleopatra, however alluring, must be neglected so long as we are struck with Roman thoughts. I do not overlook the fact that much of the dramatic effect of the play derives from the juxtapositions and conspicuous contrasts of those opposite poles of Egypt and Rome,

pock-marked as they both are. It is not a matter of separating sheep from goats, but rather of separating different kinds of goats from one another.

Our first view of Octavius (I.iv) shows him self-controlled, competent and somewhat puritanical. His opening comments upon Antony seem rather restrained condemnation if one recollects what we have seen and heard of Antony (and Cleopatra), in the three preceding scenes. Octavius alludes to Cleopatra as "the queen of Ptolemy," and inasmuch as Pompey later calls her "Egypt's widow" (II.i.37), we must infer a Shakespearean awareness of and allusion to Cleopatra's marriage with her younger brother, whom she later reportedly murdered with poison. It follows, then, that Octavius is more restrained in his language than in his implied condemnation. He speaks of Antony as "the abstract of all faults" (I.iv.9), which is also restraint compared to the descriptive possibilities in Antony's past behavior, not to mention the potentialities which will—so to speak—fruit out. In brief, the language of Octavius' opening speech foreshadows his implacable opposition to Antony. Simple Lepidus resists these judgments and would even make the faults "the spots of heaven," to which Octavius replies in his hard, laconic, absolute style, "You are too indulgent." Perhaps the actor playing Lepidus raises his eyebrows in doubt or resistance; at any rate,

Octavius proceeds to stronger and more specific condemnation (I.iv.16-25), and on the grounds that Antony's neglect of burdens of State causes them to fall on Octavius (and by implication upon the other Triumvir, Lepidus). As if in confirmation of Octavius' judgment, in comes news of Pompey's growing power and of the depredations of Menecrates and Menas (I.iv.25-51). The incompetence of Lepidus is clear and it implies his approaching superannuation. Lepidus' last speech here asks Octavius to keep him informed (I.iv.81-83), although he ought to have as good sources of information as Octavius, and therefore that speech also shows his incompetence and foreshadows his forced retirement. Octavius' answer, "Doubt not, sir, / I knew it for my bond," acknowledges his agreement with Lepidus as a fellow Triumvir, but it seems rather to imply Octavius' ensuing duplicity. The use of past tense instead of present is a further and characteristically Shakespearean hint that Octavius will abrogate that agreement and cashier Lepidus.

We next see Octavius encountering Antony in Rome. We have a brief difference as to who shall sit first in a passage which is quite free of judgment words:

Caes.   Welcome to Rome.
Ant.   Thank you.
Caes.   Sit.
Ant.   Sit, Sir.
Caes.   Nay,
   then.

                                                          (II.ii.28)

All the emotional content there must be conveyed by the facial expressions, gestures, bow (if any), and the intonations with which the words are exchanged, all of which are inevitably missing from the text. That much-fragmented line has caused some varying interpretations among critics, but we must acknowledge that the words alone are so neutral that the tone of the passage will be as the actors play it. That allowed, we must ask what manner of playing will best fit its position in the whole play. Dr. Johnson asserted resentment on Antony's part at Caesar's presumed presumption in offering him permission to sit. Malone asserted it was a mere exchange of courtesies, and M. R. Ridley has agreed. A third interpretation (and way of playing it) seems more plausible to me: whichever man sat first, while the other still stood, presumably had the higher rank, a matter of commonplace protocol both then and now. When Antony tells Caesar to sit first, he slips himself into a subordinate position, and Caesar promptly takes the superior. The incident is too trivial and too lacking in any evidence in itself to warrant such an inference, but in the next scene the soothsayer tells Antony at some length that Caesar cramps his style, that his angel "Becomes a-feared," and that his "lustre thickens" when Caesar's angel is by (II.iii.16-29). Dramaturgically this extended warning is pointless unless true. It is, more-

over, straight out of Plutarch. Between the "Sit, sir" incident and the soothsayer's warning occurs the long discussion between Antony and Caesar. Antony begins apparently aggressively: "I learn, you take things ill which are not so: / Or being, concern you not" (II.ii.29-30). But we learned earlier that Antony feels guilty over his neglect of public affairs:

> I must from this enchanting queen break off,
> Ten thousand harms, more than the ills I
>   know,
> My idleness doth hatch.
>
>   (I.ii.125-127)

> These strong Egyptian fetters I must break,
> Or lose myself in dotage.
>
>   (I.ii.113-114)

> Would I had never seen her!
>
>   (I.ii.150)

His reasons had been given at length (I.ii.175-192). When the new agreements with Caesar have been made, we see and hear again his sense of guilt over past behavior:

> Read not my blemishes in the world's report:
> I have not kept my square, but that to come
> Shall all be done by the rule.
>
>   (II.iii.5-7)

We cannot believe such a promise, not only because we all know the story and that he didn't, but also because we have just heard Enobarbus in two or three of the most famous passages in the play describe Cleopatra's elaborate Greco-Egyptian enticements and predict absolutely that Antony could not leave her (II.ii.191-240). It follows from all this that Shakespeare has portrayed Antony's guilt as a constant current in his being, and we can then see his first accusation against Caesar to be really one of self-defense. It ought to be delivered resentfully, not aggressively. Moreover, as the argument continues, Octavius seizes the initiative and puts a succession of accusations upon Antony (II.ii.38-44, 54-56, 71-74, 81-83, 88-89), to which he answers more with denials than refutation, and at length he guiltily admits his faults and asks pardon (II.ii.94-98). Upon that admission, the futile marriage with Octavia, Caesar's best trap, is proposed by Agrippa and agreed to by Antony. The relationship of underlings like Agrippa to superiors like Caesar being what they are and have always been, as we can see with Menas and Pompey (II.vii.66-73), it is impossible to imagine Agrippa's making such a proposal without having first secured Caesar's approval; moreover, Caesar himself gives the signal that opens the way for Agrippa to propose it by saying, "Yet if I knew / What hoop should hold us staunch from edge to edge / O' the world, I would pursue it" (II.ii.114-116). It is inconceivable that such a conniver should not himself have thought of marrying Octavia to Antony; and Agrippa's proposal, therefore, must in fact be Caesar's. Antony steps into the trap, and can hardly do otherwise unless he is to commit an unforgiveable affront by refusing so generous an offer and implying a preference for the trollop of Egypt over the icicle of Rome. The Soothsayer's advice to Antony is thus delivered too late for Antony and serves only to confirm the surmises of the audience. That the marriage cannot work and will cause dissention between Antony and Octavius becomes clear in the expression of Antony's own foolish expectations upon the soothsayer's exit: "He hath spoken true. / . . . I will to Egypt: / And though I make this marriage for my peace, / I' the east my pleasure lies" (II.iii.32-39). Philo was right: "this dotage of our general's / O'erflows the measure" (I.i.1-2).

Our next view of Antony and Octavius together is in parley with Pompey, and therefore it behooves us to go back to Pompey's first appearance, which occurred shortly after Caesar's (I.iv. and IIi, respectively). Pompey enters accompanied by Menas and Menecrates, with whom he is allied, as the Messenger reported to Caesar (I.iv.48-55). Pompey begins by saying that if the great gods be just, they shall assist just men— like himself, presumably (II.i.1-2). The subjunctive is ominous in that context, and we know from many previous Shakespearean portraits of self-announced righteousness that Pompey's self-righteousness may also be a bad sign. Pompey soon shows himself confident (as Brutus had been), that Antony is a poor thing, that he sits at dinner in Egypt, that Caesar is losing public support, and that Lepidus is estranged from both. Of these four assertions the first three are quite wrong and the fourth is not yet true. Mena's report that Caesar and Lepidus are in the field Pompey denies as dreaming. A man who makes such errors and in such bouquets is sure to be a loser. The audience has already seen enough to know how wrong Pompey is; that his opinion of Antony is erroneous is promptly made explicit (II.i.27-31). Pompey's only correct evaluation is that without his own opposition, the triumvirs must quarrel (II.i.44-45) but for Pompey that belief will prove a posthumous truth.

Pompey's next appearance is in his conference with Antony and Caesar— oh, and Lepidus (II. vi). Pompey speaks of "the good Brutus ghosted," and of "the all honour'd, honest Roman, Brutus," (II.vi.13, 16), and his admiration is not inappropriate, for he partakes too much of Brutus' character. There is no little self-interest in Pompey's position. His father had been worsted by Caesar, as Caesar had been worsted by Brutus, and Brutus, by Antony. In the see-saw of Roman power, Pompey remained with his father's side, and on the dubious principle that an enemy of our enemy is our friend, Pompey considers the dead Brutus his friend. His speech is too long and hashes over the past, and

laconic Octavius answers characteristically, "Take your time" (II.vi.8-23). Antony brags of their superior power (characteristically), Lepidus changes the subject to the present offers in an attempt to mediate by deflecting recriminations (also characteristically), and Octavius says, "There's the point," grimly, briefly. All four are characterized, individualized, and contrasted with each other.

Pompey's acceptance of Sicily and Sardinia as his share obliges us to doubt that with so narrow a base he could hope to maintain himself in the middle of the Mediterranean world wholly ruled by the triumvirs. We must conclude a groundless trust in Pompey, in spite of his slurs at Antony (II.vi.62-68). Notwithstanding the resentments he has displayed, Pompey invites the triumvirs aboard his galley. With the exit of the principals, the smaller fry, Menas and Enobarbus, show themselves as shadows of the great by complimenting each other upon being thieves, the pirate by sea and the soldier by land; their shaking hands is the kissing of pickers and stealers, wherefore Enobarbus says, "if our eyes had authority, here they might take two thieves kissing" (II.vi.96). But obviously there is no moral authority in this Mediterranean world to control the thieves at the top, and Menas is quite right when he presently says, "Pompey doth this day laugh away his fortune" (II.vi.102).

We are next shown the foremost men of all that world stupidly drunk: Lepidus is so drunk he must be carried off half way through the carouse (II.vii.89-91); Octavius says hardly anything, and might have been sober, except that he says he can scarcely talk straight (II.vii.122-123); Antony talks drunken nonsense (II.vii.41-45), agrees that the occasion approaches an Alexandrian feast (II.vii.95-96), desires to be dead drunk (II.vii.105-107), and needs to be steadied upon leaving (II.vii.126-128), and so surely should be presented on stage as staggering. Practical Menas sees the chance in this carouse for Pompey to win all. His proposal to cut the cable and then the throats of the drunken triumvirs is offered cautiously (II.vii.61-73), but rejected by Pompey instantly with the explanation, "Ah, this thou shouldst have done, / And not have spoke on 't! In me 'tis villainy, / In thee, 't had been good service" (II.vii.73-75). Such an excuse is the Renaissance cowardice of conscience. Pompey is portrayed as willing to profit by the crime, but unwilling to authorize or to take the blame. The fact that Menas asks is an illustration of the principle that the loyal subordinate first asks his superior before he commits a crime that may as likely injure as benefit him. If Menas had proceded to do it without having first asked, he could have expected only that such a one as Pompey would be willing to profit by the crime but would salve his conscience and public indignation with the execution of the perpetrator. Menas answers in an aside, "For this / I'll never follow thy pall'd fortunes more" (II.vii.81-82), and he is right is considering Pompey doomed: Caesar and Lepidus soon make war on Pompey (III.iv.3-4; III.p,4), who being defeated, escapes to Samos, where he has his throat cut by order of Antony, who then threatens to cut the throat of the officer who did so (III.v.18-19). Menas— one would like to say "wisely"— disappears from the play.

A contrast to Menas is promptly shown with Ventidius in Syria. We had heard briefly twice previously that he was intended for Parthia (II.ii.15; iii.40-41). Now he has won victories there, and could win more, but he holds back for a reason given at some length and as true today in dozens of vocations as ever it was in the Renaissance or Roman Military:

> Caesar and Antony have ever won
> More in their office than person: Sossius,
> One of my place in Syria, his lieutenant,
> For quick accumulation of renown,
> Which he achieve'd by the minute, lost his
>   favour.
> Who does i' the wars more than his captain can,
> Becomes his captain's captain: and ambition,
> The soldier's virtue, rather makes choice of loss,
> Than gain which darkens him.
> I could do more to do Antonius good,
> But 'twould offend him. And in his offence
> Should my performance perish.
>
> (III.i.16-27)

These generalizations have a source in Plutarch which is much more specific:

> [Ventidius] made the Parthians flie . . . Howbeit Ventidius durst not undertake to follow them any further, fearing least he should have gotten Antonius displeasure by it. Notwithstanding he led his armies against them that had rebelled . . . Antiochus, King of Commagena, . . . offered him a thowsand talentes to be pardoned his rebellion. . . . But Ventidius made him aunswere, that he should send unto Antonius, who was not farre of, and [who] would not suffer Ventidius to make any peace with Antiochus, to the end that yet this little exployt should passe in his [Antony's] name, and [so] that they should not thinke he did any thing but by his Lieutenaunt Ventidius.

A comparison of the two passages shows that Shakespeare has generalized from Ventidius in Plutarch to certain characteristics of command and power. The inclusion of the Ventidius scene does nothing to advance the plot in any way; its inclusion— when so much else had to be omitted— suggests Shakespeare was much interested in the incident, and his generalization from it suggests Shakespeare thought it true. It is not for patriotism, or empire, or national defense that such feats are done at the behest of an Antony or a Caesar, but only for the power and aggrandisement of Antony or Caesar, and a person who cannot see that truth of

power— then or now— is very likely a dupe of the calculated dissemination of fatuous ideals.

The testimony of Ventidius is followed immediately by a scene in which Agrippa and Enobarbus mimic and ridicule not only the foolishness of Lepidus, but the pretenses of Antony and Caesar. Antony is "the god of Jupiter," says Agrippa, who is part of Caesar's faction, and Enobarbus, part of Antony's, exclaims, "But as for Caesar, / Kneel down, kneel down, and wonder" (III.ii.1-20). The scene is tomfoolery, and the principal target is Lepidus, but Caesar and Antony emerge as things less than demigods in the opinions of their subordinates. In the remainder of the scene the departure of Antony and Octavia from Rome is seeded with warning to Antony: "You take from me a great part of myself; / Use me well in 't" (III.ii.24-25). But Agrippa and Enobarbus continue in asides their quizzical and skeptical comments upon the doings of the great folk (III.ii.51-59). The comments are appropriate guidance to the audience, since this marriage is broken up the next scene but one. Shakespeare has here sometimes followed Plutarch either explicitly or implicitly, and in other details he has condensed or reversed Plutarch. The most important detail is that Shakespeare only implies what Plutarch says so openly, namely, that Caesar allowed Octavia to be married to Antony so that "he might have an honest culler to make warre with Antonius if he did misuse her, and not esteeme of her as she ought to be." And again: "For Octavia, sayd they, that was maryed unto him as it were of necessitie, bicause her brother Caesars affayres so required it." The chief condensation is that considerable time elapsed between the marriage and its final open disruption, during which time Octavia leaves Athens for Italy, returns to Athens, returns to Rome, lives in Antony's house and cares for his children by herself and Fulvia. Shakespeare omits these details and the report that Caesar ordered Octavia to leave Antony's house in Rome, and that she refused until Antony himself ordered her out. Meanwhile Antony takes offense at Caesar's provocations, threatens him, is reconciled again, is offended again, rejoins Cleopatra, and in Alexandria publicly awards whole kingdoms to his and Cleopatra's children. Some of this is reported in the play, but much is not. In Plutarch Antony has given the earlier provocations, Octavius has been patient and restrained; in Shakespeare, more likely by design than as a result of the condensations, Caesar gives the provocations which cause Antony to send Octavia back to Rome (III.iv.), and that single separation is final. His dismissal of her is generous:

>   Provide your going,
> Choose your own company, and command
>   what cost
> Your heart has mind to.
>
> (III.iv.36-38)

Thus when she walks into her brother's presence, he

bursts out with no evidence, but with an instinct for political propaganda, "That ever I should call thee cast-away!" (III.vi.40). We should probably think him nothing disappointed, and the actor might throw a surprised and pleased look toward Agrippa and Maecenas. Octavia answers, "You have not call'd me so, nor have you cause," which is false in both halves, but Caesar then picks another fault at length, her unceremonious approach, which we have seen was Octavia's choice, as she acknowledges (III.vi.55-60). Octavia is trying to save her own face, which in his determination to have grievances her brother will not allow (III.vi.60-61), although he has a formidable battery of alleged grievances already assembled (III.vi.1-23), and has dismissed with specious excuses, or transparent ones— as that Lepidus was cruel (III.vi.32-34)— the better grievances that Antony has against him. Having exhibited his duplicity to the audience at some length, and also his efficiency in espionage (III.vi.65-76), Octavius recruits the high gods:

But let determin'd things to destiny
Hold unbewail'd their way. . . .
. . . . You are abus'd
Beyond the mark of thought: and the high
    gods,
To do you justice, makes his ministers
Of us, and those that love you.

                              (III.vi.84-89)

The *his* in the penultimate line certainly would be *its* in present-day usage, the antecedent of the pronoun *his* is invidentaly *justice*, but that Octavius is a minister of justice we may as certainly doubt as that Richard III is the Lord's Anointed. Octavius has traded his sister to Antony in the hope and expectation that she would be neglected or rejected and that he would thereby acquire another grievance against Antony to justify his aggressions. But Octavius had no intentions of being dependent upon the chances of such a rupture, and so he proceeded to give provocations to bring it about and to take offence in anticipation. It is a significant change from Plutarch that Caesar's provocations, which are reviewed by Antony (III.iv.1-10), took place in Plutarch *after* Octavia had returned to Rome and Antony to Cleopatra; whereas in Shapespeare's play, they are the *cause* of Antony's returning to Rome. Shakespeare thus has made Octavius less injured, less patient than he is in Plutarch, more corrupt, calculating, ruthless and predatory. He has made Antony simpler, "a plaine man, without suttletie," as Plutarch said, and something of the "plain blunt man," who could "only speak right on" (*Caesar*, III.ii.220-225), which the Antony of Julius Caesar said he was but wasn't. But Shakespeare has further improved Antony by omitting descriptions of the extremely offensive behavior which Plutarch attributed to Antony. For example, Shakespeare has Antony's seizure of Pompey's father's house mentioned twice (II.vi.26-29; vii.126-127), but nowhere is the behavior that accompanied that seizure reported in any such terms as

Plutarch used:

But setting aside the ill name he had for his insolencie, he was yet much more hated in respect of the house he dwelt in, the which was the house of Pompey the great: a man as famous for his temperaunce, modestie, and civill life, as for his three triumphes. For it grieved them to see the gates commonly shut against the Captaines, Magistrates of the citie, and also Ambassadors of straunge nations, which were sometimes thrust from the gates with violence: and that the house within was full of tomblers, anticke dauncers, juglers, players, jeasters, and dronkards, quaffing and goseling, and that on them he spent and bestowed the most parte of his money he got by all kind of possible extorcions, briberie and policie. For they did not only sell by the crier, the goods of those whom they had outlawed, and appointed to murther, slaunderously deceived the poore widowes and young orphanes . . . the holy vestall Nunnes had certaine goods and money put in their custodie . . . they went thither, and took them away by force.

Constantly elsewhere Plutarch declares of Antony or his friends, "he easely fell againe to his old licentious life . . . every one gave them selves to riot and excess"; and again, "so was he . . . to the most parte of men, cruell, and extreme. For he robbed noble men and gentle men of their goods, to geve it unto vile flatterers; who oftentimes begged mens goods living, as though they had bene dead, and would enter their houses by force"; and again, "But Antonius desire was altogether wicked and tyrannicall: who sought to keepe the people of Rome in bondage and subjection, but lately before rid of Caesars raigne." In brief, Shakespeare has debased the character and morality of Octavius and elevated the character and morality of Antony.

With the approach of Actium the behavior of Cleopatra as queen and commander of Egyptian forces becomes quasi-political. Plutarch had spoken of her enticements of Antony as "flickering," but in Shakespeare they are flamboyant and crackling from the beginning. Her principal tactic is to be adoring, complaisant and accursedly contrary by unpredictable turns: when Charmian tells her to "cross him in nothing," she answers, "Thou teachest like a fool: the way to lose him" (I.iii.9-10). Her technique works: he finds her "enchanting" and "cunning past man's thought" (I.ii.125, 143), and so with excellent reason Cleopatra has said in the first scene, "I'll seem the fool I am not; Antony / Will be himself" (I.i.42-43), i.e., they'll act a pair of fools together. The plain, blunt, triple pillar of the world is about as clever with Cleopatra as Rawdon Crawley is with Becky Sharp. Like Becky, Cleopatra reports the truth with considerable flexibility; so much so that she's rather a first cousin to a pathological liar. Nothing she says can be taken without consideration of her reasons for saying it, and the calculated lies she exhibits so casually early in the play (I.iii.1-5) continue all the way to the accounting with Seleucus (V.ii.140-157). We must, accordingly, peer around or through her speech as much as with any other character that Shakespeare has made for us.

The debate before Actium is upon whether to fight by land or sea and whether Cleopatra should be present. She enters with Enobarbus, who has opposed her participation in battle and who is already half frantic about her determination and her hostility to him for opposing her decision. "But why, why, why?" he asks, and "Well, is it, is it?" (III.vii.2,4), two popular forms of distraught indignation that are still current. Cleopatra concludes the conversation rather despotically: "Speak not against it, / I will not stay behind" (III.vii.18-19).

When Antony comes and tells her of Caesar's celerity, she answers with a rebuke of his negligence (III.vii.20-25). Apparently in an effort to mollify her he tells Canidius, "we / Will fight with him by sea," and she about-faces to rebuke him again with, "By sea, what else?" Canidius and Enobarbus both argue with Antony, Enobarbus with such arguments as paralleled the English experience with the Spanish Armada: "Their ships are yare, yours heavy" (III.vii.38), and that argument is also straight out of Plutarch, who had said, "Caesars shippes were not built for pompe, highe, and great, onely for a sight and bravery, [as Cleopatra's and Antony's were] but they were light of yarage, armed and furnished with water men" [instead of landsmen]. Antony is reduced to stubborn and stupid assertions, "By sea, by sea," and "I'll fight at sea," and Cleopatra comes to his rescue with: "I have sixty sails, Caesar none better" (III.vii.49).

With that remark we should surmise what lies behind the decision: Cleopatra wants to be present at the battle, it is she who wants the fight by sea, and her reason is the sybaritic one that her boat will be more comfortable than anything that land accommodations can provide— litters, tents, camps, horses, dust, noise and confusion. How do we know this? From her character— her voluptuousness, self-indulgence, willfulness and duplicity. What if the spectator doesn't know all that? He's free to miss it; or if it puzzles him, he can again resort to Plutarch, who says in one place, "yet for Cleopatraes sake, he [Antony] would needs have this battell tryed by sea," and in another, "But now, notwithstanding all these good perswasions, Cleopatra forced him to put all to the hazard of battel by sea: considering with her selfe how she might . . . provide for her safetie, not to helpe him to winne the victory, but to flie more easily." Even the unnamed common soldier can see how wrong the decision is (III.vii.61-66), but Antony evidently thinks him not even worth answering, and the soldier is left standing, to say in the aggrieved style of a commoner neglected because he's a commoner, "By Hercules I think I am i' the right."

He is right indeed; apparently Hercules also thought so (IV.iii.15), and the earlier aside of Enobarbus now proves prophetic:

If we should serve with horse and mares together,
The horse were merely lost; the mares would bear
A soldier *and* his horse.

(III.vii.7-9)

The politics of the remainder of the play *are* the reciprocal patterns of triumph and defeat— with little honesty emerging from either. Canidius joins six unnamed kings in defecting with all his troops to Caesar (III.x.33-35). Antony's sanguine reservations, "But if we fail, / We then can do 't by land" (III.vii.52-53), was naively oblivious of other people's ideas of their own self-interest. Antony deceives himself in thinking Caesar might allow him to remain in Egypt or to live a private man in Athens (III.xii.11-15), and he deceives himself again in thinking his army and navy hold firm (III.xiii.169-171). His supreme foolishness is in thinking Caesar might risk all against him in single combat (III.xiii.25-28). Caesar's implacable hostility to Antony and his evident intention to hunt Antony to death wherever he might go (III.xii.11-15, 19:20; V.i.37-40) leave Antony the choices of futile resistance, ignominious flight, or ignominious surrender— and death will be the certain termination of any one of those. Cleopatra, however, Caesar would save for a Roman triumph, and so the political negotiations between Caesar and Antony are replaced by those between Caesar and Cleopatra.

Caesar's first move is to attempt to separate her from Antony (III.xii.26-27), and when, after her flagrant abandonment at Actium, Shakespeare has her ask Enobarbus, "Is Antony, or we, in fault for this?" (III.xiii.2), we may surmise that Caesar's intuition is serving him well. Thidias soon arrives, having been given *carte blanche* to deceive (III.xii.26-33), and comes to Cleopatra with a face-saving opener:

Thid. He knows that you embrac'd not Antony
As you did love, but as you fear'd him.

Cleo.   O!

Thid. The scars upon your honour, therefore he
Does pity, as constrained blemishes,
Not as deserv'd.

Cleo. He is a god, and knows
What is most right. Mine honour was not yielded,
But conquer'd merely.

(III.xiii.56-62)

This dialogue is a considerable change from Plutarch, who has said, "Cleopatra began to cleare and excuse her selfe for that she had done, laying all to the feare she had of Antonius. Caesar, in contrarie maner, reproved her in every poynt." Moreover, in Plutarch Cleopatra's disowning of Antony takes place only *after* his death, at the same time as the episode with Seleucus. In advancing this detail from after Antony's death to before, and attributing its origin to Caesar's machinations, Shakespeare has complicated and subtilized it, and cynically degraded the characters of both Caesar and Cleopatra as they appear in this incident in Plutarch. How far Shakespeare's Cleopatra accepts Thidias' face-saving device is not clear. Her "0!" seems like sudden surprise, and her next answer sounds ironic, and could even be mockery if delivered that way, but Enorbarbus takes it as a straightforward lie and leaves to fetch Antony. Meantime Cleopatra continues with vague terms of accommodation and gives Thidias, as Caesar's emissary, her delicate royal hand to kiss.

In the storm of Antony's recriminations which follow, Cleopatra is always slippery, always implying he ought to properly understand her, who loves him so unreservedly, and yet she is always so non-committal that she may indeed be planning to save herself by accommodating Caesar. "O, is 't come to this?" says she, and "Wherefore is this?" and "Have you done yet?" and "I must stay his time," as he finally gets blown out, "Not know me yet?" She is not the world's most plausible candidate to play injured innocence, but she played it anyway. Antony's ravings, through which she exhibits such angelic patience, ring changes upon what he was and how the world forgets, and what *she* was, "a morsel, cold upon / Dead Caesar's trencher," although we may doubt from his own and Enobarbus' earlier testimony (II.ii.228-240) that this particular morsel was ever cold. Indeed, all through this scene Antony wrests the truth of what we know were past events (III.xiii.105-109, 116-120), blames the stars, harps on what he was and superficially seems oblivious to the fact that the authority he finds melting from him has nothing to do at all with what he, for being simply man, may be, but on the contrary derives only from power, which can exist without him, and has now passed elsewhere. Antony is quick to declare of Caesar that he lacks personal merit and derives his reputation from the achievements of lieutenants (III.xi.38-40; IV.xii.14, 48), but comparable things were said of Antony by Ventidius, of whom Plutarch had written, "Ventidius was the only man that ever triumphed of the Parthians until this present day, a meane man borne, and of no noble house nor family . . . he confirmed that . . . Antonius and Caesar . . . were always more fortunate when they made warre by their Lieutenants, then by themselves." Thus in this play the power that authority derives from appears to be based more upon prestige than upon the transcendant merit that would be necessary morally to justify the inequities of power. The prestige that appears to govern power and thence authority is shown as something of an imposition; prestige as it operates in this play is closer to its etymological meaning— delusion, illusion, juggler's trick, prestidigitation— than to its modern meaning, which is certainly naive and may be intrinsically gullible. How Antony's power has melted is explicit in the next scene when Caesar declares, "Within our files there are, / Of those that serv'd Mark Antony but late, / Enough to fetch him in" (IV.i.12-14). At the battle of Alexandria Caesar orders Antony's defected soldiers to be placed in the vanguard, "That Antony may seem to spend his fury / Upon himself" (IV.vi.10-11). We infer that troops which have revolted once may revolt again, and so they're unreliable, and so they were best used up some way, and so if one's own advantage is also served in their consumption, the benefit is double. We are then told that Caesar is suspicious of all defectors and has had one hanged outright (IV.vi.12-18).

The ultimate defection from Antony would be that of Cleopatra, and whether or not it was begun we cannot be sure. Antony's report of the movement of her fleet (IV.x.6-7), is phased in passive voice, and so we cannot tell whether he or Cleopatra had sent the order, but we must infer it was either he or she, and it is more plausible to infer the order was hers. Whichever it was, her fleet defects, and it might have done so without any order or urging from her. On the other hand, Antony asserts six times that she has betrayed him: "This foul Egyptian hath betrayed me: / My fleet hath yielded to the foe" (IV.xii.10-11); "Triple-turn'd whore, 'tis thou / Hast sold me to this novice" (IV. xii. 13-14); "Betray'd I am. / O this false soul of Egypt!" (IV.xii.24-29); "The witch shall die, To the young Roman boy she hath sold me, and I fall / Under this plot" (IV.xii.47-49); "she, Eros, has / Pack'd cards with Caesar, and false-play'd my glory / Unto an enemy's triumph" (IV.xiv.18-20); "She hath betray'd me, and shall die the death" (IV.xiv.26). Nothing dissuades him from this opinion until he receives news of her death, which, had it been true, might have been persuasive for the audience, too. As it is, we cannot tell from Plutarch whether Antony's accusation was true, and in the play Shakespeare has retained that ambiguity but heavily increased the vehemence and frequency of the accusation. When Antony storms at her fleet's defection, her answer sounds most extraordinarily hypocritical: "Why is my lord enrag'd against his love?" (IV.xii.31). Although Cleopatra speaks of Antony as "my lord" to other persons, her use of the term in direct address is uncharacteristic and implies an uncharacteristic subordination of herself; the last four words imply fault in him and innocence in herself; the third person references to him and to herself, also uncharacteristic, suggest a detachment which in turn suggests lying. Even if she was innocent of arranging for the defection of her fleet, it was visible from where they were (IV.x.4-9), and knowledge of it ought to have reached her as soon as it reached Antony.

If she already knew of it but was innocent of arranging it, she ought to have come in with woeful exclamations. If she really did not know, then the normal Elizabethan answer called for by Antony's exclamation was, "What's the matter now?" not what she says. But Shakespeare gives us no unequivocal evidence either way, easy as it would have been to do so, and we are left to weigh the possibilities against her other behavior.

During their reconciliation after the quarrel over Thidias, Cleopatra falls so strangely silent and preoccupied that Antony must recall her to what he has been saying with, "Dost thou hear, lady?" (III.xiii.172). He repeats his brags, and she answers with a mixture of encouragement and patronage: "That's my brave lord!" We cannot tell what she is thinking of, but we can see that she is not heart and soul with Antony. The defection of her fleet and her own flight to the monument follow, and Diomedes brings word to Antony:

> when she saw—
> Which never shall be found—you did suspect
> She had dispos'd with Caesar, and that your rage
> Would not be purg'd, she sent you word she was dead.
>
> (IV.xiv.121-124)

This message hardly constitutes evidence of her innocence; if one falsehood can be sent by messenger, so can other. Convincing evidence would have to be disinterested, a soliloquy or a confidence from her or from Caesar, but none is given us. Her grief over Antony's death is great poetry, and out of the silent shock of woe she answers her maid's urgent address, "Royal Egypt: / Empress," with "No more but e'en a woman, and commanded / By such poor passion as the maid that milks, / And does the meanest chares" (IV.xv.70-75).

Cleopatra's first response to Antony's death is shock, and the second is to ask, "Then is it sin, / To rush into the secret house of death / Ere death dare come to us?" (IV.xv.80-82). Caesar's first response is a tempered regret (V.i.14-48), and next, to negotiate with Cleopatra. In the same speech he tells Proculeius, "Go and say / we purpose her no shame," and also, "For her life in Rome / Would be eternal in our triumph" (V.i.61-66). This flagrant lying is not all of it at his hour of absolute triumph. He invites everyone on stage into his tent, "where you shall see / How hardly I was drawn into this war"—not how he gambled on Antony's weakness and provoked the war deliberately, as Shakespeare has shown. The inevitable myth of the virtuous victor is in process of formation.

When Proculeius appears before Cleopatra and she asks for Egypt, "mine own," Proculeius gives her soothing words without commitment (V.ii.9-34), captures her,

and supplies more soothing but deceitful words. Antony's advice to her to trust only Proculeius (IV.xv.47-48; V.ii.12-15), a detail out of Plutarch, makes Antony wrong to his dying words, however good his intentions may have been. Cleopatra's sure insight as to Caesar's intentions, that he would carry her in a triumph, is expressed with great spirit (V.ii.52-62), and confirmed not from Proculeius, who knows it, but from Dolabella (V.ii.106-110), a minor character of unaccustomed sweetness to be a minion of Caesar.

The incident with Seleucus which follows has been subjected to opposite interpretations. The bare bones of the incident are in Plutarch, where Caesar laughs at it and where the gloss declares "Cleopatra finely deceiveth Octavius Caesar as though she desires to live." This passage gave rise in the nineteenth century to the suggestion of Adolph Stahr (1864) that Cleopatra was in cahoots with Seleucus, and that her purpose was to deceive Caesar into thinking she wanted to live so that she'd have time to arrange to die in a suitable fashion. That interpretation was accepted by J. Dover Wilson and M. R. Ridley in the introductions to their respective editions. The chief difficulties with it are that Cleopatra's collusion with Seleucus is entirely inferential in both Plutarch and Shakespeare, and difficult or impossible to show in the playing, although neither objection is sufficient reason to deny the hypothesis. Whether conniving with Seleucus or not, Cleopatra is still showing herself characteristically deceitful. The only difference the denial of collusion makes is that instead of being calculatedly deceitful, she is casually so, and that latter quality is by no means out of character. It is rather a fuller revelation of her unplumbed potentials, of which one more remains.

Antony had called her a "triple-turn'd whore" (IV.xii.13), and the explanation that has been offered for that epithet is that her first turn was from Julius Caesar to Pompey, the second was from Pompey to Antony, and the third was (or Antony believed it to be), from Antony to Octavius Caesar. Plutarch gives no indication that Cleopatra played for Octavius, but in the *Roman Histories of Florus,* Bolton's translation is quite specific: "Antonius was the first of the two who slew himselfe. The Quenne kneeling at the feete of Caesar, laid baite for his eyes; but in vaine; her beauties were beneath that princes chastitie." In Daniel's *Cleopatra* (1599), she says to Octavius, "For looke what I have beene to Antony, / Thinke thou the same I might have beene to thee," of which Caesar says to Dolabella, "In deed I saw she labour'd to impart / Her sweetest graces in her saddest cheere: . . . . But all in vaine, she takes her ayme amisse."

If we look for evidence of similar tendencies in Shakespeare, it must be granted that all the evidence is so oblique that it might either be made evident or be quite obscured by the acting that accompanies the text. First, there is her apparent dealing with Caesar through Thidias, of which Granville-Barker has written, "She lends an ear to Thidias, and the message to Caesar sounds flat treason." Next, there is the defection of her fleet and Antony's consequent accusations. Third, there is her question of Dolabella after Antony's death, "Think you there was, or might be such a man / As this I dreamt of?" (V.ii.93-94). As L. J. Mills has written of this question. "It appears that she was giving him an opportunity to assure her that Caesar, now Emperor, is such a man." If so, Dolabella fails to understand or ignores what he sees, or denies it, for he says, "Gentle madam, no." Fourth, and perhaps what should be the most evident in the acting, is her farewell to Caesar. He has just said, "For we intend so to dispose you, as / Yourself shall give us counsel" (V.ii.185-186). Her farewell is, "My master, and my lord," which last is a term she had once bestowed upon Antony. If she there engages in some blandishments, smiles wistfully and kisses his hand overlong, he or any man would understand, and his answer, "Not so," is a double refusal— of her terminology and of her offer of love— and his "adieu" is meant both as the temporary departure of a conqueror and as a refusal to become a lover, but is also the long farewell of those parted by death, all of which meanings Cleopatra immediately understands. The last piece of evidence, and one which supports this interpretation of their final meeting, is after her death, lines which are Caesar's only poetry in the whole play:

> she looks like sleep,
> As she would catch another Antony
> In her strong toil of grace.
>
> (V.ii.344-346)

Certainly we should think of Octavius as thinking of himself.

As in *King Lear*, the great poetry at the tragic conclusion of the play often obscures momentarily the behavior that had produced that tragedy. The more effectively the tragic catharsis works, the less one considers all the deceitful machinations just reviewed; and conversely, the more one contemplates the machinations, the farther off the tragic catharsis and hence the dramatic essence may be felt to be. We conclude that one cannot give this attention simultaneously to both. But the play is both parts together, and only that. It is as great a love tragedy of irresponsible maturity as *Romeo and Juliet* is of irresponsible youth. As Shakespeare advanced in middle age, it is to be expected that his protagonists would also age somewhat. But a tragedy of middle-aged love need not involve a tale of politics— *Othello* doesn't— nor heroics, either. Had Shakespeare wanted to write a tragedy of middle-aged, classical and heroical figures in love, there was always the tale of Dido and Aeneas, which has all kinds of possibilities in King Cambyses' or any later vein. The choice of Antony and Cleopatra as a subject, with its very heavy emphasis upon political chicanery and deceit, is a deliberate Shakespearean choice. It continues his studies of politics at the highest levels of government, and once more what we have been shown is not at all flattering to heads of state.

Octavius is completely self-controlled, but that merit has so many inherent defects that even whether it is a merit may be questioned. He has a puritanical contempt of Cleopatra which conveniently and not incidentally serves his own interests. A man who would sell his own sister as a bait and trap to do in a friend and ally, with full expectation that the alliance will turn out as it does, stands on no eminence from which to disseminate moralistic airs. Cleopatra may be three kinds of a liar, but she has the internal spontaneity which Octavius can never even understand. His treatment of Pompey, Lepidus, alexas and Antony, and his intentions toward Cleopatra all express one impulse: his heartless and ruthless pursuit of his own power. Although Shakespeare could hardly have known the *Ricordi* of Guicciardini, the behavior of Octavius in this play illustrates the principles of the following paragraph:

> 73. Neither Alexander the Great, nor Caesar, nor the others who have been praised in this respect, ever showed mercy which they knew might spoil or endanger the fruits of their victory, because that would have been madness, but only in those cases where mercy did not threaten their security and made them the more to be admired.

That Octavius is competent to rule in his fashion cannot be denied, but that is not to say that Shakespeare's Octavius has our, Shakespeare's, or anyone's approval. His modern press has been terrible.

Antony, on the contrary, has been improved from Plutarch; his cruel and uncontrollable predation there has been muted and converted to private riot, "lascivious wassail" the envy of Octavius and posterity, gaudy nights heaped upon gaudy days, and the inexhaustible erotic safari— "Come on, my queen, / There's sap in 't yet" (III.xiii.191-192), as he no doubt grins and shakes it. Shakespeare had a Renaissance example of such a chief of state in Henry IV of France, who also came to a bad end not long after this play was written. That so self-indulgent a triumvir could be any match for so coldly calculating an Octavius is not to be thought of. In the safe and non-consequential realms of vicarious identification we can admire Antony for the poetic reasons Cleopatra gives us (V.ii.76-92), but in no lucid moment could we wish to be a citizen of the towns he gives away as the ruck of his moiety of the world.

Neither could we have much wish to be subject, like Mardian, to the whims of Cleopatra. Shakespeare's idea of the quality of her rule must be inferred from his portrait of her character. Capricious, despotic, amoral, licentious— "O happy horse to bear the weight of Antony!"— utterly possessed by her erotic appetites, seemingly, she still has self-possession enough always to seek her own immediate self-interest, to lie, cheat, swagger and swear, to be humble and sly, and to betray anyone, even Antony or her children, for her own enormously egocentric satisfactions. Shakespeare has lowered the levels of morality in both Octavius and Cleopatra from what they are in Plutarch, and he has made Antony less vicious but more foolish. If one be disposed to think well of the great and famous, Shakespeare's alterations are cynical. On the other hand, trust in the great may be fatuity, and Shakespeare's cynicism may be true realism.

To these three principals we may add the third triumvir, foolish Lepidus, and a would-be ruler, idealistic and imprudent Pompey. Not one of the five has the remotest resemblance to that Renaissance image of the perfect prince, he who was just under the angels on the Great Chain, anointed, crowned, and planted as God's vicar, most Christian, wise and just, clement, magnanimous, majestic and serene, as all the various royal rascallitie of that age commonly represented itself to its public.

SOURCES FOR FURTHER STUDY

Literary Commentary

Barroll, J. Leeds. "Shakespeare and the Art of Character: A Study of Antony," pp. 159-235. *Shakespeare Studies Annual*, No. V, edited by J. Leeds Barroll. Dubuque, IA: Wm. C. Brown Company Publishers 1969.

A thorough analysis of what distinguishes Antony from other characters. Barroll asserts that the character of Antony is defined by his own interpretation of what it means to be a soldier. In other words, for Antony, soldierly virtue includes chivalry as well as courage. However, Barroll points out, those men who serve Caesar believe that soldiers should follow policy— or a practical, Machiavellian form of warfare and strategy.

———. "The Characterization of Octavius," pp. 231-87. *Shakespeare Studies Annual*, No. VI, edited by J. Leeds Barroll. Dubuque, IA. Wm C. Brown Company Publishers, 1970.

Discusses the difficulty of settling on a single character description for Octavius Caesar. Barroll observes that unlike Antony, Octavius fails to inspire loyalty in his men. Further, Barroll suggests that for someone who likes being in control of events, Octavius is ultimately unable to control either Antony or Cleopatra.

———. "Cleopatra and the Size of Dreaming." In *Shakespearean Tragedy: Genre, Tradition, and Change, in "Antony and Cleopatra,"* pp. 130-87. Cranbury, NJ: Associated University Presses, 1984.

Analyzes the wide variety of responses— both positive and negative— to Cleopatra's character. Barroll acknowledges that Cleopatra's lack of self-understanding or of feelings of guilt might disqualify her for tragic status. Barroll locates Cleopatra's tragedy in the destruction of all of her "grandiose" plans— for herself and for Antony— and in her genuine grief at Antony's death.

Bevington, David. Introduction to *Antony and Cleopatra* by William Shakespeare, edited by David Bevington, pp. 1-70. Cambridge: Cambridge University Press, 1990.

Provides a detailed overview of the play, including date and source material and critical assessments of the characters. Bevington also focuses on the use of irony in the play— in particular, how irony sets the play's dialogue at odds with the play's action. Finally, Bevington evaluates the numerous ways in which *Antony and Cleopatra* has been performed before live audiences and includes a discussion of the difficulties of staging so elaborate a play— with its barges, battles, and monuments.

Cantor, Paul A. "Part Two: *Antony and Cleopatra.*" In *Shakespeare's Rome: Republic and Empire*, pp. 127-208. Ithaca, NY: Cornell University Press, 1976.

In his three chapters on *Antony and Cleopatra*, Cantor argues first that the play cannot be divided neatly into private versus public life; second he asserts that Antony is not "bewitched" away from Rome by Cleopatra, but that he is already aware and disapproving of Rome's faults. Third, Cantor argues that the love between Antony and Cleopatra is made possible through its very originality and tendency toward exaggeration, and that "the guiding principal of [the two lovers] in both public and private life is open hostility to stale custom." Incidentally, Cantor also argues that Antony and Cleopatra achieve marriage through death— thus turning a potentially tragic play into a comedy.

Doran, Madeleine. "'High Events as These': The Language of Hyperbole in *Antony and Cleopatra.*" *Queen's Quarterly* LXXII, No. 1 (Spring 1965): 26-51.

Interprets the play in the context of the Elizabethan fascination for hyperbolic language, or the expression of things as grandiose, perfect, and ideal. Doran concludes by suggesting that Shakespeare used hyperbole not only to satisfy his audience's tastes but also to demonstrate that the "true wonder" of human beings— of Antony and Cleopatra for example— exists not in exaggeration but in the story of their lives.

Fitch, Robert E. "No Greater Crack?" *Shakespeare Quarterly* XIX, (1968): 3-17.

Contends that we cannot mourn Cleopatra's death as tragic because it is the result of a pre-Christian struggle between power and pleasure in a world that is "coldly geopolitical" rather than genuinely loving or honorable.

Fitz, L. T. "Egyptian Queens and Male Reviewers: Sexist Attitudes in *Antony and Cleopatra* Criticism." *Shakespeare Quarterly* 28, No. 3 (Summer 1977): 297-316.

Asserts that critical approaches to the character Cleopatra have been for the most part misogynistic. Fitz explains that critics either condemn Cleopatra as "a treacherous strumpet" or celebrate her love for Antony as "transcendental." Both assessments, Fitz explains, do a disservice to the character and to the play. Fitz argues that critics need to suspend their own preconceived notions at least long enough to humanize their characterization of Cleopatra— to understand her emotions— before they can interpret the play accurately.

Harrier, Richard C. "Cleopatra's End." *Shakespeare Quarterly* XIII, No. 1 (Winter 1962):63-65.

Briefly assesses the characters of Cleopatra, Antony, and Octavius. Harrier concludes that Antony is superior to Cleopatra but that when she dies for his sake, Cleopatra raises herself somewhat to Antony's level.

Honigmann, E. A. J. "Antony versus Cleopatra." In *Shakespeare: Seven Tragedies*, pp. 150-69. London: The Macmillan Press Ltd., 1976.

Discusses the ways in which the relationship between Antony and Cleopatra changes halfway through the play. Honigmann contends that in the first half, Cleopatra dominates the action and Antony is the butt of her jokes; however, in the second half, Antony— newly ashamed by his military losses— achieves moral and theatrical superiority over Cleopatra.

Jose, Nicholas. "*Antony and Cleopatra*: Face and Heart." *Philological Quarterly* 62, No. 4 (Fall 1983): 487-505.

Argues that in *Antony and Cleopatra*, characters form the central interest of the play. Specifically, Jose discusses the characters' emotional attachments to one another, to an idea, or to their homeland as crucial to the outcome of the play.

Kuriyama, Constance Brown. "The Mother of the World: A Psychoanalytic Interpretation of Shakespeare's *Antony and Cleopatra*." *English Literary Renaissance* 7, No. 3 (Autumn 1977): 324-51.

Applies Freudian psychology to the play. Kuriyama argues that *Antony and Cleopatra* should not be read merely as a moral lesson or for its poetry. Instead, she asserts that critics should acknowledge that the play functions as a sexual fantasy which provides us the pleasure of knowing that when Antony and Cleopatra are at last "united in death," they achieve "honor," "selfhood," and "immortality."

MacKenzie, Clayton G. "*Antony and Cleopatra*: A Mythological Perspective." *Orbis Litterarum* 45, No. 4 (1990): 309-29.

Argues against those critics who suggest that the play is based on the militaristic sensibility of Roman mythology. Instead, MacKenzie argues that Shakespeare intentionally undercuts Roman mythology in *Antony and Cleopatra* and replaces it with an original mythology based on love.

Nevo, Ruth. "Antony and Cleopatra." In *Tragic Form in Shakespeare*, pp. 306-55. Princeton, NJ: Princeton University Press, 1972.

Describes the characters Antony and Cleopatra as "mutual pairs" participating equally in a tragic end— unlike Othello and Desdemona or Hamlet and Ophelia. Nevo contends that, despite scholarly complaints that Cleopatra is fickle and "devious," the Egyptian Queen is in fact faithful to her love for Antony throughout the play and she remains convinced that their love will survive after death.

Shapiro, Stephen A. "The Varying Shore of the World: Ambivalence in *Antony and Cleopatra*." *Modern Language Quarterly* XXVII, No. 1 (March 1966): 18-32.

Observes that there have been two opposing critical approaches to the characters

Antony and Cleopatra: a moralistic view that censures the two lovers; and a "transcendental" view that asserts that the pair's love is superior. Shapiro focuses on the play's dualism, arguing that the series of opposites in the play— love and war, fertility and death, Rome and Egypt— serves to draw our attention to the ambiguities in our own world.

Smith, Sheila M. "'This Great Solemnity': A Study of the Presentation of Death in *Antony and Cleopatra*." *English Studies* 45, No. 2 (1964): 163-76.

Sees the guiding force behind *Antony and Cleopatra* as the struggle of opposites: Octavius versus Antony; Rome versus Egypt; Antony versus Cleopatra. Smith demonstrates how Shakespeare skillfully maneuvers these opposites to their ultimate resolution, which is death.

Whitney, Cynthia Kolb. "The War in *Antony and Cleopatra*." *Literature & Psychology* XIII, No. 3 (Summer 1963): 63-66.

Describes the war between Egypt and Rome as one where "the world is split in half and fights itself." Whitney observes that this actual war becomes a symbol for the inner struggles of characters such as Antony, who feels torn between his loyalty for Rome and his attraction to Cleopatra. The inner struggle even affects less central characters such as Octavia, who is caught between her sense of duty to her new husband, Antony, and her love for and loyalty to her brother, Octavius.

Williamson, Marilyn. "The Political Context in *Antony and Cleopatra*." *Shakespeare Quarterly* XXI, No. 3 (Summer 1970): 241-51.

Evaluates Antony and Cleopatra as "rulers as well as

lovers." Williamson focuses on the play's politics, arguing that much can be learned about Antony and Cleopatra from their treatment of their subordinates as well as from the manner in which their subordinates view them.

Williamson, Marilyn L. "Fortune in *Antony and Cleopatra.*" *JEGP* LXVII (1968): 423-29.

Demonstrates how preeminent Fortune is in *Antony and Cleopatra*. Williamson asserts that by their changeable natures, both Antony and Cleopatra resemble the goddess, Fortune. Williamson also contends that Shakespeare relies on Fortune as a motif in the play to indicate the unpredictability of life and to underscore the point at which Cleopatra changes into someone who— after Antony's death— refuses to be ruled by Fortune.

Wolf, William D. "'New Heaven, New Earth': The Escape from Mutability in *Antony and Cleopatra.*" *Shakespeare Quarterly* 33, No. 3 (Autumn 1982): 328-35.

Acknowledges the opposing forces at work in the play: politics versus love, public versus private, Rome versus Egypt. Wolf then proceeds to point out that despite these differences, the worlds of Rome and Egypt share an important element: both are subject to violent fluctuations. With regard to Rome, Wolf observes, the change is political; with regard to Egypt, it is emotional. In both cases, Wolf asserts, the changes revolve around Antony.

Wright, Austin. "Antony and Cleopatra," pp. 37-51. In *Shakespeare: Lectures on Five Plays, Carnegie Series in English, Number Four*, by A. Fred Sochatoff et al. Pittsburgh: Carnegie Institute of Technology, 1958.

Observes that the play's central issues are politics and love. Wright views Antony as a straightforward, tragic figure but sees Cleopatra as much more complex. Cleopatra, he asserts, is "fascinating" but untrustworthy.

Media Adaptations

Antony and Cleopatra. Great Britain/Spain, 1972.
Directed by Charlton Heston. Heston stars as Mark Antony and Hildegard Neil stars as Cleopatra. Eric Porter plays Enobarbus. Available on video. 160 minutes.

Antony and Cleopatra. BBC and Time/Life, Inc., 1980.
Directed by Jonathan Miller. Starring Colin Blakely, Jane Lapotaire, and Ian Charleson. Available on video. 180 minutes.

THE COMEDY OF ERRORS

INTRODUCTION

The Comedy of Errors is considered one of Shakespeare's earliest plays, possibly his first comedy and certainly his shortest play, written sometime between 1589 and 1594, although it was not printed until 1623. The primary source of the play is the *Menaechmi* of Plautus, a Roman comic playwright, but Shakespeare also borrowed from Plautus's *Amphitruo*. From the *Menaechmi* Shakespeare took his central plot, which revolves around "errors," or mistaken identity, involving identical twin brothers. To this Shakespeare added additional characters and episodes.

Much of the criticism on the play discusses how Shakespeare complicated Plautus's plot. Shakespeare added another set of twins, servants to the twin sons of Aegeon. The story of Aegeon—his separation from his wife and one of the twin sons—is also a change from the Roman play. Shakespeare gave greater voice to the primary female characters in the play (and thus to issues of gender and the relationships between men and women), especially Adriana, who is merely a shrewish "Wife" in Plautus's play, and downgraded the role of an unnamed Courtezan. Shakespeare's selection of Ephesus for the setting of the play (the action of the play takes place in a single day in a single place) has been noted by critics as an important alteration in the play, since Ephesus was associated with sorcery, exorcism, mystery cults, and emerging Christianity. Critics tend to be in agreement that Shakespeare greatly expanded on the generally one-dimensional stereotypical characters in Plautus's play.

There was a scarcity of commentary on the play prior to the nineteenth century. Samuel Taylor Coleridge was the first to discuss the play as a unified work of art, asserting that it was a farce and therefore should not be judged by the standards applied to comedy. Some critics viewed it as an apprentice work, since it was written so early in Shakespeare's career, and few critics argued that the play displays the full range of Shakespeare's dramatic talent. More recent criticism has focused on the play's genre (its "identity" as a tragedy, farce, comedy, or a combination of these) and the way in which it explores the issues of identity, gender, and love and marriage.

PRINCIPAL CHARACTERS

Solinus: Duke of Ephesus.

Aegeon: Merchant from Syracuse traveling in Ephesus in search of his son. It is illegal for a Syracusan to travel in Ephesus; he must pay a large ransom or be condemned to death. He tells the Duke of Ephesus his tragic family tale of separation, and the Duke, sympathetic to his plight, gives him one day to gather enough money to free himself.

Antipholus of Ephesus: Twin brother of Antipholus of Syracuse, son of Aegeon and Aemilia, husband of Adriana. He is a well-known, well-respected merchant in the city of Ephesus. *(See **Antipholus of Syracuse and Antipholus of Ephesus** in the **CHARACTER STUDIES** section.)*

Antipholus of Syracuse: Twin brother of Antipholus of Ephesus, son of Aegeon and Aemilia. At the age of eighteen, he goes off to search for his long-lost brother with his servant, Dromio of Syracuse. *(See **Antipholus of Syracuse and Antipholus of Ephesus** in the **CHARACTER STUDIES** section.)*

Dromio of Ephesus: Personal servant of Antipholus of Ephesus, and the twin brother of Dromio of Syracuse. Married to Luce, Adriana's servant.

Dromio of Syracuse: Personal servant of Antipholus of Syracuse, and the twin brother of Dromio of Ephesus.

Balthazar: A merchant and business associate of Antipholus of Ephesus.

Angelo: A goldsmith hired by Antipholus of Ephesus to make a gold chain for Adriana.

Pinch: A "doctor"/conjurer. He is brought in to cure Antipholus of Syracuse of his supposed madness.

Aemilia: Abbess at Ephesus. Separated from her husband, Aegeon, in a shipwreck twenty-three years earlier, she is reunited at the end of the play with her husband as well as her long-lost son, Antipholus of Syracuse. Her appearance at the end of the play resolves the confusion surrounding the identities of her sons and their servants.

Adriana: Wife of Antipholus of Ephesus and at the center of the instances of mistaken identity between the twin Antipholi. *(See **Adriana and Luciana** in the **CHARACTER STUDIES** section.)*

Luciana: Unmarried sister of Adriana, courted by Antipholus of Syracuse. *(See **Adriana and Luciana** in the*

CHARACTER STUDIES *section.)*
Luce: Servant of Adriana and wife of Dromio of Ephesus who mistakes the Syracusan Dromio for the Ephesian Dromio.

A Courtezan: An acquaintance of Antipholus of Ephesus.

PLOT SYNOPSIS

Act I: Aegeon, a merchant from Syracuse, is apprehended in Ephesus because it is illegal for Syracusans to be in Ephesus. The Duke of Ephesus, Solinus, tells him that he must pay a ransom or be condemned to death. Aegeon then relates to the Duke his tragic tale of separation from his wife and one of his twin sons twenty-three years earlier in a shipwreck. The other son left Aegeon five years earlier with his servant (also a twin; these twins were also separated in the shipwreck) in search of his missing brother. Aegeon decided to follow him and now finds himself in Ephesus. The Duke is sympathetic to Aegeon's plight and gives him twenty-four hours to raise the money.

Unbeknownst to Aegeon, the son he is searching for, Antipholus of Syracuse, has just arrived in Ephesus with his servant, Dromio of Syracuse. Antipholus is unaware that he is in the same city as both his father and long-lost brother, Antipholus of Ephesus. Antipholus of Syracuse tells Dromio to go to their inn and guard their money since they are Syracusans in Ephesus. Dromio of Ephesus, servant to the Ephesian Antipholus, then enters and tells Antipholus of Syracuse that his wife, Adriana, wants him to come home for dinner. (Adriana is in fact the wife of his twin brother.) Antipholus, thinking that Dromio of Ephesus is his own servant, asks about the safety of the money, and when Dromio denies knowledge of the gold, Antipholus beats him. Dromio runs away and Antipholus returns to the inn.

Act II: Adriana and her sister, Luciana, engage in a lively debate on marriage. Dromio of Ephesus returns to his mistress's home, only to be scolded by her for not having brought home her husband. He is sent out again. In the meantime, Antipholus of Syracuse meets up with his Dromio, who is subsequently beaten for denying what Antipholus believes was their previous encounter. Adriana and Luciana appear, scold them for being late for dinner, and both Antipholus and Dromio of Syracuse return with the women to their home for dinner, unsure of what is happening, but willing to go along with things for the moment. Dromio guards the door of the house.

Act III: Antipholus and Dromio of Ephesus enter, accompanied by the merchant Balthazar and the goldsmith Angelo, whom Antipholus invites to his home for lunch. They are turned away at the door by Dromio, who is guarding the door from the inside. Both Adriana and her servant Luce order them away, thinking they are imposters. An angry Antipholus of Ephesus declares he will visit a Courtezan instead and give to her the gold chain he had intended to give to Adriana.

Meanwhile, Antipholus of Syracuse declares his love for Luciana, who runs from him, thinking he is her brother-in-law. Dromio of Syracuse is trying to avoid Luce, who is married to the other Dromio and mistakes Dromio of Syracuse for her husband. Antipholus decides that it is time for him and Dromio to leave Ephesus, as too many strange things are happening to them. Dromio leaves to prepare for their departure from the city. Angelo appears with the gold chain and gives it to Antipholus of Syracuse, thinking that he is his twin.

Act IV: When Angelo demands payment for the chain from Antipholus of Ephesus, he denies ever having received it. Angelo then has him arrested. At the same time, Dromio of Ephesus has been sent by his master to buy some rope, which he says he'll use to whip Adriana. Dromio of Syracuse appears, announcing to Antipholus of Ephesus that he has secured passage for them on a ship. Antipholus, thinking this Dromio is his own servant, promises Dromio of Syracuse a beating for his ridiculous remarks and orders him to go get money from Adriana to pay for his release.

Dromio of Syracuse returns with the money, but meets up with Antipholus of Syracuse instead (unbeknownst to Dromio), who is wearing the gold chain Angelo foisted upon him. Antipholus has no idea what money Dromio is talking about, of course, but attributes it to the witchcraft and sorcery for which Ephesus is known. The Courtezan then appears and, noticing the gold chain around Antipholus's neck, demands it in exchange for a ring she had given him. The Syracusans flee, thinking the woman mad, and the Courtezan goes off to tell Adriana that her husband is insane.

Meanwhile, the Ephesian Antipholus and Dromio are reunited, but Dromio has the rope he was sent to get, not the bail money. Antipholus then proceeds to beat the confused Dromio with the rope. Adriana, Luciana, and the Courtezan arrive with Doctor Pinch, whom Adriana has brought to cure her husband of his madness. Antipholus becomes more and more enraged, beats the doctor and attempts to beat Adriana. Antipholus and Dromio are subsequently tied up by a group of passersby and taken to Adriana's house for treatment by Doctor Pinch after Adriana pays for their release. Antipholus and Dromio of Syracuse appear and the group flees, thinking they are their escaped Ephesian twins.

Act V: Before the Syracusans can get to their ship,

they meet up with Angelo, who charges that Antipholus has lied to him about the gold chain. Before a fight ensues, Adriana, Luciana, and the Courtezan appear and the Syracusans flee to the safety of the nearby priory. When the Abbess (Aemilia) appears, Adriana demands that her husband be surrendered to her. The Abbess refuses. The Duke and Aegeon appear (Aegeon is being led to his execution), and Adriana appeals to the Duke. Antipholus and Dromio of Ephesus arrive on the scene, having escaped from Pinch, and appeal to the Duke as well. Charges and countercharges create much confusion, and the Duke calls for the Abbess. Aegeon sees Antipholus of Ephesus and, thinking that he is his twin, calls out to him but is met with rejection, since Antipholus has no way of knowing that Aegeon is his father. The Abbess now appears with Antipholus and Dromio of Syracuse, and all are stunned. The Abbess recognizes Aegeon and is reunited with her long-lost husband, who is pardoned by the Duke. With the confusion subsided and reunions in place, all set off for a feast in the priory.

PRINCIPAL TOPICS

Identity

The concept of identity is one of the most discussed topics in the criticism on *The Comedy of Errors,* going well beyond the obvious theme of mistaken identity. Some critics focus solely on personal identity (usually with regard to the twin brothers Antipholi or Adriana, though other characters' identities are also addressed), while others look at how public/social and private identities intersect.

It is generally acknowledged that Antipholus of Syracuse enters the city of Ephesus to make himself "whole" and find his identity, which he believes will happen when he finds his twin brother. However, the strange encounters he has (his social identity) make him question his sanity and that of others who speak to him as if they know him. Antipholus of Ephesus, on the other hand, clings to his personal identity when assailed with threats to it for reasons unknown to him. His wife, Adriana, finds her identity as Antipholus's wife threatened by the perilous course their marriage is taking. Most critics agree that the characters' "original" identities are returned to them or renewed at the end of the play, but not before the social order is seriously threatened.

Genre

In most of the commentary on the play, critics devote at least some attention to its genre or classification,

even if it is not the subject of the critical piece. It remains a topic of ongoing interest and debate. Some modern critics see the play as pure (or almost pure) farce and important in Shakespeare's canon, unlike early critics who dismissed it as merely a stepping-stone in Shakespeare's career and not worthy of much critical attention.

Commentators who find elements of tragedy and romance in the play usually point first to Aegeon's story at the beginning of the play and his impending death as keeping the play from being pure farce. Antipholus of Syracuse's wooing of Luciana, Adriana and Luciana's debate about love and marriage, and the family reunion at the end of the play are other nonfarcical elements critics discuss. Those critics who argue that the play has elements of comedy, too, and not simply farce, note that the characters in the play have more depth and dimension than would characters in a farce— they are real, not mechanized characters.

Love and Marriage

Discussion of love and marriage in *The Comedy of Errors* tends to focus on either the relationship between Adriana and her husband, Antipholus of Ephesus, or the debate between Adriana and Luciana on marriage (or both), both of which are deviations from Plautus's play. One critic argues that Shakespeare's introduction of these concepts in the play sets the stage for the romantic love so central in his later romantic comedies, maintains that that is all Shakespeare intended to do, and reads nothing further into the play. Other critics demur, citing Shakespeare's vast deviation from his Plautine source— for example, Adriana's speeches about her unhappiness (and the fact that she has a name in this play— Plautus's name for the wife of Antipholus was "Wife"), the attention given to her marriage, the reduced role of the Courtezan, and the budding love between Luciana and Antipholus of Syracuse. Other commentators explore the changing nature of male/female relationships in courtship and marriage.

Gender Issues

The topic of gender in *The Comedy of Errors* is closely aligned with the topic of love and marriage, with most of the commentary focusing on the women in the play (particularly Adriana, Luciana, and Aemilia). The critics who touch on the role of the men in the play tend to regard them with less enthusiasm than they do the women, except perhaps in the case of the Aegeon.

Some critics point to the dual nature of the women in the play— they possess "masculine" as well as "feminine" traits; they are "dominant" in courtship and "submissive" in marriage. One critic calls these "halves" of the "unified feminine principle" "outlaw" and "inlaw." Another commentator notes the division of public (commercial) and private (domestic) spheres represented in the play and the conflict that ensues between Antipholus of Ephesus and Adriana because of these spheres' seeming incompatibility.

Critics also point out the significance of Aemilia's appearance at the end of the play and the role of women in general in being catalysts in the outcome and resolution of the play.

CHARACTER STUDIES

Antipholus of Syracuse and Antipholus of Ephesus

Critics often note the similarities between the Syracusan and Ephesian Dromios, but they rarely note any similar qualities in their masters, the Syracusan and Ephesian Antipholi twins. Physically they are identical, but their personalities are vastly different. We first meet Antipholus of Syracuse as he arrives in Ephesus, a somewhat downtrodden, melancholy man in search of his long-lost brother. He believes he will somehow find his identity in his twin. Antipholus of Ephesus, on the other hand, knows exactly who he is— a well-known, well-respected businessman with a wife, home, and flourishing business. The chaos and madness that serve as foils to their reunion, which ultimately takes place in the closing scene, cause them both to confront their own identities in their interactions with the people of Ephesus. Antipholus of Syracuse is met and greeted by people he has never seen before as though they know him quite well, causing Antipholus to think that he must be mad or everyone around him has gone mad. Antipholus of Ephesus, on the other hand, finds that the people he knows or with whom he does business every day react to him as though he is someone other than himself. They recognize him as Antipholus, but as the wrong twin. His reaction to these odd events is one of fury and violence, and he, like Antipholus of Syracuse, believes that either he or everyone around him is mad. Critics generally agree that when the brothers are brought together at last in the end, we do not find them overjoyed or ecstatic; their reunion is somewhat flat. Some critics argue that their identities are secured or renewed when they are finally reunited. Others are not as sure. We do not know for certain (although it is highly probable) that Antipholus of Syracuse and Luciana will wed, and we do not know how Adriana and Antipholus of Ephesus will reconcile after all of the threats to their identities.

Most critics tend to regard Antipholus of Syracuse as the more interesting twin (at least he is the twin on which they generally focus) with a depth of character not found in Antipholus of Ephesus. They assess Antipholus of Syracuse's quest for identity as particu-

larly engaging. Some give his search psychological or Freudian undertones, arguing that it comes from a desire to be "reunited" with his mother as he was united with her as a child. He is reluctant to "merge" or "unite" completely with Luciana, even though he loves her, because he thinks he might lose his identity in the process. Antipholus of Ephesus also worries about his identity, but he is more concerned that it appears as though everyone he knows has gone utterly mad. His rejection by everyone he knows causes him to become enraged, which is, according to one critic, entirely reasonable and justified. Antipholus of Syracuse is in a dream; Antipholus of Ephesus is stuck in a nightmare.

Adriana and Luciana

In Plautus's play, the character of Adriana hardly existed— the wife of Antipholus of Ephesus was named merely "Wife" and characterized simply as a shrew. The character of Luciana did not exist at all. Thus, they are almost exclusively Shakespeare's creations in *The Comedy of Errors*. One of the most commented-upon pieces of dialogue in the play is one in which Adriana and Luciana discuss marriage, Adriana railing against the commonly held opinion that wives must be subservient to their husbands, and Luciana serving as a proponent of a wife's "proper" role. As another of Shakespeare's pairings, Adriana and Luciana revise their opinions as the play progresses, leaning more toward the other woman's point of view, and we see how their opinions are reflected in their relationships with the twin brothers.

Although in early criticism of the play Adriana was generally considered a shrew like the Plautine "Wife," most modern criticism has discarded that characterization and considers her as a more multidimensional character (although she still has her detractors). In light of the greater attention given to such issues as gender and marriage, Adriana's character has undergone reevaluation, as has the play itself. Some critics now portray Adriana as a very early voice condemning society's gender-based double standard.

Luciana is considered by at least one critic as the most complex character in the play. Most acknowledge her position next to Adriana as the voice of pious womanhood, accepting of her station in life as a woman. However, through her interactions with Antipholus of Syracuse and the Abbess (Aemilia), we see that she is not entirely satisfied with being merely a subservient wife. By the end of the play, Adriana too steps back a bit from her earlier position of condemning the restrictions marriage imposes when she is rebuked by the Abbess. At least one commentator has noted that this is not surprising, as Shakespeare was too conservative to completely reject the established system of marriage in Elizabethan society.

CONCLUSION

Although *The Comedy of Errors* is Shakespeare's shortest play, it has generated a good deal of literary criticism. Critics will likely continue to offer commentary about the play's "identity" (genre) and the popular topic of the identity problems, journeys, and resolutions of its characters. Perhaps, too, the thus far limited exploration of the characters of Aegeon and Aemilia (the Abbess) will continue. With the topics of gender and male/female relationships becoming more popular in the criticism, more commentary in these areas is likely forthcoming, now that Adriana has been "rescued" from being considered as only a "shrew." Some critics continue to see the play as an apprentice work of Shakespeare's, preferring his major works instead, but many are also finding in it much more meaning than simply a story of mistaken identities.

OVERVIEW

T. S. Dorsch

SOURCE: "Introduction," in *The Comedy of Errors*, Cambridge University Press, 1988, pp. 12-18.

[*In the following excerpt, Dorsch covers the main action and characters in the play. He notes especially that the twin Dromios are vastly different in character; that the women in the play "stand out more vividly than the men" (the Courtezan is "just the kind of girl a sensible man would look for if he had a nagging wife"); and that the Abbess (Aemilia) is a powerful presence in the play.*]

The Comedy of Errors is not only very good theatre, it is also very good reading. It is a finely-balanced mixture of pathos and suspense, illusion and delusion, love turned bitter and love that is sweet, farce and fun. The fun begins in the second scene with the entry of the Syracusan pair and is sustained with great verve and vivacity through the next three acts. It arises from the farce of mistaken identity which is the stuff and substance of the play— from all the improbabilities that result from the use of two pairs of identical twins who in the course of a single day repeatedly encounter people whom they *know* they know, but do not know. 'If we are in for improbability', said Dowden, 'let us at least be repaid for it by fun, and have that in abundance. Let the incredibility become a twofold incredibility, and it is none the worse.' The fun is of course greatly increased by our knowledge of everything that the characters in the play do not know. Even if Shakespeare did not at all times make clear in the dialogue who is who, we should know from his looks and voice who is speaking to whom. One would suppose that no producer in his senses would put on the stage two pairs of

actors who could not be told apart. The only possible surprise for us is the advent of the Abbess in the final episodes, and that should not be much of a surprise, for we have learnt from romances that if a wife disappears at the beginning she is more likely than not to reappear at the end.

The keynotes of the play are illusion and delusion. The Abbess and Egeon are the only persons who are not wholly deluded by appearances, and even they are so far deceived as not to know that all their family are alive and well, and close at hand in Ephesus; and Egeon is, naturally enough, bewildered when he is unexpectedly faced by two sons who cannot be told from each other even by a wife and two personal slaves. The illusion, like the fun, begins in the second scene when the visiting Antipholus is accosted by a slave whom he *knows* to be his own Dromio, who precipitately tells him that his dinner is spoiling and he must hurry home, and who emphatically denies that he has in his keeping money that Antipholus has entrusted to him. Newly arrived in Ephesus, he has been thinking about his long and seemingly hopeless quest, and has felt that he is

> like a drop of water
> That in the ocean seeks another drop,
> Who, falling there to find his fellow forth,
> Unseen, inquisitive, confounds himself.
>
> (1.2.35-8)

After his encounter with the wrong Dromio he recalls having been told that Ephesus

> is full of cozenage,
> As nimble jugglers that deceive the eye,
> Dark-working sorcerers that change the mind,
> Soul-killing witches that deform the body,
> Disguisèd cheaters, prating mountebanks,
> And many suchlike liberties of sin.
>
> (1.2.97-102)

The Roman-style comedy of misunderstanding is teasingly haunted by moral implications owed to the distant echoes of St Paul. The phrase 'liberties of sin' could not have come from Plautus, and suggests that those who fall under the spells of Ephesus are in need of spiritual conversion as well as material enlightenment. The mind of Antipholus of Syracuse remains 'changed' until the end of the play. A little later in the day, when Adriana claims him as her husband, he is led to wonder whether he was married to her in a dream from which he is not yet awake (2.2.173-4). His Dromio, too, is struck with a horrified wonder:

> This is the fairy land. O spite of spites,
> We talk with goblins, owls, and sprites.
>
> (2.2.180-1)

So it continues. He wonders whether he is 'in earth, in

heaven, or in hell'. When Dromio brings him money to save him from the imprisonment with which his brother is threatened, he *knows* that he is wandering 'in illusions' (4.3.36), and when, immediately after this, he is greeted as an old friend by the Courtesan, he *knows* that she is the devil (43), and Dromio agrees that she is at least 'the devil's dam'.

All the other figures in the farce are similarly bemused by error. The Duke thinks that they 'all have drunk of Circe's cup'. Antipholus of Ephesus in all his encounters thinks the wrong to be the right person. His wife more than once believes the other Antipholus to be her husband (as does Luciana), not only when she is entertaining him in her home, but even at the very end. 'Which of you two did dine with me today?' she asks (5.1.369). Luciana is surprised, and not a little shocked, when she is so warmly and elegantly courted by her brother-in-law, as she supposes Antipholus of Syracuse to be; perhaps, nevertheless, she enjoys a little quiet fun in hearing him, and in reporting him to her sister—nothing in this play is to be taken too seriously. Strangely, we are not told at the end that she is to be a wife—she and Antipholus would make a gentle and happy pair. In the theatre the swiftness of the action allows us no time to wonder at all these mistaken beliefs and weird occurrences; everywhere, as Johnson says, '*Shakespeare* approximates the remote, and familiarizes the wonderful.'

Most of Shakespeare's comedies contain pathos, separations within families, or potential tragedy. *The Comedy of Errors* is no exception. In strong contrast to Plautus's jaunty prologue, Shakespeare opens with the pathetic figure of Egeon, standing in peril of his life. Although at the back of our minds we know from the title and from our reading of romances that in the end all will be well, we must, while he is before us, feel deeply for Egeon as he tells his woeful story, and is told that, unless someone can within the day find a thousand marks to redeem him, he must die—just as we feel deeply for the later heroines who must suffer deprivation or banishment or cruelty before they are brought to happiness— Rosalind or Viola or Hermione. The pathos returns briefly in the final scene, together with a touch of suspense, when Egeon is led in with the Headsman, and again when he is bewildered by the sudden appearance of his long-lost wife and son. These moments are in keeping with all the earlier improbabilities, but they are not farcical. That they follow so hard upon the binding of the one Antipholus and the narrow escape of the other from being locked up as a madman makes the final reunion all the happier. That the close of the play should be placed in the hands of the slaves is a final incidence of fun, and, in this particular play, entirely appropriate.

It is commonly said that in farce situation is everything, characterisation little or nothing. Shakespeare knew better. In Johnson's phrase, he drew his characters, like his scenes, 'from nature and from life'. To every one of his characters he gave an individuality of his own and a distinctive voice; it is a skill that enlarges farce into comedy.

The Dromios are not, as is often said, as like as two peas. Dromio of Ephesus is the more sprightly, and the more in command of all the tricks of language that make for the comic and the witty. His opening lines are the first irruption in the play of high comedy, not only for their shock-effect on the recently-arrived Antipholus, but also in their masterly display of the rhetorical device called *anadiplosis*, by which words at the end of one line are picked up at the beginning of the next. As an introduction to Dromio, to his idiom, to the treatment that a slave expects to receive, and to the spirit of the play, the whole speech is worth quoting:

> Returned so soon? Rather approached too
>   late.
> The capon burns, the pig falls from the spit.
> The clock hath strucken twelve upon the bell;
> My mistress made it one upon my cheek.
> She is so hot because the meat is cold.
> The meat is cold because you come not
>   home.
> You come not home because you have no
>   stomach.
> You have no stomach, having broke your
>   fast.
> But we that know what 'tis to fast and pray
> Are penitent for your default today.
>   (1.2.43-52)

This playing upon words is characteristic of his voice, and, like all witty slaves, he has at his disposal a fund of proverbial wisdom. His Syracusan twin is less voluble, less ebullient; his comedy (apart from his drubbings) is more dependent on puns and proverbs. However, he shows some spirit when he is barring the entry of the Ephesians into their own house, and when he is describing Nell (3.2.77-130).

Nor are the Antipholuses, except in their appearance, alike. Weary with travel and sorrow, Antipholus of Syracuse is quiet and despondent, though quick enough, at the contrariness of slaves, to flare into anger and strike blows. When not harassed, he is gentle and courtly, given to calling ladies 'fair dame' or 'gentle mistress', and he is eloquent in his wooing— we must hope Luciana in the end said yes. The other Antipholus is more robust, ready to smash down a door (though his own) if it keeps him from his dinner. He feels a little henpecked, and is ready to seek comfort from a woman who is not his wife and to ask his goldsmith to make his excuses for him. He is embroiled in the same kinds of confusions as his twin, but reacts to them by beating slaves and not by sinking into dismay and despair; he is, or thinks he is, secure in his knowledge of Ephesus, and his knowledge that he knows everyone who needs to be known. He has for many years been held in high favour by the Duke, and is, in the opinion of his fellow citizens,

Of very reverend reputation, . . .
Of credit infinite, highly beloved,
Second to none that lives here in the city.
                                                (5.1.5-7)

He is a man of substance. He lives in a large house of two storeys ('Husband, I'll dine above with you today', says Adriana), probably with a balcony (see pp. 23-4 below), and has, for Shakespeare's purposes in 3.1, six maidservants in addition to his slave and a kitchen-maid.

The women of the play stand out more vividly than the men. The two who might have been twins— how thankful we are that they are only sisters— are more clearly differentiated than the pairs who really are twins. Adriana is temperamental; she nags her husband to the last, even complaining of him to the Abbess, but wails at great length when in exasperation he sometimes goes off to find congenial company elsewhere— after all, she keeps a good house and is herself faithful. She needs to be taught a lesson or two by her more even-tempered sister. In her worse moments she thinks Antipholus to be

deformèd, crooked, old, and sere;
Ill-faced, worse-bodied, shapeless everywhere;
Vicious, ungentle, foolish, blunt, unkind,
Stigmatical in making, worse in mind.
                                                (4.2.19-22)

When she thinks he is going to be put in jail or a madhouse, she rushes to his help and calls him 'gentle husband'. Naughty as he is, she loves him dearly, as indeed she has from the beginning, if too possessively; even her sharpest railings have come from her mouth, not her heart, as she has shown in her dialogue with Luciana at the end of 2.1, and, in so many words, in 4.2.18, 28. She will, we trust, when she has been shown her own faults, behave better in the future.

Luciana is somewhat given to preaching (as is the Abbess, but then that is her vocation) and at the same time a very agreeable and pleasantly-spoken young woman, as she was when played by Francesca Annis, with Judi Dench beside her as a not too querulous Adriana. She is of course disconcerted when Antipholus woos her so fervently, thinks that perhaps he is mad, but after her first sermon does little to stop him, and can scarcely be said to chide him as she chides Adriana. She is as anxious about her brother-in-law's welfare as her sister, and would be incapable of reviling him, as Adriana does. The gentle Antipholus knows what he is saying when he addresses her as 'Sweet mistress'.

From Dromio's graphic portrait we know all we want to know about Nell— globose, sweaty, red nose, bad of breath. Out of Plautus's courtesan Erotium Shakespeare fashioned someone entirely new. Erotium is exactly what the word courtesan means, what would at one time have been called a gold-digger, ready to clutch at cloaks or bracelets or 'brass'. Shakespeare's unnamed Courtesan is different. Of course she likes being given presents (who doesn't?) and would not have her own costly jewellery go astray, but she can scarcely be said to be rapacious, even if she is as much concerned for her lost baubles as for what appears to be Antipholus's madness. She is good company, 'of excellent discourse, Pretty and witty; wild, and yet, too, gentle' (gentle in both the modern sense and in the usual Elizabethan sense of 'well-bred', though Antipholus of Syracuse thinks otherwise)— just the kind of girl a sensible man would look for if he had a nagging wife. Her wildness is not seen, and there is no vice in her. Shakespeare chose to celebrate the loves and marriages of nice young women rather than fornication.

All the lesser figures contribute something. Doctor Pinch, Plautus's *medicus* new-apparelled, can be quickly disposed of; it is enough to quote Antipholus of Ephesus:

one Pinch, a hungry, lean-faced villain,
A mere anatomy, a mountebank,
A threadbare juggler and a fortune-teller,
A needy, hollow-eyed, sharp-looking wretch,
A living dead man—
                                                (5.1.238-42)

a magnificently Shakespearean vignette. We may note in passing that, although in his introductory stage direction he is called a Schoolmaster, in the dialogue he is always addressed, referred to, and in his pretentious way behaves, as a conjurer.

Another moment of exquisite comedy is provided by the officious and boldly-spoken Jailer; he has had the Ephesian pair carried off to prison, and is rounding off the case, when he is suddenly confronted by Antipholus of Syracuse (yet once more taken for his twin) and Dromio, with rapiers in their hands. Let the situation speak for itself:

LUCIANA God, for thy mercy, they are loose again!
ADRIANA And come with naked swords. Let's call more help
To have them bound again.
JAILER   Away, they'll kill us!
*Exeunt omnes [apart from Antipholus S. and
   Dromio S.], as fast as may be, frighted,*
                                                (4.4.138-40)

The devil-witch-courtesan, now apparently at one with Adriana, is one of those that run away as fast as may be. For the first time Antipholus and Dromio feel they have the upper hand of the terrifying creatures that beset them. 'I see these witches are afraid of swords', Antipholus drily comments, and at last Dromio 'could find it in [his] heart to stay [in Ephesus] still, and turn witch'. He is disposed to join what St Paul called 'the users of curious crafts'.

There remains a very important character, the Abbess. She, 'a virtuous and a reverend lady', is a splendid figure, a woman of great authority and, we must feel, of commanding presence; for the most part of few words, and those always to the point and peremptory. 'Be quiet, people', she says as she comes in upon a brabble, and tumult turns to mere clamour; a little later, firmly, 'Whoever bound him, I will loose his bonds.' She will not kow-tow to the Duke, as the sisters do; her power is as great as his. She will have no nonsense, has no patience with nagging wives and tells them so; Adriana has to put up with a severe scolding from her. It does not take this competent and formidable woman long to straighten out all the entanglements of the day; chaos gives way to order, confusion of mind to practical good sense. The Bible has taught her, as it has (at times) taught Luciana, to see clearly. Shakespeare wittily conjoins the idea he found in Acts 19.26, that the whole city of Ephesus was 'full of confusion', with the *epitasis*, or thickening of the plot, in Roman comedy. The Abbess offers proper Pauline counsel to those who come to hear her, and she is the *dea ex machina* who resolves the play's complications in its *catastrophe*. It is she who, in her final words, 'After so long grief, such nativity', sums up the theme of regeneration with which the play is brought to its conclusion. We rejoice with her when, after the long years, her husband and her sons are restored to her, and we wish that we could celebrate with her at her well-organised 'gossips' feast'. . . .

IDENTITY

There is not a great deal of disagreement among critics as to the importance of identity in the play. More than debating the components of a certain character's identity, critics instead offer myriad examples of how identity is manifested in the play through Aegeon, the twin Antipholi, and Adriana. **Barbara Freedman** dismisses the notion that the play is merely a farce about mistaken identities, and sees Aegeon's twin sons as representative of Aegeon's divided self, connecting the two plots of the story, and providing resolution and a new sense of self at the end of the play. **Gail Kern Paster** also notes the importance of Aegeon's personal identity; it is so powerful that the Duke grants him an entire day to save his life instead of condemning him to death outright.

Many critics discuss the identity issues facing Antipholus of Syracuse. Laurie Maguire and R. A. Foakes argue that Antipholus finds a new identity by losing himself in falling in love with Luciana, not by finding his twin, which Antipholus had thought would restore his identity. Gwyn Williams argues that his falling in love with Luciana begins the long process of finding his identity, but his belief that she has supernatural powers keeps him from entirely surrendering.

There is some disagreement as to what happens to the identity of Antipholus of Ephesus in the play. Maguire argues that this self-assured twin clings to his identity in the midst of the madness that ensues. Dorothea Kehler finds that he loses his identity and takes on Adriana's identity when he suddenly experiences what she does— what it feels like to be betrayed. As Jonathan V. Crewe, Stanley Wells, and Douglas Lanier note, appearances and recognition are important to the characters— their social environment helps determine their personal identity. This is why the idea of twins never crosses the minds of any of the characters. **Paster** and **Barry Weller** discuss the intersection of personal and social identity, **Weller** arguing that at the end of the play, personal identities are overshadowed by "corporate" or civic identities.

Barbara Freedman

SOURCE: "Egeon's Debt: Self-Division and Self-Redemption in *The Comedy of Errors*," in *English Literary Renaissance*, Vol. 10, No. 3, Autumn, 1980, pp. 360-83.

[*In the following essay, Freedman explores the concept of identity (primarily as it is evidenced in the characters of Aegeon and the Antipholi) in the play, integrating such discussions as what she sees as the plot's three-part structure, the centrality of monetary and marital debts (and their intersection), and the importance of redemption.*]

I

Virtually every good critical introduction to *The Comedy of Errors* apologizes for the play. Shakespeare was a mere youth, so the story begins, when he wrote the work, "still without too much to say about love, politics, or human nature." The generic conventions of farce provided their own peculiar restraints, since farce is a kind of drama "that not even Shakespeare could extend beyond somewhat narrow limits." Repeatedly, the reader is warned not to waste time searching for latent meanings in the text. Rather, we are advised to be grateful for what we do have: a "superb farce," a "pure comedy of event." We may value it as an "assimilation and extension of Plautine comedy," for its "symmetry and near flawlessness of . . . plot," or finally, for its rich "harmonic structure" of interrelated themes and patterns of imagery, but we should never expect this "primitive" to stand up to Shakespeare's mature comedies. Or so the story goes.

One cause of all this genial patronage appears to be an intriguing problem in criticism. Critics have been unable to resolve two major issues central to an understanding of the play as a meaningful unity: first, the purpose of the farcical confusion of the twins' identities in the main plot, and second, its relation to their father's progress in the frame plot from separation to reunion with his family, and from crime and debt to redemption. The main plot, derived from Plautus' *Menaechmi* and *Amphitruo*, is generally considered a random "rearranging [of] human puppets" in an essentially static situation, and is often compared to the farcical confusion of the four lovers in *A Midsummer Night's Dream* Critics frequently regard its opening and conclusion as arbitrary. One critic maintains that "the confusion is really the result of accidental circumstances and is as accidentally cleared up"; another muses that "the arabesques of absurdity in *The Comedy of Errors* might continue indefinitely." While it is granted that each character is, at least, forced to confront the horror of mistaken identity, it is equally observed that "no one learns more about himself or his neighbor as a result of the errors." Since "in no other play . . . is the purpose of the confusion less apparent," the work is thought to reflect a vision of a meaningless universe, its intent "no more and no less than the sheer merriment of controlled confusion."

The purpose of the frame plot, adapted from *Apollonius of Tyre*, has been less easy to dismiss, though it has proven equally obscure. Critics complain that the frame plot is poorly integrated into the rest of the play, or they weakly defend the way it humanizes the farce and "contributes an emotional tension . . . to what would otherwise have remained a two-dimensional drama." While studies of the play's themes and patterns of imagery have demonstrated its artistic unity, such approaches have failed to prove the frame plot intrinsic to the play or the main plot purposive.

To explain the relationship of *Errors'* main plot and frame plot, we must accept Shakespeare's focus on a specific context for the farcical confusion of the twins' identities, and decipher its significance. Bracketing the twins' confusion are two problems— Egeon's debt and his Syracusan son's search for a familial identity— and their resolutions, Egeon's redemption and his son's rebirth into a familial identity. The confusion of the twins, then, is *not* the problem which the play solves, just as the play's resolution is not "simply a recognition of who, physically, is who." The confusion of identity is instead a necessary step in the recreation of identity, a problem-solving device through which the frame plot is fulfilled. When we consider *The Comedy of Errors* in the context of problem-solving techniques in Shakespearean comedy, what appears as a disjunctive double plot is revealed as a fully integrated three-part structure.

Act I, scene i. The Antipholus twins separated as infants. By Francis Wheatley (1796).

In *The Comedy of Errors*, where a secondary romance plot frames the farce, we can perceive the rudimentary beginnings of the three-part structure which Shakespeare was to employ in his later comedies. The introductory scene of the play in which Egeon, while searching for his lost family, is doomed by Ephesian law to die by sundown unless he can raise an unlikely sum of money, corresponds well to the harsh world of law, the cruel and problematic reality with which so many of Shakespeare's romantic comedies commence. The main plot's nightmarish Ephesus corresponds to the improbable, fantastic, dreamlike realm of the imagination, familiar to us as a second stage in Shakespearean comedy, and perhaps best described as an example of the "second world" in fiction: an explicitly imaginative or fictional world within a work which purports to imitate reality. While *The Comedy of Errors* doesn't shift to a fantastic setting inhabited by characters capable of magical action, when Antipholus of Syracuse enters Ephesus and confusion begins, the town suddenly appears fantastical. By not removing the play's action to a magical island or forest, Shakespeare stresses the essence of nightmare: the imagined fulfillment of repressed fears and desires in everyday reality. Thus, while the irrational events in the main plot appear to us as plausible and subject to rational explanation, the events remain fantastic and horrifying to the characters. Antipholus of Syracuse's bewildered cry, "Am I in earth, in heaven, or in hell? / Sleeping or waking? mad or well advised?" (II. ii. 211-12) echoes many other Shakespearean descriptions of an essentially imaginative world. The play's conclusion, in which Egeon's problems are astonishingly solved, corresponds to the customary third phase resolution: a return to a world of law now tempered by mercy, a world of reality enriched by imaginative insight.

In such imaginative worlds as the wood outside of Athens or the Forest of Arden, the dramatic stage set before Christopher Sly or Prospero's stage and island, the customary laws of dramatic reality are suspended in favor of dreamlike, imaginative action which gives expression to the plays' problems and makes solutions possible. The functional relationship of second world to first world is the relationship of the imagination, whether in the form of dream, drama, or play, to reality. The second world is an adaptive mechanism through which problematical situations can be submitted to personal, creative re-enactment, control, and mastery.

One example of this problem-solving activity in the early comedies is the transformation of characters from the frame plot into dream-like characters equipped with superhuman powers to overcome their problems. For example, Christopher Sly's problems with the domineering alehouse wife in the introductory framework of *The Taming of the Shrew* are mastered in the main plot through the fictional Petruchio, the fantastic woman tamer in a play performed before Sly. In the frame plot of *A Midsummer Night's Dream*, Theseus has not yet conquered his Amazonian queen on the battlefield of marriage, whereas he has a chance to do so through the magical actions of the fairy king Oberon in the play's major plot. A more complex mode of problem-solving in the comedies is the decomposition of a major frame plot character into multiple, contradictory attitudes which are personified in the main plot, thus enabling an intrapsychic dialogue to ensue in the play's second world. We see this device in the Forest of Arden, where Rosalind and Orlando combat their own pessimism through the figure of Jaques, and their romantic idealism through the characters of Phebe and Silvius, before they are prepared to enter into marriage and return to society. The principle of the hero's decomposition into quasi-allegorical characters as a problem-solving device may be traced from Shakespeare's early comedies to such diverse plays as *Henry IV, Part One*, *King Lear*, and *The Tempest*.

The disjunctive double plot of *The Comedy of Errors* is the prototype of the tripartite comedies that follow, and functions according to the same problem-solving strategies. First, the main plot dramatizes a psychological space; characters are idealized or dissociated inter-

nalized objects, whose speech and actions are coded in the symbolic language of dream. Second, the relationship of main plot to frame plot, like that of second world to first world, is the relationship of creative experience to everyday reality. The main plot's function is adaptive; it restates, in symbolic form, the problem posed in the frame plot and provides a model for its solution. The complex mirroring structure of Shakespearean comedy often enables clarification of an original problem only through its restatement in the second world. Hence it is difficult at first to recognize that the actions of Egeon's sons restate and resolve his problems. One must be adept at reading backwards and forwards, equating all the problems stated until a common denominator is found which stresses the context of the frame plot (e.g., Egeon's debt equals his crime equals Antipholus of Syracuse's problem of familial division equals that which is solved by the confusion of the twins' identities). Read in this manner, *The Comedy of Errors* no longer appears to be a random and senseless farce of mistaken identities, but a carefully orchestrated psychological drama in which dissociated parts of the self are meaningfully united. The twins, as allegorical representatives of Egeon's divided state, connect main plot and frame plot issues and provide a way to resolve them. The farce of mistaken identities and punishment in the confrontation of debts doubles as a complex drama of self-redemption.

II

The Comedy of Errors dramatizes the nightmare of a sudden, inexplicable disjunction between personal and communal accounts of one's identity. Those who are most familiar proclaim one a total stranger, whereas strangers evince a mysterious familiarity. Out of this confusion of the familiar and the strange grows that sense of the *unheimlich* which we translate as "uncanny." In Freud's famous paper "The 'Uncanny,'" he argues that "the *unheimlich* is what was once *heimisch*, homelike, familiar," and maintains that the uncanny "can be traced back without exception to something familiar that has been repressed." This explains, Freud states, "why the usage of speech has extended *das Heimliche* into its opposite *das Unheimliche*; for this uncanny is in reality nothing new or foreign, but something familiar and old—established in the mind that has been estranged only by the process of repression." It is this experience of familiarity-in-strangeness which characterizes each twin's perception of the day's errors and Egeon's nightmare of non-recognition at the play's close. A recent production of *Errors* underlined this sense of the uncanny at the climax of the play's mistaken identifications. Egeon's pathetic query:

Not know my voice! O time's extremity,
Hast thou so cracked and splitted my poor
    tongue
In seven short years, that here my only son

Knows not my feeble key of untuned cares?
(V. i. 307-10)

was delivered to a winking, snickering crowd, and at each piteous lament the uncomprehending townspeople laughed the louder.

Egeon attempts to be logical about this curiously disjunctive experience and to explain phenomena that the play attributes to a fantastic comedy of errors. However much the Ephesian crowd may laugh at his attempts, the Shakespearean critic should not; for if the fantasy presented here endures, as theatrical history attests, then it must convey an archetypal experience which has significant psychological if not physical validity. Egeon's accusation that change, or "Time's deformèd hand," is the logical culprit of the mixup of identities, ties into the theory of a repression of the familiar, and may provide the source of the uncanny experience that *The Comedy of Errors* presents.

Consider, for example, the meaning of the Syracusan twin's experience. What is the meaning of a fantasy in which one is continually recognized, literally "known again" as someone else? While a logical explanation would be to posit the existence of another person who looks like oneself, a physical twin, the status of the main plot as a second world suggests the viability of a psychological twin. For the only self that looks like oneself and is not oneself, that can be remembered or "known again" by others, is a part of the self which has been lost or denied in time, a part of the self with which one no longer identifies. To the extent that the former self is repressed, we have a situation in which others "know one again" as another and one does not remember them: one is no longer who one was. Pirandello focuses on this problem of recognition in *Six Characters in Search of an Author*, when the Father complains of the Daughter's ability to freeze him into a past self with which he no longer identifies:

So we have this illusion of being one person for all, of having a personality that is unique in all our acts. But it isn't true. We perceive this when, tragically perhaps, in something we do, we are as it were suspended, caught up in the air on a kind of hook. Then we perceive that all of us was not in that act, and that it would be an atrocious injustice to judge us by that action alone, as if all our existence were summed up in that one deed. Now do you understand the perfidy of this girl? She surprised me in a place, where she ought not to have known me, just as I could not exist for her; and she now seeks to attach to me a reality such as I could never suppose I should have to assume for her in a shameful and fleeting moment of my life.

From this perspective, the Syracusan can represent a present persona confused with a past, denied persona— a part of the self with which he no longer identifies.

Yet it is this dissociated persona which the Syracusan must seek in his quest for wholeness, and which he has inadvertently found in the gaze of the Other.

Antipholus of Ephesus's experience presents a necessarily complementary but distinctly different fantasy: the perceptions of a past persona when it finds itself replaced by its double in the present. Rather than being mistaken for another, Antipholus of Ephesus is simply denied as himself, and by the very people he knows best. Bewildered at the widespread rejection he encounters, he imagines conspiracy and revenge to be its cause. Yet the actual situation is far more serious; not only are the doors of his home shut upon him, but so are the doors of his entire world. Antipholus of Ephesus is faced with the startling fact that his life is going on quite well without him— but with another version of himself in the starring role.

Again change is the logical cause of mistaken identities, yet for the Ephesian twin the community as "mirror" continues in time, along with one persona of the individual, while the persona which would be recognized has somehow escaped "time's deformèd hand." A more contemporary version of this fantasy is Washington Irving's "Rip Van Winkle," the well-known story of a henpecked husband who returns home after an afternoon's nap only to learn that twenty years have mysteriously slipped by:

Strange names were over the doors— strange faces at the windows— everything was strange. His mind now misgave him; he began to doubt whether both he and the world around him were not bewitched. Surely this was his native village, which he had left but the day before. There stood the Kaatskill mountains— there ran the silver Hudson at a distance— there was every hill and dale precisely as it had always been.

A twenty years' sleep may appear improbable and fantastic, but its logical psychological equivalent is a suddenly awakened twenty-year-old self which must confront the reality of the present. For Rip Van Winkle, as for Antipholus of Ephesus, that confrontation includes not only the horror of being shut out of one's world, but the insidious sense that one has been successfully replaced by one's double. In both situations, the double is a younger— because newer— version of the self; in Rip Van Winkle's case, it is his son who replaces him. In answer to his forlorn request:— "Does nobody here know Rip Van Winkle?"— the following conversation ensues:

"Oh, Rip Van Winkle!" exclaimed two or three; "oh, to be sure! that's Rip Van Winkle yonder, leaning against the tree."

Rip looked, and beheld a precise counterpart of himself as he went up the mountain; apparently as

Lisa Viertel as Adriana and Tony Driscoll as Pinch in GreenStage's 1999 production of Comedy of Errors.

lazy, and certainly as ragged. The poor fellow was now completely confounded. He doubted his own identity, and whether he was himself or another man. In the midst of his bewilderment, the man in the cocked hat demanded who he was, and what was his name.

"God knows," exclaimed he, at his wit's end; "I'm not myself—I'm somebody else—that's me yonder—no—that's somebody else got into my shoes—I was myself last night, but I fell asleep on the mountain, and they've changed my gun, and everything's changed, and I'm changed, and I can't tell what's my name, or who I am!"

We could accept that this double is indeed Rip Van Winkle's son, as the story tells us, were it not that twenty years cannot pass by in one nap. And we could accept that Antipholus of Ephesus and his Dromio are simply replaced by identical twins, were it not that twins are not identical within. These fantastic stories in which disjunctive selves and worlds meet are valid on a psy-

chological level; the son, the twin brother, are simply metaphors for what has been termed the "second self in time." Finally, there is a motive for Rip Van Winkle's prolonged absence which is curiously similar to Egeon's and Antipholus of Ephesus's: a nagging wife at home, and hence a marital identity from which the husband is tempted to escape.

What we are dealing with, then, is a temporal disjunction as the cause of identity confusion. Total recognition depends upon two parties remaining the same; lack of recognition occurs when neither party remains the same. Mistaken or disjunctive recognition occurs when one person has changed so drastically that be bears no resemblance to his former self—as Egeon fears he has changed physically or as we might posit he has changed psychologically. A change in time, and hence in self-concepts, can also account for the birth and confusion of the Antipholi. Either one identifies with the past and is disturbed that others in the present have forgotten who one was (Antipholus of Ephesus), or one identifies with the present and is disturbed that others relate only to a self with which one no longer identifies (Antipholus of Syracuse). What if one were to shift rapidly back and forth in one's identification with each of these perspectives? Egeon's attempt to recover home, wife, and a marital identity lost in a tempest long ago can account for just such a complex and uncanny fantasy.

When the action of the storm separated Egeon from his former life, the Ephesian twin was, literally, that part of Egeon which was lost. The Syracusan twin was the part of Egeon which remained with him to the present time. Accordingly, the Ephesian twin's distinguishing characteristics are those which differentiated Egeon's former life from his present one. Antipholus of Ephesus, like the former Egeon, is the settled, respectable citizen. Antipholus of Syracuse is the present image of his father— an unhappy sojourner. The Ephesian twin is ensconced in a familial situation, complete with nagging wife; the Syracusan is a free bachelor, seeking the domestic stability which Egeon has lost. Antipholus of Ephesus is a pragmatic businessman, recalled in Egeon's description of his former life to Duke Egeon (I. i. 39-43). Antipholus of Syracuse is the impractical romantic, hazarding all in an apparently bootless journey, much like his "hopeless and helpless" father. The Ephesian homebody is commonly accepted as the elder of the two, befitting the representative of Egeon's past, whereas the travelling Syracusan is the newer and hence younger identity. Finally, only Antipholus of Ephesus has no knowledge of his brother: as the "pre-tempest" persona, he feels unified and secure in himself. Antipholus of Syracuse, as the "post-tempest," dissociated persona, knows of his brother and seeks his identity in unity with him. Thus the woefully divided brother lodges at the Centaur, mythological symbol of self-division, and seeks symbolic death and rebirth through imagined union with his double at his lodging, the Phoenix.

This allegorical schema clarifies the relationship of the mixup of the twins' identities in the main plot to Egeon's problem in the frame plot. The tempest which divided Egeon from his wife divided his past and present, marital and single identities as well, represented by Egeon's separated twin sons. Antipholus of Ephesus is Egeon's long-lost marital identity; Antipholus of Syracuse is Egeon's present persona, willing to lose himself to find himself in reunion with his brother. The Ephesian community's mistaken identification of the Antipholi enables their proper identification with each other. Thus, out of the mistaken identifications of the traditional comedy of intrigue Shakespeare fashioned a complex psychological drama of self-integration.

III

We can see how the play works as a psychological drama in which a long-lost marital identity is sought, "mistakenly" identified with, and ultimately recovered. Curiously enough, however, that self-division, depicted in the division of Ephesus and Syracuse, is associated

with crime and unpaid debts. Self-recovery is depicted as dependent upon the payment of a series of debts, and self-integration is associated with release from crime and debt. It is a little recognized fact that the situation which functions to confuse the twins is not simply the mistaking of one for the other, but the two being so mistaken that one is recurrently debited or credited for the transactions of the other. Only when we discover the nature and validity of the debt can we explain the crime for which Egeon is arrested in the frame plot, its relation to the farcically mistaken punishment of the twins in the main plot, and its role in the miraculous redemption of Egeon by both Abbess and Duke at the play's close. Only through a close examination of the play's debts can we understand the role of the assumption, punishment, and forgiveness of debts in this comic drama of self-redemption.

There is hardly one scenario in *The Comedy of Errors* which is not concerned with debts. Egeon's search in the play's romantic frame plot has led to an actual, although apparently meaningless, monetary debt upon which his very life depends. Charged with crossing the forbidden boundary between the hostile cities of Syracuse and Ephesus, Egeon must raise an exorbitant sum of money or die at sundown. Inasmuch as we never learn the cause of the two cities' "mortal and intestine jars," the crime of crossing from Syracuse to Ephesus has no significance for us. And since Egeon has had no means of learning of this law in advance, he is innocent of criminal intent. Although we see no more of Egeon until the play's end, his two sons are repeatedly placed in similar situations of indebtedness.

Antipholus of Syracuse no sooner enters Ephesus than he is led by the device of mistaken identities to believe that he has lost all his money. Having just learned of the precarious state of Syracusans in Ephesus, Antipholus of Syracuse fears that he will incur the debt which, unknown to him, his father has contracted. His financial situation is no sooner clarified than he is mistakenly accused of marital neglect by his sister-in-law, Adriana, who claims of him the obligations of husband to wife. The substitution of marital for monetary indebtedness is significant; it leads to the first possibility of redemption in the play. Antipholus of Syracuse follows Adriana to his brother's home, where he is promised a full dinner and Adriana's forgiveness. The first pattern that emerges, then, is the association of Egeon's monetary debt with his son's potential monetary debt, in turn equated, through replacement, with a mistaken marital debt, which is promptly discharged. That Egeon's debt is acquitted through such acts leads us to question the purely monetary content of the frame plot debt as well as the mistaken nature of the debts in the main plot.

Antipholus of Ephesus's far more troubled route leads from marital to monetary indebtedness, neither of which is resolved until the play's end. We first meet him imploring Angelo, a goldsmith, to manufacture excuses and a gold chain for his wife to explain his absence from home. The acquittal is forestalled and the Ephesian's indebtedness compounded when he returns home to locked doors, only to discover that another man is paying his marital debts within. In revenge, he asks Angelo to deliver the gold chain to a courtesan with whom he will dine instead. But Angelo mistakenly presents the chain to Antipholus of Syracuse. Presented with the bill, Antipholus of Ephesus refuses payment and is promptly arrested for debt. The horror of indebtedness is underlined by the repeated failure of his attempts at bail. He mistakenly sends his brother's slave to Adriana for bail, and the slave mistakenly brings the money to his own master. His own slave returns not with bail but with the rope that was earlier required of him. Thus Antipholus of Ephesus remains helplessly in bondage, anxiously awaiting gold to redeem him, exactly fulfilling his brother's earlier fears and confronting his father's fate. The pattern here, then, is an exact reversal of Antipholus of Syracuse's misfortunes. Just as the Syracusan twin progresses from fear of actual monetary debt to payment for a mistaken marital debt, so his brother moves from fear of an actual marital debt to payment for a mistaken monetary debt. The play's initial comparison of Antipholus of Syracuse's indebtedness with his father's is also paralleled by the comparison of Antipholus of Ephesus's indebtedness with Egeon's at the play's climax. This complex pattern suggests far more than thematic harmony; it implies the essential equivalence of the three characters and their three debts.

The plot reaches a climax when Antipholus of Syracuse is again placed in debt, this time to the courtesan for the chain promised her by his brother in return for her ring. Monetary and marital debts are joined in this final image of the chain (or alternately, the ring) due a woman. The chain, like the ring, is valued both for its intrinsic monetary value and as a symbol of marital bonds. This final debt suggests the equivalence of the marital and monetary debts accrued throughout the play and hence their general validity. At this point in the plot Antipholus of Ephesus is released from the law only to be bound at home; Antipholus of Syracuse, mistaken for his brother, escapes all debts as he dashes into the Priory, and his brother escapes from his bonds at home as well. All at last meet before the Duke and Egeon, at which point the errors are clarified, Egeon is released from debt, and his family is reunited.

The series of debts of differing content and validity may be reduced to one certain, identifiable debt. The three debtors are equated through the allegorical reading of the twins as symbolic representatives of Egeon. The three debts are equated through the unity of the double plot; if the twins' confrontation of debts in the main plot effectively discharges their father's debt, then they must all be confronting the same debt. This reasoning is further substantiated by the play's curious pattern of redemption, according to which one debt is replaced by, and discharged through, a debt of differing content and validity throughout the play. There is a single, valid debt being paid off here— but what? Marital debts are paid off by money, and marriage discharges monetary debts. Is Egeon's debt marital or monetary? Insofar as all the monetary debts in the play are related to payment for marital debts, we must accord the marital debts priority. The ubiquitous chain which causes such a fuss is Antipholus of Syracuse's present to his wife, an excuse for his absence from home. If the chain cannot be paid for, however, neither can the marital debt be paid; the horror of financial obligations is here directly associated with the horror of unmet marital obligations. Egeon's obscure monetary debt is also associated with specific marital obligations, since he is charged with crossing from Syracuse to Ephesus, symbolic terms for his own single and marital identities. The debt owed in Ephesus is the debt owed one's wife, the debt that must be confronted if Egeon is to recover his past.

The play's marital debts lead back to Egeon's history and to the theme of identity as the monetary debt cannot. Adriana, the play's spokeswoman for neglected marital obligations, "mistakenly" confronts Antipholus of Syracuse with this debt:

> How comes it now, my husband, O, how
>   comes it,
> That thou art then estrangèd from thyself?
> Thyself I call it, being strange to me,
> That, undividable, incorporate,
> Am better than thy dear self's better part.
> Ah, do not tear away thyself from me!
>
> (II. ii. 118-23)

Adriana describes her husband's neglect of her in terms of his own self-estrangement. Their shared marital identity ("thou" or "me") which is "undividable" and "incorporate" has been denied by him in favor of a more attractive single identity ("thyself"). To separate from one's wife, then, is to divide oneself in two, to deny the half of one's self associated with one's wife and to deprive her of her rights in the other half. Yet it is Egeon who has been separated from his wife and hence divided into marital and single identities. It is Egeon's attempts to recover his past, to reintegrate a denied marital identity (Antipholus of Ephesus) left with his wife, that are prevented by Adriana's and the Duke's demands: payment of the remaining, present, single identity (Antipholus of Syracuse) denied Adriana. Hence separation is equated both with self-division and with crime and debt, while reunion is equated with self-integration and the payment of debts.

IV

At the point of death, Egeon is ordered to relate the story of his wanderings. He begins with his married life, and the question of Egeon's "hap" or happiness in his marriage is crucial. It can easily escape notice that the cruel fate which serves to separate husband and wife merely duplicates actions previously ascribed to Egeon's will. Egeon tells us that he was responsible for his separation from his wife, led on by the call of business. He appears to have desired to maintain that divorce, despite his protests to the contrary. He is careful to note that it was his wife, not he, who made provisions for her to follow him (a common fate of heroines in Shakespearean comedy), terms her pregnancy "pleasing punishment," and finally admits that he was unwilling to return home with her: "My wife . . . / Made daily motions for our home return. / Unwilling I agreed" (I. i. 58-60).

That unwillingness may explain Egeon's curiously passive acceptance of obstacles to his return home. When confronted with "A doubtful warrant of immediate death" (I. i. 68) in the form of a ship-tossing tempest, Egeon tells us it was a fate which he "would gladly have embraced" (I. i. 69), were it not for his family's pleas for rescue. Yet rescue of a different sort is provided, for the storm not only prevents Egeon's return home, but serves to separate husband and wife once again. Fate functions here as a disowned aspect of Egeon's will, undoing his wife's efforts to retrieve her husband and remain with him, and restoring the prior marital separation which Egeon had enforced. The woeful tale of a "helpful ship . . . splitted in the midst" (I. i. 103), of fortune's "unjust divorce" of a family (I. i. 104), of a man "severed from my bliss" (I. i. 118), is a highly elaborated and very well disguised fantasy of a man's desire to cut himself off from his previous life.

Egeon's story is the missing link which turns an arbitrary plot into a meaningfully directed fantasy. His denial of his marital identity and obligations explains his mysterious offense. It explains the use of twin sons, divided selves, to represent him. Finally, it reveals the twins' confrontation of debts throughout the play as a means of working through and resolving that original problem. The validity of the marital debt explains the apparently arbitrary harassment of an innocent man as a meaningful submission of a guilty self to the attacks of its own superego. The action of this punitive conscience is purposive as well. An acknowledgement of marital debts and a submission to self-punishment for their denial are necessary steps towards the resumption of Egeon's marital identity. Egeon's curious acceptance of harsh Ephesian punishment, and Antipholus of Syracuse's willingness to "entertain the offered fallacy" of being no less than the object of Adriana's sharp lectures on marital neglect and her threats of vengeance, are the first clues to this superego punishment

in the play. With the haunting figures of Luce, the Police Officer, and Dr. Pinch, these incarnations of a punitive conscience become grotesque caricatures, nightmarish phantoms. The sense of indebtedness, like Luce herself, is blown out of all proportion. She is the literal embodiment of the monstrous extent of Egeon's guilt and the dreadful capacity of the self for self-punishment.

That such morally punitive action should be transformed into farce is not surprising; farce derives humor from normally unacceptable aggression which is made acceptable through a denial of its cause and effect. The apparently cost-free nature of aggression in farce leads it to be characterized as a comedy of the id, yet if we distinguish between the libidinal transgressions of individual characters, and the punitive aggressive action of plots against those characters, a radical reconception of farce is possible. In *The Comedy of Errors*, as in most farces, the absurdly punitive aggression of the plot is well-disguised superego aggression. Normally unacceptable aggression is directed against the self, but made acceptable through a denial of its meaning. The actual cause of this play's obsessive punishment— Egeon's marital debt— is displaced; only the mistake, the unexpected confusion of the twins' identities, is blamed for the play's aggressive action. The effect of that aggression is similarly denied. Dromio may complain of his beatings or Antipholus of Ephesus of his treatment by cruel Dr. Pinch, but as these actions are senselessly delivered, so they are senselessly received. No one is harmed and all is forgotten in the flurry of events. The fast pace, complexity, and extraordinary subject matter of the plot further contribute to this general distortion of the sense of reality, vital to our humorous acceptance of unacceptable fantasy.

Through the genre of farce, Shakespeare transformed a private nightmare of self-punishment into a public vehicle for the pleasurable release and gratification of aggressive impulses. Equally important, farce provided an acceptable means of confronting wrongs and a pattern in which forgiveness could be won: a way of mastering, as well as releasing, feelings of guilt and aggression. The play works out the marital debt in its progression from Egeon's separation from his wife, through his son's confrontation of marital debts, to his final release from bondage and reunion with his wife. This pattern is paralleled as Antipholus of Syracuse and Luciana move from a state of aversion to marriage, to mutual love and the promise of marriage. Finally, there is a corresponding assumption of guilt for marital mishap on the wives' parts, as both Adriana and Emilia learn to accept, or at least confront, the separation of husband and wife: first, through Emilia's stay at the convent, where, as Adriana complains, the Abbess enacts "the separation of husband and wife"; next, through Emilia's lectures on the sins of possessiveness and jealousy in marriage, which draw from Adriana and admission of guilt. Both episodes work to provide the forgiveness and acceptance of marital separation necessary for the final reunion.

V

In its first recorded performance, on December 28, 1594, *The Comedy of Errors* was presented as a Christmas play for the customary Christmas revels at Gray's Inn. It was therefore perhaps not surprising to its audience that the play's theme of debts should be contained within the larger and more significant theme of redemption. Indeed, in Aristotelian terms the play may be reduced to the imitation of a single action: to redeem.

The simplest meaning of "to redeem" is "to regain or recover" something lost, whether material or immaterial. This activity is given complex comic treatment in Dromio of Syracuse's parody of learned arguments, in which he proves that there is "no time to recover hair lost by nature" (II. ii. 101-02), and at the climax of the play, where he labors to convince Adriana that "The hours come back!" (IV. ii. 55). The comic treatment of "recovery" is actually related to a more precise sense of "redeem"—"to save time from being lost"—and points to the play's major concern with the recovery of what time has stolen, "As if time were in debt" (IV. ii. 57).

Egeon's attempt to recover what has been lost in time, to redeem his past, is thwarted at the very beginning of the play. The reason given by the Duke for his arrest appears arbitrary and unrelated to his struggles:

> since the mortal and intestine jars
> 'Twixt thy seditious countrymen and us,
> It hath in solemn synods been decreed,
> Both by the Syracusians and ourselves,
> To admit no traffic to our adverse towns:
> Nay more, if any born at Ephesus
> Be seen at Syracusian marts and fairs;
> Again, if any Syracusian born
> Come to the bay of Ephesus, he dies,
> His goods confiscate to the Duke's dispose,
> Unless a thousand marks be levièd,
> To quit the penalty and to ransom him.
>
> (I. i. 11-22)

The jarring towns of Ephesus and Syracuse find their only correlation in this text in the characters of Antipholus of Ephesus and Antipholus of Syracuse, yet these characters are not enemies. Only as the twins in turn represent Egeon's contradictory personae does this interdict have meaning. The forbidden boundary between the two towns and the penalty for crossing it would seem to represent the precariousness of a split identity. If the Syracusan persona meets the Ephesian, one or the other must be destroyed, for one cannot maintain two identities simultaneously. A way out of this dilemma is provided by the thousand-mark debt,

which would seem to permit the coexistence of both identities and their ultimate integration. Yet how?

This brings us to a second sense of the word "redeem" which is really a qualification of the first. "To redeem" literally means "to buy back," to recover only "by payment of the amount due, or by fulfilling some obligation." Egeon's desire to recover his past marital identity demands his recovery of neglected marital obligations as well. He can only recover that identity by confronting those debts; therefore, one can only cross from Syracuse to Ephesus if one is prepared to pay a debt.

Egeon would seem to be prepared—psychologically if not financially. For if the solution to the problem of self-estrangement is for the present single self to confront and identify with the past marital self and its obligations, then this explains why Antipholus of Syracuse enters Ephesus, is reprehended by Adriana for neglected marital obligations, and dutifully returns home with her. Adriana's mistaken identification makes possible a meaningful psychological association. It permits the single self's assumption of a past marital identity while simultaneously maintaining its own identity. It also enables a return to one's wife and the long-due fulfillment of marital obligations. Antipholus of Ephesus is equally identified with his brother; forced upon the past are the trappings of the present, particularly its guilt. So Antipholus of Ephesus is forced into situations of debt for which he is not responsible. Through the device of mistaken identity, Shakespeare makes each twin simultaneously confront both personae; only through their mutual identification is a sense of self-continuity and, hence, self-integration possible. The play's development may be charted as the movement from a rigid, repressive sense of identity in the frame plot, through the main plot's temporary state of madness in which ego boundaries dissolve in encounter, to a new sense of self in which past and present are integrated.

A third, fourth, fifth, and sixth definition of "redeem" may be brought together to explain the climax of the play: "to ransom, liberate, free (a person) from bondage, captivity or punishment"; "to rescue, save, deliver"; "to free from a charge or claim"; and [of God or Christ] "to deliver from sin and its consequences." Adriana releases Antipholus of Ephesus from monetary debt, thereby symbolically freeing him of his marital debt, yet the play refuses to let him off so easily. He is released only to be bound by one Pinch, an exorcist, to undergo a mock purgation of his sins. Although one sort of redemption (to deliver from sin) appears to be substituted for another (to ransom), in another, quite vivid sense, the plot is denying a much longed-for release and merely continuing its guilty pattern of bondage and punishment. With Pinch's entry, the guilty conscience in control of the punitive plot becomes vividly evident and threatens to run amok. Yet Antipholus of Ephesus's cruel bondage actually serves to emphasize the finality of his ensuing release. The self is finally freed from the superego's sadistic action as Antipholus of Syracuse escapes from his bonds and revenges himself upon this pinching, punishing parasite.

The final release from self-punishment for unmet obligations is paralleled at this point in the play in Antipholus of Syracuse's actions. While his brother is attacking Pinch at home, Antipholus of Syracuse, with his Dromio, enters the marketplace with drawn rapier, frightening away Adriana and the Officer, who have threatened to bind him as well. The final mastery over self-punishment and the attendant release which characterizes this last part of the play are also represented by Antipholus of Syracuse's fortuitous escape into the Priory at this point, where neither the law nor Adriana can get at him.

The escape into the Priory heralds a new sense of release from bondage: a Christian sense of redemption which prevails to the end of the play. Just as Christian redemption is associated with a movement from father to son, from law to mercy, from bondage to freedom, from separation to reunion, and from death to rebirth, so this movement is paralleled in the text and completed at the end of the play as Egeon's sons are freed from bondage, Egeon's separated family is reunited, he is released from the penalty of death, and that death itself is replaced by his sons' symbolic rebirth. Shakespeare's decision, at the play's close, to change the twins' age from twenty-five to thirty-three, the sacred number of the years of Christ's life, further associates their rebirth with Christian redemption. As Adriana concludes:

> Thirty-three years have I but gone in travail
> Of you, my sons; and till this present hour
> My heavy burden ne'er deliverèd.
> The Duke, my husband, and my children
>   both,
> And you the calendars of their nativity,
> Go to a gossips' feast, and go with me;
> After so long grief such Nativity!
> (V. i. 402-08)

Or as the apostle Paul witnesses:

> We know that the whole creation has been groaning in travail together until now; and not only the creation, but we ourselves, who have the first fruits of the Spirit, groan inwardly as we wait for adoption as sons, the redemption of our bodies. For in this hope we were saved. (Romans 8.22-24).

A final sense of "redeem"—"to restore or bring into a condition or state"—is thus exemplified at the play's end. Yet the sons who are freed, united, and adopted by the father in *The Comedy of Errors* are reborn in a secular as well as a religious sense; their recovery presents a reorganization and rebirth of the self. The play

demonstrates how one redeems (recovers) oneself through redeeming (making payment for) one's debts in a complex process whereby one can redeem ("go in exchange for") one's alterego, and how one is thereby redeemed (released) from bondage only to share in the fruits of redemption as rebirth.

Shakespeare's association of the process of self-integration with Christian redemption may owe less to Elizabethan psychology, or even to the occasion of the play's famous Gray's Inn performance, than to the exigencies of literary form: the Christian morality play provided an obvious model for a symbolic drama of intrapsychic events. Although the morality play parallels are too extensive to be convincingly presented here, let me briefly suggest some connections. The play's grim opening, with a common man in bondage for sin, facing death, and despairing of mercy, presents a conventional portrait of natural, unredeemed man, corresponding to the Mankind figure of the morality plays. The conclusion, in which Egeon's wife emerges from the Priory in time to save him, Egeon is released from bondage, and his sins are forgiven by a merciful judge, completes the morality-patterned action from sin to Christian salvation. The main plot of the twins dramatizes the symbolic, psychological journey of the self towards the goal of redemption, centering on acts of sin and penance, including the conventional temptation and regeneration provided by the contrasting vice (the courtesan) and virtue (Luciana) figures. The twins serve as symbolic equivalents of Egeon's and Everyman's divided, contrary state, and are sharply differentiated to suggest the warring earthly and heavenly elements in Everyman's nature. The Ephesian brother's worldly interest in material and physical pleasures is throughout contrasted with the piety of his younger brother. The neglected marital identity, like the sinful aspect of man, is presented as being in need of redemption, and the single identity is associated with a spiritual agent, willing to undergo penance to redeeem its fallen counterpart.

The twins, then, can be understood on three different levels: as long-lost brothers in a family, as dissociated parts of the self, and as warring earthly and heavenly elements in the nature of Everyman. The action of the play is similarly threefold. On one level, the play is a conventional romantic comedy moving from separation, through bewilderment, to reunion and harmony of familial members and lovers. On another level, it follows a psychological formula from repression through confrontation to an integration of parts of the self. Finally, on a third level, the play's action follows a morality pattern from self-division and bondage, through penance, to redemption. . . .

A fourth reading of the twins and of the action of the play is provided by one of Shakespeare's sources: Paul's letter to the Ephesians. The story of the apostle Paul has long been accepted as a model for the play. No other source includes such elements as years of wandering, a shipwreck, the Aegean (Egeon?) and Adriatic (Adriana?) seas, Syracuse, Corinth, Ephesus and its demonic magic, revenge taken upon evil exorcists, and a conflict between law and mercy, between bondage and redemption. The significance of Paul's letter to the Ephesians, however, has yet to be noted fully. The letter's primary message, for which Paul is being held prisoner, is a call for the union of two hostile nations, Gentiles and Jews, in the body of Christ:

> For he is our peace, who has made us both one, and has broken down the dividing wall of hostility, by abolishing in his flesh the law of commandments and ordinances, that he might create in himself one new man in place of the two, so making peace, and might reconcile us both to God in one body through the cross, thereby bringing the hostility to an end. . . . For this reason I, Paul, a prisoner for Christ Jesus on behalf of you Gentiles (Ephesians 2.14-3.1)

The imagery which Paul uses—of the creation of "one new man in place of the two," of one body in which two hostile people are joined in peace and harmony—may have suggested to Shakespeare the idea of using Paul's story to depict the unity of two hostile identities within one man, one body. Shakespeare retains the two hostile nations in Syracuse and Ephesus, and joins them in the body of one common father, Egeon, by equating the two nations with the two sons and equating the two sons, in turn, with two aspects of Egeon. Thus Egeon is imprisoned for trying to unite the separated sons or selves named after these nations instead of, like Paul, the nations themselves. Interestingly enough, Paul's letter has never been cited as a source in this context, despite the fact that no other source for the play has been found which connects the frame plot of the prisoner and the main plot of the separated brothers whom the prisoner has sought to unite. No other source presents a traveller imprisoned for crossing a "dividing wall of hostility," seeking to redeem the separated stranger, attempting to "create in himself one new man in the place of the two." Finally, no other source also associates the denial of marital identity with self-estrangement—or, stated more positively, identifies one's union with and love of one's wife with the unity and love of oneself: "Even so husbands should love their wives as their own bodies. He who loves his wife loves himself. . . . 'For this reason a man shall leave his father and mother and be joined to his wife, and the two shall become one'" (Ephesians 5.28-31). Here, as in *The Comedy of Errors*, external relationships are conceived of as internalized; one's wife is envisioned as a part of oneself, whom one rejects at the cost of self-hatred and self-division.

VI

The Comedy of Errors is a surprisingly rich and complex comedy, working simultaneously on various levels and in various directions. Perhaps the best way, finally, to contain the play is to summarize briefly its view of identity. Actually, the play offers us at least three different conceptions of identity. Two of these definitions correspond to the contradictory configurations of the self embodied by the twins, while the final definition is one that resolves and integrates the former two.

The most prominent conception of identity in the play is Adriana's. According to her view, one's sense of identity is dependent upon significant relationships in one's past. What we would call the self is a composite of internalized others or relationships with others. As a sum of identifications with others, identity appears to be purely interpersonal, fixed and irreversible:

> For know, my love, as easy mayst thou fall
> A drop of water in the breaking gulf,
> And take unmingled thence that drop again
> Without addition or diminishing,
> As take from me thyself and not me too.
> (II. ii. 124-28)

Yet Adriana's view of identity only partially applies to Egeon's quest. Antipholus of Ephesus, the long-lost married brother, the long-denied marital identity, is a part of Egeon which must be accepted, yet it is only one aspect of a more complex self-image. The flaw in Adriana's argument is manifest in her language. According to Adriana, there is no "thyself," no sense of identity separable from one's identification with others. Yet her language simultaneously acknowledges a self separable from her, just as the play acknowledges an Antipholus of Syracuse separate and different from an Antipholus of Ephesus.

The contradiction in Adriana's language is the conflict of the play: the simultaneous and interdependent existence of two mutually exclusive self-concepts. Egeon's identity is not simply the sum of his past identifications with others; it is equally an agency capable of some autonomy. Antipholus of Syracuse is also an essential part of Egeon, born in Egeon's denial of the past, nurtured and sustained apart from home and wife. While this single Syracusan identity is bound to Egeon's former self, it nonetheless remains radically different from it. And, while Egeon is willing to hazard this new-forged persona to retrieve and reintegrate his former self, he is unwilling, if not unable, to abandon it. He explains his delay in seeking the son left behind, "whom whilst I labored of a love to see, / I hazarded the loss of whom I loved" (I. i. 130-31), and then relates how he followed Antipholus of Syracuse in the boy's search for his twin.

It would be as foolish to assert that Egeon's identity is found through the actual restoration of past relationships with others as it would be to assert that it is found in their denial. Egeon has neither set out in search of his beloved Emilia, his "bliss," nor does he mention ever having a desire to do so, despite the twenty-five years that they have spent in apparently needless separation. When Emilia finally does make an appearance at the play's end, Egeon's words to her are a request for his son. It is only Antipholus of Ephesus that he "labored of a love to see," and only himself (Antipholus of Ephesus) that he hazarded himself (Antipholus of Syracuse) for. Further, were Egeon truly to find himself in the renewal of past relationships, then this would be tantamount to denying his single, Syracusan identity and equating the resolution of the identity crisis with its annihilation. Rather, Antipholus of Syracuse loses himself to find himself *in relationship to* his past, not in total, self-destructive acquiescence to the past. Egeon seeks his identity in the relationship of his present to his past, not in the denial or elimination of either.

In its most basic sense, identity is the perception of self-continuity: the identification and integration of various self-concepts. Shakespeare employs the comic formula of mistaken identity in *The Comedy of Errors* to resolve a problem of self-dissociation. In the confusion of the Ephesian with the Syracusan twin, Egeon's past and present, marital and single personae are united. By the play's conclusion change is perceived as growth instead of self-division, and duality and contradiction give way to self-continuity. The twin Dromios conclude the comedy with a humorous re-enactment of the play's conflict and solution. Debating upon the subject of which brother should rightly exit through the stage door first, they finally come to an agreement: for the future, they decide, the two will "go hand in hand, not one before another" (V. i. 427-28).

Barry Weller

SOURCE: "Identity and Representation in Shakespeare," in *ELH*, Vol. 49, No. 2, Summer, 1982, pp. 345-46.

[*In the following brief excerpt, Weller explores how Antipholus of Syracuse ultimately fails in his search for the "confirmation and completion of his identity" in his twin brother. Not only is their reunion "diminished" by the second pair of twins, the Dromios, but more importantly, the "priority of corporate identities" takes precedence over personal identities. Weller uses Paul's letter to the Ephesians to show how solidarity subsumes selfhood.*]

. . . . The problems which the discovery, or recovery, of the self may raise announce themselves very conspicuously in *The Comedy of Errors*, in which one twin voyages the Mediterranean in search of the other, the brother and mirror image from whom he has been separated since infancy. The object of his search is also, one might say, himself, refracted through otherness, or a figure who is at once self and its representation. However, Antipholus of Syracuse seeks the

confirmation and completion of his identity in the very form which in other fictions has figured as a subversion of the self, a *Doppelgänger*. If the label is too redolent of nineteenth-century German romanticism, the phenomenon and the psychological dislocations it implies are less historically specific. Not every encounter of twins in Renaissance texts questions the integrity and uniqueness of the self, but unlike Viola and Sebastian, Antipholus of Syracuse and Antipholus of Ephesus cannot be said to be complementary personalities. The union of male and female attributes which is doubly signalled by the weddings and the reunion of the twins at the end of *Twelfth Night* is absent from *The Comedy of Errors*. Either each Antipholus is already self-sufficient, or their face-to-face encounter, a multiplication of nullities, can accomplish nothing. The self-important sense of metaphysical crisis which the brothers might feel at their moment of mutual encounter is diminished by the repetition of their situation between their twinned servants, the Dromios, who tilt uncanniness towards comedy.

It is not, however, only the doubling of the deuteragonists which tugs against the notion of a wholly distinct personal existence. The familial embrace with which the community of Ephesus eventually receives and reassembles the scattered members of Egeon's household intimates the priority of corporate identities over the single and limited life of the individual consciousness. Such union and reunion is of course a romance motif, but it is strengthened in the Christian context which both the play's allusive texture and the events of its resolution imply, since the supranational community of the church, as constituted by the participation of all Christians in a common creed rather than by the ecclesiastical hierarchy, is not only the most inclusive and enveloping form of fellowship which Shakespeare knew, but the one which least particularizes its members. Within it, each person belongs not as a whole but as a part. To be a member of a family or even of a society is to accept some constraints on one's autonomy; to be a member of a body is to have no true possibility of autonomy. "For we are members of [Christ's] bodie, of his flesh, and of his bones." St. Paul's language in the Epistle to the Ephesians reawakens the metaphorical sense of membership, atrophied in common usage, but for Paul the language is more than metaphorical. The continuity of our bodies with Christ's is physical; as the gloss of the Geneva Bible points out, we "are not onely joyned to him by nature, but also by the communion of substance, through the holie Gost and by faith: the seale and testimonie thereof is the Supper of the Lord."

The point, here at least, should be not so much that Shakespeare was attentive to the intricacies of Pauline discourse or even that he performed an extraordinary intertextual exercise in conflating the concerns of works as disparate as Plautus' *Menaechmi* and St. Paul's Epistle

THE COMEDY OF ERRORS

to the Ephesians. Rather, in Paul's exposition of the Christian community Shakespeare found a version of selfhood so overshadowed by the imperatives of solidarity that it represents a complete alternative and challenge to the selfhood which the character in search of definition hopes to achieve. Antipholus of Syracuse is, or hopes to be, literally self-regarding— he wants to be able to look at himself as mirrored in his brother. Measured by a Christian standard, he may be morally self-regarding as well. . . .

Gail Kern Paster

SOURCE: "The Nature of Our People: Shakespeare's City Comedies," in *The Idea of the City in the Age of Shakespeare,* University of Georgia Press, 1985, pp. 178-219.

[*In the following excerpt, Paster argues that "only by attending to the nature of the urban environment . . . can the play's deep concern with the ambiguities of personal and civic identity become fully revealed." She explores this idea primarily through commentary on Aegeon and his twin sons; specifically, how their personal identities are called into question in the social environment in which they find themselves.*]

. . . . *The Comedy of Errors, The Merchant of Venice,* and *Measure for Measure* come together by presenting urban environments faced with fundamental dilemmas, paradoxical situations whose implications call the idea of any normative urban community into severe question. In each, the city is confronted with the self-imposed necessity of enforcing a law whose consequences are so clearly inhuman that they can only make mockery of a city's reason for being. The particular logic of the comic action appears to require the city to dismantle itself, either by enforcing a monstrous law or by refusing to. Although the procedure for resolving the comic impasse differs from play to play, the end result is always to reconstitute the city for a greater inclusiveness largely achieved by means of redefinition and conversion. . .

In the three comedies that are the subject of this chapter . . . the social implications of individual behavior and circumstance are everywhere to be found, even in *The Comedy of Errors.* One of the first issues to be broached in all three plays is the noticeable tension between social identity and individual experience. Particularly apparent in *Errors* is the potential conflict between two different, separately valued kinds of identity. The first of them is clearly historical and public: a captive man is led onstage by his enemies to receive his sentence. The unnamed Syracusan merchant seems to be a political victim, forfeit for belonging to the wrong group. The relentless symmetry of this twin-filled play starts here, where the Syracusan citizen finds an enemy duke bent on using him to complete a pattern begun by "the rancorous

outrage of your Duke / To merchants, our well-dealing countrymen" (1.1.6-7). No other identity but the citizenship that dooms him (as it would doom his mirror-image, the Ephesian caught by a duke in Syracuse) would seem relevant here. Yet the duke's curiosity about a man who would trade life at home for death abroad allows the merchant to construct a powerful personal identity that so commands sympathy and pity that the desire to kill the stranger is transformed into the desire to save a fellow man. Egeon's implausible romantic story of shipwreck and separation serves not only structurally as exposition but also thematically as the creation of a personal identity that throws the predominance of his civic identity into question. The two identities could hardly be more distinct, the one betokening anonymity, hostility, and death and the other individuality, sympathy, and life.

Not only is the emotional disparity of the two identities troubling in this context; so also is the duke's obligation to divorce sympathy from judgment and see citizenship as identity. Egeon will not return to the stage until well into act 5, but we do not forget his situation . . . because his brief ambivalent experience of the two faces of Ephesus is played out in full by his twin sons. One finds himself an outcast in his own city, the relationships comprising his identity in collapse, and the other finds a mysteriously rich civic identity where none exists. . . .

By complicating social identity so early in all three plays, Shakespeare highlights the relation of the individual to a specific social environment. More important, perhaps, the environment in each case seems to contain a hazard— as yet unclear— from which the characters will not escape. Thus the wandering Antipholus no sooner steps onstage in Ephesus than he is warned to conceal his citizenship. In *The Merchant of Venice,* imagery of risk and jeopardy is all the more ominous because of Antonio and Bassanio's expressions of confidence in self and Fortune. The duke in *Measure for Measure* withdraws from his city in a haste so precipitate that it "leaves unquestion'd / Matters of needful value" (1.1.54-55). In each case, characters register a marked degree of interest either in the nature of the urban environment they are about to experience or in the power that they feel able to exercise over it. When Antonio makes no question of his power to raise money for Bassanio, we expect danger.

Admittedly, interest in their environment is not unusual in dramatic characters. What is unusual in Shakespeare is that these environments are so distinctly urban. Shakespeare insists upon the mercantile atmosphere of Ephesus and Venice; he locates the critical hazard initially in aspects of trade. A law barring traffic between trading towns like Ephesus and Syracuse is cruel and unnatural to ongoing civic life, especially when the trade war interrupts a private need as compelling as that of

Egeon and the traveling Antipholus to locate their family. The irony of Antonio's mercantilism in *The Merchant of Venice* is that it prevents him from lending to Bassanio directly (with his fortunes all at sea, Antonio has a liquidity problem) but enables him to stand security. Antonio's combination of strength and vulnerability expresses the nature of money and love. It also underscores how central Antonio's character as loving merchant is to the dynamic of Venice. And it is his opposite, Shylock (another combination of strength and vulnerability), who understands this in his ironic wordplay with Bassanio over the nature of Antonio's goodness: "my meaning in saying he is a good man, is to have you understand me that he is sufficient" (1.3.13-15). *Measure for Measure*, as we have seen, replaces the localizing detail of the other two plays with a definition of the city as idea first, rather than as place. But the play also sharply limits the individuality as presented in the first scene to that which is demanded by society— defined as "the nature of our people, / Our city's institutions"— and its need to be governed. In this play, the essential relation between self and city comes before there is any dramatically presented inner life in self or city to make that relation problematical. The valid test of Angelo's mettle can only come, as the duke knows, with direct experience of power. For us, as for Angelo, this transfer of power makes possible a direct experience of the city in 1.2.

In each play, then, the city becomes not just a resonant context for the central comic experience of the characters onstage, but an essential agent and object of change in that experience. Only by attending to the nature of the urban environment in *The Comedy of Errors* can the play's deep concern with the ambiguities of personal and civic identity become fully revealed. The "restless, schizoid condition" of the play's characters is first a feature of their environment. Thus, in seeing two Egeons where only one exists, Ephesus betrays its profound dualism, a communal dualism given literal, individual embodiment when the wandering twins step onstage.

The wandering Antipholus's first moments onstage also suggest the potential doubleness of Ephesus, for even as he is told of its dangerousness for him, he accepts a bag of gold— the gesture emblematic of the commercial exchanges at the heart of urban life. More importantly, by characterizing Ephesus as alternately welcoming and hostile, as home and alien city, Shakespeare associates the city with the closely related archetypal motifs of the pursuing double and of fraternal rivalry. Our awareness of the solution waiting at the denouement helps to distance us from the violence in the play and to see it as farce, but it should not prevent us from recognizing in the action sophisticated literary expression of primitive fears about shadows, reflections, resemblances, and name sharing which Otto Rank has given classic psychoanalytic treatment in *The Double*. Certainly the well-known Pauline associations of Ephesus

with witchcraft suggests the potential of the action for terror. The relevance of such archetypes— particularly the fraternal rivalry that we have already come to connect with the idea of the city— allows us to see how Shakespeare uses the farcical action of the doubled twins not only as a paradigm of personal self-fulfillment in family reunion, but also as a paradigm of the radical connectedness of social experience, an ideal relation of self and city which gets tested in the two later plays.

In complementary ways, both Antipholuses have incomplete relationships with the outside world here represented so ambivalently by Ephesus. In the wandering twin, melancholy subjectivity is so overpowering that it displaces social identity, causing him to perceive himself as invisible in Ephesus. The quintessential tourist, he anticipates a unilateral experience of Ephesus because he cannot imagine himself an object of Ephesian experience:

> I'll view the manners of the town,
> Peruse the traders, gaze upon the buildings,
> And then return and sleep within mine inn.
> . . . . .
>   I will go lose
> myself,
> And wander up and down to view the city.
>   [1.2.12-14;30-31]

His presumption of invisibility is particularly comic given the experience of his father. Antipholus is even more visible than Egeon, although not as the alien he feels himself to be. It is ironic that Ephesus will claim to know him at a time when he fears to have confounded himself. And it is even more ironic— virtually the comic expression of a kind of social revenge— that Ephesus's great gift of mother, brother, and father can come to him only after the city compels him to experience a complex of inexplicable social relationships. Significantly, the order of those imposed relationships moves outward from the domestic world to the world of commerce, so that the wandering Antipholus's experience has the effect of reconstructing from inside out a coherent yet persistently mysterious social self. At first the city threatens his one firm relationship with his servant— when the other Dromio calls him home to dinner. His experience of Ephesus begins, far more than our own, *in medias res:* "The capon burns," he is told, "the pig falls from the spit; / The clock hath strucken twelve upon the bell" (1.2.44-45.) His intended view of public Ephesus— manners, traders, buildings— becomes a concrete view of private Ephesus; he changes from spectator to participant. His melancholy egotism receives its first real jolt when he encounters Adriana, claiming him as her husband. The weakness of his cognitive foundations and his sense of formlessness or invisibility cause the wandering Antipholus to accede to the domestic identity being thrust upon him. His civic identity as a Syracusan provides no advantage in Ephesus. And his personal formlessness can provide no protection from a city whose undeniable solidity inheres in the homely picture of burnt capons and cold meat, the powerful conviction of the outraged wife, and her uncanny recognition of that emblem of personal form—his name. As invisibility gives way to visibility, his sense of firm reality recedes: "To me she speaks, she moves me for her theme; / What, was I married to her in my dream?" (2.2.181-82).

The resemblance of this scene to that first encounter in *Twelfth Night* between Sebastian and Olivia should clarify Shakespeare's greater interest in social nuance here. Social identity matters deeply in Ephesus, as Egeon finds out in discovering the consequences of being a stranger. His son begins to discover the consequences of being a citizen. He could not remain the invisible onlooker in Ephesus because he looks like an Ephesian; he is a twin. But being a twin in Ephesus is virtually a symbolic shorthand for existence in the city of man. Being in Ephesus not only means having a brother, but—such are this city's powers of bounty and intimacy—having his home, his wife, his community, and his dinner too. In this city one cannot take a brother's place without displacing him and those who, like the other Dromio and the two merchants, move in his company. The immediate effect of bringing the wandering Antipholus home to dinner is to lock out the resident Antipholus and to begin the gradual destruction of civic identity in him.

The comic power of the scene at the locked door derives not only from the ancient joke of cuckoldry—as is the case with the parallel scene in the *Amphitruo*—but from its flirtation with incest. The picture of a man locked out of his house and ready to break the doors down is an emblem of domestic civil war. The picture of a man ready to break down his doors because his place within has been usurped by his brother is an emblem of civic self-annihilation, the city-as-family symbolically dismantling itself with the twin disloyalties of wife and brother. The scene presents an image of archetypal fraternal rivalry as clear in its broadly comic way as the opening scene of *Titus Andronicus* where the imperial brothers challenge each other outside the gates of Rome for the right to rule within. Here, although the house certainly contains the possibility of incestuous usurpation, it also contains Luciana who stands for sexual inhibition, the peaceful resolution of conflict, and the continuing maturation of the family.

Furthermore, Shakespeare does not bring the two brothers together until their separate experiences approach equivalent portions of gain, loss, and ensuing disorientation. Although the alien Antipholus has lost a community in the search for a brother, the resident Antipholus has constructed a civic identity without firm familial foundations, without knowing he is a brother. For him, citizenship through marriage in Ephesus must always threaten incest. Thus it is significant that the persuasion the merchant Balthasar uses on the Ephesian Antipholus

not to break in should so explicitly make use of the powerful social weapon of shame—the withdrawal of community approval even into the afterlife:

> A vulgar comment will be made of it;
> And that supposed by the common rout
> Against your yet ungalled estimation,
> That may with foul intrusion enter in,
> And dwell upon your grave when you are dead.
> [3.1.100-04]

The resident Antipholus is sensitive to the twin threats of slander and scandal as his twin, having no stake in the regard of this society, would not be. The humiliation of the resident Antipholus, moreover, has been both sexual and social: being barred from his own door has not only revealed him semipublicly as a possible cuckold, but it also has made a mockery of his expansive gestures of warm hospitality to the two merchants. Psychologically, his decision to entertain his guests at the Porpentine is both understandable and realistic, as is his bravado gesture of turning over to the courtesan there the gold chain promised to his wife. His masculine self-image, in some question due to his need to invent stories to defuse her shrewishness, requires compensation for the rebuff it has suffered.

From this point of view, the courtesan plays a key role. The two sisters within the house of Antipholus represent two potential unions for his twin—an ideal one with Luciana and an archetypally destructive one with Adriana. The courtesan completes the pattern by providing the resident Antipholus with an unlawful sexual partner and an alternative, illicit household. The interconnectedness of social life in Ephesus is confirmed: locked out of his house, Antipholus occupies another. Refused by his wife, he turns to a whore—a contrast emblematic of rival cities.

It becomes increasingly evident that the presence of twins has consequences not only for the twins themselves but for the meaning of experience in the interdependent social system in which they move. The economy of structure in the play, in other words, is dramatic and social at the same time since the language and actions of everyone in Ephesus undergo divergent subjective interpretations whose coherence is known only to us. And, even for us, at times, the mirror experiences of the twins reveal an uncanny convergence of action and interpretation: thus the attraction of the wandering twin to the unmarried Luciana reflects a providential loyalty to his brother but she reproaches him for a domestic disloyalty of which his brother is in fact guilty. Luciana attempts to persuade the wanderer of the shame of open disaffection and the wisdom of duplicity:

> 'Tis double wrong to truant with your bed,
> And let her read it in thy looks at board;
> Shame hath a bastard fame, well managed;

Ill deeds is doubled with an evil word.

[3.2.17-20]

The stranger cannot be shamed as the husband could. There is broad humor and social irony in this recommendation to incest, especially since the real cause of coldness to one sister is warmth of feeling to the other. The love of the stranger is thus an act of involuntary social beneficence, a removal of the threat of incest that can only appear like madness to Luciana: "What, are you mad that you do reason so?" (3.2.53).

Thus the escalating social effects of the phenomenon of twins are first felt within the household of sisters and servants. But the ongoing life of the city quickly becomes involved in what is, in effect, a social emergency as well as a personal one. One aspect of this social emergency is, of course, factitious: differentiating the twins will point up the perversity of separating Ephesians from Syracusans; the self-protection of Ephesus will turn out to be self-denial. In a more immediate and practical sense, however, differentiating the twins is critical because civic relationships, like marital ones, depend upon the congruence of appearance and reality, upon the possibility of taking one's neighbors at face value. The multiplication of selves which threatens incest and fraternal rivalry within the family threatens the destruction of credit and the collapse of trade in the city. What the twins experience as metamorphosis, the merchants in Ephesus understand as the betrayal of trust. Indeed the two themes of metamorphosis and betrayal begin to come together at the end of act 3, when the Syracusan master and servant articulate for each other their sense of transformation at the hands of women and plan to escape or be "guilty of self-wrong" (3.2.162). The promise of dangerous enchantment which Antipholus associates with Ephesus in general and with Luciana in particular becomes tangible in the mysterious offer by Angelo the jeweler of a chain for which he refuses to accept payment. The moment is one of high comedy not only because of the consequences that we can foresee but also because it so blithely contradicts the probabilities of urban existence— the defensive stratagems that the wandering Antipholus, like other city dwellers, had accepted as axiomatic:

What I should think of this I cannot tell;
But this I think, there's no man is so vain
That would refuse so fair an offer'd chain.
I see a man here needs not live by shifts
When in the streets he meets such golden
　gifts.

[3.2.178-82]

Another source of comedy is the contrast between the traveling twin's growing bewilderment about this city and our own increasingly firm sense of the ordinariness of life in Ephesus— a sense that the growing disorder of acts 4 and 5 does nothing, really, to disturb. The interconnectedness and intimacy of the city does har-

bor a potential for destructive fraternal rivalry. And the underside of its apparent generosity to the alien twin may be a form of possessiveness: Adriana will not let him go. But we have already seen a rather idealized version of bourgeois fraternity in the exchange of courtesies between the resident Antipholus and other merchants in act 3. Concern for Antipholus's reputation prompts the merchant Balthasar's advice that he return home in the quiet of evening to find out why a wife of "her wisdom, / Her sober virtue, years and modesty" (3.1.89-90) locked him out. Antipholus attributes the jeweler Angelo's failure to meet him at the Porpentine with the chain to concern for his marriage: "Belike you thought our love would last too long / If it were chain'd together, and therefore came not" (4.1.25-26). Social experience in Ephesus also exhibits an almost perfect paradigm of trade, a bourgeois tidiness about debt, credit, and reputation which we do not find in Venice, for instance, and which only the extraordinary duplication of Antipholuses can disrupt. Angelo owes to the second merchant "even just the sum" (4.1.7) he expects to receive from Antipholus. The second merchant has refrained from importuning his debtor, "nor now I had not, but that I am bound / To Persia, and want guilders for my voyage" (4.1.3-4). The intensity of the quarrel that erupts between Antipholus and the jeweler is a measure of the sense of personal betrayal on both sides and of the authority of the mercantile code which both believe the other to have violated. They too did not need to live by shifts in Ephesus.

Ironically the civic importance and prestige of the resident Antipholus and the normality of Ephesus are clearest when the fortunes of the brothers are completely transposed and they themselves are disoriented. Just after the resident brother has been hauled off to the prison that the Syracusan twin is legally forfeit to, the wandering Antipholus attests with wonder to the fullness of his Ephesian brother's civic life:

There's not a man I meet but doth salute me
As if I were their well-acquainted friend,
And everyone doth call me by my name:
Some tender money to me, some invite me,
Some other give me thanks for kindnesses,
Some offer me commodities to buy.

[4.3.1-6]

His Dromio's punning description of the arresting officer— "not that Adam that kept the paradise, but that Adam that keeps the prison" (16-17)—is more appropriate to the antithetical experiences of the two brothers who seem to be moving about in two different cities. One city arrests you for reasons unknown, another keeps giving you something for nothing. This is the largest symmetry of the play: one city has become two, two brothers have become one. All differences between the twins— that one is a Syracusan, the other an Ephesian; that one is a melancholy loner, the other an eminent, sociable, married, and impatient Rotarian—collapse in the face of the inability of the community to distinguish them. In the course of the action, however, the effect of the identity of the brothers is paradoxically to intensify their sense of personal distinctiveness—even to the point of paranoia. The Syracusan twin, imagining himself the victim of a supernatural conspiracy, perceives the courtesan as the devil: "Satan avoid, I charge thee tempt me not" (4.3.46). His brother rages at his wife: "Dissembling harlot, thou art false in all, / And art confederate with a damned pack / To make a loathsome abject scorn of me" (4.4.99-101). For both twins now, the treachery of the city seems to be symbolized by the falseness of its women, strumpets all.

Shakespeare's point here is partly, of course, to suggest the fragility of normative social life and the essential cooperation of the community at large in objectifying individual self-perception with coherent civic identity. Also, the image of two brothers perceived as one in one city experienced as two expresses, as an idea of the city, the different kinds of self embodied in the two brothers—the one brother feeling incomplete without his twin and losing, in him, a whole city; the other feeling complete, not "twinned," thanks to the customary esteem of Ephesus yet in truth crucially deprived in a way that brings disorder to the whole community. Their antithetical experiences—of inexplicable bounty and recognition on the one hand and inexplicable shame and persecution on the other—bring both to the point of warfare against the city. The crisis between the individual and the city necessitates appeal to higher authorities represented for the stranger twin by the universal maternal sanctuary of the Abbey, for the resident twin by the duke to whom he owes his Ephesian citizenship. It is only partly true to say, as R. A. Foakes has argued, that the final scene before the Abbey reveals the participants all engaged in a private ordering of experience. What so defeats the characters and the duke as well is that they have all sought corroboration from the community for their experiences and have partly found it. Subjectivity and objectivity cannot achieve a reconciliation because the ordinary source of confirmation in comedy—the sense of the comic community—has broken down. And this has happened not because the community has been excluded from the experience of the central protagonists, but because it has been so involved.

The play finally reveals the inevitable participation of community in the most private of searches, when the only thing sought is the specific mirror of self in a twin. Here the self finds a fuller mirror in the city at large and twinship becomes not a destructive aberration that threatens all Ephesus but an intensified image of the new communal norm—a civic fraternity in which even Syracusans belong. There is no more geography at the play's close, no more Corinth or Epidamnum, no more

Syracuse and Ephesus. In its enemy city, Ephesus has recognized a twin. And the twins, by finding a family, turn the whole city of Ephesus into a feast of gossips. Ephesus, the city of man, becomes a secular image of the promise which St. Paul makes to the Corinthians: "now I know in part; but then shall I know even as also I am known" (1 Cor. 13:12). . . .

GENRE

Russ McDonald and Jack A. Vaughn argue that we should take the play for what it is—a farce. **McDonald** in particular notes that "farce" and "Shakespeare" need not be mutually exclusive terms. Vaughn argues that although the play should be classified as a farce, it is not a "simple" one because Aegeon's framing story gives the play depth. J. Dennis Huston and Robert Ornstein stop short of classifying the play as an out-and-out farce. Huston refers to the play as "nearly unmitigated farce," tempering his classification by noting the elements of tragedy (Aegeon's story) and romance (Aegeon's separation from Aemilia and his other son). Ornstein argues that Shakespeare adheres almost exclusively to Plautus's play even though he begins *The Comedy of Errors* with Aegeon's tragic tale.

Stephen Greenblatt, Ralph Berry, Maurice Charney, and David Bevington all propose taking an evaluation of the play's genre beyond farce. Greenblatt, Charney, and Bevington all take note of the play's romance elements that transcend farce—for example, the courting of Luciana by Antipholus of Syracuse and the end of separation in the reunions in the closing scene of the play. Berry argues that if the play were a farce only, it would be simply a story of mistaken identities. The play is also a comedy, as it examines how the characters react to the farcical situations in which they find themselves.

Russ McDonald

SOURCE: "Fear of Farce," in *"Bad" Shakespeare: Revaluations of the Shakespeare Canon*, edited by Maurice Charney, Fairleigh Dickinson University Press, 1988, pp. 77-89.

[*In the following excerpt, McDonald first surveys previous criticism on the play regarding its classification as a farce and its position in Shakespeare's canon. He notes that critics have tended to "elevate" the play above the "vulgar" level of farce in explaining its meaning (although its farcical elements are obvious) because it is sometimes perceived as a source of "embarrassment" in the canon. McDonald then examines "how meaning comes about in farce" through the play's "theatrical complexity," concluding that the play should be examined for what it is—a farce and a "source of wonder."*]

Zeus's sexual lapses notwithstanding, gods are not supposed to be indecorous, and a characteristic of modern Bardolatry has been its insistence on Shakespeare's artistic dignity, particularly his attachment to the approved dramatic forms. The popular image of Shakespeare as the embodiment of high culture, the author of *Hamlet* and certain other tragedies, as well as a very few weighty comedies, is merely a version of a bias that also, if less obviously, afflicts the academy. What I am talking about is a hierarchy of modes, or, to put it another way, genre snobbery. That tragedy is more profound and significant than comedy is a prejudice that manifests itself in and out of the Shakespeare Establishment: in the impatience of undergraduates who, taking their first class in Shakespeare, regard the comedies and histories as mere appetizers to the main course, the tragedies; in Christopher Sly's equation of "a commonty" with "a Christmas gambol or a tumbling trick"; in the disdain of the tourist at the Barbican box office who, finding *Othello* sold out, refuses a ticket to *The Merry Wives of Windsor;* in the decision of that Athenian student to preserve his notes from Aristotle's lecture on tragedy but not to bother with the one on comedy.

If there is a hierarchy of modes, there is also a hierarchy within modes: *de casibus* tragedy is less exalted than Greek, for example. So it is with the kinds of comedy, and the play to which I shall address myself, *The Comedy of Errors,* rests safely in the lowest rank. Farce is at the bottom of everyone's list of forms, and yet Shakespeare is at the top of everyone's list of authors. Thus, the problem I mean to examine is generated by competing hierarchies. Most literary critics have little occasion to think about farce, and those who concern themselves chiefly with the creator of texts such as *Macbeth* and *Coriolanus* do their best to avoid the form. For many years the earliest comedies were treated unapologetically as farces and Shakespeare was praised, if mildly, for his skill at contriving such brilliant and pleasing trifles. But the need to preserve his association with higher things has led in the last three or four decades to a revision of this opinion. It seems inappropriate that the cultural monument known as Shakespeare should have anything to do with a popular entertainment that we connect with the likes of the Marx brothers (Groucho and Harpo, not Karl and Moritz). Criticism resists a Shakespeare capable of wasting his time on such a trivial form.

My purpose is to suggest that Shakespeare could be "bad," but my definition differs somewhat from those of most of the other contributors to this volume. Rather than re-examine texts that may have been overvalued or seek to locate weaknesses in dramatic technique, I shall argue that Shakespeare's taste was not invariably elevated and that certain plays are less "significant" than others (or at least that they signify different things in different ways). By addressing myself to what is and is not considered "Shakespearean," I claim an interest

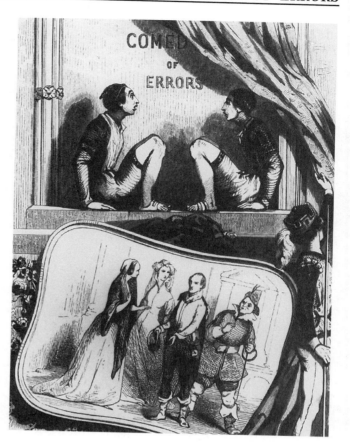

Engraving from the Verplanck edition of The Comedy of Errors *(1847).*

in one of the fundamental issues of this collection: canonicity. A work like *The Comedy of Errors* must be deformed if it is to conform to that category known as Shakespearean comedy— as a farce it is noncanonical— and such misrepresentation demands a rejoinder.

The first part of this essay surveys the evasions that critics have devised for treating Shakespeare's efforts in farce, with concentration on the dodges applied to *Errors.* The remainder, a straightforward study of that play's theatrical action, proposes to identify the playwright's strategies for the production of meaning in farce. In light of the concerns of this volume, to contend that *Errors* succeeds not as an early version of a romantic comedy or as an allegory of marriage but as an out-and-out farce is risky, for such an argument looks like yet another defense of the artistic experiments of a novice and thus seems to exemplify the very Bardolatry that many of these essays vigorously dispute. In fact, however, my aim is to establish Shakespeare's delight in and commitment to a dramatic form that has become infra dig. To recognize such a bent is to augment our sense of Shakespeare's actual range. We whitewash our subject by refusing to admit his attraction to farce and declining to explore his talent for it.

I

Suspicion of farce has fostered two main critical maneuvers, here summarized by Barbara Freedman: "The first is represented by that group of critics who know that Shakespeare never wrote anything solely to make us laugh and so argue that Shakespeare never wrote farce at all. . . . The more popular critical approach, however, is to agree that Shakespeare wrote farce, but to consider *Errors* (as well as Shakespeare's other predominantly farcical plays) to be nonsensical *insofar* as they are farce." To begin with the first group, its members are undaunted by Shakespeare's demonstrable choice of classical or Italian farces for source material: in such cases he may be seen "transcending the farce which a lesser writer might have been satisfied to make," and thus the form is mentioned so that it can be dismissed.

The most familiar and pernicious tactic of those who would dissociate Shakespeare from the vulgar category is to discuss the early plays as precursors of the mature style, as seedbeds, that is, for ideas and methods that will flower in the later comedies and even in the tragedies. (In fact, hothouses would make a better simile, since the ideas and methods are found blooming in the early play itself by the time the critic finishes.) A. C. Hamilton, for example, asserts that *The Comedy of Errors* provides a foundation for the later comedies by revealing "their basis in the idea that life upon the order of nature has been disturbed and must be restored and renewed through the action of the play." Hamilton's reticence to detect inchoate forms of particular dramatic themes from later works is not shared by Peter G. Phialas, who identifies "certain features of structure and theme, and even tone, which anticipate significant elements of Shakespeare's romantic comedies." Specifically, "*The Comedy of Errors*, though in the main concerned with the farcical mistakings of identity, touches briefly a theme of far greater significance, the ideal relationship of man and woman." This anticipatory practice amounts to reading the career backward: a play is conditioned by what follows it, and its distinctive qualities may be underrated or deformed. The prophetic approach tends to manifest itself in and to merge with the second defensive strategy.

Put simply, this way of thinking involves deepening the farces, exposing their profundity. It has become the preferred means of protecting Shakespeare against his own immature tastes or the vulgar demands of his audience, and it has attracted some eloquent and powerful advocates. Derek Traversi, for example, unites the two critical defenses, seeing *Errors* as both serious in itself and important in its tonal prefiguration of the later work. He emphasizes "the deliberate seriousness of the story of Aegeon, which gives the entire action a new setting of gravity, a sense of tragic overtones which,

elementary though it may be in expression, is yet not without some intimation of later and finer effects." In other words, the play is profound but not too profound.

That the dignifiers succeeded some time ago in making this serious position canonical is apparent in the following passage from R. A. Foakes's Introduction to the New Arden edition, published in 1962:

> These general considerations may help to illustrate the particular quality of *The Comedy of Errors*. The play has farcical comedy, and it has fantasy, but it does more than merely provoke laughter, or release us temporarily from inhibitions and custom into a world free as a child's, affording delight and freshening us up. It also invites compassion, a measure of sympathy, and a deeper response to the disruption of social and family relationships which the action brings about. Our concern for the Antipholus twins, for Adriana and Luciana, and our sense of disorder are deepened in the context of suffering provided by the enveloping action. The comedy proves, after all, to be more than a temporary and hilarious abrogation of normality; it is, at the same time, a process in which the main characters are in some sense purged, before harmony and the responsibility of normal relationships are restored at the end. Adriana learns to overcome her jealousy, and accepts the reproof of the Abbess; her husband is punished for his anger and potential brutality by Doctor Pinch's drastic treatment; and Antipholus of Syracuse is cured of his prejudices about Ephesus. Behind them stands Egeon, a prototype of the noble sufferer or victim in later plays by Shakespeare, of Antonio in *The Merchant of Venice*, and of Pericles, central figure in a play which uses more profoundly the story on which Egeon's adventures are based.

A variation of this argument is found in Harold Brooks's much-cited essay, which associates *Errors* not with a farce such as *Supposes* but with a recognition play such as the *Ion* or *The Confidential Clerk*.

Those who see Shakespeare as "transcending" farce must consent to a divorce between the "serious" issues that they elect to stress and the main business of the play. In other words, the critics analyze delicate sentiments while the characters knock heads. The discovery of gravity requires great emphasis on the frame story of Egeon, or Adriana's matrimonial laments, or the wooing of Luciana. Brooks candidly declares the incongruity between his emphasis and Shakespeare's: "The *Comedy* appeals first and foremost to laughter, as is obvious at any performance. I have dwelt on its serious themes and strands of romance because it is these that student and producer are prone to discount." One might respond that student and producer would in this case be taking their cue from the author, who was himself prone to discount the serious themes and strands of romance at this stage of his career. We should question critical means that seek to convert the early comedies into something other than they are.

The Comedy of Errors is a superlative example of dramatic farce, a simple form of comedy designed chiefly to make an audience laugh. Freedman points out that farces are almost always characterized by an "insistence on their own meaninglessness, an insistence which by no means should be accepted at face value." In other words, to regard the play as a highly developed form of farce is not to outlaw ideas. Mistaken identity is at the heart of *The Comedy of Errors*, as Antipholus of Syracuse explains in the final moments: "I see we still did meet each other's man, / And I was ta'en for him, and he for me, / And thereupon these errors have arose" (5.1.388-90). This basic formula is the source of pleasure and of meaning in the farcical comedy. My goal is to increase, if only slightly, our sense of how meaning comes about in farce, and my method for doing so is to concentrate on what an audience sees and hears in the main action. It seems reasonable to conclude—and worth pointing out, given the critical history of the text in question—that dramatic significance ought to proceed as much from the essential as from the ancillary features of a text.

II

To err is human, and one way of describing the imperfect condition of our experience is to say that we inhabit a state of division, of disunity, of separation from God, from nature, from one another. Lest this seem too portentous a beginning for a discussion of a farcical comedy, let me hasten to say that splitting (of ships, of families, of other human relations) is one of the most important of the play's patterns of action. In one sense, of course, the plot of *The Comedy of Errors* is founded on the natural division of twinship, for nature has split a single appearance into two persons. In the source play, Plautus exploits the confusion inherent in this division by geographically separating the Menaechmus brothers, and Shakespeare has increased the complexity of the original plot, as everyone knows, by doubling the twins. What is less familiar is his tactic of making the normal avenues of reconciliation into obstacle courses laid with traps and dead ends. Virtually all comedy represents characters' attempts to overcome their isolation through marriage or reconciliation, with farce throwing the emphasis on the amusing difficulties involved in such efforts. Marriage, systems of law, commerce, language—all these are forms of communion or institutions through which people seek or give satisfaction, social instruments and (implicitly) comic means for joining human beings in a happy and fruitful relation.

And yet, for all their value, these means are naturally imperfect and likely to collapse under various pressures, either of accident or human will or their own liability to misinterpretation. When they break down, the confusion that frustrates the characters delights the audience. To a great extent, the comedy of *Errors* arises from the number of barriers Shakespeare has erected and the ingenuity with which he has done so. The greatest obstacles arise in the principal characters' relations with their servants, in the arena of commerce, and in the realm of speech itself. Shakespeare generates amusing conflict by exaggerating the forces that separate people and by weakening the media that connect them.

The presence of four men in two costumes leads first to the attenuation of the normal bonds between servant and master and between husband and wife. From the twin Sosias in Plautus's *Amphitruo*, Shakespeare creates in the Dromios a pair of agents, go-betweens who link husband to wife or customer to merchant. They are extensions of their masters' wills, instruments by which each of the Antipholuses conducts business or gets what he wants. In the farcical world of the play, however, the will is inevitably frustrated as these servants become barriers, sources of confusion, gaps in a chain of communication. For Antipholus of Syracuse, lost in a strange, forbidden seaport, his one sure connection, his "bondman," seems to fail him. This treatment of the twin servants, moreover, is representative of Shakespeare's method with other characters, including Adriana, Luciana, and the Courtesan. Although the females are often said to contribute to the play's Pauline analysis of proper marriage, their primary value is as comic troublemakers. Adriana's eloquence and Luciana's charm make the two women memorable, to be sure, but they are hardly complex. Adriana's main function is to doubt her husband, to rail against his neglect, to chase him in the streets, to enlist a conjurer to minister to him; Luciana's role is to attract Antipholus of Syracuse and thereby to fuel her sister's rage.

The disintegration of personal bonds is accompanied by the weakening of the multiple commercial connections. Although the thematic importance of debts is familiar enough, it is also relevant that many of the play's amusing confrontations are grounded in thwarted commercial exchanges. Ignoring the maxim that it is best to eliminate the middleman, Shakespeare has added a host of them. Angelo the Goldsmith, Balthazar, and the First and Second Merchants are all Shakespearean inventions—businessmen, literal agents who exist to get in the way. Each functions as an additional barrier separating the twin Antipholuses, as another hedge in the maze at the center of the comedy. The Second Merchant, for instance, appears only twice and exists for no other reason than to make demands and increase the comic pressure: he has been patient since Pentecost and now needs guilders for a journey; he presses Angelo to repay the sum; Angelo must seek payment from Antipholus of Ephesus who, not having received the chain for which the money is demanded, refuses to accommodate him. In short, this importunate stranger is unnecessary: Angelo might have pursued compensation on his own initiative.

In the critical rush to find "meaning" or "tonal variety" in the addition of Luciana, Egeon, and Emilia, the structural value of the lesser auxiliary figures may be overlooked. Their untimely or mistaken demands for payment increase the confusion on the stage and damage the ties that connect them to their fellow citizens. Adriana joins the line of claimants when she tries forcibly to collect the love owed her by her husband, and her vocabulary indicates that Shakespeare has established an analogy between marital responsibilities and the cash nexus.

The setting of the comedy, as the occupations of the secondary figures remind us, is mostly the street, or "the mart," and from the beginning we observe that the business of the street is business. Most of the confrontations between characters and much of the dialogue concern the physical exchange of money or property, and other personal dealings are figured in financial terms. Egeon is a Syracusan trader unable to make the necessary financial exchange— a thousand marks for his freedom— and this fine or debt seems to have resulted from a protracted trade war. Many years before, after a period in which his "wealth increas'd / By prosperous voyages," Egeon had found himself separated from his wife by his "factor's death, / And the great care of goods at random left" (1.1.41-42). Now without family or funds, the insolvent businessman leaves the stage, whereupon Antipholus of Syracuse enters with an Ephesian merchant who tells him of the stranger's plight— "not being able to buy out his life"— and warns the young traveler to conceal his identity "lest that your goods too soon be confiscate." The citizen then returns Antipholus's bag of gold and pleads the need to pay a business call: "I am invited, sir, to certain merchants, / Of whom I hope to make much benefit" (1.2.24-25). He leaves Antipholus to his "own content, . . . the thing [he] cannot get."

This endearing soliloquy is usually said to prefigure the theme of self-understanding in the later comedies, but what is less often said is that Antipholus analyzes his dilemma in terms of self-possession: he fears that in seeking to recover his family he will "lose" himself. At the end of the same scene he frets about the loss of his treasure, worrying that Dromio "is o'er-raught of all [Antipholus's] money" and recalling the city's reputation for "cozenage," "cheaters," and "mountebanks."

The bag of gold that Antipholus gives to Dromio to deliver to the inn is the first in a list of theatrical properties that provoke farcical contention. The initial dispute occurs with the entrance of Dromio of Ephesus, to whom "the money" demanded can only be the "six-

pence that I had o' Wednesday last, / To pay the saddler for my mistress' crupper"; the "charge" is not a bag of gold but a command "to fetch you from the mart"; the "thousand marks" are not coins but bruises administered by master and mistress. As Antipholus of Syracuse worries about fraud, Dromio of Ephesus reports the misunderstanding to his mistress in a speech whose opposing clauses suggest the nature of the impasse: "'Tis dinner time,' quoth I; 'my gold,' quoth he." The metal becomes a metaphor at the end of the first scene of act 2, when Adriana speaks of reputation as a piece of enameled gold (2.1.109-15), and thus Shakespeare uses it to link the end of the scene with the beginning of the next: Antipholus of Syracuse enters puzzling over the bag of money, apparently not lost at all, whereupon his own Dromio enters, denies any knowledge of the recent dispute over the gold, and earns a beating. The pattern of confusion thus established with the thousand marks is repeated in squabbles over control of a chain, a ring, a dinner, a house, a spouse, a bag of ducats, a name, a prisoner, and a pair of strangers seeking sanctuary.

The vocabulary of these disputes is almost invariably the parlance of the marketplace: Antipholus of Ephesus and his business cronies politely debate the relative value of a warm welcome and a good meal ("I hold your dainties cheap, sir, and your welcome dear"); Nell "lays claim" to the Syracusan Dromio; to the Courtesan, "forty ducats is too much to lose"; the Officer cannot release Antipholus of Ephesus for fear that "the debt he owes will be required of me"; Antipholus of Ephesus is known to be "of very reverend reputation, . . . / Of credit infinite"; Dromio of Ephesus, declared mad and tied up, describes himself as "entered in bond" for Antipholus; and when the Abbess sees Egeon in act 5, she offers to "loose his bonds, / And gain a husband by his liberty." The great scene before Antipholus's house (3.1) becomes a dispute not just over property but over ownership of names and identity. In their efforts to get paid or to pay others back for wrongs suffered, characters often speak of "answering" each other:

Eph. Ant. I answer you? Why should I answer you?
Angelo. The money that you owe me for the chain.

(4.1.62-63)

The merchants become enraged when their customers refuse to answer them with payment; Adriana is furious that her husband will not return a favorable answer to her requests that he come home to dinner; Antipholus of Ephesus will make his household answer for the insult of locking him out; and neither Antipholus is able to get a straight answer from either of the Dromios. This financial use of "answer" links cash to language, the most complicated and potentially ambiguous medium of all.

Exploiting the pun as the linguistic equivalent of twin-ship, Shakespeare creates a series of verbal equivalents for the visual duplications of the action. Initially, it seems to me, his practice is to please the audience with repeated words and images: most obviously, he develops the conflicts by ingeniously employing the language of commerce. The normal give-and-take of business activity and family life is impaired by the mistakings of the action, and when the members of the household take Antipholus of Ephesus for a troublemaker in the street, his Dromio describes him as having been "bought and sold." The "loss" of one's good name or "estimation" is risky in this world of commerce, as Balthazar explains: "For slander lives upon succession, / For ever housed where it gets possession" (3.1.105-6). Adriana's anger at her husband leads Luciana to charge her with possessiveness, and then when Antipholus of Syracuse confesses that Luciana,

> *Possessed* with such a gentle sovereign grace,
> Of such *enchanting* presence and discourse,
> Hath almost made me *traitor* to myself,
> 　　　　　　　(3.2.158-60; italics mine)

the diction of ownership ("possessions") is cleverly modulated into that of witchcraft and madness ("possession"). This ambiguity pays its most amusing dividends when Doctor Pinch attempts to exorcise the demons from Antipholus of Ephesus:

> I charge thee, Satan, hous'd within this man,
> To yield possession to my holy prayers,
> And to thy state of darkness hie thee straight;
> 　　　　　　　(4.4.52-54)

The problems of confused identity and the loss of self-control are soon compounded by the question of freedom of action. The Dromios' lives are not their own, as they reiterate in complaining that, as slaves, they are not adequately rewarded for service. These various senses of bondage—to service, to customers, to wives, to the law, to business commitments (the Second Merchant is "bound to Persia"), to a rope—reinforce each other, especially in the last two acts, as the lines of action intersect:

> *Egeon.* Most might duke, vouchsafe me speak
> 　a word.
> Haply I see a friend will save my life,
> And pay the sum that may deliver me.
> *Duke.* Speak freely, Syracusian, what thou wilt.
> *Egeon.* Is not your name, sir, called Antipho-
> 　lus?
> And is not that your bondman Dromio?
> *Eph. Dro.* Within this hour I was his bond-
> 　man, sir;
> But he, I thank him, gnawed in two my
> 　cords.

> Now I am Dromio, and his man, unbound.
> 　　　　　　　(5.1.283-91)

Egeon, expecting to be set at liberty, is mistaken, bound by the limitations of his senses. And here Dromio, the "freedman," steals from his master the privilege of response. As mistakes are exposed and corrected, Shakespeare relies upon the commercial vocabulary that has served him from the beginning: Antipholus of Syracuse wishes "to make good" his promises to Luciana; when Antipholus of Ephesus offers to pay his father's line, the Duke pardons Egeon and restores his freedom and self-control ("It shall not need; thy father hath his life"); and the Abbess offers to "make full satisfaction" to the assembled company in recompense for the confusion of the day.

Words offer a way of resolving the divisions that the play explores, but at the same time they entail enormous possibilities for error. Given the present critical climate, some remarks about the unreliability of language are to be expected, but if words are included among the other media of exchange that Shakespeare has chosen to twist and complicate, then such a conclusion seems less fashionable than useful. Shakespeare almost from the beginning expands the wrangling over who owns what to include a series of battles over words and their significance. The two Dromios again offer the sharpest illustrations of such cross-purposes, usually in their interchanges with their masters. In the first meeting of Antipholus of Syracuse with Dromio of Ephesus, the shifts in meaning of "charge" and "marks" I have already cited represent the struggle for control of meaning that underlies the farcical action. Both servants are adept at shifting from the metaphorical to the literal:

> *Adr.* Say, is your tardy master now at hand?
> *Eph. Dro.* Nay, he's at two hands with me,
> 　and that my two ears can witness.
>
> 　　　　　　　(2.1.44-46)

When Antipholus of Syracuse threatens Dromio of Syracuse, "I will beat this method in your sconce," the servant resorts to linguistic subversion: "Sconce call you it? so you would leave battering, I had rather have it a head; and you use these blows long, I must get a sconce for my head, and insconce it too, or else I shall seek my wit in my shoulders" (2.2.34-39).

Yet the servants can speak highly figurative language as well: both describe the arresting officer in metaphors so elaborate that they baffle the auditors (4.2.32-40 and 4.3.12-30). Some of the verbal excursions resemble vaudeville turns, particularly the banter between the two Syracusans on baldness, and such jests represent verbal forms of what happens dramatically in the main action. In showing that "there is no time for all things," Dromio of Syracuse jestingly disproves an indisputable axiom, just as the errors of the main plot raise a challenge to the reality that everyone has accepted until now. This is more than what Brooks deprecatingly calls "elaborations of comic rhetoric."

The struggle over what words signify quickens as the characters sense that reality is slipping away from them. The locking-out scene (3.1) depends for its hilarity on the stichomythic exchanges between those outside (Dromio and Antipholus of Ephesus) and those inside (Dromio of Syracuse and Luce, and later Adriana). The contestants, particularly those in the security of the house, manipulate meanings and even rhyme and other sounds as they taunt the pair trying to enter, for possession of the house is apparently an advantage in the battle of words. The Dromios' attitudes toward language are almost always playful and subversive, so that even at their masters' most frustrated moments, the servants take pleasure in twisting sound and sense, as in Dromio of Ephesus's puns on "crow" ("crow without a feather?"; "pluck a crow together"; and "iron crow").

The trickiness of language can cause characters to lose the direction of the dialogue:

> *Adr.* Why, man, what is the matter?
> *Syr. Dro.* I do not know the matter; he is
> 'rested on the case.
> *Adr.* What, is he arrested? tell me at whose
> suit?
> *Syr. Dro.* I know not at whose suit he is
> arrested well;
> But is in a suit of buff which 'rested him, that
> can I tell.
> Will you send him, mistress, redemption, the
> money in his desk?
> *Adr.* Go, fetch it, sister; this I wonder at,
> *Exit* Luciana.
> That he unknown to me should be in debt.
> Tell me, was he arrested on a band?
> *Syr. Dro.* Not on a band, but on a stronger
> thing;
> A chain, a chain, do you not hear it ring?
> *Adr.* What, the chain?
> *Syr. Dro.* No, no, the bell, 'tis time that I
> were gone,
> It was two ere I left him, and now the clock
> strikes one.
>
> (4.2.41-54)

Rhetorically, the key to this passage is antanaclasis: Dromio wrests a word from Adriana's meaning into another of its senses, as with "matter" (*trouble* and *substance*), "case" and "suit" (both meaning *case in law* and *suit of clothes*), "band" (*bond* and *ruff*). The ambiguous pronoun reference in "hear it ring" illustrates the power of words to entrap: Adriana and the audience need a moment to adjust as Dromio abruptly shifts the focus from his narrative to the present.

Just as words are apt to slip out of their familiar senses, customers or husbands or servants seem to change from moment to moment. Dialogue and stage action illustrate the limits of human control as characters try to react to these confusing turns of phrase or of event. Antipholus of Syracuse, offered a wife and a dinner, can be flexible: "I'll say as they say" (2.2.214). But words may conflict with other words and realities with other realities, as the Duke discovers in seeking the undivided truth: "You say he dined at home; the goldsmith here / Denies that saying. Sirrah, what say you?" (5.1.274-75). Conflicts of personal identity, of contracts, of words, of stories, all make the truth seem elusive and uncertain.

Shakespeare's strategy of breaking the integuments that bind human beings to one another accounts for much of the mirth in *Errors* and for much of the significance as well. By interfering with familiar and normally reliable systems of relation—master to servant, wife to husband, customer to merchant, speaker to auditor—the dramatist achieves the dislocation felt by the characters and the "spirit of weird fun" enjoyed by the audience. There is, moreover, an additional verbal medium that Shakespeare has twisted to his own use, that of the play itself. The ironic bond between playwright and spectator, that relation which Shakespeare inherited from Plautus and cultivated throughout the first four acts and by which he assures us that we know more than the characters know, is suddenly abrogated when the Abbess declares her identity at the end of the fifth act: we have thought ourselves superior to the errors and assumptions of the ignorant characters, but we too have been deceived. Emilia's reunion with her husband and sons completes the comic movement of the action. This is farce, so the emphasis throughout is on the delights of disjunction; but this is also comedy, so the drama moves toward a restoration of human ties and the formation of new ones. Sentiment asserts itself in the final moments, of course, but Shakespeare does not overstate it, and the shift from pleasure in chaos to pleasure in order need not jar. The confusion must end somewhere, and it is standard practice for the farceur to relax the comic tension by devising a mellow ending to a period of frenzy.

Shakespeare attempted to write farce in *The Comedy of Errors*, and he succeeded. Certain effects and values are missing from this kind of drama: there is no thorough examination of characters, no great variety of tones, no profound treatment of ideas, no deep emotional engagement. But farce gives us what other dramatic forms may lack: the production of ideas through rowdy action, the pleasures of "non-significant" wordplay, freedom from the limits of credibility, mental exercise induced by the rapid tempo of the action, unrestricted laughter—the satisfactions of various kinds of extravagance. Indeed, farce may be considered the most elemental kind of theater, since the audience is encouraged to lose itself in play. This is bad Shakespeare in the sense that the young dramatist was content with an inherently limited mode; the play is not *Twelfth Night.* Its value is in its theatrical complexity. And yet the boisterous action does generate thematic issues. To admit that Shakespeare willingly devoted himself to farce is to acknowledge a side of his career too often neglected or misrepresented. That the author of *King Lear* was capable of writing *The Comedy of Errors* should be a source of wonder, not embarrassment.

LOVE AND MARRIAGE

Peter G. Phialas stands somewhat apart from other critics on the subject of love and marriage in *The Comedy of Errors.* He argues that the relationships between men and women in the play are not explored in any significant way, concluding that the inclusion of the contrasting male/female relationships (Antipholus of Syracuse/Luciana and Antipholus of Ephesus/Adriana) is merely a precursor of things to come in Shakespeare's romantic comedies. Ralph Berry argues that Shakespeare avoids "taking sides" in the marital troubles of Adriana and Antipholus and that overemphasizing what has been called Adriana's "possessiveness" gives too much credence to her view of love.

Marilyn French calls the "marriage relation" the "central concern" of the play. She argues that there are too many deviations from and expansions of Plautus's play to conclude otherwise. **Dorothy Kehler** agrees that Shakespeare does explore love and marriage, but that he does not provide an answer to the question, "Can love and marriage coexist?" She especially notes the powerlessness of Adriana, who is stuck in her "role" of wife at home. Laurie Maguire and Charles Brooks explore how the roles of men and women change when they transition from a courting couple to husband and wife. In courtship, the man is the worshiper; the woman is his object of love. In marriage, however, the man becomes governor and the woman the devoted wife and worshiper. It is no wonder then that Adriana and Antipholus find themselves in a marital predicament.

Peter G. Phialas

SOURCE: "*The Comedy of Errors,*" in *Shakespeare's Romantic Comedies: The Development of Their Form and Meaning,* University of North Carolina Press, 1966, pp. 10-17.

[*In this excerpt, Phialas argues that Shakespeare's use of the concept of romantic love in* The Comedy of Errors *sets the stage for its function as the "chief structural principle" of his later romantic comedies. Although, Phialas argues, love and marriage are not treated in any great depth and there is not much that is especially memorable about the relationships between men and women in the play, the fact that Shakespeare*

addresses such issues is significant in and of itself, far more so than the theme of mistaken identity.]

. . . . In *The Comedy of Errors,* it is clear, [Shakespeare] . . . essayed to express, however briefly and obliquely— by placing side by side conflicting points of view— an idea concerning love and wedded happiness. The wooing of Luciana by Antipholus of Syracuse, and her own views about marriage, are juxtaposed with the contrasting attitudes of Adriana and Antipholus of Ephesus. And thus the protestations of love addressed to Luciana by Antipholus of Syracuse serve as a counterpoint to the mutual recriminations and to the strain and unhappiness of the married pair. Although the idea which the dramatist is trying to express never achieves explicitness, and although the relationship of Luciana and her Antipholus remains unresolved, what is of great significance is that here in a farce, in what may well have been his earliest comedy, Shakespeare introduces the chief structural principle of his romantic comedies: the juxtaposition of attitudes toward love and toward the ideal relationship of man and woman.

The contrast of attitudes is introduced early in the play, in II, i, where Adriana and her sister engage in semi-formal disputation on the relations of husband and wife. Adriana, impatient and jealous, objects to her sister's "fool-begg'd patience," rejects the notion that the man should be master in the home, and wishes to curtail her husband's liberty. She blames him for everything, including her faded beauty, which she erroneously believes has driven him away:

> Hath homely age the alluring beauty took
> From my poor cheek? Then he hath wasted
>   it. . . .
> What ruins are in me that can be found
> By him not ruin'd? Then is he the ground
> Of my defeatures.
>
>   (II, i, 89-98)

Later on, believing that her husband had wooed her sister, she calls him

>   deformed, crooked, old and sere,
> Ill-fac'd, worse bodied, shapeless everywhere:
> Vicious, ungentle, foolish, blunt, unkind,
> Stigmatical in making, worse in mind.
>
>   (IV, ii, 19-22)

Here, then, is one of the causes of what Luciana calls Adriana's "troubles of the marriage bed." Adriana misconceives the proper basis of her union with her husband. In a startlingly romantic passage she recalls with pain his courtship of her which has now receded into the distant past:

> The time was once when thou unurg'd
>   wouldst vow
> That never words were music to thine ear,
> That never object pleasing in thine eye,

Beth Peterson as Luciana and Jason Engstrom as Antipholus of Syracuse in GreenStage's 1999 production of The Comedy of Errors.

That never touch well welcome to thy hand,
That never meat sweet-savour'd in thy taste,
Unless I spake, or look'd, or touch'd, or
    carv'd to thee.

(II, ii, 115-20)

The attraction she is here said to have held for her husband appears gone, and this loss is precisely what she is lamenting. It should be noted, incidentally, that his courtship had been couched in the exaggerated phrasing of the romantic lover, the hyperbolic idealizing of the sonneteer! And now, she asks,

How comes it now, my husband, O, how
    comes it,
That thou art then estranged from thyself?
Thyself I call it, being strange to me,
That, undividable, incorporate,
Am better than thy dear self's better part.

(II, ii, 121-25)

The conception of "undividable, incorporate" union of lovers seems beyond Adriana's capabilities, and in such passages we may perhaps detect a great deal more of the young dramatist himself than of his character. Nevertheless, what is significant is that Adriana, wooed in the romantic vein by her husband, and perhaps even possessed of the notion of an ideal union with him, misconceives the basis of such a union.

Adriana thinks of love in terms of possession, ownership, mastery. And this is not strange, seeing that the concrete basis of her marriage had been financial, in terms of gold in the form of dowry. And even as she may still control and even repossess that dowry, that is, take back what she has given, she insists also on possession of her husband's liberty, a possession she calls her "right." Adriana's concept of love is the right to possess, to receive and own and be master of, whereas both her sister and Antipholus of Syracuse oppose to that concept their view of love as giving. It might be added here that the financial or commercial attitude towards human relationships is reinforced by the analogous misconception which underlies the Duke's judgment on Egeon:

> Therefore, merchant, I'll limit thee this day
> To seek thy [life] by beneficial help.
> Try all the friends thou hast in Ephesus;
> Beg thou, or borrow, to make up the sum,
> And live; if no, then thou art doom'd to die.
>
> (I, i, 151-55)

The folly of possessiveness as contrasted with love's giving forms a very small part of the action. But its dramatization here anticipates the much more extensive and meaningful treatment of it in *The Taming of the Shrew* and especially *The Merchant of Venice*. In the latter play the contrast between the commercial and human relationships, between gold and love, is at the very center of the play's thought. One passage from it may illustrate the relationship between that later play and *The Comedy of Errors*, and thus demonstrate the unity and continuity of Shakespearean comedy. Before turning to that passage, let us note that in what may have been his earliest comedy, at least in the one treating of love most briefly, Shakespeare asks, however indirectly, the question: What is Love? And we should note also that that question, which is to be Shakespeare's continuing concern in the comedies, is most directly asked in *The Merchant of Venice*. "Tell me where is fancy bred," sings Nerissa while Bassanio, by some considered an ideal lover, contemplates the caskets. Within the song the reply is indirect, offering tentatively what love is not, but a more pertinent answer is given by Portia and Bassanio a moment after he has made his choice. "Fair lady," says he, kissing her, "I come by note, to give and to receive." To which she returns the notes of the ideal:

> You see me, Lord Bassanio, where I stand,
> Such as I am. Though for myself alone
> I would not be ambitious in my wish
> To wish myself much better; yet, for you
> I would be trebled twenty times myself,
> A thousand times more fair, ten thousand
>   times
> More rich. . . .

And she adds that she is happy that

> She is not bred so dull but she can learn;
> Happiest of all is that her gentle spirit
> Commits itself to yours to be directed,
> As from her lord, her governor, her king.
>
> (III, ii, 150-67)

This surrender of the self to her husband, to her "lord, her governor, her king," is precisely what Adriana rejects in her colloquy with her sister, to which allusion was made above. Though she is aware of the uniting of lovers' identities, she invokes the principle in order to justify her rights of possessing her husband. In the concluding episode she refuses to let anyone minister to him. In this she comes into conflict with Emilia, and a tug-of-war follows the refusal of each to yield to the other the man who has sought sanctuary in the abbey, who happens to be Antipholus of Syracuse, not Adriana's husband. That her concept of love as possession leading to jealousy is unacceptable and indeed dangerous is enforced upon Adriana by the abbess:

> The venom clamours of a jealous woman
> Poisons more deadly than a mad dog's tooth. . . .
> The consequence is, then, thy jealous fits
> Hath scar'd thy husband from the use of
>   wits.
>
> (V, i, 69-86)

There is no space in *The Comedy of Errors*, and perhaps neither inclination nor skill on Shakespeare's part, to pursue in detail the ideal basis for lovers' union and wedded happiness. This he was to do in the romantic comedies which followed. Nevertheless, he is able here to isolate, obliquely and in the briefest compass, one of the central conceptions of those later plays: that love does not possess, that it gives without needing to receive, for it gives to another self. "Call thyself sister, sweet, for I am thee," says Antipholus of Syracuse to Luciana.

Adriana's other misconception of the ideal union of lovers is the belief that such union is based on external beauty: that her husband has been driven away by her loss of physical attractiveness. That ideal love is not based on external beauty alone is much more directly and forcefully presented in the later comedies. And it is of especial interest to note that a much quoted passage in *The Merchant of Venice* which rejects the notion of love as possession— which opposes possession and love— likewise rejects love's concern with external beauty. "All that glisters is not gold," the Prince of Morocco is told after choosing the golden casket. But the idea is given direct and unmistakable expression in Nerissa's song as well as in Bassanio's speech which follows it.

> Tell me where is fancy bred,
> Or in the heart or in the head?
> How begot, how nourished?
>   Reply, reply.
>
> It is engend'red in the eyes,
> With gazing fed; and fancy dies
> In the cradle where it lies.
>
> (III, ii, 63-69)

And on his part Bassanio affirms that "The world is still deceiv'd with ornament," and that external beauty is but

> The seeming truth which cunning times put
>   on
> T'entrap the wisest.
>
> (III, ii, 100-1)

In *The Comedy of Errors* the idea is viewed from the other side: Adriana fears that she has lost her husband's love because her beauty is gone, and the bitterness of that loss turns into jealousy and vents itself in violent nagging. And that nagging, born of disappointment with the motion and change of things, sends our minds over a half dozen comedies to the tête-à-tête of Orlando and the disguised Rosalind in *As You Like It.* To his bookish protestations that he will love her "for ever and a day" she replies: "Say 'a day,' without the 'ever.' No, no, Orlando. Men are April when they woo, December when they wed; maids are May when they are maids, but the sky changes when they are wives. I will be more jealous of thee than a Barbary cock-pigeon over his hen, more clamorous than a parrot against rain, more newfangled than an ape, more giddy in my desires than a monkey." (IV, i, 146-53) The managing of the complex ironies here was quite beyond Shakespeare's abilities when he wrote *The Comedy of Errors.* Yet there is a palpable contact between the two plays and another instance of the unity of Shakespearean comedy. What puzzles Adriana, what in her own conduct remains beyond her awareness, is for Rosalind the most obvious fact in the nature of things. Both husbands and wives change, but their happiness need not be touched by such changes since that happiness should be based on something that remains constant: not outward beauty, not physical attraction, but inner beauty and worth.

The multiple attitudes toward love which are most skillfully woven into the fabric of *As You Like It* have no place in *The Comedy of Errors.* Here what we should note is the presence of the master-principle which controls the structure of Shakespeare's romantic comedies, namely the juxtaposition of attitudes toward love represented by different characters. This is a most significant aspect of *The Comedy of Errors,* a play dealing in the main with matters quite alien to romantic love. And it is certainly surprising to find that Shakespeare, in a severely limited space, could put in such a play so much of what was to be the chief matter of his romantic comedies. The treatment of love and the related motifs which we have noted above is elementary, lacking utterly the incisiveness as well as the ironic dramatization which we find in the later plays. But the fact remains that *The Comedy of Errors,* though in the main concerned with the farcical mistakings of identity, touches briefly a theme of far greater significance, the ideal relationship of man and woman. And it is here, rather than in the confusions of identity, that we find the element of reflectiveness and concern with something deeper than accident and the surface show of things to which we alluded at the beginning of this chapter. It is true that upon arriving at Ephesus, Antipholus of Syracuse is driven by his strange reception there to question his own identity:

So I, to find a mother and a brother,
In quest of them, unhappy, lose myself.
                                        (I, ii, 39-40)

But it is likewise true that he discovers not only his identity but a new and larger self in his love of Luciana. In her, he tells her, he has found

mine own self's better part,
Mine eye's clear eye, my dear heart's dearer heart,
My food, my fortune, and my sweet hope's
    aim,
My sole earth's heaven, and my heaven's claim.
                                        (III, ii, 61-64)

In these matters, then, *The Comedy of Errors* prefigures some of the significant features of Shakespeare's romantic comedies. It shows his general predilection for combining multiple actions into mutually qualifying relationships. More particularly, it initiates his custom of enclosing a comic action within a serious or near-tragic framing story or subplot. And most important of all it introduces into a farcical story of classical origin the theme of romantic love and attempts, in elementary fashion, to comment upon that theme by representing contrasted attitudes to it. In so doing, the play employs for the first time in Shakespeare's career the central thematic and structural characteristics of his romantic comedies.

Dorothea Kehler

SOURCE: "*The Comedy of Errors* as Problem Comedy," in *Rocky Mountain Review of Language & Literature,* Vol. 41, No. 4, 1987, pp. 230-36.

[*In this excerpt, Kehler notes that Adriana and her husband, Antipholus of Ephesus, "could pass for a well-to-do modern couple headed for divorce." She points out that part of the problem in their marriage is the "inevitable imbalance of love" between them, which is worsened by Adriana's powerlessness to change the situation.*]

.... The specific problem Shakespeare explores through the relationship of Adriana and E. Antipholus is both timeless and peculiarly modern: can love survive marriage? C. L. Barber notes [in "Shakespearean Comedy in *The Comedy of Errors*"] that, unlike Plautus, Shakespeare "frequently makes the errors reveal fundamental human nature, especially human nature under the stress and tug of marriage." Considering Shakespeare's depiction of a marriage "subjected to the very unromantic strains of temperament grinding on temperament in the setting of daily life," Barber concludes of Adriana and E. Antipholus, "No doubt their peace is temporary." Certainly, despite their classical origin, Adriana and E. Antipholus could pass for a well-to-do modern couple headed for divorce. He, successful in business but bored at home, is ripe for more entertaining companionship; she, too much at home and insecure about his attachment to her, becomes impatient and demanding. Although a divorce in law may not be a customary Ephesian alternative, a divorce of hearts within a stifling marriage is universal. In *Errors,* Adriana and E. Antipholus enact that incipient emotional divorce as a psychodrama whose *anagnorisis,* if not to them, may yet be intelligible to us.

More than any other character in *Errors,* Adriana subverts farce. Because we know her more intimately than we do her husband, she lays first claim to our interest. Although most often described as a jealous and possessive shrew, of late she is not without defenders. Marilyn French, in an illuminating reading [in *Shakespeare's Division of Experience*], sees Adriana's problem as powerlessness created by economic, political, and social structures. But if the key to Adriana's personality and predicament is powerlessness, it is powerlessness of another sort as well. The play focuses on the *emotional* structure of a marriage, depicting the almost inevitable imbalance of love between spouses— an imbalance often aggravated to the woman's disadvantage by societal conditioning and restrictions— and the plight of a woman dependent on her husband for her sole identity as beloved wife. Byron knew the world's Adrianas: "Man's love is of man's life a thing apart, / 'Tis woman's whole existence" (*Don Juan* Canto I, st. 194). [In *Shakespeare's Comic Rites,*] Edward Berry clarifies the generic issue raised by Adriana's emotional isolation and loss of identity, expressed in her neo-Platonic, Pauline speech (II.ii.119-29) on the melding of husband and wife into one soul:

> In their explorations of the self, the comedies are in some ways not unlike the tragedies, for in both genres Shakespeare consistently maneuvers his central characters into positions of psychological isolation, leaving them exposed and vulnerable both within and without. While this kind of isolation is conventional in tragedy, in comedy it is unique to Shakespeare.

While a seminal model for the heroines of Shakespeare's romantic comedies, Adriana is also a precursor of Juliet and Desdemona. For all that Adriana is a character in a play long received as farce, her nature and situation are no less tragic than comic, and this duality creates yet another generic complication of *Errors.*

Powerless over her husband's heart, Adriana grows restive and irritable, questioning the restrictions on women's freedom: "Why should their [men's] liberty than ours be more?" (II.i.10). When Luciana replies that the husband is the bridle of the wife's will, Adriana asserts, "There's none but asses will be bridled so" (II.i.14). Male supremacy turns marriage into "servitude" (II.i.26). Although for the audience these lines

imply a feminist manifesto, for Adriana they seem to hold no more lasting significance than does her threat to break Dromio's pate across. Tormented and confused, Adriana lashes out indiscriminately at all male authority, at E. Antipholus, and at an ineffectual slave; it is not sexual equality she seeks, however much she might profit from it, but only the husband she had in her spring of love:

> The time was once when thou unurg'd
>   wouldst vow
> That never words were music to thine ear,
> That never object pleasing in thine eye,
> That never touch well welcome to thy hand,
> That never meat sweet-savour'd in thy taste,
> Unless I spake, or look'd, or touch'd or
>   carv'd to thee.
>
>   (II.ii.113-18)

What Adriana cannot accept is that the honeymoon is over, that she is no longer all in all to her Antipholus. Institutionalizing desire within marriage frustrates this husband and this wife. While E. Antipholus wards off claustrophobia by lingering on the mart, despite his complaint that "My wife is shrewish when I keep not hours" (II.i.2), Adriana becomes obsessed with the conviction of her husband's infidelity, assured that to be excluded from two hours of his life is to be excluded from his heart forever. Unable to smile at grief, she becomes, in Luciana's words, one of the "many fond fools [who] serve mad jealousy" (II.i.116). In her company are Othello, Posthumus, and Leontes, who respond to suspected cuckoldry with privileged male fury. The jealous bourgeois wife merely nags, but her situation, like that of her male counterparts, can be seen as the stuff of tragicomedy or tragedy rather than farce. Implicit in *Errors* is a transgression against the codified genre.

As Adriana's eloquent "nags" reveal her fierce hunger for a caring husband, Luciana's stilted set speech on male rule dwindles in importance, becoming, if not a non-sequitur, a red herring for which critics ill-advisedly have fished:

> There's nothing situate under heaven's eye
> But hath his bound, in earth, in sea, in sky.
> The beasts, the fishes, and the winged fowls
> Are their males' subjects, and at their controls;
> Man, more divine, the master of all these,
> Lord of the wide world and wild wat'ry seas,
> Indued with intellectual sense and souls,
> Of more pre-eminence than fish and fowls,
> Are masters to their females, and their lords:
> Then let your will attend on their accords.
>
>   (II.i.16-25)

Just as Adriana's profound love for E. Antipholus undermines this speech's relevance, so the delineation of the male characters undermines its validity. "Man, more divine" is sadly represented in *Errors*. Most worthy are the loving but powerless Egeon, and Duke Solinus, who requires a miracle to enable him to tolerate foreign merchants as easily as he does native courtesans. The divinities with whom Adriana has more to do are even less awesome: the mountebank Pinch; the deluded, broken-pated Dromios; and their equally deluded, violent masters. Not surprisingly, Shakespeare bodies forth the principle of male supremacy through characters whose preeminence is dubious; Susan Snyder points out [in *The Comic Matrix of Shakespeare's Tragedies*] that the Elizabethan audience expected comedy to overturn accepted truths and customs, and [In *Shakespeare and the Nature of Women*] Juliet Dusinberre points to those Elizabethan women who rejected the status quo, even to the extent of wearing men's clothes and weapons. Dusinberre notes that both liberated women and Humanist-influenced Puritans sympathetic to women comprised a significant part of Shakespeare's audience. For the more politically, intellectually, and theologically venturesome, Adriana must have evoked more compassion than amusement.

Nevertheless, the traditional interpretation of act 2, scene 1 reminds us that Adriana's emotional problems are compounded by her social situation: "revolt against a wife's place in the cosmic hierarchy," according to Harold Brooks [in "Theme and Structure in *The Comedy of Errors*"], "is the original source of discord in Adriana's marriage." In the cosmos as envisaged by men, woman is subordinate; hence, in the social system, she readily becomes a possession. At this Adriana has not balked. By marrying E. Antipholus, Adriana has accepted the authority of both the Duke and her husband, "who I made lord of me and all I had / At your important letters" (V.i.137-38). She revolts not against her place but against lack of love; her longing to be a vine to her husband's elm (II.ii.174-76) reveals her deepest desire: to subjugate herself in marriage. It is her misfortune that, in a male-dominated society, the possession who becomes possessive is regarded as a shrew.

Adriana's error is not refusal to accept male supremacy but the nagging tongue that provides her only relief. Even when she thinks E. Antipholus is courting her sister, she admits, "My heart prays for him, though my tongue do curse" (V.ii.28). She is trapped in a painful cycle. Feeling rejected, she desires her husband all the more desperately, but her incessant recriminations, later confessed to the abbess (V.i.62-67), elicit only further rejection from E. Antipholus. He labels her shrewish and "breaks the pale" (II.i.100), having found "a wench of excellent discourse, / Pretty and witty; wild and yet, too, gentle" (III.i.109-10). "Mad jealousy" prevents Adriana from realizing how self-defeating and absurd is the attempt to moralize another into love. Although a character's blindness is fundamental to farce, Adriana's pain is so keenly felt and lyrically expressed that sympathy undercuts laughter, and the problematic aspects of marriage—and genre—assert themselves. Adriana's inability to comprehend the effect she produces upon E. Antipholus is the psychological reality behind the convention of indistinguishable twins in *Errors*. She is unable to distinguish her husband from his brother because she no longer knows her husband, having become totally engrossed in her own needs. Errors of physical identity aside, she speaks an emotional truth in her reply to Luciana:

> *Luc.* Then swore he that he was a stranger here.
> *Adr.* And true he swore, though yet forsworn he were.
>
> (IV.ii.9-10)

Adriana mistakes the newcomer for her husband because S. Antipholus is the honeymoon-lover of her heart's desire, like her husband in appearance, unlike him in spirit: sea-fresh, unspoiled by a stale marriage, trailing no minions in his wake. Most pitiful—and certainly at odds with *Errors'* farcical temper—is our realization, based on Adriana's intelligence, spirit, and capacity for love, that this out-of-control "shrew" must herself once have been "a wench of excellent discourse, / Pretty and witty; wild and yet, too, gentle"—another twin!

Despite her "venom clamours" (V.i.69), Adriana seems singularly restrained and chaste compared to her husband, a chief vehicle of farce in *Errors*. On stage, E. Antipholus strikes the Dromios (IV.iv.17,42) and Doctor Pinch (IV.iv.51), and attempts to pluck out Adriana's eyes (IV.iv.102). A messenger reports that E. Antipholus beats the maids, singes off Pinch's beard, throws pails of puddled mire on Pinch, encourages E. Dromio to nick Pinch with scissors (V.i.169-77), and vows to scorch and and disfigure Adriana's face (V.i.183). E. Antipholus compounds violence with insensitivity to his wife's feelings; by withholding love and attention he induces a jealousy that is not entirely paranoid. At his first entrance, he asks Angelo to assist him in deceiving Adriana as to his whereabouts (III.i.3-4); more important, his acquaintance with a courtesan would distress a wife as patient as Griselda. Although Luciana tries to allay her sister's fears, secretly she suspects that E. Antipholus wed Adriana for her wealth and that he likes "elsewhere" (III.ii.5-7). Although Shakespeare apparently departs from his sources, making E. Antipholus guilty of thoughtless or spiteful congeniality rather than adultery, French penetrates the underlying fable: "on the mythic level, the play deals with serious disruption: a man neglects his wife for his prostitute." Matthew would have agreed: "whosoever looketh on a woman to lust after her hath committed adultery with her already in his heart" (5.28). In fact, Shakespeare does not rule out the possibility of E. Antipholus's having committed adultery. Edward Berry suggests that "The ring [which E. Antipholus receives from the courtesan] is an appropriate symbol of the sexual and economic ambiguities in Antipholus's extra-marital relationship." In *Errors* the distinction between having the name without the game or the name with the game is not so much a matter of substantive moral difference as of genre: if E. Antipholus has fallen only in spirit but not in flesh, the sin is revocable, a comic rather than tragic error. A happy ending, or some semblance of one, remains a contingency.

Luciana's admonition and the intrigue plot collaborate to reveal a means of perhaps achieving that happy ending, if husband and wife allow themselves to be instructed. Luciana's speech on male supremacy misfires, but its introduction does not: "Why, headstrong liberty is lash'd with woe" (II.i.15). Directed at Adriana, this admonition applies with equal if not greater force to E. Antipholus. Adriana, awash in emotion, has only worsened her situation by abusing the liberty of her tongue as a quick-tempered mistress, contentious sister, and discontented wife. Her husband, abusing the liberty of his eye, has ravaged the marital peace; abusing the liberty of his hand, he is taken for mad. The woe such headstrong liberty has brought them could be alleviated through the self-government endlessly enjoined by Renaissance moralists, through the subjugation of our infected will to our erected wit. To do other is mutual madness. During her exchange with the courtesan, Adriana finds a name for her husband's fault:

> *Cour.* How say you now? Is not your
> husband mad?
> *Adr.* His incivility confirms no less.
>
> (IV.iv.43-44)

Will she realize that she too is guilty of incivility, a concomitant of headstrong liberty, of the will's mastery? Erasmus can tell us whose fault is greater: "Of an evyll husbande (I wyll well) a good wyfe may be mard, but of a good the evyll is wont to be refourmed and mended. We blame wyves falsly. No man (if ye gyve any credence to me) had ever a shrewe to his wyfe but thrughe hus owne defaute" (sig. Dii^v). Nevertheless, both the unthinking husband and the neglected, powerless wife suffer, having forfeited contentment by insisting on their own satisfactions.

The plot, undervalued for lacking an intriguer "to make the confusion delightfully purposeful," actually achieves the thematic purpose of forcing E. Antipholus to lose his identity and take on his wife's: serving mad jealousy, he feels what she feels. Thinking himself sexually betrayed—is he projecting his own guilty conscience onto her?—he discovers the pain of being "abused and dishonour'd / Even in the strength and height of injury" (V.i.199-200). In another comedy involving a shipwreck, tradewar, twins, jealousy, and madness, Malvolio, like E. Antipholus, is bound and imprisoned in darkness. The practical joke suits, for in the world

of cakes and ale, Malvolio's confusion of ambition with love and his denial of harmless pleasure mark him as insane. Shakespeare first employs this jocular punishment in *Errors,* with himself, the playwright, rather than his characters, as intriguer. For his incivility E. Antipholus suffers the treatment of a madman. (Adriana is also punished for incivility: betrayed by the abbess to her own reproof and public embarrassment). The plot holds a mirror up to husband and wife, showing them how their headstrong liberty has guided time's deformed hand in writing strange defeatures on their marriage. Of course this couple may prove no more capable of profiting from their lessons than did Malvolio. The play remains curiously open-ended.

Directors who impose a happy ending have a good case. Happiness being preferable to unhappiness, Adriana and E. Antipholus are likely to opt for it; theirs, after all, is a comic world. The audience also opts for the happy ending in comedy. Even in James Cellan Jones's BBC production, which stressed the non-farcical aspects of *Errors,* the beginning of a reconciliation is suggested as E. Antipholus places the chain about Adriana's neck. After all, Adriana and her husband have been party to a miracle, the reunion of a family sundered for a generation; to blast such unlooked for joy with self-indulgent discord touches upon sacrilege. Thanks to the miracle of reunion, their nuclear family is now extended: Adriana's isolation turns to a gossips' feast, and E. Antipholus may find wholesome recreation within his enlarged family. Ironic as it is that the only incontrovertibly happy couple has been separated for thirty-three years, even so the advice and example of loving parents may foster civility in their children.

Perhaps most important as a persuader to civility is the future of S. Antipholus and Luciana. Luciana, who makes no reply to S. Antipholus's proposal (V.i.374-76), had indicated earlier, when she mistook him for her brother-in-law, only that his words "*might* move" (IV.ii.14, italics added). The psychological reality behind the convention of indistinguishable twins for Luciana—the reason she cannot tell her would-be husband from E. Antipholus—is that, expecting no more of men than that they be "secret false" (III.ii.15), she has little motivation to sift their appearance from their reality. Her commitment phobia, as it were, may be explained by a last act in which errors of identity are clarified but errors in love are not. Luciana's sixth-act response depends on the reflection of her own future that she sees in her sister's and brother-in-law's problematic marriage. Will brother and sister, for the sake of brother and sister, learn to curb their infected wills? After the players have left the stage, will problem comedy resolve to romantic comedy?

Whether Shakespeare's personal experience of marriage accounts for this novel admixture of genres in his first comedy is an intriguing but unanswerable question. His portraits of Kate, Emilia, and Paulina suggest, however, that the stock character of the shrew proved too narrow for Shakespeare's breadth of understanding. Adriana's uncomic potential is released as Shakespeare, unlike earlier writers of shrew plays, considers the causes of shrewishness and the ordeal of a shrew. Such considerations, dictating a more realistic view of personality and marriage, take us beyond the classical pale into something rich and strange. (Later, Shakespeare's sensitivity to the stock Jew will change the generic coloration of *The Merchant of Venice.*) But whatever causes begot this generic experiment, *Errors* succeeds. The demons that frighten us the most evoke the most cathartic laughter. The difficulty of sustaining a loving relationship as nuances of feeling inexorably change is just such a demon. The farce of mistaken identities and hallucinatory situations creates the *verfremdungseffekt* that allows us to laugh when the pain of human isolation brings us closer to tears. Through generic disjunction, Shakespeare demonstrates how complex are the responses an audience can experience when Plautine intrigue bows to *genera mista,* creating, most notably, a timeless vision of dissonance in the comedy of errors we call marriage.

GENDER ISSUES

Charles Brooks and Marilyn French explore the binary nature of women in the play. Brooks argues that Shakespeare intended to show, through the characters of Adriana and Luciana, that women possess both male and female traits. Adriana's vocal dissatisfaction with her marriage represents "male dominance" and Luciana's insistence on the proper role of a wife constitutes "female submission." French also sees Adriana and Luciana as complementing one another— Adriana's resistance to submission is "outlaw" and Luciana's acceptance of it is "inlaw."

Ann C. Christensen argues that the play shows the competition between the commercial/public and domestic/private spheres. Antipholus of Ephesus is free to move about, conduct his business affairs, and meet with friends. Adriana, as his wife, is confined to the home, bored, and understandably angry when her husband will not leave his "world" for hers.

Ann Thompson notes, as many critics do, that because Shakespeare sets the play in Ephesus (a city associated with witchcraft and sorcery), it is not particularly surprising that Antipholus of Syracuse might think that Luciana is a witch, given all the strange things happening to him. What is unusual, Thompson notes, is that the "mother" is restored in the end. This is uncharacteristic of Shakespeare's early and middle comedies. Robert Ornstein takes note of the growing solidarity of the women in the play (for example, Adriana, Luciana,

and the Courtezan band together to present their case to the Duke at the end of the play) and how crucial they are to the play's outcome.

Ann C. Christensen

SOURCE: "'Because their business still lies out a' door': Resisting the Separation of Spheres in Shakespeare's *The Comedy of Errors,*" in *Literature and History, 3rd series,* Vol. 5, No. 1, Spring, 1996, pp. 19-37.
[*In the following excerpt, Christensen explores the intersection of the "home" and the "marketplace"— the private and public spheres— particularly through the characterization of Adriana and Antipholus of Ephesus. She also shows how the two realms are united at the conclusion of the play, when all misunderstandings have been resolved.*]

. . . . *The Comedy of Errors* illustrates the gendered competition regarding the functions of the domestic and the commercial spheres, which the play depicts as distinctly gendered and spatially separate, yet mutually constitutive. The husband-merchant of Ephesus appears divided between his home-life and his work, with his business associates and 'the mart' thematically and structurally opposing his wife and their home. C. L. Barber and Richard Wheeler suggest that *Errors* afforded Shakespeare a way to manage his own experience of division— between his roles as country husband, father, and son, on the one hand, and as a successful urban professional, on the other:

> the young dramatist has split himself into a stay-at-home twin, married and carrying on in a commercial world . . . and into a wandering, searching twin for whom the world of Ephesus, including the situation of marriage, is strange.

Setting to one side Wheeler and Barber's biographical approach, one infers that the sense of conflicting duties was probably common for the newly urbanized and increasingly mobile class of professional men in early modern London. Douglas Bruster, for example, argues that the propertied urban merchants gained in literary representation a 'special reputation for anxiety'. In its double plots, and in its distinct discourses of home and trade, this early comedy dramatizes the competing demands within and between the commercial and domestic spheres— a conflict which playwrights continued to explore on the Jacobean stage.

The dining table (metaphorically speaking), where the meaning of meals and mealtime is hotly debated, constitutes one crucial arena in which this competition plays itself out. Indeed the restoration of identity and the resolution of the plot devolves from Adriana's question, 'Which of you did dine with me today'? (V.i.370). For Adriana, the neglected and disgruntled wife, a family that eats together stays together or, more pertinently, sleeps together. She therefore identifies meals at home with domestic harmony, even associating the physical structure of their dwelling with her body: private, enclosed, nurturing. But, because her husband conceptualizes time and space in commercial terms, Adriana must remind him to spend time and eat meals with her at home. On more than one occasion, she sends her servant Dromio to fetch him 'from the mart, / Home' (I.i.75;IV.ii.64), eventually pursuing him herself, accosting his brother by mistake (II.ii.110 ff), and finally defying both state and church in her quest to keep him at home in her care. Adriana so believes in the prophylactic nature of her household that she blames the day's madness on her husband's absence from home where, had he 'remain'd until this time, / [he would be] Free from these slanders and this open shame' (IV.iv.66-67).

But the modern bourgeois notion of home as safe haven was neither established in Elizabethan society nor uncontested on the Shakespearean stage. The play surges forward by Antipholus of Ephesus's (hereafter, following speech tags, Antipholus E.) refusal to identify himself with home, and by the comic clashes between household and mart, inside and outside, local and stranger. Dorothea Kehler attributes the husband's centrifugal movement to his experiences of claustrophobia and boredom at home. However, a more primary struggle for domestic power and authority— a struggle to define the meanings of home, food, and family— informs those feelings. Adriana's husband wants to use their domicile to entertain business associates; so when he is unintentionally denied entry, he spurns the home and meal altogether and uses a public tavern for both business and pleasure. For spite, Antipholus E. 'eats out' with a courtesan and 'keep[s] not his hours' (III.i.2). Delinquency from meals conveys his neglect of spousal duties. This conflict has as cultural ancillary the gradual shift in early modern England from manorial socio-economic organization to that of nascent capitalism. The differences between the masculine world of commerce and law and the feminine domestic environment articulate themselves over the contested cultural form of 'dining'. *The Comedy of Errors* registers a historical moment of social transition and dislocation within the not-yet distinct public and private spheres. Forcing oppositions between desire and profit, leisure and work, women and men, Shakespeare explores contemporary anxieties attending the development of the separation of the spheres. . . .

The play's central issues of dining, time, and money punctuate the first meeting between the visiting Antipholus and his servant's twin. This encounter also shows how the 'private' life of home impinges upon and is affected by the 'public' life of commerce— how the two spheres, like the brothers and the states they trade for, are inextricably linked. Dromio E. describes the impact on the family of the master's absence:

Act IV, scene ii. Adriana, Luciana, and Dromio of Syracuse. The University of Michigan Special Collections Library.

> The capon burns, the pig falls from the spit;
> The clock hath strucken twelve upon the bell—
> My mistress made it one upon my cheek;
> She is so hot, because the meat is cold,
> The meat is cold because you come not home:
> You come not home, because you have no stomach:
>
> 　　　　　　　　(I.ii.44-49)

Along with marking the confusion over lost gold and cold meat, Dromio E. delineates the ideological and spatial opposition beneath the scene: 'My charge was but to fetch you from the mart / Home to your house . . . to dinner' (74-75).

While the play sets up such opposition between husbands and wives, the worlds of trade and home, it ultimately insists upon their ever-shifting interrelations. No definite hierarchy emerges; instead the demands of business and family alternately and farcically interfere with each other. So as we might expect, the Antipholi and their male associates— merchants, the goldsmith, and city magistrates— appear in public scenes and talk in terms of economic exchange and legal sanctions, while women converse inside, their talk focusing on 'private' topics such as marriage and family, as in Act two, scene one, when Adriana and Luciana discuss 'troubles of the marriage bed' (27), and in the beginning of Act five, when the Abbess catechizes Adriana about wifely duty.

However, these discourses are not discrete: the men's business in the mart sustains the household economy, while the household, through both consumption and (re)production, fuels the mart. Similarly, the opposing settings— borrowed from Plautus: the mart or public square and 'the house of Antipholus of Ephesus', where Adriana frets as the spit turns— coexist in a mutually constituting relation. For example, Adriana delivers her most moving speech about the sanctity of marriage at this public thoroughfare (II.ii.109-145), while their home, the Phoenix, apparently ordinarily entertains merchants, its threshold the site of a 'public scene'. Nor is the family dwelling totally distinct from the shop, but sits 'above' the business (II.ii.206)— an arrangement resembling the situations of sixteenth-century urban tradesmen. The two other loci, the Porpentine, where the courtesan serves her clients, and the Abbey, where the action is resolved in Act five, provide symbolic syntheses of public and private, being both private residences and crossroads of community.

Domestic space in *Errors* open up possibilities for community. While the more centripetal, domestic values espoused by the wives seem large enough to accommodate commercial interest in the name of the family romance, the husbands' business 'errors' or wanderings cause the division of families. Both parents and married children are separated directly or indirectly because of business trips. Egeon reports that his 'prosperous voyages' 'drew me from the kind embraces of my spouse', while she, though pregnant, joins him abroad, 'daily' urging their return home (I.i.40, 43, 59). Because of Egeon's mercantile obligations, the family has been separated once; whence wife and children too had left their home initially. Moreover, on the return voyage, which Egeon 'unwillingly' undertook, as he himself admits, a shipwreck separates them again. Like his grandfather from whom Egeon inherited the family business, and like Egeon before him, Antipholus E. seems to find embarking on 'prosperous voyages' to the mart more compelling than home-cooked meals. In certain instances, then, business forges a wedge within families: the '"husband's office" [is] neglected in pursuit of his prospering business'.

Despite the seeming incompatibility of loyalties to work and home, duplicate 'errors' in fact reunite the family, resolving confusion and clearing debts. The play constitutes economic, public, and civic bonds in relation to private, affective ties; and the interdependence of the 'separate spheres' everywhere inflects the action. For example, Adriana and Antipholus E.'s marriage is apparently a state project: not only in as much as marriage is a public institution, but also because the Duke's 'important letters' (V.i.138) had arranged the match.

Out of a sense of both civic and personal debt, the Duke had recommended Antipholus:

> Long since thy husband serv'd me in my
>   wars,
> And I to thee engag'd a prince's word,
> When thou didst make him master of thy
>   bed,
> To do him all the grace and good I could.
>   (V.i.160-164)

In a similar recognition of the personal investment in and exchange value of 'service', Antipholus E. invokes his military career:

> Even for the service that I long since did thee,
> When I bestrid thee in the wars, and took
> Deep scars to save thy life; even for the blood
> That I then lost for thee, now grant me justice.
>   (V.i.190-94)

All sorts of quids pro quo entangle personal and impersonal identifications: the merchants are all friends who employ credit and exchange money for goods; the courtesan does not give her man a gift token, but rather *trades* her ring for a gold chain of equal value; Adriana expects some recompense for her 'housewifery'; the right amount of money can buy Egeon out of legal trouble. Thus, personal and 'official' business operate on similar terms.

Nonetheless, Shakespeare portrays affective bonds more favorably than economic bonds because the former allow greater flexibility and humanity than the latter. By granting some foundation to Adriana's mistrust of her husband, Shakespeare portrays her far more sympathetically than Plautus's 'Mulier', who is simply an unreasonable shrew. Furthermore, Adriana's plight contrasts the profit-minded paranoia which drives the merchants. It is not an invisible hand that guides macroeconomy, but the long arm of the law. The enmity between the state and Syracusa frames the action and provides the model for civilian interaction: in Ephesus men do not enjoy each other's trust for long; rather, they are bound by contracts, the inflexibility of which creates mutual suspicion among partners and a hasty reliance upon public officers to settle disputes. The legal code in Ephesus is firm: it requires the Duke to 'exclude all pity' in the execution of Syracusans; it ensures that the responsibility for unpaid debt devolve upon the officers in charge of debtors (IV.iv.114-15); and it makes former friends enemies when contracts seem to be dishonored. The fact that the 'chain' which binds Balthazar, Angelo, the goldsmith, and Antipholus is credit not trust, when measured against Adriana's loyalty, compromises the humanity of mercantile associations. In a telling pun, Antipholus E. queries Angelo: 'Belike you thought our love would last too long / If it were chained together' (IV.i.25-6). As a catalyst to the recognition scene, the merchant exacts his due from Angelo, warning, 'Or I'll attach you by this officer'. In turn, Angelo remarks: 'just the sum I do owe to you / Is growing to me by Antipholus' (IV.i.6,7-8). As he hires the officers to arrest (the wrong) Antipholus, the goldsmith vows, 'I would not spare my brother in this case' (IV.i.77)—a hyperbole especially suited to this play abounding in brothers. Similarly, master turns on servant when he 'greatly fear[s his] money is not safe' (I.ii.105).

In contrast to the litigious sphere of trade, the domestic sphere in Ephesus generally keeps problems inside, as if respectful of the private nature of its commitments. For example, from the local Dromio's first speech, we imagine Adriana pacing at home, in 'fast[ing] and prayer' while awaiting her husband's return. Driven outside only reluctantly by the accretion of impatience, uncertainty, and jealousy, she initially eschews the public sphere and prefers to bypass the law and the Abbess in administering punishment, justice, or a cure for her husband's putative madness. When she snares her dinner companion in Act two, scene two, Adriana locks him in tightly: 'Dromio, keep the gate. / . . . Sirrah, if any ask you for your master, / Say he dines forth, and let no creature enter. / . . . Dromio, play the porter well' (205, 208-10). Similarly, both the Abbess and Luce, the kitchen wench of Adriana's house, stand as sentinels to defend their respective households from intrusion. Even the courtesan, that 'public woman', shows discretion in stating her grievance: when she perceives herself cheated by Antipholus, she consults his wife in the matter rather than an officer (IV.iii.87-91).

Adriana clearly exemplifies the home/body. Some critics identify her as the play's spokesperson for Protestant companionate marriage. The private family meal she offers, according to Joseph Candido, 'serves as a convenient social vehicle for the larger issue of forgiveness, and her insistence on privacy metaphorically links confidential family matters with the . . . regenerative power of the confessional'. This spiritual dimension of housewifery is nonetheless underpinned by its material basis—the furnishing of nourishment and safety, which Adriana feels uniquely qualified to provide. At first, rather than invoke the impersonal and dehumanizing legal system to 'cure' her spouse, Adriana orders him 'safe convey'd/Home to my house' (IV.iv.122-23), a wish repeated in her confrontation with the creditors and the Abbess (V.i.35, 92). But later, when physically threatened by him she hires an exorcist and then concedes to law, begging the Duke to intercede in the matter of her husband's return home. Of course, as a woman, she would lack recourse in the law within 'the late Elizabethan "sex/gender system"' that Ephesus replicates. Nor does Shakespeare provide a family outlet for Adriana's redress: unlike Plautus's 'Mulier', who calls in her father to arbitrate, Adriana relies on her own resources and hired help. Her conception of the

nuclear family—a haven safe from creditors as well as from the interventions of church and state—reflects the transition toward the separate spheres ideology. That the play elsewhere undermines this idealization of the bourgeois domicile further underlines the uneasy coexistence of ideologies and social practices. The relationship between home and marketplace is continually renegotiated in the play, as it was in Elizabethan society.

At times the household Adriana supervises nearly spoils Antipholus's mercantile ventures rather than supporting them. Although she possesses intimate knowledge of her husband's book-keeping, as when she admits surprise, 'That he, unknown to me, should be in debt' (IV.ii.48), Adriana recognizes that the marketplace poses threats to marital relations. And her husband recognizes the cost of his domestic responsibilities. Notions of family-as-obstacle unfold in Act three, scene one, where a spatial and ideological stand-off transpires concerning the function and government of the household. Antipholus E. and his cronies appear outside his home awaiting hospitable entertainment, while Adriana and her guest (the twin she mistakes for her husband) 'dine above' and forbid intrusion. A kind of Lysistradian battle of the sexes with the women and their spoils inside and the men outside trying to get in, the scene forms the climax of the play. The 'heroine', that operative symbol of domestic authority, is Luce, the enormous kitchen wench betrothed to Dromio E. and feared by his visiting twin ('She is too big, I hope, for me to compass' [IV.i.111]). In a long exchange of rhyming threats and retorts, formally extending yet undercutting the content of the men's Ephesian dialogue on 'welcome' and 'cheer' preceding it, Luce jeopardizes the foundation of her master's identity. She threatens to have him thrown into the stocks (III.i.59-60), and forces the men to 'part with neither [the cheer nor welcome]' that the householder had promised (67). Such domestic conduct is decidedly bad for business.

That this disappointed meal gets tangled up in the confusion about mercantile debts shows the deep and materially efficacious connection between men's home-lives and their public estimation in the marketplace. Discussing Adriana's behavior in terms of Antipholus's 'reputation', Balthazar reveals the dependence of commercial credit on domestic harmony, warning that '[a] vulgar comment . . . / [a]gainst [Antipholus's] yet ungalled estimation' would compromise his standing in the community (III.i.100, 102). For his part, Antipholus E. perceives the women's insubordination as a consolidated assault on his power and authority as master of the house, since he promises to punish 'my wife and her confederates' for the incident (IV.i.17). Furthermore, the men perceive female unruliness as an affront to domestic order; and they sexually encode this unruliness and associate women with feeding in the play. The husband becomes increasingly convinced that Adriana had feasted and made love to the only man she's seen with— Pinch, the schoolmaster (IV.iv.57-61). Meanwhile Luce's association with the kitchen is inseparable from her massive and threatening body, and the courtesan invites Antipholus S. to 'mend [his] dinner' at her place (IV.iii.54). His frantic, moralistic refusal of her offer: 'Avoid, then, fiend! What tell'st thou me of supping'? (IV.iii.60) makes explicit the sexual nature of dining at a woman's table, especially when compared with his earlier quest for male dinner companions (I.ii.23). Thus, it seems that men fear women's domestic control and their sexuality, both of which are related to food-provision. As we shall see, however, these fears are unfounded: Adriana wants nothing more (or less) than to administer to her husband's needs, fully accepting her proper sphere of the home, while insisting simultaneously on its sanctity and its correspondence with his business life.

The Roman source play offers some insight into this localized fear of 'feeding and dependency'. *The Menaechmi* opens with a statement about the binding effects of hospitality. As the longest speech in the play, its subject becomes a major theme. Peniculus, a Parasite on the table of Erotium (subsidized by Menaechmus, her married lover), conjectures that the way to a man's loyalty is through his stomach. He envisions a prison system based on the provision of meals:

> If then ye would keep a man without all suspicion of running away from ye, the surest way is to tie him with meate, drinke, and ease: Let him ever be idle, eate his belly full, and carouse while his skin will hold, and he shall never, I warrent ye, stir a foote. These strings to tie one by the teeth, passe all the bands of iron, steele, or what metal so ever . . .

Having cut this character from his version, Shakespeare disperses his sentiment among the male characters who flee rather than enter the bondage of feeding at women's tables. So Antipholus E. refuses to come home to dinner, while the Syracusan men renounce the women who cook and invite them to meals, calling them variously 'beastly creature', witch, devil (III.ii.88, 154; IV.iii.58).

Women as well as men recognize the contractual nature of meals— the 'strings to tie one' to the domestic sphere; and this recognition becomes the vehicle for reconciliation in the play. So Luce and the courtesan as well as Adriana and Emilia express desire, power, and protection through dining and food imagery. Adriana's lament for her neglect ranges fully through connotations of feeding, and suggests how crucially food-service defined the domestic on the Shakespearean stage and in early modern society. In language which collapses her self with her home, she complains:

> His company must do his minions grace
> Whilst I at home starve for a merry look . . .

> But, too unruly deer, he breaks the pale
> And feeds from home. Poor I am but his stale.

> (II.i.87-88, 100-1)

Adriana uses the metaphor of feeding as loving. Punning on 'grace' as the prayer before meals and the 'gracious' presence Antipholus denies her, Adriana emphasizes both the ritualized nature of meals and the enclosedness of their marriage vows which he 'breaks' by dining out. She further acknowledges the reciprocal nature of 'feeding' (the verb, like 'nurse' and 'suck', itself admits both transitive and intransitive definitions): he 'feeds' himself and his ego (and perhaps his sexual appetites) abroad, where his largess also 'feeds' the company. Meanwhile, he does not 'feed' her the recognition ('merry look') she needs, nor does he 'feed' with her. The first two lines contrast the pub(lic) 'company' with 'I at home', and construct one version of mart/ house, public/private opposition at work in *Errors*. Finally, punning on 'stale' as both whore and unappetizing food, Adriana's metaphor encapsulates the problem: the love/food she offers is no longer appetizing to her husband. By breaking the pale herself to fetch her husband, Adriana— unknowingly mirroring her mother-in-law— performs not so much an act of 'transgression' as an attempt to construct a home to contain the family. Her flight is at once remarkable and understood in the context of the play's farcical action.

The action of the play, which depends on deferring the meeting of characters crossing the same stage at different times, progresses via the presence of real or symbolic boundaries, and a sense of proper place. So, as we have seen, Syracusan merchants are out of bounds in Ephesus, and one's home ought to be off limits to strangers. Throughout her disquisition with Adriana, Luciana appears resigned to the 'bounds' that circumscribe each species and sex, and endorses the hierarchy at the top of which reigns 'Man, more divine, the master of all these' (II.i.20). Luciana's metaphysics assumes the fixed boundary between men's public roles and women's domestic duties, as she consoles her sister about Antipholus's absence from the meal: 'Perhaps', Luciana offers, 'some merchant hath invited him, / And from the mart he's somewhere gone to dinner' (II.i.4-5). She continues to argue, 'Because their [men's] business lies out o' door', they may enjoy greater 'liberty' than their stay-at-home counterparts (11). This line of argument, challenged elsewhere in the play, depends on the separation between inside and outside, home and business— fissures not yet formed, and arguably never fixed in Elizabethan society.

Angered by the double standard Luciana embraces, Adriana nonetheless endorses a type of gendered separation of the spheres, as her own identity is bound up with domestic issues. Her language borrows heavily from close-to-home imagery: taste, 'service', and eating. At

Josh Beerman as Dromio of Syracuse and Jason Engstrom as Antipholus of Syracuse in GreenStage's 1999 production of The Comedy of Errors.

one point, she accosts Antipholus S., administering a dose of marriage-tract logic that moves even the wrong audience. She first accuses her 'husband' of feeding his 'sweet aspects' to another woman. Next, she recalls a past time when they 'ate' together:

> The time was once when thou unurg'd
>   wouldst vow
> That never words were music to thine ear,
> That never object pleasing in thine eye,
> That never touch well welcome to thy hand,
> That never meat sweet-savour'd in thy taste,
> Unless I spake or look'd or touch'd or carv'd
>   to thee.

(II.ii.113-18)

This speech depicts a wife's willing service to a man who is home to appreciate it. The scenario illustrates what Karen Newman calls the 'special nearness of wives' in early modern England, their importance in the household economy and their proximity to husbands' affairs

which might threaten patriarchal control. In medieval and renaissance noble households, the meat carver was not properly a 'servant', but, possibly a function of his being entrusted with knives, he held the highest position among servers, and the privilege was often reserved for esteemed friends of the lord. Moreover, because of the nature both of the game to be served and the high occasion, the role demanded great skill and finesse. Wives fulfilled this function in middle- and upper-class households of the seventeenth century. 'When great personages shall visit' wives were expected to 'sit at an end of a table and carve handsomely', as the ninth Earl of Northumberland instructed his son in 1609. 'Let huswife be carver', Thomas Tusser charges with his characteristic and terse pragmatism. In pointing to her own carving duties, then, Adriana aligns herself with this special brand of service, skill, and trust newly designated to middle-class wives. Adriana calls for nothing radically new in their relations but rather aims to reinstate herself as Antipholus' cook, confidante, and server.

III

The only other married woman in *Errors*, Emilia endorses this domestic and meal-centred value system. Although she holds a small part in the playtext, materializing only— and at first anonymously— in the last act and discussed in Egeon's deposition (I.i), this matriarchal presence— mother, wife, abbess— looms large on stage. Like her daughter-in-law, Emilia stands firmly on the side of 'home', and, like the young wife, fights for her family's togetherness. Both she and Adriana make a religion out of their 'service' in reclaiming or sustaining their menfolk and seem prototypes of the 'domestic woman' emerging in eighteenth-century Europe described by Nancy Armstrong. Emilia is a sacrificial figure: it is she who '(almost fainting under / The pleasing punishment that women bear) / Had made provision' to follow her traveling salesman to Epidamnum; she who importunes the family's return home. Her 'incessant weepings' aboard the ship '[f]orc'd' Egeon to arrange for another voyage. Emilia, like Thaisa in *Pericles*, betakes herself to a religious retreat until such time (in her case, 33 years) as she may be restored to her role as wife and mother. When her own husband wanders, Adriana waits in fasting and prayer— the metaphor suggesting her almost religious devotion to the marriage we see her enact throughout the play.

Both Emilia and Adriana spin out practical theories of marital roles, both employing eating and consuming imagery to establish nurture as vital to the household economy and to the satisfaction of men. We have already examined Adriana's manifesto in her reminiscence of carving; in hers, Emilia acknowledges her skill in simples and medicines— knowledge she ascribes to her religious vocation, but which also fell under the auspices of 'housewifery' in the period. Their doctrines, along with Luciana's view of marriage, reflect the emergent notion of the separation of the spheres. Luciana, who understands that commercial engagements and world affairs distract men from the hearth, accepts as 'natural' the gendered division of labor and leisure, whereas the experienced wives lament this division, blaming 'other women' and scolding partners for men's distance from home. In all we note an uneasy recognition that domestic life may not satisfy men, that family matters may be incompatible with the contingencies of mercantile experience.

These problems generate further inquiry by the chief representatives of domestic life, Emilia and Adriana, who share a commitment to providing nurturing homes for their families. As the matriarch interrogates Adriana, each speaker uses the circumstances of Antipholus's dining as an indication of the state of his health and sanity, and as an index of the domestic situation itself. For example, Adriana confesses to 'urging' the subject of his fidelity '[a]t board' as well as in bed. Emilia chastens this harping habit of Adriana's with proverbial wisdom:

Thou say'st his meat was sauc'd with thy
    upbraidings:
Unquiet meals make ill digestions;
Thereof the raging fire of fever bred,
And what's a fever, but a fit of madness? . .
    .

In food, in sport, in life-preserving rest
To be disturb'd would mad or man or beast.
                    (V.i.73-76, 83-84)

The repeated emphasis on meals reveals both the mother's concern for her son's well-being and her familiarity with affairs of the hearth, while also reinforcing the centrality of nurture in the domestic economy.

Antipholus' wife and mother compete for the authorship of his cure, each invoking her feminine 'office' as justification, demonstrating a struggle for domestic authority between women in different relationships to the man of the house. Perhaps because she knows that Antipholus S. is neither mad nor married, and perhaps because of reawakened maternal duty, the abbess defends her house, her son, and her right to care for him— 'a branch and parcel of mine oath, / a charitable duty of my order' (106-107). But Adriana voices equal devotion:

I will attend my husband, be his nurse,
Diet his sickness, for it is my office,
And I will have no attorney but myself;
And therefore let me have him home with
    me.

                    (98-101)

Adriana again asserts the sanctity of the home in her desire to get him out of the hands of what seem to be strangers. Thus thwarted by the abbess, only at this point does Adriana resort to state aid in the person of the Duke. As we have seen, she has before opted to handle domestic strife privately ('And I will have no attorney but myself'), while in the commercial world contracts are enforced through officials and surrogates. Her calling upon 'official' intervention here to settle the problem heralds the final feast which celebrates the resolution; both unite private and public experience. The only festive meal hosted by a woman in Shakespeare's canon, Emilia's gossips' feast symbolically celebrates, *inter alia*, childbirth— an achievement uniquely within the province of women. Not, as in other festive comedies, a wedding feast for the presumably espoused Luciana and Antipholus S., nor a marital reunion banquet, as in the romances, 'a gossips' feast' celebrates the delayed delivery of '[her] heavy burden' (406, 403). The Duke promises, 'With all my heart I'll gossip at this feast' (408). This communal supper not only achieves official endorsement, it also promises that Adriana and Antipholus will at last eat together, and likewise transforms the vexed interrelationship of 'public' and 'private' haunting the play all along. Not exactly the romantic dinner for two that Adriana had planned, and a far cry from her husband's pub-crawls, the gossips' feast offers the *via media* between private and public dining. Here, the immediate and extended family, along with city magistrates and merchants, will feast together. With the confusion cleared up, a measure of reconciliation is possible between the young couple, augmented by Emilia's motherly (if bossy) advice to the wife.

A 'broken christening', similar to the 'broken nuptials' Carol Neely ascribes to the romances, Emilia's feast consummates the woman's part in all forms of family: her restoration to wifehood, the reunion with her children— now expanded to include Adriana and Luciana— and the rejoining of siblings, including the Dromios for whom she serves as a kind of godmother. Emilia feels re-born ('such Nativity'!) into the family romance, and her feast places wifehood, as well as motherhood and nurture, in the limelight. As social histories of childbirth indicate, from advising their kinswomen and neighbors about aphrodisiacs, to procuring their 'longings' during pregnancy, and assisting during and after childbirth, early modern women played principal roles in their community's 'reproductive rituals'. 'There were . . . aspects of birth celebrations that were essentially female rituals, in which participants were drawn from a wide social spectrum and united by gender and biological experience'. Women's protracted activities culminated in this ritual meeting. Held after and serving as a secular counterpart to the 'churching' of the young mother, the gossips' feast ritually acknowledged and 'socialized' women's reproductive power as well as their aid along the way.

Emilia's gossips' feast celebrates the newly restored community— its domestic, mercantile, and political components— at the same time as it confirms the unique achievements of women in that community. The feast is centered in private space— the abbey hitherto having been cordoned off from the town— opened up through a ritual which crosses boundaries between public and private, church and state. In the early modern period, the church publicly sanctified marriages, christened babies in baptism, and blessed women in churching— the symbolic reestablishment of the new mother into the public community. That the hostess-gossip pointedly invites men— husbands, father, brothers, Duke, merchants— to what was traditionally a private and an exclusively female affair suggests rapprochement between the otherwise gendered and separate spheres, home and commerce. The conclusion recognizes the necessary function of the domestic sphere to regenerate and ritually acknowledge the public life of a community. The meal is associated with the domestic sphere and with women: an elder woman sponsors it; presumably Luce and company will prepare and serve it; and it cel-

ebrates women's 'labor'. In accepting the invitation, the male mercantile community grants that this domestic intervention is as compelling as the 'intestine jars' which confront them in their ports, fairs, and marts. . . .

ANTIPHOLUS OF SYRACUSE AND ANTIPHOLUS OF EPHESUS

Many critics note the binary pairing of Antipholus of Syracuse and Antipholus of Ephesus, as they do with other obvious combinations (the Dromios, Adriana and Luciana, Aegeon and Aemilia). Catherine M. Shaw argues that the differences in their personalities and their relationships with women (Luciana and Adriana, respectively), "provide the distinction in tone between the high and middle comedy of the play." **William C. Carroll** notes that the "doubling" they experience through the confusion over their identities is largely a result of their conversations with other characters, particularly the Dromios, Adriana, and Luciana. Their language is transformed, just as they are.

W. Thomas MacCary and Ann Thompson explore the Freudian aspects of Antipholus of Syracuse's quest for identity, especially in relation to the "mother." Ralph Berry sees him as a precursor to Hamlet, a "spiritual" younger brother unsure of his identity in search of an elder brother who is certain about his. A. C. Hamilton finds Antipholus of Ephesus's behavior perfectly justified in the face of all that is happening to him. It is no wonder that he becomes angry when he is refused entry to his home (and thus is embarrassed in front of a business associate), falsely accused, and imprisoned.

Robert Ornstein is dubious that Antipholus of Ephesus's character has changed much if at all by the end of the play and notes that we are not witness to a reconciliation between Antipholus and Adriana. John P. Cutts argues that not only has Antipholus of Syracuse found his own identity, he now has a family identity in being reunited with his mother, brother, and father.

W. Thomas MacCary

SOURCE: *"The Comedy of Errors*: A Different Kind of Comedy," in *New Literary History*, Vol. 9, No. 3, Spring, 1978, pp. 528-34.

[In the following excerpt, MacCary examines Antipholus of Syracuse from a Freudian perspective, in terms of his relationships with Adriana, Luciana, Aemilia, and Antipholus of Ephesus. MacCary notes in particular the significance of both Adriana's and Antipholus of Syracuse's use of the phrase "drop of water" in separate conversations.]

. . . . If we were to formulate a kind of comedy which would fulfill the demands associated with the pre-oedipal period, it would have many of the aspects which critics find annoying in *The Comedy of Errors*. The family would be more important than anyone outside the family, and the mother would be the most important member of the family. Security and happiness would be sought not in sexual intercourse with a person of the opposite sex but in reunion with or creation of a person like the person the protagonist would like to become, i.e., his alter ego, or, more correctly, his ideal ego. There would be an ambivalent attitude toward women in the play, because the young child (male) depends upon the mother for sustenance but fears being reincorporated by the mother. Such fears of the overwhelming mother might be expressed in terms of locked doors and bondage, but the positive, nurturing mother would occasion concern with feasting and drinking. There might even be ambivalent situations, such as banquets arranged by threatening women, and ambivalent symbols, such as gold rings or chains, which suggest both attraction and restriction.

How much do we want to know about the pre-oedipal period? Can we really believe that certain conceptions of happiness develop in certain stages and all later experience is related back to these? To what extent is our appreciation of comedy based on our ability to identify with its protagonists? If we answer this last question affirmatively, then we must at least consider the implications of the other two. Most of us do not have twin brothers from whom we were separated at birth, so the pattern of action in *The Comedy of Errors* cannot encourage us to identify with Antipholus of Syracuse— clearly the protagonist, as I hope to show below— on the level of superficial actuality. There must be a common denominator, and thus the action of the play must remind us, by way of structural similarity or symbolic form, of something in our own experience. If a play has universal appeal, the experience recalled is more likely to be one of childhood than not, since the earliest experiences are not only the most commonly shared, but also the most formative: what we do and have done to us as children shapes all later experience. A good comedy "ends happily," which means it follows a pattern of action which convinces us that we can be happy. Happiness is different things at different periods in our lives, and if the argument on development is accepted, the greatest happiness is the satisfaction of our earliest desires. By this I do not mean that comedy should feed us and keep us warm, but rather that it should cause us to recapture, in our adult, intellectualized state, the sensual bliss of warmth and satiety.

I do not think that many critics today would label *The Comedy of Errors* a farce and dismiss it as deserving no more serious analysis. The patterns of farce, like all the patterns of action in drama, are appealing for some good reason. Clearly the comic pattern involving mis-

taken identity appeals to us because it leads us from confusion about identity— our own, of course, as well as the protagonist's— to security. The most effective version of that pattern would be that which presents to us our own fears and then assuages them, so it must speak to us in language and action which can arouse memory traces of our own actual experience of a search for identity. While it is true that this search goes on throughout the "normal" man's life, it is most intense in the early years. When Antipholus of Syracuse likens himself to a drop of water in danger of being lost in the ocean, he speaks to us in terms which are frighteningly real:

> He that commends me to mine own content
> Commends me to the thing I cannot get.
> I to the world am like a drop of water
> That in the ocean seeks another drop,
> Who, falling there to find his fellow forth,
> Unseen, inquisitive, confounds himself.
> So I, to find a mother and a brother,
> In quest of them, unhappy, lose myself.
>
> (I. ii. 33-40)

The image is based on a proverbial expression in Plautus' *Menaechmi*: "neque aqua aquae nec lacte lactis, crede me, usquam similius / quam hic tui est, tuque huius autem" ("water is not to water, nor milk to milk, as like as she is to you and you are to her") (1089-90). From a purely physical comparison, Shakespeare has developed a metaphysical conceit which has vast philosophical implications, but its immediate impact is emotional. The plight of the protagonist is felt almost physically, his yearning for his double accepted as natural and inevitable. Water itself is the most frequent dream symbol for birth, and with the mention of the mother and brother, we are set firmly in the child's world. The brother, in our own experience, is not a brother, but another self, the ideal ego which the mother first creates for us and we strive to assimilate. We are reminded of the Narcissus myth, since water can reflect as well as absorb, and Antipholus of Syracuse seeks himself in his mirror image. The water here, as ocean, is the overwhelming aspect of the mother, the mother from whom the child cannot differentiate himself. She projects to us the image of what we shall become; but it is a fragile image, and if we lose it we risk reintegration with her, reabsorption, a reversal of the process of individuation which we suffer from the sixth to the eighteenth month. Only later, when we have developed a sense of alterity, can we distinguish ourselves from the mother, and her image of us from ourselves.

Plautus, of course, does not frame his comedy of twins with a family romance the way Shakespeare does. Neither mother nor father appears; there is not even any serious romantic involvement for either twin. In fact, the negative attitude toward marriage which spreads through Shakespeare's play derives from Plautus', where the local twin lies to his wife and steals from her, and finally deserts her entirely to go home with his brother. As Shakespeare expands the cast and develops themes only implicit in the *Menaechmi*, he provides a complete view of the relation between man and wife and clearly indicates the preparation for this relation in the male child's attitude toward the mother. In Plautus we have only one set of doubles, the twins themselves, but Shakespeare gives us two more sets: the twin slaves Dromio and the sisters Adriana and Luciana. We see these women almost entirely through the eyes of Antipholus of Syracuse, our focus of attention in the play. From his first speech onwards it is from his point of view we see the action, and the occasional scene involving his brother serves only as background to his quest: he is the active one, the seeker. We meet the two sisters before he does, in their debate on jealousy, and then when he encounters them, our original impressions are confirmed. They are the dark woman (Adriana, *atro*) and the fair maid (Luciana, *luce*) we meet with so frequently in literature, comprising the split image of the mother, the one threatening and restrictive, the other yielding and benevolent. The whole atmosphere of the play, with its exotic setting and dreamlike action, prepares us for the epiphany of the good mother in Luciana, the bad mother in Adriana. Antipholus of Syracuse, who seems to have found no time for, or shown no interest in, women previously, is entranced and wonders that Adriana can speak to him so familiarly:

To me she speaks. She moves me for her theme.
What, was I married to her in my dream?
Or sleep I now, and think I hear all this?
What error drives our eyes and ears amiss?

(II. ii. 183-86)

The extraordinary aspect of his reaction, though quite natural in the context of the play's system of transferences, is that he should take for his dream the strange woman's reality: in other circumstances we might expect him to say that she is dreaming and has never really met him, but he says instead that perhaps he had a dream of her as his wife which was real. She is, then, strange in claiming intimacy with him, but not entirely unknown: she is a dream image, and he goes on to question his present state of consciousness and sanity:

Am I in earth, in Heaven, or in Hell?
Sleeping or waking? Mad or well advised?
Known unto these, and to myself disguised!

(II. ii. 214-16)

If these women were completely alien to him, had he no prior experience of them in any form, then he could have dismissed them and their claims upon him. As it is, he doubts not their sanity but his own, and wonders whether he dreams or wakes as they persist in their entreaties, suggesting he has dreamed of them before, and not without some agitation.

The exact words of Adriana's address which creates this bewilderment are, of course, very like his own

opening remarks. She seems to know his mind exactly, and this makes her even more familiar to him though strange in fact. She takes his comparison of himself to a drop of water and turns it into a definition of married love; this, then, is sufficient to drive him to distraction:

How comes it now, my Husband, oh, how
    comes it
That thou art then estrangèd from thyself?
Thyself I call it. being strange to me,
That, undividable, incorporate,
Am better than thy dear self's better part.
Ah, do not tear away thyself from me!
For know, my love, as easy mayst thou fall
A drop of water in the breaking gulf
And take unmingled thence that drop again,
Without addition or diminishing,
As take from me thyself, and not me too.

(II. ii. 121-31)

Most critics would acknowledge the central position of these two passages in the argument of the play, but they do not account for their effectiveness. The impact of the repetition is due to the reversal of the protagonist's expectations. He came seeking his mirror image, like Narcissus, his ideal ego, his mother's image of himself, and finds instead a woman who claims to be part of himself; and she threatens him with that absorption and lack of identity which he had so feared: she is the overwhelming mother who refuses to shape his identity but keeps him as part of herself. In his speech he was the drop of water; in her speech the drop of water is let fall as an analogy, but he becomes again that drop of water and flees from the woman who would quite literally engulf him.

He flees, of course, to the arms of the benign Luciana, she who had warned her sister to restrain her jealousy and possessiveness, to allow her husband some freedom lest she lose him altogether. This unthreatening, undemanding woman attracts Antipholus of Syracuse, and he makes love to her in terms which recall the two drop of water speeches:

Luc What, are you mad, that you do reason so?
Ant. S. Not mad, but mated; how, I do not know.
Luc It is a fault that springeth from your eye.
Ant. S. For gazing on your beams, fair sun, being by.
Luc Gaze where you should, and that will clear your sight.
Ant. S. As good to wink, sweet love, as look on night.
Luc Why call you me love? Call my sister so.
Ant. S. Thy sister's sister.

Luc. That's my sister.
                        Ant. S. No,
It is thyself, my own self's better part,
Mine eye's clear eye, my dear heart's dearer
  heart,
My food, my fortune, and my sweet hope's
  aim,
My sole earth's Heaven, and my Heaven's claim.
                            (III. ii. 53-64)

There is as much difference between Adriana and Luciana as between night and day: Adriana is the absence or perversion of all that is good in Luciana. It is not the difference between dark women and fair women we find in the other comedies— Julia and Sylvia in *Two Gentlemen of Verona*, Helena and Hermia in *Midsummer Night's Dream*— but much more like the difference in the *Sonnets* between the dark lady and the fair youth: on the one side we have all that is threatening and corruptive, while on the other there is truth and beauty. Again, all is a dream: Antipholus of Syracuse has seen Luciana before, in dreams, in madness, but then she was indistinguishable from Adriana, the two opposites bound up as one. Now, as if by the dream mechanism of decomposition they are separate, and he can love the one and avoid the other. He has overcome his fear of the overwhelming mother and projects now his image of the benevolent mother upon Luciana.

The relation between these two young women and Aemilia, the actual mother of Antipholus of Syracuse, becomes clear in the climactic scene. He has been given sanctuary in the priory, after having been locked up by Adriana and escaping her; Aemilia emerges, like the vision of some goddess, to settle all confusion. Her attention focuses on Adriana, and she upbraids her son's wife for the mistreatment she has given him. It is a tirade not unlike others in early Shakespearean comedy against the concept of equality and intimacy in marriage. We hear it from Katharina at the end of *The Taming of the Shrew*, and we see Proteus fleeing from such a marriage in *Two Gentlemen of Verona*, as do all the male courtiers in *Love's Labor's Lost*. In the later romances this antagonism between the man who would be free and the woman who would bind him home is equally apparent and more bitterly portrayed; e.g., Portia's possessiveness in *The Merchant of Venice* and Helena's pursuit of Betram in *All's Well*. The identification of the threatening woman with the mother in the man's eyes is developed to varying degrees in these different instances— the maternal aspect of Portia is remarkable, as are Helena's close ties to the Countess— but here it is transparent: Aemilia must instruct her daughter-in-law on the proper treatment of her son, and we see this through the eyes of Antipholus of Syracuse: he has finally been able to conquer his fear of losing his identity in his mother's too close embrace because she herself tells him that this is no way for a woman to treat him:

The venom clamors of a jealous woman
Poisons more deadly than a mad dog's tooth.
It seems his sleeps were hindered by thy
  railing,
And thereof comes it that his head is light.
Thou say'st his meat was sauced with thy
  upbraidings;
Unquiet meals make ill digestions.
Thereof the raging fire of fever bred,
And what's a fever but a fit of madness?
Thou say'st his sports were hindered by thy
  brawls.
Sweet recreation barred, what doth ensue
But moody and dull Melancholy,
Kinsman to grim and comfortless Despair,
And at her heels a huge infectious troop
Of pale distemperatures and foes to life.
                            (V. i. 69-82)

This description of madness reminds us of the mythical monsters Harpies, Gorgons, and Furies— all female, like Shakespeare's Melancholy and Despair— bitchlike creatures who hound men to madness. Clearly this entire race is a projection of male fears of female domination, and their blood-sucking, enervating, food-polluting, petrifying attacks are all related to pre-oedipal fantasies of maternal deprivation. By identifying this aspect of the mother in Adriana, he can neutralize it. Antipholus of Syracuse, then, finds simultaneously the two sexual objects Freud tells us we all originally have: his own benevolent and protective mother and the image of himself in his brother he has narcissistically pursued. . . .

William C. Carroll

SOURCE: "To Be and Not To Be: *The Comedy of Errors* and *Twelfth Night*," in *The Metamorphoses of Shakespearean Comedy*, Princeton University Press, 1985, pp. 67-79. [*In the following excerpt, Carroll discusses how Antipholus of Syracuse and Antipholus of Ephesus undergo "transformation by doubling." Antipholus of Syracuse enters a world (Ephesus) that is unfamiliar to him geographically, but the familiarity with which people greet and address him makes him wonder whether he's gone mad, is experiencing a dream, or whether some external Ephesian force is at work. Antipholus of Ephesus has a similar yet opposite experience— all that is familiar to him is now strange, which angers him and nearly drives him mad. Much of the confusion is due to the "transformations in everyday language" in their conversations with the Dromios and with Adriana and Luciana.*]

. . . . The kind of experience Antipholus of Syracuse undergoes serves as a model of transformation by doubling. He begins the play in what we deduce is an altered state: he has fallen from his customary state to being "dull with care and melancholy" (I.ii.20). This change is unexplained and troublesome, and will be reversed by the end of the play; but melancholy is soon

forgotten when madness seems to enter. As he falls
into the plot's manifold errors, Antipholus will alternate
between two theories to explain what is happening: first,
that some force external to him, in Ephesus, deceives
his eye and deludes his senses; second, that he has in
fact gone mad. The two explanations are by no means
exclusive. His long-lost twin, Antipholus of Ephesus,
will undergo a similar transformative dislocation, made
perhaps even worse because the "familiar" everyday
world he has lived in becomes completely strange. He
too enters the play already changed— estranged from
his wife Adriana, who accuses him (in the person of his
brother) of being "strange to me," and taunts him that
she has been unfaithful, because he has supposedly
avoided her for another:

> For, if we two be one, and thou play false,
> I do digest the poison of thy flesh,
> Being strumpeted by thy contagion.
>
> (II.ii.143-5)

The ideal of two becoming one, which takes on increasing suggestiveness in the play, marks only an unfortunate dislocation here. Antipholus' reply is confused,
and Luciana exclaims, "Fie, brother, how the world is
changed with you" (l. 153). The other inhabitants of
Ephesus decide more simply that no matter which
Antipholus is present, the poor fellow is mad.

As the scene proceeds, Antipholus of Syracuse lights
upon a third explanation, that he lives a dream: "What,
was I married to her in my dream? / Or sleep I now,
and think I hear all this?" (ll. 183-4). He accepts this
transformation for the time being, in a spirit of adventure, for something in him sympathetically recognizes
that error (in the root sense of wandering) is what his
own life has been, and is still the way to new revelation:

> What error drives our eyes and ears amiss?
> Until I know this sure uncertainty,
> I'll entertain the offered fallacy.
> Am I in earth, in heaven, or in hell?
> Sleeping or waking, mad or well-advised?
> Known unto these, and to myself disguised?
> I'll say as they say, and persever so,
> And in this mist at all adventures go.
>
> (II.ii.185-7, 213-17)

Mist, water, error: metamorphosis thrives in unstable
regions, and it takes some courage to step into "this
mist"— here, not the obliviousness of Bottom, but something self-conscious and risk-taking. Antipholus also
understands his position as existence in some kind of
fiction, wondering at the paradox that he may be "to
myself disguised," that he can be not himself and yet
know it at the same time.

Both Antipholi are increasingly startled by unexplained
transformations in everyday language. Faces are the

Engraving from Galerie des Personnage de Shakespeare *(1844).*

same, names the same, but nothing fits: *S. Antiph.*:
"How can she thus then call us by our names, / Unless
it be by inspiration?" (II.ii.167-8). His brother's servant
echoes him, in a now familiar trope, when he confronts
his unseen twin:

> O villain, thou hast stol'n both mine office
> and my name.
> The one ne'er got me credit, the other mickle
> blame.
> If thou hadst been Dromio today in my
> place,
> Thou would have changed thy face for a
> name, or thy name for an ass.
>
> (III.i.44-7)

Later, he rudely remarks, "A man may break a word
with you, sir, and words are but wind; / Ay, and break
it in your face, so he break it not behind" (ll. 75-6).
Words are but wind (as unstable as water) in this play
because Shakespeare has taken special pains to create
a symbolic world in which language itself, among other
things, is constantly transformed and so "fails" in the
strict constructionist sense. Nothing could be more
disorienting than a world which precisely resembles the
ordinary one except for the fact that customary language no longer operates there. The Antipholi and
Dromii believe, alternatively, that they are transformed;

that everyone else is transformed; and that their mere words have been mysteriously transformed.

Of all the words that have once been effectual but are now without stable meaning, that ordinarily establish the boundaries of identity, none is more important than one's name:

> There's not a man I meet but doth salute me
> As if I were their well-acquainted friend;
> And everyone doth call me by my name.
> Some tender money to me, some invite me;
> Some other give me thanks for kindnesses;
> Some offer me commodities to buy.
> Even now a tailor called me in his shop
> And showed me silks that he had bought for me,
> And therewithal took measure of my body.
> Sure, these are but imaginary wiles,
> And Lapland sorcerers inhabit there.
>
> (IV.iii.1-11)

The method of creating this linguistic and social dislocation— twins with the same name— is quite mechanical, as the play's detractors are always pointing out; but the effects created are anything but mechanical. The linguistic transformations are both cause and effect of the extensive psychological changes. Small wonder that at the end of the play Emilia asks everyone to "Go to a gossips' feast, and joy with me / After so long grief such nativity" (V.i.406-7). These people need not only a re-birth but also the re-naming that a christening party will provide. Antipholus of Syracuse especially needs a new beginning, his last one having failed in all ways:

> In Ephesus I am but two hours old,
> As strange unto your town as to your talk;
> Who, every word by all my wit being scanned,
> Wants wit in all one word to understand.
>
> (II.ii.149-52)

The new names at the gossips' feast will, of course, be the same as they always were, but the people, paradoxically the same outwardly, will change once again. So the gossips' feast is both renewal and repetition, since the names— what started the confusion in the first place— are and are not unique.

As identity and language begin to transform, and comfortably familiar boundaries collapse, the inevitable erotic obligato begins to sound. Pleading for her neglected sister, Luciana succeeds only in making the wrong brother (Antipholus of Syracuse) fall in love with her:

> Sweet mistress, what your name is else, I
>   know not;
> Nor by what wonder you do hit of mine;
> . . . . .
> Are you a god? Would you create me new?
> Transform me, then, and to your pow'r I'll yield.

> But if that I am I, then well I know
> Your weeping sister is no wife of mine,
> Nor to her bed no homage do I owe;
> Far more, far more, to you do I decline.
>
> (III.ii.29-30, 39-44)

Like every other Renaissance annotator faced with the powerful combination of woman, water, and metamorphosis, Antipholus next resorts to the legend of the siren to represent his experience:

> O, train me not, sweet mermaid, with thy note,
> To drown me in thy sister's flood of tears.
> Sing, siren, for thyself, and I will dote;
> Spread o'er the silver waves thy golden hairs;
> And as a bed I'll take them, and there lie,
> And, in that glorious supposition, think
> He gains by death that hath such means to
>   die.
> Let Love, being light, be drowned if she sink!
>
> (ll. 45-52)

Antipholus is not much of an Odysseus, to be sure, but the audience knows what he means. The Renaissance fascination with metamorphosis finds a perfect culmination in the related myths of Circe and the sirens— the figure of the female temptress who could transform a warrior into a Gryll or, conversely, a naive young man into a mature and worthy lover. If she was a fleshly temptress for some, she could also be (as for Antipholus) a kind of muse. She might signify lust for Homer or Ovid, or the "glorious supposition" of romantic love. This stereotyped double nature— virgin or whore— may be partly seen in Antipholus of Syracuse's two references to the siren. The first, above, is one of rapture. But near the end of the same scene, after a little more thought about his "wife" Adriana and his new love for Luciana, it all seems more difficult:

> There's none but witches do inhabit here,
> And therefore 'tis high time that I were hence.
> She that doth call me husband, even my soul
> Doth for a wife abhor. But her fair sister,
> Possessed with such a gentle sovereign grace,
> Of such enchanting presence and discourse,
> Hath almost made me traitor to myself.
> But, lest myself be guilty to self-wrong,
> I'll stop mine ears against the mermaid's
>   song.
>
> (ll. 157-65)

He is already *not* himself in this situation; but his determination to hang onto his inner self of honor, his last shred of identity, insures that his metamorphosis will remain incomplete. Clearly, the audience recognizes that there is nothing in *fact* wrong with his love for Luciana; somewhat less clearly, we see that there is something wrong instead with the entire situation. Antipholus of Syracuse will not *become* someone else, though he is mightily tempted as a way of fulfilling desire; what he doesn't realize is that he has *already* been transformed into someone else by his situation.

The Plautine convention rarely leads as deeply as Shakespeare is about to take us. He seems, in short, to have rejected the basic assumption that identical twins are identical. For dramatic purposes, the most important fact about identical twins is that they are and must be finally different. If they were *completely* identical, there would be no play. Their overwhelming similarity allows the playwright to construct a complex transformational situation, but only their difference allows it to come to dramatic life. The situation is a vivid illustration of one we will see again and again: a man resists transformation, though attracted to it; he resists it even though it could never, in human imagination, be easier to accept; and even though he resists it, it still happens. Metamorphosis appears as both change *and* stasis, then; it manifests itself simultaneously as being (remaining the same) and not-being (the metamorphosed other). The "comic horror" attached "to the notion of the *complete* identity of two human beings," as G. R. Elliot notes, underlies the play's doubling, but like any metamorphosis, which is and is not, absolute identity is only asymptotically approached, and difference, the "is not," is preserved. That Antipholus blames local "witches," finally, reminds us from Murray's accounts that the complicity of the viewing audience (onstage for now) is also required.

Antipholus of Syracuse's existential predicament finds a comic mirror in his servant's. Dromio's transformation similarly derives not only from his situation in Ephesus but also from the power of love:

> s. DROMIO. Do you know me, sir? Am I
> Dromio? Am I your man? Am I myself?
>
> s. ANTIPH. Thou are Dromio, thou art my
> man, thou art thyself.
>
> s. DROMIO. I am an ass; I am a woman's
> man, and besides myself.
>
> (III.ii.73-8)

That love transforms one, makes Dromio both himself and "besides myself," is by now a commonplace, though Dromio's capture at the hands of Nell (or Luce) seems rather desperate. After his famous comic blazon of her parts ("She is spherical, like a globe. I could find out countries in her"—ll. 114-5), Dromio leaves with the familiar animalistic fears on his mind: "And, I think, if my breast had not been made of faith, and my heart of steel, / She had transformed me to a curtal dog, and made me turn i' th' wheel" (ll. 146-7). As she is a "globe," so engulfment by her would be a total loss of self, as complete as a drop of water falling into the ocean. As in *A Midsummer Night's Dream*, the characters in *The Comedy of Errors* fear the impingement of the animal, and the lowering or abolition of human boundaries. To stop one's ears is all a mariner can do. *Not*

to be oneself, to be an "other," is as much as being an ass or a curtal dog.

As the play progresses and the "errors" multiply, the characters experience more and more transformations through situational changes in vision. Hearing that her husband's brother has wooed Luciana, Adriana begins to find her "husband"

> deformed, crooked, old and sere,
> Ill-faced, worse bodied, shapeless everywhere:
> Vicious, ungentle, foolish, blunt, unkind,
> Stigmatical in making, worse in mind.
>
> (IV.ii.19-22)

This description of course applies to her as well. From the start her shrewishness has been a given from which, we expect, she will be changed by the end of the play. The madness spreads rapidly, for S. Dromio soon describes a simple jailor as "A devil . . . a fiend, a fairy . . . a wolf . . . a hound that runs counter" (IV.ii.32-9). His master sees a routine courtesan as "the devil. . . . Avoid, then, fiend!" (IV.iii.65-6). But for all its strange occurrences, local eccentrics, and ambiguous reputation, Ephesus is after all a fairly conventional Renaissance city of commerce. The chief citizens are all merchants, and money remains their chief interest. Gold chains (and prompt payment) still take precedence over questions of the supernatural. The courtesan is not a witch but a local merchant herself; the brilliance of the play is to make her *both* things, depending— and this is crucial— on one's point of view.

The final act of *The Comedy of Errors* offers a series of contrasting perspectives. Adriana, for example, attributes her husband's sudden transformation to demonic possession (the infamous Dr. Pinch is brought in): "This week he hath been heavy, sour, sad, / And much different from the man he was" (V.i.45-6). Emilia, however, explains his changes as the result of "the venom clamors of a jealous woman . . . his sleeps were hind'red by thy railing . . . thy jealous fits / Hath scared thy husband from the use of wits" (ll. 69-86). The Abbess's version is not necessarily the whole story, though, for S. Antipholus's history shows that melancholy is widespread. Emilia, at any rate, intends to nurse him, like a mother, "With wholesome syrups, drugs, and holy prayers, / To make of him a formal man again" (ll. 104-5), as if he had in fact lost his form; to be normal is to be formal here. As the competing stories are offered, Antipholus and Dromio of Ephesus suddenly burst in with an hysterical account of their escape from Dr. Pinch. Confusion, accusation, and denial increase, and the Duke resorts, for the third time in the play, to the myth of the sorceress: "Why, what an intricate impeach is this! / I think you all have drunk of Circe's cup" (ll. 270-1). At the moment of maximum confusion on stage, when transformations and dislocations have generated the greatest chaos, discovery begins. Appropriately, the discovery must be not only an uncovering of error but also a recovery of lost names, normal perspectives, and secure boundaries to identity.

Egeon ironically initiates the discoveries with still another error: "Is not your name, sir, called Antipholus? / And is not that your bondman Dromio?" (ll. 287-8). He is both right and wrong. When E. Antipholus fails to recognize him, Egeon refers to his own transformation as an explanation:

> O, grief hath changed me since you saw me last,
> And careful hours with time's deformed hand
> Have written strange defeatures in my face.
>
> . . . . .
>
> Not know my voice! O, time's extremity,
> Hast thou so cracked and splitted my poor tongue
> In seven short years, that here my only son
> Knows not my feeble key of untuned cares?
>
> (ll. 298-300, 308-11)

Time's hand, itself both deformed and deforming, may produce metamorphoses as great as any magic; the ravages of simple mutability, "winter's drizzled snow," can change one as greatly as the pangs of jealousy or the raptures of love. Mutability may slowly achieve what transformation gains in an instant.

In trying to outdo the Plautine conventions, Shakespeare has shown remarkable ingenuity, multiplying the twins, the complex situations, and the consequent errors as much as is dramatically feasible. To engineer the resolution of his complications, Shakespeare need only bring the twins together before everyone, and then neatly "explain" all. but he has other questions on his mind, not to be disposed of mechanically, and so the ending takes some odd turns. With both sets of twins on stage, the following exchange occurs:

> ADRIANA. I see two husbands, or mine eyes deceive me.
> DUKE. One of these men is genius to the other;
> And so of these, which is the natural man,
> And which the spirit? Who deciphers them?
> S. DROMIO. I, sir, am Dromio; command him away.
> E. DROMIO. I, sir, am Dromio; pray let me stay.
>
> (ll. 332-7)

This kind of recognition scene is modeled partly on

Lylyesque or Italian pastoral drama, as I will argue more fully in discussing the ending of *Twelfth Night*. What stands out here are the rich implications of these lines. Adriana has indeed seen "two husbands," one of them mis-seen as "derformed, crooked, old and sere." The Duke makes the understandable assumption that one of the Antipholi cannot be real, but a "genius" or "spirit," with possibly sinister overtones; only one can be "the natural man." Of course, nature has given us both men—just as she will give us the "natural perspective" at the end of *Twelfth Night*— but the achievement of this play allows each Antipholus to feel that he has an attendant spirit, or perhaps is himself such a spirit. The Duke's final question, "Who deciphers them?" leads even further. No one on stage can answer him nor do the deciphering, and in fact the Dromii immediately make rival but identical nominal claims and self-assertions, as if to reveal the impossibility of answering the Duke. We might say that only the audience can decipher them, but if the actors are indeed identical twins, as in Komisarjevsky's famous production, and they are dressed the same, then how can the audience ever decipher them? In practice, they will appear as different. But we know they are different chiefly from their asides and what they say in given situations— they are different because they say they are. To "decipher" them is to be able to "read" them in a special way. The difficulty in doing this recurs throughout the final scene:

> DUKE. Antipholus, thou cam'st from Corinth first.
> S. ANTIPH. No, sir, not I; I came from Syracuse.
> DUKE. Stay, stand apart; I know not which is which.
>
> (ll. 363-5)

But standing apart won't help much. The crucial difference between them, the key to deciphering them, lies in their language; only that finally marks them apart. If the Antipholi had lost the power of speech, as Lucius and Apuleius do when metamorphosed, then they would have been, for all intents, completely identical. Here is an anomalous case where the retention of speech becomes ironic cause for further transformation. And yet names, and all language, have been revealed as generically susceptible to metamorphosis. To say "I, sir, am Dromio," is to announce and to undermine one's identity at the same time, because our names uniquely mark us and yet do not mark us. Words are but wind— our own breath and the world's.

Shakespeare turns the Plautine conventions back upon themselves, then, and in the process of challenging the tradition raises much larger questions. For the play shows us what it is like— in large part what it must *feel* like— to be and not to be at the same time. Each man acknowledges his own self, yet feels his own self violated, slipping away, its normal boundaries gone; each experiences the paradoxes of duality. On the one hand, Antipholus becomes Antipholus; on the other hand, Antipholus becomes Antipholus. When Egeon and Emilia speak of their long separation and present reunion, each twin (and certainly the audience) must recall his departure from being into not-being and his return. Amid the other reunions and re-namings in the play, this re-formation of the self is essential.

Even then, the reunion cannot be entirely unambiguous. "I know not which is which," the Duke says even now. "And are not you my husband?" Adriana wonders. Even the life-long servants remain confused:

> S. DROMIO. Master, shall I fetch your stuff
> from shipboard?
> E. ANTIPH. Dromio, what stuff of mine hast
> thou embarked?
> S. DROMIO. Your goods that lay at host, sir,
> in the Centaur.
> S. ANTIPH. He speaks to me. I am your
> master, Dromio.
>
> (ll. 409-12)

Still, even S. Antipholus' assertion is ambiguous, for it could refer to either master or either servant. The entire complication of the plot serves to focus our attention on questions of language and intention, specifically on the linguistic loss that so often accompanies metamorphosis and makes it more fearful. It is hardly a coincidence that the inn in question is the Centaur— half man, half animal, yet another example of the metamorphosed human shape.

The doubling of doubles, so baroque in its excess, represents more than a display of mechanical virtuosity on Shakespeare's part. This situational confusion also allows Shakespeare to link speech and identity, and to dramatize how this link may be served, or at least called into question, through metamorphosis. Moreover, if we identify with either Antipholus, or through some fluke of nature happen to undergo a similar experience, we will understand how, in this play at least, metamorphic doubling leads to self-alienation. In a technical sense, the Antipholi are both literally beside themselves and "mad," since the referents of their speech become dislocated from their words, and their own names and identities seem to be appropriated by some Other. . . .

ADRIANA AND LUCIANA

Among Adriana's detractors are Russ McDonald and E. C. Pettet; McDonald also finds little to praise in Luciana. McDonald assesses the value of the two women

primarily as "comic troublemakers" and little else. Adriana's role is to doubt and become angry with her husband; Luciana's job is to attract Antipholus of Syracuse (whom Adriana believes is her husband) and make Adriana angry. Pettet, while finding virtuous and admirable qualities in Luciana, concludes that Adriana is little more than the stereotypical shrew. When comparing Adriana to Shakespeare's other heroines, Charles Brooks concludes that Adriana is a shrew, albeit an intelligent one with a strong will.

Robert Ornstein, to the contrary, finds much to praise in Adriana and argues that her "powerful indictment" of the Elizabethan double standard and jealousy are hardly shrewish. She holds the marriage vow as sacred and feels defiled by what she thinks is Antipholus of Ephesus's adultery (it is never made entirely clear whether Antipholus did indeed commit adultery with the Courtezan; all that is known is that he fled to her when rejected by Adriana). It is generally considered that it is not unreasonable for Adriana to be angry and upset. Thomas P. Hennings notes that Adriana never sought political or social equality with her husband; she is concerned only with their marital unity. As Jack A. Vaughn points out, she is devoted to her husband: in the midst of all the confusion in the events of the play, she sends money to release him and later goes to bring him home from the priory when she thinks he is hiding there.

Kenneth Muir argues for considering Luciana as a more worldy woman than the one first heard from during her debate with Adriana about marriage. She does not seem overly shocked by Antipholus of Syracuse's amorous advances toward her (Muir argues that she is in fact pleased by them) when Adriana is not present (Luciana thinking that Antipholus is Adriana's husband), and requests that he at least be discreet in his indiscretions. At the end of the play, when Adriana is rebuked by the Abbess, Luciana is a loyal sister, standing up for her in public and repudiating her earlier words on the role of a wife.

Laurie Maguire explores how Adriana and Luciana work through their initial characterizations at the beginning of the play as "pagan Amazon" (Adriana) and "submissive Christian servant" (Luciana). Like the identities of the twin brothers with whom they are romantically aligned, their identities become less polar opposites and begin to merge as the play progresses. By the end of the play, Luciana is defending her sister's speech on marriage to the Abbess, and Adriana submits to being rebuked by the Abbess for her words.

Robert Ornstein

SOURCE: "*The Comedy of Errors*," in *Shakespeare's Comedies*, University of Delaware Press, 1986, pp. 29-32.

[*In this excerpt, Ornstein briefly discusses the characters of Adriana and her sister, Luciana, both of whom he terms "sympathetically drawn intelligent women." He maintains that Adriana's expectations of her husband, Antipholus of Ephesus, are reasonable, and certainly not shrewish. He assesses Luciana as not simply a pious, moralistic woman, but rather one who "knows too much about the world to have any illusions about the way men treat women."*]

. . . . There is no place in the dramatic world of *Errors* for Plautus's gluttonous Parasite or for the crass Senex, who is replaced as a sounding board for the Wife's complaints by Luciana, Adriana's sister, and later by the Abbess. The presence of these sympathetically drawn intelligent women radically alters the nature of the dramatic action because Ephesus is no longer a man's world in which women exist as household scolds or harlots, but one in which men and women are equally prominent, and the latter are more interesting and fully developed as dramatic personalities. Refusing to see her marriage as simply a domestic arrangement, Adriana regards the bond between husband and wife as intrinsic as that which links father to child. Indeed, when she speaks of her oneness with Antipholus E., it is with the same metaphor that Antipholus S. uses to describe his impossible search for his brother. For her the marriage vow is like a tie of birth and blood in that her sense of self depends on her husband's love and fidelity and she feels defiled by his adultery:

> For it we two be one, and thou play false,
> I do digest the poison of thy flesh,
> Being strumpeted by thy contagion.
>
> (2.2.142-44)

These lines evoke the noblest Renaissance ideal of love—one soul in body twain—and do not allow us to dismiss Adriana's complaints as shrewish jealousy.

The lack of any scene in which Adriana directly confronts her erring husband is striking because her misery and insistence on the inequity of her situation give *Errors* much of its emotional ballast. First she complains to her sister, then to her husband's twin, and lastly to the Abbess, but her husband is not present to hear any of these speeches. Perhaps Shakespeare feared that any direct confrontation of husband and wife would make the other farcical misunderstandings of the play seem trivial by contrast, and he was not prepared to jettison the farcical supposes that keep his plot moving. And yet he allows Adriana to make a powerful indictment of the double standard that must affect an audience even though her speech is directed to the wrong man—her husband's twin. She protests the conventional attitudes that allow men their casual philandering but condemn an unchaste wife to her husband's pitiless revenges:

> How dearly would it touch thee to the quick,
> Shouldst thou but hear I were licentious,

> And that this body, consecrate to thee,
> By ruffian lust should be contaminate?
> Wouldst thou not spit at me, and spurn at me,
> And hurl the name of husband in my face,
> And tear the stain'd skin off my harlot brow,
> And from my false hand cut the wedding-ring,
> And break it with a deep-divorcing vow?
>
> (2.2.130-38)

Although some critics have suggested that Adriana alienated her husband by a jealous possessiveness, she is not the eternally suspicious comic shrew that other dramatists portray. Her manner is never strident or undignified; her requests are never unreasonable. Balthazar, a voice of sanity in the play, speaks of her "unviolated honor," of her "wisdom, / Her sober virtue, years, and modesty"—hardly the attributes of a jealous nag. The worst that Antipholus E. can say of her is that she is shrewish if he "keeps not hours"—that is, if he is not home at a reasonable time. Even Luciana, who at first accuses her sister of "self-harming jealousy," stoutly defends her against the Abbess's intimation that her shrewishness caused Antipholus E.'s derangement. Where Plautus's husband is indifferent to his wife's continual complaints, Antipholus E. seems ignorant of his wife's unhappiness and is guilty, so it seems, of insensitivity rather than habitual infidelity. He is obtuse and quick-tempered, ready to engage in a flyting match with his servants or to tear down the gate to his house with a crowbar, but he is not loutish in the manner of his Plautine counterpart. He intended to give the necklace to his wife and presents it to the Courtesan only when he is locked out of his house. Although he is familiar with the Courtesan he does not boast of her sexual favors to Balthazar. She is, he claims, "a wench of excellent discourse, / Pretty and witty; wild and yet, too, gentle." This circumspect description does not come from the lips of a libertine; Antipholus E. is a successful businessman who uses his wife's mistreatment of him as an excuse for a night on the town. Because he is too coarse-grained and attached to his comforts to spend years in search of a lost brother, one doubts that he would understand Adriana's ideal of marriage even if he heard her pleas.

Antipholus S. is a more interesting character who not only embarks on a hopeless quest for his twin but also demonstrates his romantic temper by falling in love with Luciana at first sight. Like many later romantic heroes he is a rapturous wooer, one who has read many sonnets and knows by heart the literary language of love, the appropriate conceits and hyperboles with which to declare a boundless passion. He protests that Luciana is "our earth's wonder, more than earth divine"; nay, she is a very deity. Like many later heroines Luciana seems wiser than the man who woos her, even though she seems at first priggish in advising her sister to ac-

*Act V, scene i. Angelo, Lady Abbess, Adriana, Courtezan, Duke, Aegeon, Antipholus and Dromio of Syracuse, Antipholus and Dromio of Ephesus, etc.
Painting by John Francis Rigaud.*

cept her unhappy lot without complaint. A man is master of his liberty, she explains, and his liberty is necessarily greater than a woman's because he is the provider and must be away from the home. To this practical reason, Luciana adds the metaphysical argument that a husband is the rightful bridle of his wife's will because of his superior position in the universe. If Luciana's sermon on order and degree smells a bit of the lamp, it is nevertheless seriously offered, complete with the usual commonplaces about the hierarchy of nature that all animals recognize and obey:

> Man, more divine, the master of all these,
> Lord of the wide world and wild wat'ry seas,
> Indu'd with intellectual sense and souls,
> Of more pre-eminence than fish and fowls,
> Are masters to their females, and their lords.
>
> (2.1.20-24)

These high sentences are deflated, however, as soon as they are delivered. "This servitude," Adriana dryly re-

sponds, "makes you to keep unwed." "Not this," Luciana says, "but troubles of the marriage-bed." "Were you wedded," Adriana suggests, "you would bear some sway." Luciana's lame response is, "Ere I learn to love, I'll practice to obey," a tacit confession that she will have to school herself to the submissiveness that she claims is natural to women. When Luciana says that she would forbear a husband's wanderings, Adriana loses all patience with such pieties:

> Patience unmov'd! no marvel though she
>   pause [in marrying]—
> They can be meek that have no other cause:
> A wretched soul, bruis'd with adversity,
> We bid be quiet when we hear it cry;
> But were we burd'ned with like weight of pain,
> As much, or more, we should ourselves
>   complain.
>
> (2.1.32-37)

Inevitably Adriana has the last word because here

as elsewhere in Shakespeare's plays, platitudinous counsel and painted comforts shatter against the hard reality of suffering and anger. Moreover, Luciana is not simply a spokesman for conventional pieties; she knows too much about the world to have any illusions about the way men treat women. When Antipholus S. woos her, she is not horrified even though she thinks him Adriana's husband. Indignant at his advances, she does not, however, threaten to expose his "adulterous" (indeed, "incestuous") lust to her sister and she does not rebuff him with pious sentences. Instead she pleads with him to be circumspect in his philandering and thereby considerate of his wretched wife. She would have him be prudent if he cannot be faithful:

> If you did wed my sister for her wealth,
> Then for her wealth's sake use her with more
>   kindness;
> Or, if you like elsewhere, do it by stealth,
> Muffle your false love with some show of
>   blindness:
> Let not my sister read it in your eye;
> Be not thy tongue thy own shame's orator:
> Look sweet, speak fair, become disloyalty;
> Apparel vice like virtue's harbinger.
>
> (3.2.5-12)

On other lips this might seem Machiavellian advice, but Luciana's anger shows through her seeming acceptance of the cynical way of the world. She knows too well the emotional dependence of women on men and their willingness to deceive themselves about their marriages if their husbands will give them half a chance:

> . . . make us but believe
> (Being compact of credit) that you love us;
> Though others have the arm, show us the sleeve;
> We in your motion turn, and you may move us.
>
> (3.2.21-24)

It is remarkable that the pathos of a woman's subservience in marriage should be made more explicit in *Errors* than any other comedy to follow. The issue is not explicitly resolved in the play, but then Shakespeare never assumes the role of social critic or reformer. On the other hand, the prominence that he allows Adriana, Luciana, and the Abbess in the denouement of *Errors* makes an important if oblique comment on the relations of women and men. . . .

SOURCES FOR FURTHER STUDY

Literary Commentary

Arthos, John. "Shakespeare's Transformation of Plautus." *Comparative Drama* 1, No. 4 (Winter 1967-68): 239-53.
  Discusses how Shakespeare's *Comedy of Errors* differs from and parallels its predecessor, Plautus's *Menaechmus*.

Baker, Susan. "Status and Space in *The Comedy of Errors*." *Shakespeare Bulletin* 8, No. 2 (Spring 1990): 6-8.
  Argues that in *The Comedy of Errors*, the characters repeatedly "encounter sites and situations where the status they're prepared to play is not allowed to them," and these "spatial transgressions, dislocations, and displacements" (instances of mistaken identity) are more than simply confusion.

Barton, Anne. "The Comedy of Errors." In *The Riverside Shakespeare*, edited by J. J. M. Tobin, Herschel Baker, and G. Blakemore Evans, pp. 79-82. Boston: Houghton Mifflin Company, 1997.
  Provides an overview of *The Comedy of Errors* by comparing it to Plautus's *Menaechmi*, noting Shakespeare's additions and changes. Barton notes, for example, that Shakespeare explored more thoroughly the Syracusan Antipholus (the traveling/wandering brother), while Plautus was more concerned with the native brother.

Berry, Ralph. "'And here we wander in illusions.'" In *Shakespeare's Comedies: Explorations in Form*, pp. 24-39. Princeton: Princeton University Press, 1972.
  Provides an overview of *The Comedy of Errors*, arguing that the play should be viewed "as an anticipation of what Shakespeare is to write." Berry discusses the play's classification as both farce and comedy, the problem of identity among the characters, and the significance of the gold chain.

Bevington, David, ed. "Introduction." In *The Comedy of Errors*, pp. xvii-xxiii. New York: Bantam Books, 1988.
  Provides a brief overview of *The Comedy of Errors*, dubbing it a "superb illustration of Shakespeare's apprenticeship in comedy."

Brooks, Charles. "Shakespeare's Romantic Shrews." *Shakespeare Quarterly* XI, No. 3 (Summer 1960): 351-56.
  Discusses the characterization of Adriana in *The Comedy of Errors* and Kate in *The Taming of the Shrew* as shrewish. Brooks also uses Adriana and Kate to discuss love, courtship, and marriage in Shakespeare's romantic comedies.

Bullough, Geoffrey, ed. "Introduction." In *Narrative and Dramatic Sources of Shakespeare*, pp. 3-11. New York: Columbia University Press, 1957.
  Provides short but detailed commentary on the sources of *The Comedy of Errors*.

Charney, Maurice. "*The Comedy of Errors*." In *All of Shakespeare*, pp. 3-10. New York: Columbia University Press, 1993.
  Provides an overview of *The Comedy of Errors*. Charney includes discussion of the classical style of verse in the play.

Crewe, Jonathan V. "God or The Good Physician: The

Rational Playwright in *The Comedy of Errors*." *Genre* 15, Nos.1-2 (Spring/Summer 1982): 203-23.

Discusses the "playwright" of *The Comedy of Errors* as an omnipotent, omniscient divinity versus a healing physician.

Cutts, John P. "*The Comedy of Errors*." In *The Shattered Glass: A Dramatic Pattern in Shakespeare's Early Plays*, pp. 13-21. Detroit: Wayne State University Press, 1968.

Discusses how the characters in *The Comedy of Errors* are incapable of seeing "beyond the mirror of identical twins, to see any further than outward semblances."

Elliott, G. R. "Weirdness in *The Comedy of Errors*." *University of Toronto Quarterly* IX, No. 1 (October 1939): 95-106.

Discusses how *The Comedy of Errors* is an example of "structural excellence" and a "beautifully carved gem" through its romantic and comic "weird light."

Felheim, Marvin, and Philip Traci. "*The Comedy of Errors*." In *Realism in Shakespeare's Romantic Comedies: "Oh Heavenly Mingle,"* pp. 13-28. Lanham, MD: University Press of America, 1980.

Explores realism in *The Comedy of Errors*. The authors discuss the importance of "middle-class objects" in the play — the rope, gold chain, and ring–as well as the centrality of the concepts of order, balance, and time.

Foakes, R. A., ed. "Introduction." In *The Comedy of Errors*, pp. xi-lv. London: Methuen & Co., Ltd., 1962.

Discusses the play in three parts through a technical introduction (arguments and hypotheses regarding the play's text, date, sources, and its staging), a critical introduction (in particular, the problem of classifying the play's genre), and a stage history.

Freedman, Barbara. "Errors in Comedy: A Psychoanalytic Theory of Farce." In *Shakespearean Comedy*, edited by Maurice Charney, pp. 233-43. New York: New York Literary Forum, 1980.

Argues for a "re-evaluation of Shakespearean farce in light of a psychoanalytic theory of the dynamics of meaning in farce." Freedman also analyzes myriad definitions of farce and offers her own.

———. "Reading Errantly: Misrecognition and the Uncanny in *The Comedy of Errors*." In *Staging the Gaze: Postmodernism, Psychoanalysis, and Shakespearean Comedy*, pp. 78-113. Ithaca: Cornell University Press, 1991.

Explores such issues as the text and reader's level of awareness in *The Comedy of Errors*, how the "reading process is implicated in the principles of identity and repression," and why the instances of mistaken identity in the play are not as important as the "misrecognitions . . . that occur because of the play of character itself."

French, Marilyn. "Marriage: *The Comedy of Errors*." In *Shakespeare's Division of Experience*, pp. 77-81. New York: Summit Books, 1981.

Briefly discusses the feminine and masculine "principles" in *The Comedy of Errors* and argues that Shakespeare was deliberate in having the marriage relation take center stage in the play, and argues that the play "is devoted to the ends of the inlaw feminine principle."

Garton, Charles. "Centaurs, the Sea, and *The Comedy of Errors*." *Arethusa* 12, No. 2 (Fall 1979): 233-54.

Discusses Shakespeare's creation of the name "Antipholus" for the twin sons of Aegeon and argues that this name "becomes nodal to the patterning of the play as a whole, to its complex of themes and images, to its symbolism and its mythopoeic qualities."

Girard, René. "Comedies of Errors: Plautus— Shakespeare— Molière." In *American Criticism in the Poststructuralist Age*, edited by Ira Konigsberg, pp. 66-86. Ann Arbor: University of Michigan Press, 1981.

Discusses the use of identical twins in several of Shakespeare's plays, including *The Comedy of Errors*, as well as in the work of Plautus and Molière. Girard notes that in *The Comedy of Errors*, the use of the twins "constitutes a source of misunderstanding structurally identical with the ones caused by mimetic desire and endowed with the same dramatic possibilities."

Greenblatt, Stephen. "*The Comedy of Errors*." In *The Norton Shakespeare*, edited by Stephen Greenblatt, pp. 683-89. New York: W. W. Norton & Company, 1997.

Provides a very brief overview of *The Comedy of Errors*. Includes comparisons between Shakespeare's play and its forebear, Plautus's *Menaechmi*, as well as discussion of the loss and reacquisition of identity in the play.

Hamilton, A. C. "The Early Comedies: *The Comedy of Errors*." In *The Early Shakespeare*, pp. 90-108. San Marino, CA: The Huntington Library, 1967.

Argues that in *The Comedy of Errors* Shakespeare emphasizes plot above all else— "the plot expresses his idea of comedy and becomes the soul" of the play.

Hasler, Jörg. "*The Comedy of Errors*." In *Shakespeare's Theatrical Notation: The Comedies*, pp. 132-34. Bern: A. Francke AG Verlag, 1974.

Examines briefly the final exit of *The Comedy of Errors*.

Hennings, Thomas P. "The Anglican Doctrine of the Affectionate Marriage in *The Comedy of Errors*." *Modern Language Quarterly* 47, No. 2 (June 1986): 91-107.

Argues that the Anglican doctrine of affectionate marriage establishes the "normative pattern of the marital roles" in *The Comedy of Errors*.

Huston, J. Dennis. "Playing with Discontinuity: Mistakings and Mistimings in *The Comedy of Errors*." In *Shakespeare's Comedies of Play*, pp. 14-34. New York: Columbia University Press, 1981.

Discusses how Shakespeare "builds a plot of mistaking, self-consciously contrived," in *The Comedy of Errors*. Shakespeare does this through, for example, the false beginning of the play (where the play appears to be a tragedy or romance, not a "comedy" as the title suggests) and through the characters of Aegeon and the Duke of Ephesus.

Jardine, Lisa. "'As boys and women are for the most part cattle of this colour': Female Roles and Elizabethan Eroticism." In *Still Harping on Daughters: Women and Drama in the Age of Shakespeare*, pp. 44-46. Sussex, Eng.: The Harvester Press, 1983.

Discusses briefly how *The Comedy of Errors* "wittily ironises the consequences of the wife's maximised obligations and minimal redress."

Lanier, Douglas. "'Stigmatical in Making': The Material Character of *The Comedy of Errors*." *English Literary Renaissance* 23, No. 1 (Winter 1993): 81-112.

Discusses self-presentation as it pertains to social rank and class in Elizabethan England; how *The Comedy of Errors*, "by staging disruptions of identity-effects, is preoccupied with interrogating the curious material logic of Renaissance self-presentation"; and how analyzing the "materiality of Shakespearean character" can facilitate challenging the "traditional notion of Shakespeare's artistic 'development'" and reexamining the early comedies in light of his other work.

Levin, Harry. "Two Comedies of Errors." In *Refractions: Essays in Comparative Literature*, pp. 128-50. New York: Oxford University Press, 1966.

Compares Shakespeare's *Comedy of Errors* with its predecessor, Plautus's *Menaechmi.*

Macdonald, Ronald R. "*The Comedy of Errors*: After So Long Grief, Such Nativity." In *William Shakespeare: The Comedies*, pp. 1-13. New York: Twayne Publishers, 1992.

Provides an overview of *The Comedy of Errors*, touching on its origins; its farcical elements; how Shakespeare's use of "doubling" is "part of a larger meditation on the problem of identity, an extreme instance of the play of likeness and difference through which a workable sense of self is finally attained"; and how the play manifests elements of what Freud characterized as an oedipal struggle.

Maguire, Laurie. "The Girls from Ephesus." In *The Comedy of Errors: Critical Essays*, pp. 355-91.

Points out the many polarities and doublings in the play— characters, events, the nature of Ephesus, marriage, and the master-servant relationship. Maguire also comments on the productions of the play throughout these discussions.

Miola, Robert S. "The Play and the Critics." In *"The Comedy of Errors": Critical Essays*, pp. 3-38.

Provides an introduction to *The Comedy of Errors*, covering the play's sources; various commentary on the play's genre, characterization, and language; feminist criticism of the play and the New Historicist approach to interpreting the play; and stage and television adaptations of the play worldwide.

Muir, Kenneth. "*The Comedy of Errors*." In *Shakespeare's Comic Sequence*, pp. 15-22. Liverpool: Liverpool University Press, 1979.

Provides a brief overview of *The Comedy of Errors*, noting that "Shakespeare was feeling his way for an appropriate form and his varying success is one sign of his immaturity," another sign being the weak characterizations in the play.

O'Brien, Robert Viking. "The Madness of Syracusan Antipholus." *Early Modern Literary Studies* 2.1 (1996): 3.1-26.

Discusses madness in *The Comedy of Errors*, particularly with respect to the character of Antipholus of Syracuse, as well as Elizabethan conceptions of madness.

Parker, Patricia. "Elder and Younger: The Opening Scene of *The Comedy of Errors*." *Shakespeare Quarterly* 34, No. 3 (Autumn 1983): 325-27.

Argues that lines 78-85 of *The Comedy of Errors* have been misinterpreted by previous critics who have concluded that Shakespeare introduced an inconsistency in Aegeon's recounting of the shipwreck that separated his family.

Parrott, Thomas Marc. "Apprentice Work: *The Comedy of Errors*." In *Shakespearean Comedy*, pp. 100-108. New York: Oxford University Press, 1949.

Discusses the differences between Plautus's *Menaechmi* and Shakespeare's *The Comedy of Errors*. For example, in Shakespeare's version, there are two pairs of twins, not one, thus increasing the confusion over mistaken identity; the play ends with a reunion of the entire family; and the character of Adriana is "firmly conceived and realistically developed."

Pettet, E. C. "Shakespeare's 'Romantic' Comedies." In *Shakespeare and the Romantic Tradition*, pp. 67-100. Brooklyn, NY: Haskell House Publishers, Ltd., 1976.

Groups *The Comedy of Errors* with *The Taming of the Shrew* and *The Merry Wives of Windsor*— the "oddities" of Shakespeare's romantic comedies— arguing that it is "clearly distinguished from the majority of Shakespeare's comedies, if not their antithesis as a type of drama." Pettet also provides discussion on *The Taming of the Shrew*, *The Merry Wives of Windsor*, and the "main body" of Shakespeare's comedies, including *Romeo and Juliet* and *The Merchant of Venice.*

Salgado, Gamini. "'Time's Deformed Hand': Sequence, Consequence, and Inconsequence in *The Comedy of Errors*." In *Shakespeare Survey, Volume 25*, edited by Kenneth Muir, pp. 81-91. Cambridge: Cambridge University Press, 1972.

Discusses the importance of the movement of time (public and private time, clock-time, dream-time) in *The Comedy of Errors.*

Shaw, Catherine M. "The Conscious Art of *The Comedy of Errors*." In *Shakespearean Comedy*, edited by Maurice Charney,

pp. 17-28. New York: New York Literary Forum, 1980.
Argues that *The Comedy of Errors* is an "Elizabethan hybrid," in its drawing from Plautus and Terence, the English stage and Renaissance thought, and its "multileveling of character and narrative tone and superimposition of various layers of dramatic representation on the Latin base."

Slights, Camille Wells. "Time's Debt to Season: *The Comedy of Errors*, IV.ii.58." *English Language Notes* XXIV, No. 1 (September 1986): 22-25.
Examines one line of *The Comedy of Errors*, focusing on the interpretation of the word "season."

Smidt, Kristian. "Comedy of Errors?" In *Unconformities in Shakespeare's Early Comedies*, pp. 26-38. London: Macmillan, 1986.
Finds "signs of disturbance" in *The Comedy of Errors*, indicating that the play was perhaps revised from an earlier, longer version.

Thompson, Ann. "'Errors' and 'Labors': Feminism and Early Shakespearean Comedy." In *Shakespeare's Sweet Thunder: Essays on the Early Comedies*, edited by Michael J. Collins, pp. 90-101. Newark: University of Delaware Press, 1997.
Argues that more attention needs to be paid by feminist critics to *The Comedy of Errors* and *Love's Labor's Lost*. Thompson reviews some of the feminist literary criticism of the plays, particularly with regard to their primary female characters, and argues for a feminist production of the play.

Vaughn, Jack A. "*The Comedy of Errors*." In *Shakespeare's Comedies*, pp. 12-21. New York: Frederick Ungar Publishing Co., 1980.
Provides an overview of *The Comedy of Errors*. Vaughn includes discussion of the play's classification as a farce and the differences between Shakespeare's version and Plautus's *Menaechmi*, and he argues that Adriana is a sympathetic, multidimensional character, not a shrew.

Von Rosador, K. Tetzeli. "Plotting the Early Comedies: *The Comedy of Errors, Love's Labour's Lost, The Two Gentlemen of Verona*." *Shakespeare Survey* 37 (1984): 13-22.
Discusses the way in which the plot of *The Comedy of Errors* is one of "repeated evasion or postponement of danger," and that the "calm" after the "turbulence" is usually a result of a beating of one of the Dromios. Von Rosador also examines how Shakespeare avoids formulaic plotting. A discussion of the plots of *Love's Labour's Lost* and *The Two Gentlemen of Verona* follows.

Wells, Stanley. "Comedies of Verona, Padua, Ephesus, France, and Athens." In *Shakespeare: A Life in Drama*, pp. 52-57. New York: W. W. Norton & Company, 1995.
Provides a very brief overview of *The Comedy of Errors*, touching on its staging, its genre classification, and its approach to identity.

Williams, Gwyn. "*The Comedy of Errors* Rescued from Tragedy." *A Review of English Literature* 5, No. 4 (October 1964): 63-71.
Argues argues that *The Comedy of Errors* could have ended up being classified as a tragedy, had not the second pair of twins, the Dromios, been added. These twins "save the play as a comedy," and the farcical instances in the play revolve almost entirely around them.

CORIOLANUS

INTRODUCTION

Critics generally agree that *Coriolanus* was written in 1608, although a variety of composition dates ranging from 1605 to 1609 have been established as possible. The drama was first published in the First Folio of 1623, and this remains the only authoritative text. According to scholarly opinion this copy of the play was likely printed directly from a manuscript in Shakespeare's own handwriting with little editorial revision. The primary source for *Coriolanus* is the Greek historian Plutarch's "Life of Caius Marcius Coriolanus," included in his *Lives of the Noble Grecians and Romans*. Shakespeare most likely read this work in Sir Thomas North's English translation. In fact, as critics have often noted, *Coriolanus* derives its characters, its sequence of events, and even some of its language directly from North.

As is true of Shakespeare's work in general, the dramatist took great liberties in altering the source material for *Coriolanus*. His most significant changes include his development of the character of Menenius Agrippa, who appears only briefly in the historical source; his expansion of Volumnia's role and influence over events in the action; his emphasis on the grain shortage as the cause of citizen riots in Rome; and, most importantly, his complex portrayal of Coriolanus, whose failure in Plutarch's biography is simply the result of a defective upbringing and education.

Coriolanus has puzzled commentators throughout its critical history. Like its title character, who is the principal subject of the majority of critical discussion, the tragedy has been both admired and condemned. Generally, scholars have praised the work's lively characterization, and particularly the dramatic potency of the proud warrior's fall brought about by his rash behavior and personality. However, many early critics found the work marred by Shakespeare's harsh rhetoric, constricting imagery, and presentation of an arrogant and unsympathetic hero.

The play is usually considered Shakespeare's final tragedy, but departs from the norm of the dramatist's tragic works in its emphasis on politics. Indeed, the two most prominent modern lines of critical thought concerning *Coriolanus* relate to its political nature, as a representation of class conflict between commoners (Roman plebeians) and aristocrats (patricians), and to its psychological exploration of its principal characters and their motivations—a subject often focused on the nature of Coriolanus's relationship with his mother, Volumnia. A third and related topic of critical interest considers the ethical dimension of the play as an examination of the virtue of honor in both political and psychological contexts.

PRINCIPAL CHARACTERS

(in order of appearance)

Menenius Agrippa: Elderly Roman nobleman and friend of Coriolanus. Wise and just, Menenius gives counsel to Coriolanus and frequently speaks on his behalf to the enraged citizens of Rome. Menenius recites the fable of the belly—a simple political allegory—to the unruly Roman commoners who are threatened by famine and demand Coriolanus's execution.

Caius Marcius Coriolanus: Roman warrior. Given the name Coriolanus in honor of his victory at Corioles, Marcius is an arrogant but courageous and skilled military man. Nearly elected Roman consul, Coriolanus is exiled from Rome for his blunt claim that the commoners should have no say in his election. After his banishment, Coriolanus leads the army of a former military rival, Aufidius, to attack Rome, but is swayed by his mother's plea for mercy. He is assassinated by a group of Volscian conspirators under the direction of Aufidius. *(See **Coriolanus** in the **CHARACTER STUDIES** section.)*

Cominius: Roman consul and commander of the Roman army. Cominius's troops engage Aufidius and the Volscians near Corioles. The arrival of Coriolanus at the battle assures their triumph, and forces the defeated Volscians to retreat.

Titus Lartius: Roman general. Lartius leads his troops against the Volscian city of Corioles. His army appears to be defeated until Coriolanus fearlessly engages the Volscian soldiers. Heartened by his bravery, Lartius orders a second attack and takes the city. He then leaves the conquered Corioles in the charge of his lieutenant and joins Coriolanus and Cominius as they route Aufidius and the balance of the Volscian army elsewhere.

Sicinius Velutus: Roman tribune, an elected official

who represents the plebeians. Together with Junius Brutus, Sicinius convinces the people of Rome to withdraw their election of Coriolanus as Roman consul and to denounce him for treason.

Junius Brutus: Roman tribune. Like Sicinius, Brutus is wary of Coriolanus's power and hopes to use the patrician warrior's pride and arrogance against him.

Tullus Aufidius: General of the Volscian army. An aristocratic warrior, Aufidius is rival to Coriolanus. After being defeated on the battlefield by Coriolanus some five times, he vows revenge through treachery. Aufidius allows the banished Coriolanus to command his troops against Rome, but when the Roman warrior fails to attack, Aufidius declares him a traitor and secretly orders a group of conspirators to execute him. *(See* **Aufidius** *in the* **CHARACTER STUDIES** *section.)*

Volumnia: Roman noblewoman, mother of Coriolanus. Domineering and manipulative, Volumnia lives only to see her son win glory on the field of battle and in Roman politics. She chastises her daughter-in-law Virgilia for her fears concerning Coriolanus's safety in the wars with the Volscians. Volumnia is the only person able to convince Coriolanus to halt his attack on Rome. *(See* **Volumnia** *in the* **CHARACTER STUDIES** *section.)*

Virgilia: Wife of Coriolanus. Gentle and sensitive, Virgilia expresses her deep concern that Coriolanus may be injured in war. She weeps despairingly when her husband is exiled, and beseeches him to stay his vengeful attack on Rome. *(See* **Virgilia** *in the* **CHARACTER STUDIES** *section.)*

Valeria: A Roman lady and widow, friend of Volumnia and Virgilia. Valeria brings news of Coriolanus's victory at Corioles to the warrior's wife and mother. She also joins Volumnia and Virgilia in their efforts to halt Coriolanus's attack on Rome.

Nicanor: A Roman citizen and traitor. Nicanor happens to encounter Adrian, a Volscian, and tells him of the strange occurrences in Rome. He speaks of Coriolanus's banishment and the nobles' desire to take political power from the citizenry.

Adrian: A Volscian spy sent to find Nicanor. Adrian meets the informant by accident and learns valuable information about the chaotic state of Roman politics. He also tells Nicanor that the Volscians are preparing their army to attack Rome.

Young Marcius: Son of Virgilia and Coriolanus. He kneels before his father, under Volumnia's order, in hopes of convincing him to withdraw the Volscian forces sent to besiege Rome.

PLOT SYNOPSIS

Act I: Facing a dire shortage of food and the possibility of famine, the citizens of Rome spill into the streets demanding the death of Caius Marcius, an aristocratic general. Menenius arrives, hoping to forestall the riot and calm the unruly citizens. He recites a fable to them, in an effort to defend the aristocracy and its actions. The people remain displeased until Menenius adds that they may elect tribunes, or judges, to represent them. The arrival of the arrogant Caius Marcius threatens to enflame the mob again until news of a military threat by the Volscians, a neighboring tribe led by Tullus Aufidius, surfaces. The Roman consul, Cominius, his general, Lartius, and several senators urge Marcius to prepare for the defense of Rome. They depart and the tribunes—Sicinius and Brutus—comment on Marcius's military prowess and excessive pride.

The scene shifts to Corioles, where the Volscian senators and their military commander, Aufidius, prepare to launch an attack on Rome. Elsewhere, Marcius's mother, Volumnia, scolds her daughter-in-law, Virgilia, chiding her for fears that Marcius may be injured or killed during the fight. Volumnia imagines with joy the wounds her son will receive on the battlefield and the glory that will be bestowed upon him, upsetting Virgilia's sensitive nature. The lady Valeria enters. She speaks of young Marcius, son of Virgilia and Caius Marcius, and brings news that the Roman siege of Corioles is under way.

During the battle, Marcius's forces lose their morale and retreat. Cursing their cowardice, Marcius storms the gates of Corioles alone. Lartius and the Roman soldiers believe that Marcius has been slain, but he miraculously appears at the gates, bleeding and chased by Volscian soldiers. Rallied by their general's bravery, the Roman troops attack and capture the city. Though he is wounded, Marcius insists that he press the assault and join Cominius, whose forces are engaged with those of Aufidius. Lartius leaves Corioles in the charge of his lieutenant and catches up with Marcius, who has forced Aufidius and his men to retreat. Victorious, the Romans honor Marcius, giving him the name Coriolanus in celebration of his fearlessness at Corioles. Meanwhile, defeated once again by Coriolanus, Aufidius swears he will have revenge, even if he must resort to treachery to achieve it.

Act II: Back in Rome, Menenius verbally attacks the tribunes Sicinius and Brutus for their open hostility to Marcius (now Coriolanus). Despite the reservations of the tribunes and the people, the Roman aristocracy welcomes Coriolanus to the Capitol, nominating him to be consul—the supreme political office of Rome. Before Coriolanus can acquire the office, however, he must submit to a humbling ritual; he must go before the common people of Rome and display his battle scars. Noting Coriolanus's proud nature, the tribunes believe he will not agree to the ceremony and expect to use his arrogance to prevent him from becoming consul. After his nomination, Coriolanus indeed demands that he not be made to reveal his wounds. But the tribunes deny him this favor. Reluctantly, Coriolanus heeds the advice of his mother and decides to undergo the ceremony. Somewhat defiantly, Coriolanus asks the plebeians for their political support. They agree, and with the assistance of Menenius the election is ratified. After Coriolanus's departure, however, Brutus and Sicinius reprimand the citizens for their foolishness. Their words are heeded, and the tribunes convince the citizens of Rome to recant, nullifying Coriolanus's post as consul before final approval is made.

Act III: Word comes to Coriolanus that Aufidius and the Volscians are again clamoring for war. He also learns that the citizens of Rome have turned against him. He publicly denounces them, declaring that their opinions should not determine the outcome of a consular election. A mob forms and, under the direction of Sicinius, calls for the execution of Coriolanus. As the general prepares to defend himself he is escorted away by the aristocrats, leaving Menenius to once again placate the unruly mob. The aging aristocrat succeeds in swaying the tribunes and the people, arguing that Coriolanus should be tried for treason by the court of tribunes rather than killed outright. The mob disperses only after Menenius assures them that Coriolanus will appear before the tribunal. Menenius then informs Coriolanus, who had swiftly departed to seek the advice of his mother, of the plan. Mother and son argue, but eventually Coriolanus capitulates to Volumnia's wishes and agrees to stand trial. In court, Coriolanus appears to have regained his composure; he apologizes for his thoughtless words to the citizenry. Shortly thereafter Sicinius provokes Coriolanus's anger by calling him a traitor, and Coriolanus insults the collected multitude of plebeians. In response to this outburst the tribunes exile Coriolanus from Rome, playing to the cheers of the mob. Coriolanus arrogantly challenges them with his words and departs.

Act IV: Coriolanus withdraws from Rome, saying his farewells to family and friends. Virgilia weeps, but Volumnia expresses only her anger at the tribunes. Dressed as a beggar, Coriolanus makes his way to Antium. Meanwhile, the Volscians learn that he has been exiled and prepare for another strike against Rome. Once in Antium, Coriolanus locates Aufidius and explains his predicament. The Volscian general listens intently and accepts Coriolanus's offer to join his army. In a gesture of apparent magnanimity, Aufidius makes Coriolanus his equal as commander of his troops. Soon, news that the banished Coriolanus has joined forces with the Volscians reaches Rome. The citizens tremble and the tribunes pray that the news is false. Elsewhere, a lieutenant of Aufidius takes him aside, expressing concern

that Coriolanus's popularity with the troops has become too great. Aufidius reassures the lieutenant, guaranteeing that he will strike against the Roman when the time is right.

Act V: As Coriolanus and the Volscian forces approach Rome, Cominius attempts to intervene diplomatically but fails. He and the Roman tribunes urge Menenius to pacify Coriolanus, but the exiled general refuses to give his old friend an audience. Desperate, the Romans send Coriolanus's mother, wife, and son— accompanied by Valeria— to beg for mercy. Coriolanus allows them to speak, but refuses their entreaties. Eventually, however, he is swayed by Volumnia's words and agrees to call off his attack. Meanwhile, Aufidius sees an opening for revenge. As the Romans receive news that they will be spared the Volscian onslaught, Aufidius hatches his scheme. He informs several conspirators of Coriolanus's military withdrawal, secretly charging the general with treason. Enraged, the conspirators agree to assassinate Coriolanus for his failure to attack Rome. Coriolanus returns, and Aufidius publicly denounces him as a traitor. As the gathered crowd demands that Coriolanus be executed, the conspirators appear and kill him. Aufidius then speaks to the mob while standing on Coriolanus's dead body. He offers justifications for the murder, but acknowledges that the noble warrior should be honored with an appropriate funeral.

PRINCIPAL TOPICS

Politics and Society

One of the most prominent qualities of *Coriolanus*, and one scholars have commonly regarded as atypical of Shakespearean tragedy, is its emphasis on politics. In the dramatist's presentation of plebeians and patricians clashing in open debate over questions of authority and power, critics have identified an uncharacteristic preoccupation with public rather than private crises, with the social rather than the personal aspects of tragedy. The play's uniqueness in this respect has led many commentators to view it as a rare exposition of Shakespeare's own political views.

Various scenes in the drama reflect a preoccupation with social conflict, notably several involving Shakespeare's depiction of the Roman citizenry arising as an unruly mob; a portrayal that a few critics have asserted is characteristic of the dramatist's tendency to devalue the multitude of common men. More specifically, some critics have viewed the work as a declaration of Shakespeare's belief in the superiority of aristocratic over democratic rule. Furthermore, Menenius's metaphor of the "body politic" has sparked a great deal of interest among commentators. Early in the play, as rioting plebeians demanding food occupy the streets of Rome, Menenius steps forward to tell his fable of the belly, which presents an aristocratic perspective on the way society should be ordered. Critics see another dimension of the play's political dialogue in Coriolanus's haughty views on the inferiority of plebeians. Accordingly, many commentators see the resulting corrosion of mutual trust in the community as ultimately leading to the destructive social state that exists in the drama.

Another avenue of critical inquiry has been to interpret *Coriolanus* as a metaphorical representation of the significant social and political events that occurred in England during Shakespeare's lifetime, including riots in the Midlands over the lack of grain, Enclosure Acts that expelled small farmers from their lands, and class conflicts between commoners and aristocrats. While many of these topical interests are generally considered to have some value by scholars, most critics have demonstrated that Shakespeare was interested in portraying social interaction on a more universal scale by abstracting these events from English history and examining them in the ethical contexts offered by the analogous culture of republican Rome.

Honor and Heroism

Many critics have concentrated on the ethical component of *Coriolanus* as a drama of values and virtue. Analyzing the figure of Coriolanus, scholars have frequently viewed his uncompromising sense of personal honor and fierce integrity as the defining qualities of an aristocratic ideal under assault during the course of the play.

While many commentators acknowledge that Coriolanus's unbending personal honor is the principal reason for his heroism and god-like skill in battle, most also note that these same virtues of honor and constancy translate poorly when Coriolanus finds himself in civil society rather than on the battlefield. The warrior's aristocratic pride proves detrimental in such contexts, and manifests itself in his haughty disdain for the common people. Additionally, personal inflexibility prevents him from engaging in the give-and-take compromise so crucial to political exchange between groups holding radically different views. Thus, when Coriolanus, who measures his worth in terms of his heroic and honorable exploits in war, finds himself in the ambiguous and equally dangerous realm of power politics he reveals the seriousness of his social flaws.

Critics have also studied the destructive potential of an aristocratic conception of honor in relation to Volumnia. For the Roman matron, commentators assert, honor predominates over love, leading some to view her as the ultimate source of Coriolanus's problems. Likewise, many have investigated honor as a paradoxical virtue in a warrior society; one that, while valuable, inevitably leads to bloodshed.

Mother-Son Relationship

Focusing on psychological rather than moral or political readings of *Coriolanus*, many critics have found the relationship between Volumnia and Coriolanus to be the touchstone of the tragedy. While enumerating the similarities of these two characters, commentators have seen them as locked in a psychological struggle with one another. So-called pre-Oedipal interpretations have commonly been proposed, which examine the role of the domineering and affectionless Volumnia in determining the fate of her son. Such readings generally probe the play's imagery of nursing, which equates this process with the bloody realities of warfare. Naturally, these interpretations locate the source of Coriolanus's aggression as a displaced feeling of neglect and isolation derived from his relationship with an uncaring mother.

A related subject involves Volumnia's manipulation of Coriolanus throughout the play. Many commentators note that she is the only figure whose will is strong enough to persuade her son, and that the otherwise indomitable warrior shrinks when confronted by the disapproval of his mother. The dissonance created by this relationship and the tragic choices it prompts ultimately bring about Coriolanus's destruction. Forced to repress the uncontrolled sense of pride and honor bestowed upon him by his mother, Coriolanus must call off his attack of Rome at her request. Thereafter declared a traitor to the Volscians, Coriolanus meets his doom at the hands of Aufidius's conspirators.

CHARACTER STUDIES

Coriolanus

In the figure of Coriolanus Shakespeare presented a truly paradoxical hero. He appears cold and aloof yet undeniably passionate, scornful but noble, indomitable in battle but submissive toward his mother, steadfast but traitorous, pitiless yet ultimately merciful. Coriolanus despises the common man, and fails to see that the plebeians have any significant role to play in society. Yet, he is not political by nature. The idea of compromise does not enter in his motivations or actions. He bases his decisions on honor and the military ideals of a warrior.

Critics have frequently judged Coriolanus as unsympathetic, seeing in his motivation to protect Rome not a sense of duty, but rather expressions of his grandiose pride and warlike nature. Coriolanus is also cited for his lack of an introspective capacity or of any significant self-awareness, as well as for his inflexibility and complete inability to adequately function in ambiguous situations that require compromise. Not surprisingly, many scholars have suggested that Coriolanus brings disaster upon himself.

The degree to which Coriolanus, like other tragic Shakespearean heroes, exhibits any internal conflict also remains an object of contention. This is especially true considering the lack of soliloquies in the play, which the dramatist ordinarily employs for the purpose of expressing a protagonist's thoughts concerning his or her situation. Although a majority view has associated Coriolanus with his propensity for action rather than for thought and reflection, the investigation for evidence of his internal struggle is an ongoing line of critical study.

Volumnia

Because critics generally see Volumnia as warlike and cruel, most concur that she plays a role in her son's downfall. Many commentators attribute Coriolanus's excessive pride, his arrogance, and even his ultimate tragedy to the influence of his mother. Significantly, numerous similarities in Volumnia's character and that of Coriolanus have been observed, including their shared sense of pride, their contempt for the plebeians, and their indomitable spirits. Volumnia's spirit, however, proves superior, owing in large part to her flexibility— a quality her son severely lacks— and her ability to dissemble, allowing her to disguise her true feelings and motivations.

Volumnia's "masculine" traits— her dominance over Coriolanus and her preference for warfare over love or nurturing— are frequently discussed by critics. Some contrast her with Coriolanus in this respect and also in her belief in political necessity as superior to the warrior's ideal of honor. More recent assessments of Volumnia, however, have proposed that she possesses a certain degree of humanity. Instead of appearing cold and brutal, Volumnia is thought to possess a level of self-awareness that greatly surpasses Coriolanus's own, and is even said to display remorse for her complicity in his death.

Virgilia

Perceived as quiet, meek, and passive, Virgilia has failed to elicit more than a small amount of critical comment, although this trend has begun to change. In *Coriolanus* she speaks only about one hundred words, but her presence is felt, scholars note, in many ways, with a few commentators suggesting that she offers a significant and alternative point of view on the action of the play. In her first scene, Virgilia engages in a debate with Volumnia about heroic virtues, with Coriolanus being the natural subject of such a discussion. Significantly, Virgilia holds her own in the argument and succeeds in

expressing her feelings of dread and repulsion concerning her husband's warmaking.

When in Act II Virgilia welcomes home Coriolanus she weeps— one of the only displays of tender emotion in the entire drama— signifying her compassion and love for her husband. Later, Virgilia condemns the Roman tribunes for their banishment of Coriolanus. At this point, some critics have noted that Virgilia and Volumnia actually move toward a similar position in their attitudes toward Coriolanus and the heroic ideals he represents, in contrast to the opposing viewpoints both held at the opening of the play. In the final supplication scene, as Virgilia and others arrive to urge Coriolanus that he spare Rome, the proud warrior kneels before her. Some critics acknowledge that her sympathetic presence persuades him to halt his attack in a manner that the aggressive Volumnia cannot accomplish alone.

Aufidius

The representative figure of the Volscians, Aufidius embodies the traits of this warlike people who are in perpetual conflict with their neighbors, the Romans. Critics observe Aufidius's characterization as brave and noble, even to the degree that Coriolanus himself praises him as a worthy adversary. Aufidius confesses that he has suffered numerous battlefield defeats to the Roman warrior. His desire to emulate his noble adversary eventually fades, however, and Aufidius is left with only the desire to crush his opponent by any means necessary. Thirsty for revenge by the time the action of the play has commenced, Aufidius determines to forsake his honor in return for victory at any cost.

Critics note that Shakespeare does not depict Aufidius as a crudely evil figure. He is thought to match Coriolanus when on the battlefield, where their adversarial relationship serves to fuel the competition between Rome and Antium to the betterment of both men. However, from the moment that Aufidius determines to pursue a treacherous scheme in order to defeat Coriolanus, commentators observe a crucial turning point in his character. A changed man, Aufidius conspires with killers to dispose of Coriolanus ignobly, using the flimsy pretext that the Roman warrior has committed treachery in his refusal to attack his home city. After the execution is complete, critics note, Aufidius reveals something of his noble character again and expresses his remorse for having used such despicable methods to overcome a worthy opponent.

CONCLUSION

Coriolanus remains an anomaly among Shakespeare's tragedies. Commentators tend to agree that the source of the play's unique status is the principal character himself, whose arrogance, class pride, and violent behavior seriously undermine his role as a tragic hero. Furthermore, the irony and paradox in Shakespeare's treatment of Coriolanus have additionally limited audiences' sympathy for his downfall. For most scholars these perplexing elements of the tragedy are clear indicators that *Coriolanus* defies conclusive appraisals and escapes final and definitive analysis. Indeed, if it is the true mark of Shakespeare's genius that his works consistently resist definition, then perhaps this elusive tragedy may be, as T. S. Eliot declared, "Shakespeare's most assured artistic success."

(See also *Shakespearean Criticism*, Vols. 9, 17, and 30)

OVERVIEW

Frank Kermode

SOURCE: "*Coriolanus*," in *The Riverside Shakespeare*, Houghton Mifflin Company, 1974, pp. 1392-95.

[*In his critical introduction to Coriolanus, Kermode surveys the principal areas of interest in the play. He examines Shakespeare's departure from the primary historical source of the drama, the writings of Plutarch. He comments on the deeply flawed character of Coriolanus, whose "aristocratic loutishness," ferocity, and overdeveloped sense of* virtus— *the duty of a man— culminate in tragedy. Kermode mentions the relevance of Aristotle's dictum, "a man incapable of living in society is either a god or a beast," as it applies to the figure of Coriolanus. Kermode likewise envisions the theme of the work as the Roman warrior's inability to curb the source of his strength— his brutality on the battlefield— when dealing in the political arena, an area that requires cunning and tact rather than the raw might Coriolanus possesses in abundance. Finally, Kermode considers the subject of language in the play, including the overarching metaphor of the diseased body politic, and describes the "decorous power" of Shakespeare's verse.*]

Coriolanus is by no means a favorite among Shakespeare's tragedies. It is harsh in its manner, political in its interests, and has a hero who is not— whatever else may be said of him— presented as a sympathetic character. Wyndham Lewis was not alone in finding Coriolanus the least lovable of tragic heroes; he calls the play "an astonishingly close picture of a particularly cheerless . . . snob, such as must have pullulated in the court of Elizabeth"— a schoolboy crazed with notions of privilege, and possessed of a "demented ideal of authority." Lewis uses him to illustrate the theme suggested by his title, *The Lion and the Fox*: Aufidius plays fox to the stupid lion of Coriolanus; what stings the hero to his last fatal outburst of raw anger is a charge of disloyalty, and, significantly, the word "boy." He is an ugly political

innocent: "What his breast forges, that his tongue must vent." There is no gap between his crude mind and his violent tongue. And such men are dangerous. Yet the gracelessness of the hero and the harshness of the verse do not in themselves discredit T. S. Eliot's judgment that *Coriolanus* is Shakespeare's finest artistic achievement in tragedy; and when Shaw called it the best of Shakespeare's comedies he was perhaps making much the same point by means of a paradox: this is a tragedy of ideas, schematic, finely controlled.

The style of *Coriolanus* suggests a late date, and this is confirmed by the scanty external evidence. The simile of the "coal of fire upon the ice" (I.i.173) may have been suggested by fires built on the frozen Thames in January 1608; there had been no comparable frost since 1565. In Jonson's *Epicoene* (1609) there is what looks like another of his gibes at Shakespeare in the line "You have lurch'd your friends of the better half of the garland" (compare II.ii.101). More impressively, the play almost certainly contains allusions to serious riots and disturbances in the Midlands in 1607. In any case, *Coriolanus* could not have been written before the publication of Camden's *Remains* in 1605, since the fable of the belly (I.i.96 ff.), though mainly based on Plutarch, derives something from Camden's version of the same tale. On the whole, 1607-8 seems the most likely date. The source of the play is North's version of Plutarch's *Life of Coriolanus*, and Shakespeare follows it in his usual way— sometimes very closely, with a liberal use of North's language, sometimes altering emphases, and changing the tone and balance by omission and addition. The events are transcribed almost in Plutarch's order, and the occasional closeness of the rendering of North's text may be gauged by a comparison with the source of the speech in which Coriolanus offers his services to Aufidius (IV.v.65 ff.) and that in which Volumnia pleads with her son to spare Rome (V.iii.94 ff.). Most of the characters are substantially taken from Plutarch, though Shakespeare modifies them in many ways.

Coriolanus himself is in Plutarch "churlish and uncivil, and altogether unfit for any man's conversation"; and although Shakespeare has his own view of the significance of this aristocratic loutishness, one cannot ignore the importance to his theme of Plutarch's prefatory observations on the hero's improper education. He represents this obliquely in the scene of the Roman ladies with their talk of the young Martius (I.iii), which has no source in Plutarch; and many of the alterations he makes are calculated to develop the idea that the education and presumptions of an aristocrat can make him unfit for rule in a complex society. Coriolanus has an imperfectly viable conception of *virtus*, of the duty of a man; it takes no account of social obligations, being based on a narrower concept of military courage and honor (see III.i.318-21). Thus he is able and honorable above all others in battle; and his modesty and piety in ordinary circumstances are suited to the role of happy warrior. But the spirit of anger, licensed in war, prevents him from dealing sensibly with the plebs, and such dealing is a necessary part of aristocracy, for which prospective leaders require a proper training. Volumnia, herself harshly embracing such narrow ideals of virtue and honor, could not give him this. Coriolanus' subservience to his mother is a mark of immaturity not only in family relationships but also in elementary politics: he is the ungoverned governor, the ill-educated prince.

Shakespeare therefore makes Volumnia more fierce than she is in Plutarch, and emphasizes the powerlessness of Virgilia's pacific spirit and her inability to affect the course of her husband's life, or even her son's. Menenius is much elaborated from the source, being useful as a commentator and as a link with the tribunes; but Shakespeare characterizes him with considerable exactness in such a way as to show that the strife between his class and the common people is not by any means the sole responsibility of Coriolanus, whose friends all share some responsibility for a situation they are anxious to ameliorate by hypocritical displays of compliance.

On the other side of the political dispute, Shakespeare is also at pains to make the behavior of the people and their tribunes somewhat less responsible and more treacherous than it is in the source. In Plutarch, the plebs have real cause for political action; before the Volscian war they are oppressed by usurers, and after it by famine. Shakespeare pays more attention to the characteristic fickleness of the mob, and to their dangerous demands, than to their needs; he does not deny members of the crowd sense and even generosity, but he will not represent their factiousness as the legitimate protest of a starving populace. He also makes them cowards in war, which in Plutarch they are not. As to the tribunes, Plutarch represents them as politicians exploiting new opportunities of power, but in nothing like the same base degree as Shakespeare. For Shakespeare looked at the story not with the sentimental republicanism of Plutarch but with a predisposition to deplore the attribution of power to the people. Given a state without kings (and *Coriolanus* is set in a Rome which has only recently exiled them), the proper focus of power is in Coriolanus and his friends; but they are tragically inept in its use, and negligent of the love they owe to inferiors.

The analogy of the body politic with the human body, so prominently stated in the opening scene, is vital to an understanding of the political *données* of the play, and much more important in Shakespeare than in Plutarch, though this does not mean that Shakespeare endorses the actions of his aristocrats or of Coriolanus in his double betrayal of Rome and Corioles. Coriolanus is habitually negligent of his inferiors— Shakespeare reminds us of this when he cancels out the hero's

impulse of generosity towards a plebeian benefactor, whose name he can't remember at the important moment. In Plutarch this man is a patrician.

That there is a considerable element of political debate in the play is undoubted. Telling a story of early Republican Rome in the England of James I, Shakespeare not only modified certain Plutarchian details and emphases concerning institutions, but remembered the recent agrarian disturbances in the Midlands. Tudors and Stuarts alike feared mobs, and made propaganda against all forms of levelling; and Shakespeare's mobs, from *Henry VI* on, are dangerous beasts, in which upstart passions have taken control of reason. The risings of 1607 were part of a series of ominous events which had caused foreign observers to prophesy revolution; a royal proclamation of 1607 announced that it was "a thing notorious that many of the meanest sort of our people have presumed lately to assemble themselves riotously in multitudes." Various forms of religious communism gave the genuine grievances of some of these insurgents an ideological coloring. And a few years before *Coriolanus* there had been, in the rebellion of Essex, an aristocratic threat to state security. Essex too was an ungoverned governor; and it was said of him at the time that "great natures prove either excellently good or dangerously wicked: it is spoken by Plato but applied by Plutarch unto Coriolanus, a gallant young, but a discontented Roman, who might make a fit parallel for the late Earl, if you read his life." As in *Julius Caesar*, Shakespeare here adapted Plutarch to fit more urgent interests; he is never merely telling an old tale.

We know Shakespeare as a master of the seminal opening scene, and *Coriolanus* provides a fine example. Here begins a clash of interests and prejudices between members of one body, and the result is disease in the body politic. By the time we reach Act III we can see why Shakespeare has allowed Menenius so deliberate an exposition of his parable. In III.i the imagery of the state as a diseased body becomes dominant. Coriolanus calls the people "measles" that "tetter us" (78-79), speaks of the wars they fear as touching "the navel of the state" (123), and refers to the common people as a "bosom" (stomach) (131), so reversing the allegory of Menenius; they are a "multitudinous tongue" (156) licking up a poison that will kill the state. Meanwhile Coriolanus himself appears to the tribunes as "a disease that must be cut away" (293) and as a gangrened foot (305).

Between the opening scene and this crisis, Shakespeare has proceeded economically, even schematically. At the outset Coriolanus calls the citizens "scabs" (I.i.166); but a war intervenes, and produces a situation in which he is the master-man, and they are weak cowards. As a soldier, Coriolanus is a kind of engine of war— we hear of "the thunder-like percussion" of his sounds (I.iv.59); "before him he carries noise, and behind him he leaves

Coriolanus is banished from Rome. The University of Michigan Special Collections Library.

of war, he is noble enough to be a god; if it is the conduct of a man in civil society, he is a beast. He finds the behavior of the tribunes impossible for a nobleman to bear, and calls the people "foes to nobleness" (III.i.45); Sicinius sneeringly but accurately informs him that he needs "a gentler spirit" to "be so noble as a consul" (55-56). To him the plebs are merely necessary and ignoble "voices"; "his nature is too noble for the world" (254). But by the time Menenius says this, we have heard the words *noble* and *nobility* acquire much irony, and the patrician use of the word sometimes applies best to the behavior of the young Martius as he "mammocks" the butterfly.

The truth about the nobility of Coriolanus is most fully stated in the great speech of Aufidius at the end of the fourth act, where he finds his rival

> not moving
> From th' casque to th' cushion, but command-
> ing peace
> Even with the same austerity and garb
> As he controll'd the war.
>
> (IV.vii.42-45)

Nobility requires a proper decorum in war and also in peaceful council (the "cushion" of the Senate). In the first, it may display itself as mere "sovereignty of nature"; in the second it calls for arts of dissimulation such as Machiavelli urges upon princes for the good of their people. There is no question that men of Coriolanus' stamp ought to be obeyed; and that is why they must be properly educated to power. This was a preoccupation shared by the Renaissance with Plutarch; and although Coriolanus brings his troubles upon himself through lack of such education, we are left in no doubt that the health of the Roman body politic suffers from his absence. Rome without Coriolanus is at the mercy of its enemies; the momentary calm, the period when the citizens, unprotected by their lion, worked peacefully in their shops, was merely a dangerous illusion. "You have made good work!"

Leading the Volscians against Rome, Coriolanus, in the final movement of the play, can again behave like a god (IV.vi.90); but the only love or piety he recognizes—that excessive respect for his mother which uses up all the love he needs for good government—finally overthrows him. To put it differently, Volumnia forces him to surrender a position in which it is enough for him to be a soldier, and to plunge himself into complexities with which it is impossible for him to deal. There is no moment in the play when one feels more sympathy for him than when he recognizes the implications of this surrender; he sees that it is dangerous, "if not most mortal" (V.iii.189). The final disaster happens because Aufidius has correctly estimated the temper of Coriolanus; with a burst of his old, narrowly military nobility he combats the most dreaded of insults:

tears" (II.i.158-59). But out of his occupation of war, he feels himself reduced to a mere actor, forced to seek the suffrage of those who left him to enter the gates of Corioles alone; and it is this one-sidedness of Coriolanus that invites not only the vengeful meditation of Aufidius at the end of Act I but the fox-like stratagems of the tribunes in the next part of the play, which concerns Coriolanus in his role of suitor to the electorate.

As we have seen, the idea of the diseased body politic informs this central section, up to the banishment of Coriolanus. Health depends upon his ability to "temp'rately transport his honors" (II.i.224) from the field to the arena of politics; and the tribunes are right in thinking that he cannot— indeed, this is the theme of the tragedy. It has been intelligently suggested that Shakespeare had consciously in mind the saying of Aristotle— which circulated widely at the time— that a man "incapable of living in a society is either a god or a beast." Coriolanus evidently is thus incapable; and it is as a "lonely dragon" that he eventually is cast out from Rome into the void, though he finds again the medium of his narrow nobility in the Volscian service. Throughout the central section, up to his banishment, Coriolanus is repeatedly examined in relation to the concept of "nobility." If it consists in the licensed rage

If you have writ your annals true, 'tis there
That, like an eagle in a dove-cote, I
Flutter'd your Volscians in Corioles.
Alone I did it.

                                        (V.vi.113-16)

At the end, when our minds are charged with many ambiguous senses of the word, Aufidius grants him "a *noble* memory" (V.vi.153).

Coriolanus has been called a debate rather than a tragedy; but this is incautious. It has admittedly proved its durability as political comment (there was a famous Paris performance between the wars at which both Communists and Fascists rioted because they construed the play as propaganda against their respective causes). But it is, as is usual in Shakespeare, much more of a vivid dramatic meditation on certain political themes than a dramatized political debate; and at the heart of it is a hero. Deeply flawed, like Timon and Antony, he is also for the most part unsympathetic, harsh, and graceless; but that he is a great man, that his decision before Rome is crucial and painful— and must (as his mother explains) be in any case wrong— involves us in his fate, exactly as the Rome he "banished" was involved in it. Few plays so completely state their own theme. The skill with which Shakespeare relates the behavior of Coriolanus to his imperfect education is one instance; the brilliant invention of the scene at Aufidius' house is another, when the hero, who in departing from Rome seems to have departed from life, materializes suddenly, presenting himself in an enemy household as an inhabitant of "th' city of kites and crows" (IV.v.42) and, dressed in his poor and worn clothes, asserts his *virtus* not merely over the servants but over Aufidius and the senators of Corioles.

The verse of the play has its own absolutely decorous power. There is more to be said of the late verse of Shakespeare, as to what makes it seem "late," than talk of verse paragraphing, of weak and feminine endings, can yield. Here is verse so far from smooth that it is as if deliberately written in the vein of Hotspur's speech in *I Henry IV*. Hotspur would

         rather hear a brazen canstick turn'd,
      Or a dry wheel grate on the axle-tree,

than have his teeth set on edge by "mincing poetry" (III.i.129-32); and some of the verse of *Coriolanus* has this grating vigor. It has been observed that in this play there is an unusual degree of comment from various characters on the central figure. This is so; but it should also be observed that Shakespeare's turning inward of all the attention upon the hero (before society excludes him altogether) is a movement paralleled by that of the poetry. The verse is whirled about by the anger of Coriolanus; it clanks and thunders and revels in images of physical violence; it denies itself any more gracious

aspect. (Virgilia, the tenderest of the characters, is famous for her silence.) Decorum ("which it is the grand masterpiece to observe") was something Shakespeare had continued to learn about. He had known the long, slow pleasures of accurate rhetorical expatiation, and indulged them in *Titus*— even, perhaps, as late as *Richard II*. But with *Coriolanus* we reach an extreme where no indecorous sweetness of language intrudes upon the military violence of the theme. Students come to recognize a certain extraordinary harshness of diction and violence of imagination as characteristics of late Shakespeare. Nowhere is it more exactly reined and controlled than here. The tone is set by the opening words of Coriolanus; then others use it in celebrating his triumph ("[he] struck / Corioles like a planet"). It infects the tribunes, as in Brutus' description of the crowd (II.i.205-21); it is heard finely in the mouth of Aufidius at the end of Act IV. But it is the voice of Coriolanus, the hard tone of nobility understood as military potency. He himself hums like a battery, and so does his play. Against this noise Shakespeare counterpoints the brisk character-writer's patter of Menenius, the elegant conversation of ladies, the lively, unheroic prose of the good fellows in the crowd. But the dominant noise is the exasperated shout of the beast-god Coriolanus. The energy of it is as superb as the control. We never feel that the author allows the hero to come very close to him or to us, but in spite of his keeping Coriolanus at a critical arm's length, Shakespeare can rarely have more fully extended his powers than he does here. There is a sense in which this inhospitable play is one of the supreme tests of a genuine understanding of Shakespeare's achievement.

POLITICS AND SOCIETY

Norman Rabkin has considered Shakespeare's representation of the body politic in *Coriolanus*, and finds his vision to be deeply pessimistic. Beginning with Coriolanus's passionate sense of honor, Rabkin has argued, Shakespeare undertakes a critique of political interaction in *Coriolanus* that is the culmination of many views on human society and history offered throughout his dramas. L. C. Knights has contended that *Coriolanus* demonstrates that "public crisis is rooted in the personal," and has considered both the hero's and his mother's behavior harmful to the well-being of society. The haughty warrior's view of plebeians as inferior, as little more than objects to control, is, in the critic's opinion, destructive of the mutual respect and cooperation essential to social order.

H. M. Richmond has observed that Coriolanus cannot be held solely responsible for the dire political situation in Rome, viewing this perception as a simplification of the complex drama of conflict between aristocratic and popular political views represented in the play. James Holstun has highlighted Menenius's much studied political metaphor, his fable of the belly. Some critics have envisioned this story— which associates the aristocracy with the nourishing belly and the commoners with the lower extremities of the body— as a key to Shakespeare's view of hierarchical political order. Holstun, however, points out that the dramatist made satirical use of this Renaissance theory in order to criticize a conception of society that grants no say to the citizenry in political matters. Another commentator who has examined the fable of the belly, E. A. J. Honigmann, has perceived it as one of many examples Shakespeare employed to manipulate audience responses--in this case by presenting one possible view of social order, then later providing a critique of it.

H. M. Richmond

SOURCE: "*Coriolanus,*" in *Shakespeare's Political Plays,* Random House, 1967, pp. 218-36.

[*Below, Richmond studies political themes in* Coriolanus, *specifically, the relationship of the play's protagonist to the Roman state. Observing Coriolanus's universal contempt for the citizenry and their accusations of his treachery, Richmond nonetheless argues that the Roman warrior "proves invariably law abiding." Overall, the critic maintains that Shakespeare offered a challenge to simplified political judgments in* Coriolanus. *The critic continues by noting that in the figure of Coriolanus Shakespeare demonstrated that unbending virtue cannot govern or maintain authority over a society ruled by mob mentality.*]

Coriolanus is the last major play of Shakespeare's in which political issues are central both to the action and to the characterization. It is true that Coriolanus displays an eccentric extreme of temperament similar to that shown in *Timon of Athens,* a play in which moral and philosophical values predominate, and we can see in Coriolanus a further step in that investigation of "difficult" personalities which had already presented audiences with *Macbeth* and *Othello.* But while these last-named plays certainly have political overtones (particularly the former), the function of Coriolanus' character is inseparable from the sense of Roman society as a complex and evolving political structure. Although there are full historical foundations in Plutarch for Shakespeare's narrative and for his characterizations in *Coriolanus,* it is clear that it marks the final step in his own investigation of the fateful interaction between private judgment and public values, which had explained the sinister conspiracy of the nobles in *Henry V* through the painful study of Brutus. Brutus, however, has emerged as a paradox: a figure who is both charismatic and, at the same time, unaware both of himself and of the society around him. Coriolanus is both more extreme and more plausible. It is not simply irony that makes this supreme study of heroism come close to being the supreme study in treachery. Shakespeare demonstrates conclusively that individual excellence is at best tangential to

political supremacy, and often wholly incompatible with it. Coriolanus is a political disaster for Rome not because, as in the case of Brutus, his virtues are mingled with astounding limitations, but because his absolute integrity and his ruthless directness are both his strength in moments of crisis when the need for them is manifest, and intolerable when peace diminishes the inevitability of their logic. Just as *Othello* displays the moral disaster that inevitably awaits the superman, so *Coriolanus* is a study of his inevitably disastrous political impact.

In many ways Coriolanus, of all Shakespeare's heroes, comes closest to Aristotle's magnanimous man in Book IV of the *Nichomachean Ethics,* "who values himself highly and at the same time justly." Though Aristotle goes on to describe an ideal, it is surprising how many traits correspond to those of Coriolanus:

he will incur great dangers, and when he does venture he is prodigal of his life as knowing that there are terms on which it is not worth his while to live. He is the sort of man to do kindnesses, but he is ashamed to receive them, the former putting a man in a position of superiority, the latter in that of inferiority; accordingly he will greatly overpay any kindness done to him. . . . Such men seem likewise to remember those they have done kindnesses to, but not those from whom they have received them. . . . Further, it is characteristic of the great-minded man to ask favours not at all, or very reluctantly, but to do a service very readily. . . . It is a property of him also to be open, both in his dislikes and his likings, because concealment is a consequent of fear. Likewise to be careful for reality rather than appearance, and talk and act openly (for his contempt for others makes him a bold man, for which same reason he is apt to speak the truth, except when the principle of reserve comes in).

Scarcely an act of Shakespeare's Coriolanus fails to match this pattern, even down to the wish (I.ix.82ff.) to pay back the hospitality of his poor host, who is among the captives taken by Romans, but whose name the hero cannot remember, once his own "gratitude" has been publicly noted.

Obviously such a man is both an enormous asset to the state in emergencies, and also an enormous provocation to the citizens and democratically elected officials of anything less than a tyranny. A sense of one's own superior wisdom does not make for easy political relationships, and Shakespeare goes out of his way to establish both the transcendent military potency of Coriolanus and the moral and spiritual insignificance of those who understandably but unwisely resent his pride. Yet the crucial difference between the values of Aristotle and Shakespeare appears in the fact that, while the latter recognizes the worth of Coriolanus unreservedly, he also establishes the complete interdependence of that worth and the mediocrity of the average citizen, who lends weight, along with his fellows, to the cutting edge that Coriolanus employs to hew down Rome's enemies. Menenius' fable of the belly and the other organs (I.i.99ff.) displays the interdependence of *all* the parts of the body politic: if the citizenry cannot afford to dispense with the aristocracy, neither can the latter afford to follow the example of Coriolanus and repudiate the former, no matter how justifiably, without thereby fatally rending the fabric of the state.

Furthermore, while the prowess and the merciless realism of Coriolanus are firmly portrayed, the key to his temperament is presented with the bluntness of a case history (which in a political sense this whole play also resembles). It is fatally easy to "pluck out the heart of his mystery," for this is no tragedy of man's most inward intuitions, as is *Hamlet*, but a study of the interaction of simple political forces with conventional excellence. It is no accident that a Freudian approach rationalizes Coriolanus' bizarre consistency of character, just as it debases Hamlet's more elusive subtlety. In one of the earliest speeches of the play, one of the citizens accurately analyzes the motivations of Coriolanus for the "services he has done for his country":

> I say unto you, what he hath done famously, he
> did it to that end: though soft-conscienced men can
> be content to say he did it for his country, he did
> it to please his mother, and to be partly proud;
> which he is, even to the altitude of his virtue.
>
> (I.i.36-41)

The figure of Volumnia dominates our impression of her son, both here, in his relentless, mother-conditioned pursuit of honor, and later, in his rationalization of his seemingly arbitrary return to loyalty to Rome, when he finally spares the city from destruction at the hands of the army he is leading against those who exiled him from his native land. Coriolanus is obviously mother-fixated to an unusual degree, and we have in Volumnia yet another Shakespearean illustration of the disequilibrium that results from a woman intruding too directly—as Lady Macbeth and Cleopatra do—in affairs that are held to be proper only to men. It is thus surely intended that one be shocked by her quite unfeminine brutality in reproaching the natural apprehensions of her daughter-in-law at the thought of the bloody wounds of Coriolanus:

> Away, you fool! it more becomes a man
> Than gilt his trophy: the breasts of Hecuba,
> When she did suckle Hector, look'd not
>   lovelier
> Than Hector's forehead when it spit forth
>   blood
> At Grecian sword, contemning.
>
> (I.iii.42-6)

Even the thought of her son's death scarcely affects her: if he had died, "Then his good report should have been my son; I therein would have found issue" (I.iii.22-3). Coriolanus' heroic absolutism thus finds a plausible explanation that is denied us in the comparable case of Hotspur. Shakespeare obviously feels that the overzealous woman both displays, and induces, a too relentless concern with basic issues, which she forces to a solution at any cost. This we see not only in the negative example of Lady Macbeth, but in the worthier, yet no less fatal severity of Desdemona and Cordelia. Coriolanus is no more able to mitigate the indiscreet precision of his judgments than they are; but just as we cannot afford to dismiss the harsh truth of their observations, so we must not only credit Coriolanus with the virtue of accurate observation, we must also recognize that at no point before his exile does he depart from the strict letter of duty and civil obligation. He not only fights magnificently and reproaches his inferiors justly; he also forces himself to meet *all* the conventional requirements for election as consul, with obvious success.

It is clear that Coriolanus' exile results less from his direct provocations, than from the calculated initiatives of those, like the tribunes, whose inadequacy cannot endure the humiliating contrast provided by a hero's mere existence. Nevertheless, it is true that Coriolanus is a scathing critic of the common people. Just before his supreme feat of single-handed invasion of the city of Corioli, Coriolanus blisteringly denounces his timorous Roman troops, who have broken before the enemy's first assault:

> You souls of geese,
> That bear the shapes of men, how have you
>   run
> From slaves that apes would beat! Pluto and
>   hell!
> All hurt behind; backs red, and faces pale
> With flight and agued fear! Mend and charge
>   home,
> Or, by the fires of heaven, I'll leave the foe
> And make my wars on you.
>
> (I.iv.34-40)

The bitter threat is obviously not accidental, prefiguring as it does the ultimate result of his exile. This is imposed through the exploitation (by the shoddier elements in the Roman state) of the popular resentment at such legitimate reproaches. It is in this censorious frame of mind that Coriolanus also reacts to the enhancement of democratic representation in the Roman constitution, by the creation of popularly elected tribunes, or magistrates:

> The common file—a plague! tribunes for
>   them!—
> The mouse ne'er shunn'd the cat as they did
>   budge
> From rascals worse than they.
>
> (I.vi.43-5)

Yet, under the inspiration of his example, the Roman troops universally rally in the battle at Corioli where he earns his name, and win the compliment of their leader: "which of you / But is four Volsces" (I.vi.77-8). Coriolanus can be frank in praise as well as censure. Nor does he have an exaggerated sense of his own worth, as the citizens often imply. He sees it for what it is: by the highest standards, only what *every* citizen owes to the state. Thus he refuses any unusual reward in good faith, allying himself, like Henry V at Agincourt, with all who have fought with him against the common enemy:

> I thank you, general;
> But cannot make my heart consent to take
> A bribe to pay my sword: I do refuse it;
> And stand upon my common part with
>   those
> That have beheld the doing.
>
> (I.ix.36-40)

He thus requires of himself no less than he exacts of others, and if he has a fault it is only that of rather naively measuring others against what he frequently announces to be his own routine virtues. He is merely the good citizen in his own eyes; anyone doing less is properly censured, while he himself expects no unusual praise or reward for fulfilling his obligations. What we have in this play then is the confrontation of the mediocre by the true norm of civic responsibility. Its repudiation by the masses is a kind of political analogue to the crucifixion of Christ as a criminal; for, as we have noted, never until the climactic monstrosity of his exile does Coriolanus effectively fail in the visible discharge of his political obligations.

It is not by accident that two anonymous officers of the Roman state debate the issues and reluctantly conclude that Coriolanus cannot properly be censured for his lack of diplomacy. There is choric force in their final judgment of his status:

> He hath deserved worthily of his country: and his ascent is not by such easy degrees as those who, having been supple and courteous to the people, bonneted, without any further deed to have them at all into their estimation and report: but he hath so planted his honours in their eyes, and his actions in their hearts, that for their tongues to be silent, and not confess so much, were a kind of ingrateful injury; to report otherwise, were a malice, that giving itself the lie, would pluck reproof and rebuke from every ear that heard it.
>
> (II.ii.27-38)

This is the political situation that Shakespeare has worked to establish: the confrontation of political institutions by a hero of undisguised virtue, a Henry V without cunning. The story of their interaction displays the inadequacy of the purely ethical view of politics that was taken by the *Mirrors for Magistrates,* with which the sixteenth century had attempted to vindicate the correlation between the failure of a ruler and his disregard of Christian ethics. Coriolanus seems to initially lack the Christian virtue of mercifulness (though even this he ultimately acquires), but he transgresses against few other premises of excellence in such moralizing historians as Hall: he is deliberately made a kind of classical Henry V in all but that guilefulness in which Shakespeare suggests that the Lancastrian kings anticipated Machiavelli. Shakespeare is thus able to demonstrate plausibly that unqualified virtue is not able to function in a normal political environment. Without his guile, Shakespeare implies, Henry V would readily have fallen into conspiracies himself, as his father had always anticipated that he would (*IHIV*, III.ii.122ff.).

Nor does Shakespeare allow us any simple escape from this sinister demonstration that your innocent man is your best traitor. It is true that Coriolanus' ultimate ambition for the consulship results from his unwise assent to the full extravagance of his mother's aspirations:

> I have lived
> To see inherited my very wishes
> And the buildings of my fancy: only
> There's one thing wanting, which I doubt
>   not but
> Our Rome will cast upon thee.
>
> (II.i.214-18)

Coriolanus' own good sense somewhat drily points up the difficulty that seeking the supreme political office will present for him:

> Know, good mother,
> I had rather be their servant in my way
> Than sway with them in theirs.
>
> (II.i.218-20)

But it will not serve to quote some of Coriolanus' later speeches in order to prove that he is unworthy of such political office because of that gross contempt for the citizenry which he ultimately extends to censure of the democratically amended constitution. The fact that he has, with whatever bad grace, undergone the full rigor of popular solicitation of votes and legally secured election, is formally established by Menenius:

> You have stood your limitation; and the
>   tribunes
> Endue you with the people's voice: remains
> That, in the official marks invested, you
> Anon do meet the senate.
>
> (II.iii.146-9)

It is the unjust attempt of the envious tribunes to revoke this concluded election (II.iii.225ff.) that alone launches Coriolanus onto a denunciation of the political situation:

> This double worship
> Where one part does disdain with cause, the other
> Insult without all reason, where gentry, title, wisdom,
> Cannot conclude but by the yea and no
> Of general ignorance,— it must omit
> Real necessities, and give way the while
> To unstable slightness: purpose so barr'd, it follows
> Nothing is done to purpose.
>
> (III.i.142-9)

He derives from this understandable judgment the inexpedient conclusion that the office of popularly elected tribune should be discontinued. The tribunes' flagrant abuse of authority in recalling the consular election, while it justifies his immediate personal reaction, does not necessarily justify the broader political conclusions he draws from it. Volumnia is right to reproach him only for sacrificing the ultimate authority of the consulship merely to indulge in local resentments, however natural:

> You are too absolute;
> Though therein you can never be too noble,
> But when extremities speak. I have heard you say,
> Honour and policy, like unsever'd friends,
> I' the war do grow together: grant that, and tell me,
> In peace what each of them by other lose,
> That they combine not here.
>
> (III.ii.39-45)

The admonition is just— and it is significant that Volumnia is already losing the initiative. It is no longer the sanction of her own ambition that she invokes, but the precision of Coriolanus' own best judgments. Once again, Coriolanus proves ultimately amenable to good sense: despite his disgust at the "harlot's spirit" required (III.ii.112), he undertakes to adjust himself to the requirements of the political situation without any reservation or hesitation: "the word is 'mildly.'" (III.ii.142) It is only the willful malice of the tribunes that could cause him to break this promise, and it is hard to see how he could avoid resentment at the charge of being "a traitor to the people" (III.iii.66), in view of the near-fatal risks he has so recently borne in Rome's service. Indeed, to endure the charge would be almost as dangerous as to denounce it. It is apparent that we have here the political equivalent of Cordelia's ethical dilemma in the face of Lear's invitation to participate in her sisters' dishonest and mercenary protestations of filial devotion. The real traitors to Rome are, of course, the tribunes who (unlike Coriolanus) *have* violated the constitution; but by the viciousness implicit in

this very act they are enabled without a qualm to slander with the name of their own guilt anyone whose position threatens theirs.

Strict virtue is shown to be immediately powerless in such a situation, though it is not ultimately so— for both Cordelia and Coriolanus lead an enemy army against the homeland whose magistrates have insisted on labeling them as traitors before the event. Their accusers thus almost succeed in bringing the initially false identification to the point of realization. If one is already treated as criminal, it is the rare spirit indeed that will not ultimately live up to the charge, as Shakespeare himself observed ruefully:

> 'Tis better to be vile than vile esteem'd,
> When not to be receives reproach of being,
> And the just pleasure lost which is so deem'd
> Not by our feeling but by others' seeing.
>
> (*Sonnet 121*, 1-4)

The only effective way to meet the insidious designs of the corrupt politician at the moment of crisis is thus to duplicate them, and this Coriolanus scrupulously refuses to do in any real sense. It is in this spirit of integrity that he reverses the tribunes' sentence of exile in the paradoxical assertion to the mob, "I banish you" (III.iii.123). In a very definite sense, he is the true spirit of Rome, and where he is, civic virtue is— thus, the people he leaves are really being separated from their own true state, and, as he says, "I shall be loved when I am lack'd" (IV.i.15)— just as Cordelia is.

One cannot see how Coriolanus could have behaved otherwise without dishonesty. The political syllogism is as complete and inescapable as the ethical dilemma that confronts Cordelia in defining the relationship between a loving father and a marriageable daughter. Menenius' rueful comment on Coriolanus is true of Cordelia as well: "His nature is too noble for the world" (III.i.255). In order to avoid simplifications of this almost irresolvable tension, Shakespeare is careful to define the elements of his argument early in *Coriolanus*. On the one hand, a citizen firmly establishes the real status of the electoral power to deny the consulship that is vested in the populace:

> We have power in ourselves to do it, but it is a power that we have no power to do; for if he show us his wounds and tell us his deeds, we are to put our tongues into those wounds and speak for them; so, if he tells us his noble deeds, we must also tell him our noble acceptance of them. Ingratitude is monstrous, and for the multitude to be ingrateful, were to make a monster of the multitude; of the which we being members, should bring ourselves to be monstrous members.
>
> (II.iii.4-13)

The withdrawal of the affirmed vote is thus a monstrous act in the very terms proposed by the play, nor do Coriolanus' sentiments justify it, even though they are couched in terms directly contrary to those of the citizen's speech above:

> Better it is to die, better to starve,
> Than crave the hire which first we do deserve.
> Why in this woolvish toge should I stand
>   here,
> To beg of Hob and Dick, that do appear,
> Their needless vouches? Custom calls me to't:
> What custom wills, in all things should we
>   do't,
> The dust on antique time would lie unswept
> And mountainous error be too highly heapt
> For truth to o'er-peer. Rather than fool it so,
> Let the high office and the honour go
> To one that would do thus. I am half
>   through;
> The one part suffer'd, the other will I do.
>
> (II.iii.120-31)

There is an interesting contrast between the citizens' speciousness, and the surly assent to duty of Coriolanus' last line and a half. Shakespeare's presentation of the two patterns provides an analogy to the parable of the Two Sons (Matthew, 21:28-32). There is no doubt who here corresponds to the son who accepts his father's orders as legitimate and then fails to abide by them, and who matches the son that denounces the orders but finally obeys them. Offensive as his speech may be to democrats and constitutionalists, Coriolanus is surly but honest; more important, he proves invariably law-abiding in the long run, however unlikely this may appear, as, for example, when he is about to lead Rome's enemies into the city.

We sympathize with the citizen of whom Coriolanus crudely inquires, "I pray, your price o'the consulship?" only to get the modest reply: "The price is to ask it kindly" (II.iii.81). Improbably enough, Coriolanus finally agrees to do just that, although with a witty minimum of insincerity:

> I will, sir, flatter my sworn brother, the people, to earn a dearer estimation of them; 'tis a condition they account gentle: and since the wisdom of their choice is rather to have my hat than my heart, I will practise the insinuating nod and be off to them most counterfeitly; that is, sir, I will counterfeit the bewitchment of some popular man and give it bountiful to the desirers. Therefore, beseech you, I may be consul.
>
> (II.iii.101-10)

It is a brilliantly ironic but scarcely dishonest performance, for once neatly designed to appear gracious yet not to disavow the speaker's contempt for solicited popularity. It cleverly states the issue in a form that is true to the speaker's belief yet inaccessible to the careless audience of citizens, who at once, symbolically, commit themselves to Coriolanus, a man who here really despises them. This is a neat validation of Coriolanus' argument against the judgment of the crowd, and the ambivalence of its usual heroes. Only a man who thus covertly despises the mob can rule it. However, for all his open contempt for the new constitution, the more carefully one examines the actual behavior of Coriolanus, the harder it is to show that he is guilty of any failure to observe the law before his exile. He merely *says* shocking and ungracious things; but it is a pitiful charge against a man to say that he has intolerant opinions or mother-induced motives, if all his *acts* reveal a genuine submission to the will of the majority. If we bear this in mind, it must seem strange to make his final mercy to Rome such a theme for contemptuous criticism as it often is.

We are now in a position to resolve such problems of characterization, and the political issues raised by the last two acts of the play, acts in which Coriolanus appears to behave in a way— both traitorous and vacillating— that belies the substantial integrity of his previous behavior. There is no doubt that for a time the simpler Coriolanus surrenders to that instinct for revenge that Hamlet is subtle enough to resist from the start, even though the admonition of his father's ghost is at least as compelling an incentive as the Roman evaluation of Coriolanus as a confirmed traitor. In his overprompt reaction, Coriolanus thus makes the same mistake as Othello, confounding understandable private resentment with an objective justification for harsh punishment of the offender. As a result, Coriolanus is rapidly betrayed into the same kind of appalling dilemma as faced Macbeth: he cannot either proceed or abandon his assault on Rome, without betraying himself: "Returning were as tedious as go o'er."

The bitter irony of Coriolanus' last campaign is that he cannot win it— as his mother, reduced at last to mere wisdom, lucidly points out:

> Thou know'st, great son,
> The end of war's uncertain, but this is certain,
> That, if thou conquer Rome, the benefit
> Which thou shalt thereby reap is such a
>   name,
> Whose reputation shall be dogg'd with curses,
> Whose chronicle thus writ: 'The man was
>   noble,
> But with his last attempt he wiped it out;
> Destroy'd his country, and his name remains
> To the ensuing age abhorr'd.'
>
> (V.iii.140-8)

The only conceivable alternative to this, as she plausibly represents it, is that:

> . . . thou
> Must, as a foreign recreant, be led
> With manacles through our streets.
>
> (V.iii.113-15)

It is this pair of equally impossible alternatives that accounts for the otherwise implausible surrender of command of the Coriolian army to Coriolanus by his bitterest enemy, Aufidius. The Coriolian perceives the ultimate impossibility of Coriolanus' position and is therefore content to give way to him, because:

> When, Caius, Rome is thine,
> Thou art poor'st of all; then shortly art thou
> mine.
>
> (IV.vii.56-7)

In contemplating the solution to the dilemma achieved by Coriolanus, we must note how the whole situation irresistibly frames itself in Christian terms, which proved far less relevant to *Julius Caesar.* It appears that, the more deeply Shakespeare saturates himself in the politics of pagan Rome, the more inescapable become the terms of reference proposed to him by the New Testament. Thus, when Cominius reports the terms of Coriolanus' refusal of his pleas, he unmistakably reverses Christ's parable of the weeds in the wheat (Matthew, 13:24-30):

> I offer'd to awaken his regard
> For's private friends: his answer to me was,
> He could not stay to pick them in a pile
> Of noisome musty chaff: he said 'twas folly,
> For one poor grain or two, to leave unburnt,
> And still to nose the offence.
>
> (V.i.23-8)

The contrast with even the less liberal spirit of the Old Testament is conspicuous: Abraham's negotiations with God to spare Sodom (Genesis, 18:23-32) ultimately secure the agreement that the city will be spared if a mere ten of its citizens prove virtuous. The fiercer severity of Coriolanus is testimony to his nearly diabolical resentment. Cominius rightly presents him as a kind of pathological case: "He was a kind of nothing" (V.i.13). Coriolanus has become, as the result of his monstrous treatment, unamenable to traditional terms:

> He is their god: he leads them like a thing
> Made by some other deity than nature.
>
> (IV.vi.90-1)

As long as Coriolanus remains in this non-human state of mind, Rome is doomed by the results of its own actions. Menenius can do no more than ruefully anticipate the terms of Christianity, as the Romans' only (and, unlikely) hope:

> We are all undone, unless
> The noble man have mercy.
>
> (IV.vi.107-8)

How paradoxical such an act must appear in a pagan context is suggested when Aufidius begins to realize

that it is toward this course that Coriolanus is directing himself:

> I am glad thou hast set thy mercy and thy
> honour
> At difference in thee: out of that I'll work
> Myself a former fortune.
>
> (V.iii.199-201)

To Aufidius, it is a dangerous weakness that one's personal honor (and well-being) should be subject to a higher and often conflicting order of values, which might be deliberately preferred.

As for Coriolanus, what makes him conscious of this higher order is, of course, the self-abasement of his once lordly mother. He suddenly realizes that, if any order is to be maintained in the world, it must be at the price of surrendering the inflexible application of principle, which otherwise will end by turning the world upside-down:

> What is this:
> Your knees to me? to your corrected son?
> Then let the pebbles on the hungry beach
> Fillip the stars; then let the mutinous winds
> Strike the proud cedars 'gainst the fiery sun;
> Murdering impossibility, to make
> What cannot be, slight work.
>
> (V.iii.56-62)

The son recognizes that his mother's gesture of humility is an example to him, in his relation to his erring motherland, for which she is a kind of figure at this point. Unlike Lear or Macbeth, Coriolanus does not allow his resentment against the fallibility of the world to commit him even temporarily to a nihilistic delight in universal disorder. Exactly as he has earlier stopped short of the brink of anarchic individualism, just when it had seemed that his ideas must commit him to unqualified action against the state's traditional forms, so now he subjects his instincts and his judgment to an intuition of a higher order of behavior, which preserves the state even while he is suffering from its deficiencies. He now consciously assents to that deep humility in the face of his wrongs which he had hitherto affected resentfully from time to time through mere policy, or outside pressure. Like Hamlet, Coriolanus ends by understanding and thus mastering his predicament.

The solution of his dilemma that is arrived at by Coriolanus is at the same time adequate, paradoxical, and personally fatal:

> Behold, the heavens do
> ope,
> The gods look down, and this unnatural
> scene
> They laugh at. O my mother, mother! O!
> You have won a happy victory to Rome;

But, for your son,— believe it, O, believe it,
Most dangerously you have with him
    prevail'd,
If not most mortal to him. But, let it come.
Aufidius, though I cannot make true wars,
I'll frame convenient peace.

                (V.iii.183-91)

The speech reflects a fascinating evolution of personality in that the dashing, bellicose young leader of the first act, ever spoiling for a fight, has now evolved into a peacemaker whose personal honor and very life is to be laid down in the interest of peace, "a man by his own alms empoison'd, / And with his charity slain" (V.vi.11-12). And it must be pointed out that the terms of the treaty are in fact happy for all parties: the sack of Rome has been averted, but the Coriolian army returns home laden with spoils, and with more advantage over Rome than they had ever hoped for in the past. Aufidius is able to alienate his compatriots from Coriolanus only by preventing the terms of the treaty from being publicly proclaimed. The play thus ends on a final note of irony: Coriolanus has won for Corioli as much by peaceful methods as he had won for Rome by war— and in each case he is ultimately rewarded by bitter popular hatred. Rome, under the influence of the tribunes, execrated and exiled him; Corioli, through a similar conspiracy led by Aufidius, also turns against him, and assassinates the worthiest man among them. It thus appears that the mob cannot be governed by the purely virtuous, in either state.

Plutarch drily notes that the Coriolians paid for their folly far more dearly than did the Romans. Once Coriolanus had been murdered, the Roman resurgence began, and "the whole state of the Volsces heartily wished him alive again." Finally "the Romans overcame them in battle, in which [Aufidius] was slain in the field, and the flower of all their force was put to the sword; so that they were compelled to accept most shameful conditions of peace." Shakespeare shows us none of this, except to display the Coriolians' crude misunderstanding of the last phase of Coriolanus' career:

        His own impatience
Takes from Aufidius a great part of the blame.
Let's make the best of it.

                (V.vi.146-8)

Obviously Shakespeare has little hope of an advance or even a variation in political awareness as a result of Coriolanus' career. Yet the truth remains that Coriolanus' conduct has been a salutary example of how— even by audiences, and by generations of critics like ourselves— facts are often forgotten, so that the best may readily appear the worst. More positively, the play shows how an attempt at the greatest wrong may lead to awareness of the highest good.

Perhaps Shakespeare was also not unaware of the theme's relevance to the execution of Essex, the friend of his patron, for similarly challenging the established order. Unfortunately, Essex had few of Coriolanus' moral virtues and most of his political defects, so that his career could never stand as an epitome of the irresolvable tension between the virtues that vindicate a leader and the dubious skills by which he necessarily maintains his authority. In *Coriolanus* Shakespeare convinced himself that these opposites could *not* be reconciled; thereafter, he concerned himself chiefly with man as a complex individual primarily learning how to manage his personal relationships— often at the cost of political success. In a sense, our own responses to Coriolanus suggest why politics no longer seems worthy of interest to Shakespeare. He demonstrates that, in political affairs, men are not meaningfully interested in what others really do, but only in what they seem to be. Coriolanus is thus the great corollary of Milton's Satan: Satan appears truly heroic, yet acts with uniform destructiveness; Coriolanus perpetually appears intolerable to us, yet always acts for the best. Both are studies addressed to the purging of misjudgment from their audiences. Looking back over the similar reversals of our expectations revealed in our study of earlier Shakespearean characters, like Henry V and Brutus, we may well conclude that it is indeed just this kind of challenge to simplifying political judgments which constitutes the distinctive cathartic function of Shakespeare's political plays.

HONOR AND HEROISM

Many critics have examined the destructive potential of Coriolanus's uncompromising belief in personal honor. Charles Mitchell has equated Coriolanus's obsession with honor with his quest for political power. As Coriolanus is a man of action, his ethical perspective derives principally from his belief in the aristocratic virtue of honor even if this belief is detrimental to society as a whole. Mitchell contends that "for Coriolanus public power signifies personal honor" and the Roman "cannot concede the possibility of power's being divided between master (the aristocrat) and servant (the plebeian)." **Eugene M. Waith** has enumerated Coriolanus's godlike qualities and argued that the hero's acts of courage correspond to those of the classical Greek demi-god Hercules and that Shakespeare's work, therefore, is a "heroic drama" rather than a tragedy." D. J. Gordon has analyzed Shakespeare's critique of honor in *Coriolanus*, seeing the play as a demonstration of the destructive results that honor won in war may bring about when displaced onto civil society.

Other commentators have also recognized the negative effects of Coriolanus's heroic nature, but acknowledged Shakespeare's ironic and paradoxical use of aristocratic virtues in characterizing his protagonist. **Matthew N. Proser** has considered Coriolanus's heroic flaw of unyielding constancy, which when linked to the Roman warrior's lack of an introspective capacity worsens the chaotic situation in Rome. Phyllis Rackin has described the tragedy as a critique of the Roman ideal of *virtus*, a narrow concept of valor that prizes "masculine" traits and considers warfare superior to love. Rackin has also underscored the irony in the fact that a woman, Volumnia, is responsible for Coriolanus's rigid adherence to this limited ideal and for his rejection of the values that "bind the human community together."

Eugene M. Waith

SOURCE: "The Herculean Hero" (originally entitled "Shakespeare"), in *The Herculean Hero in Marlowe, Chapman, Shakespeare and Dryden*, 1962. Reprinted in *Modern Critical Interpretations: William Shakespeare's 'Coriolanus,'* edited by Harold Bloom, Chelsea House Publishers, 1988, pp. 9-31.

[*In the excerpt below (originally published in 1962), Waith views the figure of Coriolanus as a hero in the tradition of Hercules. Pride and anger are Coriolanus's defining characteristics, according to Waith, and lead to his tragic end. The critic emphasizes the paradoxical quality of Coriolanus's nature, and observes the method of Coriolanus's heroic characterization, which he sees as achieved through contrast with Aufidius, Volumnia, and Menenius. Coriolanus envies the nobility of Aufidius. He also lacks the sound judgment of Menenius, and is motivated by honor rather than a thirst for power—unlike Volumnia. However, Waith observes, these qualities render Coriolanus inflexible and unsympathetic, and ironically they precipitate his downfall at the moment he demonstrates a lapse in his proud nature by giving in to the demands of his mother.*]

As Coriolanus marches on Rome at the head of a Volscian army, the Roman general, Cominius, describes him thus to his old enemies, the tribunes:

> He is their god. He leads them like a thing
> Made by some other deity than Nature,
> That shapes man better; and they follow him
> Against us brats with no less confidence
> Than boys pursuing summer butterflies
> Or butchers killing flies.
>
> . . . . .
> He will shake
> Your Rome about your ears
>
> (4.6,90-94, 98-99)

To which Menenius adds: "As Hercules / Did shake down mellow fruit." In these words Coriolanus is not only presented as a god and compared to Hercules; he is "like a thing / Made by some other deity than Nature." So extraordinary is he that even his troops, inspired by him, feel themselves to be as much superior to the Romans as boys to butterflies or butchers to flies. Like Menaphon's description of Tamburlaine ("Such breadth

of shoulders as might mainly bear / Old Atlas' burthen") and Cleopatra's of Antony ("His legs bestrid the ocean"), this description of Coriolanus is central to Shakespeare's depiction of his hero. His superhuman bearing and his opposition to Rome are the two most important facts about him.

The godlike qualities of Shakespeare's Coriolanus need to be emphasized in an era which has tended to belittle him. He has been treated recently as a delayed adolescent who has never come to maturity, a "splendid oaf [John Palmer]," a mother's boy, a figure so lacking in dignity that he cannot be considered a tragic hero. The catastrophe has been said to awaken amusement seasoned with contempt. In spite of some impressive protests against this denigration, the heroic stature of one of Shakespeare's largest figures remains somewhat obscured.

That he often cuts an unsympathetic figure (especially in the eyes of the twentieth century) is not surprising. His very superiority repels sympathy, while his aristocratic contempt of the plebeians shocks the egalitarian. His pride and anger provide a convenient and conventional basis of disapproval for those who share the tribunes' view that:

> Caius Marcius was
> A worthy officer i' th' war, but insolent,
> O'ercome with pride, ambitious past all
>   thinking,
> Self-loving—
>
> (4.6.29-32)

Pride and anger, as we have seen [elsewhere], are among the distinguishing characteristics of the Herculean hero; without them he would not be what he is.

In one major respect the story of Coriolanus departs from that of his heroic prototype: Coriolanus submits to the entreaties of Volumnia and spares Rome. At this moment he is more human and more humane than at any other in the play, and it is the decision of this moment which leads directly to his destruction. Ironically, the one action of which most of his critics approve is "most mortal" to him. He is murdered not so much because he is proud as because of an intermission in his pride.

The portrait of Coriolanus is built up by means of contrasts. Some of them are absolute, such as those with the people and the tribunes. Others are modified by resemblances: the contrasts with his fellow-patricians, his enemy Aufidius, and his mother Volumnia. Such a dialectical method of presentation is reminiscent of Seneca and recalls even more precisely the technique of Marlowe in *Tamburlaine*. Something closely akin to it is used in *Bussy D'Ambois* and *Antony and Cleopatra*. In all of these plays sharply divergent views of the hero

A battle scene from the University of Washington's 1998 theatre production of Coriolanus.

call attention to an essential paradox in his nature. The technique is brilliantly suited to the dramatization of such heroes, but, as the critical response to these plays has shown, it has the disadvantage of stirring serious doubts about the genuineness of the heroism. Readers, as opposed to spectators, have been especially susceptible to these misgivings, since they had before them no actor to counter by the very nobility of his bearing the devastating effect of hostile views. Readers of *Coriolanus* seem to have adopted some or all of the opposition views of the hero's character.

The contrast between Coriolanus and the citizens of Rome is antipodal. Whatever he most basically is they are not, and this contrast is used as the introduction to his character. The "mutinous citizens" who occupy the stage as the play begins are not entirely a despicable lot. It is clear enough that they represent a dangerous threat to the established order, but some of them speak with wisdom and tolerance. For one citizen who opposes Coriolanus because "he's a very dog to the commonalty" (ll. 28-29) there is another who recalls the warrior's

services to Rome, and resentment of his pride is balanced against recognition of his lack of covetousness. These citizens, in their opening words and later in their conversation with Menenius, are neither remarkably bright nor stupid, neither models of good nature nor of malice. They are average people, and this may be the most important point about them. Their failings are as common as their virtues: in both we see the limitations of their horizons. Incapable of heroic action themselves, they are equally incapable of understanding a heroic nature. The more tolerant citizen in the first scene excuses the pride of Coriolanus by saying he cannot help it (l. 42), and hence should not be judged too harshly. In a later scene the citizens complain to Coriolanus that he doesn't love them. One of them tells him that the price of the consulship is "to ask it kindly" (2.3.81), a demand which has received enthusiastic approval from several modern critics. The citizens want the great warrior to be jolly and friendly with them, so that they may indulge in the luxury of treating him as a lovable eccentric. From the moment of his first entrance it is obvious that he will never allow them this luxury.

The first impression we are given of him is of his intemperance and his scorn of the people. Menenius Agrippa, one that, in the words of the Second Citizen, "hath always loved the people," has just cajoled them with his fable of the belly into a less rebellious mood when the warrior enters and delivers himself of a blistering tirade. The citizens are "dissentious rogues," "scabs," "curs," "hares," "geese," finally "fragments." He reminds them of their cowardice and inconstancy. But the most devastating part of his speech is the accusation that the citizens prefer to give their allegiance to a man humbled by a punishment which they will call unjust:

> Your virtue is
> To make him worthy whose offense subdues
>   him
> And curse that justice did it.
>
> (1.1.178-80)

What they cannot tolerate except in the crises of war is a greatness which lifts a man far beyond their reach.

In making his accusations Caius Marcius, as he is then called, reveals his reverence for valour, constancy and a great spirit, as well as his utter contempt for those who will never attain such virtues. We may suspect immediately what the rest of the play makes clear, that these are his own virtues. However, since they are displayed by a speech whose tone is so angry and contemptuous— so politically outrageous, when compared to the clever performance of Menenius— they are less apt to win liking than respect. We are confronted by the extraordinary in the midst of the average, a whole man amidst "fragments."

In succeeding scenes with the citizenry the indications of the first scene are developed. The battle at Corioles, where he wins his cognomen Coriolanus, is of course the key scene for the demonstration of valour, "the chiefest virtue," as Cominius later reminds the senators in describing the exploits of Coriolanus (2.2.87-88). Before the sally of the Volscians the Roman soldiers flee in miserable confusion, providing a pat example of their cowardice and bringing on themselves another volley of curses from their leader. Everything in the scene heightens the contrast between him and them. "I'll leave the foe / And make my wars on you!" he threatens; "Follow me!" (1.4.39-42). When his courageous pursuit of the Volscians into their city is followed by the closing of their gate we are presented with the ultimate contrast and an emblem of the hero's situation: he is one against the many, whether the many are enemies or fellow countrymen. As Shakespeare presents this astounding feat it borders on the supernatural. Coriolanus is given Herculean strength. The simple statement of a soldier sums it up: "He is himself alone,

/ To answer all the city (ll.51-52). Titus Lartius, supposing him dead, adds an encomium in which the qualities he has just demonstrated are converted into an icon:

> A carbuncle entire, as big as thou art,
> Were not so rich a jewel. Thou wast a soldier
> Even to Cato's wish, not fierce and terrible
> Only in strokes, but with thy grim looks and
> The thunder-like percussion of thy sounds
> Thou mad'st thine enemies shake, as if the
>   world
> Were feverous and did tremble.
>
> (1.4.55-61)

When the battle is won, the soldiers set about plundering the city; Caius Marcius, matching his valour with generosity, refuses any reward but the name of Coriolanus which he has earned. No doubt there is a touch of pride in such conspicuous self-denial, but the magnificence of the gesture is what counts. It is not contrasted with true humility but with pusillanimity and covetousness.

Coriolanus is not indifferent to the opinion of others, but he insists upon being valued for his accomplishments, and not for "asking kindly":

> Better it is to die, better to starve,
> Than crave the hire which first we do deserve.
>
> (2.3.120-21)

The question of his absolute worth— the central question of the play— is posed in an uncompromising form in the scenes where Coriolanus is made to seek the approval of the citizens. Though his reluctance to boast of his exploits, to show his wounds, or to speak to the people with any genuine warmth does not immediately lose him their votes, it has cost him the approval of many critics. In itself, however, this reluctance stems from a virtue and a major one. He refuses to seem other than he is and refuses to change his principles to suit the situation. The citizens, meanwhile, unsure what to think, first give him their "voices," and then are easily persuaded by the tribunes to change their minds. Again the contrast is pat, and however unlovely the rigidity of Coriolanus may be, its merit is plain when seen next to such paltry shifting. That it is a terrible and in some ways inhuman merit is suggested in the ironical words of the tribune Brutus: "You speak o' th' people / As if you were a god to punish, not / A man of their infirmity" (3.1.80-32). Later Menenius says without irony: "His nature is too noble for the world. / He would not flatter Neptune for his trident / Or Jove for's power to thunder" (3.1.255-57).

The greatness of Coriolanus is seen not only in his extraordinary valour and generosity but in his absolute rejection of anything in which he does not believe. In this scene he is urged to beg for something which he deserves, to flatter people whom he despises, and to conceal or modify his true beliefs. His refusal to do any of these things is manifested in a crescendo of wrath, defending his heroic integrity. The culmination is a violent denunciation of the plebeians for their ignorance, cowardice, disloyalty and inconsistency. Both friends and enemies attempt to stop the flow of this tirade, but Coriolanus rushes on with the force of an avalanche. The quality of the speech can be seen only in an extensive quotation:

> No, take more!
> What may be sworn by, both divine and
>   human,
> Seal what I end withal! This double wor-
>   ship—
> Where one part does disdain with cause, the
>   other
> Insult without all reason; where gentry, title,
>   wisdom
> Cannot conclude but by the yea and no
> Of general ignorance— it must omit
> Real necessities, and give way the while
> To unstable slightness. Purpose so barr'd, it
>   follows
> Nothing is done to purpose. Therefore,
>   beseech you—
> You that will be less fearful than discreet;
> That love the fundamental part of state
> More than you doubt the change on't; that
>   prefer
> A noble life before a long, and wish
> To jump a body with a dangerous physic
> That's sure of death without it— at once
>   pluck out
> The multitudinous tongue; let them not lick
> The sweet which is their poison. Your
>   dishonour
> Mangles true judgment, and bereaves the state
> Of that integrity which should become't,
> Not having the power to do the good it
>   would
> For th'ill which doth control't.
>
> (3.1.140-61)

It seems almost impertinent to object to the lack of moderation in this speech. In the great tumble of words, whose forward movement is constantly altered and augmented by parenthetical developments, excess is as characteristic of the presentation as of the emotions expressed, yet one hardly feels that such excess is a matter of degree. What is conveyed here could not be brought within the range of a normally acceptable political statement by modifying here and there an overforceful phrase. It is of another order entirely, and excess is its mode of being. The words of Coriolanus's denunciation of the plebeians are the exact analogue of the sword-strokes with which he fights his way alone into Corioles. Rapid, violent and unbelievably numerous, they express the wrath which accompanies heroic

valour. However horrifying they may be, they are also magnificent. Both approval and disapproval give way to awe, as they do in the terrible scenes of Hercules' wrath.

In the scenes which bring to a culmination the quarrel of Coriolanus and the Roman people the great voice of the hero is constantly surrounded by lesser voices which oppose it— the friends, who urge moderation, the tribunes, who foment discord, and the people, who respond to each new suggestion. The words "tongue," "mouth" and "voice" are reiterated, "voice" often having the meaning of "vote." We hear the scorn of Coriolanus for the voices of the many in his words: "The tongues o' th' common mouth," "Have I had children's voices?" "Must these have voices, that can yield them now / And straight disclaim their tongues? . . . You being their mouths, why rule you not their teeth?" (3.1.22, 30, 34-36, 155-56). As for the hero, we are told by Menenius, "His heart's his mouth; / What his breast forges, that his tongue must vent" (3.1.257-58), and when, shortly after, the "multitudinous tongue" accuses him of being a traitor to the people, he makes the speech which leads directly to his banishment: "The fires i' th' lowest hell fold-in the people!" (3.3.68). It is the final answer of the heroic voice to the lesser voices.

The contrast is also realized dramatically in the movement of these scenes, for around the figure of Coriolanus, standing his ground and fighting, the crowd swirls and eddies. Coriolanus and the patricians enter to a flourish of trumpets; to them the tribunes enter. After the hero's lengthy denunciation of the people, they are sent for by the tribunes. The stage business is clearly indicated in the directions: "Enter a rabble of *Plebeians* with the *Aediles*." "*They all bustle about Coriolanus.*" "*Coriolanus draws his sword.*" "*In this mutiny the Tribunes, the Aediles, and the People are beat in.*" "*A noise within.*" "Enter *Brutus* and *Sicinius* with the *Rabble* again" (3.1.180, 185, 223, 229, 260, 263).

If Shakespeare does not make the many-voiced, ceaselessly shifting people hateful, he also makes it impossible to respect them. M. W. MacCallum shows that while the people are given more reason to fear Coriolanus than they are in Plutarch, their original uprising is made considerably less justifiable. Whether or not Shakespeare reveals a patrician bias in his portrayal of them, there can be no doubt that he shares the distrust of popular government common to his time. Condescension qualifies whatever sympathy he shows.

Coriolanus cannot be condescended to. He belongs to another world, as he makes clear in his final denunciation of the people in response to their verdict of banishment:

> You common cry of curs, whose breath I hate

As reek o' th' rotten fens, whose loves I
  prize
As the dead carcasses of unburied men
That do corrupt my air, I banish you!

· · · · ·

                          Despising
For you the city, thus I turn my back.
There is world elsewhere.

                          (3.3.120-23, 133-35)

That world is the forbidding world of heroes, from which he promises his friends:

                     you shall
Hear from me still, and never of me aught
But what is like me formerly.

                          (4.1.51-53)

The tribunes are portrayed much less favourably than the people, though, surprisingly, they have eager apologists among the critics. Less foolish than the plebeians, they are more malicious. Motivated by political ambition, they provoke sedition, encouraging the plebeians to change their votes, and baiting Coriolanus with insults. When the exiled Coriolanus is marching on Rome "like a thing / Made by some other deity than nature," they appear almost as small and insignificant as the people themselves.

The contrast with these scheming politicians establishes the honesty of Coriolanus and his lack of ulterior motives. He has political convictions rather than ambitions. Though he believes that his services to Rome deserve the reward of the consulship, the wielding of political power does not in itself interest him, nor is it necessary to him as an expression of authority. He is dictatorial without being like a modern dictator. The tribunes, who accuse him of pride, are fully as jealous of their prerogatives as he is, and far more interested in increasing them. Coriolanus's nature, compared to theirs, seems both larger and more pure.

Certain aspects of this heroic nature come out most clearly in contrasts between Coriolanus and his fellow patricians. Menenius is to Coriolanus what Horatio is to Hamlet. Horatio's poise and his freedom from the tyranny of passion show him to be what would be called today a "better adjusted" person than Hamlet; yet Hamlet's lack of what he admires in his friend reveals the stresses of a much rarer nature. No one mistakes Horatio for a hero. Similarly, Menenius is far better than Coriolanus at "getting on" with people. In the first scene of the play his famous fable of the belly, told with a fine combination of good humour and firmness, calms the plebeians. When Coriolanus, after his glorious victory, objects to soliciting votes by showing his wounds in the Forum, Menenius urges, "Pray you go fit you to the custom" (2.2.146). After the banishment he says to the tribunes in a conciliating fashion, "All's well, and

might have been much better if / He could have temporiz'd" (4.6.16-17). Menenius's ability to temporize and fit himself to the custom has made him liked on all sides, but this striking evidence of political success does not guarantee him the unqualified respect of the spectator. Dennis erred only in exaggerating, when he called Menenius a buffoon.

In contrast to this jolly patrician, always ready to compromise, the austerity and fixity of Coriolanus stand out. To Plutarch, writing as a moralist and historian, it is lamentable that Coriolanus lacks "the gravity and affability that is gotten with judgement of learning and reason, which only is to be looked for in a governor of state," but though the lack is equally apparent in Shakespeare's tragedy, the conclusion to be drawn differs as the point of view of tragedy differs from that of history. Plutarch judges Coriolanus as a potential governor. He finds that a deficient education has made him "too full of passion and choler" and of wilfulness, which Plutarch says "is the thing of the world, which a governor of a commonwealth for pleasing should shun, being that which Plato called solitariness." The tragedy of *Coriolanus,* for all its political concern, is not contrived to expose either the deficiencies of the protagonist as a governor (though all the evidence is presented) or the unreliability of the plebeians and their representatives (which could be taken for granted). What Shakespeare insists on is an extraordinary force of will and a terrible "solitariness" characteristic of this hero. No contrast in the play brings these out more clearly than the contrast with Menenius.

The change in emphasis from history to the heroic is clearly evident in Shakespeare's treatment of Aufidius. In Plutarch's account he is not mentioned until the time of the banishment, when Coriolanus offers himself as a general to the Volsces. At this point, however, Plutarch states that Aufidius was noble and valiant, that the two had often encountered in battle and that they had "a marvellous private hate one against the other." From these hints Shakespeare makes the figure of the worthy antagonist, who is a part of the story of so many heroes. The rivalry is mentioned in the very first scene of the play, and is made one of the deepest motives of the hero's conduct. He envies the nobility of Aufidius,

    And were I anything but what I am,
    I would wish me only he. . . .
    Were half to half the world by th'ears, and he
    Upon my party, I'd revolt, to make
    Only my wars with him. He is a lion
    That I am proud to hunt.

                         (1.1.235-40)

To fight with Aufidius is the ultimate test of Coriolanus's valour— of his warrior's areté. And because the rival warrior most nearly shares his own ideals, the relationship takes on an intense intimacy. Shakespeare introduces Aufidius unhistorically into the battle at Corioles. We discover that although Aufidius reciprocates the feelings of Coriolanus, he is prepared after his defeat at Corioles to use dishonourable means, if necessary, to destroy his enemy, but of this Coriolanus knows nothing, nor is there any hint of it when Aufidius later welcomes Coriolanus as an ally:

> Let me twine
> Mine arms about that body whereagainst
> My grained ash an hundred times hath broke
> And scarr'd the moon with splinters.
> . . . . .
> Know thou first,
> I lov'd the maid I married; never man
> Sigh'd truer breath. But that I see thee here,
> Thou noble thing, more dances my rapt heart
> Than when I first my wedded mistress saw
> Bestride my threshold.
>
> (4.5.111-14, 118-23)

Plutarch's Aufidius makes only a brief and formal speech acknowledging the honour Coriolanus does him. Shakespeare's invention of a long speech, loaded with the metaphors of love, is the more striking at this point, since the preceding speech by Coriolanus follows Plutarch very closely indeed. The strong bond between the rival warriors is obviously important.

It is sometimes thought highly ironic that Coriolanus, who prides himself on his constancy, should be guilty of the supreme inconstancy of treason to his country. In fact, however reprehensible he may be, he is not inconstant. Shakespeare makes it clear that his first allegiance is always to his personal honour. The fickleness of the mob and the scheming of the tribunes have deprived him of his deserts, much as Agamemnon's seizure of Briseis deprives Achilles. Both this threat to his honour and an ambivalent love-hatred draw Coriolanus to the enemy whom he considers almost an alter ego.

Resemblances or fancied resemblances between the two warriors establish the supremacy of the heroic ideal in Coriolanus's scale of values, but we cannot doubt which of them more nearly encompasses the ideal. As we watch the progress of their alliance, we see Aufidius becoming increasingly jealous and finally working for the destruction of his rival even while he treats him almost as a mistress. In defence of his conduct he asserts that Coriolanus has seduced his friends with flattery, but there is no evidence to support this unlikely accusation. Malice and double-dealing are quite absent from the nature of Coriolanus.

The ill-will mixed with Aufidius's love serves another purpose than contrast, however: it adds considerable weight to his praise of Coriolanus to other characters, such as that contained in a long speech to his lieutenant:

> All places yield to him ere he sits down,
> And the nobility of Rome are his;
> The senators and patricians love him too.
> The tribunes are no soldiers, and their people
> Will be as rash in the repeal as hasty
> To expel him thence. I think he'll be to
>   Rome
> As is the osprey to the fish, who takes it
> By sovereignty of nature. First he was
> A noble servant to them, but he could not
> Carry his honours even. Whether 'twas pride,
> Which out of daily fortune ever taints
> The happy man; whether defect of judgment,
> To fail in the disposing of those chances
> Which he was lord of; or whether nature,
> Not to be other than one thing, not moving
> From th' casque to th' cushion, but com-
>   manding peace
> Even with the same austerity and garb
> As he controll'd the war; but one of these
> (As he hath spices of them all, not all,
> For I dare so far free him) made him
>   fear'd,
> So hated, and so banish'd. But he has a
>   merit
> To choke it in the utt'rance. So our virtues
> Lie in th' interpretation of the time;
> And power, unto itself most commend-
>   able,
> Hath not a tomb so evident as a chair
> T'extol what it hath done.
> One fire drives out one fire; one nail, one
>   nail;
> Rights by rights falter, strengths by strengths
>   do fail.
> Come, let's away. When, Caius, Rome is
>   thine,
> Thou art poor'st of all; then shortly art thou
>   mine.
>
> (4.7.28-57)

Surely, what is most remarkable in this account of failure is the emphasis on virtue. One thinks of Monsieur, telling Guise that Nature's gift of virtue is responsible for the death to which Bussy hastens at that very moment, led on by plots of Monsieur's contriving. In both cases the interests of the speaker are so exactly contrary to the tenor of their remarks that the character-analysis is given the force of absolute truth. Aufidius's speech has to be taken in its entirety, so dependent are its component parts on one another. Its frame is a realistic appraisal of the situation at Rome and of his own malicious purposes. Within is an intricate structure of praise and underlies the entire speech: the superiority of Coriolanus to Rome is as much in the order of nature as is the predominance of the osprey, who was thought to have the power of fascinating fish. Next comes Coriolanus's lack of equilibrium, a point which the play has thoroughly established. Aufidius then mentions three possible causes of failure, carefully qualifying the list by saying that in all probability only one was operative. Pride, the first, is presented as the natural temptation of the happy man, as it is in the medieval conception of fortune's wheel. The defect of judgment, mentioned next, recalls the contrast with Menenius, and the patent inability of Coriolanus to take advantage of his situation— to dispose "of those chances / Which he was lord of." Thus, the first cause of failure is a generic fault of the fortunate, while the second is a fault which distinguishes Coriolanus from a lesser man. The third is the inflexibility which makes him austere and fierce at all times. This is not only the most persuasive as an explanation of his troubles but is also the most characteristic of him. The comments which follow immediately— on the "merit to choke it in the utt'rance" and the virtues which "lie in th' interpretation of the time"— suggest redeeming features. They are not simply good qualities which can be balanced against the bad, but virtues inherent in some of the faults which have just been enumerated, or qualities which might be interpreted as either virtues or faults. The inflexibility is the best example. It is closely related to the other faults, to the lack of equilibrium, the pride, and the defect of judgment. Yet it is impossible to regard Coriolanus's refusal to compromise as entirely a fault. It is also his greatest strength. The concluding lines of the speech put forth a paradox even more bewildering, that power, rights and strengths often destroy themselves. Aufidius need only wait for his rival's success to have him in his power. The final emphasis falls entirely on virtue, with no mention of weakness or deficiency.

The eloquent couplet which sums up this paradox,

> One fire drives out one fire; one nail, one nail;
> Rights by rights falter, strengths by strengths
> do fail

is very like the lines . . . from Chapman's nearly contemporaneous *Tragedy of Charles, Duke of Byron:*

> We have not any strength but weakens us,
> No greatness but doth crush us into air.
> Our knowledges do light us but to err.

From this melancholy point of view the hero is only more certainly doomed than the average man.

Next to Coriolanus Volumnia is the most interesting character in the play— the Roman mother, whose influence over her son is so great and ultimately so fatal. In the first scene a citizen says of Coriolanus's services to Rome, "Though soft-conscienc'd men can be content to say it was for his country, he did it to please his mother and to be partly proud, which he is, even to the altitude of his virtue" (ll. 37-41). In the last act Coriolanus says,

> O my mother, mother! O!
> You have won a happy victory to Rome;
> But for your son— believe it, O believe it!—
> Most dangerously you have with him
>   prevail'd,
> If not most mortal to him.
>
> (5.3.185-89)

But powerful and obvious as this influence is, it should not be allowed to obscure the major differences between mother and son. Volumnia belongs to the world which Coriolanus, as hero, both opposes and seeks to redeem. She represents the city of Rome much more completely than Zenocrate represents the city of Damascus. She is by far the strongest of the forces which Rome brings to bear on him, and much of her strength derives from the fact that she seems at first so thoroughly committed to everything in which he believes. Only gradually do we discover what she truly represents.

In her first scene she is every inch the mother of a warrior, shocking timid Virgilia with grim speeches about a soldier's honour. We next see her welcome Coriolanus after his victory at Corioles, and make the significant remark that only one thing is wanting to fulfil her dreams— one thing "which I doubt not but / Our Rome will cast upon thee" (2.1.217-18)— obviously the consulship. Her son's reply foreshadows the conflict between them:

> Know, good mother,
> I had rather be their servant in my way
> Than sway with them in theirs.
>
> (2.1.218-20)

Volumnia wants power for her son as much as Lady Macbeth wants it for her husband. Coriolanus wants above all to do things "in his way."

Close to the center of the play occurs the first of the two conflicts between mother and son. There is no basis for the scene in Plutarch. It is an addition of great importance, contributing to the characterization of the principals and preparing for the famous interview in which Coriolanus is deterred from his vengeance on Rome. The issues engaged here are what separate Coriolanus from every other character.

He has just delivered his lengthy excoriation of the people, and is being urged by his friends to apologize. As Volumnia enters he asks her if she would wish him to be milder— to be false to his nature, and she, who proclaimed to Virgilia that life was not too great a price to pay for honour, gives him an answer based solely on political expediency: "I would have had you put your power well on, / Before you had worn it out" (3.2.17-18). She observes with great shrewdness, "You might have been enough the man you are / With striving less to be so," but she adds a sentence which shows that what she is advocating is politic concealment of Coriolanus's true nature:

> Lesser had been
> The thwarting of your dispositions, if
> You had not show'd them how ye were
>   dispos'd
> Ere they lack'd power to cross you.
>
> (ll. 19-23)

In the previous scene, where Coriolanus defied the people and the tribunes, the sincerity of his voice as compared to theirs was expressed in Menenius's words, "His heart's his mouth; / What his breast forges, that his tongue must vent." The same imagery is caught up here in the words in which Volumnia characterizes her attitude towards apologizing:

> I have a heart as little apt as yours,
> But yet a brain that leads my use of anger
> To better vantage.
>
> (ll. 29-31)

It is not in the least surprising that Menenius applauds this speech, as he does a later and longer one in which Volumnia urges Coriolanus to speak to the people not what his heart prompts,

> But with such words that are but roted in
> Your tongue, though but bastards and
>   syllables
> Of no allowance to your bosom's truth.
>
> (ll. 55-57)

Heart opposes the politician's brain and the orator's tongue in these speeches as honour opposes policy, even though Volumnia tries, by a specious parallel with the tactics of war, to persuade her son that honour can be mixed with a little policy and no harm done. Coriolanus, whom she accuses of being "too absolute," sees plainly that the two are not compatible:

>   Must I
> With my base tongue give to my noble heart
> A lie that it must bear?
>
> (ll. 99-101)

Volumnia has aligned herself firmly with the advocates of policy: that is, of compromise and hypocrisy. Without admitting it, she is one of the enemies of the "noble heart."

Under the stress of her passionate urging (she does not hesitate to mention that she will undoubtedly die with the rest of them if he refuses to take her advice), Coriolanus finally agrees to conceal his true nature, as Bussy, at the request of Tamyra, agrees that "policy

shall be flanked with policy." Some critics, taking a line similar to that of Volumnia, have chided Coriolanus for going from one extreme to another in his response to his mother. He says:

>   Well, I must do't.
> Away, my disposition, and possess me
> Some harlot's spirit!
>
> (ll. 110-12)

It is very difficult, however, to deny the keenness of his perception. He has agreed with great reluctance to do as his mother wishes, but he is well aware that she is asking him to betray an ideal and to sell himself.

The drama of this confrontation is infinitely heightened by our awareness that Volumnia desires more than anything else the honour of her son, though she, rather than his enemies, moves him towards the loss of it. In the following scene the tribunes are largely responsible for Coriolanus's reassertion of his heroic integrity. In words which fit into the now familiar imagery Brutus announces their strategy for provoking another outburst:

> Put him to choler straight
>   . . . . .
>   Being once chaf'd, he cannot
> Be rein'd again to temperance; then he speaks
> What's in his heart, and that is there which looks
> With us to break his neck.
>
> (3.3.25, 27-30)

The successful execution of their plan makes Coriolanus go back on his promise to dissimulate, and leads to his banishment. The city on which he turns his back to seek "a world elsewhere" is made up of his friends and his foes, but at this point in the play it is clear that they all belong almost equally to the world which he rejects.

The last two acts of the play are illuminated by the implications of the words, "There is a world elsewhere." The world which Coriolanus now inhabits is neither the world of the Romans nor that of the Volscians. It is a world of absolutes—the world, as I have already suggested, of heroes. When Cominius comes to intercede for Rome, he refuses to answer to his name, insisting that he must forge a new name in the fire of burning Rome; he sits "in gold, his eye / Red as 'twould burn Rome" (5.1.11-15, 63-64). The fierceness of his adherence to his principles has translated him almost beyond humanity. Menenius is rejected in his turn, with the comment: "This man, Aufidius, / Was my belov'd in Rome; yet thou behold'st." "You keep a constant temper," Aufidius replies (5.2.98-100). The loss of humanity is brought out again in the half-humorous description given by Menenius:

> The tartness of his face sours ripe grapes. When he

walks, he moves like an engine, and the ground shrinks before his treading. He is able to pierce a corslet with his eye, talks like a knell, and his hum is a battery. He sits in his state, as a thing made for Alexander. What he bids be done is finish'd with his bidding. He wants nothing of a god but eternity and a heaven to throne in. (5.4.18-26)

The hard metallic imagery which G. Wilson Knight has noted throughout the play is very telling in this passage. Coriolanus has steeled himself to become a Tamburlaine and administer divine chastisement, refusing to be softened by considerations of friendship.

Unlike Tamburlaine, however, Shakespeare's Herculean hero finds that in despising a petty and corrupt world he is also denying nature. Tamburlaine is obliged to accept the limitations of nature only when he is faced with death; the situation forces Coriolanus to submit sooner. As Hermann Heuer says, "'Nature' becomes the keyword of the great scene" of the hero's second conflict with his formidable mother. As he sees them approach, the battle is already engaged in his mind between nature and heroic constancy:

> Shall I be tempted to infringe my vow
> In the same time 'tis made? I will not.
>
> (5.3.20-21)

And a moment later:

> But out, affection!
> All bond and privilege of nature, break!
> Let it be virtuous to be obstinate.
>
> (ll. 24-26)

> I'll never
> Be such a gosling to obey instinct, but stand
> As if a man were author of himself
> And knew no other kin.
>
> (ll. 34-36)

Nowhere in the play is the conflict between the heroic and the human more clear-cut. Only the demigod which Coriolanus aspires to be could resist the appeal made by Volumnia and Virgilia. Tamburlaine could refuse Zenocrate before the gates of Damascus, but Marlowe made him more nearly the embodiment of a myth. Coriolanus belongs to a more familiar world and his tragedy can be put very generally as the impossibility in this world, as in the world of Bussy D'Ambois, of reliving a myth. Heroic aspiration is not proof here against the urgent reality of human feelings. Already sensing his weakness, Coriolanus begs Virgilia not to urge forgiveness of the Romans, and to Volumnia he says:

> Do not bid me
> Dismiss my soldiers or capitulate

> Again with Rome's mechanics. Tell me not
> Wherein I seem unnatural. Desire not
> T'allay my rages and revenges with
> Your colder reasons.
>
> (ll. 81-86)

There is unconscious irony in the phrase, "colder reasons," for Volumnia's appeal is nothing if not emotional. It begins and ends with the pitiable plight of Coriolanus's family— a direct assault upon his feelings and instincts. Enclosed in this context is the appeal to his honour. No longer does Volumnia urge mixing honour with policy. It is her strategy now to make the course she recommends appear to be dictated by pure honour. She suggests that if he makes peace between the two sides, even the Volscians will respect him (presumably overlooking his abandonment of their cause), while if he goes on to conquer Rome he will wipe out the nobility of his name. Honour as she now presents it is a godlike sparing of offenders:

> Think'st thou it honourable for a noble man
> Still to remember wrongs?
>
> (ll. 154-55)

The final, and successful, appeal, however, is personal:

> This fellow had a Volscian to his mother;
> His wife is in Corioles, and this child
> Like him by chance.
>
> (ll. 178-80)

Aufidius, shortly after, shows that he has understood perfectly the essential nature of the appeal:

> I am glad thou hast set thy mercy and thy
>   honour
> At difference in thee. Out of that I'll work
> Myself a former fortune.
>
> (ll. 200-202)

I have emphasized Volumnia's rhetorical strategy more than the validity of her arguments, because it is important that Coriolanus is broken by a splendid oration. Eloquence, as is well known, was highly prized by the Elizabethans, and we have seen it in Tamburlaine as a further evidence of heroic superiority. But the rhetorical training of the Elizabethans made them acutely aware of the trickiness of oratory, and eloquence on their stage could be a danger-signal as well as a badge of virtue. The case of Volumnia's appeal to Coriolanus is as far from being clear-cut as it could be. The plea for mercy and the forgetting of injuries commands assent; yet one is well aware that the nature of the injuries, and hence the validity of the vow Coriolanus has taken, are never mentioned. . . .

As it is, Volumnia's rhetoric identifies the cause of mercy with the lives of the pleaders, and Coriolanus must choose between his vow and his family. He must indeed defy nature if he resists his mother's plea. Of this she is very well aware, and she plays on her son's attachment to her just as she had done previously, when urging on him a course of moderate hypocrisy. After her victory, judgment between the conflicting issues remains as puzzling as it was before.

When Volumnia's lack of principle and her association with the political world of Rome are fully perceived, it becomes more difficult to be sure of the significance of Coriolanus's capitulation. We know from him that it is likely to be "most mortal," and we know that Aufidius will do whatever he can to make it so. We know, that is, that the hero is now a broken man, but has he been ennobled by choosing the course glorified by Volumnia's eloquence? This is not the impression made by the last scenes. MacCallum says, "Still this collapse of Coriolanus's purpose means nothing more than the victory of his strongest impulse. There is no acknowledgement of offence, there is no renovation of character." His choice is a recognition of the claims of nature, but this recognition makes possible no new affirmation such as Antony's after the bitterness of his defeat. Nature, as amoral as fecund, seems to melt the valour and stoic integrity of Antony, but in the new growth stimulated by this nature, valour and integrity appear again, transformed. To Coriolanus nature comes in the guise of a moral duty, which is also a temptation to betray his principles. The idea of fecundity is present only as Volumnia uses it for a persuasive weapon, threatening him with the horror of treading on his mother's womb. The melting that follows this persuasion leads to mere destruction. Nature, instead of opening a new way to the hero, blocks an old one and teaches him his mortal finitude.

The decision Coriolanus is asked to make is an impossible one. In the situation as Shakespeare presents it, it is almost inconceivable that he should deny the claims made by Volumnia; yet in acknowledging them he accomplishes nothing positively good. He avoids an act of shocking inhumanity and thereby surrenders control of his world to the forces of policy and compromise—the enemies of the "noble heart." Volumnia and Virgilia are hailed by the Romans, whose one thought is gratefulness to be alive. In Corioles Aufidius contrives the assassination of the hero, who is of no further use. What Coriolanus says of the scene of his submission might be applied to the entire ending of the play:

> Behold, the heavens do
> ope,
> The gods look down, and this unnatural
> scene
> They laugh at.
>
> (5.3.183-85)

For if the natural order seems to be preserved when

Coriolanus decides to spare his country, it is wrecked when the one man of principle is defeated and then murdered. The colossal folly of destroying what far outweighs everything that is preserved is sufficient to provoke the laughter of the gods.

Yet the play does not end on the note of ironic laughter. The final note is affirmation. There is no new vision to affirm and no transcendent world to which the hero willingly goes. Coriolanus will not "join flames with Hercules." What the last scene of the play affirms with compelling force is the value of what the world is losing in the death of the hero. The incident of the assassination dramatizes the essential heroism which Coriolanus has displayed throughout the action. Instead of the comfort of an apotheosis we are given the tragic fact of irremediable loss. After the success of the conspiracy even Aufidius is "struck with sorrow," and closes the play with the prophecy: "Yet he shall have a noble memory."

The handling of the assassination scene restores a much needed clarity after the puzzling ambiguities of Coriolanus's submission to his mother. Envy, meanness, and an underhand way of seeking revenge all make Aufidius the equivalent of the tribunes in earlier scenes. He baits Coriolanus in a similar way and provokes an exactly comparable self-assertion on the part of the hero. As the accusation "traitor" inflamed him before, it does so again, but here there is an interesting difference. After calling him traitor, Aufidius addresses him as Marcius, stripping him of his title of Coriolanus, and finally calls him "thou boy of tears" (5.6.84-99), referring of course to his giving in to his mother's plea. Coriolanus protests each term, but it is "boy" which raises him to the height of his rage:

> Boy! O slave!
> . . . . .
> Cut me to pieces, Volsces. Men and lads,
> Stain all your edges on me. Boy? False
> hound!
> If you have writ your annals true, 'tis there,
> That, like an eagle in a dovecote, I
> Flutter'd your Volscians in Corioles.
> Alone I did it. Boy?
>
> (5.6.103, 111-16)

What hurts most is the impugning of his manhood—his heroic *virtus*. He asserts it by the magnificently foolhardy reminiscence of his singlehanded victory over the very people he is addressing— "Alone I did it." His words recall the earlier description of him, "He is himself alone, / To answer all the city" (1.4.51-52). Shakespeare's alteration of history, making Coriolanus "alone" is one of the touches which reveals most unequivocally his heroic conception of the character. In Coriolanus the opposition of the individual might of the hero to the superior forces of nature and fate is pushed to the uttermost.

It is characteristic of Shakespeare's Coriolanus that he resents "boy" more than "traitor," for it is clear throughout that the honour and integrity to which Coriolanus is committed are intensely personal. In this respect he resembles Antony in his final moments. When James Thomson wrote his *Coriolanus* in the middle of the eighteenth century, he reversed the order of the accusations. Thomson's Tullus does not call Coriolanus "boy," but he reminds him of his capitulation and condescendingly offers to protect him from the Volscians. Coriolanus, in return, recalls his victory at Corioles, though he says nothing of being alone. Tullus then insults the Romans and finally accuses Coriolanus of being a traitor both to them and to the Volscians. To the slurs on Rome Coriolanus replies:

> Whate'er her blots, whate'er her giddy factions,
> There is more virtue in one single year
> Of *Roman* story, than your *Volscian* annals
> Can boast thro' all your creeping dark
>   duration!

This patriotic emphasis, which Thomson presumably felt necessary as a means of getting sympathy for his hero, makes all the plainer the consequences of Shakespeare's climactic emphasis on Coriolanus as an individual who can never be completely assimilated into a city, his own or another.

John Philip Kemble's acting version combined Thomson and Shakespeare. He kept the patriotic defence of Rome from Thomson, but followed it with the speeches from Shakespeare prompted by the accusation "traitor." The culmination of the interchange is once more the hero's indignant repetition of "boy!," which Kemble made memorable by his way of saying it. Slightly later, Macready was especially pleased that he could rival Kemble's success in the inflection of this crucial monosyllable. These actors, who made "boy!" the high point of their portrayal of heroic dignity, were much closer to the core of Shakespeare's character than are the critics who see him as in fact boyish and small. The whole effect of the last scene depends on a recognition very similar to Cleopatra's after the death of Antony:

> The soldier's pole is fall'n! Young boys and
>   girls
> Are level now with men. The odds is gone,
> And there is nothing left remarkable
> Beneath the visiting moon.
>
>   (4.15.65-68)

Coriolanus is angular, granitic, and hence unlovable. Antony's faults are much more easily forgiven than this obduracy. Yet of the two it is Coriolanus who more certainly commands respect and veneration.

Matthew N. Proser

SOURCE: "*Othello* and *Coriolanus*: The Image of the Warrior," in *The Heroic Image in Five Shakespearean Tragedies*, Princeton University Press, 1965, pp. 92-170.

[In the excerpted essay that follows, Proser examines Coriolanus's character and his relationship to the theme of honor, which the critic calls the "central paradox of the play." Proser finds Coriolanus's defining characteristic to be his constancy; he never changes, thus fueling his inability to perceive ambiguity and to react to it appropriately. Proser notes the purity of Coriolanus's motivations— he is heroic and honorable to the death— but that he lacks a sense of self-recognition. The critic adds that Coriolanus's honor derives only from his warrior nature and not from any sense of duty to defend his country. Likewise, his honor has little to do with the pursuit of fame, although Volumnia continually equates honor with renown. In the end, Proser observes, the plebeians, patricians, and Coriolanus all share responsibility for the disunity of Rome. However, the greatest portion of blame lies with Coriolanus and his heroic, but stubbornly constant, nature.]

. . . In *Coriolanus* the scope of the human problem is deliberately magnified beyond the personal, and the participation of the community in the tragedy is more than implied. Caius Marcius' immense military heroism and immense limitations as an individual are literally a problem of Rome. But Rome has other problems too: the division of the plebs and the patricians over the distribution of corn precedes the difficulties Coriolanus offers. Yet the two problems become inextricably related. The senate's refusal to feed the populace is congruent with and complicated by Coriolanus' refusal to "feed" the plebs any form of political, indeed, human recognition. Thus does *Coriolanus* offer a distinct correspondence between the warped relations in the body politic and the distortions in the anatomy of its main character's soul. The story of Caius Marcius is a tragedy of state . . . ; paradoxically, it is the severe inner limitations of its major character that make it such.

Coriolanus' primary difficulty as a human being is his inability to see the ambiguity either in the situations he encounters or in himself. The supremacy of his military prowess and his knowledge of what it can accomplish wall him in from the rest of mankind; his aristocratic background divides him from the "common man." "Honor" and "aristocracy" are the backbone of his existence; "And I am constant" is his most characteristic remark. This "constancy," in which he believes so devoutly, takes a number of forms. First of all, he is always "his own man," or at least he attempts to be, whether on the battlefield or in the public forum. For Caius Marcius, personal valor on the field of battle is the meaningful center of life; but if he fights well, he fights well alone, and this is never more clearly demonstrated than during the assault on Corioli's gates. The great soldier charges into the town, allows himself to be cut off from his own troops, and takes on the town's defenders by himself. Admittedly his act is audacious and heroic; nevertheless it is also foolhardy and irresponsible, a means first of all for accruing honor to his own name. Rome surely benefits from his action, but the benefit comes as a dividend, not as the principal aim.

Similarly, though Coriolanus is a member of the patrician class, his dedication is not chiefly to the ruling group in Rome, but to himself, to his own sense of dignity and honor. He can speak effectively about the anarchy which results ". . . when two authorities are up, / Neither supreme . . . ," but his refusal to buy the plebs' mercy with "one fair word" derives not from any pristine loyalty to the patrician cause (which might be better served with temperance, if not temporizing), but from his absolute loyalty to himself. After castigating the plebs for annulling his election as consul, he says to his mother:

> Why did you wish me milder? Would you
>   have me
> False to my nature? Rather say I play
> The man I am.
>
> (III.ii.14-16)

Coriolanus' "constancy," his reluctance to temporize, to play the man he is not, though from one point of view a trait which might well be admired, from another is suggestive of the persistently negative quality of his personality, a quality reinforced by his scurrility. Barring the speeches later in the play when he acquiesces to his mother's plea to spare Rome, scurrility remains his most characteristic idiom. Like his sword, it acts as a weapon both offensive and defensive in nature. It "cuts up" the plebs, but its use, passionate and vindictive, prevents constructive thinking on his part and defends him from the necessity of investigating his own moral stance. Here is Coriolanus addressing his "enemy," the people:

> Who deserves greatness
> Deserves your hate; and your affections are
> A sick man's appetite, who desires most that
> Which would increase his evil. He that depends
> Upon your favours swims with fins of lead
> And hews down oaks with rushes. Hang ye!
>   Trust ye?
> With every minute you do change a mind,
> And call him noble that was now your hate,
> Him vile that was your garland.
>
> (I.i.180-188)

Coriolanus, admittedly, has his point where the inconstant nature of the plebs is concerned. But as Second Officer says before the consular election:

> . . . he [Coriolanus] seeks their hate with greater

devotion than they can render it him, and leaves nothing undone that may fully discover him their opposite. Now, to seem to affect the malice and displeasure of the people is as bad as that which he dislikes, to flatter them for their love. (II.ii.20-25)

The intense loathing Coriolanus expresses for the plebs appears, among other things, a method of self-definition, a way of "proving" his heroic superiority over the "reechy" people. This method of self-definition, one by which he seeks to undermine the plebs in order to glorify himself, is carried over to his relationship with the senators. Here too the primarily negative quality of his character is constantly reiterated as he points out in one situation after another what he will not do, what he cannot seem, what he is not. More honorable in his own eyes than any man, Coriolanus, nevertheless, seldom tells us what he *is* (his "modesty" precludes this); honor itself is negatively defined. After Corioli he cannot bring himself to accept acknowledgment for his heroism publicly. To Cominius he says:

> I thank you, General;
> But cannot make my heart consent to take
> A bribe to pay my sword. I do refuse it,
> And stand upon my common part with
>   those
> That have beheld the doing.
>
> (I.ix.36-40)

When it comes to donning the ceremonial robe of humility as part of the consular election, he immediately refuses:

> I do beseech you,
> Let me o'erleap that custom; for I cannot
> Put on the gown, stand naked and entreat them
> For my wounds' sake to give their suffrage.
>
> (II.ii.139-142)

Nor can he repent for his surly language during the election:

> For them! [the plebs] I cannot do it to the
>   gods;
> Must I then do 't to them?
>
> (III.ii.38-39)

And when it comes to smoothing over the situation after he has completely disaffected the plebs, this too is impossible for Coriolanus:

> I'll know no further.
> Let them pronounce the steep Tarpeian death,
> Vagabond exile, flaying, pent to linger
> But with a grain a day, I would not buy
> Their mercy at the price of one fair word;
> Nor check my courage for what they can give,
> To have 't with saying "Good morrow."
>
> (III.iii.87-93)

It can be seen, therefore, that even the "fair words" Coriolanus gives himself are generally not stated directly, but must be inferred from his negative delivery of them. By such statements he implies his honor is great, but he will not say as much in so many words. His "modesty" is a case in point. Coriolanus will not boast, but his refusal to do so impresses us less as true modesty than as an attempt to hide his enormous estimation of himself. His incredible speeches to Cominius after the heroic conduct within Corioli's gates are self-conscious enough to make us feel he is posing. Surely modesty could not be responsible for such a barrage of language:

> May these same instruments, which you profane,
> Never sound more! When drums and trum-
>   pets shall
> I' th' field prove flatterers, let courts and cities
>   be
> Made all of false-face'd soothing!
> When steel grows soft as the parasite's silk,
> Let him be made [a coverture] for th' wars!
> No more, I say. For that I have not wash'd
> My nose that bled, or foil'd some debile
>   wretch,—
> Which, without note, here's many else have
>   done,—
> You [shout] me forth
> In acclamation hyperbolical,
> As if I lov'd my little should be dieted
> In praises sauc'd with lies.
>
> (I.ix.41-53)

As Cominius says, "Too modest are you; / More cruel to your own good report than grateful / To us that give you truly."

But Coriolanus can see no ambiguity in himself or in his language. At those points in the play during which he is willing to make a positive identification of himself, such as at the play's conclusion when he calls himself an "eagle," or earlier, upon his departure from Rome into exile, when he calls himself a "lonely dragon," there is no recognition that eagles and dragons (like lions or, for that matter, foxes) are predatory creatures which kill their prey, not for the sake of honor, but because it is in their nature to kill. Eagles and dragons remain for him the symbols, simple and unambiguous, of a noble ideal and of the embodiment of that ideal in himself. Similarly, invective is for him a simple reflection of the purity of his nature and his motives (while for the audience it becomes an index of his willfulness, his passion, his spitefulness, his interior defilement, and his blindness to his own human nature). Nor is there for Coriolanus any possibility of self-recognition. For the truth of the matter remains that Coriolanus *is* constant, and the image he casts is unified. Unlike Othello, he has only one occupation— that of war. Othello, for all his faults, can love, and because he can, in the end he is capable of seeing at least part

of the truth. Othello can momentarily envision the ambiguity in the role he has chosen and see the "other side of the picture." The just avenger, he finds, can be a fool: "O, blood, blood, blood!" he cries, dedicating himself to the life of violence. But recognition comes with the direct parallel, "O fool, fool, fool!" However, as Rosen states, ". . . there is no . . . journey toward painful discovery in *Coriolanus*. The Coriolanus of the first scene is the same Coriolanus at the end of the play. His opinions and attitude undergo no change." To Coriolanus, the "picture" can have only one interpretation. It is up to the audience to infer the other side.

The single image the audience receives of Coriolanus contains in fact three parts, but these parts are inseparable and cast the same shadow. There is his relationship to war, his relationship to the community, and his relationship to his mother, the quality of the first two deriving from the strength of the last. There can be no question of Volumnia's importance in Shakespeare's story of Caius Marcius. Plutarch recognizes her, but Shakespeare makes the relationship of mother and son the core of the play. In more than one respect, out of it everything develops:

> *Vol.* Thy valiantness was mine, thou suck'st it
>   from me,
> But owe thy pride thyself.
>
> (III.ii.129-130)

This judgment of Coriolanus by his mother is interesting not only because it suggests something about the intensity of their relationship, but also because it is not wholly accurate. Coriolanus' pride may not derive completely from his mother, but she is certainly involved in it. By having encouraged him to be the surpassing warrior she desires, she has helped to create the breach between him and the community which characterizes her. Coriolanus, when expressing his inability to flatter the plebs, can say, "Let them hang!" But Volumnia, despite her criticism of her son, can respond with equal vehemence, "Ay, and burn too!" Clearly, Volumnia's aristocratic separation from the Roman populace is magnified in Coriolanus. Furthermore, her ambitions for him play a significant part in his life. It is Coriolanus who stands for consul; but it is Volumnia who desires the honor for him more than he desires it for himself:

> *Vol.*   I have liv'd
> To see inherited my very wishes
> And the buildings of my fancy; only
> There's one thing wanting, which I doubt
>   not but
> Our Rome will cast upon thee.
> *Cor.*   Know, good mother,
> I had rather be their servant in my way
> Than sway with them in theirs.
>
> (II.i.214-220)

To be brief, Volumnia's aristocratic and masculine spirit informs Coriolanus' character, and the extent of her influence can be seen even in the kind of education she chose for her son. Like Othello's, but far more severely, that education limits Coriolanus' emotional possibilities, positing, as it does, physical valor as the prime value of life. In the "hardness" which results are implicit both the heroism Coriolanus attains and his moral separation from the rest of the community. Volumnia describes the education she envisioned for Caius Marcius in the following way:

> . . . When yet he was but tender-bodied and the only son of my womb, when youth with comeliness pluck'd all gaze his way, when for a day of kings' entreaties a mother should not sell him an hour from her beholding, I, considering how honour would become such a person, that it was no better than picture-like to hang by th' wall, if renown made it not stir, was pleas'd to let him seek danger where he was like to find fame. To a cruel war I sent him; from whence he return'd, his brows bound with oak. I tell thee, daughter, I sprang not more in joy at first hearing he was a man-child than now in first seeing he had proved himself a man.
> (I.iii.5-19)

The intensity of Volumnia's language surely witnesses her attachment to her son. However, perhaps it is fair to say that what appears from one point of view a positive human bond, from another assumes a negative quality. In sending her son out to fight at a time " . . . when for a day of kings' entreaties a mother should not sell him an hour from her beholding," she impairs permanently his ability to relate to the rest of mankind. Involved in soldiering, in fighting, in killing from his youth, Coriolanus persistently associates "honor" with the amount of havoc he can cause among the ranks of his "enemies." The nobility of Volumnia's sacrifice is undermined by the "hardness" in it, a "hardness" mirrored in Coriolanus' typical solution for the problems he comes to face: destruction, be it verbal or real, for his adversaries.

Honor for Coriolanus, then, lies not so much in defending his country, but in the simple fact of being a warrior. In him the military occupation of the aristocrat is disconnected from its value as a service and is made valuable in its own right— somewhat in the same manner this disconnection is made in *Macbeth*. And in battle Coriolanus is a veritable holocaust, a power all but immortal in its capacity to destroy. But if there is something "immortal" in his military prowess, by definition there is something inhuman as well, and this "inhuman" feature also develops out of the great soldier's relationship with his mother. Their bond, which should be the basis of human understanding and sympathy, is charged by Volumnia with a "divinity" in the epic sense. "Juno-like" Volumnia produces a "Mars-like" Caius Marcius,

and their bond instead of representing the kind of human interconnection applicable finally to mankind at large, restricts the two in a tight relationship that will acknowledge no connection with the common herd. The mother invests herself with more than human powers of maternal sacrifice (quite blind to the possibilities this sacrifice might lead to), and the son attempts to enact the "divine" manliness the mother delivers to him as the utmost value in life.

Nevertheless, ironically, Coriolanus' sense of honor is even more restrictive than that of his mother. The end of Coriolanus' education was to Volumnia's way of thinking not simply a question of honor, but one of fame as well. For Volumnia honor is useless unless "renown" stirs it, and it seems fair to assume that honor stirs renown as well. Thus honor and fame are interlinked, and Volumnia's ideal portrait of her son incorporates the idea of "reputation." This emphasis on renown is symptomatic of her pride, to be sure; on the other hand, to a degree it humanizes her. For Volumnia, the honor of the consulship and the fame it will bring are worth a soft word or two to the plebs:

> *Vol.*   You are too abso-
>   lute;
> Though therein you can never be too noble,
> But when extremities speak. I have heard you say
> Honour and policy, like unsever'd friends,
> I' th' war do grow together. Grant that, and tell me
> In peace what each of them by th' other lose
> That they combine not there.
> *Cor.*   Tush, tush!
> (III.ii.39-45)

But if Volumnia can admit "fame" into the complex of her values, Caius Marcius cannot; or at least he will not acknowledge such an admission. As we noticed earlier, he is incapable of accepting the praises of Cominius even when according to his own standards he deserves them; he even receives the laudatory title "Coriolanus" with the greatest reluctance. To Coriolanus, acknowledgment of a desire for fame would be in one sense the acknowledgment of a human weakness; in another it would be an admission of dependence on the rest of the world. These are both admissions Coriolanus simply cannot make.

To the degree, then, that Coriolanus claims for himself an integrity which cannot be touched by popular acclaim, he, as Volumnia says, makes his pride his own. Conversely, to the degree that Coriolanus' sense of honor is bound up with Volumnia's attempt to make her son the living image of honor, she remains the hereditary source of this pride. It is ironically appropriate, therefore, that she should be present during each of the critical moments of the play's action: when Coriolanus rebels against donning the robe of humility, when he refuses to speak the plebs fair in order to retain the consulship, and when he is about to march against Rome with the Volscian army.

Considering the importance of Volumnia's influence upon her son, it is also appropriate that she should deliver to the audience in language the commanding image of Coriolanus, the one, unstated by him, that directs his actions. She does so with the vigor and intensity we have grown to expect of her:

> Death, that dark spirit, in 's nervy arm doth lie,
> Which, being advanc'd, declines, and then
>   men die.

> (II.i.177-178)

It is a powerful image, deeply admired by Volumnia, but for the audience it is not entirely ingratiating. Nevertheless, one thing is clear— no matter how the image is interpreted, Coriolanus always fulfills it. Even when he is, in O. J. Campbell's word, "satirized," he maintains the image Volumnia has shaped for him. And in this image is reflected the perversion of relationship between mother and son which carries over to the hero's relationship with the populace. As Traversi puts it, for Coriolanus war is a "splendid and living ecstasy," and it might be added that equally for him, peace is destruction. Cominius also sets forth the image, but like Volumnia, without any awareness of its negative implications. He is speaking of Coriolanus' military heroism at the recent battle for Corioli:

> His sword, death's stamp,
> Where it did mark, it took; from face to foot
> He was a thing of blood, whose every
>   motion
> Was tim'd with dying cries. Alone he ent'red
> The mortal gate of th' city, which he painted
> With shunless destiny; aidless came off,
> And with a sudden reinforcement struck
> Corioli like a planet; now all his.
>   . . . . .
> And to the battle came he, where he did
> Run reeking o'er the lives of men, as if
> 'Twere a perpetual spoil; and till we call'd
> Both field and city ours, he never stood
> To ease his breast with panting.

> (II.ii.111-126)

This is the image of Coriolanus most admired by plebs and patricians alike, and since in Coriolanus' case action speaks louder than words, it might be said that it is the image most admired by Coriolanus himself; for it is precisely this image he enacts during the carefully developed battle scenes. It is, furthermore, the picture he would present once again in living action at the climax of the play to the city he has spent his blood

defending. Beneath the commendatory purposes of the speech, however, Cominius' purposes, lies a vision of destructiveness accentuated by the language Shakespeare puts into Cominius' mouth. This vision of destructiveness appears in such expressions as "death's stamp," "he was a thing of blood," "every motion was tim'd with dying cries," "struck Corioli like a planet," and "he did run reeking o'er the lives of men." We have here the image of the lion truly running rampant, though Cominius might be inclined to create of it a heraldic device. The horror of the scene is reminiscent of the first description received of Macbeth, that from the bleeding captain:

> For brave Macbeth— well he deserves that
>   name—
> Disdaining Fortune, with his brandish'd steel,
> Which smok'd with bloody execution,
> Like Valour's minion carv'd out his passage
> Till he fac'd the slave;
> Which ne'er shook hands, nor bade farewell
>   to him,
> Till he unseam'd him from the nave to th'
>   chaps,
> And fix'd his head upon our battlements.

> (I.ii.16-23)

But the description of Coriolanus is, at least for sheer quantity of destruction, even more impressive than that of Macbeth. Moreover, the destructive element in Coriolanus is unqualified by Duncan's gracious presence, a presence which leads the audience to believe the political and moral state of affairs at the beginning of *Macbeth* is unreservedly good and worth practically every conceivable form of defense. Considering the niggardliness of the patricians where the distribution of corn is concerned and the vacillating conduct of the plebs, it is hard to make the same statement about Coriolanus' Rome. The great soldier's impulse to destruction should be read, therefore, as a reflection of the discord in the state rather than as symbolic of the power of goodness. Indeed, Coriolanus in his very heroism seems to represent sheer power itself— an amoral force; and as things turn out he is willing to consider the use of that power not only against his enemies, but against his friends as well.

Finally, the issue of Coriolanus' "constancy" forces us to return to his language momentarily. Even the scurrility he directs against the populace is derived from his center of destruction. This scurrility does not reverse the image of the destroyer; it supports it. Aggressive, passionate and repellent, his words are meant to "annihilate" the people:

> All the contagion of the south light on
>   you,
> You shames of Rome! you herd of— Boils
>   and plagues
> Plaster you o'er, that you may be abhorr'd
> Further than seen, and one infect another

Against the wind a mile! You souls of geese,
That bear the shapes of men, how have you
    run
From slaves that apes would beat! Pluto and
    hell!
All hurt behind! Backs red, and faces pale
With flight and agued fear! Mend and charge
    home,
Or, by the fires of heaven, I'll leave the foe
And make my wars on you.

                                        (I.iv.30-40)

Although this speech should be examined in its proper context (the plebs, cowed by the Volscian forces, have begun to retreat), and admittedly Coriolanus has some justification for his disgust and rage, the extremity of his language casts some doubts on his qualifications as a military leader and reveals how far his hatred for the plebs goes. It is not every general who threatens to "leave the foe" and make war on his own men. Furthermore, the statement acts as a prediction here, for by the end of the play, he decides to make war on all of Rome for the sake of the plebs.

Coriolanus, therefore, in spite of his ultimate betrayals, remains "constant" to the very end. But our interpretation of this constancy is somewhat different from his own. To our eyes his constancy lies in this: he is always the potential killer whether defending his country or planning to destroy it. Nor does he ever probe the ambiguity in his impressive self-conception. This lack of recognition holds true in spite of his acquiescence to Volumnia's pleas for Rome at the climax of the play. If there he makes any discovery of his essential humanity, that discovery is never consciously projected outward toward the rest of mankind. Unlike the situation in *King Lear,* the hero makes no connection between the diseased and scabrous state of the world and the condition of his own soul.

But this question of recognition is important in reference to the entire state of Rome as well. What both Coriolanus and the community as a whole fail to see is that the dynamic image delineated in statements such as those by Volumnia and Cominius contains a threat to themselves as well as to their enemies. Neither the patricians nor the plebs understand how the cultivation of pure physical might, even in an outwardly acceptable military guise, in a sense prepares the soul for any violence. They do not comprehend that the strong man whose strength is his only asset lives through violence purely, though that violence be restricted to the formal patterns of war. Finally, they seem unaware that at its heart such violence is irrational and may turn, even in its being cultivated for the defense of a country, against those who enshrine it in any form.

. . . . .

The result of Coriolanus' behavior during the affair of the robe is, of course, chaos— but not only because he fails at flattery or because in his "naked honesty" he will not conform to the customs of Rome. For, as we have seen, the custom of donning the robe is not to be taken as a mere matter of form. Beneath this "vulgar display," a display which demonstrates the plebs' limitations, is something which demonstrates Coriolanus' limitations as well. Although the plebs may exhibit their "vulgar wisdoms" in demanding the ceremony without one jot abated, Coriolanus once again reveals his incapacity for accepting another class of human beings on their own terms in order to knit the state into the unity of diverse human beings it actually is. The concession to be made may be one of policy, and in his reluctance to employ policy Coriolanus may be admirable; but it is important to remember that Coriolanus' attitude toward the plebs makes the great metaphor of the body politic unworkable. There can be no true state with a man like Coriolanus at the head of government. Hence Coriolanus' behavior results in anarchy because he is incapable of recognizing that the plebs, though they may at times act like beasts, are human beings; because he is incapable of recognizing that he, though a great warrior, is a human being; and because he is incapable of recognizing that the plebs as well as the patricians are part of the state. Coriolanus' limitation turns out to be not simply a native integrity which prevents him from acting the hypocrite. It is a tremendously deep distortion of nature which can be detected in his position regarding his mother, the plebs, the state, and the world at large.

As to the plebs— they are, to be sure, not without blame. They are vacillating and hydra-headed; they do allow themselves to be used by the tribunes. On the other hand, they are intrinsically generous and give Coriolanus every chance to prove himself interested in the state and their welfare. The price for the consulship is but "to ask it kindly" and when Caius Marcius does not ask it kindly, they confer the title upon him anyway. During the scene in which Coriolanus begs their voices, they reveal a nature simple and ingratiating; however this nature is their downfall. The entire election becomes confused with the issue of "gratitude" and their mistake turns out to be the same the patricians make. During the election both parties fail to remember that Coriolanus' true function in the state is that of warrior and that his greatest potentialities do not lie in the realms of peace. Because of the plebs' generosity, and because, as Third Citizen puts it, "ingratitude is monstrous," the people choose to forget that Coriolanus hates them. Yet were the plebs thinking coherently, they would perhaps see that "gratitude" for deeds done in the quest of honor alone (whatever the benefits to the state) may not be the best credentials for public office, especially from a man clearly hostile to them.

Ironically, it is the proud and self-seeking tribunes who remind the plebs of Coriolanus' hostility. The tribunes are rabble-rousers, real "Machiavellian" foxes, and more than satisfied to see Coriolanus demonstrate his ill-will toward the plebs during the ceremonial begging for voices. His conduct provides them with a new pretext for self-aggrandizement, and they waste no time in stirring up the plebs to repudiate the election. After Sicinius and Brutus have shown the populace how Coriolanus has used them, Sicinius says to his cohort:

> To th' Capitol, come.
> We will be there before the stream o' th'
>   people;
> And this shall seem, as partly 'tis, their own,
> Which we have goaded onward.
>   (II.iii.268-271)

They are even willing to take upon their own shoulders the blame for the plebs' rejection of Coriolanus, or so they tell the people; but this willingness is no reflection of a true sense of responsibility on their part. They are looking for power any way they can get it. If there is a breach between the patricians and the people, they can use Coriolanus as a wedge to broaden the gap and slip themselves into power.

Nevertheless, the tribunes, whose motives remain anything but pure, are right, righter than anyone else, in their estimation of the danger in Coriolanus. Brutus says to the plebs:

> Did you perceive
> He did solicit you in free contempt
> When he did need your loves, and do you
>   think
> That his contempt shall not be bruising to
>   you
> When he hath power to crush?
>   (II.iii.207-211)

This Brutus, a very different sort of republican than his namesake in *Julius Caesar,* has enough basis in Coriolanus' past conduct to substantiate his judgment. Perhaps it is because the tribunes are so involved in their own self-interest that they are capable of seeing through Coriolanus. For it is they who say directly to him:

> You speak o' th' people
> As if you were a god to punish, not
> A man of their infirmity.
>   (III.i.80-82)

However, their perspicacity does not excuse their own dissentiousness. In their hunger for power they prove to be as much a threat to the state as the man they seek to have thrown from the Tarpeian Rock.

To be brief, all parties are responsible for the disunity in the city of Rome, but Coriolanus remains that disunity's commanding symbol (this, perversely enough, *because* of his "constancy"). At the same time, it is he who reveals, in an off-hand way, a recognition of his true function in the state. We have dealt with this quotation before, but for a different purpose. Coriolanus has just returned to Rome in triumph from the war with Corioli and is on his way to the capitol. His mother says:

> I have liv'd
> To see inherited my very wishes
> And the buildings of my fancy; only
> There's one thing wanting, which I doubt
>   not but
> Our Rome will cast upon thee. [the consulship.]

To which Coriolanus replies:

> Know good mother,
> I had rather be their servant in my way
> Than sway with them in theirs.
>   (II.i.214-220)

But this momentary recognition, if indeed it can be called such, is scarcely assimilated by Volumnia and not really understood by Coriolanus. Like the patricians themselves, he forgets that his value as a servant rests in his military prowess. When the patricians try to convince him to speak the crowd fair and prevent his being attached as a "traitorous innovator," they disregard the fact that Coriolanus is first and foremost a man of war whose calling is not political to begin with. Indeed, this truth is not recognized by the patricians from the outset of the play. They become as much confused by the issue of "gratitude" as do the plebs. Thus, if in electing Coriolanus consul the people fail to remember that his potentialities lie in war and that in alienating him those potentialities might well be turned against them, the senators make the same mistake. The issue of Coriolanus' repudiation, like the altercation over the gown of humility, becomes confused with "flattery" and "gratitude," and the patricians, blinded by Coriolanus' heroic image, without understanding the full significance of that image, continue to support Coriolanus in the face of popular disapproval. It is not, unfortunately, until the belated moment of Coriolanus' banishment that the senators acquiesce, the result of which is Coriolanus' total disaffection from the state. As to Coriolanus himself— in spite of his statement that he "had rather be their servant" as a soldier than as consul, his treatment by the plebs reduces all to a question of "honor" for him. He sees his wounds bleeding for Rome (although he was unwilling to reveal those wounds to the Romans), and the plebs' banishment of him, plus the patricians' acquiescence to the plebs, impel his decision to avenge himself on the city as a whole.

The question of "honor" nevertheless remains a central

paradox in the play. For in one sense Coriolanus *is* correct when he states he cannot flatter the people, that by doing this he would not be true to himself. He would lose his integrity first of all because he hates the common people, and second because he would be violating his true function in the community— the destroyer of Rome's enemies (this, given that perversely enough the people and even the patricians become Rome's enemies in their dissentiousness over the corn issue and over the public role Coriolanus is to play in the country). It is this very truth to himself that gives Coriolanus his heroic status. Like the case of Brutus in *Julius Caesar,* who is an honorable man, the honor Coriolanus seeks dishonors him. That for which under other circumstances the audience might admire him, causes the audience to condemn him. His honor so separates him from the ideal of the peaceful city that there is literally no place for him in it.

Conversely, if Coriolanus proves true to himself, it can be seen that, unlike the case of Brutus, there is never any moral conflict in him at all. He may rebel at using policy to attain his ends, but he never feels he should not hate the common people, nor does he feel that the limitation revealed by the one kind of service he can perform— that of killing— reflects a lack in himself. Thus if Coriolanus is true to his image, he is never true to what lies below that image— his own human nature. Feeling is perverted at such a deep level that all the judgments he makes against the populace, even those which are valid, turn against him and expose him as traitor to the people, traitor to Rome, traitor to Corioli, traitor to himself, and traitor to the human cause.

But he is true to his mother:

> O mother, mother!
> What have you done? Behold, the heavens do
>   ope,
> The gods look down, and this unnatural
>   scene
> They laugh at. O my mother, mother! O!
> You have won a happy victory to Rome;
> But, for your son,— believe it, O believe it—,
> Most dangerously you have with him
>   prevail'd,
> If not most mortal to him.
>
> (V.iii.182-189)

This, excluding the invective he uses at other points in the play, is some of Coriolanus' most passionate language. With it he determines to leave Rome unharmed and chooses the death Aufidius makes for him. The statement, however, opens out beyond the immediate situation. For Volumnia has most dangerously prevailed with her son throughout his life; his values, his conception of himself, so much derived from her, have led to his predicament. Coriolanus, who would not give the plebs their grain and "politically" (in both senses of the

word) feed the state, has had his human nature all but digested by Volumnia. Whatever love he most fully acknowledges is directed toward her, so that his human qualities have become isolated in her from the rest of the community. In a way they have been sacrificed for the aura of "divinity" which surrounds and unites the two. Only she, not even his wife, can make him merciful. In the close interdependency of Coriolanus and his mother are seen a kind of political and spiritual incest that reveals a distortion even in the one crucial relationship Coriolanus can demonstrably "feel" with great depth. Here Coriolanus' hidden and isolated humanity acts the part of Nemesis and mortally betrays him to the enemies he has chosen for friends— Aufidius and his army. The triplex image of Coriolanus which represents his relationship to the community, his relationship to war, and his relationship to his mother can be seen at this point, the point at which he is *most* human, to be one image, powerful and annihilating, the source of his own destruction.

But if this image, swordlike, points inward toward what is left of the feeling center of the hero's perverted humanity, it points outward too, through Rome, to Corioli. In this enemy city waits, so to speak, the same passionate mob which set Coriolanus up as consul, only to banish him. When he arrives it will welcome him with the acclaim customary for heroes and gods. But just as the tribunes had little difficulty convincing the Roman populace of Coriolanus' enmity, Aufidius, as power-seeking and envious as the tribunes, will have even less difficulty provoking the Volscian mob. Indeed, just as Coriolanus helped the tribunes in their cause, he will help Aufidius in his. The Volscian general's public accusations of "traitor" and "boy of tears" (which contain, it will be admitted, more than a suspicion of validity) impel Caius Marcius to expose himself as he has never exposed himself before. Surely now he is "most dangerously" less than modest:

> "Boy!" False hound!
> If you have writ your annals true, 'tis there
> That, like an eagle in a dove-cote, I
> [Flutter'd] your Volscians in Corioli:
> Alone I did it. "Boy!"
>
> (V.vi.113-117)

The climactic indiscretion of his words defines him clearly to the Volscian crowd as their great enemy; for they, like the Roman plebs, had apparently forgotten how Coriolanus once fought against them, although in their case the fight was military and not political. Their response is tragically appropriate in view of their memories of slaughter and carnage:

> *All the people.* Tear him to pieces! Do it
>   presently!— He kill'd my son!— my daughter:— He kill'd my cousin Marcus!— He kill'd
>   my father!
>
> (V.vi.121-123)

Aside from their capacity to create a sense of horror, these lines function in another important way. By focusing our attention upon the slaughtered members of the various Volscian families, they emphasize the major thematic issue in the play. For "families" and the distorted relationships in them have been implicit thematically throughout—from the perverted relationship of Coriolanus and his mother to the political hostilities in the state of Rome to the betrayal by Coriolanus of his own land. The personal sense of pain and anger now felt by the Volscian populace paradoxically stretches this thematic issue one step further to the universal perversion in the universal human bond: the destruction of Man by Man. And at this point we recognize that the scene as a whole has suitably drawn all participants into the primary image of destruction which characterizes the play. Both Corioli and Coriolanus are responsible for this scene of death. And behind them stand all the Romans who have made their contribution. . . . Thus in *Coriolanus*, . . . it can be seen that the enemy, the potential killer, is Man; and nobody, not the plebs, nor the patricians, nor the tribunes, nor the Volscian crowd, nor individuals like Aufidius or Volumnia or Menenius, is to escape blame for the Volscian conspirators' blood-curdling cry as they overwhelm Coriolanus in what appears an epitome of the entire play's action:

> Kill, kill, kill, kill, kill him!
>
> (V.vi.132)

Only one character may perhaps be justifiably excluded from this scene of savage death and the condemnation that goes with it. The words on the body politic might be taken from Menenius' loquacious mouth and placed in that of Caius Marcius' "gracious silence"—Virgilia, the one truly "private" character in the play, and the only character who, paradoxically, fulfills a public role in a really meaningful way. Not only is it she who can still recognize the last impulse of humanity, faint though it may be, in her husband; but it is also she who most clearly represents in her tears and silence (which are her language) the natural, quiet, inborn humanity that transcends personality—of which she appropriately has so little—and is the essential root which grows through family, through class, into the flowering state.

MOTHER-SON RELATIONSHIP

Coppélia Kahn has examined the juxtaposition of masculine and feminine in the play's combined imagery of nursing and war. According to Kahn's view, the ending of *Coriolanus* takes on an ironic tone as one realizes that Volumnia's maternal power results in the contradictions of Coriolanus's manhood and makes him an enemy of Rome, thereby bringing about his destruction. G. Wilson Knight has also focused on the relationship between the Roman matron and her son. Knight pro-

posed that the hero's failure to recognize the value of love is the source of his tragedy and that his relationship with his mother is based on shared pride rather than affection. Moreover, Knight noted, this pride ultimately causes the two characters to oppose each other. Significantly, the critic interpreted Coriolanus's yielding to Volumnia in Act V, scene iii as the triumph of love over pride.

Harold C. Goddard has scrutinized Volumnia's part in her son's ruin, focusing especially on the effects of Coriolanus's martial upbringing. Goddard argued that the hero was a "rare and sensitive" child who was molded by his warlike mother into a cruel soldier and whose gentler feelings, as well as his sense of outrage at this treatment, were transmuted into excessive pride, courage, and arrogance. Goddard also downplayed the effect of Volumnia's pleading on Coriolanus's decision to spare his native city, instead attributing this act of mercy to the presence of the hero's wife and son, who awaken in him the "innocent memories" of a time before he was "utterly crushed" by his mother's training. Along similar lines, Charles K. Hofling has provided a psychiatric diagnosis of Coriolanus, describing him as a "phallic-narcissistic personality." He presumed that the hero's principal traits—his aggressiveness, courage, and irrational temper—developed as a result of Volumnia's traumatic influence, under which he learned to seek approval only through violent behavior.

Rufus Putney has also characterized Coriolanus's warlike aggression as the result of repressed anger toward his mother that has been refocused on the citizens of Rome. Rufus finds that this dilemma comes to a climax as Coriolanus must choose between the possibility of his mother's death or of his own in her place. Likewise, Madelon Sprengnether has discerned in *Coriolanus* a complementary self-destructive pattern in which the hero unconsciously both desires and fears losing his identity to the omnipotent Volumnia. As a result, he pursues an "eroticized violence" in battle that both defines his masculinity and pleases his mother.

Rufus Putney

SOURCE: "Coriolanus and His Mother," in *Psychoanalytic Quarterly*, Vol. 31, No. 3, July, 1962, pp. 364-81.

[*Putney takes a psychoanalytic view of* Coriolanus, *emphasizing the mental drama of Coriolanus's relationship with his mother. The critic examines Coriolanus's rage—which he sees as displaced onto the citizens of Rome even though its true source is Volumnia. Coriolanus's inability to control this rage, Putney asserts, leads to his destruction. Coriolanus's psychological dilemma, then, is whether he should be true to his nature or instead subject himself to the imprisoning ideals of fame and glory imposed upon him by his mother. Volumnia's threats of suicide drive this conflict, as Coriolanus feels that ultimately he must choose between his own death or hers. Shackled by his rigidity of thought and this nearly impossible decision, Coriolanus, in Putney's opinion, selects the option of his own death by capitulating to Volumnia's demand that he not lead the Volscian army against Rome.]*

All critics, save those who think the play Coriolanus is an aristocratic manifesto or a political debate, find the relationship between Caius Marcius Coriolanus and Volumnia, his mother, the very center of Shakespeare's drama. There is relatively little difference between the comments of conventional critics like [Andrew] Bradley and [Harley] Granville-Barker and the psychoanalytically informed studies of [Jackson E.] Towne, [Harold G.] McCurdy, and [Charles K.] Hofling. In his excellent essay, Dr. Hofling fully elucidates the œdipal theme and enriches our understanding of the characters, with an insight gained from clinical experience. None of these critics has observed, however, the importance of Coriolanus's struggle to choose between his own or his mother's death, which determines the outcome of the play; nor the degree to which Coriolanus's implacable superego explains puzzling features of his behavior and reactions.

The drama opens with the rioting plebeians calling for the death of Caius Marcius, whom they rightly regard as their chief enemy. Menenius, a jolly old patrician, tries to cajole them into peace, but Marcius appears and showers vituperation on the people and their leaders. He deplores the weakness of the Senate in granting them tribunes and advocates a massacre as the most efficient way of restoring order. A messenger interrupts with news that the Volscians are in arms against Rome, and Marcius sets off with Cominius, the consul, and Lartius. He performs incredible feats of heroism, including entering alone the gates of Corioli. Not only does he refuse any reward, save the honorific epithet of Coriolanus, but he will not even accept the plaudits of the generals and soldiers.

On his triumphant return to Rome, the Senate chooses him consul, but before he can be confirmed in office he must win the assent of the plebeians. Most unwillingly he dons the traditional 'vesture of humility', but instead of begging the support of the people he gibes and jeers at them and refuses to display his scars as custom demanded. The plebeians, nevertheless, feel they cannot deny their votes to so great a hero, and their tribunes, Brutus and Sicinius, inform Coriolanus that he has fulfilled the conditions. At the instigation of the tribunes, the plebeians retract their assent, and Brutus and Sicinius intercept Coriolanus as he is going to the capitol to assume the consulship. After a furious quarrel, they seek to seize and hurl him from the Tarpeian Rock. He and his patrician supporters drive away the people and their officers. When he has gone home, Menenius and Cominius try to avert civil war by con-

ciliating the tribunes, who agree that if Coriolanus will submit himself to their judgment, he may be pardoned. At first he refuses, but his mother at length prevails, and he returns to the forum where Brutus and Sicinius wait, determined to provoke him to new wrath. He bursts forth in rage when Sicinius calls him a traitor and is sentenced to perpetual exile.

Leaving the city, Coriolanus defects to his old enemy, Aufidius, and begs to serve in the Volscian army raised to attack Rome. After overrunning the outlying districts, he brings the army to the gates of the city. There he threatens to burn Rome and to exterminate the Romans. He rejects the pleas of the Senate and of Menenius, his dearest friend, but once again his mother reduces him to submission even though he knows it will cost his life. Peace is made, and he returns to Corioli, where Aufidius and his henchmen assassinate him while he is conferring with the Volscian lords.

Coriolanus is a man whose inability to control his rage destroys him. Ostensibly his anger is directed against the plebeians and the foes of Rome, but evidence in the play supports the conclusion that his rage is displaced from its real object, his mother. In order to understand these matters, one must examine Shakespeare's development of the character of Volumnia.

In Plutarch's Life of Caius Marcius Coriolanus, the source of Shakespeare's play, Volumnia rarely appears until the climax of the story. Plutarch's only observation was to the effect that Marcius had not suffered the usual consequences of growing up without a father: 'But Marcius thinking all due to his mother, that had been also due his father had he lived, did not only content himself to rejoice and honor her, but at her desire took a wife also, by whom he had two children, and yet never left his mother's house therefore'. Shakespeare completely revised this representation of Volumnia. In contrast to Hamlet's mother who, though wanton and erring, is gracious, affectionate, repentant, and protecting, Volumnia is, as Coriolanus's mother should be, domineering, angry, proud, cruel, and harsh. She is the real tragedy of Coriolanus.

In the first act of the play Shakespeare provides the retrospective glimpse that depicts the bleak and loveless atmosphere that surrounded Coriolanus's infancy and youth. In a remarkable conversation between Volumnia and Virgilia, Coriolanus's gentle, loving wife who is grieving for her husband's absence and fearful for his safety, Volumnia says

> I pray you, daughter, sing; or express yourself in a more comfortable sort. If my son were my husband, I should freelier rejoice in that absence wherein he won honour than in the embracements of his bed where he would show most love. When yet he

was tender-bodied and the only son of my womb, when youth with comeliness pluck'd all gaze his way, when for a day of king's entreaties a mother would not sell him an hour from her beholding, I, considering how honour would become such a person, that it was no better than picture-like to hang by th' wall,' if renown made it not stir, was pleas'd to let him seek danger where he was like to find fame. To a cruel war I sent him; from whence he return'd his bows bound with oak. I tell thee, daughter, I sprang not more in joy at first hearing he was a man-child than now in first seeing he had proved himself a man (I, iii).

In reply to Virgilia's question: 'But had he died in the business, madam, how then?', Volumnia says

> Then his good report should have been my son; I therein would have found issue. Hear me profess sincerely: had I a dozen sons, each in my love alike and none less dear than thine and mine good Marcius, I had rather had eleven die nobly for their country than one voluptuously surfeit out of action (I, iii).

Surely this is not love but hostility masquerading in the garb of affection. Volumnia's ferocity is barbaric. She imagines her son in battle killing Volscians, his brow covered with blood. When Virgilia protests, 'His bloody brow! O Jupiter, no blood!', Volumnia blasts her with scorn.

> Away you fool! it more becomes a man
> Than gilt his trophy. The breasts of Hecuba,
> When she did suckle Hector, look'd not
>   lovelier
> Than Hector's forehead when it spit forth
>   blood
> At Grecian sword, contemning
>
> >   (I, iii.).

When she hears her son has again been wounded, she cries, 'O, he is wounded; I thank the gods for't' (II, i). Coriolanus has adopted her standards, but can a son love a mother who has condemned him to hardship, pain, and probable death? His resentment is implied in his words: 'My mother, you wot well / My hazards still have been your solace' (IV, i).

Volumnia's reputation as the noblest Roman matron of them all is apparently the product of outmoded idealization of motherhood. Hofling, undoubtedly the best informed of the recent commentators, writes: 'Volumnia thus is seen to be an extremely unfeminine, nonmaternal person, one who sought to mold her son to fit a preconceived image gratifying her own masculine (actually pseudomasculine) strivings. Her method, we learn from the above and other speeches, was to withhold praise and the scant affection she had to give from any achievements except aggressive and exhibitionistic ones. . . .

Volumnia does much lip service to "honor", but this attitude proves to be in part hypocritical. During the political crisis in Acts II and III, she urges her son to adopt craft and dissembling until he has won power. In other words, this woman is much more concerned about appearances than about honor or truth as things in themselves.'

There is no reason to quarrel, unless over the last sentence, with this analysis of Volumnia's character or with Hofling's classification of Coriolanus as approximating 'the phallic-narcissistic type, as originally delineated by Reich.' Uncritical dependence on Goddard's dubious theory that Coriolanus gave up his plan for vengeance against Rome because of his love for his wife probably prevented Hofling from perceiving other more important aspects of the hero's motivations.

On the surface the relations between Volumnia and Coriolanus are marked by mutual admiration and respect, but as the play progresses he becomes rebellious and defiant. The first of the two conflicts of will between mother and son occurs after he has involved Rome in civil strife by attacking the tribunes and the plebeians. Act III, Scene ii opens with Coriolanus expressing bewilderment that his mother does not approve his violence; instead, she reprimands him for his rashness. Joined by Menenius and Cominius, who combine with her in urging that he prevent civil war by submitting to the tribunes and dissemble his way into the consulship, Coriolanus resolutely spurns all pleas until Volumnia says

> >   At thy choice, then:
> To beg of thee, it is my more dishonour
> Than thou of them. Come all to ruin; let
> Thy mother rather feel thy pride than fear
> Thy dangerous stoutness, for I mock at death
> With as big heart as thou. Do as thou list.
> Thy valiantness was mine, thou suck'dst it
>   from me,
> But owe thy pride thyself
>
> >   (III, ii).

Coriolanus immediately yields. Substantially Volumnia has said, 'Very well, make your choice. What you are doing will result in my death, but your pride will have it so, and my courage is no less than yours.' Her threat he cannot face, although at this point his mother's statement is not necessarily true. It does not inevitably follow that civil war between the patricians and plebeians will result in her death. The threat of her destruction is his command. He submits because he cannot tolerate acknowledgment of his latent destructive hostility toward her.

Although Coriolanus stands out far more staunchly in Act V, when Volumnia again threatens him with her death as she appeals to him to spare Rome, ultimately he cannot withstand her repeated pressure. At the first appearance of his wife, son, and mother anxiety strikes him, but he resolves

> I'll never
> Be such a gosling to obey instinct, but stand
> As if a man were author of himself
> And knew no other kin
>
>   (V, iii).

After affectionate family greetings, Coriolanus asserts his resolution to make no peace with Rome. Volumnia, at the outset of her first long plea, seeks to arouse guilt in him by playing on his love and compassion for his family. This time she resorts to the threat of suicide.

> For either thou
> Must as a foreign recreant be led
> With manacles through our streets, or else
> Triumphantly tread upon thy country's ruin
> And bear the palm for having bravely shed
> Thy wife and children's blood. For myself, son,
> I purpos not to wait on fortune till
> These wars determine. If I cannot persuade thee
> Rather to show a noble grace to both parts
> Than seek the end of one, thou shalt no sooner
> March to assault thy country than to tread—
> Trust to't, thou shalt not— on thy mother's womb
> That brought thee to this world
>
>   (V, iii).

This time he does not immediately recoil from the possibility that he will cause his mother's death, though the danger that she will kill herself has much more directness than her earlier prophecy of doom. Does he resist now because unconsciously he senses the implied hostility in his mother's purpose and because he knows that it is a choice between his life and hers? Despite his wife's assertion that she will follow Volumnia's example, he says only

> Not of a woman's tenderness to be,
> Requires nor child nor woman's face to see
> I have sat too long
>
>   (V, iii).

With that he rises to depart. He permits his mother to detain him with a second long plea.

Some psychoanalytic criticism of Shakespeare is impaired by the exclusive attention it pays to plot rather than to close reading of the dialogue. Since Shakespeare customarily chose his dramas from existing narratives, he did not have an entirely free hand in selecting the incidents he dramatized. In this instance, a man in Coriolanus's position would surely have detained, by force if necessary, his wife, his

child, and his mother. But Shakespeare's audience would not have tolerated a change in the outcome of so well-known a legend as that of Coriolanus, even if the poet had desired to make the change. He could, however, and often did subtly alter the psychological motivations for the actions of his borrowed characters. He did so here. Volumnia first menaces Coriolanus with the ignominious reputation he will suffer if he destroys his native city. She pauses for a reply, and when none comes, she prods him futilely with, 'Speak to me, son'. Because he remains silent, she appeals to his sense of honor; that failing, she asks sharply, 'Why dost not speak?'. The next section of her speech, for which Shakespeare found no suggestion in Plutarch, affords a singular display of aggressive, domineering motherhood.

> There's no man in the world
> More bound to's mother; yet here he lets me prate
> Like one i' th' stocks.— Thou hast never in thy life
> Show'd thy dear mother any courtesy,
> When she, poor hen, fond of no second brood,
> Has cluck'd thee to the wars and safely home
> Loaden with honour. Say my request's unjust,
> And spurn me back; but if it be not so
> Thou art not honest; and the gods will plague thee
> That thou restrain'st from me the duty which
> To a mother's part belongs.— He turns away
>
>   (V, iii).

Why does he turn away. The conflict in Coriolanus must be extreme. He has always regarded himself as a patriot; yet in attacking his native city he believes in the justice of his revenge on the plebeians who sought to destroy him, and on the patricians whom he feels betrayed him. He has been a devoted, obedient, and reverent son; yet his mother is maligning him with the monstrously ridiculous charge of filial ingratitude. He turns away in anger, for how can he respond otherwise than with anger to the injustice and bitter hostility of her words?

In real life a Coriolanus would have had other choices than the one here provided of sacrificing his own life to satisfy his mother's demands. But Shakespeare, following Plutarch, could only exercise his great skill in providing satisfying motivations for the actions his source imposed upon him. The psychological and dramatic values implicit in this conflict between mother and son must have determined his decision to develop the characters in Plutarch's biography, and everything he put into the play prepares for this moment. Volumnia's motivation is complex. Rome's salvation must be uppermost. Almost as important is her concern for her son's future fame, especially as his reputation in-

Coriolanus. The University of Michigan Special Collections Library.

volves her own. To subdue him she once again employs her last weapon.

> This is the last. So, we will home to Rome,
> And die among our neighbours. Nay, behold
>   's!
> This boy, that cannot tell what he would
>   have
> But kneels and holds up hands for fellow-
>   ship,
> Does reason our petition with more strength
> Than thou hast power to deny it. Come, let
>   us go:
> This fellow had a Volscian to his mother;
> His wife is in Corioli and his child
> Like him by chance. Yet give us our dispatch:
> I am hush'd until our city be afire,
> And then I'll speak a little
>
>   (V, iii).

Coriolanus yields again not so much to her scornful words as to the repeated threat of suicide. Responsibility for that is more than he can withstand, particularly when it is joined to the challenge to order her to her death that is implied in her words, 'Yet give us our dispatch'.

The stage direction reads, 'He holds her by the hand, silent'. The speech in which he submits moves him to tears, and the tears are shed for himself. 'This unnatural scene', as he calls it, at which the gods laugh, is the spectacle of a mother condemning her son to danger and probable death. After silently holding her hand, he breaks out

>   O mother, mother!
> What have you done? Behold, the heavens do
>   ope,
> The gods look down, and this unnatural
>   scene
> They laugh at. O my mother, mother! O!
> You have won a happy victory to Rome;
> But for your son— believe it, O believe it!—
> Most dangerously you have with him
>   prevail'd,
> If not most mortal to him. But let it come
>
>   (V, iii).

In his British Academy Lecture in 1912, Bradley said, '. . . she answers nothing. And her silence is sublime.' The sublimity is currently less apparent. She has reasserted her supremacy, and there is nothing more to say. That Coriolanus can face death at her command is not surprising; that he has been doing since his youth. Faced with the choice of destroying his mother or losing his own life, he can only, though reluctantly, choose death.

Coriolanus's inexorable maternal superego decrees that he sacrifice himself. At the same time, to the force and rigidity of his superego is added the danger of acting out his matricidal impulses. His conscience is the product of absolute identification with or introjection of Volumnia, and it is fascinating to observe how well Shakespeare understood both the process of superego formation and the sadistic, self-destructive nature of such a conscience. Its genesis is most clearly revealed in an earlier passage as he is taking leave of his mother to go into exile.

>   Nay, mother,
> Where is your ancient courage? You were us'd
> To say extremity was the trier of spirits;
> That common chances common men could
>   bear;
> That when the sea was calm all boats alike
> Show'd mastership in floating; fortune's
>   blows
> When most struck home, being gentle,
>   wounded, craves
> A noble cunning. You were us'd to load me
> With precepts that would make invincible
> The heart that conn'd them
>
>   (IV, i).

These precepts and his mother's example have turned

him into the rigid personality Menenius describes after Coriolanus has brought Rome to the verge of civil war upon being denied the consulship.

> His nature is too noble for the world.
> He would not flatter Neptune for his trident,
> Or Jove for 's power to thunder. His heart's
>   his mouth.
> What his breast forges, that his tongue must
>   vent;
> And being angry, does forget that ever
> He heard the name of death
>
>   (III, i).

Menenius speaks truly although his admiration is uncritical. A little later in the play, Volumnia says, 'Anger's my meat; I sup upon myself, / And so shall starve with feeding' (IV, ii). Coriolanus, of course, has accepted his mother's violence as an appropriate mode of behavior. For him vehement plain-speaking is a compulsion of conscience that cannot be put aside.

Most interesting psychologically is the conflict between mother and son in Act III, Scene ii, when Volumnia urges him to bow to necessity and submit himself to the judgment of the tribunes. It is founded on Shakespeare's surprising understanding of the phenomenon of the child who holds to parental principles with an inflexibility that in no wise binds the parent from whom he has received them. Volumnia is opportunistic and can accommodate herself to the demands of the occasion. Coriolanus cannot, despite the urging of his mother and his friends. No character in Shakespeare's plays adheres so unwaveringly to Polonius's high-sounding but dubious maxim. 'This above all: to thine own self be true, / And it must follow as the night the day / Thou canst not then be false to any man' (Hamlet, I, iii). Volumnia has imposed upon her son a concept of himself, an ideal, that imprisons him within an iron mold that he can crack but cannot break. Throughout the scene he struggles between his desire to obey his mother and the demand of his conscience that he be true to his own nature.

Coriolanus is confused, as any child must be, at discovering the discrepancy between his mother's standards and her practice. The scene opens with Coriolanus's declaration that, no matter what the consequences, he will persist in the defiance of the plebeians that has brought Rome to the brink of civil war. The rash patrician to whom he speaks replies, 'You do the nobler'. What baffles Coriolanus is his mother's censure of his conduct. He confesses his confusion to his friend. Midway through his speech, he becomes aware that his mother has entered and he addresses her.

> I muse my mother
> Does not approve me further, who was wont
> To call them [the plebeians] woollen vassals,

> things created
> To buy and sell with groats, to show bare
>   heads
> When one but of my ordinance stood up
> To speak of peace or war— I talk of you.
> Why did you wish me milder? Would you
>   have me
> False to my nature? Rather say I play
> The man I am
>
>   (III, ii).

Impatient as one must be with his self-destructive obstinacy, one cannot but feel compassion for this bewildered man.

The argument that follows between mother and son about his returning to humble himself and placate the tribunes is wholly engrossing. During the early part of the scene, Volumnia's exhortations arouse only such laconic responses as 'Tush, tush', or 'Why force you this?'. In the face of the combined urgings of Menenius, Cominius, and his mother, he weakens and seems to accept the idea that he must do for others what he would not himself do. Understanding himself better than they do he says, 'You have put me now to such a part which never / I shall discharge to the life'. His mother presses him to yield.

> I prithee now, sweet son, as thou hast said
> My praises made thee first a soldier, so,
> To have my praise for this, perform a part
> Thou hast not done before
>
>   (III, ii).

In the first ten lines of his reply to his mother, Coriolanus bitterly expresses his sense of betrayal of himself; the degradation of himself she requires him to perpetrate.

> Well, I must do't.
> Away my disposition, and possess me
> Some harlot's spirit. My throat of war be
>   turn'd,
> Which choir'd with my drum, into a pipe
> Small as a eunuch's, or the virgin voice
> That babies lull asleep! The smiles of knaves
> Tent in my cheeks, and schoolboys' tears take up
> The glasses of my sight! A beggar's tongue
> Make motion through my lips, and my arm'd
>   knees,
> Who bow'd but in the stirrup, bend like his
> That hath receiv'd an alms!— I will not do't,
> Lest I surcease to honour mine own truth
> And by my body's action teach my mind
> A most inherent baseness
>
>   (III, ii).

To bend this steel conscience to her will, Volumnia at once accuses him of preferring her death to the sacrifice of his pride. Pride she calls it, and some there may be, but here as elsewhere he is following the only course of conduct his superego will permit. As horror of his repressed matricide exceeds his revulsion at the humiliation he must undergo, he submits and undertakes to force himself to act against his desires.

We are now prepared to understand one of the most perplexing minor problems of the play: why Coriolanus cannot accept the praise of his admirers but must habitually disparage his feats of heroism, and stubbornly conceal his wounds and scars. When Cominius, his general, starts to proclaim to the Senate Coriolanus's heroic exploits, he refuses 'To stay to hear my nothings monstered' (II, ii). He shuns all praise, especially in the scene in the first act following his victory over the Volscians. As Lartius begins to narrate to Cominius his valorous deeds, Coriolanus interrupts.

> Pray now, no more. My mother
> Who has a charter to extol her blood,
> When she does praise me grieves me. I have done
> As you have done, that's what I can; induc'd
> As you have been, that's for my country.
> He that has but effected his good will
> Hath overta'en my act
>
> (I, ix).

In another man this generous statement that the risk and the effort make all equal might be called modesty. Although Coriolanus is no braggart, one can hardly attribute modesty to this fierce, arrogant, scornful, vituperative, aggressive, lofty patrician.

The true explanation of this interesting facet of Coriolanus's personality affords another insight into Shakespeare's psychological subtlety. Volumnia provides the basis for understanding in a speech imagining her son in battle against the Volscians.

> Methinks I hear hither your husband's drum;
> See him pluck Aufidius down by the hair;
> As children from a bear, the Volsces shunning him.
> Methinks I see him stamp thus, and call thus:
> 'Come on you cowards! You were got in fear,
> Though you were born in Rome.' His bloody brow
> With his mail'd hand then wiping, forth he goes
> Like to a harvest-man that's task'd to mow
> Or all or lose his hire
>
> (I, iii).

The final simile contains the secret. Like the reaper who must mow the whole field or get no pay, Coriolanus must achieve the absolute or deserve neither reward nor praise. He is aware of his extraordinary exploits, but even they do not satisfy the exorbitant demands his conscience makes upon him. He is a truly pitiable figure. He can be contemptuous of cowardice and weakness in others, but because he can never do enough, he cannot win the gratification of self-approval. Since self-approval is lacking, he hears the praise others, even or especially his mother, heap upon him with pain rather than pleasure.

I have tried in this paper to make plain some previously unheeded aspects of the relationship between this mother and son. Specifically, there is her determination to maintain her dominance over him, even at the cost of his life. To achieve her supremacy on the two occasions when his rebellion threatens her role of Roman mother, as she conceives it, she resorts to the charge of matricide. Second, the exorbitance and inflexibility of Coriolanus's conscience force him into pain and danger without the reward of self-approval. His superego compels him to act politically in a provocative and self-defeating manner, bewilders him when he finds his mother can abandon the principles he has learned from her, and, in the end, makes him choose his own death rather than hers. Volumnia is most truly Coriolanus's tragedy; defeat is the inevitable end for the arrogant, angry, rigid man she has created.

Shakespeare clearly approached the œdipal situation in Coriolanus with a directness and bitterness impossible when he wrote Hamlet. No longer must the hero be a young 'sweet prince', 'the glass of fashion and the mold of form', a courtier, soldier, scholar. Nor is Volumnia like Gertrude, gracious, warm, affectionate, charming, penitent, devoted, who lies and makes excuses for Hamlet and whose last words are spoken to save his life. Shakespeare made Volumnia a most repulsive mother, who created a son we can admire and pity but cannot like. Shakespeare allowed her no word after she forced Coriolanus's submission. In Rome all classes hail her as the patroness and savior of the city, but in Corioli, alone among his ancient enemies, her son pays the price for her victory with the death to which she unlamentingly dispatched him. A Volscian lord orders his funeral.

> Bear hence his body,
> And mourn you for him. Let him be regarded
> As the most noble corse that ever herald
> Did follow to his urn
>
> (V, vi).

With the same cold, griefless admiration, the audience takes leave of Caius Marcius Coriolanus, Rome's mightiest warrior, the haughtiest and most irascible of her patricians. We respect him for his valor and honesty, but his uncontrolled ferocity and arrogance make him the least lovable and least loved of

Shakespeare's tragic heroes. He is the masculine counterpart and product of his mother, her victim in life and death.

With another writer there might be no more to say. But I have oversimplified Shakespeare's judgment. Coriolanus, like many other characters, is the beneficiary of Shakespeare's dramatic impartiality. And therein lies a most attractive insight into the poet's own personality. The finest spirit of modern psychotherapy is given expression by the words of the Duke in *Measure for Measure:* 'Love talks with better knowledge, and knowledge with dearer love' (III, ii). One finds characters in many of the plays speaking and acting in that spirit. One of the most extended and subtle of these instances occurs in that famous speech of Hamlet's:

> So, oft it chances in particular men,
> That, for some vicious mole of nature in
>   them,
> As, in their birth— wherein they are not
>   guilty,
> Since nature cannot choose his origin—
> By their o'ergrowth of some complexion
> Oft breaking down the pales and forts of
>   reason,
> Or by some habit that too much o'erleavens
> The form of plausive manners, that these men,
> Carrying, I say, the stamp of one defect,
> Being nature's livery, or fortune's star,—
> Their virtues else— be they as pure as grace,
> As infinite as man may undergo—
> Shall in the general censure take corruption
> From that particular fault . . .
>
> (I, iv).

It is odd that most critics have failed to recognize that Hamlet, and so presumably Shakespeare, would never join 'in the general censure', in those popular condemnations that spring from conventional morality and consequent failure of understanding. Another character Shakespeare drew who exhibits this insight and love is Lepidus in Antony and Cleopatra. Replying to Octavius Caesar's violent attack on Antony's passion for Cleopatra, he says:

> I must not think there are
> Evils enow to darken all his goodness.
> His faults, in him, seem as the spots of
>   heaven,
> More fiery by night's blackness; hereditary,
> Rather than purchas'd; what he cannot change,
> Than what he chooses
>
> (I, iv).

His genius, probably furthered by reading St. Paul, that great apostolic psychologist, brought Shakespeare this psychological tolerance. The quality finds expression in a pair of interesting comments on Coriolanus in the first scene of the play.

> *First Citizen:* I say unto you, what he hath done famously, he did it to that end. Though soft-conscienc'd men can be content to say it was for his country, he did it to please his mother, and to be partly proud; which he is even to the altitude of his virtue.
>
> *Second Citizen:* What he cannot help in his nature, you account a vice in him
>
> (I, i).

Here as elsewhere Shakespeare leaves us with the blissful uncertainty of suspended judgment. He seems to have felt, like Joseph Conrad, that one must speculate about, but can never fully explain, something so complicated as a human being. Just before the climax of this play, Aufidius, Coriolanus's inveterate enemy, ponders the mystery of his ally and adversary.

> I think he'll be to Rome
> As is the osprey to the fish, who takes it
> By sovereignty of nature. First he was
> A noble servant to them; but he could not
> Carry his honours even: whether 'twas pride,
> Which out of daily fortune ever taints
> The happy man; whether defect of judgement,
> To fail in the disposing of those chances
> Which he was lord of; or whether nature,
> Not to be other than one thing, not moving
> From th' casque to th' cushion, but com-
>   manding peace
> Even with the same austerity and garb
> As he controll'd the war; but one of these,—
> As he hath spices of them all— not all,—
> For I dare so far free him,— made him fear'd;
> So, hated; and so, banish'd; but he has a
>   merit
> To choke it in the utterance
>
> (IV, vii).

The realization reflected in these passages that man is not captain of his soul, that he is subject to intrapsychic forces beyond his conscious control, is surely the ultimate source of Shakespeare's large, liberal, humane representation of mankind.

The uncertain chronology of Shakespeare's plays makes it dangerous to yield to the temptation to connect the writing of Coriolanus with the death of Shakespeare's mother in September 1609. But this bleak treatment of the mother-son relationship most certainly brought to an end the extended self-catharsis that emerged during the eight or nine years of his great tragic period, which included Hamlet, King Lear, Othello, and Macbeth. The necessity for identifying with his heroes in order to express their passions and anguish required that the artist have access to his most strongly repressed unconscious feelings.

Emmett Wilson, Jr.

SOURCE: "Coriolanus: The Anxious Bridegroom," originally published in *American Imago*, Vol. 25, 1968. Reprinted in *'Coriolanus': Critical Essays*, edited by David Wheeler, Garland Publishing, Inc., 1995, pp. 93-110.

[*In the following essay (originally published in 1968), Wilson offers a psychoanalytic approach to* Coriolanus, *evaluating language and imagery that suggests Freudian conflicts within the play. The critic begins by analyzing the unique bodily imagery of* Coriolanus, *through which sexuality and war are thematically linked. Wilson also notes the psychological resonance of aggression in the play's family relationships. Oedipal, or incestuous, motifs appear as do Coriolanus's anxieties concerning his symbolic castration by his domineering and masculine— or "phallic"— mother, Volumnia. Wilson further explores Coriolanus's hostility toward his mother and his rebellion against her. This revolt, in turn, is characterized by the homoerotic overtones of Coriolanus's relationship with Aufidius— who also becomes a surrogate for Coriolanus's absent father— as the two men join forces to attack Rome, i.e. Volumnia.*]

In *Coriolanus*, Shakespeare adapted a plot from North's translation of *Plutarch's Lives* into an intensive exploration of a pathological mother-son relationship. It is the story of a son who attempts to rebel against his mother, to whom he has been inordinately attached. The son is ultimately destroyed when he renounces his rebellion and submits to his mother. In this paper, I wish to examine certain aspects of the play for the unconscious fantasies which may have determined the handling of the narrative material from which Shakespeare worked. In particular, I suggest that an examination of the wedding night references in the play is essential for an understanding of the work on a psychoanalytical level.

The play has sometimes been cited as peculiar among Shakespeare's works. Critics discern a "slackness" in Shakespeare's dramatic power. This slackness is supposed to be reflected in the way in which Shakespeare handled his source material. If we compare Shakespeare's adaptation with the original in North's translation, we find at several points an almost slavish closeness to the source. This dependence on North is so extensive that at first reading, the play seems little more than a simple dramatization of the plot from North. Editors have been able to make emendations and fill textual lacunae in the play by referring to North, so faithfully has Shakespeare followed his source. The later acts of the play, especially, show a marked increase in borrowing, and tend to rely almost exclusively on North. Shakespeare might, of course, have been under some merely temporal pressure to complete the play, but this marked change in the processing of the material could also have been due to the conflictual

nature of the subject matter. At any rate, Shakespeare seems to have adhered doggedly to his source in order to finish his task.

Yet, the earlier acts and the characters introduced there involve a good deal of revision and reworking of the material. Shakespeare has developed certain characters and added others, and has elaborated on the relationship of Coriolanus to the various individuals who are significant to him. Further, Shakespeare's particular choices of expression in the play are striking. The language has been called harsh. The poetry seems at times to disguise only slightly some rather grotesque ideas. As an example of the grossness of thought, consider Coriolanus' rebuke to the tribunes for their failure to control the mob: "You being their mouths, why rule you not their teeth?" These additions by Shakespeare to his source material are important for a psychological understanding of the play.

Imagery

The peculiar imagery Shakespeare has chosen tends to support the view that the theme of the play was one to which the playwright was psychologically sensitive. The images tend to fall within a narrow range. Caroline Spurgeon found these to be concerned largely with bodily functions, sickness, and loss of diseased bodily parts. Blood, and things made bloody, are constantly mentioned. Stoller calls attention to the numerous staves, pikes, rakes, swords, and other phallic equivalents. There are many references to wounds and to parts of the body, or simply to parts. Coriolanus shouts angrily to the mob, "Go get you home, you fragments!" (1.1.211).

Combat and sexuality are often linked. Battles are described in sexual images, or talk of battle provides the opportunity for a reference to sexual activity. Cominius, the Roman commander-in-chief, proudly describes some teenage battle exploit of Coriolanus as occurring at an age when he might have acted "the woman in the scene" (2.2.92). Peace is a "great maker of cuckolds" (4.5.225). Coriolanus threatens to beat the Volscians "to their wives" (1.4.41). Volumnia, his mothers, says of Coriolanus' impetuous attitude toward the mob,

> . . . I know thou hadst rather
> Follow thine enemy in a fiery gulf
> Than flatter him in a bower.
>
> (3.2.90-92)

Curiously, while Coriolanus is in battle in Act I, Volumnia and her friend go to visit a lady lying in (1.3.72).

Another significant group of images is oral. In this play of a mother-child relationship, there are frequent allusions to food, nourishment, ingestion, hunger, biting, or devouring. To note one important instance: Some servingmen are speaking of the personal rivalry between Coriolanus and his Volscian opponent, Aufidius. They recall the battle of Corioli:

> *First Serv.* Before Corioli he [Coriolanus]
> scotched him and notched him like a
> carbonado [meat cut up for cooking].
>
> *Second Serv.* And he had been cannibally given,
> he might have boiled and eaten him too.
>
> (4.5.186-89)

In some images, aggressive impulses are characteristically directed towards the interior of the body. Coriolanus' attacks on Rome are said to be "pouring war / Into the bowels of ungrateful Rome" (4.5.129). When Volumnia entreats Coriolanus to cease warring on Rome, he is said to want to tread upon his mother's womb (5.3.124). He is charged with

> Making the mother, wife and child, to see
> The son, the husband and the father, tearing
> His country's bowels out.
>
> (5.3.101-03)

This juxtaposition of aggression with the family relationships is striking, and provides unambiguous evidence of the symbolic character of the attack on Rome as an attack on those objects whom previously Coriolanus had loved. The repetition of this sort of imagery is impressive, and indicates the extent and strength of certain unconscious fantasies: the fear of being eaten, and the rage against the mother's engulfing body.

The Wedding Night

In the midst of these grotesque images of blood, aggression, and bodily destruction, there is a scene in which Coriolanus rises to intense lyric expression. In the battle at Corioli, he expresses the joy of victory, and greets his general, Cominius with

> O, let me clip ye
> In arms as sound as when I wooed; in heart
> As merry as when our nuptial day was done,
> And tapers burned to bedward!
>
> (1.6.29-32)

Here, we find an obvious reference to a specific sexual event, and an unconscious reference in the phallic burning tapers. The significance of the image is further heightened by one other reference to a wedding night. When Coriolanus joins Aufidius as an ally against Rome, Aufidius expresses *his* joy by referring to his bride on her first crossing the threshold, and he declares that he is even more rapt by Coriolanus than he was by his bride:

> Know thou first,
> I loved the maid I married: never man

Sighed truer breath; but that I see thee here,
Thou noble thing, more dances my rapt heart
Than when I first my wedded mistress saw
Bestride my threshold.

> (4.5.112-17)

Commentators have noted these two references to the wedding night. Perhaps the most insightful is Rank's brief discussion. However, the meaning of these two passages in *Coriolanus* has not been sufficiently explored. Further examination of these passages is important, for the wedding night images condense several major themes of the play.

To understand Coriolanus' reference to his wedding night, we need to examine the scene in which the reference occurs. Preceding Coriolanus' lyric recall of this event, there is a series of scenes of the battle before Corioli, in which Coriolanus is especially in danger of being deserted by his men and closed up within the gates of the enemy town. Coriolanus exhorts his soldiers to charge the Volscians when the battle first begins at the gates of Corioli. In particular, he threatens any stragglers with his "edge" (1.4.29). This threat proves insufficient. As Coriolanus follows the Volscians to the gates of their city, he still needs to urge the Roman soldiers to enter the gates with him:

> So, now the gates are ope. Now prove good
> seconds.
> 'Tis for the followers fortune widens them,
> Not for the fliers. Mark me, and do the like.
>
> (1.4.43-45)

Yet precisely before the open gates, he is deserted. The Roman response to his exhortation is:

First Sol.: Foolhardiness. Not I.
Second Sol.: Nor I.
First Sol.: See, they have shut him in.

> (1.4.46-47)

In Plutarch, when Coriolanus stormed the gates, others were with him. The complete abandonment is stressed by the soldiers: "He is himself alone, / To answer all the city" (1.4.52-53). They immediately suppose that he is dead, that he is gone "to th' pot" (1.4.48). In view of the recurrent theme of being eaten, it is very likely that those commentators are correct who suppose that the pot here is a cooking pot, and that the line means that Coriolanus has been cut to pieces.

The battle is carried by the Romans as their commander, Cominius, arrives. Coriolanus reappears, covered with blood. He sees Cominius and asks, "Come I too late?" Cominius replies, "Ay, if you come not in the blood of others, / But mantled in your own" (1.6.27-29). Coriolanus responds to the question whether he is wounded by saying that his arms are as sound as before he married, and then refers to his wedding night in an effusion of joy and enthusiasm. Curiously, Coriolanus does not give a direct answer to Cominius' question until he boasts later to Aufidius: "'Tis not my blood / Wherein thou seest me masked" (1.8.9-10).

In these scenes at Corioli, we have a battle in which the important elements are the opening and penetration of the enemy's defenses with the resulting danger of destruction to the attacker. Following the battle, there is a specific reference to the first sexual union between Coriolanus and his bride. As if to underscore the allusion to defloration, Cominius immediately after the wedding night memory, addresses Coriolanus as "Flower of warriors" (1.6.32). There is, I suggest, a symbolic parallel between the battle at Corioli and unconscious fantasies concerning the experience of the wedding night. The battle is, as it were, a symbolic re-enactment of the anxiety provoking sexual event, defloration. The battle scene at Corioli expresses the unconscious equation of coitus with a violent, damaging assault, an equation which we noted earlier in the imagery of the play. Castration anxieties aroused by coitus are heightened by the actual accompaniment of the sexual act by bleeding and a change in the female's bodily status. In the unconscious, defloration is equated with the castration of the sexual partner, and there is an associated dread of a mutilating retaliation. The feared punishment, castration, is symbolized in the battle by the danger of becoming entrapped within the gates, to be cut up and devoured. In the memory of defloration which follows the battle scenes, Coriolanus may well be attempting to deal with his terrifying discovery that he had created a sexual difference in his bride, by making her into a woman, i.e., a person who had been deprived of the phallus. Ultimately, the punishment that is dreaded for this act is a revenge by his mother on her son for having entertained these notions of assault against her body and, of course, on a deeper level, the woman who is castrated in the sexual act would be the phallic mother, Volumnia.

If I am correct in this analysis of the battle at Corioli, then the award of the name, "Coriolanus," for exploits in that battle may also be of psychological importance. For this, however, we must turn to a passage in North which has not been transferred to the play, but which may very well have influenced Shakespeare in his conception of the battle scenes. In the play, the hero receives his *agnomen*, "Coriolanus," as an honorary "trophy" for the events of the battle. The unconscious meaning of such a trophy is familiar to us as signifying the castration of the enemy and the sadistic wish to rob him of his penis. But from North's translation of Plutarch's *Life of Coriolanus*, we learn that the name could also have been given to signify, and to compensate for, an injury which the bearer of the name had received. In North, a lengthy discussion occurs on the Roman habit of according such names. In this passage North states:

Sometimes also [the Romans] give surnames derived of some mark of misfortune of the body. As Sylla, to say, "crooked-nose"; Niger, "black"; Rufus, "red"; Caecus, "blind"; Claudus, "lame." They did wisely in this thing to accustom men to think that neither the loss of sight nor other such misfortunes as may chance to men are any shame or disgrace unto them; but the manner was to answer boldly to such names, as if they were called by their proper names.

In view of this comment from North on the secondary meaning of an *agnomen* as commemorative of mutilation, there is a significant parallel to be noted between the attempt to master the psychological sequellae of mutilation by the award of a compensatory *agnomen*, and the use Shakespeare makes of the scene before Corioli as a repetition in symbolic form of an experience involving an intense fear of bodily mutilation in retaliation for forbidden sexual wishes. The same psychological mechanism would seem to be operative in the *agnomen* and in the repetition of the traumatic scene—the attempt to master a traumatic event by some compensatory maneuver after the fact. Coriolanus was wounded at Corioli, and when he stands for the consulship, Coriolanus must display the scars from the battle at Corioli, scars which mark him as having distinguished himself in the service of Rome just as much as his *agnomen* and other honors do. When Coriolanus rejects the subservient position which he had maintained to Volumnia in the first half of the play, he vehemently rejects his *agnomen* at the same time, and wants to forge another in the "fire of burning Rome" (5.1.14). There are thus some indications of a reversal of the significance of the name received at Corioli to represent Coriolanus' continued subservience to Volumnia, and his acquiescence in the role that she demanded of him.

The wound motif continues and further develops the fantasy which appears in the battle scenes at Corioli. The question of these wounds comes to dominate the scenes subsequent to the battle, and provides us with important information on the relationship between Coriolanus and his mother. The phallic castrating mother rejoices in his wounds for the purpose of going before the people: "O, he is wounded: I thank the gods for't" (2.1.107) because "there will be large cicatrices to show the people when he shall stand for his place" (2.1.132). It was a traditional requirement that all aspirants to the consulship stand before the populace and display battle wounds. Coriolanus, however, finds this custom ignominious and objectionable. The mob has from the first been presented as a cannibalistic threat to Coriolanus (1.1), and it has been suggested that the mob stands for the aggressive and dangerous aspects of the mother. Coriolanus' reluctance to display his wounds to the mob is Shakespeare's modification of his source, for in Plutarch the problem does not arise at all. Moreover, standing for the consulship is Volumnia's idea, and Coriolanus can be prevailed upon to go to the people with his wounds only at his mother's insistent cajoling and threats. Volumnia's wish to see her son as a consul, and her role in forcing him to submit to the people, give evidence of the way in which Shakespeare has adapted the plot to strengthen the dominating influence which Volumnia has over her son. Just as she had rejoiced in his wounds, the mob is to see in these same wounds evidence that Coriolanus loves and will faithfully serve Rome. Volumnia thus forces Coriolanus into a position of pleasing and placating the aggressive aspects of herself which the mob symbolizes. Coriolanus can flatter the mob only if he shows his wounds, i.e., if he shows those symbols of castration which were needed to continue in his mother's favor. The sexual nature of the display of his body to the populace is suggested when Volumnia says that it is to "flatter [his enemy] in a bower" (3.2.92). Menenius excuses Coriolanus' insolence by "He loves your people, / But tie him not to be their bedfellow" (2.2.60-61). But it is clear that this is a sexual submission, not a conquest. At the moment of capitulation to Volumnia's urgings, Coriolanus launches a torrent of petulant language showing that his position is not only ignominious but also a threat to his masculinity. To submit will make his voice "Small as an eunuch . . ." (3.2.114). Finally he begins to speak as a little boy:

> Mother, I am going to the market place:
> Chide me no more . . . Look, I am going.
> (3.2.131-2, 134)

Rebellion against the Phallic Mother

I have so far explored *Coriolanus* in those sections which express the fantasies associated with the active phase of the Oedipus complex and the expected castration by the phallic mother for entertaining aggressive impulses toward her. I now turn to the episodes in which Coriolanus rebels against the phallic mother and seeks an alternative expression of his oedipal striving. Coriolanus abandons Rome and his mother, and turns traitor to the Romans, joining with their traditional enemies, the Volscians.

Rebellion is introduced in the opening scene, in which the Roman mob is about to turn against established authority. The mob is quieted, by means of a tale of another rebellion, that of the body's members against the belly (1.1). This theme of betrayal is sustained throughout the play. In certain passages, a sexual betrayal is clearly suggested. In the scene immediately preceding Coriolanus' suit to join Aufidius and betray the Romans, a Roman traitor and a Volscian spy meet to exchange information and the following comment is made:

> I have heard it said the fittest time to corrupt a

> man's wife is when she's fallen out with her husband
>
> (4.3.26-28)

These frequent allusions to treachery and betrayal provide a background for the behavior of Coriolanus, who is at first falsely, and later with some justification, labelled a traitor. It is the false charge of treason that provokes Coriolanus and provides him with the excuse to become a traitor in fact by leading an attack on Rome at the head of the Volscian forces. When Coriolanus capitulates to his mother's entreaties in Act V and leaves off his attack on Rome, he is in the awkward position of betraying the Volscian cause which he had joined. Aufidius can justifiably charge him with treason and demand his death.

There are, in addition, some clear indications of Coriolanus' extreme ambivalence toward his libidinal objects. This ambivalence is expressed in a total repudiation and withdrawal when negative feelings have been aroused. In changing allegiance from Rome to the Volscians, Coriolanus plots the total destruction of Rome. When Coriolanus left Rome in Act IV, he was still friendly with his party in Rome, and was ready to acknowledge and express his affection for his mother and his family. In Act V, he rejects all overtures from these friends. In Plutarch, Coriolanus is milder and shrewder. He spares the goods and estates of the nobles in his war on Rome, thereby spreading party dissension in Rome. Revenge on Rome in the form of a humiliating surrender would have been satisfactory for Plutarch's Coriolanus. In Shakespeare, nothing short of the destruction and burning of Rome itself will do. Coriolanus rejects Menenius, his mother Volumnia, and his wife. At the moment that Volumnia's embassy arrives at the Volscian camp, Coriolanus resolves to "stand / As if a man were author of himself / And knew no other kin" (5.3.35-37). He had made the same resolve to Menenius earlier: "Wife, mother, child, I know not. My affairs / Are servanted to others" (5.2.75-76). This insistence on a complete rejection is characteristic of Shakespeare's Coriolanus, who seems unable to tolerate any ambiguity in situations which involve his emotional commitment.

In addition, Coriolanus views any struggle for power with extreme anxiety. He resents the newly established office of tribune. Where, in North's version, Coriolanus' objection is restrained, in Shakespeare, Coriolanus objects to the Tribuneship because

> It makes the consuls base! and my soul aches
> To know, when two authorities are up,
> Neither supreme, how soon confusion
> May enter 'twixt the gap of both and take
> The one by th'other.
>
> (3.1.108-12)

It is reasonable to suppose that the prototypes in the

unconscious of these two warring authorities are to be found in the original family situation, with parental roles presumably confused and conflicting, providing the opportunity to exploit and intensify the difficulties between the parents, and to play one off against the other.

In his soliloquy just before he goes over to the Volscians as an enemy of Rome, Coriolanus also expresses the theme of ambivalence and his concern with the struggle for supremacy:

> O world, thy slippery turns! Friends now fast
>   sworn,
> Whose double bosoms seems to wear one
>   heart,
> Whose hours, whose bed, whose meal and
>   exercise
> Are still together, who twin, as 'twere, in love
> Unseparable, shall within this hour,
> On a dissension of a doit, break out
> To bitterest enmity. So, fellest foes,
> Whose passions and whose plots have broke
>   their sleep
> To take the one the other, by some chance,
> Some trick not worth an egg, shall grow dear
>   friends
> And interjoin their issues. So with me:
> My birthplace hate I, and my love's upon
> This enemy town.
>
>   (4.4.12-24)

Here, Coriolanus anticipates the intensely homoerotic relationship into which he is about to move, when Aufidius will want to "twine" his arms around him (4.5.105). Yet he also anticipates the outcome of the trust he is about to place in Aufidius, for a moment after this extended comment on the transiency of human relationships, we see Coriolanus embraced as a bosom friend, and welcomed with greater joy than the welcome accorded a new bride, by the man who will shortly bring about his death.

Quest for a Surrogate Father

I will now examine the aspects of the play which indicate Coriolanus' attempt to institute a satisfactory expression of the passive phase of the Oedipus complex, in which he aspires to be loved by a powerful father, displacing his mother as his father's primary object.

Coriolanus' biological father remains vague in both North and Shakespeare. Yet two figures in the play serve as psychological representatives of a father to Coriolanus. One of these is the old family friend, Menenius. The other is Aufidius, who becomes an idealized father after the rejection of Volumnia.

Menenius is an apt psychological symbol for the weak and conquered father appropriate to Coriolanus' wishes

in the active phase of the Oedipus complex in which Volumnia is in the ascendancy as Coriolanus' object. Shakespeare developed the charming and complex character of Menenius almost independently of North, who gives only a few hints concerning a gentle old man who was loved by the people, and was a good choice to carry the Senate's message to a rebellious populace. But Menenius remains a weak person, especially in comparison with the stalwart Volumnia. He fawns over a letter which Coriolanus had written him, in a fashion virtually indistinguishable from the responses of the women who have also received letters (2.1). Perhaps the most masterly touch in the contrast of Volumnia and Menenius is in their parting exchange after Coriolanus has been accompanied to the gates of Rome as he goes into exile. Menenius' response to this day of emotional trials is to note that he is hungry and to arrange for dinner. Not so for Volumnia:

> *Men:*   You'll sup with me?
> *Vol:* Anger's my meat: I sup upon myself
> And so shall starve with feeding.
>
>   (4.2.49-51)

Many passages explicitly refer to Menenius as Coriolanus' father. In his embassy to save Rome, Menenius declares confidently to a guard who is preventing him from seeing Coriolanus, "You shall perceive that a Jack guardant cannot office me from my son Coriolanus" (5.2.59). It is also apparent that the relationship is erotically tinged. Menenius in his frustration shouts at the guard, "I tell thee, fellow, / Thy general is my lover" (5.2.13-14), and Coriolanus, after sending the disappointed old man away, says: "This man, Aufidius, / Was my beloved in Rome" (5.2.85-86). It would seem that Menenius adulated Coriolanus too much to be an ideal substitute for the missing father. Menenius boasts, for example, "I have been / The book of his good acts" (5.2.13-14). Also, Menenius often acts as Volumnia's agent, i.e., as a person who can appeal to Coriolanus and affect his behavior only through Coriolanus' respect and awe for his mother. As Coriolanus' anger against the mob is beginning to get out of control, Menenius attempts to restrain Coriolanus with: "Is this the promise that you made to your mother?" (3.3.87).

In opposition to the quasi-familial situation of the earlier scenes of the play in which a strong mother dominates both Coriolanus and his weak, defeated, and castrated father, there is later the alternative oedipal solution in which Coriolanus repudiates his mother, and all her symbolic representatives, to seek out the strong, masculine father. The awesome figure of Aufidius, a marked contrast to Menenius, provides the second father symbol in the play.

The turn to Aufidius involves an intense and passive homoerotic relationship, for which we have been prepared. Even while Coriolanus and Aufidius are still enemies, Aufidius was admired. Coriolanus tells us in Act I:

> I sin in envying his nobility;
> And were I anything but what I am,
> I would wish me only he.
>
> (1.1.219-221)

Passive homosexual yearnings which Coriolanus had felt for a strong father now find expression in the renunciation of Volumnia in favor of a loving relationship with the virile Aufidius. The second allusion to a wedding night occurs in Act IV, when Aufidius welcomes Coriolanus as an ally. This time, however, it is Aufidius who thinks of his wedding night. Coriolanus is clearly supplanting Aufidius' previous erotic attachment to a woman. This new and strong father is eager to accept Coriolanus, and he looks on Coriolanus as on a bride crossing the threshold, even preferring his present happiness with Coriolanus to his wedding night.

The sexual character of this turning from Volumnia to Aufidius is also shown in the banter with the servingmen in this scene:

> *Serv* How, Sir! Do you meddle with my
> master?
> *Cor:* Ay, 'tis an honester service than to
> meddle with thy mistress.
>
> (4.5.45-46)

A servingman later says that Aufidius now loves Coriolanus as a woman: "Our general himself makes a mistress of him . . ." (4.5.194).

Earlier, Coriolanus was able to express his memory of defloration anxieties as he embraced Cominius, that is, when he is protected in a homoerotic embrace he can recall the threatening heterosexual experience. Another such embrace occurs between Aufidius and Coriolanus. In both scenes containing the wedding night allusions, the same word is used for this embrace, *viz.*, "clip." Coriolanus had turned to Cominius with the words: "O, let me clip ye / In arms as sound as when I wooed . . ." (1.6.29-30). In his welcome to Coriolanus, Aufidius uses this word also:

> *Auf:*   Here I clip
> The anvil of my sword, and do contest
> As hotly and as nobly with thy love
> As ever in ambitious strength I did
> Contend against thy valor. Know thou first,
> I loved the maid I married. . . .
>
> (4.5.108-113)

In Elizabethan English, "clip" would have meant both "to embrace" and "to cut off." In this repeated word, we thus have an unconscious continuation of the theme of castration which links the two wedding night allusions.

The embrace with Aufidius involves, on the unconscious level, the necessity for undergoing castration as a precondition of the father's love. To gain the love of Aufidius, Coriolanus must reject his city, his family, his mother, he must hate his birthplace, and turn his love onto the man who had previously been his rival. It is precisely the question of what further price must be paid to be loved by Aufidius that leads to difficulties in the new role as Aufidius' minion. Earlier, we saw that Coriolanus had feared castration as a retaliation for what he had wished to do to his mother. Now he expects that he must give up his masculinity in order to be loved by the strong and virile father.

Coriolanus attempts to meet this condition, on a symbolic level. In his soliloquy he had anticipated an eventual rivalry and falling out with Aufidius (4.4.12). Passages in the play indicate Coriolanus' self-destructive tendencies which will cause his own downfall. The tribunes had recognized this self-destructive trait and used it to their advantage. Brutus hoped to make Coriolanus angry because

> then he speaks
> What's in his heart; and that is there which
> looks
> With us to break his neck.
>
> (3.3.28-30)

Aufidius' jealousy is aroused when Coriolanus becomes haughty by the honors bestowed on him by the Volscians. When Volumnia's pleas prevail and the attack against Rome is called off, Coriolanus has in effect given Aufidius sufficient reason for anger. Coriolanus sees his own downfall, although he feels helpless to control or modify the events:

> O my mother, mother! O!
> You have won a happy victory to Rome;
> But, for your son, believe it, O, believe it,
> Most dangerously you have with him prevailed,
> If not most mortal to him. But let it come.
> Aufidius. . . .
>
> (5.3.185-90)

He has betrayed the Volscians, and it is with this that Aufidius charges him, and justifies killing him.

The relationship with Aufidius is incomplete until he has made an attack on Coriolanus' body. On a deeper level, Coriolanus' death at the hands of Aufidius is also a love-union with Aufidius, which has been achieved by giving up his masculinity. By the equation of death and castration, Coriolanus has obtained the longed-for union with his father. At the moment of this attack, Coriolanus is denied his *agnomen* and condescendingly called "boy" instead. Almost the last breath Coriolanus takes is expended in his anger at this name of "boy." He boasts of his exploits at Corioli:

> 'tis there
> That, like an eagle in a dovecote, I
> Fluttered your Volscians in Corioli
> Alone I did it. "Boy!"
>
> (5.6.114-17)

In his anger, Coriolanus recalls his role at Corioli, an episode which symbolized a mutilating attack on the mother's body. This memory occurs precisely at the moment when he is to succumb to a mutilating attack by the strong father to whom he had offered himself as a love object. His identification with his mother is now complete, for he is about to be attacked and loved by his father in her stead, just as he had once desired to love her.

In summary: We may regard the earlier portions of *Coriolanus* as an articulation of the conflict found in those family constellations in which the father abdicates his function as a masculine figure for the son to identify with and to form an ego ideal. Menenius fulfilled this role symbolically in the initial situation. There is a splitting of the unconscious elements, with the defeat and castration of the father pushed into the past as an historical death, while certain aspects of the father are displaced on to Menenius in the present. In the place of a strong father, there is the ineffectual Menenius, whom Coriolanus may disregard as a feared rival for his mother.

However, Coriolanus' incestuous strivings are constantly stimulated and intensified by Volumnia in her erotization of the relationship. Coriolanus fears being engulfed by Volumnia in her ambitious designs to use him for her own goals. He is to function as her penile projection, by winning victories which will make her proud and give her opportunity to extol her blood. She would prefer military exploits to any show of tenderness:

> If my son were my husband, I should freelier rejoice in that absence wherein he won honor than in the embracements of his bed where he would show most love. (1.3.2-4)

The ego boundaries between mother and son are vague and indistinct. Coriolanus feels undifferentiated from his mother who is inimical to his development as an individual distinct from her. Coriolanus' view of his male role is thus markedly disturbed.

The sexualized attachment to Volumnia is uncomfortable because of the awareness of his hostility toward her, and of his aggressive impulses directed toward her body. Coriolanus has to deal not only with his own aggression and hatred, but also with the tendency to project this aggression on to its object in the form of

anticipated retaliation for these angry and hostile feelings. Coriolanus is operating on the phallic dichotomy of "having a penis" vs. "being castrated." These were precisely the themes involved in the wedding night reference in Act I, *viz.,* the belief that in intercourse violence is done to the woman's body, and the expectation of castrating punishment for this violence. The symbolic representation of this engulfment and destruction takes place in the battle when Coriolanus is closed off within the enemy gates and supposed dead.

Along with the fears of being castrated by the phallic mother, Coriolanus has feminine, passive wishes to submit to a strong father, even if the price is castration as a precondition for the father's love. The later portions of the play articulate this intense wish for a virile, loving father. Coriolanus joins with Aufidius to war against the mother's body, pouring war into her bowels, and treading upon her womb. Aggression towards Volumnia, which had in the earlier sections of the play been symbolically channeled on to the mob as representative of the mother, is now expressed by the massive rejection of Rome, birthplace, and mother. Aufidius and Coriolanus unite in love for one another and in mutual hatred for Rome and mother. Yet this solution is not completely successful until Aufidius is provoked to attack Coriolanus' own body, and Coriolanus achieves a love-death at the hands of the father for whom he had so ardently yearned.

CORIOLANUS

Very few critical evaluations of *Coriolanus* have been able to set aside the significance of its complex, paradoxical protagonist. **Michael Goldman**, in assessing Shakespeare's method of characterization in the play, has summarized the problematic nature of Coriolanus: he possesses a conflicting blend of heroic and ironic qualities that serve the warrior well on the battlefield, but have disastrous effects within society. Gail Kern Paster shares the consensus view that Coriolanus is presented through contrasts with other characters in the play— primarily Volumnia and Aufidius— though she notes that these individuals also have many of the aristocratic qualities he possesses in the extreme.

Elmer Edgar Stoll has judged Coriolanus differently than most Shakespearean tragic heroes. He explained that typically the Shakespearean protagonist is forced by fate, circumstances, or a villain into acts that conflict with his own beliefs and thus lead to catastrophe. According to Stoll, these forces do not operate in *Coriolanus*, since in this work the hero brings disaster upon himself. Derek Traversi has also cited conflicts within Coriolanus as the source of his tragedy. The critic has suggested that these internal struggles are meant to reflect the larger problems destroying the entire "social organism" of Rome. Emphasizing the opposing images of "vitality" and "insentience" in the tragedy's poetry, Traversi maintained that these image patterns shape the readers' perceptions of both the hero and his society. In the critic's view, Coriolanus's downfall, and by extension Rome's, derives from an irreconcilable opposition that parallels this tension in the play's language: the "continual clash" between the hero's sensibilities and his "iron rigidity."

Sailendra Kumar Sen has surveyed the variety of critical interpretations of Coriolanus's character, stating that the lack of agreement among commentators reflects one central question: whether, like Shakespearean tragic heroes, the protagonist of this play exhibits an inner conflict. Sen contended that Coriolanus indeed displays such inner turmoil, and he located specific moments in the tragedy where it is apparent. He noted, however, that the proud patrician is a man who quickly resolves such problems and never reconsiders his decisions, and thus his uncertainty repeatedly appears and disappears.

Michael Goldman

SOURCE: "Characterizing Coriolanus," in *Shakespeare Survey*, Vol. 34, 1981, pp. 73-84.

[*In the essay that follows, Goldman analyzes the character of Coriolanus and, similarly, the nature of Shakespeare's method of characterization in the play. Goldman observes that throughout* Coriolanus *various characters discuss and interpret the protagonist's character; Aufidius, for example, lists Coriolanus's flaws of pride and defective judgment. The critic notes that the assessments made by Aufidius and other figures in the play share a common theme— an overall sense of bewilderment concerning Coriolanus's problematic character. Many characters remark on the relative ease with which Coriolanus is manipulated, and while Goldman observes this fact he also highlights the hero's isolation, his nobility, and his attempt to define his own character— what Goldman calls his "self-authorship." With this last element of Coriolanus's character, the critic argues, Shakespeare presents a highly complex and paradoxical figure who exemplifies the motif expressed by Aufidius in the play that "character lies in the interpretation of time."*]

I

The trouble with characterization is that we think we know what character is, or rather we think we know where it is and what kind of discourse best describes it. We think, or at least we generally speak as if we think, that it is to be found inside people, and we answer questions about character with summaries of inner qualities. This is a reasonable procedure and, it should be stressed, not a recent one. Nevertheless, it is true that in the past 150 years or so the description has tended more and more to stress the problematical and the psychological; character is seen as elusive, a subject

for puzzle and argument, depending on the difficult and never entirely satisfactory attempt to chart the way someone's mind works. And debate about dramatic character is likely to turn on whether it is reasonable to expect this kind of novelistic presentation of character from plays, especially plays written before the nineteenth century.

It is at this point that the discussion of character in drama becomes dangerously tangled, through the operation of hidden assumptions. For the implication in the typical debate I have described is that the psychological discourse of novels and novelizing psychology is the most accurate form for describing character in what we helplessly refer to as real life. But does our experience of other people correspond more to the helpful summaries of a novel or to the un-narratized encounters of a play?

I do not mean to argue for any presumed metaphysical superiority of drama to the novel; what I wish to bring out is the potential for error in assuming that the original, as it were, of character is discursive and that drama must thus constitute a translation of that original into more foreign terms. It should be noted that my distinction applies not only to nineteenth-century novels and modern psychology, but to all discursive accounts of character, including Aristotle, Burton, or whom you will. By comparison with any mode of discursive analysis, it can at least be argued that our experience as members of a theatre audience comes closer to the way in which we apprehend character in our daily encounters. Surely our efforts to characterize our friends and enemies— even the effort to characterize them *as* friends and enemies— follows, and always to a degree haltingly, after our experience of them, experience which, in the first instance, we approach through what Francis Fergusson calls the histrionic sensibility, the art, as it were, of finding the mind's construction in the face.

The notion of characterization as description may well have had a significant influence on the study of character in drama. I think it explains why, beginning with Aristotle, critics frequently maintain that character is somehow of secondary importance in drama, the implication clearly being that it is more important elsewhere, presumably in real life. With the conception of character, as with so much else, the hidden assumptions behind our normal critical vocabulary tend to make drama parasitic on narrative, and thus to distort our understanding of the effects and methods of the dramatist from the start.

I bring up these matters because they bear very interestingly on the play I have chosen to discuss. *Coriolanus* submits the whole question of character to a remarkable analysis. To begin with a point to which I would like to devote some extended attention, it exhibits a concern unique in the Shakespearian canon with discursive characterization of the kind we recognize as distinctly modern and familiar— the nice and argumentative discrimination of psychological qualities. It contains many passages in which Coriolanus is discussed in this manner by other characters, and the effect of these characterizations is to strike the audience as increasingly inadequate to its own unfolding dramatic experience of the man.

In no other Shakespearian play do people analyse another character in the fashion they repeatedly employ in *Coriolanus*. I have in mind not disagreement or uncertainty over motivation, as in *Hamlet*, but perplexity over what we would call a character's psychological makeup. In Shakespeare we often feel the presence of such complexity, but his characters almost never comment on it. The type of question Othello raises about Iago at the end of his play— what makes him do such things?— is almost never explicitly addressed, and of course in *Othello* no answer is even hazarded, except the suggestion, immediately rejected, that Iago is a devil. Iago's own motive-hunting is just that, statements of particular reasons for enmity, rather than analysis of his mental constitution.

Hamlet is the play that seems most concerned with the subject, but even there one finds no clear-cut example. When Hamlet asserts that he has that within which passes show, he is referring to an inarticulable depth of feeling rather than some hidden aspect of his character. There is much concern with ambiguous givings out in the play, and it may well point to inner ambiguity, but no character explores the question explicitly. When Claudius says, 'There's something in his soul / O'er which his melancholy sits on brood' (3.1.164-165), his language may suggest the elusiveness to description of a complex personality, but the explicit content is either that something is bothering Hamlet or that he is up to something which, like love or ambition, is capable of simple definition and explicable as the product of an external situation, for example his father's death and his mother's hasty marriage. Perhaps more could be made out of 'I have something in me dangerous' (5.1.256), or 'Pluck out the heart of my mystery' (3.2.356), but again these are matters, at most, of resonance and implication, not explicit statement. And the examples I have just cited are the closest we ever come in Shakespeare to the discussion of character as a complex and problematic psychological essence, with the exception of *Coriolanus*.

There the discussion begins with the opening scene. Like many of Shakespeare's tragedies, *Coriolanus* opens with the eruption of a dangerous force. The mob that rushes on stage carrying staves and clubs is meant to be felt as a threat; these 'mutinous' citizens are on the verge of extreme violence. Yet suddenly, even before Menenius appears, the rebellion loses momentum. Within moments of their first appearance, the rebels pause—

to discuss Coriolanus's character.

This is the issue the second citizen has on his mind at line 12, 'One word, good citizens.' He is answered in a well-known speech by a comrade who first says of Marcius that he is proud and, after an interruption, continues:

> Though soft-conscienc'd men can be content to say
> it was for his country, he did it to please his mother
> and to be partly proud . . .

The phrase has an air of simplicity and of caricature as well, caricature both of the subject and the speaker, but it is also very much a qualification of the speaker's original confident analysis. And the uneasiness of the formulation, 'to be partly proud', which has provoked emendation and extensive commentary, suggests a difficulty in characterizing Coriolanus, even by an angry enemy who is none too scrupulous about his speech.

This kind of difficulty recurs at many moments in the play. Again, I am not talking about simple disagreement over Marcius's character, but about passages which have this habit of qualification, of instability, of attempts to specify a complex essence. The most striking example occurs in Aufidius's soliloquy at the end of act 4:

> First he was
> A noble servant to them, but he could not
> Carry his honors even. Whether 'twas pride,
> Which out of daily fortune ever taints
> The happy man; whether defect of judgement,
> To fail in the disposing of those chances
> Which he was lord of; or whether nature,
> Not to be other than one thing, not moving
> From th' casque to th' cushion, but com-
>   manding peace
> Even with the same austerity and garb
> As he controll'd the war; but one of these—
> As he hath spices of them all— not all,
> For I dare so far free him— made him fear'd,
> So hated, and so banish'd. But he has a
>   merit
> To choke it in the utt'rance.

Aufidius first poses three reasons for Coriolanus's failure to 'carry his honors even'. This latter formula, with its obscure suggestion of a difficult balancing act, initiates a meditation that keeps sliding away from fixity and clarity of analysis. Aufidius presents his three explanations as if they were mutually exclusive, but they are not. 'Pride' is the old accusation of the Tribunes, 'defect of judgement' means perhaps political miscalculation or a deeper-seated inability to calculate shrewdly, and 'nature', of course, can include the first two. But Aufidius quickly limits the application of nature to a specific failing:

or whether nature,
Not to be other than one thing, not moving
From th' casque to th' cushion, but com-
    manding peace
Even with the same austerity and garb
As he controll'd the war . . .

Then, as if he felt that none of his reasons was quite sufficient, Aufidius goes on to complete his thought in a tangle of qualifications:

but one of these—
As he hath spices of them all— not all,
For I dare so far free him— made him fear'd,
So hated, and so banish'd.

It is the passage's sole point of certainty that most gives it a feeling of bewilderment. Why is Aufidius so sure that *but* one of these causes is responsible, 'not all, / For I dare so far free him'? There can be no logical reason; Aufidius simply feels that it would be too much to accuse Coriolanus of all three failings. Why? A sense of his character, of course, which underlies the entire speech and which Aufidius has been unable to articulate. And a further sense of it seems to rise at this very point, to comment on the difficulties Aufidius is finding:

But he has a merit
To choke it in the utt'rance.

This is another line that gives editors problems. The primary meaning, I think, is that Coriolanus's merit breaks in and chokes back the account of his faults, but the 'it' is ambiguous; there is a clouding suggestion that his merits choke themselves. And of course Aufidius's own emotions seem to be registered in the verse. Coriolanus and his merits are certainly a bone in his throat. The main effect is that the attempt to characterize becomes tangled and chokes on itself.

What has been evoked here, too, is the complexity and elusiveness of the very notion of character itself. The speech delicately catches the way innate predisposition, training, feeling, and choice come together and respond to external circumstance, the shifting changes of politics, and the feelings and actions of the public world— and also how, being a public as well as a private quality, one's character is modified, in a sense created, by the responses of other people, as Marcius's is by Aufidius. Coriolanus's character has something to do with the way other people choke on it. It exists somewhere between Coriolanus and his audience.

The paradoxical impact of Coriolanus on his society is felt strikingly in Aufidius's final speech:

My rage is gone,

And I am struck with sorrow. Take him up.
Though in this city he
Hath widowed and unchilded many a one,
Which to this hour bewail the injury,
Yet he shall have a noble memory.

(5.6.147-8, 151-4)

Yet is the important word. Though Marcius has done hateful things, nevertheless he will be loved. We have with Aufidius the sensation we have with so many of Shakespeare's tragic characters— but never with Coriolanus— that it is difficult to tell where play-acting leaves off and authentic feeling begins. Is Aufidius shifting gears for political reasons here? Or is he suddenly abashed? Is he asserting that Coriolanus manages, perplexingly, to be nobly remembered, or that he will see to it that Coriolanus is so remembered, in spite of his desert? All these notes mingle in the very believable compound of envy and awe that characterizes Aufidius whenever he contemplates his great rival.

This is not the only point in the play where the notion of noble memory is associated with perplexity about characterizing Coriolanus. Many less elaborate passages have helped develop the idea. When the servingmen at Antium try to explain the mysterious quality they claim to have detected in the disguised Marcius, their language goes comically to pieces:

Second Servingman. Nay, I knew by his face that there was something in him; he had, sir, a kind of face, methought— I cannot tell how to term it.
First Servingman. He had so, looking as it were— Would I were hang'd, but I thought there was more in him than I could think.

(4.5.154-7)

Of course this is a joke, whose point is that the servingmen had noticed nothing, but this only refines the question of how a noble character is constituted. The language of the servingmen calls attention to the 'something' in Coriolanus over which his friends and enemies quarrel. Even the play's repeated use of 'thing' to describe Coriolanus suggests not only his inhumanity, as is commonly argued, but the resistance of his nature to characterization.

In the last act, Aufidius, on the verge of denouncing Coriolanus to the lords of Antium, offers to his fellow conspirators— apparently in all frankness— a further interpretation of his character, which only adds to our sense of elusiveness:

I rais'd him, and I pawn'd
Mine honour for his truth; who being so
    heighten'd,
He watered his new plants with dews of
    flattery,
Seducing so my friends; and to this end

He bow'd his nature, never known before
But to be rough, unswayable, and free.

　　　　　　　　　　　　　　　　(5.6.21-6)

Aufidius describes Coriolanus as having changed and become politically manipulative. He has no reason to deceive his listeners at this point, but his account does not square with the Coriolanus we have seen, though we understand how Aufidius may have arrived at it.

There is, moreover, a tendency in the play to keep before us the whole issue of how we characterize people— whether it be by internal attributes or external ones, by simple epithets or puzzled formulas. The three scenes of act 2, for example, have a very distinct parallel structure. This is the act in which Coriolanus, newly named, returns to Rome; and each scene begins with a prelude in which his character is debated by the people who await him. In act 2, scene 1, conversation about Marcius between Menenius and the tribunes becomes a war of rather Overburyan character descriptions, Menenius topping the tribunes by offering two 'characters', as he calls them, first of himself and then of his opponents. In the second scene of the act, the officers argue as to whether or not Coriolanus is proud and disdainful. Finally, the third scene begins with the citizens arguing over whether Coriolanus should have their voices; this prelude ends with words which sum up the aim of so much of the play's dialogue, 'Mark his behavior'. Heightening the parallelism, each scene ends with a conversation between Brutus and Sicinius in which they decide how to make political capital out of Coriolanus's impact on the people.

II

What does this interesting emphasis on character mean? Surely it suggests that the character of Coriolanus is meant to be seen as problematic, and beyond this it raises the possibility that the idea of character itself may be under scrutiny— that the play may force us to confront the question of what character is and how it is perceived. Here we must pause to examine further the peculiar relation of character and drama. Let me say a few words about how we perceive character in performance. First of all, the fictitious person we watch on stage, Hamlet, or Hal, or Othello, is not an object, but a process. He is something we watch an actor making, not the result of making but the making itself. Hamlet, in performance, is not a tenth-century or sixteenth-century prince, not even a twentieth-century one; he is in no way physically separable from the actor who plays him. Yet we perceive him as a self, a character, rather than a series of physical actions. Where is that self? It is there, on the stage; it, too, is inseparable from the actor we are watching. Yet it is not the actor's everyday self, his biographical personality. It is something he is accomplishing by acting. A character, in a play, is something an actor *does*.

We are all too likely to think of an actor's characterization as an object, a presented mask, something produced and built up by the actor's preparation, as makeup or a dossier on the character might be. Such a product might well be described by a discursive summary. But a dramatic character is an action that goes on throughout the play.

I have shifted to another meaning of the word character— that of imagined person in a drama. But the two conceptions are linked. What is the character of a dramatic character? Clearly it, too, must spring from what the actor does. And what an actor does, first of all and ceaselessly, is perform. Performance is inseparable from dramatic character. It is true that sometimes in our discussion of a play we separate the performance from the character— as for example when we object that the actor has spoken more than is set down for him. But in that case we are simply imagining a better performance, for all the words he should speak— all the words Shakespeare has written— are meant as performed words. Thus, our view of dramatic character will gain by a consideration of the performance qualities built into the role, the necessary creative action of the actor called for by the script in order to project the part.

In the case of Coriolanus, certain problems of character have always been recognized, and I think they are illuminated by attention to some of the problems of performance. That is why the play, in proper performance, gives us an impression of its hero rather different from that conveyed by a bare recital of his deeds or a bare account of his language and behaviour. We should start with the observation, particularly striking because of the great amount of discussion the character of Coriolanus receives in the play, that of all the mature tragedies this is the one whose hero seems simplest in inner constitution, a relatively narrow or immature self. Indeed, by virtue of the apparent ease with which he can be manipulated, he runs the risk of being interpreted as comic. Furthermore, many critics feel that the play's rhetoric is chill, and that this corresponds to something uninviting about both the play's ambience and its hero— a lack of warmth or generosity.

Now, though I do not think these comments give a complete picture of the response a fully imagined performance of *Coriolanus* provides, there is a degree of truth in them, and they help define a major acting problem of the role. This might be described as finding what Coriolanus means when he refers to his own 'truth' as something he is afraid of ceasing to 'honour'. Is there more to this truth than doing what his mother wants, or fighting fearlessly, or hating compliments? That is, does the role suggest a freedom and depth of personality to which the audience can sympathetically respond? To keep Coriolanus from being simply comic means finding the passion hidden in the chill rhetoric, the richness of spirit beneath the many signs of poverty.

To indicate one or two ways in which the play addresses this problem, I would like to draw attention to some qualities of performance that are required by the language of the role. Much of Coriolanus's language requires of the actor a kind of grip, a domination over complexity which is exactly the opposite of comic predictability. This grip depends on an emotional and intellectual penetration by means of which the actor maintains focus on a goal that is delayed and hidden by the movement of his speech. The histrionic action is rather like that of Coriolanus the warrior penetrating to the centre of Corioles, thrusting ahead in battle, except that it cannot be rendered as a blind pushing forward; it is not like Macbeth's 'Before my body I throw my warlike shield.' It constitutes an important part of the action which is the character of Coriolanus.

The quality of performance I am describing is largely determined by syntax. A good example may be found in act 3:

> I say again,
> In soothing them we nourish 'gainst our
>   Senate
> The cockle of rebellion, insolence, sedition,
> Which we ourselves have ploughed for,
>   sow'd, and scatter'd
> By mingling them with us, the honor'd
>   number,
> Who lack not virtue, no, nor power, but that
> Which they have given to beggars.
>
> (3.1.68-74)

If this sentence were diagrammed, one would see that it is the final pair of subordinate clauses— syntactically very subordinate indeed— which define its energy and direction. Coriolanus is primarily agitated by the idea that the patricians have given their power and virtue to beggars, and it is this which governs the notion of soothing them and is developed as sowing the seeds of rebellion. The actor must be gripped by this idea and render its presence in the speech articulate, even as he must suspend stating it till the very end. Thus the felt movement of the speech is not simply accumulative— this thing, that thing, and another— but a pursuit toward a syntactically buried point.

I think I can make this clearer by comparing another passage from act 3 with a speech from *Othello*. This is Coriolanus's climactic outburst that goes from 'You common cry of curs' to 'I banish you' (3.3.122-5). It is a swift and frightening forecast of revenge, but how different in its movement from Othello's:

> Like to the Pontic sea,
> Whose icy current and compulsive course

Ne'er feels retiring ebb, but keeps due on
To the Propontic and the Hellespont;
Even so my bloody thoughts, with violent
  pace,
Shall ne'er look back, ne'er ebb to humble love,
Till that a capable and wide revenge
Swallow them up.

(3.3.457-64)

The Othello actor must start out his passage with a desire for revenge large enough to be measured against the scope and flow of the Pontic sea. But the movement of sweep and obstruction is grandly simple. The Coriolanus actor, by contrast, must struggle forward toward the instigating idea, *You corrupt my air*, which informs the three preceding lines of imagery and comparison, and which prepares the springboard for 'I banish you':

> You common cry of curs, whose breath I
>   hate
> As reek o' th' rotten fens, whose loves I
>   prize
> As the dead carcasses of unburied men
> That do corrupt my air— I banish you.

The intricacy here can be expressed yet another way. The opening lines of the passage appear to set up a neat symmetry: 'whose breath I hate / As reek o' th' rotten fens, whose loves I prize / As the dead carcasses of unburied men', but the following phrase, 'That do corrupt my air', unbalances this symmetry and, thus, to keep the passage alive there has to be an emotional thrust through the symmetries, which allows the crucial half-line to refer back to the earlier, 'You common cry of curs'. This problem occurs repeatedly in the role. A lot of the apparent coldness of Coriolanus's rhetoric resides in the balance and opposition he is constantly striking, but very often these balances get disturbed as the speech moves on, demanding a grip that keeps the balances clear and yet enlivens them by something not at all cool or settled.

A variation on this structure occurs when an apparently concluding phrase kicks off new images, requiring a supplementary charge of energy at a position normally felt to be subordinate or merely, as it were, passive:

> What would you have, you curs,
> That like nor peace nor war? The one
>   affrights you,
> The other makes you proud.
>
> (1.1.166-8)

Here, the subordinate 'that like nor peace nor war' cannot be thrown away. The actor must pursue it with an articulation which makes coherent the balanced opposition of 'The one . . . the other'. And if we were to extend the analysis to his whole great concerto-like first appearance, in which Marcius enters at full tilt with what is in effect a long speech over and against the interjections of the First Citizen and Menenius, we would see how the larger structure echoes the tendency of the smaller and in so doing prevents our first impression of the hero from being comic. After all, what is it that keeps Marcius, with his repeated 'Hang 'em's and 'What's the matter's, from playing as a young Colonel Blimp? It is the presence of a source of emotion which governs the entire speech, pursued by Marcius through all kinds of syntactical complications and shiftingly balanced reflections on the Roman populace, and which does not surface till the very end of the sequence, when we learn that the people have been given five tribunes, which Marcius correctly sees as a source of future insurrection.

So, repeatedly, we have this construction, in which the delayed phrase may be modifier or object or even a piece of information. But the effect is regularly that what is delayed is a central source of energy and we feel it radiating through earlier phrases. Or, to put it more accurately, if even more impressionistically, we feel its radiance being pursued by the speaker down branching corridors which blaze and echo with its force. The pursuit helps establish for us a great quality of the hero—the quality of attacker. In the speeches I have described, the sense of attack comes from the pursuit of the delayed idea, the buried trigger. If it were not buried, the pursuit would not feel like attack, or at least not that magnificence of attack we associate with Coriolanus.

In the great final outburst before he is murdered, the trigger is the word 'Boy':

> Cut me to pieces, Volsces; men and lads,
> Stain all your edges on me. 'Boy'! False
>   hound!
> If you have writ your annals true, 'tis there
> That, like an eagle in a dove-cote, I
> Flutter'd your Volscians in Corioli.
> Alone I did it. 'Boy'!
>
>   (5.6.112-17)

The method I have been attempting to describe explains why that speech does not play simply as a confirmation of the Tribunes' and Aufidius's theory that Coriolanus is a manipulable figure: call him certain names and you've got him. Nor does it allow us to accept the explanation the play itself seems at times to put forward—that Coriolanus is, in fact, a boy of tears. The stimulus does not set off a mere raving reaction, but a pursuit, a kind of branching plunge, in which the whole being of the performer attacks the insult. Every phrase, 'Men and lads', 'Cut me to pieces', 'Alone I did it', 'Like an eagle', responds, separately, to 'Boy!' Each bears *toward* the word, presses in on it, ranges pieces of a multiple attack that bursts into the clear only as the offending word is finally snapped in place.

Awareness of this technique will help us with at least one crucial passage which has often been misinterpreted:

> Though I go alone,
> Like to a lonely dragon, that his fen
> Makes fear'd and talk'd of more than seen . . .
>
>   (4.1.29-31)

Most readings focus on the dragon but the fen is the point. What makes Coriolanus most like a dragon is his isolation; indeed it is not even simply the fen that is at the centre of the speech, but the power of fen-dwelling to make someone feared and talked of and hence lonely. It is not, then, a definition of his inhumanity Coriolanus gives us here, but of his felt distance from others. The dragonish qualities seem most to derive from being feared and talked of. They are, at least in part, an aspect of how society characterizes Coriolanus.

'Alone' is of course an important word in the play. But it varies greatly in meaning as Coriolanus pronounces it, and these variations are histrionic—that is, they represent differences in the way the actor projects a character through his performance of the word. In the passage just cited, 'alone' suggests isolation, but it also is coloured here, as elsewhere, by loneliness. By contrast, when Coriolanus turns on his accusers in the last act, crying, 'Alone I did it', the word means 'unaided, singling oneself out'. This is mingled with an implied insult: 'The Volsces can be beaten by one man', and a provocation: 'I take full responsibility.' It is a challenging statement of personal strength.

Now, there is another moment when the word is used in a very different sense, which is of the greatest importance for the performance of the role. And it is very different both in syntax and mood from any of the examples we have been considering. This occurs when Marcius addresses Cominius's troops after the successful assault on Corioles and before the battle with Aufidius. He asks for volunteers to follow him, and *They all shout and wave their swords, take him up in their arms, and cast up their caps.* At which point, he cries:

> O, me alone! Make you a sword of me?
>
>   (1.6.76)

This wonderful and startling line is not that of the isolated attacker, or the automaton, or the scorner of the crowd. It has a rush and a surprised pleasure we hear nowhere else from Coriolanus. It is his happiest moment in the play.

Significantly, it is presented by Shakespeare as one of a series of stage images which intricately comment upon each other. It reverses the group of images we have had a few minutes earlier, first of Coriolanus scorning the soldiers as they flee, then deserted by them, then scorning them again as they pause to loot; and it will be partially reversed, restated dissonantly, one might say, a few minutes later when he angrily denounces the same crowd as it cheers him again. Finally, it will be most emphatically reversed in the assassination scene, the only other moment in the play when Marcius allows a group of men to touch him. But now in act 1 he is elated, he accepts the praise and the physical contact of the crowd, and the word 'alone' here means singled out by others uniquely valued by people with whom he feels a bond. He is the sword of a courageous community— and the attacking hardness of the image of the sword is modified by the moment of joyous physical contact and celebration. This is the aloneness Coriolanus has felt himself bred up for, to be truly a limb of his country, a healthy limb of an heroic society; and for an instant his dream appears to come true.

III

We can appreciate some of the play's distance from Plutarch if we compare the variable implications Shakespeare gives to 'alone' with the idea of 'solitariness', which Plutarch, in North's translation, borrows from Plato to describe Coriolanus. In Plutarch, solitariness is simply a vice, an inability to deal with others, the opposite of 'affability'. Shakespeare's use of 'alone', as we have seen, suggests not only a different and far more interesting character, but a far more complex notion of how character is to be understood. In the concluding portion of this paper, I would like to focus on how the idea of aloneness in the play illuminates two closely related themes. The first is Coriolanus's own conception of character— that is, not only what kind of person he wishes to be, but also how he understands character to be created and possessed. The second is the critique of this conception of character that emerges in the course of the drama. Taken together, I think they help us understand more clearly the complex appeal of *Coriolanus* as a theatrical creation and perhaps something of Shakespeare's intention in writing the play.

Most of Shakespeare's tragic heroes entertain peculiar ideas about the relation of the self and its acts, ideas which poignantly reflect our own troubled sentiments on this bewildering subject. Coriolanus's version of this peculiarity is his notion that a man may be 'author of himself'. It is a phrase that evokes many of the same associations as his use of 'alone', and it stimulates us especially because, while it plainly reflects his gravest folly, at the same time it seems fairly to express the very authority that makes Coriolanus so much more interesting than a fool.

Perhaps no passage in the play has produced such troubled critical discussion of character as the scene in which he announces his decision to go over to the Volsces. His soliloquy seems in the most literal sense an attempt at self-authorship, at rewriting his play in the face of facts well known to the audience. Critics have

frequently noted that it is an odd speech for what it fails to say, but it is equally odd for what it says:

> Friends now fast sworn,
> . . . shall within this hour,
> On a dissension of a doit, break out
> To bitterest enmity; so fellest foes,
> Whose passions and whose plots have broke
>   their sleep
> To take the one the other, by some chance,
> Some trick not worth an egg, shall grow dear
>   friends
> And interjoin their issues. So with me:
> My birthplace hate I, and my love's upon
> This enemy town.
>
>   (4.4.12,16-24)

For Coriolanus to describe his banishment, the hatred of the Tribunes, and the accusation of treachery as 'a dissension of a doit' or 'some trick not worth an egg' is nearly incredible and suggests how far he has distanced himself from his feelings. The same may be felt in the overly neat conclusion, 'So with me', and the flat and unconvincing assertiveness of:

> My birthplace hate I, and my love's upon
> This enemy town.

This distance from feeling is one of the perils of self-authorship. And in *Coriolanus*, as in *Macbeth*, the relation between feeling, action, and full humanity becomes very important. Certainly the moment of silence with Volumnia in act 5 is reminiscent of Macduff's pause. It comes about because in act 4 Coriolanus has failed to feel his banishment as a man. He has attempted to violate the natural relation between feeling and action, and like other Shakespearian heroes he must pay for it. If it is true that the defining problem for the actor in this play is to suggest an inner action deeper than the reflexive manipulable response seen by his enemies, it is interesting that Coriolanus's crisis comes when he tries to manipulate himself. To assert that one can do anything one wants is as humanly insufficient as to assert that one is completely predictable. The creature who will acknowledge no obedience to instinct is as subhuman as the gosling.

But even more than in one's relation to one's feelings, the fallacy of self-authorship may be felt in one's relation to the outside world. Like many of Shakespeare's heroes, Coriolanus must be tutored in the connections between theatricality and life, between the private individual and the social theatre in which he plays his part and finds his audience. The lesson he learns, however, is unique to his play. If Hamlet must discover that a connection exists between play-acting and the heart of one's mystery, Coriolanus is forced to explore the relation between one's character and one's audience. We can feel this even at the very beginning of the play.

Most, if not all, Shakespearian heroes initially hold back from the opportunities for action that are first presented to them, and this is usually linked to a rejection of theatre, though it is not always so plain as Hamlet's 'I have that within which passes show', or so fearful as Macbeth's 'Why do you dress me in borrowed robes?' At first glance, Coriolanus appears not to conform to this pattern, plunging with his opening words into a denunciation of the crowd. But his opening line contains a refusal which precedes this eager engagement:

> *Menenius.*
>   . . . Hail, noble Marcius!
> *Marcius.*
>   Thanks. What's the matter, you dissentious
>   rogues . . .
>
>   (1.1.161-2)

What is Coriolanus holding back from? I would describe it as the authority, the authorship, of an audience. Menenius offers him a name, praise, a characterization: 'Noble'. It is a term Coriolanus values— in the last act, nobleness will be the quality he prays that the gods give his son. And the word 'noble' occurs more frequently in *Coriolanus* than in any other Shakespeare play. But while he may readily pray to the gods for nobility, he will not consent to be called noble, even by Menenius.

In the same way, Coriolanus seems regularly to reject *our* interest in him. And this contributes to our perception of his character as cold or unsympathetic. The problems of his act 4 transition to revenge, for example— the 'break' in characterization, the lack of transition, the flagrant inappropriateness of his remarks— constitute a defiance of the theatre audience comparable to his regular defiance of his onstage audience. Nevertheless he retains his power over both audiences— and it is clear that he *needs* them. Just as we feel an invitation to the audience in the actor's mastery of those syntactically difficult passages, or in 'O, me alone!', or the moment of silence, or the moment of assassination, or the physical release of battle— just as there are solicitations of sympathy here, enactments of aloneness which carry us along with the actor— so in his relation with the on-stage audience we see that the apparent defiance is far from complete. How else explain, for example, Coriolanus's repeated appeals to Aufidius to note how honourably he is behaving? As at Corioles, Coriolanus needs an audience to give him the name he has won. He cannot author himself alone.

This dependence of character on audience is echoed in the story of the benefactor whose name Coriolanus forgets. The point is similar to the one Shakespeare makes in *Romeo and Juliet* about the way in which names, fate, and society are interwoven. The romantic attitude is that names do not matter; what one is counts. But our name reflects a real connection between our past,

present, and future, between our selves, our acts, and our social being. Romeo *is* a Montague, and his name soon becomes that of the man who has murdered Tybalt. It matters quite as much as whether the name of the bird one hears is lark or nightingale. In the benefactor scene, Marcius has just become Coriolanus, a name which will permanently fix his relationship with Aufidius and lead to his death, and his poor friend has become a non-person because Coriolanus cannot remember his name.

Now, the relation between one's character and the behaviour of audiences is of troublesome resonance to any great artist, and I imagine Shakespeare was aware of this. At any rate, he seems as he reaches the end of the great cycle of tragedies to become specially interested in the ironies of an artistic career. In *Antony and Cleopatra*, he tells the story of a man whose gifts have equipped him for the greatest success in the practical world and who instead casts his lot with a greatness that depends wholly on the imagination, on the splendours of gesture, passion, self-dramatization— an achievement as materially insubstantial as black vesper's pageants, and which the practical world will always associate with the arts of the gypsy and the whore. In *Coriolanus* he tells the story of another man whose ruling passion suggests the situation of the artist, a man who wishes to be the author of himself, an ambition, one would think, not only artist-like, but particularly theatrical— who but an actor can change his being every day? Certainly it is an ambition easily associated with the appeal of high creativity. Who more than a great poet can make a claim to spiritual independence? Yet the theatre is, of course, the most social of the arts. Indeed, it presents in its most unpalatable and least disguised form the fact that no artist is the author of himself, but a dependent part of an inconstant multitude, which is always in some sense interpreting him. Among playwright, actors, and audience, who is the belly, who the members?

There is, it should be noted, another side to the story of the poor benefactor with the forgotten name. For it also projects a version of Coriolanus's fantasy of unconditioned power which is similar to the artist's fantasy of self-authorship. Perhaps one thinks that by being best warrior (or poet) one will gain absolute power over names— that one can command people by giving names or destroy them by forgetting them,' that one can be free of the common cry, can stand outside of society, banish the world at will, that moving others one can be oneself as stone. This is an illusion, as any poet discovers, and as Marcius discovers when he tries to forget his own name and that of friend, mother, wife, and child.

You will by now have grown tired of my saying, with Aufidius, 'And yet'. And yet I must say it again. For to end on the self-deluding aspect of Coriolanus's desire to stand alone would be to distort the play. The project of self-authorship, however mistaken, is bound up with the power and magnetism— indeed with the sympathetic appeal— of Coriolanus as a dramatic character. I think the issue here has to do with the nature of tragedy. In a sense all tragic heroes are authors of themselves. I am certain that the writer of a tragedy feels more intensely than in any other form the struggle between what he wants to make happen and what his chief character wants to do. It is true of course that any tragedy exhibits a severe sense of scriptedness, but the play would be flat and tame if we did not feel that its hero had an equally exigent sense of the script *he* wants to write, of his own authorial power. Faced with some terrible contingency, the tragic hero makes it his own necessity. Like a great actor, he makes the part he is given his own. And I think that when we argue over whether Coriolanus the character is cold and uninviting, when we ask whether his nature is fully expressed by the facts of his upbringing and the reflexes of his temper, we are asking whether he has the authority, the inspiriting freedom, of a tragic figure.

That is why the play must end, and why I wish to conclude, with Aufidius's 'Yet he will have a noble memory.' As with both Romeo and Juliet, and as with the self-authorizing ambitions of great poets, there is in Coriolanus something cherishable and indeed social about the lonely impulse which drives him. We return a last time to what I have called Coriolanus's truth. What did Shakespeare see in Plutarch's life of Coriolanus? He found there a great warrior firmly characterized as intemperately angry and hence given over to solitariness, and he accepted almost everything about him except the characterization, which is to say he accepted everything except what mattered most to his play. Shakespeare seems to have looked at Plutarch's story of the choleric superman and said, 'And yet'. Here was a man whose whole life seemed to have been devoted to a notion of character; he was, in Menenius's Overburyan sense, the very character of a Roman warrior. And yet he could decide to betray Rome. And yet, being able to betray Rome, he again could give in fatally— more than fatally, embarrassingly— to his mother's plea. Shakespeare added complexities which show Coriolanus to be determined and manipulable in the most psychologically credible way— all that family history and revealing imagery. But he also added all the details which make him less easily characterized— his moments of unexpected response, the exciting complexity of his speeches, the range of meanings he gives to the notion of aloneness, and, always, that chorus of friends and enemies inadequately, perplexedly explaining him.

To sum it up, Shakespeare insists on the problematics of characterization in *Coriolanus* because he is there peculiarly concerned with a paradox: that the distinctive quality of an individual is at once incommunicably private and unavoidably social. As such, it is situated neither entirely within our grasp or the grasp of our fellows but, fascinatingly, between us— rather like the meaning of a poem or a play— between us in our encounters on the stage of the world. Character lies in the interpretation of the time, as Aufidius puts it, and is thus susceptible to change and falsehood. And yet it is the most enduring thing about us. Perhaps this is what tragedy is about— that there is such a thing as human character. Perhaps it is only in tragedy that we feel that character as a personal possession really exists, in spite of the contradictions which surround it as a philosophical conception. At the end of *Coriolanus*, I feel that strange response which a less apologetic age would simply call tragic exaltation. And if I interpret the significance of that mood correctly, it means we feel, in spite of everything, that there is in the end something about Coriolanus which is truly his, that it characterizes him, and that for us to have shared his character, by participating in it through the process of the actor's performance, has been an experience of immense value to ourselves.

VOLUMNIA

Critical interest in the character of Volumnia has been second only to scholarly regard for Coriolanus himself. Naturally, much of the commentary focuses on their relationship, while modern interpretations have tended toward psychoanalytical accounts. Katherine Eisaman Maus has envisioned Volumnia's ferocity as socially constructed; her aggressiveness and zeal for warfare are considered unnatural in a Roman matron, and therefore must find expression elsewhere, in this case in her exaggerated masculinity and dominance over her son. William Farnham has also discussed the important role Volumnia plays in the tragedy, first, by pressing her son to do what he cannot do— that is, compromise his personal integrity— and second, by superseding his self-centered honor with the honor she possesses as his mother.

Christina Luckyj's assessment of Volumnia is indicative of a minority opinion that favors a broader conception of her role in the play. Arguing against the standard view, Luckyj has contended that Volumnia possess a full and tragic awareness of the consequences of her actions on Coriolanus, and that Shakespeare endowed her with a dynamic character that evolves throughout the course of the drama.

Christina Luckyj

SOURCE: "Volumnia's Silence," in *Studies in English Literature 1500-1900*, Vol. 31, No. 2, Spring, 1991, pp. 327-42.

[*Luckyj remarks on the complexity of Volumnia's character, viewing her as a "dynamic, powerful" figure. Responding to many past critics who have offered simple or reductive interpretations of Volumnia, Luckyj asserts the character's indeterminate nature. Initially, Volumnia is dramatized in polar opposition to Virgilia; her coldness and masculinity are emphasized and contrasted with her daughter-in-law's femininity and concern for Coriolanus. Later, Luckyj argues, Volumnia is presented less as an instrument of maternal dominance than as an evolving character with a tragic awareness of the effect her choices have had on Coriolanus's life. Luckyj traces the development of Volumnia "from the formidable virago of the first act to the powerful advocate of the last act, through the near-comic bourgeois matriarch of Act II, the 'dissembler' of Act III, and the angry, devastated mother of Act IV."*]

Volumnia's last appearance in Shakespeare's *Coriolanus* is a brief and silent one. She has just pleaded successfully with her son to spare his native city from intended destruction; her plea, we know, must result in his death at the hands of the Volscians, whose cause he has betrayed. She passes wordlessly over the stage in the company of Virgilia and Valeria as a Roman senator hails her as "our patroness, the life of Rome" (V.v.1). Academic critics take the senator's word for it; they usually see her as "the one triumphant figure that survives the play, the savior of Rome," and insist that she is not "given a moment of reflection or of recognition that [she has] caused Martius' death. . . . Coriolanus' new acknowledgement of the power of tenderness and family bonds does not change the grim world of the play; it does not even change Volumnia." While some directors do show us Volumnia's fierce delight at her son's capitulation (often— as in the 1978 and 1990 RSC productions— departing from the text to present young Martius as her next exalted victim), others have conceived of her quite differently. Following a venerable modern tradition (which includes, by my count, at least five major productions since 1954), Irene Worth rendered Volumnia's silence in the 1984 National Theatre production as mute devastation. Francis King records what he called "her finest moment": "Small, twitching smiles acknowledge the plaudits, but the eyes express a terrible desolation, since she already realises that he must die." This much-praised interpretation, integral to what was hailed as "the best Shakespeare production to emerge from the National in its 21 years," presented a "deeply thoughtful" Coriolanus who, in the supplication scene, "grows up as we watch, and becomes human, and so has to be killed." In this production, Volumnia's desolation seemed to measure her son's emotional achievement. Indeed, if Volumnia crumbles during the silent procession— as a reviewer of the 1972 RSC production put it, "her ravaged face showing no glimmer of joy, hardly of life"— we are forced to re-evaluate not only her character but her relation to Coriolanus and to the play as a whole.

Women's silences in Renaissance plays often contradict their stage interpreters. Accusing the silent Bianca of Cassio's murder, Iago claims that "guiltiness will speak, / Though tongues were out of use" (*Othello* V.i.109-10); we know that her silence conveys, not guilt, but grief. In Elizabeth Cary's *Mariam*, Pheroras remonstrates with his gentle lover Graphina, "Silence is a sign of discontent" (line 587); she tells him it shows her wonder. In Middleton and Rowley's *Changeling* DeFlores tells Beatrice-Joanna before he rapes her, "Silence is one of pleasure's best receipts" (III.iv.169); she is clearly terrified. The silence maintained initially by Cressida in the Greek camp (IV.v) may be the wanton solicitation Ulysses claims it is, or it may be desperate resistance. And the openness of women's silences in response to a proposal of marriage is notorious— from Marlowe's Zenocrate in *1 Tamburlaine* to Isabella in *Measure for Measure* and Paulina at the end of *The Winter's Tale*. That Shakespeare knew and exploited the ambiguities of feminine silence should make critics wary of too hastily judging Volumnia's.

Critical concensus on Volumnia in the play as a whole is reflected in Harold Bloom's recent statement that "Volumnia hardly bears discussion, once we have seen that she would be at home wearing armor in *The Iliad*." Yet discussion there has been, particularly among feminist and psychoanalytic critics, who usually find in her the chief cause of both Coriolanus's masculine aggression and his eventual death at the hands of the Volcians. Because his mother failed to nurture him as a mother should, Coriolanus channeled his need for nourishment into phallic aggression. Because, again, it is Volumnia who makes the case for "great nature" in the supplication scene, this fleeting hope of redeeming, "female," values is contaminated at the source. As Janet Adelman puts it,

> When Volumnia triumphs over his rigid maleness, there is a hint of restitution in the Roman celebration of her as "our patroness, the life of Rome" (5.5.1). But like nearly everything else at the end of this play, the promise of restitution is deeply ironic: for Volumnia herself has shown no touch of nature as she willingly sacrifices her son; and the cries of "welcome, ladies, welcome!" (5.5.6) suggest an acknowledgment of female values at the moment in which the appearance of these values not in Volumnia but in her son can only mean his death.

The paradox of simultaneous redemption and destruction by the mother is explained by preoedipal theory: "the mother's body becomes the locus of fantasies of both union and separation, the mother herself the representative of both plenitude and loss." Preoedipal theory, however, relies on a mother "lacking subjectivity," who is a pure construction of the threatened, longing, infantile unconscious. Stage performance emphasizes subjective agency; a Volumnia built according to this model is no more dramatically interesting than the

A scene from the University of Washington's 1998 theatre production of Coriolanus.

most hardened child-abuser. But what about a Volumnia who shows not only a "touch of nature" in the final scenes but an agonized awareness of the costs of her actions? Can we be sure that the preoedipal fantasy is Shakespeare's, and not the critic's or the director's?

In the theater, Volumnia and Coriolanus are the "two leading players," equally prominent and dramatically interdependent, so that it scarcely seems accurate to say, with Willard Farnham, that "the hero does not merely stand at the center of the tragedy; he *is* the tragedy. He brings no one down with him in his fall." Such an exclusive focus on Coriolanus alone ignores Volumnia's competing claim on our attention and suppresses vital aspects of her role. In his analysis of the 1959 Peter Hall production, Laurence Kitchin remarks that

> Volumnia, the stoical Roman matron, is too interesting a character to function merely as a symbol of antique virtue and yet not be defined as anything else. . . . If Paxinou undertook Volumnia she would no doubt find hypnotic splendour in the

old harridan, but that could only be at the expense of the title part. The alternative is to give her straight, dignified playing, as [Dame Edith] Evans did at Stratford, and let the unsympathetic elements take effect, so that she doesn't encroach on the play's main theme.

The rather unimaginative approach to Volumnia taken by Evans was clearly designed to avoid upstaging Olivier's Coriolanus. The final scenes won sympathy for the hero as a "boy' under the sway of his Roman mother." Yet to restrict the dramatic focus to Coriolanus is to ignore the play's presentation of a dynamic, powerful Volumnia. And to oversimplify Volumnia as either a castrating virago or "a symbol of antique virtue" is to miss the play's many hints at a fully developed figure with the capacity for psychic depth and change. A good deal of recent feminist criticism, by foregrounding Volumnia as mother-destroyer of her son, actually marginalizes her by denying her the full life afforded her by the text. This paper is an attempt to show that in *Coriolanus,* as Harriett Hawkins puts it, "the nature of woman would appear to be just as indeterminate, and as 'capable of transforming itself,' as the nature of man."

Volumnia's first appearance on the stage is both a shock and a relief. With a burst of tremendous energy, she ruptures the opening tableau of silent, dutiful women so idealized in Renaissance marriage manuals. As a "blood-lusting, teeth-baring" "she-wolf," she is clearly "a complete negation of Renaissance womanly virtue." But this is surely a case where in the theater, as Hawkins puts it, "moral vices may manifest themselves as dramatic virtues," and the psychological distortions of which Volumnia has so often been convicted fuel her ferocious vitality on the stage. Now this is not to return to the Romantic and Victorian Volumnia, to Anna Jameson's idealized "Roman matron, conceived in the true antique spirit." A good Volumnia for the stage is made, not of marble, but of fire— as an eyewitness account of Sarah Siddons's famous Volumnia confirms: "She came alone, marching and beating time to the music; rolling . . . from side to side. . . . Such was the intoxication of joy which flashed from her eye and lit up her whole face that the effect was irresistible." As Michael Goldman said admiringly of Gloria Foster's Volumnia for the 1980 New York production, "She gave us not the cold Roman matron, but a fierce Mediterranean matriarch, a woman who could be Lear." Indeed, after the discordant voices of the citizens and the slippery tones of Menenius, the tribunes and Aufidius, we can hear again the "tragic music" of Coriolanus in his mother's voice. It is a jangling music— the music of a military brass band— but it is also strong and rhythmic and thus brings relief. At the beginning of the play, Volumnia mirrors Coriolanus; only a critical double standard labels one a voracious matriarch, the other a proud and admirable hero.

Of course Volumnia's is not the only voice in the scene. Shakespeare begins by presenting two women who are utterly polarized— the gentle, "feminine" Virgilia and the powerful, "masculine" Volumnia. Yet the distinction soon blurs. Virgilia can also be strong and stubborn; Volumnia summons up powerful maternal feelings as support for their antithesis:

> The breasts of Hecuba
> When she did suckle Hector, look'd not lovelier
> Than Hector's forehead when it spit forth
>   blood
> At Grecian sword contemning.
>
>   (I.iii.40-43)

The speech is usually invoked to show "the source of [Coriolanus's] anger in the deprivation imposed by his mother." But Hector does to Hecuba what the Grecian sword does to Hector; the lactating breast is compared to a bleeding wound, the infant's mouth to a weapon. The metaphor, intended to show the wound as lovely

as the breast, recoils to show the breast as vulnerable as the wound. The effect of this kind of mothering on Coriolanus has often been noted; what has been less commonly observed is the vulnerability underlying Volumnia's maternal self-denial. Here Shakespeare presents us with a character who, like Lear and like Coriolanus, is both enormous in will and profoundly self-ignorant. Unlike Lear's or Coriolanus's anger, which is more obviously a defense against their intolerable need for love, Volumnia's aggression explodes from some mysterious raw origin. She is certainly not a likeable character— neither is Lear nor Coriolanus in the early scenes— but Shakespeare carefully plants the seeds of natural affection even here. Her evocation and subsequent rejection of ordinary maternal feeling limit her emotional range and restrict our sympathy for her, while at the same time contributing to her extraordinary impact on the stage. In this early scene Volumnia reveals that, like other tragic heroes, she has sufficient strength to endure change and the dramatic stature to invite it. What is more, any deviation from this colossal single-minded energy will be registered with the minutest sensitivity.

Volumnia's subsequent appearances in the play are arranged schematically: she appears in variations on the triumphal procession and the supplication scene. By arranging Volumnia's appearances in repeated situations, Shakespeare is able to suggest subtle changes in attitude that might otherwise be hidden from us by a character who, like her son, lacks introspection.

The first of Volumnia's appearances in a series of three "processions" comes early in the second act. Coriolanus is on his way back to Rome after defeating the Volscians in the battle which has earned him his name. The entire scene culminates in his triumphant welcome by Rome and his family, but its initial tone is casual and expansive, as Menenius pokes fun at the tribunes. The comic mood thus established is not interrupted but extended by the entrance of the three women. Menenius's exaggerated comparison of them with "the moon, were she earthly, no nobler" (II.i.97), draws attention by contrast to their undignified scrambling haste on the stage, implied by his descriptive question "whither do you follow your eyes so fast?" (II.i.98). Indeed, throughout the scene, Menenius's comic hyperbole guides our response to Volumnia, as she counts up everything from Coriolanus's letters home to his wounds received in battle. Volumnia's language persistently distances her from the realities of war— "wounds" are transformed into "cicatrices" (II.i.147) or "hurts" (II.i.149) earned for "the oaken garland" (II.i.124) and his "place" in the senate (II.i.148). Her final interchange with Menenius is a comic escalating calculation of wounds whose arithmetic is deliberately confusing. The scene undercuts the force of Volumnia's final grand couplet— a verbal flourish which, along with the trumpets, ushers in Coriolanus—

Death, that dark spirit, in's nervy arm doth lie,
Which, being advanc'd, declines, and then
    men die.

(II.i.159-60)

Despite the horrible encomium, Volumnia is less the terrible virago than, as a reviewer of the 1972 Royal Shakespeare Company production put it, "an exultantly bourgeois matriarch seen at her most typical when computing the number of the son's battle wounds as if they were cricket runs." The same comic tone crept into Maxine Audley's impression of the Volumnia she played in the 1979 Royal Shakespeare Company production as "a Jewish-American mother . . . like the one in *Portnoy's Complaint*." While the scene establishes Volumnia's overbearing attempt to control her son, it also humanizes her by suggesting that her *hubris* is potentially comic, a pathetic defense against life's realities.

Volumnia's illusions and defenses collapse with Coriolanus's banishment from Rome. At the beginning of the fourth act, she reappears in a scene that is an inverted echo of the earlier triumphal procession; the same group that welcomed Coriolanus's victorious return from battle now leads him into exile. Attitudes have changed with circumstances: the gloating "Jewish mother" of the previous scene now weeps with the rest of them. A confused Coriolanus enjoins his mother to "leave [her] tears" (IV.i.3), and reminds her of her "ancient courage":

    You were us'd to load me
With precepts that would make invincible
The heart that conn'd them.

(IV.i.9-11)

He tries to re-evoke the mother for whom his hazards were her "solace" (V.i.128), but is contradicted by the distraught behavior of the woman on the stage before him; the formulaic "precepts" of stoic fortitude were untried by the blow of real human loss. Volumnia's responses, whose very brevity hints at some inner struggle, move from typical rage at "all trades in Rome" (IV.i.13) to ordinary maternal solicitude:

                                      My first
    son,
Whither wilt thou go? Take good Cominius
With thee awhile; determine on some course
More than a wild exposure to each chance
That starts i' th' way before thee.

(IV.i.33-37)

The breathless rhythm of the speech shows a new awareness of life's harsh realities, as well as a new desire to soften them for her "first son." Here Volumnia and Virgilia are both "sad women" who "wail inevitable strokes" (IV.i.25-26); their shared grief is later con-

verted to shared anger. When Volumnia aggressively corners one tribune, Virgilia forces the other one to "stay too" (IV.ii.15). When Volumnia threatens both tribunes, declaring,

                        I would my son
Were in Arabia, and thy tribe before him,
His good sword in his hand,

(IV.ii.23-25)

Virgilia chimes in with, "He'd make an end of thy posterity" (IV.ii.26), and Volumnia completes her sentence: "Bastards and all" (IV.ii.27). Editorial redistribution of speeches in this scene— inspired by John Middleton Murry and followed by Brockbank's Arden edition— robs Virgilia of the angry interpolations that are clearly hers in the Folio, and creates a more violent Volumnia than Shakespeare intended. For Volumnia, the pride and anger that seemed out of place in the early scenes have become appropriate responses she shares with Virgilia to a new, harsh world of political opportunism and personal loss. When Sicinius accuses her of masculinity with his question, "Are you mankind?" (IV.ii.16) Volumnia defends the appropriateness of her behavior, replying, "Ay fool; is that a shame? Note but this fool. / Was not a man my father?" (IV.ii.17-18). As woman was born of man, she has a natural right to his anger and aggression to express her loss. "Mankind" slips into its more modern meaning of "humankind" as Volumnia begins to reconcile two warring aspects of her nature— maternal feeling and "masculine" self-assertion.

Volumnia's third appearance in a procession is also her last appearance on the stage. A modern director's instinctive rendering of her silence as despair rather than triumph finds corroboration in a text which, most scholars claim, is close to Shakespeare's "foul papers." In the previous scene, a relieved and exultant Menenius joins with the tribunes in anticipating Volumnia's triumphant return; the joyful noises of the crowd are heard offstage. In the procession itself, however, there is no entry recorded for Menenius, the tribunes, or the boisterous mob; since most of the company is probably needed to fill out the crowd in the next scene, the women are accompanied only by two senators and "other lords." One of the senators urges:

Call all your tribes together, praise the gods,
And make triumphant fires. Strew flowers
    before them;
Unshout the noise that banish'd Martius;
Repeal him with the welcome of his mother:
Cry, "Welcome, ladies, welcome!"

(V.v.2-6)

But no noisy crowd carries out the senator's commands and guides our response; as its surrogate, we can only sit in uneasy silence. The quiet of the procession contrasts with other noisy processions in the play (notably with Coriolanus's in the following scene— V.vi.71) and with Plutarch's account of the "honorable curtesies the whole Senate, and people dyd bestowe on their ladyes." The effect is both ominous and deflationary. The 1981 Stratford, Ontario, production, directed by Brian Bedford, captured the mood of this oddly untriumphant "triumph" by using a frieze of citizens on the upper stage. As Ralph Berry tells it:

> Bedford showed a cortege. Led by a grim, unsmiling Volumnia, the black-clad procession of the three women and young Martius moved rapidly across the stage. There were no words, no sounds of applause, only the electronic bells in Gabriel Charpentier's disturbing and moving soundscape. On the upper stage, a rectangle of harsh light picked out the citizens as in a film frame, the people soundlessly crying their applause for Rome's savior. The effect was ominous, tragic, heart-stopping.

If Shakespeare intended the scene to be staged less as a triumph than a dirge, a mournful Volumnia further reinforces the tension between word and image. Still wearing the dishevelled garb of the supplication scene, she casts— as a reviewer of the 1954 Old Vic production put it— "a mauve shadow on the optimism" of the senator's words, and stands in opposition to other members of her class. A terse silence shared by Volumnia and the theater audience knits them together in common resistance to any simple view of the supplication scene, confirming its complexity. And if the scene is played as a rejection of public acclaim, it brings the wheel full circle; the mother's silence recalls her son's: "No more of this; it does offend my heart" (II.i.167).

Perhaps the most striking instance of structural repetition— and one which is crucial to our understanding of Volumnia— involves the supplication scene. The scene early in the third act in which Volumnia tries to persuade Coriolanus to retract his harsh words to the plebeians is a "rehearsal"— not so much for Coriolanus's submission to the plebeians, which never in fact occurs— but for the final supplication scene. Here Volumnia tries out on her son the rhetorical strategies she will use later: emotional pleas, political arguments, and feigned rejection. She even rehearses her own future role as supplicant by showing him how to plead. Coriolanus in turn rehearses his possible responses of unyielding resistance— "I will not do't" (III.ii.120)— and utter subjection— "Mother, I am going to the marketplace" (III.ii.131). The scene is littered with references to acting, from Coriolanus's insistence on fusing role and reality in "I play / The man I am" (III.ii.15-16), to Volumnia's separation of the two in her demonstration of the "part" (III.ii.105) she wants him to play. Any hint of genuine maternal concern, of a desire to save her son from certain death off the "rock Tarpeian"

(III.i.211) is swallowed up in this metatheatrical language, which distances both characters from personal and political realities. For Volumnia makes the act of supplication into a parody of itself; her long speech, in which she acts the part of the supplicant that she would have him play (III.ii.72-86) reduces humility to theatrical posturing. Coriolanus responds appropriately to this alternative as leading only to "a most inherent baseness" (III.ii.123); after this his capitulation at the end of the scene can seem only like defeat, the ignoble surrender predicted in his own vision of "schoolboys' tears" (III.ii.116). Yet Volumnia contaminates not only Coriolanus's options but her own. She pleads with her son presumably to save his life as well as to secure him the consulship, but she presents the act of pleading as pure hypocrisy and thus makes it impossible for him either to yield with dignity to her or to settle with the plebeians.

In the final supplication scene, the idiom of the theater reappears, but this time with a difference. Earlier, Coriolanus was to play the "part" of humble supplicant and hide the reality of his inner pride; here, his pride is the "part" which, "like a dull actor," Coriolanus "forgets" (V.iii.40-41) when he begins to yield to "Great nature" (V.iii.33). In this scene, Coriolanus himself admits that his heroic self-sufficiency is merely role-playing. Indeed, it is clear from the beginning that Coriolanus will yield to Volumnia's plea: early on he cries, "I melt, and am not / Of stronger earth than others" (V.iii.28-29). The focus of the scene then shifts from Coriolanus, whose change of heart we expect, to those who have come to secure it.

In the first supplication scene (III.ii)— which has no counterpart in Shakespeare's source— Volumnia enters alone and is joined by senators and nobles; the case she presents is political rather than personal. In the later scene, Volumnia is one member of a collective of "all living women" (V.iii.97)— a collective dominated by the gentle wife who "comes foremost" (V.iii.22). Coriolanus's startling lyrical transformation of the chatty busybody Valeria into a semi-icon, "chaste as the icicle / That's curdied by the frost from purest snow / And hangs on Dian's temple" (V.iii.65-67), evokes dramatic antecedents like the pleading of the virgins before Tamburlaine (*1 Tamburlaine* V.i), and distances the mother-son encounter. No longer a political strategist, Volumnia stands in opposition to the real political presence of Aufidius and his soldiers. And, in a play in which outward appearance is seen to reflect inner essence— in which, Brockbank points out, "all qualities of the spirit have a physical manifestation"— the women's change of "raiment" (V.iii.94) for this scene is full of meaning. Volumnia's pleading rags look back to two earlier moments— to the gown of humility worn by Coriolanus when he sues for votes (II.iii), and to the beggar-like disguise he dons when he turns to Aufidius and the Volscians (IV.iv). The double analogue suggests

Volumnia's ambiguity throughout the supplication scene— her tattered garments may be at odds with her inner arrogance, as in Coriolanus's appeal for votes, or they may recall Coriolanus's reversion to the enemy, when his mean attire was "a potent visual suggestion that something in the man himself, not just in his circumstances, ha[d] changed." The latter echo may suggest that here Volumnia, like her son in Antium, bares herself to the enemy and finds herself in a situation for which her nature had never been prepared, requiring a compromise of absolute values which changes her fundamentally. The rags worn by mother and son in the last two acts connect their individual moments of crisis, when both make a choice to abandon pride and self-sufficiency and seek clemency in the bosom of the enemy— a choice of which both must later become victims.

As Volumnia begins to speak, Coriolanus anticipates and rejects the "colder reasons" (V.iii.86) he heard earlier; what he gets is not the approach that would divide heart from brain, but a verbal plea anchored in physical sensation. For, though the text of Volumnia's speech stays remarkably close to Plutarch's original, it is filled out by phrases which convey the physiological strain on the women, who "weep, and shake with fear and sorrow" (V.iii.100) at the bodily violence of Coriolanus, "tearing / His country's bowels out" (V.iii.102-103). Volumnia further identifies her own, mother's, body, with the "country" (V.iii.123) and sides with her "neighbours" (V.iii.173), in striking contrast to her earlier scorn for the people. Her equation of herself with Rome hints at penitence for personal as well as political injuries done Coriolanus when she asks, "Think'st thou it honourable for a noble man / Still to remember wrongs?" (V.iii.154-55). And some change in her perception is evident when the mother who sent her "tender-bodied" son to a cruel war desires "th' interpretation of full time" (V.iii.69) for her grandson. The bathos of Volumnia's presentation of herself as a "poor hen, fond of no second brood" (V.iii.162-63), in its absurd incongruity comes close to domestic comedy, but may also suggest her clumsy approach to new feeling. If Volumnia is a consummate rhetorician throughout the scene— thus leaving her open to suspicion— she not only echoes Plutarch's virtuous widow, but also anticipates Shakespeare's Hermione during her trial in *The Winter's Tale.* Much depends on an actress who can choose to deliver the speeches with anything from cynical manipulation to passionate conviction. But Shakespeare deliberately leaves the choice open, refusing to allow us to come to simple conclusions about Volumnia's motives. Does she still sincerely believe that peace is an alternative? It seems important that Coriolanus is finally convinced, not by the blatant emotional blackmail of the first part of Volumnia's speech, in which she outlines her dilemma and threatens suicide, but by the peace plan she sets out in the second part. Indeed, if Coriolanus senses that his yielding will prove "most mortal to him" (V.iii.189), he nonetheless goes on to implement her plan with calm self-assurance and some degree of success. A politically naive pacifist may hardly seem consistent with even a softened and changed Volumnia. But a fully cognizant Volumnia must leave us with a tangle of equally unresolved questions. Is she saving her own skin at her son's expense? Is she still the coldly patriotic virago of the first act, sacrificing Coriolanus for the sake of Rome? Or is her patriotic sacrifice made in conscious, agonized awareness of its costs for herself and her son? If so, it is a far cry from the one she gleefully imagines in Act I. Is it a sacrifice made, not for Rome, but for the young wife and child with her on the stage? Or is she committed to saving Coriolanus from his own inhumanity, even at the cost of his life? Actresses may choose to compromise and show a woman torn between hope and despair, but it seems far from Shakespeare's intention to present Volumnia as simply a primeval mother-goddess whose promise of loving union includes inevitable death for her son.

If Shakespeare leaves Volumnia's motivation complex and open-ended, he uses two major dramatic strategies to deflect her guilt. First, throughout the supplication scene, Volumnia is the instrument of a greater theatrical good. She is perceived less as "a fantasy of maternal omnipotence in which the mother seeks the death of her son" than as a necessary and positive advocate for the natural bonds which Coriolanus has tried to ignore. Second, after the supplication scene, she is rapidly supplanted by Aufidius, the real agent of Coriolanus's destruction. Indeed, Coriolanus's yielding to his mother is a sufficient, but not a necessary pretext for Aufidius's revenge— in the previous act, Aufidius had cried, "When, Caius, Rome is thine, / Thou art poor'st of all: then shortly art thou mine" (IV.vii.56-57). In the 1984 National Theatre production, which reversed "the modern tendency toward non-political interpretations of *Coriolanus* on the British stage," Volumnia emerged as a tragic figure whose "public 'Roman' front . . . almost cracked under the strain of her knowledge that she had destroyed her son" and Aufidius appeared a political opportunist, proof that "those who compromise survive; tragic heroes do not." When Aufidius ceases to be Coriolanus's homoerotic twin and becomes his foil and destroyer, Volumnia is released from her position as Coriolanus's primeval enemy and can emerge as his equal. Politics, not his mother, kills Coriolanus.

Despite hints at her deep evolution and tragic recognition, Volumnia clearly remains the overbearing matriarch who threatens her son and Coriolanus is still the "overstrained child" who simply gives in. But critics who see *only* "a child holding his mother's hand," are left with a play that forfeits its status as tragedy as well as a good deal of its power in the theater. Such an interpretation wins pity for Coriolanus as his mother's victim, but fails to arouse any concomitant fear at a dreadful choice made in favor of natural bonds. Even those critics who are prepared to accept change and complexity in Coriolanus deny them to Volumnia. While *his* silence at the end of her plea is seen as "a breaking-through into a new territory of value and of moral experience," *her* silence is an inability "to voice the sympathy, approval, or affection the moment naturally invites." Yet one wonders whether Volumnia could give a more eloquent reply than the lengthy silence which contrasts so pointedly with her previous wordy praises. And if Coriolanus here is "more of a man" and "less than ever Volumnia's son," it is a paradox that the theater cannot afford—the scene's strongest visual image is that of the bond between mother and son. On the stage Coriolanus acknowledges himself Volumnia's; if the moment has dignity as well as pathos, both characters must contribute to it. Yet whatever their differences about the complex of motives underlying Coriolanus's change of heart, most critics see Volumnia as a monumental figure incapable of change and insist that "the resolution to the conflict in Act V must be read in the light of the resolution to the conflict in Act III." Shakespeare may be using structural repetition, however, to suggest change as well as continuity in the relation between the two characters; this hypothesis is strengthened by the evidence of theatrical productions. A reviewer of the 1965 American Shakespeare Festival production remarked that "When she attempts to persuade her son that he must compromise, this Volumnia argues with a blazing temper but lets it be seen at once whence came his pride. When she leads the women to plead for mercy, she is a humble, piteous figure." A commentator on the 1979 Royal Shakespeare Company production noted that, after the first supplication scene (III.ii), "Volumnia moves back into silence until, like Lady Macbeth, she makes a powerful final appearance which is contrary to the previous movement." I believe that the text allows us to trace an evolution in Volumnia, from the formidable virago of the first act to the powerful advocate of the last act, through the near-comic bourgeois matriarch of Act II, the "dissembler" of Act III, and the angry, devastated mother of Act IV. And, though the force of Act I lies behind the impact of Act V, it has been transmuted by the play. Volumnia begins by mirroring the hero and speaking his heroic tongue, then passes into a comic, anti-heroic phase in the second and third acts, only to return to her former strength in a different way. Maynard Mack identifies this tripartite journey with the Shakespearean tragic hero. Like most of Shakespeare's tragic heroes, Volumnia places heavy demands on our sympathy. If she succeeds in securing it, she also enriches our experience of the play as a whole.

VIRGILIA

With only a relatively small presence in the play, Virgilia

has nonetheless attracted the attention of a few scholars who have seen her as thematically integral to *Coriolanus*, particularly in her role as foil to Volumnia. Catherine La Courreye Blecki has argued that Virgilia, while contrasting significantly with Volumnia, does not display meekness or passivity, as some have suggested. Rather, while she is often silent, she does contradict Volumnia when necessary. Additionally, Blecki sees Virgilia as playing a vital role in the debate over the heroic, warrior ideal with her mother-in-law.

Gail Kern Paster has seen Virgilia's silence as resistance to the aristocratic code of honor represented by the Coriolanus and Volumnia. This line of thought owes particular debt to **John Middleton Murry**, one of the first critics to comment significantly on Virgilia's character. In Murry's view, Virgilia's defining characteristic is her "gracious silence." She thus represents a powerful, nonverbal critique of the pride demonstrated by Coriolanus and Volumnia. Murry has also observed that Virgilia is perhaps the only feeling character in a play primarily concerned with heroic ideals and political abstraction.

John Middleton Murry

SOURCE: "A Neglected Heroine of Shakespeare," in *Countries of the Mind: Essays in Literary Criticism*, E. P. Dutton and Company, 1922, pp. 31-50.

[*In this excerpt, Murry considers the frequently overlooked figure of Virgilia, observing that despite the fact that she speaks scarcely more than one hundred words in* Coriolanus *she figures prominently in representing the play's theme. Murry notes Virgilia's "gracious silence" and analyzes the few passages in which she does speak. He evaluates her relationship to Coriolanus, which enables the title character's only moments of heartfelt devotion. Murry also reflects on Virgilia's silent opposition to Volumnia. For Murry, Virgilia is the dramatic embodiment of domestic love. Her character thus starkly contrasts with the proud Volumnia. Summarizing Virgilia's significance to the play, Murry writes, "in a few firm touches Shakespeare has given us a woman whose silence we can feel to be the unspoken judgment on the pride of arms and the pride of race which are the theme of the play."*]

. . . Of all the characters in *Coriolanus* one alone can be said to be truly congenial; and she is the least substantial of them all. Virgilia, Coriolanus's wife, though she is present throughout the whole of four scenes, speaks barely a hundred words. But a sudden, direct light is cast upon her by a phrase which takes our breaths with beauty, when Coriolanus welcomes her on his triumphant return as 'My gracious silence!' Magical words! They give a miraculous substance to our fleeting, fading glimpses of a lovely vision which seems to tremble away from the clash of arms and pride that reverberates through the play. Behind the disdainful warrior and his Amazonian mother, behind the vehement speech of this double Lucifer, the exquisite, timid spirit of Virgilia shrinks out of sight into the haven of her quiet home. One can almost hear the faint click of the door behind her as it shuts her from the noise of brawling tongues. Yet in her presence, and in the memory of her presence, Coriolanus becomes another and a different being. It is true we may listen in vain for other words so tender as 'My gracious silence!' from his lips. A man who has one love alone finds only one such phrase in a lifetime. But in the heat of victorious battle, when Coriolanus would clasp Cominius in his arms for joy, he discovers in himself another splendid phrase to remember his happiness with Virgilia.

Oh! let me clip ye
In arms as sound as when I woo'd, in heart
As merry, as when our nuptial day was done
And tapers burned to bedward.

And even in the anguish of the final struggle between his honour and his heart, when his wife comes with his mother to intercede for Rome, it is in the very accents of passionate devotion that he cries to Virgilia,

Best of my flesh!
Forgive my tyranny; but do not say
For that, "Forgive our Romans." Oh! a kiss
Long as my exile, sweet as my revenge!
Now, by the jealous queen of heaven, that kiss
I carried from thee, dear, and my true lip
Hath virgin'd it e'er since.

In the proud, unrelenting man of arms these sudden softenings are wonderful. They conjure up the picture of a more reticent and self-suppressed Othello, and we feel that, to strike to the heart through Coriolanus's coat of mail, it needed an unfamiliar beauty of soul, a woman whose delicate nature stood apart, untouched by the broils and furies of her lord's incessant battling with the Roman people and the enemies of Rome.

In the play Virgilia speaks barely a hundred words. But they are truly the speech of a 'gracious silence,' as precious and revealing as they are rare. She appears first (Act I., Sc. 3) in her own house, sitting silent at her sewing. Coriolanus has gone to the wars. Volumnia tries to kindle her with something of her own Amazonian ecstasy at the thought of men in battle. 'I tell thee, daughter, I sprang not more in joy at first hearing he was a man child than now in first seeing he had proved himself a man.' Virgilia's reply, the first words she speaks in the play, touch to the quick of the reality of war and her own unquiet mind.

But had he died in the business, madam;
how then?

The thoughts of her silence thus revealed, she says no

more until chattering Valeria, for all the world like one of the fashionable ladies in Colonel Repington's diary, is announced. She has come to drag her out to pay calls. Virgilia tries to withdraw. Volumnia will not let her, and even while the maid is in the room waiting to know whether she may show Valeria in, she bursts into another ecstatic vision of her son in the midst of battle, 'his bloody brow with his mailed hand then wiping.' Again Virgilia reveals herself.

His bloody brow! O Jupiter, no blood!

Valeria enters on a wave of small talk. She has seen Virgilia's little boy playing. The very image of his father; 'such a confirmed countenance.' She had watched him chase a butterfly, catching it and letting it go, again and again. 'He did so set his teeth and tear it; oh, I warrant how he mammocked it!'

Volum One on's father's moods.
Val. Indeed, la, it is a noble child.
Virg. A crack, madam.

'An *imp*, madam!' The meaning leaps out of the half-contemptuous word. Don't call him a noble child for his childish brutality. It pains, not rejoices Virgilia. Nor, for all the persuasions of Volumnia and Valeria, will she stir out of the house. She does not want society; she cannot visit 'the good lady that lies in.' She is as firm as she is gentle.

'Tis not to save labour, nor that I want love.

Simply that she is anxious and preoccupied. She will not 'turn her solemness out of door'; she cannot. Coriolanus is at the wars.

So, in two dozen words and a world of unspoken contrast Virgilia is given to us: her horror of brutality and bloodshed, her anxiety for her husband, her reticence, her firmness. She is not a bundle of nerves, but she is full of the aching fears of love. Truly, 'a gracious silence.'

She next appears when the news is come that Coriolanus has triumphed (Act II., Sc. 1). Volumnia and Valeria are talking with Menenius. She stands aside listening. He is sure to be wounded, says Menenius; he always is. She breaks out: 'Oh, no, no, no!' She retires into her silence again while Volumnia proudly tells the story of her son's twenty-five wounds. 'In troth, there's wondrous things spoken of him,' says chattering Valeria. Virgilia murmurs: 'The gods grant them true!' 'True! Pow-wow!' says Volumnia, in hateful scorn: one can see her sudden turn, hear her rasping voice. Virgilia is not one of the true breed of Roman wives and mothers. And indeed she is not. She is thinking of wounds, not as glorious marks of bravery, but as the mutilated body of the man she adores. Wounds, wounds! They talk of nothing but wounds. Virgilia suffers in silence. Coriolanus is wounded. That is a world wounded to her.

Coriolanus enters, swathed in bandages, unrecognisable. He kneels before his mother. Then he sees Virgilia, standing apart, weeping silently. These are the words of the Folio text. Only the spelling has been modernised; the punctuation has been left untouched.

> *Coria.* My gracious silence, hail:
> Would'st thou have laughed, had I come
>   coffin'd home
> That weep'st to see me triumph? Ah my
>   dear,
> Such eyes the widows in Corioli were
> And mothers that lack sons.
> *Mene.* Now the Gods crown thee.
> *Com.* And live you yet? Oh my sweet Lady,
>   pardon.
> *Volum.* I know not where to turn.
> Oh welcome home: and welcome General,
> And y'are welcome all.

The first two of these speeches and their speakers contain no difficulty. But, obviously, 'And live you yet? Oh, my sweet Lady, pardon,' does not belong to Cominius. On his lips it is nonsense. The editors have resolved the problem by giving the line to Coriolanus, and the following speech of Volumnia to Valeria. Coriolanus is supposed to say to Menenius, 'And live you yet?' then, suddenly catching sight of Valeria, to beg her pardon for not having seen her before.

We have a free hand in disposing of the line. There is no objection to Volumnia's speech being given to Valeria, whose effusive manner it suits better. But to make Coriolanus surprised that Menenius is still alive is pointless; he had no reason to suppose that the armchair hero was dead. Moreover, to make him turn to Valeria, and say, 'Oh, my sweet Lady, pardon,' is to give the great warrior the manners of a carpet knight.

Now think of the relation between Virgilia and Coriolanus; remember how her imagination has been preoccupied by his wounds; see her in imagination weeping at the pitiful sight of her wounded husband—and read the lines through without regard to the speakers. It will, I believe, occur to any one with an instinct for psychology that 'And live you yet?' takes up Coriolanus's previous words. 'Ah, my dear,' he has said, 'it is the women who have no husbands who weep as you do.' Then, and not till then, Virgilia breaks silence. 'And live you yet?' And are you really my husband? Is this thing of bandages the lord of my heart? At her sudden, passionate words, Coriolanus understands her tears. He has a glimpse of the anguish of her love. He has been an unimaginative fool. 'Oh, my sweet Lady, pardon!' This, I suggest, is the way the passage should be read:—

> *Coria.*   Ah my dear,
> Such eyes the widows in Corioli wear
> And mothers that lack sons.
> *Mene.* Now the gods crown thee!
> *Virg.* And live you yet?
> *Coria.* Oh, my sweet lady, pardon . . .
> *Val.* I know not where to turn.

And to my own mind it is an essential part of the beauty of the passage that these few lightning words of love should flash through the hubbub of Menenius's welcome and Valeria's effusive congratulations.

Virgilia appears again in the scene following Coriolanus's banishment (Act IV., Sc. 2). Here the alterations necessary are self-evident, and it is difficult to understand why they have not been made before. Again the test of reading through the short scene with an imaginative realisation of Virgilia must be applied. Again her exquisite timidity of speech must be contrasted, as Shakespeare deliberately contrasted it, with Volumnia's headstrong and contemptuous anger. It will then, I believe, be plain that of Volumnia's final words,

> Anger's my meat; I sup upon my self
> And so shall starve with feeding. Come, let's
>   go.
> Leave this faint puling and lament as I do
> In anger, Juno-like. Come, come, come,

the last two lines are addressed to Virgilia alone. Besides Volumnia herself only the two tribunes, Brutus and Sicinius, are there. The lines cannot be spoken to them. Only Virgilia remains. She is not angry, but sad, at Coriolanus's banishment, just as in his triumph she was sad, not joyful: and just as then, Volumnia scorns her for her weakness.

Now read again the Folio text, which is that of the modern editions, of lines 11-28. Volumnia meets the two tribunes who have been the prime movers in her son's banishment:—

> *Volum.* Oh y'are well met:
> Th' hoarded plague a' th' gods requite your love.
> *Mene.* Peace, peace, be not so loud.
> *Volum.* If that I could for weeping, you
>   should hear,
> Nay, and you shall heare some. Will you be gone?
> *Virg.* You shall stay too: I would I had the
>   power
> To say so to my husband.
> *Sicin.* Are you mankind?
> *Volum.* Aye, fool, is that a shame. Note but
>   this, fool,
> Was not a man my father? Had'st thou
>   foxship
> To banish him that struck more blows for

Act V, scene iii. Before the tent of Coriolanus. Coriolanus, Virgilia, Volumnia, Valeria, and others. Painting by William Hamilton, R.A. The University of Michigan Special Collections Library.

Rome
Than thou hast spoken words.
Sicin. Oh blessed Heavens!
Volum. More noble blows than ever you wise
  words.
And for Rome's good, I'll tell thee what: yet
  go:
Nay, but thou shalt stay too: I would my
  son
Were in Arabia, and thy tribe before him,
His good sword in his hand.
Sicin. What then?
Virg. What then? He'd make an end of thy
  posterity
Volum. Bastards, and all.
Good man, the wounds that he does bear for
  Rome!

It is obvious that the peremptory 'You shall stay too!' (l. 14) is not spoken by Virgilia. It is as completely discordant with her character, and with Volumnia's description of her behaviour during the scene ('this faint puling') as it is accordant with the character of Volumnia. Volumnia forces first one, then the other tribune to stay; we can see her clutch them by the sleeve, one in either of her nervous hands. At her words Virgilia interposes a sighing aside, 'Would I had the power to say so to my husband!'

It is equally clear that Virgilia cannot possibly have indulged in the brutal imagination of line 27. 'What then? He'll make an end of thy posterity.' There is no stop at the end of the line in the Folio; it runs on to the next half line; and the whole line and a half undoubtedly belong to Volumnia. A simple transposition of the rubrics is all that is needed.

Volum.   What then?
He'll make an end of thy posterity
Bastards and all.
  Virg. Good man, the wounds that he does
    bear for Rome!'

It is another sighing aside and another indication that Virgilia is haunted by the memory of those wounds she could not bear to see. Unless these asides are restored to her, and the brutal words taken away, quite apart from the violation of her character, there is no point in Volumnia's sneer at her 'faint puling.'

Virgilia appears for the last time as the silent participant in Volumnia's embassy of intercession. For the first and only time a bodily vision of her beauty is given to us, when Coriolanus cries

> What is thy curtsy worth or those dove's
> eyes
> Which can make gods forsworn? I melt and
> am not
> Of stronger earth than others.

She has no need of words to make her appeal; her eyes speak for her. She says simply

> My lord and husband!
> *Coria.* These eyes are not the same I wore in
> Rome.
> *Virg.* The sorrow that delivers us thus changed
> Makes you think so.
> *Coria.*   Like a dull actor now,
> I have forgot my part, and I am out
> Even to a full disgrace. Best of my flesh
> Forgive my tyranny; but do not say
> For that, "Forgive our Romans." Oh! a kiss
> Long as my exile, sweet as my revenge!
> Now, by the jealous queen of heaven, that kiss
> I carried from thee, dear, and my true lip
> Hath virgin'd it e'er since.

After this Virgilia speaks but a single sentence more. Volumnia ends her pleading with an impassioned adjuration to her son:—

> For myself, son,
> I purpose not to wait on Fortune till
> These wars determine: if I cannot persuade
> thee
> Rather to show a noble grace to both parts
> Than seek the end of one, thou shalt no
> sooner
> March to assault thy country than to tread—
> Trust to't, thou shalt not—on thy mother's
> womb
> That brought thee to this world.
> *Virg.*   Ay, and mine
> That brought you forth this boy, to keep
> your name
> Living to time.

Virgilia's words contain much in little space. They, her last words in the play, are the first in which she shows herself at one with her husband's mother. Always be-

fore, Volumnia has been angry, contemptuous, spiteful, malevolent towards Virgilia; and Virgilia had held her peace without yielding an inch of ground to Volumnia's vehemence. We have felt throughout that they are the embodiments of two opposed spirits— of pride and love. Not that Volumnia's pride has changed to love; it is the same pride of race that moves her, the fear of disgrace to a noble name:—

> The end of war's uncertain; but this is certain,
> That, if thou conquer Rome, the benefit
> Which thou shalt thereby reap is such a name
> Whose repetition shall be dogged with curses,
> Whose chronicle thus writ: "The man was
> noble
> But with his last attempt he wip'd it out,
> Destroy'd his country, and his name remains
> To the ensuing age abhorr'd."

But now these spirits of love and pride are reconciled; for once they make the same demand. Volumnia pleads that her son shall remember honour, Virgilia that her husband shall remember mercy. The double appeal is too strong. Coriolanus yields to it, and pays the penalty.

Not one of the readjustments suggested in this essay calls for the alteration of a single word in the text of the Folio. They consist solely in a redistribution of words among the speakers, and in the most complicated instance a redistribution of some kind has long since been seen to be necessary and long since been made. I venture to think that together they will help to disengage the true outline of one of Shakespeare's most delicate minor heroines. There was no place for a Desdemona in the story of Coriolanus; but in a few firm touches Shakespeare has given us a woman whose silence we can feel to be the unspoken judgment on the pride of arms and the pride of race which are the theme of the play.

For it is surely not against the democratic idea that Coriolanus is tried and found wanting. In spite of Signor Croce's assurance to the contrary, it is impossible to believe that the contempt for the city mob with which the play is penetrated was not shared by Shakespeare himself. The greatest writers strive to be impersonal, and on the whole they achieve impersonality; but, though they carve out an image that is unlike themselves, they cannot work wholly against the grain of their own convictions. Prejudice will out. And the loathing of the city mob which is continually expressed in Shakespeare's work and comes to a head in *Coriolanus* was indubitably his own. It is indeed less plausible to deny this than it would be to argue that at a time when his genius was seizing on themes of a greater tragic scope it was his sympathy with the anti-plebeian colour of the Coriolanus story that led Shakespeare to choose it for his play.

This is not a question of Shakespeare's political views. We do not know what they were, and we have no means of finding out. Signor Croce is thus far right. But when he goes on to assure us that it is a wild goose chase to look to discover where Shakespeare's sympathies lay in the world in which he lived, we can point to the knowledge we actually have of every great writer. We do know their sympathies. It may be an illegitimate knowledge, but the laws it violates are laws of Signor Croce's own devising. It is his own logical fiat that holds the kingdoms of the æsthetic and the practical asunder. In fact, there is no dividing line between them. A writer's predispositions in practical life do constantly colour his æsthetic creation, and every great writer who has been conscious of his activity has either confessed the fact or gloried in it.

We know that Shakespeare detested the city mob. If we care to know why we have only to exercise a little imagination and picture to ourselves the finest creative spirit in the world acting in his own plays before a pitful of uncomprehending, base mechanicals.

> Alas, 'tis true, I have gone here and there
> And made myself a motley to the view,
> Gored mine own thoughts, sold cheap what
>   is most dear.

The man who used that terrible phrase, who 'gored his own thoughts' to wring shillings from the pockets of the greasy, grinning crowd in front of him, had no cause to love them; and Shakespeare did not. He was an aristocrat, not in the political sense, but as every man of fine nerves who shrinks from contact with the coarse-nerved is an aristocrat, as Anton Tchehov was an aristocrat when he wrote, 'Alas, I shall never be a Tolstoyan. In women I love beauty above all things, and in the history of mankind, culture expressed in carpets, spring carriages, and keenness of wit.'

Shakespeare could not therefore measure Coriolanus against the democratic idea in which he did not believe; nor could he pit the patriotic idea against him, for Coriolanus was immune from a weakness for his country. It is domestic love that pierces his armour and inflicts the mortal wound. And perhaps in Shakespeare's mind the power of that love was manifested less in the silver speech of the vehement and eloquent Volumnia than in the golden silence of the more delicate woman to whom we have attempted to restore a few of her precious words.

AUFIDIUS

Critics have universally acknowledged Aufidius's secondary role in *Coriolanus*, and most define his character in relation to that of the protagonist. Charles Mitchell

has noted that to a degree Coriolanus fashions Aufidius as an ideal, and that Aufidius's actual nobility and bravery therefore cannot live up to this unrealistic projection. Ruth Nevo has contended that Aufidius's manipulation of Coriolanus proves the source of his downfall—this is typical, according to Nevo, of the pattern of Shakespearean tragedy, despite the fact the other critics have argued that Coriolanus generates his own doom.

Harley Granville-Barker has seen Aufidius as an effective counterbalance to Coriolanus. Courageous and aristocratic in Granville-Barker's view, Aufidius cannot be described as basically evil, but instead resorts to treachery only after numerous honorable attempts to defeat Coriolanus on the battlefield have failed. As Stanley Wells has observed, Aufidius also offers valuable insights into the theme of the play. Aufidius remarks, "So our virtues / Lie in th' interpretation of the time," commenting on the relativity of judgment that is one of the play's minor motifs. Wells has also noted that Aufidius provides a final comment on Coriolanus's character which insists that his fame and "noble memory" are deserved in spite of his degrading death.

Harley Granville-Barker

SOURCE: "*Coriolanus*," in *Prefaces to Shakespeare*, Vol. II, Princeton University Press, 1947, pp. 150-299.

[*In the following excerpted preface to* Coriolanus, *Granville-Barker explores the character of Aufidius, describing this "secondary hero." Granville-Barker acknowledges that Aufidius is for the most part effective as a counterpoint to Coriolanus. Aufidius is not made out to be a flat villain; he is brave and heroic, but plays a surprising role as a treacherous deceiver. Granville-Barker notes that Aufidius takes the "second-rate man's" approach by having Coriolanus put to death ignobly. Yet the critic also observes Aufidius's moments of wisdom and the final victory of common sense as the Volscian general cries, "My rage is gone / And I am struck with sorrow" above Coriolanus's dead body.*]

. . . It takes all Shakespeare's skill to make Aufidius fully effective within the space which the planning of the action allows him—and perhaps he does not wholly succeed. For a while it is not so difficult. He is admitted on all hands to be Marcius' rival and to come short of him by little. Marcius' first word of him is that

> I sin in envying his nobility,
> And were I anything but what I am,
> I would wish me only he.

He is secondary hero. And when within a moment or so we see the man himself he is telling the Senators of Corioles:

If we and Caius Marcius chance to meet,
'Tis sworn between us we shall ever strike
Till one can do no more.

Volumnia, imagining glorious things, can see her Marcius

    pluck Aufidius down by the hair . . .

In the battle the Corioles taunt the Romans with

    There is Aufidius: list, what work he makes
    Amongst your cloven army.

while to Marcius, whether far off—

    There is the man of my soul's hate, Aufidius. . .

— or within reach—

    Set me against Aufidius and his Antiats. . . .

— he is an obsession. And when they do meet and fight,
Aufidius, if bettered, is not beaten. To this point, then,
however little we may see of him, he is brought to our
minds in each succeeding scene, and is emphatically
lodged there when he is so unconsentingly rescued in
the duel with his famous enemy by "certain Volsces"
(anonymous: common soldiers presumably, therefore):

    Officious, and not valiant, you have shamed me
    In your condemned seconds.

And, since we shall not see him thereafter for some
time, this note of shame, and of the crooked passion
it can rouse in the man, is enlarged and given what
will be memorable place in a scene coming but a
little later.

            Five times, Marcius,
    I have fought with thee; so often hast thou
        beat me,
    And wouldst do so, I think, should we
        encounter
    As often as we eat.

Frank confession! But now

            mine emulation
    Hath not that honour in't it had; for where
    I thought to crush him in an equal force,
    True sword to sword, I'll potch at him some
        way
    Or wrath or craft may get him. . . .
            Where I find him, were it
    At home, upon my brother's guard, even
        there,
    Against the hospitable canon, would I
    Wash my fierce hands in's heart.

We shall certainly recall that— and be given good cause
to— when, all amazingly, the event so falls out. The
scheme of the action allows Aufidius very limited space;
but we have thus far been kept conscious of him
throughout. From now, even until he emerges into it
again, he does not go quite without mention, and we
shall have lodged in mind what he may mean to it when
he does. It is able stagecraft.

In a cruder play Aufidius and the Volsces might be
made to serve as "villains of the piece." But Shakespeare
is not painting in such ultra-patriotic black and white.
We are on the Roman side, and they are "foreigners";
so their worse, not their better, aspect is naturally turned
towards us. The victorious Romans give them a "good"
peace, Titus Lartius being commanded to send back
from their captured city

            to Rome
    The best, with whom we may articulate,
    For their own good and ours.

They, when their victorious turn comes, so we hear,

            looked
    For no less spoil than glory . . .

Shakespeare shades them somewhat. But the balance is
not unfairly held.

Aufidius, then, re-enters the action at its most critical
juncture, and to play for the moment a surprising part
in it. Here, in this wine-flushed host to the nobles of
Antium, is quite another man; and not only in the look
of him but, yet more surprisingly— suspense resolved—
in the deep-sworn enemy turned ecstatic comrade. From
that

            Nor sleep, nor sanctuary,
    Being naked, sick, nor fane nor Capitol,
    The prayers of priests, nor times of sacrifice,
    Embarquements all of fury, shall lift up
    Their rotten privilege and custom 'gainst
    My hate to Marcius.

we are at a glowing

            Let me twine
    Mine arms about that body, where against
    My grained ash an hundred times hath broke
    And scarred the moon with splinters: here I
        clip
    The anvil of my sword, and do contest
    As hotly and as nobly with thy love
    As ever in ambitious strength I did
    Contend against thy valour.

It is a turning point indeed, and doubly so; the revolution in Marcius is barely set forth before it is matched

with this. The two revolutions differ as the two men do; the one a plunging through defeat and misery from confident pride to obdurate bitterness; that in Aufidius a sudden emotional overthrow, sprung by this startling proffer, this attack upon a weakness in him which he would never think to defend. Yet there is a likeness between them too. And they are in keeping, both, with the rest of the play, its extremes of passion and their instabilities; the weathercock-swaying of the citizens, Volumnia's violence and arbitrary shifts. Marcius himself we shall see will be unable to abide by his treason to the end; and Aufidius, we shall very quickly guess, will not long sustain this unnatural change. Recurring ironies fitting into the scheme of tragic irony which informs the whole action.

This "strange alteration"— reflected too in the freakish comment of the servants— gives us a fresh, and, for the moment, an alert interest in Aufidius. From now to the end the stagecraft actuating him remains as able; and if here and there the figure seems to lack vitality, to be a little word-locked, why, livelier development of this new aspect of the man might well make more demands on the play's space than could be spared, or such a turn of inspiration as Shakespeare (even he!) has not unquestionably at command. But he does not dodge nor skip a step in the completing of the character. And, within a scene or so, to begin this, we see Aufidius again— quite disillusioned.

Thinking better of things is a dry business; and this ancillary scene, shared with an anonymous Lieutenant, will appropriately be none of the liveliest. But the matter of it is a strengthening rivet in the character scheme of the play. Aufidius' sobered reaction from his rhapsodies to the coldest common sense— hints dropped moreover of revengeful traps already laid for Marcius; Aufidius to be revenged on him for his own access of too generous folly, the hardest thing forgivable— this will redress any balance of sympathy lost between the two for the action's last phase. We have no violent swing back to the fanatically sportsmanlike hatred with which they started. On the contrary, to Aufidius is given in the scene's last speech the most measured and balanced of summarizings of his rival's qualities and failings. And for Marcius it is in this quiet reasonable accounting that his worst danger can be foreseen. Mastery in soldiership— who has ever denied him that? He has not even to exercise it now:

All places yield to him ere he sits down;
And . . .

— despite his treason; because of it indeed—

the nobility of Rome are his:
The Senators and Patricians love him too. . . .
I think he'll be to Rome
As is the asprey to the fish, who takes it

By sovereignty of nature. . . .

Aufidius, lacking just that sovereignty, could not look his own problem more fairly in the face. For, indeed, he had better know just where he has the worse of it, that being the second-rate man's due approach to getting the better of it after all. He may next encourage himself by listing— though with every scruple and reserve— Marcius' failings too: pride, temper, intolerance and the rest, and by recognizing that in this discordant world men have the defects of their qualities and the qualities of their defects; and that at best, what is more,

our virtues
Lie in the interpretation of the time. . . .

— which may prove for us or against us; and whichever way

One fire drives out one fire; one nail, one
nail;
Rights by rights founder, strengths by
strengths do fail.

Fortune, with a little patient aid, is ever ready to turn her wheel:

When, Caius, Rome is thine
Thou art poor'st of all; then shortly art thou
mine.

Both speech and scene demand of their audience close attention, closer, perhaps, than such detached argument will currently command at this juncture in a play unless it be embodied in some central, radiating figure. It is the more notable that Shakespeare should here, so to speak, be forcing his meaning through the recalcitrant lines. But his aim, it would seem, is to give a rational substance to the figure, of such a sort as will keep us and Aufidius expressively if cryptically observant through succeeding scenes while we await the due restoring of the natural open enmity between the two.

It comes with relief.

How is it with our general?

his fellow conspirators ask.

Even so
As with a man by his own alms empoisoned,
And with his charity slain.

But he is free now of his false position and on his own ground again, and the ills done him are glib upon his tongue. He must be cautiously in the right at all points:

And my pretext to strike at him admits
A good construction. I raised him, and I

pawned
Mine honour for his truth. . . .

More than so, he

took some pride
To do myself this wrong . . .

—he is fueling up with virtuous indignation, until, at the touch of a match, Coriolanus himself can be trusted to fire out in fury, no moral excuses needed. "Traitor . . . unholy braggart . . . boy of tears . . . boy!"—it is the last spark that sets all ablaze.

Aufidius' philosophic mind has not endured; nor does the one-time gallantry. "My valour's poisoned . . ."—we are back at that. He is no coward, we know; has ever been ready to fight. It is only that, now or never, he must have the best of it, and he has made all sure. So, duly provoked

The Conspirators draw, and kill Coriolanus, who falls. . . .

Upon which, though, he cannot resist it:

Aufidius stands on him

Shakespeare, in the maturity of his skill, knows how to give as much meaning to a significantly placed gesture as to a speech or more. There are two gestures here, the insolent treading of the slain man under foot, with the quick attempt in face of the shocked outcry to excuse it:

My noble masters, hear me
speak.

then the response to the reproach:

O, Tullus!
Thou hast done a deed whereat valour will weep.
Tread not upon him. Masters . . .

which can but be its shamed and embarrassed lifting, the more eloquent of Aufidius, this. The more fittingly unheroic, besides, the ending. The lords of the city have been honourable enemies.

Peace, ho! no outrage: peace!
The man is noble and his fame folds in
This orb o' the earth. His last offences to us
Shall have judicious hearing.

The sight of the outrage done him horrifies them. But as Aufidius promptly argues,

My lords, when you shall know, as in this rage
Provoked by him, you cannot, the great danger

Which this man's life did owe you, you'll rejoice
That he is thus cut off.

and, truly, as they'll in fairness soon admit:

His own impatience
Takes from Aufidius a great part of blame. . .

Common sense supervenes:

Let's make the best of it.

And Aufidius can say with truth, the man being safely dead:

My rage is gone,
And I am struck with sorrow. . . .

SOURCES FOR FURTHER STUDY

Literary Commentary

Barron, David B. "*Coriolanus*: Portrait of the Artist as Infant." *The American Imago* 19, No. 2 (Summer 1962): 171-93.
    A psychoanalytic essay that considers the subject of emotional infantilism in *Coriolanus*. Barron argues that Coriolanus's excessive dependence upon his mother has manifest itself in an adult need for achievement, which nonetheless is hindered by his inability to escape her dominance.

Blecki, Catherine La Courreye. "'The Ladies Have Prevailed': Volumnia, Virgilia, and Valeria in Shakespeare's *Coriolanus*." *San José Studies* XX, No. 1 (Winter 1994): 6-17.
    Considers the women of *Coriolanus* as a group which successfully opposes Coriolanus and the warrior ideal he represents. Blecki likewise explores the ways in which Volumnia, Virgilia, and Valeria—a mother, a wife, and a widow—question women's roles in society.

Cantor, Paul A. "Part One: *Coriolanus*." In *Shakespeare's Rome: Republic and Empire*, pp. 55-124. Ithaca, N.Y.: Cornell University Press, 1976.
    In-depth study of what *Coriolanus* reveals concerning Shakespeare's understanding of Republican Rome. Among the various topics addressed are themes of self-knowledge and of the "fundamental incompatibility between political excellence and human excellence."

Charney, Maurice. "*Coriolanus*." In *All of Shakespeare*, pp. 299-308. New York: Columbia University Press, 1993.
    Views *Coriolanus* as an abstract, ideological, and political play. Charney principally analyzes the imagery associated with Coriolanus, whom he describes as "a paradoxical hero, full of a harsh integrity and violently antidemocratic."

Coote, Stephen. *Penguin Critical Studies: 'Coriolanus.'* London: Penguin Books, 1992, 98 p.

Study of *Coriolanus* that acknowledges the play's deficiencies in comparison to many of Shakespeare's other dramas, but considers instead its powerful display of human struggle, and its strengths of dramatic tension and passion when performed on stage.

Gordon, D. J. "Name and Fame: Shakespeare's *Coriolanus.*" In *Papers: Mainly Shakespearian*, edited by G. I. Duthie, pp. 40-57. Edinburgh: Oliver and Boyd, 1964.

Explains that *Coriolanus* is substantially concerned with a critique of honor. Considering Shakespeare's sources, and the changes he made in them, Gordon evaluates the effects of Coriolanus's pride when translated from the battlefield to the city of Rome.

Holstun, James. "Tragic Superfluity in *Coriolanus.*" *ELH* 50, No. 3 (Fall 1983): 485-507.

Analyzes the metaphor of the body politic reflected in Menenius's fable of the belly, arguing that the fable should not be considered as the key to Shakespeare's perception of social order, but as part of a larger satire of an aristocratic social theory.

Honigmann, E. A. J. "The Clarity of *Coriolanus.*" In *Shakespeare: Seven Tragedies, The Dramatist's Manipulation of Response*, pp. 170-91. London: Macmillan, 1976.

Discusses *Coriolanus* as Shakespeare's final tragedy. Honigmann analyzes the fable of the belly delivered by Menenius in Act I for the light it sheds on the complex social functions of the drama. The critic also probes the development and death of Coriolanus, as well as the method of his characterization, surmising that Shakespeare constantly manipulated the perceptions of his audience, and never took a definitive stance without offering a counter-argument.

Hutchings, W. "Beast or God: The *Coriolanus* Controversy." *Critical Quarterly* 24, No. 2 (Summer 1982): 35-50.

Explores modern critical assessments of *Coriolanus* as a political play. Overall, Hutchings views character and politics as "complementary rather than antithetical in the structure of *Coriolanus*" and finds the play's concern with the conjunction of language, truth, and society as fundamental.

Kahn, Coppélia. "Mother of Battles: Volumnia and Her Son in *Coriolanus.*" In *Roman Shakespeare: Warriors, Wounds, and Women*, pp. 144-59. London: Routledge, 1997.

Studies the "interaction between mothering and warmaking" in *Coriolanus.* Kahn analyzes the imagery and sources associated with this unique juxtaposition of traditionally feminine and masculine roles, and examines its ironic results in the play.

Knight, G. Wilson. "The Royal Occupation: An Essay on *Coriolanus.*" In *The Imperial Theme: Further Interpretations of Shakespeare's Tragedies Including the Roman Plays*, pp. 154-98.

London: Oxford University Press, 1931.

Investigates the importance of *Coriolanus*'s metal, weapon, and city imagery to an understanding of both its hero and the world in which he lives. Knight also considers the relationship between Coriolanus and his mother as based upon shared pride, which proves to be the source of the protagonist's tragedy.

Lowe, Lisa. "'Say I play the man I am': Gender and Politics in *Coriolanus.*" *The Kenyon Review* VIII, No. 4 (Fall 1986): 86-95.

Probes combined political and gender conflicts operating in *Coriolanus.* Citing examples of language, metaphor, and rhetoric in the play— including the drama's psychological focus on the relationship of Coriolanus and Volumnia, and the imagery of the body politic found in Menenius's fable of the belly— Lowe focuses on the inseparable nature of the work's concern with the dynamics of male-female and class relationships.

Maus, Katherine Eisaman. "*Coriolanus.*" In *The Norton Shakespeare*, pp. 2785-92. New York: W. W. Norton and Company, 1997.

Surveys changes Shakespeare made to Plutarch's original story in writing *Coriolanus*, political debates raised in the play, and the work's intense scrutiny of Roman society and its highly restrictive patterns of masculinity and femininity.

Mitchell, Charles. "Coriolanus: Power as Honor." *Shakespeare Studies* I (1965): 199-226.

Discusses the dynamics of Coriolanus's unbending honor and his obsession for power. Mitchell examines Coriolanus's lack of feeling, his selflessness, his self-love, his rejection of praise, and ultimately his ethical inversion of good and evil.

Nevo, Ruth. "*Coriolanus.*" In *Tragic Form in Shakespeare*, pp. 356-404. Princeton, N.J.: Princeton University Press, 1972.

Maintains that *Coriolanus* fits the pattern of Shakespearean tragedy in that the fatal error of its protagonist is brought about by the manipulation of others. Nevo sees the tribunes and, later, Aufidius as manipulators, and contends that motivation for action in the play does not originate with Coriolanus, but with these schemers.

Palmer, John. "Caius Marcius Coriolanus." In *Political Characters of Shakespeare*, pp. 250-310. London: Macmillan and Co., 1945.

Explication of Coriolanus's character in political contexts which envisions the tragic climax of *Coriolanus* as "a conflict between personal pride and family affection rather than a conflict between the principles of aristocratic and popular government."

Parker, R. B. "Introduction." In *The Tragedy of Coriolanus*, edited by R. B. Parker, pp. 1-154. Oxford: Clarendon Press, 1994.

Offers information on style, sources, contemporary history, stage productions, and varying modern interpretations of *Coriolanus.*

Paster, Gail Kern. "To Starve with Feeding: The City in *Coriolanus.*" *Shakespeare Studies* XI (1978): 123-44.
Assesses Shakespeare's rendering of imagery associated with the city of Rome and the characters who inhabit it in *Coriolanus.* In addition to examining the principal characters in the play, Paster sees Coriolanus's death as a sacrifice to a greater process— "the endless tragicomic cycle of regeneration"— that allows the community as a whole to survive.

Poole, Adrian. *Harvester New Critical Introductions to Shakespeare: 'Coriolanus.'* New York: Harvester Wheatsheaf, 1988, 140 p.
Offers a close reading of *Coriolanus,* with special emphasis on its strengths in dramatic performance.

Proser, Matthew. "Coriolanus: The Constant Warrior and the State." *College English* 24, No. 7 (April 1963): 507-12.
Comments on Coriolanus's unchanging character in relation to war, community, and his mother.

Rabkin, Norman. "The Polity." In *Shakespeare and the Common Understanding*, pp. 80-149. New York: The Free Press, 1967.
Describes Shakespeare's politics, as demonstrated in his plays, as tragic. Rabkin finds the dramatist's presentation of political action in *Coriolanus* to be problematic, and determines that the play offers a critique of "the ethical status of the body politic itself."

Sicherman, Carol M. "*Coriolanus*: The Failure of Words." *ELH* 39, No. 2 (June 1972): 189-207.
Studies the theme of language in *Coriolanus,* specifically Coriolanus's fear and mistrust of words.

Spencer, T. J. B. "*Coriolanus.*" In *Shakespeare: The Roman Plays*, pp. 38-48. London: Longmans, Green, and Co., 1963.
Survey of *Coriolanus* that lauds the splendid writing of the play, but views Coriolanus as unsympathetic— a defect which causes the drama as a whole to suffer.

Stockholder, Katherine. "The Other Coriolanus." *PMLA* 85, No. 2 (March 1970): 228-36.
Contends that "the tragic focus in *Coriolanus* . . . is blurred by the protagonist's confusion of honour with a limited conception of manliness." Stockholder's interpretation highlights the ironic qualities that Coriolanus embodies, particularly the military ideals of the Roman Empire, and the destructiveness that accompanies these ideals.

Thomas, Vivian. "Sounds, Words, Gestures and Deeds in *Coriolanus.*" In *Shakespeare's Roman Worlds*, pp. 154-219. London: Routledge, 1989.
Investigates the social universe of *Coriolanus* as it is expressed through words, actions, and images, and characterized through conflict. Thomas contends that the central issue of the play is the question of values, and that while others are suited to adapt to changes in social values, Coriolanus— the "quintessential Roman"— is not.

Van Dyke, Joyce. "Making a Scene: Language and Gesture in 'Coriolanus'." *Shakespeare Survey* 30 (1977): 135-46.
Evaluates the ways in which Coriolanus expresses himself through action and gesture, and his inability to act the parts that others believe he ought to play.

Wells, Stanley. "Tragedies of Ancient Egypt and Rome." In *Shakespeare: A Life in Drama*, pp. 300-27. New York: W. W. Norton and Company, 1995.
Enumerates multiple conflicts in *Coriolanus,* including the war between the Romans and Volscians, the struggle of the Roman people against the patricians, and Coriolanus's internal strife.

Media Adaptation

The Tragedy of Coriolanus. Time-Life Video, 1983.
BBC television production of the drama. Directed by Elijah Moshinsky. Distributed by Ambrose Video Publishing. 145 minutes.

MEASURE FOR MEASURE

INTRODUCTION

The earliest authoritative text available for *Measure for Measure* was published in the First Folio edition of Shakespeare's plays dated 1623. Today, most critics accept this version of the play as a transcription of Shakespeare's "foul papers," that is, an uncorrected manuscript written in the playwright's own hand. This theory is based on the presence in the text of anomalies often found in uncorrected manuscripts, such as sparse stage directions, omitted and transposed words, and mislineations. The first recorded performance of *Measure for Measure* was on December 26, 1604, when a play entitled "Mesur for Mesur" by "Shaxberd" was performed at Whitehall before King James I and his court by "his Maiesties players," the troupe with which Shakespeare was associated from early 1603 until his retirement.

Two works have traditionally been regarded as the primary sources of *Measure for Measure*: a novella in a collection of tales entitled *Hecatommithi* (1565) by Giovanni Battista Giraldi (known as Cinthio) and George Whetstone's two-part play, *The Right Excellent and Famous Historye of Promos and Cassandra* (1578), which was based on Cinthio's novella. However, several critics have noticed significant parallels between *Measure for Measure* and *Epitia* (1583), a drama adapted by Cinthio from his novella. These discoveries have led to the generally accepted theory that Shakespeare derived the main aspects of his plot from both of Cinthio's works and used the structure of Whetstone's drama to organize the action, characterization, and themes of *Measure for Measure*. According to this hypothesis, Shakespeare drew upon the *Hecatommithi* for the Duke's magnanimous nature, his deputation of Angelo, Isabella's intellectual character and her refusal to accept Angelo's proposition, and the Duke's attraction to Isabella; in *Epitia*, Shakespeare found the conflict between justice and mercy and expanded it into a central theme in *Measure for Measure*. Finally, Shakespeare incorporated into *Measure for Measure* certain alterations of Cinthio's *Hecatommithi* which Whetstone used in *Promos and Cassandra*, such as the inclusion of a comic subplot.

Measure for Measure has fascinated and perplexed audiences and critics alike for centuries. Critical assessments have ranged from profound disappointment in the play's lack of consistency to assertions that *Measure for Measure* ranks as one of Shakespeare's greatest achievements. Scholars have in fact disagreed on virtually every aspect of the play, including its central themes and artistic unity as well as its style, genre, and characterization. Principal topics of debate have included the characterizations of the Duke, Isabella, and Angelo. Scholars have for example been divided over whether the Duke is manipulative or wise; whether Isabella is rigidly moralistic or saintly and compassionate; and whether Angelo is incomprehensibly split into two separate personalities—one respectable and the other villainous.

Recent criticism has focused on the play's effectiveness at dealing with the themes of justice versus mercy, and have argued over whether the play functions as an allegory for Christian charity versus the letter of the law. Another source of scholarly speculation has been Isabella's silence in response to the Duke's marriage proposal. Critics have argued over whether her muteness indicates acceptance or rejection of his offer, and both critics and stage directors have suggested a variety of ways of dramatizing Isabella's reaction. Finally, critics continue to debate over the genre of *Measure for Measure*. While early commentators described the play as a comedy, owing to the fact that it ends in a series of betrothals and marriages, others have called it a tragicomedy that is neatly split into a tragic first half and a comic second half. Today, most critics agree that *Measure for Measure* has earned its designation as a "problem play"—both because it leaves us with moral issues which remain ambiguous to the end, and because it refuses to be neatly classified.

PRINCIPAL CHARACTERS

(in order of appearance)

Vincentio the Duke (Duke Vincentio): Ruler of Vienna. As the play opens, Duke Vincentio is preparing to leave the city for a while, so he deputizes the puritanical Angelo to govern during his absence. In fact, the Duke does not leave Vienna after all, but disguises himself as Friar Lodowick so that he can observe undetected the way in which Angelo administers law and order. After Angelo abuses his power by trying to force Isabella to have sex with him, the Duke orchestrates a "bed-trick," whereby Angelo is ultimately forced to marry his jilted fiancée, Mariana, and Claudio is freed to marry Juliet. At the close of the play the Duke asks Isabella to marry him. (*See* **Duke Vincentio** *in the* **CHARACTER STUDIES** *section.*)

Escalus: Senior assistant to Duke Vincentio. While the Duke is away, Escalus acts as Angelo's assistant. Although Escalus has more seniority in office than Angelo has, the Duke passes over Escalus to promote Angelo as deputy— probably to test the younger man's mettle. A compassionate and honest man, Escalus is not offended that Angelo is promoted over him.

Angelo: One of Duke Vincentio's assistants (the other, more senior, assistant is Escalus). On the pretext that he must leave Vienna for a while, the Duke deputizes Angelo, giving him full powers to enforce the laws of Vienna. Angelo's first actions as deputy are to close down Vienna's brothels and to arrest and sentence to death Claudio for impregnating his fiancée, Juliet. When Claudio's sister, Isabella, begs Angelo to be lenient, the deputy becomes excited by her purity, and tries to coerce her into having sex with him in exchange for her brother's life. With Isabella's help, the disguised Duke tricks Angelo into sleeping with his jilted fiancée, Mariana, and then orders Angelo to marry her. (See **Angelo** in the **CHARACTER STUDIES** section.)

Lucio: A fashionable, dissipated gentleman and a friend of Claudio. He persuades Isabella to intercede with Angelo to save Claudio's life. Lucio inadvertently slanders the disguised Duke to his face. At the close of the play the Duke sentences Lucio first to marry a prostitute whom he impregnated and then to be whipped and hanged. Shortly afterward, the Duke limits Lucio's sentence to marriage.

Two other gentlemen (First Gentleman and Second Gentleman): Friends of Lucio. The two gentlemen are present when the brothel-keeper Mistress Overdone announces that Claudio has been arrested and sentenced to death for fornication, and they exit with Lucio to find out whether Overdone's story is true.

Mistress Overdone: She runs a house of prostitution which is closed down as a result of the newly deputized Angelo's strict enforcement of Vienna's laws. Later in the play, Elbow mentions that she has reopened her brothel under the guise of a bathhouse. She is arrested and sent to prison by Escalus.

Pompey: Although he claims to be a tapster, or bartender, Pompey Bum is actually a bawd, or pimp, who works for Mistress Overdone; he is thus part of Vienna's illicit underworld. Pompey is sent to jail for pandering and for carrying "a strange picklock." In prison, he takes a job as assistant to Abhorson, the executioner.

Claudio: Isabella's brother and Juliet's fiancé. On orders from the newly deputized Angelo, Claudio is sentenced to death for having sex with Juliet out of wedlock. Claudio asks Lucio to inform Isabella of his plight so that she will persuade Angelo to be lenient with her brother. Claudio thus sets in motion the central conflict

in the play, since Isabella's pleas ultimately arouse Angelo's lust.

Provost: Warden of the prison where Claudio is being held. In Act I, he conducts Claudio to jail. In Act II, he receives instructions from Angelo for Claudio's speedy execution. He spends much of the rest of the play helping the disguised Duke with his plan to save Claudio from death.

Juliet: Claudio's fiancée who was impregnated by him and who, like him, is imprisoned by Angelo for fornication. Unlike Claudio, Juliet is not sentenced to death— probably because she is pregnant.

Thomas (Friar Thomas): One of two friars in the play (Friar Peter is the other; Friar Lodowick is merely the Duke in disguise). The Duke reveals to Friar Thomas his plan to disguise himself as a monk so that he can secretly observe Angelo's enforcement of Vienna's laws.

Isabella: Claudio's sister. She becomes a novice of the order of Saint Clare on the same day that her brother is arrested and condemned to death for fornication. When she begs Angelo to spare her brother, the deputy insists that she have sex with him in exchange for her brother's reprieve. She refuses and is horrified when her brother pleads with her to save his life by sleeping with Angelo. She participates in the Duke's scheme to unite Angelo with his jilted fiancée, Mariana. At the close of the play, the Duke asks Isabella to abandon the life of a nun in order to marry him. (See **Isabella** in the **CHARACTER STUDIES** section.)

Francisca (a nun): A nun at the convent which has accepted Isabella as a novice. She appears at the beginning of the play, instructing Isabella on the convent's rules and privileges.

Elbow: A constable. He arrests the bawd Pompey and the foolish gentleman Froth and brings them to Angelo and Escalus for judgment. Elbow is a comic figure who tends to speak in malapropisms.

Froth: A "foolish gentleman" who, along with the bawd Pompey, is arrested by Elbow at a brothel run by Mistress Overdone, and brought before Angelo and Escalus for sentencing.

Servant: A retainer to Angelo. He announces the arrival of Isabella, who has come to plead with Angelo for her brother Claudio's life.

Mariana: Angelo's jilted fiancée. According to the Duke, Mariana and Angelo were engaged to be married until Mariana's brother, Frederick, was lost at sea along with his sister's dowry. Unwilling to marry Mariana without her dowry, Angelo nullified their engagement with the false excuse that Mariana was not a virgin. Mariana still loves Angelo in spite of his treachery, and she lives out her days secluded in a "moated grange."

Abhorson: An executioner at the prison where Claudio is being held.

Barnardine: A prisoner and hardened criminal at the jail where Claudio is being held. When the Duke arranges with the Provost to have Barnardine executed in place of Claudio, Barnardine insists that he is too drunk to die, and refuses to be executed. He is pardoned at the close of the play.

Peter: (Friar Peter): One of two friars in the play (the other is Friar Thomas). Friar Peter helps the Duke orchestrate the final scene where Angelo's hypocrisy is revealed and Mariana asserts her right to be Angelo's wife. He also performs the offstage marriage ceremony between Mariana and Angelo.

PLOT SYNOPSIS

Act I: On his departure from Vienna, Duke Vincentio deputizes Angelo to administer the laws of the city in his place, and appoints the wise "old Escalus" as Angelo's assistant. The Duke, who is concerned that he has been too lax in keeping order in the city, in fact has no intention of leaving Vienna. Instead, he plans to disguise himself as Friar Lodowick so that he can monitor the effect that the "precise" Angelo's enforcement of the laws has on the citizens; and to see whether the exercise of power causes any change in Angelo. The new deputy's first actions are to shut down all the brothels in the suburbs and to arrest and sentence to death young Claudio for impregnating his fiancée, Juliet. On his way to prison, Claudio is met by his friend Lucio, who promises to ask Claudio's sister, Isabella, to beg Angelo for her brother's life. Lucio seeks out Isabella at the convent where she has recently become a novice and tells her of Claudio's plight. Distressed at this news, she agrees to speak to Angelo.

Act II: When Escalus tries to persuade Angelo to reduce the severity of Claudio's sentence, the deputy refuses and instead instructs the Provost to have Claudio executed the next morning. Constable Elbow appears before Angelo and Escalus with the "bawd" Pompey and a gentleman named Froth in custody, and Angelo leaves it to Escalus to sort out Elbow's confusing complaint against his two prisoners. Meanwhile, Isabella arrives and pleads with Angelo for her brother's life, all the while being coached by Lucio to be more compelling in her entreaties. Aroused by Isabella's virtue, Angelo instructs her to return tomorrow for his answer. Meanwhile, the disguised Duke Vincentio visits the prison where Claudio and Juliet are being held and speaks with the loving but repentant Juliet. When Isabella meets next day with Angelo, he tells her that she must have

sex with him if she wants to save her brother. Outraged, Isabella declares that she will "tell the world aloud" about Angelo's hypocritical proposition, and he retorts that, thanks to his spotless reputation, no one will believe her accusations. Distressed and alone, Isabella refuses to submit to Angelo's blackmail. "More than our brother is our chastity," she concludes, and goes to prepare her brother for death.

Act III: Disguised as Friar Lodowick, Duke Vincentio visits Claudio in prison and reconciles him to his death sentence, but when Isabella tells her brother of the deputy's proposition, Claudio loses heart and, much to Isabella's disgust, begs her to submit to Angelo. "O Isabel! . . ." he exclaims, "Death is a fearful thing." The disguised Duke intervenes. He tells Isabella about Mariana, a lady who was once engaged to be married to Angelo but whom he shamefully rejected after her dowry was lost at sea. The Duke suggests a plan where Mariana, who still loves Angelo, would secretly sleep with Angelo in Isabella's place, thereby reclaiming her fiancé, saving Claudio's life, and preserving Isabella's chastity. Isabella gratefully agrees to this "bed-trick." Meanwhile, Pompey is arrested once more and taken to jail, and so is his employer, the brothel-keeper Mistress Overdone. Unaware that the friar is really the Duke in disguise, Lucio strikes up a conversation with him and—unwisely pretending to know the Duke well—claims that Vincentio is a fool, a drunk, and a libertine. The Duke closes Act III with a pronouncement on his deputy: "Twice treble shame on Angelo, / To weed my vice and let his grow!"

Act IV: The disguised Duke, Mariana, and Isabella meet to confirm the details of their plan. But after Angelo sleeps with the woman he thinks is Isabella, he reneges on his promise to spare her brother and instead sends a note to the Provost, instructing him to deliver Claudio's head as proof of his execution. The disguised Duke plots with the Provost to save Claudio by substituting the head of Barnardine, a drunken criminal also condemned to death, for Claudio's head. As it turns out, Barnardine is too drunk to be executed. Fortunately, a pirate who resembles Claudio has died overnight in his sleep, so it is the pirate's head which is finally sent to Angelo. Isabella appears, and the disguised Duke tells her that Angelo has broken his promise and that her brother is dead. He then instructs the grieving Isabella to condemn Angelo in public when he goes to meet the returning Duke tomorrow at the city gate. Meanwhile, Angelo is feeling guilty about his treachery, and wonders whether Isabella will dare to accuse him tomorrow in front of the Duke. He also regrets having insisted upon Claudio's execution but believes that, if he had been allowed to live, Claudio would have joined with his sister to expose the deputy's crime. "Alack," he cries, "when once our grace we have forgot, / Nothing goes right— we would, and we would not."

Act V: At the city gate, Angelo and Escalus welcome Duke Vincentio home. As instructed, Isabella accuses Angelo of being "a virgin-violator" and of murdering her brother—without as yet revealing that it was Mariana with whom he had sex. Calling Isabella insane, Angelo denies any wrongdoing. The Duke pretends to believe him and orders Isabella's arrest. Mariana arrives to declare that Angelo is by rights her husband, explaining that he slept with her, not Isabella. The Duke departs briefly, to return as Friar Lodowick and support Mariana's and Isabella's claims. Accused of bearing false witness, Friar Lodowick loses his hood as he is being arrested, and is revealed to be Duke Vincentio. The Duke orders an immediate marriage between Angelo and Mariana, then afterward sentences his former deputy to death, declaring "An Angelo for Claudio, death for death!" Although both Mariana and Isabella plead for Angelo's life, the Duke refuses to remit his sentence. All is at last resolved when Claudio is shown to be alive. The play ends as the Duke proposes marriage to Isabella, pardons Angelo, reminds Claudio to marry Juliet, and orders the troublesome Lucio to marry a prostitute "whom he begot with child."

PRINCIPAL TOPICS

Gender Roles and Sexuality

Most critics see the issues of gender roles and sexuality in the play as a power struggle between the sexes. This battle, many commentators argue, is ultimately won by the male characters. Angelo's attempted rape of Isabella and the Duke's management of the bed-trick have been discussed as methods by which the play's male characters reestablish control over the females whom they regard as disruptive or sexually overpowering. Several critics have remarked that the fear of women depicted in *Measure for Measure* was typical of the Renaissance period in which Shakespeare wrote, and that later plays by other authors were more violent in displaying the general distrust of women.

Commentators have offered varying responses to the marriages that close the play. Some argue that the Duke's orchestrated series of betrothals and weddings function as a way of reasserting male control over females. By contrast, others see the marriages as a method of restoring balance between the sexes.

Several commentators evaluate the role of female chastity in the play. Some have argued that Shakespeare both acknowledges and criticizes a double standard regarding sex outside of wedlock, wherein a woman—who was simultaneously expected to be the guardian of chastity and suspected of being a sexual temptress— was traditionally blamed for leading her lover astray. Critics

also suggest that *Measure for Measure* makes a distinction between the value of the severe, celibate chastity of the novice Isabella and the loving, emotional chastity of the faithful Mariana.

Justice and Mercy

Justice and mercy are generally regarded as central themes in *Measure for Measure*. Commentators contrast the two terms, defining "justice" as a strict and objective adherence to law and describing "mercy" as a humane, more subjective interpretation of law. Customarily, Angelo (and to a certain extent Isabella) has been regarded as a rigid upholder of justice while Duke Vincentio is considered the administrator of a justice softened or tempered by mercy. Critics have drawn attention to the Duke's admission in Act I that he has been too lax in upholding Vienna's laws as well as to his suspicion that his deputy, Angelo, will prove too harsh a judge. It is clear, critics conclude, that the play is searching for a balance between these two extremes.

Whether this balance is achieved has become a source of contention. Some commentators believe that Angelo cannot judge fairly until he has himself sinned. Others argue that one's personal experiences have nothing to do with the administration of justice. These problems reach a climax in Act V when Vincentio delivers harsh sentences on Angelo and Lucio, only to withdraw them immediately afterward. But whether the Duke has acted fairly and wisely in his administration of a justice tinged with mercy is open to debate. To reach his goal, Duke Vincentio has orchestrated the bed-trick and has led Isabella to believe that her brother is dead; many commentators are troubled by the fact that fairness is achieved at the close of the play through trickery and lies.

Structure

Whether or not *Measure for Measure* lacks unity is a difficult problem to solve. The play has been criticized for its apparently inconsistent characters as well as for its unresolved themes and unclear genre. Thus many scholars look to the play's structure for overall coherence. At least two unifying structural devices have received attention. First, it has been noted that the play consists of scenes based either on action or on conversation; the action scenes serve to further the plot while the conversation scenes give the audience time to reflect on the significance of the action.

Second, and in response to the charge that *Measure for Measure* fails to fulfill the requirements of any one genre, several critics have suggested that the play is united around its two-part structure. In the tragic first half, Claudio is sentenced to death, Isabella is threatened

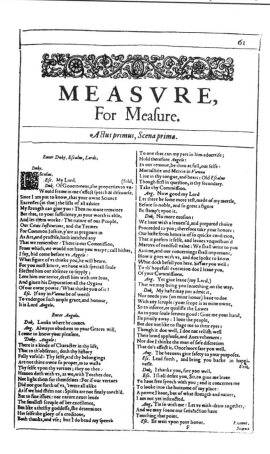

Title page of Measure for Measure *taken from the First Folio (1623).*

with rape, and Angelo has fallen from his rigid moral principles. In the comedic second half, Duke Vincentio steps in to judge Angelo, to save Claudio from death and Isabella from rape, and to unite the group in multiple marriages. Thus, some commentators observe, the play achieves unity as a tragicomedy.

CHARACTER STUDIES

Angelo

In the play, Angelo has a reputation for rigid self-control and for supporting a strict moral code. Escalus considers Angelo to be "most strait in virtue." The Duke describes his deputy as "precise," or puritanical. Dissolute Lucio complains that Angelo is so cold and prudish that his blood "is very snow-broth" and claims that the deputy controls his passions by fasting and studying. Angelo himself argues that people must see others punished before they themselves are willing to behave, and that being lenient with criminals only makes them disrespectful of law and order.

Critics have observed that despite these testimonials to his strictness, Angelo's apparent goodness and self-control are subject to doubt early in the play— even *before* he propositions Isabella. In Act I, for example, the Duke explains that part of his reason for deputizing Angelo with full authority to govern Vienna is to discover whether such power will corrupt this "seemingly" incorruptible man. And well before his sister ever meets Angelo, Claudio casts doubt on the purity of the deputy's motives by complaining that Angelo must have resurrected the "neglected" law against fornication simply because he hopes to make a name for himself. Later in the play, the Duke reveals that Angelo was once engaged to a gentlewoman named Mariana, but when her brother and her dowry were lost at sea, Angelo abandoned Mariana, "left her in her tears, and dried not one of them with his comfort," and, in order to break his engagement, he accused Mariana of being unchaste. When they try to persuade Angelo to be merciful with Claudio, both Escalus and Isabella reason that if Angelo were ever tempted, he might fall like anyone else. When Angelo finally does fall, he compounds his offense with hypocrisy.

Several critics have observed that *Measure for Measure* is, among other things, a play about self-knowledge. They remark that at the start of the play, Angelo is a poor ruler because he has no understanding of his own weaknesses and, by extension, his connections with the rest of humanity. By the end of the play, some commentators suggest, Angelo has been forced to acknowledge his own capacity for guilt and as a result will become a more merciful leader. On the other hand, some critics point out that in his last speech in the play, Angelo is still demanding to be executed rather than pardoned for the crimes that he has committed— he is, therefore, as rigid in his thinking as he ever was.

Duke Vincentio

Duke Vincentio has been called a godlike figure who solves potentially tragic dilemmas and who turns the play into a Renaissance comedy, complete with multiple marriages and a happy ending. According to this interpretation, the Duke is in full control of the close of the play. What's more, he triumphs in his attempt to replace absolutism with moderation when he exposes and then forgives Angelo's crimes, and when he teaches Isabella to be more tolerant and sympathetic of others to the extent that she joins Mariana in pleading for the life of her enemy Angelo.

The Duke has also been described as a puppeteer who abuses his power and takes advantage of his anonymity as Friar Lodowick to run people's lives. This interpretation focuses on the problematical aspects of the play. It takes issue, for example, with the Duke's orchestration of the bed-trick and of the phony executions, both of which involve honest people such as Isabella, Mariana, and the Provost in dishonest acts.

The interpretation of the Duke as a manipulator also underlines his blunders. Despite his efforts, Duke Vincentio's puppets do not always behave according to plan. Lucio, for example, continually ruffles the Duke's dignity with his insinuations, and repeatedly interrupts discussions and revelations—even at the close of the play. As for Angelo, after the bed-trick (during which the deputy thinks he has slept with Isabella) he unexpectedly breaks his promise to save Claudio and instead renews his order for Claudio's swift execution. When Vincentio tries to solve this glitch by substituting the condemned criminal Barnardine's head for that of Claudio, the drunken Barnardine refuses to be executed. When Angelo's villainy is at last exposed, the deputy begs for death, and continues to do so even after the Duke has ordered his marriage to Mariana and has forgiven him for his crimes. Finally, it has been pointed out that the Duke chooses to marry Isabella despite the fact that she has clearly decided to become a nun. In this light, her silence in response to his offer of marriage at the close of the play is not regarded as a tacit acceptance of his proposal, but as unwillingness to conform to this part of Duke Vincentio's plans.

Isabella

Isabella's behavior in the play has been the subject of negative as well as positive assessments. It has been pointed out that she gives up too easily in her efforts to persuade Angelo to spare her brother, and that Lucio has to remind her again and again to argue her case more forcefully. Critics have also asserted that Isabella's ideas about right and wrong are too extreme and that she mistakenly assumes that everyone shares her beliefs—when in fact, the only other character who believes in absolutes (absolutists follow the theory that something is either right or wrong, good or evil, but never in-between) is her adversary, Angelo. Critics argue further that Isabella is coldly insensitive in her treatment of the terrified Claudio—angrily rejecting him after he begs her to sleep with Angelo, and even suggesting that her brother is illegitimate since, according to her, he is too dishonorable a person to be her father's son.

Finally, the character of Isabella has been criticized for inconsistencies in her behavior. For example, her willingness to participate in the "bed-trick" (when Mariana secretly sleeps with Angelo in place of Isabella) contradicts the young novice's ardent belief in honesty. Those critics who view Isabella in a favorable light argue that she is forced to cope as best she can in a society where she has very little power. They point out that initially, Isabella is tolerant of Claudio and Juliet's predicament, and that her views become inflexible only after she is

frightened by Angelo's lust. Before she has spoken with Angelo, and in response to Lucio's news that Juliet is pregnant by Claudio, Isabella declares suggests that the two lovers should marry. Later, when she tries to persuade Angelo to be lenient, she tells him that nothing is as admirable as mercy.

Critics sympathetic to Isabella also note that although she is ultimately saved from being raped by Angelo, she is nevertheless discouraged by her society from leading the convent life she has chosen: At the end of the play, the powerful Duke Vincentio proposes marriage to her, and although Isabella does not respond to his proposal, some commentators believe that we are left with the assumption that she will marry him.

CONCLUSION

Measure for Measure is a disturbing play for critics, directors, and audiences alike. While the play raises a variety of compelling issues—the extent to which mercy should temper justice, the nature of power and the need for self-knowledge; the relationship between men and women and the definition of gender roles and human sexuality—none of these questions appears to be answered definitively by the close of the play. Angelo seems to be as inflexible as ever; Isabella is silent in the face of the Duke's marriage proposal; the Duke has used subterfuge to accomplish his aims; and Mariana is married to someone who doesn't want her. Is this, commentators ask, the stuff of tragedy or comedy? How, directors wonder, should Isabella's silence be staged? What are we to think of the Duke's behavior—is it manipulative or full of wisdom? Such issues continue to be hotly debated. Ultimately, we are left to conclude that the questions raised by *Measure for Measure*—and our own varied responses to them—are more worthwhile than any one answer the play might otherwise provide.

OVERVIEW

Northrop Frye

SOURCE: "Measure for Measure," in *Northrop Frye on Shakespeare*, edited by Robert Sandler, Yale University Press, 1986, pp. 140-53.

[Frye uses the title of Measure for Measure *to organize his essay around some fundamental components of the play: characterization, theme, and genre. He demonstrates, for example, how the play measures one character against another (such as Angelo versus Claudio) and one theme against another (such as justice versus mercy, or "a justice that includes equity and a justice that's a narrow legalism"). Frye also looks at the Duke's role as stage manager in the drama that occurs between Isabella,*

Angelo, and Mariana, and concludes by remarking on the ways in which Measure for Measure *"proceeds upward" from potential tragedy to fulfill the requirements of comedy through marriage, forgiveness, and reconciliation.*]

Most critics link the title of this play with a verse from the Sermon on the Mount: "Judge not, that ye be not judged: for with what judgment ye judge, ye shall be judged; and with what measure ye mete, it shall be measured to you again." The phrase is a common one, and was used by Shakespeare in an earlier play, but the link with this quoted passage seems to be clearly there, and suggests that this play is concerned, like much of *The Merchant of Venice,* with the contrast between justice and mercy. Only it doesn't talk about Christians and Jews; it talks about the contrast between large-minded and small-minded authority, between a justice that includes equity and a justice that's a narrow legalism. The title also suggests the figure of the scales or balance that's the traditional emblem of justice. The play seems to me very closely related to the late romances, and that's why I'm dealing with it here, although it's earlier than *King Lear* and *Antony and Cleopatra.*

The story used in the play has many variants, but the kernel of it is a situation where a woman comes to a judge to plead for the life of a man close to her, husband or brother, who's been condemned to death. The judge tells her that he'll spare the man's life at the price of her sexual surrender to him. In some versions she agrees and the judge double-crosses her, having the man executed anyway. She then appeals to a higher judge, king or emperor, who (in stories where it's a husband she'd pleaded for) orders the judge to marry her and then has him executed. All these elements of the story are in Shakespeare's play, but he's redistributed them with his usual infallible instinct for what fits where.

The versions closest to his play are a long (two-part), crowded, rather cumbersome play called *Promos and Cassandra,* by George Whetstone, which goes back to 1578, and a story in a collection by an Italian writer who used the name Cinthio, a collection that also seems to have provided, whether in the original or in a French translation, the source of *Othello.* Shakespeare used such collections of stories a good deal: one reason, and we'll see in a moment why it is a reason, is that a lot of the stories are very close to being folk tales; in fact a lot of them are folk tales that the author has picked up somewhere and written out. This play, as most critics recognize, has three well-known folk-tale themes in it: the disguised ruler, the corrupt judge and the bed trick.

If we look at the first of these themes, the disguised ruler, we run into a difficulty that's central to this play. The Duke of Vienna, Vincentio, feels that his town is getting morally out of hand, especially in its sexual permissiveness, so he disappears, leaving a subordinate named Angelo to administer a law very strictly providing the death penalty for adultery. Our reactions to this may be very unfavourable to the Duke. Surely he's being a coward when he runs away from his responsibilities, leaving someone else to administer an unpopular and perhaps sick law because he's afraid of spoiling his nice-guy image (at least, that's more or less the explanation he gives); he's being incompetent in putting Angelo in charge instead of his more conscientious and humane colleague Escalus; and he's a sneak to come back disguised as a friar to eavesdrop on the consequences of what he's done. But whether our reactions are right or wrong, they clearly seem to be irrelevant to the play. Why are they irrelevant? We can see that Lear is being foolish when he abdicates, and our knowledge of that fact is highly relevant: what's different here?

I haven't any answer to this right now, except to say that this *is* a different kind of play: I have first to explain what I think is going on. We saw in *King Lear* that when the king abdicates, his kingdom is plunged into a lower level of nature, and when Lear has reached the bottom of that, on the heath with the Fool and Poor Tom, he starts to acquire a new kind of relation to his kingdom, where he feels his affinity with the "poor naked wretches" he prays to. Because *King Lear* is a tragedy, this doesn't get far before Lear is involved with other things, like madness and capture. In *Measure for Measure* what happens as a result of the Duke's leaving the scene is not that we descend to a lower order of nature, but that we're plunged into a lower level of law and social organization. The Elizabethans, like us, attached great importance to the principle in law called equity, the principle that takes account of certain human factors. Angelo is out simply to administer the law, or rather *a* law against fornication, according to legalistic rules.

Authority is essential to society, but what we called in *King Lear* "transcendental" authority, with an executive ruler on top, depends on the ruler's understanding of equity. If he hasn't enough of such understanding, authority becomes a repressive legalism. Legalism of this sort really descends from what is called in the Bible the knowledge of good and evil. This was forbidden knowledge, because, as we'll see, it's not a genuine knowledge at all: it can't even tell us anything about good and evil. This kind of knowledge came into the world along with the discovery of self-conscious sex, when Adam and Eve knew that they were naked, and the thing that repressive legalism ever since has been most anxious to repress is the sexual impulse. That's why a law making fornication a capital offence is the only law the abdicating Duke seems to be interested in.

In the framework of assumptions of Shakespeare's day, one was the doctrine in the New Testament that the law, as given in the Old Testament, was primarily a symbol of the spiritual life. The law in itself can't make people virtuous or even better: It can only define the lawbreaker. You're free of what Paul calls the bondage of the law when you absorb the law internally, as part of your nature rather than as a set of objective rules to be obeyed. Under the "law" man is already a criminal, condemned by his disobedience to God, so if God weren't inclined to mercy, charity and equity as well as justice, nobody would get to heaven. This is what Portia tells Shylock in *The Merchant of Venice,* where Shylock symbolizes the clinging to the "bond" of the literal law that was the generally accepted view of Judaism in England at the time. It's a very skewed notion of Judaism, naturally, but there were no Jews legally in England then, and so no one to speak for another point of view. *Measure for Measure,* I suggested, deals with the same target of narrow-minded legalism, but without the very dubious attachments to assumed Christian and Jewish attitudes. What Jesus attacked in the Pharisees is as common in Christianity as it is anywhere else, and Angelo's breakdown illustrates the fact that no one can observe the law perfectly. Portia's point is repeated by Isabella when she says to Angelo: "Why, all the souls that were were forfeit once" (II.ii. 73).

I've often referred to the ideology of Shakespeare's day, the set of assumptions his audience brought into the theatre with them. Every society has an ideology, and its literature reflects the fact. But I don't think any culture is really founded on an ideology: I think people first of all make up stories, and then extract ideas and assumptions from them. The Christian ideology of Shakespeare's day, as of ours, was a derivation from Christian mythology; that is, the story that Christianity is based on. Our word "myth" comes from the Greek *mythos,* meaning plot, story, narrative. The Christian myth, the complex of stories it tells, is, we said, structurally closest to comedy. Critics a hundred years ago said that *Measure for Measure* was a play in which Shakespeare was trying to discuss serious issues like prostitution and the theory of government, but couldn't get far because of censorship and other obstacles. Of course he couldn't have got far with such themes: the assumption is that he wanted to discuss them, and that's an assumption I very much distrust. Other critics think the play is a kind of dramatic exposition of Christian doctrines and principles. I distrust the assumption in that even more. I think Shakespeare uses conceptions taken from the ideology of his time incidentally, and that we always have to look at the structure of the story he's telling us, not at what gets said on the way. That is, as a dramatist, he reflects the priority of mythology to ideology that I've just spoken of. Further, he reflects it increasingly as he goes on. Because of this, his later plays are more primitive than the earlier ones, not, as we might expect, less so. They get closer all the time to folk tales and myths, because those are primitive stories: they don't depend on logic, they don't explain things and don't give you room to react: you have to listen or read through to the end. That's what

brings *Measure for Measure* so close to the romances at the end of Shakespeare's productive period, both in its action and in its mood.

Well, it's time we got to the second theme, the crooked judge. We saw from *A Midsummer Night's Dream* how often a comedy begins with some kind of irrational law— irrational in the sense that it blocks up the main thrust of the comic story, which somehow manages to evade or ignore it. Usually such a law is set up to block the sexual desires of the hero and heroine, and sometimes it isn't really a law, but simply the will of a crotchety parent who lays down *his* law. Sometimes, instead of the law, we start with a mood of deep gloom or melancholy, and that's the main obstacle the comic action has to scramble over. *Twelfth Night,* for example, begins with Duke Orsino overcome with love melancholy— at least he thinks he is— and Olivia in deep mourning for a dead brother. These elements in comedy are those connected with the corrupt judge theme in *Measure for Measure.* The ugly law is scowling at us from the beginning, and Angelo's temperament, in both his incorruptible and his later phases, ensures that there will be enough gloom.

Angelo, to do him justice (we can't seem to get away from that word), expresses strong doubts about his fitness for the post. Nonetheless he's put in charge of Vienna, ready to strike wherever sex rears its ugly head. He has a test case immediately: Claudio is betrothed to Julietta (I call her that for clarity), and betrothal in Shakespeare's time could sometimes be a fully marital relation, complete with sexual intercourse. Claudio and Julietta have got together on this basis, but have failed to comply with all the provisions of the law about publicizing the marriage. So he's guilty of adultery, and has to have his head cut off. Lucio, a man about town, is horrified by this, not because he's a person of any depth of human feeling, but because he sees how enforcing such a law would interfere with his own sex life, which is spent in brothels. So he goes (at Claudio's urging, it is true) to Claudio's sister, Isabella, who is almost on the point of becoming a novice in an order of nuns, to get her to plead with Angelo for her brother's life. Isabella is not very willing, but Lucio finally persuades her to visit Angelo, and accompanies her there.

Before this happens, though, there's a broadly farcical scene in which a dimwitted constable named Elbow comes into the magistrate's court presided over by Angelo and Escalus, with a charge against Pompey, who is a pimp and therefore one of the people the newly enforced law is aimed at. The scene seems to be pure comic relief, but it establishes three important points. First, Angelo walks out on the proceedings before long and leaves Escalus to it: his speech on doing so ends with the line "Hoping you'll have good cause to whip them all" (II.i. 136). Angelo despises the people before him so much that he can't bother to listen to their meanderings. The phrase from the Sermon on the Mount, "Judge not, that ye be not judged," comes to mind. What it surely means, among other things, is: If you despise other people for their moral inferiority to yourself, your own superiority won't last long; in fact, it's effectively disappeared already. Second, even Escalus can hardly figure out who did what to whom, so we wonder about the ability of law ever to get hold of the right people, or understand what is really going on about anything. Third, while Claudio, who is a decent man, is going to be beheaded, Pompey, who at least is an avowed pimp (and incidentally quite proud of it), is let off with a warning.

We may notice another feature of the scenes with the bawds: very little is said about the relatively new and then terrifying disease of syphilis; it's clearly in the background, but it stays in the background. "Thou art always figuring diseases in me," says a fellow patron to Lucio, "but . . . I am sound" (I.ii. 49). That isn't because Shakespeare felt reticent about the subject: if you think he did, take a look at the brothel scenes in *Pericles*. But to pull down houses of prostitution because of the danger of syphilis would give the law in this play a more rational motive than Shakespeare wants to assign to it. He's no more out to justify the law than to attack it: he merely presents the kind of hold that such law has on society, in all its fumbling uncertainty and lack of direction.

We're ready now for the big scene with Angelo and Isabella. I've suggested to you that when you're reading Shakespeare you might think of yourself as directing a performance, which includes choosing the kind of actors and actresses that seem right for their assigned parts. If I were casting Angelo, I'd look for an actor who could give the impression, not merely of someone morally very uptight, but possessing the kind of powerful sexual appeal that many uptight people have, as though they were leading a tiger on a leash. If I were casting Isabella, I'd want an actress who could suggest an attractive, intelligent, strongly opinionated girl of about seventeen or eighteen, who is practically drunk on the notion of becoming a nun, but who's really possessed by adolescent introversion rather than spiritual vocation. That's why she seems nearly asleep in the first half of the play.

If the setting of the interview weren't so sombre, with a man's life depending on the outcome, the dialogue would be as riotously funny as the strange case of Elbow's wife. Let's resort to paraphrase. Isabella: "I understand you're going to cut my brother's head off." Angelo: "Yes, that is the idea." Isabella: "Well, I just thought I'd ask. I have to go now; I have a date with a prayer." Lucio: "Hey, you can't do that! Make a production of it; weep, scream, fall on your knees, make as big a fuss as you can!" So Angelo and Isabella start manoeuvring around each other like a couple of

knights who are in such heavy plate armour that they can't bend a joint. The effect is that of a sombre Jonsonian comedy of humours. The humours in this case are two forms of predictable virtue, in people paralyzed by moral rigidity. We've already heard Isabella telling a senior nun that she would like her convent to be as strict and rigid as possible; we've heard Angelo saying out of his shell of righteousness:

'Tis one thing to be tempted, Escalus,
Another thing to fall.

(II.i. 17-18)

Isabella goes into general maxims about the beauty of combining strength with gentleness, and Angelo, genuinely bewildered, says: "Why do you put these sayings on me?" (II.ii. 134). But something keeps them going; Isabella gets increasingly interested in her role, another meeting without Lucio is arranged, and eventually the serpent of Eden thrusts itself up between Justice in his black robes and Purity in her white robes, and tells them both that they're naked.

At least, I'm pretty sure that the serpent speaks to them both, although of course it doesn't get through to Isabella's consciousness. Her overt reaction, when she finally understands what Angelo is proposing, is simply horror and outrage. But I wonder if she isn't suppressing the awareness that she's much more attracted to Angelo than she would consciously think possible, and that in her gradual warming-up process Angelo has done more warming than Claudio. However that may be, she goes off to visit Claudio in the prison and tells him that he will now have to die, not to fulfil the demands of the law, but to save his sister's honour, which naturally he will do with the greatest willingness. She's utterly demoralized to discover that Claudio is very unwilling to die, and quite willing to have her go along with Angelo to preserve his life. To paraphrase once again: "But it's my chastity," screams Isabella. "Yes, but it's my head," says Claudio. Isabella then explodes in a furious tirade (in which, incidentally, a Freudian listener would hear a strong father fixation, even though the father does not exist in the play). She pours all the contempt on Claudio that her very considerable articulateness can formulate, tells him that the sooner he dies the better, and even that "I'll pray a thousand prayers for thy death" (III.i. 145). She's awakened out of all her dreams, and the world around her that her awakened eyes see is a prison. A real prison, not the dream prison she'd like her convent to be.

So far the action has been fairly unrelieved tragedy for the major characters. The Duke has disappeared. The Friar, not generally known to be the Duke, is a prison chaplain, or seems to be functioning as one. His opening gambit as Friar doesn't seem to have much promise: it's a speech addressed to Claudio, telling him to "be absolute for death," that he should welcome death because if he lives he may get a lot of uncomfortable diseases. It is doubtful that any young man was ever reconciled to immediate death by such arguments: certainly Claudio isn't. The terror of death he expresses to Isabella, in the wonderful speech beginning "Ay, but to die, and go we know not where," shows that the Friar's consolations have left him untouched. Angelo has betrayed his trust; Claudio is about to die; Isabella's dreams of a contemplative spiritual life, free of the corruptions of the world, are shattered forever.

We notice that as we go on we feel less and less like condemning people, because of the steady increase of a sense of irony. We can't condemn Claudio for his fear of what he feels to be, despite Isabella and the Friar, a totally undeserved death; we can't condemn Isabella for turning shrewish when she feels betrayed by both Angelo and Claudio. As for Angelo, he now knows what it's like to fall as well as to be tempted. As almost an incarnation of the knowledge of good and evil, he's in a state of schizophrenic war with himself, the newly born impulse to evil determined on its satisfaction, the repudiated impulse to good despising, hating, and being miserably humiliated by its rival. This sense of a dramatic irony replacing an impulse to make moral judgments again points to the limitations of law, or at least of this kind of law.

It was generally accepted in Shakespeare's day that the writing of a play was a moral act, and that the cause of morality was best served by making virtue attractive and vice ugly. Whetstone's play, mentioned earlier, says this in its preface, and Hamlet endorses the same view. No doubt *Measure for Measure* accomplishes this feat too in the long run, but in the meantime we wonder about the dramatic pictures of virtue and vice that we've had. Angelo is certainly not more likable as a hypocritical fraud than he was in his days of incorruptibility, but he seems somehow more accessible, even more understandable. Perhaps we can see, if we like, that what finally broke him down was not Isabella's beauty, and not even his own powerfully repressed sexuality, but the combining of the two in a sadistic position of authority over a supplicating girl. But Isabella, in her invulnerable virtue, would not be anyone's favourite heroine, and, at the other extreme, there's Lucio, who retains something about him that's obstinately likable, though he's clearly a basket case morally, and Barnardine, whose vitality makes it pleasant that he gets away with his refusal to be beheaded.

In any case, the action in the prison scene reaches a complete deadlock, with Claudio still begging Isabella to do something to help him, and Isabella telling him in effect, in every possible sense, to go to hell. Then the disguised Duke steps forward to speak to Isabella, and the rhythm abruptly switches from blank verse to prose (III.i. 150).

This is the most clearly marked indication of structure, I think, that we've yet reached in any of the plays we've talked about. The play breaks in two here: the first half is the dismal ironic tragedy we've been summarizing, but from now on we're in a different kind of play. One of the differences is that the Duke in disguise is producing and directing it, working out the plot, casting the characters, and arranging even such details as positioning and lighting. So it's really a play within a play, except for its immense size, a half play that eventually swallows and digests the other half. Within the Duke's own conventions, he's playing with real-life people, like those nobles who used to play chess games using their own servants for pieces. In anything like a real-life situation, such a procedure would almost certainly meet with disaster very quickly, like Lear staging his love test. But in *Measure for Measure*, where we're in the atmosphere of folk tale, our only reaction is to see what comes next. It'll all work out just fine, so don't you worry.

The first element in this new play that the Duke produces is the story of Mariana, who provides a close parallel and contrast to the Claudio situation, and one which involves Angelo. Angelo had previously been engaged to a lady named Mariana, who still loves him, but the engagement fell through because the financial arrangements weren't satisfactory. According to the way the law works things out, Angelo's uncompleted engagement leaves him a person of the highest social eminence, whereas Claudio's uncompleted betrothal leaves him a condemned criminal. So much for the kind of vision the knowledge of good and evil gives us: even if Angelo had remained as pure as the driven snow, the contrast in their fates would still be monstrous. The way the Duke proposes to resolve this situation is the device of the bed trick, where Isabella pretends to go along with Angelo's proposal and assign a meeting, but substitutes Mariana in her place. It sounds like a very dubious scheme for a pious friar to talk a pious novice into, but something in Isabella seems to have accepted the fact that she's in a new ball game, and that the convent has vanished from her horizon.

I've talked about the affinity of this play with folk tales, and we can't go far in the study of folk tale without coming across the figure of the trickster. The trickster may be simply mischievous or malicious, and may be associated with certain tricky animals, like the fox or the coyote. But in some religions the trickster figure is sublimated into a hidden force for good whose workings are mysterious but eventually reveal a deep benevolence. There are traces of this conception in Christianity, where a "providence" is spoken of that brings events about in unlikely and unexpected ways. I don't want to labour the religious analogies, because they're structural analogies only: if we try to make them more than that, they get very misleading. I think the Duke in this play is a trickster figure who is trying to turn a tragic situation into a comic one, and that this operation involves the regenerating of his society: that is, of course, the dramatic society, the cast of characters. A trickster, because, while tragedy normally rolls ahead to an inevitable crash, comedy usually keeps something hidden that's produced when it's time to reverse the movement.

Let's go back to King Lear and his abdication. I said that when he's reached the bottom of his journey through nature, he discovers a new awareness of the "poor naked wretches" of his kingdom. He abdicates as "transcendental" ruler and takes on another identity in an "immanent" relation to his people, especially the suffering and exploited part of his people. As I said, this theme can't be completed in a tragedy, but a comedy like *Measure for Measure* can take it a bit further. Duke Vincentio opens up, by leaving his place in society, a train of events headed for the bleakest and blackest tragedy. By his actions in disguise, he brings the main characters together in a new kind of social order, based on trust instead of threats. I'm not talking about the moral of the play, but about the action of the play, where somet'ing tragic gradually turns inside out into something comic.

The trickster element in him comes out in the fact that his schemes involve a quite bewildering amount of lying, although he assures Isabella that there's no real deception in what he does. He starts by telling Claudio privately, in the prison, that Angelo is only making trial of Isabella's virtue. He gets Isabella to agree to the bed trick scheme, which necessitates lying on her part; Isbella is told the brutal lie that Claudio has been executed after all; he gives such strange and contradictory orders to Angelo and Escalus about his return that they wonder if he's gone off his head; his treatment of that very decent official, the provost of the prison, would have a modern civil servant heading for the next town to find a less erratic boss. Whenever he remembers to talk like a friar, he sounds sanctimonious rather than saintly. We have only to put him beside Friar Laurence in *Romeo and Juliet* to see the difference between a merely professional piety and the real thing.

There are two or three references in the play to frightening images that turn out to be harmless: an indulgent father's whip, a row of extracted teeth in a barber shop, and, on the other side, Angelo's "We must not make a scarecrow of the law" (II.i. 1). In this play most of the major male characters are threatened with death in some form; the two women are threatened with the deaths of others. Yet in the long run nobody really gets hurt: even the condemned criminal Barnardine is set free, except that he has another friar attached to him. A pirate in the prison who died of natural causes has his head employed for some of the deceptions, that's all. It's an ancient doctrine in comic theory that one of the standard features of comedy is what's called in

Greek the *basanos,* which means both ordeal and touchstone: the unpleasant experience that's a test of character. This seems to be why the Duke starts off with his "Be absolute for death" speech to Claudio in the prison. He doesn't seriously expect Claudio to be reconciled to death by hearing it, but it leaves him with a vision of seriousness and responsibility for the whole of his life that will make him a proper husband for Julietta and ensure that he doesn't drift off into being another Lucio. Sounds far-fetched, but you won't think that an objection by now.

Angelo, of course, gets the bed trick deal, which is a popular device in literature. Shakespeare used it again in a comedy that's usually thought of as a companion piece to this one, *All's Well that Ends Well.* Even the Bible has such a story, when Jacob, who wanted and expected Rachel, woke up to find Leah in his bed instead. Jacob's society being polygamous, he got them both in the long run, but in Shakespeare's bed trick plays the device is used to hook a man to a woman he ought to be married to anyway. It's one of the devices for the middle part of a comedy, the period of confused identity in which characters run around in the dark, as in *A Midsummer Night's Dream,* or the heroine puts on a boy's clothes. One thing it represents in the two comedies where it occurs is the illusory nature of lust, in contrast to genuine love. Angelo's lust tells him that he wants Isabella and doesn't want Mariana, but in the dark any partner of female construction will do, and on that basis his wakened consciousness can distinguish between what he wants and what he thinks he wants. For Angelo the bed trick is the agent both of his condemnation and of his redemption. When his deceptions are uncovered in the final scene, he welcomes the death sentence as the only thing appropriate for him: he's still a man of the law, even if his conception of law has matured. Mariana is the spark plug of the second half of the play: without her steady love for Angelo, no redeeming force could have got started. It nearly always happens in Shakespearean comedy that one of the female characters is responsible for the final resolution. Her importance, I think, is marked by the fact that when we meet her we hear a song, no less, and a very lovely song, in this grim clanking play.

But of course Isabella is the Duke's staged masterpiece. After being instructed how to act, she brings her accusation against Angelo, and there follows a great to-do about not believing her and a stretching of tension to the limit. Eventually Angelo is publicly humiliated, ordered to marry Mariana, and condemned to death immediately afterward. Mariana's pleas for his life are rejected, so she turns to Isabella. Isabella's speech corresponds dramatically to Portia's speech on mercy in *The Merchant of Venice,* but the latter is a rhetorical set speech: Portia after all is a lawyer, or pretending to be one. Isabella's speech is short, thoughtful, painfully improvised, as the rhythm shows, and full of obvious fallacies as a legal argument. She is also making it at a time when she believes that Angelo has swindled her and had her brother executed after all. The essential thing is that the woman who earlier had told her brother that she would pray a thousand prayers for his death is now pleading for the life of the man who, as she thinks, murdered him, besides attempting the most shameful treatment of herself. People can't live continuously on that sort of level, but if one's essential humanity can be made to speak, even once in one's life, one has a centre to revolve around ever after. The Duke is so pleased that he announces that he is going to marry her, though later he speaks of proposing to her in a private conference.

The final confrontation is with Lucio, and that one is perhaps the strangest of all. Lucio was the spark plug of the first half, as Mariana is of the second: without his efforts on Isabella, all the Duke's schemes would, so far as we can see, have ended in nothing but a dead Claudio. Yet he is the only one of the Duke's characters (apart from Barnardine, whose inner attitude is unknown to us) on whom the Duke's benevolent trickery makes no impression whatever. The Duke transfers to him the penalty he assigned to Angelo: Lucio is to marry the whore he has made pregnant, then executed. The threats of whipping and hanging are ignored by Lucio, and he doesn't seem to notice that they are remitted, but he protests strongly against the violation of his comfortable double standard. He seems to be possessed by a peculiarly shabby version of the knowledge of good and evil. What is "good," or at any rate all right, is what other fashionable young men do. Slandering a prince is all right because it's only the "trick," the fashion; visiting whorehouses likewise. But of course the whores are "bad" women.

And yet the final scene would be much poorer without him: he gets all the laughs, and the Duke's rebukes of him are simply ineffective bluster. He represents in part the sense of vestigial realism that we still have, the part of ourselves that recognizes how unspeakably horrible such snooping and disguised Dukes would be in anything resembling actual life. His slanders are forgiven, perhaps because he was describing the kind of person he would admire more than he does the actual Duke. And while the bulk of what he says is nonsense, one phrase, "the old fantastical Duke of dark corners" (IV.iii. 156) is the most accurate description of him that the play affords.

The title of the play is quoted by the Duke when he speaks of the retribution in the law: "An Angelo for a Claudio, life for life" (V.i. 407). This is the axiom of tragedy, especially revenge tragedy, with its assumption that two corpses are better than one. From there, the action proceeds upward from this "measure for measure" situation to the final scene with which Shakespearean comedy usually ends: the vision of a renewed and regenerated society, with forgiveness, reconciliation and the pursuit of happiness all over the place. Forgiveness and reconciliation come at the end of a comedy because they belong at the end of a comedy, not because Shakespeare "believed" in them. And so the play ends: it doesn't discuss any issues, solve any problems, expound any theories or illustrate any doctrines. What it does is show us why comedies exist and why Shakespeare wrote so many of them. And writing comedies may be more valuable to us than all the other activities together, as we may come to realize after the hindsight of three or four hundred years.

GENDER ROLES AND SEXUALITY

The issues of gender role and sexuality are closely connected in *Measure for Measure*. Critic **Ronald Huebert** discusses the ways in which the male characters' "manliness" is formed by their sexual education combined with self-knowledge. Claudio, for example, exhibits the manly virtue of courage when faced with death for impregnating Juliet; however, when tempted with the possibility of reprieve— even at his sister's expense— he manfully comes to terms with the fact that his courage is not proof against temptation. By contrast, Huebert describes Angelo's rigid morality as "a caricature of genuine manliness" and asserts that the deputy achieves real manliness only after he openly acknowledges his own transgressions and learns to recognize his own sexual desires.

For many scholars, gender role and sexuality depend upon the nature of power in the play— how power is defined and who it is that wields it. **David Sundelson** remarks that for characters such as Duke Vincentio and Angelo political and sexual power are virtually one and the same. For Duke Vincentio, sense of self and masculinity depend upon his correcting the moral laxness of Vienna without humiliating himself with possible failure. Sundelson observes that both the Duke and his deputy, Angelo, display a fear of women that pervades the play in the form of sexual imagery. Angelo, for example, becomes frightened as Isabella's assertive plea for her brother's life begins to weaken his resolve. The Duke, meanwhile, feels overwhelmed by Mariana's powerful love for Angelo. Both men, Sundelson argues, try to use their political power to reassert themselves against what they see as the potentially devastating effects of female power. Thus, Angelo claims authority over Isabella by demanding that she trade sex for her brother's life; the Duke reestablishes his own will by managing Isabella and Mariana in the dubious "bedtrick" and by prolonging Isabella's grief over the supposed execution of her brother.

Alberto Cacicedo suggests that the male characters' fear

of female power is in fact a fear of female sexuality that was symptomatic of the Renaissance. Sexual promiscuity in *Measure for Measure*— and by analogy, in Renaissance England— was the fault of women who tempted men (such as Angelo) into weakness. According to Cacicedo, marriage in England and at the end of the play was a "necessary evil" that forced women back into their subordinate role. Harry V. Jaffa, by contrast, sees marriage as an instrument for renewing the balance between genders that was disturbed by the Duke's unwillingness to assert moral authority and by Isabella's insistence on celibacy.

Linda Macfarlane and Juliet Dusinberre view the female characters in *Measure for Measure* as powerless. Macfarlane argues that Isabella, for example, is in "a no win situation" when confronted by male power: on her own, she has no defense against Angelo's exertion of his sexual and political power but must turn to another male— the Duke— for protection. Dusinberre remarks that when couples participated in unwedded sex in Renaissance England, the woman was always regarded as the guiltier of the two; she asserts, however, that Shakespeare criticized this double standard in *Measure for Measure* by posing the negative, celibate chastity of Isabella against the positive, spiritual chastity of Mariana.

David Sundelson

SOURCE: "Misogyny and Rule in *Measure for Measure*," in *Women's Studies*, Vol. 9, 1981, pp. 83-91.

[Sundelson focuses on the male characters' insecurity regarding their masculinity in Measure for Measure. *Sundelson argues that in the play, there is the fear that loss of power can cause a man to lose his sexual identity. Thus the Duke protects his masculinity by working from the sidelines— allowing his stand-in Angelo rather than himself to be made a fool of publicly. Angelo, on the other hand, demonstrates his fear of women when he tries to force himself upon Isabella. Sundelson argues that in this case, Angelo is afraid that a woman's "pretty face and . . . confident tongue" can weaken and emasculate a man— a fear that is violently expressed against women in later plays of the period.]*

When Hamlet welcomes the Players to Elsinore, he pays special attention to one of them. "What, my young lady and mistress! by'r lady, your ladyship is nearer to heaven than when I saw you last by the altitude of a chopine. Pray God your voice, like a piece of uncurrent gold, be not cracked within the ring" (II.ii.429-33). Although the repetition of "lady" and the bawdy puns ("cracked," "ring") may betray a certain uneasiness about what is female, Hamlet can joke comfortably enough about a farewell to it, about a boy actor who will soon be unable to play a woman's role. For Shakespeare, the movement from androgyny to a clearer, more certain

masculinity is evidently not disturbing.

What can be very disturbing indeed is the idea of reversing this movement. The idea haunts *Measure for Measure*; at its heart are grave fears about the precariousness of male identity and, linked to them, fears of the destructive power of women. Together, these fears explain much of what seems most puzzling about the play. Take for example its central problem: the behavior of Duke Vincentio. To mention only two of the questions it raises, why does he entrust Angelo with power, and why does he allow Isabella to believe that her brother is dead? I want to show that the answers to these questions are related. *Measure for Measure* fuses anxieties about political and sexual power, and I believe that the Duke's actions, which have struck readers as mysteriously benign or haphazard or even perverse, belong instead to the coherent defensive strategy of a shrewd prince and an insecure man. The Duke does treat his subjects as puppets, as Empson remarks, but not simply "for the fun of making them twitch."

The executioner Abhorson is a convenient emblem of the play's preoccupations. With his highly suggestive name ("abhor," "whore," "whoreson") and his pride of office, his ax and his assistant the bawd, he reflects a network of fantasies about power, sex, degradation and punishment. Only the Deputy learns all the connections in the network, learns how easily the throneroom can become the bedroom or the block. But even Escalus, kindly and disinterested as he is, finds that power brings out an impulse in him that smacks of Angelo's ugly proposition: "Pray you, my lord, give me leave to question; you shall see how I'll handle her . . . I will go darkly to work" (V.i.270-7). Judicial office is dangerous to hold; as if to avoid being compromised by working darkly, Elbow's neighbors pay him to serve their terms as constable.

Instead of buying a surrogate as they do, the Duke appoints one.

I have on Angelo impos'd the office:
Who may in th' ambush of my name strike home,
And yet my nature never in the fight
To do in slander.

(I.iii.40-3)

"Ambush," "strike," and "fight" make government aggressive and violent. "To do in slander" is unclear (the text may be corrupt), but the phrase adds an erotic dimension to the power the Duke is unwilling to wield. If the fear of sadistic impulses, of the temptation to let the body politic "straight feel the spur" (I.ii.151) is one reason for his abdication, he also dreads humiliation, the moment when "the rod / Becomes more mock'd than fear'd" (I.iii.26-7) and "Liberty plucks Justice by the nose" (I.iii.29). He seems to equate rule and exhibition— "to stick it in their children's sight / For terror" (I.iii.25-6)— and ranges nervously from one vulnerable appendage to another. To save his nose from plucking, he confers on Angelo "all the organs / Of our own power" (I.i.20-1) in the hope that his double, "one that can my part in him advertise" (I.i.41), will perform the exhibition for him, and with more vigor than he himself is willing to risk: "In our remove, be thou at full ourself" (I.i.43).

"Part" suggests both a role and an organ, but Angelo finds that to advertise his parts is to jeopardize them. While he gives every sign of being the aggressor with Isabella, her very approach makes his heart "unable" (II.iv.21) and, even worse, "dispossesses" all his "other parts / Of necessary fitness" (II.iv.22-3). "I would to heaven I had your potency, / And you were Isabel" (II.ii.67-8), the lady exclaims in their first interview, and a similar notion of exchange or androgyny surfaces in Pompey's answer when the Provost asks if he can cut off a man's head: "if he be a married man, he's his wife's head; and I can never cut off a woman's head" (II.ii.2-4). With a joke, Pompey can pluck the flower, safety, from the nettle, danger, but in Angelo's second meeting with Isabella, uncertain sexual identity becomes more and more unsettling.

We see the uncertainty in the deputy's description of his desire as "the strong and swelling evil / Of my conception" (II.iv.67); the metaphor seems male and female at once. Similarly, a wish for passivity lies beneath his assault. "Teach her the way" (II.iv.19) he says when Isabella returns, as if he wanted to be seduced, and complains openly: "your sense pursues not mine" (II.iv.74). If at first Isabella has "too tame a tongue" (II.ii.46) to affect him, she soon grows more assertive, and her increasingly penetrating rhetoric corresponds to Angelo's growing doubt. She begins to boast of "true prayers, / That shall be up at heaven and enter there" (II.ii.152-3), and in her second visit threatens to attack the Deputy "with an outstretch'd throat" (II.iv.152). "How might she tongue me" (IV.iv.23), he worries, and her later denunciation realizes his worst fears.

These warnings of female potency make Angelo's violence seem like a defense, as if he resorted to rape so as not to confront his own weakness.

> *Angelo*   Be that you are,
> That is, a woman; if you be more, you're
>   none.
> If you be one— as you are well express'd
> By all external warrants— show it now,
> By putting on the destin'd livery.
> *Isabella*   I have no tongue but one: gentle my
>   lord,
> Let me entreat you speak the former language.
> *Angelo*   Plainly conceive, I love you.
>   (II.iv.133-40)

Love has nothing to do with the case, of course; the nightmare intensity of this dialogue comes from its barely suppressed anxieties. "If you be one," Angelo says, and the doubt persists; he fears that Isabella may really be a man. She tries to convince him that she hides nothing beneath the "external warrants" of her gender— "I have no tongue but one"— but the reassurance is not enough, and "gentle my lord" is hardly tactful at such a moment. She must wear the "livery" that announces submission and, more important, "plainly conceive": only by bearing a child can she dissolve Angelo's fear that their encounter has made him a woman.

In the light of Angelo's ordeal, the rules of Isabella's convent seem designed to protect men more than women.

> When you have vow'd, you must not speak
>   with men
> But in the presence of the prioress;
> Then, if you speak, you must not show your
>   face;
> Or if you show your face, you must not speak.
>   (I.iv.10-13)

Men must not confront the double danger of a pretty face and a confident tongue, and the play as a whole reinforces these rules by keeping a tight rein on female energy and initiative. No Portia or Rosalind wears male clothing. Isabella is quite dependent on the Duke and needs Lucio's urgent coaching— "You are too cold" (II.ii.56)— in her interview with Angelo. Juliet and Mariana are conspicuously submissive. Mariana even apologizes for listening to music— sad music at that— and introduces convent discipline into her marriage: "I will not show my face / Until my husband bid me" (V.i.171-2). As needy or compliant as they are, however, the women still threaten. "O, I will to him and pluck out his eyes" (IV.iii.119), Isabella cries when she learns of Angelo's perfidy. Describing Mariana, the Duke begins with pity and ends with something close to fear: "His unjust unkindness, that in all reason should have quenched her love, hath, like an impediment in the current, made it more violent and unruly" (III.i.240-4). Mistress Overdone— "Overdone by the last" (II.i.199) of her husbands, according to Pompey— has in fact survived all nine of them. "Women?— Help, heaven!" (II.iv.126) Isabella exclaims; like Pompey's joke, her remark leaves the weaker sex's identity in doubt and gives an ironic turn to her wish that "a more strict restraint / Upon the sisters stood, the votarists of Saint Clare" (I.iv.4-5).

This nervousness helps to explain the play's considerable misogyny. Its expressions range greatly in intensity and self-consciousness; they include Lucio's casual reference to Mistress Kate Keepdown, who has borne him a child, as "the rotten medlar" (IV.iii.171) and Elbow's

Engraving from Galerie des Personnages de Shakespeare *(1844).*

malapropism: "My wife, sir, whom I detest before heaven" (II.i.68). Less humorous is Angelo's metaphor when he predicts what will happen to Isabella if she tries to accuse him: "you shall stifle in your own report, / And smell of calumny" (II.iv.157-8). Angelo must bear the pain of recognizing that his own sexuality is inseparable from his wish to annihilate women, although self-awareness at least gives him a certain moral stature: "Shall we desire to raze the sanctuary / And pitch our evils there? O fie, fie, fie!" (II.ii.171-2).

Far more painful to Isabella than his attempted extortion, ironically— and it is perhaps the central irony in the play, the one that makes us most uneasy— is her protracted torment at the hands of the Duke, who never for an instant admits that he has anything at heart but her good. He lets Isabella believe that her brother has been executed, and, as if that were not enough, accuses her of madness and drives her uncomfortably close to it by pretending not to believe her denunciation of the deputy. "Look," the Duke tells the Provost, "th' unfolding star calls up the shepherd" (IV.ii.202-3). He invites us to regard him as that kindly guardian, guided by a star, but his rationale for lying to Isabella suggests that the lamb this shepherd tends best is himself— Lucio's epithet "sheep-biting" (V.i.352) is appropriate in more ways than one.

She's come to know
If yet her brother's pardon be come hither;
But I will keep her ignorant of her good
To make her heavenly comforts of despair
When it is least expected.

(IV.iii.106-10)

Isabella has wished for her brother's death— "Take my defiance, / Die, perish!" (III.i.142-3)— and the lie punishes her for that wish, in fairy tale fashion, by pretending to grant it. The lie also feeds the rage which can make Isabella so threatening, directs it once again at Angelo, and enables the Duke to dispel it and belittle its power: "This nor hurts him, nor profits you a jot. / Forbear it therefore; give your cause to heaven" (IV.iii.123-4). What happens is not unlike an exorcism: a woman's hidden and unpredictable menace is exposed and then tamed by the controlling wisdom of her husband to be.

The Duke proposes to Isabella only after explosions at the Deputy and Claudio have exhausted her rage, and he makes sure that Angelo will marry Mariana, whose love is so violent and unruly. With a deputy to act out the play's most dangerous fantasies, both aggressive and passive, the Duke is free to define his own identity in safer terms. Concealing the truth about Claudio will let the Duke restore him to his sister as if resurrecting him from the dead. "To make her heavenly comforts" thus reveals a cold-eyed view of how to resemble a god and cloaks in piety a questionable but psychologically useful act. The synthetic miracle will earn Isabella's perpetual gratitude, but this strategy, surely, is at the heart of our disappointment in their union. It establishes control where we hope for playfulness and freedom, fixes permanently what ought to be flexible, and defines a hierarchy— patron and debtor— which precludes any marriage of true minds. It makes us feel, in short, that Isabella leaves one sort of convent only to enter another.

The Duke's method with his other subjects is much the same; the purity of his own motives is his constant theme, even with Barnardine, Pompey, and Abhorson for an audience. He speaks to the Provost of "yonder generation" (IV.iii.89) as if he weren't a part of it himself, and the calculated strangeness, so unlikely in a comic hero, is essential to his manner. "Not of this country," as he tells Escalus, but on "special business from his Holiness" (III.ii.210-14), he seeks to rise above the messy domains of human sexuality and power, to assume, like some Christian knight-errant, a sanctity not available to ordinary men: "trust not my holy order, / If I pervert your cause" (IV.iii.147-8). Crucial here is the pun on "order": the masquerade defines his power in terms which will persist long after he has ceased to play the friar. He wants obedience without recourse to the spur, and the note of piety hallows what would otherwise be only a prince's bidding. In addition, this "most bounteous sir" (V.i.442), as Isabella learns to call him, finds a novel strategy: he rules by forgiving. As the play ends he pardons not only the obvious offenders Angelo, Claudio, Lucio, and Barnardine, but the Provost, Escalus, and Isabella as well. It is startling to hear Isabella, after all her needless suffering, ask forgiveness for having "employ'd and pain'd / Your unknown sovereignty" (V.i.385-6), but such is the power of his spell.

Measure for Measure leaves us nevertheless with mutually exclusive resolutions: a Duke both retiring and worldly, who sounds like an altruist but serves only himself. "Your friar is now your prince" (V.i.380), he tells Isabella, but the transformation is incomplete; he clings to both roles at once, as his language sways doubtfully between courtliness and piety.

> As I was then,
> Advertising and holy to your business,
> Not changing heart with habit, I am still
> Attorney'd at your service.
>   (V.i.380-83)

The Duke's weakness at least makes him a reassuring husband for Isabella— no threats of rape are likely from a man who "can do you little harm" (III.ii.162), even if he is the "more mightier member" (V.i.236) Angelo perceives behind Mariana's accusation. But what are we to think of a bridegroom who referred earlier to "the dribbling dart of love" (I.iii.2) and whose most passionate words, even now, are "Dear Isabel, / I have a motion much imports your good" (V.i.531-2)? Such excessively modest overtures are hardly the occasion for comic rejoicing. Indeed, if Isabella's plea for the deputy's life balances her wish for Claudio's death, the anxieties about women are too strong to be completely resolved. Angelo has tried once to define a woman in a limited, reassuring way— "if you be more, you're none"— and the attempt continues in the Duke's catechism of Mariana.

> *Duke*   What, are you married?
> *Mariana* No, my lord.
> *Duke*   Are you a maid?
> *Mariana* No, my lord,
> *Duke*   A widow, then?
> *Mariana* Neither, my lord.
> *Duke*   Why, you are nothing then;
>   neither maid, widow, nor wife!
>   (V.i.172-9)

Once again, we see the play's fearfulness about women and its willingness to obliterate their mystery ("You are nothing") rather than embrace it, features which anticipate the explosion of violence against them in subsequent Jacobean drama.

Ronald Huebert

SOURCE: "Taking the Measure of Manliness," in *Dalhousie Review*, Vol. 63, No. 1, Spring, 1983, pp. 125-34.
[*Huebert looks at Shakespeare's definition of manliness in his plays in general and in* Measure for Measure *in particular and concludes that, judging from such characters as Pompey, Claudio, Lucio, and Angelo, Shakespeare settled on courage, accountability, honesty, and earthiness as the qualities of manhood. Huebert argues that while all four of these characters achieve a degree of manliness by the end of the play the Duke, by contrast, fails to prove himself.*]

In choosing a title for this essay I've taken the liberty of referring casually to *Measure for Measure*, by first name only, and I've suggested that manliness is the particular question that interests me as I read it. To prevent false expectations, I should admit that I'm not proposing a feminist interpretation of the play, and I'll have little to say about the notoriously double standard which everyone in Shakespeare's Vienna seems to take for granted. I'm not offering a phenomenology of sexual experience in the play. Nor am I going to set out anything in the way of new evidence (from seldom-read letters, commonplace books still in manuscript, or plays of the period so obscure as to be neglected by everyone but the over-achievers of Elizabethan studies). All of these would be worthwhile objectives, but I've decided not to follow other beckonings in the interests of getting somewhere with one simple question: namely, what are the implicit standards for judging manliness of character or behaviour in *Measure for Measure*?

If the play had been written either by [Christopher] Marlowe or [Ben] Jonson, the answer to this question wouldn't be what it is. Marlowe, I'm convinced, would have made Claudio into something altogether more splendid than Shakespeare did. Claudio earns his place in the plot by being sexually impetuous, and is then placed in the awkward position of having to define his attitude towards a system of authority that condemns him. What Marlowe could have done with such an opportunity for defiant rebellion can be suggested by remembering what he in fact did with Piers Gaveston or Doctor Faustus or Leander. Jonson, conversely, would have made something altogether more grotesque out of Angelo. Perhaps the closest analogue in Jonson's plays to Angelo's dilemma is the position of Zeal-of-the-land Busy as he confronts the pleasures of Bartholomew Fair. He knows that eating pig is an abomination, especially if you enter the tents of the wicked to do it, but this doesn't prevent him from washing down two-and-a-half of Ursula's dripping man-sized portions with a pailful of Mooncalf's ale. For Jonson, Angelo's puritan hypocrisy would have been the signal for a satiric performance of uninhibited virtuosity.

In Marlowe's plays, manliness is an ideal that asserts itself by soaring above the ordinary; in Jonson, it's a position of stability from which the masquerades of the world can be seen for what they are. Shakespeare seems at times to share Marlowe's view of the matter (to judge by Cleopatra's requiem for Antony), at other times Jonson's (to judge by Hamlet's confidence in Horatio). But in Shakespeare as in life, it's easier to deduce the precise meaning of a standard from conspicuous failures than from celebrated successes. And for this purpose I'm going to comment briefly on two flagrant offenders: Romeo and Macbeth.

The streets of Shakespeare's Verona are bursting with young men who have something to prove. Tybalt's way of achieving manhood is to carve out a reputation as Prince of Cats— a title which stands in constant need of defence by swaggering once it has been established. Mercutio's method is to simulate the knowing weariness of the man of the world. Cassius Clay before he changed his name; Bob Dylan before whatever it was that happened to him. Romeo's experience looks blissfully normal by comparison: he's in the process of becoming a man by learning the difference between infatuation and love. And, even if love is what absorbs him, it doesn't detract from the respect he has earned from his peers. If Tybalt sends a challenge, Benvolio knows that "Romeo will answer it" (II.iv.9). That's not quite what happens when the fighting begins, but I think it's clear that Romeo shows more courage in trying to stop the fight than either of the combatants. And when he does draw his weapon, the mighty Prince of Cats goes down.

But these acknowledged marks of manliness (bravery, self-restraint, physical daring) are in one sense less than what Romeo needs. After his banishment, while hiding in the Friar's cell, Romeo falls to the ground in a seizure of adolescent despair. The Nurse bustles in to find him in the same predicament as Juliet: "Blubbering and weeping, weeping and blubbering" (III.iii.86). While the Nurse and Friar Laurence are making practical arrangements to preserve his future, Romeo is threatening suicide. He deserves the rebukes both of his elders offer. "Stand, and you be a man," says the Nurse (III.iii.87). The Friar expands this shrewd advice into a moving sermon on manliness:

> Art thou a man? Thy form cries out thou art.
> Thy tears are womanish, thy wild acts denote
> The unreasonable fury of a beast. . . .
> Thy noble shape is but a form of wax
> Digressing from the valour of a man.
>
> (III.iii.108-26)

The Romeo who needs these exhortations is still lovable, perhaps even understandable, but not admirable. In this scene he's a failure by the very standards he has earlier been able to uphold.

Macbeth's failure happens for the opposite reasons: he loses not the ability to stand up but the willingness to bend. At the outset Macbeth is winning all of the rewards that fall to models of manliness: victory in battle, admiration from his best friend, congratulations and caresses from his wife, promotion, trust, adulation. But he has not lost either the gentleness of spirit that marks him out as a real hero, or the ability to stop the crescendo of applause for the purpose of asking moral questions. Lady Macbeth knows that his nature "is too full o'th'milk of human kindness" (I.v.17) to allow him to kill in cold blood. So with ferocious determination she goads and challenges and manipulates him, using a variety of rhetorical pitches all of which lead to her most provoking question, "Are you a man?" (III.iv.57). He tries to silence her by affirming his moral position: "Pr'ythee, peace. / I dare do all that may become a man" (I.vii.45-6). But she won't hear his answers. She dazzles him with histrionics, torments him with the thought of cowardice, threatens him with sexual deprivation. He can move ahead only after he's accepted her shallow interpretation of manliness, which he does in the form of an equivocal compliment:

> Bring forth men-children only!
> For thy undaunted mettle should compose
> Nothing but males.
>
> (I.vii.73-5)

To accept this view amounts to killing or excluding everything else; dominance at any cost means that Macbeth can't keep the things he really wants: "honour, love, obedience, troops of friends, / I must not look to have" (V.iii.25-6). But by the time he says these words it is too late. The arbitrary code of manliness which Macbeth learned from his wife has become habit, and he sees no alternative but to keep on butchering until someone butchers him.

The hollowness of the code Macbeth adopts is beautifully counterpointed by the case of Macduff. Here too is a man of action and courage. When Macduff leaves for England without so much as a farewell note, Lady Macduff complains (understandably) that "He wants the natural touch" (IV.ii.9). But this is precisely untrue. Just as Macbeth loses his gentleness at the prompting of his woman, so Macduff reveals his own fully developed humanity in relation to his family. While the revolutionary forces are assembling in England, Macduff receives the news of his great loss. Malcolm wants to turn private grief at once into a battle cry: "Dispute it like a man," he urges (IV.iii.220). Macduff is still absorbing the horror and the hurt and the unspeakable sense of loss. He falters, repeats himself, disbelieves, curses. And he does accept Malcolm's challenge, with a qualification:

> I shall do so;
> But I must also feel it as a man.
>
> (IV.iii.220-21)

Here if anywhere in the play is the distinction between the rampantly destructive machine nicknamed "manliness" and the deeply coherent sense of courage which deserves the name. Lady Macbeth's question ("Are you a man?") gets its complete answer only here. Yes, if I can also feel it as a man.

To return to the comparison I suggested earlier, it would appear that the assumptions Shakespeare makes about manliness are neither as idealistic as Marlowe's nor as tough as Jonson's. If you prefer an assessment more flattering to Shakespeare, you might say that Shakespeare's manliness is more flexible than Marlowe's, more chivalrous than Jonson's, more generous than both. In the closing scene of *Measure for Measure,* just after Mariana has become a bride, she's told that she'll soon be a widow. Judged by his own system of pure precision, Angelo will have to die. As Angelo's widow, Mariana will be entitled to his property and this, the Duke assures her, ought to be enough "To buy you a better husband" (V.i.423). But Mariana won't be satisfied with anything less than a real man. "O my dear lord," she says to the Duke, "I crave no other, nor no better man" (V.i.423-4). She kneels, begs, argues, persists:

> They say best men are moulded out of faults,
> And, for the most, become much more the
>   better
> For being a little bad. So may my husband.
> (V.i.436-8)

On the face of it, this looks like dubious moral theory and a recipe for a disastrous marriage. Only by laundering a great deal of the evidence against Angelo can you come up with the notion that he's been "a little bad." But Mariana's plea is based on something deeper than a clear-sighted review of the evidence. She's desperately in love with Angelo, and the years of waiting have intensified her need. As the Duke explains, the betrayal by Angelo "that in all reason should have quenched her love, hath, like an impediment in the current, made it more violent and unruly" (III.i.241-4). Now that she's slept with Angelo at last (and married him too, as luck would have it), she feels for the first time the blessedness of having the man she wants. Not the perfect man, just the man she wants. And, convicted of demonstrable sensuality, Angelo somehow seems a lot more manly than he did when his reputation for icy correctness was intact. I'm going to return to the question of Angelo's manliness before long, but since his is a difficult case, I want to deal first with the other sexual offenders in *Measure for Measure.* They are— in the order of ascending complexity— Pompey, Lucio, and Claudio.

In a world where people are willing to mortify themselves and execute others in the name of abstractions, it's reassuring to meet somebody like Pompey. He has the kind of authority that comes from knowing who he is: "Truly, sir, I am a poor fellow that would live" (II.i.220). It's this willingness to live at the level of the flesh that gives Pompey his greatness, expressed largely in terms of the comic advantage he holds in the confrontations with Escalus and Elbow. When Escalus tells him that the law isn't going to tolerate promiscuity, Pompey answers with a question that implicitly defends the body against the tyranny of the soul: "Does your worship mean to geld and splay all the youth of the city?" (II.i.228-9). This isn't the only question that might be asked of the law in Vienna, but it's an honest one. In a good production, Pompey will get a chorus of approving laughter on this line— laughter in which the spectators are congratulating him, in effect, for cutting through all the sanctimonious twaddle about the dangers of too much liberty and the dignity of the great legal symbols. To put it another way, Pompey gets his authority from direct contact with experience. Escalus gets his from Angelo, who gets it from a Duke who's nowhere to be found, who gets it from a statute on sexual behaviour which has been asleep for either fourteen or nineteen years (nobody seems quite sure which). Even if the statute were a holograph in God's handwriting, the transmission of the manuscript is (as usual) a history of early neglect and subsequent corruption. Against these dubious claims, Pompey has every right to defend himself as a poor fellow who wants to live.

Pompey enters the play under the accusation of sexual misconduct. Elbow's dignity as a husband has been offended because Pompey has done something to his wife (the judicial inquiry makes the nature of the deed progressively less clear). As the constable of his parish, Elbow thinks he can get legal redress for Pompey's action. While the absurdity of the case is unfolding, like the gigantic silk banner which used to be the handkerchief in the clown's pocket, Angelo leaves. Absurdity is among the things he can't abide. So Escalus is left in charge, and he sees through both the accuser and the accused. When he learns that Elbow has held seven consecutive terms as constable, he's disturbed: "Are there not men in your ward sufficient to serve it?" he asks (II.i.263-4). Despite his naive charm, Elbow isn't a sufficient man by any standards. Despite his record as a pimp and his habitual irreverence, Pompey (on his own terms) is. He escapes with a warning which he intends to follow "as the flesh and fortune shall better determine" (II.i.250-51). To be at the mercy of the flesh and fortune is not what the complete man might aspire to, but it's the best a poor fellow who wants to live can afford.

Lucio manages to put together a plausible semblance of manliness. If Pompey follows the promptings of the flesh out of habit, Lucio does the same out of allegiance to a theory. He's a libertine. A very likeable one, in fact, who can say clever things like, "thy head stands so tickle on thy shoulders, that a milkmaid, if she be in love, may sigh it off" (I.ii.161-3), or "'tis my familiar sin, / With maids to seem the lapwing, and to jest / Tongue far from heart" (I.iv.31-3). Among the women who owe their happiness to this praiser of his own potency is Kate Keep-down, once the recipient of Lucio's promise to marry her, now the mother of his one-year-old. At the end of the play Lucio is forced into facing responsibility just as Angelo is. First, he'll have to marry the woman whose child he fathered. "The nuptial finished," says the Duke, "Let him be whipp'd and hang'd" (V.i.510-11). The threat of hanging doesn't seem to bother Lucio, or at least it's upstaged by the larger insult of being married "to a whore," as he puts it; "good my lord," he begs, "do not recompense me in making me a cuckold" (V.i.511-15). I think the threat of hanging is only a threat (as it is in Angelo's punishment), because the Duke continues to insist that marriage is Lucio's inescapable penance, while adding: "Thy slanders I forgive, and therewithal / Remit thy other forfeits" (V.i.517-18). So, when Lucio is led off to prison, it's to await the execution of nothing more serious than his long-overdue reunion with Kate Keep-down and family. For Lucio, that's a serious blow nonetheless; it hurts him where he's most vulnerable. It's a blow to the unfettered manhood he's been proclaiming as his only principle.

The other man who fathers a child out of wedlock is Claudio. Morally, Claudio's sex-life begins on the pattern set for him by Lucio: with a promise of marriage to Juliet. It's pregnancy that forces the distinction, best expressed in the domesticated chivalry of Victorian language, between the man of character and the cad. Claudio does the decent thing in standing by Juliet, whom he describes as "fast my wife" (I.ii.136), and whom he would gladly marry if her tiresome relatives could settle their bickering about the dowry. It may be the integrity of his response to Juliet's pregnancy that wins Claudio his reputation for special worth. Mistress Overdone, whose views shouldn't be taken lightly where the point at issue is manliness, gives Claudio her loudest praise: "There's one yonder arrested and carried to prison, was worth five thousand of you all" (I.ii.56-7). And the Provost, after dutifully making the arrest, describes his prisoner as "a young man / More fit to do another such offence, / Than to die for this" (II.iii.13-15).

Under the shadow of a death sentence, especially in his confrontation with Isabella, Claudio faces the hardest test of his manliness. For Isabella the solution is clear enough, as she indicates in the one line from the play that has found a life of its own as an ironic proverb: "More than our brother is our chastity" (II.iv.184). Armed with such fierce conviction, she's horrified when Claudio doesn't simply applaud her decision. "Death is a fearful thing," he says (III.i.115), and, realizing that it's within her power to rescue him, he begs her to change her mind:

> Sweet sister, let me live.
> What sin you do to save a brother's life,
> Nature dispenses with the deed so far
> That it becomes a virtue.

> (III.i.132-5)

This argument provokes a retort from Isabella more scathing than anything she's said to Angelo. Her speech beings with "O, you beast!" and ends with "No word to save you" (III.i.135-46). Between these unrelenting extremes is a withering assessment of his valour: "Wilt thou be made a man out of my vice?" What Marlowe's Faustus referred to as "manly fortitude" should, on Isabella's terms, be enough to ensure that her brother be willing to give his life to the cause of absolute purity.

I'm not going to concern myself with Isabella's motives, or the arguments for and against her choice. Whatever they are, she's being unfair to Claudio. He's not a coward. In conversation with the supposed Friar Lodowick (really the Duke, of course), he resigns himself to the universal human fate: "Let it come on" (III.i.43). And to Isabella, before she's explained the terms of Angelo's proposal, he's equally brave:

> If I must die,
> I will encounter darkness as a bride
> And hug it in mine arms.

> (III.i.82-4)

But there's an understandable impatience in these lines. The "If" is haunting Claudio's mind like the flickering trunk of a palm tree between vertical bars of desert heat. Yes, yes, I'll die bravely if I have to, but please don't prolong this test of my courage if there's anything else to report. Manliness doesn't prevent Claudio from sharing a bottom-line instinct with Barnardine, who announces quite sensibly that he drank too much last night to face the ordeal of execution today, or with Pompey, who knows that he's a poor fellow who wants to live.

Angelo stands over the rest of society, "Dressed in a little brief authority" (II.ii.119), brittle rather than tough, self-absorbed rather than self-assured, a caricature of genuine manliness. "I would to heaven I had your potency," Isabella says to him during their first interview (II.ii.67). But almost as soon as she's said the word, she limits its meaning to the official one: the power to judge. Angelo's professionalism is impeccable. He has the kind of perfect record that makes you wonder if he's not hiding something. And once he's in control, it's obvious that his reputation has been won at the expense of everything that matters more. When the Provost asks him what's to be done "with the groaning Juliet" (II.ii.15), for example, Angelo's reply— "See you the fornicatress be remov'd" (II.ii.22)—is a desecration of woman in her sacred state. Anyone as obsessed with power as Angelo is will have little patience with the chivalry of sexual behaviour. That's why his rejection of Mariana, though legally clean, has more in common with Lucio's treatment of Kate Keep-down than with Claudio's treatment of Juliet.

Morally, Angelo is the perfect example of Jonson's view, as recorded in *Discoveries,* that "Too much pickednesse is not manly." It's obvious from the plot that his fastidious legalism hurts and threatens to hurt other people. What it does to him is equally damaging. "It is certain," says Lucio, "that when he makes water, his urine is congealed ice; that I know to be true. And he is a motion ungenerative; that's infallible" (III.ii.105-8). This would be vulgar instead of funny if it didn't ring true. Angelo has bruised the body to pleasure the soul. In doing so, he's come perilously close to losing his manliness. His dealings with Claudio, Elbow, Pompey, Juliet, and Mariana show him up as little more than the "ungenitured agent" that Lucio imagines him to be (III.ii.167-8).

It's the habit of renunciation that has made Angelo what he is. That's why he feels threatened as soon as he knows that he's responding to Isabella's presence not with professional severity but with lust. "O fie, fie, fie, fie!" he says shortly after she's left him; "What dost thou, or what art thou, Angelo?" (II.ii.172-3). And as he waits for her to return, he knows he'd pawn his "gravity" for the "idle plume" he now desires (II.iv.9-11). The rest of Angelo's part in *Measure for Measure* is a painful education in the rudiments of manly behaviour. He thinks he can have a night's indulgence— secretly— and then return to the austerity of his professional routine. But he finds that "This deed unshapes me quite" (IV.iv.18). He's made himself vulnerable in ways that he won't understand completely until the Duke reveals all at the close.

And as his own brittleness begins to soften, Angelo starts to wonder about the feelings of others. He has "A deflower'd maid" on his hands now (IV.iv.19). What will "her tender shame" (IV.iv.21) prompt her to do or prevent her from doing? Angelo's answers aren't yet the ones a manly lover might give. But at least he's asking the questions. And he's come a long way from the days when a woman who slept with a man could be dismissed as a "fornicatress." As for Claudio, "He should have lived," Angelo now admits (IV.iv.26), though he fights this admission as soon as he makes it with as much legal jargon as he can remember. Still, "Would yet he had lived" (IV.iv.30). What Angelo is going through is the kind of education in manliness described by Mariana in her plea at the end of the play. He's beginning to understand the sense in which all men, including himself, are "moulded out of faults."

If I can risk a few premature conclusions, I'd say that the standard of manliness in *Measure for Measure* is like the pattern in Marlowe's plays in that it celebrates

personal desire. If Claudio gets "possession of Julietta's bed," as he puts it (I.ii.135), that's because he's bold enough to go after what it is he wants. But desire in Shakespeare has its social as well as personal character, partly because it promises (or threatens) fertility. If Claudio sleeps with Juliet, that's a private matter of course, until everyone in Vienna starts making it into a public matter. In *Edward II,* society punishes desire in just the way that Angelo would like to but can't. I'd also say that Shakespeare's manliness is like the Jonsonian pattern in the sense that it places value on the kind of integrity that comes from self-knowledge, and scorns the rigidity of merely mechanical behaviour. The most Jonsonian image in the play is the "angry ape" (II.ii.121) which Isabella holds up to Angelo as a mirror of his false manliness. But the suggestion that manliness itself is "moulded out of faults"— this is a more tolerant and less exacting view than either Marlowe or Jonson would allow.

I'm aware that *Measure for Measure* includes a major icon of manliness whom I've mentioned only in passing. The Duke, in my scheme, remains an unsolved problem. I shall invoke only one production of *Measure for Measure*— the one directed by John Barton for the Royal Shakespeare Company in 1970— and I'd like to introduce the Duke's problem by recalling what happened in the final moments of this interpretation. The Duke approached Isabella with outstretched arms on the words, "Dear Isabel" (V.i.531), and looked invitations at her during the next few lines, ending with, "What's mine is yours, and what is yours is mine" (V.i.534). Then he waited, and waited, and waited. At last Isabella slowly turned away from him and, without looking back, made her exit at stage left. The Duke spoke the final couplet— about referring to "our palace" (V.i.535)— with understandable sadness. Then, slowly, he made his exit stage right.

I don't think for a moment that anything comparable to this happened at the Globe in 1604. But I think the unconventional ending chosen by the RSC does point up a serious difficulty, namely, that the Duke has done nothing, dramatically, to deserve Isabella's hand in marriage. While he's busy testing everyone else's manliness, his own remains untried. Lucio claims that, despite the Duke's previous record as a womanizer, "He's now past it" (III.ii.176). I'd like to be able to dismiss this as the most cutting of Lucio's "slanders" against the Duke, but I can't be satisfied quite so easily because Lucio is demonstrably perceptive about the sexual behaviour of just about everyone else. I'm aware that one can invent various symbolic marriages for this pair, perhaps embellishing them with stage directions borrowed from the tradition of the morality play: *"Here Courtly Liberty, being now past it, taketh Chaste Vigilance by the hand, and leadeth her in a sprightly measure to the music of Sellinger's Round."* Still, it doesn't feel like a real courtship. And it's infuriatingly true that, in response to the

Duke's proposal, Isabella says nothing. It's Angelo who says that the Duke has been omnipresent, "like power divine" (III.i.367). Perhaps. But in theatrical terms, he has spent most of the play fulfilling Lucio's description of him as "the old fantastical duke of dark corners" (IV.iii.156).

I suppose it's an egalitarian perversity that prompts me to suppose that dukes, like other men, should have to prove themselves. If so, I think it's an attitude encouraged by a play in which the man who judges turns out to be moulded out of the very faults he won't admit to himself or allow to his fellow men.

Linda Macfarlane

SOURCE: "Heads You Win Tails I Lose," in *Critical Survey*, Vol. 5, No. 1, 1993, pp. 77-82.

[*Macfarlane argues that in the world of* Measure for Measure, *women are effectively powerless because the only power they supposedly possess—sexual—is defined and limited by men. Men, on the other hand, are seen to possess the power to govern, accumulate wealth, and set moral standards. Macfarlane suggests that this discussion of the nature of men and women is relevant to today's society.*]

In *Measure For Measure* Isabella is placed firmly in a no win situation. Even on the threshold of a convent, at the very moment of making a clear statement about her vocation, her desires and her sexuality, she is not safe. She is plucked back into the outside world to bear the responsibility for the sexual urges, misdemeanors and fantasies of four men.

As Lucio approaches to plead for Isabella's intervention in her brother's cause his greeting sexualises her: 'Hail, virgin— if you be, as those cheek roses / Proclaim you are no less!' Lucio clearly identifies Isabella by her sexuality and his subsequent encouragement of her in the face of her imminent failure to win over Angelo supposes she must use her sexuality if she is to succeed. He assumes that Isabella's assertion that she will 'bribe' Angelo is an offer of sex. He suggests that she 'had marred all else!' a statement which indicates at this early stage in the play the limited possibilities perceived by men for women. In fact Isabella's 'bribe' is to be 'with true prayers'. Lucio is unable to do other than he does— the exchange he envisages is part of the parcel of assumptions about women which this play foregrounds.

It is with this 'parcel of assumptions' that this essay is concerned. As the play explores matters of power, justice and mercy, it chooses to do so through a revelation of gender relations which makes it deeply relevant to a twentieth-century audience. Attitudes to female sexuality and choice are a particular focus and are clearly signalled in the opening moments of the play when Isabella's choice of a convent life is being totally disregarded— in fact, is not even considered.

Angelo, of course, shares Lucio's assumptions and the fascination with Isabella's virgin state. It is her purity which makes her desirable and for Angelo, who sees sex as something corrupt and corrupting, to have that which is untouched holds its own attraction. This point about the desirability of the sexually inexperienced is made when Angelo, torn by his desires and wracked by his hatred of sex, questions himself:

> What is't I dream on?
> O cunning enemy, that, to catch a saint,
> With saints dost bait thy hook! Most dangerous
> Is that temptation that doth goad us on
> To sin in loving virtue. Never could the strumpet,
> With all her double vigour, art and nature
> Once stir my temper; but this virtuous maid
> Subdues me quite.
>
> (II. ii. 178-85)

It is noticeable that for all the emphasis on virtue and saintliness it is Isabella's lack of sexual experience, made clear in the contrast between 'maid' and 'strumpet', which stirs Angelo's temper. He is unable to envisage a state of chastity or purity which is sexual. There is nothing between abstinence and prostitution. This points to one of the many double binds women find themselves in: to be sexually active is to be suspect, to be a virgin is to be desirable and therefore potentially sexually active and potentially suspect. Either way women lose. Either way they are sexualised.

Claudio's demands of his sister are couched in a language which presumes her power: 'sweet sister, let me live:' and heaps all the responsibility for his life (or death) onto her shoulders. Her power to save him is vested at this juncture totally in her assent or refusal to use her sexuality.

Isabella is reduced by the attitudes of Lucio, Angelo and Claudio to a sexual being at the very point in her life when she has chosen abstinence from sex as a way of life. Isabella is reduced, not because sexual activity is essentially reductive, but because all other aspects of identity are being denied her.

The demands made of Isabella's sexuality do not end here. At the end of the play her mentor, the Duke, who in his guise of friar has ostensibly taken a vow of chastity which should guarantee Isabella's freedom from predation and respect for her own choice of vocation, exerts another pressure, again sexual and invites (commands?) marriage. This it must be noted in spite of the assurance given earlier to the Provost that 'My mind promises with my habit no loss shall touch her by my company.' (III. i. 178-80). It must be asked why it is felt necessary to give this assurance. It is as if, by being female, Isabella is automatically 'at risk' and that this 'risk' entails some form of taking or having by which she will be diminished in some way, hence the idea of 'loss'. The Friar/Duke is at least conscious of the state of things even as he professes the purity of his intentions. His words also make clear that the agent of the supposed 'loss' would not be Isabella herself. As has already been noted, the Duke's words to the Provost prove meaningless.

Isabella and male attitudes to her are placed at the centre of the play, thus audiences are forced to face their own attitudes to female sexuality. Many directors of the play have shown us an Isabella actively or unconsciously encouraging Angelo's advances. This has usually to be done by some surreptitious glance or coy movement or even, in one recent production, by the removal of Isabella's headcovering by Angelo as she abased herself at his feet. Whilst one would not like to deny directors interpretive powers, it is clear that such an interpretation owes much to the deep-seated belief that when women say no they mean yes and nothing at all to the evidence of the text. The text makes the Isabella/Angelo situation unambiguous. Angelo is attracted by Isabella's aloofness and she is prepared to bribe only with prayers. If Angelo finds all this attractive then he must, as he clearly does, accept the responsibility and look to himself:

> What's this? What's this? Is this her fault or
>   mine?
> The tempter or the tempted, who sins most?
> Ha, not she. Nor doth she tempt; but it is I
> That, lying by the violet in the sun,
> Do as the carrion does, not as the flow'r,
> Corrupt with virtuous season.
>
> (II. ii. 162-7)

The emphatic positioning of 'I' at the end of the third line of this quotation makes the point unequivocally that the tempter is imbued with the power to tempt by the tempted. That Angelo is responsible and accepts responsibility for his own feelings is clear and further, having named Isabella as tempter, he then restates his position, 'Nor doth she tempt'. He knows who is the agent in this particular act of temptation even if others have been less clear.

What has been ignored by all the male characters is Isabella's choice of vocation. Her decision to become a nun assumes sexual abstinence as part of a way of life, but this has been disregarded as unimportant not only within the play, but by a body of opinion which has focused on Isabella as some sort of fanatic with a neurotic attachment to her virginity. The judgment is turned on the woman who in asserting her freedom to choose is held responsible for her brother's death— this

in spite of the fact that she is being manipulated and pressured by men, especially Angelo, who have alternatives open to them. She is sexualised, marginalised and depersonalised as remorselessly by such criticism as she is by Lucio, Claudio, Angelo and the Duke.

One of the points the play illustrates so well is that Isabella's freedom to choose is severely limited by male versions of her, all of which limit her identity to that which is simply sexual. The issue of choice between Claudio's life and Isabella agreeing to Angelo's demands, though central to the play, is often subsumed in the spurious argument about whether Isabella would be giving up much if she agreed to Angelo's demands. Roughly stated the argument runs, 'what's a one off sexual encounter against a man's life?' The play is not merely asking this question. Those who reduce the issue to this align themselves clearly with those who collectively pressure Isabella and collectively disregard her version of herself and her version of personal integrity. They also miss much that is revealed by the play's probing of attitudes to sexuality, both male and female, but especially of male attitudes to women as wholly and only sexual. For if we project ourselves imaginatively into the situation where Isabella has gone to Angelo and if we approve her going though we know how unwillingly she goes, we are accepting that female sexuality should be traded to satisfy the tyrannical desires of the rich and powerful. If we accept this state of affairs then who should we really be judging?

The reduction of the issue to a simple choice between enforced sex and a man's life disregards Isabella's version of herself. She does not split off her sexuality from the rest of herself. It is an integral part of herself— in fact this attitude to the self as somehow integrated leads her to offer her life for Claudio's life. It leads her to assert: 'I have spirit enough to do anything that appears not foul in the truth of my spirit.' (III. i. 208). What is emphasised here is a self which has the potential to be faithful to its own idea of truth. The argument centres on a notion of integrity of ideal and action in which there can be no split between what is believed and what is done, between one's sexual self and the rest.

In spite of, or perhaps because of this version of herself, Isabella does not judge others' sexual behaviour. Her immediate response to the news of Juliet's pregnancy reveals this: 'O let him marry her.' (I. iv. 48). What she does judge is Angelo's abuse of power and Claudio's fear of death. Her passionate outburst as she scorns Claudio's pleading for life comes from the torment of being caught in an intolerable situation. The intemperate nature of her response and her abhorrence at what she is being asked to do is surely understandable. It should be emphasised that it is the idea of buying her brother's life with loveless and enforced sex that Isabella finds abhorrent, not sex itself. It is the context which revolts Isabella. As a woman of Christian commitment and absolute faith it should not surprise us that she has no fear of death. To Isabella death is preferable to the shame of such an exchange as Angelo has suggested. In her desperation she makes the mistake of expecting her brother to have the same response as she does.

So what is Isabella's real 'crime'? Is it simply that she chooses a way of life which includes sexual abstinence as one of its aspects? Those of us who do not make this choice may well ask why we feel threatened by those who do— why, when someone expresses abhorrence at the idea of loveless enforced sex, we feel free to judge that person, usually female, as somehow abnormal. In Isabella's case this 'defect' has also been given the label frigidity, which is another sexual category applied to women, though in the situation we are dealing with it is difficult to see that the term has any meaning.

Perhaps it would be more helpful if we were to see Isabella's choice as a form of sexual freedom. After all, it is no less a sexual freedom than sexual activity in its various forms; both are circumscribed as are all notions of free choice. Indeed some might see sexual activity as the greater evil, leading, as our male writers have often shown us, to a tension between desire and the ability to cope with that desire. Such agonisings have long been the subject of male writings in the form of novels, poems, plays, jokes and films. Angelo in this play is but one example. His appallingly inadequate response to his desire for Isabella is to degrade rather than celebrate sexual desire, to be inwardly tormented into self-hatred and to outwardly disregard the otherness of Isabella. Whatever our views about the 'value' of individual sexuality, whether we cherish and celebrate it by being sexually active or by sexual abstinence or whether, like Angelo, we fear and mistrust it, what is abhorrent is not only that Isabella is expected to 'give up' that which she has chosen to 'protect', but that her attitude to her own sexuality as an integral part of herself is being scorned.

At the moment when the play produces absolute alternatives, it mercifully avoids the choice. The Isabella—Marianna swap is an avoidance not a negation of the situation which has been vividly presented to us. It conveniently prevents Isabella from having to face the consequences of her decision— whatever that ultimately might have been, for there were many options available. The closure in the play prevents the audience from witnessing one of the awful alternatives— the death of a man about to become a father or the sexual humiliation of a woman against her own clearly expressed wishes, almost literally on the threshold of a convent. The closure prevents the dramatic following through of either alternative, but it does not prevent the imaginative engagement with what the play has

opened up.

The swap is a necessary dramatic convention and represents that moment when the play ceases to be an exploration of the attitudes to sexuality it has hitherto disclosed and imposes on itself a schematic resolution to its own problem. Having turned away from the great difficulty it has set itself the play returns to its beginning, coming full circle in the final dénouement as Isabella is propositioned by the Duke and faces once again her earlier dilemma, albeit in the form of marriage.

Isabella's failure to reply, her collapse into silence, may signal her utter disbelief and exhaustion or her resignation at the turn events have taken. It may also show that Isabella has learned to use one of the few sources of female power, silence. To reserve at least one's thoughts to oneself denies the power of knowing to others. It may also bring us back symbolically to the earlier entry into the silent and enclosed order of nuns at the play's opening or to a beginning in which Isabella's silence represented her initial inability to plead with Angelo. In any case we have learned that both her silence and her articulate pleadings, her quick-witted rhetoric and her logical arguments have got her precisely nowhere. In not answering the Duke she makes no commitment, but, ironically, places herself in the position of the woman who says nothing and can therefore mean anything.

Isabella has nowhere to turn in this play. Even as she and Marianna manipulate events to get Isabella off the hook they are indebted to the Duke for suggesting and enabling the course of action they plan to follow. It is a course of action in which power is defined in a peculiarly female form, that is the use of sex and supported by another, deceit. The very framework which enables also reveals the limits of female power and clearly reminds us that for the women in this play there is no other power available. The convenient willingness of Marianna only serves to highlight the helplessness of her situation while at the same time revealing the limited nature of the control she and Isabella have over their own lives.

As a result of the machinations of the Duke and the actions of the two women, Marianna is secure in the knowledge that she will at last be married— a state which represents one of the options open to women in the play, the others being whoredom, institutionalised chastity or pregnancy outside of marriage. All are defined by sex.

Isabella represents the female struggle to define and decide her own project for herself. If the site of the struggle is to be the limited spectrum of female choices offered in the play, all of which are delineated by particular versions of female sexuality, then she has to function within that world. When she does threaten to expose some of the corrupt structures which uphold it she is constrained by the obvious power relations between Angelo, the embodiment of state power and herself, a woman wishing only to escape the world to enter a convent. Her total defeat by Angelo, who represents one form of male power, is only prevented by her total dependence on that other powerful male, the Duke. This play shows very forcefully what is the nature of the limits placed on female choices and by whom those choices are defined. It seems Isabella would have been safe from the predations of the males only if she had become a fully fledged nun. It says much that Isabella's decision to express her sexuality in her own way could not be respected unless supported by the external and protective walls of an institution— the convent enclosing its order of nuns. It says more when we consider that this freedom is enclosed by a male sanctioned institution.

JUSTICE AND MERCY

Justice and mercy play pivotal roles in *Measure for Measure*. Justice is defined by most critics as an objective adherence to the letter of the law and in fact, **Joel Levin** uses the term "law" in place of the term "justice." Mercy, on the other hand, is described as a charitable and tolerant interpretation of the law. Levin uses the term "equity" in close conjunction with the term "mercy"; both he and Wilbur Dunkel point out that the Duke, as the representative of mercy in the play, and Angelo, as the standard-bearer for justice, each prove inadequate to solving the problems of the corrupt Viennese society. Dunkel and Levin contend that the answer lies in combining justice with mercy; additionally, they suggest that this solution occurs at the close of the play when the Duke "both condemn[s] and allow[s] a wrong" by sentencing and then forgiving the transgressions of Angelo, Claudio, and Lucio.

The relationship between justice and mercy is taken a step farther by Robert Grams Hunter and Rolf Soellner, both of whom argue that Angelo cannot judge others fairly until he himself has sinned, and that once he thinks he has "deflower'd" Isabella and put Claudio to death, he begins to understand guilt; as a result, they explain, Angelo will discover his own humanity, along with the virtue of charity towards other people's weaknesses. David Thatcher rejects Soellner and Hunter's thesis as inconsistent. While he agrees that Angelo should be condemned for his attempted rape of Isabella and for his rigid enforcement of unreasonable laws, Thatcher contends that "natural guiltiness," or a judge's own guilt, is not sufficient reason for that judge to be merciful towards someone else who has committed the same crime. Further, Thatcher suggests that the issue of "natural guiltiness"— that is, the moral gray area be-

tween enacting justice versus granting mercy— is what makes *Measure for Measure* a "problem play."

Finally, **Linda Anderson** broadens the discussion of justice and mercy to include revenge. She disagrees with those critics who describe the theme of *Measure for Measure* as the triumph of mercy over justice and revenge and instead observes that revenge works as an instrument of justice and mercy. In other words, the Duke disguises himself so that he can protect the rights of innocents such as Isabella and Mariana even while he tricks the guilty such as Lucio and Angelo into calling revenge down upon themselves. Thus by the close of the play, all three concepts have merged as the Duke "takes revenge against wrongdoers, establishes justice for everyone, and extends a limited forgiveness to Angelo and Lucio not because they deserve it, but because his power, wisdom, and magnanimity allow him to be generous."

Linda Anderson

SOURCE: "Problem Comedies," in *A Kind of Wild Justice: Revenge in Shakespeare's Comedies*, University of Delaware Press, 1987, pp. 156-68.

[*In this excerpt from her study of the pervasiveness of revenge "as a useful social instrument in Shakespeare's comedies," Anderson reminds us that the Duke temporarily leaves Vienna in Angelo's hands not only to correct the city's excessive vices but also to test Angelo's ability to wield power fairly. Further, Anderson observes that as Isabella is forced to make decisions regarding her chastity, her brother's life, and Angelo's hypocrisy— and as the Duke himself steps in to draw the play to a close— the concept of revenge is intermingled with the concepts of justice and mercy to the extent that the three become "almost indistinguishable" from one another.*]

None of Shakespeare's titles is more suggestive of revenge than *Measure for Measure*. Although the phrase itself may mean no more than strict justice, it recalls the Old Testament law often cited as vengeful:

> . . . thou shalt paye life for life,
> Eie for eie, tothe for tothe, hand for hand,
>   fote for fote,
> Burning for burning, wonde for wonde,
>   stripe for stripe.
>
> (Exod. 21:23-25)

This is the spirit in which the Duke uses the phrase:

> The very mercy of the law cries out
> Most audible, even from his proper tongue,
> "An Angelo for Claudio, death for death!"
> Haste still pays haste, and leisure answers
>   leisure;

Like doth quit like, and *Measure* still *for Measure.*

(5.1.407-11)

Yet the phrase itself is from quite another context:

Judge not, that ye be not judged.
For with what judgement ye judge, ye shal
be judged, and with what measure ye
mette, it shal be measured to you againe.

(Matt. 7:1-2; see also Luke 6:37-38)

That the Duke in judging Angelo for judging Claudio should condemn him with a paraphrase of a biblical injunction condemning judging suggests a more complex irony than merely that "the ending of the play, then, really contradicts the title." Although a traditional objection to the play is that Angelo escapes any real revenge, revenge is not absent from the play but is so intertwined with justice and mercy that what are elsewhere separate and even opposing qualities become, in *Measure for Measure*, almost indistinguishable.

The standard reading of the play, based on the Duke's explanation to Friar Thomas (1.3.19-43), is that Vincentio intends Angelo to (re)enforce the "strict statutes and most biting laws" of Vienna "to strike and gall" the citizens. But this is not what the Duke says to Angelo; rather, he links severity and leniency:

Mortality and mercy in Vienna
Live in thy tongue and heart.

(1.1.44-45)

Your scope is as mine
own,
So to enforce or qualify the laws
As to your soul seems good.

(1.1.64-66)

Since the Duke does not tell Angelo to be severe, but tells Friar Thomas that this severity is his aim in temporarily abdicating, if we take his words at their face value we can only assume that his knowledge of Angelo's character leads him to believe that Angelo will not err on the side of mercy. Although he is certainly correct in that belief, it has been asserted that the Duke fails to understand his deputy's character and is thus responsible for Angelo's actions.[20] Not only does it seem rather harsh to condemn the Duke for accepting Angelo's character as Angelo presents it, but such a reading ignores another of Vincentio's purposes. In deputizing Angelo, the Duke has made it clear that he has no respect for a fugitive and cloistered virtue:

Angelo:
There is a kind of character in thy life,
That to th' observer doth thy history
Fully unfold. Thyself and thy belongings

Are not thine own so proper as to waste
Thyself upon thy virtues, they on thee.
Heaven doth us as we with torches do,
Not light them for themselves; for if our
virtues
Did not go forth of us, 'twere all alike
As if we had them not.

(1.1.26-35)

Not only does the Duke wish to make use of Angelo's virtue for the good of the state, he wishes to observe how Angelo's professed character is affected by power:

. . . Lord Angelo is precise;
Stands at a guard with envy; scarce confesses
That his blood flows; or that his appetite
Is more to bread than stone: hence shall we see
If power change purpose: what our seemers
be.

(1.3.50-54)

Angelo's trial begins with his judgment on Claudio, who enters not merely arrested but exhibited publicly through the streets at Lord Angelo's "special charge." Claudio at first seems resigned to a just punishment for an admitted crime:

Claudio: Thus can the demigod, Authority,
Make us pay down for our offense by weight
The words of heaven: on whom it will, it
will;
On whom it will not, so; yet still 'tis just.
Lucio: Why, how now, Claudio? whence
comes this restraint?
Claudio: From too much liberty, my Lucio,
liberty:
As surfeit is the father of much fast,
So every scope by the immoderate use
Turns to restraint. Our natures do pursue,
Like rats that ravin down their proper bane,
A thirsty evil, and when we drink we die.

(1.2.119-30)

But having explained the extenuating circumstances of his offense (1.2.145-55), Claudio's tone changes. Although still admitting that he broke the law, he expresses feelings of persecution:

And the new deputy now for the Duke—
Whether it be the fault and glimpse of new-
ness,
Or whether that the body public be
A horse whereon the governor doth ride,
Who, newly in the seat, that it may know
He can command, lets it straight feel the spur;
Whether the tyranny be in his place,
Or in his eminence that fills it up,
I stagger in—but this new governor
Awakes me all the enrolled penalties

not Angelo would equate his situation with Claudio's, he calls down vengeance upon his own head if he ever commits Claudio's offense:

> When I, that censure him, do so offend,
> Let mine own judgment pattern out my
>   death,
> And nothing come in partial.
>
> (2.1.29-31)

Our opinion of Angelo's severity is influenced by that of the other characters who enforce the laws in Vienna. Not only does Escalus plead for and pity Claudio, but the Justice remarks that "Lord Angelo is severe" (2.1.282) and the Provost risks Angelo's anger by questioning the order for execution (2.2.7-14) and comments to himself on Claudio's state:

> Alas,
> He hath but as offended in a dream!
> All sects, all ages smack of this vice, and he
> To die for't!
>
> (2.2.3-6)

These characters serve to support the opinion that "Angelo (the name is patently ironical: he puns on it himself) is law or legalism, rather than justice. His hard, prim, precise ruling by the book is not felt to be just, because his rule makes all offences the same size; and to think of incontinence or fornication as if it were murder does violence to all normal human feelings" (Rossiter 1961, 121). In a minor key, however, Angelo's severity triumphs over his legalism when he expresses his hope for punishment in the case against Pompey and Froth, which he does not bother to hear:

> I'll take my
>   leave,
> And leave you to the hearing of the cause,
> Hoping you'll find good cause to whip them
>   all.
>
> (2.1.135-37)

Isabella, at first, seems to find it difficult to argue with Angelo. Admitting that Claudio's offense is

> a vice that most I do abhor,
> And most desire should meet the blow of
>   justice
>
> (2.2.29-30)

she is easily swayed by Angelo's statement that his function is to punish criminals; declaring it a "just, but severe law" (2.2.41), she would abandon Claudio to his fate, if it were not for Lucio. Her succeeding (though unsuccessful) arguments are rather an odd mixture. She first suggests that Angelo might pardon Claudio "and neither heaven nor man grieve at the mercy" (2.2.50); to this, Angelo replies that he will not. She then argues that mercy is the greatest ornament of

Act II, scene iv. Angelo and Isabella. By Robert Smirke (1797).

> Which have, like unscour'd armor, hung by
>   th' wall
> So long that nineteen zodiacs have gone round
> And none of them been worn; and for a
>   name
> Now puts the drowsy and neglected act
> Freshly on me— 'tis surely for a name.
>
> (1.2.157-71)

Our next glimpse of Angelo is likely to incline us to Claudio's latter view. Angelo's first argument in favor of executing Claudio is not that the punishment fits the crime but that the ultimate penalty is needed *pour encourager les autres*. When Escalus argues for mercy and suggests that in a similar situation Angelo himself might have acted similarly, Angelo rejects the argument (2.1.1-31). Not until later in the play does the irony of this rejection become clear: "Moreover— and it is one of the dramatist's most subtle and original uses of parallelism— Claudio's relation to Juliet had been almost of a piece with that of Angelo to Mariana. But where the one for worldly reasons left his already affianced bride in the lurch, the other with generous impetuosity had preferred disregard of an outward form to heartless desertion. Thus Claudio's transgression is in itself most venial, and Angelo is the last man justified in visiting it with condign penalties" (Boas 1896, 362). Whether or authority, and that if their positions were reversed Angelo would have sinned as did Claudio, but Claudio would not have condemned him for it; Angelo asks her to leave. She then pleads as a Christian:

> Why, all the souls that were were forfeit once,
> And He that might the vantage best have took
> Found out the remedy. How would you be
> If He, which is the top of judgment, should
> But judge you as you are? O, think on that,
> And mercy then will breathe within your lips,
> Like man new made.
>
> (2.2.73-79)

Angelo replies that "It is the law, not I, condemn your brother" (2.2.80), and Isabella again shifts her ground, first requesting a reprieve and then asking "Who is it that hath died for this offense?" (2.2.88). Angelo responds that the reawakened law, enforced, will prevent future evils. When Isabella asks him to "show some pity" (2.2.99), he equates that quality with justice:

> I show it most of all when I show justice;
> For then I pity those I do not know,
> Which a dismiss'd offense would after gall,
> And do him right that, answering one foul wrong,
> Lives not to act another.
>
> (2.2.100-104)

But Isabella replies to this with another equation, asserting that what Angelo calls justice is in fact tyranny (2.2.106-9, 110-23, 126-28, 130-31, 134-36), adding,

> Go to your bosom,
> Knock there, and ask your heart what it doth know
> That's like my brother's fault. If it confess
> A natural guiltiness such as is his,
> Let it not sound a thought upon your tongue
> Against my brother's life.
>
> (2.2.136-41)

This argument now seems to affect Angelo, although he has already heard it from Escalus and rejected it (2.1.8-31). But we soon learn that it is not Isabella's varied pleas that justice be tempered with mercy that have affected Angelo's professed conviction that harsh justice for Claudio is mercy for Vienna. Angelo's final speech in this scene reveals how her arguments have touched him: "Isabella has insisted that there is a natural, sexual man hidden below Angelo's exterior of virtue. And at her bidding the sexual man steps forth with a ve[n]geance" (Stevenson 1966, 42). Realizing this, Angelo (in soliloquy) completely reverses his previous argument:

> O, let her brother live!

> Thieves for their robbery have authority
> When judges steal themselves.
>
> (2.2.174-76)

Finally, he sounds the first note of vengeance in the play with his invocation of the tempter who seeks to avenge his fall on mankind:

> O cunning enemy, that to catch a saint,
> With saints dost bait thy hook!
>
> (2.2.179-80)

With these lines Angelo, the villain of the piece, reveals that he feels himself a victim of diabolical revenge. But since he attributes the revenge to his righteousness, it is difficult to feel much sympathy for him even before he begins plotting his crimes.

At their second meeting, Angelo and Isabella continue to debate justice and mercy even though the subject of the argument has widened to include Isabella's chastity as well as Claudio's life. Isabella, however, is concerned now with divine justice, rather than the divine mercy she invoked in their previous argument, while Angelo concentrates on earthly concerns:

> *Angelo:* Which had you rather, that the most just law
> Now took your brother's life, [or,] to redeem him,
> Give up your body to such sweet uncleanness
> As she that he hath stain'd?
> *Isabella:* Sir, believe this,
> I had rather give my body than my soul.
> *Angelo:* I talk not of your soul. . . .
>
> (2.4.52-57)

Angelo insists that divine justice is earthly cruelty, that there might be "a charity in sin" (2.4.63), but Isabella insists on maintaining distinctions:

> *Isabella:* Better it were a brother died at once,
> Than that a sister, by redeeming him,
> Should die for ever.
> *Angelo:* Were not you then as cruel as the sentence
> That you have slander'd so?
> *Isabella:* Ignomy in ransom and free pardon
> Are of two houses; lawful mercy
> Is nothing kin to foul redemption.
>
> (2.4.106-13)

Ultimately, their debate results in threats of revenge:
> *Isabella:* Ha? little honor to be much believ'd,
> And most pernicious purpose! Seeming, seeming!
> I will proclaim thee, Angelo, look for't!
> Sign me a present pardon for my brother,
> Or with an outstretch'd throat I'll tell the

world aloud
What man thou art.

(2.4.149-54)

Angelo: Redeem thy
  brother
By yielding up thy body to my will,
Or else he must not only die the death,
But thy unkindness shall his death draw out
To ling'ring sufferance.

(2.4.163-67)

While Angelo's righteousness crumbles, we see the disguised Duke combining justice and mercy by trying Juliet's repentance (2.3.21-36) and counseling Claudio to be absolute for a death that the Duke's presence insures he will not suffer (3.1.5-41). Moreover, this presence, and in particular the Duke's eavesdropping on Claudio and Isabella, may direct our opinion of her passionate outburst against her brother's plea that she yield to Angelo.

Various critics have found repugnant Isabella's conviction that "more than our brother is our chastity" (2.4.185). But the Duke, our principal standard of ethics in the play, expresses no such repugnance; on the contrary, he describes Isabella as "having the truth of honor in her" and tells her "the hand that hath made you fair hath made you good" (3.1.164, 180-81). As for the possibility that she is affected by "her recoil from her rage at Claudio" (Stevenson 1966, 46), there is no evidence of it; not only has she previously threatened to expose Angelo, but before the Duke proposes his plot and assuming that Claudio will already have been executed, she tells Vincentio "But O, how much is the good Duke deceiv'd in Angelo! If ever he return, and I can speak to him, I will open my lips in vain, or discover his government" (3.1.191-94). If Isabella suffers any loss of innocence, it is due to the discovery of evil in Angelo and cowardice in Claudio; both discoveries make her justifiably angry, but they do not affect her virtue, which, as the Duke says, is bold (3.1.208). As for the "duplicity" of the plot, the Duke has answered the question before it was asked: "the doubleness of the benefit defends the deceit from reproof" (3.1.257-58).

The deceit is particularly interesting for the multiplicity of purposes it serves, as the Duke suggests more than once (3.1.199-204, 251-55). It allows the Duke to provide justice for Mariana and Angelo, mercy for Claudio, and pleasure for himself, in addition to allowing Isabella revenge on Angelo by turning his own scheme against him. The rightness of the plot is reinforced by the various episodes in the remainder of act 3, in which we see the Duke act justly toward various transgressors. After attempting in vain to persuade Pompey of the error of his ways, he concludes

Correction and instruction must both work
Ere this rude beast will profit.

(3.2.32-33)

Similarly, he tries to dissuade Lucio from slandering the Duke and, failing that, challenges him to stand by his slanders when the Duke returns (3.2.116-57). Finally, he comments on Angelo and on his own plans:

If his own life answer the straitness of his proceeding, it shall become him well; wherein if he chance to fail, he hath sentenc'd himself.

(3.2.255-57)

Craft against vice I must apply.
With Angelo to-night shall lie
His old betrothed (but despised);
So disguise shall by th' disguised
Pay with falsehood false exacting,
And perform an old contracting.

(3.2.277-82)

The Duke's use of craft is further justified when Angelo compounds his tyranny with treachery, refusing to pardon Claudio after all (4.2.120-26). Driven to further shifts to save Claudio, the Duke also tries to deal both justly and mercifully with "the magnificent and horrible Barnardine" (Rossiter 1961, 166), seeking to advise, comfort, and pray with him before his deserved execution (4.3.50-52). But being unwilling to damn Barnardine's soul, he is compelled to spare him.

But though Barnardine is spared, Isabella is not, for the Duke tells her that Claudio has been executed. His excuse for this cruel lie—

But I will keep her ignorant of her good,
To make her heavenly comforts of despair,
When it is least expected

(4.3.109-11)

—is hardly convincing. A more likely explanation for such behavior from a character who throughout the play tests and interrogates others is that he is preparing to test Isabella. The actual test, however, will not take place until the last act. Although Isabella's reaction to the news of her brother's death—"O, I will to him [Angelo], and pluck out his eyes!" (4.3.119)—is that of a stage revenger rather than a novice nun, it meets, in tenor if not in immediate action, with the Duke's full approbation:

              If you can pace your wisdom
In that good path that I would wish it go,
And you shall have your bosom on this
  wretch,
Grace of the Duke, revenges to your heart,
And general honor.

(4.3.132-36)

Revenge is likewise on Angelo's mind. Apprised of the Duke's return and of his proclamation that citizens craving redress of injustice may petition him upon his arrival, he is forced to consider, although he rejects, the possibility that Isabella may avail herself of this opportunity. Further, he explains his reason for proceeding (as he thinks) with Claudio's execution:

> He should have
> liv'd,
> Save that his riotous youth with dangerous
>   sense
> Might in the times to come have ta'en
>   revenge,
> By so receiving a dishonor'd life
> With ransom of such shame.
>
> (4.4.28-32)

Just as the Duke administers to Isabella

> a physic
> That's bitter to sweet end
>
> (4.6.7-8)

so to Angelo he administers praise that will make the blame to come more bitter (5.1.4-8, 9-16). After Isabella has made her accusation, he twists the knife further, pretending to disbelieve what he knows— in intent, at least— to be true and expressing an opinion of Angelo's character that— though popularly thought true— he knows to be false:

> By heaven, fond wretch, thou know'st not
>   what thou speak'st,
> Or else thou art suborn'd against his honor
> In hateful practice. First, his integrity
> Stands without blemish; next, it imports no
>   reason
> That with such vehemency he should pursue
> Faults proper to himself. If he had so
>   offended,
> He would have weigh'd thy brother by
>   himself,
> And not have cut him off.
>
> (5.1.105-12)

The Duke's behavior toward Angelo is compounded of justice, mercy, and revenge. It is just to make him suffer the mental anguish that he has inflicted on Claudio, Isabella, and Mariana. Like the criminals the Duke advised in his role as a friar, Angelo can receive mercy only after he has been made to feel true remorse. Finally, the entire plot against Angelo, with its disguises, accomplices, and presentation to him first of Isabella's false charge (which he believes to be true) and Mariana's true charge (which he believes to be false), is a classic revenge. Angelo is hoist with his own petard— caught doing what he condemned Claudio for doing, although he thought he was doing something much worse.

Although the Duke is entrapping Angelo, and allowing Lucio to entrap himself, we can feel little sympathy for them because of their shameless persistence in their evil ways. Angelo, still believing he can bluff his way out of the case against him, calls down the law's vengeance on his own head, even though he is perceptive enough to see that his secret is out and that several people are plotting against him:

> I did but smile till now.
> Now, good my lord, give me the scope of
>   justice,
> My patience here is touch'd. I do perceive
> These poor informal women are no more
> But instruments of some more mightier
>   member
> That sets them on. Let me have way, my
>   lord,
> To find this practice out.
>
> (5.1.233-39)

Similarly, Lucio attempts to cover his own guilt by slandering an innocent friar (and thereby, although he doesn't know it, again slandering his prince). It is therefore appropriate that, urged on by Angelo, "when Lucio plucks off the Friar's hood and discovers the Duke, the impudent buffoon also accomplishes his own exposure" (Oscar James Campbell 1943, 130)— and Angelo's.

Although both Angelo and Lucio recognize that they are caught, they react very differently to the knowledge. Lucio merely remarks "This may prove worse than hanging" (5.1.360), while Angelo begs to be punished:

> O my dread lord,
> I should be guiltier than my guiltiness,
> To think I can be undiscernible,
> When I perceive your Grace, like pow'r divine,
> Hath look'd upon my passes. Then, good
>   Prince,
> No longer session hold upon my shame,
> But let my trial be mine own confession.
> Immediate sentence then, and sequent death,
> Is all the grace I beg.
>
> (5.1.366-74)

The Duke, having given Mariana justice by marrying her to Angelo, seems willing to grant Angelo's request for immediate execution, but he phrases the sentence in such a way as to reassure the audience that death will not be allowed to mar the ending of this comedy. "An Angelo for Claudio, death for death!" (5.1.409) would be strict justice; but in fact no death has occurred, and it would therefore be unjust to execute Angelo. As Isabella says, in another context:

> His act did not o'ertake his bad intent,
> And must be buried but as an intent

That perish'd by the way. Thoughts are no
  subjects,
Intents but merely thoughts.

(5.1.451-54)

But at this point in the play, neither Angelo nor Isabella knows that Claudio is still alive. In addition to drawing out Angelo's punishment, the Duke seems to be testing Isabella's reaction to her brother's "murderer," although he is subtle about it. When Mariana asks Isabella to join her in pleading for Angelo's life, the Duke maintains that for her to do so would be so unnatural as to call down (or, in this case, up) supernatural vengeance:

Against all sense you do importune her.
Should she kneel down in mercy of this fact,
Her brother's ghost his paved bed would
  break,
And take her hence in horror.

(5.1.433-36)

Isabella nevertheless does join Mariana in her pleading, but her charity changes nothing, since the Duke continues to uphold Angelo's death sentence and Angelo himself professes to prefer death to mercy (5.1.455, 474-77). It is not until Claudio is revealed to be alive that the Duke pardons Angelo, and the "quickening" in the latter's eye indicates, presumably, that he has resigned himself to life (5.1.494-95).

Yet even as he forgives Angelo, Claudio, and Barnardine, the Duke declares

I find an apt remission in myself;
And yet here's one in place I cannot pardon.

(5.1.498-99)

Since Lucio's crime seems to us far less serious (and far more amusing) than Angelo's, this statement and the Duke's later speeches concerning Lucio have been taken by some critics as indications that Vincentio is vengeful rather than just in this case. In fact, however, the Duke behaves toward Lucio very much as he has toward Angelo, allowing him to suffer the apprehension of justice for his crimes and then extending mercy. Even the punishment that Lucio suffers is merely justice to the woman he has wronged.

If the Duke is more vindictive in his threats to Lucio than in those to Angelo, it may be excused on a number of counts. Angelo has, up to the point of his "temptation" by Isabella (and excluding his treatment of Mariana), been reputed a righteous man; even his condemnation of Claudio, although harsh, is within the law. It is difficult to imagine Lucio being able to plead a previous good character, and his victim, the Duke, is apparently entirely innocent of the accusations Lucio makes against him. Angelo's wicked designs remain merely "intents"; Lucio, on the other hand, actually commits the crime of "slandering a prince." Finally, Angelo professes remorse and craves punishment; Lucio makes excuses and seeks to avoid punishment. At the end of the play, there is hope that Angelo may truly reform; Lucio, like Barnardine, is forgiven because of the virtue of the Duke, not because he has deserved forgiveness or because we can even imagine him deserving it.

The play as a whole, and particularly the ending, have provoked a variety of critical responses. Oscar James Campbell, who sees the play as a satire on hypocrisy—as embodied by Angelo—and libertinism—as embodied by Lucio—finds the ending false: "the play does not end as a satire should. Angelo is exposed but not ejected from the play with a final burst of derision. . . . Angelo deserves not a wife, but scornful ridicule" (1943, 125). If we assume that the "darker" aspects of the play do, in fact, indicate a satirical intention, this may be a valid criticism, but not every critic is willing to make such an assumption: "however much incidental gloom or bitterness may be there, the themes of mercy and forgiveness are sincerely and not ironically presented" (Tillyard 1950, 139). Knight takes an entirely different angle, viewing Angelo and Lucio as neither satiric figures nor objects of mercy but, in some degree, the heroes of the piece: "The punishment of both is this only: to know, and to be, themselves. This is both their punishment and at the same time their highest reward for their sufferings: self-knowledge being the supreme, perhaps the only, good" ([1930] 1949, 94-95). Finally, Chakravorty sees the play as a statement that mercy is superior to justice: "Punishment is the function of justice and belongs to the State which is an impersonal machinery; mercy or forgiveness, on the other hand, is the function of a superior ethic and belongs only to the individual" (1969, 259).

None of these positions seems to me to be completely accurate. *Measure for Measure* does not appear to be any kind of sustained satire. Angelo is not, at least at the beginning, entirely without merit, and even Lucio behaves well in trying to help his friend Claudio and urging Isabella on against Angelo. Although there are elements of the puritan in Angelo and of the swaggerer in Lucio, neither character is merely a conventional type; they are too individual to be the straw men of satire. On the other hand, there is no direct evidence that either character attains self-knowledge, except insofar as Angelo learns that he is not proof against temptation; Lucio merely attains self-pity. Although mercy is certainly a theme in the play, it is not presented in isolation or in opposition to justice or revenge. Rather, what the Duke achieves at the end of the play is a balanced combination of these three qualities, in which malefactors are lured by the devices of the stage revenger into betraying themselves, threatened with the force of justice, and finally pardoned. Angelo and Lucio do not get off without suffering or

322

without making at least some restitution; Isabella does not declare that she loves Angelo, nor the Duke that he loves Lucio. The Duke alone is able to extend mercy (though others can ask for it), but he does not do so by nullifying justice. Rather, by applying "craft against vice," he takes revenge against wrongdoers, establishes justice for everyone, and at last extends a limited forgiveness to Angelo and Lucio not because they deserve it, but because his power, wisdom, and magnanimity allow him to be generous.

Joel Levin

SOURCE: "The Measure of Law and Equity: Tolerance in Shakespeare's Vienna," in *Law and Literature Perspectives*, edited by Bruce L. Rockwood, Peter Lang Publishing, Inc., 1996, pp. 193-207.

[*Levin clarifies the distinction between "law" and "equity"—explaining that while law gives a civilization a set of impartial rules by which to govern its people, equity allows for the subjective but necessary qualities of mercy, fairness, and tolerance. Levin then examines how* Measure for Measure *treats the issues of law and equity by revealing through the course of the action that each is inadequate without the other; for example, at the start of the play the Duke's Vienna is described as libertine and ungovernable, but during the course of the play, Angelo's Vienna is shown to be unfairly rigid. Levin points out that by the end of the play, there are signs that the Duke's notion of equity and Angelo's (and Isabella's) notion of the rule of law will be combined and thus tempered by one another to create a better form of government for Vienna.*]

Legal history often appears to be little more than a contest between law and equity. Law's defenders hold that individuals cannot be trusted to reach the right decision outside formal, firm, knowable, fixed, reliable rules. Equity's defenders argue that rules can hardly account for the diversity of social situations which are governed by them or for the need for creativity, mercy, individuality, and perceived justice which constitute the mix often labeled "equity". Notions as ancient and universal as "the rule of law" and "a government of rules not men" suggest a wariness, all too terribly and shamefully justified, of unfettered equity. Yet, the history of autocracies from Rome through the Soviet Union indicates the shortcomings of rules without equity or, more exactly, how little protection is afforded by sure and definitive standards bereft of equity and fairness.

No legal system more completely formalized the dichotomy between law and equity than Shakespeare's 17th century England. The national law courts— King's Bench, Common Pleas and Exchequer— applied the legal rules, and often served as a bulwark against unfettered power: both at the county and the national level. However, rules were often harsh on one hand and ineffective on the other. Relief could be sought in separate courts with their own judges, applying a different law: the law of equity. For example, if a mortgage contract allowed a creditor both to retain the real estate and keep all funds if a debtor missed even one payment, the debtor could go to the Chancellor in the equity courts and receive an "equity of redemption" to regain the overcharges (or, more or less, the excess principal). Similarly, if property were required to be sold and the seller refused, equity could order to have done what ought to be done, and imprison indefinitely the recalcitrant seller. The division between law and equity was, significantly, carried over into a division of both bench and bar.

The friction between law and equity is apparent as Shakespeare's *Measure For Measure* opens. The Duke of Vienna, wounded by criticisms of his leniency and individualistic remedies in administering the city, announces he will leave Vienna indefinitely. While absent, the city will be governed by his stern deputy, Lord Angelo, "a man of stricture and firm abstinence" (1.3.12). Angelo will provide an antidote to the lax rule of the Duke, who admits

> We have strict statutes and most biting laws,
> The needful bits and curbs to headstrong
>   weeds,
> Which for this fourteen years we have let slip,
> Even like an o'ergrown lion in a cave,
> That goes out not to prey. Now, as fond
>   fathers,
> Having bound up the threat'ning twigs of
>   birch, only to
> Stick it in their children's sight
> For terror, not to use; in time the rod
> Becomes more mocked than feared; so our
>   decrees,
> Dead to infliction, to themselves are dead,
> And Liberty plucks Justice, by the nose;
> The baby beats the nurse, and quite athwart
> Goes all decorum.
>
> (1.3.19-31)

The Duke remains in Vienna, though disguised as a friar, and observes Angelo's arrest of Claudio for fornication with the now pregnant Juliet. Angelo sentences Claudio to death, despite Claudio's assertion that

> Thus stands it with me: upon a true contract
> I got possession of Julietta's bed.
> You know the lady, she is fast my wife,
> Save that we do the denunciation lack
> Of outward order. This we came not to,
> Only for propagation of a dower
> Remaining in the coffer of her friends,
> From whom we thought it meet to hide our
>   love
> Till time had made them for us.
>
> (1.2.148-156)

Frank Corrado as the Duke and Laura Patterson as Escalus in Act I, scene i of the San Jose State University's 1997 production of Measure for Measure.

Isabella, Claudio's sister, delays taking her vows as a nun in order to plead with Lord Angelo for mercy. After some hesitation and indecision, Angelo suggests that should Isabella give up her virginity to him—that is, commit the very crime for which he is sentencing Claudio—he would release Claudio. After initially rejecting this blackmail offer, Isabella is convinced by the Duke in his priestly disguise to agree, but to substitute (in a darkened place) Angelo's jilted former fiancé, Mariana. This masquerade works and Angelo unknowingly consummates his relationship with Mariana, but nevertheless reneges on his agreement and orders Claudio executed. However, Angelo is unmasked at the end by the Duke, who has conveniently saved Claudio from death and suggests a courtship might begin between the Duke and Isabella. Meanwhile, Angelo's fate is determined jointly by the Duke and Isabella: he both condemns Angelo to death and orders him to marry Mariana, but then allows Isabella to pardon him from the first edict.

This tidy solution carried out, the play nevertheless raises dramatic and moral questions, and has engendered sharp criticism. Is the Duke's leaving merely a device to show how personally invaluable he is to the governance of the city? Is fornication not only to be unpunished but in fact rewarded? Are the positive laws of the state meaningless? Why should Angelo, guilty of corruption, rape, and attempted murder, be pardoned? In fact, why should a priest's advice, even a fake noble one, be to encourage the deflowering of Mariana? How satisfying is a conclusion allowing Mariana's marriage to Angelo, especially as a happy ending to a comedy? Most suspiciously, how convincing is what Coleridge called a "painful play" and "hateful work", where abuse of power, licentiousness, fornication, weakness of the will, and deceit is left unpunished; where the characters are variously weak (Angelo and Claudio), self-righteous and morally rigid (Isabella), a braggart, liar and opportunist (Claudio's friend, Lucio), or morally opportunistic and willing to ignore the moral precepts and social norms of the day to obtain their ends (Mariana and the Duke)? Particularly, how satisfying is this play when considered that it was immediately preceded by "*Othello*" and immediately succeeded by "*King Lear*" and "*Macbeth*"?

The answer to these concerns, and the defense of the play, lies with understanding how Shakespeare used equity to ameliorate the harshness of traditional rules and to allow for an idea new to societies emerging from the early Renaissance: the idea of tolerance. The Duke is established as a teacher (or "Doctor," as the masters of equity jurisprudence were sometimes called) who wished to demonstrate the need for rule by equity, although a peculiar form of it. The society needed to be shown the consequences of positive law without equity, and of an administrator who applies rules without thought of fairness. The primary teaching device becomes the law of the marriage contracts, and the principal teacher the ambiguous and deceitful character of Angelo. However, neither the applicable legal rules nor the actual equities of the situation can be taken as the entire explanation of either the play's or the Duke's strategy. As a matter of law, the contracts fail technically, and as a matter of equity they fail for immorality. Rather, in the play the contracts serve as dramatic props to establish justice through an unfolding demonstration of an emerging idea of toleration.

I. The Dilemma of The Contracts

Let us look briefly at the marriage contracts, or rather, the facts behind them. Claudio and Juliet would be married but for some difficulty with Juliet's family providing the dower. In every other way, they treat each other as husband and wife. The legal rules operate as a bar, but it is a guiding principle of equity that it generally declares as done what ought to be done. Angelo and Mariana provide the converse. Mariana's dowry, too, is lost. But the prevention of the marriage is due to the greed of one of the parties to the marriage— the grasping Angelo— and not to the outside force of a recalcitrant family. When Mariana's brother dies at sea, she loses her brother, her fortune and her one loyal betrothed, Angelo.

> She should this Angelo have married; was affianced to her by oath, and the nuptial appointed: between which time of the contract and limit of the solemnity, her brother Frederick was wracked at sea, having in that perished vessel the dowry of his sister. But mark how heavily this befell to the poor gentlewoman: there she lost a noble and renowned brother, in his love toward her ever most kind and natural; with him, the portion and sinew of her fortune, her marriage dowry; with both, her combinate husband, this well-seeming Angelo.
>
> (3.1.217-228)

There is no legal bar to their marriage. Nothing is being held back by the family, if there is one aside from her

late brother. Yet a free-ranging equity would defeat the purpose of the terms of the original agreement.

If the two near-contracts of marriage both fail for want of a dower, the character differences lie in the reaction of the potential grooms. Both brides wish to continue the romance, with Mariana pining for Angelo and Juliet bedding with Claudio. Angelo, however, refuses to have any more to do with Mariana, and in fact

> Left her in her tears, and dried not one of them with his comfort; swallowed his vows whole, pretending in her discoveries of dishonor: in few, bestowed her on her lamentation, which she yet wears for his sake; and he, a marble to her tears, has washed with them, but relents not.
>
> (3.1.229-234)

The failed contracts involve, conversely, illegality (the fornicating couple) and injustice or inequity (the estranged couple). In both cases, the marriages were prevented by a lost dower, or more simply, by the lack of money. The ultimate beneficiary of the dower is *de facto* the intended husband who requires it, and thus, in the financial sense, the moral high ground belongs to Claudio. But in terms of the societal respect, the official opinion is

> If any in Vienna be of worth
> To undergo such ample grace and honor,
> It is Lord Angelo.
>
> (1.1.22-24.)

Crucial, then, to the Duke's demonstration of the justification of equity is not merely his appointment of Angelo as the strict defender of the rule of law. It is seeing Angelo as the reneger of his promises who has made use of technical defenses to extricate himself from a financially unprofitable bargain. The Duke observes Angelo's flawed character, and if unsure what form it will take once unleashed, allows it free reign for further revelation.

The plot, then, is set in motion when the formal political system is headed by a legal formalist. Angelo's behavior constitutes, in fact, the plot. He condemns Claudio to death unfairly, with the unfairness arising not so much because fornication appears (to our eyes), at best, a minor offense, or because the misbehavior in engaging in sexual conduct without marriage is due to extrinsic and arbitrary circumstances concerning a family reluctant to grant a dower; but because the sentence is so suddenly, harshly and violently imposed without a hint of notice. Claudio appears the victim because the law which springs to life does so at his expense, almost *ex post facto*.

Why, however, is the elaborate facade of the Duke's leaving the city, Angelo's promotion to the sovereignty, the Duke's wearing a friar's garb, the condemnation of

Claudio, and the deceptive coupling of Angelo and Mariana necessary to show that the rarely enforced laws on the books should remain unenforced? The answer is that equity, while a corrective to the tyranny of bad legal rules, could not be put directly in the service of fornicators and those wronged by greedy but not breeding former betrotheds. That is, equity originated from a religious moral code which condemned non-traditionally legitimate sexual practices on the one hand, and gave little comfort to those unable to fulfill the terms of an unexecuted contract on the other. Even modern notions of equity which are stripped of their religious justifications and structures (although equity's voice almost never reverberates without deafening theological echoes) do not necessarily endorse fornication and contract breach.

II. The Inadequacies of Equity and Mercy

Equity, then, is not enough. There is no suggestion that the rules of Vienna are bad, wrong, improper, illegitimate, immoral, discriminatory, unfounded, indefensible, arbitrary, capricious, or barbaric. In fact, rejudged by the civil sovereign turned holy man they might even be right. Shakespeare uses a cleric of a church not known for smiling on sexual relations outside marriage to devise two plots contrary to canon law: encouraging (via Angelo) and pardoning (via Claudio) fornication.

In fact, the entire plot might be seen as establishing, in a primitive way, the idea of tolerance. To tolerate an act is not necessarily to endorse or approve it. Rather, an act might consistently be tolerated and condemned at the same time by the same person. The notion of tolerance is relatively recent in political theory, and has been justified by a whole host of reasons equally recent in origin: the autonomy of the person, the limited power of the state, the notion of individual rights, the marketplace of ideas, and a general rise in cultural, moral, political, and spiritual relativism. None of those reasons would appear compelling to an Elizabethan. Instead, the 17th century observer, if unhappy with the political and legal structures he or she faced, would not need to compromise, but to choose a new (and probably equally intolerant) set of rules or principles. The choice would not be whether to forgive or tolerate fornication but whether to endorse it.

The traditional analogue to what we now consider toleration is, of course, mercy. Mercy allows us to condemn the act but pardon the actor. A large part of the role of the women in the play is to articulate the case for mercy. (Mercy is often portrayed as a peculiarly feminine virtue). Initially, Claudio's friend Lucio enlists Isabella in the plot to save her brother, telling her

> . . . All hope is gone,
> Unless you have the grace by your fair prayer

to soften Angelo.

> . . . . .
> . . . Go to Lord Angelo,
> And let him learn to know, when maidens
>   sue,
> Men give like gods, but when they weep and
>   kneel,
> All their petitions are as freely theirs
> As they themselves would owe them.
>   (1.4.65-67, 79-84)

Isabella, in fact, makes the traditional appeal for mercy, which gains the traditional response.

> *Isabella.* I do beseech you, let it be his fault,
> And not my brother.
> . . . . .
> *Angelo.* Condemn the fault, and not the actor
>   of it?
> Why, every faults condemned ere it be done.
>   (2.2.35-36, 38-39)

Mercy tends to be a somewhat clumsy devise, whereby the pleader needs both to join in the condemnation and beg in an unflattering manner. Moreover, in such cases there is usually no good reason for mercy, except the plea "that we all are weak, so let's not be too harsh." This is exactly the reason suggested by Isabella, and deserved (more or less) the response of Angelo.

> Those many had not dared to do that evil,
> If the first that did th' edict infringe
> Had answered for his deed."
>
>   (2.2.91-93)

No special reason is given why Claudio should be spared, and given how clear was the law and how widespread the (perceived) problem of licentiousness, punishment (if less harsh punishment) appears reasonable. If the Duke were sitting in Angelo's place, he would have had few, if any, attractive options when an appeal of mercy were made. Claudio's act was open, continuing, likely to be repeated, well-known and clearly in violation of the law. The attractiveness of mercy as a remedy lies in its ability to take care of the *sui generis* case. Almost every special reason for special treatment in such cases is lacking here, and the Duke would be hard pressed to justify mercy without undermining the law itself.

Dramatically, then, mercy must be tried and must fail. The slippage between law and equity can then give a foothold to tolerance. The legal rules are not judged to embody tainted values, and the equitable principles can not be put in the service of impious and sexually immoral claimants. Yet the requirement of mercy needs to be fulfilled: condemn the act but tolerate the actor.

If mercy is inappropriate, and the law is not in need of repair, then allowing the wrong-doing to exist is the only remedy. The Duke accomplishes this by double negation. The act of banning Angelo is discredited.

III. The Concept of Governmental Tolerance

Governmental tolerance, in its full-blooded form, has (at least) four elements: lack of punishment of the offender, an indication by authority of the problematic nature of enforcement against such offenders generally, a policy of curbing such enforcement, and rights in the offender to carry out the offending activity.

These four elements might variously be labeled the elements of mercy, leniency, weak tolerance, and strong tolerance. It is the suggestion of weak tolerance in the play which is a relatively new concept, and which is the concept raised by the slippage between law and equity.

The slippage might be seen as follows:

The legal rules concerning marriage contracts, sexual conduct, and criminal punishment are always valid, never directly attacked, but never lauded. Equitable principles—fairness, *lex talionis* (appropriate punishment for an offense, where the greater the offense, the greater the punishment) and enforcement and completion of inchoate and unperformed contracts—offer a remedy but not one guaranteed or formal. The equitable principles operate as a wide-spread standard by which to judge the law, but insufficiently weighty to convert it. The point of *Measure For Measure* is, then, to legitimize the role of equity by allowing it to operate as part of the governing structure. Equity, though, in the special form of a head of government who acts as a private detective to uncover hypocrisy and investigate police facts remains indispensable. As such, it remains indispensable. More dependable would be a concomitant attitudinal shift, where the lessons of equity are used to curb the hardness of received rules. "Tolerance" would be the name of such an attitude.

Mercy and leniency are the traditional province of equity. Equity, at least in English courts and in Shakespeare's version of Viennese equity, would be rooted in a Christian idea of morality, even if that idea passed first through neo-Platonist and then Aristotelian filters. Mercy operates independently of the culpability of the actor under such ideas. Any person, regardless of the evil he has done, can qualify. Leniency is a stronger concept and suggests that the mercy is not pure, but justifiable. Clearly, the entire drama of *Measure For Measure* suggests good reasons for not enforcing the rules. Put simply, whatever the general validity of the rules, they would be unfair if applied here. For example, it is clear Shakespeare wants the audience to agree that Mariana should have been married to Angelo, and Juliet to Claudio, although the contractual promises of a dowry were not met. This is true even though such promises were not, at least to the Elizabethan mind, indefensible

preconditions of performance.

The dispensation, and correcting of such wrongs without challenging the rules, comes in the form of mercy. The clearest act of mercy occurs when the rules themselves are the least likely to cause objection to their strict enforcement: where, for example, they would call for a severe penalty to be given to Angelo for any number of felonious acts: *i.e.,* extortion, blackmail, and the beasts of power and (apparent) murder. Isabella makes a plea for mercy, nonetheless. No reason is given and none need be for mercy. However, as Angelo himself made clear earlier, the law itself cannot provide for mercy.

Law itself can not be, or traditionally has not been, lenient. Either a rule applies or it does not, and the consequences of such rules also apply in an all-or-nothing manner. The chief local spokesman for rules, and a man who is clearly cognizant of their violation when they get in his way, is Lord Angelo. When the law turns against him, Angelo's speech is that of a hypocrite caught, but not one hypocritical about rules

> O my dread Lord,
> I should be guiltier than my guiltiness,
> To think I can be undiscernible,
> When I perceive your Grace, like pow'r divine,
> Hath looked upon my passes. Then, good prince,
> No longer session hold upon my shame,
> But let my trial be mine own confession.
> Immediate sentence then, and sequent death,
> Is all the grace I beg.
>
> (5.1.369-377)

A rule-oriented, common-law partisan here is unable to seek a remedy to save himself in equity. Certainly, Angelo is an individual whose moral depravity would allow him to make any viable argument for self-preservation, if only he knew of a legitimately persuasive one. It is left to Isabella to introduce an equitable notion of leniency to save him. Leniency does not require disregard of rules, it merely suggests that there are times when there are better reasons for following equitable principles than for obeying legal rules. Isabella argues for the life of the man whom she thinks has killed her brother not by suggesting that all rules should be followed, but by saying that her

> . . . brother had but justice
> In that he did the thing for which he died.
> (Act V, Sc. I, Lns. 451-452.)

Equity does not invalidate the rules, but merely justifies non-enforcement in a particular situation. In so doing, it can also suggest the possibility of a generalized theory of non-compliance, which may encompass a category (or assortment) of acts which, though illegal, fail to justify judicial sanction.

IV. Protecting Bad Intentions

Of course, it is just such a notion of tolerance which arises from this complicated interplay of law and equity. By the play's end, all is outwardly restored as before, without any wide-spread attack on the validity of the rules, and yet with a clear notion that they would not be enforced. The underlying misconduct which is considered morally reprehensible throughout the play, and which is itself never justified, is thus no longer banned. There is, of course, no change in the *de jure*, statutory law, at least in the criminal code. Rather, the reader is left with the impression that such misbehavior, while not being approved, will undoubtedly be tolerated. Isabella suggests this first by pointing out that while there may be evidence of misbehavior, which is reprehensible, it is basically not the concern of the state, the public, or the law:

> His act did not o'ertake his bad intent,
> And must be buried but as an intent
> That perished by the way. Thoughts are not
>   subjects,
> Intents but merely thoughts.
>
> (5.1.454-457)

Here, "not subjects" means not subject to law. Protected are bad intentions, a relatively modern notion about tolerating free thought and giving the individual sovereignty. Suddenly, there is a right of privacy with regard to matters of the mind and heart. As long as there was not extra, overt, additional action, there should be no basis for legal intervention.

This notion of weak tolerance is strengthened by the final speech of the play. There, the Duke allows all to return to their former position without any thought of subsequent punishment. Instead, thanks are given to various characters, accolades and directions for the future are passed out (joy to Mariana, love to be bestowed by Angelo, thanks to the senior advisor Escalus) and, in general, a suggestion that everyone should return home without fear:

> So, bring us to our palace, where we'll show
> What's yet behind, that's meet you all should
>   know.
>
> (5.1.541-542)

The concept of tolerance, then, triumphs, but only through guises, private pleas, and indirection. There is no overt triumph for equity as overruling the legal rules. These rules stay in place, their harshness the *de facto* standard. The Duke never establishes any right to do the "wrong thing"—the test of a truly tolerant authority—and never authorizes equitable excuses for failing to follow the rules. The behavior remains illegitimate, fornication is never considered excusable, yet the Duke himself encouraged the act. It was his idea, after all, to permit Angelo's scheme to trade a night in bed with Isabella for her brother Claudio's life to go forward, and the Duke adds to the deception when he suggests that Mariana substitute for Isabella. Whatever the injustice of Angelo's failing to wed Mariana, the plot portrays the Duke, a secular ruler, exploiting his role as a religious figure, to have an unmarried, presumptively virginal, woman engage in a sexual union with Angelo:

> . . . Go you to Angelo; answer his requiring with a plausible obedience; agree with his demands to the point; only refer yourself to this advantage; first, that your stay with him may not be long; that the time may have all shadow and silence in it; and the place answer to convenience. This being granted in course—and now follows all—we shall advise this wronged maid to stead up your appointment, go in your place. If the encounter acknowledge itself hereafter, it may compel him to her recompense: and here, by this, is your brother saved, your honor untainted, the poor Mariana advantaged, and the corrupt deputy scaled. The maid will I frame and make fit for his attempt. If you think well to carry this, as you may, the doubleness of the benefit defends the deceit from reproof. What think you of it?
>
> (3.1.247-264)

The defense for this impropriety, this "deceit", is the "doubleness of the benefit". The formal, juristic mechanisms are insufficient to cure the situations, but the ideas inherent in the legal and equitable concepts allow this kind of circuitous remedy. The target of the remedy is the person who is the embodiment of the rules, Angelo, and he is clearly to be taught a lesson. As the Duke stated earlier, this is in order to "heal the rupture and cure the dishonor."

For the traditionalist, it might be argued, equity is embodied in the head of state. The power to dispense pardons, commute sentences, exempt citizens from rules which apply to others, and order (natural) justice generally belongs to the king, or here, the Duke. What the Duke does is not more private in matters of justice than in other matters of state. The head of Elizabethan and Stuart equity, after all, was the monarch's chief advisor, the Lord Chancellor. Thus, it might be argued by a traditionalist, the acts of the Duke in dispensing rough and *sui generis* justice to his subjects constitutes equity as usual. This argument misses two points: first, even though England shows the least reliance on natural law as a system in Europe, a large, even cumbersome, equity judiciary and bar existed, with a life apart from that of the monarch; and second, announcements in equitable courts had precedential value, had influence with all the bench and bar, and were intended to be judicial announcements with a general force and effect. By not using the tainted Angelo or the judicious Escalus in the process of resolving the disputes and problems of the city, the Duke fails to make the leap from a weak and budding tolerance to a right grounded in precedent not to have the state intrude in private matters.

"Strong tolerance" in the form of formalized rights is not established in the Duke's Vienna by the actions portrayed in the play, but may be on the horizon. Authority has publicly intervened to both condemn and allow a wrong, creating a fact on the ground that may be the beginning of the authorization of strong tolerance. The story of the travails of Claudio, Mariana, Angelo, Isabella, Juliet and the Duke give rise to this possibility.

STRUCTURE

Anthony Caputi and **Gregory W. Lanier** tackle the problem of locating unity in a play as complex as *Measure for Measure*. Both assert that any consistent pattern to the play depends on its structure. Caputi, for example, remarks that while themes such as Christian ethics, atonement, and mercy run through the play, none of them is expansive enough to unify all of the dramatic plots and subplots. Further, Caputi argues that Shakespeare intentionally scattered his major characters "irregularly" in order to indicate that character development was not the central issue in the play. Caputi notes that what stands out in *Measure for Measure* is the unusual structure of the acts and scenes: while some are filled with action, others— particularly Act V— level out to long stretches of conversation. Caputi suggests that Shakespeare relied on the long conversational scenes to give his audience time to reflect on his principal focus— that civilization may stumble but it is bound to recover— which is what it does as the play draws to a close.

Gregory W. Lanier on the other hand observes that the play divides into halves— the first comic and the second tragic— so that structurally as well as thematically the play falls into the genre of tragicomedy. Lanier notes that it is left to the Duke to shift the play from its tragic to its comedic structure as he works behind the scenes, advising Isabella and Mariana and stage-managing the bed-trick. Lanier also notes that many of the play's tragic scenes are mirrored in the second half of the play by their direct comic opposites. Ultimately, Lanier explains, what the Duke and the structure of the play anticipate is Isabella's transformation from someone desiring revenge for the apparent execution of her brother to someone willing to forgive Angelo for his heinous crimes. This "tolerance" or "moderation" on Isabella's part signals the end of extremes which mark the play's tragic first half, thus allowing the action to shift into the multiple marriages which characterize comedy.

Anthony Caputi

SOURCE: "Scenic Design in *Measure for Measure*," in *JEGP*, Vol. LX, 1961, pp. 423-34.

[*Caputi argues against the idea that an "ethical pattern" or set of moral themes such as justice, mercy, or Christianity organizes* Measure for Measure. *Further, he does not believe that the play is organized around any particular character or characters. Instead, he asserts that the play is intentionally structured for dramatic effect around "long, slowly developing scenes" which clearly resolve themselves in the last act into a positive view of civilization.*]

Much of the best criticism of *Measure for Measure* has focused on what one critic has called the "ethical pattern of the play." Critics have by no means agreed on the nature of that pattern or its function, but an impressive number have agreed that the play is governed structurally by a conceptual scheme. The strength of this criticism derives from the fact that the play is unusually rich in ideas— particularly ideas about law and Christian doctrine. Yet to grant that these critics have properly identified the play's subject matter is not to accept their assumption about the play's structure: that an "ethical pattern" determines it, that a single or even multiple thesis about the law, Christian justice, mercy, or atonement can or ought to account for every detail of character, every placement of scene, and every fleeting allusion to the order of St. Clare. Whatever its value, this approach to the play reveals an unmistakable weakness in its inability to deal with the total play without at some point invoking special responses dependent on a jurist's knowledge of Elizabethan law or elaborate theories of revision or textual corruption.

Indeed, something in the nature of this criticism has prevented a conclusive answer to the most basic question about the play: What kind of play is *Measure for Measure*? Is it, as Hardin Craig insists, "gloomy and unpropitious"? Or is it, as R. W. Chambers argues, a paean to Christian forgiveness? Or is it, as one reviewer said of the recent production at the American Shakespeare Festival, "Lovely, rollicking, grand farce"? This question can probably never be answered with the certainty with which one might answer a similar question about a Plautine farce. Yet perhaps a fresh approach to the question can be undertaken if, while keeping what critics of the play's "ethical pattern" have said of its subject matter, we abandon their assumption about its structure and examine the play as a dramatic entity, one that achieves its peculiar power largely through a dramatic pattern. Such an approach inescapably emphasizes the large units from which the play is built rather than particular speeches, the general lines of development rather than nice points of theology and law. But in the process it directs attention to that dynamic unity so essential to a play's capacity to move an audience to a particular state of thought and feeling.

And perhaps that is where the emphasis belongs.

Actually, the dramatic pattern of *Measure for Measure* is clearer than it might otherwise be, because of the rather clumsily joined seams that have prompted universal claims of textual corruption. This unfinished quality has left exposed an unusually clear outline of tensions and movement. Clues to this pattern are most easily found in two fairly obvious, if neglected, features of the play: Shakespeare's sporadic use of important characters and the dramatic design of certain scenes. In *Measure for Measure* Shakespeare has used his principal characters so irregularly as to imply unmistakably that character was not his primary concern. Angelo, for example, though extremely important early in the play, drops out of it between the end of Act II and IV.iv. The Duke, though he emerges in III.i to dominate the action, plays a rather slight part before Act III. Isabella, though a center of interest through III.i, becomes largely instrumental to the intrigue thereafter. And Mariana, though crucial to the action, is hardly prominent at all, indeed is not even mentioned until the end of III.i. The dramatic design encountered in key scenes is, perhaps, even more closely linked to the dramatic pattern that we are seeking to clarify. It is strange that so little has been made of the unusual design within scenes. Though the play has the usual five acts, almost three of them are given over to long scenes in which very little happens, scenes in which, instead of action, we get an inordinate amount of talk. After Act I, in which the action advances very rapidly, Act II settles down to a series of rather static interviews. First we have the long scene in which Escalus examines Pompey and Froth, then the long scene of Angelo's first interview with Isabella, then the short scene involving the Duke and Juliet, and then the long scene of Angelo's second interview with Isabella. And the same is true of most of Act III. Only at the end of Act III does the action regain speed and variety to press into Act IV, where events move very rapidly. But in Act V the action again levels out, this time into one long trial scene.

Clearly any attempt to describe the structure of *Measure for Measure* must come to terms with these structural peculiarities. That they are what they are by intention seems beyond question: they are far too prominent to be the result of carelessness or a botched text. And that they are closely related to each other seems no less clear. It is altogether likely, in a play where great attention has been given to long, slowly developing scenes, often involving no more than two characters, that important characters will drop out of sight for long intervals. Thus Angelo does not appear from the end of Act II to the end of Act IV. He is a central character in his major scenes with Isabella, but almost irrelevant in Act III, where Claudio's interviews with the Duke and Isabella hold the stage. Thus the Duke appears only briefly in Act II, since here every resource is drawn upon to heighten the effect of Angelo's inter-

views with Isabella. And thus Isabella, after her big scenes in Acts II and III, becomes an instrumental character since interest subsequently centers in the Duke.

If we begin with the observation, then, that *Measure for Measure* gives unusual prominence to long, slowly developing scenes— indeed, that more than half of the play consists of such scenes— surely it would not be unreasonable to suppose that they contribute heavily to the play's power. An examination of these scenes reveals that all, with the notable exceptions of the short scene between the Duke and Claudio (III.i) and, for different reasons, the last act, are similar in structural outline in that all resemble informal debates or disputations. Because they are conversational and spontaneous, they are, of course, different from the formal debate. But, like all debates, they typically involve two characters who articulate, carefully and at some length, *opposing positions*.

This feature alone has important implications for *Measure for Measure*. Clearly, in scenes wherein characters argue something at length, as compared with scenes— like the banquet scene in *Macbeth*— in which events develop rapidly and unexpectedly, the dual effect is that they draw the audience's critical faculty into play and insist upon a certain critical distance. But this feature, if pressed further, leads to still more important observations. If we compare the scenes in question (excepting, again, the Duke's scene with Claudio and the last act), we discover that in none of them are the opposing positions reconciled. On the contrary, all end in unresolved states of conflict: characters meet, talk, discover differences of opinion, discuss their differences, and part only after having heightened the tension expressed by their disagreement. Moreover, if we compare the opposing positions expressed in these scenes, we also find a certain consistency among them. In each the conflict involves one character who takes, essentially, the position of civilized man with confidence in his codes and decorums, and a second character who takes, essentially, the position of natural man with a vivid sense of his frailties and imperfections. In II.i, Escalus speaks for civilization and Pompey for the "poor fellow that would live"; in II.ii, Angelo defends the law while Isabella defends natural man against it; in II.iv, Angelo and Isabella change roles; and, subsequently, Claudio, the Duke, and Lucio take their turns. As the argument develops and the positions crystallize, they become increasingly irreconcilable. We are made distinctly aware that the positions taken by the characters are drawing apart until, at the end of each scene, the situation seems hopelessly stalemated— far worse than it was at the beginning.

Of course even this general description requires some qualification. However stalemated Escalus and Pompey seem at the end of their scene, obviously their scene is qualitatively very different from Angelo's scene with

Isabella. By setting aside the low-life scenes for a moment, however, we can see that all the other pertinent scenes are designed to convey a vivid impression of the incompatibility of civilized and natural man, to bring before us in almost paradigm form a dramatized challenge to civilized or moral life. By communicating an awareness of the inadequacy of law and decorum to man's condition and, conversely, an awareness of man's inadequacy to his laws and codes, these scenes generate a disturbing sense of the very precarious foundations on which civilized life is built— what, for the purposes of this play, can be called a distinct sense of moral distress.

In view of the prominence of these scenes in the first three acts and of the qualitatively comparable scene in Act IV, in which the Duke waits for Claudio's pardon only to learn that Angelo is capable of depths he dreamed not of, we can tentatively infer that the dramatic pattern of the first four acts of *Measure for Measure* is calculated to make us feel much of what the Duke feels in III.ii, that "there is scarce truth enough alive to make societies secure, but security enough to make fellowships accursed: much upon this riddle runs the wisdom of the world" (ll. 219-22). This speech offers the play's most explicit statement about the represented condition of civilized life, the most direct glance at the disparity between what man fondly aspires to and what he is. To support this description of the play's power in more detail, however, we must go back to the scenes that dramatize this perception, and particularly to the details of design within scenes that control the sense of moral distress. We can then consider how the last act is designed to dispel it.

It is relevant, first, to look at two conspicuous loose ends in the pattern thus far described. The long scene involving Escalus, Froth, and Pompey in II.i plainly dramatizes the typical conflicting positions and plainly shows them to be irreconcilable; but surely we do not respond to this scene with anything like distress. And if we say that the famous scene between the Duke and Claudio generates a sense of distress, we must admit that in this instance the distress does not proceed from marked disagreement. However consistent with the dramatic pattern thus far discerned, these scenes also deviate from it; and they deviate with good purpose.

The structural analogy between the Escalus-Pompey scene and the other interview scenes provides an important insight into the function of the low-life characters in the play. Actually, the analogy is hardly limited to this scene: throughout the play Pompey, Mistress Overdone, and Barnardine are at odds with law and morality. In other words, throughout the play they dramatize a conflict like that dramatized rather painfully in the scenes involving Angelo, Isabella, Claudio, and the Duke. Yet certainly we do not respond to the conflict as they dramatize it with feelings any more

serious than a sense of exhilarating incongruity, perhaps even of exhilarating futility. By and large, we are in sympathy with what they represent, however much we may resent it. They are the eternal yardbirds of civilized life, who, like Pompey Bum, will always muddle through to the easiest jobs— even in prison. They represent the intractability of human nature: its refusal to submit to laws and codes, indeed, in the case of Barnardine, its contemptuous defiance of them. Moreover, these low-life offenders have their counterpart among the representatives of law and order: Elbow, with his genius for getting things wrong side to, is unmistakably a comic variation on Escalus and Angelo. The scenes involving these characters provide a comic exhibition of the precariousness of civilized foundations that counterpoints the more serious dramatization of the other scenes. They furnish a kind of comic obbligato that prevents the feelings of distress aroused from becoming too intense, and tempers these feelings with complexity of outlook. To put the matter another way, the low-life scenes control the quality of the other interview scenes by putting them in a framework that adds comic dimensions to otherwise serious exhibitions of moral disorder; they dramatize what must always be funny from the detached point of view of the comic muse: the hilarity of man's high designs.

The Duke's great scene with Claudio, on the other hand, is nothing if not serious. Traditionally, it has given critics trouble because it is almost too serious, because it expresses so gloomy a view of life as to be out of keeping with the long-range optimism of the Christian doctrine everywhere in evidence. But the scene also poses difficulties of a much less subtle kind. At this point in the play we have no evidence that Claudio, who has not appeared since Act I, will not face death courageously; and though we find it normal that a friar would console a condemned man, we are surprised to learn that so impressive a consolation comes to nought in the next scene, where Claudio seems to have forgotten everything the Duke as friar has said. Perhaps the first point to be made about this scene, accordingly, is that it has a very slight function in the chain of episodes: it in no significant way advances the action. Its function, rather, seems to be to intensify the peculiar power of the scenes immediately preceding and following it. Coming just after Isabella's scenes with Angelo and just before her scene with Claudio, this scene, and especially the Duke's elaborate consolation, serve chiefly to focus the energies generated up to this point, to heighten the play's pervasive sense of the insecurity of human affairs.

> Reason thus with life:
> If I do lose thee, I do lose a thing
> That none but fools would keep: a breath
> thou art,
> Servile to all the skyey influences,
> . . . Merely, thou art death's fool,

Engraving from Galerie des Personnages
de Shakespeare *(1844).*

. . . Thou art not noble,
. . . Thou'rt by no means valiant,
. . . Thou art not thyself,
. . . Happy thou art not,
. . . Thou art not certain,
. . . If thou art rich, thou'rt poor,
. . . Friend hast thou none,
. . . Thou has nor youth nor age,
But as it were an after-dinner's sleep,
Dreaming on both . . .
. . . and when thou art old and rich,
Thou hast neither heat, affection, limb, nor
   beauty,
To make thy riches pleasant. What's yet in
   this,
That bears the name of life? Yet in this life
Lie hid moe thousand deaths; yet death we fear,
That makes these odds all even.

(III.i.6-41)

This is not a tragic perception of insecurity, qualified, as it is, by the low-life characters and seen, as it is, with considerable detachment. But it is the dominant perception, and one that emphasizes the detached sobriety rather than the gaiety of comedy.

In our inspection of other scenes, we need not deal here with the short scenes, like those met chiefly in Acts I and IV. They clearly have the main function of laying down the probabilities of action and character necessary to support the play's big scenes. Scenes as important as those involving Angelo and Isabella in Act II, however, require detailed examination. Both characters have prompted considerable comment, and perhaps no Shakespearean character has occasioned so much disagreement as Isabella. The traditional alternatives for her—that she is either an exalted ideal or a travesty on womanhood—seem violently extreme and dangerously simple. It is probable that Shakespeare's contemporaries found much to admire in her intensity of purpose, her quickness of mind and aptness of tongue, and her courage. It is doubtful, however, that even they were meant to warm to her decision to save her chastity by permitting her brother to die. On the contrary, apparently Shakespeare has consciously forced this dreadful choice on her—dreadful because neither alternative is satisfactory—and, in order to scale down her attractiveness somewhat, has made her put this choice in unusually cold, succinct, almost painfully simple terms.

Better it were a brother died at once,
Than a sister, by redeeming him,
Should die forever.

(II.iv.106-108)

Then Isabel live chaste, and brother die;
More than our brother is our chastity.

(II.iv.184-85)

        Dost thou think, Claudio?
If I would yield him my virginity,
Thou mightst be freed.

(III.i.96-98)

Unquestionably, Shakespeare has very carefully scaled her down in other ways. Lucio's speeches in I.iv and II.ii help to adjust our attitude toward her. In the nunnery scene (I.iv) he begins with a parody, "Hail, virgin," and continues with tongue in cheek. Despite all attempts to read his praise of her literally ("I hold you as a thing enskied and sainted"), there is nothing in his character or in his subsequent description of her to justify the reading. Obviously, he does not fool Isabella, who replies, "You do blaspheme the good, in mocking me" (l. 38). Then later, during Isabella's first interview with Angelo (II.ii), Lucio's remarks, "You are too cold" (ll.45, 56), serve unmistakably to underline this shortcoming in her. For all Isabella's admirable qualities, the truth is that she is out of her element in the world of Lucio, Angelo, and even Claudio. Her most stirring quality is the cold fire she suggests when arguing law and morality. Though we view her with sympathy and admiration, we do so with considerable detachment.

Angelo is a far simpler matter than Isabella. In Acts I and II we have every reason to believe reports that he is a man of strictest virtue. Indeed, Shakespeare carefully withholds all information about Mariana until late in III.i, so that we may believe these reports. In Act II we see him take a position on the question of Claudio and withstand firmly the successive assaults made on it by Escalus (II.i), the Provost (II.ii), and Isabella (II.ii). Up to this moment he is a kind of abstract extreme, a point of view with respect to the problems that have developed. After he has succumbed to Isabella's physical attractions, he is the only character whom we know through introspective soliloquies. (The Duke speaks soliloquies, but they consist of choral comments on the state of society.) Yet even this interest in Angelo's character is very carefully controlled: just when he is becoming most interesting, he drops out of the play for almost two acts, and our attention is whisked away to Claudio, Isabella, the Duke, and Mariana. Like Isabella, he is distinctly subordinate to a larger design that invites us to view him with fascination, but with a fairly detached, critical fascination.

When Isabella appears before Angelo in II.ii, both characters represent extremes: Isabella is as much as possible like a nun without actually being one, and Angelo (partly because Shakespeare has withheld all information about Mariana) is very like a monk. In this juxtaposition alone consists a great deal of the interest of this and their second interview, especially when toward the end of this scene their relations take so sensational a turn. The structural interest of the scene lies in the development of the conflict between them, a development that Lucio and the Provost very carefully accentuate. At the beginning of II.ii, Isabella takes the most difficult of positions for one pleading for Claudio's life: she admits that she hates Claudio's sin to the point of being reluctant to plead for him. Angelo, on the other hand, takes a position that even at the outset seems impregnable: he implies that he could do something, but he "will not do't" (l. 57). With these positions established, much of the suspense of the scene proceeds from the attempts to reconcile them. We hope that Isabella will win Angelo over; but she is only half-hearted and he immovable. Only gradually does she catch fire, and then, as she drives narrow wedges into his argument and their positions seem to draw together, the scene builds to the shocking disclosure that she has succeeded only in arousing his desire for her. This sensational turn throws open a whole new set of possibilities, and in the second interview Angelo and Isabella take entirely new positions, though every bit as irreconcilable as the first.

The second interview builds in much the same way, but rests on different devices. Here the suspense is produced and sustained first by Isabella's apparent failure to understand Angelo's proposal. When she has understood it and rejected it, tension continues to mount as he becomes firmer and finds that he can charge her with inconsistency, while she attacks him, with increasing heat, for baseness. The acceleration of tempo and excitement is again, we should notice, correspondent to the intensifying antagonism between the points of view represented. At the end of the scene we are aware not only that they are farther apart than before, but also that there seems to be no satisfactory compromise for the conflict they have dramatized.

Following the next scene—the interview between the Duke and Claudio—the scene between Isabella and Claudio is in structure and effect very like the Angelo-Isabella interviews. Here the suspense is sustained by Isabella's reluctance to reveal Angelo's proposal and her decision. At this point she serves to develop in the audience a new apprehensiveness, in that she, too, has had her confidence shaken: she has come to fear for Claudio's sense of honor, for the genuineness of his commitment as a civilized man. Yet despite all her caution, the characteristic disparity of positions develops, to emerge clear in Claudio's declaration that "Death is a fearful thing" (l. 115).

Taken as a group, these scenes trace the dominant dramatic pattern of the first two-thirds of the play, and lead to the explicit impasse of the scene in Act IV where the Duke's first plan is upset by Angelo (IV.ii). In the main they convey a distinct perception of the flimsiness of civilized life: of the distressing inadequacy of man's efforts at civilization and of the comic incongruity of his pretensions to it. But our description of the play's dramatic pattern is hardly complete until we consider the Duke's role in all this, and the ways in which the long final scene dispels this serio-comic distress.

The Duke's role is sufficiently important to consider at some length. After his brief appearances in Acts I and II, he emerges in III.i to dominate the action. Thereafter, he is either eavesdropping from some dark corner or deliberately ordering events: making arrangements with Isabella, Mariana, the Provost, and Friar Peter. To see the importance of his presence in the scenes from III.i to the end, we need only consider what we know because of his disguise that the characters in the play, except for Friar Peter, do not know. Most significantly, we know that the Duke *is* in disguise, that he is observing everything, and that he is capable at any moment of averting disaster. Surely the chief result of this knowledge is our confidence that Angelo cannot succeed, that the action is destined for a favorable outcome. The Duke's disguise, then, serves chiefly to control the sense of distress aroused and to lead, with probability, to its dispersion in the last act. After his emergence in III.i, this sense of distress gradually diminishes as he takes an increasingly prominent hand in the action. As we are assured that he intends to avert catastrophe, our awareness of moral disorder gradually gives way to an awareness that the characters perceive moral disorder where, in fact, it does not have absolute sway. The emergence of this reassurance is very carefully controlled— particularly through the Duke— until in the last act the machinery of the plot is thrown into reverse: where in the first four acts the characters have continually met with worse developments than they— or we— have expected, in the last act they continually meet with better.

A corollary function of the Duke's disguise is that it also diminishes the long-range melodramatic suspense that could have proceeded from these otherwise very melodramatic scenes in favor of fixing our attention on the moral quality of the action. Suspense in this play is not built on such questions as "How will this turn out?" Because of the Duke, we know or, at least, are reasonably certain about how it will turn out. Instead, we are invited to attend closely and critically to what is happening at the moment in scenes contrived to generate a short-range suspense of their own. The Duke's disguise, accordingly, is yet another part of the general pattern calculated to encourage us to view the separate events of the play critically.

Having quietly rearranged everything to his satisfaction, the Duke simply sits back in Act V to let the intrigue work itself out. Clearly the primary function of Act V is to cause our sense of distress to yield to a sense of reassurance, to supplement our perception of the precariousness of civilized foundations with the perception that with understanding man can regulate, if not remedy, his difficult situation; indeed, he can occasionally achieve the poetic justice that the Duke in his temporary omniscience manages at the end of the play. It is, finally, a sense of assurance that, however precarious the foundations of civilized life, man will somehow sustain it.

This reassurance proceeds from the last act in a number of ways, some of which involve solid evidence for it, others of which are little more than artifice. To begin with, it proceeds from the reversed pattern of developments already mentioned. More important, and more conspicuously, it proceeds from the leisurely exposure and punishment of Angelo and even of Lucio. If the last act is long for any reason, it is because the Duke is so unhurried about exposing Angelo. Instead of denouncing him immediately, as well he might, he permits him to extend himself as completely as possible. And after he has exposed him, he prolongs his anguish by permitting him to believe that he is to die for Claudio's death. This leisureliness is important. To relieve the intense antipathy that has been built up against Angelo and still conclude the play with forgiveness for him, Shakespeare had to dramatize his punishment. To do this, he had to entangle Angelo so profoundly in the Duke's web that at the moment of the Duke's unhooding Angelo disgraces himself publicly and

completely. At this moment, Angelo's overwhelming sense of failure is almost adequate to expiate the crimes that he actually succeeded in committing.

Lucio, on the other hand, is a rather different matter. As many have observed, he is something of a scapegoat in the sense that, though he deserves his punishment, it seems in part contrived to relieve feelings of righteous indignation aroused in other quarters. However true this may be, Lucio serves chiefly at this point to support our growing assurance of the efficacy of law, not only by providing the Duke with an occasion to exercise it, but partly by providing him an opportunity to identify and punish its most serious enemy in the play. For all Lucio's lightheartedness, his is in many ways the low point of cynicism in the play: unlike Pompey and Barnardine, he is a man in whom we expect beliefs; yet he has none. He has no serious loyalties and no capacity for guilt or repentance because he is incapable of a serious commitment of any kind. There is, accordingly, a subtle justice in the Duke's active disapproval of him that has very little to do with the Duke's personal pique. In one sense Lucio's punishment represents the finest adjustment, though hardly the most important, that the just forces make toward the end of the play.

At any rate, the length of this final act is necessary to strengthen the sense of confidence and assurance we have felt all through it so that these feelings are sufficiently strong to be dominant at the end. The marriages serve simply to support these feelings. That they do not produce the rejoicing produced by an *As You Like It* means no more than that Shakespeare did not intend them to. *Measure for Measure* is, throughout, a play in which our concern about the characters' fortunes is distinctly subordinate to our concern about the fortunes of civilization. It is civilization as it is at issue in the careers of Isabella, Claudio, Angelo, the Duke, Pompey, Barnardine, and others that chiefly enlists our attention and engages our feelings.

It is doubtless for this reason that so many critics have been drawn to an abstract analysis of the play's ideas. No one would deny that the play abounds in ideas. But however important, they do not alter the fact that, no less than *King Lear* or *Twelfth Night*, *Measure for Measure* is, structurally, a dramatic rather than an intellectual persuasion and that, as such, its capacity to move an audience to an enlightened state of feelings depends largely on the direction and control of its dramatic pattern. It is only this kind of pattern that can put the marriages at the end in a reasonable perspective, a perspective in which they are not required to complete a conceptual formulation, but serve quite simply and effectively to support the affirmation of faith in civilization on which the play closes. By viewing the play from this point of view we do not solve all problems, it is true, but we do eliminate many pseudo-problems by making dramatic sense of a play that never asked to be a dark intellectual puzzle.

Gregory W. Lanier

SOURCE: "Physic That's Bitter to Sweet End: The Tragicomic Structure of *Measure for Measure*," in *Essays in Literature*, Vol. XIV, No. 1, Spring, 1987, pp. 15-36.

[*Lanier disagrees with those critics who see* Measure for Measure *as a structural failure with an unsatisfying, tacked-on ending. By contrast, he contends that Shakespeare intentionally divided the play into halves, with the first eight tragic scenes linked to the last eight comic scenes by one intermediary scene. Lanier explains that Angelo's "transgressions" (displayed in his hypocritical behavior toward Claudio, Isabella, and Mariana) inform the play's tragic first half while Isabella's "tolerance" (displayed when she begs the Duke to spare Angelo's life) is responsible for the play's comic second half. Ultimately, Lanier argues that the split between tragic and comic is in fact what gives* Measure for Measure *the very unity that many scholars believe the play lacks.*]

In 1949 E. M. W. Tillyard bisected *Measure for Measure* into potentially tragic verse and dissolutely comic prose; some years earlier G. Wilson Knight asserted that the symbolic sequence of transgression, judgment, and redeeming mercy provides an innate structural integrity. This polarity in critical responses has proved to be nearly as enduring as the play itself. Cynthia Lewis provides a short summary of this division in her recent article:

> Readers who, like Harriett Hawkins, find the play's ending "not only aesthetically and intellectually unsatisfying, but personally infuriating," usually see *Measure for Measure* as split in tone, structure, and viewpoint. . . . On the other hand, many readers see *Measure for Measure* as unified. Arthur Kirsch, who sees *Measure* as a radically Christian play, concludes that the Duke's secret plotting represents the hidden workings of Providence. . . .

Lewis' argument, based on a consideration of "Duke Vincentio not as a plot device or a Providential figure, but as a human character," is a solid and welcome answer to a number of recent excoriations of *Measure for Measure*. Richard Wheeler's assessment is, perhaps, more indicative of the prevailing voice:

> The ending of *Measure for Measure* does not "play-out" earlier developments, it plays them down; it looks back to the previous action with an averted, mystifying gaze that has its emblem in Vincentio's anxiety-denying movement from one character and one issue to another in the final scene. The failure of these characters (and these issues) to respond to him—as in Isabella's silence and the silence of Claudio and Angelo—mirrors Shakespeare's inability to find an ending that responds fully to the whole action. The kind of integration of inner impulse with external reality that is established in a successful play, and which provides a paradigm for the comic action of *As You Like It*, is not achieved in *Measure for Measure*. . . . Instead of clarifying either positively or negatively, the relations between comic art and experience, Shakespeare seeks unearned reassurance in a comic ending that cannot fully acknowledge previous developments in *Measure for Measure*.

I strongly disagree with Wheeler's statement that *Measure for Measure* fails to provide an ending that "responds fully to the whole action," and I do not believe that the "integration of inner impulse with external reality" defines a successful play. Rather than judging this controversial play by noting its failure to fit into a preconceived notion of what it *should* be, I think it would be more fruitful to examine the play's disposition, to see what the structure of the play itself reveals. *Measure for Measure* is, structurally, a tragicomedy. It is a juxtaposition of two dramatic modes, tragedy and comedy, carefully poised to create a cohesive, resonant unity.

But we need not allegorize *Measure for Measure* into a redemptive pageant with the Duke as Christ-like regisseur to discover its unity. To do so, in fact, obscures the structural division fundamental to the play's essence. The structure of *Measure for Measure* is, indeed, sharply divided: eight tragic scenes cast the characters into catastrophe: a medial scene wrenches the action about; eight comic scenes restore social harmony. Moreover, as Tillyard noted, the shift from tragedy to comedy precisely coincides with a shift from verse to prose. Spatially, as Northrop Frye has said, *Measure for Measure* presents "a dramatic diptych of which the first part is a tragic and ironic action apparently heading for unmitigated disaster, and the second part an elaborate comic intrigue which ends by avoiding all the disasters." We should, then, approach *Measure for Measure* as we would approach a diptych altar painting: we should look for correspondence, balance, resonance, and continuity of theme between structural elements while comprehending the essential contrast between and separation of halves. The integrity of *Measure for Measure* is created through just such a correspondent balance of discontinuous parts. A careful equipoise of antithetical elements informs the play's intrinsic structure; contrast, not similarity, is the dominant mode. The tragic actions, textures, and themes that initiate the play find their measure and fulfillment in the inclusive comic denouement. A fundamental resonance binds tragic fragmentation to comic cohesion and achieves a unified balance through the correlation of contrasting parts, and the main element of that resonance is the temperance introduced into the play's action by the Duke.

The first half of *Measure for Measure* carefully establishes a tragic pattern—the conflict of inflexible wills that leads to the disintegration of social order. Claudio tenaciously clings to a "weary and loathed worldly life" regardless of the cost; Angelo indulges the tyrant of his "sensual race," assured of exploiting his office without retribution; Isabella, by steadfastly preserving her chastity, drives the play towards the tragic resolution of violation or violent death. But comedy lurks in the shadows. When Isabella, Claudio, and Angelo have locked themselves into tragic confrontation, the "mad fantastical Duke of dark corners" steps forward and conjures a comic ending. With "cold gradation and well-balanced form," the Duke tempers conflict into concord, thereby recreating stability in Vienna. Significantly, the Duke's method is recognizably comic. The disguises, deceptions, substitutions, and choreographed spectacles he employs are counterparts to Rosalind's festive manipulations, not Iago's vicious plots. The action and texture of the play invert once the Duke applies "Craft against vice." The play initially sweeps us along with concern for the bloodshed, outrage, and death which threaten the characters but concludes with festive, ceremonial, and almost ritualistic marriages. And that emblematic inversion is the essence of Shakespearean tragicomedy. As the play progresses we should be aware that Shakespeare is gently coercing us to subordinate our engagement with the feelings of the characters to our comprehension of their emblematic movement within the larger pattern of the play's dramatic structure.

Claudio's arrest for his affair with Juliet— perhaps a benign form of sexual license but transgression nonetheless in Angelo's eyes— initiates the tragic movement. The opposition of liberty to restraint provides the pattern for succeeding tragic complications in the play:

> *Lucio.*   Whence this restraint?
> *Cla.*   From too much liberty, my Lucio. Liberty,
> As surfeit, is the father of much fast;
> So every scope by the immoderate use
> Turns to restraint.
>
>   (I.ii.116-20)

Surfeit causes restraint with an almost binary exclusiveness. Claudio, unaware of moderation, expresses his dilemma in antithetical terms: surfeit vs. fast, scope vs. restraint. Further, the remainder of Claudio's speech implies that humans are naturally intemperate, unwilling and unable to control their appetites:

>   Our natures do pursue,
> Like rats that ravin down their proper bane,
> A thirsty evil; and when we drink, we die.
>   (I.ii.120-22)

Man is not merely frail but severely flawed, a slave to his rapaciousness and doomed to actively seek his "proper bane." Such a description, emphasizing both the appetite's abrogation of the reason and the inevitable destruction that results from that imbalance, pre-

sents man as a tragic figure, a life-long calamity who, fallen, can only fall further. Claudio's rhetoric establishes the tragic model followed not only by himself but by other characters in *Measure for Measure*. In each case the character moves away from moderate actions towards excessive reactions, whether it be to excessive restraint (Isabella and, initially, Angelo) or excessive liberty (Claudio, Lucio, and the fallen Angelo). Without proper government to curb the pursuit of the "thirsty evil," disintegration on both the individual and social levels inexorably occurs.

A spreading dissolution of the Viennese community is evident quite early in the play, and it is firmly linked to Claudio's excessive libertinism. What appears to be on the periphery of the tragic concerns in *Measure for Measure*, the comedy of Lucio and his companions, contains a second pattern central to the play's tragedy:

> *Lucio.*   Thou conclud'st like the sanctimonious pirate, that went to sea with the Ten Commandments, but scrap'd one out of the table.
> *2 Gent.* 'Thou shalt not steal'?
> *Lucio.*   Ay, that he raz'd.
> *1 Gent.* Why, 'twas a commandment to command the captain and all the rest from their functions: they put forth to steal.
>
>   (I.ii.7-14)

The pirate captain proves an apt example for Lucio and Pompey, even for Claudio and Angelo. Each had a "function" to follow; each dismisses the law as his convenience (we may read appetite) demands. Lucio habitually flaunts the statutes prohibiting fornication and slander to pursue his moment's fancy. Pompey swears that pandering would be a lawful trade "If the law would but allow it" (II.i.224) and refuses correction, promising to follow Escalus' advice "as the flesh and fortune shall better determine" (II.i.250-51). Neither character will allow any law to impede the indulgence of their "flesh and fortune"; their resolute devotion to gratification demonstrates the accuracy of Claudio's simile comparing man to rats. Claudio also exhibits this disregard for the law, admitting that he lacked the denunciation of "outward order" when he took possession of Juliet's bed (I.ii.138). And, lest we are hastily inclined to exonerate that mutually committed offense, we must admit that Claudio and Juliet's sexual relationship parallels Lucio's escapade with Kate Keepdown. The more chilling resonance, however, links Pompey to Angelo. Pompey would have the law allow pandering; Angelo will have it allow rape. When Angelo determines to give his "sensual race the rein" (II.iv.159), he fulfills the pattern started by Lucio's joke about the sanctimonious pirate. Angelo is in the position to raze any law from the table; he can fulfill Pompey's wish and force the law to allow any transgression he fancies. No law alone sufficiently deters man's natural tendency to glut his appetite. In Pompey's words, "they will to't" unless one manages to "geld and splay all the youth of the city" (II.i.227-30). Again the language and logic are binary, entertaining only the extremes of indulgence or eradication. What began as comic by-play becomes a major tragic theme, an indication of the tightly conceived balance between comic and tragic elements. Man's innate impulses drive him to gratify his animalistic appetites, and his reason, the law over his body, is swept aside. Man's proper balance seeks a median between ascetic denial and unrestrained sensuality. Hence, proper government would seek to temper desires, to channel excess into appropriate vessels. "Firm abstinence," however, is as dangerous as "sharp appetite," and as Lucio and Claudio are guilty of excessive liberty, there are those guilty of excessive restraint— Angelo and Isabella.

An icy reserve cloaks Angelo from his first entrance. The Duke's famous "heaven and torches" (I.i.27-47) speech is less remarkable for its Biblical allusions than for its penetrating characterization of Angelo. The image distinguishes an outer, radiant charity from an occult self-absorption, and firmly links Angelo to those who inordinately husband their resources. The Duke later articulates this implied duality:

> Lord Angelo is precise;
> Stands at a guard with Envy; scarce confesses
> That his blood flows; or that his appetite
> Is more to bread than stone.
>
> (I.iii.50-53)

Angelo's controlled appearance is the antithetical complement to Lucio's licentious behavior. Yet the Duke suggests a kinship between them, that stubborn self-control thinly covers the blood and appetite Angelo must possess. Unfortunately, Angelo remains blind to his hypocrisy, and, thinking himself the paragon of humanity, imposes his unnatural restraint on the inhabitants of Vienna.

Once he has assumed the Duke's position, Angelo governs with the inflexible severity of a self-appointed and self-righteous saint. The rigid standard of austerity becomes Angelo's measure of justice:

> You may not so extenuate his offence
> For I have had such faults; but rather tell me
> When I that censure him do so offend,
> Let mine own judgement pattern out my
>   death,
> And nothing come in partial.
>
> (II.i.27-31)

Angelo's response to concupiscence is eradication, in Pompey's terms to "geld and splay all the youth of the city," including himself. This repression presents the antitype to Claudio and Lucio's pattern. Imposed restrictions based on inhuman self-denial cannot elimi-

nate the offenses of sexual license since that desire is ingrained in man's nature. The infliction of "stricture and firm abstinence" (I.iii.12) only further emphasizes the opposition of license to restraint. Moderation is required, but Angelo's justice does not recognize a *via media*.

Although the Duke has admonished Angelo to "enforce or qualify the laws / As to [his] soul [seemed] good" (I.i.65-66), Angelo wields strict enforcement, tyrannically demanding that all adhere to his personal asceticism. And Claudio rightly complains that Angelo's sword of justice cuts capriciously:

> Thus can the demi-god, Authority,
> Make us pay down for our offence by weight.
> The words of heaven; on whom it will, it
>   will;
> On whom it will not, so; yet still 'tis just.
>
> (I.ii.112-15)

The conflation of just authority with the inscrutable, perhaps arbitrary, design of heaven is striking. It seems that Angelo, swollen in his power, elevates temporal and limited prerogatives to a level beyond their normal scope. Angelo sees himself as the "demi-god, Authority," a posture confirmed by Escalus:

> . . . my brother justice have I found so severe that
> he hath forced me to tell him he is indeed Justice.
>
> (III.ii.246-48)

The stringent puritanism Angelo professes allows him to tyrannize with a righteous indifference. Angelo claims to judge with an immaculate perception, mistakenly combining the immutable justice of providence with the petulant (and maybe malevolent) authority of man. Significantly, Angelo betrays his limitations, seizing only "What's open to justice" (II.i.21)— Claudio's simple and benign case— while impatiently leaving Escalus to sort out matters with the obfuscating Pompey. Juxtaposed, these two judgments point up the haphazard nature of Angelo's oppression. The "words of heaven" do not fall where they will; only the whims of a self-deceived deputy do.

Angelo is not the only character whose self-deception unnaturally restrains the appetite. Isabella denies her humanity as well. Whereas Angelo assumes affected gravity and precise control to restrain his impulses, Isabella relies on the seclusion of the convent to avoid her sexuality. Immediately after the Duke laments the lapse of strict statutes in Vienna, we find Isabella about to embrace even stricter regulations. Moreover, though the rules of the convent are stringent, Isabella thinks them lax. This dissatisfaction seems over-zealous, and one may conclude that Isabella desires to proscribe the world, or perhaps just the male sex, with consecrated walls. Isabella, wishing for a "more strict restraint /

Upon the sisterhood, the votarists of Saint Clare" (I.iv.4-5), and Angelo, imposing his puritanic law without mitigation, pursue the same ideal. Both demand an unyielding and religiously based code that would prohibit all illicit (and most licit) sex. Both "rebate and blunt [their] natural edge / With profits of the mind, study, and fast" (I.iv.60-61), and expect the same from others. But neither the puritan's gown nor the nun's habit can unconditionally suppress the "wanton stings and motions of the sense" (I.iv.59). Their repressions are only momentary, and we should expect their sexual desires to erupt violently.

The Duke has previously hinted that Angelo's self-deceptions may not last: "Hence shall we see / If power change purpose, what our seemers be" (I.iii.53-54). We are not then surprised that Angelo succumbs to his blood's appetite when he meets Isabella. What should be emphasized, though, is how Shakespeare chooses to present this action. Shakespeare depicts Angelo's fall into concupiscence in explicitly tragic terms, signaled by the fragmented internal landscape of the psychomachia. The calm smugness of Angelo's assertion, "'Tis one thing to be tempted, Escalus, / Another thing to fall" (II.ii.16-17), markedly contrasts with the frantic search for identity a few lines later:

> Can it be
> That modesty may more betray our sense
> Than woman's lightness? Having waste
>   ground enough,
> Shall we desire to raze the sanctuary
> And pitch our evils there? O fie, fie, fie!
> What dost thou, or what are thou, Angelo?
> Dost thou desire her foully for those things
> That make her good?
>
> (II.ii.168-75)

The "strong and swelling evil" (II.iv.6) of Angelo's innate desires will no longer submit to restraint. Clearly, the rise of Angelo's blood indicates his position as the play's tragic protagonist, and we expect his fall from his false seeming to initiate a series of violent incidents. Indeed, by choosing to give "his sensual race the rein" (II.iv.159), Angelo converts tyrannous restraint into licensed tyranny. Angelo's attempt to extort sexual intercourse from Isabella fulfills Pompey's wish. As the "demi-god, Authority," Angelo allows whatever transgression he desires, confident that the outward "austereness of [his] life" (II.iv.154) shall overweigh Isabella's accusations. And as Angelo undergoes tragic fragmentation, so does his society: "Thieves for their robbery have authority, / When judges steal themselves" (II.ii.176-77). Angelo's attempt to restrain the world in his own image fails, and Vienna becomes a society where faults are still

> . . . so countenanc'd that the strong statutes
> Stand like the forfeits in a barber's shop,

> As much in mock as mark.
>
> (V.i.318-20)

Though Angelo is determined not to make a "scarecrow of the law" (II.i.1), his repression does not eradicate license from Vienna.

As the play's action then shifts from the court to the prison, the play's tragic texture is distinctly felt. Angelo and Isabella now stand in diametric conflict: Angelo demands Isabella's chastity and Isabella will not yield. Yet the same obsession with sensuality that leads Angelo to give up his restraint leads Isabella to excessively restrain her sexuality, as her rejection of Angelo reveals:

> . . . were I under the terms of
>   death,
> Th' impression of keen whips I'd wear as
>   rubies,
> And strip myself to death as to a bed
> That longing have been sick for, ere I'd yield
> My body up to shame.
>
> (II.iv.100-04)

A noble sentiment, but couched in unfortunate images. Isabella has long safeguarded her chastity with inordinate compulsion, and when Claudio suggests she yield to Angelo, Isabella's response becomes a perverse sexual hysteria:

> O, you beast!
> O faithless coward! O dishonest wretch!
> Wilt thou be made a man out of my vice?
> Is't not a kind of incest, to take life
> From thine own sister's shame? What should
>   I think?
> Heaven shield my mother play'd my father fair:
> For such a warped slip of wilderness
> Ne'er issued from his blood. Take my defiance,
> Die, perish! Might but my bending down
> Reprieve thee from thy fate, it should proceed.
> I'll pray a thousand prayers for thy death,
> No word to save thee.
>
> (III.i.135-46)

No one, I think, condemns Isabella for resisting Angelo's immoral pressure. But the frenzied viciousness of those last four lines damns her. Isabella is in "probation of a sisterhood" (V.i.75); to pray for the death of her brother at the least contradicts the duty of her Christian charity. The last remaining social bond— between brother and sister— violently rips apart. The choices Angelo, Isabella, and Claudio have made create a series of forces moving inexorably towards tragic conflict. The only options are dilemmatic. Isabella either sacrifices her chastity and moral sanctity or Claudio dies. Since either action is irreversible, both would satisfy the logic of the play's tragic structure. The binary opposition that pervades the play leads to tragedy's brutal choice: rape or death. And lacking the necessary dramatic indications for a possible alternative, we can only ponder which shall occur.

Thus the tragic impetus of *Measure for Measure* swells, capped by Isabella's furious outburst. The elements of the play are precisely arrayed on either side of the gulf separating liberty from restraint, the increasing dismemberment of order demanding a violent and irrevocable action to complete the tragic structure. Comedy, however, ensues. The "old fantastical Duke of dark corners" (IV.iii.156) steps forth and assumes control of the play's action, converting tragedy into comedy.

The Duke's emergence as the director of *Measure for Measure*'s action marks the shift from tragic to comic panel in the plays diptych structure. His appearances had been brief and intermittent; after he approaches Juliet his presence on stage is almost continuous. The metamorphosis of tragedy into comedy requires a catalyst, and the Duke alone possesses the freedom and authority to effect that change. The Duke's secular authority in Vienna stands without question. His "terror" is only lent to Angelo, and he resumes it with stunning elan during the comic reversal. Moreover, the Duke's adoption of a friar's robe, along with the clerical habits he appropriates (shriving Juliet, confessing Claudio and Mariana), indicates at least a partial assumption of ecclesiastical authority as well. But more important than his ethical role as head of church and state is the Duke's freedom of movement, more exactly his freedom of influence. Only the Duke ranges across all the strata of Vienna's social levels, contacting (and manipulating) characters from Mistress Overdone and Abhorson to Escalus and Angelo. As we observe the Duke initiate his design, we become aware of his role as the play's chief manipulator, placing each piece in meticulous order to realize the conclusion he creates. To assert that the Duke envisions a comic ending, though, perhaps oversteps the boundaries of the direct evidence in the play. *Measure for Measure* lacks the number of revealing soliloquies *Hamlet* conditions us to rely on for glimpses of motivation. The accumulated evidence of the Duke's actions must provide most of our insight. From the opening of the play the Duke seems to be striving to alter the tendencies of his subjects:

> I say, bid come before us Angelo.
> What figure of us, think you, he will bear?
> For you must know, we have with special soul
> Elected him our absense to supply;
> Lent him our terror, drest him with our love,
> And given his deputation all the organs
> Of our power.
>
> (I.i.15-21)

Certainly the "special soul" that elects Angelo reveals a complex purpose in the Duke's mind, especially since he passes over the more reliable (and better suited) Escalus. The Duke may expect Angelo's renowned rigor to effectively check the license in Vienna (I.iii.35-43), yet he also suspects that rigor to be fallacious (I.iii.53-54). By dressing Angelo in borrowed "terror" and "love," the Duke disguises Angelo in a manner analogous to the comic disguises of *As You Like It* and *Twelfth Night* where disguise becomes a means by which identity is discovered, not hidden. Viola's "man's attire" (*TN* I.i.SD) evokes the actual humanity hidden behind the refined facades Orsino and Olivia erect; Rosalind's "doublet and hose" (*AYL* III.ii.215) elicit a natural gentility from Orlando's tongue-tied rusticity. Further, the disguises allow Rosalind and Viola insight into their identities as well. Viola learns of her role in the play's concatenation of "place, time, and fortune" (*TN* V.i.250), and Rosalind learns that her feminity makes *As You Like It*'s "doubts all even" (*AYL* V.iv.25). Similarly, Angelo's assumption of "absolute power and place" (I.iii.13), surrounded with images of dressing, provides the spark of self-awareness that leads to his recognition of the "strong and swelling evil / Of [his] conception" (II.iv.6-7). The consequence of Angelo's perception, the "monstrous ransom" proposed to Isabella, indicates a potentially tragic result from a comic motif. But the Duke's freedom to "Visit both prince and people" (I.iii.45) supplies the means to forestall tragic consequences if the Duke exercises sufficient ability and foresight.

By disguising himself as a friar, the Duke places himself in a position to direct the action covertly, subtly guiding Vienna's inhabitants towards proper government. This direction has two purposes: to avert Angelo's abuses, and to re-erect the true authority that lapsed fourteen years earlier. Importantly, the method the Duke adopts corresponds to the advice on ruling given by James I in the *Basilicon Doron*. "I neede not to trouble you with the particular discourse of the foure Cardinall vertues, it is so troden a path; but I will shortly say vnto you; make one of them, whiche is Temperance, Queene of all the rest within you." To govern properly in Vienna or London is to exert temperance. Temperance supplies the means by which *Measure for Measure*'s tragedy is converted into comedy since it permits the binary oppositions that have informed the tragic structure to be avoided. The death sentence Angelo decrees for Claudio appears tyrannous (and not just to us, but to Escalus and the Provost as well) because it lacks sensible moderation: "Vse Iustice, but with suche moderation, as it turne not in Tyrannie: otherwaies *summum ius*, is *summa iniuria*." The strictures of the law must be tempered when the circumstances demand or else only dilemmatic options can occur, options which, as we have seen, have only tragic resolutions. We are certainly meant to contrast the rigor of Angelo's inflexible judgments and their inevitable tragic potential for both accused and accuser with the Duke's mitigation. Angelo informs Escalus:

You may not so extenuate his offence
For I have had such faults, but rather tell me,
When I that censure him do so offend,
Let mine own judgement pattern out my
    death,
And nothing come in partial.

                       (II.i.27-31)

Again we hear Angelo's characteristic division of the problem. One either remains spotless and lives, or slips and dies: "'Tis one thing to be tempted, Escalus, / Another thing to fall." The Duke's perception of justice is strikingly different: "I find an apt remission in my self" (V.i.496). The Duke can afford to remit forfeits because he is a man of temperance. Escalus' appreciation for the Duke's moderate temper is, in fact, the most accurate evaluation of the Duke's nature in the play:

> *Duke.* I pray you, sir, of what disposition was
>   the Duke?
> *Esc.* One that, above all other strifes,
>   contended especially to know himself.
> *Duke.* What pleasure was he given to?
> *Esc.* Rather rejoicing to see another merry,
>   than merry at anything which professed to
>   make him rejoice. A gentleman of all
>   temperance.

                       (III.ii.225-30)

As J. W. Lever notes, "the true ruler or judge was not the most holy or zealous of men, but he whose reason and moderation exalted him above mere pity and passion." Under the Duke's moderate direction the dilemmatic impasses created by Angelo are resolved. The Duke's temperate method provides the *peripeteia* which inverts the tragic oppositions into comic concordance. The Duke deflects the tragic possibilities of Isabella's rape or Claudio's death, and, by deflecting these possibilities, admits comic resolutions.

Only after he overhears Claudio and Isabella shriek to an impasse does the Duke begin to exert his influence and alter the direction of the play's action. For his first device the Duke pulls a convenient Mariana out of his cowl. Mariana's introduction marks a significant change in the play's dramatic architecture. The first two acts of *Measure for Measure* proceed with a smooth verisimilitude in presentation that rivals *Lear* or *Othello* or *Coriolanus*. Shakespeare sculpts the action with an exact eye on the probability of event and character and refrains from staining the dramatic reality of the play. Angelo's tyrannous behavior arises naturally from the combination of his persona and circumstance, just as Isabella's fervid determination to stay chaste and Claudio's plaintive desire to stay alive arise naturally from theirs. But the precipitant introduction of a character who just happens to have a previous connection with Angelo, and who just might be willing to "stead up

[Isabella's] appointment" (III.i.251) with Angelo, smacks of contrivance. I do not, however, think this mars the play. Rather, the introduction of elements without consideration to their plausibility (like the concurrent shift from verse to prose) indicates a transformation in the representational mode. In the second half of *Measure for Measure* Shakespeare abandons the careful causality he used to create the tragic tensions, choosing to allow fortuitous coincidence to establish the critical outlines of the structure. After the crisis in the prison— with Mariana suddenly materializing, then passing undetected in Angelo's bed, and with heaven itself providing a convenient head when no suitable substitute could be obtained— *Measure for Measure* reads much like *Cymbeline* or *Pericles*. The playwright's interest here lies not with psychological veracity, but with the movement of emblematic characters within the denotative structure of the action. Shakespeare chooses to present a suggestive pattern rather than a realistic probability. As *Measure for Measure* progresses, characterization becomes subservient to form and each character's importance becomes a function of his position in the play's architectural pattern. Mariana, for example, inverts the established pattern of tragic excess into a new comic form. Mariana's love has lost its proper management: "[Angelo's] . . . unjust unkindness, that in all reason should have quenched her love, hath, like an impediment in the current, made it more violent and unruly" (III.i.240-43). The image of the flood exactly captures the indomitable violence of passion that staggered Angelo. Further, reason's inability to withstand or control sexual impulses indicates the severe need for proper direction. Mariana's state parallels Angelo's but lacks the potential for tragic results. More importantly, her presence provides the balance for Angelo's excess. The flows of desire that plague both characters are channeled; the impediments that augment their excessive tendencies are removed. Bringing Angelo and Mariana together curbs the intemperate license in both:

> We shall advise this wronged maid to stead up
> your appointment, go in your place. If the encounter acknowledge itself hereafter, it may compel him
> to her recompense; and by this is . . . the poor
> Mariana advantaged, and the corrupt deputy scaled.

                       (III.i.250-56)

Thus Mariana measures (the primary sense of the Duke's "scaled") Angelo by functioning as Angelo's comic antithesis. Angelo's sexual impulses, consciously restrained, erupt without control and force him to attempt a brutal crime. Conversely, Mariana's desires, though frustrated, emerge beneath the Duke's temperate guidance and are channeled toward the social balance implied by Shakespeare's favorite image of social harmony— marriage. Mariana's importance to the play's structure derives, therefore, from her pivotal position in the pattern. Her willingness to accept Angelo averts Isabella's tragic violation and anticipates the inclusive comic denouement.

We know that Mariana's presence can temper, perhaps even redeem Angelo; we are less certain about Isabella. Isabella's need for moderation, though, is certain. Her psychomachia is less overt than Angelo's, but the sensual imagery that creeps into her language indicates an inordinate sexual repression, and the vehement tirades she lashes Claudio with betray her quick temper. The Duke himself assumes the task of instructing Isabella in her own humanity. Although he could inform Isabella of Claudio's preservation from Angelo's treachery, the Duke chooses not to, preferring to

> . . . keep her ignorant of her good,
> To make her heavenly comforts of despair
> When it is least expected.
>
> (IV.iii.108-10)

We first notice that the Duke defers the revelation until a more dramatic moment, just as he delays the public acknowledgement of Angelo's tryst with Mariana until the moment for proper recompense. This postponement is partly structural—Shakespeare desires to include as much as he can in the comic recognition for maximum theatrical effect. But another, perhaps more fundamental, reason remains. Isabella must be purged of the tendency towards tragic excess, just like Angelo and everyone else. Isabella lacks the Christian charity, even the Christian reflection, a future votarist of St. Clare should habitually exhibit. Isabella's ire surfaces clearly when the Duke tells her that Claudio has been executed: "O, I will to him and pluck out his eyes!" (IV.iii.119). The Duke trenchantly replies: "This neither hurts him, nor profits you a jot. / Forbear it therefore: give your cause to heaven" (IV.iii.123-24). Heaven should have had Isabella's cause immediately. Her novice's habit notwithstanding, Isabella demonstrates neither temperance nor charity. Before the Duke gives her "heavenly comforts," she will learn both.

The most perspicuous indication of the Duke's desire to employ "cold gradation and well-balanc'd form" (IV.iii.99) is his single soliloquy. True authority and proper government emanate from the moderate balance of remission and repression:

> He who the sword of heaven will bear
> Should be as holy as severe:
> Pattern in himself to know,
> Grace to stand, and virtue, go:
> More nor less to others paying
> than by self-offences weighing.
>
> (III.ii.254-59)

These lines are the central expression of the "philosophy of balance and correspondence on which the play is founded." They speak of an equitable temperance, of the just measure of rigor and mercy, and of divine standards and human frailty. Extreme positions, either Angelo's repression or Lucio's license, fundamentally imbalance the social structure. And it remains imperative for the representative of heaven's authority to establish and maintain that balance. We notice that the poetry itself supports this conclusion. The octosyllabic couplets (the only verse in a goodly stretch of prose, a definite indication of its importance) are paired, signalling its formal symmetry. Further, the couplets contain carefully counterpoised units: severity and holiness, the individual and society, knowledge and the action springing from that knowledge. And if we follow the soliloquy through, we discover tragedy and comedy balanced in the same fashion:

> Craft against vice I must apply.
> With Angelo tonight shall lie
> His old betrothed, but despised:
> So disguise shall by th' disguised
> Pay with falsehood false exacting
> And perform an old contracting.
>
> (III.ii.270-75)

The craft of an artist employing devices counteracts the vices leading to tragedy. Beneath the comic motif of mistaken identity—which is the essence of Mariana's substitution for Isabella—we again find the pattern of tragic potentialities forestalled by a figure who creates comic possibilities. The "falsehood" of Mariana's disguise, by consummating the "old contracting" of their betrothal, prepares for the marital festivities that conclude the play and that presage new birth, not death. Angelo's impulses continue to trap him into committing tragic actions (he sends the warrant for Claudio's death to hide his culpability), but he will be forced into a comic resolution by the pattern of the play, now firmly under the Duke's temperate control.

The comedy of *Measure for Measure* culminates in Act V. A "physic / That's bitter to sweet end" (IV.vi.7-8), the pageant functions as a purge and restorative, negating the consequences of the tragic impulses without eliminating the memory of them. This carefully plotted episode is the comic counterpart to the major action of Act II—Isabella's attempt to rescue Claudio from Angelo's decree, and Angelo's extortionary demand. The contiguity between the acts is furthered by the exact recurrence of theme: Angelo is guilty of Claudio's offense, and Angelo's sentence becomes the crucial focus of the pivot from tragedy to comedy. The contrast between locales is a less obvious but critical correlation between Acts II and V. Angelo and Isabella confer privately, within chambers; the Duke ensures his proceedings are both public and well attended. Act V is best regarded as a spectacle of justice, complete with actors (the Duke, Friar Peter, the Provost, and, to a point, Isabella) who have prepared parts. The Duke arranges the entire event so that the denouement becomes an emblematic performance of temperate government.

Speaking as if he were playing the part of a prologue, the Duke ceremoniously opens the pageant of justice in Act V. The painstaking formality echoes the careful protocol of the play's opening lines, thus signalling a completion of one cycle of the play's action: the Duke resumes the authority he lent Angelo and ends his surreptitious direction of events. Although Shakespeare's genius for characterization still obtains, this scene is the structural antithesis to the plausible tragedy of Acts I and II. The characters' actions are subservient to the comic pattern, and though occasional moments of spontaneity indicate partially realistic events, complex psychological motivations are replaced by symbolic postures. The Duke even blocks the initial actions as if he were a stage manager. His gestures ("Give we our hand," and "Come Escalus, / You must walk by us on our other hand" [V.i.17-18]) lend a masque-like stateliness to the episode. Moreover, the Duke's language reveals a preoccupation with dramatic artifice:

> O, but your desert speaks loud, and I should
> 　wrong it
> To lock it in the wards of covert bosom,
> When it deserves with characters of brass
> A forted residence 'gainst the tooth of time
> And razure of oblivion. Give we our hand,
> And let the subject see, to make them know
> That outward courtesies would fain proclaim
> Favours that keep within.
>
> 　　　　　　　　　　　　(V.i.10-17)

The language indulges in rich grandiloquence and vibrant imagery, qualities unknown in the Duke's pedestrian prose of the previous two acts. It is almost as if Act V metamorphoses into a royal entertainment staged for our edification and delight. Further, as we might expect in a royal masque, the elegant poetry contains a duality of purpose. The Duke extends courteous greetings and thanks but also darkly denounces the hypocrisy of external appearance belying internal reality. We note the oppositions between a "covert bosom" and "characters of brass," between "outward courtesies" and inwardly kept "Favours." The Duke presages a revelation of Angelo's occult behavior which has become deadly only because of its need for secrecy. The entire pageant, indeed, is designed to "let the subject see, to make them know" of Angelo's duplicity. But the Duke intends only recognition of, not retribution for, that duplicity. The Duke's comic craft has averted the tragic impulse; to demand punishment for Angelo's transgressions would only revert comedy to tragedy. Moderation of actions remains the Duke's goal, and by publicly exposing Angelo's vicious and unrestrained disposition, the Duke may guide him (and his subjects) to conduct his life in a more temperate fashion.

The action of Act V unfolds reiteratively: previous scenes and textures, once tragic, are now recast as comedy. Isabella's histrionic demand for "Justice! Justice! Justice! Justice!" (V.i.26) inverts her previous plea

for mercy before Angelo (II.ii.49ff). Although Angelo's treacherous behavior has ensured our approval of Isabella's fervent demand for redress, the scene communicates none of the deadly impact that surrounds the contest for Claudio's life. Act V's structure allows only a spurious and dramatic threat to Angelo's life, just as the structure of *The Merchant of Venice* permits Shylock only to menace Antonio without ever placing him in danger of actual bloodshed. We know Claudio to be safe; Angelo, therefore, is safe. A second inversion maintains this comic perspective. Isabella has implored Angelo, and most eloquently, to show Claudio mercy:

> Why, all the souls that were, were forfeit once,
> And He that might the vantage best have took
> Found out the remedy. How would you be
> If He, which is the top of judgement, should
> But judge you as you are? O, think on that,
> And mercy then will breathe within your lips,
> Like man new made.
>
> 　　　　　　　　　　　　(II.ii.73-79)

The appeals to the elements that normally constitute the comic perspective— the common heritage of man and his shared suffering, the redemption and acceptance of the fallen, the general allusion to the reconstituted man in St. Paul's "man new made"— increase the tragic pitch in the first acts because there they are denied. Conversely, Isabella's desire for strict rigor— ". . . for that I must speak / Must either punish me, not being believ'd / Or wring redress from you" (V.i.31-33)— increases our expectation of a festive resolution, since reprisals do not sort with our understanding of the comic structure here pertaining. As long as the Duke is present we realize that the intensity of these pre-arranged conflicts is undercut by our awareness of a larger pattern which contains and determines the particular actions. The subliminal comic structure tempers our reaction to momentary dynamics and prevents us from seriously considering a tragic resolution even though the urge to appraise events in dilemmatic terms recurs in Isabella's language:

> 　　　　　　　　　　'Tis not impossible
> But one, the wicked'st caitiff on the ground,
> May seem as shy, as grave, as just, as absolute,
> As Angelo; even so may Angelo,
> In all his dressings, caracts, titles, forms,
> Be an arch-villain.
>
> 　　　　　　　　　　　　(V.i.55-60)

But the antitheses here sound histrionic. The *ad hominem* attack lacks the trenchant applicability of Claudio's assessment of man's condition. Comparing Angelo to the "wicked'st caitiff on the ground" overstates; Isabella's virulence strains the credibility of the accusations. And, were her estimate accepted, it would lead only to the eradication of a single figure rather than the restoration

Act IV, scene ii. Abhorson, Pompey, and Provost.

like haste.
Away with him.

(V.i.405-14)

The Duke's condemnation of Angelo resounds with the tragic textures characteristic of Angelo's judgments. Again, and most clearly, we are confronted with an extreme solution: death for death; Angelo for Claudio. To exercise this *lex talionis* would return us to tragic themes. Man's faults manifested and condemned— and "We are all frail" (II.iv.121)—lead only to death. Or, to borrow Hamlet's piercing rejoinder to Polonius, "Use every man after his desert, and who shall scape whipping?" (*Hamlet* II.ii.524-25). Angelo is guilty, just like Claudio, of the "violation / Of sacred chastity" (V.i.402-03), and though his conduct is more vicious than Claudio's, and I believe it is, still it is presented in this play as paradigmatic of the human condition. The majority of the characters in *Measure for Measure*— Lucio, Pompey, Mistress Overdone, Froth, Angelo, Claudio, Juliet, Mariana—exhibit this infirmity to various degrees. We, with the Duke, must remember the truth of Lucio's statement:

> Yes, in good sooth, the vice is of a great kindred;
> it is well allied; but it is impossible to extrip it
> quite, friar, till eating and drinking be put down.
>
> (III.ii.97-99)

If the vice cannot be eradicated, perhaps, as the Duke has just said, "severity" can "cure it" (III.ii.96), but surely all that can actually be done is that the vice can be controlled by temperance.

Isabella's reaction to Angelo's sentence provides the archetype for the comic resolution of *Measure for Measure*. Stability and order are achieved through forgiveness and moderation, through controlling the impulses that lead man to ravin down his proper bane. The Duke's caution to Mariana indicates the impulses that Isabella must control:

> Against all sense you do importune her.
> Should she kneel down in mercy of this fact,
> Her brother's ghost his paved bed would
>   break,
> And take her hence in horror.
>
> (V.i.431-34)

But the anger and desire for revenge that had governed Isabella earlier gives way to temperance and the capacious redemption characteristic of Shakespearean comedy. Isabella's request that Angelo receive mercy crystalizes the dramatic nature of tragicomedy, the structure in which tragedy can become comedy. Just as Angelo's transgressions are paradigmatic of the iniquities in Vienna, so must Isabella's tolerance be of comic temperance:

> Look, if it please you, on this man

of an entire society. If we accept Isabella's judgment that Angelo is unredeemable, then his execution is inevitable. But the Duke intends inclusion, and Angelo's death would forbid a concordant resolution.

The Duke's feigned rejection of Isabella's suit, Lucio's interjections, Mariana's tale of a night with her lawful husband, and the disguised Duke's charges of corruption all prepare for the comic reversal. Once Lucio unmasks him, the Duke firmly and finally assumes direct control over the comic resolution. In order to move from an extreme position to a medial, thereby establishing a pattern for temperate behavior, the Duke assumes the position of unwavering, strict justice:

> The very mercy of the law cries out
> Most audible, even from his proper tongue:
> 'An Angelo for Claudio; death for death.
> Haste still pays haste, and leisure answers
>   leisure;
> Like doth quit like, and Measure still for
>   Measure.'
> Then, Angelo, thy fault's thus manifested,
> Which, though thou would'st deny, denies
>   thee vantage.
> We do condemn thee to the very block
> Where Claudio stoop'd to death, and with

condemn'd
As if my brother liv'd.

(V.i.442-43)

In that instant Isabella overcomes the binary options that had propelled the characters in *Measure for Measure* towards tragedy. Isabella bridges the opposition between Claudio's death and Angelo's life with the inclusive possibility "as if," the fountainhead of simultaneous conceivability from which temperance springs. If one can contemplate the consequences of both extremes, one also discovers the path of moderation between. Mercy extended to one who "should slip so grossly, both in the heat of blood / And lack of temper'd judgment afterward" (V.i.470-71) forms the example of moderate conduct for a world much too predisposed to thrust itself heedlessly into the harsh and deadly shocks that the flesh is heir to. To convert potential tragedy into comedy requires the momentary temperance needed to deter the impulse leading to death and disintegration. Isabella illustrates that temperance and demonstrates its virtue to the characters and audience.

And though it may be identified as such, that temperance is not exactly mercy. Mercy freely pardons; temperance instructs and corrects. As the Duke remarks with regard to Pompey, "correction and instruction must both work / Ere this rude beast will profit" (III.ii.31-32). Those who are sufficiently wise take the emblematic action of Act V as instruction; those who are not (Pompey, Mistress Overdone, Lucio) receive correction. Pompey and Mistress Overdone are removed from their salacious occupations. Lucio is checked, like Angelo, with marriage even though no one expects Lucio to settle into blissful domesticity with Kate Keepdown. Perhaps the humiliation will serve the place of "pressing to death, / Whipping, and hanging" (V.i.520-21). His marriage, like the remission of the "other forfeits," is emblematic. Lucio represents that portion of humanity "on whose nature / Nurture can never stick" (*The Tempest* IV.i.188-89). Shakespeare seems acutely aware that a darkness unredeemable lurks in the human soul: all men possess Calibans which they must acknowledge theirs. Fortunately, admitting their existence often leads to the ability to control them.

I cannot overstate the importance of the concluding marriages to the structure of *Measure for Measure*. Marriage is Shakespeare's most pervasive and most hopeful symbol of concordant social integration. By closing *Measure for Measure* with a recessional of betrothed and married couples Shakespeare appeals to our recognition of the denotation of this forceful dramatic device. What had begun as tragedy concludes with the comic crystalization of a new society, best described by Frye:

. . . a new social unit is formed on the stage, and the moment that this social unit crystalizes is the moment of the comic resolution. In the last scene,

when the dramatist usually tries to get all his characters on the stage at once, the audience witnesses the birth of a renewed sense of social integration. In comedy as in life, the regular expression of this is a festival, whether a marriage, a dance, or a feast.

Shakespeare repeatedly relies on marriages to represent the triumph over divisive forces in his plays. We only need to remember the endings of *A Midsummer Night's Dream, The Two Gentlemen of Verona, The Merchant of Venice, Much Ado About Nothing, As You Like It,* and *Twelfth Night* to conclusively demonstrate that argument. And like the marriages in those plays, the marriages in *Measure for Measure* are less important as psychological realities than as emblematic pairings. Lucio and Kate indicate libidinous impulses momentarily checked. Claudio and Juliet, perhaps the most believable of the pairings, signal the danger of unrestrained and excessive impulses, and how the stability of marriage may rectify the previous intemperance. The marriages of Mariana to Angelo and Isabella to the Duke reinforce that same lesson. I suspect that Shakespeare meant his audience to recognize the social harmony multiple marriages suggest, and I suspect that Shakespeare meant his audience to recognize the attendant triumph of comedy over tragedy as well.

Measure for Measure divides into two structural units that can be described as the progression of locales: the descent from the Duke's chambers to the prison, and the corresponding ascent from the prison to the street. The descent, marked by an increasing polarization that results, finally, in fragmentation, contains the recognizable motifs of tragic conflict. An affair that should signal pastoral harmony is unexpectedly pulled towards untimely death:

Your brother and his lover have embrac'd;
As those that feed grow full, as blossoming
time
That from the seedness the bare fallow brings
To teeming foison, even so her plenteous
womb
Expresseth his full tilth and husbandry.

(I.iv.40-44)

But Angelo's machinations promise the unnatural truncation of that cycle, not its natural completion:

[Angelo], to give fear to use and liberty,
Which have for long run by the hideous law
As mice by lions, hath pick'd out an act
Under whose heavy sense [Claudio's] life
Falls into forfeit: he arrests him on it,
And follows close the rigour of the statute
To make him an example.

(I.iv.62-68)

The profit of Claudio's "full tilth and husbandry" is

that his life "Falls into forfeit." Thus procreation begets death. But the tragedy of this movement must be circumvented. A second assignation and its "blossoming time" averts the earlier tragedy. The description of Mariana's meeting place is the comic counterpart to the tragic panel:

He hath a garden circummur'd with brick,
Whose western side is with a vineyard back'd;
And to that vineyard is a planched gate,
That makes his opening with this bigger key.
(IV.i.28-31)

The overtones of this tryst are antithetical to Claudio and Juliet's affair— Angelo contemplates rape. The result, however inverts that potential and establishes comic stability. The substitution of Mariana for Isabella preserves the comic resolution from Angelo's deadly intentions. Mariana's contact with Angelo, in a setting of hushed fecundity that links their encounter to the fertility of Claudio and Juliet's love, is the seed of comic structure. Mariana craves "no other, nor no better man" (V.i.424), and accepts Angelo without qualification:

They say best men are moulded out of faults,
And, for the most, become much more the
   better
For being a little bad. So may my husband.
(V.i.437-39)

That acceptance is the essence of the comedy of *Measure for Measure*, just as Angelo's admission, "Blood, thou art blood" (II.iv.15), is the essence of its tragedy. But the two parts stand in concordant correspondence, not isolation, and are joined by strong and pervading resonances. *Measure for Measure* is divided, but Tillyard, and later Wheeler, failed to consider how that very division gives the play structural unity. And, I believe, few playwrights have ever created a tragicomedy of *Measure for Measure*'s unified magnificence, the perfect balance of tragedy's "bitter physic" and comedy's "sweet end."

ANGELO

Numerous critics have evaluated the dual nature of Angelo— how it is reflected in the play's structure and how it represents the concerns of Renaissance society. **Leo Kirschbaum** goes so far as to observe that *Measure for Measure* presents us with "two strikingly disparate characterizations" of Angelo that cannot easily be combined to form a single, unified character. At the beginning of the play, Kirschbaum observes, Angelo "is a keen if hard protector of orderly society" whose fall from grace after meeting Isabella is in keeping with the downfall of such tragic figures as Othello or Macbeth. However Kirschbaum points out that after Act II, the Angelo we see is a grasping, "small-minded" man no

longer capable of tragic actions but instead reduced to jilting his fiancée over a lost dowry. In light of this discrepancy, Kirschbaum speculates that, for Shakespeare, the overall impression that the play makes was more important than the continuity of any one character; Shakespeare, Kirschbaum contends, wanted the closing act of *Measure for Measure* to be theatrical rather than tragic.

Harold Fisch, Darryl F. Gless, and Rolf Soellner also discuss the change in Angelo's character, but they regard it as the direct result of his own behavior. Fisch observes that Angelo has a Puritanical personality that causes him to adhere rigidly to the laws pledged to his care as well as to employ ruthlessly the power that the laws afford him; Angelo's personality undergoes a change when his possession of power turns to the abuse of power and he tries to rape Isabella. Fisch suggests that Angelo is transformed a final time when he is forced to acknowledge his transgression and do "penance" by fulfilling his pledge of marriage to Mariana. Gless and Soellner stress that the change in Angelo's character occurs when he gains self-knowledge: in other words, when he learns that he is as sinful as those on whom he passes judgment.

Leo Kirschbaum

SOURCE: "The Two Angelos," in *Character and Characterization in Shakespeare*, Wayne State University Press, 1962, pp. 119-26.

[*Kirschbaum suggests that the change in the structure of* Measure for Measure *is the result of a change in the characterization of Angelo. At the beginning of the play, Kirschbaum notes, Angelo is cruel and inflexible, but this is tempered somewhat by the fact that he is also noble in his consistent adherence to the law. Kirschbaum contends that, in order to shift the play away from tragedy, Shakespeare was obliged to recreate Angelo for the final half of the play, turning him into a character who is no longer noble but who is instead "small-minded, mean, calculating, (and) vindictive."*]

Not even Mary Lascelles' *Shakespeare's Measure for Measure* (1953), which is an almost word-for-word perception and analysis of the play, handles, or for that matter even recognizes, the problem I intend to deal with now, that of two strikingly disparate characterizations of the same character.

That Shakespeare, for the sake of the whole, for the sake of the entire impression which he wants a play to make, for the sake of the particular impression which he wants a play to make at a particular moment, could introduce a new motive for a particular character's actions, even at a relatively late or very late stage of the drama's progress, is proved by the clear insertion of Hamlet's ambition in the last act of his play. And that critics have noticed the phenomenon, whether they have brought good evidence to support their claims or not, is indicated by certain pages of L. L. Schücking's *Character Problems in Shakespeare*, wherein he attempts to substantiate his hypotheses that there are two Julius Caesars and two Cleopatras out of which no unified character analysis in the Bradleyan manner can be extracted. The example of Angelo, however, is definitive. It is impossible to bring the two divergent portrayals together. And one must assume that Shakespeare's change of the well-known story because of which the sister's virtue is not sacrificed forced the shift in Angelo's character, which is so well concealed that— to my great astonishment!— not even perceptive auditors and critics have noticed it.

Up to his exit at the end of 2.4, Angelo is a character who might vie with Macbeth in the split between his compulsive desires and his conscience. Frightening he is, even sadistic— as is implied by his treatment of Claudio, his blunt assertiveness to the decent and human-hearted Provost, and his abrupt dismissal of Elbow's "criminals," hoping they will all be whipped— contrast this last with the understanding tolerance of his fellow magistrate, Escalus. But Angelo here in these scenes is by no means an ignoble figure. He may lack empathy, but his view of law and justice is not despicable. This is a difficult play; Shakespeare does everything he can to show that a harsh attitude toward concupiscence may exist in heaven but not on earth. And determination is even further muddled by the friar Duke's harshness towards Juliet for the same "sin" which he later encourages Mariana to commit and Isabella to aid. Nevertheless, it would be impossible for an enlightened jurist to impugn Angelo's statements to Escalus or to Isabella. Let us look at some of these. Escalus says in 2.1:

> Ay, but yet
> Let us be keen and rather cut a little,
> Than fall and bruise to death. Alas, this
>   gentleman
> Whom I would save had a most noble
>   father.
> Let but your honor know,
> Whom I believe to be most strait in virtue,
> That in the working of your own affections,
> Had time cohered with place or place with
>   wishing,
> Or that the resolute acting of your blood
> Could have attained th' effect of your own
>   purpose,
> Whether you had not sometime in your life
> Erred in this point which now you censure
>   him,
> And pulled the law upon you.

To which Angelo replies:

> 'Tis one thing to be tempted, Escalus,

> Another thing to fall. I not deny
> The jury passing on the prisoner's life
> May in the sworn twelve have a thief or two
> Guiltier than him they try; what's open made
>   to justice,
> That justice seizes; what knows the laws
> That thieves do pass on thieves? 'Tis very
>   pregnant
> The jewel that we find, we stoop and take't
> Because we see it; but what we do not see
> We tread upon, and never think of it.
> You may not so extenuate his offense
> For I have had such faults; but rather tell me,
> When I that censure him do so offend,
> Let mine own judgment pattern out my
>   death
> And nothing come in partial. Sir, he must
>   die.

Angelo's speech not only defends the integrity of the law but even admits the possible defalcation of the lawmaker and law enforcer. This is great utterance, and there is nothing in the least pernicious about it. Similarly, although our hearts go out wholly to Isabella in mercy in 2.2, yet the Angelo who says

> The law hath not been dead, though it hath
>   slept.
> Those many had not dared to do that evil
> If that the first that did th' edict infringe
> Had answered for his deed. Now 'tis awake,
> Takes note of what is done, and like a
>   prophet
> Looks in a glass that shows what future evils,
> Either new, or by remissness new-conceived,
> And so in progress to be hatched and born,
> Are now to have no successive degrees,
> But, ere they live, to end.

is a keen if hard protector of orderly society. We should remember that a merciful God is also an all-knowing One: man in his hopes and fears for the future must perforce be, fortunately or unfortunately, legalistic.

When and as Angelo falls, he falls as a great man. He is tempted not as a Lucio, to engage in momentary sport, but as a noble victim of a completely uncontrollable emotion. This is not lechery; this is the complement of the strong rigidity that has hitherto guided him. He like his counterparts Coriolanus, Othello, Lear, and Macbeth is swept on to irresponsibility by a force that in its strength shows that it is outside reason. The essence of the situation is magnificently phrased by Angelo himself when in an aside he states that he is "that way going to temptation / Where prayers cross." Consider the word *love* in the following soliloquy that ends 2.2:

> From thee: even from thy virtue.

What's this? what's this? is this her fault or
    mine?
The tempter, or the tempted, who sins
    most?
Ha!
Not she, nor doth she tempt; but it is I
That, lying by the violet in the sun,
Do as the carrion does, not as the flower,
Corrupt with virtuous season. Can it be
That modesty may more betray our sense
Than woman's lightness? Having waste
    ground enough,
Shall we desire to raze the sanctuary
And pitch our evils there? O fie, fie, fie!
What dost thou? or what art thou, Angelo?
Dost thou desire her foully for those things
That make her good? O, let her brother
    live:
Thieves for their robbery have authority
When judges steal themselves. What, do I
    love her,
That I desire to hear her speak again,
And feast upon her eyes? what is't I dream
    on?
O cunning enemy that, to catch a saint,
With saints dost bait thy hook: most
    dangerous
Is that temptation that doth goad us on
To sin in loving virtue. Never could the
    strumpet
With all her double vigor, art and nature,
Once stir my temper; but this virtuous
    maid
Subdues me quite. Ever till now,
When men were fond, I smiled and
    wondered how.

Angelo does not say merely that he lusts after Claudio's sister; he says that he *loves* her. The appetite here is the opposite of momentary lust. It is the ruthless compulsion that makes of Maugham's *Of Human Bondage* and even sometimes of the cheapest opera an artifact that has disturbing credibility. This is what drives Romeo and Juliet together.

Seized by this emotion Angelo confronts Isabella in 2.4. His admissions are illuminating. "We are all frail," he says; "Plainly conceive, I love you"; and again, your brother "shall not [die], Isabel, if you give me love." (It is the sublimity of Shakespeare's irony that not until this moment of intimate non-intimacy do the two call each other by their names!) The very beat and tautness of his lines show a ruthless but not small, a savage but not cheap, villain:

          Answer me tomorrow,
Or, by the affection that now guides me
    most,
I'll prove a tyrant to him. As for you,

Say what you can, my false o'erweighs your
    true.

After 2.4 Angelo makes no appearance until two full acts later, until 4.4, which is just upon the beginning of the last scene and act. Already as we know he is in the grip of the plot which will expose him. And the Angelo of the last scene is by no means the caught figure of Macbeth or Othello. He is there because he has to be the pawn of the theatricality that Shakespeare has invented. He has neither bulk nor credence. He is there to be exposed and then married and then freed. One might truly say that after 2.4 the great Angelo whom I have tried to describe in the first two acts has no part in the play. And I think one of the reasons why is not far to seek. Beginning with 3.1.204 the former Angelo disappears and a new Angelo replaces him:

Duke: . . . Have you not heard speak of Mariana, the sister of Frederick, the great soldier who miscarried at sea?

Isabella: I have heard of the lady, and good words went with her name.

Duke: She should this Angelo have married, was affianced by her oath, and the nuptial appointed: between which time of the contract and limit of the solemnity, her brother Frederick was wracked at sea, having in that perished vessel the dowry of his sister. But mark how heavily this befell to the poor gentlewoman: there she lost a noble and renowned brother, in his love toward her ever most kind and natural; with him the portion and sinew of her fortune, her marriage dowry; with both, her combinate husband, this well-seeming Angelo.

Isabella: Can this be so? Did Angelo so leave her?

Duke: Left her in her tears, and dried not one of them with his comfort; swallowed his vows whole, pretending in her discoveries of dishonor; in few, bestowed her on her own lamentation, which she yet wears for his sake; and he, a marble to her tears, is washed with them but relents not.

Let us hazard reasons why the second Angelo— small-minded, mean, calculating, vindictive— has to enter the play.

In order to get Isabella off the hook Shakespeare has to employ "the bed-trick." Somebody else must substitute for Isabella in the garden that night. Since the coming together of Mariana and Angelo has to be legally and religiously acceptable, the bed-trick has to be advised by a friar. This can only come about by having had Angelo break a betrothal contract. One cause for breaking the contract could have been Angelo's finding a new love. But although Shakespeare can add demeaning traits to the old Angelo, he cannot without peril totally contradict the old Angelo. Now one of the most marked characteristics of the former Angelo was his initial non-amorous nature. Thus the only recourse for Shakespeare was to have the Angelo-Mariana betrothal broken because Angelo did not get the dowry he expected. The motive, in other words, for the rupture was avarice. But there is nothing in the early Angelo that prepares us for this miserliness. Furthermore, although his refusing Mariana comfort goes along with the sadism which I have remarked, his pretence that Mariana was dishonorable is, I think, also denied by our impression of the original Angelo. That he would be thus cheap and mean does not seem possible. This avaricious and small-minded creature, a jilting Angelo, is a far cry from the noble, if too noble for his own good, character who inhabits the play in the first two acts.

When Angelo changes, the play changes. What has been hitherto almost a deterministic sequence of events between a man and a woman becomes a theatrical trickery the virtues of which I would not deny. Nevertheless these are easier virtues than those which possess the great tragedies, effective as they too are on the stage.

Hence I do not think I am wrong in assuming that the shift that most people feel in *Measure for Measure* from a great drama to a great theatrical and ideological drama is occasioned as much as anything by the fact of the two Angelos.

DUKE VINCENTIO

Darryl F. Gless describes Duke Vincentio as a godlike figure who, thanks to his use of disguise, appears omniscient to the other characters of the play and who closes the play by administering justice to all and awarding "true praise where it is due." Carolyn E. Brown and Robin Grove see the Duke in a negative light. Brown, for instance, turns to the relationship between Vincentio and the dissipated but perceptive Lucio for evidence supporting *Measure for Measure*'s designation as a "problem" play. Brown explains that although the Duke appears superficially to be virtuous, and although his manipulations of Isabella, Mariana, and Angelo end happily, nevertheless his conversations with and harsh sentencing of Lucio reveal a troubled and sublimated personality. Grove criticizes the Duke for the lack of self-perception he reveals in believing that he is capable of judging others. Grove also describes the Duke's manipulations at the close of the play as cruel.

By contrast, **William A. Freedman** views Duke Vincentio as a benign character and "moral spokesman" who succeeds at his ultimate goal which is to guide Vienna back toward merciful justice. Like Gless, Freedman contends that the Duke displays godlike abilities

but Freedman insists that the character nevertheless retains his humanity; **Melvin Seiden** sees a somewhat different duality in Vincentio's characterization. Seiden describes the Duke as shy and scholarly on the one hand and splendidly manipulative on the other, but argues that these differences only add to the entertainment value of Shakespeare's play. Richard A. Levin tries to put the debate concerning the Duke's inconsistent nature to rest by looking at the character from a psychological point of view. Levin suggests that Vincentio appears to be inconsistent because "his conscience is troubled": after all, he has instructed Mariana in the morally dubious bed-trick and is therefore, as Carolyn E. Brown has pointed out, sensitive to Lucio's perceptive barbs. Unlike Brown, however, Levin concludes that the Duke's moral ambiguity fulfills Shakespeare's purpose for the play, which is to reserve judgment on others even if his characters do not.

William A. Freedman

SOURCE: "The Duke in *Measure for Measure*: Another Interpretation," in *Tennessee Studies in Literature*, Vol. IX, 1964, pp. 31-38.

[*Freedman refutes the commonly held view of the Duke as inconsistent and inhuman, countering this viewpoint with the argument that Vincentio is in fact consistently "concerned with . . . his reputation and public image." Freedman remarks that reputation serves as an important theme in the play along with mercy and justice, so that appropriately, as the most powerful character in the play, the Duke brings these themes to the forefront at the close of* Measure for Measure *by displaying a very human concern for his reputation and authority in Vienna even while he teaches his subjects the importance of tempering justice with mercy.*]

Undoubtedly one of, if not the, most enigmatic of all Shakespeare's so-called "problem plays" is *Measure for Measure*. Much ink has been spent over the very intention of the play and over the related question of the abundance of the tragic element in this supposed comedy. Perhaps, however, one of the most controversial aspects of the play is the character of the Duke. Vincentio is commonly written off by many critics as an egregiously inconsistent, even non-human, character. Professor Mark Parrott describes the controversy and offers a not unpopular solution, as follows:

> Pages have been written . . . about the Duke. He has been blamed as derelict in duty; he has been extolled as an earthly Providence watching over wayward children. All this is beating the wind; the Duke is not a living man at all, but a *deus ex machina* devised by Shakespeare to steer the action through storm and stress into the final heaven. He is a mere bundle of inconsistencies; he does not like to stage himself in people's eyes, yet he indulges in a most spectacular bit of self-revelation; he preaches a long sermon to Claudio to prepare him for death when he is fully purposed to save the boy's life. If we

cease to analyze his character we may overlook its inconsistency and admire the art with which Shakespeare makes him serve the end for which he was designed.

Parrott's analysis, it seems to me, is correct in everything but its two major points: that the Duke's character is beset with inconsistencies, and that he is in fact not a living man at all. So far as I know, no analysis of the Duke thus far has satisfactorily reconciled the problems he presents, and it will therefore be the purpose of this paper to offer a resolution to the question of the Duke's character. I shall try to show, to be more specific, that the Duke, if we try to understand him as a man who is concerned with, nay solicitous after, his reputation and public image, emerges as a quite consistent, quite human delineation, and one reflects in this aspect of his character one of the principal themes of *Measure for Measure*.

Much of the difficulty about the Duke arises from the fact that he, of all the characters lifted from Shakespeare's source— Whetstone's *Promus and Cassandra*— undergoes the most radical alteration. He appears in the Whetstone play, and in the Cinthio novel from which it was first derived, only towards the end. The earlier character does not, as the Duke does, permeate the entire work. In Whetstone, the Duke, there a king, merely sends his delegate to the city of Julio for the purpose of administering justice. The King himself is not seen until the latter part of the play, where he is told of the delegate's abuses of authority and metes out merciful justice. The fact that the Duke in *Measure for Measure* is a far more active participant in the drama, that he in fact manipulates the action to a considerable degree, has given rise to the conviction that he is the *deus* in Shakespeare's machine. His presence throughout assures us that despite the tragic appearance of events, all will work out well. The Duke thus abates the seriousness found in the sources and makes *Measure for Measure* more palatable as comedy. But by means of his enlargement of the Duke's role, Shakespeare has done far more to his source than this. He has magnified a latent theme in Whetstone's drama, namely that of reputation, and has made the Duke contribute out of his humanity toward the evocation not only of the theme of mercy, but to this secondary theme as well.

The theme of reputation, implicit in the dramatic situation, but made explicit in Whetstone only in Cassandra's (here Isabella's) case, touches crucially in *Measure for Measure* virtually every major character. Angelo is of course virtue untested; and his reputation, about which everyone has something to remark, proves undeserved. Angelo admits to taking pride in his gravity, an index of his own consciousness of his public image; and he bases his trust in Isabella's secrecy in his supposed violation of her chastity on the grounds first, that his reputation for rectitude will render incredible any accusations to the contrary, and second, that Isabella will

not wish to undermine her own repute. Isabella is naturally thinking largely of her reputation as well as her soul when she rejects Angelo's proposition. And in his substitution of Mariana for Isabella in the controversial "bed trick," Shakespeare not only lightens the play's tragic load, but places Isabella in direct contrast with Angelo as virtue tested and proved and reputation deserved. In fact, the putative Puritanism of Angelo and the genuine chastity of Isabella are greatly magnified from the Whetstone play (Cassandra is no novice in Whetstone) to heighten this contrast.

Similarly, the reputations of Claudio "who was worth five thousand of you all," and Juliet, for the violation of whose chastity Angelo has condemned him, are likewise considered. Juliet, observes the prison provost, "falling in the flames of her own youth, / Hath blistered her report." Too, the reputation of Mariana is examined and guaranteed before she consents to the substitution. And Angelo confesses at the end to having "disvalued" her reputation by breaking off his earlier engagement to her.

The comic figures also contribute richly to the theme of reputation and respectability in their characteristic medium of malapropism. In a nineteen-line comic sequence involving Pompey and Elbow, and concerning the repute of the latter's wife, the word "respected" appears no fewer than eight times, consistently misused for, among other things, "suspected" or "ill-reputed."

Elb. First, an it like you, the house is a respected house; next, this is a respected fellow; and his mistress is a respected woman.

Pom By this hand, sir, his wife is a more respected person than any of us all.

Elb. Varlet, thou liest! Thou liest, wicked varlet! The time is yet to come that she was ever respected with man, woman, or child.

Pom Sir, she was respected with him before he married with her.

Escal. Which is the wiser here, Justice or Iniquity? Is this true?

Elb. O thou caitiff! O thou varlet! O thou wicked Hannibal! I respected with her before I was married to her! If ever I was respected with her, or she with me, let not your worship think me the poor Duke's officer. Prove this, thou wicked Hannibal, or I'll have mine action of battery on thee.

(Act II, Sc. 1, ll. 170-188)

The Duke's extraordinary consciousness of and concern for reputation, his own and that of others, is first made clear in Act I, Scene 3, where he explains to the friar his motives for delegating his power to Angelo and assuming a friar's habit to observe the consequences. As ruler of Verona he has, in his leniency, allowed the statutes of the city to go unheeded, the result being a somewhat anarchic wantonness. "Liberty plucks justice by the nose." Yet when the friar suggests that it is the Duke's responsibility to remedy the situation himself, his answer is twofold— both revelatory of this aspect of his character. First,

> Sith 't was my fault to give the people scope,
> 'T would be my tyranny to strike and gall
>> them
> For what I bid them do; for we bid this be
>> done,
> When evil deeds have their permissive pass
> And not the punishment. Therefore indeed,
>> my father,
> I have on Angelo impos'd the office;
> Who may, in th' ambush of my name, strike
>> home,
> And yet my nature never in the fight
> To do it slander.
>
> (Act I, Sc. 3, ll. 35-43)

And second,

> . . . Lord Angelo is precise,
> Stands at a guard with envy, scarce confesses
> That his blood flows, or that his appetite
> Is more to bread than stone; hence shall we see,
> If power change purpose, what our seemers
>> be.
>
> (Act I, Sc. 3, ll. 50-54)

In the first place, then, the Duke seems to regret his current reputation, but at the same time is concerned that his name not be stained in the process of restoring order to his city. Secondly, he is interested in discovering whether Angelo's reputation for staunch rectitude, so much stronger than his own, be truly deserved. If we keep in mind the Duke's dissatisfaction with the public image he has thus far created of himself along with his desire to restore order without injuring his name, we may have a key to many of his otherwise quite puzzling actions.

The Duke's expressed concern for reputation, far from ending with his explanation to the friar, underscores and in fact accounts for almost everything he speaks and does. It is he who, in the guise of the friar, assures Mariana that her reputation will not suffer in the substitution. Also in the friar's habit he asks after himself of Escalus, his second deputy, for no reason, it would seem, other than that he simply wants to know how he is regarded. The very disguise he has chosen, it is well worth noting, is relevant to the Duke's character. In assuming the guise of a friar, he takes one not only well suited to his function as dispenser of mercy and the play's moral spokesman, but one which at the same time com-

mands the veneration he desires. Further, the Duke's insistence to both Claudio and Isabella that Angelo's proposition was merely a deliberate testing of the latter's virtue ties the theme of reputation to another of the play's central questions, that of life *versus* honor. This latter is the real question posed to both Isabella and Claudio by Angelo's heinous offer. But the Duke, attempting to relieve them of the burden of their decision, mitigates the importance of their choice, tells them that Angelo would have executed Claudio anyway, and characteristically puts the questions in terms of the testing of reputation.

As with most of Shakespeare's characters, however, Vincentio is most self-revelatory in his soliloquies. The Duke has only three such speeches, and it is crucial to the understanding of his character that two of them concern themselves exclusively with the problem of repute and that it is a significant part of the third. The first of these, in Act III, Scene 2, follows the departure of Lucio, a wanton and a "fantastick," who has just left off a slanderous denunciation of the Duke thinking he addressed but an ordinary friar. He has berated the Duke as a lecher, a drunkard, and a "very superficial, ignorant, unweighing fellow," and when he leaves, the Duke reflects:

> No might nor greatness in mortality
> Can censure scape; back-wounding calumny
> The whitest virtue. What king so strong
> Can tie the gall up in the slanderous tongue?
>
> (Act III, Sc. 2, ll. 196-199)

It is interesting in this context to note that the Duke here implicitly associates himself with considerable "might" and "greatness," with the "whitest virtue," and with a "king." This is fully in character, for the Duke was careful to refute in its turn each of Lucio's calumnies and to defend himself as a "scholar, a statesman, and a soldier" (the virtues of the Renaissance man and, as Horatio tells us, of Hamlet). In the same way, he is certain to inform all of the recipients of his benevolence that that is exactly what they are receiving. He is but a friar now, but he is already planning his great unveiling, and he is careful to plant the seeds of proper gratitude and respect.

The second of the Duke's soliloquies closes out the same scene and comes when he is in full possession of the scope of Angelo's inhumanity. The soliloquy outlines the nature of the lesson the Duke has learned in the course of the play and is concerned primarily with the doctrines of mercy and measure for measure— that he who would administer justice should be "more nor less to others paying / Than by self-offences weighing." But located neatly in the middle of this twenty-two line monologue are eight lines integrally related to the question of public versus true image:

> Twice treble shame on Angelo,

To weed my vice and let his grow!
O, what may man within him hide,
Though angel on the outward side!
How may likeness made in crimes,
Making practice on the times,
To draw with idle spiders' strings
Most ponderous and substantial things!

                    (Act III, Sc. 2, ll. 283-290)

The Duke's final soliloquy occurs in the very next scene, Act IV, Scene I. It is spoken while Isabel has gone off with Mariana to advise her of the proposed substitution. The speech, however, seems to have no immediate provocation, a fact which only serves to emphasize still more the Duke's preoccupation with the subject of reputation, most particularly his own. Isabella and Mariana having made their exits, he repines:

O place and greatness! millions of false eyes
Are stuck upon thee: volumes of report
Run with these false and most contrarious
     quests
Upon thy doings; thousand escapes of wit
Make the the father of their idle dream
And rack thee in their fancies.

                    (Act IV, Sc. 1, ll. 60-65)

In the light of this major aspect of the Duke's character, two of the play's major problems may be cleared up: first, the Duke's seeming inconsistency of character, and second the rancor with which he regards the calumnies of Lucio.

As for Lucio, the Duke finds, even amid all his bestowals of mercy, including one to Antonio, a would-be executioner, that,

. . . here's one in place I cannot pardon
You sirrah, that knew me for a fool, a coward,
One all of luxury, an ass, a madman,
Wherein have I so deserv'd of you,
That you extol me thus?

                    (Act V, Sc. 1, ll. 504-508)

Ultimately, Lucio too is pardoned and relieved of his sentence of whipping first and hanging after, but the Duke does compel him to marry a punk he has gotten with child. Marrying a punk, Lucio complains, is "pressing to death, whipping, and hanging." "Slandering a prince deserves it," answers Vincentio. Little, I think, need be said in explanation of this verdict. One so sensitive of his name and so concerned with improving it as the Duke has revealed himself to be could hardly be expected to react otherwise.

The seeming inconsistencies in the Duke's character, when looked at in the light of the interpretation I have been suggesting, actually represent little difficulty. The two inconsistencies named by Parrott, and I think the two most likely to appear irreconcilable are: "he does

not like to stage himself in people's eyes, yet he indulges in a most spectacular bit of self-revelation; he preaches a long sermon to Claudio to prepare him for death when he is fully purposed to save the poor boy's life. Both of these seeming contradictions, and indeed virtually all of the questionable activities in which the Duke engages throughout the course of the play, can be explained in the light of the same concern for public image and reputation. His statement that "I love the people but do not love to stage me to their eyes" is easily explained. The remark is offered to Angelo as an account for his delegation of power, and it follows his insistence that he is in a hurry so urgent that it "leaves unquestioned matters of needful value." This insistence is of course, as we later discover, quite untrue— there is no such urgency; and on the same grounds, we may place as little credence in the statement in question: he can hardly be expected to provide Angelo with the true account which he gives the friar. The second inconsistency is reconciled if we consider that almost from the start, the Duke has been planning, to put it bluntly, to shine in the big final scene. This explains in large part his allowing Claudio to persist in his belief in his impending execution. It is also largely responsible for his soliciting the Provost's secrecy about the substitution of another's head for Claudio's, his decision to leave Isabella in the dark about the fact that her brother actually lives, his advice as the friar to Isabella to accuse Angelo before the Duke, his pre-arranged publicly announced return to Vienna, and finally his letter to Angelo and Escalus to "proclaim it in an hour before his entering, that if any crave redress of injustice, they should exhibit their petitions in the street." (Act IV, Sc. 4, ll. 9-12.) The Duke simply postpones all revelation of his good news for the final moment when he, as Duke and in plain view of his subjects, can make all known. Angelo having failed, the Duke must restore order and obedience to Vienna. But as he earlier told the friar, his reputation for laxity would have made sudden rigourousness seem tyrannical. A public device, such as the final scene is, represents the Duke's attempt to restore order to his subjects on the basis of an increased respect for their sovereign as well as an increased understanding of the nature of true justice. Only this, it seems to me, can account in full for the Duke's manipulation of the final scene in such a way as to make himself the public administrator of mercy in seven consecutive instances: Escalus, Isabella, Bernardine (a murderer), Claudio, Angelo, Lucio, and the Provost. This last, it should be noted, he himself accuses with full knowledge of his subject's innocency and to no apparent end other than its allowing him to grant a further pardon.

In spite of all this, I am not trying to make of the Duke a petty miscreant. I am not trying to deprive him of his status as the play's moral spokesman nor of the quality of mercy in which he so richly abounds. That is why I have said that his concern for his reputation only partly accounts for these manipulations. They can also be accounted for by his desire to make public the arch injustice of Angelo and to provoke both him and his victims to an understanding of the necessity of mercy. This latter, however, is hardly a satisfactory account if it is forced to stand alone. The Duke, it would seem, has gone to lengths too unsavory even for such a noble purpose. Nevertheless, the play retains its moral; it retains its lessons of measure for measure, and the need for a justice tempered by mercy. But this moral achieves greater substance from the fact that it is delivered not by an inconsistent, inhuman, mechanical *deus*, but by a man led by his weaknesses as well as his virtues to proclaim it aloud.

The Duke is, as everyone has said, a *deus ex machina*— at least in that he manipulates in large part the action of the play. But he manipulates the action as he does, not as a mechanical device, but as a particular kind of individual character with particular kinds of needs and desires. The Duke is a consistent human being who adds out of his humanity a substance to the theme of reputation and to the moral and drama of *Measure for Measure*.

Melvin Seiden

SOURCE: "The Duke As Politician," in Measure for Measure: *Casuistry and Artistry*, The Catholic University of America Press, 1990, pp. 16-24.

[Seiden identifies two different and contradictory personalities of the Duke: one, a "shy and diffident" scholar who shuns contact with his people; and the other, a "man who relishes both the hidden power of the dramatist and the excitement of acting." Seiden asserts, however, that since these two conflicting roles are treated separately in the play and with equal authority by Shakespeare, neither undercuts the Duke's ultimate ability to bring merciful justice to Vienna, nor does either diminish the power of Shakespeare's play to entertain us—particularly in the second half, where the action is effectively stage-managed by the Duke.]

If by its title *Measure for Measure* implies a quantified equality, a moderate and orderly apportioning of whatever it is that is going to be measured out, it delivers on that promise: the play does indeed arrive at a series of carefully considered and symmetrical resolutions that are cut to measure. In still another sense, the fifth act is about the kind of measuring that adds up to tit for tat: old scores are settled and just desserts earned. But in the process of arriving at the moral symmetry that emerges in the final moments, virtually everything and everyone has been unbalanced, unmeasured, unsettled. Besides, so many variables enter into the calculations— into the measuring that seeks to make legal, moral, and political judgments— that even wise Duke Vincentio may have forgotten some of them.

From the beginning this duke of dark corners takes extreme and radically incompatible positions. It is one thing to delegate a monarch's authority to a trusted and honored deputy precisely because one trusts him and believes in his virtues:

> Angelo,
> There is a kind of character in thy life,
> That to th' observer doth thy history
> Fully unfold.
>
> (I.i.28ff.)

It is quite another to endow an underling with power because his virtues are not credible and there are good reasons for not trusting this paragon of rectitude. If the duke's words in this ambiguous speech are not the panegyric they appear to be but hint at an intention to expose Angelo's shamming of virtue, then Vincentio is playing a duplicitous game. Here, at the outset, perhaps, is what we might call homeopathic measuring: if Angelo's imminent evil is disguised behind a show of virtue, then the duke will camouflage his hostile intentions behind a display of admiration.

And yet, when the duke ends his eulogy of Angelo with the words "But I do bend my speech / To one that can my part in him advertise," we are as likely as Angelo to take them at face value. Nothing hints at insincerity and deviousness; the praise sounds genuine and we have no reason at this point to suspect Vincentio of underhanded tactics. Which is it, then, trust or mistrust that accounts for the way in which the duke speaks to his deputy in the opening colloquies?

As the action progresses and the duke offers more explanations for his abrupt abdication and delegation of power to Angelo, each new piece of evidence conflicts in some way with one of the previous motives, and as we try to reconcile one with the other, we begin to suspect that each of the duke's postures is independent of the other. When in the opening lines of the play he tells Angelo, "your own science [expertise in government] / Exceeds . . . all advice / My strength can give you" (I.i.5ff.), he means what he says; when he seems to be praising Angelo, he must again be taken to mean what he says; but when, later, he is doubtful and suspicious (in I.iii) and introduces a new and contradictory motive— "Hence shall we see, / If power change purpose, what our seemers be" (ll. 53-54)— that dubiety is neither more nor less important an intention than any of the others; each of the duke's explanations stands in discrete integrity, and none negates any of the others. In the world of *Measure for Measure* rigid and exaggerated attitudes— trust, admiration, mistrust, and contempt— are not modified or tempered. They are abandoned and others, no less intense or extreme, replace them.

In the third scene the duke explains to Friar Thomas

The "bed trick" with Gene Carulho as Angelo from the the San Jose State University's 1997 production of Measure for Measure.

why he has been negligent in enforcing the laws of the realm. He admits that because "'twas my fault to give the people scope, / 'Twould be my tyranny to strike and gall them" (ll. 35-36). Angelo, as the duke's surrogate, can accomplish the task of reawakening the sleeping law without damaging the duke's good name. To this argument a stern moralist might reply that the duke's desire to avoid the role of tyrant by a belated revival of the antifornication law only compounds the error of allowing the law to be "like an o'ergrown lion in a cave, / That goes not out to prey" (ll. 22-23). Vincentio expresses himself here in a revealing way: "I have on Angelo imposed the office," he says, "Who may in the ambush of my name, strike home . . ." (ll. 40-41). We may suspect that it is, however, Angelo who is being ambushed; when in the closing lines he gives us a glimpse of the future that sounds like a threat—"Hence shall we see, / If power change purpose, what our seemers be"—we may infer that Angelo is being entrapped. We may want to see Vincentio as finally and truly tipping his hand when he ends the third scene with these portentous words and then read back into his earlier speeches a Machiavellian duplicity.

The Vincentio of the third scene is dubious; he mistrusts someone who "scarce confesses / That his blood

flows, or that his appetite / Is more to bread than stone" (I.iii.51ff.). He seems duplicitous. How strange that the duke, in the course of explaining to Angelo (I.i.65ff.) the reasons for making Angelo his surrogate, should describe himself as a reluctant ruler, someone who was not cut out for the hurly-burly of public life.

> I love the people,
> But do not like to stage me to their eyes.
> Though it do well, I do not relish well
> Their loud applause and Aves vehement. . . .
>
> (I.i.68ff.)

If we think of the vivid Americanism "pressing flesh," the sort of mixing with and being swallowed up by the crowd that politicians like Hubert Humphrey and Lyndon Johnson seemed to revel in, we get a good picture of what is abhorrent to Vincentio. Again, to Friar Thomas, he makes virtually the same point—"I have ever loved the life removed" (I.iii.8)—so the distaste for the noise and crowds of politics must be genuine. Vincentio's is a point of view closely associated with the contempt for the political mob expressed most notably by Coriolanus but also found in *Julius Caesar.*

Angelo, surprisingly, shares his master's refined distaste for the multitude. He expresses his political— but we might call it a visceral— repugnance while in the throes of a violent epiphany of self-hatred. He has asked Isabella to return for a second meeting in which she will have an opportunity to plead for her brother's life. Angelo, for his part, will have a chance to tell her without equivocation or euphemism that he wants her sexually and is willing to barter away Claudio's death sentence for her favors. Here, in act 2, scene 4, Angelo echoes Vincentio's patrician politics. Hearing that Isabella has arrived, Angelo describes the rush of "blood [that] thus muster[s] to my heart"; by association, he leaps from the idea of breathlessness to the idea of suffocation in a tableau in which "foolish throngs" huddle around the "one that swoons" and thus, in their well-intentioned solicitude, cut off the air needed by the one who has fainted. And from this image of a crowd, ignorant and undisciplined, however kind its collective heart, Angelo moves to the political example:

> And even so
> The general subject to a well-wished king
> Quit their own part, and in obsequious
> fondness
> Crowd to his presence, where their untaught
> love
> Must needs appear offense.
>
> (II.iv.26ff.)

Leaving aside the glancing allusion to King James, the purpose of this passage is to reinforce the duke's aristocratic principles. If for Angelo these are principles, they are entertained as intensely as feelings; if they are prejudices, they are expressed with all the sobriety and thoughtfulness of principles. A wise ruler refuses to be a crowd pleaser, and one good reason for eschewing popularity is given here: the crowd one panders to may, in all its "obsequious fondness," do harm even when it does not intend to do so. It is not just that Angelo, like the duke, has a delicate political stomach that cannot abide the "stinking breaths" of the rabble, a phrase attributed, predictably, to Caius Marcius Coriolanus, archenemy of the people. The People is a dangerous sociopolitical animal, always potentially a hydra-headed mob, even when it has good intentions.

When the duke voices his diffident and qualified "love [of] the people" and his dislike of "Their loud applause," he connects his diffidence to the empowering of Angelo, assuring the somewhat reluctant deputy, "Your scope is as mine own, / So to enforce or qualify the laws / As to your soul seems good" (I.i.65ff.). When Angelo, later, expresses his more censorious version of the duke's political diffidence, he reinforces the bond between Vincentio and himself. Angelo is the duke's man; his job is the duke's neglected job; his sexual, legal, and political principles are the duke's— at least at the outset. We may find it easier to see Angelo as a perverter of everything that Vincentio stands for, but that stark opposition between the beneficent ruler and his delinquent underling is too simple and too melodramatic even for this splendidly melodramatic play. If Angelo were the democrat his principles do not allow him to be, he might not be so assiduous an enforcer of the antifornication law. If Angelo's sexual morality allowed him to take an easygoing— we might call it a Lucio-like— view of fornication, he might not have espoused the politics of a Coriolanus; Angelo's sexual morality and his political ideas are all of a piece; and that perfectionist, absolutist point of view, that contemptuous scorn of collective and individual folly, is also Vincentio's. It is more intense in Angelo, more a violent and self-destructive passion in the surrogate than in the man who may have been his mentor. Nevertheless, there can be no evading the fact that the duke and his deputy are bonded by a set of shared moral assumptions. Angelo's echoing of Vincentio's political attitudes makes the point overtly.

Later in the play Vincentio's political fastidiousness is connected to his personal morality. To the disguised Vincentio, Escalus describes this "gentleman of all temperance" as "One that, above all other strifes, contended especially to know himself" (III.ii.245ff.). This glimpse of the duke's high standards suggests that he aspires nobly to the status of philosopher-king. The duke seems to be more philosopher than king. Alas (we may be tempted to say) for Vienna, for poor Claudio, the victim of the punitive regime inaugurated by Angelo; alas for Vincentio, who would rather study than rule, would rather be the stern judge of his own merits and failings than applauded by an ignorant and "vehement"

crowd. Such sympathy is misdirected. The duke's unwillingness to be soiled by popularity— which is to say, his distaste for the politics of democracy— is not a defect but a virtue. We may want to blame Vienna's endemic corruption on the negligence, even the self-indulgence of a monarch who seeks Socratic wisdom at the expense of public duties, but the play does not come to that severe judgment. On the contrary, Vincentio demonstrates the goodness of his character as a man by the austerity of his private and political principles.

It is not difficult to debunk— shall we say *deconstruct?*— the character of the duke. His every motive and move, peered into with a cold, analytical eye, raises suspicions about him. The bed trick whereby Vincentio, disguised as a friar, arranges for the jilted bride Mariana rather than Isabella to sleep with Angelo is only one, though the most notorious, case in which our everyday morality does not square with that of the duke. We shall have more to say about the interplay between morality and opportunism in a later discussion. At this point it is necessary to state a simple, dogmatic, but nevertheless inescapable principle: *One cannot deconstruct the character of the duke without also deconstructing the play.*

In *Richard II* a stage image is used by the duke of York to describe the fall of Richard and the rise of the new king, Bolingbroke:

> As in a theatre the eyes of men
> After a well-graced actor leaves the stage
> Are idly bent on him that enters next,
> Thinking his prattle to be tedious,
> Even so, or with much more contempt, men's eyes
> Did scowl on gentle Richard.
>
> (V.ii.23ff.)

The fickle mob of the streets becomes the capricious audience in a theater. Bolingbroke then, like a shrewd and calculating actor, knows how to use the streets as a stage, how to "upstage" poor Richard and thus steal the affection and popularity that once belonged to him.

> Mounted upon a hot and fiery steed . . .
> Bareheaded, lower than his proud steed's neck,
> [Bolingbroke] Bespake them thus; "I thank you, countrymen."
>
> (V.ii.8ff.)

In the pseudohumble Bolingbroke Shakespeare gives us a picture of the politician as actor; the horse has become a prop, a visual effect to heighten the "impact" of all this feigned modesty. In politics appearance is more potent than reality; it is better to be thought humble than to possess that virtue genuinely but not be judged to be so by public opinion, an idea that Shakespeare might have found voiced in *The Republic* by Socrates' shrewd antagonist Thrasymachus or by Machiavelli, except that Elizabethan and Jacobean England did not read Old Nick, as we know, but only his philosophical and religious enemies.

Vincentio tells Angelo, even though "I love the people, / [I] do not like to stage me to their eyes." We must, of course, accept this as self-insight, as a simple truth. However, there is an antithetical truth, which is that the whole of the fifth act is a staged play in which Vincentio, the anonymous playwright, plays the lead in the role that might be called "The Gullible Judge"; he is director as well in the minidrama he has enacted in front of the city gate by actors who will eventually understand that Vincentio, like Shakespeare, has been manipulating them for his own artful purposes.

We want to unify the shy and diffident Vincentio who retreats from the public arena with the man who relishes both the hidden power of the dramatist and the excitement of acting. We would like to be able to reconcile what almost seems two antithetical Vincentios, one modest and uncertain, the other bold, manipulative, and full of the confidence that comes with the catbird seat. Can we? Not easily, and not without doing violence to the integrity of each of the elements in the makeup of the duke. And so we must accept the contradiction, understand that there are two (and possibly more) Vincentios. Insofar as he is to be seen as a monarch who finds the contemplative life more appealing than the active, Vincentio's first role in the play is that of the decent and honorable man who should not be taxed for the degeneracy that afflicts his dukedom. He has been negligent, yes, but in a good cause, spiritual enlightenment, and we must not be any harder on Vincentio than he is on himself. Insofar as it is given that Vienna's disease must be cured by almost any judicial or social medicine that can be found, Vincentio assumes a role quite different from that of the shy fellow who "ever loved the life removed" (I.iii.8). In the role of improvising physician, he devises one ad hoc stratagem after the other in his effort to purge Vienna. Beneath the disguise of the friar there is the disguise of the good doctor, and beneath that, the most potent and determining of Vincentio's many personae, the dramatist who acts a role in a play of his own devising. Each role, each persona, each identity has its own authenticity, must command our uncynical assent, but cannot be made to fit into a smoothly "realistic" portrait.

Is Duke Vincentio too scrupulous to be a successful ruler? Yes. Is he too unscrupulous to be the ideal man Escalus takes him to be? Yes. Must we decide— more important, must Shakespeare decide— which is the authentic Vincentio? No. Vincentio's scruples are admirable in themselves, and thus we should not give too much importance to the admittedly bad consequences of these praiseworthy scruples. On the other hand,

Vincentio's clever but unscrupulous manipulations, like those of his only begetter, William Shakespeare, give us so much pleasure, divert and astound us so consistently, that the delight they afford is indeed an end that justifies the means.

A duke who, as Sir Thomas Browne expressed it in speaking of Christian faith, lives "in divided and distinguished worlds" is part of the pattern in which unequivocal and even radical values are asserted but then jettisoned so that new ideas, equally powerful but incompatible with those they replace, may be given their brief moment.

ISABELLA

Carolyn E. Brown evaluates the conflicting critical attitudes to Isabella's character, noting that while some scholars regard Isabella as "saintly," others condemn her as shrewish. Brown asserts that a psychological assessment of Isabella reveals that she is a complex character who unconsciously harbors incestuous feelings for her brother and a fascination with sexual masochism. Bernice Kliman describes Isabella as youthfully innocent; further, Kliman observes that Isabella is a "poor debater" and an inexperienced rhetorician who must depend on the Duke for a resolution to her troubles. By contrast, **Amy Lechter-Siegel** and Marcia Riefer consider Isabella to be highly articulate. However, both Lechter-Siegel and Riefer remark that because the novice's speeches pose a threat to the established male authority, they become fewer and less persuasive until Isabella is at last reduced to what Riefer regards as a powerless silence at the close of the play. Barbara J. Baines directly refutes Riefer's argument, contending that Isabella remains a powerful force throughout thanks to her chastity. Baines argues that in a "diseased state" such as Vienna, where sexual license is rampant, chastity is regarded as a formidable cure, and one that is respected by characters as different as the Duke and Lucio.

Critics disagree about the significance of Isabella's silence in response to the Duke's proposal of marriage at the close of the play. Baines and Lechter-Siegel suggest that it is a mute sign of passive resistance to the Duke's offer. Laura Lunger Knoppers observes that Isabella's silence has traditionally been regarded as "happy consent" to marriage but that it may in fact signal the Duke's success at remodeling the novice into an "obedient" and "ideal wife." Karl F. Zender suggests that since the play closes as a conventional comedy should— with several couples either married or betrothed, then it is likely that Isabella's silence indicates assent. On the other hand, Zender also observes that the end of *Measure for Measure* is hardly festive: none of the couples speaks affectionately to one another, and one of the couples—Juliet and Claudio—doesn't interact at all. Therefore, Zender notes, Isabella's own silence may not be as acquiescent as it seems. Maureen Connolly McFeely puts Isabella's silence within its historical context. She argues that while modern audiences would probably interpret Isabella's unresponsiveness as an indication that she has chosen to remain celibate, Renaissance comic conventions and Renaissance social standards (which preferred silent obedience in women) called for Isabella's mute acceptance of the Duke's offer.

Amy Lechter-Siegel

SOURCE: "Isabella's Silence: The Consolidation of Power in *Measure for Measure*," in *Reconsidering the Renaissance: Papers from the Twenty-First Annual Conference*, edited by Mario A. Di Cesare, Medieval & Renaissance Texts & Studies, 1992, pp. 371-80.

[*Lechter-Siegel observes that scholarly assessments of Isabella as morally rigid and therefore fortunate to have been "saved" from the convent through "moral education" and by the Duke's marriage proposal are inaccurate because they stem from each critic's personal "value judgments" rather than from Renaissance history or the play itself. By contrast, Lechter-Siegel argues that Isabella does not in fact change her moral views, nor does she agree to marry the Duke. Instead, Lechter-Siegel asserts that Isabella's articulate speeches in the first half of the play threaten the Duke's absolutist control of the state and that the Duke himself represents England's absolutist monarch, James I. Because they pose a threat to the fictional state represented in the drama as well as to the actual state of England, Isabella's subversive comments must be "contained" through marriage at the close of the play; however, Lechter-Siegel argues that Isabella's resulting silence does not indicate that she has necessarily abandoned these subversive views.*]

In act 1 of *Measure for Measure*, the novice Isabella first appears on stage in obedience before a religious authority of whom she requests a life of severe asceticism. In Isabella's first major speech, she makes closely reasoned pleas for the Christian principle of mercy. By contrast, in act 5 Isabella appears in supplication before a secular authority and first makes emotional and then poorly reasoned pleas for the secular principles of justice and equity. In the final scene, the novice, who had requested a cloistered life of chastity and severe simplicity, anticipates a public life of marriage and courtly opulence. A character who is first described to the audience as an eloquent and persuasive speaker is, in the final moment of the play, silent.

What transpires between acts 1 and 5 to bring about this reversal? Can we view Isabella as a developing dramatic character whose desires change from the beginning to the end of the play? Many critics imply that we can and argue that this alteration is a happy

development brought about under the Duke/Friar's tutelage and testing. Some critics argue that Isabella receives a "moral education": she realizes that she was too severe at the start in refusing so resolutely to show mercy for her brother by sacrificing her chastity. Other critics argue that Isabella receives a sexual education: Anne Barton, for example, argues that "beneath the habit of the nun is a passionate girl afflicted with an irrational fear of sex which she has never admitted to herself." Similarly, many see the Duke's marriage proposition as a felicitous ending: [Geoffrey] Bullough notes [in *Narrative and Dramatic Sources of Shakespeare*], "Isabella yields and thereby proves herself too valuable to the world to immure herself in a convent."

The problem with all these views, it seems to me, is that they are value judgments imposed from outside based on the critic's assessment of moral, or sexually healthy, or socially beneficial behavior and that they do not consider the ending in terms of Isabella's own behavior and expressed desires. If we consider these, there seems to be nothing in the play which leads us to conclude that she gains a new moral or psychic awareness or that her desires change from the beginning to the end. She never considered the concept of mercy to require that she commit a mortal sin, nor does her final plea for mercy at the end encompass that idea. And there is no hint, in word or deed, that Isabella develops any burgeoning awareness of her own sexuality. Finally, in the end, she does not willfully "yield" to the proposition of marriage; rather, in the face of command masquerading as a proposal, Isabella is silent.

Thus, if we cannot see Isabella as a developing dramatic character for whom the ending is a satisfactory resolution, we must look for the function of her character and the significance of the resolution elsewhere. I suggest that we see Isabella less as a character than as a representative of certain ideas. I am in agreement with Marcia Riefer, who has traced the process by which Isabella becomes increasingly directed by the patriarchal control of the Duke until her voice is "literally" lost. Riefer persuasively argues that the anomalous ending represents "the incompatibility of sexual subjugation with successful comic dramaturgy." I would like both to build on and to shift significantly the focus of that position by arguing that the Duke/Friar represents not generalized patriarchal control, but rather historically specific Jamesian-style control as James I outlines his concept of absolutist authority in the *Basilikon Doron*. In this context, Isabella can be understood to represent two specific challenges to Vincentio's absolutist position. First, in her adherence to religious authority, Isabella resists the secular control of the state; and second, in her adherence to virginity, she resists the social control of the Duke as both a private and public patriarch. Further, as a highly articulate spokesperson of these ideas, her rhetoric is especially threatening to the state. If we understand Isabella in this way, we can understand her "development" as a process of containment whereby the challenges she represents are eliminated in the play's resolution.

Such a reading is based on already extensive scholarship which argues for the interrelationship of *Measure for Measure*, the *Basilikon Doron*, and James I and which maintains an identification of the Duke/Friar with King James. First, I wish to add to this scholarship by arguing that the *Basilikon Doron* can be read as James's program for consolidating religious, secular political, and social power and that *Measure* can be read as a parallel text in which the same program is reproduced. Second, I wish to show how the process of containment is reflected in the Duke's ability to transform and to control Isabella's speech.

James opens the *Basilikon Doron* with a sonnet which defines his divine right style of rule. It begins:

God giues not Kings the stile of *Gods* in
    vaine,
For on his Throne his Scepter doe they swey.

This idea is echoed again when he urges his son "to know and love that God . . . for that he made you as a little GOD that sit on his Throne, and rule ouer other men."

James's program for the consolidation of religious, secular political, and social power in a divine right monarch is benignly couched as advice to his son on the proper behavior of a king in his three roles of good Christian, of good ruler, and of model virtuous social being— roles which correlate to the three areas of monarchal power. I would argue that it is by the consolidation of power through the use of these three roles that James attempts to establish his absolutist position, and it is further by the elimination of all challenges to this consolidation that James seeks to sustain this position. The treatise also reflects James's perception of the obstacles to this consolidation and his extreme anxiety over these.

Because the Renaissance notion of sovereignty demanded that all people must obey the sovereign without question *unless* his demands directly contradicted God's orders, it is natural that it was the power of the church (whether Anglican, Protestant, or Catholic) which would pose the greatest threat to a monarch who saw a special divinity in his rule. In the *Basilikon Doron*, James seems to perceive the challenge to his divine right position coming from two sources: the first threat comes from those who would accuse him of insufficient religiousness; and the second comes from religious leaders who would assert the priority of *their* authority over the monarch's.

His greatest anxiety is over the Anabaptists who show"

contempt for the civil Magistrate," and who advocate that "Christian Princes . . . be resisted." These kind of men, James writes, "I wishe my Sonne to punish, incase they refuse to obey the Law, and will not cease to sturre up rebellion." The divisiveness created by the Anabaptists furthermore increases the power of the Catholics (Papists) to challenge the authority of the state. James exhorts his son to suppress the power of church leaders in a language which dramatically conveys both the extent of his anxiety and his absolutist stance: "as well as yee repress the vain Puritaine, so not to suffer proude Papall Bishops . . . so *chaine them with such bondes* as may preserve that estate from creeping to corruption" [emphasis mine].

James begins the second book of the *Basilikon Doron* with an image which marvelously suggests the consolidation of religious and secular control in the person of the king: "But as ye are clothed with two callings so must ye be alike careful for the discharge of them both: that yee are a good Christian so yee may be a good King." "Clothed with two callings" describes the Friar/Duke of *Measure* who is literally so clothed, and thus by his person contains both appeals to independent religious authority (made by Isabella) and claims of independent secular authority (made by Angelo). The Duke/Friar has not only to contain these competing elements, but also to reintegrate them into society through marriage, and he arranges these marriages through the third role James describes in the *Basilikon Doron*— his social role as both private and public patriarch of the realm.

In the *Basilikon Doron* James notes that a good king acts, in relationship to his subjects, "as their naturall father, and kindley Master." In this role, James would undertake the arrangement of marriages as an absolutist strategy of social control in order to consolidate his political position. In *Measure*, Duke Vincentio is, of course, the quintessential arranger of marriages. Also, James's remarks on marriage and the choice of a wife in the *Basilikon Doron* reflect how the double-edged quality of the new Protestant conception of marriage allowed the private and public patriarch to assume more direct power over women than he previously had. The Protestant marriage gave for the first time in history priority to married chastity over Catholic asceticism and virginity. While many have seen this as a happy development for women, others have realized that, to the degree that the power of the priest was diminished, to an equal degree, the power of the family patriarch was increased. In the Duke's proposal to Isabella after his dramatic unhooding by Lucio, Shakespeare provides a compelling *visual* representation of this very transformation from the priority of virginity to the priority of married chastity and of the quite literal transference of power from the priest (or friar) to the husband.

As a natural father, James could claim to be a Father

to the realm more convincingly than could Elizabeth claim an analogous personal leadership role before him. The Duke in *Measure for Measure* uses marriage in the end to contain all subversive elements in the society, to suppress any challenges to his divine right position, and, in good comedic fashion, to reintegrate everyone back into his society— creating a union directed by a monarch who has gained control through the consolidation of his secular political, religious, and social roles.

Finally, I would like to suggest that in the *Basilikon Doron*, James perceives the threat to his control expressed through "slander." Those who would accuse him of irreligiousness or question his religious authority he accuses of "famous libels," "iniurious speaches," and dishonorable "inuectiue" against all Christian princes and maintains that the "malicious lying tongues of some haue traduced me." His anxiety is so great that he advises his son, again in absolutist language, that the "remedie" for "vnreuerent speakers" is to "stop their mouthes from all such idle and vnreuerent speeches." Although it is Lucio who most persistently represents the threat of slander, and it is Lucio's mouth which most obviously will not be stopped, Isabella too threatens and eventually does slander Angelo. Because her rhetoric challenges the power of the state, the Friar first directs, then effectively stops, her speech.

To reiterate, I have argued that Isabella challenges the Duke/Friar's absolutist position in two ways. First, by invoking religious authority over secular (in her arguments to the Duke's representative, Angelo), she challenges the secular political control of the state; second, by choosing virginity, she resists the social control of the monarch as patriarch of the realm. Now, I would like to argue that the play enacts the containment of those challenges and that the process of containment can be traced by following Isabella's changing discourse: first, Isabella generates reasoned arguments which challenge the state; next, under the Duke/Friar, her language is directed by the state; and finally, her speech is contained by the state.

In the early scenes of the play, Claudio says of his sister, "she hath prosperous art / When she will play with reason and discourse / And well she can persuade" (1.2.184). The first time we see Isabella she stands before a nun of whom she requires not a lesser, but a stricter restraint within the already strictly ascetic order of St. Clare. Further, we learn in this scene that once Isabella enters the order she must take a vow of silence forbidding her to speak to and be looked upon by men at the same time. Interestingly, while Isabella will *freely admit* to the imposition of silence in obeisance to religious authority, she will, in the meantime, use her arts of language brilliantly in the next scenes to challenge and inadvertently threaten secular authority.

In her first encounter with Angelo, Isabella challenges

his secular authority by using logical appeals which show proficiency in close reasoning and the ability to make clear distinctions. She presses her case by making eight reasoned pleas. Each time she makes an argument based on Christian principles, Angelo counters with an argument based on secular legal authority. Thus, a dialectic movement is set up between these two sources of power. Finally, Isabella audaciously challenges Angelo's position by daring to project herself (woman and novice) into the role of the head of state: "I would to heaven I had your potency, And you were Isabel" (2.2.71). This bold assertion is based on her sense of power as a follower— and perhaps to a certain extent as a representative— of religious authority. In her final pleas, Isabella challenges the very legitimacy of secular authority itself, deploring the tyrannous exercise of power by "proud men dressed in a little brief authority" (2.2.118). Having reminded him that his authority is not absolute (an argument that implicitly interrogates the Jamesian absolutist position), she tells him to look inside himself. This argument inadvertently leads to Angelo's realization that her words have compelled him to love her and to his (quite liberal) loss of control. There is thus a correlation suggested here between loss of sexual control and loss of political control. Both the content and manner of Isabella's speech threatens the control of the representative of the state, and the rest of the play is concerned with containing that threat. Importantly, between Isabella's and Angelo's first and second meetings the Duke/Friar makes a brief appearance which seems to have little dramatic purpose. However, his appearance can function as a visual synthesis of the religious/secular dialectic, and thus it rehearses the ultimate consolidation of religious and secular power in the person of the monarch at the end of the play.

In her second meeting with Angelo, Isabella is forced from the offensive position of challenging secular authority to the rhetorically weaker defensive position of resisting that authority's attempts to possess her sexually. Again, the dialectic is resumed with Angelo invoking the authority of the state in order to propose that Isabella exchange her virginity for her brother's life, while she invokes the religious principle that death is better than eternal damnation. Her integrity of speech is maintained when Angelo suggests she respond in a more "womanly" way; she answers, "I have no tongue but one . . ." (2.4.139). When Angelo presses further, she threatens slander: "Sign me a present pardon . . . / Or . . . I'll tell the world aloud / What man thou art" (2.4.152-85). But Angelo's retort that no one will believe her suggests that the punishment for the slanderer is rhetorical powerlessness: "you will stifle in your own report and smell of calumny" (2.4.158-59). This scene signals the beginning of the process by which Isabella's strength of speech is undermined.

When in the next scene the brother whom she trusts

implies that she should submit, her rhetoric breaks down to a vituperative and aggressive hurling of epithets. This change suggests a breakdown of what one critic has called that "strong self" constituted by her rhetoric. We might assume that Isabella, fleeing from Claudio, is rushing back to the convent when the Duke/Friar suddenly appears before her and bids a word. She responds, "What is your will?" (3.1.152). Humiliated by the forces of secular authority, she is anxious to cleave to religious authority, and when the Friar suggests a plan, she consents: "Show me how good father" (3.3.238). At this point in the play we see not a development of Isabella's personality but a shift in her position from one of powerful and articulate resistance to secular authority to (though unbeknownst to her) submission to it. From now on the Duke/Friar maintains control over Isabella by making her believe Claudio is dead and then by scripting a scenario which requires her to announce publicly that she is a violated virgin— a remarkable request considering both her integrity of speech ("I have no tongue but one") and her vocation of chastity. As Riefer points out, despite Isabella's reluctance "to speak so indirectly" (4.6.1), she gives over rhetorical control when she vows to the Duke/Friar, "I am directed by you" (4.3.137).

In act 5, Isabella's rhetoric demonstrates a changed relationship to the state. Whereas the use of close reasoning in support of mercy describes her first encounter with Angelo, here she is making a pathetic appeal for justice— the secular principle she renounced in act 1. Regaining her capacity for reasoned argument, however, she presses her charges against Angelo with careful distinctions and analogies once again: "'tis not impossible / But one, the wicked'st caitiff on the ground, / May seem as shy, as grave, as just, as absolute, as Angelo . . ." (5.1.52-55). Ironically, her strong discourse constitutes slander, and the Duke— consistent with the Jamesian absolutist position— must contain the slander by imprisoning Isabella. This is a very interesting moment, for here we see the Duke constructig a threat to secular authority (in the role consigned to Isabella), and then through his consolidated secular/religious authority containing that threat. It will be marriage, not imprisonment, that is the final mode of containment; but, I would argue, the imprisonment of Isabella makes the final solution of marriage seem benevolent by contrast.

This same process of constructing the threat in order to contain it occurs again when Vincentio re-presents himself on stage as the Friar who slanders the Duke. Here he constructs a challenge by religious authority, not only to secular authority (as was the case with Isabella's challenge), but to divine right monarchy. Again a dialectic is played out between the "Friar" and Escalus (5.1.305) in which the Friar claims religious authority is not subject to monarchy ("The Duke / Dare no more stretch this finger of mine than he / Dare rack his own. His subject I am not" [5.1.313-15]). The Friar's

challenge, which so compellingly echoes the threats James perceives from churchmen in the *Basilikon Doron*, is once again contained by Escalus, who accuses the Friar of "slander to the state" and orders his imprisonment.

At this point, Lucio unhoods the Friar to expose the Duke. At last, the consolidation of religious and secular power in the person of the Jamesian divine right monarch is visually represented in this brilliant coup de théâtre. Angelo confirms his divinity: "I perceive your Grace, like power divine" (5.1.369). But what of Isabella to whom he entreats, "Come hither, Isabel, / Your friar is now your prince"? When secular power (embodied in Angelo) was re-presented as religious power (embodied in the Friar) Isabella bent to its will. But after she cleaved unto religious authority, that authority represented itself once again as divine right absolutist authority. This visual transformation, suggestive of a magician's sleight, brilliantly conveys *how* Isabella comes under the sway of the state. *That* she comes under its sway is demonstrated in her final plea for Angelo.

In this plea, Isabella argues for mercy, but instead of grounding this argument on Christian principles as she had earlier, she now grounds it on the secular principle of equity: "His act did not o'ertake his bad intent / And must be buried but as an intent / That perish'd by the way" (5.1.450-54). While secular law makes a distinction between intent and action, theological law *does not;* an argument by Christ would see Angelo's transgression as a serious violation of God's law. Furthermore, Isabella's argument is illogical, for Angelo did not only intend to engage in illicit sex, but, in sleeping with his fiancée, he actually did the very same thing Claudio did. Isabella's inability to make that distinction, when her forte all along has been the ability to perceive distinctions, represents the final dissolution of that "strong self" constituted by her rhetoric.

In the final consolidation of power, the Duke uses the Jamesian social role of patriarch in order to reintegrate his citizens into society through marriage. But the Duke's use of marriage is an absolutist strategy which can be at variance with individual desire. Lucio makes this clear when he tells the Duke, who directs him to marry a whore, that he'd rather be whipped: "Marrying a punk, my lord, is pressing to death, whipping, and hanging" (5.1.522-23). The Duke replies, "Slandering a prince deserves it" (5.2.524). That the imposition of marriage is an absolutist strategy in this play, in contrast to most Shakespearean comedies, is suggested by the fact that of those who are married off in the end, fully half— Angelo, Lucio, and Isabella— do not desire it.

The problematic "deus ex machina" ending which troubles many critics becomes singularly appropriate if the play is understood as one about "ideas" more than about "characters" and about specifically Jamesian ideas— as these are articulated in *Basilikon Doron*— of

Act V, scene i. Varrius, lords, Angelo, Escalus, Lucio, citizens, Isabella, Peter, Mariana, and Provost.

consolidating secular political, religious, and social power by ruling (as the Duke/Friar does) in "the stile of *Gods*." The very contrivance of the ending, wherein the events do not seem to evolve naturally and dramatically from the desires of the individual characters, but rather are imposed from without (by a kind of god from a machine), suggests the very style of authoritarianism and absolutism which, I have maintained, the play is "about."

Isabella's silence at the end of *Measure for Measure* has provided a challenge for theatrical directors of the play. Jonathan Miller's National Theatre production had Isabella turn away in horror at the Duke's proposal of marriage; by extreme contrast, another recent production had Isabella throw off her veil in a celebratory and liberating gesture. While Miller's interpretation is consistent with Isabella's "dramatic character," it contradicts the play's movement toward comic resolution. On the other hand, the second interpretation, while true to the play's movement towards resolution, is so totally contrary to Isabella's character that it altogether lacks

dramatic veracity. Shakespeare gives us neither Miller's nor any other response from Isabella. He gives us silence. It is "silence," argues Pierre Macherey, that "the critic must make speak." Isabella's silence speaks most convincingly, I believe, as an expression of the Jamesian Duke/Friar's successful containment of voices which challenge his absolutist claims to authority. However, containment does not imply any simple or comfortable acquiescence by those voices. Rather, speechlessness can also be interpreted as a *refusal* to assent positively to the control of an "other." It is for this reason, I believe, that Isabella's silence reverberates in our minds long after the play is done.

SOURCES FOR FURTHER STUDY

Literary Commentary

Bache, William B. "The Ethic of Love and Duty." In *"Mea-*

sure for Measure" as Dialectical Art, pp. 1-12. Lafayette, IN: Purdue University Studies, 1969.

Argues that *Measure for Measure* is a realistic play about the "brutality" of life. Bache focuses on the religious overtones in the play and the manner in which its central characters struggle to find the right way to live in the face of life's difficulties.

Baines, Barbara J. "Assaying the Power of Chastity in *Measure for Measure*." *Studies in English Literature* 30, No. 2 (Spring 1990): 283-301.

Asserts that the character Isabella is not as powerless as numerous critics believe she is. Baines observes that chastity is a unique instrument of power in a society that has become as corrupt as the Duke's Vienna has, so that the chaste novice Isabella is someone whom the other characters cannot afford to ignore.

Brown, Carolyn E. "*Measure for Measure*: Isabella's Beating Fantasies." *American Imago* 43, No. 1 (Spring 1986): 67-80.

Suggests that Isabella provokes sharply conflicting reactions from scholars— some of whom regard her as a positive character while others see her as unpleasantly negative. Brown approaches Isabella's character from a psychological point of view as an ambivalent, "complex character" who subconsciously entertains masochistic and incestuous sexual fantasies even while she "aspires to a saintly life."

———. "*Measure for Measure*: Duke Vincentio's 'Crabbed' Desires." *Literature and Psychology* XXXV, Nos. 1 & 2 (1989): 66-88.

Focuses on the Duke's interview with Lucio in Act II, Scene ii. Brown observes that this short meeting reveals much about Vincentio's problematical character— including the fact that this superficially virtuous ruler has a cruel streak, which he hides from himself.

Cacicedo, Alberto. "'She Is Fast My Wife': Sex, Marriage, and Ducal Authority in *Measure for Measure*." *Shakespeare Studies* XXII (1995): 187-209.

Emphasizes gender issues and the role of women in Shakespeare's time. Cacicedo examines the play in light of Renaissance society's ambivalent feelings toward women and the Renaissance view of marriage as a necessary evil.

Dunkel, Wilbur. "Law and Equity in *Measure for Measure*." *Shakespeare Quarterly* XIII, No. 3 (Summer 1962): 275-85.

Examines the play from the point of view of its Renaissance audience and the highly theatrical King James I. Dunkel argues that justice (that is, the rule of law) tempered with equity (that is, mercy) was an important concern for Shakespeare's England and that audiences would be sensitive to the fact that until the final act of this comedy, the Duke dispenses mercy without justice and his deputy, Angelo, dispenses justice without mercy.

Dusinberre, Juliet. "Introduction." In *Shakespeare and the Nature of Women*, pp. 1-76. London: The Macmillan Press Ltd., 1975.

Provides an overview of Renaissance feminism as it is reflected in the literature of the time— particularly in Shakespeare's works. Dusinberre argues that in *Measure for Measure*, Shakespeare made clear his objection to the sexual double-standard that demanded that women bear most of the blame for being unchaste.

Fisch, Harold. "Shakespeare and the Puritan Dynamic." *Shakespeare Survey* 27 (1974): 81-92.

Looks at the nature of Puritanism in three of Shakespeare's plays, including *Measure for Measure*. Fisch contends that as a Puritan, Angelo is corrupted by his love of power even as he acknowledges that his religion is at odds with earthly power.

Gless, Darryl F. "Duke Vincentio: The Intermittent Immanence of Godhead." In *"Measure for Measure," the Law, and the Convent*, pp. 214-55. Princeton, NJ: Princeton University Press, 1979.

Analyzes the character of the Duke in terms of the tests he imposes on the other characters in the play. Gless describes Vincentio as "a little image of God" who dispenses divine justice, resolves Vienna's failings, and engineers the play's conclusion.

Grove, Robin. "A Measure for Magistrates." *The Critical Review*, No. 19 (1977): 3-23.

General discussion of character in Shakespeare's plays. Grove includes a particular focus on Duke Vincentio and his role in shaping the outcome of the action in *Measure for Measure*; Grove sees the Duke as self-important and insensitive.

Hawkins, Harriett. "'The Devil's Party': Virtues and Vices in *Measure for Measure*." *Shakespeare Survey* 31 (1978): 105-113.

Focuses on the religious issues that contribute to the status of *Measure for Measure* as a "problem play." Hawkins asserts that applying a religious interpretation to the play does not resolve its ambiguities since religious disagreement, ambiguity, and debate existed during Shakespeare's time; further, Hawkins suggests that Shakespeare purposely filled the play with "unanswered questions and unsolved problems," and that these questions themselves are more important than any answers to them would be.

Hunter, Robert Grams. "Measure for Measure." In *Shakespeare and the Comedy of Forgiveness*, pp. 204-26. New York: Columbia University Press, 1965.

Defines the relationship between humanity and justice as it is presented in *Measure for Measure*. Hunter argues that in the play, rigid "Justice must learn from Iniquity" (in the same way that the overly strict Angelo learns from his own weaknesses) in order to understand the virtue of charity.

Jaffa, Harry V. "Chastity as a Political Principle: An Interpretation of Shakespeare's *Measure for Measure*." In *Shakespeare as Political Thinker*, edited by John Alvis and Thomas G. West, pp. 181-213. Durham, NC: Carolina Academic Press, 1981.

> Examines the thematic concerns of *Measure for Measure*. Jaffa points out that at the beginning of the play, there exist two extremes in Vienna— celibacy and lechery— and that the action of the play is resolved when marriage becomes a viable force in the city.

Kirsch, Arthur C. "The Integrity of *Measure for Measure*." *Shakespeare Survey* 28 (1975): 89-105.

> Defends *Measure for Measure* against those critics who consider it a failure. Kirsch asserts that the play in fact achieves unity through its religious themes and biblical references.

Kliman, Bernice W. "Isabella in *Measure for Measure*." *Shakespeare Studies* XV (1982): 137-48.

> Discusses the problematical nature of Isabella's characterization. Kliman departs from most critics when she describes Isabella as "a poor debater," and explains that this flaw in Isabella serves to focus the audience's attention on the importance of the Duke's role in the play.

Knoppers, Laura Lunger. "(En)gendering Shame: *Measure for Measure* and the Spectacles of Power." *English Literary Renaissance* 23, No. 3 (Autumn 1993): 450-71.

> Focuses on the role of women in *Measure for Measure*. Specifically, Knoppers argues that Isabella's silence at the end of the play indicates that she has been coerced into obedience but not into approbation by the Duke's proposal of marriage, and that thus the play remains problematical as a comedy.

Levin, Richard A. "Duke Vincentio and Angelo: Would 'A Feather Turn the Scale'?" *Studies in English* 22 (1982): 257-70.

> Examines Duke Vincentio in relation to the other, morally rigid, characters in the play— Angelo and Isabella. Levin suggests that if we look at the Duke "as a psychologically plausible character" rather than as a symbol or instrument for dispensing final judgment, then we will understand that he possesses very human, contradictory traits: those of goodness and moral weakness.

McFeely, Maureen Connolly. "'This Day My Sister Should the Cloister Enter': The Convent as Refuge in *Measure for Measure*." In *Subjects on the World's Stage: Essays on British Literature of the Middle Ages and the Renaissance*, edited by David G. Allen and Robert A. White, pp. 200-16. Newark: The University of Delaware Press, 1995.

> Speculates on how Renaissance audiences reacted and how modern audiences should react to Isabella's silence in response to the Duke's proposal of marriage at the end of the play. McFeely concludes that since "Renaissance society idealized silence and obedience" in women, then Isabella's lack of a response would have been regarded as acquiescence; modern audiences, on the other hand, would be influenced by Isabella's insistent refusal throughout the play to give up her virginity.

Pinciss, G. M. "The 'Heavenly Comforts of Despair' and *Measure for Measure*." *Studies in English Literature* 30, No. 2 (Spring 1990): 303-13.

> Applies Protestant theology to *Measure for Measure*. Pinciss demonstrates how the central characters in the play each undergo self-despair as a necessary prerequisite to spiritual understanding.

Reifer, Marcia. "'Instruments of Some More Mightier Member': The Constriction of Female Power in *Measure for Measure*." *Shakespeare Quarterly* 35, No. 2 (Summer 1984): 157-69.

> Examines the role of Isabella in the play. Reifer sees Isabella as an important transitional character in Shakespeare's body of plays, appearing as she does— articulate but restricted— between the self-reliant female characters of Shakespeare's comedies and the female "victims" of his tragedies.

Soellner, Rolf. "Measure for Measure: Looking into Oneself." In *Shakespeare's Patterns of Self-Knowledge*, pp. 215-36. Columbus: Ohio State University Press, 1972.

> Discusses the themes of justice and mercy in the play as well as the role of Angelo. Soellner argues that the behavior of the character Angelo demonstrates that people do not function effectively or fairly as judges until they have been forced to judge themselves.

Thatcher, David. "Mercy and 'Natural Guiltiness' in *Measure for Measure*." *Texas Studies in Literature and Language* 37, No. 3 (Fall 1995): 264-84.

> Examines *Measure for Measure* as a "problem play" and discusses the issue of justice versus mercy. Thatcher argues that Angelo is right in asserting that "natural guiltiness"— that is, the fact that the judge of someone else's crime might well have committed the crime himself or herself— is not a valid argument in favor of acquittal.

Zender, Karl F. "Isabella's Choice." *Philological Quarterly* 73, No. 1 (Winter 1994): 77-93.

> Discusses Isabella's options concerning Angelo's proposition and the Duke's proposal. Zender suggests that Isabella's decision not to test her word against Angelo's by revealing his hypocrisy is the result of her own preference for silence. On the other hand, Zender observes that Isabella's silence at the end of the play when presented with the Duke's marriage proposal and when she would in all probability prefer to remain celibate is required by the play's designation as a comedy.

RICHARD II

INTRODUCTION

It is generally believed that Shakespeare wrote *Richard II* during the mid-1590s. Many scholars maintain that the play could not have been written before late 1594 or early 1595, since it was not until this time that a poem thought to be one of Shakespeare's primary sources was listed in the Stationers' Register. (The Stationers' Company was an association of manufacturers and sellers of books. They kept a register of the titles of works to be printed and published.) The poem was an epic written by Samuel Daniel entitled *The Civil Wars. Richard II* itself was not listed in the Stationers' Register until August 29, 1597.

In addition to Samuel Daniel's poem, in which there are many parallels to *Richard II*, Shakespearean scholars identify several other works from which Shakespeare may have drawn in writing *Richard II*. Viewed as the most significant of these sources is Raphael Holinshed's *Chronicles of England, Scotlande, and Irelande* (1587). Holinshed offers an account of the historical Richard II's reign, deposition, and assassination. Shakespeare freely appropriated this source material in many ways, including in the area of characterization. Gaunt, for example, is depicted by Holinshed as greedy and ruthless, whereas Shakespeare portrays him as a wise and patriotic nobleman. For the plot sequence, Shakespeare adapted Edward Hall's *The vionon of the two noble and illustre famelies of Lancastre and York*. Additionally, scholars suggest that Shakespeare's sympathetic or pitying attitude toward Richard may have been derived from several French sources.

Richard II earned a reputation among Elizabethan audiences as a politically subversive play. In 1601, supporters of the Earl of Essex, who would the next day (February 7) mount an unsuccessful rebellion against Queen Elizabeth, paid Shakespeare's company to put on a special performance of the play. Queen Elizabeth was compared to Richard, because of her lack of an heir and due to what some subjects viewed as her inclination toward heavy taxation and indulgence of her favorites. Sixteenth-century critics often viewed the play as a politically dangerous commentary on the monarchy, and it was not until the eighteenth century that the play began to generate literary, rather than political, interest.

The main issues in the play are all rather inter-related and focus on the nature of kingship; whether Richard is deposed by Bolingbroke or deposes himself; and the characterization of Richard and Bolingbroke. The play examines the conflict between the legal and divine right to rule, and the effectiveness of the ruler. Richard is believed to be the legal, rightful ruler of England, ordained by God. Yet he is also shown to be a weak and ineffective king who focuses more upon the appearances, rather than the responsibilities, of kingship. Bolingbroke acts decisively, and arguably, with moral justification. He also is backed by the support of the people. It is unclear whether or not Shakespeare favored Richard and the divine right to rule over Bolingbroke and the effective use of political power, wielded with the consent of the people. Similar debate surrounds the issue of Richard's deposition. Does Bolingbroke truly force Richard to give up the crown, and has he been plotting to do so all along? Or does Richard timidly and without much cause surrender the kingship to Bolingbroke? The questions are debated by critics who find support for both arguments within the play.

A related issue is the characterization of both Richard and Bolingbroke. Some find Richard's weakness sympathetic, others find it despicable. Those who pity Richard's weakness maintain that he may be weak, but he is not evil. He is, however, influenced by evil advisors who offer bad counsel. Richard's supporters also point out that he is, in fact, the rightful king. Others contend that Richard's weakness and ineffectiveness are harmful to England, a fact to which Richard is oblivious. Richard is often accused of being overly concerned with himself, his personal gain, and the luxuries he enjoys as king. Additional counts against Richard include his role in the death of Gloucester, the banishment of Bolingbroke, and the confiscation of Gaunt's estate. Critical estimation of Bolingbroke is likewise divided. He is viewed as a traitor and usurper by some. Others maintain that his actions are justified and in fact save England from ruin. While he illegally returns to England after he has been banished, he has in fact been illegally disinherited by Richard. For most of the play, he is silent about his own motivations, and it is alternatively argued that he is driven by political ambition or by noble intentions.

PRINCIPAL CHARACTERS

(in order of appearance)

King Richard II of England: Richard is the title character and the ruler of England. He banishes Mowbray and Bolingbroke and confiscates Gaunt's land after the duke dies. When Bolingbroke returns from exile, Richard relinquishes his crown to him. The deposed King Richard is then imprisoned and later killed. *(See* **Richard** *in the* **CHARACTER STUDIES** *section.)*

Gaunt (John of Gaunt, Duke of Lancaster): Gaunt is York's brother and Richard's uncle. Despite his loyalty to his king— Gaunt refuses to avenge the death of his brother, Thomas Woodstock, the Duke of Gloucester, because the assassination had been ordered by King Richard— when Gaunt dies in Act II, scene i, his loyalty to his country prevails. Gaunt condemns the way Richard has "leas'd out" the country for his own financial gain.

Bolingbroke (Henry, Duke of Herford, afterwards King Henry IV of England): Bolingbroke is Gaunt's son and King Richard's cousin. Richard banishes him and seizes Gaunt's estate, which rightfully belongs to Bolingbroke. Bolingbroke returns from exile with an army. After Bolingbroke takes Richard into custody, Richard claims he is willing to give up his crown to Bolingbroke, which Richard eventually does. At the end of the play, Bolingbroke promises to make a pilgrimage to the Holy Land to atone for the death of Richard. *(See* **Bolingbroke** *in the* **CHARACTER STUDIES** *section.)*

Mowbray (Thomas Mowbray, Duke of Norfolk): Bolingbroke accuses Mowbray of embezzlement and murdering Thomas Woodstock, Duke of Gloucester. Richard orders a trial by combat between Bolingbroke and Mowbray, but calls it off and banishes both of them instead. It is later reported that Mowbray has died in exile.

Duchess of Gloucester: The widow of the murdered Thomas Woodstock, Duke of Gloucester. She pleads with her brother-in-law Gaunt to avenge her husband's death, but Gaunt refuses. In Act II, scene ii, York is told that the duchess has died.

Lord Marshal: He is the administrator of the trial by combat Richard has ordered between Bolingbroke and Mowbray. When Richard calls off the trial, the marshal states his wish to accompany Bolingbroke and see him off as he leaves England.

Aumerle (Duke of Aumerle, afterwards Earl of Rutland): York's son and cousin to Richard and Bolingbroke. Aumerle is loyal to King Richard and is accused in Act IV, scene i, of conspiring to kill Thomas Woodstock, Duke of Gloucester. After Richard is deposed, Aumerle plots with the Abbot of Westminster and the Bishop of Carlisle to assassinate Bolingbroke. The plot is discovered by York. Aumerle is pardoned by Bolingbroke, but is demoted from Duke of Aumerle to Earl of Rutland.

Bushy (Sir John Bushy): An advisor and favorite of King Richard. When Bolingbroke returns to England, Bushy and Green fear that Richard will be usurped, and the two men flee in fear of their lives. They are captured and executed by Bolingbroke.

Bagot (Sir John Bagot): Also a counselor and favorite of King Richard. Instead of being executed like Bushy and Green, he is taken to parliament to accuse Aumerle in the conspiracy against Thomas Woodstock, Duke of Gloucester.

Green (Sir Henry Green): Another advisor and favorite of King Richard. Green counsels Richard to go to Ireland to suppress an uprising there, but later claims it would have been better if Richard had not left, since Bolingbroke has returned to England. Green and Bushy are executed by Bolingbroke.

York (Edmund of Langley, Duke of York): Richard and Bolingbroke's uncle, brother of Gaunt, and father of Aumerle. Like Gaunt, York is loyal to king and country, but is outraged by Richard's confiscation of Gaunt's estate. When Bolingbroke returns from exile, York, who has been appointed regent while Richard is in Ireland, tells Bolingbroke that he would have him arrested if his own forces were not outnumbered by Bolingbroke's. Following Richard's deposition, York's loyalty is transferred to the new king (Bolingbroke), and when the plot of Aumerle against Bolingbroke is discovered, York rushes to warn Bolingbroke.

Northumberland (Henry Percy, Earl of Northumberland): Father of Harry Percy (or Hotspur), and supporter of Bolingbroke. He, Ross, and Willoughby criticize Richard in Act II, scene i. Northumberland disrespects King Richard in several instances, referring to him only as Richard and refusing to kneel before him. In Act IV, scene i, Northumberland insists that Richard read aloud the charges against him.

Queen Isabel: King Richard's wife. She chastises Richard for surrendering to imprisonment and argues that he should attempt to retain his dignity and remain a king in spirit even if he is no longer in fact the king.

Ross (Lord Ross): A supporter of Bolingbroke, he conspires with Northumberland and Willoughby for Bolingbroke's return from exile.

Willoughby (Lord Willoughby): A supporter of Bolingbroke, he conspires with Northumberland and Ross to enable Bolingbroke's return to England.

Percy (Henry Percy, also known as Harry Percy or Hotspur): Like his father, he supports Bolingbroke. He has a larger role in *Henry IV, Part One* (the play that follows *Richard II*), in which he becomes the enemy of King Henry (Bolingbroke) and his son.

Berkeley (Lord Berkeley): While Richard is in Ireland and York is acting as regent, York sends Berkeley to ask Bolingbroke why he has illegally returned to England.

Salisbury (Earl of Salisbury): A supporter of Richard. In Act II, scene iv, he implores the Welsh Captain to desert Richard. Northumberland later announces that Salisbury has died rebelling against the new king (Bolingbroke).

Welsh Captain: The leader of Richard's troops in Wales, the Captain tells Salisbury that since no word from Richard has been received, except rumors that he has died, he and his troops will not stay and fight for Richard.

Bishop of Carlisle: Loyal to Richard, Carlisle firmly believes in the divine right of Richard to rule. Carlisle speaks out against Bolingbroke and is arrested by Northumberland. He conspires with the Abbot of Westminster and Aumerle to assassinate Bolingbroke. After the plot is discovered, Bolingbroke gives the bishop a relatively light sentence.

Scroop (Sir Stephen Scroop): A supporter and ally of Richard who informs King Richard that the people have turned against him, that Richard's advisors Bushy and Green have been killed, and that York has joined Bolingbroke.

Gardeners: The gardener and his assistant appear in Act III, scene iv. Queen Isabel overhears the men discussing how England has fared under Richard's rule. They describe England as a garden surrounded by a sea wall, tangled with weeds, and infested with caterpillars (Bushy, Bagot, and Green), who have given the king bad advice.

Fitzwater (Lord Fitzwater): A nobleman in parliament who supports Bagot's claim that Aumerle is responsible for the Duke of Gloucester's death. Bolingbroke, after becoming King Henry IV, rewards Fitzwater for helping to gather and execute Bolingbroke's enemies.

Surrey (Duke of Surrey): When Aumerle is accused by Fitzwater of murdering the Duke of Gloucester, Surrey defends Aumerle.

Abbot of Westminster: In Act IV, scene i, Northumberland tells Westminster to take custody of the Bishop of Carlisle, who has just spoken out against Bolingbroke. At the end of this scene, the abbot, the bishop, and Aumerle conspire to assassinate Bolingbroke. Harry Percy later reports that the abbot has died.

Duchess of York: Wife of the Duke of York and Aumerle's mother, she tries to protect Aumerle when his plot against Bolingbroke is discovered.

Exton (Sir Pierce of Exton): Exton assassinates Richard in his prison cell. He believes that he is following Bolingbroke's wishes, for in Act V, scene iv, Exton quotes Bolingbroke as asking "'Have I no friend that will rid me of this living fear?'" (line 2). Exton concludes that as he is the king's friend, he will eliminate Bolingbroke's enemy, Richard. But Henry condemns Exton for the murder.

Groom: A former employee of Richard, he visits Richard in prison and tells Richard that Bolingbroke, after his coronation, rode Richard's favorite horse.

Keeper: The keeper of the prison in Pomfret castle where Richard is being held, he brings Richard his last meal, which has been poisoned by Exton. Richard refuses to eat it and attacks the keeper before being murdered.

PLOT SYNOPSIS

Act I: King Richard presides over a conflict between Bolingbroke and Mowbray. Bolingbroke has accused Mowbray of misappropriation of funds and of murdering the Duke of Gloucester. Richard and Gaunt advise the men to settle their affairs peacefully, but they refuse, and Richard sets a date for trial by combat. Meanwhile, the Duchess of Gloucester pleads with Gaunt to avenge her husband's death, but Gaunt refuses, claiming that Richard himself ordered the assassination. When the trial by combat is about to ensue, Richard halts the proceedings and instead banishes Mowbray for life, and Bolingbroke for ten years. When Richard sees Gaunt's distress at the sentence, he reduces Bolingbroke's banishment to six years. Richard tells Aumerle that he dislikes that Bolingbroke is popular with the commoners. The king's advisor, Green, counsels Richard to attend to a possible uprising in Ireland. To raise money for the trip, Richard plans to lease royal lands. At the end of the act, Richard is called to the bedside of Gaunt, who is dying.

Act II: On his deathbed, Gaunt condemns Richard's poor governing of England and advises Richard to change his ways. Once Gaunt is dead, Richard confiscates his land to finance the war against Ireland. York counsels Richard that Gaunt's estate rightfully belongs to Gaunt's banished son, Bolingbroke. Richard leaves for England, appointing York regent in his absence. In the meantime, Queen Isabel discovers that Bolingbroke has defied his banishment by returning to England, and that he has the support of other nobles and their armies. Outnumbered by Bolingbroke's forces, York sends the queen to safety and retreats to Berkeley castle. Bushy, Bagot, and Green, as the king's favorites, flee fearing that Bolingbroke might take action against them. Bolingbroke arrives at Berkeley castle, telling York that he has come to claim his inheritance. Richard's forces in Wales, meanwhile, have deserted upon hearing rumors that Richard had died.

Act III: Bushy and Green are captured and executed by Bolingbroke. Richard returns to England and discovers that his Welsh troops have deserted him and joined Bolingbroke's forces. Bolingbroke has also won the favor of the people of England and of York. Upon receiving the news, Richard dismisses his own troops and retreats to Flint castle. Accompanied by York and Northumberland, Bolingbroke arrives at Flint castle and sends Northumberland with his demands to Richard: that his banishment be repealed and that his estate be restored. Convinced that Bolingbroke intends to depose him, Richard surrenders and is taken to London. At York's estate, Queen Isabel and her attendants overhear the gardeners comparing England under Richard's rule to an untended garden. They predict that the king will be deposed.

Act IV: Bagot is brought in front of parliament to be questioned about Gloucester's murder and Richard's role in it. Bagot accuses Aumerle and Bolingbroke suggests that Mowbray be returned from banishment to help settle the issue. It is revealed that Mowbray is dead. York appears and announces King Richard's willingness to give up the kingship to Bolingbroke, who accepts the offer. The Bishop of Carlisle objects, but he is arrested for treason and remanded to the custody of the Abbot of Westminster. Bolingbroke orders that Richard be brought in front of parliament. While Richard appears to formally abdicate his crown, he refuses to read aloud the charges against him. Richard asks to leave and Bolingbroke sends him to the Tower of London. At the end of the scene, the abbot, the bishop, and Aumerle plot to assassinate Bolingbroke.

Act V: As Richard is being led to the Tower, Queen Isabel waits in the street to see him. He tells her he is resigned to his fate and she reproaches him for his easy surrender. Northumberland tells Richard he will be taken instead to Pomfret castle, and the queen and king share a final parting. York discovers his son Aumerle's plot and rushes to inform Bolingbroke. The Duchess of York tells Aumerle to plead for Bolingbroke's mercy. In a meeting with his noblemen, Bolingbroke (now King Henry IV), is interrupted by the York family. Aumerle pleads for his life, York condemns his son's treason, and the duchess intercedes for her son to be pardoned. Bolingbroke does pardon Aumerle but punishes the others involved in the plot. Exton says he has overheard Bolingbroke wishing Richard was dead and decides to assassinate Richard. In his cell at Pomfret castle, Richard considers his fate. Exton arrives with two other men to murder Richard. Before being killed by Exton, Richard kills the two men who have accompanied Exton. When King Henry (Bolingbroke) learns of the deed, he condemns Exton and vows to make a pilgrimage to the Holy Land as an act of penance for Richard's murder.

PRINCIPAL TOPICS

Kingship

Shakespeare's examination of kingship in *Richard II* focuses mainly on the conflict between the legal and divine right to rule, and the effectiveness of the ruler. Many critics agree that in *Richard II*, King Richard is legally the rightful king; that he is commonly recognized by other characters in the play as having the divine right to rule; and that despite these rights, King Richard does not show himself to be an effective ruler. It is this opposition between Richard's right to rule and his failure to do so effectively that is the subject of much critical debate. In addition to examining this conflict within the play, some critics conjecture that the way in which Shakespeare presents these issues reflects his thoughts on the rule of the monarch who served during Shakespeare's lifetime: Queen Elizabeth. It has been noted that Bolingbroke and Richard both represent aspects of kingship which can be related to Queen Elizabeth: Bolingbroke acts like a ruler and has the popular support of the people, whereas Richard holds the right to rule. Additionally, the historical Richard II was often compared to Queen Elizabeth in the later years of her reign, as she, like Richard, had no heirs and the problem of succession was on the minds of the people. Due to the similarities between both Bolingbroke and Richard to Queen Elizabeth, some feel that Shakespeare felt compelled to render both Bolingbroke and Richard in a sympathetic manner. The audience is drawn to Bolingbroke's power and kingly air, and has a sense that he has been unjustly banished and disinherited. At the same time, we may feel pity or sympathy for Richard. He is viewed by many to be weak, but not evil, and he receives bad counsel from corrupt advisors. Additionally, he *is* the rightful king, even though it is argued that he deludes himself into thinking that having the noble appearance and rights of a king override his responsibility to his people. Some critical commentary suggests that Shakespeare did not favor either view of kingship, and that he presented both Bolingbroke and Richard in an ambiguous manner so as to explore both sides of the issue.

Just as critics have debated the question of whether or not Shakespeare advocates the rights of the king over the king's effectiveness, others have questioned whether the divine right overrides the sovereign's legal obligations. Is Richard above the law, since he and many other characters believe he has been ordained by God to be king? Some critics have noted that even while characters such as Gaunt and York acknowledge Richard's divine right to rule, the same characters also recognize that Richard has failed to act like a king. The play cites several instances where Richard breaks the law: he is implicated in the death of Gloucester, and he breaks the inheritance laws by confiscating Gaunt's estate rather than allowing the transfer of Gaunt's money, land, and title to his son Bolingbroke. It has been suggested that while the commonwealth may have held that its king is sanctioned by God *and* the law, the people had no procedure for compelling a king to abide by the law. The result of Richard's disobeyance of the law, despite the fact that he is not legally punished, is that he loses the support of his people, and he gives his subjects the license to break the law themselves. Bolingbroke does just that when he returns illegally from exile. The nature of kingship is further examined when a king (Bolingbroke) ascends the throne with the support of the people but without legal or divine sanction.

Language, Imagery, and Symbolism

Often examined as a way of highlighting important themes in *Richard II*, the language, images, and symbolism used in the play are all complex and rich in meaning. Some critics have noted the way these elements reflect the theme of Richard's fall, and Bolingbroke's corresponding rise. Words and images that evoke the sense of rising and falling are used heavily throughout the play, in word pairs—such as "ascend" and "descend," "high" and "low," and "sky" and "earth"—and in images such as ladders, scales, and buckets in a well, one rising and one falling. Another set of images used includes those related to the elements of nature: fire, water, earth, and air. Richard is initially associated, as the sun-king, with fire and Bolingbroke with water, as a flood, until their fortunes are reversed. The shift in the elemental imagery underscores the transfer of power from Richard to Bolingbroke. Other critics have shown that images related to growth and vegetation similarly emphasize the passage of power from the old and sterile ruler (Richard) to the young and fertile Bolingbroke. Additionally, commentators have noticed Biblical images and parallels that suggest the fall of humanity in the characters of both Richard and Bolingbroke.

Other critics have focused specifically on the play's language. A common observation among critics is that in many ways, such as the contrast in the play between formal, rhymed verse and blank verse, the play emphasizes that a distance exists between words themselves and their true meaning. Others suggest that this discrepancy between language and reality is dramatized through the character of Richard, who loses his faith in the power of language and learns that words do not express fact, but only desires or wishes, that the word "king" itself does not give the one who bears that name the authority of king.

Ceremony and Play-Acting

Richard II's emphasis on ceremony and role-playing has been examined by a number of critics. Richard seems to be *playing* the role of king, more concerned with the nobility of his appearance than with the reality and responsibilities of kingship. Some critics have argued that the play suggests that kingship itself is a sham, that a great gulf exists between the appearance of royal authority and the reality of political power. Others contend that the play is *about* playing, that Richard and Bolingbroke both produce or set the scenes in which they appear. Another critic examines the effect of the somewhat comic, farcical scenes—in which Aumerle's plot against Bolingbroke is discovered and announced to Bolingbroke—on the rest of the play's treatment of ceremony and play-acting. It is argued that rather than mocking the seriousness and gravity of the play, this comic interlude forces the audience to rethink and more deeply value the ceremonial displays of kingship which surrounds the interlude.

The way many characters in the play use ceremonies or theatricality as a mask to conceal their true nature and intentions is also another area of study. It has been observed that Richard, for example, makes use of theatrical antics and language as a diversionary tactic in order to avoid going through with "unkinging" himself and to continue to deny the reality of what is happening. He refuses to read the charges against him as Northumberland demands (in Act IV, scene i), claiming that his eyes are filled with tears, he is blinded by them. He seems to be evading the truth about his crimes against the state, but at the same time, he says he sees in himself a traitor.

CHARACTER STUDIES

Richard

Critical assessments of King Richard II vary widely, ranging from condemnation of Richard for betraying his royal office to sympathy for a weak but rightful ruler. Some critics have commented that while Richard views himself in a sentimental manner, it would be wrong for the audience to do so as well. They maintain that although Bolingbroke's rebellion is illegal, kingship is both sacred as well as a heavy burden that one must earn the right to endure. Richard's character is unsympathetically reviewed by commentators for transgressions both large and small. The king is thought by many characters to have ordered the death of Gloucester. Additionally, Richard orders both Mowbray and Bolingbroke to be banished, and then proceeds to confiscate the estate of Bolingbroke's father Gaunt after Gaunt's death. Legally, the estate and title belong to Bolingbroke. Also noted is Richard's rather sarcastic, flippant treatment of Bolingbroke and Mowbray and his insolent attitude displayed to his uncles, York and Gaunt. Accused of being more concerned with the appearance and ceremonies of kingship than with his

Matt Bernhard as Lord Ross, Landon Wine as Northumberland, and Jeff Beauvoir as Willoughby in GreenStage's 1998 production of Richard II.

responsibilities, Richard creates chaos in his kingdom as a result of both negligence and abuse of power, some critics maintain. They also contend that Richard deposes himself. He is often seen as self-absorbed and self-deluded into thinking that because he is legally and divinely ordained as king, he is not subject to human frailty, that he is above the law.

On the other hand, Richard is viewed much more sympathetically by other commentators. They maintain that while Richard is weak, he is not evil. Rather, in his weakness he is influenced by the evil counsel of his advisors, Bushy, Bagot, and Green. Although he is not an effective ruler, he is nevertheless the rightful ruler, sanctioned by both the law and God. Some critics also assert that after Richard is no longer king, he realizes the gulf that exists between the name "King" and the authority that the name represents. He is also finally moved to act rather than simply talk about what has happened to him: when his assassins arrive, he manages to kill two of them before he himself is slain. Some have compared him to King Lear, arguing that in his

final moments he comprehends the extent of his own responsibility for the events that have occurred.

Bolingbroke

Like Richard, Bolingbroke is viewed with alternatively sympathetic and unsympathetic eyes. He is seen either as a traitor and a usurper, or as morally justified in taking the crown from an ineffective king. Some note that just as Richard falls politically but experiences a spiritual rise, Bolingbroke rises politically but undergoes a spiritual decline when he seizes the crown belonging to Richard. Bolingbroke is sometimes viewed as a manipulative opportunist, a true politician with a clear sense of his goals. Often Bolingbroke is accused of engineering Richard's downfall and forcing his abdication.

Despite being charged by some critics with rebellious ambition, Bolingbroke is defended by others. Some say he is silent regarding his motivations; we never know what he intends. Others suggest that Bolingbroke makes his illegal return from exile either to reclaim his father's estate and title, or to claim his right as a subject to be ruled by a responsible king. The same critics also give moral justification to Bolingbroke's execution of Richard's advisors, stating that his actions are directed toward the good of the commonwealth, whereas Richard's have always been directed toward his own self-interest. Bolingbroke is often seen as a man of action, compared to Richard who is prone to self-pitying reflection. Many acknowledge Bolingbroke to be a pragmatic, realistic man, better equipped to rule than Richard. In the opinion of many commentators, Richard deposes himself and is not strong-armed into surrender by a ruthless Bolingbroke.

CONCLUSION

Richard II is a play filled with political controversy. The conflict between Richard and Bolingbroke and all they represent remains unresolved in more than one sense. Critics will continue to debate whether Richard is weak or evil, overthrown or self-deposed, and whether Bolingbroke's motivations are political or personal and whether he is a usurper or the man who saved England from ruin. Similarly, the conflict lives on within Shakespeare's tetralogy, for although Richard dies at the end of *Richard II*, his prophesy that under Bolingbroke's rule civil unrest will plague England is made manifest in *Henry IV, Parts One* and *Two*. The tensions are only temporarily laid to rest in *Henry V*.

OVERVIEW

A. L. French

SOURCE: "Who Deposed Richard the Second?," in *Essays in Criticism*, Vol. XVII, No. 4, October, 1967, pp. 411-33.

[*In the essay that follows, French analyzes the characters and structure of* Richard II, *maintaining that the play presents an inconsistent rendering of one of the key events in the play— the deposition of Richard. French states that in the first half of the play, there is little to indicate that the king will be deposed, but in the second half of the play, other characters clearly view Richard as having been deposed.*]

A couple of years ago I saw a competent amateur performance of *Richard II*. As it happened I had not read the play for some time, and I naturally approached it with certain assumptions in mind— assumptions derived ultimately, no doubt, from scholars such as Tillyard. But as I watched, I first felt puzzled, then irritated, and finally astonished. The play was not making sense in the only way in which (I had thought) it *could* make sense; nor did it seem to be making sense

in any other way. Afterwards, I re-read the piece, to see where I or the actors had been stupid; but to my further surprise I found that the puzzlement I had felt was quite justified. The blur was not in the performance and not in my mind, but in Shakespeare's play. The present article is an attempt to describe this blur.

The assumptions we take to *Richard II* are, I have said, derived from Tillyard and others. The most important one is that Richard was deposed by Henry Bolingbroke, who by his action involved England in a century of unrest and civil war which was only brought to an end at last by Henry VII. This is in fact the interpretation not only of *Richard II* but also of the eight main Histories that Tillyard proposed over twenty years ago; and it has dominated scholars' and critics' thinking ever since. It is still current. In 1963, for example, Kenneth Muir remarked that 'we are warned over and over again that Richard's deposition is a sin which will be punished by the horrors of civil war' (introduction to Signet Classics ed., p. xxix); while in 1964 Andrew Cairncross repeated that in Henry VI's time the 'original crime— the deposition and murder of Richard II by Henry IV— was still unexpiated' (introduction to Arden ed. of *3 Henry VI*, p. 1). Now, there is no particular reason why this account of Histories should be wrong: if Tillyard found it in Edward Hall's Chronicle, Shakespeare could have found it there too; and since it is a nice neat account, he may well have made use of it. Indeed, in History plays apart from *Richard II*, Shakespeare more than once refers to Richard's deposition. In *2 Henry VI*, for example, Richard Duke of York tries to convince Salisbury and Warwick of his title to the throne, and in the course of his argument refers to Richard II

> Who, after Edward the Third's death, reigned as king
> Till Henry Bolingbroke, Duke of Lancaster,
> The eldest son and heir of John of Gaunt,
> Crowned by the name of Henry the Fourth,
> Seized on the realm, deposed the rightful king,
> Sent his poor queen to France, from whence she came,
> And him to Pomfret, where as all you know,
> Harmless Richard was murdered traitorously.
> (*2HVI*, II. ii. 20-27)

Here it is assumed as a fact that Richard was deposed; though whether it is as *important* an assumption as E. M. W. Tillyard made out is another question entirely. The Henry VI plays were written before *Richard II*; but in *1 Henry IV*, written after it, the charge that Richard was 'deposed' is repeated— by the very Northumberland who, in *Richard II*, helped to procure the crown for Bolingbroke. He talks of the time when

> the unhappy King—
> Whose wrongs in us God pardon!— did set forth

Upon his Irish expedition;
From whence he intercepted did return
To be deposed, and shortly murderéd.
                                    (*1HIV*, I. iii. 148-152)

And in *Richard II* itself, Richard makes the same accusation. When in the 'deposition scene' Northumberland tries to make him sign a confession of his 'grievous crimes', Richard retorts that if Northumberland's own crimes were 'upon record', he would

> find one heinous article,
> Containing the deposing of a king.
>   (IV. i. 233-234)

When Richard bids farewell to his queen, he asks her to 'tell the lamentable tale of me', the result of which will be that

> some will mourn in ashes, some coal-black,
> For the deposing of a rightful king.
>   (V. i. 49-50)

Nevertheless, the assumption that, in *Richard II*, the King is deposed by Henry Bolingbroke is, in my view, not wholly borne out by the text of the play. You may ask: if that is the case, how comes it that almost everyone takes away from the piece the impression that this is what in fact happens? The answer to this question will (I hope) emerge from my critical scrutiny of the text; and we shall be led right into the imaginative blur in the play— a blur that seems to me far more crucial than the oddities which commonly worry critics (e.g. Woodstock's murder, or Richard's blanks and benevolences). The business of the deposition is of course connected with the puzzle about Bolingbroke's motivation: so I shall discuss both issues, and shall proceed more or less chronologically.

Our difficulties begin towards the end of II. i. After Richard has departed for Ireland, Northumberland, Ross and Willoughby are left by themselves, and begin a diatribe against Richard's rule (he has just confiscated Gaunt's estates). England is going to the dogs, and they wonder what they can do to save her. Total wreck is unavoidable, says Ross. Not so, says Northumberland, arrestingly if obscurely—

> Not so, even through the hollow eyes of
>   death
> I spy life peering; but I dare not say
> How near the tidings of our comfort is.
>   (II. i. 270-272)

Ross and Willoughby understandably ask what he means, and he replies that he has just heard that Bolingbroke and many others have set sail from Brittany and mean to land in the north. He goes on:

If then we shall shake off our slavish yoke,
Imp out our drooping country's broken
  wing,
Redeem from broking pawn the blemished
  crown,
Wipe off the dust that hides our sceptre's
  gilt,
And make high majesty look like itself,
Away with me in post to Ravenspurgh.
                                    (291-296)

Asked to comment on the kind of metaphors we find here, we would probably say, disparagingly, that they are simple, conventional, emblematic— typical, in short, of the young Shakespeare and the early 1590s. True enough, as long as we add that, in the given context, the metaphors are very obscure indeed. The phrase 'shake *off* our slavish yoke' suggests getting rid of the king, but it is not clear whether 'imp out' means '*engraft* new feathers' (i.e. strengthen England by removing the people who are misleading Richard), or 'engraft *new* feathers' (i.e. substitute someone else for Richard). The same sort of difficulty arises over 'redeem' and 'wipe off'— nor are we sure in the latter case whether the gilt/guilt pun is a hit àt Richard's (?assumed) complicity in Woodstock's murder. The penultimate line could mean either that they must make Richard 'look' more kingly, or else that they must put another, more kingly, monarch in his place. Northumberland, in fact, is talking in riddles so far as the audience is concerned, though his fellow lords seem to be quite satisfied with his meaning. We do not know whether he means to seat Bolingbroke on the throne, or whether he only wants to use him to force Richard to reform— and, as a matter of historical fact (which Shakespeare could have found in Holinshed) Richard had been restrained in this way before, by the so-called 'appellants' between 1387 and 1389.

The difficulties continue in the next scene, which brings the news of Bolingbroke's arrival and the desertion of the people to him. At line 40 Greene comes in and tells the Queen, Bushy and Bagot what has happened; he refers to Bolingbroke as an 'enemy', says he comes 'with uplifted arms', and reveals that many powerful lords have 'fled to him'. When York enters (at 72) he says that Bolingbroke and his followers have come to make Richard 'lose at home', repeats that many nobles have deserted, and adds that 'the commons [are] cold' and may revolt. At line 104 he is wondering how he can get 'money for these wars', and a moment later asks the favourites to go and muster men. Thus the impression we have at this point is that Bolingbroke has come back to get, by force of arms if need be, something— but what? The favourites, too, towards the end of the scene (122 *ad fin*), are full of foreboding, and clearly expect a conflict; but at no juncture do we gather *what* they think Bolingbroke is after.

The opening of the next scene looks as though it might be going to give us an answer, but our expectations are raised only to be disappointed. We see Bolingbroke come in with Northumberland, and we probably expect— reasonably enough— that their words will reveal something of their plans and intentions. Not a bit of it: they pass the first few moments of the scene in mutual compliment, Northumberland spending seventeen lines congratulating Bolingbroke on the excellence of his conversation. We never learn what this 'fair discourse' was about. Vital information is withheld in a way that seems capricious; and as a result when Bolingbroke and Northumberland confront Richard in the third Act, we remain ignorant whether they have concerted their plans, or even whether they have any plans. It is curious that, if Shakespeare was the Tudor propagandist he is alleged to be, he should have missed this very easy opportunity of showing his Tudor audience how wicked Bolingbroke was. It is odder still that, as a competent dramatist, he should have missed his chance to suggest at least *something* about the working of Bolingbroke's mind.

At line 70 Bolingbroke says for the first time why he has come back: when Berkeley addresses him as 'My Lord of Hereford', he retorts that his name is Lancaster,

And I am come to seek that name in
    England.

This is his story, and he sticks to it with dogged pertinacity right up to the point in Act IV where, *after* York has told him that Richard has adopted him heir 'with willing soul', he exclaims 'In God's name, I'll ascend the regal throne' (IV. i. 113). At no point before this does Bolingbroke give the least hint that he is aiming at the crown. We may conjecture that this was what was 'really' in his mind all along, but that is a kind of guesswork irrelevant to the highly conventional art of which Shakespeare was a master; such speculations would probably never have crossed an Elizabethan's mind. But the fact that in *Richard II,* forewarned though we are, some such questions do persistently occur to us, suggests that Shakespeare may be misusing his conventions rather than using them.

To return to II. iii. York comes in at line 80, and implies that Bolingbroke is a traitor ('I am no traitor's uncle'). It turns out (89 f.) that 'traitor' indicates only that Bolingbroke has come back from banishment without permission and, moreover, in arms. A little later York repeats the charge:

Thou art a banished man, and here art come,
Before the expiration of thy time,
In braving arms against thy sovereign.
                            (II. iii. 109-111)

When we see this in the theatre it is especially noticeable that York, who at this point does not know why Bolingbroke has returned, obviously assumes it is only

to reclaim his rights. Not till York has finished his speech does Bolingbroke tell him that

As I was banished, I was banished Hereford;
But as I come, I come for Lancaster.
                            (112-113)

And Bolingbroke goes on to give a passionately reasoned account of his wrongs which has the ring of profound conviction, in the sense that we feel the man's whole being is engaged, that he is not dissembling or being politic. If Shakespeare had meant us here to suspect that Bolingbroke was being disingenuous he could easily have suggested it. He does not. Bolingbroke is unique among Shakespeare's ambitious men (if he *is* an ambitious man) in that he is never given an opportunity to open his mind to us; long before Shakespeare wrote this play he let the go-getting Lords in *Henry VI* disclose their ambitions— Suffolk and York, for instance. But so strong is Bolingbroke's feeling in the speech we have discussed (and in his later words at III. i. 16-27) that we arguably have what is in effect a self-revelation. York takes his nephew's words at face value; so do we. Northumberland now chimes in:

The noble Duke hath sworn his coming is
But for his own; and for the right of that
We all have strongly sworn to give him aid.
And let him ne'er see joy that breaks that
    oath!
                            (147-150)

What is interesting here is that 'but' in the second line, the implication being that someone might suspect, or does suspect, that Bolingbroke is concerned with much more than 'his own'; perhaps Northumberland is voicing what he conceives to be York's unspoken fear, only, of course, in order to allay it. Yet this is such a small point that it goes unnoticed in the theatre; and even in the study it is far too small for us to be able to argue that Northumberland had already thought of getting rid of Richard. Bolingbroke finally asks his uncle to accompany him to Bristow castle, which is held by the favourites (the 'caterpillars of the commonwealth'), and York replies:

It may be I will go with you; but yet I'll
    pause
For I am loath to break our country's laws.
                            (167-168)

What does York mean by breaking the 'country's laws'? Does he refer to the illegal execution of the favourites (whom Bolingbroke has 'sworn to weed and pluck away'), or does he mean the mere act of keeping company with a traitor? This is again a trifling matter, but again we cannot be sure. At least we note that York seemingly does not object to Bolingbroke's high-handed action over the favourites, any more than he does in the scene where they are about to be executed (III. i); so it seems dubious for Peter Ure to call the execution an 'act of quasi-regal authority' (Arden ed., p. lxvii). If it was meant to be seen as anything so decisive, York would surely have been allowed to make a fuss.

I pass now to the first of the three crucial scenes which bring together my two themes— Bolingbroke's motives and the nature of Richard's fall. The scenes are III. ii, III. iii and IV. i.

Returning from Ireland, where he has heard from Bagot of Bolingbroke's expedition, Richard talks about 'rebels', 'treacherous feet', 'usurping steps' and 'foul rebellion', referring to Bolingbroke as the 'sovereign's foe'. In his second long speech (III. ii. 36 f.) he says that when the sun is hidden

> Then thieves and robbers range abroad
> unseen
> In murthers and in outrage boldly here,

but when the sun comes out,

> Then murthers, treasons, and detested sins . . .
> Stand bare and naked, trembling at them-
> selves.

He goes on to identify Bolingbroke as 'this thief, this traitor'. It is not clear at first how far we are meant to identify the emblematic robbers and murderers with Bolingbroke; but the last phrase clinches the matter. Richard is suggesting— the first time anyone definitely does so— that Bolingbroke is after the crown. This interpretation of his admittedly oblique words is confirmed by his explicit use, a few lines later, of the verb 'depose':

> The breath of worldly men cannot depose
> The deputy elected by the Lord.
>
> (56-57)

The idea has now entered his head, and we note that it has done so *before* he hears the disastrous tidings brought by Salisbury and Scroope— that is, he does not yet know that his own forces are weak. When he learns that the Welshmen have dispersed, he asks 'is my kingdom lost?' and, a moment later, 'strives Bolingbroke to be as great as we?' In the long speech provoked by the news of the favourites' death, he says:

> Let's choose executors and talk of wills.
> And yet not so— for what can we bequeath
> Save our deposed bodies to the ground?
>
> (148-150)

This use of 'deposed' (which, standing alone, could arguably mean just 'laid aside': *O.E.D.*, s.v. 'depose',

2a) links up with the 'sad stories of the death of kings', because some kings 'have been deposed' (156-7). By the end of the scene Richard has convinced himself that he is about to be supplanted by Bolingbroke. He goes so far as to discharge his remaining followers, and with these words:

> let them hence away,
> From Richard's night, to Bolingbroke's fair
> day.
>
> (217-218)

Thus, so far as the audience are concerned, it is Richard himself who first expresses the idea that his crown is at stake.

In the next scene Bolingbroke and Richard finally meet, though at first through Northumberland. At the start York rebukes Northumberland for not saying '*King* Richard', and a bout of punning follows:

> *North.* Your grace mistakes; only to be brief,
> Left I his title out.
> *York*   The time hath been,
> Would you have been so brief with him, he
> would
> Have been so brief with you to shorten you,
> For taking so the head, your whole head's
> length.
> *Bol.* Mistake not, uncle, further than you
> should.
> *York* Take not, good cousin, further than
> you should,
> Lest you mistake: the heavens are o'er our heads.
> *Bol.* I know it, uncle; and oppose not myself
> Against their will.
>
> (III. iii. 10-19)

The suggestion is that York suspects Bolingbroke wants to take wrongly something beyond what he has declared; possibly the crown. But it is no more than a suspicion on York's part, and in any case Richard knows nothing of this suspicion either now or later. Moreover if 'take not' is intended as advice to Bolingbroke, it is advice which he unswervingly follows. The whole exchange, dominated as it is by York's hideously unamusing puns, has an uncertain tone and a debatable effect. Likewise, it is hard for the actor who plays Bolingbroke to know what tone to take in his long speech (31 f.): should the fivefold repetition of 'King Richard' be sarcastic or not? It is a problem for the reader too, since the tone of the speech could well reveal what is 'in' Bolingbroke's mind over and above what he chooses to say. And yet so far as one can see no irony is intended: the manner is ceremonially flat, recalling the sort of verse we find in Act I. Only once does any strong feeling show through. Bolingbroke has asked Northumberland to tell Richard that he returns from exile with no object beyond recovering his rights, but if they are not granted—

> If not, I'll use the advantage of my power
> And lay the summer's dust with showers of
>   blood
> Rained from the wounds of slaughtered
>   Englishmen—
> The which, how far off from the mind of
>   Bolingbroke
> It is such crimson tempest should bedrench
> The fresh green lap of fair King Richard's land,
> My stooping duty tenderly shall show.
>
>   (42-48)

Bolingbroke feels a positive delight in making the threat, but checks himself immediately; moreover when Northumberland later repeats to Richard the substance of what Bolingbroke has said (103 f.) he leaves out the threat. Bolingbroke goes on:

> Be he [Richard] the fire, I'll be the yielding
>   water;
> The rage be his, whilst on the earth I rain
> My waters—on the earth, and not on him.
>
>   (58-60)

At first it sounds as though he intends to play a passive role; but there seems to be a pun on rain / reign (noted by Muir but not by Ure or Dover Wilson) which makes us think again. Shakespeare has built in two contradictory pointers as to Bolingbroke's intentions, and leaves us wondering whether he can be said to have a coherent state of mind at all. We are again pulled up short a little further on:

> See, see, King Richard doth himself appear,
> As doth the blushing discontented sun
> From out the fiery portal of the East,
> When he perceives the envious clouds are bent
> To dim his glory and to stain the track
> Of his bright passage to the occident.
>
>   (62-67)

We have met this problem before: what is the relation between metaphor and fact? Bolingbroke is comparing Richard to the sun and himself to the clouds; but what does 'dim' mean in terms of political actuality? It could be translated either as 'make less' or as 'extinguish altogether'—a slight distinction, but one that makes all the difference between correction and deposition ('stain' seems to imply the former alone). Is the uncertainty Bolingbroke's or Shakespeare's? Since there is no evidence elsewhere that Bolingbroke has any intention of removing the king, we must conclude, tentatively, that it is Shakespeare's. The uncertainty is pervasive throughout this scene, even in minor details: for example, York's reply to Bolingbroke's lines quoted above begins 'Yet looks he like a king. . . . ' It would be fruitless to try and decide whether 'yet' refers purely to time or whether

it means 'nevertheless'; in other words, whether or not York is now half-admitting that in some minds there is the idea that Richard may not be king for much longer.

At any rate, Richard now shows just how kingly he can be; in the long speech to Northumberland, Bolingbroke's emissary, he is genuinely *regal* for the first and only time in the play. Despite the firmness and dignity of his words, however, his mind is full of thoughts of deposition; he says

>   show us the hand of God
> That hath dismissed us from our steward-
>   ship;
> For well we know no hand of blood and
>   bone
> Can gripe the sacred handle of our sceptre,
> Unless he do profane, steal, or usurp.
>
>   (77-81)

He accuses the rebels of lifting 'vassal hands against my head' and threatening the 'glory of my precious crown', and ends with a vivid evocation of the horrors of the civil war which will take place in the future as a result of Bolingbroke's present actions. Northumberland, in his reply, goes to great pains to quash Richard's notion that Bolingbroke is after the throne, or that there will be civil war, now or later. He reports Bolingbroke as swearing by all he holds sacred that

> His coming hither hath no further scope
> Than for his lineal royalties, and to beg
> Infranchisement immediate on his knees,
> Which on thy royal party granted once,
> His glittering arms he will commend to rust,
> His barbéd steeds to stables, and his heart
> To faithful service of your Majesty.
> This, swears he as he is a prince, is just;
> And, as I am a gentleman, I credit him.
>
>   (112-120)

As with much of the play's verse, the tone of this is hard to disengage: the verse is so flat, and frankly so undistinguished, that an actor could extract from it almost any tone of voice he liked. He could make Northumberland sound sincere, or sarcastic, or cautious—for instance he could say 'lineal royalties' neutrally, or else emphasise the 'lineal', thus conceding Richard's fears only to pooh-pooh them. It is not merely that Shakespeare is asking us to work hard and pay close attention; he is also (it seems) asking us to make up his mind for him.

Richard, at all events, takes Northumberland's words at their face value, and his reply has an unmistakable note of relief:

> Northumberland, say thus the king returns:

His noble cousin is right welcome hither,
And all the number of his fair demands
Shall be accomplished without contradiction;
With all the gracious utterance that thou hast
Speak to his gentle hearing kind commends.

(121-126)

It sounds as though his fears, which have been building
up since the beginning of III. ii, have been allayed. And
though he at once turns to Aumerle, hating himself for
his self-abasement, it seems that what he has in mind
is the repeal of Bolingbroke's banishment rather than
anything more radical:

O God! O God! that e'er this tongue of
  mine,
That laid the sentence of dread banishment
On you proud man, should take it off again
With words of sooth!

(133-136)

Yet he still has forebodings, though he expresses them
obliquely:

O that I were as great
As is my grief, or lesser than my name!
Or that I could forget what I have been!
Or not remember what I must be now!

(136-139)

The last 'what': is he 'now' going to be a king whose
royal prerogatives have been circumscribed, or is he
going to cease being a king at all? Again we have the
feeling that the words spoken correspond only approximately to what is 'in the character's mind', and that we
do not quite know how to take them. Perhaps the
safest explanation here is that Richard has a strong
streak of the masochist in him, and that he gets positive pleasure from making his plight appear worse than
it really is— though we do not even know what it 'really' is, since we have no idea what is in Bolingbroke's
mind and his motives remain utterly obscure. It is *hindsight* that makes us guess he wanted the crown.

Northumberland now returns from Bolingbroke but,
before he has a chance to report Bolingbroke's reply,
Richard bursts out:

What must the king do now? Must he
  submit?
The king shall do it. Must he be deposed?
The king shall be contented. Must he lose
The name of king? a God's name, let it go.

(143-146)

His pendulum has swung to the extreme of self-abasement; but it has done so without the slightest provocation
from external events. His outburst could, I suppose, be
triggered off by a particularly bellicose demonstration from

the soldiers whom Bolingbroke (49-53) ordered to march
up and down. Yet there is no stage-direction to this effect
in the Quartos or the Folio; whereas in a comparable
scene in *3 Henry VI* the Folio has the very explicit direction 'He stamps with his foot, and the Soldiers show
themselves' (I. i. 169). From our text of *Richard II*, we can
only suppose that Richard's outburst is the culmination of
the hysteria which has been mounting ever since line 133
(nor would a threatening demonstration accord with
Bolingbroke's habitual caution). As far as Richard is concerned, the situation remains just as it was seventy lines
before, when he made that dignified speech to
Northumberland, who returned the conciliatory reply
quoted in part above. Yet when he addresses
Northumberland, who has come back from Bolingbroke,
he talks about 'King Bolingbroke' (173), and adds 'Down,
court! down, king!' (182).

Up to this point, then, there is little evidence to suggest
that the Bolingbroke faction have ever given a thought
to deposing Richard: Shakespeare puts all the talk about
deposition into Richard's own mouth. Indeed, it would
not be fantastic to wonder whether Shakespeare did
not intend us to see Richard as suggesting the idea to
Bolingbroke. At all events, that is a more tenable theory
than that Bolingbroke forces it on Richard.

When the King finally meets his cousin face to face, it
is still Richard who keeps harping on the crown.
Bolingbroke kneels to him, but Richard, pointing to his
crown, says

Up, cousin, up; your heart is up, I know,
Thus high at least, although your knee be
  low.

(194-195)

He twists Bolingbroke's protestation that 'I come but
for mine own', retorting 'Your own is yours, and I am
yours, and all'. Bolingbroke again protests:

So far be mine, my most redoubted lord,
As my true service shall deserve your love,

and again Richard plays on the words:

Well you deserve. They well deserve to have
That know the strong'st and surest way to get.

(196-201)

Finally Richard acknowledges, or half-acknowledges, Bolingbroke as his 'heir', and adds

What you will have, I'll give, and willing too,
For do we must what force will have us do.

(206-207)

He has capitulated; capitulated not to force (as he says)
nor to persuasion, not to York or Northumberland or

Erin Day as the Duchess of York and Ken Holmes as York in GreenStage's 1998 production of Richard II.

Bolingbroke, but to himself. No 'force' is necessary. This is not the case in Holinshed, where Northumberland, solemnly promising Richard safe-conduct, ambushes him and takes him prisoner (Holinshed, 500/2/13; quoted by Bullough, *Narrative & Dramatic Sources of Shakespeare*, III, 402-3). For Shakespeare's Richard the mere *show* of force, mounted (so far as the audience know) to gain a strictly limited objective, is more than enough. Thus he has precisely fulfilled the prophecy made by the dying John of Gaunt:

> O, had thy grandsire with a prophet's eye
> Seen how his son's son should destroy his
>   sons,
> From forth thy reach he would have laid thy
>   shame,
> Deposing thee before thou wert possessed,
> Which art possessed now *to depose thyself.*
> (II. i. 104-108)

Richard has done just that: at no-one's prompting but his own, he has deposed himself.

The reason why people have accepted without question the view that Richard was deposed by Bolingbroke is, perhaps, that it is Richard's own view. We have, in fact, a case rather like that of *Othello*, where (as Dr. Leavis pointed out long ago) the traditional view of Othello has been much the same as Othello's. Yet the case here is more difficult; for as the quotations from other Histories at the beginning of this essay show, Richard's view of himself is the one which, elsewhere, Shakespeare apparently accepts. Moreover in *2 Henry IV*, Henry—the former Bolingbroke—says to his son:

> God knows, my son,
> By what by-paths and indirect crook'd ways
> I met this crown. . . .
> (*2HIV*, IV. v. 184-186)

It is easy enough, armed with Richard's remarks about himself and with references to him in other Histories, to read back into *Richard II* the notion that Bolingbroke was the guilty party and that Richard, though not blameless (over favourites, finances, and Woodstock), was deprived of his office by force. This is in fact the assumption that critics have habitually started from. What I question is whether it represents a true and accurate response to Shakespeare's play— never mind about the other Histories, the Tudor Myth, and the National Epic. Bearing in mind such doubts, let us go on to look at the 'deposition scene'.

After the bitter quarrel in which four men accuse Aumerle of having caused Woodstock's death (an episode which adds a further touch of confusion to the already vague attitude the play has taken to Richard's complicity therein), York enters with news from Richard:

> Great Duke of Lancaster, I come to thee
> From plume-plucked Richard, who with
>   willing soul
> Adopts thee heir, and his high sceptre yields
> To the possession of thy royal hand.
> Ascend his throne, descending now from
>   him,
> And long live Henry, fourth of that name!

> (IV. i. 107-112)

One incidental detail of the message is intriguing: how are we supposed to take 'with *willing* soul'? Those who want to share Richard's view of things must turn York into a sycophant, which he is surely too honest to be. If, on the other hand, my reading is correct, we must take the phrase quite literally, and after all Richard, at the end of III. iii, *was* 'willing'.

The Bishop of Carlisle now breaks in with an impassioned objection to the whole proceeding. What is remarkable about this well-known speech is that it contains no reference to the *deposing* of Richard (though it does mention the dire consequences of crowning Bolingbroke); its emphasis is rather on *judging* him:

> Would God that any in this noble presence
> Were enough noble to be upright *judge*
> Of noble Richard! then true noblesse would
> Learn him forbearance from so foul a wrong.
> What subject can *give sentence* on his king?
> And who sits here that is not Richard's subject?
> Thieves are not *judged* but they are by to hear,
> Although apparent guilt be seen in them,
> And shall the figure of God's majesty,
> His captain, steward, deputy elect,
> Anointed, crownéd, planted many years,
> Be *judged* by subject and inferior breath,
> And he himself not present?

> (117-129)

This is a baffling speech, because at this stage no-one has proposed to judge Richard. Nobody has publicly suggested that he is unfit to reign; no-one but himself has proposed he should step down. It is not till nearly one hundred lines later that Northumberland tries to get him to sign a schedule of his 'grievous crimes'— that is the first we learn of his being formally accused of anything, and consequently, in terms of this play, the first occasion on which he could possibly be 'judged'. Commentators do not seem to notice this: the Arden editor, for instance, compiles a note on Elizabethan beliefs about the right of a subject to judge his king, without ever asking himself what Carlisle is talking about. The only explanation for the oddity must lie *outside* the play— in an Old Play, or the Chronicles. In fact there is a perfectly good explanation in Holinshed (512/2/29; Bullough, op. cit., III, 410-11), but Shakespeare chose not to use it. One can of course argue that 'the audience knew their history inside out' (thus several critics); but if they did, why did Shakespeare elsewhere go to such pains to explain legal and constitutional issues— as he does for example in the hundred-line disquisition on the Salic Law in *Henry V* (I. ii), or in Richard Duke of York's lengthy statement of his claim to the throne in *2 Henry VI*, previously mentioned, a claim which has already been expounded at tedious length by Mortimer in *1 Henry VI* (II. v)? We must conclude that when he wrote *Richard II* Shakespeare was not quite sure what he was trying to do.

When Richard comes in he starts play-acting, and in response to one of his fantasies Bolingbroke, with some impatience, says

> I thought you had been willing to resign.

('Willing' picks up York's use of the word at 108.) Richard replies:

> My crown I am, but still my griefs are mine.
> You may my glories and my state depose,
> But not my griefs; still am I king of those.
> (190-193)

Perhaps it is the familiarity of this dying fall that blinds us to the fact that Richard is engaging in double-think: he admits he is 'willing' to resign his 'crown', but at once charges Bolingbroke with having 'deposed' him! And, as we saw earlier, he charges Northumberland too with 'deposing' him (234). In reply to another reminder from Bolingbroke, Richard equivocates:

> Ay, no; no, ay; for I must nothing be.
> Therefore no 'no', for I resign to thee.
> (201-202)

He is having his cake and eating it: extracting the maximum pleasure from seeing himself in the role of a deposed king, and also from protesting that he should never have been deposed in the first place. And it is in this self-regarding role that he throws out the account of what has happened which has become the official version. He now resigns the office of king with deliberate and knife-twisting formality (203-222). Northumberland asks him to read and sign the list of his crimes,

That, by confessing them, the souls of men
May deem that you are worthily deposed.

(226-227)

The surprising thing here is that Northumberland has fallen into Richard's own terminology and view of the situation— a view which Northumberland has not held before, which only Richard has ever put forward (but see my comment on the Garden scene, below). I do not think that Shakespeare is being subtle, though it would be attractive to argue that Richard has hypnotised the tough Earl as well as many willing critics. Two other explanations are possible. One is that Shakespeare simply nodded— which is not an explanation at all. The other is that he suddenly realised, at this late stage, that he could not write the sort of play he had set out to write, that it was a practical impossibility for him to present on the Elizabethan stage a Richard so much at odds with the official one (who was political dynamite anyway). He therefore started to make the play's 'truth' correspond with Richard's personal 'truth', and scattered hints of the Ricardian view throughout the play. Unfortunately he did not go back and remove the non-Ricardian view which holds good till nearly the end of Act III. I do not pretend to know why he started to write about a Richard who abdicated rather than being deposed. Perhaps he was genuinely confused about the deposition business— and it *is* terribly confusing, whether you go to Holinshed or to modern historians (see, for example: Anthony Steele, *Richard II* [1941], 1962, pp. 263-85; May McKisach, *The Fourteenth Century* [Oxford History of England, vol. V], 1959, pp. 492-6; E. F. Jacob, *The Fifteenth Century* [O.H.E., vol. VI], 1961, pp. 10-17). If professional historians who have access to all surviving documents dealing with the events of 1399 make heavy weather of them, we shall not perhaps be surprised if Shakespeare did too.

At all events Shakespeare's change of mind comes out almost disarmingly in the Garden scene (III. iv). It intervenes between the Flint Castle scene and the 'deposition scene', and prepares the way for the latter in a manner that has apparently gone unnoticed. The gardener, his 'man' and the Queen all refer to deposition. The gardener's mate asks

What, think you the king shall be deposed?

and the gardener answers

Depressed he is already, and deposed

'Tis doubt he will be.

(III.iv.67-69)

The Queen breaks in and demands

Why dost thou say King Richard is deposed?

This exchange follows on from the long analogy between the commonwealth and a garden— an analogy which it is reasonable to call choric and conventional. The trouble is that the personae are then used to give an apparently disinterested (because choric) account of Richard's fall in terms of his *being* deposed— the gardener's use of the passive voice very subtly slips in the Ricardian view where we might expect such a commentator to take the play's view. This is not dramatic craftsmanship, it is dramatic craft— sleight of hand. And it is this legerdemain [trickery] which has ensured that readers take away from *Richard II* a view which is largely confined to the latter part of the play and which is completely inconsistent with what has gone before. Shakespeare has to work increasingly hard as the play progresses to attract the audience's emotional regard to Richard and repel it from Bolingbroke; readers have proved curiously eager to sentimentalise Richard in the way that Richard sentimentalises himself (again we are reminded of *Othello*). Self-dramatising self-pity can always attract sympathy, of course; but whereas Othello's self-regard is skilfully 'placed', in *Richard II* Shakespeare, having left so late his effort to put Richard in a favourable light, simply cannot afford to qualify our sympathy. Hence, no doubt, the sugared poignancies of the exchanges between Richard and his Queen (V. i), the words of York to his wife (V. ii. 23 f.), and the grotesque elaboration of Richard's soliloquy in prison (V. v).

Now there were, even for the most orthodox Elizabethan, two quite different ways of looking at Richard's fall. As it happens Shakespeare dramatised them elsewhere. In *3 Henry VI* there is a bitter debate between the Yorkist and Lancastrian factions about Henry VI's title to the throne. Part of it runs as follows:

Henry Tell me, may not a king adopt an heir?
York What then?
Henry An if he may, then am I lawful King;
For Richard, in the view of many lords,
Resigned the crown to Henry the Fourth,
Whose heir my father was, and I am his.
York He rose against him, being his sovereign,
And made him to resign his crown perforce.

(*3HVI*, I. i. 135-142)

Each man here naturally takes the line that serves his own interests: Henry wants to prove his title good, York the reverse. Nevertheless the episode does suggest that there could be genuine doubt in an Elizabethan mind about Richard's fall. (It further suggests, incidentally, that long before *Richard II* Shakespeare could and did stage a deposition scene in which the participants thrashed out the complex issues thoroughly— the debate goes on for about 140 lines.)

But the fact that there *could* be genuine doubt does not, I think, exculpate Shakespeare in *Richard II*. The trouble is not that he merely dramatises the doubt, for this could imply that however many subjective 'truths' there are, the play as a whole comprehends them, organises them, sees them from a coherent point of view. This happens in *Othello* where, although there are as many 'truths' as there are personae, the play gives us a truth which transcends any single character's truth. No, the trouble with *Richard II* is that it suffers from what we might call double vision, giving us one truth in one place, and another in another, with apparently equal weight and conviction. It leaves us to settle matters, but does not contain within itself the evidence by which alone we could do so.

Some critics have found *Richard II* unsatisfactory in this general way, but for other reasons: A. P. Rossiter, for example (in *Angel with Horns*), thinks that Richard's financial misdemeanours and his hinted complicity in Woodstock's murder are left very obscure, and that the York-Aumerle scenes in Act V are incoherent. With some reservations I agree; but Rossiter still does not seem to me to put his finger on the play's central weakness, for the shortcomings he lists do not, perhaps, amount to a very formidable indictment; and they certainly do not in themselves explain why the overall impression produced by an attentive reading or witnessing of the piece is one of bafflement and irritation at the way our sympathies are tampered with. If we concentrate on the question which forms the title of this essay, we can at least give a more cogent account of this impression— an account which ties in, as we have seen, with Shakespeare's uncertain handling of Bolingbroke, and indeed with the worries that Rossiter felt without being able to organise fully.

But such an account calls into question more than the merits or demerits of *Richard II*. It also casts the gravest possible doubt on the orthodox reading of the eight main Histories as demonstrating God's punishment for England's sin of deposing her lawful King. I have elsewhere shown that in the earlier tetralogy (i.e. *1, 2* and *3 Henry VI* and *Richard III*) Shakespeare makes only passing reference to the fate of Richard II, and that the 'sin' which England is expiating is no single or simple thing. We can now add that the later tetralogy (*Richard II* to *Henry V*) presents what is historically the first term in the whole series, *Richard II*, in a fundamentally confused way. So we are perhaps entitled to ask whether Shakespeare really is the Celebrator of the Tudor Myth. Surely, at least in the best Histories— *Richard III* and *Henry IV*— he is a very great deal more than that; so much so that to talk in terms of the Tudor Myth is

merely reductive. In any case, it is about time that we started to read the plays Shakespeare actually wrote, rather than the ones written for him by historical critics. To read *Richard II* is, at all events, what I have been attempting to do. If it has turned out to be a lesser thing than orthodox taste has made it (examining bodies never tire of setting it), the blame will, I hope, be laid where it belongs: on the capable shoulders of William Shakespeare.

Maurice Charney

SOURCE: "Richard II," in *All of Shakespeare*, 1993, pp. 160-69.

[*In the following essay, Charney briefly discusses the content of the plays in the* Henriad *tetralogy. The* Henriad *tetralogy is a series of four plays:* Richard II; Henry IV, Part One; Henry IV, Part Two; *and* Henry V. *Charney then explores the primary themes and characters in* Richard II *and comments on the relevancy of key scenes to events occurring in Shakespeare's England.*]

Richard II is the first play of the Major Tetralogy, followed by the two parts of *Henry IV* and *Henry V*. Shakespeare learned a great deal from writing the four plays of the Minor Tetralogy (the three parts of *Henry VI* and *Richard III*), which were probably completed in 1592 or 1593. *King John*, which was probably written just before *Richard II*, has many stylistic affinities with it, both plays make important use of the divine right of kings. We can date *Richard II* fairly confidently to 1595, and the other three plays of the Major Tetralogy follow in the next three or four years.

It is curious that the events of the Major Tetralogy exactly precede those of the Minor Tetralogy, which begins with the death of Henry V in 1422 and covers the Wars of the Roses to its conclusion at Bosworth Field in 1485. It looks as if Shakespeare wanted first to establish the origins of the Tudor line and the way that Henry, Duke of Richmond (later Henry VII), providentially ends the Wars of the Roses and unites the houses of York and Lancaster. The Major Tetralogy is much more concentrated historically, beginning with the quarrel of Bolingbroke and Mowbray in 1398 and ending with the triumph of Henry V over France and his marriage to Katherine, daughter of the French king and queen, in 1420. The Major Tetralogy is more self-consciously a four-part unit than the Minor Tetralogy, with many more interconnections, echoes, and anticipations.

The events in *Richard II* are compressed into only two years, from 1398 to 1400, which helps give the play a feeling of tragedy, by concentrating so strongly on Richard's fall and creating the sense of a quick-moving and almost fateful action. Richard's hubris, insolence, presumption, and perhaps just foolishness make his fall inevitable, but once it is clear that he can no longer remain king, the play unleashes a tremendous flood of feeling for Richard in adversity. This is Shakespeare's first history play to invoke so powerfully the analogy between the fallen king and Christ in extremis. This sense of sorrow for Richard evokes tragic feelings of sympathy and compassion. We forget whatever Richard has done to bring his fate upon himself and think only of his torment and his sufferings.

More than any other Shakespeare history play, *Richard II* goes to great lengths to invoke the doctrine of the divine right of kings, which was popular in the Tudor program of homilies to be read aloud in churches. The heinous sin of Richard's deposition and murder and the ascent of Bolingbroke to the throne as Henry IV are not really resolved until the Wars of the Roses end in the victory of the Earl of Richmond in 1485, who comes to the throne as Henry VII, the first Tudor. . . .

It is necessary to insist so strongly on the divine right of kings in *Richard II* in order to appreciate the magnitude of Henry IV's transgression. The Bishop of Carlisle's prophetic speech right before Richard's deposition looks forward to the bloody events of both tetralogies and is a forecast of English history in the fifteenth century:

> And if you crown him [Bolingbroke], let me
>   prophesy—
> The blood of English shall manure the
>   ground,
> And future ages groan for this foul act . . .
>   (4.1.136-38)

Bolingbroke as "subject" cannot "give sentence on his king" (121), since the king is the anointed of God. As God's scourge, Bolingbroke is sure to bring an evil doom on himself and on England, which will "be called/ The field of Golgotha and dead men's skulls" (143-44).

The argument of divine right is all that Richard can offer to defend himself, and the conflict is lost before it ever begins. When Richard returns from Ireland to safeguard his kingdom against Bolingbroke, who has landed at Ravenspurgh, he speaks largely in "divine right" rhetoric, which his followers see as a counsel of despair:

> Not all the water in the rough rude sea
> Can wash the balm off from an anointed
>   king,
> The breath of wordly men cannot depose
> The deputy elected by the Lord.
>   (3.2.54-57)

Richard's sense of the forces of Nature being mar-

shaled against the enemy of God seems ludicrous to his troops. He protests: "Mock not my senseless conjuration, lords" (23), but the King's approach to impending danger is entirely wrong.

Richard's invocation to "my gentle earth" (3.2.12) is unmilitary in the extreme: "But let thy spiders, that suck up thy venom, / And heavy-gaited toads lie in their way" (14-15). To this Richard continues to add supposedly baleful images: "Yield stinging nettles to mine enemies" (18). It is this "conjuration" of senseless things that his lords are mocking, and Carlisle tells him gently: "The means that heavens yield must be embraced / And not neglected" (29-30). The army of Bolingbroke is unlikely to be defeated by venomous spiders, heavy-gaited toads, and stinging nettles.

According to the Renaissance doctrine of the King's two bodies, the king as a public figure has a sacred body identified with the body politic, but as a private man his body is fragile and vulnerable. Richard argues on both sides of the divine right paradox. When he considers himself as a person, he is subject to all the weaknesses of mortal man, and he is far from having the invulnerable image of a king:

> I live with bread like you, feel want,
> Taste grief, need friends— subjected thus,
> How can you say to me, I am a king?
>   (3.2.175-77)

In the pun on *subjected*— "made a subject" and "subjected to," or "liable"— lies the heart of the paradox. Richard is moving to an acute awareness of his loss of identity, by giving up the kingship he surrenders the essence of his being and he declines to anonymity and nothingness. The issue of identity becomes of crucial importance in Shakespeare's later tragedies, such as *Othello*, when Othello declares that his "occupation's gone" (3.3.354) or *Antony and Cleopatra*, when Antony "cannot hold this visible shape" (4. 14. 14).

The important theme of Richard's identity reaches its climax in the deposition scene, when he understands that by giving up his kingship he is giving up everything, including his sense of self:

> I have no name, no title,
> No, not that name was given me at the font
> But 'tis usurped.
>   (4. 1. 254-56)

He seeks total annihilation in his wish-fulfillment imagery:

> O, that I were a mockery king of snow,
> Standing before the sun of Bolingbroke,
> To melt myself away in water drops!
>   (259-61)

This scene anticipates Hamlet in many places, especially Hamlet's first soliloquy:

> O that this too too solid [as in Folio] flesh
>   would melt,
> Thaw, and resolve itself into a dew . . .
>   (*Hamlet* 1. 2. 129-30)

Some lines later, after Richard sends for a mirror and throws it down in disgust, he exclaims:

>   My grief lies all within,
> And these external manners of laments
> Are merely shadows to the unseen grief
> That swells with silence in the tortured soul.
>   (4. 1. 294-97)

These lines clearly anticipate Hamlet's sense of isolation in the Danish court in the same context I quoted before: "But I have that within which passes show; / These but the trappings and the suits of woe" (*Hamlet* 1. 2. 85-86). Both Richard and Hamlet feel a painful contrast between outward seeming and inward reality. They are both courting the annihilation of self.

Richard's contemplating his face in the mirror is like Hamlet's contemplating mortality in the skull of Yorick, the king's jester. It is interesting that Richard parodies Doctor Faustus's famous invocation of Helen of Troy in Marlowe's play (1592):

>   Was this face the face
> That every day under his household roof
> Did keep ten thousand men? Was this the face
> That, like the sun, did make beholders wink?
>   (4.1.280-83)

He rejects the image of his face by shattering the looking glass, thus seeking the anonymity he has been flirting with from the beginning of his griefs.

At the end of the play before he is murdered at Pomfret Castle, Richard has a long soliloquy meditating on themes of time, life and death, and his own identity. He takes up again the "nothing" theme that echoes throughout the play, as it does in *King Lear,* and that here signifies the king's awareness of his own impending death. He imagines himself as an actor, coping with a difficult reality by moving quickly between different identities: "Thus play I in one person many people, / And none contented" (5.5.31-32). Shifting between king and beggar, Richard is finally "unkinged by Bolingbroke, / And straight am nothing" (37-38). From here it is only a quick move to the final step of the reasoning: that no man "With nothing shall be pleased, till he be eased / With being nothing" (40-41). Despite the urgency of death, Richard cannot resist the pleasing cadence of the internal rhyme ("pleased-eased"), he also manages to kill two of his executioners.

The critical question whether Richard is a poet manqué [unsuccessful, unfulfilled] or an actor manqué is a deceptive one because Richard is poetical and histrionic [dramatic] in playing his part as a king, especially a deposed king. Hamlet seems actually to be a friend of the traveling players, which Richard is not. Nor has Richard written at least a dozen or sixteen lines to be inserted into the *Mousetrap* play, nor does he declaim with bravado the Dido and Aeneas play as Hamlet does. But Richard poetizes actively throughout his play and indulges in elaborately ingenious poetic figures called "conceits."

Something grotesque in these excessively worked out images mingles with Richard's grief to create a sense of hysteria, as in the following:

> Or shall we play the wantons with our woes,
> And make some pretty match with shedding
>   tears,
> As thus, to drop them still upon one place,
> Till they have fretted us a pair of graves
> Within the earth, and, therein laid, "there lies
> Two kinsmen digged their graves with
>   weeping eyes",
> Would not this ill do well?
>   (3.3.163-69)

The image is extremely literal in its visual requirements, which are uncomfortably specific. That is why, once again, the imagery misfires and the onlookers think it ridiculous: "Well, well, I see / I talk but idly, and you laugh at me" (169-70). In Elizabethan parlance, *idly* means both lazily and foolishly. Richard is mocking his own poetical style in the manner of Touchstone in *As You Like It,* who lays it down as gospel that "the truest poetry is the most feigning" (3.3.18-19).

Henry Bolingbroke, the son of John of Gaunt, becomes the model for Shakespeare's political figures: the unheroic, practical man who manages to survive, while more committed and more ideological persons all are doomed to an early death. Bolingbroke is neither poetical nor histrionic, but Richard envies him his ability to win political favor easily and spontaneously. Even before his return to England, Richard fears "his courtship to the common people" (1.4.24). Bolingbroke is essentially a political creature with no natural eloquence like Richard, but with an uncanny sense of the right gesture:

> Off goes his bonnet to an oyster-wench;
> A brace of draymen bid God speed him well,
> And had the tribute of his supple knee . . .
>   (31-33)

Unlike Tamburlaine or Richard III, Bolingbroke has no grandiose visions of kingship, and he proceeds step by step without revealing, even to himself, his ultimate objective. We have to believe that when he returns to England from exile he comes only to claim his rightful inheritance from his dead father, Gaunt, and not to depose Richard and be king himself. Yet events move with incredible swiftness and inevitability, and when Bolingbroke condemns Bushy and Green, two of "The caterpillars of the commonwealth" (2.3.166), in act 3, scene 1, he is already acting like the king, who doesn't need any specific legal warrant. Bolingbroke prepares us remarkably for Claudius in *Hamlet* and perhaps also for Macbeth.

In the final scene of the play Bolingbroke resembles Macbeth remarkably in the equivocation he practices with himself. To Exton, who murders Richard II at Pomfret, Bolingbroke speaks only the ambiguous words of guilt:

> They love not poison that do poison need,
> Nor do I thee; though I did wish him dead,
> I hate the murderer, love him murderèd.
>
> (5.6.38-40)

This is essentially the Henry IV of the next two plays in the tetralogy: crafty, ineloquent, guilty, and well meaning. If Henry weren't so troubled in spirit, we would think him a gross hypocrite for making pronouncements like the following: "Lords, I protest, my soul is full of woe, / That blood should sprinkle me to make me grow" (45-46).

But Henry does nothing to prevent blood from sprinkling him and he does nothing to conceal his open complicity. He vows here what he vows time and again in the two later plays: to "make a voyage to the Holy Land, / To wash this blood off from my guilty hand" (5.6.49-50), but we are sure that he has not the slightest intention to make this voyage of contrition and expiation. This is not part of his style. He mourns over the "untimely bier" (52) of Richard II, even though it was he himself who had him murdered. Unlike Richard III Bolingbroke is not sardonic, but his sincerity is suspect as a public pronouncement, not a personal commitment.

His avalanche of couplets in his final scene reminds us that *Richard II* was written right around the time of *Romeo and Juliet* and *A Midsummer Night's Dream*, both of which it resembles in its lyric extravagance and its use of set pieces of eloquence. The dying Gaunt's vision of England is presented as an antithesis to the corruption and decay of England under Richard's misrule. Gaunt, expiring, speaks like a "prophet new inspired" (2.1.31) of "This blessed plot, this earth, this realm, this England" (50). It is an extraordinary patriotic effusion, but England is "now leased out . . . / Like to a tenement or pelting farm" (59-60). *Farm* is a derogatory word used three times in this play to indicate Richard's outrageous financial exactions. To "farm" the realm is to sell for cash the

right to collect royal taxes, such as on crown lands and on customs. This is combined with "blank charters" (1.4.48), in which favorites of the king could write in whatever sum they pleased as an exaction on the nobles, and "benevolences" (2.1.250), or forced loans, to create Richard's "rash fierce blaze of riot" (33). Like a tragic protagonist, Richard is preparing his own fall.

The Garden Scene (3, 4) has often been discussed as an internal, choral commentary on the play, but its literal, allegorical quality allies it with early Shakespeare. Later, Shakespeare will embody his meanings much more intrinsically in the dramatic action rather than in symbolic set pieces. The Gardener lectures his servants pedantically about the analogy between the garden commonwealth and the body politic. With the Queen and her Ladies as audience, the Gardener expatiates on the political implications of gardening:

> O, what pity is it
> That he had not so trimmed and dressed his land
> As we this garden!
>
> (3.4.55-57)

This scene is easy to teach but it doesn't represent Shakespeare at his best.

At the end of the scene, however, the Gardener speaks a touching soliloquy in couplets:

> Here did she fall a tear; here in this place
> I'll set a bank of rue, sour herb of grace;
> Rue even for ruth here shortly shall be seen,
> In the remembrance of a weeping queen.
>
> (3.4.104-7)

We are reminded inevitably, as by so much else in this play, of *Hamlet*, particularly the mad Ophelia's distribution of flowers: "There's rue for you, here's some for me. We may call it herb of grace o' Sundays. O, you must wear your rue with a difference" (*Hamlet* 4.5.181-83).

One incident that hangs over *Richard II* and is mentioned repeatedly in the play is the murder of Thomas of Woodstock, Duke of Gloucester and Richard's uncle, in 1397. These events are treated in the anonymous play *Woodstock* (sometimes called the first part of *Richard II* since it deals with the period 1382 to 1397, before Shakespeare's play opens), which was probably written before Shakespeare's play. *Richard II* begins in 1398 with the quarrel between Bolingbroke and Thomas Mowbray, the Duke of Norfolk, who was clearly implicated in Gloucester's death at Calais, probably under orders from Richard. The scene between Bolingbroke and Mowbray is confusing, since the men trade accusations that seem equally powerful. Bolingbroke claims that Mowbray sluiced out Gloucester's

Engraving from Galerie des Personnages de Shakespeare *(1844).*

> innocent soul through streams of blood;
> Which blood, like sacrificing Abel's, cries
> Even from the tongueless caverns of the earth
> To me for justice and rough chastisement . . .
> (1.1.103-6)

We never learn for sure about Mowbray's role in this murder, but we are never allowed to forget Richard's complicity.

In the next scene, the Duchess of Gloucester asks Gaunt to take revenge for his brother's murder, but Gaunt refuses. This is the first we hear of the doctrine of the divine right of kings, which is so important in the play. Gaunt says directly that the King,

> God's substitute,
> His deputy anointed in His sight,
> Hath caused his [Gloucester's] death . . .
> (1.2.37-39)

He adds that "God's is the quarrel" (37), for Gaunt as a subject "may never lift / An angry arm against His minister" (40-41). This makes the issue of Gloucester's murder explicit in the play. Before his death Gaunt accuses Richard directly of murdering his uncle:

> That blood already like the pelican

> Hast thou tapped out and drunkenly caroused:
> My brother Gloucester, plain well-meaning
> soul . . .
> (126-28)

This is almost at the end of Gaunt's long and prophetic death speech, in which he seems to curse Richard: "Live in thy shame" (135).

The issue of Gloucester's death comes up again in act 4, scene 1, when Bagot specifically accuses Aumerle, the son of the Duke of York (Gaunt's brother), of having killed Gloucester on orders from Richard. Bagot is joined in his accusations by Fitzwater, Percy, and others, but what is important is that this is the beginning of the deposition scene and the accusations of murder provide a context for the judgment of Richard by Bolingbroke. Richard is not such an innocent as he makes himself out to be. In his grief he makes no effort at all to defend himself, but merely expatiates on his tragic and alienated condition. The fallen king appears powerfully as a suffering individual, lyric, meditative, and philosophical in adversity.

Richard II is one of the most politically explosive of Shakespeare's plays. The Deposition Scene (most of act 4, scene 1), in which Richard abdicates the throne, was never printed during Queen Elizabeth's lifetime and first appeared in the Fourth Quarto of 1608. This is potentially seditious material for which one could be summoned before the Star Chamber. We know that the Essex conspirators got Shakespeare's company to put on a special performance of *Richard II* on the eve of their totally disastrous rebellion on February 8, 1601. Presumably, they thought that the Deposition Scene would be good propaganda for the overthrow of Elizabeth, who thought of herself as Richard II: "I am Richard II. Know ye not that?" (E. K. Chambers, *William Shakespeare,* vol. 2, p. 326). Bolingbroke is clearly labeled as a dangerous usurper in this play and in both parts of *Henry IV,* constantly anxious about his cloudy title to the throne. His son, Prince Hal, who becomes Henry V, continues these perturbations, and the issue is settled definitively only at the end of *Richard III,* when the Earl of Richmond defeats Richard at Bosworth Field and becomes Henry VII. As part of the royal myth, the Tudors take the stain off the English throne.

KINGSHIP

Richard II presents several aspects of kingship, including the notions of the legal right to rule as king, the divine right to rule, and the effectiveness of one's rule as king. The "divine right" of kings refers to the notion that the right to rule is ordained by God, not by the popular consent of the people. **Lewis J. Owen** observes that the characters of Richard and Bolingbroke each represent an important aspect of kingship in relation to Queen Elizabeth. Richard stands for the divine right to rule and Bolingbroke represents effective, "kingly" leadership. Owen argues that Shakespeare takes care in the play to treat both Richard's and Bolingbroke's claim to the throne sympathetically. Our sympathy for Richard is generated by three factors, Owen states. The first is the fact that Richard is surrounded by "evil" advisors. Owen notes that while to modern readers this may seem like a flimsy excuse, Elizabethans would have been more likely to judge a monarch less harshly than we would if that monarch made poor decisions based on the advisement of corrupt counselors. Another factor Owen cites is Richard's own personal weakness. Again, Owen observes that Elizabethans would have been more sympathetic to a ruler who was weak, rather than one who was evil. The final factor that Owen believes draws the audience's sympathy to Richard is that he is in fact the rightful king. Bolingbroke, on the other hand, is shown to be a king by his deeds, Owen comments.

Similarly, **Donna B. Hamilton** analyzes the issues of Richard's legal and divine right to rule. Hamilton questions whether or not the king is above the law because he is ordained by God. In discussing the scenes in which Richard fails to abide by the laws of the commonwealth, Hamilton observes that Richard is believed by other characters to be implicated in the death of Gloucester, and that Richard breaks the laws of inheritance when he seizes Gaunt's estate. Legally, Gaunt's money, land, and title belong to his son, Bolingbroke, whom Richard banishes. Hamilton maintains that as king, Richard has the responsibility to obey the laws, and his failure to do so harms the people, results in the loss of popular support, and gives his subjects the license to similarly ignore the law. With Bolingbroke's ascension to the throne, Hamilton shows, another aspect of kingship is brought forth: that of the threat to the commonwealth when the king (Bolingbroke) bears no legal or God-given right to the throne.

Lewis J. Owen

SOURCE: "Richard II," in *Lectures on Four of Shakespeare's History Plays*, Carnegie Institute of Technology, 1953, pp. 3-18.

[*In this essay, Owen examines the conflict between Richard's legal and divine right to be king, and his failure to act as king. Owen also reviews the relevance to the play of Elizabethan views on kingship. Additionally, Owen highlights the several factors related to Richard's kingship that draw the audience's sympathy to Richard.*]

There are, among others, two immediately apparent ways in which to understand and evaluate any literary work. One is to apply to its form and content some absolute critical standards, independent of time and place; the other is to accept the particular conventions or standards within which the work was conceived and to judge it, so to speak, on its own terms. The extent to which either of these two approaches becomes applicable depends, of course, upon the nature of the work being considered; and it is certainly true that a work usually becomes what has loosely been called "great literature" to the extent that it transcends its own particular circumstances and arrives at some aspect of universal human truth. But neither approach, it seems to me, can be entirely complete without the other. As long as a work of literature is conceived by a particular person of a particular time and place, it will never be completely free of the conventions within which its author lived. It may seek to approach universal truth, but it can never do so except through particular circumstances.

This dependence for final meaning upon an understanding of particular circumstances is especially true of dramatic art, which by its very nature— its dependence upon special actors and a special audience— becomes more entangled with the conventions of its own times— its manners, its language, its popular beliefs— than does any other literary form. No other has to rely for its final presentation upon so unpredictable a middle man as the actor; no other makes so direct and immediate appeal to a contemporary audience.

To the extent that this kind of understanding is, in some degree, essential for any play, it becomes especially so for the plays of Shakespeare, separated from us as he is by some 350 years. And just as this understanding is generally necessary for all of his plays, it becomes particularly so for some. All his plays, for instance, pose for most of us certain problems of language. The nature and structural conventions of Elizabethan blank verse, as well as the particular words and idioms involved, require from us more attention than the perfectly familiar language of, say, Bernard Shaw or Arthur Miller. The references to mythology and even to the Bible are often unfamiliar. Often the terms of moral responsibility, though we accept the notion of moral responsibility itself, are hard to understand. In short, there are in all his plays certain things which have become, through the passage of years, unfamiliar to us but which we must understand as he and his audience understood them before the plays can have for us their full meaning. Perhaps those plays are the greatest which, admitting some dependence, depend the least upon "qualifying conventions" for their total meaning. If this be so, then Shakespeare's histories cannot rank with his tragedies, whose backgrounds and issues are eternal. For, as Mr. Dover Wilson remarks, in all ten of Shakespeare's English histories, both dramatist and audience are less concerned with the fortune of the principal characters than with the sanity and health of the whole state of England. The characters are seen and appraised in relation to a political background and political issues which were still actual for the Elizabethan spectators. It is hardly necessary to observe that these backgrounds and issues are not still actual for us today, and herein lies the bar to any easy understanding of Shakespeare's histories.

This is not to say that nothing is to be got out of these plays without intimate knowledge of the Elizabethan period and heritage. Shakespeare was too great a writer to depend entirely upon such particulars. Without knowing anything of the period it is possible to be both entertained and instructed by them. But from my own experience I am convinced that some knowledge of the sort makes the entertainment more entertaining and the instruction more meaningful. Hence,... I should like to preface my discussion of *Richard II* with a brief consideration of why Shakespeare turned to English history and then selected the particular area of that history which he did.

Shakespeare came to London from Stratford about 1590, just two years after the English fleet had defeated the Spanish Armada. This sea victory produced a tide of English nationalism which has probably never been surpassed. The fifteenth century had been torn with civil strife, as the two noble houses, Lancaster and York, fought for possession of the throne of England. Lancaster had won the war at the Battle of Bosworth in 1485, and a Lancastrian, Henry the Seventh, had ascended the throne. But since he took for his wife a woman from the House of York, the civil war seemed to be healed by something stronger and more lasting than simply a military victory. And so it proved, for from these two, Henry of Lancaster and Elizabeth of York, sprang the Tudors— of whom the most famous were Henry the Eighth and his daughter, Queen Elizabeth herself. Once again the English had a lasting dynasty of monarchs, and under their steadying influence there began to grow a solidifying national unity and national pride, whose high point was the defeat of the Armada in 1588. England had achieved a national awareness and a taste for international power; and it was natural that the writers of the time should look more eagerly than ever to English history for their subjects.

It was also natural that Shakespeare, a newcomer to the London stage, should turn, along with his contemporaries, to a subject so currently popular. The first assurance of immediate success is always the selection of a popular theme; no one, as I have suggested, depends more upon immediate success than a writer for the stage; and no playwright is less able to flaunt the importance of popular success than the indigent newcomer. It is not hard to understand why a great part of Shakespeare's early plays are English histories.

The four plays with which we will be dealing in these

talks have, however, a more special significance than simply the fact that they all are drawn from English history. First, there is a tight chronological sequence which binds them together; one leads directly into the next, and in each there are passages which anticipate the plays to come or recall the ones already over. Secondly, the nature of this chronological unity is the rise of the House of Lancaster, as Bolingbroke, Duke of Lancaster, seizes the throne from Richard the Second, becomes in turn Henry the Fourth, and then passes the crown to his son, Henry the Fifth. This action immediately precedes the war between Lancaster and York, of which I have already spoken, and it was more than a haphazard selection from English history; for it was from these Lancastrians that the Tudors were descended. Thus, for the Elizabethan audience, the plays had a more particular significance than even the glorification of England, for they pointed to Queen Elizabeth herself.

The glorification of Elizabeth's ancestors, then, was the first reason that Shakespeare turned for his subject matter to this particular period of English history. But such a topic, though it could have provided chronicle history, could not have provided the stuff of dramatic history without a second reason, different from but not unrelated to the first. The English, at the same time that they were proud of England's past, were concerned about England's future. By the time that Shakespeare was writing his history plays, Elizabeth had already been on the throne for thirty-five years. Unlike some women, she could not be expected to last forever, and never having married, she had provided no heir to the throne. Her subjects saw an imminent end to the relative tranquility of the Tudor line. The question of succession haunted them, for it was this very question which had led to the bloodshed of the civil wars between York and Lancaster just a little more than a century before.

And with the succession in doubt, they turned beyond that question to the subject of kingship itself. Who, first of all, had the right to be king, and once a king was rightly and justly crowned, could he do wrong? There were of course conventional answers to this possible paradox; but to Shakespeare it suggested a source of dramatic conflict which was both timely and, to the Elizabethan world at least, universal. Within the context of Elizabeth's ancestry he could study the delicate problem of the ruler who must forget neither his divine right nor his temporal obligations. Just as the chronological sequence of events provides a physical unity in these plays, so this study of kingship provides a spiritual unity. The last three plays of this tetralogy are studies of kings who try to compensate by means of kingly actions for an absence of real divine right to the throne. *Richard II* is the study of a king who believes that his right to be a king relieves him of the responsibility of acting like one.

It has been traditional to affirm that Shakespeare's history plays have little meaning for a modern audience because they deal with a problem that is so specifically Elizabethan. But just as our understanding of the background and issues of the plays will help us better to understand the plays on their own terms, so it should make it possible for us to begin to abstract from them some universal truth, some meaning that is as real for us now as it was for the Elizabethans. The implications of kingship are not so far removed from our own lives as we might think. Its specific terms are, of course, very different. From medieval times, through the reign of Elizabeth, and well into the seventeenth century, there persisted the notion that kings were ordained by God, and that their subjects owed them the absolute obedience due to what amounted to a series of Christs on earth. Richard, indeed, continually compares his betrayal to that of Christ; he refers to his apparently treacherous friends as Judases and to his judges as Pilates. But remove the idea of divine ordination and substitute for it any higher moral right, and in its larger sense the Elizabethan problem of kingship becomes the quite universal problem of keeping the delicate balance between obligations to any conflicting powers. A similar problem in modern times might be, I suppose, the conflicting obligations of a public servant to the party which put him in power and to the people whom he is supposed to serve. The level of the issue has been lowered, but its essence has not really changed. To make the drama of Richard the Second come alive we need only to accept, in the same way that we accept the idea of Fate in Greek tragedy, the idea of divine sanction of kings. From that point on the tragedy of Richard can become meaningful beyond its own terms.

Richard the Second is a king who has the greatest theoretical but the least practical claim to his throne. It is through the discrepancy between these two claims that the dramatic conflict is established, first, within the character of Richard himself, and second, between Richard and Bolingbroke, Duke of Lancaster, who represents most strongly those qualities of kingly nature which Richard lacks.

To make this conflict effective, it was first necessary to establish very thoroughly Richard's divine right to the throne. Historically his claim could not be doubted, and the Elizabethans were well aware of this. From the time of William the Conqueror, the line of inheritance had been unchallenged. Richard was the grandson of Edward the Third by Edward's eldest son, and not even his most active enemies would accuse him of holding the throne unlawfully. Throughout the play this right is consistently underscored by Richard himself and by others: by Richard to remind his enemies that he cannot be deposed, or even opposed, and by his advisors to remind him that as a divinely ordained king he should more properly understand the duties of the king. Early in the play, the Duchess of Gloucester is urging her brother-in-law, old John of Gaunt (the father of Bolingbroke), to take some action against King Richard, who has been largely responsible for the murder of her husband. But Gaunt, although he is Richard's uncle and recognizes besides how just her accusations against the King are, will not strike out against God's anointed, even to avenge a murdered brother.

> God's is the quarrel; for God's substitute,
> His deputy anointed in His sight,
> Hath caus'd his death; the which if wrongfully,
> Let Heaven revenge; for I may never lift
> An angry arm against His minister.
>
> (I, ii, 37-41)

Similarly, at the end of Act II, the Duke of York, another of Richard's uncles, refuses to join the group of nobles who are determined to oppose Richard's will and force him to return to Bolingbroke those lands which he confiscated at the time of Gaunt's death.

> My lords of England, let me tell you this:
> I have had feeling of my cousin's wrongs
> And labour'd all I could to do him right;
> But in this kind to come, in braving arms,
> Be his own carver and cut out his way,
> To find out right with wrong— it may not be;
> And you that do abet him in this kind
> Cherish rebellion and are rebels all.
>
> (II, iii, 140-147)

These references to Richard's divine ordination can be vastly multiplied by even a cursory reading of the play. They appear on every hand and come from every mouth.

But the statements by John of Gaunt and the Duke of York are particularly significant. These two old men, Richard's uncles and the last of Edward's sons, represent the old order, an order whose kings were kingly in fact as well as theory. Their position thus served a double function; it made them acutely conscious of their duty to the King, while at the same time, by immediate contrast with their own father, it made them more painfully aware of Richard's own shortcomings. It also gave them a license to speak which was not officially shared by the younger members of the court. Hence, we hear from those same two who most clearly acknowledge the divinity of Richard's right, the sharpest rebukes for his failure properly to fulfill the obligation which goes with that right. Although he will not act against Richard, York will speak most strongly against him, to his face, when he confiscates the dead Gaunt's property to support his own ruinous Irish Wars. He lists the King's injustices, and enforces them with an exceedingly unflattering comparison with his own father, Edward the Third.

His face thou hast, for even so look'd he,
Accomplish'd with the number of thy hours;
But when he frown'd, it was against the
    French
And not against his friends. His noble hand
Did win what he did spend and spent not
    that
Which his triumphant father's hand had won.
His hands were guilty of no kindred blood,
But bloody with the enemies of his kin.
O Richard! York is too far gone with grief,
Or else he never would compare between.
                                  (II, i, 176-185)

But even stronger than York's rebuke is that of Gaunt, who, on his sick bed, has the sanction not only of rank and age, but the license of one who is about to die. And for the Elizabethans— perhaps even for us— his statement has besides its inherent force the prophetic ring of a last confession; it partakes of that mythical ability to see most clearly just before all vision, all sense of sight is lost; and, following hard upon what is perhaps the greatest national panegyric ever written, it points out finally, completely, the vast discrepancy between Richard's duty and his performance, and underlines it by emphasizing the nobility of the country which through his incompetence is being so neglected.

It is the beginning of the second act of the play. Gaunt, who in the first act has refused to lift his hand or voice against the King for either the banishment of his son or the murder of his brother, will no longer stifle his urgent feelings about England or about the King.

Methinks I am a prophet new inspir'd
And thus expiring do foretell of him:
His rash fierce blaze of riot cannot last,
For violent fires soon burn out themselves. . .
.
This land of such dear souls, this dear dear
    land,
Dear for her reputation through the world,
Is now leas'd out, I die pronouncing it,
Like to a tenement or pelting farm.
England, bound in with the triumphant sea,
Whose rocky shore beats back the envious
    siege
Of wat'ry Neptune, is now bound in with
    shame,
With inky blots and rotten parchment bonds.
That England, that was wont to conquer others,
Hath made a shameful conquest of itself.
                            (II, i, 31-34, 57-66)

And when Richard comes to see him, secretly hoping that Gaunt will die so that he can seize his lands, Gaunt speaks no less pointedly to him. Richard, he says, and not he, is the one who is dying:

Now He that made me knows I see thee ill;
Ill in myself to see, and in thee seeing ill.
Thy death-bed is no lesser than thy land
Wherein thou liest in reputation sick;
And thou, too careless patient as thou art,
Commit'st thy anointed body to the cure
Of those physicians that first wounded thee.
                                  (II, i, 93-99)

These statements by characters in the play, most particularly those by Gaunt and York, thus establish explicitly both Richard's divine right of office and his failure to act like a king. But this idea, which is so important if we are going to understand, first, Richard's personal tragedy, and second, the terrible problems of Bolingbroke as he tries to establish himself and his heirs on the throne, is emphasized by Shakespeare in two other ways: by the nature of his imagery, and by the nature and actions of Richard himself.

The Elizabethans were always quick to see a parallel between the world of men and the world of nature. They first of all believed that there was a connection between the affairs of men and the affairs of nature— that tranquility or turbulence in one would be reflected in the other. Hence the storm on the heath to match the storm in Lear's soul, and the strange perturbations of nature after the murder of Duncan by Macbeth. They believed, too, that natural phenomena could prophesy as well as reflect happenings in the world of men, as in the strange portents in *Julius Caesar,* or the fatal conjunction of the stars in *Romeo and Juliet.* And finally, they saw very readily a parallel between the hierarchy of nature and that of men. It is this last parallel which is used most particularly in *Richard II,* and while its purpose is the same as that served by Gaunt and York, its method is often different. The statements of the two Dukes were always explicit; the suggestions of the natural imagery are, more often than not, implicit; and the effect of the irony is usually more powerful than the blunt directness of the Dukes. The comparisons are to both animate and inanimate nature; Richard is compared both to the lion and to the sun. The comparison or contrast is sometimes, of course, quite straightforward, as when the Queen chides the deposed Richard for not acting like the lion who, even dying, thrusts forth his paw

And wounds the earth, if nothing else, with
    rage
To be o'erpower'd; and wilt thou, pupil-
    like,
Take the correction, mildly kiss the rod,
And fawn on rage with base humility,
Which art a lion and the king of beasts?
                                   (V, i, 30-34)

Similarly explicit is Salisbury's brief speech about Richard's return from Ireland:

Ah, Richard, with the eyes of heavy mind
I see thy glory like a shooting star
Fall to the base earth from the firmament.
Thy sun sets weeping in the lowly west,
Witnessing storms to come, woe, and unrest.

(II, iv, 18-22)

This foreshadows almost exactly Richard's coming down to the base court of Flint Castle to parley with Bolingbroke. In these two instances can be clearly seen the distinction between what Richard should be like and what he is. It is in moments when the distinction between the substance and the show is not so clearly perceived that the subtle irony acts most powerfully. The unwillingness of those about him to see what is so obvious to us suggests the immeasurably strong influence of Richard's divine protection. York reluctantly admits the difference when Richard appears on the battlements of Flint Castle to open the parley with Bolingbroke:

Yet looks he like a king! Behold, his eye,
As bright as is the eagle's, lightens forth
Controlling majesty. Alack, alack, for woe,
That any harm should stain so fair a show!

(III, iii, 68-71)

Even now, when all is almost lost, York clings to the hope that the show will carry Richard through. And just before this speech of York's, Bolingbroke himself has said:

See, see, King Richard doth himself appear,
As doth the blushing discontented sun
From out the fiery portal of the east,
When he perceives the envious clouds are bent
To dim his glory and to stain the track
Of his bright passage to the occident.

(III, iii, 62-67)

But just as York has hinted that Richard's was a seeming show, so Bolingbroke's image very quickly suggests that this sun has passed its zenith and is moving to the occident, "to set weeping in the lowly west." It remains for Richard himself to be the only one completely deceived by the nobility of his appearance. It is this fair seeming which has been the be-all of his court life up to the time of his deposition; it is the absence of this gorgeous show and the contrasting bleakness of his prison domain which most preoccupies him when he is no longer king.

This very naivete, this absence of any real perception, deplorable as it may seem, first establishes for him the sympathy necessary to his tragedy. The strength of this negative quality in eliciting sympathy is based on two very unusual phenomena. First, the Elizabethan audience, anyway, could not wholly reject a man whose belief, however naive and unrealistic, was essentially just. Weak in action as he was, Richard's claims to being the lion, to being the sun, could not be refuted. They were given to him by God. But this singular situation was not in itself enough. The audience could have had little sympathy for a man who failed to live up to the obligations of his divine right if they had felt that he was conscious of the discrepancy between the two and was willfully refusing to do anything about it. They could tolerate his weakness only because it was in terms that they could sympathize with, because his naivete was genuine, not pretended. But if he had been a poor king without being naive, or had been naive in a belief that was groundless, Richard could not have become a sympathetic, and hence not a tragic, figure.

It is clear, I think, how important an appreciation of the Elizabethan notion of kingship becomes. For it explains, first of all, the great issues and tensions which form the fabric of the play, and it makes understandable and meaningful the particular pattern of Richard's life within this fabric. Without the strange admixture of truth and delusion, his naivete would become ridiculous, and his weakness and inadequacy would become criminal. The fact that neither possibility is ever quite realized explains whatever stature Richard has as a protagonist; but the consistently implied imminence of these possibilities provides a dramatic tension and a dramatic ambiguity which are essential to a play having in effect— and particularly in the eyes of an Elizabethan audience— two protagonists: Richard, who represents the divinely ordained king, and Bolingbroke, who represents the first in a line of monarchs that leads directly to Elizabeth. Thus the fall of Richard must not seem so unjust as to condemn the legitimacy of Elizabeth's claim to the throne, nor must the rise of Bolingbroke seem so just as to set at naught the notion that kings are ordained by God and cannot be deposed by men. Richard and Bolingbroke, in short, each represented an aspect of kingship which was essential to Elizabeth. Richard was king by God, and Bolingbroke became a king by deed. The right of the latter had indirectly placed her on the throne; but it was the right of the former that kept her there. We thus have two protagonists, neither of whom must lose his stature at the expense of the other; and Shakespeare accomplishes this ambiguity of sympathy by the clever contrasting of two themes— public and private lives.

The political fall of Richard is accompanied by a corresponding growth in his personal stature; the political rise of Bolingbroke, on the other hand, is marked by a deterioration of his personal stature. In neither case does the change in personal character match in extent the reversal of public fortune; but it is sufficiently strong to modify the conclusions about the political change which must have been reached had they not been counter-pointed by considerations of personal character. It would be wrong, of course, to expect that these changes in character should take place except in terms of the personalities of the two men as they have been established during the early part of the play. To have done otherwise, Shakespeare would have had to sacrifice truth to device. But accepting the restricted limitations within which it was reasonable that the character of the two men might change during the year between Richard's deposition and his death, a considerable change, it seems to me, can be discerned.

Richard, as we have seen, is a curious admixture of weakness and naivete; his uncertain nature is perhaps best illustrated by his actions at the beginning of the play, when he tries to reconcile the hot-blooded Bolingbroke and Mowbray, who have come before him with countercharges of disloyalty to the King. Richard, who will do anything, who will even compromise honor, in order to avoid strife, seeks to reconcile them, quoting his own doctors who say that "this is no month to bleed." He orders them to throw down the gages, which each has accepted from the other as a challenge to public combat. Both Bolingbroke and Mowbray refuse; and Richard attempts to be firm:

> Rage must be withstood;
> Give me his gage. Lions make leopards tame.
> (I, i, 173-174)

That he is a lion in imagination only, he himself almost immediately admits, as he inadvertently acknowledges his own impotence:

> We were not born to sue, but to command;
> Which since we cannot do to make you
>   friends,
> Be ready, as your lives shall answer it,
> At Coventry, upon Saint Lambert's day.
> There shall your swords and lances arbitrate
> The swelling difference of your settled hate.
> (I, i, 196-201)

But the King is inconstant even in this decision. Just as the two are about to meet in the lists, he changes his mind again, throws down his warder to stop the combat, and banishes both Bolingbroke and Mowbray in order, as he says, not

> To wake our peace, which in our country's cradle
> Draws the sweet infant breath of gentle sleep.
> (I, iii, 132-133)

Obviously unable to cope with the spirited nobles of his realm, Richard withdraws from this vital element of English life, and surrounds himself with obsequious [servile] sycophants [self-seeking flatterers]. But bad as their influence is for Richard and for England, they do in a large measure draw the blame for the misrule away from the King and attach it to themselves. It was customary in medieval and Tudor times to side-step any direct censure of a divine king by simply saying that he

had been misled by evil advisors. Thus the king became guilty not of evil actions, but of poor judgment and choice. A modern audience will, of course, accept this evasion of responsibility much less readily than the Elizabethans; but knowledge of the tradition may modify somewhat our attitude toward Richard. Gaunt and York are the two ministers whose advice he should have followed; instead, he associated with "the caterpillars of the commonwealth," Bagot, Bushy, and Green, whose evil influence ate at the fair flower of the realm. Because of them, Richard's flaw, according to those about him, was weakness rather than evil. Taking advantage of his weakness, his flatterers led him to the series of unscrupulous acts which we have already heard listed by Gaunt and York. For us, this juggling of responsibility does not completely exonerate Richard, but for those who were quick to catch at any way by which to avoid direct censure of the King, this consideration greatly softened their attitude toward him.

This was the attitude of others toward Richard. His attitude toward himself and his position sprang directly from the two characteristics I have mentioned. His naivete was a combination of unwillingness and inability to distinguish between illusion and reality. He exaggerated the essential right of his position and closed his eyes to the dishonesty and unscrupulousness of his acts. His court was full of pageantry, but either his weakness forestalled action, or his unscrupulousness prompted wicked action.

We have seen how the others, like York and Bolingbroke, saw or at least hinted at the irony in the comparison of Richard to the king of beasts or the lord of the heavens. But it was Richard himself who indulged in the most extensive of these comparisons, and yet it was he alone who never suspected that fair show and seeming were not enough. The irony of his situation reaches its climax in Act III when, bereft of his power, he still fancies that his divine presence alone will put to flight the rebellious nobles.

> Discomfortable cousin! know'st thou not
> That when the searching eye of heaven is hid
> Behind the globe, that lights the lower world,
> Then thieves and robbers range abroad
>   unseen
> In murders and in outrage boldly here;
> But when from under this terrestrial ball
> He fires the proud tops of the eastern pines
> And darts his light through every guilty hole,
> Then murders, treasons, and detested sins,
> The cloak of night being pluck'd from off
>   their backs,
> Stand bare and naked, trembling at themselves?
> So when this thief, this traitor, Bolingbroke,
> Who all this while hath revell'd in the night
> Whilst we were wand'ring with the antipodes,
> Shall see us rising in our throne, the east,
> His treasons will sit blushing in his face,

Not able to endure the sight of day,
But, self-affrighted, tremble at his sin.
Not all the water in the rough rude sea
Can wash the balm off from an anointed
    king;
The breath of worldly men cannot depose
The deputy elected by the Lord.
For every man that Bolingbroke hath press'd
To lift shrewd steel against our golden crown,
God for his Richard hath in heavenly pay
A glorious angel; then, if angels fight,
Weak men must fall, for Heaven still guards
    the right.

                (III, ii, 36-62)

But this is pitiful, not bitter irony. For Richard's notion was true, no matter how unrealistic. And in the light of the essential truth of his belief, his self-indulgence and self-pity become more understandable than they ever could be if they were based on a completely absurd or unsympathetic notion of his own right.

These three factors, his evil advisors, his own weakness, and his essential right to the crown, hold in partial abeyance any direct antagonism to Richard while he is on the throne; once he is deposed, once his weakness no longer has the power to allow evil actions, they become positive forces which draw sympathy to him. His right to rule seems all the stronger when he no longer wears the crown. Stature which was impossible for him as king becomes possible for him as a man. Thus Richard, who has never completely lost sympathy, achieves a temporary dignity in his last minutes when, moved to action at last, he kills two of the men come to murder him, before he is struck down. The dramatic force of this last act, however brief, cannot be overestimated.

Richard's stature as a tragic figure is thus maintained, despite an extended overindulgence in self-pity, which would ordinarily alienate the sympathy of the audience. For his reflections on his own state have the substance of truth, and are, besides, ennobled and heightened by Shakespeare's poetry; his evil actions are attributable not entirely to evil intentions but partly to limited perceptions and to misuse of a power which is truly his; his misuse of power is, in turn, more the fault of wicked friends who have taken advantage of his weakness and egoism; and his own actions at the end give momentary evidence of a nobility which until then has been lacking. This is not to say that Richard can match the greatness or dignity of Hamlet or Lear; but in terms which the Elizabethans would accept, he achieves a tragic stature.

This explanation cannot, however, obscure the fact that Richard was not a good king. His seizure of Gaunt's land was manifestly unjust, and the injustice became the means by which Bolingbroke, at the outset of the play, achieved the sympathy of a rising protagonist. And as long as Bolingbroke merely opposed the illegal acts of the King, and not the King himself, he could keep the sympathy of the nobles and of the audience. That was his original aim when he returned with an army from exile. Go, he says, and thus deliver to the King:

Harry Bolingbroke
On both his knees doth kiss King Richard's
    hand
And sends allegiance and true faith of heart
To his most royal person, hither come
Even at his feet to lay my arms and power,
Provided that my banishment repeal'd
And lands restor'd again be freely granted.

                (III, iii, 35-41)

But Richard himself immediately perceives the truth. "Your heart," he says to the kneeling Bolingbroke, "is up, I know, thus high at least," and he touches his own head. Not content with the restoration of his property, Bolingbroke reaches for the crown as well. At this point both the public and private fortunes of Richard and Bolingbroke cross. Politically, Richard's fall is matched with Bolingbroke's rise; but privately their fortunes are reversed. Bolingbroke's hands are no longer clean; he is guilty of the Greek *hybris,* the sin of pride and ambition; and Richard, in becoming the unjustly deposed king, plucks to himself the sympathy which until then has lain largely with Bolingbroke. If Richard gains both sympathy and a semblance of dignity at the end of the play, Bolingbroke, in taking the crown, has taken unto himself and to his heirs the curse so vehemently pronounced by the Bishop of Carlisle:

What subject can give sentence on his king?
And who sits here that is not Richard's
    subject? . . .
My Lord of Hereford here, whom you call
    king,
Is a foul traitor to proud Hereford's king;
And if you crown him, let me prophesy,
The blood of English shall manure the
    ground,
And future ages groan for this foul act.
          (IV, i, 121-122, 134-138)

So we come to the strangely ambivalent conclusion to this play, and the ambivalence was possible only because the primary concern was not for any single human being, but for the whole realm of England. Both Richard and Bolingbroke were in a measure innocent, and in a measure guilty. Richard was a legitimate king, but his rule was ruining England. If England was to live, he must be destroyed; but, paradoxically, this necessary destruction of God's divine instrument must then be punished. Thus, the ensuing plays about Henry the Fourth and Henry the Fifth become, among other things,

David Dodge as Richard II and J. Bretton Truett as Bolingbroke in GreenStage's 1998 production of Richard II.

a study of the suffering and expiation of the House of Lancaster. The civil wars and filial troubles of Henry the Fourth, constantly referred to as punishments for his sin, are gradually worked out; and when Henry the Fifth, like his great-grandfather Edward the Third, turns away from civil wars to wars of conquest in France, he prays before his great battle finally to be absolved from the sins of his family.

> O, not to-day, think not upon the fault
> My father made in compassing the crown!
> I Richard's body have interred new,
> And on it have bestow'd more contrite tears,
> Than from it issu'd forced drops of blood. . .
>
>   More will I do;
> Though all that I can do is nothing worth,
> Since that my penitence comes after all,
> Imploring pardon.
>   (*Henry V*, IV, i, 310-314, 319-322)

His victory at Agincourt seems pretty clearly to be

God's answer.

Donna B. Hamilton

SOURCE: "The State of Law in Richard II," *Shakespeare Quarterly*, Vol. 34, No. 1, Spring, 1983, pp. 5-17.

[*In the essay that follows, Hamilton studies the concept of a "law-centered kingship" in* Richard II, *suggesting that despite Richard's divine right to rule, he is not above the law. Nevertheless, Hamilton demonstrates, in many ways Richard acts as if he is free from having to answer for his own illegal action. In conclusion, Hamilton observes that when Bolingbroke becomes king, another issue of kingship is raised, as Bolingbroke possesses only popular support, not the legal or divine right to rule.*]

Near the end of the speeches of warning and instruction that Gaunt delivers on his deathbed to the wayward Richard II, one encounters the passage,

> Landlord of England art thou now, not king,

Thy state of law is bondslave to the law.

                                        (II.i.113-14)

[All references to Shakespeare's plays are from the *Arden Shakespeare* editions, including Peter Ure, ed., *King Richard II* (London: Methuen, 1956) and A. R. Humphreys, ed., *The Second Part of King Henry IV* (London: Methuen, 1967)]

Although it is evident that Gaunt is expressing displeasure with Richard, the substance of his complaint has not always been clear. A. P. Rossiter, for example, has described the passage as "hopelessly obscure." At issue is the relationship between king and law. To understand Gaunt's speech one must sort out the distinction the old man is drawing between landlord and king.

When this passage is glossed in modern editions of the play, the readings nearly always suggest that the second line stands in apposition to the first, presumably repeating in different words what the first line says. A consequence of this assumption is the interpretation that Gaunt is accusing Richard, as J. Dover Wilson says, of having "diminish[ed] the royal prerogative." Citing J. C. Smith, Wilson offers the following paraphrase of the second line: "Your legal status as king ('in all causes supreme') is now amenable to the common law like that of any other mortgagee." Similarly G. L. Kittredge, basing his reading on the glosses of Samuel Johnson and Edmund Malone, writes, "Your legal status is no longer that of supreme King of England by divine right; for you are now as subject to the law in regard to the whole realm as any landlord is with reference to his private estate when he has given a lease of it." The Arden, Pelican, and Riverside editions of the play all offer essentially the same explanation.

These glosses raise problems because their phrasing, particularly the references to supremacy, seem incompatible with certain notions about kingship to which recent historians have drawn our attention. These notions include the recognition that a king who ruled by divine right was also, in theory and in practice, subject to the law; he was to rule according to the law, and his power derived from the law. Glosses that derive their authority from nineteenth-century scholarship proceed on the assumption that the king is not subject to the law; they suggest, therefore, that the lines in question present Richard as having declined from a condition of supremacy to one in which he is subject to the law. What I wish to show in the following pages is that, on the issue of king and law, *Richard II* reflects the views of the playwright's own time, as historians now understand those views.

I

To arrive at a better reading of Gaunt's speech, it is necessary to recognize at the outset that the relationship of the lines to each other is not that of apposition. Rather, they express a paradox: a king who acts like a landlord instead of a king becomes in some sense a slave.

Some of the best help for these lines is available in that storehouse of political thought, *De Republica Anglorum* (1583), by Thomas Smith. Smith's definition of commonwealth has as its core a statement about the proper relationship between a king and his people. In his description of what that relationship *should* be, Smith includes a comment about what it should *not* be, namely the kind of relationship that existed between a Roman landlord and his slaves:

> A common wealth is called a society or common doing of a multitude of free men collected together and united by common accord & covenauntes among themselves, for the conservation of themselves as well in peace as in warre. . . . And if one man had as some of the olde Romanes had. . . . V. thousande or L. thousande bondmen whom he ruled well . . . yet that were no common wealth: for the bondman hath no communion with his master, the wealth of the Lord is onely sought for, and not the profit of the slave or bondman. For as they who write of these things have defined, a bondman or a slave is as it were . . . but the instrument of his Lord, as . . . the saw, the chessyll and gowge is of the charpenter. Truth it is the charpenter looketh diligently to save, correct and amend all these: but it is for his own profit, and in consideration of him selfe, not for the instruments sake . . . and there is no mutuall societie or portion, no law or pleading betweene thone and thother.

For Smith, the keystone of a commonwealth is not the king's royal prerogative [an exclusive right or privilege], his power, or his supremacy, but the well-being of those he rules. By contrast, a landlord sees his people as slaves, as the means by which he enlarges himself; they exist only to increase his wealth and profit. Their well-being is of concern only in the sense that they must be kept in good condition, like tools, if they are to function efficiently in fulfilling the tasks he has for them. And because they have no value except insofar as they are useful to him, they can make no demands upon him, can claim no rights: "There is no mutuall societie or portion, no law or pleading betweene thone and thother."

Just as it is clear in Smith's discussion that this relationship between landlord and people is antithetical to the idea of a commonwealth, so is it clear in the line by Gaunt— "Landlord of England art thou now, not king"— that he would prefer to see Richard behave like a king, not a landlord. Significantly, the issue for Gaunt is not the matter of the king's royal prerogative, but the well-being of those the king rules. As Gaunt has told York before Richard enters the scene, Richard's "insatiate . . . consuming" rule poses a grave threat to all that

England is and represents, both at home and abroad. In overtaxing the commons, in using blank charters to gather larger revenues, Richard has managed to reduce a demi-Paradise "to a tenement or pelting farm." The profit of the ruler, not that of the people, is being advanced. For Richard to act like a landlord is not to diminish the royal prerogative, then, but to act as though the royal prerogative allows a king to do anything he wishes.

For an interpretation of the monarchy of Richard II which coincides with this point of view Shakespeare need have gone no farther than *The Mirror for Magistrates*, Raphael Holinshed's *Chronicles*, or the anonymous *Woodstock*, if indeed that play preceded Shakespeare's. . . .

III

In Shakespeare's *Richard II*, the view that Richard's activities are bad because they harm the commonwealth is nearly everywhere present. In addition to Gaunt's references to Richard as landlord, there are regular references to the rights and desires of the commons. Such references furnish a significant background against which to consider a king who speaks of his people as "slaves" deserving no respect, no "reverence" (I.iv.27), a king who taxes his subjects beyond their means and who disregards the laws and customs of inheritance when he determines to "Take Herford's right away" (II.i.195). In this atmosphere of neglect and abuse Northumberland's announcement that he and others are launching an effort to "shake off our slavish yoke" (II.i.291) sounds less like the language of an ambitious nobleman and more like the protest of a subject concerned about violations of his rights.

If Richard's failure at rule has consequences for the people, it also has consequences for Richard. One is his loss of popular support. How significant that loss is seems clear from the response Richard makes to the news that the Welsh have deserted him. Richard explains to Aumerle why he has suddenly grown "so pale":

> But now the blood of twenty thousand men
> Did triumph in my face, and they are fled;
> And till so much blood thither come again,
> Have I not reason to look pale and dead?
>   (III.ii.76-79)

In equating the blood of twenty thousand men with the blood that should be in his face, Richard is acknowledging that in a very important sense a king is, or should be, one with the people— mystically joined to them and, indeed, comprised of them. This emphasis is one not usually associated with Shakespeare's plays, and particularly not with *Richard II*, a history play which has sometimes been thought of as a storehouse of materials on divine-right theory. It may be instructive, then, to note that such ideas are also available in so standard and respectable a source as *De Laudibus Legum*

Angliae (1470) by John Fortescue. Comparing the body politic and the natural body, Fortescue explains that just as the heart and blood give life to the natural body, "sembably in a bodye politike the intent of the people is the first lively thing, having within it bloud, that is to say, politike provision for the utilitie and wealth of the same people, which it dealeth furth & imparteth as wel to the head as to al the members of the same body wherby the body is nourished & maintained." The lifeblood that flows to the king from the people also flows from them to the laws, which, according to Fortescue, comprise "byndyng" sinews that allow the body to function properly (sig. Dviii'). Because the people are the heart and blood of the commonwealth, the source both for laws and for the king, Fortescue says that ultimately the king, the head of the body politic, receives a measure of his "power of the people," a situation that makes it possible to "measure the power, which the king therof may exercise over the lawe and subjectes of the same" (sig. Ei').

This understanding of the composition of the body politic extends the implications of *Richard II*'s many references to the people who are leaving Richard. As they depart from him, the life in his body diminishes. The twenty-thousand Welshmen are but a small wound compared to the paleness and death that come over Richard's kingship when the politic body's other members, the "white-beards . . . boys . . . beadsmen . . . distaff-women . . . young and old" (III.ii.112-19), withdraw their support. The new recipient of that support is, of course, Bolingbroke, whom Richard had once mocked for giving himself over to the people's "hearts" (I.iv.25). Misconceiving the consequences of Bolingbroke's favor with the people, Richard has failed to recognize that the "reverence" he thought Bolingbroke uselessly "did throw away on slaves" was in reality a gesture that added life, first, to Bolingbroke's legal cause and, later, to his growing political power.

The idea that Richard's failure to rule properly has drained the lifeblood from his rule is similar to the notion implicit in the "bondslave" line. As we have seen, the line preceding— "Landlord of England art thou now, not king"— defines the nature of Richard's failure. This line— "Thy state of law is bondslave to the law"— states the consequences of that failure, the paradox that a king who treats others as slaves will eventually lose his power over them, not augment it.

IV

To understand how this may be so, it is necessary to examine the notion current in Shakespeare's time, but with roots that sixteenth-century lawyers understood to reach back to Henry of Bracton, that the law makes the king. This notion is important to bear in mind when one considers either Richard II or Bolingbroke-Henry IV, because both are kings whose right to rule comes under question. The concept comes into *Richard II* most explicitly when York, following Richard's announcement that he plans to seize the deceased Gaunt's "plate, his goods, his money, and his lands," warns the king that failing to heed the laws of inheritance is akin to undermining the very laws upon which his right to the throne depends: "Take Herford's rights away, and take from time / His charters, and his customary rights . . . For how art thou a king / But by fair sequence and succession?" (II.i.195-99). Through this reminder that the law makes Richard king, York is warning Richard that royal disregard for the law gives license for subjects to disobey the law. Even worse, York says, Richard's disobedience puts him in the precarious position of a ruler acting in the absence of any authority— separating himself from that which gives him power in the first place. In delivering such a warning, York takes a position similar to that expressed by Richard's contemporary, John Gower. In his discourse on the education of kings, in the seventh book of *Confessio Amantis,* Gower says:

> What Kinge of lawe taketh no kepe
> By lawe he may no royalme kepe.
> Do lawe away, what is a kynge?
> Where is the right of any thynge
> If that there be no lawe in londe?

The most influential English legal authority to define the king in this manner was Bracton, upon whom Gower, Fortescue, and many of their successors, including Richard Hooker and Francis Bacon, relied. As Bracton had written in his thirteenth-century treatise *De Legibus et Consuetudinibus Angliae,* "law makes the king. Let him therefore bestow upon the law what the law bestows upon him, namely rule and power. For there is no *rex* where will rules rather than *lex.*" These are complicated sentences open to various application and interpretation. What is of first importance to this essay is that here is a set of ideas all mutually dependent on one another, inseparable from one another. The law makes the king; the law makes the king powerful; and the king is to rule by law.

In *De Laudibus,* after declaring that the king "at the time of his coronation . . . is bound by an othe to the observaunce and keeping of his owne lawe," John Fortescue explains that to rule by law "is no yoke, but liberty and great securitie not onely to the subjectes, but also to the kinge" (sig. Kvii'). If the king does not rule by law, does he become more powerful? No, Fortescue says; he trades what liberty and security he has for the yoke of impotence. Ironically, he puts himself in a position analogous to that of a slave, one who has in effect no ability to plead to the law or make the law plead for him. As Quintilian had observed, "A slave cannot acquire his freedom without the consent of his master; a man assigned for debt can acquire it by paying his debt without the consent of his master being necessary. A slave is outside the law; a man

assigned for debt is under the law." Defined by law and made powerful by law, a king forfeits his very freedom if he attempts to function "outside the law." If he thinks that abuse of law, which amounts to abuse of the relationship between king and people, will make him more powerful, he is deceived. To abuse the law is, in effect, to unavail himself of his authority; if he acts outside the law he soon finds that his relationship to the law deteriorates to that of a bondslave.

All of this Bracton knew. And this is what Gaunt means in *Richard II* when he defines Richard's situation as that of a landlord and a bondslave.

V

I should like now to consider the opening three scenes of the play, examining one issue central to those scenes to show how they prepare for the moment when Gaunt assesses Richard as a landlord-bondslave.

In the opening scenes of the play, where Richard is king and Bolingbroke is subject, the issue that might be said to provide the conceptual basis for the action is the inviolability the Crown enjoys by virtue of the royal prerogative. By illustrating the power a king can wield if he chooses, the scenes also reflect some of the relationships between the concept of the king as an official made by law and under the law and the concept, more often used as a by-word for discussions of *Richard II,* that the king derives his power from God and is under God. For our purposes, the most important elements in that relationship are suggested by the sentences immediately preceding Bracton's assertion that "law makes the king." They include the famous Bractonian explanation that the king is *"non . . . sub homine sed sub deo et sub lege."* According to Bracton, "The king has no equal within his realm. Subjects cannot be the equals of the ruler, because he would thereby lose his rule . . . because he would then be subjected to those subjected to him. The king must not be under man but under God and under the law, because law makes the king."

In making clear that the king is more powerful than the subject, Bracton's compact phrases helped future generations in their efforts to establish, among other things, a legal basis for the king's possession of extraordinary powers— his power to dispense with law, for example, and to determine cases according to equity. These provisions gave the king a degree of authority thought necessary to ensure that a condition of justice and well-being was maintained in the state. Power to dispense with the law or, through equity, to correct the law, was given so that the king could better fulfill the ultimate intention of the law, which was to protect and preserve the commonwealth. By virtue of his being clearly defined as above his subjects, moreover, the king had the advantage of increased security. His superiority was of a sort that made it impossible for him to be brought to trial; he could not be sued. Or, as is often said, he was not amenable to the law.

Despite these prerogatives, however, the king was still to be regarded as under the law. It was by law that he possessed prerogatives, and it was presumed that, in his use of these special powers, he would always exercise the kind of self-restraint that would keep his rule in the interest of the common-wealth and within the intention of the law. Just a few lines after declaring the king *"non sub homine,"* Bracton goes on to say that the king must will "himself to be subjected to the law" even as had Jesus Christ, "lest his power remain unbridled." . . .

A problem that could develop under such principles is the one dramatized in the three opening scenes of *Richard II.* For the royal prerogative of immunity from prosecution could result in a situation whereby a king guilty of an illegal act would be free of having to answer for it. The commonwealth had no institution or procedure to compel a king to act in conformity with the law or to punish him for violating it.

In the first scene of the play, then, when Bolingbroke accuses Mowbray of treason, he is taking the only action he can against a king who is guilty of having ordered the murder of Gloucester, but whose prerogative renders him immune from trial. With Richard occupying such an invulnerable position, the most Bolingbroke could accomplish would be to bring to trial the subordinate who exercised Richard's will in the matter. Hence Bolingbroke's action against Mowbray.

In the second scene of the play this context sheds light on Gaunt's reply to the angry and despairing Duchess of Gloucester, who wants satisfaction for her husband's murder. Gaunt is as aware as Bolingbroke that no legal action can be taken against the King. If Richard is ever to be punished, that punishment must come from God:

> God's is the quarrel—for God's substitute,
> His deputy anointed in his sight,
> Hath caus'd his death; the which if wrongfully,
> Let heaven revenge, for I may never lift
> An angry arm against His minister.
>
> (I.ii.37-41)

In reminding the Duchess that the King's authority derives ultimately from God and that the King is above his subjects, Gaunt is reflecting an understanding of the royal power and royal prerogative which coincides with the Bractonian assumptions we have been considering.

In the third scene Richard exercises his royal prerogative by halting the trial by combat and sentencing the combatants himself. The reason he gives for his action is that he wishes to avoid bloodshed. But the sentencing is also convenient for Richard, allowing him to get

rid of both the man who played henchman for him and the man who sought to expose the King and his henchman.

While there is a sense in which the king's prerogative can be described as being provided by law to place the king above the law, his being always also under the law makes it possible for him to be judged according to the law. The opening scenes of *Richard II* call for the audience to render a judgment against Richard not only because he is implicated in a murder, but also because in both his scenes of confrontation with Bolingbroke and Mowbray (and most obviously in the second), Richard can be viewed as exercising the royal prerogative for his own self-interest rather than for the good of the commonwealth. Even though the prerogative that keeps Richard from being brought to trial makes him punishable by God alone, then, it is nevertheless true that Richard is still susceptible to criticism for not having bridled himself, as Bracton would have insisted, so that all his acts, including his use of the royal prerogative, would be in conformity with the law. Instead of accepting his responsibility to serve and execute the law, Richard has become "unstaid" (II.i.2). As a king "wanting the manage" of himself (III.iii.179), he has created conditions that promote the unruliness of others.

VI

A similar judgment of Richard will be offered in the garden scene (the scene immediately preceding the deposition), another place in the play where the responsibilities of a God-given and a law-made kingship are set forth. This scene provides an occasion for recalling that one whose authority is stronger because it is from God as well as from the law not only accepts the advantages of great power when he accedes to the throne; he also assumes responsibility for fulfilling the demands of both God and the law. The king is empowered, but he is also obligated—to trim and dress the land, to "Keep law and form and due proportion" (III.iv.41). And just as Adam, whom God had "set to dress" another garden, was cast out from that paradisal setting when he sought to satisfy his own desires instead of God's commands, so Richard's failure in stewardship to God and the law presages his expulsion from the sea-walled garden that is John of Gaunt's "other Eden."

Following the display, in Act I, of the ways in which Richard abuses his power, much of the rest of the play points, as does the garden scene, to the consequences of those abuses—consequences which nearly always involve Bolingbroke. Bolingbroke's re-entry into England is one of the first. That return must be judged illegal because it defies the order of banishment. But it also serves as a reminder that Richard has furnished his subjects with a precedent for side-stepping the law.

Moreover, because some of Richard's abuses have been particularly at Bolingbroke's expense, the latter's return directs attention quite specifically to the consequences of Richard's disregard of a subject's rights under the law. Before leaving England, as York has reminded Richard, Bolingbroke had hired attorneys to secure his inheritance in the event of his father's death. When access to legal aid is denied him and the right to his inheritance is threatened, the banished Bolingbroke enters the country to maintain that which he believes to be his, according to his status under the law: "I am a subject, / And I challenge law; attorneys are denied me, / And therefore personally I lay my claim / To my inheritance of free descent" (II.iii.132-35). By refusing to buckle under as someone with no right to plead for justice under the law, Bolingbroke is expressing much the same sentiment as that of Northumberland's determination to "shake off our slavish yoke." For a commonwealth to exist, there must be, as Smith said, "a mutual societie" with "law or pleading between thone and thother."

VII

As Bolingbroke's status in the realm changes from that of subject to that of king, *Richard II* prompts an audience to think of yet other aspects of kingship. The central issue for Bolingbroke's rule, and one to which every play in the rest of the second tetralogy will return, is the threat to the realm when the king is not legally titled. Historically, great care was taken by Bolingbroke and his supporters to make Richard II's deposition and Henry IV's accession appear legal. Technically, Richard's power was given, not taken away; he deposed himself publicly in the presence of Parliament, a detail whose significant presence in *Richard II* Ernest Talbert has emphasized in his analysis of references to Parliament in the stage directions for the deposition scene. Nevertheless, because the deposition is an interruption of the tradition of legal succession, Bolingbroke's power exists without the clear sanction of either the law or God, a point the Bishop of Carlisle addresses when he declares,

> And shall the figure of God's majesty
> His captain, steward, deputy elect,
> Anointed, crowned, planted many years,
> Be judg'd by subject and inferior breath. . . .
> My Lord of Herford here, whom you call king,
> Is a foul traitor to proud Herford's king.
> (IV.i.125-28, 134-35)

Bacon, in the Case of the Post-Nati, explains that "toward the king himself the law doth a double office . . . the first is to intitle the king. . . . The second is . . . to make the ordinary power of the king more definite and regular" (p. 646). Richard's transgressions are against the latter provision of the law, Bolingbroke's against the former. Conse-

quently, Bolingbroke's power rests almost solely on public support, an element so sorely lacking in Richard that the authority which God and law had given him was undermined. Richard himself describes the precariousness of Bolingbroke's reign in his prophecy to Northumberland:

> thou shalt think.
> Though he divide the realm and give thee half,
> It is too little, helping him to all;
> He shall think that thou, which knowest the way
> To plant unrightful kings, wilt know again . . .
> To pluck him headlong from the usurped throne.
> (V.i.59-65)

Bolingbroke is in the one position that Bracton said a ruler could least afford: "Subjects cannot be the equals of the ruler, because he would thereby lose his rule. . . . The king must not be under man."

It is, then, with a certain sad irony that one observes Bolingbroke demonstrating his capacity for rule. He announces his intention of returning Norfolk's lands to him, and he exercises the royal prerogative in a manner that benefits a subject when he acquits Aumerle of treason. The presence of some qualifications for kingship is not always sufficient compensation, however, for the absence of others. Thus it seems fitting that a play which begins with scenes recalling the murder Richard ordered should end with scenes referring to the murder of Richard. Unwilling to accept those aspects of kingship in which law is sovereign, both Richard and Bolingbroke separate themselves from that which makes the power of kings secure. Fortescue's conclusion that the king who refuses to rule by law thereby loses his freedom (sig. Kvii) is thus aptly illustrated by the fates of both Richard and Bolingbroke. In their closing scenes (V.ii and V.iii), both kings are prisoners of guilt.

VIII

The concepts of law that define king and commonwealth in *Richard II* and guide the audience's assessment of Richard's reign are the same standards that many of Shakespeare's contemporaries used to assess their own monarch and society. The presence of such concepts in *Richard II* would seem, then, to be incompatible with interpretations that consider the play to be about the passing of a period with a less modern kingship than that of the Renaissance, or interpretations that consider the play to be about the destruction of an era characterized by a kind and degree of order that could never be recreated. On the contrary, the presence of these ideas about law and commonwealth in *Richard II* suggests that the dramatist saw in Richard's story an example of something that had happened once in England, and might happen again. Richard's story was a meaningful one for Shakespeare's own time, and the dramatist enacted it in a manner that allowed it to reflect the social and political ideals his own time revered.

Realizing that the concept of a law-centered kingship is central to *Richard II* has implications both for the way one interprets this play and for the way one assesses its place in the second tetralogy. The political ideals that many of Shakespeare's contemporaries upheld appear in *Richard II* primarily through a succession of negative examples. In the English history plays that follow, the same assumptions prove pertinent, prompting an audience to apply the same standards in *1* and *2 Henry IV* and in *Henry V* as it assesses the degree to which the commonwealth is presented in terms of an ideal state of law. When the tetralogy is looked at from this point of view, a most important moment is the one in *2 Henry IV* when Hal, making his first entry as Henry V, announces to the Lord Chief Justice that he now takes him as his "father." That gesture indicates that Hal correctly comprehends what a king is and what a commonwealth should be:

> You shall be as father to my youth,
> My voice shall sound as you do prompt mine
>   ear,
> And I will stoop and humble my intents
> To your well-practis'd wise directions.
>   (V.ii.118-21)

In acknowledging that he is under the law and in promising to act accordingly— and then in proceeding to banish the lawless Falstaff and summon Parliament— Hal offers assurance that his rule will be a responsible one and that he will always consider himself to be "busy for the commonwealth" (V.ii.76). Obviously Falstaff is wrong when he assumes, upon hearing that Hal is king, that "the laws of England are at my commandment" (V.iii.132-33). Rather, the laws will now be sovereign over king and subject alike. The days of having a landlord for a king, or a subject with as much power as the king, are finally past.

LANGUAGE, IMAGERY, AND SYMBOLISM

The language of *Richard II* and the images and symbols it contains can help illuminate the significance of the play's themes. **Arthur Suzman** and Andrew Gurr both examine the ways in which the imagery highlights important themes and supports the action of the play. Suzman argues that the play is primarily concerned with the fall of Richard and the rise of Bolingbroke. A parallel theme, Suzman states, is the spiritual rise of Richard, which follows his political fall, and the spiritual fall of Bolingbroke, precipitated by his political rise. The imagery of the play reflects this theme of rise and fall. The action of the play as well, Suzman notes,

is closely linked with this imagery. In almost every scene, the imagery of rise and fall is used, Suzman explains. Word pairs such as "ascend" and "descend" or "sky" and "earth" are often employed to emphasize rising and falling, and images such as ladders or "two buckets in a well" are used for the same purpose. Suzman traces the usage of such language and imagery from the play's beginning to end, noting that one of the scenes where this language and imagery is powerfully employed is Act III, scene iii, when Richard, standing high on the battlements, looks down on Northumberland and Bolingbroke below. Richard has told Bolingbroke that he shall acquiesce to his demands. Richard then descends from the battlements to Bolingbroke's "base court" (III.iii.180). Bolingbroke kneels before Richard, but Richard replies, "Up, cousin up— your heart is up, I know . . ." (III.iii.194). Suzman notes that with these and the next several lines, the "climax of the play has passed."

Gurr studies the imagery of the play in a different way, observing that the images used in *Richard II* are related to the four elements: earth, air, fire, and water. Richard as king, for example, is associated with the sun and fire, Bolingbroke with a flood, or water, until Bolingbroke becomes king and takes over the sun imagery. Gurr emphasizes that as the play progresses, the shifting of these elemental images makes clear that the balance of power has shifted from Richard to Bolingbroke. Gurr also analyzes the language of the play, specifically focusing on the use of formal, rhymed verse compared to the usage of blank verse. The contrast between blank verse and the formality of rhymed verse, Gurr argues, represents the play's concern with the gulf between the words used and the meaning they represent.

Arthur Suzman

SOURCE: "Imagery and Symbolism in Richard II," in *Shakespeare Quarterly*, Vol. VII, No. 3, Summer, 1956, pp. 357-70.

[*In the following essay, Suzman argues that the main theme of* Richard II *is the political fall of Richard and the rise of Bolingbroke. This theme, Suzman states, is paralleled by Richard's spiritual rise and Bolingbroke's spiritual fall. The play's imagery and symbolism are used as a method of presenting this "dual theme of rise and fall," Suzman maintains. Suzman closely analyzes the play's language, imagery, and symbolism to show that the action of the play is tightly linked with its imagery.*]

The fall of Richard and the rise of Bolingbroke provide the central theme of Shakespeare's tragedy, *The Life and Death of King Richard the Second*. As William Hazlitt observes: "The steps by which Bolingbroke mounts the throne are those by which Richard sinks

Act V, scene i. Northumberland, Richard II, the Queen, soldiers, and attendants. By M.L. Ralston.

into the grave." Spiritually, one might add, as Richard rises, so Bolingbroke declines. This dual theme of rise and fall provides in turn the dominant imagery and symbolism of the play, indeed, it may justly be described as its *leitmotif* [a theme associated throughout a drama with a particular idea or person].

Perhaps in no other of Shakespeare's plays do imagery and action so closely correspond. The recurrent imagery of rise and fall goes far beyond a purpose of mere description. Throughout, it has a significance beyond its immediate context and bears a striking relationship to the central dramatic theme.

The imagery, in the language of Wolfgang Clemen (*The Development of Shakespeare's Imagery*) is functional and organic and plays a decisive part both in expressing the dramatic theme and in characterization.

This close relationship in *Richard II* between the action of the play and its iterative imagery appears somehow to have escaped attention in the numerous writings on Shakespearian imagery. Even Richard D. Altick, in his detailed study, *"Symphonic Imagery in Richard II"* (*PMLA*, LXII) makes no specific mention of the repeated use throughout the play of the imagery and symbolism of rise and fall, or of its constant relationship to the underlying theme of the tragedy.

E. M. W. Tillyard, in his *"Shakespeare's History Plays"* (1946) emphasizes the marked ceremonial character of *Richard II;* indeed, he describes it as the most formal and ceremonial of all Shakespeare's plays and points out that the very actions tend to be symbolic rather than real and the language that of ceremony rather than of passion. "In *Richard II",* he writes, "with all the emphasis and the point taken out of the action, we are invited again and again, to dwell on the sheer ceremony of the various situations."

Almost throughout, however, the very ceremony itself, no less than the elaborate poetic language in which it is clothed, is symbolic or suggestive of this central theme of rise and fall.

This ceremonial, expressed in varying forms, but always with the same underlying symbolic motif, occurs in the play on four significant occasions: firstly, in the opening scene, at Windsor Castle, when Bolingbroke and Mowbray throw down their gages; next, before the lists at Coventry (I.iii), when the King throws down his warder— "His own life hung upon the staff he threw"; thirdly, at Flint Castle (III.iii), when the King, surrendering to Bolingbroke, descends to the "base court" from the castle walls; and, finally, in the deposition scene at Westminster Hall (IV.i), when Richard hands his crown to Bolingbroke and later, at the close of the scene, when he dashes the mirror to the ground where it lies "crack'd in a hundred shivers".

There is scarcely a scene in the play where the imagery of rise and fall does not occur. The dual imagery is achieved usually by means of antitheses— contrasting ideas of rise and fall being expressed by the use of pairs of words such as: "ascend", "descend"; "up", "down"; "high", "low"; "sky", "earth". Occasionally, the mere subject matter itself, such as "scale", "ladder", "two buckets in a well", suggests the two-fold imagery. Pregnant phrases, such as "jauncing Bolingbroke" and "plume-pluck'd Richard", convey in a word the changing fortunes— ascending or descending— of the characters.

The play is rich in colorful metaphor suggestive of the images of the rising Bolingbroke and the falling Richard. Thus, of Bolingbroke— "How high a pitch his resolution soars"; "The eagle-wing'd pride of sky-aspiring and ambitious thoughts"; "How far brought you high Hereford on his way?"; "Great Bolingbroke, mounted upon a hot and fiery steed, which his aspiring rider seemed to know". And, of Richard— "I see thy glory like a shooting star fall to the base earth from the firmament. Thy sun sets weeping in the lowly west"; "Down, down I come, like glist'ring Phaethon."

The thesis that Shakespeare secures the unity of each of his greatest plays not only by the plot, by linkage of characters, by the sweep of Nemesis, by the use of irony and by appropriateness of style, but by deliberate repetition through the play of at least one set of words or ideas in harmony with the plot, is propounded by F. C. Kolbe (*Shakespeare's Way: A Psychological Study*). "It is like the effect of the dominant note in a melody", writes Kolbe. "In some of the plays there are two such sets of ideas and then one is seen to be the dominant and the other the tonic."

Writing of *Richard II*, Kolbe states there are in the play four inter-woven strains, Sorrow, Life-blood, Inheritance, and England, and that the leading idea in the play is "England's Heritage of Blood and Woe". This, he adds, is in reality the key chord of the whole octave of plays from *Richard II* to *Richard III*.

A review of the imagery and symbolism in *Richard II* strikingly supports Kolbe's general thesis, for it reveals a deliberate repetition throughout the play of one set of words or ideas in harmony with the plot, namely, the dual theme of rise and fall, reflecting the conflict between the two protagonists, Richard of Bordeaux and Henry Bolingbroke, Duke of Lancaster.

The play opens, it will be recalled, at Windsor Castle where Henry Bolingbroke, Duke of Hereford (son of "old John of Gaunt, time-honour'd Lancaster") and Thomas Mowbray, Duke of Norfolk, both "high-stomach'd and full of ire", have been summoned before the King "to appeal each other of high treason". In the opening scene, as already mentioned, the imagery of rise and fall is expressed symbolically. Bolingbroke hurls his gauntlet at Mowbray's feet, challenging him to stoop and take it up. Mowbray takes up the gage and duly throws down his, which Bolingbroke, in turn, takes up. This ceremonial, accompanied by language appropriate to the symbolism, provides, as it were, an overture to the central theme of rise and fall.

Thus, Bolingbroke, answering Mowbray's charge:

> Pale trembling coward there I *throw* my gage,
> Disclaiming here the kindred of the king,
> And lay aside my *high* blood's royalty,
> Which fear, not reverence, makes thee to
>   accept. . . .
> If guilty dread have left thee so much strength,
> As to *take up* mine honour's pawn, then
>   *stoop*.
>
> (I.i.69ff.)

[All textual references are to the Cambridge Shakespeare *Richard II*, edited by John Dover Wilson (1939). The italics are my own.]

Mowbray replies:

> I take it *up*, and by that sword I swear,
> Which gently laid my knighthood on my
>   shoulder,
> I'll answer thee in any fair degree,
> Or chivalrous design of knightly trial:
> And when I *mount*, alive may I not *light*,
> If I be traitor or unjustly fight!

When Bolingbroke returns to the charge, accusing Mowbray of plotting the death of the Duke of Gloucester whose blood, he says, cries to him for "justice and rough chastisement", the King significantly exclaims: "How *high a pitch* his resolution *soars!*" (I.i.109). Richard, calling upon Mowbray to answer the charge, proclaims his impartiality. "Such neighbour nearness to our sacred blood", he vows,

> Should nothing privilege him nor partialize

The *unstooping* firmness of my *upright* soul.

(I.i.120-121)

Ineffectually, the King seeks to reconcile his quarrelsome subjects, and then calls on John of Gaunt:

Good uncle, let this end where it begun,
We'll calm the Duke of Norfolk, you your son.

(I.i.158-159)

The theme continues:

Gaunt. To be a make-peace shall become my age,
Throw down, my son, the Duke of Norfolk's gage.
K. Richard. And, Norfolk, *throw down* his.
Gaunt. When, Harry? when?
Obedience bids I should not bid again.
K. Richard. Norfolk, *throw down*, we bid, there is no boot.
Mowbray. Myself I *throw*, dread sovereign, at thy foo'
My life thou shalt command, but not my shame.

(I.i.160 ff.)

The combatants remain unmoved. Richard, addressing Bolingbroke, again commands: "Cousin, *throw up* your gage, do you begin", and Bolingbroke replies:

O God defend my soul from such *deep* sin!
Shall I seem *crest-fallen* in my father's sight?
Or with pale beggar-fear impeach my *height*
Before this out-dared dastard? ere my tongue
Shall wound my honour with such feeble wrong,
Or sound so *base* a parle, my teeth shall tear
The slavish motive of recanting fear,
And spit it bleeding in his *high* disgrace,
Where shame doth harbour, even in Mowbray's face.

(I.i.187 ff.)

The same symbolism recurs— but with deeper significance— when Bolingbroke and Mowbray next appear, as commanded, on Saint Lambert's Day before the Lists at Coventry, their swords and lances "there to arbitrate the swelling difference of their settled hate".

Bolingbroke approaches the Lord Marshal, exclaiming: "Lord marshal, let me kiss my sovereign's hand, And *bow my knee* before his majesty." The King descends from his throne and ironically proclaims: "We will *descend* and fold him in our arms. Cousin of Hereford, as thy cause is right, So be thy fortune in this royal fight."

Bolingbroke replies:

As confident as is the *falcon's flight*
Against a bird, do I with Mowbray fight.

(I.iii.61-62)

Turning to his father, John of Gaunt, he adds:

O thou, the earthly author of my blood,
Whose youthful spirit in me regenerate
Doth with a twofold vigour *lift me up*
To reach at victory *above my head* . . .
Add proof unto mine armour with thy prayers. . .
.

The heralds announce their respective combatants; the Lord Marshal commands, "Sound, trumpets; and set forward, combatants." A charge is sounded. As the combatants are about to join battle, the Lord Marshal cries out, "Stay, stay, the king hath *thrown* his warder *down!*"

This dramatic moment presages the fall and death of Richard. In the later play of *2 Henry IV* the incident is thus recounted, in the same symbolic language, by Thomas Mowbray's son:

Then, then, when there was nothing could have stayed
My father from the breast of Bolingbroke . . .
O, when the King did *throw* his warder *down*,
(His own life hung upon the staff he threw!)
Then *threw* he *down* himself and all their lives
That by indictment and by dint of sword
Have since miscarried under Bolingbroke.

(IV.i.123 ff.)

Bolingbroke and Mowbray are banished. John of Gaunt dies, foretelling that Richard's "rash fierce blaze of riot" cannot last. Richard, to replenish his coffers for his Irish wars, seizes Gaunt's possessions, thereby, as the Duke of York prophesies, "plucking a thousand dangers on his head and losing a thousand well-disposed hearts."

The King departs for his Irish wars. The King gone, Bolingbroke returns to England from banishment. The very news of Bolingbroke's return is expressed in language which heightens the image of his rising fortunes. Thus, Northumberland announces he has received intelligence that Harry, Duke of Hereford and others "With eight *tall* ships, three thousand men of war Are making hither . . ." (II.i.286). Green thus informs the Queen: "The banish'd Bolingbroke repeals himself, And with *uplifted* arms is safe arriv'd, At Ravenspurgh" (II.ii.49 ff.). The tidings are thus brought by Scroop to the King:

Like an unseasonable stormy day,
Which makes the silver rivers drown their shores,

As if the world were all dissolved to tears;
So *high* above his limits *swells* the rage
Of Bolingbroke, covering your fearful land
With hard bright steel.

(III.ii.106 ff.)

The image of the sagging fortunes of the King is portrayed by York (himself torn between conflicting loyalties) when he complains:

Here am I left to *underprop* his land.

(II.ii.82)

        . . . all is
uneven,
And everything is left at six and seven.

(II.ii.123)

Richard's followers, meanwhile, having heard no tidings from their King, would disperse, but Salisbury begs them stay but another day. In the Captain's reply, the theme of the fall and doom of Richard is now given out in a minor key of foreboding:

'Tis thought the king is dead; we will not stay.
The bay-trees in our country are all withered,
And *meteors* fright the fixed stars of heaven,
The pale-faced moon looks bloody on the earth,
And lean-looked prophets whisper fearful change,
Rich men look sad, and ruffians dance and leap—
The one in fear to lose what they enjoy,
The other to enjoy by rage and war:
These signs forerun the death or *fall* of kings . . .
Farewell. Our countrymen are gone and fled,
As well assured Richard their king is dead.

(II.iv.7 ff.)

Salisbury takes up this theme and soliloquizes:

Ah, Richard! with the eyes of heavy mind
I see thy glory like a *shooting star*
Fall to the *base* earth from the firmament.
Thy sun *sets* weeping in the *lowly* west,
Witnessing storms to come, woe, and unrest.
Thy friends are fled to wait upon thy foes,
And crossly to thy good all fortune goes.

Richard returns to England. As he sets foot on his native soil, symbolically he stoops to touch the earth—to do it favor with his royal hands. "I weep for joy", he says,

To stand upon my kingdom once again:
Dear *earth,* I do salute thee with my hand,
Though rebels wound thee with their horse's
    hoofs:
As a long-parted mother with her child
Plays fondly with her tears and smiles in
    meeting;

So, weeping, smiling, greet I thee, my *earth,*
And do thee favour with my royal hands.

(III.ii.5 ff.)

This earth shall have a feeling, and these stones
Prove arméd soldiers, ere her native king
Shall *falter* under foul rebellion's arms.

(III.ii.24 ff.)

Richard fondly believes that when the traitor Bolingbroke

Shall see us *rising* in our throne, the east,
His treasons will *sit* blushing in his face
Not able to endure the sight of day,
      . . . . .
For every man that Bolingbroke hath pressed
To *lift* shrewd steel against our golden crown,
God for his Richard hath in heavenly pay
A glorious angel; then, if angels fight,
Weak men must *fall,* for heaven still guards
    the right.

(III.ii.50 ff.)

Richard's mood of self-confidence is but short-lived. When Salisbury tells him he has returned a day too late, that his Welsh followers "Are gone to Bolingbroke, dispers'd, and fled", he pales. Aumerle has but to remind him he is king— "Comfort, my liege, remember who you are", and Richard's self-confidence is restored; dejection gives way to elation and he exclaims:

I had forgot myself, am I not king?
. . . Look not to the *ground,*
Ye favourites of a king, are we not *high?*
High be our thoughts. I know my uncle York
Hath power enough to serve our turn. . . .

(III.ii.83 ff.)

Yet no sooner is he told of the execution of Bushy, Green, and the Earl of Wiltshire than he once again falls into a mood of deep dejection. His plaintive outburst of self-pity re-echoes, but now in inversion, the theme of his earlier words— "Look not to the ground, Ye favourites of a king, are we not high?":

. . . Of comfort no man speak:
Let's talk of *graves,* of worms, and epitaphs,
Make dust our paper, and with rainy eyes
Write sorrow on the bosom of the *earth* . . .
Let's choose executors and talk of wills:
And yet not so, for what can we bequeath,
Save our *deposéd* bodies to the *ground?*
Our lands, our lives, and all are Bolingbroke's,
And nothing can we call our own, but death;
And that small model of the barren *earth,*
Which serves as paste and cover to our bones.
For God's sake, let us *sit* upon the *ground,*
And tell sad stories of the death of kings—
How some have been deposed, some slain

400

in war,
Some haunted by the ghosts they have
  deposed, . . .
Cover your heads, and mock not flesh and
  blood
With solemn reverence, throw away respect,
Tradition, form, and ceremonious duty,
For you have but mistook me all this while:
I live with bread like you, feel want,
Taste grief, need friends— subjected thus,
How can you say to me, I am a king?
                              (III.ii.144 ff.)

When Richard hears that York has "joined with Bolingbroke and all his northern castles yielded up", he discharges his followers and with Aumerle seeks refuge in
Flint Castle.

In the following scene, Bolingbroke, York, Northumberland, and their forces appear on the plain before the
Castle. Bolingbroke bids Northumberland go to the
"rude ribs" of the ancient castle and "thus deliver" to
the King:

> Henry Bolingbroke
> On both his *knees* doth kiss King Richard's
>   hand,
> And sends allegiance and true faith of heart
> To his most royal person: hither come
> Even at his *feet* to *lay* my arms and power;
> Provided that my banishment repealed
> And lands restored again be freely granted;
> If not, I'll use the advantage of my power,
> And *lay* the summer's dust with showers of
>   blood,
> *Rained* from the wounds of slaughtered
>   Englishmen,
> The which, how far off from the mind of
>   Bolingbroke
> It is, such crimson tempest should bedrench
> The fresh green lap of fair King Richard's land,
> My *stooping* duty tenderly shall show.
>   (III. iii. 35 ff.)

A parley is sounded. King Richard appears on the battlements. Northumberland stands below. Richard looks
down, waiting, in vain, for obeisance to his royal person. Addressing Northumberland, he says:

> We are amazed, and thus long have we stood
> To watch the fearful *bending* of thy *knee,*
> Because we thought ourself thy lawful king:
> And if we be, how dare thy joints forget
> To pay their awful duty to our presence?
>   (III. iii. 72 ff.)

"Tell Bolingbroke", he says,

> That every stride he makes upon my land

Is dangerous treason: he is come to open
The purple testament of bleeding war.
                              (III. iii. 92 ff.)

Richard's mood of defiance soon gives way to one of
resignation, and he bids Northumberland tell
Bolingbroke that "all the number of his fair demands
shall be accomplished."

As Northumberland retires, Richard again vacillates and
asks of Aumerle:

> We do *debase* ourself, cousin, do we not,
> To look so poorly and to speak so fair?
> Shall we call back Northumberland and send
> Defiance to the traitor, and so die?
>   (III. iii. 127 ff.)

"Let's fight with gentle words", counsels Aumerle, "Till
time lend friends, and friends their helpful swords."
Richard, conscious of his deep humiliation, exclaims:

> O God! O God! that e'er this tongue of
>   mine,
> That *laid* the sentence of dread banishment
> On you proud man, should *take it off* again
> With words of sooth! O, that I were as great
> As is my grief, or lesser than my name!
>   (III. iii. 133 ff.)

As Northumberland returns from Bolingbroke, Richard
in a flood of pathetic self-pity and helplessness, delivers
those poignant lines, which yet again re-echo the theme
of the earth and of graves. The imagery again matches
his mood of utter dejection.

> What must the king do now? must he
>   submit?
> The king shall do it: must he be deposed?
> The king shall be contented: must he lose
> The name of king: a God's name let it go:
> I'll give my jewels for a set of beads:
> My gorgeous palace for a hermitage:
> My gay apparel for an almsman's gown:
> My figured goblets for a dish of wood:
> My sceptre for a palmer's walking-staff:
> My subjects for a pair of carvéd saints,
> And my large kingdom for a little *grave,*
> A little little *grave,* an obscure *grave,*
> Or I'll be *buried* in the king's highway,
> Some way of common trade, where subjects'
>   feet
> May hourly *trample* on their sovereign's *head;*
> For on my heart they tread now whilst I live:
> And *buried* once, why not upon my *head?*
> Aumerle, thou weep'st (my tender-hearted
>   cousin!),
> We'll make foul weather with despiséd tears;
> Our sighs and they shall *lodge* the summer corn,

And make a dearth in this revolting land:
Or shall we play the wantons with our woes,
And make some pretty match with shedding
    tears?
As thus to drop them still upon one place,
Till they have fretted us a pair of *graves*
Within the *earth,* and therein laid . . . there lies
Two kinsmen digged their *graves* with weeping
    eyes!
Would not this ill do well? Well, well, I see
I talk but idly and you laugh at me. . . .
Most mighty prince, my Lord
    Northumberland,
What says King Bolingbroke? will his
    majesty
Give Richard leave to live till Richard die?
You *make* a *leg,* and Bolingbroke says 'ay'.
                                (III. iii. 143 ff.)

Throughout the scene, Richard's alternating moods of
defiance and dejection, hope and despair, provide a
rhythmic undertone to the imagery of rise and fall
which now reaches a climax. The very setting heightens
the imagery. Richard stands aloft on the battlements,
looking down; Northumberland and Bolingbroke stand
below, looking up.

In the following lines the word "down" is repeated no
fewer than six times, and the word "base" recurs five
times:

Northumberland. My lord, in the *base* court he
    doth attend,
To speak with you, may it please you to
    come *down?*
K. Richard. Down, *down* I come, like glist'ring
    Phaethon:
Wanting the manage of unruly jades. . . .
In the *base* court? *Base* court, where kings
    grow *base,*
To come at traitors' calls, and do them grace.
In the *base* court? Come *down? Down* court!
    down king!
For night-owls shriek where *mounting* larks
    should sing
                                (III. iii. 178 ff.)

As the King descends, Bolingbroke kneels. The theme
is resumed, but in lighter and sarcastic vein:

Fair cousin, you *debase* your princely *knee,*
To make the *base* earth proud with kissing it:
Me rather had my heart might feel your love,
Than my unpleased eye see your *courtesy:*
Up, cousin, *up*— your heart is *up,* I know,
Thus *high* at least, although your knee be *low*
                                (III. iii. 190 ff.)

"My gracious lord, I come but for mine own", retorts

Bolingbroke; and Richard replies:

Your own is yours, and I am yours and all.
What you will have, I'll give, and willing too,
For do we must what fate will have us do. . .

Set on towards London, cousin, is it so?
                                (III. iii. 197 ff.)

"Yea, my good Lord", answers Bolingbroke; and Richard ends: "Then I must not say no."

The struggle is over. The climax of the play has passed.
The imagery of rise and fall now takes on a new note.

The scene changes to the Duke of York's garden at
Langley. In the interchanges between the Queen and
her ladies and the gardener and his men, the whole
tempo is slowed down; the iterative imagery is now
more measured, more elaborate and is in allegorical
form. Thus the gardener to his two men:

Go, bind thou up yon *dangling* apricocks,
Which like unruly children make their sire
Stoop with oppression of their prodigal
    weight,
Give some supportance to the *bending* twigs,
Go thou, and like an executioner
Cut off the heads of too fast growing sprays,
That look too *lofty* in our commonwealth—
All must be *even* in our government.
                                (III. iv. 29 ff.)

Again, referring to the King, he says:

He that hath suffered this disordered spring
Hath now himself met with the *fall* of leaf:
The weeds that his broad-spreading leaves did
    shelter,
That seemed in eating him to *hold* him *up,*
Are *plucked up* root and all by Bolingbroke.
                                (III.iv.48 ff.)

The conversation between the gardener and his men
continues thus:

First Servant. What, think you then the king
    shall be deposed?
Gardener. Depressed he is already, and deposed
'Tis doubt he will be. . . .

The Queen, overhearing their conversation, comes forth
and addresses her gardener in words which continue
the imagery, again in allegorical form:

What Eve, what serpent, hath suggested thee
To make a second *fall* of curséd man?
Why dost thou say King Richard is deposed?
Dar'st thou, thou little better thing than earth,

Divine his *downfall?*

The gardener, in his reply, uses the metaphor of Bolingbroke, in the one scale, weighing down Richard, in the other, pointing the declining fortunes of the one and the ascending fortunes of the other. The idiom changes but the imagery persists:

> King Richard, he is in the mighty hold
> Of Bolingbroke: their fortunes both are *weighed:*
> In your lord's *scale* is nothing but himself,
> And some few vanities that make him *light;*
> But in the *balance* of great Bolingbroke,
> Besides himself, are all the English peers,
> And with that odds he *weighs* King Richard *down.*

Act IV opens with the historic deposition scene at Westminster Hall where Bolingbroke, the Lords Spiritual and Temporal, and the Commons are assembled. York's announcement of the King's abdication stresses in almost every line the two-fold imagery of rise and fall:

> Great Duke of Lancaster, I come to thee
> From *plume-pluck'd* Richard, who with willing
>   soul
> Adopts thee heir, and his *high* sceptre yields
> To the possession of thy royal hand:
> *Ascend* his throne, *descending* now from him;
> And long live Henry, of that name the
>   fourth!
>
> (IV. i. 107 ff.)

Proudly Bolingbroke exclaims: "In God's name, I'll *ascend* the regal throne."

From this moment, as Richard grows in spiritual stature, so Bolingbroke declines, and the imagery now reflects this spiritual transformation in the two central characters of the play.

The Bishop of Carlisle, alone of those assembled, raises his voice in protest, calls Bolingbroke a foul traitor and prophesies that if they crown him—

> O, if you *raise* this house against this house,
> It will the woefullest division prove
> That ever *fell* upon this cursèd earth.
>
> (IV. i. 145 ff.)

For his pains, Northumberland orders Carlisle's arrest for capital treason. "Fetch hither Richard", orders Bolingbroke, "that in common view he may surrender."

York returns with Richard, guarded and stripped of his royal robes; officers follow, bearing the crown and sceptre. "Alack," cries Richard,

> Why am I sent for to a king,

> Before I have *shook off* the regal thoughts
> Wherewith I reigned? I hardly yet have
>   learned
> To insinuate, flatter, *bow*, and *bend* my knee:
> Give sorrow leave awhile to tutor me
> To this submission.
>
> (IV. i. 162 ff.)

As Richard takes the crown, he calls on Bolingbroke:

> Here, cousin, seize the crown;
> Here, cousin,
> On this side, my hand, and on that side,
>   thine.
>
> (IV. i. 181 ff.)

Victor and vanquished stand face to face, each holding the crown; Richard about to be unkinged, Bolingbroke soon to be enthroned. The poetic imagery of rise and fall— accentuated by the tenseness of the drama— now reaches sublime heights as Richard exclaims:

> Now is this golden crown like a *deep well*
> That owes two buckets, filling one another,
> The emptier ever *dancing* in the air,
> The other *down*, unseen, and full of water:
> That bucket *down*, and full of tears, am I,
> Drinking my griefs, whilst you *mount up on*
>   *high.*
>
> (IV. i. 184 ff.)

"I thought you had been willing to resign", protests Bolingbroke, and grief-stricken Richard replies:

> My crown I am, but still my griefs are mine:
> You may my glories and my state *depose*,
> But not my griefs; still am I king of those.

As the dialogue proceeds, the theme of rise and fall recurs, contrapuntally, as it were:

> *Bolingbroke.* Part of your cares you give me
>   with your crown.
> *K. Richard.* Your cares *set up* do not *pluck* my
>   cares down.
> My care is loss of care, by old care done,
> Your care is gain of care, by new care won:
> The cares I give, I have, though given away,
> They tend the crown, yet still with me they
>   stay.
> *Bolingbroke.* Are you contented to resign the
>   crown?
> *K. Richard.* Ay, no; no, ay; for I must
>   nothing be:
> Therefore no 'no', for I resign to thee. . . .
> Now mark me how I will *undo* myself:
> I give this *heavy weight* from off my *head,*
> And this unwieldy sceptre from my hand,
> The pride of kingly sway from out my heart;

> With mine own tears I wash away my balm,
> With mine own hands I give away my crown,
> With mine own tongue deny my sacred state,
> With mine own breath release all duteous
>   oaths:
> All pomp and majesty I do forswear;
> My manors, rents, revenues, I forgo;
> My acts, decrees, and statutes, I deny:
> Long mayst thou live in Richard's *seat* to sit,
> And soon *lie* Richard in an *earthy* pit. . . .
> God save King Henry, unkinged Richard says,
> And send him many years of sunshine
>   days. . . .
> What more remains?
>
>   (IV. i. 194 ff.)

Northumberland demands that Richard read out the accusations against himself,

> That, by confessing them, the souls of men
> May deem that you are worthily deposed.
>   (IV. i. 226-227)

Richard protests:

> Mine eyes are full of tears, I cannot see:
> And yet salt water blinds them not so much,
> But they can see a sort of traitors here.
> Nay, if I turn mine eyes upon myself,
> I find myself a traitor with the rest:
> For I have given here my soul's consent
> T' *undeck* the pompous body of a king;
> Made glory *base*; and sovereignty, a slave;
> Proud majesty, a subject; state, a peasant.

Northumberland intervenes, "My Lord,— " and Richard retorts:

> No lord of thine, thou *haught*, insulting man,
> Nor no man's lord; I have no name, no title;
> No, not that name was given me at the font,
> But 'tis *usurped*: alack the heavy day,
> That I have worn so many winters out,
> And know not now what name to call
>   myself!
> O, that I were a mockery king of snow,
> Standing before the sun of Bolingbroke,
> To *melt* myself away in water-drops!

Richard commands a mirror, "That it may show me what a face I have, Since it is bankrupt of his majesty" (IV. i. 266-267). He gazes in it and laments:

> No *deeper* wrinkles yet? hath sorrow struck
> So many blows upon this face of mine,
> And made no *deeper* wounds?
>   (IV. i. 277 ff.)

As Richard dashes the mirror to the ground he exclaims:

> A brittle glory shineth in this face,
> As brittle as the glory is the face,
> For there it is, cracked in a hundred shivers. . . .
> Mark, silent king, the moral of this sport,
> How soon my sorrow hath destroyed my
>   face.

Richard's final dramatic gesture in the deposition scene strikingly symbolizes his own disintegration.

Walter Pater, in his essay, *"Shakespeare's English Kings"* (1889) likens the scene in which Richard divests himself of his crown and sceptre to "an inverted rite, a rite of degradation, a long agonising ceremony in which the order of the coronation is reversed." The imagery and ceremonial symbolism of the scene reflect this inversion.

As the dramatic deposition scene draws to a close, Richard begs leave to go. "Whither?" asks Bolingbroke, and Richard tauntingly replies, "Whither you will, so were I from your sights." On Bolingbroke's curt command: "Go, some of you convey him to the Tower", Richard is led away. With Richard's parting thrust, the imagery takes on a sardonic twist:

> O, good! convey? conveyers are you all,
> That *rise* thus nimbly by a true king's *fall.*
>   (IV.i.317-318)

As Richard is led through the streets of London, we see the final meeting and parting with his Queen, who sadly awaits him on his way to "Julius Caesar's ill-erected tower". At his approach, she tenderly exclaims:

> But soft, but see, or rather do not see,
> My fair rose wither. . . .
>   . . . Thou most beauteous
>   inn,
> Why should hard-favoured grief be lodged in
>   thee,
> When triumph is become an alehouse guest?
>   (V.i.7 ff.)

Richard, still the absorbed spectator of his own tragedy— to borrow a phrase from John Palmer's *Political Characters of Shakespeare*— replies:

> Join not with grief, fair woman, do not so,
> To make my end too sudden. Learn, good
>   soul,
> To think our former state a happy dream,
> From which awaked, the truth of what we are
> Shows us but this: I am sworn brother,
>   sweet,
> To grim Necessity, and he and I
> Will keep a league till death. . . .   Hie thee

Act V, scene ii. York's description of the arrival of Bolingbroke and Richard II in London. By James Northcote.

to France,
And cloister thee in some religious house.
Our holy lives must win a new world's *crown,*
Which our profane hours here have *thrown
down.*

The Queen retorts:

What, is my Richard both in shape and mind
Transformed and weak'ned? hath Bolingbroke
deposed
Thine intellect?

Northumberland appears on the scene. "My lord, the mind of Bolingbroke is chang'd", he tells Richard, "You must to Pomfret, not unto the Tower." Richard, addressing himself to Northumberland, uses yet another vivid metaphor to point the imagery, not merely of the mounting Bolingbroke, but of Northumberland, the means whereby Bolingbroke ascends the throne:

Northumberland, thou *ladder* wherewithal

The mounting Bolingbroke *ascends* my throne,
The time shall not be many hours of age
More than it is, ere foul sin *gathering head*
Shall break into corruption.

(V.i.55 ff.)

Northumberland is unmoved. "My guilt be on my head, and there an end. Take leave and part, for you must part forthwith." The Queen pleads with Northumberland: "Banish us both and send the king with me." "That were some love, but little policy— " is Northumberland's curt retort.

In the subsequent play of *2 Henry IV,* Richard's prophetic admonition is recalled by Bolingbroke, now King Henry IV:

. . . . But which of you was by—
You, cousin Nevil, as I may remember—
When Richard, with his eye brimful of tears,
Then checked and rated by Northumberland,
Did speak these words, now prov'd a prophecy?

'Northumberland, thou *ladder* by the which
My cousin Bolingbroke *ascends* my throne'
(Though then, God knows, I had no such
   intent,
But that necessity so *bow'd* the state,
That I and greatness were compell'd to kiss):
'The time shall come', thus did he follow it,
'The time will come, that foul sin, *gathering
   head,*
Shall break into corruption': so went on,
Foretelling this same time's condition,
And the division of our amity.

(III.i.65 ff.)

We finally see Richard, in solitude, in the dungeon of Pomfret Castle. His poignant soliloquy, "studying how he may compare the prison where he lives unto the world", is interrupted by the entry of his former Groom. Even in this brief interlude, which momentarily seems to bring the light of the outside world into the gloom of the dungeon, the imagery of rise and fall, now charged with pathos, recurs. The Groom recounts how it yearned his heart when he beheld, in London streets, on coronation day, Bolingbroke mounted on "roan Barbary", Richard's fiery steed. "Rode he on Barbary?" asked Richard; "Tell me, gentle friend", he asks pathetically, "How went he under him?" And the Groom replies, "So proudly as if he disdained the ground", and Richard exclaims:

So proud that Bolingbroke was on his back. . . .
Would he not *stumble?* Would he not *fall
   down,*
Since pride must have a *fall,* and break the
   neck,
Of that *proud* man that did *usurp* his back?
Forgiveness, horse! why do I rail on thee,
Since thou, created to be awed by man,
Was born to *bear?* I was not made a horse,
And yet I *bear* a *burthen* like an ass,
Spurred, galled and tired by *jauncing* Boling-
   broke.

(V.v.84 ff.)

The tragedy draws to a close. The Groom departs and Richard's Keeper brings in his food. "Taste of it first", bids Richard, "as thou art wont to do." The Keeper declines: "My lord, I dare not. Sir Pierce of Exton commands the contrary." Striking his Keeper, Richard exclaims: "The devil take Henry of Lancaster and thee! Patience is stale, and I am weary of it."

Exton and his men, who have come to rid Bolingbroke of his "living fear", rush in. Richard is struck down. In his dying words, Richard gives expression to a final image, that of his own apotheosis:

Mount, mount, my soul! thy seat is up on
   high,

Whilst my gross flesh *sinks downward,* here to
   die.

(V.v.111-112).

RICHARD

King Richard has met mixed reviews from audiences and critics. His character has generated pity and sympathy as well as disdain and condemnation. In an essay reprinted in the Overview section, A. L. French observes that Shakespeare seems to treat Richard in two different ways in the play. In the first half of the play, there is little indication that Richard will be deposed by Bolingbroke, French argues, but in the second half of the play, other characters seem to be of the opinion that Richard has in fact been deposed. Yet Richard deposes himself, French stresses. French states that it is as if Shakespeare presents two different truths in the play (that Richard will not be and has not been forcefully deposed by Bolingbroke, and that he has indeed been unjustly deposed), rather than presenting a consistent truth throughout.

To others, Richard appears to be presented more consistently. Lewis J. Owen, in an essay reprinted in the Kingship section, examines the ways in which Shakespeare's characterization of Richard drew, if not the sympathy of modern audiences, at least that of Elizabethan audiences. Owen observes that Richard is shown to be a weak king who falls prey to evil advisors but is nevertheless the rightful ruler. Owen also states that although Richard falls politically, he grows personally, and that the opposite happens to Bolingbroke. As some evidence of Richard's growth, Owen points to the fact that Richard is finally moved to act when he kills two of the men that have come to assassinate him, before he is murdered himself.

Other critics offer a different interpretation of Richard. **Lois Potter** maintains that while Richard is often viewed as a virtuous character, especially toward the play's end, he in fact displays both irony and duplicity throughout the entire play. These traits are more obvious in the play's first half, for example when it is suggested that despite the short sentence Richard has placed on Bolingbroke's banishment, the king might not allow him to return at all. Later in the play, in Act IV, scene i, when Bolingbroke is attempting to conduct a ceremony designed to emphasize the legality of the transfer of power from Richard to himself, Richard thwarts the proceedings through irony and ambiguous statements. Potter notes for example that when Northumberland tries to get Richard to read the charges against him, Richard "in a well-timed burst of hysteria, avoids having to read the articles." Richard says he will read his sins from a mirror, where he can see his transgressions written on his face. But Richard smashes the mirror, Potter explains, because it lies: he sees no sins, only the face of a king. Potter's examples stress that Richard is not the poor, weakling king many have made him out to be, but rather a clever, duplicitous, and defiant king who is unresigned to giving up his crown.

Jack R. Sublette presents yet another view of Richard. Sublette traces Richard's systematic abuse of power throughout the play. Focusing on Richard's role in Gloucester's murder, and on Richard's banishment of Bolingbroke and subsequent confiscation of Gaunt's estate, Sublette emphasizes that through such abuses of power, Richard creates the disorder that pervades the rest of the play. Richard's most significant abuse of power is his abdication of the crown, Sublette notes. Not only does Richard disrupt the natural order of inheritance in doing so, but he prophesies that if Bolingbroke becomes king, generations of Englishmen will suffer as a result; and still he relinquishes the crown to Bolingbroke.

Lois Potter

SOURCE: "The Antic Disposition of Richard II," in *Shakespeare Survey*, Vol. 27, 1974, pp. 33-41.

[*In this essay, Potter asserts that Richard is often viewed as a sympathetic, virtuous character by the end of the play, despite his misdeeds. Potter argues, however, that Richard is in fact consistently ironic and duplicitous throughout the entire play. Potter supports this contention through an analysis of the play's language, showing how certain types of language correspond with the respective weakness or power that Richard or other characters possess at a given point in the play.*]

Many critical studies of *Richard II,* and a surprising number of productions, start from a furious assumption: that Shakespeare wrote, and asked his leading actor to star in, a long play dominated by a character whose main effect on the audience was to be one of boredom, embarrassment, or at best contemptuous pity. If Richard's part is not a good one, the play is simply not worth seeing; and 'good', in theatrical terms, means not necessarily virtuous but interesting. I want to argue that Richard is in fact rather less virtuous than has often been thought, and, just for that reason, a 'better' dramatic character.

Much of our difficulty with the play is a difficulty of knowing what moral connotations to attach to its highly rhetorical language. It is useful to be reminded by R. F. Hill that 'apparently self-conscious control of language does not, of itself, indicate dispassion and triviality in character', especially since he goes on to show that self-conscious language is by no means confined to Richard. Yet there is no doubt that elaborate language is used as a substitute for action and, to that extent, is a symbol of weakness. 'Give losers leave to talk' is an Elizabethan proverb, and in the first two acts of the play the long speeches do in fact belong to the 'los-

ers'— Mowbray, Gaunt, York, the Duchess of Gloucester, *and* Bolingbroke. They all talk too much, seldom content with one simile where three or four will do (even Bolingbroke's rejection of the consolations of language is itself couched in a series of rhetorical repetitions); they all become despondent in adversity, rejecting all attempts to comfort them; and three of them (the Duchess of Gloucester, Mowbray, Gaunt) prophesy, correctly, that they are soon to die. This is the style which, in the second half of the play, is associated with the defeated king and his supporters. It is foreshadowed, even before Richard's return from Ireland, by the fanciful dialogue of the Queen and the favourites as well as by the Welshmen's prophecies of death and disaster.

Yet, though such language may be a sign of weakness in those who speak it, it is itself extremely powerful. This is largely because of its evocation of patriotic and religious sentiments, on which most of the emotional and poetic force of the first two acts depends. It may be disregarded by the other characters but it works on the audience, and the same is true when Richard starts speaking this language halfway through the play.

The other kind of power, later associated with the 'silent king' Bolingbroke, is at first displayed only by Richard. He declares in the opening scene that 'We are not born to sue but to command' (I, i, 196), [References are to the Arden edition of the play, ed. Peter Ure (London, 1956)] and his reactions to the eloquence of others are either impatient— 'It boots thee not to be compassionate' (I, iii, 174); 'Can sick men play so nicely with their names?' (II, i, 84)— or deflationary, as when he asks 'Why, uncle, what's the matter?' after York has spent twenty-two lines trying to tell him (II, i, 186). His few long speeches, such as the description of Bolingbroke's behaviour to the common people and the formal banishment of the two appellants, are almost the only ones in this part of the play that do not make the director reach for his blue pencil. The banishment speech, indeed, may look at first as if it needs shortening, but in performance its rhetoric has an obvious dramatic effect; Richard keeps the two men in suspense during fifteen lines of sonorous clauses— 'For that', 'and for', 'and for'— and then drops his bombshell in the simple phrase 'Therefore we banish you our territories' (I, iii, 139). His shorter utterances, too, are very like the language which, when it appears in connection with Bolingbroke, we associate with confidence, efficiency and power. His reception of Gaunt's death—

> The ripest fruit first falls, and so doth he;
> His time is spent, our pilgrimage must be;
> So much for that
>
> (II, i, 153-5)

— can be compared with Bolingbroke's reaction to Mowbray's, when, as Kenneth Muir has pointed out, he also 'changes the subject in the middle of a line'. Similarly, Richard's flippant-sounding jingle,

> Think what you will, we seize into our hands
> His plate, his goods, his money and his
> 　　lands,
>
> 　　　　　　　　　　　　　　(II, i, 209-10)

falls into the same rhythm as Northumberland's couplet in the final scene:

> The next news is, I have to London sent
> The heads of Salisbury, Spencer, Blunt, and
> 　　Kent.
>
> 　　　　　　　　　　　　　　(V, vi, 7-8)

The change which Richard undergoes in the second half of the play may be explained in terms of language and decorum, but this is not much help to the actor who has somehow to reconcile the two halves. The commonest solution is to play the first two acts in the light of the other three. A foppish or wicked Richard may spend the first scene eating sweetmeats, talking with his favourites, or making clear that he is the real murderer of Gloucester, while a more pathetically conceived Richard may appear in Christ-like make-up, looking frail and helpless among the brawny peers who will obviously be making mincemeat of him within the hour. It has even been argued that such interpretations are necessary: as one reviewer of the 1964 Stratford production put it, in the first part of the play 'Shakespeare only does half the job, and, unless he is helped, we listen amazed at old Gaunt's dying protest about the king's "rash, fierce blaze of riot". What riot?'

Nicholas Brooke has rightly objected to actors trying too hard to establish Richard's personality before Shakespeare lets it emerge in I, iv. His description of this personality— 'a cold politician with atheistic tendencies . . . cheap however witty'— seems to me fair enough, except perhaps that it underrates the effectiveness of cheap wit in a formal setting and audience readiness to sympathise with the character who uses it (compare Shakespeare's *other* King Richard). Professor Brooke feels that our awareness of the real Richard confuses our response to the cosmic and political themes which he embodies and expresses; I should prefer to say that the interest of Richard's character lies in his ability to *use*, and not simply to embody, the emotional associations of these themes. This use only gradually becomes conscious and, like Hamlet's antic disposition, co-exists with a capacity for emotional involvement. But irony and a suggestion of duplicity are present in Richard throughout the play.

For the point about Richard's terse style in the opening scenes is that it is also enigmatic; his carefully balanced speeches to Mowbray and Bolingbroke do not, unless

slanted by the production, help the audience to decide which of the challengers is right (indeed, we never know). Hence, the difference in their punishments seems not retributive but arbitrary, especially when, simply because Gaunt looks unhappy, four years are casually lopped off Bolingbroke's exile. The latter's response,

> How long a time lies in one little word!
> Four lagging winters and four wanton springs
> End in a word— such is the breath of kings,
>
> 　　　　　　　　　　　　　　(I, iii, 213-15)

introduces the themes, which Gaunt will take up at more length, of time, breath, and the destructive power of kings. But, taken on its own, it suggests rather oddly that Richard has not restored but killed four years of life. A darker purpose is in fact confirmed by the next scene, where the king's first 'private, words express a doubt,

> When time shall call him home from banish-
> 　　ment,
> Whether our kinsman come to see his
> 　　friends.
>
> 　　　　　　　　　　　　　　(I, iv, 21-2)

In other words, he may never repeal Bolingbroke after all. Perhaps the 'hopeless word of "never to return"', which Richard breathes against Mowbray (I, iii, 152), is likewise *only* a word, another sign that the breath of kings can blow hot and cold.

Evidence of duplicity in Richard's character could have been provided for Shakespeare by Holinshed, who lists among the thirty-three articles alleged against him the charge that his letters were written in a style 'so subtill and darke that none other prince once beléeued him, nor yet his owne subiects'. Equivocation— setting the word against the word— is a common practice of the Machiavellian ruler in drama (compare Mortimer's use of the 'unpointed' message in *Edward II*), and in the later scenes of the play Bolingbroke himself is not free from a suspicion of it. Hence his almost comic difficulty in finding a form of words which will convince the Duchess of York that he really has pardoned Aumerle. Her nervousness is understandable, since her husband has just made the helpful suggestion, 'Speak it in French, king, say "pardonne moy"' (V, iii, 117). But in fact I get the impression throughout the play that Bolingbroke is genuinely trying to say what he means. There is, for instance, a vast difference between his sharp words to his peers,

> Little are we beholding to your love,
> And little look'd for at your helping hands,
>
> 　　　　　　　　　　　　　　(IV, i, 160-1)

and Richard's way of putting the same thing, when York has insisted that both Gaunt and Herford love him well:

Right, you say true; as Herford's love, so his;
As theirs, so mine; and all be as it is.
                                        (II, i, 145-6)

This kind of irony reveals rather than conceals the speaker's emotions, which is why it is often taken as a sign of weakness. But it also enables him to avoid stating his intentions, and thus, as we shall see, to give a great deal of trouble to Bolingbroke.

The transitional scene at Barkloughly Castle is unusual in its lack of this irony. Richard not only takes over the emotionally charged rhetoric which has hitherto been associated chiefly with his opponents, he also takes on their role as spokesman for England and the Church. From the moment when he greets the English earth, it is he alone who embodies the spirit of Mowbray's lament for his native tongue, Bolingbroke's 'English ground, farewell', and Gaunt's famous purple passage. At the same time the presence of Carlisle reminds us that Richard consistently has the support of the Church, something which his successor never gets. This is unhistorical— Holinshed describes the prominent part taken by the Archbishop of Canterbury on Bolingbroke's behalf— and seems to be deliberate. In the early part of the play the values of Church and State are united in frequent evocations of the figure of the Crusader in the Holy Land and the warrior upholding the truth in single combat. Our last vision of this kind of harmony, now already in the past, comes in Carlisle's account of the death of Mowbray who has fought under the colours of 'his captain Christ' (IV, i, 99). Henry IV will never make his intended Crusade, churchmen are frequently involved in rebellions against him, and it is not until the reign of Henry V that Shakespeare again shows Church and State reconciled.

But their values cannot be reconciled in any case. Richard's behaviour at Barkloughly Castle is often taken as an undignified oscillation between two equally reprehensible states of mind, futile rage and morbid despair. It seems to me rather a bringing out into the open of a conflict between the equally valid but contradictory roles of king and Christian. Richard's moods of defeatism, though Carlisle condemns them, can be interpreted as an attempt to achieve that Christian resignation which, in the *Mirror for Magistrates* view, is the only refuge for the victim of Fortune's wheel. Reviewing the 'sad stories of the death of kings', he describes them as 'all murthered' (III, ii, 155-60), because no death can ever be 'natural' for men who have been led to think of themselves as immortal. The failure to bear in mind their own mortality is the chief crime of which the speakers in the *Mirror* accuse themselves; it is also the only sin which Richard lays to his own charge. Hence the special sense given to 'flattery' in the play: Bolingbroke actually receives much grosser adulation than Richard (especially in II, iii), but the latter says that he is being flattered even when the mirror shows

him a beauty that is really his, because it fails to show the ultimate truth about the transitoriness of that beauty. Similarly, at the end of the Barkloughly scene, he seems to equate all forms of comfort with flattery. As York said earlier, 'Comfort's in heaven, and we are on the earth' (II, ii, 78), and 'that sweet way I was in to despair' (III, ii, 205) may be sweet because, in one sense, it is the way to salvation.

On the other hand, as the exchanges of defiances, gages, and insults throughout the play remind us, the concepts of nobility and kingliness are not necessarily Christian. Mowbray and Bolingbroke refuse to accept counsels of patience in I, i, while Gaunt, in the scene that follows, opposes Christian patience to his sister-in-law's exhortations to think of family honour and revenge. Her response—

Call it not patience, Gaunt, it is despair . . .
That which in mean men we intitle patience
Is pale cold cowardice in noble breasts.
                                        (I, ii, 29-34)

— is similar to what the Queen says to Richard at their parting:

The lion dying thrusteth forth his paw
And wounds the earth, if nothing else, with
    rage
To be o'erpow'r'd, and wilt thou, pupil-like,
Take the correction mildly, kiss the rod,
And fawn on rage with base humility,
Which art a lion and the king of beasts?
                                        (v, i, 29-34)

The Barkloughly castle scene is difficult to play because the Lion King and the Christian are juxtaposed too often and too abruptly. But this is not to say that the roles are not sincerely played. They have to be, if the scene is to work at all. The reason why Richard is unironic here is that he believes, although we know otherwise, that effective action is still possible; his responses are real responses. To say that Richard is an actor giving a performance is irrelevant: all good dramatic parts allow actors to behave like actors. But to ask an actor to play the part of an actor giving an unconvincing performance is theatrical suicide. No one can possibly take any interest in the future history of a character shown to be as hollow as his crown. Fops are minor figures in drama, and rightly so.

It is when Richard is completely cut off from the possibility of effective action that he begins to make use of the roles of king and Christian for his own purposes; their contradictions no longer matter, because he is concerned only with their effect. The Lion King makes his last gesture when he asks,

Shall we call back Northumberland and send

Defiance to the traitor, and so die?
                              (III, iii, 129-30)

But he chooses instead to follow the advice of Aumerle:

No, good my lord, let's fight with gentle
  words,
Till time lend friends, and friends their
  helpful swords.
                              (III, iii, 131-2)

As has been pointed out, this is 'an intention of plain duplicity'. Words are a weapon for Richard, as well as a form of emotional release, and a closer look at his confrontations with Bolingbroke will show that he does in fact fight very skilfully with them.

In the first of these scenes, III, iii, Richard first makes an impressive speech in the kingly style, then sends a 'fair' (and, as he at once indicates, a lying) message to Bolingbroke, then (possibly for Northumberland's ears as well as Aumerle's) indulges in a fantasy of despair which plays 'idly', as he says, with traditional Christian symbols. To Northumberland, the sarcastic speeches which follow seem the words of 'a frantic man'. Yet when Richard re-enters the 'base court' he does not sound frantic. He picks up his own words, 'Down, down I come' and 'In the base court?' as he addresses Bolingbroke:

Fair cousin, you *debase* your princely knee
To make the *base* earth proud with kissing it . . .
Up, cousin, *up* . . .
                         (III, iii, 190-1, 194)

Bolingbroke and the rest treat him gently because he seems so helpless; he is then able to show up their gentleness as hypocrisy by hinting that he knows what they are really after. It is possible to argue that his anticipation of Bolingbroke's intentions makes Richard an accomplice in his own destruction; it is possible similarly, to say that Lear makes his daughters into monsters by treating them as such before they have done anything more unfilial than complaining about his hundred knights. But this seems to me too 'psychological' an approach to the plays. Richard does not, like a predestinating God, make things happen because he foresees them. He foresees them because they are going to happen, and because his awareness of the situation is both a convenient dramatic shorthand (if an event is accepted as inevitable, Shakespeare does not have to explain the precise practical means by which it comes about) and a means by which he can dominate the action.

Typical of the way in which he uses words to transform weakness into strength is his exploitation, at Flint Castle and in Westminster Hall, of conceits on tears. We dislike this sort of language nowadays, so it is tempt-

ing to describe as mere self-indulgence Richard's images of making 'foul weather with despised tears' (III, iii, 161), digging a pair of graves with them (III, iii, 165-9), being weighed down with them like a bucket in a well (IV, i, 184-9), and washing away his royal balm in them (IV, i, 207). What all these fantasies emphasise is the power of something which is normally taken to be a symbol of helplessness. The comparison of himself and Bolingbroke to two buckets in a well derives, in its rising-falling pattern, from the idea of Fortune's wheel and the 'Down, down I come' and 'Up, cousin, up' of III, iii. But in his insistence that he outweighs his cousin, who is able to rise so high only because he is essentially hollow, Richard also echoes and reverses the 'balance' image which the Gardener had used to the Queen:

Their fortunes both are weigh'd;
In your lord's scale is nothing but himself,
And some few vanities that make him light.
But in the balance of great Bolingbroke,
Besides himself, are all the English peers,
And with that odds he weighs King Richard
  down.
                              (III, iv, 84-9)

What we see throughout the deposition scene is that Richard alone, in his potently symbolic role as the Man of Sorrows, can in fact outweigh Bolingbroke and the peers.

The chief irony of this scene is one of which Richard himself is quite well aware: only a king can judge a king, and therefore it is he who must depose himself, yet the very fact that he is in this humiliating position is also a proof of his kingship which nothing can eradicate. He makes as much capital as possible from this two-edged predicament. Bolingbroke, in response apparently to Carlisle's plea, sends for Richard to perform in public what (according to York) he has already agreed to in private. The intention is, first, that the king should be seen to abdicate voluntarily and thus free his successor from the guilt of usurpation, and, second, that he should prove that he is 'worthily deposed' by reading out the articles which contain the charges against him. Richard does neither of these things.

Instead, he continues to employ the technique which we first saw at the end of the Flint Castle scene, that of giving with one hand and taking back with the other:

Well you deserve. They well deserve to have
That know the strong'st and surest way to
  get.
                              (III, iii, 200-1)

What you will have, I'll give, and willing too,
For do we must what force will have us do.
                              (III, iii, 206-7)

His first speech in Westminster Hall shows the same teasing ambiguity:

> God save the king! although I be not he;
> And yet, amen, if heaven do think him me.
>
> (IV, i, 174-5)

Urged to resign the crown, he invites Bolingbroke to 'seize' it. The series of quibbles which follows has a serious purpose. By claiming, for instance, that he is willing to resign his crown but not the cares that go with it he is transforming a sacramental object into a piece of metal, a 'heavy weight from off my head' (IV, i, 204). He may formally 'undo' himself, in language that seems as thorough as Bolingbroke could wish, but his very exaggeration is suspicious. The renunciation culminates in his insistence that by losing the crown he loses his life since the one is so completely identified with the other. Later he virtually takes everything back when he condemns himself and everyone else as traitors for their part in the ritual undoing. The stress throughout has been on the unalterable fact of his kingliness.

He also, by a well-timed burst of hysteria, avoids having to read the articles. He promises to read his sins, not from the paper Northumberland is brandishing, but from the mirror where he can see them written on his face. But the mirror shows him no sins; it reveals the face of a king. He smashes it because it lies about his situation, the true situation of all men, even kings. Thus, in drawing Bolingbroke's attention to 'the moral of this sport', he may be offering a warning as well as a further statement of the power of sorrow (IV, i, 290-1).

His last gesture is a trick, and apparently a rather pointless one. He will, he says,

> beg one boon,
> And then be gone, and trouble you no more.
>
> (IV, i, 302-3)

But what he begs in fact is permission to be gone. The request is a further move in the power-struggle, both because Richard is able to leave without having read the articles and because he forces Bolingbroke to show his intentions at last by sending him to the Tower. In his parting shot—

> O, good! Convey! Conveyers are you all,
> That rise thus nimbly by a true king's fall.
>
> (IV, i, 317-18)

— he seizes on the unfortunately chosen word 'convey' (which was slang for 'steal') and adds, I think, a characteristic pun on 'true king' (a 'true man' was the opposite of a thief). It is a good exit, but what he wins is not simply a moral victory; by making it clear that he is not willing to resign the crown and still considers

himself the rightful king, he has opened the way for just such a conspiracy as we see taking shape at the end of the scene.

Stanley Wells has pointed out the parallel between the ending of the deposition scene and that of II, i. There, too, mere words—those of the dying Gaunt and York— seem to have no effect, yet the scene ends with three onlookers deciding to take action on behalf of an apparently hopeless cause. Richard's pun on 'convey' links the two still further, since it was his own theft of Gaunt's lands which started the rebellion against him. That the rebellion against Bolingbroke is later discovered and crushed does not alter the effect of the rebels' words, coming as they do immediately after the 'woeful pageant'. It is too simple to treat the deposition scene as a triumph of silent, powerful Bolingbroke over verbose, weak Richard. Language *is* a source of power in the play, even though there is also an awareness of its inadequacy. Though Richard's rhetoric successfully appeals to the spectators' reverence for the symbol of England and the Church, the nobles and churchmen who rally to his cause are defeated in a way that is clearly providential: Aumerle has no sooner said that he intends to be in Oxford 'If God prevent it not' (V, ii, 55) than York notices the seal hanging out of his son's doublet. And the less admirable motives which make the old man gallop away to reveal the plot do not detract from his conviction that Bolingbroke's usurpation, however shocking, must somehow be part of a divine plan.

Shakespeare does not attempt to explain this paradox, but he continues to explore it in the last act of the play, largely through the opposing kinds of language he gives to Richard. On the one hand, the deposed king becomes more formal and rhetorical than ever before. After the ceremonial unkinging, which he later describes as a divorce between him and his crown (V, i, 71-2), comes his equally ritualistic parting with the Queen, when he 'unkisses' his contract with her in an exchange of hearts which is also a marriage with sorrow. Even his dying words are formal, a divorce of soul from body:

> Exton, thy fierce hand
> Hath with the king's blood stain'd the king's own land.
> Mount, mount, my soul! thy seat is up on high,
> Whilst my gross flesh sinks downward, here to die.
>
> (V, v, 109-12)

The speech echoes and unites several dominant images of the play: the rising-falling pattern, the sacrificial blood watering the earth, and the stain which cannot be washed away. Richard shows complete certainty both of his kingly status and of his own salvation; Exton, similarly,

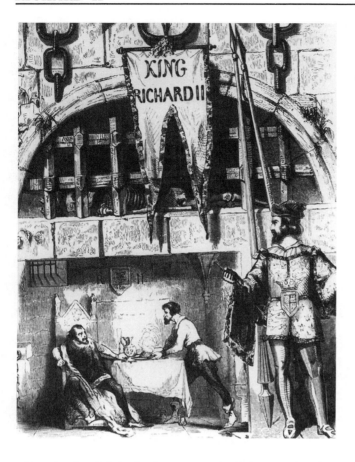

Engraving from Galarie des Personnages de Shakespeare *(1844).*

accepts the view that he himself is damned forever. We have seen the death of a symbol, not a human being.

But alongside this ritualistic King of Sorrows Shakespeare also gives us intriguing glimpses of the other Richard: sharp-tongued, self-mocking and quite unresigned. The pointed realism of his words to Northumberland in V, i, is fully in keeping with his constant anticipation of Bolingbroke's moves, and I am sure the Quartos are right to give him, and not Northumberland, the cynical reply to the Queen's request that the two of them be banished together: 'That were some love, but little policy' (V, i, 84). The symbolic representative of England has little discernible affection for his people ('A king of beasts indeed' [V, i, 35]), and, as the prison soliloquy shows us, God's representative on earth is unsure of his own salvation. Unlike the saintly Henry VI with his crown of content, Richard finds that 'no thought is contented' (V, v, 11) and he now sees death not as the way to 'a new world's crown' (V, i, 24) but as 'being nothing' (V, v, 41). The images in which he personifies his own thoughts all tend irresistibly toward the grotesque, whether they are quibbling over scriptural contradictions, plotting an impossible escape, or, like beggars in the stocks (not Stoic philosophers, or even the hermit that he once imagined himself), trying to resign

themselves to fate. His playing with words, far from providing a consoling substitute for reality, nearly drives him mad. Yet, despite the desire for human love which comes through at the end of the soliloquy, his immediate reaction to the unexpected appearance of the Groom is a stale pun on 'royal' and 'noble'. The familiar tone of this little episode is almost immediately followed by the outbursts against the keeper and the murderers, in which the dominant note seems one of relief that he at last has an object on which to release his pent-up energies. There is relief for the audience as well, not only in the violent action which follows five acts of fighting with words alone, but also in the sheer arrogance of Richard's reaction: 'How now! what means death in this *rude* assault?' (V, v, 105). Nevertheless, one can see why his dying speech had to be modulated into a different tone.

The formality of that speech, and its rhyming couplets, are taken up at once by Exton, establishing the simplified, symbolic view of Richard ('As full of valour as of royal blood' [V, v, 113]) which is to prevail in the final scene. However uninspired poetically, the alternation of speeches reporting the downfall of Henry's enemies with bathetic thank-you couplets from Henry is dramatically effective in that it prepares the entry of Exton, whom the king emphatically does *not* thank. Moreover, Henry's forgiveness of Carlisle, which ought to be the climax of the scene, is immediately and ironically nullified by the appearance of the coffin which, though it contains 'the mightiest of thy greatest enemies' (V, vi, 32), is a source not of triumph but of consternation to him. 'A god on earth thou art', was the Duchess of York's phrase after he pardoned Aumerle (V, iii, 134), but Exton's act has identified him irrevocably with Pilate, wishing in vain both to pardon his victim and to wash the blood off his hands. As Reese has pointed out, 'thy buried fear' (V, vi, 31) has a double meaning, indicating not only an end to fears but a permanent source of them in the coffin of the murdered king. The presence of that coffin lends dignity and resonance even to the stiff couplets of Henry and Exton; in particular, the phrase 'Richard of Burdeaux' has a shock effect which is curiously moving in the theatre. Henry's last speech calls upon the familiar national and religious symbols and attempts to channel potentially dangerous emotions into the ritual of court mourning and the promise of a Crusade. But it is fitting that irony and ambiguity should hang over this solemn ending and that the 'silent king' in the coffin should still present a threat. Richard dominates the scene in his silence as he had dominated it before with words.

Jack R. Sublette

SOURCE: "Order and Power in Richard II," in *Ball State University Forum*, Vol. XXII, No. 1, Winter, 1981, pp. 42-51.

[In the following essay, Sublette contends that Richard abuses his power and as a result creates the disorder that occurs in the play. Sublette demonstrates that in the play's opening scenes "ordered disorder" exists under Richard's command, but after Richard seizes Gaunt's estate, events follow that cause the apparent order to clearly become disorder, and this disorder dominates the rest of the play.]

Much of the disorder represented in William Shakespeare's *Richard II* and the subsequent plays in the *Henriad— 1 Henry IV, 2 Henry IV,* and *Henry V*— occurs as a direct result of Richard's violation of the natural cycle of time. *Richard II* dramatizes a sequence of events in which the natural order of time and succession is violated and in which men then struggle to restore order. Through struggling in an existence framed with time, King Richard acquires self-knowledge. Theodore Spencer writes that the violation and subsequent restoration of order are common dramatic themes:

> Such is the general plan of all Shakespeare's historical plays, as it was . . . of all drama that has deep roots in the beliefs and conventions of its time. An existing order is violated, the consequent conflict and turmoil are portrayed, and order is restored by the destruction of the force or forces that originally violated it.

Because of the political setting in *Richard II*, the concepts of order and power are closely connected as Shakespeare explores human activities and values. This paper examines the imagery in *Richard II* which reflects Shakespeare's treatment of order and power at the various levels of life— in the individual, the family, the social and political groups, the state, and the universe.

Richard II begins with a paradox of ordered disorder in the quarrel between the contending British lords, Mowbray and Bolingbroke, who come before the King to present their charges and counter-charges of guilt. The fact that the King is present to hear the quarrel between Mowbray and Bolingbroke suggests that an orderly system of justice exists in the kingdom. However, Richard fails to fulfill his role of arbiter. Bolingbroke's accusations against Mowbray for misappropriating military funds and plotting the death of the Duke of Gloucester emphasize the seriousness of the present conflict and the extent of the disorder which plagues the kingdom. Stressing the need for revenge, Bolingbroke accuses Mowbray of murdering the Duke of Gloucester: ". . . blood, like sacrificing Abel's, cries / Even from the tongueless caverns of the earth / To me for justice and rough chastisement" (I. i. 104-106).

Historically appropriate, this image alludes to the archetypical example of a brother's murdering his own brother, for as actual history asserts and as John of Gaunt and the Duchess of Gloucester are about to testify, King Richard, not Mowbray, is responsible for the murder of his own uncle. In history, Gloucester and his supporters, known as the Lords Appellant, who included both Bolingbroke and Mowbray, had earlier secured the execution or exile of several of Richard's friends. In personifying the grave of Gloucester, this initial image suggests both the disorder of the land in which "tongueless caverns" speak and the continuity and cyclical nature of human life in which death does not represent the finality of one's existence. Although Gloucester is dead and although the act of killing him is past, the voice of Gloucester, the need for justice, and the reality of the murder still exist. The King who should settle this quarrel between two of his subjects simply complicates, probably because of his own guilt, the existing disorder. To Bolingbroke and Mowbray, Richard entreats:

> Let's purge this choler without letting blood.
> This we prescribe, though no physician.
> Deep malice makes too deep incision.
> Forget, forgive, conclude and be agreed.
> Our doctors say this is no month to bleed.
>
> (I. i. 153-57)

This image, drawn from medicine, shows Richard's distorted view of his own role. As king, Richard should be the physician to his kingdom, but his interpretation of his "sacred blood" and of his role as monarch by divine right concentrates on the privileges rather than the obligations and responsibilities of kingship. The accepted method to purge the choler-infected land would be to let blood, but because Richard suffers from a similar infection, he foolishly refuses to accept the monarchical responsibilities that would bring about the necessary healing of his state. The King's professional negligence is confirmed in the "garden scene." A physician, a gardener, and a king have a similar obligation to provide the necessary services for the patient, the garden, and the kingdom. These caretakers are responsible for bodies which are subject to change, growth, disease, and excesses. Paradoxically, physicians, gardeners, and kings must sometimes destroy part of what they care for in order to maintain order and health and to effect a cure. Impotent to create health with the prescription of his commands, the King decides to allow Bolingbroke and Mowbray to lance their own boil of contention: "There shall your swords and lances arbitrate / The swelling difference of your settled hate" (I. i. 200-01). Richard has unknowingly delegated his own authority. Ironically, although Richard thinks that this is no time for blood-letting, both his previous action and his current behavior effect deadly blood-letting for him and his kingdom.

Shakespeare intensifies the disorder which Gloucester's murder and Richard's inept behavior have revealed with the Duchess of Gloucester's hyperbolic prayer for more disorder, which she feels will bring about revenge on

Mowbray for his part in her husband's death:

> Oh, sit my husband's wrongs on Hereford's
>   spear,
> That it may enter butcher Mowbray's breast!
> Or if misfortune miss the first career,
> Be Mowbray's sins so heavy in his bosom
> That they may break his foaming courser's
>   back
> And throw the rider headlong in the lists,
> A caitiff recreant to my cousin Hereford!
>
>   (I. ii. 47-53)

Because Richard does not allow the actual combat between Bolingbroke and Mowbray to occur, the Duchess of Gloucester's hopes for Mowbray's misfortunes have no opportunity to materialize. Her picture of the heaviness of guilt from an individual's sin anticipates the mood of the reign of Richard II. In fact, Shakespeare depicts characters throughout the *Henriad* who suffer from guilt. The feeling of guilt sits very heavily in the mind of Henry IV. In addition to the Duchess, Richard II, Henry IV, and Falstaff all end their lives with grief. The *Henriad* dramatizes life in a kingdom where several principal characters find their old age rewarded not with a feeling of accomplishment and satisfaction but with sorrow and grief.

Ironically, as Mowbray prepares for the tournament with Bolingbroke which he will not be permitted to pursue, he describes his inner mood and feeling:

> Never did captive with a freer heart
> Cast off his chains of bondage, and embrace
> His golden uncontrolled enfranchisement,
> More than my dancing soul doth celebrate
> This feast of battle with mine adversary.
>
>   (I. iii. 88-92)

Actually, Mowbray is about to replace his freedom with external banishment. The image in the last line of the passage above also foreshadows a time when feasting will become supplanted with battles. At no time in the *Henriad* does the reader see the characters preparing for a happy and joyous feast. The image intensifies the lack of genuine mirth and festivity throughout the *Henriad.* Even in the *Henry IV* plays, the scenes with Falstaff suggest a distorted humor. Mowbray's preparation for single combat, which sets a kind of mood and pace for the remainder of the *Henriad,* anticipates others like Prince Hal and later King Henry V, King Henry IV, and the Percys who plan and equip themselves for war.

The proposed joust between Mowbray and Bolingbroke represents a kind of ordered ceremony, but it is disrupted and prevented from being completed. Even though Richard prevents the combat between his two subjects, his reasons for doing so suggest rather spe-

cious thinking stemming from the idea of disturbing the peace. The King fears that strife between Mowbray and Bolingbroke will awaken peace:

> . . . peace, which our country's cradle
> Draws the sweet infant breath of gentle sleep—
> Which so roused up with boisterous untuned
>   drums,
> With harsh-resounding trumpets' dreadful
>   bray,
> And grating shock of wrathful iron arms,
> Might from our quiet confines fright fair peace,
> And make us wade even in our kindred's
>   blood.
>
>   (I. iii. 132-38)

To keep peace sleeping, the King banishes Mowbray forever and Bolingbroke for ten years, a sentence which he soon reduces to six years. Harold Goddard insists that a careful examination of this speech renders it very damaging to Richard's character. According to Goddard, Richard is linguistically skillful enough to disguise the lack of meaningful content in his words:

> The central figure is that of Peace, an infant, asleep in its cradle, England. But why should a professed lover of tranquility like Richard wish to keep peace asleep? Obviously, when peace sleeps, war and domestic turmoil have their chance. Don't awaken peace, says Richard, lest she frighten out of our land . . . [sic] and to our logical consternation we discover that what this aroused infant peace is to scare into exile is, of all things, peace itself.

In Goddard's view, Richard's idea of peace as a being which is subject to both waking and sleeping makes no sense. Goddard's assessment is severe, but the speech does give an accurate picture of Richard's idea of peace. To Richard, peace is simply the absence of war. Real peace represents much more; actual peace exists not when peace lies asleep but when it is awake with all of the activity in the kingdom designed not only to perpetuate the absence of war but to create a climate of healthy growth, vitality, honesty, and justice. Richard's kingdom in which he has effected his uncle's execution and seemingly avoided civil disruption by employing the powerful "breath of kings" is a peaceful, ordered country only superficially and temporarily.

Richard's banishment of Mowbray, the one who has perhaps carried out the King's commands, anticipates the exile of Exton by Henry IV at the end of the play. In an attempt to establish a superficial order, both Richard and Henry IV punish men who have followed the wishes of their superiors. The severity and impropriety of the banishments soon become clear in the words of those affected. Because he must abandon his native language, Mowbray feels that his tongue cannot function properly:

And now my tongue's use is to me no more
Than an unstringed viol or a harp,
Or like a cunning instrument cased up
Or, being open, put into his hands
That knows no touch to tune the harmony.

(I. iii. 161-65)

This poignant image depicts the feelings of a man who has been loyal to his king, the same king who claims to desire peace and order. In the language of a pragmatic idealist, John of Gaunt advises his banished son to assuage the grief of his exile by imagining that he is the king, that he flees a pestilence, and, in general, that exile is a desirable fate (I. iii. 279-91). In addition to foreshadowing the day when Bolingbroke will return to become king and to speaking truthfully about the infected kingdom, Gaunt counsels his son that in order to be able to tolerate his life, he must view the world from a completely unrealistic perspective, one which totally reverses the actual situation. Although Bolingbroke explicitly denies the usefulness and expediency of his father's advice, the effects of Bolingbroke's banishment confirm Gaunt's counsel. In a land which is farmed out because of the King's excesses and in a country ruled by a king who prays for physicians to kill rather than heal so that this same king can illegally confiscate an inheritance, life is so disordered that it is difficult to distinguish between idealism and realism. In fact, what seems to be the most unlikely— for example, Bolingbroke's becoming king— often becomes fact.

John of Gaunt mentions another reversal in his famous description of England under the rule of Richard. To Gaunt, Richard has destroyed the essence of the British kingdom:

This land of such dear souls, this dear dear
    land,
Dear for her reputation through the world,
Is now leased out, I die pronouncing it,
Like to a tenement or pelting farm.

(II. i. 57-60)

Gaunt's words, in contrast to the present, look back to the days of his father, Edward III, and perhaps to the time of his own regency. In one sense, this speech merely represents Gaunt's lament for his own lost youth and the passage of time. But his image of the blighted and blotted England leased out proves to be more than an old man's mourning for the loss of a former time. His depiction of the corrupted kingdom has already been partially verified by Richard's immoral greed and will be confirmed by Richard's action upon Gaunt's death. In addition to characterizing England as a leased out farm, Gaunt's words identify the debasement and corruption in the position and role of kingship itself. In an image which recalls Richard's comment about Gaunt's physician, Gaunt reminds Richard that he, being a sick ruler, commits his "anointed body to the cure /

Of those physicians that first wounded thee" (II. i. 98-99). Under the command of Richard, England is a land in which the physicians kill, the King is a landlord subject to the laws, and the royal family is reduced to a pelican-like existence in which the young spill the blood of their elders in order to strengthen their own positions. In Richard's kingdom, those like Mowbray and Gaunt who threaten his seemingly secure, divine-right position become either "an unstringed viol" or "a stringless instrument" (II. i. 149). In terms of the imagery, Mowbray and Gaunt represent silent men like unstringed or stringless instruments, which cannot be played upon.

Very little time passes before the apparent order displayed in the beginning of *Richard II* dissolves into open disorder. Upon Richard's seizing Bolingbroke's inheritance and leaving for Ireland, Northumberland advocates to Willoughby and Ross a course of insurrection to remedy the troubled kingdom:

. . . we shall shake off our slavish yoke,
Imp out our drooping country's broken
    wing,
Redeem from broking pawn the blemished
    crown,
Wipe off the dust that hides our scepter's
    gilt,
And make high majesty look like itself[.]

(II. i. 291-95)

Because of the chaotic nature of Richard's kingdom, the rebels ironically substitute one "slavish yoke" for another which is equally enslaving and a "blemished crown" for another one which they have helped stain. Besides being an apt description of England, Northumberland's conception of the country as a broken wing predicts the kind of images Shakespeare will use to portray the people who inhabit the kingdom of Henry IV and Henry V. Many of the subjects living in the disordered kingdom become less like human beings and more like animals as the imagery in the *Henriad* shows.

With the King having gone to Ireland, Bolingbroke having returned to England, and some of Richard's chief supporters having fled to Bolingbroke, the Duke of York, feeling that the time itself is sick (a symbol of disorder), expresses his feeling about the nature of life on earth: "Comfort's in Heaven, and we are on the earth, / Where nothing lives but crosses, cares, and grief" (II. ii. 78-79). York's pessimistic view of life on earth is a direct result of Richard's effect on his kingdom. York is right to differentiate between life on earth and life in a more orderly existence beyond earth. In doing so, he exemplifies man's search for order in a world of change, flux, and confusion. However, this belief that man's earthly existence is composed exclusively of "crosses, cares, and grief" substantially distorts life. York generalizes about life from his own position: he is saddened by one brother murdered, by another newly dead, by a nephew banished, and by the death of the Duchess of Gloucester; he is commanded by another nephew, who is also his king, to be Lord Governor of England; he is deprived of the support of the Percys and Lords Ross, Beaumond, and Willoughby and of financial assistance; and, he is weakened by his own age. York's "crosses, cares, and grief" are, indeed, "a tide of woes / [that] Comes rushing on the woeful land at once" (II. ii. 98-99).

York's affliction and distress cause him to be confused. He finds himself in a position which he has not effected but with which he must contend:

> If I know how or which way to order these
> affairs
> Thus thrust disorderly into my hands,
> Never believe me. Both are my kinsmen.
> The one is my sovereign, whom both my
> oath
> And duty bids defend. The other again
> Is my kinsman, whom the King hath
> wronged,
> Whom conscience and my kindred bids to right.
>
> (II. ii. 109-15)

This speech focuses on one of the basic conflicts of the play— opposing loyalties— and also anticipates York's loyalty at the end of the play to the new King in conflict with his own son's opposition to Henry. York's situation indicates his position on the wheel of fortune. The confusion which is almost overpowering in York's life and the disorder which prevails in the English kingdom occur because both York and Bolingbroke act irresponsibly, illegally, and immorally and because human life is subject to the ever-turning wheels of fortune and time. Even if man's task on earth amounts to "numbering sands and drinking oceans dry" (II. ii. 146), his worth and his character as a human being are determined by the use of his moral capacities in his actions, no matter how insuperable his task may seem.

Under York's regency, Richard's kingdom continues to be a land infected by "caterpillars" like Bushy, Bagot, and Green. The extent of Richard's disordered rule is shown in the Welsh Captain's report of omens which have caused the Welsh forces to desert Richard:

> The bay trees in our country are all withered,
> And meteors fright the fixed stars of heaven.
> The pale-faced moon looks bloody on the
> earth,
> And lean-looked prophets whisper fearful
> change.
> Rich men look sad and ruffians dance and
> leap,
> The one in fear to lose what they enjoy,

> The other to enjoy by rage and war.
>
> (II. iv. 8-14)

The Captain's words indicate the presence of a cosmic turmoil which parallels and which is the direct result of man's life on earth. This image depicts the nature of man's earthly existence on a macrocosmic scale. The accuracy of the omens materializes when Bolingbroke sentences Bushy and Green to execution. In order to counteract Bolingbroke's cleansing actions, Richard, upon his return from Ireland, exhorts his native soil to come alive, to starve the rebels, and to function as a part of his army:

> But let thy spiders, that suck up thy venom,
> And heavy-gaited toads lie in their way,
> Doing annoyance to the treacherous feet
> Which with usurping steps do trample thee.
> Yield stinging nettles to mine enemies,
> And when they from thy bosom pluck a
> flower,
> Guard it, I pray thee, with a lurking adder,
> Whose double tongue may with a mortal touch
> Throw death upon thy sovereign's enemies.
>
> (III. ii. 14-22)

These are the words from a King who has proclaimed his love of peace. The picture of England which Richard portrays in this speech actually suggests an exact description of the country as it now exists. Richard has already become the "lurking adder" with a "double tongue" in an unhealthy kingdom which is full of spiders, toads, and poison. In a land functioning with an orderly system of succession by which the eldest son inherits his father's title, land, and wealth, Richard, who is supposedly the protector and defender of the country's laws, has usurped Bolingbroke's rightful inheritance. His entreaty for the total transformation of a kingdom into a poisonous menagerie ironically works for his own downfall. The King might have been less severe in his desire for the defeat of one who returns, albeit illegally, from exile to claim his inheritance.

Richard's rash and irresponsible mode of thinking and acting is further exemplified when he calls Bushy, Green, and the Earl of Wiltshire villains, vipers, dogs, snakes, and three Judases and when he commands "Terrible Hell [to] make war / Upon their spotted souls for this offense" (III. ii. 133-34). Although these men are misleaders of a king, they have been faithful to their king. Perhaps their souls are spotted but not for the offense which Richard claims. Richard's kingdom is so disordered that even he as its leader cannot distinguish faithful caterpillars from disloyal dogs and Judases. In fact, Richard's allusion to Judas in describing his followers indirectly implies a comparison between himself and Christ, an analogy so inappropriate and improper that it accentuates the chaotic state of the English kingdom under Richard's rule. Later, when brought before

Bolingbroke to read the list of crimes and accusations, Richard compares his subjects to Judas and himself to Christ. This time the comparison seems more realistic and more effective than his earlier mention of Judas in arousing the reader's pity for him. After York acquiesces to the "tide of woes," Richard finds himself in the same swift metaphorical stream. He, too, succumbs: "A king, woe's slave, shall kingly woe obey" (III. ii. 210). The image of woe as a stream is appropriate not only for the suggestion of the comparison with the traditional stream of time but also for the realistic depiction of the powerful forces which affect man in the various roles which he plays, particularly in the role of king.

Even though Richard prophesies that if Bolingbroke takes the crown, many Englishmen will die for generations to come, he further inverts and perverts the order of his kingdom by agreeing to exchange his role of king for that of a peasant:

> I'll give my jewels for a set of beads,
> My gorgeous palace for a hermitage,
> My gay apparel for an almsman's gown,
> My figured goblets for a dish of wood,
> My scepter for a palmer's walking-staff,
> My subjects for a pair of carved saints,
> And my large kingdom for a little grave,
> A little little grave, an obscure grave.
>
> (III. iii. 147-54)

Rather than simply giving to Bolingbroke what is his, Richard irresponsibly assents to surrender the crown. Ironically, Shakespeare suggests that until Richard recognizes that he is only a human being, just a peasant, he will never be able to assume the role of king.

In Pomfret Castle, he will finally come to this realization. He has become king without becoming a man; therefore, he loses his crown. In his symbolic descent from the balcony of Flint Castle to the court below to meet Bolingbroke, Richard acknowledges the inappropriateness of his action:

> Down, down I come, like glistering Phaeton,
> Wanting the manage of unruly jades.
> In the base court? Base court, where kings
>   grow base,
> To come at traitors' calls and do them grace.
> In the base court? Come down? Down, court!
>   Down, King!
> For night owls shriek where mounting larks
>   should sing.
>
> (III. iii. 178-83)

Despite the accurate description in this image of Richard's act, the words emphasize the inappropriate behavior of the King. Richard, who should have taken the role of Phoebus, not Phaethon, once had had the

power to manage the kingdom so that both the owls and the larks could sing their respective songs at the proper times. Because he misused that power, he has lost it. Like the jewels, palace, gay apparel, goblets, scepter, subjects, and kingdom which Richard catalogues as being physical and material possessions of the king, power is also a part of the royal entourage, an abstract part which, when not properly exercised, becomes as easy to lose as the crown itself. Richard's assessment of power politics makes this point: "They well deserve to have / That know the strong'st and surest way to get" (III. iii. 200-01). Even though this political philosophy accurately depicts the action of the remainder of the *Henriad*, it ignores the established and orderly system of rightful and legal succession. Perhaps knowing the strongest and surest way to achieve power, as Bolingbroke and his son obviously do, establishes one's possession of it in one sense, but Shakespeare, in contrast to Richard, seems to suggest that there is more to acquiring power than political and military knowledge. Richard's failure to recognize a higher principle of order than political shrewdness and power and, consequently, his violation of that higher order brings chaos to his kingdom. Without realizing the seriousness of his act, Richard surrenders, indicating his recognition of a force which he cannot control. For Bolingbroke, the acceptance of the crown indicates a lack of understanding of his role. Richard, Bolingbroke and York yield to what seems, vis-a-vis the powerful forces confronting them, the most natural course of action. The actions of men—Richard, weakened by his misuse of power and loss of military support; Bolingbroke, weakened by growing greed; and York, weakened by old age—inflict further disorder on the English kingdom.

At the end of Act III, the gardener and the two servants in the Duke of York's garden delineate in careful detail and on a microcosmic scale, in contrast to the Welsh Captain's depiction on a larger scale, the extent of Richard's neglect of his kingdom and the consequential harm and destruction. The gardener explains to the two workmen that a gardener's job is to tend the garden. Symbolically, in losing control of his garden-kingdom, Richard allowed those subjects who seemed to support him to destroy him. The "other Eden, demi-Paradise" of which John of Gaunt proudly spoke had become a garden full of weeds:

> . . . our sea-walled garden the whole land,
> Is full of weeds, her fairest flowers choked up,
> Her fruit trees all unpruned, her hedges
>   ruined,
> Her knots disordered, and her wholesome
>   herbs
> Swarming with catterpillars[.]
>
> (III. iv. 43-47)

In addition to affirming the lack of needed order in the state, this image identifies Richard with the disordered kingdom and identifies him as a man, an identity which Richard himself does not fully realize until his imprisonment in Pomfret Castle. Shakespeare includes this identification in this earlier scene of political allegory.

As they did after the conflict between Bolingbroke and Mowbray at the beginning of the play, civil bickering and disruption continue in the English kingdom after Bolingbroke assumes power. Even before Richard is officially deposed and Henry IV crowned, several British subjects in the presence of Bolingbroke accuse each other of lies and guilty acts (IV. i. 1-85): Aumerle is opposed by and opposes Bagot, Fitzwater, Hotspur, and a Lord; Surrey and Fitzwater oppose each other. Like Richard, Bolingbroke defers the settlement of the opposing claims to a later time. The Bishop of Carlisle warns Bolingbroke about the woeful nature of a future time if Bolingbroke takes the crown:

> Peace shall go sleep with Turks and infidels,
> And in this seat of peace tumultuous wars
> Shall kin with kin and kind with kind confound.
> Disorder, horror, fear, and mutiny
> Shall here inhabit, and this land be called
> The field of Golgotha and dead men's skulls.
>
> (IV. i. 139-44)

For his truthful words, Carlisle is arrested for treason. With Carlisle's arrest, disorder, horror, and fear already inhabit England in the space of very little time; mutiny will occur before very much more time passes. The actions of Richard and Bolingbroke are, as the Abbot of Westminster proclaims, "A woeful pageant" (IV. i. 321).

After Richard's formal deposition, his Queen reproves him for the manner in which he accepts his new position without a struggle. The Queen suggests that Richard should imitate the dying lion:

> The lion dying thrusteth his paw
> And wounds the earth, if nothing else, with rage
> To be o'erpowered. And wilt thou, pupil-like,
> Take thy correction mildly, kiss the rod,
> And fawn on rage with base humility,
> Which art a lion and a king of beasts?
>
> (V. i. 29-34)

Neither the Queen nor Richard yet fully realizes that Richard has already severely wounded the earth, for which both Richard and his kingdom now suffer. Richard's reply to his wife, "A king of beasts, indeed. If aught but beasts, / I had been still a happy king of men" (V. i. 35-36), indicates that he does not fully comprehend the reasons for the loss of the crown and power. Having apparently forgotten his remark that "Lions make leopards tame" (I. i. 174), Richard blames his subjects for being animals. In addition to the tradi-

tional symbol of the lion as the English king, the image of Richard as the king of beasts tacitly suggests his kinship with those whom he rules. A "happy king of men" should recognize that he, as well as his subjects, is just a man. Ironically and unfortunately for Richard and his kingdom, Richard has become a beast who is a king of beasts without first becoming a man and a king of men. When he comes to this realization, he has already lost his kingdom.

Part of the disorder in the realm has occurred because of Richard's faulty vision. Throughout his reign, he was both short-and thick-sighted. With the crown removed from his head, his vision begins to sharpen and to clear. On his way to Pomfret Castle, Richard looks into the future and accurately predicts the destiny of the English kingdom. Specifically, he warns Northumberland about his future relationship with the new King:

> Northumberland, thou ladder wherewithal
> The mounting Bolingbroke ascends my throne,
> The time shall not be many hours of age
> More than it is, ere foul sin gathering head
> Shall break into corruption. Thou shalt think,
> It is too little, helping him to all.
> And he shall think that thou, which know'st the way
> To plant unrightful kings, wilt know again,
> Being ne'er so little urged, another way
> To pluck him headlong from the usurped throne.
>
> (V. i. 55-65)

Later when Henry wonders how Richard was able to be accurate in his prediction, the Earl of Warwick says simply that because Richard was a careful observer of human nature, he was able to forecast one subject's behavior on the basis of his past actions. Warwick is correct in his assertion, but Richard has not always been a careful observer of human nature. Richard's accurate predicion about disorder in the English kingdom represents a healthy change in his vision and a growing sense of order in his own mind. Had Richard been able to observe and to think clearly earlier, he would still be king in fact as well as in name. Tragically and realistically, this knowledge comes to Richard only with very painful experience. Even though order comes to the mind and sight of England's former king, disorder increases in the land ruled by the usurper. Later, when Richard is imprisoned at Pomfret Castle, he will be able to look back and view his past clearly.

Immediately following Henry's coronation, disorder in the kingdom surfaces at a very basic level. York finds that his son Aumerle is a member of a conspiracy planning to murder the new king. Upon this discovery, York, despite his wife's contrary protests, decides to inform King Henry of Aumerle's plan and guilt. Turmoil exists also in the royal family. To the news of his father's triumph, the new king's oldest son irreverently responds that "he would unto the stews" (V. iii. 16). Perhaps with thoughts of his own son in mind, Henry pardons Aumerle, the son of another apparently honorable man. The point is that his reign begins with fathers and sons opposing each other. In addition to the appearance of familial disorder at the end of *Richard II,* Henry sees his power growing as it feeds on the human blood of Oxford, Salisbury, Blunt, Kent, Brocas, Seely, the Abbot of Westminster, and King Richard II. A kingdom fertilized with the blood of its own subjects and its own king perpetuates a woeful pageant.

The imagery of order and power in *Richard II* illustrates the fact that the *Henriad* represents more than simply a dramatized presentation of political philosophy. In addition to a continual relationship with time, man seeks an ordered existence which he believes parallels the nature of the universe. *Richard II* explores in detail one man's use of power and his loss of it with the attendant growth of disorder. Because of chance and the orderly process of succession, Richard finds himself heir to the English throne, a position which allows him certain privileges, which provides him an inordinate amount of power, and which lays certain responsibilities and obligations on him. As king, Richard neglects his responsibilities; he wastes and abuses his power. He fails to recognize the true source of his power and its limitations. As a result of his irresponsible acts, he loses his royal power and finally his life, but not before he acquires some knowledge of his identity. His knowledge arrives too late to mitigate the growing disorder in the kingdom. Because of chance and because of his own political competence, Bolingbroke assumes Richard's power, but he fails to restore the lost order because of his illegal usurpation. Despite the fact that Henry effects an appearance of order with the official deposition of Richard, and with his own coronation processional, and with the king established as commander of the royal army, England under his rule becomes a land of pretense, counterfeit, and disease. Shakespeare uses the role of monarch as the central dramatic position for the exploration of order and power. He portrays both Richard II and Henry IV as kings who fail to acknowledge their identity as human beings before they assume the role of king. Richard selfishly abuses the royal power and allows the entire kingdom to become disordered. As a result of Richard's inappropriate actions, he loses his power, but he does gain a realistic sense of his own identity before he dies.

BOLINGBROKE

Although Bolingbroke accepts a crown that legally belongs to Richard, Bolingbroke is often seen in a heroic light, as the man who rescues the kingship and the commonwealth from Richard's weak and ineffective hands. Critics such as Lewis J. Owen (whose essay appears in the Kingship section) and Arthur Suzman (whose essay appears in the Language, Imagery, and Symbolism section) argue that despite Bolingbroke's political rise, he experiences a personal or spiritual decline. Owen explains that Bolingbroke loses dignity when he takes the crown which is rightfully Richard's.

Barbara J. Baines argues that while some critics have attacked Bolingbroke, Shakespeare presents him in a favorable, sympathetic manner. The play itself does present both sides of Bolingbroke, Baines notes, that of Bolingbroke who acts the king through his deeds, and that of Bolingbroke the traitor. Baines suggests that the former, sympathetic attitude is given more weight in the play. Baines argues that Richard loses the crown (in fact deposes himself) as a result of his disregard for the laws of the commonwealth, that he disinherits himself through his role in Gloucester's death and his confiscation of Gaunt's estate. Although some critics feel that Bolingbroke does not make his motivations known, Baines argues that he returns not to regain his inheritance (his father Gaunt's estate) but to claim his right as a subject to be ruled by a responsible king. Bolingbroke's actions, such as the execution of Richard's advisors as well as Bolingbroke's desire to journey to the Holy Land to atone for Richard's death, are all informed by his sense of moral responsibility, Baines asserts.
C. G. Thayer, on the other hand, focuses on Bolingbroke's silence. In many instances, Thayer observes, the audience is left to make assumptions about Bolingbroke's actions, but we are not told what he is thinking or what his plans are. Thayer suggests that since the historical Richard II was often compared with Queen Elizabeth in the later years of her rule, perhaps Shakespeare was being cautious by not making Bolingbroke's motivations more explicit, by not suggesting that his actions were justified or that Richard's downfall was God's will.

Barbara J. Baines

SOURCE: "Kingship of the Silent King: A Study of Shakespeare's Bolingbroke," in *English Studies*, Vol. 61, No. 1, February, 1980, pp. 24-31.

[In the essay that follows, Baines analyzes what she identifies as Shakespeare's sympathetic portrayal of Bolingbroke, stressing that the dominant theme of the play is not Bolingbroke's ambition, but Richard's incompetence. Baines traces Bolingbroke's actions throughout the play, demonstrating the moral justification for his decisions and activities.]

Few, if any, characters in the Shakespeare canon evoke such diverse and strong emotional response as the key figures of the second tetralogy: Richard II, Bolingbroke, and Hal. They are of course fascinating psychological portraits, but their special appeal derives from the political and moral issues which they dramatize. Together they present Shakespeare's courageous exploration of the controversial subject, kingship: the right to reign, the use and abuse of power, and the reciprocal responsibility of sovereign and subject. In these three kings whose fortunes and identities are inextricably linked, the playwright dramatizes the formidable conflict between political necessity and Christian morality. This conflict, which gives the plays their singular vitality, is part of what Michael Manheim has defined as the 'weak-king dilemma' and what Moody Prior, relying on Friedrich Meinecke, has called the dilemma of *raison d'état*. That Bolingbroke's behavior often demonstrates Machiavelli's precepts of political necessity has been irrefutably demonstrated in the past and again recently. But the significance of this behavior in the minds of Bolingbroke and his creator has never been satisfactorily resolved. The complexity of the political-moral issues of the tetralogy is, therefore, most evident in this ambiguous, keystone figure who, like his heir, demonstrates the cardinal virtues requisite of a king. Bolingbroke's triumph, through the glory of his heir, is made possible by a pragmatic acceptance of the tenuous balance between the claims of political necessity and Christian ethics. I hope to demonstrate that Shakespeare's attitude toward Bolingbroke is much more sympathetic than critics have been willing to acknowledge and that this sympathy underscores the playwright's very realistic attitude toward kingship.

We know of course that the Tudor establishment, like Richard, expounded the theory of the divine right of kings and the incontestability or virtual infallibility of the king body politic. The Tudor concept of kingship and the subject's obedience is so pervasive and eloquently expressed that, as G. R. Elton notes, 'theories of kingship which stressed the rights of subjects and the dominance of law have tended to be overlooked in the dazzling light of God-granted authority'. But the fact remains that these conflicting theories did exist, and it is not likely that Shakespeare would have overlooked them. The struggle between Richard and Bolingbroke for the crown shows clearly that he did not. *Richard II* presents both the Lancastrian sympathetic interpretation of Bolingbroke's motives and actions and the Yorkist view of Bolingbroke as hypocrite and despicable traitor. Robert Ornstein has recently pointed out that Holinshed, Shakespeare's primary source, presents essentially a Yorkist view, one that stresses the principle of legitimacy too strongly to have been much comfort to the Tudor monarchs and thus had to be qualified or balanced by the playwright with the Lancastrian view. For many readers the fascination and pathos evoked by Richard in the last two acts tend to overshadow the Lancastrian argument. I would like to argue here that the justification of Richard's deposition, if we consider the entire tetralogy and give adequate attention to the first three acts of *Richard II*, is more important to an accurate assessment of the political statement of the plays than the tragic suffering of Richard. In light of the complexity of conflicting ideas about kingship, the singular nature of Bolingbroke— the morally accountable Machiavellian prince— takes on new significance.

How Bolingbroke acquires the crown is of course a crucial issue in any assessment of the character. Richard II loses the crown because he denies the principle and laws upon which his right to the crown rests. York, who, along with Gaunt, supports the theory of the divine right of kings, points out that Richard denies his own legal right when he denies Bolingbroke's rightful inheritance. The destruction of the hereditary order in the duchy of Lancaster prefigures the destruction of the hereditary order in larger England. It is Richard, not Bolingbroke, who causes this destruction. Richard has disturbed the old order of possession by insisting that possession of the crown means possession of Gaunt's estate. Ironically enough, he discovers that he must live by the new order of possession which he has himself created and sanctioned. The crown and the Lancastrian estate do in fact go hand-in-hand— not because Bolingbroke is a usurper but because Richard has inadvertently disinherited himself through a series of crimes. Disregard for royal blood, for the offspring of King Edward, has already become a practice before the action of the play begins, in the cruel murder of Thomas Woodstock, Duke of Gloucester. The strongest condemnation of Richard, 'Landlord of England art thou now, not king, / Thy state of law is bondslave to the law', calls to mind the worst of his sins as they are depicted in the anonymous *Woodstock*. Accordingly, Richard's fate and the justice of that fate are clearly prophesied by the dying Gaunt:

> O, had thy grandsire, with a prophet's eye,
> Seen how his son's son should destroy his
>   sons,
> From forth thy reach he would have laid thy
>   shame,
> Deposing thee before thou wert possessed,
> Which art possessed now to depose thyself.
>   (II.i.104-8)

What Gaunt is describing here is not usurpation but self-deposition. Moreover, he considers the act already accomplished ('Landlord of England art thou *now*, not king') before Bolingbroke's return from exile. Richard's crimes, not Bolingbroke's, dictate Gaunt's final address to Richard not as king but as 'my brother Edward's son' (II.i.124).

Bolingbroke receives the crown as a result of his morally sanctioned demand for his inheritance. The first crucial question, then, in an evaluation of Bolingbroke's policy and ethics is whether or not he has a right to return to

England to claim and defend his inheritance. Even as a loyal supporter of the establishment, York reveals that he is torn between two loyalties: one to the state, the other to his conscience:

> . . . Both are my kinsmen.
> Th'one is my sovereign, whom both my oath
> And duty bids defend; t'other again
> Is my kinsman, whom the king hath
>   wronged,
> Whom conscience and kindred bids to right.
>   (II.ii.111-15)

What is significant here is that duty and oath of office (aspects of political necessity) speak for Richard, whereas conscience speaks for Bolingbroke. To York's blustering accusations (II.iii.87-111) Bolingbroke appeals to the obligation of kinship, but what is more important, he asserts his right by law:

> I am denied to sue my livery here,
> And yet my letters patents give me leave.
> My father's goods are all distrained and sold;
> And these, and all, are all amiss employed.
> What would you have me do? I am a subject,
> And I challenge law. Attorneys are denied me,
> And therefore personally I lay claim
> To my inheritance of free descent.
>   (II.iii.129-35)

But the rigidly idealistic York insists that the end, however justifiable, will not in this case justify the means. He will not exonerate Bolingbroke's attempt 'to find out right with wrong'. At the same time, York can offer no viable alternative to Bolingbroke's action; to the pragmatic question, 'What would you have me do?' he has no answer. This failure best explains York's impotence and the metaphoric appropriateness of his intention to remain 'neuter' (1. 159). The impotence of York (who is, after all, the King's Regent) underscores the necessity of the course taken by Bolingbroke.

Although Bolingbroke's action is morally justified, his motives and intentions remain a mystery; he never confides in the audience or in another character. There is ample evidence that Bolingbroke, from the beginning, anticipates the necessity of restricting drastically or else abolishing altogether Richard's authority. The idea of merely reforming or limiting Richard's power would hardly seem feasible to the realistic Bolingbroke. He knows that Richard is an absolutist and that any form of resistance or criticism would not be tolerated. The fact that Richard is responsible for the death of Gloucester is from the beginning no secret in the Lancaster household. Bolingbroke knows, therefore, that his challenge to Richard's faithful servant Mowbray is, in fact, a challenge to Richard himself. Richard evidently recognizes the thinly disguised challenge when he accuses Bolingbroke of 'sky-aspiring and ambitious

Act V, scene v Exton, Richard II, and servant. By Abraham Cooper (1826).

thoughts' (I.iii.130). The only easy way out is the unjust banishment of both men. The sudden, dramatic, and unjust decision to banish both lords is, in Bolingbroke's consciousness, sufficient example of Richard's intolerable abuse of absolute power. Compromise and reconciliation, therefore, could hardly seem a likelihood in Bolingbroke's mind when he returns from France.

It is highly probable, then, that the silent Bolingbroke at this early point— that is, before Richard confiscates the Lancaster estate— already intends a final confrontation with Richard. The time sequence of Act II, scene i, is deliberately ambiguous. It is impossible to tell whether Bolingbroke has had time to receive the news of the confiscation of his inheritance before he sets sail from Brittany with the eight tall ships. The confiscation of the Lancaster estate may not be the primary cause for Bolingbroke's return, but certainly it is a primary factor in Richard's self-deposition. Bolingbroke's defense of his refusal to accept banishment (II.iii.113-36) is fundamentally an accusation of Richard rather than an explanation of his own motives.

Part of the ambiguity of Bolingbroke's motives and intentions derives from the role of resistance which he has chosen. From the beginning he prepares for what he knows will be Richard's ultimate mistake; the eight tall ships are waiting. Whether or not they actually sailed before Bolingbroke received news that Richard had confiscated the Lancastrian estate is ultimately of little importance. Bolingbroke has already been denied justice at the moment of his banishment, and he knows that Richard will continue, in some form or other, the pattern of injustice. When he returns to claim his rights, he is claiming more than his title and property. He is claiming the right which, according to one theory of kingship, every Englishman has— the right to be governed by a responsible king.

Bolingbroke does not reveal his plans because he still is not certain how far his confrontation will have to go or should go; a great deal depends upon how Richard behaves. There is no reason to believe that Bolingbroke is being hypocritical when he assures York that he does not intend to oppose himself against the will of heaven (III.iii.18-19). He does not define at this point what he thinks the will of heaven is because he does not know; Richard's behavior will, to a great extent, clarify the question. In the crucial confrontation scene (III.iii), Bolingbroke quickly kneels before Richard and declares, 'My gracious lord, I come but for mine own'. But Richard recognizes (as we should by now) that what Bolingbroke's 'own' is has not been defined by Bolingbroke; certainly among other things it includes the right to just government. Richard answers, 'Your own is yours, and I am yours, and all'. The reality of the situation is ultimately shaped by the mind of Richard, not by the action of Bolingbroke. Richard's followers have tried to direct his mind away from the madness of despair toward constructive action against Bolingbroke. But the prophecy of old John of Gaunt, who described Richard as one 'which art possessed now to depose thyself', proves to be an accurate statement of the will of heaven.

Another crucial matter to be dealt with in any evaluation of Bolingbroke is his execution of those 'caterpillars of the commonwealth', Bushy and Greene. This action has been interpreted as Machiavellian political necessity to assure the capitulation of Richard (Ribner, pp. 181-2). One certainly cannot help recalling this execution scene when much later Bolingbroke on his deathbed alludes to the 'by-paths and indirect crooked ways' to the throne (*2 Henry IV,* IV.v.184). But if we look closely at the situation in *Richard II* we see that the playwright has created ample grounds to justify Bolingbroke's behavior. By their own admission Bushy and Greene have emptied the purses of the commons (II.ii.129-32) and earned their hatred. The straightforward nature of Bolingbroke's statement of intention 'to weed and pluck away' the King's parasites and the assumption that he will have the Regent's authority supporting him (II.iii.162-6) imply a strong moral justification for his judgment and execution of the King's men. York certainly voices no objection to the idea that these men deserve to be executed. His reluctance apparently again concerns Bolingbroke's methods: 'It may be

I will go with you; but yet I'll pause, / For I am loath to break our country's laws' (II.iii.168-9). York freely chooses to go with Bolingbroke because he realizes that although Bolingbroke's methods may be questionable, the end result, the good of the commonwealth, is not.

More important than York's response to Bolingbroke's ministration of justice is that of his gardener in the emblematic garden scene (III.iv). The gardener's man asks:

> Why should we, in the compass of a pale,
> Keep law and form and due proportion,
> Showing, as in a model, our firm estate,
> When our sea-walled garden, the whole land,
> Is full of weeds, her fairest flowers choked up,
> Her fruit trees all unpruned, her hedges ruined,
> Her knots disordered, and her wholesome herbs
> Swarming with caterpillars?
>
> (40-7)

This question does more than simply define the emblematic correspondences; it suggests that order on a secondary or personal level (within 'the compass of a pale') has little meaning when there is no order on the primary or national level (within 'the sea-walled garden'). The question implies that there is very little motivation to achieve moral order on the personal level when none exists on a national level. The gardener is able to satisfy this complaint and affirm the necessity for private order because Bolingbroke has acted to restore national order. It may well be that on his deathbed Bolingbroke still has the blood of Bushy and Greene on his hands, but their execution is clearly a part of the establishment of order and justice in the kingdom, without which the sea-walled garden would go to ruin.

Bolingbroke's ministration of justice continues with an effort to identify those involved in the murder of Gloucester (IV.i). This scene, which parallels the opening scene of the play in which Richard presides over the challenge brought by Bolingbroke against Mowbray, dramatizes Bolingbroke's sincere desire for the truth but even more clearly reveals that Bolingbroke already wields the power of arbitrator and judge, the power of *de facto* king. Bolingbroke's willingness to hear and weigh all evidence and his willingness to repeal Mowbray's banishment sharply contrast with the whimsical, capricious behavior of Richard in the earlier comparable situation. The disruptive intrusion by York to announce that Richard has abdicated and declared Bolingbroke his heir suggests clearly that the right to power goes hand-in-hand with the ability to use it properly. This point is made again through Bolingbroke by the gratitude and respect shown York, the mercy shown Aumerle (V.iii.59-66), and the tolerance shown Carlisle (V.vi.24-29).

Thus the dominant theme of *Richard II* is the incompetence of Richard, not the ambition of Bolingbroke. We sympathize with Richard, the man, in Acts IV and V, but earlier in the play we see Richard, the King, in the cold light of his incompetence and crimes. The comparison which Richard draws between himself and 'glistering Phaeton' (III.iii.178-79) is intended as a criticism of 'unruly jades'— those who challenge the king's authority. The comparison, however, turns ironically on Richard, since in the myth it is Phaeton's presumption and incompetence which threaten the cosmic order. Richard discovers that he is but a mortal— that he is neither sun-god nor Christ. In the mirror episode (IV.i) the myths which Richard has created fade in the harsh light of truth. He sees in the mirror not the image of the king body politic but the image of a simple man. The image in the mirror is a much more accurate reflection of Richard's sins than any confession which Northumberland could draw up. The recognition of his mortal face forces an acknowledgment that Richard has unfortunately never made during his reign. The history he reads in the glass is one of folly: 'Was this the face that faced so many follies / And was at last outfaced by Bolingbroke?' (IV.i.285-86). In this moment of truth Richard does not use the word 'usurped' or 'deposed' but instead uses the word, 'outfaced', which is an accurate description of Bolingbroke's behavior and an important indicator of the author's attitudes toward both characters.

Richard's incompetence is stressed also by Shakespeare's deviation from his main source. In Holinshed's account of Richard's fall, Northumberland captures Richard by tricking him into an ambush. Richard is then firmly persuaded by advisors to agree to a peaceful abdication. In Shakespeare's play Richard rejects the course of resistance offered by Aumerle and Carlisle and retires to Flint Castle, where he quickly and without advice acknowledges Bolingbroke as king. Shakespeare's Richard clearly has an alternative to abdication. The alternative would require that he acknowledge the injustice of some of his decisions. But Richard, obsessed with the idea of his divine right and virtual infallibility, cannot bend to such a compromise. Since Richard will not change, his abdication is essential to the well-being of the nation. Its strategic location between Richard's surrender at Flint Castle and Bolingbroke's acceptance of the crown at Westminster makes the emblematic garden scene again crucial. The gardener may be sympathetic with the fallen king, but his main point and the point of the scene is that the garden must be tended. Bolingbroke understands this fundamental principle of kingship; Richard does not— at least not in time to save his crown.

Bolingbroke's competence as it contrasts with Richard's incompetence does not go unnoticed by the conservative York. As he observes the unfolding of events,

York moves from suspicion and censure, to ambivalence, finally to complete acceptance of Bolingbroke as rightful sovereign. He can with good conscience shift his allegiance from Richard to Bolingbroke because Richard 'with willing soul' has adopted Bolingbroke as his heir (IV.i.108). York is willing to accept Bolingbroke as king for still another and perhaps more important reason. He realizes that fortune favors Bolingbroke; he has the support of the lords and the parliament and has found no positive resistance in Richard. Circumstances therefore indicate to York that Bolingbroke truly has not opposed the will of heaven. Since in Act V, scene ii, York is alone in his own home with his wife, he has no reason for saying something which he does not truly believe. He describes the joyous reception of Bolingbroke and the public contempt for Richard. Moved to compassion by Richard's suffering, he nevertheless concludes

> That, had not God for some strong purpose steeled
> The hearts of men, they must perforce have melted,
> And barbarism itself have pitied him.
> But heaven hath a hand in these events,
> To whose high will we bound our calm contents.
> To Bolingbroke are we sworn subjects now,
> Whose state and honour I for aye allow.
> (V.ii.34-40)

York's loyalty to Bolingbroke— a loyalty which York considers divinely sanctioned— is put to the supreme test by Aumerle's involvement in the conspiracy to murder Bolingbroke.

York's providential view of Richard's fall and Bolingbroke's rise is reinforced years later by Bolingbroke's interpretation of the events and his motives for accepting the crown:

> Though then, God knows, I had no such intent
> But that necessity so bowed the state
> That I and greatness were compell'd to kiss . . .
> (*2 Henry IV*, III.i.72-74)

Compelling necessity was his motive, not ambition. When Henry IV contemplates Northumberland's treachery, he remembers that Richard accurately predicted the situation. Warwick explains that Richard foresaw Northumberland's treachery, not because he had any supernatural perception or influence, but because he comprehended an easily discernible pattern in Northumberland's nature. The disorder which Bolingbroke faces as king is a result of a constant principle in human nature. Necessity cries out in the case of Northumberland's treachery, as it did in the case of Richard's incompetence, and Bolingbroke prepares himself once more to meet that political necessity (*2 Henry IV*, III.i.92-94). The point of Northumberland's rebellion is not that rebellion begets rebellion, but that a king proves his competence and thus his right to rule by his capacity to deal with rebellion.

But with all of his competence, Bolingbroke is still a human being, subject to weakness and sin, even in his role as king. In a moment of weakness he voices his wish for Richard's death. Exton, who makes the wish a reality, reminds Bolingbroke, 'From your own mouth, my lord, did I this deed' (*Richard II*, V.vi.37). Bolingbroke does not deny this assertion, nor does he try to justify Richard's murder on the grounds of political necessity. As a morally responsible individual, Bolingbroke acknowledges his guilt and promises expiation: 'I'll make a voyage to the Holy Land, / To wash this blood off from my guilty hand' (V.vi.49-50). Unlike Machiavelli's model prince, Bolingbroke acknowledges the importance of reconciling political necessity with Christian morality. That he hopes to achieve expiation and at the same time 'busy giddy minds with foreign quarrels' does not imply religious hypocrisy, but a pragmatism consistent with the nature of this character. What is important is his refusal to dismiss the moral issue altogether and his awareness that all of his actions will be judged by the failure or success of his reign and by his capacity to perpetuate his reign through his heir. . . .

C. G. Thayer

SOURCE: "The Silent King: Providential Intervention, Fair Sequence and Succession," in *Shakespearean Politics: Government and Misgovernment in the Great Histories*, Ohio University Press, 1983, pp. 62-70.

[*In the following excerpt, Thayer examines Bolingbroke's silence regarding the motivations for his actions. Thayer suggests several reasons why Shakespeare omitted such crucial information and suggests that the result of such omissions is that Shakespeare "cleans up" the image of the historical Bolingbroke.*]

One of the most striking facts about the Bolingbroke of *Richard II* is that at critical points he does not tell us what he is thinking about or what he plans to do. He takes important actions that must certainly have been based on hard decisions— or so it would seem; but the decisions we hear him utter are almost redundant: "In God's name I'll ascend the regal throne" (IV.i.113); "On Wednesday next we solemnly set down/Our coronation" (IV.i.249-250). But he has been acting king since act III, scene i at least (the sentencing of Bushy and Greene). He has no soliloquies and no confidants in *Richard II* (and only one real soliloquy and two confidants in *Henry IV*, Warwick and Westmoreland, with whom he mainly discusses his son, not affairs of state). Unique among the great Shakespearean, Jonsonian, and

Marlovian conspirators, tragic or comic, he keeps his motives and decisions to himself, so much so that we might be justified in asking to what extent he is actively engaged in a conspiracy at all. It would be unreasonable to require stage conspirators to confide in their victims, but they all confide in audiences in soliloquies or inform them through talk with their fellow conspirators or, like Claudius in *Hamlet*, reflect on their crimes and on what they have gained or lost by them. Shakespeare obviously found political conspiracy of more than routine interest, and he represented some fascinating ones on the stage; but Bolingbroke seems almost to be engaged in a private conspiracy of silence.

We assume that Bolingbroke has something definite in mind when, in the first scene of *Richard II*, he accuses Mowbray of a staggering array of treasons, the murder of Gloucester being the most important. No doubt we can safely assume that he is somehow getting at Richard, who bears the major guilt in Gloucester's death; and we naturally assume that Bolingbroke knows about Richard's guilt, since everyone else seems to. But these are merely assumptions based on hindsight: Bolingbroke himself says nothing about Richard's responsibility until act IV. To most of us it is simply inconceivable that Bolingbroke's charges are directed solely against Mowbray, but nothing in the play's opening scene tells us anything else. We are, perhaps, invited to guess at what he actually has in mind when he makes his accusation; but he doesn't talk about it, not even with his father, before going into exile, even though, in view of what has been happening, Gaunt might have expressed some curiosity about what his son has been up to. Gaunt was conspicuously present when the charges were made ("Old John of Gaunt, time-honoured Lancaster"— I.i.1), yet when father and son part for the last time (at the end of I.iii), the talk is about the sorrows of exile and how to lighten them. These facts are particularly striking in view of the substance of act I, scene ii— the absolute necessity of passive obedience. Presumably, Gaunt has not perceived what his son has been up to, and we should therefore be cautious in making our own assumptions.

It is important to remember that the King's responsibility for Gloucester's death was so clearly established in the chronicles and in *Woodstock* (an understandably anonymous play much more openly emphatic than Shakespeare's play in its condemnation of Richard) that it can hardly have been a mystery to many people watching the play.

Again, and even more important, at the end of act II, scene i when we learn from Northumberland that the just-disinherited Bolingbroke is returning from exile equipped for an invasion ("eight tall ships, three thousand men of war" [II.i.286]), it does not require great subtlety of mind to see that he must have decided to do what in fact he does. Both Hall and Holinshed describe widespread hatred of Richard and a movement to recall Bolingbroke, a movement so vast as to suggest something more like a popular mandate than a plot. Yet in the play, all, or almost all, is silence. We don't know when Bolingbroke decided to return or the details of his decision, in spite of that decision's overwhelming importance. Shakespeare maintains silence on the subject when anyone who could read might well have known the story and might well have been puzzled by the omissions. The conditions of Bolingbroke's decision should be of consuming interest, and that interest is systematically frustrated. One may argue that actions speak louder than words, but on this subject some words would clarify something that we must assume Shakespeare did not want to clarify. A major part of the action of four plays arises from a decision, made in Brittany, by a principal character; and about the circumstances of that decision, as opposed to its outcome, we really know nothing— hence all the guesswork, some of it demonstrably bad.

In fact, we don't know when he made his decision— before or after his father's death and his own disinheriting— although it is possible that on this matter we can make something like a passable assumption. The problem is familiar: we learn that Bolingbroke is on his way home at the end of the same scene (II.i.277 f.) that contains the death of Gaunt and the disinheriting of the man who was his rightful heir "by fair sequence and succession." We are shown a good reason for Bolingbroke to return, and then we learn that he has embarked before (presumably) that reason existed. At least that's the way it looks to most readers, and perhaps that is the way it sounded to contemporary audiences. But Shakespeare's chronological games are notorious, like those of most of his fellow playwrights, and I do not think it is self-evident that Shakespeare intends his audience to see Bolingbroke jumping the gun: at this point, it is almost a relief to know that he is on his way. Perhaps this is why Shakespeare has Northumberland specify "eight tall ships, three thousand men of war." Holinshed, in his amiable way, repeats conflicting reports: "fifteen lances" or "not past threescore persons" or the force specified by Northumberland (Hosley, pp. 76-77). In view of the outrage just perpetrated by Richard, eight tall ships and three thousand men of war seem appropriate. Bolingbroke's return with fifteen or thirty chums would be less likely to raise the spirits. It is certainly possible that "Shakespeare's strategy makes Bolingbroke's return morally ambiguous," but I suspect that an audience is less likely going to be troubled by the chronology and what it implies than is the curious reader. One other odd detail: when Bolingbroke arrives, the text does not give us the impression that he has an army with him; he *appears* to have arrived more or less alone, although we must no doubt assume that he didn't. Then, as in Holinshed, his friends begin to gather— not all of them the sort of friends one would choose if the choice were

wider. The information that he is coming with an army indicates that Richard will have his work cut out for him; if we then get the impression that Bolingbroke arrives alone, there will be a clear contrast with Richard on his return from Ireland, with Richard's friends forsaking him as rapidly as Bolingbroke's assemble. (The most specific statement about a popular uprising comes, briefly, from Scroope, III.ii.104-120. It's interesting to hear about, but we don't see it— one of many instances of Shakespeare's version of show-and-tell, not-show-and-tell, show-and-not-tell.)

Even if we assume, however, that Bolingbroke has embarked for England before hearing of his father's death and his own disinheriting, there is on the face of it nothing particularly surprising about his return (unless surprise must spring from violations of Tudor notions of obedience), just as there was nothing notably just about his banishment— Richard's alternative to a duel that would have actually settled something. The banishment was no doubt legal enough, but in King Richard's England, under the circumstances associated with his notions of kingship, legality and justice aren't necessarily the same, just as positive laws generally have no necessary and automatic connection with considerations of right and wrong. At worst, Richard's grand larceny provides a *post hoc* justification for Bolingbroke's decision to return home (just as the Dauphin's providential tennis balls provided King Harry the fifth with a legitimate reason to go to war with France— they are a challenge to a duel and as such are a good deal more convincing a motive than is Canterbury's exposition of the Salic Law, which may justify a claim on the French throne but not a war to make the claim good). Everyone has seen that Bolingbroke has extraordinary luck at key points on his way to the crown (e.g., Richard's proximity, in Flint Castle). Whatever his original intentions in returning from exile with a small army and navy, Richard or God or providence provided a nearly unanswerable argument. If he intended to return as a rebel with ambitions for the crown, Richard, by his unadvised violation of fair sequence and succession, has made him a rebel with a cause, a cause with which almost anyone else can easily sympathize.

It is precisely when Richard casually, and with some lack of sensitivity, disinherits his cousin and ignores York's instructive protests that one is likely to run definitively out of patience with him. And it is in that scene that we learn just how serious his situation is likely to become, just how swift and condign [well-deserved] the retribution is likely to be. Shakespeare has made it easy for any member of an audience to regard Northumberland's good news as providential— just as both Hall and Holinshed thought they saw the hand of providence at work in the rise of Bolingbroke and the fall of Richard (Hosley, p. 81). However we interpret the timing of events in act II, scene i, it is clear enough that Richard has misbehaved prodigiously and that hot vengeance is on the way, and that point, I think, is underscored by Bolingbroke's silence. We can guess all we want about his specific reasons for returning, but Shakespeare makes such guessing more or less irrelevant. It would have been another matter if he had shown the Archbishop of Canterbury negotiating a coup with Bolingbroke (as historically he did) or Bolingbroke sitting down to discuss strategy with the Duke of Brittany or Sir Thomas Erpingham, but that is exactly what he does not show us. Bolingbroke does not even discuss strategy with Northumberland; when the time comes, he simply sends him to Richard with an unanswerable ultimatum.

We may ask why Shakespeare is so reticent about specifying the idea of providential intervention since Hall and Holinshed have already led the way. But they were not writing a tendentious play about the justifiable deposition of a rightful king. And after giving us an almost interminable list of Richard's shortcomings as king, Holinshed can say, with his characteristic lovable idiocy, that Richard "was a prince the most unthankfully used of his subjects of any one of whom ye shall lightly read" (Hosley, p.89). Perhaps Holinshed thought such a *pro forma* protestation was necessary, although it certainly doesn't amount to much; but in any case, he was writing an enormous and not wholly exciting chronicle in rather soporific prose, not a play for the public stage, about a king who was compared with Elizabeth during the later years of her reign. Some of Bolingbroke's silences are probably Shakespeare's as well (and, as we know, the deposition scene was omitted from the first two quartos of the play), understandable and discreet silences. If people are comparing Elizabeth with Richard, one had better not specify that Richard's fall was providential.

There is another possible reason for considerable caution on this subject. As we have seen, Robert Persons paid his negative compliments to the idea of the King's Two Bodies in *A Conference about the Next Succession to the Crown of England* (1594). In the same work, he describes how providence manifests itself through rebellion against tyrannical or incompetent rulers and then often provides better rulers than those deposed. In all Christian realms, princes have been deposed

> for just causes, and . . . God hath concurred and assisted wonderfully the same, sending them commonly very good kings after those that were deprived, and in no country more than in England it selfe, yea in the very lyne and familye of this king Richard, whose noble grandfather king Edward the third was exalted to the crowne by a most solemne deposition of his predecessor king Edward the second, wherefore in this point there can be little controversie. [p. 62]

And

> I know not whether every man here have considered the same, to wit that God hath wonderfully concurred for the most part, with such judicial acts of the commonwealth agaynst their cruel Princes, not only in prospering the same, but by giving them also commonly some notable successor in place of the deposed, thereby to justify the fact, and to remedy the faulte of him that went before. . . . God disposeth of kingdomes and worketh his wil in Princes affayres as he pleaseth. [pp. 33-34]

It seems to me that Shakespeare takes the same view, differing perhaps on a very minor point: God sent a king as good as a king could be under the circumstances and that king was succeeded by one of Persons's and Shakespeare's "very good kings," a wonderful concurrence and assistance in a judicial act of the commonwealth. I assume that Shakespeare was familiar with some of Persons's work (it certainly caused a sensation when it appeared in England), but he needn't have gone to Persons for the view that the first two Lancastrian kings were superior to Richard II.

But Shakespeare is not wholly silent on the subject of providential intervention: he does raise it once, in York's familiar account of Bolingbroke's and Richard's riding into London. The crowd received Bolingbroke with cheers, but not Richard:

> No man cried "God save him!"
> No joyful tongue gave him his welcome home,
> But dust was thrown upon his sacred head;
> Which with such gentle sorrow he shook off,
> His face still combating with tears and smiles,
> The badges of his grief and patience,
> That had not God for some strong purpose steel'd
> The hearts of men, they must perforce have melted,
> And barbarism itself have pitied him.
> But heaven hath a hand in these events,
> To Bolingbroke are we sworn subjects now,
> Whose state and honor I for aye allow.
>
> (V.ii.28-40)

This passage, with its seemingly perfunctory concluding couplet, is often attributed simply to York's weakness, but since he has been established throughout the play as a kind of reflector for audience responses to both Richard and Bolingbroke, I see no reason why he should be deprived of that function now, even though he is shortly to be involved in a spectacle of low comedy. Richard is an object of pity, but God had "some strong purpose," and "heaven hath a hand in these events." If we can believe York here, we can easily enough believe that the same agencies, under the general rubric of providence, had also been at work earlier, all along, since all those other events prepared the way for this sad but necessary sight. To pity Richard is not to wish him to resume his throne.

Another silence is rather different from the ones just discussed. The so-called Doncaster oath was to be of some importance historically. Holinshed tells us, in his engaging way, that when Bolingbroke returned from exile he swore (at Doncaster) to Northumberland, Sir Henry Percy (Hotspur), and Westmoreland "that he would demand no more but the lands that were to him descended by inheritance from his father and in right of his wife" (Hosley, p. 77). "Moreover, he undertook to cause the payment of taxes and tallages to be laid down, and to bring the King to good government" (p. 77). One detects a certain inconsistency here. More important, this account follows one in which the same historian describes how "divers of the nobility, as well prelates as other, and likewise many of the magistrates and rulers of the cities, towns, and commonalty . . . devised, with great deliberation and considerate advice, to send and signify unto Duke Henry [Bolingbroke], . . . requiring him with all convenient speed to convey himself into England; promising him all their aid, power, and assistance if he, expelling King Richard as a man not meet for the office he bore, would take upon him the scepter, rule, and diadem of his native land and region" (Hosley, p. 76). After *that*, the Doncaster oath doesn't amount to much, and in *1 Henry IV* it is used against the King only by men who might be described as having interested motives.

Maybe it was politically discreet for the historical Bolingbroke to swear his oath in public to the magnates who were to help him to the throne. It was even more discreet for Shakespeare's Bolingbroke to do nothing of the sort. His only comment on that subject is to York: "As I was banish'd, I was banish'd Herford; / But as I come, I come for Lancaster" (II.iii.112-113)— an ambiguous statement, perhaps, but no oath, and since the founder of the Tudor dynasty claimed, not with total candor, to be of Lancastrian (as well as Arthurian) descent, and therefore to be restoring the house of Lancaster to the throne, a statement like "I come for Lancaster" could have its own peculiar and complex resonances. The Doncaster oath put the historical Bolingbroke in the wrong since it is well known that all politicians must and do keep their promises. For Shakespeare's Bolingbroke, such an oath would be not only untrue but also superfluous: you don't invade your native country without some notion of putting yourself in charge. Shakespeare, therefore, has Northumberland allude to the oath, with no great precision of language, at II.iii.147-150 and III.iii.103-120, and Northumberland is a notable liar, here and in the two plays that follow. (For Bolingbroke he is a useful liar but a liar anyhow.) Shifting the blame to Northumberland is another way in which Shakespeare cleans up

the historical Bolingbroke. In *Richard II* and *1 Henry IV* the Doncaster oath becomes a fiction of Northumberland's, not a lie of Bolingbroke's. The whole business is worth some reflection: Shakespeare cleans up Bolingbroke, but he is to be seen, obviously enough, in the context of human political standards, not of impossible moral absolutes. As with his son, the measure by which he is to be judged is human, nothing else. There are, of course, different kinds of politicians— Richard and Bolingbroke, for example.

SOURCES FOR FURTHER STUDY

Literary Commentary

Baker, Herschel. "*Richard II*." In *The Riverside Shakespeare*, edited by G. Blakemore Evans, pp. 800-04. Boston: Houghton Mifflin Company, 1974.

> Discusses the sources Shakespeare used to write *Richard II* and offers a brief introduction to the play's plot, main themes, and characters.

Black, James. "The Interlude of the Beggar and the King in *Richard II*." In *Pageantry in the Shakespearean Theater*, edited by David M. Bergeron, pp. 104-13. Athens: University of Georgia Press, 1985.

> Maintains that the comic interlude in which Aumerle's plot against Bolingbroke is discovered does not undercut the play's seriousness but rather emphasizes that seriousness through contrast.

Clare, Janet. "The Censorship of the Deposition Scene in *Richard II*." *Review of English Studies* XLI, No. 161 (February 1990): 89-94.

> Examines the evidence supporting the theory that the deposition scene was censored out of contemporary productions of *Richard II* for its political subversiveness.

Cohen, Derek. "The Containment of Monarchy: *Richard II*." In *Shakespeare's Culture of Violence*, pp. 10-29. New York: St. Martin's Press, 1993.

> Explores the effect on the monarchy of the assassinations and revolution in *Richard II*.

Friedman, Donald M. "John of Gaunt and the Rhetoric of Frustration." *ELH* 43, No. 3 (Fall 1976): 279-99.

> Challenges the traditional reading of Gaunt's deathbed speech, which is typically viewed as a patriotic set-piece that supports orthodox Tudor political doctrine.

Frye, Northrop. "The Bolingbroke Plays (*Richard II*, *Henry IV*)." In *Northrop Frye on Shakespeare*, edited by Robert Sandler, pp. 51-81. New Haven: Yale University Press, 1986.

> Offers a brief discussion of the lineage of those English monarchs relevant to *Richard II* and the rest of the

tetralogy. Frye then examines Shakespeare's presentation of the claims to the throne of the houses of York and Lancaster, and the legitimacy of the Tudor line. Frye emphasizes that Shakespeare's concern in *Richard II* is not really history, but rather the "personal actions and interactions of the people at the top of the social order."

Gurr, Andrew. Introduction to *King Richard II*, by William Shakespeare, pp. 1-52. Cambridge: Cambridge University Press, 1984.

Provides a detailed overview of the play, including discussion of the date of composition of the play; the influence of and references to contemporary history; the sources from which Shakespeare drew; the play's structure, imagery, and language; and staging issues.

Hunter, Edwin. R. "Shakspere's Intentions Regarding King Richard II." In *Shakspere and Common Sense*, pp. 31-48. Boston: The Christopher Publishing House, 1954.

Examines Shakespeare's characterization of Richard II, arguing that Shakespeare intended Richard's dominant characteristics to be "a bent for self-dramatization" and "a theatrical habit of mind," which, in several scenes "comes dangerously near to the grotesque."

Jensen, Pamela K. "Beggars and Kings: Cowardice and Courage in Shakespeare's *Richard II*." *Interpretations* 18, No. 1 (Fall 1990): 111-43.

Focuses on Richard's fall and Bolingbroke's rise to power, charging that Richard's abuse of power "provokes Bolingbroke's challenge," and that Richard gives in to Bolingbroke without attempting to defend himself.

Kehler, Dorothea. "King of Tears: Mortality in *Richard II*." *Rocky Mountain Review of Language and Literature* 39, No. 1 (1985): 7-18.

Studies the "death-centered world" of Richard, arguing that our own fears of death often prevent us from thoroughly examining the sympathy Richard draws.

MacIsaac, Warren J. "The Three Cousins in *Richard II*." *Shakespeare Quarterly* XXII, No. 2 (Spring 1971): 137-46.

Analyzes the relationships and power struggles among Richard and his cousins, Aumerle and Bolingbroke.

Maus, Katharine Eisaman. "*Richard II*." In *The Norton Shakespeare: Based on the Oxford Edition*, edited by Stephen Greenblatt, pp. 943-51. New York: W. W. Norton & Company, Inc., 1997.

Offers an overview of the play, discussing Shakespeare's sources, the play's relation to Elizabethan history and views, and the play's plot, themes, and characters.

Moore, Jeanie Grant. "Queen of Sorrow, King of Grief: Reflections and Perspectives in *Richard II*." In *In Another Country: Feminist Perspectives on Renaissance Drama*, edited by Dorothea Kehler and Susan Baker, pp. 19-35. Metuchen, N.J.: The Scarecrow Press, Inc., 1991.

Studies the significance of Queen Isabel in *Richard II*, examining the way in which she both emphasizes important issues in the drama and serves as a "mirror of Richard." Moore maintains that through Isabel, we are allowed a new understanding of Richard's experience.

Palmer, John. "Richard of Bordeaux." In *Political Characters of Shakespeare*, pp. 118-79. London: Macmillan and Co., Limited, 1945.

Analyzes the political significance and ramifications of *Richard II*, maintaining that the political aspects of the play are often overlooked, as the drama is often seen as Richard's personal tragedy.

Pye, Christopher. "The Betrayal of the Gaze: *Richard II*." In *The Regal Phantasm: Shakespeare and the Politics of Spectacle*, pp. 82-105. London: Routledge, 1990.

Explores the relationship in *Richard II* between the power of the kingship and theatricality, examining in particular the uses Richard makes of theatrical speeches and antics.

Rackin, Phyllis. "The Role of the Audience in Shakespeare's *Richard II*." *Shakespeare Quarterly* 36, No. 3 (Autumn 1985): 262-81.

Contends that the audience perceives the action of the play in two different ways. They are sometimes required to take a "long, historical view of the action" and are sometimes encouraged to see the action as "insistent, present reality."

Reese, M. M. "*Richard II*." In *The Cease of Majesty: A Study of Shakespeare's History Plays*, pp. 225-60. London: Edward Arnold Publishers, Ltd., 1961.

Examines the kingship and character of Richard, as well as the plot of the play. Reese also presents a brief analysis of other characters in the play.

Media Adaptations

King Richard the Second, BBC, 1978.
Directed by David Giles and starring Derek Jacobi, John Gielgud, Jon Finch, and Wendy Hiller. 157 minutes.

Richard II, Bard Productions, 1982.
Directed by William Woodman. Videotape distributed by Shakespeare Video Society. 172 minutes.

SONNETS

INTRODUCTION

We do not know when Shakespeare composed his sonnets, though it is possible that he wrote them over a period of several years, beginning, perhaps, in 1592 or 1593. Some of them were being circulated in manuscript form among his friends as early as 1598, and in 1599 two of them—138 and 144—were published in *The Passionate Pilgrim,* a collection of verses by several authors. The sonnets as we know them were certainly completed no later than 1609, the year they were published by Thomas Thorpe under the title *Shake-speares Sonnets.* Most scholars believe that Thorpe acquired the manuscript on which he based his edition from someone other than the author. Few believe that Shakespeare supervised the publication of this manuscript, for the text is riddled with errors. Nevertheless, Thorpe's 1609 edition is the basis for all modern texts of the sonnets.

With only a few exceptions—Sonnets 99, 126, and 145—Shakespeare's verses follow the established English form of the sonnet. Each is a fourteen-line poem in iambic pentameter, comprising four sections: three quatrains, or groups of four lines, followed by a couplet of two lines. Traditionally, a different—though related—idea is expressed in each quatrain, and the argument or theme of the poem is summarized or generalized in the concluding couplet. It should be noted that many of Shakespeare's couplets do not have this conventional effect. Shakespeare did, however, employ the traditional English sonnet rhyme-scheme: *abab, cdcd, efef, gg.*

Shakespeare's 154 sonnets, taken together, are frequently described as a sequence, and this is generally divided into two sections. Sonnets 1-126 focus on a young man and the speaker's friendship with him, and Sonnets 127-52 focus on the speaker's relationship with a woman. However, in only a few of the poems in the first group is it clear that the person being addressed is a male. And most of the poems in the sequence as a whole are not direct addresses to another person. The two concluding sonnets, 153 and 154, are free translations or adaptations of classical verses about Cupid; some critics believe they serve a specific purpose—though they disagree about what this may be—but many others view them as perfunctory.

The English sonnet sequence reached the height of its popularity in the 1590s, when the posthumous publication of Sir Philip Sidney's *Astrophel and Stella* (1591) was widely celebrated and led other English poets to create their own sonnet collections. All of these, including Shakespeare's, are indebted to some degree to the literary conventions established by the *Canzoniere,* a sonnet sequence composed by the fourteenth-century Italian poet Petrarch. By the time Shakespeare wrote his sonnets, there was also an anti-Petrarchan convention, which satirized or exploited traditional motifs and styles. Commentators on Shakespeare's sonnets frequently compare them to those of his predecessors and contemporaries, including Sidney, Sir Thomas Wyatt, Henry Howard, Earl of Surrey, Samuel Daniel, and Edmund Spenser.

The principal topics of twentieth-century critical commentary on the sonnets, however, are their themes and poetic style. Analyses of formal elements in the poems include examinations of the rhetorical devices, syntax, and diction Shakespeare employed here. The multiple and indefinite associations of his words and phrases have proved especially intriguing—and problematic—for scholars as well as general readers. The complexity and ambiguity of Shakespeare's figurative language is also a central critical issue, as is the remarkable diversity of tone and mood in the sequence. Shakespeare's departures from or modifications of the poetic styles employed by other sonneteers have also drawn a measure of critical attention.

Many of Shakespeare's themes are conventional sonnet topics, such as love and beauty, and the related motifs of time and mutability. But Shakespeare treats these themes in his own, distinctive fashion—most notably by addressing the poems of love and praise not to a fair maiden but instead to a young man, and by including a second subject of passion: a woman of questionable attractiveness and virtue. Critics have frequently called attention to Shakespeare's complex and paradoxical representation of love in the sonnets. They have also discussed at length the poet-speaker's claim that he will immortalize the young man's beauty in his verses, thereby defying the destructiveness of time. The themes of friendship and betrayal of friendship are also important critical issues, as is the nature of the relationship between the speaker and the youth. The ambiguous eroticism of the sonnets has elicited varying responses, with some commentators asserting that the relationship between the two men is asexual and others contending that it is sexual.

Because these lyrics are passionate, intense, and emotionally vivid, over the centuries many readers and commentators have been convinced that they must have an autobiographical basis. There is, however, no evidence that this is so. Nevertheless, there has been endless speculation about what these sonnets may tell us about their creator, and researchers have attempted to identify the persons who were the original or historical models for the persons the speaker refers to and addresses. The fact remains, however, that we do not know to what degree Shakespeare's personal experiences are reflected in his sonnets. Nor do we know with any measure of certainty whether the persons depicted in these poems are based on specific individuals or are solely the product of Shakespeare's observation, imagination, and understanding of the human heart.

CHARACTERS

There are no "characters" in Shakespeare's sonnets as the term is usually understood in literary analysis. None of the figures who appear or are referred to in the sequence is given a proper name. Specific details about physical features or demeanor are noticeably scarce. For the sake of convenience, many modern commentators have adopted some form of the designations used here, but these names do not appear in the sonnets.

The Poet: This phrase denotes the speaker of the sonnets as distinguished from the man who wrote them. The Poet is a complex and contradictory figure. He appears to be generous and long-suffering— even self-effacing— yet he also expresses anger and pride. The Poet describes himself as older than his friend and mistress, but he gives few indications of what his age may be. Furthermore, he calls himself a liar, which raises doubts about his reliability as a reporter. This is important because it is only through the Poet that we know anything about the other figures in the sonnets. *(See* **The Poet** *in the* **Character Studies** *section.)*

The Friend: He is characterized as younger than the Poet, of superior or aristocratic rank, and not married. The Poet describes him as unusually beautiful, and at times his inner virtue seems to match his outward nature. On other occasions he appears cold, narcissistic, even morally corrupt. Sometimes he returns the Poet's love, yet he is also accused of having a sexual relationship with a woman— perhaps the one who is the Poet's mistress. *(See* **The Friend** *in the* **Character Studies** *section.)*

The Dark Lady: She is specifically called "dark" only once, but it seems she has dark hair and eyes. Her social rank or status in society is not specified. She may be a married woman, though the Poet refers to her as his "mistress." He alternately describes her as ill-favored and attractive, and characterizes her as sensual, tyrannical, and playful. He further alleges that she has betrayed him by seducing his young friend. *(See* **The Dark Lady** *in the* **Character Studies** *section.)*

The Rival Poet(s): Sonnets 21, 78-80, and 82-86 refer to a competitor or competitors for the Friend's favor and patronage. The Poet describes his rival(s)' verses as more ornate and artificial than his own, and he represents them as a threat to his relationship with the Friend.

NARRATIVE

Shakespeare's sonnets do not describe or enact a clear sequence of events, nor do they follow a straightforwardly logical or chronological order. They allude to only a few specific actions, and even these are presented in general rather than particular terms. The setting too is generalized, with no reference to any specific locale. There is a sense of time elapsing as the sonnets portray developments in the speaker's relationships with the young man and the woman, but there is only one suggestion about how long either of these associations lasted.

In Sonnets 1-17— the most coherent group in the sequence and often referred to as the "procreation sonnets"— the speaker urges a young man of aristocratic birth to marry and have children so that his unusual beauty will be preserved for the ages. The last three sonnets in this cluster hint at another possibility of forestalling the destructiveness of time: the Poet will immortalize the Friend's beauty in his verses. This idea is more fully developed in Sonnets 18 through 26, where the Poet makes extravagant claims about the fame and durability of his verses but also expresses humility about his art. In addition, new motifs are introduced, particularly the possibility of a physical or sexual relationship between the Poet and the Friend (Sonnet 20), and the existence of a rival poet (Sonnet 21). Beginning with Sonnet 27 and continuing thereafter, it appears that while the Poet was away from his Friend, his mistress seduced the young man. There is a suggestion in Sonnet 40 that the youth similarly betrayed the Poet on another occasion. Sonnets 28 through 126 depict a recurring cycle of contrition and coldness on the part of the Friend, and forgiveness, understanding, praise, and reproach on the part of the Poet. In these verses the Poet alternates between confidence in his art and in his friendship with the young man, and doubt and anxiety that either of these will prove to be of lasting value. For example, in Sonnets 32, 76, 87, 105, and 108, the speaker expresses his fears about the worth and originality of his poetry, and in Sonnets 71-74, he questions whether he will be remembered after his death. Sonnets 27-28, 43-45, and 97-99 suggest that there may have been more than one period when the Poet and the Friend were estranged. And in Sonnets 78-80 and 82-86, the speaker refers again to another poet or poets who are vying for the young man's attention and patronage.

Sonnets 127-54 portray the Poet's relationship with the woman known as the Dark Lady. There is even less of a sequential story line here than in the first 126 sonnets. The Poet's attitude toward his mistress— and himself— shifts radically from one poem to the next. He teases her, insults her lusty sensuality, accuses her of repeated infidelities, praises her unfashionable dark beauty, upbraids himself for his own carnal desires, and plays bawdily on the numerous meanings of "will." As with the majority of the sonnets to the young man, the Poet's conflicting thoughts and emotions do not follow any logical sequence. Critics disagree about whether either of these two sections of Shakespeare's sonnets comes to a close with a sense of finality or resolution.

PRINCIPAL TOPICS

Themes

Human love— in a variety of manifestations— is a principal focus of Shakespeare's sonnets. Commentators have called attention to the many different kinds of love expressed in these verses: spiritual and erotic, parental and filial, love that ennobles and love that corrupts. They point out that these verses explore the paradoxical nature of human passion from different perspectives, sometimes idealizing love and sometimes treating it sardonically. Many critics emphasize Shakespeare's innovative and unique treatment of the traditions of courtly and Petrarchan love. They compare the Renaissance ideal of human love— a relationship in which earthly and heavenly desires are balanced and complementary— with the sonnets' representation of these desires as polar opposites.

In Shakespeare's sonnets, critics have argued, love is sometimes presented as an inspiration for transcendent art, with the lover claiming that he can eternalize his beloved's worth and beauty by enshrining them in his poetry. Thus love and art can unite to triumph over time and its destructive effects. Love in the sonnets is also represented as an impulse that can help a person realize the noblest virtues of human nature: patience, understanding, selflessness, and forgiveness. Yet some commentators maintain that the sonnets' depiction of self-effacing love represents a satire on the servile lover of sonnet tradition, who willingly assumed the role of abject servant and devoted himself to obeying his mistress's every wish. Critics have pointed out that love in the sonnets sometimes manifests itself as infatuation, turning the lover's head and blinding his judgment. It is also represented, particularly in Sonnets 127-52, as lust or carnal desire, a passion that corrodes the soul and debases the lover. Yet as critics point out, some of the Dark Lady sonnets wittily and exuberantly portray sensual love as a vital expression of human nature. Love is also represented as friendship, and some commentators have read the relationship between the Poet and the Friend in terms of the classical notion that an intimate friendship between two men has greater intrinsic value

than a sexual relationship between a man and a woman.

Over the centuries, commentators have alternately denied, confronted, accepted, and celebrated the ambiguous eroticism of the sonnets. One seventeenth-century editor changed all the masculine pronouns and adjectives into their feminine counterparts so that the beloved of Sonnets 1-126 became a woman. Eighteenth- and nineteenth-century editors and commentators struggled with the implications of the use of masculine address in the central portion of the sequence. Twentieth-century critics are divided on the issue of whether the relationship between the Poet and the Friend is sexual. But virtually everyone agrees that whatever the nature of that relationship, it sheds no light on the personal life of the author of the sonnets. Stephen Booth's pronouncement on what is termed the biographical fallacy has been frequently cited by other critics: "William Shakespeare was almost certainly homosexual, bisexual, or heterosexual. The sonnets provide no evidence on the matter."

In Shakespeare's sonnets, an important theme associated with love is betrayal of love. Most commentators agree that although the Poet accuses the Dark Lady of sexual infidelity, he is far less concerned about her faithlessness than he is about the Friend's. As critics have noted, the Poet fears that the young man will prove inconstant, yet he tries to suppress his doubts and trust the youth. When the Friend betrays him, the Poet attempts to justify and excuse his infidelity, then reproaches the young man for his deception and himself for believing in the youth. Several commentators remark that the shock of betrayal is intensified because the Poet is convinced that there is a direct symmetry between the young man's outward appearance— his extraordinary beauty— and his inner self; when the Poet realizes there is disparity rather than correspondence, he is desolate. Nevertheless, commentators generally agree that the Poet's love for the young man is sustained to the end— though perhaps it becomes tempered by a more realistic appraisal of his friend's true nature.

Several critics have asserted that narcissism is an important motif related to the principal theme of love. In their judgment, many of these verses underscore the sterility and deceptiveness of self-love and emphasize the belief that "To give away yourself keeps yourself still" (Sonnet 16). This motif is perhaps most evident in the so-called "procreation sonnets" (1-17), where the Poet urges the young man to marry and beget children so that his beauty and virtue will be replicated in succeeding generations of his family. But critics have pointed out that the sonnets equate self-love with barrenness in other ways as well. A narcissistic view of one's natural gifts as personal assets rather than attributes to be shared with others is also sterile: hoarding one's treasures rather than using them is the same as wasting them, for time will ultimately consume them. Moreover, some commentators observe, the sonnets warn that self-love inevitably traps the narcissist into believing what false friends and lovers tell him about himself.

Narrative and Dramatic Elements

Assessments of narrative elements frequently begin by pointing out that the order in which Shakespeare's sonnets appear in most modern editions follows the one established by Thomas Thorpe in the original publication of these verses in 1609. We do not know if Shakespeare had any hand in this publication, and thus we cannot know if this is the order in which he intended them to be read. Many scholars, believing that a coherent story would emerge if the sonnets were rearranged, have revised the order. However, none of these rearrangements has gained significant acceptance by other critics and commentators.

Countless summaries of the narrative line of Shakespeare's sonnets have appeared in print. These range in length from one sentence to thirty pages or more. Critics generally agree that there are few traces of a traditional plot in the sonnets. Indeed, most commentators remark on the absence of a definable progression of events, specific actions, and indications of time and place. And recently, critics have considered the possibility that some of the sonnets in the first group (1-126) may be addressed to the Dark Lady. Since we cannot be sure to whom many of the sonnets refer, we cannot trace the course of a developing— even if illogical— narrative. Indeed, critics argue, the sequence focuses not on a series of events but on the speaker's thoughts and emotions.

From about the middle of the nineteenth century to the present, Shakespeare's sonnets have frequently been read as a series of dramatic monologues. Thus many commentators describe the sonnets as "dramatic" in that they provide immediate emotional contact between the speaker and his reading audience. Furthermore, some critics view the tensions that the speaker describes between himself and his young friend, and between himself and his mistress, as essentially dramatic in nature. However, some critics argue that the sonnets are nondramatic in that they seem to take place in an eternal present.

Language and Imagery

The linguistic inventiveness of the sonnets is one of their chief characteristics. Critics have noted that the language is dense and complex, rich in significance, contradictions, overtones, and echoes. They have also remarked that Shakespeare's vocabulary, imagery, and diction are inseparable from the various themes or topics within each poem. Some commentators have argued that the ambiguity of Shakespeare's language is a reflection of his ambivalent attitude toward the subjects of his poetry. Others have evaluated the wide range of tone in the sequence, pointing out the often abrupt shifts from playfulness to derision, intensity to detachment, ecstasy to despair. Studies of the sonnets' elaborate verbal patterns have focused on such elements as alliteration and assonance, syntax, neologisms, punning and other forms of wordplay, as well as Shakespeare's use of paradox and antithesis.

The figurative or metaphorical language of the poems is a chief topic of critical interest. There is widespread agreement that the imagery of Shakespeare's sonnets is functional rather than ornamental. Imagery often serves as a unifying agent between individual sonnets, creating a formal pattern which links together poems that are otherwise discontinuous in logic or topic. Commentators have often remarked on the multiple associations of a single image, arguing that readers should not try to find one meaning— in this rich mixture of connotations— that is more significant than the others. Images drawn from nature appear frequently throughout the sequence, particularly with reference to the passing of the seasons and the cycle of growth and decay. Other important metaphorical patterns are linked to treasure or riches, corruption and disease, scarcity and abundance, and the effectiveness of procreation and poetry as means of immortalizing beauty and defying time.

CHARACTER STUDIES

The Poet

Most late twentieth-century critics maintain that the Poet is the principal focus of the sonnets as well as the most significant figure. In their judgment, the sequence depicts a mind torn between conflicting thoughts and emotions as the speaker deals with the central issues of human existence: love and friendship, birth and death, self-knowledge and self-delusion, sin and virtue, the vagaries of fortune, and the ravages of time. Many commentators view the Poet as prone to misjudge both himself and the Friend. Others contend that he willfully avoids facing the truth about the young man's nature and conduct— either because he continues to love the youth or because he doesn't want to acknowledge the malignant effect of this relationship on himself. Most agree that the sonnets depict a man who is struggling to make sense of his life and bring order out of chaos.

Many critics have explored what they see as the Poet's moral, ethical, or intellectual confusion. They emphasize the dilemma he faces in remaining constant to a beloved who has proved inconstant. They note that he appears to be both generous and self-interested. They highlight the contrast between the occasions on which he proudly affirms the power of his poetry and the instances when he expresses grave doubts about both the value of art and the worth of his own verses. Such inconsistencies have been variously explained. Some commentators allege that if the sonnets were reordered the poet could be shown progressing steadily from one state of mind to the next rather than fluctuating back and forth throughout the sequence. Others view this wavering between confidence and uncertainty as a function of the discrepancies in age and social rank between the Poet and the Friend. Still others see it as a realistic portrayal of the quandary facing a man whose beloved is simultaneously attractive and loathsome.

Many critics disparage what they regard as the Poet's servile attitude toward the Friend. Others condemn his relationship with the Dark Lady, remarking that the Poet seems unable to break away from a relationship that he finds degrading. The Poet's passivity or hesitancy to take action is frequently noted. To some critics, he seems trapped in a state of reflection, beset by fears and anxieties. Several commentators point out that the Poet repeatedly says he is a liar—though some maintain that he is himself the principal victim of his dishonesty. In connection with this, many critics caution that since the Poet represents himself as an unreliable witness, we should not assume that what he says about the Friend and the Dark Lady is necessarily true or accurate. Indeed, his descriptions of the other figures in the sequence may reveal as much about himself as about those he describes.

The Friend

Commentary on the Friend is a mixture of biographical speculation and literary analysis. For hundreds of years, researchers have attempted to determine whether there was a specific person on whom Shakespeare modeled the young man of the sonnets. Many searches have begun with the enigmatic dedication of the 1609 edition of the poems to "Mr. W. H.," described as "the only begetter of these ensuing sonnets." Some scholars have contended that "begetter" means that "Mr. W. H." provided the publisher with the text of Shakespeare's sonnets. Others believe that "Mr. W. H." alludes to the youth who inspired the poems, and over the centuries, an impressive array of possible candidates has been proposed. At the top of the list are Henry Wriothesley, Earl of Southampton (1573-1624), and William Herbert, Earl of Pembroke (1580-1630). Most late twentieth-century commentators believe that the issue of who "begat" the sonnets will never be resolved and is, moreover, irrelevant. Instead they focus on the picture of the Friend that the Poet provides us. And it is important to remember, they point out, that the only perspective we have on this young man is the Poet's constantly changing point of view.

Critics have variously viewed the Friend as aloof, sensitive, vulnerable, impulsive, and inscrutable. Many have empha-

sized his essential egotism. The opening sonnets celebrate his physical beauty, but subsequent ones question his integrity and faithfulness, and increasingly he is portrayed as arrogant and self-important. Commentators have remarked that the treatment of the Friend throughout the sonnets is characterized by a remarkable lack of specificity: his beauty is generalized rather than particularized, and all we hear or see of his speech and actions is through second-hand reports. The Poet accuses him of a grave fault—seemingly of a sensual nature—but this fault is never particularized. Some critics stress the Friend's accomplishments, his grace, and his beauty. Others focus on his pride, his susceptibility to flattery, and his apparent rejection of the Poet.

The Dark Lady

Commentary on the Dark Lady often deals more with the speaker's frame of mind in Sonnets 127-52 than with the woman herself. And as with the Friend, much of what has been written about her is principally concerned with whether she has a historical antecedent. Mary Fitton, a lady in waiting to Queen Elizabeth, is high on the list of candidates. Others include Luce Morgan, a London brothel-keeper, and Emilia Lanier, a woman whose virtue was apparently regularly compromised. Again as with the Friend, most critics doubt that we will ever know if there was a "real-life" prototype of the Dark Lady. However, few believe that if we did, this would affect our responses to the poems that allude to her.

The Dark Lady of Shakespeare's sonnets is even more shadowy than the Friend. There is general agreement that she is lusty and seductive, and that the Poet is irresistibly drawn to her. Commentators suggest that although the Poet loves her—or has loved her in the past—he also despises her. She has apparently seduced the Friend while carrying on an affair with the Poet, but the extent of her promiscuity—indeed, whether she is married and therefore an adulteress—is not evident to all readers. Several critics have evaluated the Dark Lady sonnets in the context of literary conventions, arguing that these verses represent a parody of Petrarchan lovers by depicting a mistress who has neither virtue nor beauty. Over the centuries, many commentators have identified the Dark Lady with a debased form of love. However, late twentieth-century studies, especially those written from a feminist perspective, have been more sympathetic, challenging the accuracy or reliability of the Poet's account of her and calling for an appraisal that takes into account his obvious bias.

CONCLUSION

Contradictions and uncertainties are implicit in Shakespeare's sonnets. Both individually and as a collection, these poems resist generalities and summations. Their complex language and multiple perspectives have given rise to a number of different interpretations, all of which may at times seem valid— even when they contradict each other. Few critics today read the sonnets as personal allegory. Indeed, most commentators assert that speculation about what these verses may imply about Shakespeare's life, morals, and sexuality is a useless exercise. The speaker is as closely identified with each reader as he is with the writer who created him. His confused and ambiguous expressions of thought and emotion heighten our own ambivalent feelings about matters that concern us all: love, friendship, jealousy, hope, and despair.

(See also *Shakespearean Criticism*, Vols. 10, 40, and 51.)

OVERVIEW

Maurice Charney

SOURCE: "The Sonnets," in *All of Shakespeare*, Columbia University Press, 1993, pp. 388-99.

[*In this concise appraisal of various issues associated with Shakespeare's sonnets, Charney pays particular attention to Shakespeare's development of the sonnet form and the effectiveness of his concluding couplets. Charney also discusses the motifs of time and mutability, the presence of both lyric and dramatic elements in the sequence, and the poet-speaker's reflections on his creative powers.*]

Thomas Thorpe published 154 Sonnets by Shakespeare followed by *A Lover's Complaint* (also said to be by Shakespeare) in 1609. Unlike the texts of *Venus and Adonis* and *The Rape of Lucrece*, the printed text has many obvious errors, and Shakespeare clearly did not proofread it or see it through the press. Although the *Sonnets* seem to have an authoritative manuscript behind them, they were certainly not published with Shakespeare's knowledge or permission. Sonnets usually circulated in handwritten "books" among one's private friends and acquaintances. It was not considered necessary or even desirable to publish them.

The great vogue of sonnet writing was in the 1590s, and we know from Sonnet 104 that three years had passed since the poet first saw his "fair friend," which makes it likely that the writing of the *Sonnets* occupied at least three years in the 1590s, probably the early 1590s. Some of the *Sonnets* may have been written in the early 1600s, but the bulk of them are associated with Shakespeare's ingenious, heavily conceited, and self-consciously rhetorical style of the early and mid-1590s. In 1598 Francis Meres mentions in *Palladis Tamia* Shakespeare's "sugred sonnets among his priuate friends," an obvious compliment to his elegant style, although we may have some doubts about *sugred* as a term of praise. In 1599 two Sonnets, 138 and 144, were printed in a slightly differ-

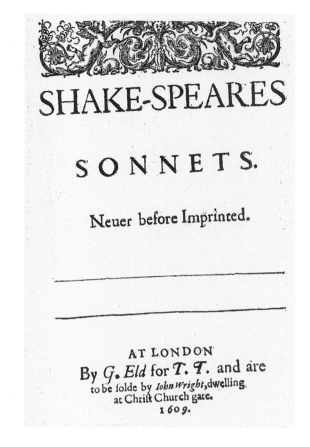

Title page of the 1609 edition of Shakespeare's Sonnets.

ent form in *The Passionate Pilgrim*.

The *Sonnets* were dedicated to "Mr. W. H." as "the only begetter," but it is hard to know whether this is the poet's or the publisher's dedication. It is unlike the formal dedications of *Venus and Adonis* and *The Rape of Lucrece* to the Earl of Southampton, and it may be that Mr. W. H. is the only begetter in the sense that he made his manuscript copy of Shakespeare's *Sonnets* available to the publisher. There has been endless and mostly fruitless biographical speculation about the *Sonnets*, and even more elaborate autobiographical guessing about Shakespeare's own personal relation to the experience described in the *Sonnets* and to characters in the *Sonnets* such as the Friend, the Dark Lady, and the Rival Poet or Poets. There is no independent confirmation in other writing or records of the time of anything factual that is said in Shakespeare's *Sonnets*. We would expect, at the least, some outside confirmation of the Rival Poet's activities: his sonnets to the friend or to the lady, or some account of his love life. It is curious that in the elaborately punning Sonnets 135 and 136 it seems that Shakespeare, the Dark Lady's husband, and the Friend are all named Will. This is convenient because *will* is also a word for carnal appetite and lust.

We know nothing definite about the historical identity of the Dark Lady and the Friend. The *Sonnets* seem to be strongly homoerotic, but in terms of Petrarchan love conventions, the Platonic idea of friendship offers a much higher ideal than heterosexual love, as we can see plainly in the opening sequence between Leontes and Polixenes in *The Winter's Tale* or in the friendship of Palamon and Arcite (and Emilia and Flavina) in *The Two Noble Kinsmen*. Leontes' fiendish jealousy seems to be generated, like Original Sin, from sexuality itself, as Hermione his wife so keenly recognizes. Sexual love is represented repeatedly in the *Sonnets* as a source of grief and enslavement, nowhere more strongly than in Sonnet 129, "Th' expense of spirit in a waste of shame."

Sonnet 20 seems to lay out clearly the distinction between an ennobling love between two male friends and the potentially debasing sexual love between a man and a woman. The Friend has "A woman's face, with Nature's own hand painted" and is "the master mistress of my passion." Nature first created him "for a woman," but then "fell a-doting, / And by addition me of thee defeated." Nature's "addition" seems to be clearly a penis, as we learn from the punning couplet close:

> But since she pricked thee out for women's
>   pleasure,
> Mine be thy love, and thy love's use their
>   treasure.

There is a clear distinction between the noble "love" and the lesser "love's use," or intercourse. We learn later that the Dark Lady has seduced the Friend and engaged him in a sexual relationship (Sonnets 35, 40, 41, etc.). Sonnet 20 makes a sharp distinction between noble friendship and physical love. Sex is excluded from the relation with the Friend.

The Shakespearean or English sonnet is derived from the Earl of Surrey and has three quatrains (rhyming abab, cdcd, and efef) with a concluding couplet (gg) all in iambic pentameter. Most of the sonnets have fourteen lines, although there is one (Sonnet 99) of fifteen, with an introductory first line, and one of twelve (Sonnet 126), which has six couplets. There are vestiges of the Italian sonnet in Shakespeare, in which an octave is set against a sestet. The octave of two quatrains contrasts with the sestet, which consists of a quatrain and a couplet considered as a single unit. These are relatively uncommon in Shakespeare, although Sonnet 18 has the feeling of an Italian sonnet: it has three quatrains and a couplet, but the third quatrain has a different logical movement from the first two. The feeling of a distinct sestet is continued through the triumphant couplet:

> So long as men can breathe or eyes can see,
> So long lives this, and this gives life to thee.

This couplet provides an upbeat ending.

The most problematic feature of the Shakespearean sonnet is the couplet close, which is sometimes disappointing because it is so epigrammatic, so didactic, so much like a neat summary tacked on to a poem that doesn't need it. There are many feeble couplets, for example the one in Sonnet 37:

> Look what is best, that best I wish in thee.
> This wish I have, then ten times happy me!

This seems like mere filler for a sonnet that is clearly not one of the best, but is nevertheless complex, about a poet "made lame by Fortune's dearest spite," who shares in his friend's "abundance." This certainly doesn't indicate that the poet is literally "lame," and the couplet doesn't do justice to the poetic reasoning of the three previous quatrains.

The couplet works wonderfully well in Sonnet 73, and is generally successful when it has an element of dramatic surprise, like a punch line. In Sonnet 19 the couplet comes upon us as a sudden peripeteia to the irresistible powers of "Devouring Time":

> Yet do thy worst, old Time; despite thy wrong,
> My love shall in my verse ever live young.

This couplet introduces an alternative with its "Yet" and "despite" that comes upon us as a hidden truth. Sonnet 65 is similar. Against "sad mortality" and his "spoil of beauty" there is no protection, except for the miracle of poetry trumpeted in the couplet:

> O, none, unless this miracle have might,
> That in black ink my love may still shine
>   bright.

The couplet form lends itself in the *Sonnets* (and in Shakespeare's plays, too, especially scene-ending couplets) to bold and emphatic statement. Sonnet 56 is not particularly memorable, but its couplet ending vibrates with promise and new possibility. The poem is an appeal to "Sweet love" to "renew thy force," presumably in a period of absence or neglect. The "Return of love" is connected syntactically with the couplet:

> Or call it winter, which being full of care,
> Makes summer's welcome thrice more wished,
>   more rare.

A series of five accented syllables beginning with *thrice* in the last line is driven home with the unusual fourth-beat caesura, or mid-line pause, after *wished*. *More rare* soars in a way that redeems the entire poem.

Time is the most frequently repeated concept and image in the *Sonnets*. This is the pervasive Renaissance theme of mutability, and the poet presents various ways to defy Time. The first seventeen Sonnets constitute the most distinctive unit of the whole sequence, which is arranged more or less logically by similarity of theme. We don't, of course, know who devised the ordering of the *Sonnets* or what relation the sequence has to date of composition. The first seventeen sonnets all urge the young friend to marry and to reproduce his beauty in children. This is the familiar doctrine of use that is part of Venus's argument to Adonis in *Venus and Adonis* and that echoes the often-repeated parable of the talents in Matt. 25: 14-30. Man is the steward, not the owner, of his good qualities and possessions, and he is obligated to put his natural gifts to use for the benefit of others. If you are beautiful, you must make use of your beauty (as money accumulates "use" or interest) by having children on whom to bestow your god-given gifts.

The beginning of the first sonnet announces the immortality of beauty through propagation:

> From fairest creatures we desire increase,
> That thereby beauty's rose might never die.

You are not allowed to be in love with yourself and waste your substance in "niggarding," or hoarding, to be "contracted to thine own bright eyes" and feed "thy light's flame with self-substantial fuel." This is to make "a famine where abundance lies," that is, the potential abundance that comes from creating children to perpetuate one's beauty. Children are like "flowers distilled" (Sonnet 3), or perfume, that defies the tyranny of Time.

Another way to wage war against Time is to write verse, which confers a kind of immortality upon the Friend. This is a repeated theme in the *Sonnets*. Posterity and poetry both do battle against oblivion. Nature is a destroyer of beauty, but poetry is immutable and guarantees that "thy eternal summer shall not fade" (Sonnet 18). In Sonnet 65 there is a series of unanswerable questions about Time, one in each of the first two quatrains, and two in the third:

> O, fearful meditation, where, alack,
> Shall Time's best jewel from Time's chest lie
> 　　hid?

Presumably, "Time's best jewel" is the beautiful Friend, whom the Poet is trying to conceal from the ravaging hand of Time, who threatens to seize him and put him in his chest. How can "beauty hold a plea" against the rage of Time? The only solution to this "fearful meditation" is the miracle of poetry: "That in black ink my love may still shine bright." The immanence and immortality of poetry are postulated as a defense against the ravages of Time.

Two sonnets dwell specifically on music, 8 and 128, but the musicality of the *Sonnets* as a group is striking. The slow, sad lyrical effects are the most impressive, and they lend themselves to being set to music (as many

sonnets have been). Sonnet 30 is best remembered as supplying C. K. Scott Moncrieff with the English title for Proust's *A La Recherche du Temps Perdu*. It is artful in its heavy use of alliteration and its legal / commercial imagery. In the first quatrain, "remembrance of things past" is summoned to appear at the "sessions of sweet silent thought," in which the poet presumably sits in judgment on the events of his own life. The predominance of s-sounds in the opening line immediately establishes a mood of reverie and meditation— the sibilants are associated with sleep, as in the colloquial expression *a few z's*, meaning a short nap. "My dear Time's waste" continues the most repeated theme in the *Sonnets* of Time the Destroyer. The memorializing of the second quatrain presents a mournful threnody for "precious friends hid in death's dateless night," "love's long since canceled woe," and "th' expense of many a vanished sight."

The sonnet is an elegy to death, the expiration of love, and the gradual disappearance of all that is lovely and beautiful. There is a sense in the third quatrain that "grievances foregone" can never be forgotten and that "The sad account of fore-bemoanèd moan" must be paid anew as if it had never been paid before. The music of the three quatrains is an almost perfect elegy for "remembrance of things past," but the couplet is jarring and facile:

> But if the while I think on thee, dear friend,
> All losses are restored and sorrows end.

It is as if a mere thought of the "dear friend" is enough to cancel the previous three quatrains. This is one of the most disturbing and inappropriate couplets in the *Sonnets*. We are soon to learn of many negative and unfavorable aspects of the "dear friend."

Sonnet 73 is similar to Sonnet 30 in its elegiac tone and in its meditation on man's mortality. It does not use such deliberate alliteration, but its prominent caesuras, or midline pauses, slow the rhythm down, especially in the three caesuras of line 2:

> That time of year thou mayst in me behold
> When yellow leaves, or none, or few, do hang
> Upon those boughs which shake against the
> 　　cold . . .

The numerous accented syllables in the fourth line also slow down the movement of the poem practically to a funeral dirge: "Bare ruined choirs where late the sweet birds sang." "Bare ruined choirs" and "sweet birds sang" are all heavily accented without any intervening unaccented syllables. The autumn of the first quatrain is matched by twilight in the second, with black night and sleep, which is described as "Death's second self." In the third quatrain, the embers of the fires of youth match autumn and twilight as images of death. The fire consumes "that which it was nourished by." In this sonnet, the couplet is a perfect conclusion to the somber mood and adagio movement of the first three quatrains:

> This thou perceiv'st, which makes thy love
>   more strong,
> To love that well which thou must leave ere
>   long.

Love is intimately connected with death, and the idea of mutability and mortality should serve to make love more intense.

The *Sonnets* are obviously related to the plays, but generically there are important differences between lyric and dramatic expression. The wooing sonnet in *Romeo and Juliet* (1.5.95ff.), for example, is a playful and witty part of the early courtship of Romeo and Juliet— they answer each other— but it would be inappropriate later in the play. If we consider specific sonnets in relation to plays, it is clear that Sonnet 66 looks ahead to *Hamlet* in its account of "The slings and arrows of outrageous fortune" (3.1.58), especially in the third quatrain:

> And art made tongue-tied by authority,
> And folly (doctorlike) controlling skill,
> And simple truth miscalled simplicity,
> And captive good attending captain ill.

Hamlet's "sea of troubles" includes

>   the whips and scorns of time,
> Th' oppressor's wrong, the proud man's
>   contumely,
> The pangs of despised love, the law's delay,
> The insolence of office, and the spurns
> That patient merit of th' unworthy takes . . .
>   (*Hamlet* 3.1.70-74)

Despite verbal similarities in the catalogues of ills, in Hamlet's "To be, or not to be" speech they are part of an intolerable strain that includes the possibility of suicide. In Sonnet 66 the cry for "restful death" is rejected in the couplet close because it would isolate the poet from his love. The sonnet itself is a self-contained logical unit that ends by rejecting the possibilities of the first three quatrains. It has no relation to a highly characterized speaker or to a specific point in the dramatic action.

Even if radical differences exist between the *Sonnets* and the plays, the best sonnets still use dramatic devices that are similar to those in the plays. The sonnets that are most appealing seem to be those that explore a strong sense of turmoil and perturbation and that consequently offer poignant, often negative, characterizations. Sonnet 94 is powerfully dramatic— not theatrical in the sense of any imagined scenes— in its characterization of the Friend as cold, disdainful, and unattached. Despite all the ear-

lier sonnets on the doctrine of use and the insistence on man's stewardship rather than absolute possession of his beauty, in the octave the Friend ironically claims to be one of those who are "the lords and owners of their faces" rather than "stewards of their excellence." He is "Unmovèd, cold" and husbands "nature's riches from expense." The opening line, "They that have pow'r to hurt and will do none," is so frightening because the powerful Friend is affectless, lacedemonian, and uninvolved. Therefore his beauty is like a flower that suffers "base infection," and that is why, finally, "Lilies that fester smell far worse than weeds." The lily pretends to be a nobler flower than a weed, and hence its possibilities of corruption are more extreme. The Friend is characterized in this and many of the surrounding sonnets as incapable of real love.

A comparably dramatic sonnet is 129 about the Dark Lady, who appears in Sonnets 127-52. She is much more specifically sexual than any of Shakespeare's dramatic heroines, including Cleopatra and Cressida, and she seems to enslave the Poet (and his Friend, too) in an irresistible but shameful intensity of lust, such as Tarquin's self-defeating lust in *The Rape of Lucrece*. Sonnet 129 is not directly about the Dark Lady, but about her demonic effect on the Poet, who doesn't know how "To shun the heaven that leads men to this hell." Active lust involves "Th' expense of spirit," or the expenditure of seminal fluid, "in a waste of shame," which may pun on *waste* and *waist*. Until ejaculation, male lust follows the pattern of Tarquin, who seems to be arguing with another self that he doesn't recognize: lust "Is perjured, murd'rous, bloody, full of blame, / Savage, extreme, rude, cruel, not to trust." The spondaic thrust of the last line carries some of the metrical and phonetic harshness of the meaning. Lust is deceptive and self-defeating: "Enjoyed no sooner but despisèd straight" and "A bliss in proof, and proved, a very woe." The stark alternatives make this a very dramatic sonnet, as if lust is entirely outside a man's power to control. The Dark Lady is therefore both the heaven and the hell of the Poet.

The personal anguish of Sonnet 129 is displaced in the witty, mannered, sexual puns of Sonnet 151, "Love is too young to know what conscience is." It is as if the Poet has finally mastered the "sensual fault" (Sonnet 35) and "Lascivious grace" (Sonnet 40) of earlier poems, and he can proceed to the "sensual feast" (Sonnet 141) without any trepidations or pricks of conscience. The Poet willingly betrays his soul to his "gross body's treason," and "flesh" (specifically the penis) doesn't wait for any further excuses, "But, rising at thy name, doth point out thee, / As his triumphant prize." The double entendres on erection— *reason, rising, pride, stand,* and *rise and fall*— resemble Shakespeare's early comedies. Lust is no longer an excruciating torment, but rather an entertainment. The couplet cadence is playful:

> No want of conscience hold it that I call

Her "love" for whose dear love I rise and fall.

This is a good example of a couplet that really concludes the three preceding quatrains and seems to answer the opening proposition of the sonnet. I am not offering the ingenious Sonnet 151 as an example of one of Shakespeare's best sonnets, but it does provide a contrast to the ferocious energy and reckless mood of Sonnet 129.

The wittiest sonnet is undoubtedly 130, which is endlessly quoted although it is not at all characteristic of Shakespeare's entire sequence. It stands out because it satirizes the very Petrarchan conventions upon which Shakespeare so firmly depends. Specifically, it ridicules the accepted clichés of a woman's beauty that were made so much fun of in *Love's Labor's Lost* and Shakespeare's early comedies. The Dark Lady, by definition, doesn't fulfill the Nordic criteria of beauty established in the 1590s: exceptionally white skin, brightly rosy cheeks, and brilliantly blonde hair, which standards were met more vividly by cosmetics than by nature. As Hamlet complains to Ophelia: "I have heard of your paintings, well enough. God hath given you one face, and you make yourselves another" (*Hamlet* 3. 1. 143-45). The Dark Lady, then, has eyes that "are nothing like the sun," presumably in clarity and brilliance. She lacks the classic war between the white and the red in her cheeks:

> I have seen roses damasked, red and white,
> But no such roses see I in her cheeks.

Her lips are not as red as coral nor her breasts white as snow. They are, in fact, "dun" colored, or dark and swarthy, like Cleopatra's, another Dark Lady, who shows a "tawny front" (*Antony and Cleopatra* 1.1.6) and is sunburned, "with Phoebus' amorous pinches black" (1.5.28). The Dark Lady is a practical and seemingly unromantic figure: her breath "reeks," her speaking voice is not very musical, and "when she walks" she is unlike a goddess because she "treads on the ground."

The couplet conclusion, however, is in an entirely different and unexpected tone:

> And yet, by heaven, I think my love as rare
> As any she belied with false compare.

The soaring assertion and affirmation in the couplet is out of keeping with Sonnet 129, "Th' expense of spirit in a waste of shame," that immediately precedes it. This should give us pause about making exact autobiographical claims for Shakespeare's *Sonnets*. We don't know who arranged the poems in their present order— perhaps it was the printer, or perhaps he was only following the sequence of his manuscript— but there are some striking inconsistencies of tone and mood. The Dark Lady is hardly the same figure in Sonnets 129 and 130, nor do her sexual attractions seem to match in Sonnets 129 and 151.

We are struck by Shakespeare's skepticism about his own powers as a poet and a dramatist. He is excessively deferential to the Rival Poet or Poets, who are also writing sonnets to the Friend and the Dark Lady. His "poor rude lines" (Sonnet 32) are "exceeded by the height of happier men"— "happier" in the sense of more gifted. The "proud full sail" of the Rival Poet's "great verse" has "struck me dead" and swallowed up "my ripe thoughts in my brain," as if their womb became their tomb (Sonnet 86). This undercuts in some important way the power of the Poet to confer immortality on the love object through his poetry.

Shakespeare feels himself unable to cope with the newer and more refined style of such poets as John Donne and the Metaphysicals, who wrote what the Elizabethans called "strong lines." In Sonnet 76, Shakespeare complains that his verse is "barren of new pride," "far from variation or quick change," but "still all one, ever the same." He cannot seize the moment and use "new-found methods" and "compounds strange." The explanation is rather facile: "I always write of you," "So all my best is dressing old words new." We feel that the Poet is dissatisfied with the fact that "every word doth almost tell my name," but he doesn't know how to shift into a more innovative style.

The Poet expresses even stronger dissatisfaction with his public career as a playwright and actor, in which he feels trapped. In a striking image from daily life:

> And almost thence my nature is subdued
> To what it works in, like the dyer's hand.
> (Sonnet 111)

Like Macbeth's, the dyer's hand is "incarnadine" (*Macbeth* 2.2.61), and "all great Neptune's ocean" (59) cannot change its color. Shakespeare is engaged in a profession to please the public, and "public means" breed "public manners." From this obvious cause comes the fact that "my name receives a brand." In the previous sonnet (110), Shakespeare apologizes to the Friend that he has made himself "a motley," or clown dressed in a motley, parti-colored costume, "to the view," and "Gored mine own thoughts, sold cheap what is most dear." In other words, he has betrayed his innermost thoughts to the public scrutiny of the theatrical public. I am not assuming that this is an autobiographical statement of utmost sincerity, but merely that it is an essential part of the fictional persona (and personas) created in the *Sonnets*. If Shakespeare is the most unrevealing and paradoxical English Renaissance author in his plays, there is no convincing reason to believe that he bares his heart in the *Sonnets*. The very directness of the revelations should put us on our guard.

It is unfortunate that Shakespeare's *Sonnets* have attracted a mass of biographical speculation different from that expended on the plays. Some of the same questions haunt all of Shakespeare's works, both dramatic and nondramatic: the ambiguous nature of art, revealing and concealing at the same time; the tendency to dramatize experience, as if "All the world's a stage, / And all the men and women merely players" (*As You Like It* 2.7.138-39); and, most comprehensively, the fictionalizing of human experience on the assumption that we enact and represent a reality that we create in our minds from our own histrionic imagination. The *Sonnets* share these qualities with Shakespeare's other works, especially those of the earlier 1590s. They can't be dealt with autonomously as if they were written by a poet separate from the man who wrote the plays.

THEMES

A prominent theme of Shakespeare's sonnets is the paradoxical nature of love, and many commentators have discussed this issue. **David Lloyd Stevenson,** for example, emphasized the literary conventions that shaped Shakespeare's depiction of human passion. In Stevenson's judgment, the poet made use of conventional romantic sentiment but rejected the traditional notion of idealized love. Instead, he argued, Shakespeare emphasized the irrationality of human love— the conflicting impulses of aversion and attraction that are characteristic of the experience of sexual desire. Anthony Hecht and Marion Bodwell Smith also addressed the question of the sonnets' depiction of love as contradictory or paradoxical. Hecht noted that these verses exploit the traditional philosophical notion that the antagonism between soul and body can be resolved when sacred and profane love are brought together in an ideal relationship. Smith similarly evaluated the theme of love in the sonnets in the context of Renaissance philosophy, concluding that Shakespeare disavowed the notion that love could encompass both spiritual and physical values. Instead, the critic maintained, the sonnets portray the two faces of love as polarities: in the verses to the youth, love is a joining of souls, but in the ones involving the Dark Lady, love is enslavement of the body. **Stephen Spender** considered the conflict in the sonnets between the appearance of love and the actual experience of it. He suggested that the Poet is committed to reconciling the disparity between the outward semblance of love in the Friend and the young man's corrupt inner nature.

Critics agree that as the sonnets gradually reveal the Friend's true nature, the Poet must find a way to deal with the betrayal of love. **M. M. Mahood** highlighted the Poet's frequently expressed fears that the young man is treacherous and deceitful, and that he is destined to be unfaithful. But Mahood also argued that the Poet's love endures: even when the Friend repu-

diates him, she remarked, the Poet assures him of his continuing affection. Hilton Landry focused on the Poet's response to betrayal in Sonnets 92-96, finding in this series a variety of reactions, including fear, irony, ambivalence, and concern for the young man's well-being. Kenneth Muir also saw irony and ambivalence in the Poet's reactions to his friend's faithlessness, but in addition he detected disgrace and shame.

Several critics have maintained that in addition to deceitfulness, the Friend is guilty of self-love. **Philip Martin** proposed that Shakespeare's treatment of the youth's narcissism is unusually complex. Self-love, the critic argued, is portrayed as a destructive alliance with "devouring time," for by concentrating on himself the Friend will inevitably lose his essence instead of perpetuating it through procreation and love of others. In a psychoanalytic reading of the sonnets, Jane Hedley contended that the Poet himself is caught up in narcissism. She asserted that by loving a youth of incomparable beauty, the Poet is able to recapture an idealized image of himself— one that has been eroded as he has grown older. Similarly, **Stephen Spender** discussed the affinity between the narcissistic young man and the Poet who seeks to immortalize his beauty. In Spender's judgment, both men regard the Friend's beauty as a "unique value" that must be preserved, and in their shared determination to achieve this, they become one.

Discussions of the nature of the relationship between the Poet and the Friend often raise the question of whether it is represented as love-in-friendship or whether it has a sexual component. Kenneth Muir, for example, interpreted Sonnet 20— a verse that is at the center of this controversy— as the Poet's frank admission that his feelings for the young man are erotic as well as spiritual. Marion Bodwell Smith, on the other hand, suggested that Shakespeare's sequence traces the development— and dissolution— of love-in-friendship, as the Poet moves from confidence to doubt and from despair to an acceptance of the contradictions inherent in human love. Anthony Hecht called attention to the fact that from the classical era through the Renaissance, male friendship was seen as an advanced form of human relations— that is, superior to heterosexual love. Hecht suggested that from this perspective, Shakespeare's sonnets constitute an inquiry into the truth of that notion. Reading the sonnets in the context of the period in which they were written, Paul Innes described social and cultural norms governing relationships between men in the English Renaissance. He noted that the system of literary patronage deepened the gap between aristocratic benefactors and socially inferior writers. Calling attention to the connection between "the language of love and the discourse of patronage" in the sonnets, Innes suggested that one of the Poet's greatest fears is that if the young man rejects his love, he will lose the social and monetary benefits he presently enjoys.

David Lloyd Stevenson

SOURCE: "Conflict in Shakespeare's Sonnets," in *The Love-Game Comedy*, AMS Press, 1966, pp. 174-84.

[*Stevenson analyzes the unique perspective on love expressed in the Dark Lady sonnets, arguing that they reveal a profound appreciation of the paradoxical nature of human passion. Stevenson maintains that although other sonnet writers had dealt with the discrepancy between idealized love and the actual experience of it, Shakespeare's sardonic treatment of lust and romantic sentiment in the Dark Lady verses is distinctive and original.*]

Shakespeare . . . presents the sixteenth-century quarrel over the nature of love from a point of view peculiarly his own. This presentation of love in his sonnets is important because it is very like that found in his comedies of courtship. Within the narrow limits of their fourteen lines, he expresses with intensity and candor the highly individualized version of lovers' difficulties which is comic and implicit in his love-game comedies.

Shakespeare expresses the familiar sentiments of the courtly or Petrarchan lover in very few of his sonnets. In Sonnet CXXVIII he elaborates a metaphor in which he wishes he were the nimbly leaping jacks of the spinet his lady is playing, that he might also "kiss the tender inward" of her hand. In Sonnet CXXXII he writes a playful, romantic compliment. He toys with the time-honored conceit of the eye and the heart, concluding that since his mistress' eyes are black, they are mourners for the love sickness caused in him by her heart. In Sonnet CXLV, the lightest of the three, he plays with his mistress' exclamation, "I hate," for the length of the sonnet, closing it with the quick about face,

> "I hate" from hate away she threw,
> And sav'd my life, saying— "not you."

Conversely, in only two sonnets does Shakespeare concern himself with what had been a major problem to Sidney and Drayton— the unreality of the conceits which served to describe the traditional romantic ideal of beauty. In the one (Sonnet CXXVII), Shakespeare suggests that his mistress lacks the fair complexion and golden hair required of the ideal lady of romance.

> In the old age black was not counted fair,
> Or if it were, it bore not beauty's name;
> But now is black beauty's successive heir.

In the other sonnet (Sonnet CXXX), in a line by line analysis, he calls attention to the disparity between his mistress' attractions and those which poetic convention decreed that she should possess. This sonnet is the familiar one beginning, "My mistress' eyes are nothing like the sun."

With these few exceptions, Shakespeare does not give

romantic sentiment direct lyric expression in his sonnets. Nor does he present the usual conflict between romance and a new, humanistic skepticism. Moreover, Shakespeare is too objective to react against Petrarchism in the sharply satiric way of Marston and Donne, and he does not try to avoid the difficulties of lovers by following the Renaissance Platonists in spiritualizing love. Least of all does he escape from love by retreating to the sixteenth-century equivalent of monastic morality— Puritanism. The truth is that the majority of his lyrics begin where other Elizabethan poetry leaves off. They both recognize and explain the paradoxical nature of love. They acknowledge in a sardonic fashion the presence of inevitable contradictions in experienced passion. His sonnets record his effort to exploit the conventions of romantic sentiment, but not the idealizing spirit of which they are a product.

Shakespeare expresses his comprehension of the interplay of an idealizing tendency and cold fact in a number of different ways. In one sonnet (CXXXI) he employs terms of half-complimentary, half-scornful acceptance of his lady's physical imperfections. The poem is a perfectly clear statement of the complementary halves of love. To his "dear doting heart," he says, his lady is "the fairest and most precious jewel." Others have challenged her beauty, he admits, and

> To say they err I dare not be so bold,
> Although I swear it to myself alone.

Therefore, he tells her,

> A thousand groans, but thinking on thy face,
> One on another's neck, do witness bear
> Thy black is fairest in my judgment's place.

A similar perception, that this idealized portrait of his lady is contradicted by the reality of her deeds, is expressed in the sonnet (CL) which opens,

> O! from what power hast thou this powerful
>   might,
> With insufficiency my heart to sway?

There is so much graceful redemption in the "very refuse" of her deeds, he cries,

> That, in my mind, thy worst all best exceeds.

And he concludes, turning the contradictions of love upon himself in derision:

> If thy unworthiness rais'd love in me,
> More worthy I to be belov'd of thee.

In several of his sonnets he further examines the difference between ideal love and the less than ideal reality of his mistress. He uses, in ironic fashion, the old descriptive psychology of passion and its origins in the flame of the eye. Thus he cries,

> O me! what eyes hath Love put in my head,
> Which have no correspondence with true sight.

And he concludes, again in self-mockery, that the eyes of a lover are blinded with his tears of despair. It is they which blur tawdry aspects of his passion till the discrepancy between them and his ideal is all but invisible.

> O cunning Love! with tears thou keep'st me
>   blind,
> Lest eyes well-seeing thy foul faults should
>   find.

Shakespeare uses this same figure of the self-deceptive eye, but more bitterly, more in self-castigation, when he asks of Love,

> Why of eyes' falsehood hast thou forged hooks,
> Whereto the judgment of my heart is tied?

Shakespeare often deliberately turns his back upon Petrarchan conventions. He elaborates in caustic fashion his mistress' departure from the prescribed appearance and behavior of the lady of romance. He cries that he has perjured himself far more than she. She has merely her

> . . . bed-vow broke, and new faith torn,
> In vowing new hate after new love bearing.

But as her lover he has

> . . . sworn deep oaths of thy deep kindness,
> Oaths of thy love, thy truth, thy constancy;
> And, to enlighten thee, gave eyes to blindness,
> Or made them swear against the thing they see;
>   For I have sworn thee fair; more perjur'd I,
>   To swear against the truth so foul a lie!

However, Shakespeare presents most graphically the contradictory impulses that go to form the experience of love, not through ironic use of familiar metaphors of poetry, but by a description of the attraction and repulsion of sexual desire. Thus, in Sonnet CXLVII he exhibits the same wretched consciousness of the power of physical love to destroy an ideal as he did in *The Rape of Lucrece*. The mere sexual impulse

> . . . is as a fever, longing still
> For that which longer nurseth the disease.

He uses the figure of Reason, the physician whose prescription has been ignored, abandoning the lover to incurable dilemma.

> Past cure I am, now Reason is past care,

And frantic-mad with evermore unrest.

A similar, though more generalized, presentation of the inadequacy of lust either to satiate itself or to come up to its imagined delight is the subject of Sonnet CXXIX. Desire is

> A bliss in proof,— and, prov'd, a very woe;
> Before, a joy propos'd; behind, a dream.

. . . Shakespeare here reduces the paradox to its essentials. But he does not, . . . deny the romantic expectations of love or, . . . deny its carnality. He acknowledges, on the contrary, the irrationality of human passion.

> All this the world well knows; yet none knows
>   well
> To shun the heaven that leads men to this hell.

Most of Shakespeare's sonnets to a dark lady describe in various ways and in varying degrees of derision his understanding of the conflicting forces which form the experience of love. In a few sonnets, however, he goes beyond recognition of these forces to suggest (as did John Donne) that the discordant elements of love must be accepted as essential parts of a unified experience. Shakespeare, in Sonnet CXLII, proposes one way of easing man's disappointment when he discovers that sexual experience is not to be identified with complete spiritual felicity. His lady has questioned his love for her because of his past infidelity. He replies that her own life has not been of the sort to give her the right to criticize his.

> O! but with mine compare thou thine own
>   state,
> And thou shalt find it merits not reproving;
> Or, if it do, not from those lips of thine.

He suggests that they can strike some kind of balance between the dismal fruition of their love and their extravagant hopes only through pity for each other. If she "root pity" in her heart for him, she, in turn, may receive pity from those

> Whom thine eyes woo as mine importune thee.

Otherwise,

> If thou dost seek to have what thou dost hide,
> By self-example mayst thou be denied.

With less mockery, Shakespeare expresses a similar conciliatory idea in Sonnet CLI. He builds up an elaborate phallic metaphor to describe the triumph of sexuality in love despite the knowledge (conscience) that his lady, as well as he, has been a "gentle cheater." The mere recognition of their unillusioned views of each other, their mutual skepticism, does not inevitably destroy his pride in possessing her.

> No want of conscience hold it that I call
> Her "love" for whose dear love I rise and fall.

Shakespeare repeats this propitiatory gesture in a clearer fashion in another sonnet. He first acknowledges the insincerities of both parties to love.

> When my love swears that she is made of
> truth,
> I do believe her, though I know she lies,
> That she might think me some untutor'd youth
> Unlearned in the world's false subtleties.

Then he concludes that tranquility is best served by a resigned accommodation of oneself both to illusion and to fact.

> O! love's best habit is in seeming trust,
> And age in love loves not to have years told:
> Therefore I lie with her, and she with me
> And in our faults by lies we flatter'd be.

It would be difficult to find in any other Elizabethan poet a more frank acknowledgment not only that there are paradoxes involved in love, but also that they define love. In Donne alone is there anything comparable, but in his poetry an intellectual skepticism pervades his attitude of disillusionment, and a philosophic detachment his dispassionate balancing of contradictory impulses. Shakespeare arrives at a conclusion like that suggested by Donne, but usually by an approach that is quite different, by an emotional reaction to experience. In one of Shakespeare's sonnets, however, an intellectual skepticism does triumph. In this one sonnet is found his nearest lyric approach to the comic spirit dramatized by his love-game comedies. He presents his lady with the ironic suggestion that she pretend to be faithful to him, that she merely play the role of romantic mistress.

> If I might teach thee wit, better it were,
> Though not to love, yet, love, to tell me so;—
> As testy sick men, when their deaths be near,
> No news but health from their physicians
> know.

And the last line of this sonnet, which repeats this concept, does so by echoing familiar courtly love phraseology.

> Bear thine eyes straight, though thy proud heart
> go wide.

Shakespeare's sonnets are not written outside the Petrarchan tradition, nor do they ignore romantic sentiment. Indeed, as has been seen, he makes constant use of the inherited language of love, with its symbols the eye and the heart. It is merely that in his sonnets he does not use the usual metaphors and conceits as a Petrarchan or as an anti-Petrarchan. He succeeds in evoking the innermost essence of his emotions, and thus can make no easy use of conventional materials. He reshapes them, not in rebellion against a romantic attitude, but as part of a sardonic commentary on the contradiction between idealized and experienced passion. The customary Elizabethan poetic conceits fail to convey all that Shakespeare wishes to say about love. He expresses a much more profound understanding of what had hitherto been presented in most sixteenth-century writings as the conflict of a systematized romanticism with reality. The contradictory attitudes and emotions which his sonnets display are presented with so much more apparent conviction that they appear to be not so much a generalized comment on a common problem as a highly personal comment on an individual one.

This fact is illustrated further in a few sonnets which are concerned solely with the attraction and the repulsion of sexual desire. Here the thought seems distant from that usually found in Elizabethan love poetry. But these sonnets are related to the sixteenth century by the fact that they display a mood of bitter recoil from romantic sentiment. Recourse to obscenity is, in fact, a way of making rebellion against one's own ideals seem tolerable. It is an attempt to drown out the insistent voice of hopeless disenchantment. Such erotic blasphemy gives significance, for example, to such a metaphor as the one from Sonnet CXXXV,

> Wilt thou, whose will is large and spacious,
> Not once vouchsafe to hide my will in thine?

By insisting that the physical consummation of love is a gross and undignified act its psychic, intangible import is derided. This descent to the phallic is an attempt to reduce love to its elements and thereby to free oneself from the penalties of a softly idyllic mood which has carried one too far from reality. It is paralleled by all the jealous or frustrated lovers in Shakespeare's plays. It is Hamlet's treatment of Ophelia, Leontes's of Hermione, and the basis of one of the most harrowing scenes in all literature, Othello's treatment of Desdemona as his whore.

Shakespeare's sonnets mirror lovers' difficulties in a highly individualized fashion. What John Donne was doing intellectually, Shakespeare was doing in a more intuitive way. He was turning the exaggerated conflict between an idealized sentiment and a skepticism engendered by humanistic thought back into an expression of a conflict more fundamental to the human being. . . . Shakespeare often appears to be describing the contention between a personally imagined perfection of amorous experience and experience itself. In his sonnets the courtly and Petrarchan symbols of love are partially transmuted. The wheel has nearly come full circle. What began in Provence as a systemized exaltation of love, in

Shakespeare's lyrics to a dark lady begins to break down into the confusion inherent in the quarrel between an individual's own imagination and his own experience of reality.

M. M. Mahood

SOURCE: "Love's Confined Doom," in *Shakespeare Survey*, Vol. 15, 1962, pp. 50-61.

[*In her examination of the friendship between the speaker and the young man he addresses, Mahood focuses on the Poet's growing fear that his friend will betray him. She maintains that most of the sonnets from 33 to 124 represent the Poet's various attempts to deal with what he increasingly sees as inevitable: his friend will prove treacherous. Mahood also compares Shakespeare's development of the themes of deception and betrayal of friendship in the sonnets with his treatment of these motifs in several plays—especially his depiction of the relationships between Antonio and Bassanio in* The Merchant of Venice, *and Hal and Falstaff in* 1 *and* 2 Henry IV.]

I

The present trend of criticism is bringing Shakespeare's poems and his plays together. A dramatic element is recognized in short poems of many kinds— Shakespeare's sonnets, Keats's odes, the lyrics of Yeats. Like plays they attempt to give through some fiction (the truest poetry is the most feigning) form, and so meaning, to experiences whose real-life occasions are now lost to us and are, in any case, none of our business. A sonnet cannot help in the interpretation of a play, nor can the play throw any light on the sonnet's meaning, if the two works are thought of as belonging to different grades of imitation; if the sonnet, for example, is a snippet of biography or a poetic exercise. But if the two kinds of poetry are regarded, despite their differences in magnitude, as products of the same imaginative process, then our reading of the one can illumine our understanding of the other. In particular, these cross-references can lead us to a fuller understanding of the main theme of the sonnets: the complex and profoundly disturbed relationship of the poet with the friend to whom most of the sequence is addressed.

Sonnet XXXIII provides an example of the elucidation that such cross-references can afford:

Full many a glorious morning have I seen
Flatter the mountain-tops with sovereign eye,
Kissing with golden face the meadows green,
Gilding pale streams with heavenly alchemy;
Anon permit the basest clouds to ride
With ugly rack on his celestial face,
And from the forlorn world his visage hide,
Stealing unseen to west with this disgrace:
Even so my sun one early morn did shine

With all-triumphant splendour on my brow;
But out, alack! he was but one hour mine;
The region cloud hath mask'd him from me now.
    Yet him for this my love no whit disdaineth;
    Suns of the world may stain, when heaven's sun staineth.

It is not at all easy, in reading this, to grasp what the friend has done— if the clouds represent some blot on his reputation with the world at large, or the relationship of poet and friend has been clouded by the friend's unkindness. Is the clouding involuntary or deliberate? The grammatical structure of the second quatrain leaves us in doubt whether the sun hides his visage, stealing away in shame, or whether, untouched himself, he simply permits the clouds to hide it. 'Celestial' implies that the friend, like the sun, belongs to the immutable order of heavenly bodies who are not themselves affected in any way by the rack of clouds passing below them in the sublunary world's insubstantial pageant. Yet if the friend merely allows his glory to be eclipsed and is himself in no way blemished it is hard to see what Shakespeare intended by 'disgrace', since the word whenever used by him (with the possible exception of 'And then grace us in the disgrace of death' in *Love's Labour's Lost*, where it can mean 'disfigurement') has a derogatory meaning. 'Stain' also is a teasingly imprecise word. It can mean to darken, or even to eclipse or to be eclipsed (as in *Antony and Cleopatra*, III, iv, 27), though a much commoner meaning is to blemish or to become blemished.

If we turn to the plays for parallels in thought, diction or imagery which may throw light on Shakespeare's intention in sonnet XXXIII, we are immediately struck by two passages which bear a close resemblance to the second quatrain of the sonnet. When Richard II appears on the walls of Flint Castle, Hotspur exclaims

See, see, King Richard doth himself appear,
As doth the blushing discontented sun
From out the fiery portal of the east,
When he perceives the envious clouds are bent
To dim his glory and to stain the track
Of his bright passage to the occident.

To which the Duke of York adds

Yet looks he like a king: behold, his eye,
As bright as is the eagle's, lightens forth
Controlling majesty: alack, alack, for woe,
That any harm should stain so fair a show!
                    (III, iii, 62-71)

The verbal resemblances between this and sonnet XXXIII are close, but no closer than others to be found in a passage of *Henry IV, Part I*. Hal, parting from his Eastcheap companions, lets the audience into the secret

Queen Elizabeth I.

Upon my smiles.

(III, ii, 410-12)

The context is one of betrayal; however hard Wolsey seeks, like the poet in sonnet after sonnet (for example, XXXV, which is closely connected with XXXIII and in which 'Thy adverse party is thy advocate') to justify the King, every audience is perturbed by Henry's treachery. The use of 'gild' is significant. Shakespeare nearly always employs the word in a derogatory sense to suggest the brilliance that masks corruption: 'England shall double gild his treble guilt'; 'men are but gilded loam'; 'the gilded puddle'; 'gilded tombs do worms infold'. Goneril [in *King Lear*] is 'this gilded serpent'. Even a seemingly neutral use of the word turns out to be ambiguous. When Antony sends a jewel to Cleopatra after his parting with her, the queen greets the messenger with the words

coming from him, that great medicine hath
With his tinct gilded thee.

(I, v, 36-7)

Gold is cordial. Antony is life-giving, 'sovereign' like the sun. Yet at this moment he is bound for Rome and marriage with Octavia. A mainspring of the play's action is Cleopatra's uncertainty as to whether Antony is dust a little gilt or gilt o'er-dusted. This is exactly the uncertainty in which the poet of the sonnets stands in relation to his friend.

'Alchemy', like 'gild', was not a word which necessarily implied deception to the sixteenth-century reader. But it too is used by Shakespeare in contexts of betrayal. As J. W. Lever has shown [in *The Elizabethan Love Sonnet*] there is a meaningful resemblance between the opening of sonnet XXXIII and the lines in *King John* in which the King, having treacherously abandoned the cause of Constance and her son Arthur by agreeing to the French match, declares of the marriage day

To solemnize this day the glorious sun
Stays in his course and plays the alchemist,
Turning with splendour of his precious eye
The meagre cloddy earth to glittering gold.

(III, i, 77-80)

Even more interesting is the way the word is used in *Julius Caesar:*

O, he sits high in all the people's hearts:
And that which would appear offence in us,
His countenance, like richest alchemy,
Will change to virtue and to worthiness.

(I, iii, 157-60)

Although Cassius gives warm assent to this 'right well conceited' description of Brutus, the play itself leaves us in lasting doubt over the effect of such alchemy. Does

of his relationship with them:

Yet herein will I imitate the sun,
Who doth permit the base contagious clouds
To smother up his beauty from the world,
That, when he please again to be himself,
Being wanted, he may be more wonder'd at,
By breaking through the foul and ugly mists
Of vapours that did seem to strangle him.

(I, ii, 220-6)

In the first passage the sun image is used of a weak man who, for all his show of controlling majesty, is controlled by his subjects; in the second, of a strong man who conceals his true nature for reasons of policy. This contrast heightens rather than solves the contradictions of sonnet XXXIII. But fortunately the plays also offer a number of parallels with the sonnet's magnificent opening quatrain which may take us a little further in understanding the poem.

The first of these is in *Henry VIII*, when Wolsey, disgraced by the King ('That sun, I pray, may never set!'), laments that

No sun shall ever usher forth mine honours,
Or gild again the noble troops that waited

it in fact turn the assassination into a golden deed, or does it only gild over the conspirators' guilt? Public virtue, Shakespeare hints here and elsewhere in the plays, never cancels out private wrong, and the noblest Roman of them all is branded with the lasting reproach of *Et tu, Brute.*

To Coleridge the opening of sonnet XXXIII represented one mark of the poetic imagination at its best: its ability to transfer a human and intellectual life to images of nature [*Biographia Literaria*]. Just as Venus' sense of loss at Adonis' departure is precisely matched by the experience of watching a shooting star vanish in the night sky, so Shakespeare finds in the treacherous overclouding of a bright summer's day the exact image for his disappointment in his friend's deliberate coldness. This disappointment is not the almost impersonal regret felt by Hotspur and York at Richard's weaknesses; it is the personal pain that Henry V could give his old companion, Falstaff. So much is suggested by the beginning of sonnet XXXIV—'Why didst thou promise such a beauteous day', where the hurt is scarcely healed by the tears the friend sheds. 'And they are rich and ransom all ill deeds' may well be spoken with deep irony to the man who thinks his patronage can pay for his unkindness. For in italicizing the word 'Flatter' in his quotation, Coleridge unerringly indicated the tone of sonnet XXXIII and the succeeding sonnet. Flattery forebodes treachery. What Shakespeare dreads in his friend is not the folly of youth—that he is almost eager to condone—but the cold strength of maturity.

II

If Thorpe's arrangement of the sonnets has any significance, sonnet XXXIII represents the first cloud across the friendship, and the poet never subsequently speaks with the simple trust that we find, say, in sonnet XXIX. When Shakespeare later made use of the image of the rising lark which supplies the unforgettable sestet of that sonnet, he gives it a bitter setting; [in *Cymbeline*] it becomes the incidental music to Cloten's attempt to corrupt Posthumus' wife. And when, within the sonnet sequence itself, Shakespeare returns in sonnet XCI to the theme of love's riches as compensation for the world's neglect—'And having thee, of all men's pride I boast'—the final, misgiving couplet quite alters the sonnet's effect:

> Wretched in this alone, that thou mayst take
> All this away and me most wretched make.

Another sonnet concerned with the friendship's value is the forty-eighth, which contrasts the care the poet has taken to stow away his material wealth on leaving for a journey with the way his most precious possession of all, the friend himself, is left 'the prey to every vulgar thief':

> Thee have I not lock'd up in any chest,
> Save where thou art not, though I feel thou
> art,
> Within the gentle closure of my breast,
> From whence at pleasure thou mayst come and
> part.

The lingering monosyllabic line 'Save where thou art not . . . ' is heavy with mistrust. Such a mistrust is experienced by the Helena of *A Midsummer Night's Dream*, whose affection has been so freely and foolishly given and who still cannot quite believe, when all the mistakes of a midsummer night are over, that Demetrius is hers:

> And I have found Demetrius like a jewel,
> Mine own, and not mine own.
>
> (IV, i, 195-6)

The motif of a treasure in a casket which occurs several times in the sonnets is of course an integral part of *The Merchant of Venice.* Here the critics draw our attention to one particularly close parallel. Bassanio, making his choice of the leaden casket, moralizes over the way the world is still deceived with ornament:

> So are those crisped snaky golden locks
> Which make such wanton gambols with the
> wind,
> Upon supposed fairness, often known
> To be the dowry of a second head,
> The skull that bred them in the sepulchre.
>
> (III, ii, 92-6)

Sonnets LXVII and LXVIII also protest at the deceptions of the time, which are held to accord ill with the friend's 'truth'. His beauty is his own as beauty was in the days

> Before the golden tresses of the dead,
> The right of sepulchres, were shorn away,
> To live a second life on second head;
> Ere beauty's dead fleece made another gay.

The poet's intention seems to be that both Bassanio and the friend should stand for truth in a naughty world. Sonnet LXVII in fact strengthens this connection by saying that nowadays Nature is bankrupt—'Beggar'd of blood to blush through lively veins'; and Bassanio's wealth, he tells Portia, all flows in his veins. But though he is frank enough to tell her this when he first comes wooing he does not then tell her what he later confesses, that he is 'worse than nothing' and that he is in fact indebted to Antonio for coming like a day in April 'To show how costly summer was at hand'. It is unfashionable at present to regard Bassanio as a fortune-hunter, yet in this same scene Gratiano puts the facts of the matter honestly enough when he says 'We are the Jasons, we have won the fleece'. If generations of critics have been perplexed by the discrepancies between Shakespeare's apparent intentions in portraying Bassanio and the character who emerges from the play, the reason may be that Shakespeare's presentation of the character is related to a real-life discrepancy between what he wishes his friend to be and what he fears he is. So in the sonnets, with their many verbal parallels to *The Merchant of Venice*: Shakespeare strains in sonnet LXVII and sonnet LXVIII to dissociate his friend from the corruption of the times and in sonnet LXIX blames those times for adding to his friend's fair flower 'the rank smell of weeds'; yet the collection as a whole shows him to be haunted by the fear that his friend is all the time a lily that festers.

Such a re-reading of *The Merchant of Venice* in the light of the sonnets helps us towards an answer to the question with which the play opens: why is the Merchant himself so sad? Already in the first scene Antonio hints at the true source of his sadness:

> My ventures are not in one bottom trusted,
> Nor to one place; nor is my whole estate
> Upon the fortune of this present year:
> Therefore my merchandise makes me not sad.
>
> (I, i, 42-5)

Discriminatory stress here falls on *bottom, place, merchandise;* Antonio has not entrusted all his wealth to one ship, but he has entrusted all his affection to one man and is obsessed by thoughts of the hazards he runs in this venture. In the story, as Shakespeare shapes it out of the casket tale and the tale of the cruel bond, Bassanio is faithful to Antonio, whose fears are therefore groundless. But they are none the less real to the audience. Antonio begins as he ends, the odd man out, awakening in the audience a sympathy which is extraneous to the play's general effect and so quite different from any emotions which Shylock may arouse. In Antonio's readiness to stake all for his friend, his parting from him, his letter, his willing resignation, we find the dramatic expression of that 'fear of trust' at which Shakespeare hints also in Bassanio's speech on ornament, and which runs through so many sonnets to find, perhaps, its most eloquent expression in sonnet XC:

> Ah, do not, when my heart hath 'scaped this
>   sorrow,
> Come in the rearward of a conquer'd woe;
> Give not a windy night a rainy morrow,
> To linger out a purposed overthrow.
> If thou wilt leave me, do not leave me last,
> When other petty griefs have done their spite,
> But in the onset come; so shall I taste
> At first the very worst of fortune's might.

The same fear of trust may be the case of a similar disproportion in another of Shakespeare's middle comedies, *Twelfth Night*. The Antonio of that play feels for Sebastian a devotion which belongs to an altogether different order of experience from the Duke's infatuation with Olivia or Olivia's mourning for her dead brother. Viola's silent passion comes within reach of it, and for this reason she is deeply moved by Antonio's reproaches to her for not yielding his purse (a situation handled with cheerful heartlessness in *The Comedy of Errors*). Bewildered as she is by this meaningless demand, she can recognize his anguish of disillusion, an anguish oddly misplaced in Illyria:

> Let me speak a little. This youth that you see
>   here
> I snatch'd one half out of the jaws of death,
> Relieved him with such sanctity of love,
> And to his image, which methought did
>   promise
> Most venerable worth, did I devotion . . .
> But O how vile an idol proves this god!
> Thou hast, Sebastian, done good feature shame.
> In nature there's no blemish but the mind;
> None can be call'd deform'd but the unkind:
> Virtue is beauty, but the beauteous evil
> Are empty trunks o'erflourish'd by the devil.
>
> (III, iv, 393-404)

Two persistent themes of the doubting sonnets— the youth's beauty, promising 'most venerable worth' and the poet's worshipping devotion— are to be found here, and Antonio's speech of further reproach in the last act adds another: the contrast between the speaker's spend-thrift affection and the friend's careful calculations of the risks involved:

> His life I gave him and did thereto add
> My love, *without retention or restraint,*
> All his in dedication; for his sake
> Did I expose myself, pure for his love,
> Into the danger of this adverse town;
> Drew to defend him when he was beset:
> Where being apprehended, his false cunning,
> *Not meaning to partake with me in danger,*
> Taught him to face me out of his acquaintance,
> And grew a twenty years removed thing.
>
> (V, i, 83-92)

This relationship of Antonio to Sebastian stands up like a great inselberg of eroded experience in the green landscape of comedy. And in a history play of the same period, *Henry V,* surprising prominence is given to the theme of trust betrayed, in Henry's eloquent reproaches to the traitor Scroop. The loosely episodic construction of the play is not injured by the stress Shakespeare lays on an incident which is briefly treated by the chroniclers. But this emphasis once again suggests that Shakespeare was haunted by the fear that his self-possessed friend would one day repudiate him:

> O, how hast thou with jealousy infected
> The sweetness of affiance! Show men dutiful? . . .

Free from gross passion or of mirth or anger,
Constant in spirit, not swerving with the blood,
Garnish'd and deck'd in modest complement,
Not working with the eye without the ear,
And but in purged judgement trusting neither?
Such and so finely bolted didst thou seem:
And thus thy fall hath left a kind of blot,
To mark the full-fraught man and best indued
With some suspicion. I will weep for thee;
For this revolt of thine, methinks, is like
Another fall of man.

(II, ii, 126-42)

Among the sonnets, sonnets XC-XCIV, a sequence of mounting mistrust which most of the rearrangers leave undisturbed, and which culminates in the much-discussed 'They that have power', come very close in theme and tone to Henry's speech. Sonnet XCIII speaks, with all the bitterness of *Twelfth Night's* Antonio, of the youth's deceptive beauty, and like Henry V the poet here associates outer fairness and inner corruption with original sin; so calamitous and yet so inescapable does the friend's betrayal appear to him:

But heaven in thy creation did decree
That in thy face sweet love should ever dwell;
Whate'er thy thoughts or thy heart's workings
  be,
Thy looks should nothing thence but sweetness
  tell.
How like Eve's apple doth thy beauty grow,
If thy sweet virtue answer not thy show!

III

The sonnets we have hitherto discussed are among the least conventional in the sequence. In many of the more conventional ones, however, it is noticeable that Shakespeare is making use of the convention to relieve or to escape from his intolerable doubts of his friend's loyalty. Thus one of the oldest themes which the sonnet absorbed from medieval love poetry, the poet's abject self-abasement before the god-like nature of the friend or mistress, eases the poet's dread of betrayal by supplying a justification for it. Such a rationalization of fear is found, alongside the melancholy which the fear induces, in Shakespeare's depiction of Antonio in *The Merchant of Venice*. His words at the trial—

I am a tainted wether of the flock,
Meetest for death: the weakest kind of fruit
Drops earliest to the ground; and so let me:
(IV, i, 114-16)

are as movingly unconvincing as is sonnet LXXXVIII:

With mine own weakness being best
  acquainted,
Upon thy part I can set down a story

Of faults conceal'd, wherein I am attainted,
That thou in losing me shalt win much glory.

Glory of this kind is won by Hal at the end of the second part of *Henry IV* when he repudiates Falstaff; and there are several sonnets in which the relationship between the young, handsome and conspicuous friend seems closely to parallel that of the Prince of Wales and his reprobate old companion. Of these sonnet XLIX comes nearest to the culminating scene of *Henry IV, Part II*:

Against that time, if ever that time come,
When I shall see thee frown on my defects,
When as thy love hath cast his utmost sum,
Call'd to that audit by advised respects;
Against that time when thou shalt strangely
  pass
And scarcely greet me with that sun, thine eye,
When love, converted from the thing it was,
Shall reasons find of settled gravity,
Against that time do I ensconce me here
Within the knowledge of mine own desert,
And this my hand against myself uprear,
To guard the lawful reasons on thy part:
  To leave poor me thou hast the strength of
    laws,
  Since why to love I can allege no cause.

At the end of the play, love is converted from the thing it was when Hal, succeeding to the throne, declares 'I have turned away my former self' and takes as his new counsellor the strength of laws in the person of the Lord Chief Justice. If we take, from the back of the gallery or the back of history, a long view of the Hal-Falstaff relationship, the rejection is justified. But the sonnet gives us a sombre close-up of the matter from the viewpoint of the rejected companion, in which cold prudence shows itself in the 'advis'd respects' (a phrase already used of majesty in *King John*) and in the profit-and-loss calculations with which the friend casts his utmost sum. The reasons of settled gravity serve, to borrow a telling phrase from sonnet LXXXIX, 'to set a form upon desired change'. Gravity belongs to the court and in particular to the Lord Chief Justice who tells Falstaff 'There is not a white hair on your face but should have his effect of gravity'. 'What doth gravity out of his bed at midnight?' Falstaff asks when a nobleman of the court comes to summon Hal to a reckoning with his father; and gravity is dismissed by levity while the scene of reckoning is played out as an Eastcheap farce. But in the charade, Falstaff is soon turned out of the role of Hal's father; and the royal resolution— 'I do, I will' with which Hal encounters Falstaff's plea not to banish honest Jack is put into effect when the new-crowned Henry V passes 'strangely'. The Lord Chief Justice follows, to waken Falstaff rudely from his long dream in which he, and not the Lord Chief Justice, will replace Hal's father—

Thus have I had thee, as a dream doth flatter,
In sleep a king, but waking no such matter.
(*Sonnet* LXXXVII)

In the play as well as the poems, Shakespeare seeks to exorcize the haunting fear of betrayal by showing such betrayal to be justified in the light of prudence, a cardinal virtue, and of policy, the wisdom of governors. But the reproach of disloyalty remains, breaking out in the sonnets through ambiguous words and phrases, and perplexing for centuries the audiences of *Henry IV*.

Readers who are distressed by the self-abasing tone of such sonnets may turn with relief to those that make use of a contrary convention and promise the friend immortal life in the poet's verse. Yet many of these 'eternizing' sonnets are not so much the expression of confidence as of fear, the same persistent fear of the friend's treachery. In anticipation of that betrayal, the poet tries to perpetuate his friend in his verse as he now is and while he is still the poet's friend. He seeks 'To make him seem long hence as he shows now' (sonnet CI). But what he seems and shows may be quite other than what he actually is, and some of these sonnets are as profoundly ironic as the Duke's words to Angelo in the last act of *Measure for Measure*, when the deputy still appears 'unmoved, cold, and to temptation slow':

O, your desert speaks loud; and I should
  wrong it,
To lock it in the wards of covert bosom,
When it deserves, with characters of brass,
A forted residence 'gainst the tooth of time
And razure of oblivion.
(v, i, 9-13)

Because the characters of brass may ultimately speak of the friend as someone very different from the man the poet knows, the poet insists on his power to perpetuate him in his verse, not as a paragon of all the virtues— in fact we are told very little about the young man, as all Shakespeare's biographers have cause to complain— but simply as the poet's friend—

But you shall shine more bright in these
  contents
Than unswept stone besmear'd with sluttish
  time.
(*Sonnet* LV)

Sluttish time not only neglects the gilded monuments but actually besmears them; the poet is fighting to preserve his friend against 'all-oblivious *enmity*' and beyond that, it may be conjectured from the same sonnet's ambiguous final couplet, from the ultimate truth of his nature which the poet dreads to see discovered:

So, till the judgement that yourself arise,
You live in this, and dwell in lovers' eyes.

So too in the greatest 'eternizing' sonnet, the Ovidian sonnet LX, Time appears as the enemy not only of the youth's beauty but of his virtue too. Time feeds on the rarities of Nature's truth, and the eclipses which fight here against the glory of maturity can be, as they are in sonnet XXXIII, the darkened reputation which comes even in a man's lifetime from 'envious and calumniating time'.

The ravages of Time are the subject of sonnet LXIV— 'When I have seen by Time's fell hand . . .'. But here there is no promise of an immortality in verse to offset the melancholy close:

Ruin hath taught me thus to ruminate,
That Time will come and take my love away.
  This thought is as a death, which cannot
  choose
  But weep to have that which it fears to lose.

Commentators on this sonnet are much struck by the resemblance between its second quatrain and the speech of King Henry in *Henry IV, Part II* beginning 'O God! that one might read the book of fate'. Both passages picture the sea's encroachment upon the land and the land's upon the sea. It is worth following Henry's speech in the play a little further, to see what application he makes of the image:

O, if this were seen,
The happiest youth, viewing his progress
  through,
What perils past, what crosses to ensue,
Would shut the book, and sit him down and
  die.
'Tis not ten years gone
Since Richard and Northumberland, great
  friends,
Did feast together, and in two years after
Were they at wars it is but eight years since
This Percy was the man nearest my soul,
Who like a brother toil'd in my affairs
And laid his life and love under my foot.
(III, i, 53-63)

Time will also come and take Shakespeare's love away— by death perhaps, although in the natural course of things the poet would die the earlier; the *Henry IV* passage shows rather that Time may take him away as it took Northumberland from Richard and has taken Hotspur from Henry. Here again then destructive time is equated, as Derek Traversi has said [in *Approach to Shakespeare*], with the 'necessary flaw at the heart of passion'.

So the millioned accidents of time creep in, the poet says in sonnet CXV, between men's vows and 'Divert strong minds to the course of altering things'. In this last sonnet, however, the vicissitudes of time are made to serve a new turn of thought by explaining how it has been possible for the poet's love to increase. This sonnet therefore belongs with those that make use of a third conventional idea of love poetry and of the sonnet in particular, the constancy of the poet's love. Whatever the friend may do, the poet's affection will last for ever and a day. There is thus a natural transition from this sonnet to the boast of sonnet CXVI that love is not love 'Which alters when it alteration finds'. Sonnets CVII and CXXIV also belong to this group, and when, after all that has been written about these two difficult poems, one rereads them in their place in the sequence it is hard to see how the 'love' they celebrate could ever have been taken to mean the friend himself and not Shakespeare's affection for the friend. The 'confin'd doom' of CVII can surely only mean the limits which cynical on-lookers have set to Shakespeare's friendship, limits suggested perhaps by a knowledge of the friend's true nature. But in defiance of these prophecies, the poet claims his love is not 'the child of state'—

> It fears not policy, that heretic,
> Which works on leases of short-number'd
>   hours.

The friend's love may well be diverted from its true allegiance by policy; he has already revealed himself as a calculating young man, and the time may come when he will cast his utmost sum and, knowing his estimate, will reject the poet. But in contrast the poet's love stands 'hugely politic'; it embraces the whole state of existence and to him it is inconceivable that he could ever 'leave for nothing all this sum of good'—

> For nothing this wide universe I call,
> Save thou, my rose; in it thou art my all.

Sonnet CIX, from which these lines are quoted, presents the poet 'like one that travels' bringing 'water for my stain'. Verbally it closely parallels the passage in *Henry IV, Part II* from which T. W. Baldwin [in *The Literary Genetics of Shakespeare's Poems and Sonnets*] begins his study of the relationship between the poems and the plays:

> *Falstaff.* But to stand stained with travel, and sweating with desire to see him; thinking of nothing else, putting all affairs else in oblivion, as if there were nothing else to be done but to see him.
>
> *Pistol.* 'Tis 'semper idem', for 'obsque hoc nihil est:' 'tis all in every part.
>
> (v, v, 25-31)

In this of course Falstaff's devotion is anything but disinterested, and I have already suggested that it is one of Shakespeare's ways of evading the fear of trust to present Falstaff as a character who deserves the dismissal he gets. But Falstaff does not alter where he alteration finds. He believes that he will be sent for

soon at night and when that last hope is gone, Falstaff himself has nothing left to live for: 'The king hath killed his heart.'

IV

In suggesting that the deep fear of love's confined doom and the various ways of coming to terms with that fear— by accepting the justice of the doom, by stressing poetry's power to escape devouring time and by protesting the poet's own unchanging loyalty— are the motive forces of most of the sonnets between XXXIII and CXXIV, and an important element in several of Shakespeare's middle plays, I have run the risk, especially where the plays are concerned, of appearing to be a biographical speculator. But while I am convinced the fear of trust is a factor to be reckoned with in our reading of the poems and plays, I would not suggest following this clue out of the text and into Shakespeare's life. We know too little about the labyrinthine processes by which experience is tranformed into the work of art. The warning of a Victorian editor of the sonnets, Robert Bell, is apposite: 'the particle of actual life out of which verse is wrought may be, and almost always is, wholly incommensurate to the emotion depicted, and remote from the forms into which it is ultimately shaped'. Some trifle light as air may have rendered Shakespeare the man jealous of a friend's affection and so created the tormented 'I' of the sonnets as well as the two Antonios and certain aspects of Falstaff.

If the recognition of the 'fear of trust' as a strong element in the sonnets and middle plays throws no clear light on Shakespeare's biography, it might be expected to help in the critical evaluation of these works. But here we meet a long standing difference of opinion between those critics— they are mostly practising poets like Yeats, Auden and Empson— who hold that poetry should be the clear expression of mixed feelings and those others, and they include some of the best commentators on the sonnets, who feel that ambiguities of tone and verbal meanings constitute a defect because they indicate the poet has insufficiently realized his experience in a poetic form. For these critics the lack of moral explicitness in, say, *The Merchant of Venice* and *Henry IV* will always be a blemish on these plays, and they are likely to prefer *Integer vitae* [the upright life] to 'They that have power', or the perfect control of 'When in disgrace with fortune . . . ' to the sounding imprecision of 'Not mine own fears . . . '. If I here stop short of an evaluative conclusion to these few observations on the Sonnets and middle plays, it is not because I feel such evaluations can be dismissed as a matter of taste, but because they need a definition of critical principles that lies outside the scope of the present essay. And even when we are furnished with such principles we are likely to find that in critical evaluation, as in biographical inquiry and other activities of scholarship, we may come to the pericardium, but not the heart of truth.

Philip Martin

SOURCE: "Sin of Self-Love: the Youth," in *Shakespeare's Sonnets: Self, Love and Art*, Cambridge University Press, 1972, pp. 15-43.

[*Martin concentrates on Sonnets 1-17, where, he contends, the principal themes of all the sonnets involving the young man are subtly introduced. In this group, the critic notes, the speaker simultaneously praises and censures the youth's self-absorption. Though he agrees that the young man's self-love is justified, he also points out that by refusing to marry and have children the youth is, in effect, cooperating with time in the destruction of his beauty. Martin also calls attention to the intimate connection between themes and language in the sonnets, illustrating this with a careful analysis of the relationship between the diction, syntax, and figurative language of Sonnet 1 and the ideas expressed there.*]

Anyone who reads the Sonnets must notice how often and how variously they speak of self-love. It is there from the start. The order of the Quarto may be disputed, but surely not the position of Sonnet 1. For the sequence could have no opening so completely Shakespearean as this. Here, as in those dialogues between minor characters which open many of the great plays, the chief themes are quietly asserted: the youth's beauty, the destructiveness of time, the choice to be made between defying time and co-operating with it.

> From fairest creatures we desire increase,
> That thereby beauties *Rose* might never die,
> But as the riper should by time decease,
> His tender heire might beare his memory:
> But thou contracted to thine owne bright eyes,
> Feed'st thy lights flame with selfe substantiall
>   fewell,
> Making a famine where aboundance lies,
> Thy selfe thy foe, to thy sweet selfe too cruell:
> Thou that art now the worlds fresh ornament,
> And only herauld to the gaudy spring,
> Within thine owne bud buriest thy content,
> And tender chorle makst wast in niggarding:
>   Pitty the world, or else this glutton be,
>   To eate the worlds due, by the grave and
>   thee.

What particularly corresponds here to the first scenes of the plays is the pitch of the poetry, the understatement of its manner. This is a deliberately minor sonnet as compared, say, with 'Not marble, nor the guilded monuments' or 'Let me not to the marriage of true mindes'. It is not elevated, it is not one of the great moments of the sequence, yet it is indispensable. And while it is, like Sonnet 144 ('Two loves I have of comfort and dispaire'), an obviously thematic sonnet, it does not merely state its themes, it embodies them in a respectably complex poetic texture. Restrained as it is, it has the true Shakespearean richness of suggestion. And to read it

aloud will show how beautifully timed its long crescendo is; how much the aural shape of the poem, its 'music' in the popular sense, is a part of that other 'music of poetry' which Eliot speaks of: the patterning of diverse, even discordant elements into a unified meaning.

Self-love may be servitude, self-love may be freedom: this is what a great many of the Sonnets say, some throwing the emphasis on one possibility, some on the other. In Sonnet 1 it falls on the first: self-love, as the poet sees it in the youth, is nothing less than a complicity with 'devouring Time'. But the point is made both tellingly and winningly; praise and condemnation balance each other. This is a poetry which keeps something in reserve and never raises its voice unless it has to. The 'thou' of the poem is not mentioned a moment too soon, and the harshest word applied to him, 'glutton', is held back until the second last line, where the rhythm gives it a surprising force. But it would be well to look more closely at this sonnet to see what it establishes, not only in the way of themes, but also of modes of language; for in both respects (which are in any case intimately related) it is a genuine introduction to the poems that follow.

The first line intimates a concern with 'creatures', beings subject to a mightier power (though that is not yet insisted on); and by assonance and alliteration 'creatures' and 'increase' are linked in the poetry as they should be (the poem implies) in life. 'Thereby' in line 2 points back, more than syntactically, to 'increase' and to the 'creatures' from which it proceeds. As an image, 'beauties *Rose*' needs no more force than it has, being used as a commonplace for beauty perpetually flourishing, withering and being reborn. The line goes on to introduce the ideas of *dying* and of *never dying*, and thus to make the first reference to immortality. In line 3 the suggestions of 'as . . . should' are ambiguous. The line points to what *must* happen in the nature of things, with which it seems prepared to acquiesce: that 'the riper should by time decease' is fitting. But (the next line adds) only if there is an heir. And this changes the meaning of 'as' from 'because' to 'while' in both its senses: firstly as referring to time (while one life is declining, another rises in its stead) and secondly as marking a contrast (on the one hand, death; on the other, new life patterned on the old). And together the two lines juxtapose 'riper' and 'tender'. 'Riper' has the usual Shakespearean associations of maturity and acceptance ('Ripeness is all'), and there may be an implication, coming partly from the even movement of the line, that the acceptance is that of the parent as well as of people generally (the 'we' of the poem): for him it is a 'well-contented day', or it will be if an heir survives it. And a 'tender' heir: the word implying youth (the first blades of grass, the first shoots on a bough), and also human affection, the grateful love of children towards those who have given them life, and whose memory they are glad to 'beare'. The delicate forwarding movement of the language is difficult to suggest in critical prose: it is so much more deftly many-sided than any description can be. As Mrs Nowottny remarks [in "Formal Elements in Shakespeare's Sonnets: Sonnets I-VI"], in discussing the fugal form of Sonnet 4, 'critical analysis, which cannot reproduce the simultaneousness of the original, must labour heavily behind, discussing first the development of each part and then their interaction.' . . . But even such an attempt may suggest how one line leads inevitably into the next, and in no mechanical or predictable way; how even the second half of a line may realize a further stage of the process established in the first. The furthering may be achieved, as we have seen, by an ambiguous phrase or by a pun on a single word: 'beare', for instance. Essentially the line in which this occurs is concerned with issue: an heir who will carry on the parent's line. But the poetry does not separate biology from the rest of life. 'Beare his memory' conveys the two ideas that in his love the heir consciously cherishes the memory of his father, that in himself he *is* the memory of his father, whose image can be seen in him by those (like the poet perhaps?) who knew the father; and that naturally the son will wish to carry on his memory, his *and* his father's, by begetting children of his own.

The first quatrain, then, creates a sense of natural and inevitable order, a necessary enchainment of one generation with the next and the next: father, child, and the unconceived who must be brought to birth. This quatrain states the thesis both of this sonnet and of at least the sixteen poems which follow it. I would point again to the quietness of this opening: a softly-spoken but in no way tentative statement of an idea which (the tone leads us to feel) no one is likely to deny. There is tact here (or is it tactics?); and there is, too, an expansive movement within the quatrain. The first line provides a starting-point as quiet and gentle as possible, but each line seems to mount on the rising curve of the one before it, and the gradually mounting wave of the four lines together sweeps us slowly but powerfully into the second quatrain. If the first states a thesis the second shows its immediate application. We know we have reached the point of reference with the first words: 'But *thou*'. And yet in the next words the gentleness of the poem's manner, or manners, is still apparent. No ringing denunciation, at least not yet. Instead:

> But thou contracted to thine owne *bright eyes*,
> Feed's thy *lights flame* with *selfe substantiall fewell*,
> Making a famine where aboundance lies.

Half of the effect of these lines is of praise for the youth. Beyond doubt the compliment is intended: his eyes *are* bright. If it is becoming clear that he falls short of his end, the lines intimate also the wealth of his endowments. It is *almost* pardonable, certainly understandable, that he should live as he does, with such eyes, such abundance, to 'court an amorous looking-

glass'; the poetry, pursuing this vein of compliment, might almost seem to be saying that the youth is, as he thinks, 'selfe substantiall'. Yet in this process the self is being consumed. And the vein that runs counter to that of praise emerges strongly in the third line with the heavy stress on 'famine'; so that the negative is already set against the positive at the climax of the quatrain and the centre of the poem. Quite effortlessly the poetry holds in one hand the two terms of the contradiction: in 'Making a famine where aboundance lies', the rhythmic antithesis between 'famine' and 'aboundance' weighs praise against blame, blame against praise, and in a manner to suggest that an abundance which 'lies' unused must turn to a famine equally great; a destruction equal to the power destroyed. The quatrain ends with a paradox which, through a lessened subtlety, creates I think a slight anticlimax even while it drives the point home; yet the two strands are retained, of criticism and compliment, or rather, perhaps, of appeal: 'Thy selfe thy foe, to thy *sweet* selfe too *cruell*'.

This double insistence is carried through into the third quatrain. The beloved is 'now the worlds fresh ornament': 'fresh' on the one hand meaning new, young, vital, and on the other implying, with some help from 'now', that possibly the world has had other such ornaments before, and will lose this just as it lost those: You won't always be beautiful. And (say the next two lines) if I call you 'herauld to the gaudy spring' I mean that while you seem to promise new life and growth, in fact you frustrate it: 'within thine owne bud buriest thy content'. Not that the verse makes any crude opposition: the youth *is* the world's fresh ornament *and* he buries his own content. 'Content' means 'all that he contains', which of course includes the power to beget children, and at the same time it means his 'contentment', now and more especially in the future, and the contentment which he could give to others. 'Bury' has something of the sense it has in 'burying one's talents' or 'burying one's head in the sand' as well as conveying the more important, more direct meaning that the youth is making an end, and so a grave, of that which is properly the beginning of new life, his 'owne bud'. We are offered a paradox which underlies most of the sonnets, and all of the sonnets on this theme: that to concentrate on your self is to lose it. For it can't be kept: if it is not given away it will be taken away. The friend may be a bud, but he can flower only in another. To swerve from this is to make waste in niggarding: to squander one's substance through sheer meanness, or to be guilty of a kind of gluttony. Now in the couplet we are made to see new meaning in the word 'feed' of line 6. There it referred to the fuelling of a fire. Here the reference is human: gluttony means eating more than one needs, and perhaps what others need; so to consume oneself is to consume what, in one's issue, belongs to the world. It is 'to eate the worlds due' just as the grave swallows us; it is in fact, as the closing phrase suggests, to be in league with the grave, to assist in what it is doing anyway. And with 'Pitty the world' the practical implications of the twice-used 'tender' are made explicit in a new context: as there exist mutual obligations of love between parent and child, so there is a relation between the individual and the world. *This* individual, at least, has a duty not to deprive it of its proper food.

It should be clear, then, what sort of questions the sonnet raises and in what terms the language puts them, what life it makes them live. The more one looks at this poetry the more one sees the real complexities which underlie the deceptively smooth surface. In this it is a fitting start to a sequence where again and again the attentive reader must pause and ask, 'Just what is being said here? Is this affirmation or questioning? Or both, from different points of view?' In Sonnet I it is not just the equivocality of attitude which is characteristic of so many later sonnets: it is the slyness of tone which goes with this attitude and reveals it. The blade is sheathed in silk. Not praise alone, nor blame alone; not one and then the other; but both at once. And this is not a clever balancing-act or parrying of experience, nor an attempt to stand outside or above it: it is a recognition of many-sidedness, of the need to give full weight to the various and sometimes conflicting elements which may be present simultaneously in human affairs. The result is an art which is, like life, difficult to read completely, an art which attends to the variousness of an experience and creates the equivalent of this in language. But Shakespeare is not simply noting or recording experience; his art is not merely mimetic, a secondary thing depending on mechanical fidelity to its subject-matter. On the contrary, it is freely creative, autonomous, and while its complex living patterns of meaning correspond with patterns of experience outside art, they exist here in their own order. If, in this sense, things happen here as they do in life, the poetry rarely compels attention to its significance by any striking gesture (mention of Donne should make this clear): the meaning or complex of meanings can be missed if one is too hurried to watch closely, to be attentively still. This is, as I shall argue later, a poetry born of 'negative capability', and it requires this gift in the reader also. To a remarkable extent it is a poetry for contemplation: it can be fully comprehended only by pondering line and phrase, turning them this way and that as they themselves turn. In this it strikingly resembles the poetry of [T. S. Eliot's] *Four Quartets*, which likewise can be possessed only through a deep and contemplative listening of the whole being, and not less through an attentiveness to all the possibilities of individual words and phrases.

I should like to glance more quickly at the rest of the sonnets in this first group of seventeen. It is a critical commonplace that many of the Sonnets fall into groups which can be compared to the musical form of theme and variations. This can certainly be said of Sonnets 1-17. One sonnet may amplify an idea from an earlier one; the next may extend it into a new area, a new aspect of

the general concern; and throughout the set the main themes and images will be seen continually forming and re-forming in patterns like the dancers in a grave ballet.

While Sonnet I states the themes for the sonnets immediately following and also for the sequence at large, touching on the questions of what Time does to us and what we can do to resist him, it does this incompletely: the themes are announced, but they have still to be developed. The gradual unfolding, even naming, of various related aspects of the whole concern takes place in Sonnets 2-17, and by the time we have read them through we have been introduced to all the main subjects which will be discussed in the 126 sonnets addressed to the youth. They are questions which occur also in the sonnets to the mistress, but less directly and, of course, with the addition of others.

Murray Krieger [in *A Window to Criticism*] remarks on

> Shakespeare's brilliant method of creating constitutive symbols in one sonnet and, having earned his right to them there, transferring them whole to another sonnet, with their full burden of borrowed meaning, earned elsewhere, taken for granted. Thus a creative symbol in one sonnet becomes a sign, one of the raw materials, in another . . . The critic can treat the single poem as an aesthetic unit while still using it as an explicative instrument to reveal the interrelation among the sonnets that creates the oneness of their total symbolic system, their unified body of metaphor.

Something like this happens in the tightly-organized group under discussion now. It is common to find a phrase or image, used in one sonnet, repeated by a later one in a new context and so extended. Sometimes the earlier use is the establishing one and the meaning in the second case is largely borrowed from that; sometimes the new context throws a new light on the earlier image or even turns into an image what was merely a 'sign' before. Then, too, there may be repetition with little or no development, but used as a method of relating one phase of the total exploration of the theme to an earlier, and perhaps a later one. All of these seventeen poems have in common the one idea, that the youth must marry and have children. But they have more in common than that: they are related poetically, and in quite complex and intricate ways.

To give some examples. Sonnet I warns the youth not to '*eate* the worlds due, by the *grave* and thee'; in Sonnet 2 his continued singleness would be 'an *all-eating* shame'; in Sonnet 6 the 'eate' and 'grave' of I are echoed, if faintly, in 'To be deaths conquest and make wormes thine heire'. Again, 'beare his memory' from I is recalled at the end of 3: 'But if thou live remembred not to be', where 'remembred', according to Krieger's law, borrows the metaphoric force of the previous passage. To take a more complicated case, the 'wast in *niggarding*' of I is picked up in the 'beautious *nigard*' of 4, and this idea is extended throughout 4 in financial terms, which in turn receive a backward glance in 6: 'That use is not forbidden usery'. Again, notice the transition from Sonnet 2 to Sonnet 3:

> If thou couldst answere this faire child of mine
> Shall sum my count . . .

> Looke in thy glasse and tell the face thou
>   vewest,
> Now is the time that face should forme an
>   other.

In the first passage '*this* faire child' puts the child there, in an imagined situation, to be pointed out as his father's image. In the second the image is merely the one given back by the glass; yet, says the poet, there is a moral there too. These lines may at first seem to lack sharpness but on a closer reading they work quite subtly: the friend is to tell his mirrored face that that face, itself one kind of image, must create another, the face of a son. The mirror, then, is more than a mirror, it can also be a window. And indeed in Sonnet 3, 'glass' is made to change its meaning in just this way. The turning-point comes in lines 9-10:

> Thou art thy mothers glasse and she in thee
> Calls backe the lovely Aprill of her prime.

The poetry has progressed by stepping backwards in time. The friend is to his mother (the mirror image of her youth) what the poet would have a son be to the friend. 'Glasse' here still means mirror, though now the image is a living one and the gazer, rather than looking *into* the glass at the closed system of self and reflection, is almost looking *through* the glass: at another being, and one who recalls past youth. And so the modulation to the next two lines is achieved:

> So thou through windowes of thine age shalt
>   see,
> Dispight of wrinkles this thy goulden time.

'Windowes', unlike mirrors, offer escape or at least a prospect of the larger world: solace for 'age' with its very physical 'wrinkles'.

Yet another example of imagery threading through a group of sonnets begins here in Sonnet 3 and carries us forward to 5 and 6. 'Glass', as well as meaning 'mirror' and 'window', can also mean a vessel, and Sonnet 5, after hinting noncommittally (in 'The lovely gaze where every eye doth dwell') at the first two, finally introduces the third; but not before a new context of imagery has been formed, natural and seasonal, tactile as well as visual:

> For never resting time leads Summer on

> To hidious winter and confounds him there,
> Sap checkt with frost and lustie leav's quite
>   gon.
> Beauty ore-snow'd and barenes every where.

After 'sap checkt with frost' in particular, we are prepared for the lines which follow:

> Then were not *summers distillation left*
> *A liquid prisoner pent in walls of glasse,*
> Beauties effect with beauty were bereft . . .
>   But *flowers distil'd* though they with winter
>   meete,
>   Leese but their show, their substance still
>   lives sweet.

The next sonnet carries this on and unites it with a suggestion from Sonnet 3, the poet's fear lest the friend 'beguile the world, unblesse some mother'. After that, 'make sweet some *viall*' in 6 suggests both the child and the woman who bears him.

And again, what is said of 'hidious winter' in 5 is condensed by 6 in the opening metaphor of 'winters wragged hand' and expanded by much of the imagery of 12 and by the reference in 13 to 'the stormy gusts of winters day/ And barren rage of deaths eternall cold'. It is clear that the concerted effect of these passages is to build an impression of winter and of the destruction it represents. Indeed, the whole pattern of repetition and extension throughout these sonnets forms a rich carpet of suggestion, a texture of reiterated but varied persuasion. There are, too, interruptions of this pattern which further elaborate the whole design: poems like 4, 7 and 14 which confine themselves to working out a single conceit and play little part in the give-and-take with other sonnets.

Three other features of the group should be noticed. One is the poet's attitude, which begins by being completely self-effacing, and, in fact, remains largely so; it is not until the end of Sonnet 10 that he makes any claim for a relationship between himself and the youth, and then it is far from strong: 'Make thee an other selfe *for love of me*'. The poet's sense of the youth's value is everywhere apparent before and after this, but it is conveyed with tact, with a servant's remoteness. Only in this couplet and in the couplet of 13 is there any approach to greater intimacy:

> O none but unthrifts, *deare my love* you know,
> You had a Father, let your Son say so.

The point is, however, that the closer relationship seen in later sonnets (18-126) is already foreshadowed here, like so much else.

Secondly, the general imaginative movement in this first group is an expansive one. This seems to be involuntary as well as deliberate. While Sonnet I seems to know quite certainly what it is doing, one may feel that the sequence steadily moves outward in sonnet after sonnet to a wider awareness of what was implied in that starting-point. The increasing exploration of the human themes in natural and seasonal terms is one sign that Shakespeare's imagination is broadening and deepening the range of meanings hinted at in the opening sonnet.

Thirdly, it is here that poetry is first mentioned and its role asserted. The group considers not one but two means of transcending time and death, in a gradual discovery of new corridors of possibility. Sonnet 12 ends:

> And nothing gainst Times sieth can make
>   defence
> Save breed to brave him, when he takes thee
>   hence.

But later poems in the group qualify that: they speak of that other form of imitation with which the poet is by his nature concerned. The way has been prepared for this by the mirror, window and vial metaphors already discussed. From the 'image' in the mirror, the 'flowers distil'd', it is no distance to art seen as a means of distilling beauty and defeating time. The image of art as a distilling is seldom prominently used later, but it underlies quite naturally all the assertions that poetry will immortalize the beloved. For the present the claims are fairly modest ones; certainly they are weighed against others. Sonnet 15 ends:

> And all in war with Time for love of you
> As he takes from you, I ingraft you new.

And in the manner already established, this theme is developed through the rest of the group and is carried over the bridge formed by Sonnet 18 into the larger sequence. Sonnet 16 refers slightingly to the poet's 'barren rime', 17 to the disbelief with which that 'rime' may meet:

> And your true rights be termed a Poets rage,
> And stretched miter of an Antique song.

18, more hopefully, speaks of 'eternall lines':

> So long as men can breath or eyes can see,
> So long lives this, and this gives life to thee.

In the couplet of 15, the image, with overtones of Saint Paul, is of a new life created by grafting that of the beloved into language; *this* posterity at least, for what it is worth, the poet can promise. But the next sonnet immediately puts it in perspective:

> But wherefore do not you a mightier waie
> Make warre uppon this bloudie tirant time?
> And fortifie your selfe in your decay

> With meanes more blessed then my barren
>   rime?

Here and elsewhere the poet who speaks in the Sonnets is fully prepared to admit the limitations of his power. Presumably he would have agreed with D.H. Lawrence's remark that *lives* were more important than anything else, even works of art; and one remembers G. Wilson Knight's remarks about 'breath' in his discussion of the statue scene in *The Winter's Tale*. Commenting on Leontes' 'What fine chisel/Could ever yet cut breath', he says [in *The Crown of Life*]: 'However highly we value the eternity phrased by art (as in Yeats' "monuments of unaging intellect" in *Sailing to Byzantium* and Keats' *Grecian Urn*), yet there is a frontier beyond which it and all corresponding philosophies fail: they lack one thing, breath. With a fine pungency of phrase . . . a whole world of human idealism is dismissed'. The same realization is clear in the Shakespeare of the Sonnets: he sees that selves, persons, are the ultimate goals of love: who in his senses would prefer a poem to his friend's living child? It is in this context that 'rime' may seem 'barren', 'poor', a 'stretched metre'. The poet's estimate of his poetry is generally marked by humility, or perhaps we should say realism. . . . [For] the moment his attitude is best summed up in the couplet of Sonnet 17:

> But were some childe of yours alive that time,
> You should live twise, in it and in my rime.

NARRATIVE AND DRAMATIC ELEMENTS

There is little question that Shakespeare's sonnets are essentially lyrical—that is, short verses expressing thoughts or feelings. There is critical debate, however, about the extent to which they contain narrative or dramatic elements. Most twentieth-century commentators find little more than a skeletal "story" in these verses. Kenneth Muir, for instance, summarized what he termed "the basic facts" of the sonnets in a single sentence. He reminded readers that these verses do not represent a novel in poetic form, yet he also acknowledged that Shakespeare convinces us that the sonnets are sincere expressions of the speaker's emotions, from one day to the next and from year to year. **Heather Dubrow** (1981) stressed the fact that only rarely do the sonnets relate a chronological sequence of events. She called attention to the lack of specific references to time and place, and to the scarcity of sonnets that describe something that actually happens to the Poet, the Friend, or the Dark Lady.

Dubrow also addressed the question of dramatic elements in the sonnets. She suggested that these poems are profoundly dramatic in that they bring before us, immediately and intensely, the conflicted mind of the speaker. The dramatic confrontation is not between external forces, she argued, but between the speaker's competing or contradictory thoughts and emotions, and this struggle is conveyed through monologues or meditations that resemble, to some degree, soliloquies in plays. G. K. Hunter similarly maintained that Shakespeare's sonnets bring readers into direct contact with the speaker's suffering and, through their poignancy and immediacy, evoke the same feelings of pity and terror elicited by tragic drama. **Michael Cameron Andrews** agreed with Dubrow that the sonnets are essentially lyrical, but he maintained that they are dramatic in the sense that they constitute a dynamic portrayal of a mind at war with itself. He argued that these poems vivify the tempestuous flow of conflicting emotions in the speaker's mind as he tries desperately to resolve— through justification, pretense, self-deception, and other subterfuges— the discrepancy between his idealized vision of the Friend and the knowledge that the young man has deceived him.

Heather Dubrow

SOURCE: "Shakespeare's Undramatic Monologues: Toward a Reading of the *Sonnets*," in *Shakespeare Quarterly*, Vol. 32, No. 1, Spring, 1981, pp. 55-68.

[*Though she acknowledges the presence of narrative and dramatic elements in Shakespeare's sonnets, Dubrow asserts that most of these poems are interior monologues in the lyrical mode. Shakespeare's principal concern is to convey the speaker's anguish and confusion, she suggests, and to heighten our experience of his thoughts and emotions. Dubrow argues that the unusually generalized setting of these sonnets and the lack of a story help increase readers' identification with the speaker by universalizing his experience. Moreover, she notes that while the problems created by the behavior of the Friend and the Dark Lady are vivid and immediate, they themselves remain shadowy figures. These characteristics make Shakespeare's sonnets unique in comparison with those of his contemporaries, she remarks, as does his unusual use of the couplet: instead of summarizing the ideas and arguments of the preceding quatrains in the last two lines, he frequently introduces new thoughts here, thus underscoring the speaker's self-doubts and anxieties.*]

> There is, it seems to us,
> At best, only a limited value
> In the knowledge derived from experience.
> The knowledge imposes a pattern, and falsifies.
> For the pattern is new in every moment
> And every moment is a new and shocking
> Valuation of all we have been.
> T.S. Eliot, "East Coker"

We assume that the non-dramatic poetry of a great playwright will in fact be dramatic in many senses of that complex term. And we assume that when a writer who, among his manifold gifts, is a skilled storyteller chooses to write sonnets, at least some of them will be narrative.

Those presuppositions help to explain why, despite all the other controversies about Shakespeare's *Sonnets*, certain concepts are so repeatedly and so uncritically brought to bear on interpretations of these poems. We are regularly informed, for example, that they are "dramas" or "stories," a view reflected in the frequency with which critics of the *Sonnets* include the word "dramatic" in the titles of their studies and then proceed to comment on the "plots" and the "characters" that they find in the sequence. But in literary criticism, as in so many other human activities, we are prone to see what we expect to see, and nothing else. While Shakespeare's *Sonnets* evidently do include certain dramatic and narrative elements, in focusing on that aspect of them we have overlooked a more revealing and more surprising fact: that many of the characteristics central to other dramatic and narrative poetry, including other Renaissance sonnet sequences, are signally absent from Shakespeare's *Sonnets*.

I

A comparison of Shakespeare's Sonnet 87 with two other works that also concern a leavetaking will highlight his approach to the genre. The famous lines of Drayton's *Idea* 61 demonstrate how a poem in what is essentially a lyric mode can become dramatic:

> Since ther's no helpe, Come let us kisse and
>   part.
> Nay, I have done: you get no more of Me,
> And I am glad, yea glad with all my heart,
> That thus so cleanly, I my Selfe can free,
> Shake hands for ever, Cancell all our Vowes,
> And when We meet at any time againe,
> Be it not seene in either of our Browes,
> That We one jot of former Love reteyne;
> Now at the last gaspe, of Loves latest Breath,
> When his Pulse fayling, Passion speechlesse lies,
> When Faith is kneeling by his bed of Death,
> And Innocence is closing up his Eyes,
>   Now if thou would'st, when all have given
>   him over,
>   From Death to Life, thou might'st him yet
>   recover.

Rather than describing the episode in which the lovers part, Drayton enacts it. We are asked to believe (and, thanks to his skill, the illusion is persuasive) that we are actually witnessing the speaker bidding farewell to his lady. We are as conscious of her implicit but powerful presence as that speaker is himself. And we are conscious, too, that what the poem claims to enact is a specified and unique moment in time. To be sure, Drayton briefly uses allegory to distance us from that moment— but his main reason for establishing such a distance is to create a foil against which his final appeal to the woman will seem all the more immediate.

Though Petrarch's *Canzonière* CXC is primarily concerned with rendering certain states of mind— the poet's joy at the beauty of Laura and his intense sorrow at her loss— he evokes those states by telling a story:

> Una candida cerva sopra l'erba
>   Verde m'apparve, con duo corna d'oro,
>   Fra due riviere, a l'ombra d'un alloro,
>   Levando 'l sole, a la stagione acerba.
> Era sua vista si dolce superba,
>   Ch'i'lasciai per seguirla ogni lavoro;
>   Come l'avaro che 'n cercar tesoro
>   Con diletto l'affanno disacerba.
> 'Nessun me tocchi.' al bel collo d'intorno
>   Scritto avea di diamanti e di topazi;
>   'Libera farmi al mio Cesare parve.'
> Et era'l sol gia volto al mezzo giorno;
>   Gli occhi miei stanchi di mirar, non sazi;
>   Quand'io caddi ne l'acqua, et ella sparve.

Petrarch's poem may be visionary and mystical, but like other narratives it is firmly anchored in time. It has a clear beginning, middle, and end: at the opening of the poem the speaker sees the deer, then he admires her, and then he loses her.

Shakespeare wears his rue with a difference:

> Farewell, thou art too dear for my possessing,
> And like enough thou know'st thy estimate.
> The charter of thy worth gives thee releasing;
> My bonds in thee are all determinate.
> For how do I hold thee but by thy granting,
> And for that riches where is my deserving?
> The cause of this fair gift in me is wanting,
> And so my patience back again is swerving.
> Thyself thou gav'st, thy own worth then not
>   knowing,
> Or me, to whom thou gav'st, else mistaking;
> So thy great gift, upon misprision growing,
> Comes home again, on better judgment making.
>   Thus have I had thee as a dream doth flatter,
>   In sleep a king, but waking no such matter.
>   (Sonnet 87)

The opening word, "Farewell," suggests that this sonnet is going to enact a parting in much the same way that Drayton's does; and the third quatrain does in a sense tell a story. Yet Shakespeare's poem is not necessarily a rendition of a particular event that takes place at a particular moment: one cannot tell whether the parting is in the process of happening or has already occurred. For Shakespeare's primary concern is not to imitate an incident in which a lover says farewell but rather to evoke the lover's reflections on the process of parting. And Shakespeare's sonnet differs from Drayton's in another and no less significant way: while most of the assertions in Drayton's sonnet are addressed to the beloved, most of those in Shakespeare's are not. In the

couplet, for example, Shakespeare's speaker seems to be brooding on his experiences rather than either enacting them or announcing their significance to the person he has loved.

The characteristics of that couplet and of the sonnet in which it figures recur throughout Shakespeare's sonnet sequence. The narrative, dramatic, and lyrical are not, of course, necessarily exclusive of each other, either in general or in Shakespeare's sonnets in particular. In his sequence as a whole, and not infrequently within a single sonnet, we do encounter instances of all three modes. Sonnets 153 and 154, for example, are certainly narrative according to virtually any definition of that term; the entire sequence is indubitably dramatic in the sense that it vividly bodies forth the speaker himself, developing and drawing attention to the nuances of his character. Nevertheless, it is not the presence of certain narrative and dramatic elements but rather the absence of others that is most striking when we read Shakespeare's sequence and most telling when we juxtapose it with the sonnets composed by many other Renaissance poets.

II

One of the clearest and most important indications that the majority of the *Sonnets* are in certain senses neither narrative nor dramatic is that they do not include a temporal sequence of events, as does, for example, Petrarch's "Una candida cerva sopra l'erba." As we read Shakespeare's *Sonnets,* we witness tortuous shifts in the speaker's emotions and judgments, but very seldom do we encounter a chronological progression of occurrences. Instead, his monologues take place in the kind of eternal present that is usually a mark of lyric poetry. Characteristically, they generalize about an event that recurs frequently rather than focusing on one instance of it: "When I consider everything that grows" (Sonnet 15, line 1); "When to the sessions of sweet silent thought / I summon up remembrance of things past" (Sonnet 30, lines 1-2). In another sense, too, the sonnet sequence that so vividly evokes the horrors of time is not itself rooted in time: Shakespeare's poems seldom refer to datable real incidents or even to incidents that occur at a specific, though symbolic, moment. Petrarch alludes to the date of his meeting with the real woman who was transformed into Laura and the date of her death, and his sequence may also have complex symbolic relationships to the calendar. Spenser's sonnets are apparently keyed to the seasons. One of Daniel's refers to a trip to Italy. But in Shakespeare we find very few such references. To be sure, in one poem the speaker does suggest that he met his beloved three years before; but nowhere else does he allude to time in so specific a way. And Shakespeare is no more specific about place. We know that Sidney's Stella takes a ride on the Thames, while Shakespeare's *Sonnets* never mention a particular locale.

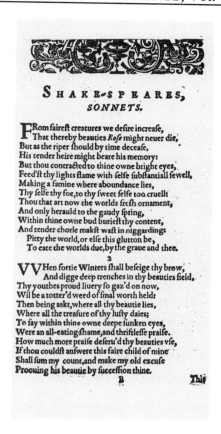

First text page of Shakespeare's Sonnets (1609).

The omission of such allusions to place and time is all the more suggestive in light of Shakespeare's repeated—one is almost tempted to say frenetic— puns on "will." Like Sidney's play on "rich" or his adoption of the pseudonym "Astrophil," these puns are evidently intended to remind us that the poems in question are closely linked to autobiographical experience. One would presume that the same attitudes that lead a poet to pun on, and hence draw attention to, his own name might well encourage him to refer to specific dates and places. But this Shakespeare chooses not to do.

The lack of temporal perspective in most of the *Sonnets* reflects the absence of anecdotal sonnets. With only a handful of exceptions, Shakespeare's sequence omits not only the mythological stories that so frequently grace the sequences of other sonnet writers but also non-mythological allegories like Spenser's *Amoretti* LXXV ("One day I wrote her name vpon the strand"). Moreover, Shakespeare seldom chooses to narrate an incident that happens to the lovers, as, say, Sidney does in *Astrophil and Stella* 41 ("Having this day my horse, my hand, my launce"). It is as uncharacteristic of Shakespeare to begin a sonnet with "One day" as it is characteristic of Spenser to do so.

A sonnet that does not narrate an anecdote may, of course, be anchored in a specific event or situation nonetheless: it can be the outgrowth of an occurrence which, though not recounted systematically, is referred to frequently and specifically in the course of the poem. Many readers have assumed that the vast majority of Shakespeare's *Sonnets* are "situational" in this sense. But in point of fact comparatively few of them are. In some of Shakespeare's monologues the reflections are inspired not by a particular situation but by a general problem; thus in Sonnet 94 the speaker evokes a certain kind of personality, and Sonnet 129 is an anguished consideration of the nature of lust. Because poems like these rely so heavily on generalizations, critics regularly describe them as interesting exceptions to Shakespeare's approach elsewhere in the sequence. They are, however, merely extreme instances of their author's tendency to detach the speaker's emotions and speculations from an immediate situation.

Some poems in the sequence imply that a specific incident may lie behind the speaker's reactions but omit any discussion of details. We learn little about the "forsaking" to which Sonnet 89 alludes, for example, or the reasons for the parting described in the absence sonnets. As we read Sonnet 35 we do not know what the "sensual fault" to which it refers may be, or even whether "fault" indicates a particular lapse or a general character trait. If we try to enumerate the situations on which Shakespeare's *Sonnets* are based, we find that our list is short and the events on it shadowy. The poet encourages the Friend to marry; there is a period of separation, and there are one or more quarrels; the Friend is praised by another poet; the Friend betrays the speaker with the Dark Lady. By contrast, in *Astrophil and Stella,* a sequence about two-thirds the length of Shakespeare's, the situations include a stolen kiss, Stella's illness, her ride on the Thames, an absence, a quarrel, Astrophil's triumph in a tournament, and many more.

III

If most of Shakespeare's *Sonnets* do not tell stories, neither do they enact dramas in the way that, say, Drayton's *Idea* 61 does ("Since ther's no helpe, Come let us kisse and part"). And yet the reader becomes involved in these poems. One Shakespearean has attempted to explain why: "By setting up a system of tensions between forces presented as persons, Shakespeare's sonnets engage the reader's interest in a manner akin to the dramatic" [G. K. Hunter, "The Dramatic Techniques of Shakespeare's Sonnets" (1953)]. It is true that some of the *Sonnets,* notably the poems addressed to Time, do operate this way. But most do not: Shakespeare's *Sonnets* embody the tension of conflicting forces, but those forces are more often internalized within the speaker than dramatized as characters.

Though the Friend and the Dark Lady dominate the speaker's thoughts, in some important respects they do not function as active participants within the *Sonnets.* The problems engendered by their behavior are frighteningly immediate, but the characters themselves are not. Except for the fact that the young man is attractive and the lady is dark, we do not know what they look like. Unlike the main characters in most sonnet sequences, they are never assigned names, even fictional ones, even in those poems that refer to them in the third rather than the second person. The epithets by which they are addressed serve, if anything, to distance us further from them. When, for example, Shakespeare opens Sonnet 56 on the command, "Sweet love, renew your force," he establishes an unresolved ambiguity about whether the poem concerns his beloved or the abstract quality of love, or both. When he directs an apostrophe to "Lascivious grace" (Sonnet 40, line 13), he initially seems as much to be brooding on the abstraction that the epithet expresses as to be talking to a person who has been reduced (or who has willingly reduced himself) to the state expressed by that oxymoron. Similarly, only once (Sonnet 34, line 13) in 154 sonnets does Shakespeare allude to the movements or gestures of the beloved in a way that suggests that he is physically present and actually listening to the speaker. Contrast *Astrophil and Stella* 31, which so unequivocally sets up the fiction that Astrophil is in the presence of the moon, or *Astrophil and Stella* 47, whose "Soft, but here she comes" (line 13) so effectively signals Stella's arrival.

It is a truth as significant as it is neglected that the Friend and the Dark Lady are not quoted directly within the poems. Despite all his experience in writing plays, Shakespeare chooses not to create the kind of dialogue on which such poems as *Astrophil and Stella* 54 ("Because I breathe not love to everie one") or *Idea* 24 ("I heare some say, this Man is not in love") or even *Amoretti* LXXV ("One day I wrote her name vpon the strand") are based. On those rare occasions when the words of the beloved are recorded, they are presented in a form that distances us from the statements and their speakers: the poet either uses indirect discourse to report what the beloved has said ("When my love swears that she is made of truth" [Sonnet 138, line 1]) or predicts what he or she is likely to say rather than what has actually been said ("O then vouchsafe me but this loving thought: / Had my friend's muse grown with this growing age" [Sonnet 32, lines 9-10]).

If the lovers remain shadowy in the sonnets addressed to them, so too do the other characters who occasionally appear. We know surprisingly little about the Rival Poet himself, though we learn much about his impact on the speaker's emotions. When Shakespeare chooses to refer to society's reactions to his love, he characterizes it vaguely as "all tongues" (Sonnet 69, line 3) rather than evoking specific figures like the nymphs who berate Astrophil. Time is personified, of course, but it generally functions more as a threat looming over the speaker than as an active character. Even in Sonnet 19,

the poet only anticipates the effects of "Devouring time" on his beloved, whereas Spenser is engaged in fighting with the waves (and Donne actually invites his "Busie old foole" into his bedroom). It is revealing, moreover, that the kinds of characters who populate other sequences and create miniature dramas by arguing with the speaker are totally absent from Shakespeare's poems. The ladies who are Laura's companions, the cynical friend who berates Drayton, the court nymphs who criticize Astrophil— no figures like these appear in Shakespeare's *Sonnets.*

Nor is Shakespeare prone to replace them with internalized characters. Though the morality tradition influences his sequence in other ways, only rarely does he depict the conflicts within his speaker as allegorical personages engaged in a confrontation. Many of his sonnets concern a debate between opposing forces such as reason and passion; but very few evoke that debate through allegorical characters like those that figure so prominently in *Astrophil and Stella.*

Most of the sonnets are not narrative, then, in the sense that the speaker is not recounting a story to the reader or to any other implied audience. And they are not dramatic in the sense that we are not witnessing a confrontation that occurs at a specific place and time between a speaker and a particular listener, or even between two clearly distinguished personages within the speaker. Instead, it is the lyric mode that predominates. Some of the poems resemble an internalized meditation, others a letter, others a monologue that the beloved hears but apparently does not respond to.

The soliloquy immediately presents itself as a parallel to and an inspiration for Shakespeare's unusual approach to the sonnet, and in certain respects the comparison is an illuminating one. The speaker in Shakespeare's *Sonnets* often seems to be thinking aloud, to be at once speaking audibly and meditating. But, as the passages that I have cited suggest, in one crucial way the *Sonnets* differ from the soliloquies that are so frequently embedded in their author's plays: the soliloquy normally takes place at a unique moment and is often provoked by a clearly defined event that has preceded it, whereas most of the *Sonnets* are signally lacking in those types of particularization.

IV

Most readers have found the differences between Shakespeare's sonnets and those of his contemporaries puzzling. Several of the most idiosyncratic qualities of Shakespeare's *Sonnets* stem from the poet's decision to shape so many of them as lyrics in the sense of subjective reflections. Thus his couplets, which fail to provide the reassuring summaries we have been told to expect at the end of a "Shakespearean sonnet," can best be understood if we remember the mode in which

Shakespeare is generally writing. As long as we think of the *Sonnets* as dramas or stories, we will be conditioned to expect their couplets (like those of many other sonneteers) to be reasoned statements of objective truths: we will expect them to function rather like the chorus's commentary in a play or the narrator's judgments in a novel. When, however, we recognize that so many of the *Sonnets* are internalized monologues, we are in a position to observe that one purpose of Shakespeare's couplets is to reflect the chaos in the speaker's mind, a purpose to which a couplet that merely summarized the preceding twelve lines would prove inadequate.

Some of Shakespeare's couplets resolve difficult problems too neatly, an impression intensified by the tidiness and balance inherent in the couplet form. Thus, for instance, "Pity me then, dear friend, and I assure ye, / Ev'n that your pity is enough to cure me" (Sonnet 111, ll. 13-14) does not persuade the reader that the diseases of the heart chronicled in the previous twelve lines can be cured as readily as the speaker hopes. The jingly rhyme increases our sense that the speaker is whistling in the dark, our sense that the couplet is merely another vain attempt to solve his dilemmas.

Other couplets offer responses that seem inappropriate reactions to what has come before. Once again we are more aware of the stresses that make the speaker seek reassurance than of the reassurance that the couplet, if only by virtue of its innately epigrammatic tone, claims to provide. The quatrains of Sonnet 33, for example, draw attention to the wrongs that the poet has suffered at the hands of his beloved:

> Full many a glorious morning have I seen
> Flatter the mountain tops with sovereign eye.
> Kissing with golden face the meadows green,
> Gilding pale streams with heav'nly alchemy,
> Anon permit the basest clouds to ride
> With ugly rack on his celestial face,
> And from the forlorn world his visage hide,
> Stealing unseen to west with this disgrace.
> Ev'n so my sun one early morn did shine,
> With all triumphant splendor on my brow;
> But out alack, he was but one hour mine,
> The region cloud hath masked him from me
>   now.
>
> (ll. 1-12)

Here Shakespeare develops the metaphor of the sun in a way that emphasizes its guilt and hence by implication that of the Friend. Thus "Flatter" (line 2) and "Gilding" (line 4) have connotations that are at the very least ambiguous: flattery can be sycophantic, and gilding can be deceptive. The sort of couplet that these quatrains lead us to expect is something like "I thought our love an everlasting day / And yet my trust thou didst, my love, betray." If we try to read the poem through with this couplet tacked on the end, we find that the unca-

nonical lines fit the spirit of the poem. If, on the other hand, we read the sonnet through with the couplet that Shakespeare did in fact write— "Yet him for this my love no wit disdaineth; / Suns of the world may stain when heav'n's sun staineth" (ll. 13-14)— we become uneasy. Shakespeare's speaker is trying to fool himself; he takes one conceivable moral from the metaphor (the Friend's betrayal is justified by that of the sun) and neglects the more central one that the reader has been observing (the Friend, like the sun, has been culpably deceptive).

Similarly, the many couplets that offer an unexpectedly pessimistic interpretation of the issues in the poem suggest the impingement of new facts— especially new apprehensions and doubts— on the speaker's troubled consciousness. Sonnet 92, for instance, ends "But what's so blessèd-fair that fears no blot? / Thou mayst be false, and yet I know it not" (ll. 13-14). Just as an unexpected fear enters the speaker's mind and disturbs the peace he has been attempting to achieve, so an unexpected idea enters the couplet and disturbs its potential function as a neat summary of the preceding quatrains.

All of these couplets are a response to the fundamental paradox that confronted Shakespeare as he wrote the *Sonnets*. The sonnet is, as so many of its readers have remarked, one of the most orderly of literary forms; it is tightly structured and compact. Its couplet is the most orderly and ordering of its elements. No matter what the content of the couplet, in contrast to the syntactical and metrical complexities of the preceding quatrains it will often sound like an easily achieved truism. Frequently, too, the convictions expressed in the couplet will be so epigrammatic that they mirror and intensify the impression of assurance that the very form conveys.

The experiences evoked by Shakespeare's *Sonnets* are, however, unusually tumultuous even in a genre that specializes in psychological torment. As we have seen, in a number of ways his sonnets focus our attention on the speaker's chaotic reactions. We would no more expect a man who is wrestling with the kinds of unresolved contradictions plaguing Shakespeare's speaker to express them in the carefully structured and epigrammatically decisive lines of a couplet than the Elizabethans would have expected a madman in a play to speak in verse. Like the poet in Donne's "The Triple Fool," we assume that grief brought to numbers cannot be so fierce.

Rather than ignoring or struggling to overcome these characteristics of his form, Shakespeare exploits them. The reader comes to view the sentiments in many of the couplets not as objective summaries of the problems that the quatrains have been exploring, but rather as yet another symptom of the anguish and confusion that those problems have caused. As we have seen, those couplets that abruptly reverse the ideas in the quatrains and thus disturb the way the sonnet form generally functions reflect the process by which troubling new thoughts disturb the speaker's emotions. Such couplets are the formal equivalent of the turmoil in the lover's heart. Similarly, those couplets that seem deliberately to oversimplify experience effectively mirror the speaker's vain attempts to resolve the conflicts in his own mind: he often appears to turn to the couplet with relief, to find in its easy absolutes of hope or despair (and the straightforward syntax in which these emotions are expressed) a welcome alternative to the torturing ambivalences with which he has been wrestling (and the tortuous syntax in which he has expressed them).

Though Shakespeare's couplets often resemble soliloquies in their evocations of a mind brooding on experience, those that oversimplify complex realities differ from most Elizabethan soliloquies in the unreliability of their reflections: the speaker is lying to himself and hence to us. On first reading we may be confused or even deceived into taking the lines at face value, much as the figure delivering them is himself confused or deceived. That speaker is in a sense compounding his lies by the very act of presenting them through the vehicle of an epigrammatic couplet. For in the sonnets in question that prosodic form itself functions deceptively: we have come to expect from it, not the unreliable and subjective half-truths or untruths that we may in fact encounter, but unexceptional verities. We may therefore be seduced by the very nature of the couplet form into momentarily believing the speaker's assertions.

Shakespeare's couplets explore and often exemplify an issue with which the whole sequence is very concerned: our predilection for deceiving ourselves and others. The Dark Lady uses her artfulness to lie verbally to her lover ("When my love swears that she is made of truth, / I do believe her though I know she lies" [Sonnet 138, ll. 1-2]), while the Friend's physical appearance is itself a kind of visual lie. The behavior of the Friend and the Dark Lady is contagious in this as in so many other regards, for the speaker himself comes to use art (in many senses of that term) to twist or destroy the truth. Some of the speaker's lies are offered in the service of his lovers, for whom he undertakes the process he describes in Sonnet 35: "Myself corrupting salving thy amiss, / Excusing thy sins more than thy sins are" (ll. 7-8). But the most disturbing of the deceptions in the sequence are the speaker's self-deceptions. By shaping so many of the poems as internalized lyrics, Shakespeare provides a forum for his speaker's repeated attempts to lie to himself. Sometimes a whole poem represents his effort to impose a more comforting but fallacious interpretation on a reality that, as the reader uneasily recognizes, demands a different response. At other times the couplet undercuts the neat but false interpretation in the quatrains. Most often, however, it is the couplet itself that contains the lie. The main reason that several of the most complex sonnets in our language end with couplets that are simple or even simplistic is that the pat

answers in those lines demonstrate the habits of self-deception that repeatedly lead the speaker, like his companions, to distort his perceptions, his morals, and his language. In sonnets like these, the couplet form itself becomes a symbol of our cursed rage for order, our tendency to simplify and sanitize our experience, even at the expense of truth.

V

Their emphasis on the lyrical rather than the narrative or dramatic also helps to explain another characteristic of Shakespeare's *Sonnets:* how immediately and how intensely they evoke the speaker's feelings. The reader need channel little or none of his attention to an exposition of a situation or an exploration of the beloved's psyche: he focuses instead on the poet-lover himself. For example, the impact of Sonnet 12, at first glance a comparatively impersonal poem, in fact stems not merely from its vivid depiction of time's ravages but also from its moving evocation of its speaker's sensibility:

> When I do count the clock that tells the time,
> And see the brave day sunk in hideous night,
> When I behold the violet past prime,
> And sable curls all silvered o'er with white,
> When lofty trees I see barren of leaves,
> Which erst from heat did canopy the herd,
> And summer's green all girded up in sheaves
> Borne on the bier with white and bristly beard;
> Then of thy beauty do I question make
> That thou among the wastes of time must go,
> Since sweets and beauties do themselves
>   forsake,
> And die as fast as they see others grow,
>   And nothing 'gainst time's scythe can make
>   defense
>   Save breed to brave him when he takes thee
>   hence.

In one sense this sonnet is a carefully documented argument. The quatrains, which present a series of facts marshaled to support the thesis in the sestet, function as part of a syllogism (all sweets and beauties die; you yourself are a sweet and beauty; therefore you will die). But in presenting this case the poem repeatedly directs our attention to the mind brooding on it: like Marvell's "To His Coy Mistress," this lyric is as much concerned with the speaker's thoughts about death as with ways of combatting that inevitable but unendurable fact. The first five lines contain no fewer than four verbs referring to the speaker's processes of cognition ("do count" ..."see" ..."behold" ..."see"), three of which are preceded by the personal pronoun "I." The anaphora in lines one and three ("When I") further heightens the emphasis on the speaker's sensibility. "Then of thy beauty do I question make" (l. 9), which follows these two quatrains, contains in microcosm the characteristics that we have been noting, for one may gloss those words in two ways: (1) I ask you a question ("thy beauty" functioning as synecdoche in this interpretation) or (2) in my own mind I raise a question about your beauty. Even while communicating with the beloved, then, the speaker also seems to be communing with himself. As he considers the beloved's behavior, therefore, the reader is also led to concentrate on how that behavior affects the speaker.

While a thorough affective study of the *Sonnets* would demand a separate essay, one important truth about the reader's responses is clear: the primary effect of the lyrical mode of these poems is to intensify our identification with the speaker. And one reason our identification becomes so deep is that these sonnets are far more universal than those by any other English poet (with perhaps the interesting exception of Wyatt). As we have observed, they are not linked to particular dates or seasons or places. More important, because the events and situations to which Shakespeare alludes are presented only sketchily, we can readily relate the *Sonnets* to our own lives; we are not conscious of local details that do not conform to our own experiences.

Above all, we identify closely with the speaker because the emotions and reactions we experience when reading the poems are very similar to the emotions and reactions the poems are about. Like the speaker, we are confused by ambiguities in language and in the situations language is exploring. When we read Spenser's *Amoretti* VIII ("More then most faire, full of the liuing fire") we have few doubts about the judgments being passed on the lady; when we read Sonnet 94, however, we have, and I suspect are meant to have, few certainties. We are forced to keep thinking about the issues being raised, to keep re-examining the charged and ambiguous words of the poem.

Like Shakespeare's speaker, his readers try to find oases of order and stability in the tumultuous world of the *Sonnets*. The speaker reaches out for the overly simple answers expressed in his couplets in a way that is not unlike the way we reach out for a reordering of the *Sonnets* that would lessen their complexities and explain their ambiguities. If it is true that the *Sonnets* are the record of meditations, it is equally true that they encourage meditation in their reader far more than most poetry does. Since we are not offered neat answers, we, like the speaker, keep brooding on the questions that have been raised.

VI

The nature of Shakespeare's *Sonnets* reflects the nature of the experience they evoke. Most of them are lyric rather than narrative or dramatic because they concern a world in which narrative and dramatic modes would be inappropriate. One reason so few of these poems reflect a chronological sequence of events is that their speaker is trapped in brooding rather than acting or

even being acted on. His mind is tormented with calamities that the future may bring (his beloved will betray him, Time will destroy even this most precious of mortals) or that the present, unbeknownst to him, may already hold (his two friends may have already been unfaithful to him, the beloved may be morally stained). And these calamities are rendered more painful by the fact that the speaker is powerless, whether to prevent those disasters that the future may hold or to be certain that those the present may contain have not in fact come to pass:

> Yet eyes this cunning want to grace their art;
> They draw but what they see, know not the
>   heart.
>
> (Sonnet 24, ll. 13-14)

> And even thence thou wilt be stol'n, I fear.
>
> (Sonnet 48, l. 13)

In dramas, including the miniature version of drama that a sonnet can embody, characters often commit definite actions; in narratives, even fourteen-line narratives, usually definite events occur. But, as the passages above suggest, the dominant mood of Shakespeare's *Sonnets* is fearful anticipation and troubling suspicion, not clear-cut events. Narrative and dramatic modes would not have been as suited to evoking such a milieu.

Just as Shakespeare's decision to omit certain narrative and dramatic elements from his *Sonnets* aptly expresses his speaker's painful inaction, so it expresses the uncertainties suffered by that speaker and by the reader who is so intimately involved with him. If presented within the intense and concentrated form of the sonnet, both the narrative and the dramatic modes tend to suggest moral and epistemological certainties. When sonnet writers use mythological allegories, for example, they generally do so in order to make some simple but significant point about love; Cupid's tricks may remind us that love is deceptive, and Venus' fickleness that women are untrustworthy. Similarly, in narrating an event involving a lover and his mistress, sonneteers usually establish some important facts about the participants, such as the lady's unremitting and unremorseful chastity. And when sonnets imitate a dialogue between opponents, the two figures generally argue neatly antithetical positions. A victory for one position or the other, or possibly a synthesis of both, is achieved by the end of the sonnet. Even if the poet-lover himself remains trapped in his moral dilemma, a sequence relying extensively on narrative and dramatic modes can establish important verities. Thus *Astrophil and Stella* as a whole documents truths about Neoplatonism that Astrophil can only imperfectly grasp.

In so frequently avoiding the narrative and dramatic in his *Sonnets*, Shakespeare declines to provide the kinds of ethical truths and moral certainties that those modes can generate. He is achieving in formal terms the types of moral confusion he is exploring thematically. Just as the experience of the reader mirrors that of the speaker in these poems, so form mirrors content to an extent unusual in even the greatest art.

Michael Cameron Andrews

SOURCE: "Sincerity and Subterfuge in Three Shakespearean Sonnet Groups," in *Shakespeare Quarterly*, Vol. 33, No. 3, Autumn, 1982, pp. 314-27.

[*Andrews maintains that many of the sonnets involving the young man are dramatic in the sense that they are profoundly dynamic depictions of a mind at war with itself. Focusing on Sonnets 33-35, 40-42, and 87-96, Andrews traces the speaker's continuing struggle to avoid confronting the reality that he has been corrupted by his relationship with the young man. In the sonnets that directly address the youth as well as in those that function as interior monologues, Andrews sees a sharp contrast between the sentiment on the surface and the one that runs beneath it. In the critic's judgment, the moments when the speaker is totally honest with himself about his friend's deceitfulness are so painful that they must be quickly covered up and denied through elaborate strategies of exoneration, insincerity, and self-deception.*]

Early in *Sincerity and Authenticity* [1971], Lionel Trilling comments on the "implicit pathos" of Polonius' final adjuration to Laertes [in *Hamlet*]: "Who would not wish to be true to his own self? True, which is to say loyal, never wavering in constancy. True, which is to say honest: there are to be no subterfuges in dealing with him." But as Trilling sadly observes, "We understand with Matthew Arnold how hard it is to discern one's own self in order to reach it and be true to it."

> Below the surface-stream, shallow and light,
> Of what we *say* we feel— below the stream,
> As light, of what we *think* we feel— there flows
> With noiseless current strong, obscure and
>   deep,
> The central stream of what we feel indeed.

In the Sonnets, as in our lives, words, thoughts, and feelings are often at variance. In the sonnets to the young man, the speaker passes from what may be called sincere delusion to efforts to rationalize or palliate what the eye cannot help perceiving. In the later poems in this group, particularly those I shall consider, we often encounter lines conspicuously deficient in poetic conviction. Are we to say that Shakespeare, despite himself, could do no better? It seems to me, as to Philip Edwards [in *Shakespeare and the Confines of Art* (1968)], that Shakespeare's "bad" poetry in the Sonnets is intentional. And one of its uses is the dramatic one of calling attention to instances in which the speaker is not expressing what he actually feels. I do not, of course, mean that the Sonnets are dramatic in most of the usual senses of that

term; indeed, as Heather Dubrow has recently emphasized [in "Shakespeare's Undramatic Monologues"], they are generically lyrical, not dramatic:

> . . . we are not witnessing a confrontation that occurs at a specific place and time between a speaker and a particular listener, or even between two clearly distinguished personages within the speaker. Instead, it is the lyrical mode that predominates. Some of the poems resemble an internalized meditation, others a letter, others a monologue that the beloved hears but apparently does not respond to.

Shorn of particularity, highly subjective, these poems give us only the voice and point of view of the speaker. Nonetheless, many of the Sonnets are dramatic in a special sense— their intensely kinetic rendering of "the passions of a mind" [Stephen Booth, "Shakespeare in California" (1976)] in conflict with itself. Poems which, regarded purely as poetry, would be flawed sonnets, may be superb "dramatic" addresses or "meditations," combining unconscious or deliberate subterfuge with moments when the "central stream" of feeling pulses in the verse. In other sonnets, seeing and saying are for the most part neither disjunctive nor self-deceiving; in them the almost intolerable is confronted, not merely glimpsed. Yet there is perhaps no sonnet in which the speaker, having passed from ignorance to knowledge, can look at the friend without at some point flinching from the truth.

But who is this speaker? To use terms like sincerity and subterfuge implies the existence of someone to whom they can apply. In Professor [Kenneth] Muir's view, "the Sonnets, although not directly autobiographical, do at least reflect the poet's experience" ["The Order of Shakespeare's Sonnets" (1977)]. We have, I believe, no grounds for discounting the possibility of a strong autobiographical element— though Shakespeare, on the evidence of his plays, experienced much that he had not lived. But "reflect" is surely the appropriate word. A poet does not write "autobiographical sonnets," however much they may reflect his life. The poetic presentation of the self is in some measure the freeing of the self, the translation of life to art. One becomes a character in a poem. And Shakespeare, dramatist as well as poet, is native and indued to this kind of imaginative activity. Whatever the autobiographical basis of the Sonnets (and the question may be as irrelevant as it has been unanswerable), the Shakespeare of the Sonnets is no longer Shakespeare, but a dramatic character at one remove from his creator. The sincerity of this character, the speaker, may be gauged by what he says, and how. He is the imagined presence behind the actual words.

There is no need to discuss the ideal value with which the speaker invests the young man. The friend "becomes . . . a symbol of living perfection" [Douglas Bush, "Introduction" to the Sonnets in *William Shakespeare: The*

Complete Works, gen. ed. Alfred Harbage (1969)]; "the friendship takes on a symbolic value . . . becoming the emblem of hope in a changing and discouraging world of unrealized desires" [Edward Hubler, *The Sense of Shakespeare's Sonnets* (1952)]. No one could doubt the sincerity of most of the sonnets which appear to celebrate him. Yet the young man proves, of course, something less than the embodiment of Truth and Beauty (Sonnet 14); and Beauty, where Truth is not, has in the Sonnets a special horror.

I

Often the movement from insincerity to honest anguish is dramatic, either within a sonnet or within a linked group. In Sonnets 33-35, for example, there is at first an effort at exculpation:

> Full many a glorious morning have I seen
> Flatter the mountain tops with sovereign eye,
> Kissing with golden face the meadows green,
> Gilding pale streams with heavenly alchemy;
> Anon permit the basest clouds to ride
> With ugly wrack on his celestial face,
> And from the forlorn world his visage hide,
> Stealing unseen to west with his disgrace:
> Even so my sun one early morn did shine
> With all-triumphant splendor on my brow;
> But, out alack, he was but one hour mine,
> The region cloud hath masked him from me now.
>   Yet him for this my love no whit disdaineth;
>   Suns of the world may stain when heaven's sun staineth.

But even here the weight of felt experience subverts what is said—and perhaps thought—to be true. The sonnet expresses disillusionment and loss. To say that the friend "was but one hour mine" is, like Hamlet's telescopings of time, to use the natural language of one for whom time is the medium of betrayal. The idealized friend has proved a son of the world—as the pun bleakly intimates, more common than he seems. As he moves among the base companions who now surround him, there is no reason to expect him to "imitate the sun . . . By Breaking through the foul and ugly [clouds]" (*1 Henry IV*, I. ii. 185, 190). For the sun functions here as a symbol, not merely of vicissitude, but of the contamination of the beautiful. Today's cloud-choked sun may be tomorrow's glorious morning; but that is rarely true of the moral life of sons of the world. And if the friend should return in "all-triumphant splendor," as if nothing had happened, the illusion of love's security would not. We are left with a sense of *stain.*

Sonnet 34 begins as if the speaker were impatient with the insincerity of pretending to accept the friend's conduct. He abandons the effort, implicit in the use of "he," to stand somewhat apart from the emotions expressed. Address becomes direct, intimate:

> Why didst thou promise such a beauteous day
> And make me travel forth without my cloak,
> To let base clouds o'ertake me in my way,
> Hiding thy brav'ry in their rotten smoke?
> 'Tis not enough that through the cloud thou break
> To dry the rain on my storm-beaten face,
> For no man well of such a salve can speak
> That heals the wound, and cures not the disgrace:
> Nor can thy shame give physic to my grief;
> Though thou repent, yet have I still the loss:
> Th' offender's sorrow lends but weak relief
> To him that bears the strong offense's cross.
>   Ah, but those tears are pearl which thy love sheeds,
>   And they are rich and ransom all ill deeds.

The colloquial vigor and plain-speaking stance, like the shift from "he" to "thou," make this seem an eruption of the emotions buried in the previous sonnet. The image of the sun is divested of its glory—the promise of a beauteous day hardly corresponds to the "sovereign eye" and "heavenly alchemy"—and is eclipsed by other figures after line six. The tone, moreover, is directly reproachful: Why did you make me trust you, then do this to me? To lack one's customary defenses is to suffer the more. For the emphasis here is on the speaker's sense of being wounded rather than on the sullying of an ideal. Though separation is less complete than in Sonnet 33 (sunny glances do pierce the clouds), the speaker has suffered a storm of grief. Far from working with "heavenly alchemy," the friend's commiseration dries his tears but leaves "disgrace," "grief," a painful sense of "loss."

After these tersely aphoristic lines, the couplet, which reverts to the language of conventional romantic hyperbole, must come as a shock. It is as if the speaker, fearing he has gone too far, attempts to give the friend's tears a value beyond what they actually possess. But the anguish expressed in the previous lines has too intense a reality to be asserted away by a couplet—certainly not by one which must impress us as more mechanical than felt. And if the speaker believes what he says, he is the more deceived; quite obviously, it is not what he *feels.*

In Sonnet 35, also in the form of direct address, the same emotional territory is re-surveyed, and a different conclusion reached. Reversing Sonnet 34, the speaker begins as if in exculpation; but as in Sonnet 33, deep misgivings lurk beneath seeming acceptance:

> No more be grieved at that which thou hast done:
> Roses have thorns, and silver fountains mud;
> Clouds and eclipses stain both moon and sun,
> And loathsome canker lives in sweetest bud.

All men make faults, and even I in this,
Authorizing thy trespass with compare,
Myself corrupting, salving thy amiss,
Excusing thy sins more than thy sins are;
For to thy sensual fault I bring in sense
(Thy adverse party is thy advocate)
And 'gainst myself a lawful plea commence;
Such civil war is in my love and hate
　　That I an accessary needs must be
　　To that sweet thief which sourly robs from
　　me.

What could sound more simple than the opening line? It is as if enough tears had fallen to wash away (or seem to wash away) the sins of the past. But we soon discover that this is not the reason tears are to be avoided. The friend is not to grieve because imperfection is an inescapable consequence of the natural condition. So stated, the idea is logically unexceptionable, if magnanimous. But in fact the first five-and-a-half lines give us something incomparably more complex. There could scarcely be a more untroubled way of accepting the friend's human imperfection than the proverbial "roses have thorns" analogy. It is extremely flattering to the friend; but it is also somewhat incongruous. The thorns of a rose serve as protection. They do not make the flower less beautiful, or less worthy to be admired; though an oblique reminder of the Fall, they are not a symbol of corruption. The second image, "and silver fountains mud," is— and sounds— more unpleasant: beneath the beautiful is found something common and potentially sullying. In the next two lines the note of disgust becomes more pronounced. The moon and sun are *stained*— a return to the imagery of Sonnet 33— "And loathsome canker lives in sweetest bud." How different from the cheerful "nobody's perfect" "Roses have thorns" of line two. As a defense for misconduct, it clearly will not serve.

And such, indeed, the speaker realizes, feeling his way even as he attempts to formulate adequate excuses. Suddenly, in disgust, he turns on himself for "Authorizing thy trespass with compare." As Patrick Cruttwell observes [in *The Shakespearean Moment* (1960)], there is a notable shift in style: in place of the pointed sententiousness of the opening quatrain one suddenly encounters poetry that is "terse, subtle, complex to the point of obscurity . . . finding its imagery not in the 'poetical' of roses and fountains, but in the world of law courts and politics." In Professor Cruttwell's view, "this abandonment of the poetical diction corresponds to the complex fullness of what has to be said." I would modify Cruttwell's statement by saying that the first quatrain has its own subtlety and complexity: its style is entirely successful for a self-deceived effort to defend the indefensible. Without the contrast between surface and depth it could not be what it is. The rest of the sonnet, which voices feelings previously no more than intimated, is equally well suited to expressing corrosive self-aware-

ness. "[C]ivil war is in my love and hate," and the speaker acknowledges that he has perverted reason on behalf of "that sweet thief which sourly robs from me." We have reached, to alter Johnson's phrase, the instability of truth. Here is no shuffling.

II

In Sonnets 40-42, all in the form of direct address, there is a good deal of shuffling. Sonnet 40 begins with a desperate attempt to justify the friend's infidelity; the nature of his theft, implicit in Sonnet 35, is now made explicit:

Take all my loves, my love, yea, take them all:
What hast thou then more than thou hadst
　　before?
No love, my love, that thou mayst true love
　　call;
All mine was thine before thou hadst this
　　more.
Then, if for my love thou my love receivest,
I cannot blame thee for my love thou usest;
But yet be blamed if thou this self deceivest
By wilful taste of what thyself refusest.
I do forgive thy robb'ry, gentle thief,
Although thou steal thee all my poverty;
And yet love knows it is a greater grief
To bear love's wrong than hate's known injury.
　　Lascivious grace, in whom all ill well shows,
　　Kill me with spites; yet we must not be foes.

The first line, as abject as it is dramatic, has the authority of authentic anguish. After such an outcry we do not need to be told *why* the friend can "Take all my loves." But between it and the couplet we encounter desperate sophistries which obviously do not convince the speaker. The movement of lines 2-7, slowed by frequent repetition and feminine rhyme, testifies to the violence of the emotions the speaker strives to transmute to studied reasonableness. He cannot blame his friend for using "my love" as his own "if [it is done] for my love." But "if," of course, equivocates; and in what follows the speaker gives up the line of defense he has chosen. "But yet be blamed if . . ." (l. 7) initiates the imputation of guilt, but does so while attempting to preserve an idealized sense of the friend: he is to be blamed if, in being false to the speaker, he is also being false to himself. Paradoxically, what the speaker hopes for is insincerity in sin: for if the friend is really what his actions imply, what hope remains? It is this latter possibility, most evident in the couplet, which dominates the rest of the sonnet. The "gentle thief" is forgiven and not forgiven; the speaker will "bear love's wrong" because he must. In the couplet, the promise of line one is fulfilled in language utterly naked of defense:

Lascivious grace, in whom all ill well shows,
Kill me with spites; yet we must not be foes.

The oxymoron quivers with peculiar horror. But along with this appalling insight into the friend's nature is an acknowledgment, stripped of all self-respect, that any suffering is preferable to losing him. In the immense sadness of the final phrase the worst is glimpsed.

Sonnets 41 and 42 draw back from this abyss, and continue the futile efforts at self-deception. Sonnet 41, the more intense and dramatic, is— like Sonnets 35 and 40— a self-correcting monologue:

> Those pretty wrongs that liberty commits
> When I am sometime absent from thy heart,
> Thy beauty and thy years full well befits,
> For still temptation follows where thou art.
> Gentle thou art, and therefore to be won;
> Beauteous thou art, therefore to be assailed;
> And when a woman woos what woman's son
> Will sourly leave her till she have prevailed?
> Ay me, but yet thou mightst my seat forbear,
> And chide thy beauty and thy straying youth
> Who lead thee in their riot even there
> Where thou art forced to break a twofold truth:
>   Hers, by thy beauty tempting her to thee,
>   Thine, by thy beauty being false to me.

Of the tone of the opening we may say, in [Randall] Jarrell's phrase, that the "dishonesty is so transparent / It has about it a kind of honesty" [*The Complete Poems* (1969)]. The friend's betrayal is not susceptible to being so characterized: "pretty wrongs," "liberty," and "sometime absent" leave no doubt as to the speaker's real feelings. The friend's conduct is appropriate for one of his age and beauty, because (and here the tone turns ominous) "still temptation follows where thou art." And what man can resist temptation? As the structure of lines five and six implies, this one yields before he is even assailed ("gentle" in this context may remind us of the chamber-visitors in Wyatt's "They flee from me"). Who can say no when a woman woos— and to say "woman's son" makes refusal sound like ingratitude to the sex. Then, abruptly, the speaker expresses what he thinks and feels: among the "pretty wrongs" is infidelity with the speaker's own mistress. What was termed liberty is really "riot." And the beauty of the friend, tempting and provoking temptation, has effected a double breach of truth. By beauty the speaker is undone.

Sonnet 42 begins in comparable sincerity, but does not maintain it. Instead of the transparent dishonesty of the first lines of Sonnet 41, we encounter a totally unpersuasive exercise— a kind of pseudo-*tour de force*— in sophistic argument:

> That thou hast her, it is not all my grief,
> And yet it may be said I loved her dearly;
> That she hath thee is of my wailing chief,
> A loss in love that touches me more nearly.

Loving offenders, thus I will excuse ye:
> Thou dost love her because thou know'st I
>   love her,
> And for my sake even so doth she abuse me,
> Suff'ring my friend for my sake to approve her.
> If I lose thee, my loss is my love's gain,
> And, losing her, my friend hath found that
>   loss:
> Both find each other, and I lose both twain,
> And both for my sake lay on me this cross.
>   But here's the joy! my friend and I are one;
>   Sweet flattery! then she loves but me alone.

All the abusing and approving, then, is for his sake. But even the joyless joy of this "sweet flattery" is preferable to confronting the truth. The couplet, however, surprises by what it does not say. The friend, whose loss touches the speaker more nearly, is not the subject of the final line. There is no pretense that the speaker and his mistress are one, and that the friend's infidelity may thus be regarded as testifying to the love it seems to violate.

III

I come now to the last of the three groups I wish to consider, the "estrangement sonnets" (Sonnets 87-96). Here, as we might expect, the interplay of sincerity and subterfuge may be observed in its most intense and fascinating forms.

Sonnets 87-92 may be dealt with briefly, as an induction to Sonnets 93-96. In Sonnet 87, for twelve lines a "farewell" to one "too dear for my possessing," the speaker seeks to camouflage his real feelings with legal imagery and a coolly ironic tone. In the couplet, however,

> Thus have I had thee as a dream doth flatter,
> In sleep a king, but waking no such matter.

we hear a different voice. The image, which attests to the enormous value the friend has had, also intimates that he never really gave himself. What the speaker possessed, he now realizes, never existed except in his own mind.

If Sonnet 87 is, but for the couplet, more self-protective than sincere, Sonnets 88 and 89 embody a different kind of falseness. The speaker in Sonnet 87 uses irony as a defense; its astringency attests to his self-awareness. There is no possibility of deception here: we realize at once that the speaker is assuming one of the most familiar of "deliberate disguises." But in Sonnets 88 and 89 we encounter something more subtle. Sounding the very base-string of abnegation, the speaker presents himself as love's martyr; under the guise of selflessness, he attempts emotional blackmail. The insidious attractiveness of this tactic has already been apparent, particularly in Sonnet 71:

No longer mourn for me when I am dead
Than you shall hear the surly sullen bell
Give warning to the world that I am fled
From this vile world, with vilest worms to
    dwell.
Nay, if you read this line, remember not
The hand that writ it, for I love you so
That I in your sweet thoughts would be forgot
If thinking on me then should make you
    woe. . . .

In Sonnet 88, the speaker is less sentimental and more aggressive. The first quatrain sets the tone:

When thou shalt be disposed to set me light
And place my merit in the eye of scorn,
Upon thy side against myself I'll fight
And prove thee virtuous, though thou art
    forsworn.

The speaker, in short, makes the most of his role: he looks like the innocent flower, but is the serpent under it. The sudden uncoiling of the self, so notable here, is repeated in the couplet:

Such is my love, to thee I so belong,
That for thy right myself will bear all wrong.

Sonnet 89, which is utterly abject throughout, serves as a foil for Sonnet 90. Its last line— "For I must ne'er love him whom thou dost hate"— is a fair indication of the speaker's lack of conviction.

In Sonnet 90 we are back in the real world of felt emotion:

Then hate me when thou wilt; if ever, now;
            . . . . .
If thou wilt leave me, do not leave me last,
When other petty griefs have done their spite,
But in the onset come: so shall I taste
At first the very worst of fortune's might;
    And other strains of woe, which now seem
    woe,
    Compared with loss of thee will not seem so.

The speaker says nothing fraudulently self-effacing; he speaks of the pain of loss, not of justifying the friend's conduct. In the image of Sonnet 34, he ventures forth without his cloak.

Sonnet 91 ends in a confession of vulnerability: the speaker is "Wretched in this alone, that thou mayst take / All this away and me most wretched make." But in Sonnet 92 he expends much ingenuity on dispensing with this formidable truth. According to the argument, the friend is his "For term of life" because his own life will immediately cease if friendship is withdrawn. This idea is developed in such pallid language that one is

never in danger of believing the speaker means what he says. "O, what a happy title do I find, / Happy to have thy love, happy to die!" sinks no roots into living experience. But in the couplet— and shockingly, after such a tissue of artifice— the speaker opens his mind with brutal directness:

But what's so blessèd-fair that fears no blot?
Thou mayst be false, and yet I know it not.

It is with this recognition that Sonnet 93 begins:

So shall I live, supposing thou art true,
Like a deceivèd husband; so love's face
May still seem love to me though altered new,
Thy looks with me, thy heart in other place.
For there can live no hatred in thine eye;
Therefore in that I cannot know thy change;
In many's looks the false heart's history
Is writ in moods and frowns and wrinkles
    strange:
But heaven in thy creation did decree
That in thy face sweet love should ever dwell;
Whate'er thy thoughts or thy heart's workings
    be,
Thy looks should nothing thence but sweetness
    tell.
    How like Eve's apple doth thy beauty grow
    If thy sweet virtue answer not thy show!

The sonnet recapitulates much that has been both active and implicit in earlier sonnets. The friend's involvements, sometimes confronted in their intrinsic painfulness but often at least partially rationalized, are here likened to marital infidelity. A kind of sacrament has been profaned; but the speaker has his human claims too, his possessiveness. For, whether or not we are to imagine physical consummation, this is sexual jealousy, an emotion that, in Helen Gardner's phrase, "involves the whole personality at the profound point where body meets spirit." ["The Noble Moor" (1963)]. The young man's beauty, once seen as emblematic of his moral and spiritual qualities, is perceived as a mask behind which any vileness may lie concealed. Whatever his inner qualities, he will appear all "sweetness." And this, with wonderfully mordant irony, is said to be the work of heaven. In the first line of the couplet, however, there is neither irony nor indirection. The friend's beauty is like that of "Eve's apple"— and then the speaker equivocates— "If thy sweet virtue answer not thy show." Though the sonnet began supposititiously, its language leaves no doubt as to what the speaker believes to be true. The saving "if" (rather than "since") shows him attempting to extricate himself from the full implications of what he has said. Yet, given the disturbing idea that what the young man shows is invariably beautiful, one cannot help imagining a vast disparity. The image of the fair fallacious fruit, primal temptation itself, is a natural one.

IV

Sonnet 94, though closely linked to the sonnets in this group, is set apart by its seeming detachment. There is no reference to the speaker or his friend; the abstract "they" replaces "you" or "thou":

> They that have pow'r to hurt and will do none,
> That do not do the thing they most do show,
> Who, moving others, are themselves as stone,
> Unmovèd, cold, and to temptation slow;
> They rightly do inherit heaven's graces
> And husband nature's riches from expense;
> They are the lords and owners of their faces,
> Others but stewards of their excellence.
> The summer's flow'r is to the summer sweet,
> Though to itself it only live and die;
> But if that flow'r with base infection meet,
> The basest weed outbraves his dignity.
>   For sweetest things turn sourest by their
>   deeds;
>   Lilies that fester smell far worse than weeds.

Few of the Sonnets seem less dramatic than this extraordinary poem. Yet it is nonetheless, I think, to be understood as a dramatic meditation, analogous within its context to the "To be, or not to be" soliloquy in *Hamlet*. In each instance, apparent detachment masks intense involvement: to generalize is to escape, however briefly, from the tyranny of the personal. Neither Hamlet nor the speaker confronts the painful particulars. But what has struck at the mind and heart to occasion such reflections?

The sonnet describes, in the octave, people almost wholly different from the friend. Power to hurt he has in abundance; and the speaker has suffered. In Sonnet 96, moreover, the speaker talks of what the friend might do:

> How many lambs might the stern wolf betray
> If like a lamb he could his looks translate!
> How many gazers mightst thou lead astray
> If thou wouldst use the strength of all thy
>   state!

(ll. 9-12)

Here "pow'r to hurt" appears both in the wolf-as-lamb image and in the vaguer— but still sinister— assertion that the friend might lead many gazers astray if he wished to "use the strength of all [his] state." Not doing what one most shows sounds far more disquieting. And what the friend has "shown" is, I think, the critical question. If the friend's virtue answers his show— that is, his physical appearance— the line cannot apply to him: he would exemplify proper concordance, not a praiseworthy discrepancy between appearance and reality. But there is another way of showing. As Stephen Spender has remarked [in "The Alike and the Other" (1962)], the friend creates a "double impression":

> What we see are two things, characteristics which the poet doubtless found present in the real young man, but which are so idealized that it is difficult to form a realistic picture from them: and opposite to this, references to the friend's lascivious faults, coldness, falsity, and his ill reputation, a kind of counter-image held up before his eyes as a terrible example.

Setting aside biographical speculation, we may agree that the friend, like a Renaissance perspective drawing, produces a double impression: his looks imply one thing, his conduct another. And if, despite all evidence to the contrary, his conduct has been misinterpreted (or he can be shamed into amending it), the speaker would have reason to rejoice. There is of course falseness, both in the general proposition regarding the virtue of those who "do not do the thing they most do show," and in the speaker's belief that the friend may be one of them. But how much better for the friend to be virtuous after all than for him to be, as Sonnet 96 implies, masterly in predation.

The speaker continues the argument in similarly strained terms, for his desire to reconcile what he has perceived of the friend with at least the possibility of virtue commits him to what would otherwise seem a kind of mock-encomium. Readers are right, I believe, to detect irony along with apparent commendation: to be "as stone," "cold," hardly sounds like the way to "merit heaven's graces." But as Sonnet 95 emphasizes, the friend is guilty of precisely opposite defects:

> That tongue that tells the story of thy days,
> Making lascivious comments on thy sport,
> Cannot dispraise but in a kind of praise;
> Naming thy name blesses an ill report.
> O, what a mansion hath those vices got
> Which for their habitation chose out thee,
> Where beauty's veil doth cover every blot
> And all things turns to fair that eyes can see!
>   Take heed, dear heart, of this large privilege;
>   The hardest knife ill used doth lose his edge.

(ll. 5-14)

The changeless beauty of the friend, so prominent in Sonnet 93, is here shown for what it is: there is no question of "if." And what the veil covers is rampant sexuality. In view of the "deceived husband" image (also Sonnet 93), we may suspect that the speaker is thinking of the friend's profligacy when he praises those who "do not do the thing they most do show" (both *do* and *thing* have sexual senses too well established to require documentation). Since the friend's "sport" is what Sonnet 129 calls "Th' expense of spirit in a waste of shame," there is something to be said for "husband[ing] nature's riches from expense." And if the peculiarly non-active beings praised in the octave are (surely with some irony) the "owners of their faces," the corresponding image in Sonnet 95 makes vices possess the bodily "mansion" of the young man: given the alternative, the former must seem preferable. But of course the image is, in its immediate context, repellent: it suggests deceptiveness, the ability to hide whatever one does not wish the world to see. This quality, unlike the others that the "they" of the octave possess, has characterized the friend from the start. In conjunction with his beauty, it is his most striking attribute; do what he will, his face will never give him away. But the real "lords and owners of their faces," the speaker insists, are men of another sort, these almost passionless unmoved movers.

It has escaped few readers that this has been a singularly wintry recommendation. The speaker, who obviously has little relish for these paragons of attenuated humanity, cannot praise but in a kind of dispraise. His mind, however, is on the friend, so profusely endowed in all seeming, who squanders nature's riches. Sterile self-mastery is set against the friend's misuse of the excellence entrusted to him by nature or heaven.

The uncorrupted flower of the sestet requires little comment. Unlike Eve's apple, it is what it seems. And as in the octave, the contrast is between what appears to be incomplete participation in life (living and dying to itself) and actions that are reprehensible. The subverted flower, like the friend, meets "with base infection." So expressed, the flower's plight differs in one essential from that of the friend: for how is one to blame a flower for letting itself suffer blight? But the speaker is willing to sacrifice logic in order to make his point. Thus, in the couplet, the festering of lilies symbolizes the way "sweetest things turn sourest by their deeds." It is through what one *does* that corruption comes. The "sweet thief" of Sonnet 35 has turned sour.

In Sonnet 95, as we have seen, the speaker abandons obliquity and addresses the friend directly. The first quatrain, which I have not quoted, employs the image of the corrupted flower:

> How sweet and lovely dost thou make the
>   shame
> Which, like a canker in the fragrant rose,
> Doth spot the beauty of thy budding name!
> O, in what sweets dost thou thy sins enclose!

But neither here nor in Sonnet 96 can the speaker refrain from ending on a note of insincerity. The couplet of Sonnet 95, "Take heed, dear heart, of this large privilege; / The hardest knife ill used doth lose his edge," is a palpably fraudulent effort to treat what obviously arouses moral horror (not to speak of jealousy) in a spirit of levity. In Sonnet 96, the speaker strives to seem far more disinterested than he actually is. And his language shows it. The friend might, if he wished, mislead many: "But do not so; I love thee in such sort / As,

thou being mine, mine is thy good report"—as if the friend's reputation, rather than his deeds, were at the heart of the matter. What the speaker sees and feels, in short, renders him incapable of total sincerity.

V

Arnold's image of the three-leveled stream, with which we began, is of course too simple and too orderly to suggest the full complexity of experience—the speaker's or our own. "After all," Kafka asks in a letter written in 1913, "who knows within himself how things really are with him? This tempestuous or floundering or morasslike inner self is what we really are. . . ." Knowing what we do of suppression and repression, not to speak of the conscious role-playing that is a consequence of intense self-awareness, we recognize how hard it is to be veridical, "simply true." And as Robert M. Adams trenchantly observes [in *Bad Mouth: Fugitive Papers on the Dark Side* (1977)], "Even to protest the difficulty of truth is to betray it; for one's protest implies special exalted standards, and there's no one of us who doesn't live snugly enough in the enseamed, sweaty security of a thousand prudent, approximate lies." With respect to the young man, the speaker's deepest feelings are fundamentally ambivalent—an ambivalence corresponding to the double impression the young man creates. There is no "noiseless current strong, obscure and deep," but a turbulent confluence of conflicting emotions. Never in these sonnets do we encounter anything like the edged self-awareness, combined with awareness of the other, that we find in some of those sonnets to or about the mistress—nothing comparable, for instance, to Sonnet 138: "When my love swears that she is made of truth / I do believe her, though I know she lies." In the sonnets we have been considering, the price for such an insight comes too dear. The speaker—our double, our brother—cannot bear very much sincerity; when we think we have found where truth resides, we probably have found only where it lies.

LANGUAGE AND IMAGERY

There is widespread agreement that in Shakespeare's sonnets both verbal and stylistic patterns are closely linked to themes and topics. **Philip Martin,** for instance, argued that these poems characteristically display an intimate connection between themes and linguistic modes. Calling attention to the pattern of repetition and extension that occurs throughout Sonnets 1-17, Martin suggested that in addition to iterating the idea that the youth must marry and have children, this group of verses opens the way for all the central themes of Sonnets 1-126. Jane Hedley emphasized the regular appearance of ambiguity, obsessive repetition, contradiction, and specious argument in Sonnets 1-126. She linked this verbal pattern to the Poet's frequent shifts between identification with and estrangement from the young man.

There is also a consensus that the words and images in Shakespeare's sonnets have multiple meanings and associations. Stephen Booth compiled an exhaustive commentary on the many connotations, nuances, and references in almost every line of the 154 sonnets. He also offered encouragement to modern readers, asserting that Shakespeare's original audience would have been as challenged or bemused by the poet's words and phrases as we are. Philip Martin recommended that readers proceed slowly through a sonnet in order not to miss the network of meanings embedded in each lyric; this is "a poetry for contemplation," he advised, that can only be fully understood by carefully considering each line and phrase. Hilton Landry offered a close reading of Sonnet 94, remarking that this verse has been interpreted in many different ways. The language is so allusive, he argued, that the poem must be read in the light of those that precede and follow it, in order to locate some context for its richness, complexity, and subtlety.

Among the many critics who have discussed images and metaphors in the sonnets— and their connections with thematic issues— are **Winifred M. T. Nowottny**, James Dawes, Arthur Mizener, Neal L. Goldstien, and **Anne Ferry**. Focusing on the first six sonnets, Nowottny demonstrated that within an individual sonnet various images may at first seem unrelated, but closer examination shows that they are connected to images in adjacent verses. Shakespeare used imagery not merely for its beauty, she argued, but as a means of integrating different parts of his sequence and as a way of intensifying the expression of the speaker's experience. In an examination of images that represent mutability and constancy, Dawes similarly noted the unifying effect of the imagery in Shakespeare's sonnets. Clusters of images that recur throughout the sequence function as substitutes for a traditional narrative or plot, weaving together different parts of the sequence, he contended. Mizener analyzed Shakespeare's compound metaphors, calling attention to the rich blend of connotations in many of them. No one meaning stands out from the others, he declared, or claims our exclusive attention; instead, we must see them all simultaneously. Goldstien directed readers' attention to various forms— and associations— of money imagery in the sonnets, noting that while Shakespeare often uses riches as a synonym for sexuality, he also frequently links treasure and beauty. Goldstien argued that these ambiguous or contradictory associations underscore the poet's profoundly ambivalent attitude toward love. Ferry assessed the significance of Shakespeare's immortalizing metaphors or conceits, particularly in Sonnet 15. Through metaphors that associate immortality with art and vegetation, she argued, the poet accentuates the principal idea of the poem: that he is at war with time. Ferry also pointed out that the use of the present tense in this sonnet represents another expression of the poet's attempt to control time.

Finally, both **Winifred Nowottny** and Douglas L. Peterson have offered analyses of the prevalent styles in the sonnets. Both of them commented on the frequent juxtaposition of an artificial or ornate style with a more direct or simpler one. Nowottny pointed out that the artificial style predominates when the speaker is most self-conscious; by contrast, when he expresses his feelings more sincerely, the style tends toward the commonplace. Peterson focused on the Dark Lady and Rival Poet sonnets, concluding that the verses in both these groups demonstrate that Shakespeare found the traditional plain style employed by some sonnet writers just as insincere and exaggerated as the overly eloquent mode used by others.

Winifred M. T. Nowottny

SOURCE: "Formal Elements in Shakespeare's Sonnets: Sonnets I-VI," in *Essays in Criticism*, Vol. II, No. 1, January, 1952, pp. 76-84.

[*Nowottny examines in detail the relation between diction, syntax, and imagery in the first six sonnets of Shakespeare's sequence. Particularly in Sonnets 5 and 6 she finds a carefully crafted organization of formal elements that enhances the development of the principal motifs in this group: beauty as a physical attribute and beauty as a treasure or inheritance that must be accounted for. Nowottny maintains that this harmony of ideas and style is sustained throughout the collection.*]

Despite Shakespeare's own description of his sonnets as being 'far from variation or quick change', they have proved to be remarkably resistant to generalizations. It is, however, the purpose of this article to suggest that there is one generalization that can be made about them; one, moreover, that affords a point of view from which it is always helpful to regard them: namely, that the *Sonnets* reveal Shakespeare's strong sense of form, and that it is with respect to their form that the peculiar features or striking effects of individual sonnets may best be understood. There are in the *Sonnets* so many experiments with form that it would be difficult to lay down at the outset a definition of 'form' at once comprehensive and precise, but the meaning of the term as it is used here will be sufficiently indicated by describing 'form' as 'that in virtue of which the parts are related one to another', or indeed as 'that which manifests itself in the relationships of the parts'. What is important for the purposes of this article is not the precise definition of form, but rather the indication of elements which commonly contribute to the manifestation of form. At the present day, the most illuminating criticism of individual sonnets is characterized by its concentration on imagery, and though it is true that imagery in the *Sonnets* is of great importance, it is not of exclusive or even of paramount importance. In this article I shall try to show that in Shakespeare's sonnets imagery is subordinated to the creation of the form of the whole and that imagery itself is at its most effective when it supports or is supported by the action of formal elements of a different kind.

Sonnets I-VI of the 1609 Quarto afford illustration. Shakespeare is often praised for his power of using imagery as an integrating element, yet in these sonnets it is evident that he has sacrificed the integration of the imagery of the individual sonnet to larger considerations of form; this sacrifice has features which show that it is in fact a sacrifice and not the ineptitude of a novice in sonnet-writing. In Sonnet I, the degree to which the images assist the organization of the poem is slight indeed. Almost every line has a separate image, and these images are heterogeneous (for instance: 'Beauty's rose'— 'heir'— 'contracted'— 'flame'— 'famine'— 'foe'— 'herald'— 'buriest'— 'glutton'). The relation between the images is, for the most part, a relation *via* the subject they illustrate; it is not by their relations to one another that the poem is organized. This, however, is not ineptitude. The separateness, the repetitiveness (in that there is no increasing penetration of the object, but only an ever-renewed allegorization) and the regularity (a single new image in each of the first twelve lines) give this sonnet the character of a litany. If Sonnet I is indeed in its rightful place, there would seem to be here a recognizable decorum of form in the poet's electing to open by a litany of images a sonnet-sequence which makes extended use of each. Further, the hypothesis that in Sonnet I there is a decorum of form which to the poet seemed more important than the congruity of images within the individual sonnet, is borne out by some features of Sonnets II-IV. The imagery of Sonnet II falls into two distinct parts connected by a modulation. In the first quatrain there is a group of images all referring to the beauty of the face; in the third quatrain a very different group, not visual like the first, but moral or prudential, relating to beauty considered as treasure, inheritance, and a matter for the rendering of accounts; the intervening quatrain is entirely devoted to a modulation from one type to the other:

> Then, being ask'd where all thy beauty lies,
> Where all the treasure of thy lusty days,
> To say, within thine own deep-sunken eyes,
> Were an all-eating shame and thriftless praise.

(In this modulation the visual and the prudential— 'beauty' and 'treasure'— are formally balanced, and the 'deep-sunken' unites the eyes and the treasure in a single imaging epithet.) This careful four-line modulation suggests that Shakespeare was well aware of the virtue of relating images one to another as well as to the object they convey; yet the very necessity for a modulation here derives from the remoteness from one another of the two types of imagery. Here again the discrepancy finds its justification in larger considerations of form: namely, in the relation of Sonnet II to Sonnets III and IV. Sonnet III takes up and expands the first quatrain

Henry Wriothesley, Third Earl of Southampton.

of Sonnet II, turning as it does upon the beauty of the face ('Look in thy glass, and tell the face thou viewest . . . '), and Sonnet IV takes up and expands the third quatrain of Sonnet II, turning as it does entirely upon beauty as treasure, inheritance and a matter for the rendering of accounts. It is further to be observed that Sonnets V and VI repeat this pattern, V dealing with visual beauty in visual terms, and VI dealing with 'beauty's treasure' in a long-sustained conceit drawn from usury. Would it be fanciful to suggest that the infelicity of the usury conceit in Sonnet VI reflects the difficulty the poet found in bringing this little sequence to a formally symmetrical conclusion?

In each of these six sonnets, features of the individual sonnet are illuminated by a consideration of the design of the whole group. But since we have no external warrant of the correctness of the 1609 order, the case for Shakespeare's sense of form must further be argued on grounds affording independent corroboration. This is found in Sonnet IV where, though the imagery chosen relates the sonnet to its fellows, the development of that imagery within the sonnet is a self-contained exercise in abstract form. The sonnet must be quoted and discussed in full.

> Unthrifty loveliness, why dost thou spend
> Upon thyself thy beauty's legacy?

Nature's bequest gives nothing, but doth lend,
And, being frank, she lends to those are free.
Then, beauteous niggard, why dost thou abuse
The bounteous largess given thee to give?
Profitless usurer, why dost thou use
So great a sum of sums, yet canst not live?
For, having traffic with thyself alone,
Thou of thyself thy sweet self dost deceive.
Then how when nature calls thee to be gone?
What acceptable audit canst thou leave?
    Thy unus'd beauty must be tomb'd with thee,
    Which, used, lives, th'executor to be.

Here we have a sonnet in which, patently, there is a high degree of organization. Firstly, the imagery of financial matters is sustained throughout. Secondly, there is within this integrated scheme a number of strongly marked subsidiary systems. The most immediately striking, which may therefore be cited first, is the ringing of the changes in lines 5-8 on 'abuse'— 'usurer'— 'use', which is taken up in the couplet by 'unus'd', 'used'. Another marked system is that of the reflexive constructions associated with 'thee': 'spend upon thyself'— 'traffic with thyself'— 'thou of thyself thy sweet self dost deceive', taken up in the couplet by 'thy . . . beauty . . . tomb'd with thee'. That these are deliberate systems, not inept repetitions, is proved by the way in which they interlock in the couplet: 'unus'd' is, in the first line of the couplet, linked with 'thy beauty . . . tomb'd with thee', and this contrasts with the second line of the couplet, where there is a linking of 'used', 'executor', and 'lives', to produce the complete formal balance in thought, diction and syntax, of

    Thy unus'd beauty must be tomb'd with thee,
    Which, used, lives, th'executor to be.

This formal balance is of course closely related to the thought of the sonnet: Nature, which lends beauty in order that it may be given, is contrasted with the youth, whose self-regarding results in a usurious living on capital alone, which is a negation of Nature and of life; these paradoxes of the thought make possible the correspondences and contrasts of the verbal systems. What is remarkable is the way in which the poet evolves from this material an intricate and beautiful form which is very close to the art of fugue. Like the fugue, its effect resides in the interaction of the parts; critical analysis, which cannot reproduce the simultaneousness of the original, must labour heavily behind, discussing first the development of each part and then their interaction. We may note, then, that 'Unthrifty loveliness', with which the sonnet opens, is, as it were, a first blending of those two distinct voices, 'why dost thou spend upon thyself' and 'Nature's bequest'. The second quatrain blends them again in 'beauteous niggard', which is itself an inversion, formally complete, of 'unthrifty loveliness', and moreover an inversion which leads on to the extreme of 'profitless usurer'; further, the movement towards the

judgment represented by 'profitless usurer' has all the while been less obtrusively going on in the verbs as well as in the vocatives ('spend'— 'abuse'— 'yet canst not live'). Then, with 'yet canst not live', the sonnet brings out the second voice, that reflexive (and self-destructive) action announced in 'spend upon thyself', but kept low in the first eight lines, maintaining itself there only by the formal parallels of 'why dost thou spend'— 'why dost thou abuse'— 'why dost thou use'. This voice now emerges predominant in 'For, having traffic with thyself alone', and this voice in turn reaches its extreme of formal development in the line 'Thou of thyself thy sweet self dost deceive'. The remaining lines bring the two voices to a sharp contrast with 'nature calls thee to be gone' (where 'nature' and 'thee' achieve a syntactical nearness embodying a conflict of opposed concepts, and this conflict-in-nearness is fully stated in the complete formal balance of the couplet). In this rough analysis of the blending of the voices in this sonnet, much has had to be passed over, but now we may go back and point to the incidental contrast and harmony of 'beauteous niggard' with 'bounteous largess'; to the transition, in the pun of 'canst not live', from usury to death (which leads on to the contrast in the couplet); to the felicity of 'audit' in line 12, which is relevant not only to all the financial imagery that has gone before, but also to the rendering of an account when life is at an end; to the subtle conceptual sequence of 'unthrifty loveliness' (the fact of beauty), 'beauteous niggard' (the poet's reproof), 'profitless usurer' (the youth's own loss), and finally, 'unus'd beauty' (the whole tragedy— of beauty, of the poet, and of the youth— in the hour of death). Thus this sonnet, which in its absence of visual imagery has little attraction for the hasty reader, reveals itself to analysis as having an intricate beauty of form to which it would be hard to find a parallel in the work of any other poet.

Though Sonnet IV is a *tour de force* in the handling of form, Sonnet V is even more important to the critic who would make much of formal elements, in that it has a quality which sets it apart from the preceding four: a quality the average reader might call seriousness or sincerity. Here Shakespeare deals with Time and Beauty (and for the application of these to the particular case of the youth requires Sonnet VI, linked to V by 'Then let not . . . '). The evident artifice of Sonnets I-IV (emblematic imagery, conceits, punning and patterned word-play) gives place in Sonnet V to language which, though it is of course figurative, derives its figures from that realm of common experience in which processes conceived philosophically by the mind have in fact their manifestations to the senses: from the seasons which figure Time, from the flower and its fragrance which figure Beauty and Evanescence. In short, the poem appeals to us in that realm of experience where we are all, already, half poets. Yet despite this change from the 'artificial' to the 'sincere', this poem too derives much of its strength from its formal design. This design is simple but perfect. The easy continuous process of Time is stated in lines themselves easy and continuous:

> Those hours that with gentle work did frame
> The lovely gaze where every eye doth dwell,

and in the next two lines, which suggest that this process implies a coming reversal, the reversal is still a thing of the future and is indicated not by any change in the movement but only by the verbal contrasts between 'gentle' and 'will play the tyrant' and between 'fairly' and 'unfair'. So the continuous movement flows uninterrupted through these lines and on into the fifth:

> For never-resting time leads summer on

but in the sixth line,

> To hideous winter and confounds him there

the reversal so casually foretold in the first quatrain becomes, by the violence of 'hideous winter' and 'confounds' and by the change of tense, a present catastrophe, and the movement of the fifth and sixth lines taken together perfectly corresponds to the sense: the running-on movement of summer is checked by 'hideous winter' and again by the heavy pause at 'there'. The next two lines embody perfectly, by sound and imagery as well as by sense, this checking and reversal:

> Sap check'd with frost and lusty leaves quite
>   gone,
> Beauty o'ersnow'd and bareness everywhere.

(Particularly subtle is the way in which the alliteration of 'lusty leaves' gives place to that of 'beauty' with 'bareness'.) Now in the remaining six lines the poet in his turn attempts a reversal, and the beauty of the form is to be seen in the way in which he now uses the two kinds of movement already laid down in the sonnet (the one of flowing, the other of checking). What he does is to *transfer to Beauty* the flowing movement of Time, and then to *arrest* Beauty in a state of permanent *perfection;* this he does by the long flowing movement, ending in arrest and permanence, of the line,

> Then, were not summer's distillation left . . .

This triumphant transfer to Beauty of the movement formerly associated with Time, is of a piece with the imagery of the next line ('A liquid prisoner pent in walls of glass'), where Beauty's distillation is at once arrested ('prisoner', 'pent') yet free ('liquid') and visible ('glass'); this image of course reverses the implications of the earlier images of winter, where the sap was checked with frost and beauty was o'ersnow'd. Thus the movement of the first eight lines proves to have been designed not merely to make the sound repeat the sense, but rather to lay down formal elements whose reversal enables the poet to reverse the reversal implicit in Time.

Similarly, the image of distillation is seen to be not merely an illustration of the concept of preserving Beauty, but also an answer to the image of winter's freezing of the sap and obliteration of Beauty. Clearly, the formal elements of Sonnet V are part of the poetic logic: the movement, as much as the imagery, is a means of poetic power. It is because of this that the study of formal elements in the Sonnets is not an arid academic exercise. Such a study can help one to arrive at a fuller understanding of Shakespeare's means of communication and a fuller possession of those poetic experiences with which the Sonnets deal.

This article has dealt only with the first six sonnets of the 1609 Quarto. These six sonnets are not exceptional in their successful handling of form; from the whole range of the *Sonnets* many examples more subtle and more striking might have been chosen but it seemed to me best, in order to argue the case for Shakespeare's interest in form, to make no arbitrary selection, but simply to begin at the beginning and scrutinize what is to be found there. The findings warrant a much greater attention to formal aspects of the *Sonnets* than is at present customary. The result of such an attentiveness to Shakespeare's handling of form is the discovery that the greater the immediate effect of a sonnet, the more surely does it prove, upon examination, that the effects rest no less upon the form than upon the appeal of the sentiments or of the imagery (as, for instance, in the famous Sonnet CXVI, 'Let me not to the marriage of true minds . . .'). Again, it will be found that many of the sonnets which are not commonly held to be of the finest, reveal an unsuspected depth and strength when they are, after scrutiny of their form, revalued. It is upon this last point that particular stress may well be laid, for it is here that one becomes aware of new possibilities for the interpretation of Shakespeare's language, not only in the poems but also in the plays. A close study of the language of the *Sonnets* makes it clear that, great as was Shakespeare's ability to use imagery not only for its beauty but also for its integrating power, he possessed in even greater measure the power to make the formal elements of language express the nature of the experience with which the language deals.

Anne Ferry

SOURCE: "Shakespeare," in *All in War with Time: Love Poetry of Shakespeare, Donne, Jonson, Marvell,* Harvard University Press, 1975, pp. 3-63.

[*Ferry analyzes Sonnet 15 in the context of the speaker's claim that through the medium of language he can defeat time and immortalize his beloved in verse. She illustrates how, in this sonnet, Shakespeare seems to suspend the inevitable process of death and destruction by generalizing time in terms of particular verbal comparisons— especially metaphors of gardening and vegetation. She also describes the way Shakespeare's use of the present tense and a dispassionate tone disengages the speaker and the young man from the ordinary sequence of time.*]

The speaker in Shakespeare's Sonnet 15 declares himself to be "all in war with Time for loue of you," the friend whose precious quality he would preserve from mortality. Throughout the first one hundred and twenty-six poems in the collection we find sonnets concerned with this struggle. The speaker varies in the attitudes he takes toward it, challenging or lamenting time's power, in tones arrogant or despairing, detached or resigned. His preoccupation with its destructiveness is evident from the first poem urging the young man to father a child, that his beauty might not "by time decease." Beginning with Sonnet 15, the lover who feels himself to be time's enemy is explicitly and repeatedly identified as an artist whose weapon in love's battle is his poetry.

The figure of the poet-lover dominates English lyrics during the later sixteenth century. Poets of this period, ultimately influenced by Petrarch but also by the French, characteristically introduce the lovers in their poems as poets, inspired to write or made tongue-tied by their feelings, eternizing, praising, persuading, complaining in verse, or comparing their beloveds to beauties celebrated in other poems. *Astrophil and Stella*, the earliest English sonnet sequence and of measureless influence, begins with three poems spoken by a lover struggling to find a literary language in which to write about his feelings, and throughout elaborates on the speaker's role as poet-lover. Following Sidney (and Petrarch), Spenser, Daniel, and Drayton, as well as many of their imitators, begin their sequences with poems explicitly "about" writing love poetry: Spenser's lover addresses his completed book of sonnets which he imagines the lady will read.

Shakespeare's collection (perhaps because it is a collection rather than a sequence) does not begin with a lover who identifies himself explicitly as a poet, though he is pre-eminently an appreciator of beauty, but elsewhere it adopts all the conventional postures of the poet-lover; expands or alters them; even introduces the (perhaps autobiographical) motif of a rival who is also a poet. Shakespeare's uses of the figure are distinctive because they are more pervasive and more various and therefore point us toward his most central concerns in the sonnets. The poet whose verse is love's weapon against time declares the nature of his own power in that struggle and so defines his conception of the nature and power of poetry.

The earliest declaration is Sonnet 15, which appears in the midst of the opening group of related sonnets where the speaker urges a young man to immortalize his beauty by reproducing it in a child. Although connected to the poems in this group by images of time as the enemy of youthful beauty, this sonnet opens new interests which are pursued with many variations throughout the rest of Sonnets 1 to 126.

Sonnet 15 is the first to identify the lover explicitly as an artist, and the first of many to do so by adapting the convention of the eternizing conceit—"I ingraft you new"—immediately recognizable to readers of Italian, French, and English love sonnets as a metaphor for the poet's power to immortalize his beloved in verse. Allusions to this convention occur more often in Shakespeare's than in any other group of English sonnets. His poet-lover, obsessed with the effects of time, refers to the traditional promise so often and with such variousness, so frequently asserts, questions, modifies, finally even attacks, ridicules, and condemns it, that its recurrent uses may be one of the principal reasons why readers tend to think of the speakers in these poems as one personality. So much emphasis accumulates that Shakespeare's changing uses of the eternizing conceit can point to ways we may define his changing concerns about love and also about poetry in the sonnets.

In Sonnet 15 the poet's promise to preserve his beloved from time's decay, although he vows it in full and sad awareness of mutability, is finally asserted with a confidence supported by his ways of manipulating the language of the poem. These devices are characteristic of a *kind* of poetry, found more often among the lower-numbered poems in the collection, which is designed to support the eternizing conceit, or the attitudes associated with its appearance. The assumptions implicit in this kind of sonnet are first consciously argued in Sonnet 15:

> When I consider euery thing that growes
> Holds in perfection but a little moment.
> That this huge stage presenteth nought but showes
> Whereon the Stars in secret influence comment.
> When I perceiue that men as plants increase,
> Cheared and checkt euen by the selfe-same skie:
> Vaunt in their youthfull sap, at height decrease,
> And were their braue state out of memory.
> Then the conceit of this inconstant stay,
> Sets you most rich in youth before my sight,
> Where wastfull time debateth with decay
> To change your day of youth to sullied night,
>   And all in war with Time for loue of you
>   As he takes from you, I ingraft you new.

The language is designed to persuade us, as well as the friend addressed directly in line 10, that an assertion may be true which we know to be contrary to fact. We know that all creatures in the temporal world must decline and eventually die as surely as we know that day must change to night and that seasons pass. The speaker even seems to insist on this knowledge, by his sadness in contemplating how brief and precarious is living "perfection," and by the way he ponders with lavish illustration the fate of "euery thing that growes." Yet the very language in which he dwells on the inevitable waste wrought in the much-loved world by time is his instrument for arguing and so promising his friend that he can defeat its universal power with his art.

The speaker's authority to challenge time is expressed most obviously by the detachment in his tone throughout most of the poem. We recognize it in the leisure he initially enjoys to "consider" and "perceiue," and in the generality and Latinate objectivity of his diction. We hear it in the ways his considerations seem to exclude him from the unconscious life of "euery thing that growes" or of "men as plants," toward whom he feels kindly pity for their vaunting in ignorance of their fate. We find it in his role as spectator which joins him in "secret" knowledge with the stars who also "comment" on the vast scenes presented for their entertainment by the ever-shifting "showes" of the mortal world. This tone of detached sympathy is itself achieved in contradiction of fact, for in fact the speaker as well as his friend belongs to the category "men," and so is subject to time. The authority expressed in his detachment must therefore depend on the ways in which his language manipulates the inescapable facts of temporal experience. The language of the sonnet itself must demonstrate, by its essential characteristics and their peculiar effects, the power of the poet at war with time.

It does so in part by making the passage of time a subject for contemplation while excluding its process, insofar as possible, from the language itself. There are no changes of tense in the poem. "When I consider" exists in the same expansive present with "euery thing that growes / Holds in perfection" and "Where wastfull time debateth" or "To change your day of youth." The prominent series, "When . . . When . . . Then," with which successive quatrains opens, is essentially not a temporal but a logical pattern. "When" and "Then" do not mark stages in a narrative of consecutive events but terms in a syllogism whose structure dictates the design of the poem. Of course, in any argument there is a sense of advance or development, created by a sequence of logically connected points, as the speaker proceeds from one term to that which necessarily follows from it. Even more prominently, as this poet-lover unfolds his argument, his involvement grows, his feelings deepen and change, so that we hear a dramatic development as well as a sequential argument. Yet the ordering principle is different in kind and in its effects from that of a narrative recounting a temporal sequence of events whose succession is dictated by the order in which they happened. For it begins with the opening proposition and is derived from it, so that it seems to develop according to logical necessity. Within this order there are no references to single events, happening at specified moments in time, although the poet does speak of activities, his own or in the world he considers. In our experience outside of poems, actions are events which take place at particular times and in temporal sequence, but within the language of the sonnet all action is gen-

eralized and made to take place in the continuum of the argument. That is to say, the activities of "euery thing that growes," of "this huge stage," of "men as plants" are not presented as particular events in the speaker's remembered experience of individual times in his past, but as general illustrations of his major and minor premises. They point to his deduction, not by the inevitable passage of time, but by the direction of his own argument. In the language of the conclusion, it is not time which impels him to recognize how his meditation applies to his friend, but his own operations as observer and as poet:

> Then the conceit of this inconstant stay,
> Sets you most rich in youth before my sight,
> Where wastfull time debateth with decay
> To change your day of youth to sullied night.

Here he perceives his friend's subjection to cruel changes, not because time has already wrought those changes and so forced his admission, but because his own verbal comparison has reminded him, as it actively "Sets . . . before my sight" the decline of "men as plants," that his friend will, like plants and men, cease to be. Yet even this painful recognition, forced upon him by the workings of his own comparison, does not ultimately destroy the speaker's control over his unfolding argument. That is, because the metaphorical action is performed by his own "conceit," it seems to operate according to philosophical or verbal laws rather than the cruel dictates of time. Because the act performed by his "conceit" is to set the youth before his "sight" like a scene on a stage or a subject of formal debate, both the friend and the speaker's "conceit" of his subjection to time seem of a different order from temporal experiences. They are like illustrations in an argument, which are also metaphors in a poem, existing outside of time within the verbal order that creates them.

The verbal order of Sonnet 15, which is in part logical and also, as we shall see more fully, metaphorical, is completed by the poet-lover's vaunting of his own power in the battle with time:

> And all in war with Time for loue of you
> As he takes from you, I ingraft you new.

This promise is made in the same present tense used by the poet all through the sonnet. It is designed to lift the destructive action of time, the poet's opposing action, and the fate of the friend out of temporal sequence and to incorporate them in the continuous present of the poem.

The conjunction "And" joins the couplet to the preceding quatrains as an additional conclusion of the syllogism: "When . . . When . . . Then . . . And." In this sequence "And" does not have primarily narrative suggestions of "then the next thing happens after" but has rather the meaning of "an additional conclusion is the following." The speaker therefore makes two deductions from his initial premises:

> When I see that every thing growing in the temporal world including "men as plants" must "decrease" and die, then I see you who belong to that category must "decrease" and die, and I renew you.

Acceptance of this second conclusion, as a possibility contrary to the facts of the timebound world, depends on the design of the poem, which is logical, we have seen, but also metaphorical.

In his last words, "I ingraft you new," the speaker identifies himself figuratively as a gardener, and his means of combating time as grafting. This art he devotes to the preservation of his friend who, like a plant, is continually diminished by time. We are prepared to accept this claim by the ways in which the poet's metaphorical language all through the sonnet has directed us to think of time's power as it acts on vegetative life. To be sure, his first consideration— "euery thing that growes / Holds in perfection but a little moment"— applies to all living beings. It includes men as well as other natural creatures, but by using the verb "grows" to define the existence of "euery" undifferentiated "thing" he has already begun to speak of "men" as "plants." The second quatrain is therefore the minor premise of his syllogism and the extension of his metaphor. Here he calls attention to the comparison by explicitly naming its terms— "men as plants"— and then elaborating it by describing the flourishing and wilting of human and vegetative life in the same vocabulary. The working-out of the "conceit" points to the poet's means for rescuing his friend. Perceived in vegetative terms, his friend's "day of youth" is bound to "decrease" and die, but because he has been transformed into a plant, his existence in time, comparable with day and night, may be seen to belong to nature's cyclical pattern of decline and renewal— "As he takes from you, I ingraft you new"— and therefore like a plant he can escape individual mortality.

We are therefore able to accept the possibility of this second conclusion within the order created by the language of the poet, although our experience in the world outside the poem has taught us that man cannot be rescued from time's destruction by any human skill. Because the speaker's metaphor makes us perceive his friend as a plant, it makes possible the conclusion that like a plant his declines do not have the finality of human deaths and like a plant he can be renewed by grafting. The emphasis is less on the friend's power of survival, however, since as a plant he is made to seem fragile and helpless, than upon the speaker's manipulation of it by his ability to "ingraft." As a gardener he uses his knowledge and skill to make of a beautifully passive natural creature a new, more enduring creation, blooming as he has artfully designed within the whole order of his garden domain.

That life-giving knowledge and skill is shown in his capacity to "consider" the facts of experience in time, to transform them into the "conceit of this inconstant stay" (a phrase which, through the pun on "stay," itself seems to arrest the passage of time) and so to create a nontemporal order, where sequence is ruled by philosophical necessity. The language of the poem is therefore a demonstration of what the couplet bravely claims, the poet's power through his art to combat destruction by time. It persuades us to accept the possibility of his final assertion contrary to fact, and to recognize his authority to assert it despite his own sad awareness of mutability. This authority is earned by his triumph over time, which he admits to achieve strictly within the design of the poem, his garden world. Although his assurance here is saved from complacency by his tender appreciation of his friend's "day of youth" and by his sorrow that time "takes from" that brief perfection, it allows the tone of detached sympathy with which he first considers the fate of "euery thing that growes" and the confidence with which he eventually engages the power of his art "all in war with Time."

THE POET

For many commentators, the speaker's expression of his tortured thoughts and feelings represents the chief interest of Shakespeare's sonnets. The Poet has been variously described as enigmatic, self-deluded, inconsistent, and servile. Both **Philip Martin** and **John Klause** have tried to explain his deferential attitude to the young man. In Martin's judgment, the Poet exchanges the self-effacing demeanor of the early sonnets once he and the Friend have achieved a relationship of greater intimacy. By contrast, Klause has argued that the Poet's self-deprecation is one of the strategic ploys he uses as he tries to teach the youth the meaning of love. In Klause's estimation, the Poet's other strategies include flattery, rebuke, forgiveness, and lies.

The Poet's dishonesty— his distortion of the truth or evasion of it— has attracted a large measure of critical attention. **Heather Dubrow** (1981) has argued that this characteristic reflects the Poet's moral confusion and underscores the general absence of truth and certainty in the sonnets. Furthermore, she suggested that our wavering confidence in his truthfulness influences our responses: sometimes we identify with him, but when we doubt his honesty we become more detached. Whether the Poet is deceiving himself as well as his audience is a central critical issue that has been addressed by a number of commentators. Emily E. Stockard, for example, maintained that when he can no longer deny the reality of his friend's desertion, the Poet adopts a strategy of consolation designed to isolate him from that reality; thus he claims to find comfort in the Friend's absence, even though he knows that this strategy is based on illusion. **Michael Cameron Andrews** argued that in the sonnets to the young man, the Poet is initially unaware of the Friend's true nature, but when the young man's duplicity becomes evident, the Poet devises a series of expedients to rationalize or justify what he cannot bear to confront. From Andrews's perspective, the Poet is caught up in a profound struggle as he tries to hide his feelings from himself.

Other critics who have considered the issue of the Poet's self-deception include **Philip Edwards** and James Winny. Focusing on the Dark Lady sonnets, Edwards argued that here the Poet desperately tries to make sense of his life— to understand why a man would betray the nobler aspects of his nature and be ruled by base instinct. Edwards traced the Poet's various attempts, all grounded in self-deception, to portray carnal desire as something other than a degradation. Also directing his attention to Sonnets 127-51, Winny maintained that these poems depict the Poet struggling with the recognition of his mistress's unworthiness on the one hand, and his inability to resist her on the other. In Winny's opinion, the Poet judges himself as harshly as he judges the Dark Lady.

John Klause

SOURCE: "Shakespeare's *Sonnets:* Age in Love and the Goring of Thoughts," in *Studies in Philology,* Vol. LXXX, No. 3, Summer, 1983, pp. 300-24.

[*Though many commentators have disparaged the Poet's frequent self-abasement and his seeming inconsistency, Klause regards these as part of the speaker's strategy to create and preserve the affection of a young man who is neither lovable nor aware of what love means. Thus in his role as guide and instructor, the Poet employs whatever tactic will serve his purposes: flattery, rebuke, sophistry, forgiveness— even lies. Klause reads the final sonnets to the Friend as indications that despite the Poet's loving patience and selflessness, his attempts to teach and motivate the young man have been unsuccessful. The critic also discusses the candor of Sonnets 127-52. In Klause's judgment, the Poet despises the Dark Lady and knows he's a fool for desiring her.*]

To call the man whose travail is recorded in Shakespeare's *Sonnets* a protagonist may seem to grant him a status beyond his desert. Of a protagonist we expect at least that he struggle for or against something and that in his exertions, even when he is inconsistent, he prove himself a coherent personality. Shakespeare's Poet, it has been suggested, does neither.

Yvor Winters once complained [in "Poetic Styles Old and New" (1959)] of a "servile weakness" in the Poet. And indeed, one is tempted to underscore evidence of an emotional and moral supineness in a man who is everywhere full of self-denigration: "To leave poor me thou hast the strength of laws, / Since why to love I can

allege no cause" (49.13-14), who envisions himself a "sad slave" without personal prerogatives, existing to serve through his presence or absence the pleasure of a sovereign Friend and living vicariously through him (57; 37.1-4); who allows his Friend moral obliquity, which he will rationalize for his master even when he is himself its victim: "Suns of the world may stain, when heaven's sun staineth" (33.14); who professes to have no rights, not even to pardon the injury inflicted on him (58.9-14); who blesses the Friend who steals his mistress ("sweet thief," "gentle thief" [35.14; 40.9]), and will then find more blame in himself for excusing the crime than in his Friend for committing it (35); who stumbles after his Lady like a "babe" after its mother, "crying" for attention (143); who knowingly, helplessly acquiesces in the falsehood necessary to keep a wildly irrational love alive: "Therefore I lie with her, and she with me, / And in our faults by lies we flattered be!" (138.13-14). It is no wonder that critics have proceeded beyond the view that the Poet is sometimes "trapped" into inertia, to the conviction that, in some poems at least, he exhibits "an almost masochistic humility" [Giorgio Melchiori, in *Shakespeare's Dramatic Meditations* (1976)] or a "masochistic generosity." [R. P. Blackmur, "A Poetics for Infatuation" (1962)].

But is the Poet ever consistent enough to be described as passive or prostrate? His art and his self-confidence are alternately feeble and potent: his rhyme is now "barren" (16.4), now "pow'rful" (55.2). He acknowledges that "nothing 'gainst Time's scythe can make defense / Save breed" (12.13-14); yet he promises his Friend:

> But thy eternal summer shall not fade.
> . . . . .
> So long as men can breathe or eyes can see,
> So long lives this, and this gives life to thee.
>
> (18.9, 13-14)

The Poet humbly confesses his verse to be plain— even monotonous and unadventurous (76), a "worthless boat" beside his Rival's "tall building . . . of goodly pride" (80.11-12). He nonetheless takes pride in his "true plain words," which are free from the "strained touches rhetoric can lend" (82.12, 10).

> So is it not with me as with that Muse
> Stirr'd by a painted beauty to his verse,
> Who heaven itself for ornament doth use,
> And every fair with his fair doth rehearse,
> Making a couplement of proud compare
> With sun and moon, with earth and sea's rich gems,
> With April's first-born flowers, and all things rare
> That heaven's air in this huge rondure hems.
>
> (21.1-8)

This from the same Poet who compares his love to "a

summer's day" and the "eye of heaven" (18.1, 5); to "the lily's white," the "sweet" of the "violet," and "the deep vermilion in the rose" (98.9-10; 99.1-3); to Helen and to Adonis (53); and, by implication, to the triune God himself (105). The Poet's love seems self-abnegating in the extreme:

> If you read this line, remember not
> The hand that writ it, for I love you so,
> That I in your sweet thoughts would be forgot,
> If thinking on me then should make you woe.
>
> (71.5-8)

But this love candidly pleads for "recompense" (23.11). It is generous in granting the beloved independence: "Thee have I not lock'd up in any chest" (48.9). Or perhaps it is not:

> So am I as the rich whose blessed key
> Can bring him to his sweet up-locked treasure,
> The which he will not ev'ry hour survey.
>
> (52.1-3; cf. 75.3-8)

The lover who proves that love must be forever changing, growing (115), then insists that "it is an ever-fixed mark" (116.5) and in the next breath admits his own inconstancy (117). A voice remorseful ("Alas, 'tis true, I have gone here and there" [110.1]), self-convicted of "transgression" (120.3), can suddenly turn defiantly proud of its essential righteousness:

> On my frailties why are frailer spies,
> Which in their wills count bad what I think
>   good?
> No, I am that I am, and they that level
> At my abuses reckon up their own;
> I may be straight though they themselves be bevel;
> By their rank thoughts my deeds must not be
>   shown.
>
> (121.7-12)

These psychological somersaults may seem too spectacular and unconnected to be turned by a character in a dramatic *praxis* or action— hence the impulse of many cirtics to abandon story in favor of idea.

Some, however, have tried to face squarely the problem of the protagonist. They have challenged the portrait of the supine lover in either of two ways: by appeals to irony or to an ethical code.

The Poet's profession of vassalage, it is said, should not always be understood naively:

> Being your slave, what should I do but tend
> Upon the hours and times of your desire?
> I have no precious time at all to spend,
> Nor services to do, till you require.
>
> (57.1-4)

Here and elsewhere one may find the words heavy with equivocation, called upon to express simultaneously devotion and reproach. "I am utterly yours. 'So true a fool is love,' I have no needs but yours. Indeed!" And where the expressions of "self-naughting" are ingenuous, they are not the whines of servile helplessness but, in an almost religious sense, the effects of an active heroism (what Milton was to call "the better fortitude / Of patience and heroic martyrdom" [*Paradise Lost*, 9.31-2]). "I may not evermore acknowledge thee' (36.9), "No longer mourn" (71.1), and "Although thou steal thee all my poverty" (40.10) spring "from a region in which love abandons all claims and flowers into charity." C. S. Lewis's formulation of this view has become classic:

> The self-abnegation, the 'naughting', in the *Sonnets* never rings false. This patience, this anxiety (more like a parent's than a lover's) to find excuses for the beloved, this clear-sighted and wholly unembittered resignation, this transference of the whole self into another self, without the demand for a return, have hardly had a precedent in profane literature. In certain senses of the word 'love', Shakespeare is not so much our best as our only love poet [*English Literature of the Sixteenth Century*].

The question of the Poet's consistency is also addressed under two assumptions: either that the problem would dissolve if the true "order" of the Sonnets were known, or that the contradictions, real enough in themselves, are precisely the kind we might expect of a complex human being in turbulent love affairs. Thus a plausible story may be seen to lurk in the *Sonnets,* and a plausible protagonist; and both can be discovered if only art may be rearranged to suit the logic of life or the illogic of life allowed to invade the ritual of art.

There is merit in all of these views. But aside from the obvious fact that at some points one may be incompatible with another (the lover either abandons all claims or ironically does not, is consistent or is not), none of these solutions is sufficiently cogent or comprehensive to escape major objections. Irony is a quality of mind, not of character, and may be found in a spirit morally feckless. A lover's ironic protest against his friend's faithlessness hardly qualifies as an "action." We might remember Carlisle's admonition to Richard II:

> My lord, wise men ne'er sit and wail their
>   woes,
> But presently prevent the ways to wail.
>
> (R2, III.ii.178-9)

If the Poet's self-naughting is genuine (and we shall see that it is not as straightforward and radical as Lewis proposed), it may in the abstract be deemed heroic and wise. But the Poet's generosity towards this particular Friend is in some ways less charity than connivance. The freedom granted from "claims" (insofar as it *is* granted) is the opportunity to receive with ingratitude, to ignore, forget, steal, and betray with impunity. Rearrangement may bring the *Sonnets* closer to a plausible sequence; but there is no authority to guarantee that Shakespeare's is one of those "likely" stories that are all too rare in and out of fiction. Furthermore, true contradictions will not be resolved by shuffling. And if they are allowed to stand, either an explanation must be found for the Poet's inconsistency or he must be judged helplessly, pointlessly wayward.

Discovering a rationale for inconsistency is not, in fact, an impossible task. We may see that irony and ingenuousness coexist in a lover whose self-martyrdom is at once real and strategic, generous and self-interested, noble and tainted, variable and utterly single-minded. In order to do so, we must dwell upon the implications of two facts about the Poet, to which he calls attention and which are so obvious that we tend to take them for granted: he is old and he is a liar.

The Poet's age in Shakespeare's *Sonnets* is not merely a hackneyed, implausible convention. Petrarch's reference to his own "weary spirit," "wrinkled skin," "decaying wit and strength" (Sonnet 81) had indeed inspired many of his successors (like Samuel Daniel, Richard Barnfield, and Michael Drayton—the eldest of whom was thirty-one years old at his work's first printing) to pose as superannuated in all but "desire." But the counterfeit silver hair and furrowed brows of most of these sonneteers could not disguise the youth of the passion which they portrayed. Theirs were "the propositions of hot blood and brains." Like many youthful suitors, their lovers were young enough in sensibility to look upon desire and its sublimation as the only important facts of life. Even where the lovers' attitudes were reflective, the reflection, though sometimes deep, was narrowly channeled—as it tends to be if a young person decides that the problems surrounding love must be addressed before the rest of life can be attended to. When Shakespeare's Poet speaks of his age, however, we sense no discrepancy between his psychology and his pose.

> my glass shows me myself indeed,
> Beated and chopp'd with tann'd antiquity.
>
> In me thou seest the glowing of such fire
> That on the ashes of his youth doth lie.
>
> she knows my days are past the best.
>   . . . . .
> And age in love loves not t' have years told.
>   (62.9-10; 73.9-10; 138.6, 12)

Whatever his chronological age (he regards "forty winters" as an "antiquity" [2.1]), the Poet everywhere speaks from the perspective of a man who has weathered life. The disparity in years between him and his "lovely boy" (126.1), between him and the lady before whom he tries

to suppress the "simple truth" of his age (138.8), colors almost every motive and action in the relationships to which the *Sonnets* refer.

That an older man should speak in sonnets, with the benefit of experience, is not a situation we would expect after reading Shakespeare's plays, where sonnet-lovers, mostly young, are almost invariably treated with condescension. In *Two Gentlemen of Verona* "wailful sonnets" are by definition "serviceable," little more than devices for a young man to use who would "lay lime to tangle" a lady's "desires" (III.ii.68-70). The poetical flights of the wooers in *Love's Labour's Lost* are products of immature, insincere, uneducated sentiment, which must be chastened; its language made more "honest" (V.ii.413). Orlando's "odes" and "elegies" in the forest of Arden are harmless and touching enough; they are also ridiculous, and Rosalind is right to call the young poet a "fancy-monger" in need of "good counsel" (*AYL*, III.ii.361-4). The romantic intensity of Romeo and Juliet, who speak in a sonnet at their first meeting and kiss on the couplet (*Rom*, I.v.93-106), is no less callow for being genuine; and use of "the numbers that Petrarch flowd in" (at which an overwise Mercutio sneers [II.iv.38-9]) marks the couple for trouble who take the sonneteers' hyperboles too seriously. As a form, then, the sonnet does not promise Shakespeare much. He takes it away from the young, however, among whom it has been abused, doing so not simply to parody an institutionalized silliness, but to give "age in love" its proper voice. This voice is both consistent, true to the character from whom it issues, and inconsistent, as it must be to achieve the character's ends.

If the Poet in Shakespeare's *Sonnets* "loves not t' have years told" (138.12), he is forever telling his age anyway—not only by calling attention to his physical decline ("That time of year thou mayst in me behold" [73]), but by consistently revealing in himself the attitudes and preoccupations of a man whose "days are past the best" (138.6). He lives with memories of "precious friends hid in death's dateless night" and can "weep afresh love's long since cancell'd woe" (30.6-7). He speaks with nostalgia of a past when standards were simpler but higher, nobler, than those of a sophisticated present. "In the old age," in "days long since, before these last so bad," when hours were "holy," beauty was unambiguously "fair" (67.14; 68.9; 127.1); "antique" pens were as eloquent as modern ones—for all their "new-found methods" and "compounds strange"—are inarticulate (106.7; 76.4). The "time-bettering days" of this age of progress (82.8) have amassed a rich harvest of "new-fangled ill" (91.3). The Poet also dwells much upon the future—that is to say, the little time he has left, the "twilight" (73.5) from which he can already contemplate his death (71) and wish for it (66). He often raises issues of time and eternity with his Friend, who seems too young to be seriously concerned about them (see 77, especially). The Poet's many exhortations to the Friend to achieve immortality through procreation and his offers to the youth of an immortality in verse spring more from his own obsessions than from attention to the other's frame of mind.

It is understandable that a man who feels his living substance devoured by time, or rather "transfix[ed]," "mow[n]," "beated," "chopp'd," "crush'd," "drain'd," and "consum'd" (19.1; 60.9, 12; 62.10; 63.2, 3; 73.12), is most sensitive to "accounts" owing and owed, honored and neglected. Tallies become extremely important when supplies run short. Seeing himself in the growing shadow of extinction, the Poet allows his imagination to be filled with commercial and legal metaphors, which, though on occasion used ironically to remind a lover that love should not be mercenary, are in general approved analogies. Having long grappled with the world and provided a life for himself by "public means" (of which, one must admit, he sometimes seems ashamed [111.4]), the Poet naturally looks to the courts and the marketplace for a vocabulary to express his sense of (his own or another's) threatened or waning personal treasures, his understanding of love's privileges, rights, obligations, audits, losses, expenses, and "use" (e.g., 4, 21, 30, 49, 67, 74, 79, 87, 120, 122, 126, 134, 142, 146). In this respect Shakespeare's economic and judicial motifs are more functional than those of most of his predecessors and contemporaries among sixteenth-century love-poets.

The Poet's social status requires his deference to the Friend as to a superior. The older man bears the "canopy" for the young person of eminence (125.1), relies on him for patronage in competition with a rival (76-86). Love, of course, demands its own kind of obsequiousness (125.9), and, with whatever ironic demurrals, the Poet becomes the loved one's "slave" (57, 58). But age gives the elder the inclination and the right to treat the youth as a son in need of a father's care. Thus, running counter to the voice of dependency in the *Sonnets* (with a wholly plausible inconsistency) is that of the preceptor, who tries to teach his charge the value of a family, the lessons of time, and definitions of love; of the patient, concerned parent, ever ready to "play the watchman" for his loved one's sake, even when his love is betraying him (61.12); of the doting parent, quick to make excuses for the youth's "pretty wrongs" (41.1); of the protector, who vows to bear his Friend's heart, keeping it "so chary / As tender nurse her babe from faring ill" (22.11-12), and who pleads with the Lady who has enslaved his "sweet'st friend":

> My friend's heart let my poor heart bail
> Whoe'er keeps me, let my heart be his guard.
>   (133.4, 10-11)

Even when the Poet speaks in words of self-pity he does not relinquish the paternal mantle:

> As a decrepit father takes delight

> To see his active child do deeds of youth,
> So I, made lame by Fortune's dearest spite,
> Take all my comfort of thy worth and truth.
>   (37.1-4)

In weakness he maintains his authority.

The Poet's affair with the Dark Lady, like Antony's with Cleopatra, is rather a combat between powers who are equals if not in age (the Poet seems older) then in stature. Adults stepping out of earshot of the youth who plays a part in both their lives, they must settle the issue of his possession themselves, with their own kind of frankness (133-4). Indeed, although age in love may feel compelled to hide its years (138), it speaks for the most part with a cynical honesty about itself and its object. The Poet's bawdy jokes and insults at his mistress's expense are the humorously bitter quips of a man tired of the illusions used by romance to dignify lust.

> No want of conscience hold it that I call
> Her "love" for whose dear love I rise and fall.

> Wilt thou, whose will is large and spacious,
> Not once vouchsafe to hide my will in thine?

> In nothing art thou black save in thy deeds,
> And thence this slander as I think proceeds.
>   (151.13-14; 135.5-6; 131.13-14)

The Poet is old and wise enough to see clearly that he perjures his eye in forcing it to swear its object lovable (152.13). Age will sin no less than youth, but it may be doomed to suffer a livelier appreciation of the preposterousness of its evil and the vileness of its guilt.

> What merit do I in myself respect,
> That is so proud thy service to despise,
> When all my best doth worship thy defect,
> Commanded by the motion of thine eyes?
>   But, love, hate on, for now I know thy mind:
>   Those that can see thou lov'st, and I am blind.

> Th' expense of spirit in a waste of shame
> Is lust in action.
>   (149.9-14; 129.1-2)

The very fact of the Poet's age, then, continually insisted upon, is the source of two of the great incongruities in the *Sonnets:* that an older man has become "vassal" to a youth much inferior to him in insight and (though the elder is no saint) moral character; that (as seems most likely) this same man lives in open-eyed thrall to a passion which, as the young Hamlet believed, is supposed to be conquered by time:

> Ha, have you eyes?

You cannot call it love, for at your age
The heyday in the blood is tame, it's humble,
And waits upon the judgment, and what
    judgment
Would step from this to this?

                                (*Ham*, III.iv.67-71)

Since love in all its forms is rarely scrupulous in observing rules of logic, common sense, or common expectation, we must acknowledge the incongruities to be part of a constant truth about human nature.

Some of the inconsistencies in the *Sonnets*, however, are too refractory to be accounted for by the Poet's forthright revelation of his age. In order to see how he might consciously and therefore plausibly be responsible for many of them, we must understand how in age he has become mendacious.

The Poet's attitude towards the truth is a complicated one. Defined as something more than the "correspondence" of thought and fact (148.2), truth has for him a moral dimension—as fidelity ("I will be true" [123.14]) and authenticity ("Without all ornament, itself and true" [68.10]). With goodness and beauty truth is a transcendental value, the goal of human striving, and when found in a person occasions the highest compliment (105). Departure from such truths is either madness or a criminal betrayal. Yet a certain kind of verity, the Poet believes, is no more than a bland literalness, which as his practice indicates may be improved by hyperbole. Historical "records" he knows to "lie"; not only may the writers of history be in error, but "what we see," the facts themselves (123.11). This is not the kind of truth that will win one to its service. And devotion to another may lead a lover to abandon the truth in forsaking himself:

    Speak of my lameness, and I straight will halt,
    Against thy reasons making no defense.

                                        (89.3-4)

The Poet thinks he has grounds for appealing to the "virtuous lie" against a truth that is "niggard" (72.5, 8).

Shakespeare's plays often portray with some approval an idealism that is not too saintly to compromise itself. Tricksters like Prince Hal and Duke Vincentio [in *Measure for Measure*] become morally ambiguous in their resort to deception; but their diminution is the price exacted by a wicked world, perverse in its paradoxes, for the achievement of good. The sanctity of absolutists like Isabella [in *Measure for Measure*] and Cordelia [in *King Lear*] is always splendid but not in every respect benign. If the world would be spiritually poor without martyrdom, it would be poorer still if it lacked the flawed but elementary moral successes of a flexible soul like Helena, the heroine of *All's Well that Ends Well*, who is mundane enough to banter with the crass Parolles on

his own terms, who can imagine that "virtue's steely bones" may look "bleak i'th' cold wind" (I.i.103-4), who deceives her way to justice and love.

There is, in fact, a strong kinship between Helena and the Poet of the *Sonnets* which ought not to go overlooked in favor of more obvious parallels between male characters from the plays and the sonneteer. The middle-aged Antonio of *The Merchant of Venice* hazards himself for the prodigal young Bassanio, as does the sea-captain Antonio for the young Sebastian in *Twelfth Night*. But Helena, if not the same age or sex as the older male friends, is their equal in devotion and in other respects much more like the figure in the poems. Not old herself she yet has the older generation on her side—the King, the Countess, Lafew—and acts as a representative of a past whose nobility threatens to become attenuated in "these younger times" (I.ii.46). She is a poet, author of a sonnet in the Shakespearean form (III.iv.4-17), which sounds familiar notes of self-denigration and selfless love:

    He is too good and fair for death and me,
    Whom I myself embrace to set him free.

In Bertram Helena loves a man superior to herself in rank but who is, though of a "well-derived nature" (III.ii.88), so far beneath her in moral stature that she must strive mightily to overcome his iniquity and to make him, not only her lover, but an object worthy of her love. (Whether or not she succeeds, of course, is a "problem.") As a woman rendered "inferior" by social conventions (the Poet of the *Sonnets* suffers a lowliness dictated by other social codes) she must be active in secret to pursue her goals; and secrecy involves lying and deceit.

The lies of the Poet are not so spectacular as a fabricated death-notice or a bed-trick, but they are just as real and just as purposeful. They are of several kinds. One may deny the "simple truth" to another person: "I lie with her, and she with me" (138.8, 13). One may also try to deny it to oneself, to make, as Macbeth says, "The eye wink at the hand" (I.iv.52). The Poet has been accused of such attempts at self-deception, and the charge seems substantiated in his own professed resolve:

    So shall I live, supposing thou art true,
    Like a deceived husband, so love's face
    May still seem love to me, though alter'd new.

                                        (93.1-3)

He would lie to himself about the extent of the Friend's devotion and innocence, rationalize the Friend's obvious treachery, perjure his own eyes to love a formidably worthless Lady. As Macbeth's case reminds us, however, an acute mind cannot easily un-know a momentous, insistent truth already in its possession. In acknowledging that he sees himself lying, the Poet proves that he has not escaped an inconvenient knowledge. He is a manipulator of lies, not their victim, for his prevarications are primarily rhetorical.

Reading most of the *Sonnets* as rhetoric rather than as drama or meditation (although rhetoric may of course grow out of meditation and play its part in a dramatic action) may drastically alter our approach to the poems. Such a reading makes less crucial the search for a linear plot and helps to explain contradictions that would remain even in a definitively established sequence of events. It may also affect significantly our estimate of the Poet's character. A rhetorician's design upon an audience (here, the Friend or Lady), his concern to teach or to move, may lead him to suppress or falsify history, his own motives, or his own condition. There is no need to trace a developing awareness in the Poet if, as his age and experience suggest, he knows most of the truth from the beginning, allowing only as much or as little of it into each poem as will serve his ends.

His purpose in the poems to the Friend, like Helena's in her dealings with Bertram, is to win the love of a man who must be made lovable and taught how to love. In the very first sonnet of a group which is almost universally believed to pertain to the early stages of the relationship the Poet reveals something of his method:

> From fairest creatures we desire increase,
> That thereby beauty's rose might never die,
> But as the riper should by time decease,
> His tender heir might bear his memory:
> But thou, contracted to thine own bright eyes,
> Feed'st thy light's flame with self-substantial fuel,
> Making a famine where abundance lies,
> Thyself thy foe, to thy sweet self too cruel.
> Thou that art now the world's fresh ornament,
> And only herald to the gaudy spring,
> Within thine own bud buriest thy content,
> And, tender chorl, mak'st waste in niggarding:
>   Pity the world, or else this glutton be,
>   To eat the world's due, by the grave and thee.
>
>   (1)

No less aware of the friend's self-absorption here ("Within thine own bud buriest thy content") than he is later ("The summer's flowr is to the summer sweet, / Though to itself it only live and die" [94.9-10]), the Poet withholds an explicit condemnation (plainspeaking, it is clear, would do no good) and attempts to make use of this trait in his argument. "Don't violate the logic of your narcissism," he suggests. "Produce another *self.*" There is criticism in the subtle plea to the young man that he become a different kind of "glutton" than he already is, but the irony is too sugar-coated to alienate a vain sensibility ("to thy sweet self too cruel," "tender chorl"). The rhetorician's flattery is offered on the premise that the youth will be moved to go out of himself, and thus "give the world its due," only by an ignoble appeal to his pride. The world needs, has a right to the "fairest creatures."

This exhortation is hardly calculated to bring the youth immediately to a state of heroic virtue. But the Poet, proceeding with the tolerance or patience that his own long lifetime of imperfection has taught him, is willing to settle for the slightest improvement, even if purchased with debased currency, in his pupil's art of giving. And whether or not the Poet was commissioned by a concerned parent to write the sonnets advocating marriage and begetting, it is in his own interest to encourage the young man whom he loves, or will love, to learn self-surrender. In order to teach this, the Poet must persevere, as the illogic of love urges him to do, in his concern for a Friend who over time comes to wound him deeply ("Kill me with spites, yet we must not be foes" [40.14]) and must direct his pleas and arguments by expediency.

What is expedient will change from moment to moment in a relationship that spans three years or more (104) and suffers a number of significant reversals. Flattery will alternate or combine with, displace or yield to, rebuke as quickly as the Poet feels they must to suit his purpose. So will "strained rhetoric" to "true plain words." Thus in Sonnets 33-5 the Poet's initial reaction to an injury done him is to accept it, even to prettify the wrong, for to do otherwise would be to lose the malefactor:

> The region cloud hath mask'd him from me now.
>   Yet him for this my love no whit disdaineth:
> Suns of the world may stain, when heaven's sun staineth.
>
>   (33.12-14)

The irony in "no whit" and in the outrageous analogy between the two suns cannot be doubted. Yet the criticism is muted until the Poet feels it opportune to ask plainly and in anger, "Why didst thou promise?" (34.1). "Base clouds" then lose their "brav'ry," becoming "rotten smoke" (34.3-4); the Poet speaks with a frankness and an authority not heard before:

> Though thou repent, yet I have still the loss,
> Th' offender's sorrow lends but weak relief
> To him that bears the strong offense's cross.
>
>   (34.10-12)

But of what use is this naked blade of truth if it severs the bonds that love would keep whole? The Poet allows "tears" to "ransom all ill deeds" (34.13-14) (or pretends that they do) not because the injured man has melted before the penitent's weeping, but because he would keep the possibility of love alive. Forgiveness, hollow-sounding as it is, will by fiat prevent a breach, while

Eminent by-gone performers of Shakespeare's characters: From top, first row, left to right, Betterton, Garrick, and Macklin; second row Pritchard, Siddons; third row, Cooke, Henderson, and Kemble.

providing an example of selfless devotion and proving the forgiver worthy to be loved. The Poet goes so far as to take upon himself the "sin" of "excusing" his Friend's "amiss" (35), relinquishing the brief authority that injured innocence had given him; for the Friend probably could not abide an extended awareness of his moral inferiority.

In these poems, then, are two great violations of the truth: the lies required by forgiveness and the lies told in self-diminishment. The Poet resorts to them here and throughout the *Sonnets* because to utter them is the only way to render them unnecessary— or rather, the only means allowed by a love that will not abandon its object. The lies are told in an irregular pattern. Retreat from the truth is made for the sake of an ultimate advance toward it, and the forward pressure diminishes or increases as circumstances change.

The conflict is especially tense after the Friend has seduced or been seduced by the Poet's mistress. "Take all my loves, my love, yea, take them all" (40.1). Outrage is tempered even as it is voiced, directed at "my love." A specious casuistry absolves the thief: "All mine was thine, before thou hadst this more. . . . I cannot blame thee"

(40.4, 6), then absolution is invalidated: "But yet be blam'd" (40.7); then reaffirmed: "I do forgive thy robb'ry, gentle thief" (40.9); and allowed to stand, with a reminder to the sinner that forgiveness is heroic:

> And yet love knows it is a greater grief
> To bear love's wrong than hate's known injury.
>   (40.11-12)

The pattern is repeated in Sonnets 41 and 42: extenuation of "pretty wrongs"; a change of mind expressed in a bitter sexual joke: "Ay me, but yet thou mightst my seat forbear"; renewed forgiveness: "Loving offenders, thus I will excuse ye," attached to a reminder that the injured party lies on a "cross" and that forgiveness is gratuitous, since its rational grounds are the feeblest of logic:

> But here's the joy, my friend and I are one;
> Sweet flattery! then she loves but me alone.
>   (41.1, 9; 42.5, 12, 13-14)

The sign of a more thorough forgiveness would be a more complete forgetfulness, and this the Poet tries to demonstrate to the Friend. Some of the *Sonnets* have seemed to many readers to be out of place because the Poet speaks in them in apparent unawareness of events which previous poems have recounted. In Sonnet 48, for example, not long after suffering his Friend's infidelity, the Poet anticipates losing what has already been lost: "thou wilt be stol'n, I fear." In Sonnet 70 he speaks of the youth's "pure unstained prime":

> Thou hast pass'd by the ambush of young days,
> Either not assail'd, or victor being charg'd.
>   (70.9-10)

These poems may well be out of order. It is just as likely, however, given the Poet's practice elsewhere, that he is passing over the truth in forgiveness and compliment. The Friend may have strayed, but he was not definitively "stol'n"; he was indeed "assailed" (41.6), and if not a "victor" in every battle, triumphant in the campaign as a whole. In the Poet's eyes, the young man's prime was "unstained," the scarlet of his sins made white as snow. The same fiction, after all, is used by the Poet when, after a period of separation (estrangement?) (97-8), love no longer "new" (102.5), he celebrates the Friend's "truth" (101.2; 105.9) as though he had never cause to question it, or had not questioned it in fact (41.14). Then, confessing a guilt of his own, hoping that the forgiven sinner has learned the lesson of such generous deceit, he pleads with the Friend for a similar favor: "o'er-green my bad" (112.4).

The lies of self-diminishment, more varied than those spoken in the name of forgiveness, are as undeviatingly aimed at creating, preserving, and educating love. The "sad slave" describes his vassalage as a reproach to the master who abuses him (57-8). In the altruist's self-naughting there is surely a plea for sympathy:

> No longer mourn for me when I am dead
> Than you shall hear the surly sullen bell
> Give warning to the world that I am fled
> From this vile world with vildest worms to
>   dwell;
> Nay, if you read this line, remember not
> The hand that writ it, for I love you so,
> That I in your sweet thoughts would be forgot,
> If thinking on me then should make you woe.
> O, if (I say) you look upon this verse.
>
> (71.1-9)

If the Poet really wished to be "forgot," he would not write and keep reminding his Friend to read. Much of the Poet's self-criticism is offered in the hope that it will be protested. The author who boasts of his "pow'rful rhyme" (55.2) and prides himself on the honest humility of his verse (82) does not in competition with a rival intend to convince his Friend that his own Muse is "tongue-tied" (80.4; 85.1) or that his "numbers are decay'd" (79.3); he seeks affirmation.

> Thus wisdom wishes to appear most bright
> When it doth tax itself; as these black masks
> Proclaim an enshield beauty ten times louder
> Than beauty could, display'd.
>
> (*MM*, II.iv.78-81)

A young lover may try to win the admiration of a lady by parading his vigor, his potential, or his achievement, as Astrophil does in his forty-first sonnet after he "obtain'd the prize" at a tournament. An older man will have to be loved for different reasons: not for his prowess, but for his tenderness, understanding, constancy, generosity, what is called in *A Lover's Complaint* "the charity of age" (70), and in spite of his growing infirmities. The Poet, far from attempting to hide his debility, is forever proclaiming it, for it cannot be hidden and can at least be turned to modest account in flattering the Friend's sense of his own potency or virtue:

> As a decrepit father takes delight
> To see his active child do deeds of youth,
> So I.
>
> This thou perceiv'st, which makes thy love
>   more strong,
> To love that well, which thou must leave ere
>   long.
>
> (37.1-3; 73.13-14)

Weakness, however, is not of itself attractive. To prove that discrepancy in age does not matter, that love

> Weighs not the dust and injury of age,
> Nor gives to necessary wrinkles place,

> But makes antiquity for aye his page,
>
> (108.10-12)

the Poet distinguishes himself in selfless dedication. If he is "nothing worth" (72.14), his whole energy will go to promoting and proclaiming the worth of his Friend, whose interests supersede the poor lover's own:

> Bending all my loving thoughts on thee,
> The injuries that to myself I do,
> Doing thee vantage, double-vantage me.
> Such is my love, to thee I so belong,
> That for thy right myself will bear all wrong.
>
> (88.10-14)

Nevertheless, the Poet does not relish or thrive on self-diminishment. His admission that he can "allege no cause" for his Friend to love him can hardly be ingenuous. The *Sonnets*, the self-naughting ones especially, offer a multitude of causes and, at least indirectly, ask the beneficiary of so much giving for a return. The "slave" would be made an equal. The eulogist would have his own worth affirmed. The constant lover would be shown loyalty. The trespasser would have his own trespasses forgiven even as he has forgiven a deep betrayal. Sonnet 120 is an open attempt to teach reciprocity: "if you were by my unkindness shaken / As I by yours, y'have pass'd a hell of time" (as the memory of *my* agony tells me).

> But that your trespass now becomes my fee,
> Mine ransoms yours, and yours must ransom
>   me.
>
> (120.5-6, 13-14)

One cannot easily inspire gratuitous forgiveness except by granting it, and the Poet has already offered it in full measure.

Since the Poet has continued to love his Friend despite "love's wrong" (40.12), the recompense he seeks is for an action that, despite its place in rhetorical arguments, is essentially unfeigned. Forgiveness is itself genuine. But it involves lying; and so does moral education. We may suspect that in Sonnet 62 the self-incriminator plays with the truth in order to challenge a complacent egotism that rarely gives.

> Sin of self-love possesseth all mine eye,
> And all my soul, and all my every part.
>
> (62.1-2)

Although the Poet is not immune to pride, his confession and repentance before a young man who seems distinguished for narcissism is probably an invitation to follow a salutary example. We may also wonder if the Poet's contritions after he has "rang'd" and "made old offenses of affections new" (109.5; 110.4) are purposely exaggerated. They follow a separation for which the

Friend seems responsible (87-96); and when a man goes elsewhere after being rejected, he would hardly have cause to consider himself unfaithful. It is probable that the friendship can be repaired at this point only if the Poet assumes a guilt he never knew and allows himself to be forgiven. Only thus may virtue be "rewarded."

Other gambits are available to the resourceful lover, and the Poet makes use of them without regard for their consistency, which is far less important to him than results. In the midst of all his sophistries, he sometimes risks forthrightness— an undisguised sermon:

> Oh how much more doth beauty beauteous
> seem
> By that sweet ornament which truth doth give!
> (54.1-2)

or a direct calling to account:

> For thee watch I, whilst thou dost wake
> elsewhere,
> From me far off, with others all too near;
> (61.13-14)

or a less direct (because attributed to the "world") yet daring insult:

> But why thy odor matcheth not thy show,
> The soil is this, that thou dost common grow.
> (69.13-14)

His avowals of selflessness are interrupted by a reference to his desperate *needs:* "So are you to my thoughts as food to life" (75.1). When overtures seem to fail, he utters a "Farewell" (87), but of course does not immediately depart. He mingles with pleas for sympathy an angry challenge:

> Then hate me when thou wilt, if ever, now,
> Now while the world is bent my deeds to
> cross.
> (90.1-2)

All of these episodes are desultory steps in an experiment that fails. If the final sonnets addressed to the Friend (97-126) are in anything close to chronological sequence, they suggest a story that ends in the preceptor-lover's acrimonious defeat. Sonnet 97 refers to an "absence" which may have resulted from the friendship's temporary collapse. The previous sonnet, following upon statements of candid reproach (93-5), seems to represent a climactic complaint and a breaking off. The Poet has sensed that his Friend is trying to "steal [him]self away" (92.1), is seeking ways to let the rejected lover down easily ("there can live no hatred in thine eye, / Therefore in that I cannot know thy change" [93.5-6]). Although the Poet determines to live like a "deceived husband," supposing his love to be "true" (93.1-2), he

knows the truth of his abandonment and proclaims to the Friend, who has "pow'r to hurt, and will do none":

> The summer's flow'r is to the summer sweet,
> Though to itself it only live and die,
> But if that flow'r with base infection meet,
> The basest weed outbraves his dignity:
> For sweetest things turn sourest by their
>   deeds;
> Lilies that fester smell far worse than weeds.
> (94.1, 9-14)

That is, the Friend may soothe his conscience with the thought that his kind appearance will not reveal a treachery which will therefore do no harm. But such a grand deception is impossible. When lilies fester, they smell— all the more foully for being so fair. In Sonnet 95 there is a sardonic warning: "The hardest knife ill us'd doth lose his edge." And in Sonnet 96, where the Friend is close to becoming a "stern wolf," betraying innocent lambs, the Poet urges:

> But do not so, I love thee in such sort,
> As thou being mine, mine is thy good report.
> (96.13-14)

This couplet repeats word for word that of Sonnet 36, where it had the meaning: "Do not honor me publicly, for by so doing you detract from your own reputation. For you to be honored is all that I need." In the later poem, the words have a different sense: "Do not lead innocents astray. Since my love has so closely identified me with you, I would share your dishonor." The repetition and reversal are an economical means both of reminding the Friend of a longstanding devotion and of asserting that love will no longer tolerate perfidy.

The Poet marks his return to the Friend after the "absence" by pouring forth extravagant compliments as though no breach had occurred (97-9). The Friend, apparently resentful of long inattention, is not easily soothed; and the Poet strains to apologize for his reticence or his silences and to prove that they are not irredeemable (100-3). He returns to some of the old eulogistic themes (104-7), now, however, manifesting an impatience with them. When previously he had spoken with the youth about the true (or the good) and the beautiful, it was often to remind him that beauty had to earn the honor of goodness (e.g., 54; 68-70). Now, faced with the Friend's insistent and inordinate appetite for praise, the eulogist offers him the kind of excessive tribute that ought to embarrass any recipient. The true, the good, and the beautiful,

> "Fair," "kind," and "true" have often liv'd
> alone,
> Which three till now never kept seat in one.
> (105.13-14)

A special significance has been given to what becomes the Friend's epithet, "a god in love" (110.12)— "hallowed" be his name (108.8). "What's new to speak, what now to register," after this (108.3)?

But the Friend's mind is not to be swayed from what he perceives to be the Poet's infidelity, however vague a crime it may be; and the young man whose majesty has been wounded must be reassured, confessed and apologized to, and flattered (109-14). He is given what he wants. A silly bit of sophistry (115), however, (like Donne's "Loves Growth") proving that love can be both full and growing, ends with a double-edged couplet that hints at the Poet's exasperation: "Love is a babe, then might I not say so, / To give full growth to that which still doth grow" (115.13-14)— one interpretation of which is: "I've had to lie in order to give our love a chance." Sonnet 116 ("Let me not to the marriage of true minds") advances closer to the truth, for it describes the objective ideal ("Love alters not") measured against which no love is perfect:

> If this be error and upon me proved,
> I never writ, nor no man ever loved.
>
> (116.13-14)

"And if this be *not* error, no man has loved. At any rate, I have not, nor have you; for we both have strayed." Such is the implied coda if the poem is written (as the context suggests) in response to the Friend's charges of inconstancy. This frankness is returned to, with less indignation, in Sonnet 120, after three pieces of half-serious casuistry which set out a faulty "logic" of forgiveness; and thereafter the tone of pleading disappears. Sonnet 121 betokens a new era of truth-telling that will be short-lived, for it marks love's "doom and date."

> I am that I am, and they that level
> At my abuses reckon up their own.
>
> (121.9-10)

The Poet will no longer denigrate or apologize for his imperfect love. He has thrown away the Friend's book, or "tables," and its "tallies," for he does not need them to remind him of his obligations (122.1, 10). His contrition has yielded to pride in his integrity: "No! Time, thou shalt not boast that I do change" (123-4). Love's law is "mutual render, only me for thee"; and he has given from his side all that he can (125.12). Since the Friend has not done and will not do so, despite all the Poet's efforts to teach and to move him, the only words that remain to be spoken are those of a sadly bitter twelve-line *envoi*, addressed to a "boy" who remains "lovely" and a boy, and who is left with a somewhat ungenerous reminder (there is no final forgiveness) of the important word whose higher meaning he has failed to learn:

> [Time's] audit (though delay'd) answer'd must be,
> And her quietus is to *render* thee.
>
> (126.1, 11-12, emphasis mine)

It is not clear that all of the poems which follow those addressed to the Friend are rhetorically directed to another person. "Th' expense of spirit in a waste of shame" and "Poor soul, the center of my sinful earth," are meditations that require no audience; and those sonnets in which the Poet speaks to the Lady (or ladies) do not reveal the same complex purposes as those in the larger group. "Lust in action" does not need the help of subtle or heroic lies; indeed, as we have already noted, except in the suppression of the "simple" truths of age and infidelity (138) this passion is better served by a witty, prurient, sometimes brutal honesty.

But candor may serve a rhetorical purpose, upon which we may reflect briefly. The Poet freely insults both the Lady and himself: she is only ambiguously beautiful (127, 130, 131, 137, 141, 147) and a slut ("the bay where all men ride" [137.6]); he, a fool, whose eyes and judgment desire has blinded (137, 148) and who loves his foolishness too much to become wise. These indignities yoke the two together in a corrupt complicity which, the argument goes, they might as well enjoy:

> *Will* will fulfill the treasure of thy love,
> Ay, fill it full with wills, and my will one.
>
> (136.5-6)

Insults also serve either as threats or as compliments, to be presented as occasion demands. The dishonored Lady is pushed toward compliance by being reminded that she is not worth an extended effort (142). Or she is "flattered" by learning the extent of her power to degrade her lover's mind and conscience (149).

There are other kinds of appeal in these poems: to the Lady's pity (139), to her fear of detraction (140), to her sense of humor (143). In constructing a piece of Donne-like casuistry for her (151), the Poet compliments her wit. Not all is rhetorical game, however. The sonnets which pray for the Friend's release arise out of a pathetic helplessness in the Poet, which, he knows, no amount of pleading can remedy, for the Lady is "covetous" and the Friend only fictitiously "kind" (133.3-4; 134.3-6). The sufferer addresses only to himself the vulgar humor which this helplessness evokes in him:

> I guess one angel in another's hell.
>　Yet this shall I ne'er know, but live in doubt
>　　Till my bad angel fire my good one out.
>
> (144.12-14)

In his complaints to the woman whom he despises yet craves, his reproaches are on occasion scathing enough to undermine any ulterior purpose in the rhetoric: "the bay where all men ride"; "the very refuse of thy deeds" (151.6);

> Nor are mine ears with thy tongue's tune
>   delighted,
> Nor tender feeling to base touches prone,
> Nor taste, nor smell, desire to be invited
> To any sensual feast with thee alone.
>
> (141.5-8)

And his reflections on lust (129) and mortality (146) stand self-contained, the former in its own fierce disgust, the latter in its longing for a transcendent purity.

There is no sign in the second group of sonnets that the Poet simply moves from rhetorical assault to introspective meditation. He is never unaware of the moral and psychological truths in his case, and he adverts to them as he will. Having spun no great lies to be unraveled, these poems come to no conclusion. They portray in a credible randomness conflicts which, as the platonism of one sonnet acknowledges, will not be resolved until "there's no more dying" (146.14).

The Poet once admits to his Friend that in public displays "I have . . . Gor'd mine own thoughts" (110.1-3). Whatever its meaning in context, the phrase may be seen as relevant to the speaker's private story as well, suggesting that he has "wounded" his thoughts in a denial of his knowledge; that he has made them parti-colored (as "gores," or wedges of cloth, turn motley a fool's breeches); and that he has dishonored them (a heraldic "gore" was "a shaped area interposed between two charges, and was used as a mark of cadency or abatement of honour" [W. 6. Ingram and Theodore Redpath, eds., *Shakespeare's Sonnets*) This admission itself may, as has been suggested, involve a goring of thought, but its use as a tactic does not detract from its basic truth. To his Friend the Poet offered his mind in a pastiche. To his Lady he presented the oblation of a stabbed and bleeding conscience, still alive to see but too weak to move a Will to action. On each count he has suffered an "abatement of honour." He feels himself shamed by "Th' expense of spirit" to which the wounding of his moral judgment has led. And in the "virtuous" lies which he told for the noblest of causes, it is impossible to separate heroism from ignominy. His fatherly concern, loving affection, patience, forgiveness, and long-suffering were all real; yet these virtues had to be devious (age in love knew how to be) to express themselves. Altruism was sometimes put to "use," flattery dispensed, wrongs publicly countenanced, truth suppressed, as love sacrificed some of its integrity that it might exist. And the sacrifice was also real. Unlike Helena's character, which was much more protected by appearing in an adult fairy tale, this liar's "nature" was "subdu'd / To what it work[ed] in, like the dyer's hand" (111.6-7)— and in vain, for the end which required but

could not justify the means was lost. One might say in condescension that the Poet was proud and foolish to believe that he could ever succeed in creating love almost *ex nihilo;* and in saying so, such is Shakespeare's achievement in portraying a human dilemma in its bewildering complexity, one would be both correct and ungenerous. It is simpler to insist on what should now be evident, that the character whose situation has been examined here was neither an abjectly submissive nor an implausible protagonist.

THE FRIEND

Commentators frequently maintain that the young man of the sonnets is an indistinct figure, presented suggestively rather than concretely. David R. Shore, for example, agreed with others that there is a remarkable lack of visual specificity about him: the speaker praises the Friend's extraordinary beauty but doesn't tell us what he looks like. Similarly, J. B. Leishman remarked that we don't know how tall he is or the color of his eyes and hair; nor do we ever see him in the midst of some activity where he displays the charms and graces the Poet ascribes to him. **Heather Dubrow** (1981) further noted that the Friend never functions as an active participant in the sonnets. In addition to being nameless and shadow-like, he has no voice of his own, she pointed out. The speaker either reports what the young man has said or predicts what he's likely to say. In Dubrow's judgment, this contributes to a sense of detachment— a failure of engagement— between the reader and the Friend.

A number of critics have proposed that the Friend is a profoundly contradictory figure. **Stephen Spender,** for instance, described him as having a double or divided nature. On the one hand, Spender observed, there is the Poet's idealized portrait of the Friend as a youth of incomparable beauty and worth, yet we are also shown a young man who is cold, selfish, proud, and decadent. Though **Hallett Smith** focused on the sonnets' depiction of the Friend's merits and beauty, he also remarked that the young man is capable of slighting the Poet and even rejecting him. With a less sympathetic view of the Friend, **John Klause** emphasized the youth's inferior judgment and character. From Klause's perspective, the young man has not yet learned how to love or how to be worthy of love. Also suggesting that the Friend is a contradictory figure, **Michael Cameron Andrews** remarked on the disparity between the youth's attractive appearance and his offensive behavior. In Andrews's judgment, the Friend's unusual beauty masks a "rampant sexuality," and his most prominent attribute is deception.

Several commentators have called attention to a significant change in the relationship between the Poet and the Friend after Sonnets 1-17. **Hallett Smith** proposed that Sonnet 18 signals that the Poet's friend has become his beloved. Kenneth Muir also noted a distinct change in relations between the two men after Sonnet 17; furthermore, he argued that in Sonnet 20 the Poet recognizes that his love for the young man is erotic as well as spiritual. Robert Crosman interpreted Sonnets 1-17 as reflecting a period when the Poet and the Friend were establishing a personal association— one that would grow from friendship and patronage to a union of kindred souls, linked by mutual sympathy and understanding.

Stephen Spender

SOURCE: "The Alike and the Other," in *The Riddle of Shakespeare's Sonnets,* Basic Books, 1962, pp. 91-128.

[*Spender— the distinguished English poet and critic— suggests that the young man of the sonnets possesses a double or divided nature. Sometimes the Friend's mind and heart appear to be as beautiful as his outward form, but on other occasions he is cold, selfish, arrogant, and dissolute. The Poet reacts to this basic disparity in various ways, Spender observes, ranging from objectivity and irony to bitterness and despair. Spender also discusses what he sees as the Friend's narcissism. He suggests that the Poet's determination to preserve the young man's beauty in his verses reveals that he endows it with the same inestimable value as does the young man himself.*]

Clearing our minds of preconceptions, if we read the sonnets simply accepting what they tell us about [the young man], what impression would we get? The first thing that would strike us is, I think, that he has opposite characteristics. He is divided between his ideal nature, corresponding to his outward beauty, and his actual behavior, which is shown to be cold, self-seeking, proud, and corrupt.

On the one hand the poet reiterates the theme of "kind and true" and "For nothing this wide universe I call, / Save thou, my rose; in it thou art my all" (109). On the other hand the rose is cankered (95):

> How sweet and lovely dost thou make the
>   shame
> Which, like a canker in the fragrant rose,
> Doth spot the beauty of thy budding name!

On the one hand the young man is pure essence; on the other hand he is essence tainted at the source.

Shakespeare was, of course, addressing the sonnets to the friend. He was not making a word portrait of him, and we attempt to deduce his character from things written to him, about him. What we see are two things, characteristics which the poet doubtless found present in the real young man, but which are so idealized that it is difficult to form a realistic picture from them: and, opposite to this, references to the friend's lasciviousness, sensual faults, coldness, falsity, and his ill reputation, a kind of counter-image held up before his eyes as a terrible example. One cannot but be reminded of the scene in which Hamlet holds up before his mother's eyes "the counterfeit presentment of two brothers," one with "a station like the herald Mercury," the other "like a mildew'd ear."

From reading the sonnets and making my own deductions— which may be very different from those of other readers— the picture I have is of a person who produced in the minds of others the double impression of the self-fixated. The doubleness in such people consists essentially in their being loved, but being unable to love back in return, through the cold self-sufficiency and self-attachment which is the result of their very beauty. They like to be loved partly because being loved is reflected self-admiration, but partly also because they would themselves perhaps like to love and think that through being loved they may learn to do so. The combination of beauty, coldness, and desire to learn to love, gives them a kind of purity. But in their behavior they may be corrupt because they accept, with involuntary indifference, whatever love they get, though they retain the air of perpetual seeking. What they are genuinely seeking is those qualities which they lack. When such a person is loved by an artist, he has the attraction of being an empty vessel, a blank page into which the admirer can read his own ideal.

[Bernard] Shaw points out that however much Shakespeare may have suffered on account of the dark lady, it is wrong to regard him as a victim. She can hardly have been happy reading about herself in 127, 130, and 138. The same holds good for the young man, whose behavior the sonnets analyze and excoriate. From the internal evidence of the sonnets he sometimes tried to answer accusation with counter-accusation. In 120 the poet admits in lines close to doggerel:

> For if you were by my unkindness shaken
> As I by yours, you've pass'd a hell of time,
> And I, a tyrant, have no leisure taken
> To weigh how once I suffer'd in your crime.

There are critics who idealize the young man and others who abhor him. But the poet's attitude to the friend is hardly discussed; and there is surely an element of unfairness in putting pressure on him to be something that he is not, and of then turning on him because he has failed to be the ideal. The poet seems often as much in love with the picture in his mind of the arranged relationship of complete mutuality as with the young man, who has to fit into this picture.

Yet so long as the poet continued to write sonnets I think that he must have believed in some ultimate quality of pure being which resided in the young man, under the misbehavior and the falsity. Even after bitter disillusionment he reverts to the purity of the original concept; in 105, for example:

> Kind is my love to-day, to-morrow kind,
> Still constant in a wondrous excellence.

So the sonnets express the conflict between idealization of the young man as the living equal of the poet's imaginings, and the realization that he is different from this. Sometimes the difference is analyzed as betrayal, sometimes the poet endeavors to find a basis on which he can accept it and yet retain the relationship. Sonnet 36 is an extreme example of acceptance of difference, in which he admits that their ways must be separate: "Let me confess that we two must be twain" and yet their "undivided loves are one." He invents metaphors for the relationship which suggest a rethinking of what it really is or must be. In 37, it is of father and son, and, indeed, where the young man fails, it tends to shift from the pattern of mutuality to that of a son whose errors are seen and suffered and forgiven by a loving father. In 33, contemplating the withdrawal of the "sun" into the "region cloud," the poet resumes the pun in the couplet with:

> Yet him for this my love no whit disdaineth;
> Suns of the world may stain when heaven's sun
>   staineth.

In 93, desperation drives the poet to the metaphor of a "deceived husband"; and frequently he is a slave who tends upon, and waits for, his lord.

Whether one thinks, as I do, that Shakespeare continued, in spite of everything, to love and (like a forgiving father) believe in the young man, or that the disillusionment of realization led to his regarding him only (or with very little qualification of charitable feeling) as a subject for irony, affects one's interpretation of the very important 94, "They that have power to hurt and will do none."

After a very close analysis, William Empson concludes (in *Some Versions of Pastoral*) that this sonnet expresses almost total contempt for the friend. The contempt is qualified only by the poet discovering, through his pretending to praise what he does not admire, "a way of praising W.H. in spite of everything."

It is not possible here to argue my way through Empson's close analysis, for which I have great respect. My disagreement with him is not in disputing his interpretation of references and complexities of meaning in particular phrases, but because I think that, through the irony and the realization, there seems to me a note of exhortation which still clings to belief, and which arises from a love that endures. In a word, I would say the sonnet found "a way of *loving* in spite of everything," rather than, or as well as, a way of praising. The love is cruel, but praise would be nothing except cruel and contradictory, since it means praising what the poet did not regard as praiseworthy. If it is praise, the sonnet is, as Empson notes, an "evasion." But if it is love, it is more in the nature of a desperate warning.

My argument is clear if I say that the two last lines of the previous sonnet (93), "How like Eve's apple doth thy beauty grow, /If thy sweet virtue answer not thy show!" are more exhortatory than condemnatory. The poet still clings to the hope that even if while the young man's face shows nothing but sweet love (" . . . heaven in thy creation did decree /That in thy face sweet love should ever dwell") his heart (unlike others whose false hearts show in the "wrinkles strange" of their faces) may be false— that even so, he can, by an effort of willing truth, make inner being conform to the outward appearance of love. The kind of exertion required is not of making a lie true, but of making what is true, which has for some perverse reason become falsified, revert to its real nature, become true again. It is an argument based on love which appeals to the imagination to realize in action the truth which exists. It is a creative attitude different from a modern irony, though of course it uses irony. In fact it is very much the type of argument which Hamlet uses to his mother when, showing her the pictures of her two husbands, he appeals to her to use her eyes (her inner eyes) in order to make a choice which is imposed on her simply by her seeing which is false and which is true.

Condensing the argument of 94, the desperate appeal, based on a cool appreciation of the young man's nature, seems to me of this kind: "If you are cold and self-centered as I have now come to realize you are, then you may perhaps participate in the power, justice, and virtue of those who are detached from passion, but who nevertheless control the lives of others; but to be like them, you must have the virtue of coldness which is chastity. You are, after all, more like the funereal lily than the generous rose; but remember that when the cold are false, their corruption is far more evil than that of the warm." The thought is perhaps that the warm, being essentially more alive (and not like stone) go on being capable of self-renewal and repentance.

This is very much the attitude that a father, himself believing in the personal values of human relations and love and imagination, might feel toward a much-loved son, whom he discovered to be of a cold nature, but possessed of beauty and power to entrap others. The father does not cease to love his son, but begins to realize that his moral character will be ruined, unless he match his power with scrupulousness, his coldness with chastity. Otherwise the corruption of his personality will be worse than that of a person who is lascivious but warm-hearted, and because warm-hearted, capable of contrition and change.

The sonnet expresses, of course, a change of attitude, coming— as 93 and 95, the sonnets on each side of it, show— from a shock of realization of the deep corruption of the young man.

That the powerful are praised has surprised many readers. Previously, although a world of power has been taken for granted, it has not been discussed; it has remained the background to personal relations. But suddenly the poet expresses his admiration for the cold and powerful. If one remembers once again that the sonnets are one side of a dialogue, this is not so surprising. Number 94 was written perhaps during a phase when the poet was most critical of the friend's character. Surely, the friend may have said to the poet: "The truth is that your sorts of people are not mine. The people I admire are the great and powerful, and I want to belong to them." In this case the sonnet may be seen as taking up the theme, accepting, with whatever undertones of bitterness and despair, that the friend might belong to this other world, but using the acceptance as another way of hammering in the lesson of pure being.

Although 94 expresses such a shift from personal to public values, from the imagination to the world of power, the thematic material introduced in the sestet, which indicates the presence of the young man, remains the same as in earlier sonnets.

In fact the poem takes the form of a general statement about the virtues of the great and powerful, in the octave and then, in the sestet, applies this to the young man.

The octave is, as it were, a different voice, not quite that of the poet, but to which the poet assents, indeed lends his gift, stating a case in the strongest and most favorable terms.

The case is that those who are great and powerful and who, although they might do so, do not use their power to cause others pain— those who, while making others act, remain immovable themselves, and are untempted, incorruptible— merit their position. There is a feeling of rendering unto Caesar that which is Caesar's. There is irony, but there is also assent. Angelo, in *Measure for Measure*, is admired so long as he remains cold and powerful. It is when he becomes lascivious and corrupt that he appears far worse than the carnal sinners on whom he sits in judgment.

In the first line of the sestet the young man appears in a guise with which we have been made familiar very early on, in fact in the first sonnet, where we read of the young man, " . . . thou, contracted to thine own bright eyes, / Feeds't thy light's flame with self-substantial fuel." Here he is the summer's flower, "to the summer sweet, /

Though to itself it only live and die." The position is restated. In the first sonnet the self-sufficient lovely boy is asked to marry. Later he is asked to love the friend. Now he is being warned that perhaps he would do well to model himself on the coldly powerful, since he is himself cold. But if he does so, let him remain like them, solitary, chaste. If he does not do so, the lily (which he has chosen to become rather than the rose to which he has previously been compared) will, festering, "smell far worse than weeds."

Doubtless there is irony here, and bitterness, but what seems to me the strongest feeling is a despairing acceptance of the young man's coldness combined with an equally despairing warning.

The first seventeen sonnets are usually . . . regarded as being outside the main series. They are so, but they are also a kind of prelude, and throw light on the character of the friend.

Here, when the poet is exhorting the friend to marry, he also makes very apparent the reasons why he should not do so. They are that he is concentrated on, almost married to, his own image. The arguments used to persuade him to marry are that a son would provide, as it were, a mirror projecting the image of that beauty which culminates in his face now, into the future (13):

O, that you were yourself! but, love, you are
No longer yours than you yourself here live.

So while the friend is warned of the dangers of "having traffic with thyself alone," the poet nevertheless shares with him the view that he is the paragon. The poet puts himself at the young man's side fighting for the cause which is that a means should be found to perpetuate his beauty exactly as it now is. The poet offers two means of achieving this result. One is fathering a child, and the other, which plays an even more persistent part in the sequence, is the poetry. Sonnet 17 unites these two themes in the culminating couplet:

But were some child of yours alive that time,
You should live twice; in it and in my rhyme.

So that while the poet dutifully uses the poetry to urge the friend to marriage, his verse itself is advertized as a means of achieving the same result as a son might do. In a manner of speaking, both child and poetry are mirrors of the young man's own face.

The modern reader may well be tempted to condemn the obvious narcissism of the friend, which Shakespeare exploits so much as argument. But it should be noted that Shakespeare does not appear to condemn it, though he may, later, deplore its callous effects. But he is in complete agreement with the friend as to his beauty, as though it is a value which both share, the young man having his face, and the poet having his poetry, which he identifies with the lovely boy. The poet has an attitude towards the young man's beauty which seems exactly the same as that of the young man himself. Both regard it as a unique value which must by every means possible be preserved.

The young man's narcissism— which, versed in modern psychology, we are apt to condemn— may indeed have been precious to the poet. For it is very difficult in the world of the sonnets to draw a line between the young man's self-regard— which the poet supports— and the claims that the poet makes for his immortal verse. To us, the readers, they may seem very different, but given the extraordinary aesthetic cult of the young man's external appearance, which is central to the sonnets, they may seem the same thing. Again and again the argument is put forward that the poetry is the immortalization of the young man's beauty. The boy's beauty has the inestimable virtue of being life. The virtue of the poetry is as a perpetuating mirror which freezes on its bright surface the fleeting image which will die. The attraction of the young man is that of all life, made incarnate in an incomparable beauty of form.

Narcissus fell in love with himself, but the water in which he gazed at his reflection surely also fell in love with his image. The mirror is in love with the mirrored because it becomes the gazer— that which the gazer never succeeds in doing himself. The poet through his poetry can retain the beauty which the friend himself is bound to lose. Moreover, the poet is changed into the beauty of the youth by virtue of retaining that image in his heart (22):

> My glass shall not persuade me I am old,
> So long as youth and thou are of one date . . .

Most critics are puzzled by the insistence of the poet on the contrast between his "chopped antiquity" and the young man's beauty and youth. Nothing is really less surprising. For a relationship which is based on the idea of identity is inevitably upset by dissonances. So the great and perhaps excessive insistence on the immortality of the poetry in these poems is a claim made not for the poet but for the friend. It is he who is going to survive in these lines, we are told through many variations (63):

> His beauty shall in these black lines be seen,
> And they shall live, and he in them still green.

So the poet was occupied in giving back, by the means of his poetry, the image of the friend to himself. To us this bargain seems unequal, because all we have of the young man is the written words, which are Shakespeare's self. We should remember, though, that for the poet, the matter was different. He was taking life in its miraculous complexity and giving back words. The fact that the words are so marvelous is due (or may have seemed to him due) to the fact that the living reality was of such extraordinary value. Occasionally, for example, in 53, we experience the impact of million-faceted flesh, worshipped as the moment of beauty never matched in all past time:

> What is your substance, whereof are you made,
> That millions of strange shadows on you tend?

The mirror image constantly occurs in the sonnets. There is also implicitly the idea of two mirrors reflecting one another with rays that reach into infinity. When the "lovely boy" looks into the friend's poetry, he sees not only his own image, but that the physical presence of the poet has been changed into that beauty.

Perhaps the significance of the narcissism of the friend may be that if the narcissist has a character that requires a mirror, the artist also requires a mirror of life in which to see his art. As Hoelderlin observed in *Socrates and Alcibiades*, "often in the end the wise pay homage to the most beautiful." The world of art or thought which fills the mind of genius is essentially lonely. He finds it least of all reflected in the minds of other artists, and the public. He seeks it therefore in the beautiful, particularly among those in whom nature seems to have flowered spontaneously without the interruption of too much intellectual process. The narcissist, in his self-cultivation (Montherlant describes the poet as one who gives himself up to "noble self-cultivation") may appear to have an affinity with the artist. The narcissist might be described as a living poem going in search of a poet.

At the same time, the discovery that the narcissist is vulgar, that his self-absorption and isolation do not prevent his belonging to the "region cloud," that he will look in any broken fragment of glass to see the same reflection of himself, is inevitable. But there was a time in the sonnets when the young man's beauty seemed of the season which is fresh in nature and which was also incomparably fresh in Shakespeare's poetry.

The failure was that of the poet to discover his own inner being mirrored— as it should have been— in the young man's external beauty, and leading there to the love in which they shared their being. The poetry is a plea to him to be true to his own appearance, and in doing this, true to the poet's imagination.

Hallett Smith

SOURCE: "Personae," in *The Tension of the Lyre: Poetry in Shakespeare's Sonnets*, Huntington Library, 1981, pp. 13-41.

[Smith surveys the personality of the Friend and his relationship with the Poet as these are generally represented in Sonnets 18-126. What is most distinctive about the Friend, the critic pro-

poses, is that he is an ideal subject for courtly love poems; in addition, he seems to be blessed with as much virtue as physical beauty, and, at least for a time, he returns the love bestowed on him by the Poet. With respect to the Friend's fault or flaw, Smith considers what this might be and concludes that whatever its nature— and no matter how grievous it is— the Poet will always try to justify it and exonerate the young man.]

It has been said that in the first seventeen sonnets "Shakespeare wrote not so much as if he were in love himself, but as if he were trying to persuade a friend to love and marry; they describe, as it were from the outside, the fruits of love" [John Russell Brown, in *Shakespeare and His Comedies*]. It has also been noticed by many readers that the first group of sonnets advocates prodigality, urges procreation, and tries to influence a young man about whom the reader can gather almost nothing except that he is a bachelor. He has no "character" or personality; he is physically beautiful and should therefore pass on that beauty to succeeding generations. Not to do so would be not only miserly but also a sin against nature and against the heritage he has from his ancestors.

The focus is very different in the sonnets numbered 18-126 in 1609. The Fair Friend is now the beloved of the speaker; he has a personality and a character. The sonnets express over and over again a moral concern about him. Prodigality is not encouraged, it is deplored. Great attention is paid to "inward worth" without neglecting "outward fair" (16.11). Even the conventional praise which promises to confer immortality is different. No longer is there a half-serious rivalry between a son and poetry to perpetuate the beauty of the young man. Poetry has won the contest; it is now the "mightier way" to make war upon that bloody tyrant, Time (16.1-2).

Sonnet 18 is fuller, more confident, more resonant than its comparable poem in the first series, "When I consider everything that grows" (15). It begins by displaying the speaker as "a poet whose art is the creation of metaphor." [Anne Ferry, in *All in War with Time*].

Shall I compare thee to a summer's day?
Thou art more lovely and more temperate:
Rough winds do shake the darling buds of
  May,
And summer's lease hath all too short a date;
Sometime too hot the eye of heaven shines,
And often is his gold complexion dimm'd,
And every fair from fair sometime declines,
By chance or nature's changing course
  untrimm'd:
But thy eternal summer shall not fade,
Nor lose possession of that fair thou ow'st,
Nor shall Death brag thou wand'rest in his
  shade,
When in eternal lines to time thou grow'st.
  So long as men can breathe or eyes can see,
  So long lives this, and this gives life to thee.

The promise of immortality through verse is a commonplace of classical and Renaissance poetry. But Shakespeare's use of the word "summer" drifts from the literal to the figurative in a very subtle way. When Titania, Queen of the Fairies, introduces herself to the transformed Bottom, she says

I am a spirit of no common rate;
The summer still doth tend upon my state;
And I do love thee, therefore go with me.
  A Midsummer Night's Dream (III, i, 154-56)

And the soliloquy which opens *Richard III* begins

Now is the winter of our discontent
Made glorious summer by this son of York.

The literal summer has its all too brief a time; its weather is sometimes too hot, or perhaps cloudy; but the Fair Friend's *eternal summer* shall not fade, or become less fair, or die, because poetry preserves it. In another mood, reflecting on the transience of beauty, Shakespeare calls the Fair Friend "beauty's summer" (104.14).

The most important thing about the Fair Friend addressed in the sonnets after 17 is that he is the perfect subject for poetry. He is more consistent, more reliable, more permanent than a summer's day because of the poetry about him. This brings the poet and the Fair Friend into a far more intimate relationship than existed between the bachelor and the advocate of marriage in the first seventeen sonnets. As Rosalie Colie put it [in *Shakespeare's Living Art*], "Clearly, the relation of poet to this friend is based on poetry; poetry is not only the conventional instrument of appeal to patron, friend, and lover, the conventional voice in beauty's praise; but poetry is also the poet himself, ingrained in his personality and thus marking (the dyer's hand) all his human realizations and relations."

As a subject for poetry, the Fair Friend is inexhaustible. "How can my muse want subject to invent" asks Sonnet 38, "While thou dost breathe, that pour'st into my verse / Thine own sweet argument?" Sonnet 76 maintains that the poet has no other subject: "O know, sweet love, I always write of you, / And you and love are still [always] my argument." In Sonnet 79 the poet declares that the subject exceeds his poetic powers: "I grant, sweet love, thy lovely argument / Deserves the travail of a worthier pen." This modesty is traditional, and though it may seem inconsistent with the claims made for immortality through the poet's pen, readers of Shakespeare's sonnets (and indeed some parts of the plays) must be prepared to abandon logic when the occasion requires.

In other collections of Elizabethan sonnets, most of which can be called sequences with better justification than this one can, the beautiful person celebrated is a woman. Sometimes she is a real person; Sidney's Stella is Penelope Devereux, Lady Rich. Sometimes she is an invention, as Giles Fletcher's Licia is. Into which class the Fair Friend falls is quite uncertain. There have been many real persons suggested for the role, but all of these suggestions are wasted effort if, as is quite possible, the Fair Friend is an invention of the poet's. On this subject there is no certainty; the theories flare up and fade out, get lost among the shadows; the poetry remains.

It does matter, of course, what sort of figure the sonnets are addressed to— those which are clearly addressed to someone else, not to the poet himself and not to nobody. First of all, the Fair Friend has one quality in common with the heroines of Elizabethan sonnet cycles addressed to women: he is beautiful. But unlike the ladies of the other sonneteers, he loves the poet: Sonnet 25 contrasts the situation of the poet with that of people who can boast of public honor and proud titles, with great prince's favorites, with military heroes— all of whom may lose what they most enjoy.

> Then happy I that love and am beloved
> Where I may not remove, nor be removed.

But the Fair Friend's beauty is not all external. He is said to have surpassing "worth" or virtue:

> Yet what of thee thy poet doth invent
> He robs thee of, and pays it thee again.
> He lends thee virtue, and he stole that word
> From thy behavior. . . .
>
> (79.7-10)

At times the poet has failed to do justice to his worth:

> And therefore have I slept in your report,
> That you yourself, being extant, well might
>   show
> How far a modern quill doth come too short,
> Speaking of worth, what worth in you doth
>   grow.
>
> (83.5-6)

Sometimes this worth or virtue is identified with constancy, which is, of course, natural enough in love poetry:

> In all external grace you have some part,
> But you like none, none you, for constant
>   heart.
>
> (53.13-14)

A recent critic finds "worth" to signify something about poetry: "Throughout the sonnets, the paradox of poetry turns on the question of 'worth.' Even in his most disillusioned moods when thoughts of the world's corruption lead him to anticipate his own decay and death,

Shakespeare never forgets the power of art to redeem life." [John D. Bernard, "'To Constancie Confin'de': The Poetics of Shakespeare's Sonnets"]. Finally, I think, "worth" is an aspect of love that is fundamentally mysterious, as in the proclamation that love is

> the star to every wand'ring bark
> Whose worth's unknown, although his highth
> be taken.
>
> (116.7-8)

The Fair Friend is younger than the poet: "My glass shall not persuade me I am old / So long as youth and thou are of one date /. . . . How can I then be elder than thou art?" (22.1-2, 8). He is of superior rank: "Lord of my love, to whom in vassalage / Thy merit hath my duty strongly knit" (26.1-2).

In fact, the poet is sometimes apprehensive that close association with him may cause social embarrassment or disgrace to the Fair Friend:

> I may not evermore acknowledge thee,
> Lest my bewailëd, guilt should do thee shame,
> Nor thou with public kindness honor me,
> Unless thou take that honor from thy name.
>
> (36.9-12)

He carries this attitude to the extreme of warning the Fair Friend not to mourn for him after his death, lest the "wise world" mock him for caring about one so lowly (71 and 72).

Yet for all his "worth" and constancy, the Fair Friend is capable of snubbing the poet, of rejecting him as Prince Hal, newly become King Henry V, rejected his old crony Falstaff:

> Against that time when thou shalt strangely
>   pass
> And scarcely greet me with that sun, thine eye,
> When love converted from the thing it was
> Shall reasons find of settled gravity . . .
>
> (49.5-8)

As M. M. Mahood says [in *Shakespeare's Wordplay*], this quatrain is "the rejection of Falstaff in little. The parallel is strengthened by the sun image (as in Hal's 'Yet herein will I imitate the sun') and by the way *gravity* calls to mind the Lord Chief Justice's reproach to Falstaff." She continues to characterize the Fair Friend as "a brilliant, prudent, calculating egotist."

Sonnet 87 ("Farewell, thou art too dear for my possessing"), . . . is one of several in which the Fair Friend has rejected the poet or in some way broken with him. Sonnet 88, which begins

> When thou shalt be dispos'd to set me light,

Shakespeare performing before Queen Elizabeth and her court.

And place my merit in the eye of scorn,

promises casuistically that the speaker will take the side of the Fair Friend and so win glory because he indeed belongs to the Fair Friend. Sonnet 89 likewise embraces the reason why the poet has been abandoned:

Say that thou didst forsake me for some fault,
And I will comment upon that offense;

He will, he promises, side with the Fair Friend against himself:

For thee, against myself I'll vow debate,
For I must ne'er love him whom thou dost
　　hate.

Sonnet 90 is closely linked, arguing that the Friend should hate him now, if ever, "Now while the world is bent my deeds to cross"; the Friend's abandonment should come first, in the vanguard of the other troubles, because in

comparison the other troubles will then seem light.

These sonnets have a common theme and they share the same rhetorical strategy. But just as, in the plays, dialogue may lead up to and prepare for a soliloquy, so these sonnets, addressed to a *persona*, can be viewed as preliminary to the meditative Sonnet 94, "They that have power to hurt and will do none." This sonnet generalizes; it is a "fearful meditation," connected of course with the commonplace, *optimae corruptio pessima* [the worst corrupts the best]. But it should be understood as a reverie after the speeches of Sonnets 87, 88, 89, and 90 have been made.

What else do we know of the fault or the flaw of the Friend? Sonnets 33-35 portray it in a favorite Shakespearean metaphor, that of the sun being obscured by clouds. It is used, we recall, by Prince Hal in his soliloquy notifying the audience that he will emerge from the cloud of dissipation now covering him and shine as a true prince should. Sonnet 33 is one of the most eloquent:

Full many a glorious morning have I seen
Flatter the mountain tops with sovereign eye,
Kissing with golden face the meadows green,
Gilding pale streams with heavenly alcumy,
Anon permit the basest clouds to ride
With ugly rack on his celestial face,
And from the forlorn world his visage hide,
Stealing unseen to west with this disgrace:
Even so my sun one early morn did shine
With all-triumphant splendor on my brow,
But out, alack, he was but one hour mine,
The region cloud hath mask'd him from me
    now.
    Yet him for this my love no whit disdaineth:
    Suns of the world may stain, when heaven's
    sun staineth.

The structure shows a clear division between octave
and sestet. The sound texture is very rich, displaying
alliteration and assonance not only within lines but across
them. The movement is steady and regular, broken only
by the exclamations in line II. The rhyme words are
firm and strong, modified by the feminine rhyme in the
couplet. The sonnet is an example of a rhetorical figure which Puttenham describes [in *The Arte of English
Poesie*] as "the figure *Paradiastole*, which . . . we call the
Curry-favell, as when we make the best of a bad thing . . .
as, to call an unthrift, a liberall gentleman: the foolish-
hardy, valiant or couragious: the niggard, thriftie . . .
moderating and abating the force of the matter by craft,
and for a pleasing purpose."

Sonnet 34 is more severe, even though the Friend seems
to have repented:

Why didst thou promise such a beauteous day,
And make me travel forth without my cloak,
To let base clouds o'ertake me in my way,
Hiding thy brav'ry in their rotten smoke?
'Tis not enough that through the cloud thou
    break,
To dry the rain on my storm-beaten face,
For no man well of such a slave can speak
That heals the wound, and cures not the
    disgrace;
Nor can thy shame give physic to my grief,
Though thou repent, yet I have still the loss,
Th' offender's sorrow lends but weak relief
To him that bears the strong offense's [cross].
    Ah, but those tears are pearl which thy love
    sheeds,
    And they are rich, and ransom all ill deeds.

This is addressed directly to the Fair Friend, in contrast
to the meditative Sonnet 33; it is full of personal pronouns. There is no structural division after line 8, though
the imagery changes after line 6 from weather to medicine. However, there may be a link between the rain-
drops on the poet's face and the tears on the Friend's.

The poem gains strength from a concentrated vocabulary including *disgrace, shame, grief, loss, sorrow,* and *cross.*
The idea of a wound that could be cured by a salve but
leaves a disgrace has led some editors to refer to Tarquin
as he leaves Lucrece's bed:

Bearing away the wound that nothing healeth,
The scar that will despite of cure remain.
                                            (731-32)

Sonnet 35, the last of the little series on the Friend's
fault, continues the exculpation of the friend and accordingly is another *Curry-favell*, but it also confesses the
casuistry of the poet, which the rhetorical figure
Paradiastole was not supposed to do. This emphasis on
the self consciousness of the poetry itself is very characteristic of Shakespeare, though it has baffled some of
the critics and expositors:

No more be griev'd at that which thou hast
    done:
Roses have thorns, and silver fountains mud.
Clouds and eclipses stain both moon and sun,
And loathsome canker lives in sweetest bud.
All men make faults, and even I in this,
Authorizing thy trespass with compare,
Myself corrupting, salving thy amiss.
Excusing [thy] sins more than [thy] sins are;
For to thy sensual fault I bring in sense—
Thy adverse party is thy advocate—
And 'gainst myself a lawful plea commence.
Such civil war is in my love and hate
    That I an accessary needs must be
    To that sweet thief which sourly robs from
    me.

The opening words, "No more be griev'd" give us
warning that platitudes are to follow, as in all attempts
to offer consolation to a grieving person. A good example is Claudius' exhortation to Hamlet in I, ii, 87-117
of that play. The second quatrain involves the speaker
in the fault making: it is a fault to justify a fault. From
line 9 we learn that the Friend's fault was sensual, and
the poet brings in "sense" or reason to justify it. . . . The
identification of the fault as sensuality puts this sonnet
into the company of Sonnets 40-42; in the first of these
the Fair Friend is called "Lascivious grace, in whom all
ill well shows," but these sonnets are apparently out of
place in the 1609 order and seem to belong with the
Dark Lady sonnets. . . . The couplet of Sonnet 93 is
perhaps germane:

How like Eve's apple doth thy beauty grow,
If thy sweet virtue answer not thy show!

Sonnets 67 ("Ah, wherefore with infection should he
live") and 68 ("Thus is his cheek the map of days out-
worn") accuse the Friend of artificiality and reflect the
bias against cosmetics and extravagant dress which seems

almost a personal trait of Shakespeare. But the following sonnets, 69 ("Those parts of thee that the world's eye doth view") and 70 ("That thou are blamed shall not be thy defect") are more specific about the Fair Friend and his reputation in the world. People who praise his beauty also look into his character:

> [Thy] outward thus with outward praise is
>   crown'd,
> But those same tongues that give thee so thine
>   own,
> In other accents do this praise confound
> By seeing farther than the eye hath shown.
> They look into the beauty of thy mind,
> And that in guess they measure by thy deeds,
> Then, churls, their thoughts (although their eyes
>   were kind)
> To thy fair flower add the rank smell of weeds:
>   But why thy odor matcheth not thy show,
>   The [soil] is this, that thou dost common
>   grow.
>
> (69.5-14)

. . . . Line 12 takes us back, quite directly, to Sonnet 94, with its reference to those who "rightly do inherit heaven's graces / And husband nature's riches from expense" and of course to the smell of weeds. Even more closely does it approach the two following sonnets, 95 ("How sweet and lovely dost thou make the shame") and 96 ("Some say thy fault is youth, some wantonness") whose first lines suffice to show the nature of the fault in the friend. From the poet's point of view, however, the fault is mainly important because it is the poet's business to defend and justify it.

THE DARK LADY

As many critics have pointed out, Sonnets 127-52 generally portray the speaker's mistress in a disparaging way. J. B. Leishman noted that not only does the Poet despise her, he loathes himself for loving this woman who has enslaved his young friend. **Philip Edwards** compared the warm and charming description of the woman in Sonnet 130 with the subsequent depiction of her as "an agent of damnation" from whom the speaker turns away in disgust. By comparison, **John Klause** argued that the Poet continues to desire her despite his revulsion, and their mutual depravity keeps them together. In his important essay on the Dark Lady, James Winny pointed out that most of the speaker's descriptions of her suggest, rather brutally, that she is fickle, ill-favored, and cruelly contemptuous of his feelings. And yet, as Heather Dubrow (1987) and others have remarked, negative appraisals of the woman are frequently followed by positive ones. Dubrow maintained that the speaker's inconsistent portrait of his mistress should make us wary of trusting his judgment and forming any definitive interpretations about her character.

Similarly, **S. Schoenbaum** suggested that because the disclosures about the Dark Woman are obscure and contradictory, and because the speaker's hostility toward her is so apparent, it is difficult to draw reliable conclusions about her. M. L. Stapleton has recently argued that the Poet's description of his mistress is neither accurate nor reliable. We must always keep in mind, she warned, that the Dark Lady is entirely a creation of the Poet's voice— and he is a self-admitted liar. Kenneth Muir is one of several critics who have emphasized the bitterness and anger in many of the Dark Lady sonnets, but Muir also pointed out that this mood changes swiftly and frequently as the speaker turns from attacking or insulting her to begging for her kindness or forgiving her transgressions.

Many commentators— including Douglas L. Peterson, Katharine M. Wilson, and James Winny— have read the Dark Lady sonnets as a satirical treatment of Petrarchan sonnet conventions. Peterson maintained that Shakespeare's verses mock the Petrarchan ideal of the fair beloved and parody the traditional sonnet modes of praise, complaint, and plea. Wilson, on the other hand, asserted that the Dark Lady sonnets specifically satirize the artificiality of sonnets written by Shakespeare's English predecessors and contemporaries. Reading the Dark Lady series as a subversion of conventional attitudes toward love in the Petrarchan tradition, Winny identified several targets of Shakespeare's satire, including the lover's devotion, his beloved's moral perfection, and the ennobling power of love.

Philip Edwards

SOURCE: "The Sonnets to the Dark Woman," in *Shakespeare and the Confines of Art*, Methuen, 1968, pp. 17-31.

[*Seeking an explanation for the different moods and tones in Sonnets 127-52, Edwards proposes that these reflect the Poet's struggle to exorcise his feelings of hopelessness by expressing them in verse. In the critic's judgment, the Dark Lady represents carnal love— a debilitating and contaminating passion that degrades the Poet and imperils his soul. The Poet fully comprehends the threat this liaison poses, Edwards contends, yet he cannot extricate himself from the bondage of sexual desire. Caught in this dilemma, he experiments with a variety of poetic perspectives, searching for one that will make sense of his predicament and allow him to transcend it.*]

The characteristic of the Dark Woman sonnets is that the suggestion of a 'real' relationship is created, running beneath poems which, sometimes ostentatiously, show their failure to crystallize and comprehend this relationship. It is the impression of failure which provides the evidence of the 'real' relationship. It is like defining God by negatives, showing the inability of language to describe Him. We may often enough indulge our fancy about the real relationship which lay behind some love poem and imagine that in life things were not quite as the poet has put it. But love poems do not usually make the effort to hint at a discrepancy; the sense of life is what most of them try to give. I suggest that the most profitable way to read the Dark Woman sonnets is to think of Shakespeare watching his creature-poet at work. The sonnets, strung along a thin line of narrative about wooing, conquest and disgust, are a poet's ordering of his own life, his answering 'the daily necessity of getting the world right'; and Shakespeare is observing his grim failure. As the affair intensifies from courtship to consummation to bitterness, Shakespeare's ironic detachment from his creature becomes less and less, but a distance is maintained throughout.

Each of the first four sonnets is a posture; each introduces a particular kind of artistic ordering which is to be followed up later. Sonnet 127, 'In the old age black was not counted fair', proves that the dark woman is beautiful and is the first of a number of courtship poems in which the sonneteer, delighting in his own poetic wit, denies the distinction between ugliness and beauty, and hence, by traditional symbolism, denies the distinction between evil and good. The second poem, 'How oft when thou, my music, music play'st', is one of those classed as 'independent' by Professor [Brents] Stirling. It seems to me the very necessary introduction of the purely conventional wooing-poem. The humble lover watches his mistress at her music, envies the keys which touch her hand and pleads for the gratification of a kiss. To explode this world of sighing poetry-love, there follows the great sonnet on lust (129):

Th' expense of spirit in a waste of shame
Is lust in action; and till action lust
Is perjured, murd'rous, bloody, full of blame,
Savage, extreme, rude, cruel, not to trust;
Enjoyed no sooner but despisèd straight;
Past reason hunted, and no sooner had,
Past reason hated as a swallowed bait
On purpose laid to make the taker mad.
Mad in pursuit, and in possession so;
Had, having, and in quest to have, extreme;
A bliss in proof, and proved, a very woe;
Before, a joy proposed; behind, a dream.
  All this the world well knows; yet none knows well
  To shun the heaven that leads men to this hell.

Magnificent though this sonnet is, taken by itself, it gains a special force from its position. The early sonnets in this sequence, before the reversal in 137, provide a study in self-deception, and the evidence for this is sonnet 129. Here the poet has a momentary vision of himself as a madman, here he sees his courtship as the longings of lust for its reward of self-loathing. Every wooing-poem which follows this is coloured by it; the

poet who has had this vision of what he is doing in seeking the favours of the dark woman goes on writing poems which 'convince' him that he is in no danger, poems in which he is able to smother his moral sense in his delight in his own poetic skill. Far from being an ending to the sequence, the sonnet on lust finds its proper place near the beginning. It poses the question to which the sequence as a whole finds that there is no answer; why does a man willingly poison himself?

In the fourth sonnet, 'My mistress' eyes are nothing like the sun', the poet explores the possibilities of the common anti-petrarchan convention.

My mistress' eyes are nothing like the sun;
Coral is far more red than her lips' red;
If snow be white, why then her breasts are
  dun;
If hairs be wires, black wires grow on her head.
I have seen roses damasked, red and white,
But no such roses see I in her cheeks;
And in some perfumes is there more delight
Than in the breath that from my mistress
  reeks.
I love to hear her speak, yet well I know
That music hath a far more pleasing sound;
I grant I never saw a goddess go:
My mistress, when she walks, treads on the
  ground.
  And yet, by heaven, I think my love as rare
  As any she belied with false compare.

At first, this sonnet seems to be a direct attempt to cut through the nonsense of 128 and to come to a 'real' relationship. Rejecting idiotic comparisons, it seems a sane and human acceptance of a woman for what she is. The poet's love seems truer and warmer in its independence of poetic flattery. For the reader to see the poem only in this way, however, is to slip into the very trap which Shakespeare wants to show his poet falling into. Who is the woman who is contemplated so humanly, so warmly, so confidently? The Dark Woman, who is shortly to be shown as an agent of damnation. When we read this poem in its proper context, we can see that the final couplet conveys a double impression. First we congratulate the poet on the honesty of his love which needs no lying comparisons to assist it. Then we reflect on the continuous play in these sonnets between fairness-beauty-virtue and darkness-ugliness-vice, and we wonder whether a sophistical confusion between these two poles is not at work here too. Because all women, however beautiful, are 'belied' by being compared with goddesses, are all women equally beautiful and equally worthy of love? The poet has a right to love whom he will, and to accept a plain woman is no crime, but in so far as the ground of his acceptance is the equality of women as non-goddesses, he shows himself insensitive to the distinction (symbol of a moral distinction) between ugliness and beauty. Shakespeare does not say outright that the woman is ugly; students are taught that 'reeks' does not imply halitosis or garlic. But no one can read the poem without a sense of considerable unattractiveness in the dun breasts, black hair, pallid cheeks and breath which, if it is not sour, is not exactly sweet. The sonnet may be seen as a parody of the usual anti-petrarchan sonnet in which the poet rejects ornamental comparisons because true beauty needs no such aids. While showing that a woman gains nothing from false flattery the poet implies that physical demerits (the emblems of spiritual demerits) are of no account with him. With the gallantry of his wit, he once more confounds all distinction between women. To understand what the lover really achieves in this sonnet, we can turn to any of the later poems, sonnet 150 for example:

To make me give the lie to my true sight
And swear that brightness doth not grace the
    day.

The ugliness of the woman is made obvious in the subtle poem which follows (131). The poet jokes that in spite of her unpromising face, his mistress must be a conventional beauty because she tyrannizes over his heart like the heroine of any ordinary sonnet-sequence. He again denies distinction ('Thy black is fairest in my judgement's place') and tells us outright, for the first time, of the woman's viciousness:

In nothing art thou black save in thy deeds,
And thence this slander, as I think, proceeds.

What a great joke it is for him to be in love (if that's the word) with an ugly woman of dubious character and to be able to prove her as fair as the fairest— and, by means of the proof, insult her.

Sonnet 132 carries the jesting on and deepens the sense of ugliness. Conventional comparisons, rejected in 130, are trotted out with an accent which cleverly degrades the woman as they seem to praise her.

And truly not the morning sun of heaven
Better becomes the grey cheeks of the east,
Nor that full star that ushers in the even
Doth half that glory to the sober west
As those two mourning eyes become thy face.

The denial in this poem is emphatic, 'Then will I swear beauty herself is black', and the denial is promised as a consequence of her granting him 'pity'. The denial of value is a price he is willing to pay for the satisfaction of his lust.

The 'triangle' sonnets, which follow, are important in reminding us at this stage of the existence of the other kind of love and of the contamination of the higher by the lower kind. The two poems make the woman's 'black deeds' more real as they describe her promiscuity and

draw her as a demon whose loathsome magnetism enslaves her victims. The extraordinary 'will' sonnets, 135 and 136, show what wit can do to turn what is dreadful into amusement; the lover's plea for pity is advanced in a crudely physical way. His arguments for being admitted to her favours are at the level of mutual sexual satisfaction; he equates his whole being with his carnal desire and his virility:

And then thou lovest me, for my name is Will.

He is still laughing at the joke as he unites with the woman he knows the worst of in a congress whose emotional and spiritual consequences he has already foreseen in sonnet 129. The climax of the sequence— the 'kiss' sonnet of discreeter series— is sonnet 137. At the moment of fruition, there is immediate and overpowering revulsion.

Thou blind fool, Love, what dost thou to mine
    eyes
That they behold and see not what they see?
They know what beauty is, see where it lies,
Yet what the best is take the worst to be.
If eyes, corrupt by over-partial looks,
Be anchored in the bay where all men ride,
Why of eyes' falsehood hast thou forged hooks
Whereto the judgement of my heart is tied?
Why should my heart think that a several plot
Which my heart knows the wide world's
    common place?
Or mine eyes seeing this, say this is not,
To put fair truth upon so foul a face?
    In things right true my heart and eye have
    erred,
    And to this false plague are they now
    transferred.

The question, why does a man betray himself and swallow the bait?, continues for the rest of the sequence, but in the end there is no answer to give beyond the simple statement that it has happened.

The sequence continues with a series of sonnets written in bed. The rapid alterations of mood, the contradictions in viewpoint, may seem bewildering, but they are by no means an indication that the order is haphazard. The mood as a whole is of restless conflict in the single attempt to write the poem that makes the unbearable look bearable. Sonnet 138 ('When my love swears that she is made of truth / I do believe her though I know she lies') tries to follow the pattern of conciliation used in the sequence to the young man— not to insult and despise but to recognize and accept one's own imperfections as well as those of one's partner. But the resolution has a very hollow sound; they will lie to each other and each will pretend to believe the other, for 'love's best habit is in seeming trust'. On this thin surface they will try to build, but all that they have with which to build is sexual pleasure:

> Therefore I lie with her and she with me,
> And in our faults by lies we flattered be.

In 139, he shows himself afraid of his own facility for consoling himself by writing down specious excuses for the woman. The mood is very similar to the mood of sonnet 35 in which the poet begins to pour out tired exculpatory analogies on his friend's behalf, and then pulls himself up in disgust at his own lack of moral courage. In sonnets 141 and 142, the word 'sin' enters for the first time, and the poet sees his suffering as condign punishment. Orthodox moral judgement of himself and his mistress as adulterers brings a new perspective into the sequence.

Sonnets 143, 144, 145, 146 seem to me to be of central importance. Two of them are very weak, the other two are very powerful. Indeed, in 145 ('Those lips that Love's own hand did make') we have one of the worst of all the sonnets, and in 146 ('Poor soul the centre of my sinful earth') one of the best. But when he is writing badly, Shakespeare does so intentionally, not for the first or the only time (we may think of the sonnets given to the young nobles in *Love's Labour's Lost*). In each of these sonnets, Shakespeare— or rather his poet— tries to make the peculiarly unhappy fact of his predicament conform to a different poetic 'idea'; he tries out different objectifications of the intolerable position he finds himself in— and none of them 'works'. Sonnet 143, a study in whimsical self-derision, turns the lover into a neglected baby crying for the mother who is chasing a hen. If this ludicrous image for deserted lover and predatory female lowers the poet, the poem yet provides in the rounded movement of its own logic the promise of consolation:

> But if thou catch thy hope, turn back to me
> *And play the mother's part,* kiss me, be kind.

The next sonnet in the group is 'Two loves I have of comfort and despair', which we have already discussed. Like the lust-sonnet, it gains extra depth from its position, rudely cancelling out the propositions of a weak preceding sonnet. It is followed in its turn by a remarkable song (145). A characteristic and understandable note on this appears in the Harbage and Bush 'Pelican' edition of the Sonnets: 'The authenticity of this sonnet, in tetrameters and rudimentary diction, has been questioned, with considerable show of reason; in any case, it is not in context with the adjacent sonnets.' The Ingram and Redpath edition says:

> These trivial octosyllabics scarcely deserve reprinting. Some editors have considered the poem spurious on account of its feeble childishness. It would seem arbitrary, however, to rule out the possibility that one of Shakespeare's trivia should have found

its way into a collection not approved by him.

> Those lips that Love's own hand did make
> Breathed forth the sound that said 'I hate'
> To me that languished for her sake;
> But when she saw my woeful state,
> Straight in her heart did mercy come,
> Chiding that tongue that ever sweet
> Was used in giving gentle doom,
> And taught it thus anew to greet:
> 'I hate' she altered with an end
> That followed it as gentle day
> Doth follow night, who like a fiend
> From heaven to hell is flown away.
> 'I hate' from hate away she threw,
> And saved my life, saying 'not you'.

It can surely be argued that this absurd song *does* fit the place it is given. The idea of the woman's hate, as opposed to coldness or indifference, was first introduced in 142 and is continued here and in later sonnets. The metaphor of heaven and hell makes a direct link with the preceding 'two loves' sonnet and with the mortification-sonnet which follows next. I suggest that this despised poem should be taken as a satirical picture of a poet smoothing out life's problems, whistling to keep his spirits up. All's well that ends well; the fiend flies out of the window. The feebleness of the poem is an exaggerated comment on the weakness of poetry as a means of arranging one's life or even portraying it. Yet, exaggerated as it is, it does make a comment on poetry as a whole. It uses a magic which is quite patently ineffectual, but it draws our attention to poetry as a kind of magic which may or may not work. The poem which follows is a particularly powerful poem. Although, as with two earlier poems I have mentioned, it gains extra force from exploding a namby-pamby predecessor, I believe we must also say that it is coloured by its predecessor. The mortification-sonnet is akin to the song in being a poet's attempt to relieve the pressures on his life through the perspective of art.

> Poor soul, the centre of my sinful earth,
> [Fooled by] these rebel pow'rs that thee array,
> Why dost thou pine within and suffer dearth,
> Painting thy outward walls so costly gay?
> Why so large cost, having so short a lease,
> Dost thou upon thy fading mansion spend?
> Shall worms, inheritors of this excess,
> Eat up thy charge? Is this thy body's end?
> Then, soul, live thou upon thy servant's loss
> And let that pine to aggravate thy store;
> Buy terms divine in selling hours of dross;
> Within be fed, without be rich no more:
>   So shalt thou feed on Death, that feeds on men,
>   And Death once dead, there's no more dying then.

That mortification of the pride of the flesh and a life turned towards God can be an answer to the attack of the female devil ('there's no more dying then') is ruled out by the next sonnet—

> My love is as a fever longing *still*
> For that which longer nurseth the disease.

('still' is at least as likely to have here its modern meaning as the older meaning of 'always'.) Death is not dead: 'I desperate now approve / Desire is death.' Sonnet 146 does not put the claims of religion any the less nobly because it does not serve the poet as more than a transient insight into what might be. It may seem a greater poem because of its hint of tragedy in that a man should know what this poem knows and yet be unable to avail himself of what the poem offers. And I certainly do not think that its value is lessened if we see it as one of a series of poems in a *dramatic* sequence in which the hero, a poet, restlessly turns to different poetic images of his own troubles.

The wild music of the few remaining sonnets puts them among the greatest writing of Shakespeare. There is never a last word. The poet accepts his incurable condition as a madness in 147, but then he goes on to degrade himself in anger (149 and 150), blaming *her* for entangling him:

> If thy unworthiness raised love in me,
> More worthy I to be belov'd of thee.

The obscene sonnet 151 tries vainly to find refuge in the idea that there being nothing nobler in man than his sexual desire, he might find contentment in simply being the woman's drudge. Sonnet 152 ends with yet another repetition of the inexplicable:

> And, to enlighten thee, gave eyes to blindness,
> Or made them swear against the thing they see;
>   For I have sworn thee fair; more perjured
>   eye,
> To swear against the truth so foul a lie.

After this, the sequence evaporates in two perfunctory sonnets on the theme of Cupid's brand heating a well.

> Past reason hunted, and no sooner had,
> Past reason hated as a swallowed bait
> On purpose laid to make the taker mad.

The story of the poet and the dark woman is not some isolated adventure. Shakespeare is writing about sexual desire, and he portrays it as a degradation that a man cannot withstand. What is perhaps not improperly called the fear of desire is partly submerged in Shakespeare's earlier plays but it reappears at the turn of the century and in almost every play from *Measure for Measure* onwards there is an acknowledgement of the supposed disjunction between the marriage of minds and the union of bodies. In the last plays there is much that is perplexing on this subject. What we have read in the Sonnets helps to explain the chiaroscuro of Marina in the brothel [in *Pericles*], Polixenes' vision of childhood innocence, [in *The Winter's Tale*] and the anxiety of Prospero's spirits to keep Venus out of the wedding masque. [in *The Tempest*]. Auden was right to conclude his essay on the sonnets [introduction to the Signet edition of the sonnets (1964)] with the address to all-enslaving Venus from Shakespeare's last offering, *The Two Noble Kinsmen.*

At the moment what concerns us is not Shakespeare's 'attitude to sex' but his attitude towards art. The drama of the Dark Woman sequence is not alone the drama of the curse of the granted wish, but the drama of the poet groping to materialize his emotions in verse. Shakespeare sets poetry the task of describing a certain kind of hopelessness and he shows poetry pulling like a tidal current away from hopelessness towards resolution of one kind or another. Although individual poems, however brilliant, may be 'failures' in that they are shown to be separated from the life they pretend to record, the cumulative effect of the sequence is success of the highest order, not failure.

S. Schoenbaum

SOURCE: "Shakespeare's Dark Lady: A Question of Identity," in *Shakespeare's Styles: Essays in Honour of Kenneth Muir*, edited by Philip Edwards, Inga-Stina Ewbank, and G. K. Hunter, Cambridge University Press, 1980, pp. 221-39.

[*Noting that most of what has been written by commentators about the Dark Lady is speculation about whether she can be identified with a historical person, Schoenbaum summarizes what the sonnets themselves tell us about her. Little can be derived, he points out, from the mostly enigmatic clues in Sonnets 127-52: she has dark hair and eyes, and a complexion that is not light; she is not conventionally attractive; she has a lusty sexual appetite and is perhaps married; and she has a volatile temperament. Schoenbaum also briefly discusses Sonnets 153 and 154, where he finds a suggestion that the speaker has contracted a venereal disease as a result of his affair with the Dark Lady.*]

> My mistress' eyes are nothing like the sun;
> Coral is far more red than her lips' red;
> If snow be white, why then her breasts are
>   dun;
> If hairs be wires, black wires grow on her head.
> I have seen roses damasked, red and white,
> But no such roses see I in her cheeks;
> And in some perfumes is there more delight
> Than in the breath that from my mistress
>   reeks.
> I love to hear her speak, yet well I know
> That music hath a far more pleasing sound;

I grant I never saw a goddess go—
My mistress when she walks treads on the
   ground.
   And yet, by heaven, I think my love as rare
   As any she belied with false compare.

                      (Sonnet 130)

It was, I believe, Aldous Huxley who once spoke of the imbecile earnestness of lust. Shakespeare can certainly be earnest on the subject; witness the tremendous sonnet (just preceding the one quoted) in which, in an explosively forceful series of self-lacerating modifiers, he excoriates a passion that post-coitally he despises, and which yet tyrannises over body and spirit. But Sonnet 130 reflects another mood; the lover is at once clear-eyed and high spirited. His mistress's attractions can survive his own denigration of them. So she withstands the anti-Petrarchan assault of the three quartets— the reference to disagreeable breath seems especially devastating in an age of oral hygiene— to assert her allure, and attendant mystery, in a concluding couplet that draws its special force from *not* being dependent upon romantic illusion.

This is the Dark Lady who, more than three and a half centuries ago, sauntered into the best-loved sequence of lyric poems in the language. They describe with a playwright's art how she captivated the poet, against his reason, and seduced the golden youth he adored. One of the great sorceresses of literature, she has since added innumerable readers to the tally of her conquests. . . .

Familiar as the poems are, it may be well to begin by piecing together what we can about the Dark Lady from the revelations, sometimes obscure or contradictory, that they afford. She makes her entrance obliquely, a felt presence rather than a directly introduced member of the dramatis personae. 'Base clouds' suddenly overcast a sunny day. Somehow the poet's friend has given offence. We hear of a wound, of disgrace and shame, and of penitent tears. The trespass, the next sonnet (35) reveals, was theft, and the fault 'sensual'. Five poems later the nature of the larceny becomes clearer, although not yet explicit. 'Take all my loves, my love', the poet cries, 'yea, take them all.' It seems that the friend has taken Shakespeare's mistress.

At last, in Sonnet 41, indirections cease, the circumlocutions of tact and poetical conceit give way; what has happened is starkly stated:

    Gentle thou art, and therefore to be won,
    Beauteous thou art, therefore to be assailed;
    And when a woman woos, what woman's son,
    Will sourly leave her till she have prevailed?

So she— whoever she is— has taken the role of aggressor, and the beauteous friend has succumbed. It is an interesting triumph. The lovely boy is high-born, the poet's patron, and of ambiguous masculinity. Nature has fashioned him to be a woman, and given him a woman's face; but rather spoilt things for the heterosexual poet by outfitting her exquisite creation with a male organ. The emotional and psychological weight of these poems resides in the relationship between the two men. The woman who has come between them is still only a shadow— or cloud.

Later she comes into her own. In Sonnet 127 we meet her properly and for the first time learn about the colouration that sets her apart. Black wires grow upon her head, Sonnet 130 adds, and 'If snow be white, why then her breasts are dun', which the Oxford Dictionary helpfully defines as 'of a dull or dingy brown colour; now *esp.* a dull greyish brown, like the hair of the ass and mouse'. If the Dark Lady is beautiful, hers is an unfashionable beauty; but some question emerges as to whether she is beautiful by any standard:

    In faith, I do not love thee with mine eyes,
    For they in thee a thousand errors note.

This is 141; just two sonnets earlier the poet has commended her 'pretty looks'. Are all these poems, one may wonder, addressed to the same woman? Or is it merely that we are witnessing a lover's varied moods? The old adage holds that beauty lies in the eye of the beholder; perhaps the report shifts, not the object reported. It is one of many puzzles.

Elsewhere we tread on firmer ground. We learn that the lady is musical, and (in Sonnet 128) catch a charming glimpse of her seated at the virginals. Perhaps she sings as she plays. Her fingers dance over the wooden keys, the jacks leaping nimbly up to kiss the inside of her hand. Her lover, envying the jacks, kisses his mistress on the lips. It is rather like a seventeenth-century Dutch genre painting.

Other poems show the Dark Lady as a *belle dame sans merci*, tyrannising over her lover. She breaks her bed-vow— does this mean she is married, as most have assumed, or merely that she has broken a vow made to her lover when they were in bed together? About her sexual appetite and promiscuity, however, there is no question; she is 'the bay where all men ride'. Even when with the poet she humiliates him by eyeing other men. Older than his mistress— 'my days', he laments, 'are past the best'— and consequently insecure, he wearily accepts her infidelities, and deludes himself into crediting 'her false-speaking tongue'. The word *lies* furnishes an opportunity for rueful word-play:

    Therefore I lie with her, and she with me,
    And in our faults by lies we flattered be.

Will, another key word, could mean 'carnal desire or appetite'. It might also signify the male or female geni-

Shakespeare's contemporaries. Clockwise from top: Ben Jonson, Fletcher, Drayton, Shirley, Massigner, Beaumont, and (center) Spencer.

talia. And of course the poet's name was Will. He plays with all these meanings simultaneously in Sonnet 135, where (in the 1609 quarto) the word *will* is italicised—with an uppercased *W*— seven out of the thirteen times it appears:

> Whoever hath her wish, thou hast thy Will,
> And Will to boot, and Will in over-plus;
> More than enough am I that vex thee still,
> To thy sweet will making addition thus.
> Wilt thou, whose will is large and spacious,
> Not once vouchsafe to hide my will in thine?

The only thing virginal about this lady is the musical instrument she fingers so fluently.

In an extraordinary sonnet (151) the poet contemplates her powers of conjuration over another instrument, which stands erect at the mere mention of her name: 'flesh stays no farther reason, / But, rising at thy name, doth point out thee / As his triumphant prize'. What are we to make of a mistress who can be thus addressed? Was she, as some have thought, a common prostitute? Standards of propriety of course vary with the times and with individuals; one man's grossness is another's refreshing candour. If we may occasionally

lament the loss of past reticences, a flesh-and-blood Shakespeare is perhaps preferable to the impassive statuary of the culture-worshippers who wend their pious way to the Stratford shrines and cough through a performance at the Royal Shakespeare Theatre. We do well every now and then to remind ourselves that Shakespeare, father of three, had a penis.

The 144th Sonnet sets in perspective the complex triangle involving Poet, Fair Youth, and Dark Lady:

> Two loves I have, of comfort and despair,
> Which like two spirits do suggest me still;
> The better angel is a man right fair,
> The worser spirit a woman coloured ill.
>   . . . . .
> But being both from me, both to each friend,
> I guess one angel in another's hell.
>   Yet this shall I ne'er know, but live in doubt,
>   Till my bad angel fire my good one out.

This seems straightforward enough: Hell fits nicely into a scheme that includes good and bad angels, saint and devil, and gains here another dimension by alluding to the game of barley-break, in which the last couple playing found itself 'in hell'. But hell was also a cant word for the female organ; hence the sexual innuendo of: 'I guess one angel in another's hell.' The last line possibly harbours a grimmer allusion. 'To fire out', which meant originally 'to smoke a fox out of its den'— cf. *King Lear,* V, iii, 23: 'fire us hence like foxes'— also signified 'to communicate a venereal disease'.

A similar allusiveness may help to explain the otherwise puzzling last two poems of Shakespeare's sonnet sequence. These, as a recent critic [James Winny, in *The Master-Mistress: A Study of Shakespeare's Sonnets* (1968)] sums up,

> are generally looked upon as an appendix not connected with the story, which Shakespeare or the printer added simply to enlarge the collection. Both tell a fanciful story about the origins of a medicinal spring, brought into being when a nymph extinguished Cupid's torch in a well, which 'took heat perpetual' from this fire.

'I, sick withal, the help of bath desired', the poet reports, 'and thither hied, a sad distempered guest.' The Greek Anthology, the ultimate source of these poems, makes no reference to the curative powers of the waters. As early as the eighteenth century, a commentator queried, 'Whether we shall read *Bath* (i.e. the city of that name)?' Bath is still celebrated for its medicinal hot springs, the fountains of the town proudly displaying the dubious motto, 'Water is best.' Although in Shakespeare's day it had not yet become a fashionable spa, Elizabethans sought out the waters of Bath for curative purposes. . . . True, the word *bath* is not capitalised, or placed in italics, in Sonnets 153 and 154 in the 1609 edition, as are other proper nouns (*Cupid, Dian's*); but one cannot expect nice distinctions to be scrupulously maintained by a typesetter unchecked by authorial supervision. A topographical identification is in any event not required: there were other spas, and the reference may point, not to natural springs, but to the sweating tubs, filled with hot water, used by the victims of venereal infection. Some such allusiveness seems to be indicated by the sexual innuendoes of these two sonnets.

'I, my mistress' thrall, / Came there for cure', Shakespeare concludes in the last lines of his last sonnet, but the waters appear to have vouchsafed no cure, only the awareness that: 'Love's fire heats water, water cools not love.' Thus, ingloriously does the cycle end. If this reading is correct, and underneath their fanciful surface Sonnets 153 and 154 reveal the unpleasant medical consequences of an illicit affair, they perhaps afford an autobiographical clue to the sex-nausea that so many critics have remarked on in *Hamlet, Troilus and Cressida,* and *King Lear.*

Whatever the merits of such speculation, the Dark Lady is (within the limits of lyric poetry) as vitally realised a dramatic creation as Cressida, with her wanton spirits looking out from every joint and motive of her body, and some have wondered whether both portraits were drawn to life from the same sitter. Never mind; we have enough to occupy us with the Dark Lady on her own, although the information is not always so clear cut as either one would wish or some have surmised. To sum up: she is younger than the poet, musical, raven-haired and raven-eyed, dark-skinned (how dark is not clear), and either unattractive or unconventionally beautiful, depending upon the viewer and the viewer's mood. She is certainly seductive, gives free rein to her appetite, may be married, and is possibly infected with venereal disease. In character she is a *femme fatale*: proud, fickle, overbearing, and deceitful. No wonder scholars have sought to find for her a local habitation and a name.

SOURCES FOR FURTHER STUDY

Literary Commentary

Allen, Michael J. B. "Shakespeare's Man Descending a Staircase: Sonnets 126 to 154." *Shakespeare Survey* 31 (1978): 127-38.

Emphasizes the contribution of each poem in the Dark Lady group to the dramatic coherence of this series. The inconsistent narrative in this section overturns conventional expectations of chronology, Allen maintains, allowing readers to focus on these sonnets' depiction of the transitory and unpredictable nature of human experience.

Booth, Stephen. "Commentary." In William Shakespeare, *Shakespeare's Sonnets,* pp. 135-538. New Haven: Yale University Press, 1977.

The most complete compilation of the likely meanings of words and phrases in Shakespeare's sonnets. Booth provides multiple glosses rather than, as most editors, a single one, so that readers may become aware of "all the meanings, contradictions, echoes, and suggestions" inherent in Elizabethan diction and idiom. He also remarks that Shakespeare's modes of expression and phrasing would have been just as troublesome for his contemporaries as they are for modern readers.

Crosman, Robert. "Making Love Out of Nothing At All: The Issue of Story in Shakespeare's Procreation Sonnets." *Shakespeare Quarterly* 41, No. 4 (Winter 1990): 470-88.

Reads the subtext of Sonnets 1-17 as the poet's invention of a relationship of increasing intimacy with the young man through the medium of poetry. Crosman uses the French term autofiction— referring to a genre that comprises both historical and fictional elements— to describe Shakespeare's entire sonnet sequence, which he characterizes as a self-portrait of "the artist as lover."

Dawes, James. "Truth and Decay in Shakespeare's Sonnets." *Cahiers Elisabethains* 47 (April 1995): 43-53.

Asserts that Shakespeare's sonnets represent a dialectic between certainty and doubt, as the speaker alternately expresses his belief in the truth of love and art and then represents such faith as illusory. Dawes traces the opposition of constancy and mutability in word clusters and images throughout the sequence, with special attention to Sonnets 53, 95, and 105.

Devereux, James A. "The Last Temptation of Shakespeare: The Sonnets and Despair." In *Renaissance Papers 1979,* edited by A. Leigh Deneef and M. Thomas Hester, pp. 29-38. Southeastern Renaissance Conference, 1980.

Proposes that the basic structural principle of Shakespeare's sonnets is the struggle— similar to the contest between good and evil angels in medieval morality plays— for possession of the poet's soul. Devereux also reviews traditional attitudes toward the sin of despair and finds echoes of these in Sonnets 140, 146, and 147.

DuBrow, Heather. "'Conceit deceitful': The Sonnets." In her *Captive Victors: Shakespeare's Narrative Poems and Sonnets,* pp. 169-257. Ithaca: Cornell University Press, 1987.

A comprehensive analysis of the relation between form and content in Shakespeare's sonnets. In Dubrow's judgment, Shakespeare undermines conventional Petrarchan and anti-Petrarchan rhetorical patterns— including equivocal use of praise and blame, excusing or justifying faults, lack of finality or closure, avoidance of flattery, and the "ugly beauty" motif— to reflect the sonnet speaker's paradoxical position as both a masterful manipulator of language and emotions and their unwitting victim.

———. "'Incertainties now crown themselves assur'd': The Politics of Plotting Shakespeare's Sonnets." *Shakespeare Quarterly* 47, No. 3 (Fall 1996): 291-305.

Challenges conventional wisdom about the addressees, narrative line, and two-part structure of Shakespeare's sonnet sequence. Dubrow maintains that since many of the poems are not specifically addressed to the Friend, the Dark Lady, or anyone else, and since there is no convincing evidence that Shakespeare intended the sonnets to be arranged in the order in which they are traditionally presented, readers are free to construct "any number of narratives" from the sequence.

Goldstien, Neal L. "Money and Love in Shakespeare's Sonnets." *Bucknell Review* 17, No. 3 (December 1969): 91-106.

Argues that the imagery of riches and wealth in the sonnets is deeply ambiguous, reflecting the poet's complex perspective on money and what it stands for. Goldstien notes the different uses of financial terms in numbers 1-17, the Dark Lady section, and several other sonnets, where materialism is variously associated with beauty, love, sexuality, and wickedness.

Grundy, Joan. "Shakespeare's Sonnets and the Elizabethan Sonneteers." *Shakespeare Survey* 15 (1962): 41-49.

Points out similarities— and significant distinctions— between Shakespeare and his fellow-sonneteers. Grundy contends that, in general, Shakespeare puts greater emphasis on his beloved and less on his own suffering than do his contemporaries, that he is less concerned with what the world thinks of him, and that he is more conscious of the dilemma of how to praise without seeming to flatter.

Hecht, Anthony. "The Sonnet: Ruminations on Form, Sex, and History." *Antioch Review* 55, No. 2 (Spring 1997): 134-47.

A collection of thoughts on several different topics. Hecht reviews the differences between English and Italian sonnet forms; sexual ambiguity in medieval courtly love poems; the customary view, from antiquity up through the Renaissance, that close friendship between men was a nobler relationship than love between the sexes; and medieval and Renaissance notions of the relationship between sacred and profane love.

Hedley, Jane. "Since First Your Eye I Eyed: Shakespeare's *Sonnets* and the Poetics of Narcissism." *Style* 28, No. 1 (Spring 1994): 1-30.

A psychoanalytic assessment of rhyme, repetition, and wordplay in the sonnets, with particular attention to Sonnets 33-37, 40-42, 66-72, and 91-96. Hedley maintains that these devices help carry out the "dream work" project of keeping the narcissistic love relationship between poet and friend alive by continually destabilizing it and then reviving it in new contexts.

Hunter, G. K. "The Dramatic Technique of Shakespeare's Sonnets." *Essays in Criticism* III, No. 2 (April 1953): 152-64.

Emphasizes the immediacy and expressiveness of Shakespeare's sonnets. Hunter dissects the way the poet reworked conventional themes and rhetorical devices to give voice to human feelings and thus engage readers in the emotional situations he described. The critic also contrasts these poems with the essentially nondramatic sonnets of Spenser, Sidney, and Donne.

Innes, Paul. "The Young Friend." In *Shakespeare and the English Renaissance Sonnet*, pp. 108-37. New York: St. Martin's Press, 1997.

Analyzes Shakespeare's sonnets— particularly 18-95— in the context of the historical circumstances under which they were produced. Focusing on the patriarchal structure of English Renaissance society and relations between poets and literary patrons, Innes reads these sonnets in terms of gender relations and class distinctions. He contends that from the poet's perspective, the young man's superior social position is both fortunate and threatening.

Kay, Dennis. "The *Sonnets* and *A Lover's Complaint*." In *William Shakespeare: Sonnets and Poems*, pp. 96-152. New York: Twayne, 1998.

An overview that addresses a variety of issues, including the literary and cultural contents of the English Petrarchan sonnet; current textual and bibliographical scholarship of Shakespeare's sonnets; whether Shakespeare's verses constitute a formally arranged sequence; homosexual love in the sonnets vis-à-vis early modern culture; other sonnet collections and literary models on which Shakespeare may have drawn; and responses to Shakespeare's sonnets over the centuries.

Landry, Hilton. "The Unmoved Movers: Sonnet 94 and the Contexts of Interpretation." In *Interpretations in Shakespeare's Sonnets*, pp. 7-27. Berkeley: University of California Press, 1964.

A reading of Sonnet 94 in relation to the six that precede it and the two that follow it. Landry views the first eight lines of Sonnet 94 as an admission that the loss of the speaker's friend, which was threatened in Sonnets 87-93, has become actuality. The critic interprets the final six lines as a parable warning the friend of his vulnerability to corruption: the turn of events that the poet describes in Sonnets 95 and 96.

Leishman, J. B. "Shakespeare's Sonnets on Love as the Defier of Time." In *Themes and Variations in Shakespeare's Sonnets*, pp. 102-18. London: Hutchinson, 1963.

Proposes that in Sonnets 115-125, the poet affirms that what he has truly loved in his friend is not his youthful, external beauty but what that love has meant to him. Leishman regards these sonnets as a spiritual or visionary expression of belief in the transcendence and timelessness of love.

Mizener, Arthur. "The Structure of Figurative Language in Shakespeare's Sonnets." *Southern Review* V, No. 4 (Spring 1940): 730-47.

Defends the complexity and logical inconclusiveness of Shakespeare's figures of speech. In a close reading of Sonnet 124, Mizener asserts that here, as in other examples of Shakespeare's finest verses, the poet imbued individual words and images with multiple connotations, all of which are of equal significance; no single association may be emphasized at the expense of the others, the critic contends, if the reader wishes to appreciate the rich complexity of Shakespeare's figurative language.

Muir, Kenneth. "Commentary." In William Shakespeare, *Shakespeare's Sonnets,* edited by Kenneth Muir, pp. 45-87. London: George Allen & Unwin, 1979.

Divides the sonnets into nine sections and highlights the central and subordinate themes in each group. Muir's overview of the entire sequence also includes a discussion of imagery and wordplay, as well as the contrasts and linkages within single sections and between one group and the next.

Neely, Carol Thomas. "Detachment and Engagement in Shakespeare's Sonnets: 94, 116, and 129." *PMLA* 92, No. 1 (January 1977): 83-95.

A line-by-line analysis demonstrating how Shakespeare achieves the effect of motionlessness and impersonality in these three sonnets. The moments when the speaker appears to have controlled a painful emotion or resolved an issue are only transitory, Neely argues, for all three sonnets are followed by verses as full of conflict as those that precede them.

———. "The Structure of English Renaissance Sonnet Sequences." *ELH* 45, No. 3 (Fall 1978): 359-89.

An overview of the structural similarities and differences between English and Italian sonnet sequences. Neely discusses the English sonneteers' modifications of the primary strategy— the division into two unequal parts— developed by Dante and Petrarch, and she also calls attention to their different ways of beginning and ending a sequence. Her survey includes the major sonnet sequences of Sidney, Spenser, Shakespeare, and Milton as well as the minor ones of Watson, Barnes, Drayton, and Daniel.

Peterson, Douglas L. "Shakespeare's Sonnets." In *The English Lyric from Wyatt to Donne,* pp. 212-51. Princeton: Princeton University Press, 1967.

Evaluates the sonnets in the context of both the plain and courtly poetics developed by Shakespeare's predecessors and contemporaries. Throughout his analysis of such stylistic elements as sound and syntax, meta-

phorical language, paradox and antithesis, Peterson emphasizes Shakespeare's freshness and originality— even as he notes that the poet's graceful compliments and verbal ingenuity are distinctive traits of the well-established courtly tradition.

Platt, Michael. "Shakespearean Wisdom?" In *Shakespeare as Political Thinker,* edited by John Alvis and Thomas G. West, pp. 257-76. Durham: Carolina Academic Press, 1981.

An exploration of the subject of the first line of Sonnet 94— "*They* that have pow'r to hurt and will do none"— in relation to the nature and value of dramatic art. Platt suggests that in this sonnet Shakespeare is addressing himself: a dramatist who has the ability to move others yet who must use his natural gifts not in a life of action and deeds but in solitude, where he may come to understand himself and thereby all humanity.

Shore, David R. "'So Long Lives This': Turning to Poetry in Shakespeare's Sonnets." *English Studies in Canada* 14, No. 1 (March 1988): 1-14.

Maintains that Sonnet 18 expresses Shakespeare's belief that through his poetry he can recreate not the individual beauty of his Friend but rather the human experience of beauty for generations of imaginative readers. Shore urges that this sonnet be read in conjunction with numbers 15-17 in order to apprehend fully Shakespeare's faith in the power— and the limitations— of poetry to defeat time.

Smith, Marion Bodwell. "The Poetry of Ambivalence." In *Dualities in Shakespeare,* pp. 53-78. Toronto: University of Toronto Press, 1966.

Analyzes Shakespeare's ambivalent treatment of love and art in the sonnets. Smith identifies a progressive moment in the sequence, from a search for absolutes in the early parts, to acknowledgment of differences and imperfections in the middle sections, and the poet's ultimate acceptance of the contradictions of life. Smith remarks that as Shakespeare's perspective on what is true in love and poetry becomes less simplistic, his use of paradox and ambiguity increases.

Stapleton, M. L. "'My False Eyes': The Dark Lady and Self-Knowledge." *Studies in Philology* XC, No. 2 (Spring 1993): 213-30

Focuses on the persona of "Will," the speaker of Sonnets 127-54, and the accuracy of his account of the Dark Lady. Stapleton asserts that Will is a liar and an antifeminist whose descriptions of his mistress are not just inconsistent but unreliable as well.

Stockard, Emily E. "Patterns of Consolation in Shakespeare's Sonnets 1-126." *Studies in Philology* XCIV, No. 4 (Fall 1997): 465-93.

Examines the different strategies of argumentation employed by the poet as he searches for comfort in the face of the inevitable loss of love. As each traditional means of consolation fails him, Stockard contends, the speaker tries to redefine the problem to fit another mode of rationalization, but ultimately he acknowledges that all explanations are illusory and self-deceptive.

Wilson, Katharine M. "The Dark Lady." In her *Shakespeare's Sugared Sonnets,* pp. 81-144. London: George Allen & Unwin, 1974.

Reads the Dark Lady poems as Shakespeare's parody of the artificial language and themes of other English sonneteers. Wilson illustrates her argument with extensive comparisons of the Dark Lady sonnets with the courtly love verses of Constable, Watson, Daniel, Barnes, Wyatt, Sidney, and others.

Winny, James. "The Dark Lady." In *The Master-Mistress,* pp. 90-120. London: Chatto & Windus, 1968.

A frequently cited essay on the Dark Lady sequence that treats these sonnets as both an exploration of the speaker's emotional life— his struggle to understand his powerlessness to resist a passion he increasingly recognizes as morally worthless— and a satiric undermining of conventional Petrarchan attitudes toward love. Winny notes that the progress of the relationship between the poet and the woman is not at all straightforward, and he finds even less of a narrative here than in the poems that involve the young man.

Media Adaptations

Shakespeare's Sonnets. Caedmon Audio, 1963, 1996.
120 sonnets. Read by Sir John Gielgud. 2 cassettes. ISBN 0-69450-770-9.

The Complete Sonnets of William Shakespeare: With "A Lover's Complaint" & Selected Songs. Dove Books Audio, 1996.
154 sonnets, *A Lover's Complaint,* and songs from Shakespeare's plays. Read and performed by Roscoe Lee Browne (narrator), Christopher Cazenove, Vanessa Redgrave, Elliot Gould, Alfre Woodward, and Michael York. 2 cassettes. ISBN 0-78710-650-X.

William Shakespeare: The Sonnets. HighBridge Classics, 1996.
154 sonnets. Read by Simon Callow. 2 cassettes. ISBN 1-56511-137-0.

William Shakespeare: The Sonnets. Naxos AudioBooks, 1997.
154 sonnets. Read by Alex Jennings. 3 cassettes. ISBN 9-62634-645-0.

THE WINTER'S TALE

INTRODUCTION

Most scholars agree that Shakespeare wrote *The Winter's Tale* in late 1610 or early 1611. The play's first known performance occurred at the Globe Theatre on May 15, 1611. Scholars have made speculative attempts at a more accurate dating of the play's composition, but such theories have not gained widespread acceptance. What most critics do agree upon is that the style and themes of *The Winter's Tale* clearly link the play to Shakespeare's other late romances. They conclude that *The Winter's Tale* is therefore a product of Shakespeare's final period of play writing, and that the play was most likely composed after *Cymbeline*, which is believed to have been written in 1609-10.

The primary source for *The Winter's Tale* is a novel by Robert Green entitled *Pandosto; or, The Triumph of Time*, which was first published in 1588. The novel was reprinted a number of times after 1607 as *Dorastus and Fawnia*. In *Pandosto*, the title character is driven by passionate jealousy to drive away his friend and banish his infant daughter. This results in the deaths of Pandosto's wife and young son. Although this basic format closely parallels *The Winter's Tale*, Shakespeare did make some significant alterations to his source. Leontes's jealousy is quite sudden, compared with that of Pandosto. In Greene's novel, Pandosto is presented with an array of circumstantial evidence before his jealousy erupts. Also, the characters of Paulina, Autolycus, and the figure of Time are entirely Shakespearean creations. Other additions to the source include Shakespeare's sheep-shearing scene (Act IV, scene iv), and the statue scene (Act V, scene iii). Perhaps the most drastic alteration to Greene's novel is the restoration of both Perdita and Hermione to Leontes. In Greene's story, Pandosto's wife truly does die, and Pandosto commits suicide after learning that Fawnia, whom he has attempted to seduce, is in fact his long-lost daughter.

Little is known about the reactions of seventeenth-century audiences and critics to *The Winter's Tale*. Simon Forman wrote the first known account of the play in the form of a journal entry in which he summarizes the play's plot. Forman was most impressed by the character of Autolycus. Ben Johnson, Shakespeare's contemporary and rival, noted with displeasure a geographical inaccuracy in the play, which also appeared in Shakespeare's source, Greene's *Pandosto*. Both Greene and Shakespeare write about the seacoast of Bohemia, which in fact, was a landlocked country. (Today, Bohemia is a region in Western Czechoslovakia and was formerly a part of Austria.) John Dryden considered *The Winter's Tale* to be one of Shakespeare's failed plays, along with *Pericles, Measure for Measure*, and *Love's Labour's Lost*. All of these plays, Dryden comments, are based on impossibilities, or so poorly written that the comic parts do not result in laughter, nor do the serious parts produce concern.

The action of the play is generated by Leontes's jealousy. Perdita's banishment, Mamillius's death, and Hermione's supposed death are all effects of Leontes's jealous rage. It is not surprising then, that many scholars and students of the play focus on the question of whether or not Leontes's jealousy is improbable. Few would argue that the king's reaction is justified, but some maintain that Leontes's jealousy is not a sudden and rash reaction, but rather has been building for some time and is present from the play's beginning. Others have analyzed Leontes's jealousy as one aspect of a personality that is obsessed with childhood.

Other issues that have generated critical commentary center on the play's combination of tragic, comic, and pastoral elements; on the debate between art and nature in the play; and on the dramatic effect and meaning of Hermione's restoration. Some critics find that the pastoral and comic elements of the play help to alleviate the tragic aspects; others argue that the pastoral elements are dark and disturbing in many ways. Two scenes in the play focus specifically on the art versus nature controversy: Act IV, scene iv, in which Polixenes and Perdita discuss the merits of cross breeding or grafting in flowers; and Act V, scene iii, where the "statue" of Hermione is revealed to be Hermione herself. These scenes are either read as evidence that Shakespeare was arguing that art *is* nature, or alternatively, that art is necessary to "mend" or perfect nature. In the last scene of the play, Paulina presents Hermione's statue and commands her to "descend" and reveal herself. Some commentators view this scene and the fact that Hermione has concealed herself for sixteen years as highly unlikely. They assert that Hermione's restoration was a cheap stage trick, designed to delight the audience but possessing little literary value. Others stress that Hermione's concealment is entirely justified, and that her restoration at the play's end is moving and significant.

PRINCIPAL CHARACTERS

(in order of appearance)

Archidamus: A Bohemian lord. He appears in the first scene and tells Camillo that Bohemia could not offer its guests the same magnificence that Sicilia has offered to the Bohemian entourage. He also speaks of the bond between Leontes and Polixenes.

Camillo: A Sicilian lord and Leontes's trusted advisor. He is ordered by Leontes to poison Polixenes, but instead informs Polixenes of Leontes's plot against him. Camillo guides Polixenes from Sicilia and accompanies him to Bohemia. Sixteen years later, Camillo laments his lost friendship with Leontes. After Camillo and Polixenes discover Florizel's relationship with Perdita, Camillo advises the young couple to flee for Sicilia. At the play's end, Leontes selects Camillo to be Paulina's husband.

Polixenes: King of Bohemia, boyhood friend of Leontes. Polixenes announces that after a nine-month stay in Sicilia, he must return to Bohemia. He refuses Leontes's request that he extend his visit, but after Hermione entreats him as well, he agrees. Polixenes flees for Bohemia when Camillo informs him that Leontes suspects Polixenes and Hermione are having an affair. Sixteen years later, Polixenes is infuriated by his son Florizel's desire to wed a young shepherd girl, who is really Perdita, Leontes's daughter.

Leontes: King of Sicilia, boyhood friend of Polixenes. Leontes suddenly becomes convinced that Hermione and Polixenes are intimately involved. In his jealousy, he plots to poison Polixenes and imprisons Hermione. In his mother's absence, Mamillius dies. Leontes also banishes his infant daughter, sending her to a remote area of Bohemia to live or die. Following Mamillius's death, it is announced that Hermione, whom Leontes has convicted of adultery, has also died. After presuming Hermione to be dead for sixteen years, Leontes is reunited with her and with his daughter in the last act of the play. *(See* **Leontes** *in the* **CHARACTER STUDIES** *section.)*

Hermione: Leontes's wife, the Queen of Sicilia. At Leontes's request, Hermione successfully entreats Polixenes to extend his visit in Sicilia. As a result, Hermione is tried and convicted of adultery, despite the fact that the oracle has exonerated her. Hermione conceals herself for sixteen years. She next appears in the last scene of the play, when a statue of her apparently comes to life. *(See* **Hermione** *in the* **CHARACTER STUDIES** *section.)*

Mamillius: Young son of Leontes and Hermione. When Leontes becomes convinced of Hermione's infidelity, he removes Mamillius from his mother's presence. Mamillius becomes sick and dies.

Antigonus: A Sicilian lord, husband of Paulina. Antigonus opposes Leontes's treatment of Hermione and Hermione's infant daughter. When threatened by Leontes's charge of treason, Antigonus takes the baby to Bohemia and abandons her. Before doing so, he

places a bundle next to her. The bundle proclaims the baby Perdita's true identity. With a storm coming, Antigonus heads for the ship waiting for him, but is pursued and devoured by a bear.

Paulina: Wife of Antigonus. Paulina speaks out boldly against Leontes's treatment of Hermione and the baby Perdita. After Hermione's apparent death, Paulina refuses to let Leontes forget about his wife or his actions. She advises Leontes not to remarry. In the last scene, Paulina presents the "statue" of Hermione. Leontes, Hermione, and Perdita are then reunited. *(See* **Paulina** *in the* **CHARACTER STUDIES** *section.)*

Jailer: Having custody of Hermione after Leontes's sends her to prison, the jailer refuses to allow Paulina to see Hermione. He does however let Paulina speak with Emilia, Hermione's lady-in-waiting. He eventually agrees to allow Paulina to take the baby Perdita from the prison.

Emilia: Lady-in-waiting to Hermione. Emilia accompanies Hermione to prison and tells Paulina that Hermione has given birth to a baby girl. Emilia agrees with Paulina's plan to take the baby to Leontes.

Perdita: Daughter of Leontes and Hermione. As a baby, Perdita is abandoned by Antigonus at the request of her father. She is given her name, which means "the lost one" by Antigonus, who dreams that Hermione appears to him and instructs him to so name the child. Perdita is raised in rural Bohemia by the shepherd who discovers her. After sixteen years have passed, Perdita falls in love with Polixenes's son Florizel. Perdita escapes with Florizel to Sicilia after Polixenes learns of their relationship.

Cleomines and *Dion*: Sicilian lords. Cleomines and Dion are sent to Apollo's temple in Delphi to bring back the proclamation of the oracle, the god Apollo's revelation. The oracle's proclamation is thought to contain the truth concerning Leontes's accusation against Hermione, yet Leontes dismisses this revelation, which exonerates Hermione.

Mariner: The mariner captains the ship which transports Antigonus to Bohemia. Worried about the threatening storm, the mariner pleads with Antigonus to be quick. The mariner is drowned when the storm sinks his ship.

Shepherd: Perdita's adoptive father. He finds Perdita after Antigonus has abandoned her and raises her as his own. At the end of the play, he is made a gentleman.

Clown: Son of the Shepherd. He recounts to his father the shepherd that a bear has eaten a man (Antigonus), and that a ship has sunk in the storm. At the end of the play, the Clown is made a gentleman.

Time: The Chorus, appearing at the beginning of Act IV as the personification of Time. Time informs the audience that sixteen years have passed since the last scene.

Autolycus: A rogue, rover, and thief. He picks the clown's pocket and successfully robs a number of people at the sheep shearing festival. Autolycus trades clothes with Florizel at Florizel's command, enabling the prince and Perdita to escape to Sicilia. He also directs the old shepherd and his son to Sicilia, where they reveal the truth of Perdita's identity. *(See* **Autolycus** *in the* **CHARACTER STUDIES** *section.)*

Florizel: Son of Polixenes. Florizel falls in love with Perdita, whom he believes to be a shepherd's daughter. In disguise, Florizel speaks to his also-disguised father and informs him of his plan to marry Perdita. In response to Polixenes's rage and at Camillo's advice, Florizel and Perdita flee to Sicilia. In Sicilia, Perdita's true identity is revealed. Known to be of royal birth, Perdita is now free to marry Florizel.

Mopsa: A shepherdess. She is the Clown's sweetheart, and she dances with him at the sheep shearing festival. After the Clown buys sheet music from Autolycus, Mopsa, Dorcas and Autolycus sing a ballad together.

Dorcas: A shepherdess. She dances at the sheep shearing festival and is eager to buy ribbons Autolycus. After the Clown buys sheet music from Autolycus, Mopsa, Dorcas and Autolycus sing a ballad together.

PLOT SYNOPSIS

Act I: In Sicilia, King Leontes attempts to persuade his boyhood friend, King Polixenes of Bohemia, to extend his nine-month visit. Polixenes objects, stating that he has pressing business at home. Leontes then requests that his wife Hermione intercede. At the pregnant Hermione's insistence, Polixenes agrees to stay. Leontes then reveals that he believes Hermione and Polixenes to be secretly having an affair. After questioning his advisor Camillo about his suspicions, which Camillo does not believe, Leontes orders Camillo to poison Polixenes. Camillo agrees, but later informs Polixenes of Leontes's plot instead. Polixenes assures Camillo that in Bohemia, the Sicilian lord would enjoy the same status and privileges he now knows, and Camillo agrees to guide Polixenes and his entourage out of Sicilia.

Act II: Leontes learns that Camillo has betrayed him and Polixenes has fled. The report fuels Leontes's jealous rage. He confronts Hermione, accusing her of adultery. Leontes removes Mamillius from Hermione's presence and sends his wife to prison. Antigonus objects to Leontes's actions but Leontes dismisses him. The King sends Cleomines and Dion to consult the

oracle at Apollo's temple at Delphi; the messengers are to return with the oracle's proclamation regarding the truth about Hermione and Polixenes. After Hermione gives birth to a baby girl, the child is taken by Paulina, Antigonus's wife, to Leontes in the hopes that the sight of the baby will soften Leontes's attitude toward Hermione. Paulina is a strong advocate for the baby and Hermione, and Leontes accuses Antigonus of being hen-pecked for being unable or unwilling to silence his wife. After Paulina departs, Leontes demands that Antigonus take the baby to some remote destination and abandon her.

Act III: Hermione is brought to trial on the charge of adultery. After offering words in her own defense, in which Hermione claims her innocence, Cleomines and Dion return with the oracle's proclamation: "Hermione is chaste" (III.i.132). Leontes, however, pronounces the oracle false. At this point, a servant enters and announces that Mamillius has died. Hermione is escorted from the room after fainting, and Leontes asks that she be ministered to. Leontes privately asks for the god Apollo's forgiveness, and promises to make amends to Polixenes. Paulina then enters to announce that Hermione has died of grief. At the end of Act III, Antigonus abandons the baby girl in a remote part of Bohemia, leaving a bundle with her, which contains money and her true identification. Fleeing an oncoming storm, Antigonus exits, "pursued by a bear" (III.iii.58). A shepherd discovers the baby, and his son reports having seen a ship sink off the coast and a bear devouring a man.

Act IV: The act opens with Time proclaiming that sixteen years have passed since the end of Act III. In the Bohemian court, Camillo tells Polixenes that he wishes to visit Leontes, but Polixenes convinces Camillo to remain in Bohemia. Polixenes and Camillo attend the sheep shearing festival at the home of the old shepherd who has raised Perdita. Perdita is dressed as the mock queen of the festival, and Florizel is dressed like a rustic. The audience learns that they are in love, and that Florizel intends to keep the relationship a secret from his father. Polixenes and Camillo enter in disguise, and eventually discover Florizel's secret. Polixenes scolds Florizel, and threatens to scar Perdita and punish her shepherd father as well. At Camillo's urging, Florizel and Perdita escape to Sicilia. The shepherd and his son, who are aided by Autolycus, follow them. Autolycus is hoping to reveal Perdita's true identity to Florizel and thereby profit from this revelation himself.

Act V: In Sicilia, Leontes's advisors urge him to remarry in order to conceive an heir. Paulina reminds Leontes of part of the oracle's prediction, that Leontes would have no heir unless his lost child was found. After Paulina scolds Leontes for betraying Hermione's memory, he agrees not to marry unless Paulina finds him a suitable wife. Soon after Florizel and Perdita arrive, a servant announces that Polixenes and Camillo have also returned to Sicilia, and that Polixenes is holding the shepherd and the clown captive. Polixenes also demands that Florizel and Perdita be arrested. In a series of events, many of the play's complexities are now untangled. Primarily, Perdita's true identity is discovered, Perdita and Leontes are reunited, and Polixenes and Leontes are reconciled. The shepherd and his son are elevated to the status of gentleman for raising Perdita. Perdita requests to see the statue of her mother, which she is told is in Paulina's possession. Paulina presents the statue, and everyone is amazed at how lifelike it is. Paulina then commands that Hermione descend from her pedestal; the queen is alive. After Hermione addresses her long lost daughter, Leontes announces that Camillo and Paulina will marry. The group exits to discuss the events of the past sixteen years.

PRINCIPAL TOPICS

Pastoral Elements

A pastoral is a poem or play dealing with shepherds and rural life. Within the conventional treatment of pastoral themes, this rural way of life is idealized. In *The Winter's Tale*, the pastoral scenes or "pastoral interlude" as it is often referred to, begins in Act III, scene iii, when the action of the play shifts from Sicilia to Bohemia. In Act IV, which begins with Time announcing that sixteen years have past, the interlude continues through the last scene of this act. With the passage of time and the movement from the Sicilian court to the Bohemian countryside comes a movement from the tragedy of the first three acts to comedy. The lightness of comedy reaches into the play's final act, in which the pastoral characters journey to the Sicilian court. The pastoral scenes, with their rustic figures, festival, singing and dancing, serve as a sharp contrast to the more somber and cold world of the Sicilian court. Despite this contrast, the pastoral world is not free from the darkness that looms over the courtly world in Sicilia. Commentary on the pastoral scenes focuses heavily on the fact that, unlike the conventional pastoral, Shakespeare's pastoral is not completely idyllic. In the pastoral world, a terrible storm threatens as Antigonus arrives in Bohemia with the baby Perdita. Before Antigonus can escape to his ship he is chased and later devoured by a bear. Polixenes's angry outburst in Act IV, scene iv, is also cited as another indication that all is not ideal in this pastoral setting, especially since his rage is reminiscent of Leontes's wrath against his wife. Leontes's anger, it will be remembered, sets into motion the events causing the abandonment of the baby Perdita, the death of Mamillius, and the presumed death of Hermione. Other elements in the pastoral scene

which tarnish the idealism of the pastoral vision include the suggestion that perhaps the old shepherd who raised Perdita is motivated by greed, the hint that Perdita and Florizel are on the verge of losing their innocence, and the presence at the sheep shearing festival of the thieving Autolycus, as well as that of Camillo and Polixenes, royal individuals foreign to the pastoral setting.

Despite such aspects darkening the lightness of the pastoral interlude, many commentators have noted how the pastoral setting and characters nevertheless engender a feeling of hopefulness. Perdita, some have observed, is portrayed as an idealized pastoral figure, and in her attitude toward life she helps the audience to embrace the view of time that Shakespeare presents. (Some critics see Shakespeare's view of time as eroding and destructive, in that it moves persistently forward. Others note that it is only after the passage of time—sixteen years— that healing and reconciliation occur in this play.) Additionally, Perdita and the pastoral scenes themselves celebrate the possibility of familial and societal restoration. Perdita is a pastoral figure though of noble birth, and through her return families and friends are reunited and reconciled.

Art and Nature

The debate between art and nature was a common one in Shakespeare's time and in fact had been argued since antiquity. Within this debate, art is understood to be the applying of human intervention, imagination, or knowledge to what nature has created. The central issue is whether or not art can or should perfect nature. Can art make what is natural appear to be more natural? A common point brought up in early debates and relevant today is the notion of using cosmetics to achieve a "natural," fresh look by hiding one's natural imperfections. In two scenes in particular in *The Winter's Tale*, this debate is taken up once again. The first scene is Act IV, scene iv, in which Perdita and a disguised Polixenes analyze the practice of cross breeding of flowers. The statue scene, Act V, scene iii, in which a statue of Hermione is revealed to be Hermione herself, is the other scene in which this debate is revisited. Critical commentary on these scenes focuses on explicating the stances taken up by Perdita and Polixenes and on attempting to determine where Shakespeare may have stood on the issue. In the discussion between Polixenes and Perdita, Polixenes states the view that art *is* nature. One may speak of art perfecting nature, but in a sense, this really means that nature is perfecting itself. Perdita objects to the art's deceptive, imitative, and artificial nature. It has also been noted that Perdita does not object to the practice of art itself, but to the impulse behind its practice, that is, the desire to produce something more attractive than what nature has created. Many critics have noted the dramatic irony of these speeches. While Polixenes expresses the value of marrying "wild" stock to more noble flowers, he takes the opposite view where his son Florizel is concerned, staunchly opposing the marriage of a royal prince to a shepherd girl. Similarly, Perdita defends the view that differing stock should not be interbred; at the same time, she is (to her knowledge) a rustic country girl seeking to marry a prince. While many critics agree on the ironic tone of these speeches, one has pointed out that perhaps these lines are not as ironic as many make them out to be. Just because a person believes something is right for flowers, does not mean he needs to consistently apply this belief to himself or his children. In any event, Perdita is of noble blood; art is not necessary to perfect her nature to make her worthy of marriage to Florizel. It is often pointed out as well that in the statue scene, what seems to be art in the form of Hermione's statue, is in fact nature; the statue *is* Hermione. Some critics have concluded that Shakespeare either adheres to the view that art is, in itself, nature, or that the playwright does not advocate the primacy of art or nature.

Others have found that the play seems to say that art is necessary to perfect, or "mend" nature. In Act IV, scene iv, Perdita presents flowers to Polixenes and Camillo. The flowers are meant to be appropriate to the men's ages, as seasons of the year were viewed as corresponding to the seasons of a person's life. Perdita appears to see through Polixenes disguise, for she apologizes for not having the appropriate flowers for his age, those blooming in late summer, or appropriate for late middle age. The reason she has no such flowers are because these flowers are grown by the procedure of grafting or cross-breeding, which Perdita finds to be unnatural. The metaphor some critics see in this exchange is that artificially bred flowers are those which correspond to an age in a man's life. Art must be employed to produce such flowers, and is therefore necessary to mend nature and to allow man to pass from one season of life to the next. Similarly, it is often held that art's interference is necessary for Leontes to move on in his life. Human intervention interferes with the natural order in several ways. Camillo interferes by influencing Florizel to take Perdita to Sicilia. Paulina interferes by counseling Leontes in his repentance, and in advising him not to marry again. Hermione pretends she is dead and then is later restored. By this reading of events, human intervention upon nature or natural order is necessary to bring about the play's happy ending.

Gender Issues

The relationship between gender roles and power is often explored in *The Winter's Tale*. The societies of Sicilia and Bohemia in the play are patriarchies. A patriarchal society is one in which a father, or father-figure, represents the society's supreme authority. Com-

mentary on this subject often centers around Leontes's effort to maintain his power, as well as on the role of women within Leontes's patriarchy. Patriarchal power is passed on from father to son. It has been suggested that Leontes's jealous attack on Hermione stems from his fear of disturbing the patriarchal succession. In order to produce male heirs to his power, Leontes needs his wife to be faithful to him. The transfer of male power is further disabled when Leontes fails to properly care for his son Mamillius. Hermione has not been able to care for her son since she has been imprisoned and kept apart from Mamillius. As a result, Mamillius dies. Patriarchal power is also upset through the character of Paulina. She challenges Leontes, pleading on behalf of Hermione and the baby Perdita. Although she is dismissed by Leontes, whereas male courtiers who have challenged him have been tolerated, Paulina later develops a level of control over him. After berating him repeatedly for his actions, Paulina becomes Leontes's confessor and advisor, counseling him to repent his sins and not to remarry. Despite Paulina's power, patriarchal authority appears to be stronger. Leontes and Polixenes reconcile, notably before the reconciliation takes place between Hermione and Leontes. As male bonds are renewed, Leontes also announces that Paulina will marry Camillo. Some critics note that while Leontes has learned to view women with some respect, Paulina, Hermione, and Perdita are transformed from threatening figures who challenge male authority into nurturing, supportive figures. By the play's end, the women are restored to their "proper" places within the patriarchy.

Commentators also observe that the women who challenge male power in the play are all slandered. Hermione is accused of being an adulteress, and she is punished for it, losing both of her children in the process. Also, Leontes names Paulina a "mankind witch" (II.ii.68). Perdita, too, is accused of witchcraft, when Polixenes claims that Perdita has seduced Florizel. Polixenes calls her "fresh piece / Of excellent witchcraft" (IV.iv.422-23). It has been suggested that what seems to be male anxiety about female sexuality, both in the play and in Shakespeare's England where there were strict laws regulating female behavior and sexuality, is really male fear of female power.

CHARACTER STUDIES

Leontes

In Act I, scene ii, of *The Winter's Tale*, Polixenes, after a nine-month stay in Sicilia, is preparing to depart for home. Leontes unsuccessfully requests that Polixenes stay, and then asks his wife Hermione to implore their guest to extend his visit. Hermione succeeds, and shortly after Leontes is convinced that his friend and his wife are having an affair. His jealousy explodes suddenly and seemingly without cause, confounding students and scholars alike. Some commentators view Leontes's jealousy as a weakness inherent in his character. Similarly, some say that Leontes is by nature a coarse, physical, and sensual man. While his jealousy may be irrational, they say, it is not unnatural. Another approach is sometimes taken in the examination of Leontes's jealousy as an aspect of his character. Some critics suggest that Leontes is hampered by his obsession with his childhood. This produces in him a tendency to view the world narrowly, to be rash and petulant, to make sweeping judgements based on limited experience with human nature, and to fail to properly attend to his wife's emotional needs. Others contend that this inexplicable jealousy is a flaw in Shakespeare's dramatic construction, one of many such improbabilities in the play, some commentators maintain. Despite some critical admonition against reading too much into the text, still other commentators believe that Leontes's jealousy is actually not abrupt, but has been present from the beginning of the play. When Leontes consults with Camillo about the matter of Hermione's supposed infidelity, Leontes seems to indicate that he has witnessed Polixenes and Hermione together, prior to the occasion where Hermione convinces Polixenes to stay. In I.ii.284-86, Leontes, speaking of Hermione and Polixenes, asks Camillo, "Is whispering nothing? / Is leaning cheek to cheek? Is meeting noses? / Kissing with inside lip?" When Hermione is successful in detaining Polixenes, Leontes takes this as evidence of their guilt, confirmation of his long-simmering suspicion.

Leontes's jealousy has often been contrasted with that of Shakespeare's Othello. Whereas Othello's jealousy increases gradually and is fed by Iago's insinuations against Desdemona, the development of Leontes's jealousy is not portrayed in *The Winter's Tale*. Some say that this is due to Shakespeare's greater interest in the effects, rather than the cause of Leontes's jealousy. Similarly, it has also been suggested that Leontes himself should not be treated realistically, or analyzed as man. Rather, Shakespeare's focus was on jealousy as a force of evil in the play, and Leontes serves primarily as a vehicle for introducing this force into the play.

Hermione

Hermione's moral goodness has seldom been impugned. Many critics extol her virtues, among them honesty, patience, and dignity. In the opening scenes she is shown to be vivacious and happy, even assuming when Leontes first confronts her with her supposed infidelity that he is joking. Tested by Leontes's insane jealousy, she sheds her formerly light-hearted nature, and is given the opportunity to demonstrate the strength of her character. The trial scene (Act III, scene ii), in which Hermione

defends herself against Leontes's accusation of adultery, is often used to demonstrate Hermione's moral strengths. Hermione realizes that the power of the words she speaks in her own defense depend upon how they will be received by Leontes, who has already attacked her reputation. Nevertheless, she proceeds to argue for the nobility of her reputation, asserting herself as the daughter of a king and the mother of a prince. She next answers the formal charges brought against her, noting that Leontes commanded her to appeal to Polixenes. Her final argument defies Leontes's threat of death. Hermione answers that given all she has lost, including her children and her reputation, she would welcome death. Despite Hermione's honesty and eloquence, Leontes is not swayed. When Hermione hears that Mamillius has died, she faints, and it is later announced that she is dead.

The ensuing sixteen-year exile of Hermione, combined with her "resurrection" at the end of the play has been the object of much critical debate. Some scholars view her long absence and the illusion that her statue comes to life as two of the plays glaring improbabilities. Others explain her absence by claiming that her highly principled nature lead her to conceal herself from her husband, who was responsible for the loss of both her children, as well as her reputation. It is also suggested that the extended absence was necessary for her to completely forgive Leontes. Hermione, after stepping down from her statue-like position in the play's last scene, addresses only Perdita. To her long-lost daughter, Hermione reveals that the oracle gave her hope that Perdita lived, and that is why Hermione has "preserved" herself (V.iii.126-28). While commentators often criticize the coming-to-life of Hermione's statue as a cheap stage trick, and as so highly improbably as to mar the scene and the whole play, others praise the effect Shakespeare creates. The fact that Hermione is not in fact dead receives no foreshadowing. Additionally, Antigonus and Mamillius have both died very real deaths in the play, giving the audience no reason to believe that Hermione lives. For these reasons, it is explained, Hermione's restoration is all the more stunning, powerful, and satisfying.

Paulina

Paulina is closely linked to Leontes, and she is often studied in this capacity. At the same time, she is considered a pivotal character in her own right. Her relationship to Leontes is described in terms of stock characterization; she plays the shrew to Leontes's tyrant. In this capacity, some critics observe, Paulina helps to soften the way the audience perceives Leontes. It would be easy to judge Leontes and despise him throughout the entire play. However, when Leontes plays the henpecked, scolded victim of Paulina's harsh and much-repeated accusations, the effect of seeing the two char-

A party scene in Sicilia from the Stratford Festival's 1986 production of The Winter's Tale.

acters in these roles is intended to be somewhat comic. Additionally, the situation also creates a sense of sympathy for Leontes. Commentators suggest that the effect of the stock characterization of Paulina and Leontes is to use the comedy and sympathy aroused to forestall the audience's judgement of Leontes. It is also stressed that despite Shakespeare's placement of Paulina in the role of the shrew, she remains a credible character. Other critics have noted that Paulina does not simply become Leontes's confessor in the latter portions of the play. Rather, she transforms the "shrew" role; her words to Leontes serve as the voice of his conscience.

In addition to the way in which Paulina's character influences Leontes and the audience's perception of Leontes, Paulina is also examined as an active player in the plot, as well as a keen observer of other characters and important events. Additionally, it is noted that Paulina is in many ways the play's stage director; her intervention makes things happen. She guides Leontes's penance and convinces him not to remarry. In this capacity, she is described as a voice of hope. She wishes to see Leontes and Hermione reunited, and to do this, she must insure that Leontes remember Hermione and what he has done. Paulina also assists in keeping Hermione's secret and directs the action of the last scene of the play, in which she reveals that the "statue" of Hermione is Hermione herself. Paulina does not stand passively by in this scene; she engineers its spectacle, presenting the statue to Leontes, ordering music to be played and commanding Hermione to step down from her pedestal.

Playing a key role in defying Leontes's authority, Paulina is not afraid to speak out against him. She is labeled a "mankind witch" for doing so, an insult that implies she practices in sexual perversity and forbidden arts. In refusing to succumb to masculine power, she is viewed as something less than, or other than a woman. After Mamillius's death, however, Leontes alters his behavior toward Paulina, accepting both her strength and the verbal punishment for his tyranny that she dispenses.

Autolycus

Autolycus has received generally favorable reviews as a comic character. He is described as charming, funny, and a welcome realistic element in the pastoral world. Apparently viewed by many as relatively harmless, Autolycus claims to prefer cheating to robbery, as it is less dangerous. He proves himself to be a good showman and con-man, selling cheap trinkets to customers and singing them bawdy ballads before slitting their purses. Directly involved in the plot on two occasions, Autolycus does some good in spite of himself. He trades clothes with Florizel at Florizel's command, enabling the prince and Perdita to escape Polixenes's wrath. Also, Autolycus directs the old shepherd and his son to Sicilia, where they reveal the truth of Perdita's identity. It may be noted that he does so, however, hoping to profit from the revelation about Perdita's identity himself. Other critics have found that Autolycus is not simply a source of comedy, a loveable rogue. He is in fact, still a thief. His victimization of the shepherd and the clown is often viewed as a comic event. However, the shepherd and his son are not just rustic bumpkins, as some assume. They posses their own simple dignity, and as objects of Autolycus's thieving designs, they arouse some sympathy, not just laughter. Another dark side to Autolycus is shown to be his parallel with Leontes. In Act IV, scene iv, the disguised Autolycus threatens the clown with torture, and seemingly does so with considerable relish. This abuse of power is seen as a parallel to the similar threats Polixenes has made earlier in the scene to Perdita and Florizel, and also as a parallel to Leontes's own abuse of power, which leads to the death of Mamillius, the abandonment of Perdita, and the apparent death of Hermione.

CONCLUSION

With its mixture of tragic, comic, and pastoral elements, *The Winter's Tale* is found to be many things to many people: entertaining, problematic, meaningful, frivolous. Nevertheless, Shakespeare's dramatization of the effects of jealousy and the possibility of reconciliation even after much time has passed continue to draw scholars and students to this play.

OVERVIEW

Jack A. Vaughn

SOURCE: "'The Winter's Tale,'" in *Shakespeare's Comedies*, Frederick Ungar Publishing Co., 1980, pp. 201-211.

[In this essay, Vaughn offers an introduction to The Winter's Tale, *commenting on the date the play was written and the source material Shakespeare used. Vaughn discusses in more detail the structure, plot, characters, and themes in the play. Additionally, Vaughn notes that many critics focus on inconsistencies in the play, but Vaughn himself views these problems as minor.]*

In *The Winter's Tale* (1610-11) Shakespeare brought to near perfection the form of tragicomic romance— the genre with which he had been experimenting in *Pericles* and *Cymbeline*. This play is the most successful of the three, particularly in terms of theatrical viability. *The Winter's Tale* can be a deeply affecting work on the stage when well acted and directed with sensitivity.

Shakespeare's source for this play was a fictional romance by Robert Greene called *Pandosto, the Triumph of Time*, published in 1588. It provided the basic ingredients that Shakespeare required in fashioning his tragicomic plot: the oracle of Apollo, a shipwreck, an abandoned infant of royal blood, recovery of lost royalty, and so on. Many such elements appear also in *Pericles* and *Cymbeline*, but never in those plays with the degree of narrative credibility, structural unity, and theatrical power as are found in this play. *The Winter's Tale* is romantic in the best Elizabethan sense of the word, "dealing with love in people of high estate, events controlled by supernatural agency and by chance, and heroic adventure in both courtly and arcadian settings."

The play's title provides a clue as to the sort of story we can expect. A "winter's tale" is an old wives' tale— a story of perilous adventures, of "sprites and goblins," told but to while away a winter's evening. And as the young prince Mamillius tells us: "A sad tale's best for winter" (II, i). Ultimately, of course, the tale ends happily, but it contains considerable sadness along the way, including the death of Mamillius himself.

It is the nature of the genre that tragicomic romance necessarily includes some rather implausible and even farfetched story elements, and critics have been quick to point out this play's shortcomings in that respect. How, for example, could Paulina have successfully hidden Hermione away for sixteen years? Why does Hermione say that Paulina told her of the oracle (V, iii) when she herself had heard it read (III, ii)? How can we accept the anachronisms of the Emperor of Russia and the Renaissance painter Julio Romano in a pre-Christian setting? And should not Shakespeare have known that Bohemia has no seacoast? All of these "defects" are, of course, trivial. Such minor inconsistencies may emerge in the reading, but they vanish on the stage. And that is the ultimate test of any drama.

Structurally, *The Winter's Tale* is divided into three main parts. The first part runs through Act III, scene ii, and is an almost totally self-contained drama. By itself, it constitutes a Greek tragedy in miniature, ending with Leontes' realization of his tragic error after the deaths of his queen and son. The single unresolved thread of plot that leads to the second part is the casting out of the infant princess by Antigonus; that is the episode (III, iii) with which the second part begins. This central section of the play provides a pastoral interlude in Bohemia and ends at the conclusion of Act IV. The third part then takes us back to Sicilia for the recovery of the lost princess Perdita and her happy reunion with Leontes and the "resurrected" Hermione. In the progress of this action, sixteen years of dramatic time are presumed to have passed.

Time plays an important role in each of Shakespeare's last four romances; the passage of time serves as a reconstructive or conciliatory influence. In this play especially time is essential in effecting both growth and decay. Time provides the soil that nurtures change, allowing the maturation of Perdita and burying the sorrows caused by Leontes' mad jealousy. The subtitle of the source story by Greene is significant: "The Triumph of Time."

In *Cymbeline* and *The Tempest* time in the story has passed before the play begins; past events are recounted through narrative exposition. In *Pericles* and *The Winter's Tale*, however, the early events of the story are presented on stage, necessitating an interruption in the flow of events. *The Winter's Tale* especially has been criticized for the frankly artificial way in which Shakespeare disposes of sixteen years: the speech, in rhymed couplets, of "Time, as Chorus" at Act IV, scene i:

> I, that please some, try all, both joy and
>   terror
> Of good and bad, that makes and unfolds
>   error,
> Now take upon me, in the name of Time,
> To use my wings. Impute it not a crime
> To me or my swift passage, that I slide
> O'er sixteen years and leave the growth
>   untried
> Of that wide gap.

This major time lapse in the structuring of the plot, although it violates neoclassical ideals of unity, serves a useful purpose in *The Winter's Tale*. It enhances the play's appeal in the theater. How intriguing it is to see both the passionate young Leontes and the older, repentant Leontes; the young Hermione abused, then the mature Hermione serene and triumphant; the dual figures of Paulina, of Camillo, of Polixenes! Much of the theatrical appeal of *The Winter's Tale* would be lost if we were merely to hear recounted in narration the tragic events that constitute the first section of this play. Shakespeare's handling of dramatic time and plot structure here is unconventional—perhaps even "unliterary"—but it makes for first-rate theater.

The tragicomic method of *The Winter's Tale* is quite different from that of *Pericles* and *Cymbeline*. The comic aspect of *Pericles* is minimal and resides almost solely in its happy denouement. The serious and comic elements of *Cymbeline* are fully integrated, occurring simultaneously. In *The Winter's Tale* the tragic action is confined to the first part of the play, while the comic material dominates the second and third parts. The first part of the play is almost unrelievedly solemn, but for the occasional innocent chatter of Mamillius. The tragic tone prevails until Act III, scene iii, a scene that Shakespeare used to good effect in bringing about a transition from the tragic to the comic.

This transitional scene, although set in Bohemia, opens with an extension of the tone and plot of Sicilia: the soliloquy by Antigonus, in which he recounts the visitation of Hermione's ghost. The soliloquy itself signals a shift in tone; its language, unlike the fairly realistic verse of the first part, is fanciful and extravagant. Hermione's ghost, we hear, approached Antigonus "in pure white robes," and, "gasping to begin some speech, her eyes / Became two spouts." After chastising him for casting out the babe, "with shrieks, / She melted into air." The tone of the soliloquy is that of a "winter's tale," spooky and fanciful.

Antigonus' soliloquy is brought to an abrupt conclusion by what is perhaps the most famous stage direction in Shakespeare: *"Exit, pursued by a bear."* However much we may pity the fate of poor Antigonus, the visual effect of this exit is undeniably comic—especially so if the "bear" is an actor in an animal suit. (Sir Arthur Quiller-Couch suggested that Shakespeare conceived this exit to take advantage of an actual trained bear, available from the Bear-Pit in Southwark, near the Globe Theatre.)

The appearance of the bear provides a hilarious piece of visual comedy, which is then quickly followed by the appearances of the Shepherd and the Clown—the former to discover the abandoned princess and the latter to describe the drowning of the sailors and the death of Antigonus in the clutches of the bear. The Clown's description is grotesquely comic as he tells how the "bear tore out his shoulder-bone" and how the "poor gentleman roared and the bear mocked him." Finally the Clown leaves his father to go see "if the bear be gone from the gentleman and how much he hath eaten. . . . If there be any of him left, I'll bury it." By this point Antigonus is no more than a memory, the audience is laughing heartily, and the gaiety of Bohemia is upon us.

Once the scene has shifted to Bohemia, the play never again returns to the tragic tone of the first part, although there are some dark moments in the pastoral scene (IV, iv). Polixenes' angry denunciation of his son's love for Perdita and his threat to disinherit the prince briefly cast a shadow on the jollity of the sheep-shearing festivity. But for the most part Bohemia is a happy place. And the final return to Sicilia is even happier with its joyful reunions and reconciliations.

Although it draws upon the same fanciful story elements of fictional romance that render *Pericles* and *Cymbeline* rather farfetched, *The Winter's Tale* is surprisingly realistic in many respects. Its language and versification especially contribute to the effect of realism. Nearly a third of the dialogue is in prose, and there is no rhyme in the verse passages (the songs and Time's speech excepted). Moreover, the meter of the play's blank verse is unobtrusive; broken lines, incomplete sentences, and involved syntax occur regularly. The people of this play speak as though their minds were at work:

> ARCHIDAMUS. Wherein our entertainment shall shame us we will be justified in our loves; for indeed—
>
> CAMILLO. Beseech you,—
>
> ARCHIDAMUS. Verily, I speak it in the freedom of my knowledge: we cannot with such magnificence— in so rare— I know not what to say.
>
> (I, i)

There is realism, too, in Shakespeare's rendering of the Sicilian court. This is no fairy-tale kingdom like those of *Pericles* and *Cymbeline*. There is an emphasis upon domesticity in Leontes' court. Paulina henpecks her husband Antigonus and feels free even to rail at the king if occasion serves (II, iii). Leontes plays with his son and wipes some dirt off his nose (I, ii). Hermione is pestered by her little boy (II, i) but entertains his childish prattle. The Sicilia scenes convey the sense that their characters— Leontes, Camillo, Paulina, Antigonus, Hermione— know and respond to one another as people, not as picture-book kings and queens.

The realistic tone is not, however, confined to Sicilia. The rustic scenes in Bohemia also go beyond the artifice of conventional pastoral romance. The sheepshearing celebration of Act IV, scene iv (the longest single scene in Shakespeare), is not simply the arcadian idyll of so many pastoral romances. It is, rather, a fairly realistic picture of a contemporary Elizabethan festivity. In reference to this scene, E. M. W. Tillyard has written: "Shakespeare never did anything finer, more serious, more evocative of his full powers, than his picture of an earthly paradise painted in the form of the English countryside."

It is true that Florizel and Perdita, in their roles of disguised and undiscovered royalty, respectively, play conventional parts in the sheepshearing scene. But they play against the dominant mood of the festiv-ity— the mood established by the Clown and his two bickering girlfriends Mopsa and Dorcas, by the dancers and musicians, by the old fussbudget Shepherd, and, most importantly, by the roguish Autolycus, confidence man par excellence.

Autolycus (roughly "very wolf") is a true original. Like Jaques in *As You Like It*, he is always there but really does nothing to advance the plot. He recalls Feste (*Twelfth Night*) in his singing, his jesting with the audience, and his freedom from personal ties with the other characters. He bears some kinship with Sir John Falstaff (*Henry IV*) in that he considers lying and cheating to be normal modes of behavior. He is a self-proclaimed rogue and thief:

> My traffic is sheets; when the kite builds, look to lesser linen. My father named me Autolycus; who being, as I am, littered under Mercury, was likewise a snapper-up of unconsidered trifles. With die and drab I purchased this caparison, and my revenue is the silly cheat.
>
> (IV, iii)

He then proceeds to prove his claim by picking the pocket of the dull-witted Clown. This scene provides a delightful opportunity for slapstick; it must be seen to be appreciated.

Autolycus and his low-comedy antics help to counteract the fairy-tale tone of *The Winter's Tale* and emphasize the realistic background before which the other characters play. The last scene (V, ii) with Autolycus, in which he humbles himself before the Shepherd and the Clown, serves as a thematic underscoring of Leontes' humility in the play's moving final scene. (It has been suggested, in fact, that Shakespeare intended the roguery of Autolycus to be the comic counterpart of the malevolence of Leontes in the tragic action.)

The jealousy of Leontes is probably the least realistic and most purely conventional feature of *The Winter's Tale*. Much has been written of the implausibility with which his jealous suspicions abruptly overtake him, as well as of the tenacity with which he clings to them against all reason. The question of plausibility would not have arisen, however, with the Jacobean audience, who understood well the literary convention of "hornmadness" (irrational fear of being cuckolded).

Leontes has been compared to Othello, but the two are quite different. In *The Winter's Tale* there is no villainous conniver such as Iago to spur the hero to jealousy. Leontes' passion is self-induced and self-sustained. It is to be understood as a sickness— a madness that deprives its victim of the ability to reason. Bertrand Evans called Leontes "Shakespeare's lone example of unqualified self-deception."

Aside from his jealous passion, Leontes is characterized with consistency and with some degree of realism. He is not a great man, not a story-book king like Cymbeline. He behaves more like a husband and father than a ruler, and he shows human failings by his immaturity, bad temper, and feelings of persecution. Despite his irrational behavior in the first part of the play, Leontes is normally well liked by his courtiers. Camillo is a faithful friend to him and prefers to flee rather than acquiesce to his temporary madness. Paulina's seeming shrewishness is motivated by a fervent desire to bring her sovereign and friend back to his senses, and in the latter part of the play she is still affectionately (if a trifle naggingly) ministering to him. Hermione, in the face of Leontes' outrageous accusations and cruelty to her, never once abandons her love for him.

The reappearance of Hermione in the play's final scene is one of the most amazing bits of theatrical legerdemain [sleight of hand; trickery] in Shakespeare. Whatever its implausibility at the level of realism, it creates a stunning effect in the playing and provides a supreme moment of wonder and spirituality to which no audience can fail to respond.

There is no similar instance in Shakespeare's plays of an audience's expectations being deliberately led astray— no other event so devoid of preparation or foreshadowing. (In *Much Ado about Nothing*, Hero is said to have died after the altar scene, but the audience knows that she is alive. Not so with Hermione.) It is not simply that the audience is allowed to believe Hermione dead; we are repeatedly made to believe it.

Paulina tearfully and convincingly reports Hermione's death in Act III, scene ii, immediately after the queen has swooned and been carried from the courtroom. When the First Lord expresses incredulity, Paulina responds: "I say she's dead: I'll swear't. If word nor oath / Prevail not, go and see." At the close of the scene Leontes exits, presumably to view the body: "Prithee, bring me / To the dead bodies of my queen and son: / One grave shall be for both." In the very next scene Antigonus recounts the visitation of Hermione's ghost. Every reference to Hermione gives positive assurance that she has indeed died.

It is not until the first scene of Act V that a few hints of Hermione's survival begin to surface. Paulina has exacted from Leontes a promise never to remarry "unless another, / As like Hermione as is her picture, / Affront his eye." If he is to remarry, states Paulina, his new bride "shall be such / As, walk'd your first queen's ghost, it should take joy / To see her in your arms." In the following scene the Third

Gentleman speaks of the statue of the dead queen, sculpted by Julio Romano who "so near to Hermione hath done Hermione that they say one would speak to her and stand in hope of answer." The Second Gentleman then tells of Paulina's daily visits over the past sixteen years to the house where the statue is kept. By this point the spectator may begin to suspect that some unusual and significant event will center on this mysterious statue.

It is not until the statue is revealed, however, that the audience knows that Hermione lives. There is no stagecraft that can make us believe we behold a statue, once the actress playing Hermione is revealed. All those on stage (except, of course, Paulina and Hermione herself) are deceived, but we are not. And that is precisely Shakespeare's intention. His management of theatrical effect here is masterful. From the moment the curtain is drawn aside until Hermione steps down from her pedestal, some eighty lines of dialogue are spoken— approximately four or five minutes of playing time. This is the time during which the audience, now at last superior in knowledge to the characters, anticipates the "resurrection" of Hermione and the reconciliation that must surely follow. It is an interval of pure suspense, during which the dramatic tension builds. Had we known all along of Hermione's preservation, the emotional effect of this moment would be dissipated. Shakespeare has concentrated and intensified our anticipation of Hermione's rebirth. When it finally comes, to the accompaniment of solemn music, so comes our joy; the tears fall freely. No one who has experienced this moment in the theater can question its affective power, its spirituality, and its supreme joy.

The reunion of Hermione and Leontes, too profoundly moving for words, is effected in a silent embrace; her single speech is to her daughter Perdita:

> You gods, look down
> And from your sacred vials pour your graces
> Upon my daughter's head! Tell me, mine own,
> Where hast thou been preserved? where lived? how found
> Thy father's court? for thou shalt hear that I,
> Knowing by Paulina that the oracle
> Gave hope thou wast in being, have preserved
> Myself to see the issue.

In this final scene Shakespeare's principal theme— reconcilement— is made manifest in the most moving of actions. It is a theme that is stated also in *Pericles* and *Cymbeline*, but not so powerfully or affectingly as in *The Winter's Tale*. Through the healing ministration of "this great gap of time," "that which is lost [is] found," past sins are forgiven and sorrows forgotten, and we are shown a world redeemed—a world "in which the sins of the fathers are not visited on the children." . . .

PASTORAL ELEMENTS

From Act III, scene iii, through the end of Act IV, the action of *The Winter's Tale* takes places in the rural, pastoral setting of Bohemia. With this shift in scenery comes a shift from tragedy to comedy. Conventionally, the pastoral mode idealizes the rural way of life, yet **Peter Lindenbaum** and **Thomas McFarland** observe that in *The Winter's Tale*, Shakespeare's presentation of the pastoral world is somewhat less than ideal. Lindenbaum demonstrates that although Perdita is presented as an idealized spokesperson of pastoral life, the presence in the pastoral world of devastating storms, man-eating bears, and rustic characters who are not particularly intelligent or chaste, tarnishes the idyllic pastoral vision. A pastoral interlude, McFarland states, set within a work entitled *The Winter's Tale*, suggests from the beginning that ambivalence or sadness will tarnish the light, carefree pastoral vision. McFarland goes on to identify other features of the play that taint the happiness of the pastoral, including the death of Mamillius and the apparent death of Hermione, as well as the motifs of hatred and broken faith. Thomas Allen Nelson and Rosalie L. Colie have made similar criticisms. Nelson argues that the pastoral interlude contains dark elements, such as the suggestion that the old shepherd who raises Perdita is motivated by greed. Colie also comments that *The Winter's Tale* does not embrace the "delight which the pastoral myth offers its believers." Nevertheless, Lindenbaum and McFarland both note the ways in which the pastoral scenes and characters mediate the earlier tragedies of the play and help to bring about the play's happy ending. Lindenbaum states that through Perdita, the "representative of the country," and through the attitude of life she expresses, Shakespeare presents a view of time's destructiveness which the audience is allowed to celebrate rather than fear. Through the pastoral scenes, McFarland maintains, the possibility for the restoration of a happy society is emphasized.

Peter Lindenbaum

SOURCE: "Time, Sexual Love, and the Uses of the Pastoral in 'The Winter's Tale,'" in *Modern Language Quarterly*, Vol. 33, No. 1, March, 1972, pp. 3-22.

[In the essay that follows, Lindenbaum examines the pastoral elements of the play, noting how pastoral life in Bohemia offers a sharp contrast to the world of the Sicilian court. Lindenbaum argues that although Perdita is presented as an idealized figure and serves as the primary spokesperson of the pastoral world and its values, the pastoral world itself is not romanticized. Lindenbaum maintains that Shakespeare presents a view of time as destructive, but through his depiction of pastoral life and Perdita's attitude toward life, we, the audience, are able to accept such a view of time in a calm, perhaps even an enthusiastic manner.]

Time in *The Winter's Tale* is not merely cited as a force man has to reckon with in his life, but is even given its moment on stage. It appears in the middle of the play as a personified figure in what is first of all a brilliant solution to the potentially difficult dramatic problem of accounting for a gap of sixteen years in the action. In keeping with the final outcome which is to develop in the play, this Time is a thoroughly benevolent and polite chap, anxious to please and careful not to offend: he wishes the audience may never spend its time less agreeably than it does while watching the play. He speaks in slightly archaic rhymed verse and himself admits to being old-fashioned; but even while admitting that, he in effect warns that he is not one to be snickered at or ignored. His admission comes in lines which show that he sees himself not merely as a Chorus— the role assigned to him by the Folio's stage direction— but as the author of the play in which he appears:

> Let me pass
> The same I am, ere ancient'st order was,
> Or what is now receiv'd. I witness to
> The times that brought them in; so shall I do
> To th' freshest things now reigning, and make stale
> The glistering of this present, as my tale
> Now seems to it.
> (IV.i.9-15 New Arden Edition of *The Winter's Tale*, ed. by J. H. Pafford (London and Lambridge, MASS., 1963).

He is Shakespeare's agent in calling attention to the deliberate departure from realism in the play, to the ways in which the play is like an old tale or romance. But at the same time he is also asserting the play's realistic bias. For he notes the similarity between the world of his play and the world outside the play; he claims not only that he controls the lives of his characters but that his power extends over the audience as well; he can and will make the "glistering present" in which the audience finds itself just as stale and old-fashioned as this play. Benevolent and good-natured as he is, then, he reminds the audience of his very real power, of his ability to please some but try all, to make and unfold error, and to "o'erthrow law, and in one self-born hour / To plant and o'erwhelm custom" (IV.i.8-9).

Most modern critics of *The Winter's Tale* have been unwilling to grant Time the amount of power in the play's world that he claims for himself. The "triumph of time"—to borrow the subtitle from Shakespeare's source—usually seen is one which amounts to a triumph over time. For the play presents a fall and a redemption which is climaxed by a return to life of a figure apparently long dead. And a lost child is found again and is reconciled to her father in a scene which onlookers witness as if they were hearing of "a world ransomed, or one destroyed" (V.ii.15). This redemptive scheme, along with the high frequency of obviously theological terms, especially that of "grace" applied to Hermione and Perdita, has made the play particularly subject to allegorical and theological interpretation. S. L. Bethell, for instance, sees the play as adumbrating the Christian scheme from the fall of man to his ultimate restoration in heavenly bliss. A different but parallel interpretation looks instead to the seasonal references in the play and finds it a reflection of the pagan fertility myth: the play begins in winter and ends in summer; Perdita herself refers to Proserpina when she is handing out flowers; and she and Florizel are as welcome in Sicily "As is the spring to th' earth" (V.i.151). Both of these interpretations of the play—as embodying the Christian scheme of man's fall and redemption, or as re-enacting the pagan fertility myth's cycle of death and rebirth—lead almost inevitably to the assertion that time is finally not important in the play and has been conquered, either by Christ or by great creating Nature.

Certainly there are resonances of both the vegetation myth and the Christian drama of redemption in the play, and I am not about to deny that this scheme of death and rebirth or fall and redemption is to be found in it. Leontes does sin against Hermione by doubting her chastity and fidelity, and he commits blasphemy against heaven by denying that there is any truth in Apollo's oracle, acts for which he is evidently punished by the loss of his son and the apparent loss of his daughter and wife. He goes through a period of "saintlike sorrow" or penance under the tutelage of a figure significantly named Paulina; and when he awakes his faith, he is rewarded with the miraculous return of his "gracious" wife, Hermione. Yet Shakespeare points out that the Hermione who is redeemed is sixteen years older than the woman Leontes accused of infidelity. And no matter how much of a miracle Hermione's resurrection appears to be when it is played on stage, Shakespeare is careful to present us with a more prosaic explanation of how and why she has survived all these years: a gentleman of the court notes that Paulina has visited her "removed house" two or three times a day since Hermione's apparent death (V.ii.104-107), and Hermione herself tells us that she has remained alive so as to see the daughter who the Oracle gave her reason to believe had survived (V.iii.125-28). The recognition by Leontes himself that Hermione has more wrinkles now than she did sixteen years earlier forces us to the realization that Time has not been routed

after all. In the soliloquy in IV.i, Time notes that he is the same as he was "ere ancient'st order was"; he is, then, beyond the control of his own ravaging power. But he is the only figure in the play who is. The final scene, despite its emphasis on the marvelous and the miraculous, does not bring its characters back to the point at which they began. And a full and accurate reading of *The Winter's Tale* must recognize the contradictory conceptions within the play of time being triumphed over and of time still triumphing and having its inevitable eroding effect on man's life and strength.

Just as there are two contradictory conceptions of time in the play, so are there two patterns or structures accommodating them. Beneath or running counter to the symbolic scheme of death and rebirth, or fall and redemption, is a simpler scheme of a steady development or growth. This second structure does not postulate an ideal state, then a fall, and then a redemption in which time's effects are suddenly reversed or nullified, but rather entails a direct movement from what might best be called a state of disease to one of health. It is a structure that the differing versions of pastoral in the play mark out or adumbrate. There are two major glimpses of Arcadia or Arcadian retreats in the play: the picture of Polixenes' and Leontes' pastoral youth presented in I.ii and the sheepshearing scene of IV.iv. The two conceptions of Arcadia are very different, and in their difference lies much that the play as a whole has to tell us. For while the first of these pictures of pastoral life is described in Edenic terms and is remembered with fondness by Polixenes, and presumably by Leontes as well, the action of the whole play brings us to a recognition that there is something basically wrong with that picture, with Polixenes' attitude toward it, and, by extension, with Polixenes' whole attitude toward life and the world of time around him. A trip to the real countryside becomes a crucial step in the education or cure of Polixenes, Leontes, and, to the extent that he resembles his elders, Florizel. As this second structure, what I would call its "pastoral structure," accommodates the conception of time moving relentlessly forward, it also helps to account for the great amount of realistic detail to be found in a play so often viewed as "symbolic" or as an allegory.

When in the second scene of the play Polixenes is asked by Hermione to describe his and Leontes' youth together, he calls upon imagery from the pastoral world to convey the particularly innocent quality of their experience:

> We were as twinn'd lambs that did frisk i' th'
>   sun,
> And bleat the one at th' other: what we
>   chang'd
> Was innocence for innocence. . . .
>
>   (I.ii.67-69)

It is not just any pastoral scene he is evoking, however, but a specifically Edenic one, for the picture he presents is one that denies the effects of time and the fall on the two young princes. The denial of time occurs in lines describing how he and Leontes felt when they were still young:

> We were, fair queen,
> Two lads that thought there was no more
> behind,
> But such a day to-morrow as to-day,
> And to be boy eternal.
>
> (62-65)

Such an attitude is typical of youth perhaps, and is by no means objectionable. More troublesome though is the way Polixenes *now* looks upon that past experience, for as he continues his description, he betrays a wish to be a child again and live in what he considers to have been an unfallen state:

> we knew not
> The doctrine of ill-doing, nor dream'd
> That any did. Had we pursu'd that life,
> And our weak spirits ne'er been higher rear'd
> With stronger blood, we should have
> answer'd heaven
> Boldly 'not guilty', the imposition clear'd
> Hereditary ours.
>
> (69-75)

Not only is he giving vent to escapist sentiments in this speech, but he is on unsure theological ground as well. For the "hereditary imposition" he refers to here can only be original sin, and he is suggesting that had he and Leontes remained in their childhood state, they would have escaped that taint. With the reference to "stronger blood," he is implying further that it was sexual passion which brought about their fall from grace, an implication Hermione is quick to seize upon. She humorously challenges Polixenes with "By this we gather / You have tripp'd since" (75-76), thus inviting him to be more explicit, and he complies:

> O my most sacred lady,
> Temptations have since then been born to 's:
> for
> In those unfledg'd days was my wife a girl;
> Your precious self had then not cross'd the
> eyes
> Of my young play-fellow.
>
> (76-80)

But Polixenes is being slightly careless with his words and is still not completely aware of some of the implications of his own statements. In effect, he is accusing Hermione of being the cause of Leontes' fall from grace, while at the same time he uses courtly formulas and refers to her as "my most sacred lady."

Hermione, on her part, shows that she is more aware of those implications, and she takes Polixenes to task for them. Her initial outburst to this explanation of Polixenes is the cryptic "Grace to boot!" (80), the spirit of which might best be expressed by a paraphrase like "Some thanks we get!" A more literal translation, though, would read "Grace in addition to the bargain," and by the remark Hermione could well be pointing to the discrepancy in being addressed as "sacred" while being called a satanic or Eve-like temptress. But she does not stop here; for the moment apparently accepting Polixenes' definition of sexual love as sin, she announces that she is perfectly willing to assume responsibility for the "fall" Polixenes describes:

> Of this make no conclusion, lest you say
> Your queen and I are devils. Yet go on;
> Th' offences we have made you do, we'll
> answer,
> If you first sinn'd with us, and that with us
> You did continue fault, and that you slipp'd
> not
> With any but with us.
>
> (81-86)

Throughout this extremely gay and lighthearted interchange, Polixenes has been unconsciously betraying a disapproval or even a fear of sexual love. It is a fear that Hermione clearly does not share. For in telling Polixenes to go on, she even welcomes the charge of being a devil or temptress, if it is only her participation in sexual love which makes her an offender. With such a definition of sin as that of Polixenes being applied by a prosecutor, she is confident of her ability to account for her actions before her judge. Her own implication here is that she does not consider sexual love between marriage partners as itself a sin. Just as a moment earlier she questioned Polixenes when he suggested that he and Leontes might have escaped the taint of original sin, so here she is on firmer theological ground than he is.

Hermione's manner since she began talking with Polixenes has been that of one who is confidently and wittily, yet warmly, cutting through the veneer of complex and courtly expression to the real meaning to be found beneath. Her remark, "By this we gather / You have tripp'd since," for instance, reduces to a stark, explicit statement Polixenes' implication about his and Leontes' present moral state. If we are willing to grant that "Grace to boot" is more than a casual expletive, we can see the phrase as a mark of the same habit of mind. It was her ability to see through polite expression and the use of words simply to create an impression which earlier told her that Polixenes did not really have to leave for home just yet. Correctly seeing the use of the feeble and rather unmasculine oath "verily" as betokening a lack of real commitment to an immediate return, she proceeded to trap him into agreeing to stay on longer. And at the end of the dialogue with Polixenes, she turns these same powers of perception on to the examination of her husband's words. When she tells Leontes that Polixenes will stay on, and is complimented with "thou never spok'st / To better purpose" (88-89), she queries the remark, implying that it is overstated; she will not rest until she hears the full and explicit truth from Leontes:

> *Leon.* Hermione, my dearest, thou never spok'st
> To better purpose.
> *Her.*   Never?
> *Leon.*   Never but once.
> *Her.* What! have I twice said well? when was't
>   before?
> I prithee tell me: cram 's with praise, and make's
> As fat as tame things: one good deed, dying
>   tongueless,
> Slaughters a thousand, waiting upon that.
> Our praises are our wages. You may ride 's
> With one soft kiss a thousand furlongs ere
> With spur we heat an acre.
>
> (89-96)

Such a speech as this last gives evidence not only of Hermione's wit, but also of her essential health. She is apparently belittling women in the speech, and when she says "cram 's with praise, and make 's / As fat as tame things," the primary level of her metaphor equates women with pets that one feeds. But she is eight months pregnant and plainly pleased with herself as she speaks these words, and the very exuberance, bordering on harshness or even grossness, of the word "cram" here expresses what we might call the very opposite of squeamishness. Unlike Polixenes, she is fully willing to accept the flesh and all that some might consider the gross part of man's nature. Her demand to be made fat and her later suggestion of being ridden by a man are a far cry from the *repressed* mode of sexual innuendo: they are openly and enthusiastically sexual.

The fear of sexual love that Polixenes, on the other hand, betrays in this scene amounts to an inadvertent confession that he and Leontes simply could not deal with sexual passion without disastrous results. That confession is given immediate verification in the sudden outbreak of Leontes' perverted sexual passion, his jealousy. While there is no direct evidence from the text that Leontes overhears the interchange between Hermione and Polixenes, that interchange is in several ways closely connected with Leontes' sudden seizure. Leontes later objects to private conversations between Hermione and Polixenes, conversations which he claims involve paddling of palms, pinching of fingers, and practiced smiles (I.ii.115-16), and this interchange between the two is the only one we see. And it is only after, and right after, this conversation between Hermione and Polixenes that we come upon the first definite sign of Leontes' jealousy— his aside of "Too hot, too hot!" (108). It is not unreasonable to assume

that it is the conversation between Hermione and Polixenes about the princes' Edenic youth, whether Leontes overhears that conversation or not, which provides the immediate stimulus for the outburst of Leontes' sexual jealousy. And I would argue further that the attitude toward sexual love that Polixenes expresses in that conversation is a more distant but basic cause of that outburst and of Leontes' disease. With the definitions of innocence, sin, and the fall which Polixenes gives in that interchange, it is not surprising— in fact it is almost inevitable— that one or the other of the princes should be subject to an uncontrollable outburst of misplaced sexual feeling. The sufferer in this case happens to be Leontes, while it was Polixenes who expressed the fear and distrust of sexual experience; but the two princes are in many ways similar, and there is every reason to believe that Polixenes' feelings about his youth and loss of innocence represent those of Leontes as well.

In the opening scene of the play, we are told that the two princes were "trained together in their childhoods, and there rooted betwixt them then such an affection which cannot choose but branch now" (I.i.22-24). Derek Traversi has pointed to the double and contradictory use of "branch" in this sentence, conveying the meaning both of "the unity of living growth" and "a spreading division within that growth." But "affection" also has multiple meanings in this context. Its principal use here is to point to the strong emotional attachment the princes have for one another. Yet it can suggest also that the two princes have the same emotional make-up. A stronger suggestion of this and of their similar attitude toward their youth is to be found later in I.ii, when Leontes himself brings up the subject of his childhood:

> Looking on the lines
> Of my boy's face, methoughts I did recoil
> Twenty-three years, and saw myself unbreech'd,
> In my green velvet coat; my dagger muzzl'd
> Lest it should bite its master, and so prove,
> As ornaments oft do, too dangerous.
>
> (153-58)

Leontes, like Polixenes, quite understandably looks back to his youth as a time of joy and safety, and he is quite consciously expressing a wish to be back in that happier period; he too wishes he could stop time's movement. But the lines denote something else as well. First of all, the reference to his "muzzl'd dagger" has definite sexual suggestions, and if we follow them out, we can find the idea expressed that the male sexual organ was originally only an ornament, not designed to be used, but potentially very dangerous to its possessor. Leontes is no doubt largely or totally unaware of this meaning in his lines; he is, he thinks, talking about his dagger, though that in itself is evidence that at some level of his consciousness he is unwilling, even while thinking of him-

Brian Bedford as Leontes, Rod Beattie and Peter Hutt as Lords, James McGee as an Attendant, Gregory Wanless as a Lord, and Martha Henry as Paulina in the Stratford Festival's 1978 production of The Winter's Tale.

self as "unbreech'd," to confront the fact of his own sexuality. While he may not himself intend any comment on his early sexual experience or fear of it here, the lines with their buried sexual meaning do associate Leontes with the fear and distrust of sexual love which Polixenes voiced a moment earlier in his conversation with Hermione.

In addition, there is a general parallel in the actions of Polixenes and Leontes. As Traversi has noted, Polixenes' furious attack on Perdita in IV.iv is the exact complement to Leontes' outburst earlier in the play: Polixenes' threat to scratch Perdita's beauty with briars (IV.iv.426) is strikingly similar in its violence to Leontes' brutality against Hermione and even the young Perdita. Other critics have noted that this parallel is part of a structural similarity between the two halves of the play. After a sixteen-year gap, Polixenes participates in much the same sequence of actions as Leontes did earlier. The outbursts of rage in both figures follow immediately upon the presentation of a picture of life in a pastoral world, and the result of each outburst is that Perdita is put at the mercy of the sea; Camillo is each time called upon to advise and help the victim of the tyrannous rage. The effect of the structural parallelism and the similarity in the actions, sentiments, and temperaments of Polixenes and Leontes is to make the two characters virtually interchangeable. It is the general and emphasized similarity between the two princes which makes it possible to say that Polixenes' visit to Arcadia is an essential part of the education and regeneration of Leontes, who himself never leaves the court. And this similarity makes it all the safer to assume that Polixenes speaks for Leontes as well, when he yearns for an existence unaffected by time's movement and provides that definition of primal innocence which implies that sexual love could be no part of man's experience in his unfallen condition.

Just as Leontes has his complement in Polixenes, so does Hermione have a complement, in the second half of the play, in her daughter Perdita. The word "grace" with its many meanings appears very frequently in the play, most often to denote a quality in Hermione: Leontes, looking back to the past, refers to his presumably dead wife "as tender / As infancy and grace" (V.iii.26-27); it is a word frequently on Hermione's own lips (I.ii.80, 99, 105), and when she goes off to prison, she announces that her action is for her "better grace" (II.i.122). When Time reintroduces Perdita, sixteen years older than the babe we have just seen left on the coast of Bohemia, he uses the same term to describe the daughter as was used for the mother: Perdita is "now grown in grace" (IV.i.24). Perdita, who has been raised in the country, is by no means as sophisticated as her mother: unlike Hermione, for instance, she is made uncomfortable by praise. But she shares her mother's distrust of courtly rhetoric and extravagant statement, and she has Hermione's ability to examine such expression critically. When Camillo very lamely flatters her with "I should leave grazing, were I of your flock, / And only live by gazing" (IV.iv.109-10), she, after the manner of her mother, rebukes him for his words by reducing them to their literal meaning instead of accepting them merely as a vague compliment:

> Out, alas!
> You'd be so lean that blasts of January
> Would blow you through and through.
>
> (110-12)

Perdita consistently shows that she, like her mother, is quite able to acquit herself well in conversation and debate.

The most important similarity between Perdita and Hermione, though, is their attitude toward sexual love. Hermione's willingness to acknowledge being a devil in the definition of the fall that Polixenes provides in I.ii implies that she accepts sexual love as a good and natural practice for man. Perdita brings back to the earth not only spring for Leontes, but that attitude toward sexual love as well. She is the repository of Hermione's thoughts in the next generation, and, while thoroughly chaste and modest, she is particularly frank and open about her sexual desires. And they are desires which exist not in a timeless world but in a time-governed one. It is the insistence on time passing and on the full acceptance of sexual love which most differentiates Perdita's pastoral vision from Polixenes' vision of his "Eden" earlier in the play. Whereas Polixenes sought to stop time and be free of sexual passion, Perdita fully accepts the first and rejoices in the second.

Her consciousness of time is shown to us initially in her words and actions as she distributes flowers to the various guests at the sheepshearing feast. It was her desire to find flowers appropriate to each recipient which involved her in the famous debate with Polixenes on nature and art. She first gave Polixenes

and Camillo the winter flowers of rosemary and rue, which were chosen, Polixenes assumes, as a gift suitable for aged men (IV.iv.78-79). Concluding from Polixenes' remark that he was insulted by this initial offer, Perdita goes on to explain why she gave them flowers betokening old age:

> Sir, the year growing ancient,
> Not yet on summer's death nor on the
> birth
> Of trembling winter, the fairest flowers o'
> th' season
> Are our carnations and streak'd gillyvors,
> Which some call nature's bastards: of that
> kind
> Our rustic garden's barren; and I care not
> To get slips of them.
>
> (79-85)

These lines are frequently misread as a reference to the present time of the scene as being not yet on summer's death nor on the birth of winter. But the time of this scene is most likely late June, when sheepshearing feasts traditionally take place; and these lines are simply an explanation of why Perdita could not give Polixenes and Camillo the late summer flowers that would have been more appropriate for them: because the fairest late summer flowers suggest to her unchastity and work by an artist's hand, she does not have any of them in her garden. After the debate with Polixenes she proceeds to give Polixenes and Camillo midsummer flowers instead— hot lavender, mints, savory, marjoram, and marigolds— and in handing them over is consciously flattering her guests for a moment:

> these are flowers
> Of middle summer, and I think they are
> given
> To men of middle age. Y'are very welcome.
>
> (106-108)

And following this, she turns to Florizel and her younger friends and expresses a desire to give them flowers of spring. In her choice of and reference to flowers, Perdita has been moving gradually backward in time— from winter to late summer to middle summer to spring. In this backward movement, she is re-enacting or recapitulating in small the redemptive scheme of the play as a whole. But at the very moment that time is symbolically redeemed by Perdita's actions and words, Perdita herself reasserts the concept of time as constantly moving forward. For she has to admit that she does not have those spring flowers she would like to hand out, and she points to a way, then, in which she is *unlike* Proserpina:

> Now, my fair'st friend, [*To Florizel*]
> I would I had some flowers o' th' spring,
> that might

Become your time of day; and yours, and
  yours,
    [*To Mopsa and the other girls*]
That wear upon your virgin branches yet
Your maidenheads growing: O Proserpina,
For the flowers now that, frighted, thou let'st
  fall
From Dis's waggon!

                                    (112-18)

There is a strong note of melancholy here and of regret over the fact that she cannot really bring spring
back to the earth. In handing out her flowers, Perdita
is very conscious of the limitations placed on man's life
by time's movement.

Perdita would appear, for the moment, to be like
Polixenes in seeking a life in which one would not be
limited by time's inevitable movement onward. But while
Polixenes moved from a vision of a timeless world to
a desire to retreat and avoid sexual involvement, Perdita
quickly snaps out of her melancholic mood and moves
instead to a triumphant assertion of her dedication to
active, living, sexual love:

Per.   O, these I lack,
To make you garlands of; and my sweet friend,
To strew him o'er and o'er!
Fla.   What, like a corpse?
Per. No, like a bank, for love to lie and play on:
Not like a corpse; or if— not to be buried,
But quick, and in mine arms.

                                    (127-32)

She pauses on "or if" most likely because she has in
her mind struck upon the root meaning of "corpse";
she would very plainly, then, be thinking about love
which makes full use of the body.

There is, no doubt, a smile on Florizel's face as he
teases Perdita with his question "What, like a corpse?"
But the question points to a way in which Florizel has
not yet reached Perdita's level of appreciation of the
type of love she advocates. He is generally, next to her,
a rather unsure figure. Like his father, when he wants
to give the highest possible praise to something, he
places it beyond time's control; in expressing his love
for Perdita, he in his own way tries to deny time and
make her action eternal:

                    What you do,
Still betters what is done. When you speak,
  sweet,
I'd have you do it ever: when you sing,
I'd have you buy and sell so, so give alms,
Pray so, and, for the ord'ring your affairs,
To sing them too: when you do dance, I wish
  you
A wave o' th' sea, that you might ever do

Nothing but that, move still, still so,
And own no other function. Each your doing,
So singular in each particular,
Crowns what you are doing, in the present
  deeds,
That all your acts are queens.

                                    (135-46)

G. Wilson Knight has commended this speech as a
praiseworthy "striving after eternity," and another critic
has called it "one of the most moving passages in the
whole of Shakespeare." The sentiment expressed is
beautiful, but if Shakespeare had wanted us to accept
these lines without qualification, he probably would not
have had Perdita object to them. Perdita has earlier
had to chide Florizel for his extremes in dressing her
up as the goddess Flora for the feast (1-14), and here
she finds his words too extravagant. His praise gives
evidence of a verbal art which she distrusts and which
disguises what she takes to be his true nature:

        O Doricles,
Your praises are too large: but that your youth,
And the true blood which peeps fairly
  through 't,
Do plainly give you out an unstain'd shep-
  herd,
With wisdom I might fear, my Doricles,
You woo'd me the false way.

                                    (146-51)

Even in her mild rebuke, she retains her wit. For she
knows very well that Doricles is a prince and not simply an unstained shepherd. But prince and representative of the court and its art that he may be, Florizel
eventually justifies Perdita's confidence and trust in
him. At the moment he must choose between his succession and his love, he stands by Perdita; and in doing
so he allies himself with all of nature as well:

            It cannot fail, but by
The violation of my faith; and then
Let nature crush the sides o'th' earth together,
And mar the seeds within! Lift up thy looks:
From my succession wipe me, father; I
Am heir to my affection.

                                    (477-82)

It was Leontes' diseased "affection" (I.ii.138-46) which
so blinded him to the truth and caused him to commit
the unnatural act of seeking the death of his own seed,
Perdita. It is a mark of Florizel's health here that he
can rely upon and dedicate himself fully to just those
emotions and passions which Polixenes and Leontes
found so dangerous and disruptive. For Florizel *not* to
follow the dictates of his "affection" would, in his view,
be as bad as marring all the seeds germinating in the
earth. He is speaking in overly exalted terms perhaps,
but there is some reason to take his exclamation seri-

ously. Perdita has by this time— as a result of her stand in favor of unadulterated nature in the nature and art debate, her distribution of flowers, and her identification with Flora— been fully associated with nature and natural life. On this level of association and symbol, Florizel in standing by her *is* helping to insure nature's continuance from generation to generation. And in allying himself with nature and the country as opposed to the court, Florizel is assuming, for his own, the vision of human life in which time has a definite effect and in which sexual love or affection plays a good and vital role.

Though born at court, Perdita is the chief spokesman for the pastoral world in the play. She is clearly an idealized figure. The other country figures, with their banter, their dances, and their delight in song, present a picture in sharp contrast with the world of the court of Acts I-III. But the natural world, with its storms and its hungry bears, is not portrayed merely as an idyllic haven in the play. Bohemia, in fact, provides one of Shakespeare's harsher pastoral landscapes: the bear of this play succeeds in satisfying its hunger, whereas the lion of *As You Like It* did not. And Shakespeare is careful, as he was in *As You Like It* also, to show that living close to nature does not automatically or necessarily make a person intelligent, sensitive, healthy, attractive, or chaste. Autolycus at his first entrance sings of tumbling in the hay with country beggar women (IV.iii.12); and though Perdita speaks of her friends who "wear upon your virgin branches yet / Your maidenheads growing" (IV.iv.115-16), her foster brother has evidently tripped with several and has not yet retired from the field (239 ff.). The rustic shepherds are like sheep themselves, unthinking easy prey for that wolf Autolycus, who enjoys his own kind of sheepshearing feast. The country figure besides Perdita who possesses the most dignity is the Old Shepherd, her reputed father. He is differentiated from the rest by being given poetry rather than prose to speak, and that poetry shows him to be hospitable, warm, and genial, with a firm love of the land and of tradition. Unaware of the true identity of either Perdita or Florizel, he at first warmly approves of the match. But at the moment Polixenes unmasks, the old man is selfishly concerned only for his own neck. And after his meteoric rise in social status, he becomes just as comic a butt for laughter as his mindless son. Perhaps more damaging yet is the fact that he is used to provide a parody of Polixenes' response to the onset of sexual passion in youth. His solution of how to deal with that passion has simplicity to recommend it, but that is about all; he would merely eliminate the years between ten and twenty-three from young people's lives:

> I would there were no age between ten and three-and-twenty, or that youth would sleep out the rest; for there is nothing in the between but getting wenches with child, wronging the

ancientry, stealing, fighting. . . .

(III.iii.59-63)

He is primarily expressing his anger at the young men who have been hunting in bad weather and have driven two of his sheep away from the flock, but his words here are enough to present on a totally comic level one of the major concerns of the play.

With such rustics as these in it, Shakespeare is plainly not offering up the country as an escape from, or as a blissful alternative to, life at court. And Perdita's attitudes toward sexual love and time's movement cannot simply be called those of the country, since she is the only one in the country to voice them. Further, it is not absolutely necessary that one go to the country to find and develop a vision like that of Perdita; Hermione possessed that vision without ever having left the court. But Shakespeare, while not romanticizing the country, is calling up all the usual associations of life in the country, with its beauty, peace, and health, so as to marshal them behind Hermione's vision and to give force and greater attractiveness to those views he wishes to endorse. By having a specifically country figure as well as Hermione hold those views, he is suggesting that Hermione's attitude toward sexual love is good, proper, healthy, and perfectly natural to man, an attitude, then, he would easily arrive at were his own mental balance and life in the complex world to allow him to do so. The trip to the country with the discovery of Perdita's insistence on time's movement and attitude toward sexual love presents the final repudiation of Polixenes' definitions of innocence, sin, the fall, and even of the ideal human existence— those definitions and attitudes which were so closely connected with, and even the ultimate cause of, Leontes' diseased outburst of sexual jealousy.

While the trip to the country is only one of two possible ways the play presents as a means of moving from the disease of Acts I-III to the health and happiness of the conclusion— the other way being the path of penance Leontes follows at court under the moral guidance of Paulina— the action of the final scene is thoroughly imbued with the lessons taught by the country. The recognition that Hermione's statue has wrinkles which Hermione herself did not have sixteen years earlier reasserts the vision of time presented by Perdita when she confesses to her inability to bring back spring and to distribute spring flowers out of season. The play ends with a rather stark insistence on time passing. When the statue first moves, Polixenes raises the question of what exactly Hermione has been doing all these years (V.iii.114-15). As Hermione begins to answer it and explain to her daughter why she kept herself alive, she is interrupted by Paulina with:

> There's time enough for that;
> Lest they desire (upon this push) to trouble

Your joys with like relation.

(128-30)

Had the question been pursued further, it might well have proved embarrassing for Paulina and for Shakespeare. But Shakespeare, by having Paulina interrupt Hermione here, is not simply trying to hurry quickly over a dramatic weakness. By intentionally raising and then not answering Polixenes' question fully, Shakespeare manages to enforce upon our consciousness just how terribly wide a gap of time sixteen years can be.

And finally, the concluding scene offers yet another of the instances in the play in which a character expresses a wish to halt time's and life's movement, only to be corrected or rebuked for that wish. Leontes and Perdita both, when they see Hermione's statue, desire simply to stand there and gaze at it for twenty years (V.iii.84-85). Polixenes proved to be misguided in desiring to return to a realm in which he could be "boy eternal," and Florizel was gently chided for desiring a Perdita constantly repeating the same action, like a wave of the sea. Here, time moving onward brings Leontes and Perdita greater joy than the single moment made eternal. For in the place of a statue, a work of art set in a timeless dimension, Leontes and Perdita are presented with a Hermione warm with life. Polixenes, in his description of his youth, expressed a distrust of his own "blood," by which he meant his passions and particularly sexual passion. In the sheepshearing scene, the word "blood" for Perdita referred to a quality in Florizel that she could rely upon to express his true feelings when she could not trust his extravagant words (IV.iv.148); Florizel's "true blood," then, was cause for confidence and trust. For Leontes in this final scene, the fact that Hermione's statue appears to have veins which bear blood (V.iii.65) becomes cause first for wonder and then, when verified, for rejoicing. "Blood" at this point means not simply the passions but one's lifeblood, that fluid whose movement makes one a living being. The use of the term here is understandable enough and to be expected, but it helps to point out that Polixenes, in his distrust of his own blood and in his wistful look back toward the past and childhood, was denying life. The final scene of the play is a celebration of life. It is, in fact, life itself which Paulina calls Hermione's redeemer when she bids the apparent statue descend from its pedestal:

Come!
I'll fill your grave up: stir, nay, come away:
Bequeath to death your numbness; for from
  him
Dear life redeems you.

(V.iii.100-103)

"Life" in this final scene clearly means life as it exists in a moving world, in a world ruled by time. It is Shakespeare's considerable achievement in The Winter's

Tale that he can bring us to accept the view of time as constantly moving forward and hence as eroding and destructive, and to accept it not with resignation or depression but with equanimity, confidence, and even enthusiasm. And it is primarily his picture of life in a pastoral setting and the attitude toward life expressed by Perdita, as representative of the country, which enable us to do so.

Thomas McFarland

SOURCE: "We Must Be Gentle: Disintegration and Reunion in 'The Winter's Tale,'" in *Shakespeare's Pastoral Comedy*, Chapel Hill: University of North Carolina Press, 1972, pp. 122-45.

[In this essay, McFarland traces Shakespeare's treatment of pastoral elements in The Winter's Tale. *McFarland identifies the ways in which the normally light and carefree pastoral vision is undercut by sadness and ambivalence throughout the play. The first several acts of the play focus on death, attack childhood happiness, and present Shakespeare's emphasis on "human faithlessness," McFarland argues, while the pastoral scenes offer the possibility that society can be reconciled and restored to happiness.]*

"*A* sad tale's best for winter." The melancholy words of the doomed child Mamillius (2.1.25) set the tone, and ordain the comic reality, of *The Winter's Tale.* For demonic forces are loose within this play, and the redemption provided by pastoral is as bittersweet as the idea of winter's beauty itself. Indeed, the very conception of a winter pastoral evokes an ambivalence; the Ovidian golden age was specifically one where "ver erat aeternum"— spring was eternal. A pastoral simplification of winter, no matter what its beauty, must incorporate something less than the perfect fulfillment of the paradisal vision. . . .

In *The Winter's Tale,* death, and other aspects of diminished being that herald it, dominate the first three acts. In its motifs of restlessness, sudden hatred, troubled journeys, deadly pursuit, and broken faith, the play in these acts affirms the bitter cosmos of *Pericles.* And death is everywhere: in the King's intentions toward Polixenes, in his attitude toward Hermione's baby, in the wasting away of Mamillius, in the seeming death of Hermione, and, most grotesquely, in the devouring of Antigonus. The sixteen-year hiatus between the third and fourth act, which so fascinated Coleridge, and which so utterly repudiates the dramatic unities of the French classical mode, is a sign of the play's tormented wrenching of comedy out of its normal symmetries, and is also a psychological necessity. For only a new generation, and many years to soften old hatred, can make acceptable a comic resolution to the madness of Leontes.

The first enunciation of his inner rage erupts, startlingly, into a seemingly ideal social situation of happy marriage and longtime friendship. Indeed, if this play looks back, in its pastorally redeemed fourth and fifth acts, to a torment sixteen years gone, such curious preoccupation with the past is not unique. For the torment of Leontes, and the destruction it causes, themselves look back to a still earlier time when pastoral bliss was the norm. As Northrop Frye says, "We begin with reference to an innocent childhood when Leontes and Polixenes were 'twinned lambs,' and then suddenly plunge from the reminiscence of this pastoral paradise into a world of superstition and obsession" (*A Natural Perspective: The Development of Shakespearean Comedy and Romance* [New York and London, 1965], p. 114).

This play, in fact, attacks pastoral bliss at its very heart, for childhood is the persistent object of the action's dramatic rage. Leontes repudiates the childhood friendship he bore for Polixenes, frightens the boy Mamillius to death, rejects the infant Perdita and abandons her to die. His rejection of his newborn child shockingly epitomizes his madness. Emilia notes that Hermione "is, something before her time, deliver'd. . . . A daughter, and a goodly babe, / Lusty and like to live" (2.2.25-27). Paulina, relying on society's universal love for children, says, "I'll show't the King, and undertake to be / Her advocate to th' loud'st. We do not know / How he may soften at the sight o'th' child" (2.2.38-40). But this tactic only elicits a language of the most twisted and grotesque hatred: "Give her the bastard"; "Take up the bastard; . . . giv't to thy crone"; "This brat is none of mine"; "My child! Away with't! . . . take it hence, / And see it instantly consum'd with fire"; "Shall I live on to see this bastard kneel / And call me father? Better burn it now / Than curse it then" (2.3.73, 75-76, 92, 131-33, 154-56).

Scarcely less grotesque is his altered decision to stop just short of murdering the infant:

> You, sir, come you hither.
> You that have been so tenderly officious
> With Lady Margery, your midwife there,
> To save this bastard's life—for 'tis a bastard,
> So sure as this beard's grey—what will you
>   adventure
> To save this brat's life? . . .
>   We enjoin thee,
> As thou art liegeman to us, that thou carry
> This female bastard hence; and that thou bear it
> To some remote and desert place, quite out
> Of our dominions; and that there thou leave it,
> Without more mercy, to its own protection
> And favour of the climate. As by strange
>   fortune
> It came to us, I do in justice charge thee. . . .
> That thou commend it strangely to some place
> Where chance may nurse or end it.
>
> [2.3.157-82]

The attack on childhood signifies everything that is sick, inhuman, antisocial, and opposed to the express values of the paradisal vision. Leontes's rage, indeed, erupts like lava from a nether region, and in its intensity, its awesome suddenness, suggests vast subliminal depths of torment and anguish. Often noted as one of the most startling of all dramatic volte-faces, the change from mellow friendliness to seething hatred never loses its power to shock. We retrace the process:

> POLIXENES.   . . . I have
>   stay'd
> to tire your royalty. . . .   No longer stay.
> LEONTES. One sev'night longer.
> POLIXENES. Very sooth, to-morrow.
> LEONTES. We'll part the time between's then. . . .
> Tongue-tied our Queen? Speak you.
> HERMIONE. I had thought, sir, to have held
>   my peace until
> You had drawn oaths from him not to stay.
>   You, sir,
> Charge him too coldly. . . .
> LEONTES. Well said, Hermione. . . .
> HERMIONE.   Not your gaoler,
>   then.
> But your kind hostess. Come, I'll question
>   you
> Of my lord's tricks and yours when you were
>   boys.
> You were pretty lordings then!

And this elegant and archetypal situation, of a husband and wife entreating an old friend to prolong a visit, expands in its good feeling to include an Edenic claim of more happiness than life, its childhood paradise lost, can sustain:

> POLIXENES.   We were, fair Queen,
> Two lads that thought there was no more
>   behind
> But such a day to-morrow as to-day,
> And to be boy eternal. . . .
> We were as twinn'd lambs that did frisk i' th'
>   sun,
> And bleat the one at th' other. What we
>   chang'd
> Was innocence for innocence; we knew not
> The doctrine of ill-doing, nor dream'd
> That any did. Had we pursu'd that life,
> And our weak spirits ne'er been higher rear'd
> With stronger blood, we should have answer'd
>   heaven
> Boldly "Not guilty," the imposition clear'd
> Hereditary ours.
>
> [1.2.14-75]

But the Pelagian thought of heavenly innocence in this our life is ironically and mightily rebuked by the eruption from the Augustinian depths of man's corrupt and fallen nature:

LEONTES.   Is he won yet?
HERMIONE. He'll stay, my lord.
LEONTES. At my request he would not.
Hermione, my dearest, thou never spok'st
To better purpose.

                                        [1.2.86-89]

And after some banter Hermione answers:

Why, lo you now, I have spoke to th' purpose
    twice:
The one for ever earn'd a royal husband;
Th' other for some while a friend.

                                        [1.2.106-8]

Then she gives her hand to Polixenes, and Leontes, aside, utters those words of agonized hatred that give the lie to all optimism about human affairs:

                              Too hot, too hot!
To mingle friendship far is mingling bloods.
I have tremor cordis on me; my heart dances,
But not for joy, not joy. This entertainment
May a free face put on; derive a liberty
From heartiness, from bounty, fertile bosom,
And well become the agent. 'T may, I grant;
But to be paddling palms and pinching fingers,
As now they are, and making practis'd smiles,
As in a looking-glass; and then to sigh, as 'twere
The mort o'th' deer.

                                        [1.2.108-18]

The sexual fury and disgust that seethed in Hamlet when he thought about Claudius and his mother are echoed in these words; and as Leontes goes on, he begins to croak in the tones of Othello's Iago-induced prurience and suspicion:

                              Is whispering nothing?
Is leaning cheek to cheek? Is meeting noses?
Kissing with inside lip? Stopping the career
Of laughter with a sigh?—a note infallible
Of breaking honesty. Horsing foot on foot?
Skulking in corners? Wishing clocks more swift;
Hours, minutes; noon, midnight? And all eyes
Blind with the pin and web but theirs, theirs
    only,
That would unseen be wicked—is this noth-
    ing? . . .

                                        [1.2.284-92]

The most persistent theme in all Shakespeare, in fact, is that of human faithlessness. It is the very substance of the history plays, the most tormented preoccupation of the tragedies, the chief ingredient of the bitterness in the middle and late comedies, all haunted by the theme of sonnet 92: "Thou mayst be false, and yet I know it not." Othello's suspicions, like those of Leontes, are in the instance unjustified, but they derive motive power from the high probability of a young wife's betrayal; and Othello is, indeed, betrayed, by his friend Iago if not by his wife Desdemona, just as Desdemona, though faithful to her husband, betrays her father. Elsewhere the probability of betrayal is more directly realized. The pain suffered by Troilus corresponds to his actual betrayal by Cressida, and the language of that play mocks all human idealism as alternating between illusion and treachery. Indeed, when Shakespeare deals with the ideas of loyalty and broken faith, the betrayal of human commitment is far more often represented as simple fact than as mistaken suspicion. The betrayal of friendship by Rosencrantz and Guildenstern, of love by Ophelia, of wifehood by Gertrude, of brotherhood by Claudius—these motifs form the central meaning of *Hamlet*. Macbeth's betrayal of Duncan, Enobarbus's of Antony, Rome's of Coriolanus, Caesar's of Rome and the conspirators of Caesar, Angelo's of the Duke, Prince Hal's of Falstaff, and above all, Lear's betrayal by his daughters—these and other instances testify to the prevalence of the themes of betrayal and broken faith in Shakespeare's art. . . .

The mysterious rage of Leontes is another expression of this persisting view of the probability of baseness in human relationships. The dual potentiality of man, either to be like the animals or like the angels, was often insisted on by Shakespeare's philosophically minded predecessors in the Renaissance. As Pomponazzi, for instance, says, "Man is clearly not of simple but of multiple . . . nature, and he is to be placed as a mean between mortal and immortal things. . . . And to man, who thus exists as a mean between the two, power is given to assume whichever nature he wishes" (*De immortalitate animae*, Cap. I.). Leontes's rage, following so suddenly on the benign scene appropriate to comedy, is a sort of reflection of the Renaissance emphasis on man's multiple possibility. To it, moreover, must be added darker thoughts, from Augustine and Calvin, about man's inherent corruption. All such thoughts receive their validation from experience: in Shakespeare's life, about which we can only speculate, or in our own, about which we can be certain.

The eruption of Leontes's suspicion represents a kind of absolute standard of the anticomic; and it is therefore the means by which the magnetic attraction of people to one another, the comic cohesiveness, is reversed. Things fall apart. Society disintegrates under the blasting reality of Leontes's rage. Polixenes the friend becomes Polixenes the fugitive. Camillo the loyal retainer becomes Camillo the traitor, rather than accept Leontes's command and remain as Camillo the murderer. Antigonus the trusted counselor becomes Antigonus the doomed wanderer. Mamillius the prince and heir becomes Mamillius the pining child. Hermione the faithful wife becomes Hermione the accused whore and Hermione the prisoner—finally, Hermione the seeming-dead. And all these things are wrought by Leontes's

paranoid rage. As Paulina tells him in the cathartic
moment of truth:

> That thou betray'dst Polixenes, 'twas nothing;
> That did but show thee, of a fool, inconstant,
> And damnable ingrateful. Nor was't much
> Thou wouldst have poison'd good Camillo's
>   honour,
> To have him kill a king—poor trespasses,
> More monstrous standing by; whereof I reckon
> The casting forth to crows thy baby daughter
> To be or none or little, though a devil
> Would have shed water out of fire ere done't;
> Nor is't directly laid to thee, the death
> Of the young Prince, whose honourable
>   thoughts—
> Thoughts high for one so tender—cleft the heart
> That could conceive a gross and foolish sire
> Blemish'd his gracious dam. This is not, no,
> Laid to thy answer; but the last—O lords,
> When I have said, cry "Woe!"—the Queen, the
>   Queen,
> The sweet'st, dear'st creature's dead; and ven-
>   geance for't
> Not dropp'd down yet. . . .
>   But, O thou tyrant!
> Do not repent these things, for they are heavier
> Than all thy woes can stir; therefore betake thee
> To nothing but despair. A thousand knees
> Ten thousand years together, naked, fasting,
> Upon a barren mountain, and still winter
> In storm perpetual, could not move the gods
> To look that way thou wert.
>   [3.2.182-211]

The cleansing release afforded by Paulina's denunciation is some measure of the amount of desolation caused
by Leontes's maddened thoughts. Such a lengthy and
bitter excoriation is necessary to discharge the outrage
that Leontes's actions have provoked; and it prepares
the way for the possibilities of comic reclamation. Having
delivered herself of her counterrage, Paulina subsides
into an attitude more inviting to the prospect of ultimate reconciliations:

>   Alas! I have show'd too much
> The rashness of a woman! He is touch'd
> To th' noble heart. What's gone and what's past
>   help
> Should be past grief. Do not receive affliction
> At my petition. . . . Now, good my liege,
> Sir, royal sir, forgive a foolish woman.
>   [3.2.217-24]

The volcanic flow of Leontes's rage having erupted
and subsided by the second scene of the third act, the
action of the play moves in place (to the seacoast of
Bohemia) and in time (sixteen years) to allow further
cooling to occur. The last symbol of the molten world

is the grotesque exit of Antigonus, the babe Perdita
now safely deposited on the shore:

>   A savage clamour!
> Well may I get aboard! This is the chase;
> I am gone for ever. [*Exit, pursued by a bear.*]
>   [3.3.57-59]

The bear, which appears as suddenly and ferociously as
the rage of Leontes, clears the coast for a new entrance—one equally unlikely in a sea's environment—
that of a shepherd. And at that moment the balm of
pastoral begins to be applied to the burning wounds
inflicted by the action so far. As the clown reports the
sinking of the ship at sea, and the death of Antigonus
on land ("how the poor souls roar'd, and the sea mock'd
them; and how the poor gentleman roared, and the
bear mock'd him" [3.3.96-98]), the shepherd replies
with words that justify the play's division into two worlds
of space and time:

> Now bless thyself; thou met'st with things dying,
> I with things new-born. Here's a sight for thee;
> look thee, a bearing-cloth for a squire's child!
>   [3.3.109-12]

The first two scenes of the fourth act establish the
passage of sixteen years, and connect the new present
with the past by means of the conversation between
Polixenes and Camillo. At the beginning of the third
scene, Autolycus appears, singing the carefree words
that we recognize as the symbol of transformation to
the ideal realm of pastoral:

> When daffodils begin to peer,
>   With heigh! the doxy over the dale,
> Why, then comes in the sweet o' the year;
>   For the red blood reigns in the winter's pale.
>   [4.3.1-4]

The figure of Autolycus, the pastoral thief, serves in
some ways the same function as Jaques in *As You Like
It*. Like Jaques, Autolycus indicates a slight falling off
from the golden ideal. Such an indication is a reminder,
however harmless, of the searing possibilities opened
up by Leontes. The division of the two worlds of space
and time, though it must be sharp, cannot be absolute;
continuity of theme and interest must be preserved.
The child Mamillius lost in the first world finds a
counterpart in the babe Perdita saved for the second;
the rage of Leontes finds a counterpart in the activity,
harmless though it be, of Autolycus. Unlike Jaques,
however, Autolycus is not a cerebral critic of the pastoral world, but a kind of life-force, which reinforces
the theme of "things new-born" at the same time that
it prevents us from wholly forgetting the troubles that
accompany remembrance of the past. Though benign,
he is nonetheless a thief, which is not socially acceptable; so his role confirms the hint of malaise found in

the conception of winter, rather than spring, as the pastoral matrix. But he sings, and proves, that "red blood reigns in the winter's pale." Traversi speaks well on this matter:

> Autolycus, indeed, has a part of his own to play in the complete conception. His comic function is that of one who is regarded as a little apart from the main structure, whose behaviour is in some sense irreducible to the social values of the play, calculated to throw upon the symbolic symmetry itself a touch of relativity, a sense of the incalculable individuality of the processes of life. . . . The key to Autolycus, and to his peculiar position in the action, can, indeed, be defined in the phrase from his own song that "the red blood reigns in the winter's pale." The reference to winter implies at once a contrast and a point of reference. It connects the episode now before us with the play's title, and establishes a relationship between the birth of spring in the heart of winter and the affirmation of the warm, living "blood" of youth against the jealousy and care-laden envy of age, an affirmation shortly to be confirmed in the contrast between the young lovers and their elders. In Autolycus himself, of course, this outpouring of spontaneous life moves on the margin of social forms. It has indeed a predatory aspect comically expressed in his first action, the picking of the Clown's pocket; but this itself is, to some degree, a devaluation of his victim's newfound riches and the social pretensions which these have aroused in him (*Shakespeare: The Last Phase* [New York, n.d.], pp. 138-39).

It should be noted, furthermore, that the picking of the Clown's pocket mockingly prefigures the "sheep-shearing" scene that follows.

That scene represents one of the most concentrated expressions of pastoral ever achieved by Shakespeare. Its essence lies in the extended imagery of the giving of flowers; for by giving flowers here, healing blossoms are strewn over the entire desert seared by Leontes:

> PERDITA.   You're welcome, sir.
> Give me those flow'rs there, Dorcas. Reverend
>   sirs,
> For you there's rosemary and rue; these keep
> Seeming and savour all the winter long.
> Grace and remembrance be to you both!
> And welcome to our shearing.
>
> [4.4.72-77]

The tropes of welcoming, of giving, of grace, all float in upon these words; and the perfumed scent and beautiful sight of flowers are heaped, almost overpoweringly, over the vast desolate anxiety established by the play's beginning:

> POLIXENES.   Shepherdess—
> A fair one are you—well you fit our ages

> With flow'rs of winter.
> PERDITA.   Sir, the year growing ancient,
> Not yet on summer's death nor on the birth
> Of trembling winter, the fairest flow'rs o' th'
>   season
> Are our carnations and streak'd gillyvors,
> Which some call nature's bastards. Of that kind
> Our rustic garden's barren; and I care not
> To get slips of them.
> POLIXENES.   Wherefore, gentle maiden,
> Do you neglect them? . . .
> Then make your garden rich in gillyvors
> And do not call them bastards.
>
> [4.4.77-99]

The torment of Leontes's earlier ravings about his supposed "bastard" child is transformed into the loveliness of flowers and the acceptance of kings. And Perdita provides more fragrance and color:

>   Here's flow'rs for you;
> Hot lavender, mints, savory, marjoram;
> The marigold, that goes to bed wi' th' sun
> And with him rises weeping; these are flow'rs
> Of middle summer, and I think they are given
> To men of middle age. Y'are very welcome.
>
> [4.4.103-8]

And from the cornucopia of symbolic well-being, in seemingly inexhaustible abundance, issue flowers that blanket and perfume all things:

>   Now, my fair'st
>   friend,
> I would I had some flow'rs o' th' spring that
>   might
> Become your time of day— and yours, and
>   yours,
> That wear upon your virgin branches yet
> Your maidenheads growing. O Proserpina,
> For the flowers now that, frighted, thou let'st
>   fall
> From Dis's waggon!— daffodils,
> That come before the swallow dares, and take
> The winds of March with beauty; violets, dim
> But sweeter than the lids of Juno's eyes
> Or Cytherea's breath; pale primroses,
> That die unmarried ere they can behold
> Bright Phoebus in his strength— a malady
> Most incident to maids; bold oxlips, and
> The crown-imperial; lilies of all kinds,
> The flow'r-de-luce being one. O, these I lack,
> To make you garlands of, and my sweet friend,
> To strew him o'er and o'er!
>
> [4.4.112-29]

That Shakespeare here achieves a kind of absolute in the invocation of symbolic bliss is attested by Milton's reworking of "O Proserpina, / For the flowers now that, frighted, thou let'st fall / From Dis's waggon" into his description of the Garden of Eden itself:

> Not that fair field
> Of *Enna*, where *Proserpin* gath'ring flow'rs
> Herself a fairer Flow'r by gloomy *Dis*
> Was gather'd
> . . . might with this Paradise
> Of *Eden* strive. . . .
>
> [*Paradise Lost*, 4.268-75]

Milton's lines also equate the splendor of Eden with the quintessence of pastoral, for his reworking of Shakespeare's Proserpina-and-Dis passage immediately follows a specifically Ovidian and Virgilian description of Eden as the golden world:

> Thus was this place,
> A happy rural seat of various view:
> Groves whose rich Trees wept odorous Gums
>   and Balm, . . .
> Flow'rs of all hue, and without Thorn the Rose: . . .
> The Birds thir quire apply; airs, vernal airs,
> Breathing the smell of field and grove, attune
> The trembling leaves, while Universal *Pan*
> Knit with the *Graces* and the *Hours* in dance
> Led on th' Eternal Spring. Not that fair field
> of *Enna*. . . .
>
> [*Paradise Lost*, 4.246-69]

The introduction of *"Pan"* and "Eternal Spring" identifies Milton's Eden as more than analogously or accidentally the golden world.

Milton thus renders homage to Shakespeare's pastoral vision as evoked by the flower passages in the fourth act of *The Winter's Tale*. Elsewhere he pays his respects in another way. The "pale primroses, / That die unmarried" provide the code by which Shakespeare's catalog of flowers becomes interchangeable with the catalog set forth in *Lycidas*:

> Bring the rathe Primrose that forsaken dies,
> The tufted Crow-toe, and pale Jessamine,
> The white Pink, and the Pansy freakt with jet,
> The glowing Violet,
> The Musk-rose, and the well attir'd Wood-
>   bine,
> With Cowslips wan that hang the pensive
>   head,
> And every flower that sad embroidery wears. . . .
>
> [*Lycidas*, 142-48]

The homage appears even more explicit in light of the fact that Milton, in the first draft of his poem, used the word "unwedded" rather than the word "forsaken."

Milton's instinct for the essence of the pastoral feeling here joins with his understanding of its central use: to soften the harshness of actuality, especially to soften the fact of death. The delicately mourning flowers in *Lycidas* are specifically requested "To strew the Laureate Hearse where *Lycid* lies." The same function is obliquely suggested in *The Winter's Tale*. When Perdita concludes the passage with the words "To strew him o'er and o'er!" Florizel says:

> What, like a
>   corse?
> PERDITA. No; like a bank for love to lie and
>   play on;
> Not like a corse; or if— not to be buried,
> But quick, and in mine arms. Come, take
>   your flowers.
> Methinks I play as I have seen them do
> In Whitsun pastorals.
>
> [4.4.129-34]

Flowers used not to mitigate death but to affirm life and love endorse the change from the devastation wrought by Leontes's rage to the restoration of a happy society by means of "things new-born." That Leontes's rage in this play, as opposed to the hegemony of rage in *Timon of Athens*, will be merely an interlude between the pastoral bliss of Leontes's and Polixenes's childhood and the pastoral bliss established by the fourth act, is in any case suggested in the shepherd's very first words when he appears as the harbinger of the pastoral mood:

> I would there were no age between ten and three
> and twenty, or that youth would sleep out the rest;
> for there is nothing in the between but getting
> wenches with child, wronging the anciency, steal-
> ing, fighting—
>
> [3.3.59-62]

The "in the between" implies that the woeful events of the play are merely an interval. But the *Lear* situation is in fact here reversed: the wrongs are not done by children to elders, but, as noted above, by elders to children and the ideal of childhood. Leontes makes life impossible for Mamillius, rejects Perdita, repudiates his childhood friendship. This motif, of jealous eld encroaching upon young life, thrusts itself so powerfully into the play that not all its traces are erased even by the perfumed therapy of fourth-act pastoral. Polixenes, disguised at the sheepshearing, reveals himself in order to threaten his son Florizel:

> [*Discovering himself*] Mark your divorce, young
>   sir.
> Whom son I dare not call; thou art too base
> To be acknowledg'd— thou a sceptre's heir,
> That thus affects a sheep-hook!
>
> [4.4.409-12]

And he threatens also the youthful beauty of Perdita:

                    And thou, fresh piece
Of excellent witchcraft, who of force must know
The royal fool thou cop'st with—
SHEPHERD.   O, my heart!
POLIXENES. I'll have thy beauty scratch'd with
    briers and made
More homely than thy state. For thee, fond
    boy,
If I may ever know thou dost but sigh
That thou no more shalt see this knack— as
    never
I mean thou shalt— we'll bar thee from
    succession;
Not hold thee of our blood, no, not our kin. . . .
                    And you, enchantment,
Worthy enough a herdsman— yea, him too
That makes himself, but for our honour
    therein,
Unworthy thee— if ever henceforth thou
These rural latches to his entrance open,
Or hoop his body more with thy embraces,
I will devise a death as cruel for thee
As thou art tender to't.

                                    [4.4.414-33]

Although it echoes the authoritarian and kin-dissolving assaults of Leontes, Polixenes's wrath is filtered through the magic fact of pastoral, as is shown by his acknowledgments of Perdita's charm and even by his threats to have her beauty "scratch'd with briers." It is, however, the persistence of this threat of age against youth, muted by flowered loveliness though it is, that authenticates the equivocal role of Autolycus. Indeed, he explicitly recognizes himself as somehow prefiguring, keeping open as it were, the same disharmonies as those arising from authoritarian age:

So that in this time of lethargy I pick'd and cut most of their festival purses; and had not the old man come in with a whoobub against his daughter and the King's son and scar'd my choughs from the chaff, I had not left a purse alive in the whole army.

                                    [4.4.604-9]

With such strains of disharmony still running through it, the world established by the pastoral healing of the fourth act is just a better human society, with all the variegations of daily life, rather than a paradise. Even so, as Bertrand Evans says:

From the point of view of the management of awarenesses, the most complex and most effective scene in *The Winter's Tale* is IV.iv— the sheep-shearing. Bedecked with rural trappings, alive with shepherds and shepherdesses, seeming-shepherds and seeming-shepherdesses, bright with costumery, spectacular to the eye, resonant with music, song, and the babble of voices, a feast for eye and ear— this

is a pastoral scene like no other. The sparkling lyrics of Autolycus— inkles, caddises, cambrics, lawns. Why, he sings 'em over as they were gods or godtwelve Satyrs: all this would be abundance if there were nothing more (*Shakespeare's Comedies* [Oxford, 1960], p. 300).

And all the inhabitants of the pastoral environment contribute towards the joyous society achieved in the fifth act. Even the shepherd and the clown join in. They decide to take to Polixenes the "fardel" that proves Perdita's ancestry ("Show those things you found about her, those secret things" [4.4.684-85]). Cozening them out of the fardel, along with their money, Autolycus then decides himself to complete their reconciling mission ("To him will I present them. There may be matter in it" [4.4.825-26]).

In a larger movement, at the end of the fourth act and throughout the fifth act, the tide of separation that had borne so many figures away from the destroyed happiness of Sicilia reverses itself, and with gathering wonder the play begins to draw together into a renewed and purged community the scattered members of the earlier group. Florizel and Perdita, determined to save their love, decide to flee from Polixenes's rule:

FLORIZEL. Not for Bohemia, nor the pomp
    that may
Be thereat glean'd, for all the sun sees or
The close earth wombs, or the profound seas
    hides
In unknown fathoms, will I break my oath
To this my fair belov'd. . . .
                            I am put to
    sea
With her who her I cannot hold on shore.
                                    [4.4.480-91]

The resonant dignity of his language seems all-encompassing in its affirmation of trust, loyalty, and coming together; in its rejection of the divisiveness of authoritarian rage. Camillo converts the random idea of flight into the specific idea of reunion:

                        . . . make for Sicilia,
And there present yourself and your fair
    princess—
                        . . . Methinks I
    see
Leontes opening his free arms and weeping
His welcome forth; asks thee there "Son,
    forgiveness!"
As 'twere i' th' father's person; . . .
                                    [4.4.535-42]

And Camillo, speaking aside, indicates still further agency in the great bringing together:

What I do next shall be to tell the King
Of this escape, and whither they are bound;

　　　　　　　　　　　　　　　　　　　　[4.4.652-53]

So once more the figures of the play take ship over "the profound seas" of space, time, and separation. The repeated voyagings link this play more closely to *Pericles* than to any other of Shakespeare's comedies. Although a certain fantasticalness— as in the oracle (3.2.130-33) or in the matter of Hermione's supposed statue coming to life— seems to link *The Winter's Tale* to the forced solutions of *Cymbeline*, the resemblance to *Pericles* is much closer. For not only do the motifs of danger and restless voyaging suggest those of *Pericles*, but the tones of the two plays are almost identical in the affirmations of joy with which they both conclude. Both involve multiple reconciliations, after separation and supposed death, of father with daughter and of husband with wife. Both, after their existential wanderings, recognize their mutual happiness in language of startling intensity— an intensity that we associate more with tragic exhilaration than with comic benignity:

> PERICLES. O Helicanus, strike me, honour'd sir;
> Give me a gash, put me to present pain,
> Lest this great sea of joys rushing upon me
> O'erbear the shores of my mortality,
> And drown me with their sweetness. O, come
> 　　hither,
> Thou that beget'st him that did thee beget;
> Thou that wast born at sea, buried at
> 　　Tharsus,
> And found at sea again!
> 　　　　　　　　　　　　. . . I embrace you.
> Give me my robes. I am wild in my beholding.
> O heavens bless my girl! . . .
> 　　　　　　　　　　　　[*Pericles*, 5.1.189-222]

And Pericles's reunion with his child Marina is followed by his reunion with his wife Thaisa:

> THAISA. 　　　　　　Now I know you better.
> When we with tears parted Pentapolis,
> The King my father gave you such a ring.
> 　　　　　　　　　　　　　　[*Shows a*
> *ring.*]
> PERICLES. This, this! No more, you gods! your
> 　　present kindness
> Makes my past miseries sports. You shall do
> 　　well
> That on the touching of her lips I may
> Melt and no more be seen.
> 　　　　　　　　　　　　[*Pericles*, 5.3.37-43]

The conclusion of *The Winter's Tale*, doubling its happiness, like *Pericles*, into separate reconciliations of father with daughter, and then of husband with wife, shares the same exalted tone of wonder and renewed joy. The associated tyranny of winter and age is broken by the arrival of youth and spring: "Welcome hither, / As is

the spring to th' earth," says Leontes in greeting Florizel and Perdita (5.1.151-52). No longer the persecutor of the young, but their advocate instead, Leontes agrees to speak for the lovers to Polixenes; and Polixenes, already cognizant of Perdita's true birth, dissipates his own authoritarian rage in a matching acceptance of the youthful pair. Unlike *Pericles*, the play reports these happy events— and the reunion of the two kings— rather than presents them dramatically, with the result that in addition to the joy of those directly involved, society at large participates in their gratification. The language of the anonymous gentlemen reporting the reunions is saturated with joy and wonder: "A notable passion of wonder appeared in them . . ." (5.2.15-16); "Did you see the meeting of the two kings?" "No." "Then have you lost a sight which was to be seen, cannot be spoken of. There might you have beheld one joy crown another . . . their joy waded in tears. . . . Our king, being ready to leap out of himself for joy of his found daughter . . . then asks Bohemia forgiveness; then embraces his son-in-law. . . . Now he thanks the old shepherd. . . . I never heard of such another encounter, which lames report to follow it and undoes description to do it" (5.2.39-56). Although the gentleman insists that the sight "was to be seen, cannot be spoken of" Shakespeare's way of speaking of it could scarcely be surpassed by seeing it.

> FIRST GENTLEMAN. Are they returned to the
> 　　court?
> THIRD GENTLEMAN. No. The Princess hearing
> 　　of her mother's statue, which is in the
> 　　keeping of Paulina— . . . thither with all
> 　　greediness of affection are they gone, and
> 　　there they intend to sup.
> SECOND GENTEMAN. Shall we thither and with
> 　　our company piece the rejoicing?
> FIRST GENTLEMAN. Who would be thence that
> 　　has the benefit of access? Every wink of an
> 　　eye some new grace will be born.
> 　　　　　　　　　　　　　　[5.2.90-107]

And this tone, not merely of benignity, but of astonished delight, is taken up by other minor figures. All separations are ended, all sunderings redeemed into brotherhood:

> CLOWN. . . . for the King's son took me by
> 　　the hand, and call'd me brother; and then
> 　　the two kings call'd my father brother;
> 　　and then the Prince, my brother, and the
> 　　Princess, my sister, call'd my father father.
> 　　And so we wept. . . .
> 　　　　　　　　　　　　　　[5.3.134-38]

In golden reverberation the shepherd says, "we must be gentle, now we are gentlemen" (5.2.146).

The mystical joy, the dramatic juxtaposition of motifs

of separation and reunion, the coming together of father and daughter, suggest, in both *Pericles* and *The Winter's Tale*, the end of *King Lear*. But where *Lear* is true to the tragic fact of death, though the language nevertheless holds out the possibility of heavenly reunion, both comedies retreat into their genre's typical artificiality and typical reluctance to face the reality of death. They thereby achieve a unique position in Shakespeare's art, for they combine tragic intensity with comic well-being. The combination in each case is achieved at a certain cost, that of probability, but the cost is debited to comedy's special account with the artificial.

Both that artificiality and its attendant tone of tragically intense joy are displayed in the statue scene that concludes *The Winter's Tale.* Boldly accepting, despite its wild implausibility, the idea that a person might be able to pass as a statue, the play then builds upon this initial artificiality, with no further recourse to improbability. All other improbabilities are not only accounted for, but actually transformed into the probable:

> LEONTES.   But yet, Paulina,
> Hermione was not so much wrinkled, nothing
> So aged as this seems.
> POLIXENES.   O, not by much!
> PAULINA. So much the more our carver's
>   excellence,
> Which lets go by some sixteen years and makes
>   her
> As she liv'd now.
>
> [5.3.27-32]

And the realism of the situation is further emphasized:

> LEONTES. Would you not deem it breath'd, and
>   that those veins
> Did verily bear blood?
> POLIXENES.   Masterly done!
> The very life seems warm upon her lip.
> LEONTES. The fixure of her eye has motion
>   in't,
> As we are mock'd with art.
> PAULINA.   I'll draw the
>   curtain.
> My lord's almost so far transported that
> He'll think anon it lives.
>
> [5.3.64-70]

This teasing realism in which life is made to seem like stone, and stone to suggest life, indicates the true function of the statue scene. One of the deepest of all mysteries is that of the difference between thought and thing, between mind and matter. Much of human desire is and always has been a longing to animate the inanimate. We need discuss neither anthropological formulations such as Tylor's animism, nor the speculations of philosophers: Strato's hylozoism, Leibniz's monadology, or, with reference to the separation of

thought and thing, Sartre's *pour soi* and *en soi*, or Coleridge's persisting question, "what is the difference or distinction between THING AND THOUGHT?" We need not invoke such matters because the realization of the difference between thought and thing, and the desire to animate the inanimate, are part of the fabric of all men's awareness. The longing to reconcile the two realms, and the knowledge of their utter difference, reach their greatest urgency at that almost universally suffered moment when a human being, living, stands beside the loved statue that is a corpse and experiences the abyss of separation between the living and the inanimate. Furthermore, a recurring strain of experience and statement in our culture recognizes that cruelty, or human uncaringness, somehow removes life from the realm of the animate and gives it to that of the inanimate. The use of force, as Simone Weil has argued, makes a person into a thing; certain criminal acts, as Coleridge saw, seem to forfeit their perpetrator's humanity and turn him into a thing. And common metaphorical usage equates a cruel heart with a heart of stone. "I am asham'd," says Leontes: "Does not the stone rebuke me / For being more stone than it?" (5.3.37-38). Moreover, the state of being stone is also used as a metaphorical recognition of human deficiency in feeling, as in Lear's anguished outcry: "Howl, howl, howl, howl! O, you are men of stones!"

Conversely, the change of stone to humanness represents a profound fulfillment of human hopes. If blood did come from a stone, then all the world would be different. Some of the deepest dreams of magic have to do with the animation of statues. Augustine, in his *De civitate Dei*, attacks Hermes Trismegistus, as Frances Yates says, "for praising the Egyptians for the magic by which they drew . . . spirits or demons into the statues of their gods, thus animating the statues, or making them into gods" (*Giordano Bruno and the Hermetic Tradition* [Chicago, 1964], p. 10). So Paulina is at pains to say that the statue's "actions shall be as holy as / You hear my spell is lawful" (5.3.104-5), and she insists on the distinction between her power of animation and that of black magic:

>   If you can behold
>   it,
> I'll make the statue move indeed, descend,
> And take you by the hand, but then you'll
>   think—
> Which I protest against—I am assisted
> By wicked powers.
>
> [5.3.87-91]

But setting aside the question of "unlawful business" (5.3.96) as does Paulina, it is clear that the animation of an inanimate body represents one of the pinnacles of human hopes. "Do you see this?" asks Lear as he looks on the dead Cordelia, "Look on her, look, her lips, / Look there, look there!" But his thought that he sees life on dead lips is, in the harsh world of tragedy, a final illusion of madness; and Lear joins Cordelia by dying himself rather than by her coming back to life. *The Winter's Tale*, however, rests secure within the magic boundaries of comedy. Leontes's illusion of life upon dead lips is there miraculously transformed into reality:

> LEONTES.   Let no man mock me,
> For I will kiss her.
> PAULINA.   Good my lord,
>   forbear.
> The ruddiness upon her lips is wet;
> You'll mar it if you kiss it; stain your own
> With oily painting.
>
> [5.3.79-83]

But Leontes's proposal marks the conclusion of the statue's stoniness and the regaining of humanity:

> PAULINA.   Music, awake her: strike.
> 'Tis time; descend; be stone no more; approach;
> Strike all that look upon with marvel. Come;
> I'll fill your grave up. Stir, nay, come away.
> Bequeath to death your numbness, for from him
> Dear life redeems you.
>
> [5.3.98-103]

And as the stone of the statue, like the stone of Leontes's heart, comes again to life and mutual happiness, the play exults not only in the achievement of new society, but in the symbolic conquest of death. In religious supplication and wonder Leontes's words repudiate his initial wrong; to the restored Hermione and the fraternal Polixenes he says:

> What! look upon my brother. Both your
>   pardons,
> That e'er I put between your holy looks
> My ill suspicion.
>
> [5.3.147-49]

Even Paulina, the widow of the devoured Antigonus, is restored to the blessedness of marriage by being matched with Camillo, the formerly rejected counselor. And her benediction, ringing with the special strain of intense gladness finally achieved in this play, signalizes the holy reclamation of all its survivors into the state of joy: "Go together, / You precious winners all; your exultation / Partake to every one" (5.3.130-32). Where all are winners, all go together, and all partake of exultation, there is found that social happiness that constitutes the aim and dearest hope of comic action.

ART AND NATURE

There are two scenes in *The Winter's Tale* in which the debate between art and nature is dramatized. One is in

Engraving from Galerie des Personnages de Shakespeare *(1844).*

Act IV, scene iv, when Polixenes and Perdita discuss the merits of the horticultural art of grafting flowers to create hybrids. The other scene is the last scene of the play, in which Hermione's "statue" is revealed to be Hermione herself. **Edward William Tayler** examines in detail the exchange between Polixenes and Perdita. In his interpretation of Polixenes's argument, Tayler explains that to Polixenes, art *is* nature, that when one speaks of art perfecting nature, what is really meant is that nature perfects itself. Tayler shows that Perdita argues against the deceitful and artificial elements of art. Both speakers, Tayler notes, argue against their best interests. Polixenes does not want his royal son to marry a shepherd girl, but his horticultural argument stresses the value of grafting nobler flowers to "wild" stock. Perdita, on the other hand, who thinks she is a rustic shepherd girl, seeks to marry the noble Florizel, but her argument strenuously emphasizes the importance of keeping stock pure by not grafting different classes together. In the end, Tayler observes, Perdita is discovered to be of noble birth anyway. What Shakespeare seems to be saying, Tayler argues, is that nature does not need to be "civilized" by art if it is "royal Nature." Tayler also maintains that the statue scene— in which what *seems* to be art (the statue of Hermione) is in fact nature (the statue *is* Hermione)—

emphasizes that Shakespeare blends art and nature without committing to the primacy of either art or nature. **Maurice Hunt**, in his analysis of the significance of the ages of Leontes and Polixenes, also examines the horticultural exchange between Polixenes and Perdita. While Perdita argues against the artificiality of grafting flowers, that is, against art interfering with nature, Hunt states that the flowers produced by such interference would have produced those appropriate to be given to a man of Polixenes's age. Hunt suggests that Shakespeare is here emphasizing the need for art to "mend" nature in order for man to pass through the seasons of life. Robert Egan presents a similar view, maintaining that the "fictive, illusionary art" of man is necessary to restore the order of nature. Egan explains how nature's order has been violated, both by Leontes's condemning of Perdita, and by Perdita's denial of her true nature when she shirks the role of queen at the festival. Man's art, Egan asserts, is employed through the "artistic intentions" of Camillo, who advises Florizel to take Perdita to Sicilia. By Camillo's interference, Perdita's, and Hermione's, restorations are insured.

Edward William Tayler

SOURCE: "Shakespeare's 'The Winter's Tale,'" in *Nature and Art in Renaissance Literature*, Columbia University Press, 1964, pp. 124-41.

[In the following essay, Tayler contends that the symbols and patterns used in The Winter's Tale *emphasize Shakespeare's interest in the philosophical problem of the apparent opposition between nature and art. Tayler demonstrates the way in which the movement of the play flows through cycles of "harmony and alienation," and "integration and disruption." As the play progresses, Tayler states, the view that nature is superior to art seems to dominate. Tayler concludes, however, that through the character of Perdita, and scenes such as Perdita's exchange with Polixenes and the statue scene in which Hermione is "resurrected," Shakespeare's emphasis seems to be that "art itself is nature."]*

. . . [T]he "symbolic" pattern of *The Winter's Tale*, turning on images of the seasons, of birth and death, of the sea as destroyer and savior, works together with the conceptual pattern of Nature and Art.

The division between Nature and Art occupied Shakespeare throughout his career. It is implicit in the pastoral episodes of *As You Like It*, and even as early as *Venus and Adonis* he is toying with the conventional notion of strife between Nature and Art in painting:

> Look, when a painter would surpass the life
> In limning out a well-proportioned steed,
> His art with nature's workmanship at strife,
> As if the dead the living should exceed.
> (ll. 289-92)

And in reference to a painting of the siege of Troy in *The Rape of Lucrece*:

> A thousand lamentable objects there,
> In scorn of nature, art gave liveless life.
> (ll. 1373-74)

The association of "art" with death and "nature" with life persists even so far as the "dead likeness" of Hermione in *The Winter's Tale;* and the commonplace pairing of Nature and Art is alluded to in play after play, reappearing at some length in *Timon of Athens*, shortly before the writing of the last romances. In the opening scene that advertises the main concerns of that play, the Poet and the Painter are discussing an example of the Painter's work, and the Poet is amiably self-important in traditional terms:

> I will say of it,
> It tutors nature. Artificial strife
> Lives in these touches, livelier than life.
> (I.i.36-38)

Such statements are commonplace, and despite some attempt at variation the similarity of wording implies that Shakespeare produced such literary detritus from his memory on demand, without thought and without effort, as the appropriate occasion presented itself.

Although Shakespeare's use of the division in his allusions to the fine arts is entirely traditional, Nature and Art represented a vital and living problem for him in the ethical speculations of the last plays. In *Cymbeline* the beginnings of what is to be an intense preoccupation may be glimpsed in one of the major ethical contrasts of the play— between the King's stepson, Cloten, and his real sons, Guiderius and Arviragus. Cloten is the product of the "art o' th' court" that Belarius, the guardian of the real sons, continually disparages. Guiderius and Arviragus, having been brought up in savage surroundings apart from the court, represent the triumph of Nature untutored by Art. As Belarius explains it:

> O thou goddess,
> Thou divine Nature, how thyself thou
>   blazon'st
> In these two princely boys! They are as gentle
> As zephyrs blowing below the violet,
> Not wagging his sweet head; and yet as rough,
> (Their royal blood enchaf'd) as the rud'st wind
> That by the top doth take the mountain pine
> And make him stoop to th' vale. 'Tis wonder
> That an invisible instinct should frame them
> To royalty unlearn'd, honour untaught,
> Civility not seen from other, valour
> That wildly grows in them but yields a crop
> As if it had been sow'd.
> (IV.ii.169-81)

The opposition between Nature and Art is not absolute for Shakespeare— he allows the Princes to express an awareness that courts may be in many respects superior to caves— but throughout the terms have been manipulated in such a way as to provide a main theme of the romance. As far as the Princes are concerned, Shakespeare agrees with Spenser and the courtesy books in making Nature more powerful than nature; and thus it is appropriate that Nature unaided by Art should figure in the reconciliation scene at the end of the play. Granted the thematic value of the terms, remarks like those of Belarius' attain in context a force beyond that which may be assigned to a commonplace. In *Cymbeline* statements about Nature and Art have become part of the dramatic design, so that they function, perhaps a little creakily, as part of the plot and not merely as isolated allusions.

By the time of *The Tempest* the process has been developed and intensified, passing from the relatively derivative use of the division to a more subtle and skillfully articulated study of the traditional opposition of Nature to Art. Frank Kermode's elegant Introduction to *The Tempest* takes full account of Nature and Art and there is no need to rehearse his arguments here; although one may grow restive at his identification of Caliban as the central figure of the play, against which all the other characters are measured, it nevertheless seems clear that Kermode is right in contending that the "main opposition is between the worlds of Prospero's Art, and Caliban's Nature." Hence there is little to be gained by pursuing this survey: enough has been said to establish Shakespeare's interest, early and late, in Nature and Art and to provide a context for detailed consideration of *The Winter's Tale*, the play that exploits most fully the relationship between the philosophical division and the pastoral genre.

Beneath the romance trappings of *The Winter's Tale* the critics have seen a pattern that, reduced to its essentials and stated in relatively neutral language, is based on cycles or alternations of harmony and alienation, of integration and disruption. Harmony, symbolized in the friendship of Leontes and Polixenes, receives initial emphasis in the first scene as Camillo remarks, perhaps a little ambiguously: "They were train'd together in their childhoods; and there rooted betwixt them then such an affection which cannot choose but branch now." In the next scene Polixenes sounds the same note as he recalls for Hermione what it was like to be "boy eternal" with her husband, Leontes.

> We were as twinn'd lambs that did frisk i' th'
>   sun
> And bleat the one at th' other. What we
>   chang'd
> Was innocence for innocence; we knew not
> The doctrine of ill-doing, nor dream'd
> That any did. Had we pursu'd that life,

> And our weak spirits ne'er been higher rear'd
> With stronger blood, we should have
>   answer'd heaven
> Boldly, "Not guilty," the imposition clear'd
> Hereditary ours.

> (I.ii.67-75)

The idea of carefree harmony and the connotations of spring and birth are in this particular passage subordinated to the theological terms. The harmony recalled by Polixenes is a vision of the integrity of man in Eden, free of the taint of original sin— an association reinforced by the wit of the following lines as he and Hermione joke about the boys having "first sinn'd with" the queens, the implication being that the innocence of former days was lost because of woman.

This is not allegory, of course, nor is *The Winter's Tale* a covert recapitulation of the Fall of Man. But the web of allusion in these lines provides a frame of reference within which the main events of the play can receive meaning: the speech introduces the vision of the green world, the ideal of past harmony, and associates it with birth, innocence, spring, even with the Garden of Eden. To speak technically, this is the "integrity" of Nature before the Fall.

The vision of the Garden, however, is brief and not easily sustained. As Shakespeare's audience was well aware, the harmony of Eden had been lost to man so that his "stronger blood" was no longer free of the hereditary "imposition." Consequently the Elizabethan audience was better prepared than Shakespeare's modern critics for Leontes' sudden and unmotivated jealousy, the towering excess of passion that, appearing in the same scene with Polixenes' speech of remembered bliss, obliterates the initial mood of harmony and introduces the chaos and death for which Leontes is finally to do penance.

Leontes is a man, his Nature impaired by the Fall, so that he is *non posse non peccare*, not able not to err. The terrible consequences of Leontes' passion— alienation from Polixenes and Camillo, the death of his son, the death of `, the apparent deaths of his daughter and wife— form the main burden of the play until the Chorus of Time that introduces Act IV. Meanwhile the members of Shakespeare's audience have seen the result of an excess of passion and have been able to judge the action in the terms, moral and theological, most meaningful to them. The first phase of the cycle is complete; harmony and integration have been replaced by alienation and disruption.

The pivotal point of the play lies where it should, toward the end of Act III; as in *Pericles* and *The Tempest* it involves a storm at sea, the archetypal image of birth and death. The young shepherd (the clown) witnesses the destruction of the ship and the death of Antigonus, but at the same time the old shepherd comes across the living babe whose restoration figures in the fulfillment of the oracle. The scene thus recalls the disruption and chaos of the earlier action and at the same time anticipates the restoration of harmony in the last act. As the old shepherd puts it, saying more than he understands: "Now bless thyself! thou met'st with things dying, I with things new-born" (III.iii.116-18).

Act IV includes the pastoral interlude and, as we have come to expect, the main references to the controversy over Nature and Art. Florizel, the son of Polixenes, has fallen in love with the shepherdess Perdita whom we know to be the daughter of Leontes, marooned by his order during a transport of jealousy. The child has grown up without benefit of Art, and yet her demeanor, like that of the Princes in *Cymbeline*, reflects the irrefragable excellence of royal blood. Throughout the word "queen" is applied to her, for as Florizel says:

> Each your doing,
> So singular in each particular,
> Crowns what you are doing in the present
>   deed,
> That all your acts are queens.
>
> (IV.iv.143-46)

Both royal children are for the moment disguised as shepherds, the difference being that Florizel knows his true birth whereas Perdita does not. And while they masquerade as pastoral figures, Shakespeare takes care to have us associate the children with more than purity of blood.

Florizel's name— it does not appear in Shakespeare's source— is clearly allegorical, and the association with Flora receives further emphasis in the Prince's description of Perdita in her role as queen of the sheepshearing:

> These your unusual weeds to each part of
>   you
> Do give a life— no shepherdess, but Flora
> Peering in April's front! This your sheep-
>   shearing
> Is as a meeting of the petty gods,
> And you the queen on't.
>
> (IV.iv.1-5)

Despite the wide difference in (apparent) birth, Shakespeare makes it clear that there is no intention of exercising *droit du seigneur*; Florizel's "youth" and "blood" are as idyllic and pure as his pastoral surroundings, as Perdita herself recognizes even when his praise of her is so extravagant as to seem suspicious:

> Your praises are too large. But that your
>   youth,
> And the true blood which peeps so fairly

> through't,
> Do plainly give you out an unstain'd shep-
>   herd,
> With wisdom I might fear, my Doricles [i.e.,
>   Florizel],
> You woo'd me the false way.
>
> (IV.iv.147-51)

Florizel makes it explicit:

>   my desires
> Run not before mine honour, nor my lusts
> Burn hotter than my faith.
>
> (IV.iv.33-35)

In short, Shakespeare has taken care to lend Florizel and Perdita the qualities that his audience associated with pastoral figures— idyllic innocence and artless Nature.

The value of Perdita's artlessness is particularly emphasized. Her intellectual simplicity cleaves directly to the heart of a problem, a quality that leads Camillo to acknowledge that he

>   cannot say 'tis pity
> She lacks instructions, for she seems a
>   mistress
> To most that teach.
>
> (IV.iv.592-94)

And her modest demeanor does not prevent her from making the pastoral comparison between country and court explicit in referring to Polixenes' rage at discovering his son in love with a "shepherdess":

> I was not much afeard; for once or twice
> I was about to speak, and tell him plainly
> The selfsame sun that shines upon his court
> Hides not his visage from our cottage, but
> Looks on alike.
>
> (IV.iv.453-57)

Even this satiric cut— it is in no sense "democratic"— is of the kind common in pastoral. So far in Shakespeare there is no more than what may be expected from the bucolic tradition: spring, youth, innocence, idyllic love, and the assumption that Nature is superior to Art. But when we have understood the exact function of the pastoral episode in relation to the play as a whole, in relation to its dramatic structure and to its underlying alternation of harmony and disintegration, we will be in a better position to see the individual uses to which Shakespeare has put the traditional materials of Nature and Art.

The pastoral episode immediately precedes the last act, the time of reconciliation and reintegration. The court of Sicily— where the action of the play began— is now the scene of an elaborate series of discoveries in which poetic and other justice is rendered all around. A number of exchanges between Paulina and Leontes have assured the audience that the king is truly repentant; the theological note, sounded so persistently and quietly throughout the play, once more assumes a prominent function, as in the words of Cleomenes:

> Sir, you have done enough, and have perform'd
> A saint like sorrow. No fault could you make
> Which you have not redeem'd; indeed, paid
>   down
> More penitence than done trespass. At the last,
> Do as the heavens have done: forget your evil;
> With them, forgive yourself.
>
> (V.i.1-6)

Redemption is indeed at hand.

Florizel and Perdita, fleeing Bohemia and the anger of Polixenes, appear at the Sicilian court; and Leontes, in words that recall the pastoral interlude, welcomes the lovers as a change from the winter of his discontent: "Welcome hither / As is the spring to th' earth" (V.i.151-52). The "unstain'd" youth of Florizel and Perdita, their "true blood," symbolizes the restoration of harmony, the coming of spring to the wasteland, and the purification of the "stronger blood" of their fathers that is impaired by the stain of original sin. Perdita, she who was lost, is found, and discovered to be the daughter of the King; Leontes and Polixenes are once more united in friendship; the way is cleared for the young lovers; Hermione is restored to Leontes during the famous (or notorious) statue scene; and the extraordinary network of repeated words and phrases— youth and age, spring and winter, Nature and Art, birth and death, innocence and sin, Nature and Grace, blood and infection, and so on— is resolved in a series of brilliant puns, in the paradoxical wit of the last scenes. The second phase of the cycle of alienation and harmony, of disruption and reintegration, has been completed.

Enough has been said so that the function of the pastoral scenes in this cycle of— to put it theologically— Fall and Redemption is perhaps obvious. Without these scenes the play would be structurally and symbolically defective, for they reflect, at the appropriate point in the action, the harmony with which the play began: the qualities that Leontes and Polixenes were said to have had as boys are those which Shakespeare gives in turn to Perdita and Florizel. And even the imagery of "twinn'd lambs," together with the assumption of innocence unimpaired by original sin, that Shakespeare uses in describing the young princes accurately reflects pastoral conventions; Shakespeare chose appropriately if not "originally" in this respect.

The imaginative force of the paradisiacal intimacy that once existed between Polixenes and Leontes is therefore essentially similar to the pastoral harmony that is now associated with Perdita and Florizel, and it is therefore proper that the two moments in the Garden balance each other structurally, the one preceding disruption and the other preceding integration. Moreover, the two moments serve a similar moral function in the play. In the cycle of disruption and integration the moments of childhood innocence and pastoral integrity provide the audience, in essentially similar ways, with visions of ideal order in terms of which the rest of the action may be meaningfully understood. The pastoral episode is consequently not merely a decorative interlude but the structural and symbolic prelude to the restoration of harmony in the last act.

Shakespeare's use of pastoral as the expression of an ethical ideal, of a simple world by which the more complex one might be judged, is strictly traditional, and yet it is a little more complicated than my statements so far might imply. Shakespeare's idealization of shepherd life, for example, does not extend much beyond Perdita who is, like Pastorella in *The Faerie Queene*, of shepherd nurture but not of shepherd nature. And while the old shepherd, that "weather-bitten conduit of many kings' reigns" (V.ii.61-62), is allowed to display a certain amount of rude dignity, the Mopsas and Dorcases of Shakespeare's pastoral world are bumpkins, foils for that snapper-up of unconsidered trifles, Autolycus. Perdita's royal blood manifests itself despite her surroundings and not because of them. For Shakespeare, then, shepherds may serve as exemplars of virtue if they are royal shepherds, and Nature may do without the civilizing influence of Art if it is royal Nature. Toward ordinary shepherds Shakespeare's attitude is realistic and gently satirical; his tolerant humor recalls Theocritus but is a long way from Vergil's delicate enthusiasms.

Shakespeare's attitude toward the division between Nature and Art is at least as complicated, but analysis begins most conveniently with his knowledge of traditional materials. Certainly he was aware of the long-standing association of pastoral with Nature and Art, for his pastoral episode includes a fairly thorough debate on the subject. Camillo and Polixenes, disguised, appear at the sheepshearing to investigate the truth of the rumored liaison between Florizel and some humble shepherdess. Polixenes and Perdita discuss flowers, but matters of cultural propriety are always near the surface of what is ostensibly a horticultural argument.

These speeches are worth quoting at length because of their explicit relevance to my thesis, their complex character, and their importance as conceptual statements of the ethical concerns of the play. Perdita begins by apologizing for presenting these men of "middle age" with winter flowers; she has no fall flowers because she will not grow "nature's bastards," and the discussion immediately turns into a highly technical debate on Nature and Art.

Per.   Sir, the year growing ancient,
Not yet on summer's death nor on the birth
Of trembling winter, the fairest flow'rs o' th'
    season
Are our carnations and streak'd gillyvors,
Which some call nature's bastards. Of that kind
Our rustic garden's barren, and I care not
To get slips of them.
Pol.   Wherefore, gentle maiden,
Do you neglect them?
Per.   For I have heard it said
There is an art which in their piedness shares
With great creating nature.
Pol.   Say there be.
Yet nature is made better by no mean
But nature makes that mean. So, over that art
Which you say adds to nature, is an art
That nature makes. You see, sweet maid, we
    marry
A gentler scion to the wildest stock
And make conceive a bark of baser kind
By bud of nobler race. This is an art
Which does mend nature— change it rather; but
The art itself is nature.
Per.   So it is.
Pol.   Then make your garden rich in
    gillyvors,
And do not call them bastards.
Per.   I'll not put
The dibble in earth to set one slip of them;
No more than, were I painted, I would wish
This youth should say 'twere well, and only
    therefore
Desire to breed by me.

                  (IV.iv.79-103)

The speeches are obviously meant to be significant in relation to the entire action of the play; they are not merely decorative commonplaces, but their function has never been fully explained.

There is a possibility that Shakespeare intended the actor portraying Polixenes to speak his lines in such a way that the audience will take the horticultural reasoning as a trap, as a device by which Polixenes hopes to expose Perdita as a scheming wench who is after that "bud of nobler race," Florizel. But it is Perdita who first commits herself against "nature's bastards," and Polixenes' tone, now deliberative, now authoritative, does not appear to support such an interpretation. The King seems pretty clearly to be reasoning in earnest.

Admittedly, the contention that an Art that changes Nature is in fact Nature may seem at first blush sophistical, calculated to make a young girl betray her desires for the "gentler scion." Yet Polixenes' stand is perhaps the most dignified and carefully argued in the whole history of possible opposition between Nature and Art. Like Aristotle and Plato, Polixenes points out

that the "art itself is nature." Aristotle had argued in the *Physics* that when we claim that Art perfects Nature we do in fact mean in the last analysis that Nature perfects herself: "The best illustration is a doctor doctoring himself: nature is like that." And Plato in the tenth book of the *Laws* had maintained that the good legislator "ought to support the law and also art, and acknowledge that both alike exist by nature, and no less than nature." Although Polixenes' argument may appear sophistical, it is in fact an orthodox statement of the "real" significance of the ancient opposition.

There is of course nothing new in the mixture of horticultural and social vocabularies either, but the implications of the mixture in Polixenes' argument are shockingly unorthodox:

        You see, sweet maid, we marry
   A gentler scion to the wildest stock
   And make conceive a bark of baser kind
   By bud of nobler race.

Translated into purely social terms— Shakespeare's equivocal vocabulary forces the audience to consider the social implications— the argument of Polixenes seems to call for a program of egalitarian eugenics [improvement in the type of offspring produced], a program equally shocking, one suspects, to Polixenes and to the Elizabethan audience. Especially in the given dramatic situation, for the King is at this moment disguised as a shepherd expressly to prevent his "gentler scion" from marrying a "bark of baser kind."

Perdita has throughout revealed a Spenserian appreciation of "degree," and now her reply to Polixenes rejects his (implied) social radicalism along with his horticultural orthodoxy:

            I'll not put
   The dibble in earth to set one slip of them;
   No more than, were I painted, I would wish
   This youth [Florizel] should say 'twere well,
     and only therefore
   Desire to breed by me.

Perdita's uneasiness in her "borrowed flaunts" (IV.iv.23), her modest conviction that she is, "poor lowly maid, / Most goddess-like prank'd up" (IV.iv.9-10), has culminated in her final identification of Art with deceit, with false imitation, with "painted" womanhood— a kind of Art morally and otherwise inferior to Nature. Her position is, indeed, as venerable as that of Polixenes, appearing in such diverse places as Plato's concept of imitation in the fine arts, in Castiglione's view of cosmetics, and in virtually the whole of the pastoral tradition. Yet neither Polixenes nor Perdita may be taken to represent Shakespeare's final word on the division between Nature and Art. The two traditions are both philosophically "respectable"; dramatic propriety alone requires that Polixenes maintain the court position and Perdita hold to the pastoral belief in the absolute dichotomy between the two terms.

If Shakespeare's "own" position must remain for the moment conjectural, it is at least possible to understand what he is doing with the ancient division between Nature and Art. Clearly he is using it *dramatically*, as an oblique commentary on the action of the play. Less obvious is his use of the conceptual terms of the division to reflect the major ethical concerns of the play, using them to sum up with dramatic irony the ethical and social questions of *The Winter's Tale*.

With Perdita, for example, the debate becomes a comment on the way Shakespeare has characterized her. She is given to us as the creation of Nature who, despite her lack of Art, is "mistress / To most that teach"; she is completely incapable of deceit, and her charming sensuousness is tempered by a clear perception of decorum, of her proper place in the order of things. At the same time her role in the sheepshearing is the creation of Art; her "unusual weeds" make her a "goddess," a "queen," but since these "borrowed flaunts" are deceitful, she resolves finally to "queen it no inch farther" (IV.iv.460). Thus Perdita's stand on the ancient debate accurately reflects her character; it is perfectly consistent with the manner in which she is dramatized. It is this and more. In addition it anticipates ironically the discoveries of the last act, for although Perdita at this point appears to be arguing (in horticultural terms) against a marriage with Florizel, her words describe unwittingly but exactly the final situation of the two lovers: in the last act it will be revealed that Perdita is a "queen" by Nature rather than by Art, that her "borrowed flaunts" are hers by right. At the time when she takes her stand on the question of Nature versus Art, she is by Nature what she conceives herself to be by Art.

Her speech to Polixenes is therefore effective in two main ways: on the one hand it accents her pastoral status as a figure of Nature, free of the corruption and taint of Art, suggesting the Nature of Eden; on the other hand the speech anticipates obliquely the last act of the play in which she and the other characters (the spectator is of course already aware of the dramatic irony of her speech) will understand that Florizel's metaphorical praise— "all your acts are queens"— represents truth on the literal as well as the figurative level.

Polixenes' argument similarly sets up reverberations far beyond the limits of his speech and the immediate context. Polixenes, like Perdita, seemingly argues against his own best interests, for his resolution of the opposition between Nature and Art apparently sanctions the marriage of a noble to a commoner, the "bud of nobler race" to a "bark of baser kind." Thus, as far as

Shakespeare and the audience are concerned, it is still another opportunity for dramatic irony; again the spectator is aware of more in a character's words than the character himself. Polixenes appears conscious only of the horticultural application of his words while the spectator is in a position to see that, in the case of Perdita, the "art itself *is* nature." Thus, Polixenes is also "right," even in the social sense of his words, though he cannot yet see that the queenliness of Perdita's "nature is made better by no mean / But nature makes that mean." It is only in the last act that the disagreement between Perdita and Polixenes is transcended and resolved in the general restoration of harmony.

The last act is worth looking at in connection with Nature and Art because Shakespeare returns to the subject, this time in the sphere of the fine arts, in an attempt to resolve the paradoxical contrarieties generated out of the debate between Perdita and Polixenes. That which was lost has been found in the person of Perdita, and the two kings are reunited. All that remains is for the dead to rise as in *Pericles:* the "dead" Hermione is still lost to Leontes. Her improbable restoration in the statue scene has been condemned as a vulgar concession to popular taste and cited as an example of the triviality of the romance form. Such criticism quite misses the point, for it ignores the ground swell of harmony and alienation that informs the play and, even more pertinently, it neglects Shakespeare's preoccupation with Nature and Art.

Properly assessed, the "unrealistic" quality of the statue scene is beside the point. Here as elsewhere in the last romances Shakespeare's respect for "truth" lies in the intensity of his verse and in the underlying pattern of the plays. If the statue scene is improbable, it nevertheless conforms with fidelity to the cycle of alienation and harmony, and the verse of this scene possesses a rare imaginative integrity. All the crucial words of the play— summer and winter, "infancy and grace," Nature and Art, life and death— come together in the last scenes in a series of reckless paradoxes. Paulina speaks to the statue:

> Bequeath to death your numbness, for from him
> Dear life redeems you.
>
> (V.iii.102-3)

The time of Hermione's "better grace" has arrived; her stepping down from the pedestal means harmony, forgiveness, restoration, redemption.

The role played by Nature and Art in this larger resolution is perhaps obvious. Clearly a statue represents Art, and in this case the statue represents living Art, or Nature. Such distinctions were equally clear to Shakespeare, and his language shows that he also expected his audience to have in mind the traditional opposition between the terms. We first hear of the statue from the Third Gentleman, whose description is marked by the ancient division and avails itself of the ancient analogy:

> . . . a piece many years in doing, and now newly perform'd, by that rare Italian master, Julio Romano, who, had he himself eternity and could put breath into his work, would beguile Nature of her custom, so perfectly he is her ape.
>
> (V.ii.103-8)

The artist is the ape of Nature, his imitation practiced so perfectly that he almost outdoes Nature, his final aim being *naturam vincere*. We have already seen the same notion in *Venus and Adonis*, the *Rape of Lucrece*, and *Timon*; it is the cliché of iconic poetry of the period, summed up in Cardinal Bembo's epitaph on Raphael: "Nature feared that she would be conquered while he lived, and would die when he died." It is in this tradition of friendly contest between Art and Nature that Paulina invites praise of her "statue":

>   Prepare
> To see the life as lively mock'd as ever
> Still sleep mock'd death,
>
> (V.iii.18-20)

and it is in this tradition that Leontes praises it:

> The fixure of her eye has motion in't,
> As we are mock'd with art.
>
> (V.iii.67-68)

Art has successfully imitated Nature, or so it seems to those who do not know that Paulina has preserved Hermione alive.

The symbolic value of the scene is clear: as with Perdita, the imitation or "mock" of Nature turns out finally to be Nature after all. What seems to be Art is in fact Nature, fulfilling Polixenes' assertion that the "art itself is nature" and confirming Perdita's belief in the supremacy of "great creating nature." The statue scene is with all its improbability a dramatic embodiment of Shakespeare's preoccupation with Nature and Art; it transcends the earlier disagreement between Perdita and Polixenes, for the opposition between Nature and Art dissolves in the pageantry of the statue's descent.

The traditional division lies at the center of *The Winter's Tale*. It is used conceptually and as an instrument of dramatic irony in the pastoral episode, and it appears symbolically as part of the total resolution of Act V. Nevertheless, Shakespeare does not seem to be as far committed to the division as Spenser. Although both poets take full advantage of the association of the literary genre with the philosophical division and although both use the pastoral as "an element in the harmonious

solution of a longer story" about the court, in Shakespeare the division lacks much of the didactic immediacy it possesses in Spenser. The virtue of courtesy must be placed properly in the order of nature, and Spenser uses Nature and Art to achieve this didactic end; he is thinking *with* the established terms more than he is *about* them. Perhaps because *The Winter's Tale* is less obtrusively didactic, Shakespeare thinks *about* the terms more than he does *with* them, finding in Nature and Art opportunities for witty debate and verbal paradox; perhaps because of his lack of absolute commitment he can afford to extract from various and conflicting interpretations the full dramatic value of the philosophical division. In *The Winter's Tale* the traditional terms represent, through dramatic irony, a conceptual summation of the ethical and social interests of the play, and in the last act they form a main part of the elaborate series of paradoxes culminating in the statue scene— the pun made flesh.

Maurice Hunt

SOURCE: "The Three Seasons of Mankind: Age, Nature, and Art in 'The Winter's Tale,'" in *Iowa Journal of Research*, Vol. 58, No. 3, February, 1984, pp. 299-307.

[In this essay, Hunt maintains that the debate in the play between art and nature is informed by a study of the ages of Leontes and Polixenes. Hunt demonstrates how age is significant in some of Shakespeare's other plays and shows that the age of Leontes and Polixenes can be determined by various references in The Winter's Tale. *Next, Hunt focuses on the pastoral scene in the play in which Perdita presents the disguised Polixenes with the gift of flowers. She appears to see through his disguise, Hunt suggests, in that she apologizes for not having the appropriate flowers to give him (Her gift of flowers is meant to reflect the age of the gift's recipient.) The reason Perdita gives for not having flowers appropriate for late middle age is that such flowers are those which are not found in nature, but which are grafted, or artificially developed by man, and Perdita does not approve of such techniques. Hunt explains that such flowers would have represented the age of Polixenes most accurately, and states that in this sense art is needed to "mend" nature, in order to allow man to pass through the seasons of life.]*

Pastoral nature in *The Winter's Tale* stresses the symbolic importance of Leontes' and Polixenes' age, while their age, in turn, illuminates the relationship between art and nature. In the pastoral scene (IV.iv), Shakespeare bases a threefold scheme of mankind's ages upon the progress of the seasons. Within this scheme, Perdita's gifts of flowers help define Polixenes' character and that of Leontes by extension. Critics have only partly understood the significance of Perdita's floral tributes, primarily because they have not calculated Leontes' and Polixenes' late age. Once this age is placed within a natural context, we can more fully appreciate the dramatic value of grafting— of art's special mending of nature. Traditionally, numerology gave schemes of mankind's seven ages their value. Plotting Polixenes' and Leontes' ages within a conventional grid of mankind's years can indicate, by contrast, Shakespeare's unorthodox design of the human lifetime.

While the use and significance of numerology can be profitably studied in such works as Spenser's "Epithalamion" and Dante's *Commedia,* they are discussed in Shakespeare's plays at great risk. Shakespeare's skepticism and the essentially non-allegorical nature of his work account, in large part, for the relative absence of numerical symbolism in his drama. Nevertheless, figures occasionally carry special meanings in his plays. In *King Lear,* for example, the repeated one hundred and zero— the cipher— do represent states of existential wholeness and nothingness. Recently, John E. Hankins has argued that Shakespeare assigned ages to certain characters— among them Juliet, Kent, Iago, and Miranda— which correspond to key years within a basic Renaissance scheme of mankind's seven ages. [*Background of Shakespeare's Thought* (Hamden, Connecticut: Archon Books, 1978), pp. 61-67. . . . [The seven ages of man include:] 1 to 7 years, *Infantia;* 7 to 14 years, *Pueritia;* 14 to 21 years, *Adolescentia;* 21 to 28 years, *Juventus;* 28 to 49 years, *In Statu Virili* (Man's Estate); 49 to 63 years, *Senectus* (Age); 63 to 70 or 77, *Decrepita Aetas* (Decrepit Age).] Since the key years marked the passage from one of the seven ages to another, they were considered, according to Hankins, to be momentous and often turbulent and life-threatening. Thus Iago's emotional upheaval can be attributed, in small part, to his stormy journey, at age twenty-eight, from Youth (*Juventus*) to Man's Estate (*In Statu Virili*).

Whatever the case, Shakespeare often did give his characters ages which either reinforce or ironically qualify important ideas in the plays. Fourscore and upward, Lear has crawled to the natural limit fixed by the Psalmist; he can readily bid "the wind blow the earth into the sea, / Or swell the curled waters 'bove the main" (III.i.5-6), for at this boundary of age chaos begins its reign. Approaching fourscore, Old Adam, on the contrary, still stands within nature's confine. "Though I look old, yet I am strong and lusty" (*AYL* I.iii.47), he maintains. His redemptive action— providing Orlando with the means for freedom from Oliver's bondage and accompanying him to Arden— clearly contradicts the senility of Decrepit Age, which Jaques has cynically portrayed as being "sans teeth, sans eyes, sans taste, sans everything" (*AYL* II.vii.163-66). In general, Jaques' Seven Ages highlight themes in *As You Like It.* In *The Winter's Tale,* Shakespeare continues to give his characters ages pertinent to motifs in the play. Understanding the relevance of art for age depends initially upon calculating Leontes' age at crucial moments in the play.

From references to the ages of different characters in *The Winter's Tale,* Leontes' approximate age can be determined. In Act I, Leontes reveals that he is twenty-three years older than his son, Mamillius:

> Looking on the lines
> Of my boy's face, methought I did recoil
> Twenty-three years, and saw myself unbreech'd,
> In my green velvet coat. . . .
>
> (I.ii.153-56)

Hence calculating Leontes' age at the beginning of the play depends upon fixing that of Mamillius. In Act V, Paulina declares that Mamillius and Florizel were born within a month of one another:

> Had our prince
> (Jewel of children) seen this hour, he had
> pair'd
> Well with this lord: there was not full a
> month
> Between their births.
>
> (V.i.115-18)

By disclosing Florizel's age, Shakespeare makes possible the computation of Mamillius' and Leontes' years. When Florizel first enters his court late in the play, Leontes indicates the prince's present age:

> Were I but twenty-one,
> Your father's image is so hit in you,
> His very air, that I should call you brother,
> As I did him. . . .
>
> (V.i.125-28)

In order to be Florizel's peer, Leontes must wish himself to be twenty-one; Shakespeare encourages his viewer to assume that this is the prince's present age. Florizel's and Mamillius' earlier age can be determined in the light of a remark made by Time the Chorus. Time conveniently informs the viewer that sixteen years elapse between the turmoil in Sicilia and the events dramatized in the latter half of the play (IV.i.4-7). Florizel and Mamillius thus must be roughly five years old when the young Leontes makes his compelling speech about recoiling twenty-three years to idyllic childhood. The king must be approximately twenty-eight years old when maddening jealousy overwhelms him and approximately forty-four when he penitently awaits the arrival of Florizel and his mistress.

Does Leontes' later age qualify him to be the winter king? In Sonnet 2, Shakespeare wrote:

> When forty winters shall besiege thy brow,
> And dig deep trenches in thy beauty's field,
> Thy youth's proud livery, so gazed on now,
> Will be a totter'd weed of small worth held.
>
> (ll.1-4)

In light of this poetry, the viewer may wonder what relevance Polixenes' image of ruinous age has for the two kings. When Florizel refuses to include his father in his proposed wedding party, Polixenes asks:

> Is not your father grown incapable
> Of reasonable affairs? is he not stupid
> With age and alt'ring rheums? Can he speak? hear?
> Know man from man? dispute his own estate?
> Lies he not bed-rid? and again does nothing
> But what he did being childish?
>
> (IV.iv.398-403)

Senility can grotesquely resemble childhood, mocking a major value of the play. In the introductory scene, childhood miraculously appears capable of remedying age. Camillo informs Archidamus that Mamillius is

> a gallant child; one that, indeed, physics the subject, makes old hearts fresh: they that went on crutches ere he was born desire yet their life to see him a man.
>
> (I.i.38-40)

Concerning the crippled men and women, Archidamus asks, "Would they else be content to die?" Camillo replies, "Yes; if there were no other excuse why they should desire to live." And the Bohemian courtier concludes: "If the king had no son, they would desire to live on crutches till he had one" (I.i. 41-45). Polixenes, nevertheless, powerfully reminds us, in the quotation from Act IV, that age can be childish, challenging the belief that the child within the man renews failing spirits. For Polixenes, however, the challenge is immaterial. Florizel's reply to his father's questions reveals that Decrepit Age does not rule Polixenes:

> No, good sir;
> He has his health, and ampler strength indeed
> Than most have of his age.
>
> (IV.iv.403-05)

Clearly, Polixenes' rage over his son's secret love does not spring from physical impotence. An inability to tolerate Time's growth and natural branching (represented here by Florizel's leaving of his father for a wife) appears to be its source. In this respect, Polixenes is Leontes' double, for the Sicilian king's madness proceeds, in one sense, from his failure to give up a boyhood friendship for his married bond. Leontes' male affection and sexual love disturbingly blend when he imagines that Polixenes and Hermione intimately unite.

Throughout *The Winter's Tale*, Polixenes and Leontes often appear to be alter egos. As boys, the two kings, according to Leontes, frisked as "twinned lambs" do; the phrase appears to cover a multitude of shared traits.

Shakespeare extends the identification to cover Leontes' and Polixenes' ages. Leontes' speech about reverting to age twenty-one in order to call Florizel his brother— as he once did Polixenes— would have no meaning were the kings not roughly the same age. One can thus assume that both kings are in their mid-forties during the Bohemian episodes. Polixenes' icy rage disrupts Perdita's festival even as Leontes' wrath chills his court. Both can be spiritual, if not physical, winter kings. Their clutching to the past, heard in the refusal to give up any part of youthful experience, typifies spiritual aging. David Brailow's judgment on Prospero also applies to Leontes. "The desire to withdraw from reality, to create a golden world of his own fancy, is in itself reminiscent of the longing of the *senex* for the imagined good old days and of his failure to adapt to the . . . world." Leontes' cold, leaden language, blighting festive events like his original wooing of Hermione (I.ii.101-04), flows from an "old heart"— one which requires "freshening."

While the age of forty-four or forty-five can be located within the seven-fold Renaissance scheme, the result is not illuminating. Nonetheless, the physical age of Leontes and Polixenes is symbolically meaningful, and the clue to that meaning lies in a theory of pastoral to which we now turn. Drawing upon the *Kalendar of Shepardes,* an almanac popular in the sixteenth and seventeenth centuries, William O. Scott has argued that the four-phase movement of the natural seasons best comments upon Leontes' and Polixenes' age and upon Perdita's gifts of flowers to the Bohemian king and to Florizel. In the *Kalendar,* the natural year represents a lifetime: February through April typifies Youth; May through July Strength; August through October Wisdom; and November through January Age. "It is easy at once to fit this scheme of the seasons and human life to some of the major characters in *The Winter's Tale.* The youthful lovers Florizel and Perdita are surrounded by flowers and spring-time, and in the winter of his life the aging Leontes is penitent." Since "Polixenes, like Leontes, is of the winter generation," Scott believes that Perdita's gift of rosemary (remembrance) and rue (penitence) is perfectly apt for the moral situation of an aging king. . . . While Polixenes' mood may be termed wintry, we have seen that neither he nor Leontes has actually entered the winter of his years.

Rather than four seasons, Perdita (and Shakespeare) mention only three— spring, summer, and winter:

> Sir, the year growing ancient,
> Not yet on summer's death nor on the birth
> Of trembling winter, the fairest flowers o' th' season
> Are our carnations and streak'd gillyvors
> Which some call nature's bastards. . . .
>
> (IV.iv.79-83)

Perdita's omission of autumn can be regarded as evidence of her fierce purity; she will have nothing to do with a season whose flowers are "bastards." Nevertheless, Shakespeare on other occasions failed to mention autumn, describing summer suddenly becoming winter.

In the above passage, Perdita presumably is referring to the autumnal equinox in late September, when day and night are of equal length. Within the astrological context, summer abruptly becomes winter as Libra replaces Virgo on or near September twenty-third. The idea was a Renaissance commonplace. George Sandys, for example, in his commentary on the tenth book of Ovid's *Metamorphosis* writes:

> . . . the Naturalists call the upper Hemisphere of the Earth, in which we inhabit, *Venus;* as the lower *Proserpina:* Therefore they made the Goddesse to weepe, when the Sun retired from her to the sixe winter signes of the Zodiacke; shortning the daies, and depriving the earth of her delight and beauty: which againe he restores by his approach into *Aries.* . . . So the Winter wounds, as it were, the Sunne to death, by deminishing his heate and lustre: whose losse is lamented by *Venus,* or the widdowed Earth, then covered with a vaile of clowds. . . . But when the Sun returnes to the Aequator, *Venus* recovers her alacrity; the trees invested with leaves, and the earth with her flowrie mantle. . . .

Sandys' fable strikingly resembles the myth of Ceres and Proserpina, which F. D. Hoeniger has found informing *The Winter's Tale.* More importantly, Sandys provides a contemporary context for understanding Perdita's reference to the seasons. Shakespeare portrays mankind's lifetime as a development from spring through summer directly to winter. In the light of this scheme, twenty-three is a significant number in *The Winter's Tale.* For example, that is the number of years that Leontes imagines himself to regress in order to find lost innocence. Twenty-three is the number of days required for Cleomenes and Dion to obtain Apollo's oracle, which sets the terms for the play's resolution (II.iii.197-98). Moreover, the Old Shepherd believes that "three-and-twenty" is the age at which youth casts off its vices (III.iii.59-67). Within the biblical span of threescore and ten years, twenty-three most precisely separates the spring from the summer of a man's or woman's life. Doubled, the age most nearly divides the summer from the winter. Nearing the age of forty-six, Leontes and Polixenes approach summer's death and the birth of trembling winter.

Understanding the place of the kings' approximate age within mankind's three seasons helps the viewer to appreciate Perdita's welcoming of her guests by giving them complimentary flowers and herbs. Polixenes and Camillo have disguised themselves in white beards in order to spy upon Florizel at the festival. Perdita thus initially gives them herbs symbolic of the December when the soul should prepare its spiritual accounts. Polixenes capitalizes

Engraving from Galerie des Personnages de Shakespeare *(1844).*

upon her gift of rosemary and rue to fix his false identity:

> Shepherdess—
> A fair one are you— well you fit our ages
> With flowers of winter. . . .
>
> (IV.iv.77-79)

Perdita responds to this speech by explaining that, when the year grows ancient, carnations and gillyflowers are the fairest blossoms, and that she abhors them because they are hybrids created by the (to her mind) unnatural process of grafting. Perdita's words have an apologetic tone. She appears to be explaining why she does not have the flowers corresponding to Polixenes' actual age. In *The Winter's Tale,* disguises often are ineffective. For example, Perdita never does think of Florizel as "Doricles," while the Shepherd and his son, the Clown, easily see the rogue beneath Autolycus' guise as a rich courtier. Perdita subconsciously penetrates Polixenes' disguise and perceives the man of late summer beneath it. After their memorable debate about the relationship of art and nature— a debate in which the viewpoint of each speaker will be ironically qualified— Perdita again appears to apologize to Polixenes for her aversion to grafting. In this instance, her apology takes the form of a second gift of flowers:

Per.   I'll not put
The dibble in earth to set one slip of them;
No more than, were I painted, I would wish
This youth should say 'twere well, and only
    therefore
Desire to breed by me. Here's flowers for
    you:
Hot lavender, mints, savory, marjoram,
The marigold, that goes to bed wi' th' sun
And with him rises, weeping: these are
    flowers
Of middle summer, and I think they are
    given
To men of middle age. Y'are very welcome.
                                        (IV.iv.99-108)

These flowers are not given to nameless characters, presumably shepherds, attending the festival. Perdita has been addressing Polixenes and Camillo, and her gift appears in the context of her speech to them. It would be strange theater for Perdita inexplicably to break off her reply to Polixenes, quickly bestow some flowers upon anonymous bystanders, and then abruptly return to the disguised men. Camillo reacts to her words as though he had been given midsummer flowers:

I could leave grazing, were I of your flock,
And only live by gazing.
                                        (IV.iv.109-10)

By giving Polixenes winter herbs and midsummer flowers, Perdita doubly emphasizes her failure to produce the natural symbols for Polixenes' true time of life. It has often been noted that Perdita, in her giving of flowers, reverses the natural course of the seasons. She progresses from winter through midsummer to spring, where she luxuriates in the daffodils and violets that she would give Florizel— if she had them. Ernest Schanzer observes that "sheepshearings in Shakespeare's day always took place around midsummer"— a time which J. H. P. Pafford fixes in late June. By giving Camillo and Polixenes flowers of midsummer, Perdita may be "consciously flattering her guests for a moment." Such flattery would stem from her belief that she has been too insistent concerning artifice, possibly offending the strangers. In any case, Perdita has only the unspectacular herbs of winter, present year-round, and the flowers of midsummer. Unaided nature cannot fulfill human wishes which transcend its rigidly fixed patterns. Neither king nor prince receives a symbolic tribute suitable for his time of life.

Art must mend nature if each age of man is to bloom fully, realizing a latent potential. Carnations and streaked gillyflowers do bloom until the first frosts; as a gift, they are wonderfully apt for reflecting Polixenes' still present virility and reminding him of it. While Polixenes' wrath might reveal a wintry moral mood, for which the rosemary and rue are appropriate, his age still reflects

the year's prime and so qualifies for the beautiful hybrids. Polixenes' year— his lifetime— is *growing* ancient; Perdita's phrase captures a certain ripeness made possible by aging— the aging toward death. During Polixenes' and Leontes' time of life, the midsummer powers do not come as robustly or as easily as they once did. They must be grafted to an older stock.

Such a grafting occurs, for example, when Perdita's radiant beauty causes the man of September to blossom again. When Florizel learns that Polixenes has pursued him to Leontes' court, he begs his host to intercede for him:

                            Beseech you, sir,
Remember since you ow'd no more to time
Than I do now: with thought of such affec-
    tions,
Step forth mine advocate: at your request,
My father will grant precious things as trifles.
                                        (V.i.217-21)

Recollecting his youthful affections, Leontes replies:

Would he do so, I'd beg your precious
    mistress,
Which he counts but a trifle.
                                        (V.i.222-23)

Leontes' recollection leads him to experience sensual desire. His words are not merely courteous; for a moment (but only for a moment), he covets the lovely Perdita. Shakespeare adapts the motif of incest that mars Greene's *Pandosto* and makes the concept serve an enlightened end. The artisan Apollo through his providence, his bringing together of Leontes and Perdita, is mending nature. In this case, a certain wildness, a youthful passion represented by Perdita, is being married (grafted) to an aging king— the gentle scion:

                            This is an art
Which does mend nature— change it rather—
    but
The art itself is nature.
                                        (IV.iv.95-97)

Apollo's art thus makes possible a natural rebirth. Paulina calls attention to Leontes' efflorescence by criticizing his desire for Perdita:

                            Sir, my liege,
Your eye hath too much youth in 't; not a
    month
'Fore your queen died, she was more worth
    such gazes
Than what you look on now.
                                        (V.i.223-26)

"I thought of her, / Even as these looks I made," the

king replies. By thinking of Hermione as he desires Perdita, Leontes unknowingly prepares himself for loving his soon-to-be-reborn wife. When he can fully experience his recovered love by embracing Hermione, the providential grafting—the mending of nature by art—is most wonderful. The man of latest summer who stands near the ominous pale of winter gains a *vita nuova*. As a force in *The Winter's Tale*, Time is almost Apollo's equal. Hermione's wrinkles do disturb Leontes in the statue scene, and Perdita does find herself empty-handed when she tries to reverse the inevitable course of the seasons. Reared by strong blood, Adam's heir cannot regress to a childhood state of innocence; age must be acknowledged and accommodated. Only then can the man of September become a marvelous hybrid, fully realizing the grace of his season.

GENDER ISSUES

One of the main issues related to gender as it is examined by critics of *The Winter's Tale* is the issue of power. **Peter B. Erickson** points out that in this play, one of the central motifs is the need for the maintenance and renewal of patriarchal power. Erickson traces the way in which Leontes's patriarchy adapts from one characterized by tyranny into one in which women are treated respectably. First, Erickson demonstrates that in the absence of Hermione, the father-son relationship, which serves as the primary basis for the transference of patriarchal power, fails under Leontes's care. Mamillius, Leontes's son, dies. Another influence on the balance of patriarchal power is identified in the character of Paulina. In the control she develops and asserts over Leontes, the balance of patriarchal power is upset. However, Erickson states, the brother-brother relationship between Leontes and Polixenes, however damaged by Leontes's accusations, remains resilient. The two men are able to reconcile, and notably, Erickson observes, the reconciliation between Leontes and Polixenes precedes that of Leontes and Hermione. As for the role of women within the patriarchy, Erickson argues that by the play's end, Leontes has learned to value women, seeing them as sanctified. At the same time, the women's roles become less threatening and more nurturing. Erickson concludes that the role of women in the play is significant, but narrow and confined within the emotional and institutional structures established by men. M. Lindsay Kaplan and Katherine Eggert take another approach in examining the gender roles in the play. These critics discuss the way in which male fears and anxiety about female sexuality, in Shakespeare's England and in the play, may be viewed as "a displaced version of anxiety about female authority." The slander suffered, for example by Hermione, accused of being an adulteress, and Paulina, described as a witch, the critics suggest, reflects male fears about female power. Kaplan and Eggert also propose that the play in a sense takes a "feminist stance" against the laws against women in Shakespeare's time, suggesting that the play offers a tentative critique of the politics of gender.

Peter B. Erickson

SOURCE: "Patriarchal Structures in 'The Winter's Tale,'" in *PMLA*, Vol. 97, No. 5, October, 1982, pp. 819-28.

[In the following essay, Erickson explores the emphasis in The Winter's Tale *on patriarchy. Erickson traces the transformation of patriarchy in the play from a crude, tyrannical form to one in which women are treated more benevolently and valued. In this discussion, Erickson shows how the father-son relationship so crucial to the transfer of patriarchal power fails when Leontes fails to nurture his son in Hermione's enforced absence. Erickson also demonstrates how several other factors—including Paulina's assertion of power over Leontes, and the resiliency of the brotherly bond between Leontes and Polixenes—influence the strength of the patriarchal system. By the play's end, Erickson states, Leontes has learned to view women as sanctified and deserving of his respect, but at the same time, the women lose some of their power, shifting from a threatening role to one of nurturing and reassurance.]*

A critical assessment of *The Winter's Tale* can benefit greatly from a focus on the particular ways that sexual politics shapes the interaction of characters. Here "sexual politics" refers to the characters' assumptions about what it means to be masculine or feminine and to the relative power that accrues to these implicit definitions of gender. Patriarchy forms one basis for the relations within the play, and the need to maintain and renew it amounts to a central motif. The dramatic action consists partly in the fashioning of a benign patriarchy—in the transition from a brutal, crude, tyrannical version to a benevolent one capable of including and valuing women. *The Winter's Tale* enacts the disruption and revival of patriarchy. The male-oriented social order undergoes a series of challenges and crises that reveal how unstable it is until it can be reestablished on a new basis.

The most obvious disturbance in male control is the abrupt manifestation of Leontes' alienation from Hermione. Hermione's visible pregnancy activates a maternal image that seems in and of itself to provoke male insecurity. Leontes' apposition, and thus connection, of "bounty" with "fertile bosom" suggests the maternal role in which he is casting his wife:

> This entertainment
> May a free face put on, derive a liberty
> From heartiness, from bounty, fertile bosom,
> And well become the agent; 't may—I grant.
> (1.2.111-14)

To adapt Melanie Klein's language, what is called into

question here is the "good breast" ("fertile bosom"): the "bounty" provided by maternal "entertainment" is suddenly suspect and inherently untrustworthy. Once the "free face" of nurturance appears to be a mask falsely "put on," Leontes' belief collapses and his own facial composure disintegrates. Polixenes reports that Leontes "hath on him such a countenance / As he had lost some province and a region / Lov'd as he loves himself" (1.2.368-70). Leontes cannot even follow Camillo's advice to pretend that all is well: "Go then; and with a countenance as clear / As friendship wears at feasts, keep with Bohemia / And with your queen" (343-45). Leontes' aggressive doubt renders "friendship" and "feasts" impossible, and the image of festivity does not reappear until the pastoral scene from which Leontes is absent (4.4).

I. "Interchange of gifts": Gift Giving as a Male Institution

Even before a woman enters the picture, the play dramatizes a problem in male institutions: the opening phase (from 1.1.1 to 2.2.27, when Leontes turns in frustration to Hermione) shows a strain in the politics of male "entertainment" (1.1.8). The verbal exchange between Camillo and Archidamus (1.1), which anticipates the similar exchange (at the beginning of 1.2) between the two men they represent, reveals an uneasiness beneath the elaborate surface politeness. The tension stems from the disparity in the two kings' munificence; mutuality is threatened because the two cannot give equally. Archidamus insists, despite Camillo's efforts to dissuade him, that Bohemia cannot match Sicilia's "magnificence" (12) and that therefore "our entertainment shall shame us" (8). (The play will simply omit the awkward moment of Polixenes' reciprocating Leontes' entertainment: Leontes' visit never takes place, except insofar as Perdita ironically and surreptitiously receives Bohemia's pastoral bounty in her father's stead.) Camillo tries to remove entertainment from the realm of calculation and to view it as pure generosity and love: "You pay a great deal too dear for what's given freely" (17-18). Yet he does not succeed, as the direct exchange between Leontes and Polixenes shows.

In retrospect we note a sharp contrast between past and present circumstances. In Polixenes' paradisal version of his childhood friendship with Leontes, the two traded "innocence for innocence" (1.2.69). This mode of exchange has now been replaced by an "interchange of gifts" (1.1.28), which is expanded to "entertainment," a general display of largesse, when Polixenes' visit temporarily ends "separation of their society" (26). The defects in this form of exchange emerge at the sensitive point when the visit draws to a close. The intricacies of protocol express contentiousness as much as affection. Polixenes, echoing Archidamus, announces his inability to repay (1.2.3-9). Both giving and accepting become obligatory as Leontes' insistence on his liberality grows into an imposition. The barely suppressed

tension in the situation comes out in the odd language: "We are tougher, brother, / Than you can put us to 't" (15-16); "which to hinder / Were (in your love) a whip to me; my stay, / To you a charge and trouble" (24-26). Leontes gets his way, but he also gets this "trouble." In Marcel Mauss's formulation, "charity wounds" the recipient; but Leontes' charity wounds Leontes himself.

The initial discord is a product of male interaction rather than of female intrusion. When Leontes draws his wife into this competitive situation, she expresses the preexisting mood in a playful and heightened way, speaking vividly and openly about the emotional ambivalence of the guest-host relation. Her wit is quite blunt about the coerciveness of courtesy: "Force me to keep you as a prisoner, / Not like a guest: so you shall pay your fees / When you depart, and save your thanks" (52-54). Hermione succeeds in breaking the stalemate between the two men because Polixenes is receptive to any woman who can call forth his courtly reflex gesture (56-59). "O my most sacred lady" (77) is the automatic response to woman regarded as the source from whom it is blessed to receive. Although Polixenes' response to women is inconsistent, as Hermione quickly points out (80-82), there is a familiar method in his inconsistency. While Renaissance men aspire to the ideal of the whole man, women are typically divided into opposite extremes, perfection and evil. Thus Polixenes calls Hermione "sacred" at the same time as he implies that women are "devils" (82) who spoil idealized male bonds (67-79). The logic of the play is to excise this antifeminist tendency by eliminating the negative view of woman and magnifying the positive one.

In the final scene Hermione becomes the "most sacred lady" who restores the image of "bounty" (113) that Leontes so drastically questions. The play achieves this restoration by distinguishing male and female kinds of gift giving. Male gift giving is institutionalized, though it has its "natural" source in the pastoral image portrayed by Polixenes. Female bounty, in contrast, is analogous to nature, grounded in giving birth and nurturance to infants. The three women in the play appear to function not according to the logic Mauss outlines but, rather, with the liberality that Wind attributes to the three graces (26-41, 113-21).

These two structures of giving are illustrated by the two kinds of innocence in which they originate. Polixenes asserts the pastoral innocence of his and Leontes' friendship— insulated from women: "What we chang'd / Was innocence for innocence" (1.2.68-69). Once this friendship is poisoned by Leontes' suspicion, another form of innocence emerges in connection with the birth of Perdita. Paulina sees the baby as "pure innocence" (2.2.39). Hermione defends herself by association with her daughter— "My poor prisoner, / I am innocent as you" (26-27)— and protests that her baby "is from my breast / (the innocent milk in it most innocent mouth)

/ Hal'd out to murther" (3.2.99-101). Here is the "fertile bosom" that Leontes' delusory mistrust negates. Finally, the oracle confirms that the child is an "innocent babe" (134). The plot formula contained in the phrase "if that which is lost be not found" (134) suggests that the recovery of Perdita means recovery of the values associated with her: the mutually reinforcing innocence of the newborn and of the maternal bounty symbolized by literal nurturance ("innocent milk"). To summarize, we can say that the plot involves the hopeless corruption of the giving instituted in male entertainment, the reconstitution of the concept of entertainment through festive occasions that center on women (on Perdita in 4.4, on Paulina and Hermione in 5.3) and serve as analogues of maternal nurturance, and the eventual return of entertainment to male control.

II. The Father-Son Relation

The father-son relation is fundamental to patriarchal organization because it implies male control of reproduction. The mother is ordinarily included only as the vehicle that bears the father's successor. Leontes expresses this view in his first response to Florizel (who will become his own heir): "Your mother was most true to wedlock, Prince, / For she did print your royal father off, / Conceiving you" (5.1.124-26). This mirroring of the father in the son provides the basis for the transmission of property, values, and the self (since the son reincarnates the father). It ensures the continuity and self-perpetuation of patriarchal order. The son is the lifeblood of the system, its source of rejuvenation: "I very well agree with you in the hopes of him; it is a gallant child; one that, indeed, physics the subject, makes old hearts fresh. They that went on crutches ere he was born desire yet their life to see him a man" (1.1.37-41).

It is of course essential that the child be male: "If the King had no son, they would desire to live on crutches till he had one" (45-46). The opening scene sets us up for the loss of Mamillius, a loss that in a negative way underscores the need that he could have filled. The political implications of Mamillius' potential as "an unspeakable comfort" (34) are drawn out when Camillo reminds Leontes that any plan of action must be judged by its consequences for Mamillius ("Even for your son's sake" [1.2.337]), when the oracle poses the threat that Leontes may "live without an heir" (3.2.135), when the lords argue that Leontes should remarry "for royalty's repair" (5.1.24-34), when Leontes himself laments that he is "issueless" (5.1.174).

The patriarchal use of the father-son relation is shown to be problematic. The equation of father and son on which patriarchal continuity depends is the very one that destroys Mamillius. Having apparently lost Hermione and Polixenes, Leontes is left with an emotional vacuum that he tries to fill by turning to Mamillius.

Mamillius becomes his new "twinn'd lamb" (1.1.67), as Leontes invokes the father-son identification enshrined in patriarchal succession and uses it to escape from the intolerable and genital present:

> Looking on the lines
> Of my boy's face, methoughts I did recoil
> Twenty-three years, and saw myself unbreech'd
> In my green velvet coat, my dagger muzzled,
> Lest it should bite its master, and so prove
> (As ornament oft does) too dangerous.
>   (1.2.153-58)

In thus sanctioning his "recoil," Leontes reverses the equation that promotes continuity: instead of the son's becoming the father, the father becomes the son, swallowing up Mamillius in the process.

Leontes' use of his son as a narcissistic reflector on whom to project his own anxieties becomes the pattern for his actions. After concluding that "I have drunk, and seen the spider" (2.1.45), Leontes immediately moves to protect Mamillius from oral contamination by separating mother and son: "Give me the boy. I am glad you did not nurse him" (56). Leontes' use of Mamillius as an unacknowledged mirror image is again evident in his diagnosis of his son's disease:

> To see his nobleness,
> Conceiving the dishonor of his mother!
> He straight declin'd, droop'd, took it deeply,
> Fasten'd and fix'd the shame on't in himself,
> Threw off his spirit, his appetite, his sleep,
> And downright languish'd.
>   (2.3.12-17)

This description fits the revulsion Leontes feels on "conceiving" Hermione's "dishonor." He has opened the scene complaining of symptoms similar to those of his son, including insomnia: "Nor night, nor day, no rest" (1). He fails completely in his attempt to nurture his son. Preoccupied with himself, he cannot see that his son's "languish" and loss of "appetite" stem from maternal deprivation, which causes the boy's death.

The news of Mamillius' death punctures Leontes' delusion (3.2.146-47), as the oracle's announcement does not (140-41), because it carries the jolt of recognition based on the equation of father and son: this death hits home. Leontes' repentance continues this identification through ritual worship of the maternal dyad: "Prithee bring me / To the dead bodies of my queen and son. / One grave shall be for both" (234-36). It is out of this rejoined symbiotic unit that Leontes will recreate himself: "Once a day I'll visit / The chapel where they lie, and tears shed there / Shall be my recreation" (238-40). His acceptance of Paulina's punishment and guidance provides a living parallel to the buried image: Leontes plays the role of obedient son to mother Paulina, who dictates a period of "fasting" to compensate for the oral deprivation Leontes imposed on Mamillius (211). The play's final scene reenacts the symbiotic unity that Leontes now mourns. Because Hermione lives, Leontes can eventually take the place of the son who has been sacrificed for the father's sacrilege against maternity.

The father-son motif, with all its political implications, is repeated in the conflict between King Polixenes and Prince Florizel in act 4. Polixenes explicitly links his paternal position with Leontes' and states their common unhappiness: "Kings are no less unhappy, their issue not being gracious, than they are in losing them when they have approv'd their virtues" (4.2.26-28). As set up in the second scene of act 4, the Polixenes-Florizel conflict teasingly echoes that between Henry IV and Hal. But the two princes are drawn from the court by quite different antiworlds: Hal dallies with Falstaff in a tavern, but Florizel pursues a woman in a green world, where the Falstaff role is dispersed between the benign figures of Autolycus and Camillo.

Florizel poses a clear-cut threat to patriarchal order. Though Perdita readily acknowledges the image of the father by her expressions of fear (4.4.18-24, 35-37), Florizel is absolute in his commitment to her as against his father: "Or I'll be thine, my fair, / Or not my father's" (42-43). Florizel proves true to his word when he resolutely refuses to consult his father about his choice in marriage (392-416) and when he ultimately renounces his paternal inheritance: "From my succession wipe me, father, I / Am heir to my affection" (480-81). In rejecting his birthright, Florizel violates the principal tenet of patriarchy, loyalty to the father. As Polixenes indicates, the father "should hold some counsel / In such a business" as his son's marriage (409-10) because a father's "joy is nothing else / But fair posterity" (408-09).

In his initial rage, Polixenes disowns Florizel: "Whom son I dare not call" (418). But he quickly tempers this extreme position in order to maintain the bond with his son. He makes disinheritance conditional. A kind of patriarchal defense mechanism goes into operation to protect Polixenes' self-interest, deflecting the full force of his anger from Florizel, in whom he has a great investment, to Perdita, who is both female and lower-class. By gently rejecting the either/or thinking on which Florizel's defiance of his father is based, Camillo becomes the architect who puts patriarchy back together again— a feat I examine in section 4.

III. Reversal of Sexual Roles as a Threat to Male Control

The axioms underlying patriarchal order include the hierarchy not only of father over son but also of male over female. Since patriarchy distributes power according to sexual roles, Paulina's illegitimate assertion of power upsets the system. She is automatically labeled "masculine" for usurping male prerogatives: "that audacious lady" (2.3.42) is by Leontes' definition "A mankind witch!" (68).

Leontes is equally concerned about Paulina's husband, who fails to prevent her independent stand: "He shall not rule me" (50). Like Mamillius, Antigonus is a screen on whom Leontes projects his anxieties. We should hear Leontes' accusations against Antigonus as self-accusations and self-doubts: "What? canst not rule her?" (46); "Thou dotard, thou art woman-tir'd; unroosted / By thy Dame Partlet here" (75-76); "He dreads his wife" (80). Leontes' decision not to burn the baby, his willingness to "let it live" (157), coincides with his decision to punish Antigonus: "You that have been so tenderly officious / With Lady Margery, your midwife there, / . . . what will you adventure / To save this brat's life?" (159-63). In the long run, Leontes himself learns to be "tenderly officious." In the short run, he assigns "adventure" to Antigonus. Leontes thus delegates his problems to Antigonus, who, like a scapegoat, takes on the suffering that Leontes would have had to go through if the play were a tragedy. "O, the sacrifice," marvel the visitors to Apollo's temple (3.1.6). In the play as a whole, Mamillius and Antigonus are sacrificed to exorcise Leontes' wrath, to propitiate [appease] the terrible mother created by Leontes' fears.

Paulina conforms to this fear by, in effect, impersonating the mother figure that haunts Leontes. In adopting Perdita's cause, Paulina becomes a foster mother, a surrogate for the imprisoned Hermione. The maternal link between Hermione and Paulina, emphasized by Paulina's carrying the baby on stage, helps to explain Leontes' extreme reaction. Paulina continues the mother-child image from which Leontes is estranged: he sees Paulina's nurturance ("I / Do come with words as medicinal as true" [36-37]) as a poison he must resist at all costs.

From the standpoint of sexual politics, the relation between mother and son is a special one not easily integrated into patriarchal order. The reversal of sexual roles to which Leontes strenuously objects in the Paulina-Antigonus relation is normal in the mother-infant bond. In theory, the husband's power over the wife contains and restrains the mother's power over the male child. But this set of checks and balances breaks down if the husband's anxiety leads him to adopt son-like postures (as I argue that Leontes does). In practice, the general patriarchal attitude is "the less said about mothers, the better." Hal is the prototype of what this attitude can achieve when it works. In the best of all possible patriarchal worlds, mothers would be unnecessary. Hence the explicit fascination with that figment of the male imagination, the man not "of woman born." This fantasy defines a supermanliness that makes other men recognize their vulnerability and admit, "[I]t hath cow'd my better part of man" (*Macbeth* 5.8.18). *The Winter's*

Tale, however, insists on motherhood and therefore requires some accommodation to it.

We see the tenuous beginnings of this accommodation when, after Paulina leaves without the baby, Leontes partially relents, as if her departure had activated some area of self-restraint. First, Leontes modifies his response to Paulina, "Whom for this time we pardon" (2.3.173). Second, he changes his approach to the baby: "That thou may commend it strangely to some place / Where chance may nurse or end it" (182-83). The infant's survival is made to hinge on "nursing." Leontes' decree is a metaphor for the capriciousness of maternal nurturance; yet he no longer rules out the possibility of care. This step can thus be regarded as his tentative attempt to test the nurturance he has so precipitously denied to Mamillius and to himself. Although Shakespeare's pastoral ensures that the nature evoked as "some remote and desert place" (176) will be provident, Leontes must do penance, which takes the form of entrusting himself to the care of the woman (Paulina) whom he has previously resisted. There is even a sense in which he had always expected this outcome: "I charg'd thee that she should not come about me: / I knew she would" (43-44). Not only has he been certain that Paulina could be depended on to come after him, perhaps (like Lear) his deepest desire is to be chased and caught by "kind nursery."

IV. Brothers and Brotherhood

The two key relationships on which patriarchy depends are father-son and brother-brother. While the former is hierarchical, the latter implies equality, and therein lies its value. Patriarchy cannot rest on the father-son relation alone, because of the need for an ideal male love that can transcend hierarchy and dissolve the tensions created by hierarchy. In *The Winter's Tale* the principal image of brothers is found in Leontes and Polixenes, the original "best brothers" (1.2.148) who at the end can again address each other as "Dear my brother" (5.3.53). But brotherhood, under Camillo's direction, is generalized to the entire network of male relations.

As the connecting link between Leontes and Polixenes, Camillo preserves the possibility of their friendship. His mediating role is suggested in act 4, scene 2, where men's need for one another is plangently articulated, pulling Camillo in two directions. In a replaying of act 1, scene 2, Polixenes anxiously promises Camillo largesse in an effort to suspend his departure. Again a language of payment and calculation demonstrates the emotional bond: "which if I have not enough consider'd (as too much I cannot), to be more thankful to thee shall be my study, and my profit therein the heaping of friendships" (4.2.17-20). But Leontes also needs Camillo: "the penitent King, my master, hath sent for me, to whose feeling sorrows I might be some allay" (6-8). To avoid the new rupture that might result from these ardent, competing claims, Camillo waits until he can "frame" an enabling fiction that will satisfy both needs at the same time (4.4.509, 662-67). Once presented with the opportunity to devise this plan, Camillo vividly expresses his longing for Leontes: "Purchase the sight again of dear Sicilia / And that unhappy king, my master, whom / I so much thirst to see" (511-13); "in whose company / I shall re-view Sicilia, for whose sight / I have a woman's longing" (665-67; "Sicilia" here may be taken as referring to king as well as country). In the context of male ties, the oral and sex-role imagery can be spoken without embarrassment.

Camillo's resolution goes into effect immediately, mending the patriarchal breach between Polixenes and Florizel before it can get out of control and do irreversible damage. In a series of astute moves, Camillo leads Florizel to accept reconciliation with his father in fiction so that it can later occur in fact. In introducing his "advice" to Florizel (505), he has already reconnected father and son: "Well, my lord, / If you may please to think I love the King, / And through him what's nearest to him, which is / Your gracious self, embrace . . ." (520-23). Camillo presses this opening further by imagining Leontes' equation of son with father (549-50), by making the "color" of Florizel's visit that Florizel has been sent by Polixenes (555-56), and by creating a script through which Florizel internalizes Polixenes: "that he shall not perceive / But that you have your father's bosom there, / And speak his very heart" (562-64). Camillo's plan succeeds even before it is carried out, as is indicated by Florizel's manner of accepting it: "Camillo, / Preserver of my father, now of me, / The medicine of our house . . ." (585-87). This conception of one male "house" to which both father and son belong predicates the resolution that quickly follows.

The final act of *The Winter's Tale* is organized as a series of reconciliations, of which the Leontes-Hermione reunion— crucial as it is— is only one. As Barber emphasizes, Leontes' reconciliation with Polixenes precedes the recovery of Hermione (65-66). While the male reconciliations in the first two scenes of act 5 do not complete the play's work, they impress us with how much men achieve through male relationships. The male network is solid and copious enough not only to withstand the impact of Hermione's return but to supply replacements for Mamillius and Antigonus. Leontes' delusion has resulted in their deaths, but the principle of the identity of "brothers" within the patriarchal system generates adequate substitutes in Florizel (male heir to Leontes) and Camillo (husband for Paulina). The primary indication of the resilience of male bonds in this play is that Leontes does not have to give up his friendship with Polixenes to regain Hermione. The patriarchal context provides both a basic confidence in encountering women and a frame to contain the experience.

V. The Role of Women

Hermione, Paulina, and Perdita are strongly linked with one another. Like the three graces described by Edgar Wind, they seem to have been "unfolded" into three separate characters who can be "infolded" as the facets of a single figure. This figure is the natural bounty imaged by women's bearing and suckling children, as is made clear at the moment when Perdita is born (2.2). Having been rejected by Leontes, Hermione is forced to withdraw into what becomes a separate female society: "Beseech your Highness, / My women may be with me, for you see / My plight requires it" (2.1.116-18). An impressive female solidarity emerges as Paulina joins mother and newborn daughter as "midwife" (2.3.160). She links gender and nature, in the context of reproduction, by proclaiming: "The office becomes a woman best" (2.2.29-30) and "This child was prisoner to the womb, and is / By law and process of great Nature thence / Freed and enfranchis'd" (57-59). Perdita will instinctively express her allegiance to this female alliance in her defense of a "great creating Nature" (4.4.88).

Each of the women takes on the role of hostess, which is an extension of maternal nurturance. Hermione is "your kind hostess" (1.2.60). As "mistress o' th' feast," Perdita is quickly educated into the role of a maternal feeder with a never-ending supply of goods and attentiveness:

> Fie, daughter, when my old wife liv'd, upon
> This day she was both pantler, butler, cook,
> Both dame and servant; welcom'd all, serv'd
>   all;
> Would sing her song, dance her turn; now
>   here,
> At upper end o' th' table, now i' th' middle . . .
>
> (4.4.55-59)

Even Paulina, who seems least likely to assume the role, conforms to the pattern by becoming hostess in the final scene, which is held in her "poor house" (5.3.6). Of course Paulina has spectacular refreshments to offer, but they are modeled on the original image of maternal nurturance, as Leontes' expression of satisfaction suggests: "O, she's warm! / If this be magic, let it be an art / Lawful as eating" (109-11). Caring for infants is thus extrapolated to include caring for adult men. While it is better to have men regard women as enablers than as disablers, we should note that the final harmony between men and women is based on women's acting as caretakers.

The dramatic principle of *The Winter's Tale* has often been described as a logic of transformation. This transformation is of two kinds: the miraculous change in Leontes as he relinquishes his view of women as degraded and learns to see them as sanctified and the parallel but less noticed transformation in the women as they shift from threatening to reassuring figures. While the removal of the threat permits the joyous happy ending, it also occasions a loss, since the women suffer a contraction of power.

Hermione most vividly illustrates the reductive side effects of the play's logic of transformation. In her first appearance she is vibrant, feisty, forceful, but once accused of infidelity she adopts a stance of patience and stoic passivity (2.1.106; 3.2.31). This resignation would be intolerable were it not that the accused woman is in effect split into two women: Paulina is invented to express the angry, active side of the female response to Leontes' outrage. When at last Hermione is revived, her original vitality and vivacity are not recovered. The "feminine" characteristics she incarnates at the end are not the "feminine" qualities she displayed at the outset. She is warm and wrinkled, but she is also thoroughly idealized according to her earlier self-effacing gesture: "This action I now go on / Is for my better grace" (2.1.121-22).

The constriction in Hermione's behavior is tacitly present from the beginning. Early in the play she asserts her power—"a lady's 'verily' is / As potent as a lord's" (1.2.50-51)—and exposes the pretension of Polixenes' nostalgic "boy eternal" (65). Yet ultimately her witty performance calls attention to the limits of her role. Her response to Leontes is exuberant, challenging, but also sarcastic:

> What? have I twice said well? When was't before:
> I prithee tell me; cram's with praise and make's
> As fat as tame things. One good deed dying
>   tongueless
> Slaughters a thousand waiting upon that.
> Our praises are our wages.
>
> (1.2.90-94)

Hermione can mock and make fun of her role, but she can neither transgress nor change it. The sarcastic undertone of her wit suggests a sense of frustration, of being trapped. She provokes Leontes into naming what constrains her—the conventional utterance by which she made herself her husband's possession: "I am yours for ever" (105). When she loses Leontes' "favor," "the crown and comfort of my life" (3.2.94), she submits her case to an earlier patriarchal authority:

> The Emperor of Russia was my father.
> O that he were alive, and here beholding
> His daughter's trial! that he did but see
> The flatness of my misery, yet with eyes
> Of pity, not revenge!
>
> (3.2.119-23)

This appeal to the benign father provides a microcosm of the play's resolution: it points ahead to Leontes' conversion from vengefulness to benevolence and establishes the female commitment, not to independence, but to patriarchal power properly used.

Playing the role of dutiful daughter, Perdita continues this motif of female subordination. She readily enters into her socialization as the all-providing female; she instinctively attends to the prerogatives of paternal power; and though she touches briefly on the egalitarian implications of nature, she hesitates to confront Polixenes directly on the issue and quickly accepts the class distinctions that make her "dream" impossible (4.4.443-50). The reconciliation of father and daughter precedes that of husband and wife partially because the former provides a comfortable and stable means of recovering a positive feminine image. The father-daughter relation is clearly hierarchical and therefore less threatening to the male, as Perdita's compliant radiance confirms.

Paulina is less of an exception to the general rule of female obedience than she appears to be. Her challenge to Leontes' tyrannical authority is sharp, but it is also limited. Since her anger is in the service of the maternal function, she does not seriously violate the code for appropriate gender behavior. Despite Leontes' accusation that she is a "mankind witch" (2.3.68), she appoints herself to defend Hermione and the infant because "The office / Becomes a woman best" (2.2.29-30). Given Leontes' delusion and Hermione's repression, Paulina's assertive action is justified; moreover, she is clearly working in Leontes' best interests, as he ultimately acknowledges: "Thou canst not speak too much, I have deserv'd / All tongues to talk their bitt'rest" (3.2.215-16). Finally, her domineering role is only temporary. At the end she removes the mask of punitive and demanding mother, resuming her normal place when she accepts a second marriage, which Leontes arranges for her.

In the last scene Hermione changes from art object to particularized human being as she "descends" and "is stone no more" (5.3.99). Although this rite is important, we overstress it if we do not also perceive that she remains an icon. If Hermione is a living, directly accessible secular madonna, all the better. Because Hermione's and Leontes' respective roles as all-giving and all-worshiping are fixed, their newly won mutuality is stereotypical. The exchange comprises Hermione's conferring sustenance and forgiveness on Leontes and his conferring appreciative idealization on her. His idolatry, however, needs to be placed in its larger context of patriarchal ideology, for such worship does not prevent Leontes from resuming political control.

In good tragic form, Hermione initially suggests that Leontes can never undo the consequences of his deluded accusation: "You scarce can right me throughly, then, to say / You did mistake" (2.1.99-100). The tragic conclusion having been averted, Hermione's surrogate,

Paulina, prepares to reward Leontes because he has "paid home" (5.3.4). In *King Lear*, the tension between accountability and forgiveness breaks in favor of the former. Cordelia's "No cause, no cause" is not permitted to withstand the ruthless working out of consequences for which Lear in large part must be held responsible. In *The Winter's Tale*, accountability is superseded and ultimately suspended through the mediation of women: an apparently "free" bounty prevails. Yet the commercial metaphor is still needed to describe the final transaction by which female bounty is extrapolated from the image of maternal nurturance and converted into male bounty, whose circulation is the basis of benevolent patriarchal order. In this sense, the patriarchal body politic is founded on the female body. Hermione blesses her daughter with the nurturance that she had previously been forced to withhold: "You gods, look down / And from your sacred vials pour your graces / Upon my daughter's head" (121-23). Yet the nurturance is displaced, attributed to what we may assume to be a male-controlled heaven under the reign of Zeus or his son Apollo (both of whom are invoked by Florizel [4.4.27-31]). The moment, furthermore, is treated as an interlude that leads to patriarchal closure. In the final speech, Leontes returns to the role of dispenser of bounty and director of entertainment.

An ultimately positive attitude toward procreation is one of the main reasons for the joyous resolution of *The Winter's Tale*. In this late romance, Shakespeare achieves the genuine reconciliation of procreation and art that is missing in the *Sonnets*. Moreover, it is a reconciliation that favors procreation. While Shakespeare is certainly not apologetic about the artistic construct represented by the last scene, he is humble about his art. There is a sense in which he has given nature a position superior to that of art. In the final paragraph of a superbly formulated essay on transformation in the late romances, Barber sheds light on the conclusion of *The Winter's Tale* by adapting a line from *Pericles* and applying it "to the dramatist himself: 'He that beget'st her that did him beget.'" Thus one can conclude that in Hermione Shakespeare recreates and celebrates the mother who gave birth to him. I should like to return to the original line and its stress on female agency— "She that beget'st him . . ."—in order to emphasize that she also rebegets him. My view is that (though the dramatist obviously created Hermione) Shakespeare's main locus in the final scene is Leontes. Like Leontes, Shakespeare is in the position of declaring and displaying his "faith" (5.3.95). He too depends on Hermione for rebirth and rescue (for which Prospero must turn more uncertainly to the audience). In a paradoxical but not merely rhetorical sense, Shakespeare submits to his own creation and receives its bounty.

To use a phrase spoken prematurely in act 5 but resonant beyond its immediate context, Shakespeare can be seen as "forgiving himself" (5.1.6) in relation to women.

What would allow him this forgiveness after such tragic knowledge is his placing himself in a different relation to his art. While the sonnets of immortality often aspire to an aesthetic realm that excludes natural forces, mastery of a more inclusive art requires relinquishing this ideal by relaxing, as it were, the artistic grip. In this new kind of art, Shakespeare aligns himself with nature and women; procreation becomes a model for an artistic process that can lead beyond tragedy. Yet it is a mistake to leap from this observation to the conclusion that Shakespeare was paying homage to women. Such an unwarranted leap is the essence of the sentimental reading of the play, but Shakespeare's tribute to women is complex and deceptive because patriarchal strictures minimize and hedge the risks attendant on his apparent openness to women. What the sentimental reading of *The Winter's Tale* overlooks is that female roles, though significant, are narrow and fixed, arranged to be consistent with the emotional needs and institutional structures of men. Men do not, through a simple identification, adopt the values of nurturance they have had to learn from women; rather, men appropriate these values as they translate them into ongoing patriarchal institutions that place limits on women, albeit in a benign and harmonious atmosphere.

VI. Conclusion

In *Antony and Cleopatra*, even those of us who are sympathetic to Cleopatra's "dream" of "an Emperor Antony" (5.2.76) are forced to acknowledge the reality principle— no matter how paltry we would like to consider it— that qualifies her artful suicide. While *Antony and Cleopatra* has to answer to the demands of both transcendence and reality, the resolution of *The Winter's Tale* appears not to be pulled in these two directions but to partake of a world made safe for the total fulfillment of transcendence. Yet, as I have argued, the concept of patriarchy helps to reveal the reality principle operating at the end of *The Winter's Tale*.

The reality principle that qualifies Antony and Cleopatra's achievement is indicated not only by the external facts of their suicides and of Caesar's power but by internal aspects of their relationship. Not everything in the relationship can be transformed. In the midst of Cleopatra's apotheosis, the maternal image that explicitly manifests itself is not what we might have expected or wished for: "Peace, peace! / Dost thou not see my baby at my breast, / That sucks the nurse asleep?" (5.2.308-10). Cleopatra's equation of baby and poisonous asp undercuts the nurturant fulfillment, and the poetic atmosphere cannot wholly conceal this negation. Though the context is different, I find this evocation of the maternal breast as disturbing as the allusions by Lady Macbeth and Volumnia. The logic of transformation in *Antony and Cleopatra* is finally incomplete and imperfect because the negative image of the mother-infant bond cannot be absorbed. This unassimilable

residue enforces an intrinsic limit that is more significant than external circumstances in causing us to have reservations that distance us from Antony and Cleopatra. Much as we are tempted to turn *Antony and Cleopatra* into a late romance, Cleopatra's image of the breast foils us. At this point, Shakespeare's subsequent work appears to offer a welcome way out: we shift quickly from the conclusion of *Antony and Cleopatra* to that of *The Winter's Tale*. But in making this shift, I want to qualify the assurance it is usually seen as providing, the assurance that Shakespeare won through to an entirely positive image of maternal nurturance.

Cleopatra and Hermione both preside over a conclusion that consists in the woman's giving herself completely. But, while *Antony and Cleopatra* may give us "new heaven," *The Winter's Tale* gives us "new earth," creating a real world fully conducive to transcendence, a world in which the logic of transformation proceeds unimpeded to the total fulfillment lacking in the earlier play. The rite that Paulina arranges in the last scene of *The Winter's Tale* celebrates the nurturant life that Cleopatra in her final performance is forced to give up. In seeking the "fire and air" of an imaginary heaven and relinquishing her "other elements" "to baser life" (5.2.289-90), Cleopatra renounces what *The Winter's Tale* calls "Dear life" (5.3.103). The "Dear life" that "redeems" Hermione includes an actual family. The absent Antony and the asp, however intensely imagined as "husband" and "baby," cannot compare with Leontes and Perdita, who are present to receive Hermione's life-giving "blessing." Yet it would be incorrect to end on an exclusively optimistic note. The contrast between the two plays is not so one-sided. The gains in fulfillment in *The Winter's Tale* are achieved at a cost— the imposition of restrictive definitions of gender. To attain the climactic harmony of *The Winter's Tale*, Shakespeare retreats from the experiment in androgyny in *Antony and Cleopatra* and returns to a traditional conception of polarized sexual roles. The mutuality between men and women dramatized in *The Winter's Tale* is schematic compared with the vibrant (though troubled) give-and-take enacted by Antony and Cleopatra. I conclude that the contrast between the tragedies and the late romances is relative rather than absolute; the romances continue in a different form the exploration of tragic motives, and the late plays remain stubbornly problematic.

LEONTES

Criticism of Leontes's character focuses heavily on the issue of his jealousy, which seems to explode in Act I, scene ii, after Hermione persuades Polixenes to extend his stay. **Roger J. Trienens** notes that often, critics view Leontes's jealousy as either a flaw inherent in Leontes's nature, or, as highly improbable, and therefore a weakness in Shakespeare's dramatic construction. Both views, Trienens maintains, assume that Leontes's jealousy arises nearly instantaneously. Trienens argues that on the contrary, Leontes's jealousy is displayed from the play's beginning. When Leontes asks Hermione to implore Polixenes to stay longer, Leontes is seeking proof for the suspicions that have been developing for some time. **Michael Taylor** takes another approach, suggesting that Leontes's jealousy and impulsive actions are based in his "primal innocence." Taylor describes Leontes as "an innocent in the worse sense . . . who looks at the world and sees reflected there his own hysterical forebodings." This primal innocence explains Leontes's rash, petulant behavior, and his habit of making broad judgements based on his limited knowledge of human behavior, Taylor argues. Taylor indicates that by the play's end, Leontes's primal innocence has been replaced by a new, more mature version, which incorporates art and nature, the intellectual and the physical. Along with this new innocence comes new dangers, Taylor seems to suggest. John P. Cutts's critique of Leontes is similar to that of Taylor. Cutts maintains that Leontes suffers from a "boy eternal" complex, which affects his relationship with both Hermione and Polixenes. Cutts explains that Leontes seems obsessed with his childhood, "when he stood heir to men's greatest expectations of him. . . ." The dominant theme of the first scene of the play, Cutts observes, is Leontes's boyhood and his relationship with Polixenes. Furthermore, in Leontes's description of his prenuptial wooing of Hermione, and in Hermione's expression of her need to be praised and kissed, Cutts sees further evidence of Leontes's "boy eternal" complex. Leontes still has not matured enough to properly woo Hermione; the wooing, Cutts says, is one-sided, as it is in the final scene of the play. When Hermione is restored, it is she who woos Leontes, hanging about his neck. Leontes, however, still treats Hermione like a statue, yet he is revived by his reconciliation with Polixenes, his boyhood friend. Like Peter Erickson, in his essay on gender issues, Cutts suggests that the reconciliation of Polixenes and Leontes takes precedence over that of Hermione and Leontes.

Roger J. Trienens

SOURCE: "The Inception of Leontes' Jealousy in 'The Winter's Tale,'" in *Shakespeare Quarterly*, , Vol. 4, No. 3, July, 1953, pp. 321-26.

[In the following essay, Trienens examines Leontes's apparently sudden and unfounded jealousy in Act I, scene ii, of The Winter's Tale. *Trienens observes that most critics view Leontes's jealousy as either a weakness in Leontes's nature, or as improbable, and a flaw in Shakespeare's construction of the play. Unsatisfied with such interpretations, Trienens highlights the problems with both views before presenting his own. Trienens argues that Leontes's jealousy does not appear suddenly, but*

Act II, scene iii. By W.M. Craig. Leontes, Antigonus, Lords, servants, Paulina, Perdita.

rather is demonstrated from the play's beginning.]

Much of the criticism of *The Winter's Tale* hinges upon the characterization of Leontes and upon his startling outburst of jealousy in Act I, scene ii. Most critics have assumed that Leontes is in a normal state of mind when this scene begins but that he suddenly becomes jealous when Hermione persuades Polixenes, the visiting king, to remain longer in Sicily. Yet this has seemed a very inadequate cause for suspicion, because Hermione, however graciously, merely obeys her husband's command. Therefore these critics have generally tried to account for his sudden jealousy in one of two ways. Either they have explained it as manifesting a weakness inherent in Leontes' nature, a weakness which makes him respond to a most trifling cause for suspicion, or else they have simply called it an improbability and hence a flaw in the dramatic construction.

Each of these views has certain drawbacks which I should like to point out before citing what I consider to be a true interpretation. Harold C. Goddard, in *The Meaning of Shakespeare*, illustrates the view that Leontes' jealousy is an inherent characteristic; for he attributes it to "emotional instability." He believes that Leontes becomes instantaneously the victim of an insane jealousy for no other reason than the trifle that his friend from boyhood . . . agrees to stay at the solicitation of Leontes' wife. Within a matter of minutes, we might almost say of seconds, he is so beside himself that he is actually questioning the paternity of his own boy and his mind has become a chaos of incoherence and sensuality. Unmotivated, his reaction has been pronounced by critic after critic, and so it is, if by motive we mean a definite rational incitement to action. But there are irrational as well as rational incitements to action, and what we have here is a sudden inundation of the conscious by the unconscious, of which the agreement of Polixeness to prolong his visit is the occasion rather than the cause.

The psychology of the unconscious here seems to mitigate the moral indictment which early critics like Coleridge frequently level against Leontes. In comparing *Othello* with *The Winter's Tale*, Coleridge describes Othello as a noble person who is not easily jealous, whereas he describes Leontes as an ignoble person who suffers from such faults as "grossness of conception" and "selfish vindictiveness" and who is therefore easily given to jealousy. Lady Martin expresses the same view when she writes, "Shakespeare has therefore dealt with Leontes as a man in whom the passion of jealousy is inherent; and shows it breaking out suddenly with a force that is deaf to reason, and which stimulated by an imagination tainted to the core, finds evidences in actions the most innocent. How different is such a nature's from Othello's! . . ."

For Leontes to be considered naturally jealous, as these critics imagine, certain obstacles would appear insurmountable. Leontes has been married for several years before manifesting jealousy and he has been tolerating the company of Polixenes for nine months. Surely if he were naturally jealous he would have betrayed his weakness in some manner before. Yet the opening scene, the discussion between Archidamus and Camillo, is clearly designed to put the audience in the same frame of mind as the characters in the play, who are astonished when such a man as Leontes turned out to be jealous. Shakespeare treats Leontes sympathetically, as in the talk with Mamillius, and he treats him as a noble rather than as a base character. It is true that Leontes succumbs to jealousy without the assistance of an Iago or an Iachimo; but at the close of the play, having suffered a purgatory of grief, he appears worthy of the reconciliation with Hermione.

Thus the alternate view that Leontes' sudden jealousy is simply an improbability would seem preferable. Hudson expresses this view, saying, "In the delineation of Leontes there is an abruptness of change which strikes us, at first view, as not a little a-clash with nature; we cannot well see how one state of mind grows out of another; his jealousy shoots comet-like, as

something unprovided for in the general ordering of his character." In his introduction to the *New Cambridge Shakespeare* edition Quiller-Couch further emphasizes the artistic ineptitude: "In *Pandosto* (we shall use Shakespeare's names) Leontes' jealousy is made slow and by increase plausible. Shakespeare weakens the plausibility of it as well by ennobling Hermione— after his way with good women— as by huddling up jealousy in its motion so densely that it merely strikes us as frantic and— which is worse in drama— a piece of impossible improbability. This has always and rightly offended the critics. . . ."

This interpretation is reasonable, at least, since it does not contradict the most obvious facts of Leontes' characterization; yet one would naturally wish to discredit it, since it is damaging to the artistry of the play. It may seem the better of the two customary views. But fortunately both of these views may be shown to be incorrect because they are both based on a mistaken assumption; on the assumption, namely, that Leontes' jealousy rises almost instantaneously. One critic, John Dover Wilson, has contradicted this assumption in a brief note to the *New Cambridge Shakespeare* edition:

> . . . The problem of this scene is to determine at what point Leontes first becomes jealous. My own belief is that the actor who plays him should display signs of jealousy from the very onset and make it clear, as he easily may, that the business of asking Polixenes to stay longer is merely the device of jealousy seeking proof.

It is my hope in the present article to support Wilson's belief with arguments that will convince the reader of its validity.

The other critics would have us believe that Leontes is not beset with jealousy when scene ii begins and that his passion must therefore rise in the brief period between line 1 and line 108 when he expresses his feelings in an aside. Moreover some critics shorten the period still further. According to Coleridge, for example, the words "At my request he would not" (line 87) reveal the commencement of Leontes' jealous fit. Coleridge believes that even in lines 43-45,

> yet, good deed, Leontes,
> I love thee not a jar o' th' clock behind
> What lady she her lord,

Hermione sets Leontes' allegedly inherent jealousy "in nascent action." These lines, says Coleridge, should be accompanied, "as a good actress ought to represent it, by an expression and recoil of apprehension that she had gone too far." But only Wilson has forthrightly asserted that Leontes is already experiencing jealousy at the very beginning of the scene. Now in the source of *The Winter's Tale*, Greene's *Pandosto*, the jealousy of the king is quite plausible. For in the narrative form of the story it seems natural that over a period of time he should become increasingly suspicious while he observes his queen and the visiting king enjoying each other's company. Quiller-Couch, in the passage we have read, states that in the process of dramatizing it Shakespeare rendered the story improbable. Yet it is also possible to assume that at the beginning of scene ii the action of the play is identical with that of the novel. If we can impose the novel on the play—that is, if we can read the opening of the scene as if Leontes were already jealous—then we should be able to relieve our minds of the charge that the plot is at this point faulty.

As a matter of fact, a textual analysis of the scene will confirm such a reading. Let us assume that Leontes has watched with increasing anxiety the familiarity that has grown up between Hermione and Polixenes during the latter's long visit. Why then would Leontes wish to detain Polixenes? Probably not in order to exact revenge, because his suspicion has not yet developed into a conviction. It seems more plausible that like Othello he simply cannot bear to doubt and that he is intent upon ascertaining the truth, which he could not easily do if Polixenes were to depart. In view of this situation it would be natural if in his attempt to detain Polixenes with a show of courtesy, Leontes failed to communicate himself with appropriate warmth. And indeed, his words seem remarkably terse and laconic in relation to the situation as it seems on the surface. In their total effect they give more the impression of blunt refusal than of courteous persuasion. Having managed to say little himself, Leontes addresses these curt words to Hermione: "Tongue-tied our Queen? Speak you." She has noticed the inappropriateness of his speech which is apparent even in the printed text and which should be quite obvious in the stage delivery. Yet she does not suspect the anxiety which affects his speech any more than, up to this point, does the audience. Nor can she suspect how her success in persuading Polixenes will unsettle his mind; but that it immediately does produce such an effect is made clear by Leontes' pointed comment, "At my request he would not." If his mind were not already given to jealousy this swift reaction would be incredible. Therefore why should we not assume that he was already jealous? If we weigh the probabilities I think we ought to conclude that Shakespeare, although not overtly revealing his jealousy before the aside, has written this scene on the premise that Leontes is jealous at its very beginning and even for some time antecedent to it.

When Leontes expresses jealousy in his aside, he does not betray the astonishment of one who has just been surprised into a passion; but instead he speaks with a careful eye for detail as he observes the behavior of Hermione and Polixenes. He has taken the event which has just passed as evidence of guilt, and he has already turned his attention towards other evidence. In fact it is a measure of the advanced stage of his suspicion that

he can think in such unemotional terms about what he sees. Instead of exclaiming, "What does this mean?" or "Can it be true?" he speaks only as if he were confirmed in his suspicion: "My heart dances, but not for joy, not joy."

After the aside, Leontes succeeds for a while in concealing his jealousy from the other characters as before; but the audience gets a better measure of his passion from the conversation with his boy, Mamillius. What distinguishes scene ii, as it progresses, from any of Leontes' previous experiences is that the seeming confirmation of his doubts rapidly unbalances his mind. Further indication that his suspicions are not entirely new comes when Leontes finally discloses his jealousy to Camillo. For then he implies that it is based not only upon Hermione's success in persuading Polixenes, but upon that in conjunction with many previous observations:

> Is whispering
> nothing?
> Is leaning cheek to cheek? Is meeting noses?
> Kissing with inside lip? stopping the career
> Of laughter with a sigh?—a note infallible
> Of breaking honesty;—horsing foot on foot?
> Skulking in corners? wishing clocks more
> swift?
> Hours, minutes? noon, midnight? . . .
>
> (284-290)

He is accustomed to observing such appearances. Insofar as they are real (we need not accuse Hermione of serious impropriety), they certainly have not all impressed his mind within the last few minutes or even hours. And still later in the scene, when Polixenes asks Camillo how Leontes came to be jealous, Camillo does not mention the incident which merely intensified the passion. He replies,

> I know not; but I am sure 'tis safer to
> Avoid what's grown than question how 'tis
> born.
>
> (432-433)

Wilson's theory, which he set forth in 1931, has not gained the support or even the attention that it deserves and critics like M. R. Ridley, E. M. W. Tillyard, G. B. Harrison, and Hardin Craig have continued to discuss Leontes' characterization along the lines of earlier criticism. On the other hand, Mark Van Doren seems to follow Wilson in his discussion of the play, especially when he states that Leontes "opens his whole mind to us" in the aside. But if he accepts Wilson's interpretation he does not assert the fact, much less give reasons for doing so. Thomas Marc Parrott is one critic who has struck out on a fresh path:

> It may repay us to follow the action of the play and to observe Shakespeare's use of the tragi-comic tech-

nique of surprise and spectacle. It opens gaily with the portrayal of the old friendship of the two kings and with Hermione's playful pressure on Polixenes to defer his departure, but the first surprise comes swiftly with the revelation of her husband's jealousy. No auditor, unless aware that Shakespeare was dramatizing Greene's novel, could have expected this. The sudden unmotivated passion of Leontes has often been denounced by critics, but Shakespeare had no desire to write *Othello* over again. The jealousy of Leontes, unlike that of the Moor, is causeless, self-centered, and recognized by all others in the action as morbid self-delusion.

Parrott differs from critics like Quiller-Couch because in comparing the play with its source he emphasizes the surprise element instead of the supposed improbability. However, he too regards Leontes' jealousy as a "sudden unmotivated passion."

S. L. Bethell, in his book *The Winter's Tale, A Study*, has noticed Wilson's theory and attempted to refute it. His argument appears in an appendix entitled "Leontes' jealousy and his 'secret vices,'" where he also attempts to refute Wilson's other theory that Leontes himself had sinned before the opening of the play. I will not enter into this second dispute except to say that I do not believe that Leontes had led a sinful life either. But surely these two ideas are not interdependent; for as I have already argued, Shakespeare treats Leontes as a worthy character and Leontes becomes jealous because of the morbid condition of mind in which his situation has placed him. Bethell's argument is principally based on Leontes' comment after Hermione and Polixenes go into the garden:

> I am angling now,
> Though you perceive me not how I give line.
> (180-181)

He believes that if Shakespeare gives this conventional indication of Leontes' state of mind here, it is improbable that he should have used the "relatively naturalistic technique" at the beginning of the scene. But if we accept Parrott's idea that Shakespeare used a *surprise* technique, this argument loses its force because the same surprise cannot happen twice. Moreover, the striking presentation of Leontes' jealousy is characteristic of Shakespeare's genius— his plays are remarkable for their dramatic openings— and by developing the contrast between the general opinion of Leontes' happiness and his true state of mind Shakespeare reiterates one of his favorite themes, that appearances are deceiving.

The Winter's Tale is complementary with *Othello* in that it takes jealousy as its premise and traces its consequences for a man who avoids death, whereas the earlier play traces the inception and growth of jealousy leading up to a tragic incident. In *The Winter's Tale* Shakespeare is thus satisfied only to hint at the question of "how 'tis

born." After scrutinizing the text we can picture to ourselves how Leontes first became jealous. However, we should realize that Shakespeare omits this matter in order to turn our attention to the estrangement which inevitably follows; for *The Winter's Tale* is essentially a study of estrangement and reconciliation. If jealousy is the premise of this play it does not have to rise instantaneously. Yet if Shakespeare were to have described its development dramatically he would have had to introduce matter irrelevant to his theme— as Parrott says, he would have had to write *Othello* over again. And if he had immediately disclosed the secret of Leontes' jealousy to the audience he could hardly have begun the play in so surprising and effective a manner.

Michael Taylor

SOURCE: "Innocence in 'The Winter's Tale,'" in *Shakespeare Studies*, Vol. XV, 1982, pp. 227-41.

[In this essay, Taylor examines the character of Leontes as an "innocent" figure. Taylor demonstrates that the play's opening scenes, in their focus on childhood innocence, prepare the audience to view Leontes "as an innocent in the worse sense." That is, Leontes is shown to be a person who fails to look at the world objectively, but instead sees reflected in the world his own dark suspicions and paranoia. After tracing Leontes's "primal innocence" throughout the play, Taylor argues that by the play's end, this primal innocence is replaced by a new and more mature type of innocence, in which both intellect and passion, nature and art, are combined. In his reference at the end of the essay to William Blake's "spiritual vision," Taylor implies that this new type of innocence may be problematic and may be, in some ways, just as dark and troublesome as the primal innocence which hampers Leontes throughout much of the play.]

Dominated by Leontes' ravings, the first act of *The Winter's Tale* appears to be the fiery prelude to a tragedy of jealous passion, the flights of Camillo and Polixenes to Bohemia at the act's end an intimation of more dismal fates to come. Polixenes can see only too clearly the reasons why Leontes' wrath will be immoderate:

> This jealousy
> Is for a precious creature. As she's rare,
> Must it be great; and as his person's mighty,
> Must it be violent; and as he does conceive
> He is dishonored by a man which ever
> Professed to him, why, his revenges must
> In that be made more bitter.
> (I.ii.449-55 [*William Shakespeare: The Complete Works*, ed. Alfred Harbage (Baltimore: Penguin, 1969).])

Polixenes' logically irresistible analysis of his predicament— as much a manifestation in linguistic terms of the engaged mind as Leontes' outbursts of the crazily disengaged— contains no hint that we have left behind the tragic world of *King Lear* in favor of one more romantically conceived. Polixenes' prediction carries an indisputable authority. Yet the play's true status as a tragicomedy is startlingly and ingenuously revealed in the first scene of the next act when, out of the blue, Antigonus makes a judgment of Leontes' behavior to end the scene on a very different note from the one sounded so funereally by Polixenes. After Leontes has made a furious exit, following fruitless attempts to raise up everyone else to his own frenzied state, Antigonus with remarkable sangfroid [composure] confides to us that they are all more likely to be raised up "To laughter, as I take it, / If the good truth were known" (II.i.198-99).

If when the good truth is known it will produce laughter, derisive and cleansing, what will in the meantime produce violent recrimination is a bad deception; the one, for example, by which Leontes deceives himself into thinking that his wife has slept with his closest friend, Polixenes. To Leontes, the bad deception is the bad truth. Time and again he insists petulantly on the accuracy of his knowledge, on its dismal validity. His interpretation of the ways of his world has all the innocence of the recent convert to a simplistic faith, as well as the hysterical insistence. Although Camillo "cannot name the disease" (I.ii.384), he can see what a tenacious hold it has on its victim and his understandable ignorance of the cause of Leontes' behavior has been echoed not quite so understandably by generations of critics despite the background that Shakespeare provides for it.

In the play's second scene, Hermione playfully interrogates Polixenes about the time he spent as a youth with Leontes; she is especially (and ominously) intrigued by accounts of "my lord's tricks" (I.ii.61). Equally playfully, Polixenes declares that what as boys they were "trained together" (I.ii.21) in was a golden naiveté, a pastoral innocence, in which

> We were as twinned lambs that did frisk i'
>   th' sun,
> And bleat the one at th'other. What we
>   changed
> Was innocence for innocence; we knew not
> The doctrine of ill-doing, nor dreamed
> That any did.
>
> (I.ii.67-71)

Although tupping old rams have replaced frisking lambs in the landscape of Leontes' mind, he still retains the innocent ignorance of which Polixenes speaks, as though his adult incoherences were a version of his youthful, equally uncommunicative, bleating. The Arcadia of Polixenes' nostalgia seems just as unreal: a benign landscape beyond responsibility, where time, like the waves of Florizel's sea, "moves still, still so" in a perpetual

renewal of delight, where "there was no more behind, / But such a day tomorrow as to-day" (I.ii.63-64). It does not seem unlikely that someone who experienced his childhood in such a state of joyful ignorance should, as an adult, misinterpret his wife's generous affection for an honored guest: to be obsessively and exclusively aware of the doctrine of ill-doing as an adult might very well entail as little knowledge of human nature as to be blissfully ignorant of such a doctrine as a child.

Although the conversation between Polixenes and Hermione never quite loses its veneer of courtly gallantry, it becomes more pointedly ominous. Pursuing his joke's conclusion, Polixenes fastens the blame for the loss of their boyhood innocence on the "temptations" of the women in their lives; and while Hermione takes his jesting in good part, she makes it clear that she understands his inference perfectly well: "Of this make no conclusion, lest you say / Your queen and I are devils" (I.ii.80-91). She prolongs their courtly encounter by offering Polixenes marriage's monogamous contract as a casuistic justification for his fallen condition:

> Th'offences we have made you do we'll
>   answer,
> If you first sinned with us and that with us
> You did continue fault and that you slipped
>   not
> With any but with us.
>
> (I.ii.83-86)

It is at this significant moment that Leontes, who has been silent and presumably otherwise engaged for the previous fifty lines or so, intercedes, to complete Hermione's last line of verse with the impatient enquiry, "Is he won yet?"

His intervention at this point raises the question of how much, if anything, he has overheard of the tag end of his wife's remarks. There is no indication in the text; what Leontes says next need not involve a change of mood. Most actors seize the opportunity, however, for a highly charged rendering of such flat statements as "At my request he would not" (I.ii.87), and the play's New Cambridge and New Arden editors both suggest that Leontes overhears those last especially equivocal lines of Hermione, inevitably misinterpreting them. Even in the theater then (perhaps especially in the theater) Leontes' outbreak of jealousy a few lines later comes as no real surprise, though its intensity never fails to shock. And I agree with William Matchett when he argues that it would have come as no real surprise to us even had Shakespeare not allowed Leontes the circumstantial evidence of Hermione's ambiguities, or, for that matter, our brief glimpse into that backward of time where idyllic ignorance so childishly frisked. Hermione's visibly pregnant condition, the news that Polixenes has been in Sicilia for nine months, and our awareness of the narrative conventions governing such a triangle, would surely be adequate preparation. Everything else, including the premonitory punning that Matchett discerns . . . , thickens the texture of the experience for us, and intensifies its credibility. Polixenes' nostalgic desire "To be boy eternal" (I.ii.65) performs these functions by invoking a past that has as much premonitory significance as anything spoken about the present. As Lindenbaum notes, Polixenes childishly "yearns for an existence unaffected by time's movement and provides that definition of primal innocence which implies that sexual love could be no part of man's experience in his unfallen condition." . . .

Primally innocent Leontes still manages to be. Despite the obvious power that he now wields as a king, and despite the poetry of his lamentations, he often strikes us (and members of his court, too) as a small child in hysterical bouts of contumacy against parental authority: the eternal boy at his most spiteful and petulant. Little wonder that Paulina treats him as though he were a wayward son: in her scornful view he indulges "needless heavings" (II.iii.35), "Fancies too weak for boys, too green and idle / For girls of nine" (III.ii.179-80). As the first wave of inane suspicion sweeps over him, he follows Polixenes in a sentimental evocation of himself as a child, mirrored now before him in his son, Mamillius, whose innocent presence increases his peevishness at the same time that it reminds Leontes of his former innocent self:

> Looking on the lines
> Of my boy's face, methoughts I did recoil
> Twenty-three years, and saw myself unbreeched,
> In my green velvet coat, my dagger muzzled
> Lest it should bite its master and so prove
> As ornaments oft do, too dangerous.
>
> (I.ii.153-58)

Such dangerous-sounding nostalgia— the phallic dagger, the winsome "green velvet coat"— is matched by the dangerous nonsense of his concurring with Polixenes that their sons cure in them thoughts that would make thick their blood. Nothing could be further from the truth. Rather, his behavior illustrates the wisdom of Bacon's maxim that "Children sweeten labours; but they make misfortunes more bitter." Mamillius' presence intensifies Leontes' thickening thoughts, reminding him not only of his innocent youth but of his years with Mamillius' mother that he had until so recently thought just as innocent.

All this harping on childish innocence in these opening scenes prepares us to see Leontes as an innocent in the worst sense, one who "does nothing / But what he did being childish" (IV.iv.394-95), who looks at the world and sees reflected there his own hysterical forebodings. All he knows about human nature he expresses in a number of vulgar truisms based upon some kind of loose, undifferentiating overview that bundles everyone

together. Until his change of heart in the middle of the play Leontes never ceases to startle us with the number and intensity of his assured judgments about Polixenes and Hermione in particular and human behavior in general. Unaware of his primal condition, he speaks as though he were the Delphic Oracle he later rejects. Encountering opposition, Leontes' rage knows no restraint: he speaks a language that no one understands, is "in rebellion with himself" (I.ii.358), obeys a cogitation (to use his own pedantic term), infected as though he had drunk and seen the spider (II.i.45). Throughout his excesses, the pedantic language of cogitation mingles uneasily with expressions— often unconscious— of furtive or violent sexuality. Even before he expresses— or thinks that he has reason to express— his suspicions about his wife, he speaks in such a way as to alert us to the violence and corruption within him, as in this disturbing description of the ardor of his wooing:

> Why, that was when
> Three crabbed months had soured themselves
> to death
> Ere I could make thee open thy white hand
> And clap thyself my love.
>
> (I.ii.101-04)

Later, he lingers over his accounts of his wife's suspected sexual activities as though deriving some kind of perverse pleasure from them. "To your own bents dispose you" (I.ii.178) he says to Hermione and Polixenes, revealing his own unconscious bent to be cuckolded. In his conversation with Polixenes, Camillo perfectly catches his master's voyeuristic conviction of Hermione's guilt:

> He thinks, nay, with all confidence he swears,
> As he had seen't or been an instrument
> To vice you to't, that you have touched his
> queen
> Forbiddenly.
>
> (I.ii.412-15)

On the evidence of his language alone, we might agree with C. T. Neely that Leontes' primal innocence "springs from a pre-rational, pre-linguistic state of consciousness characterized by its 'indeterminacy.'" She goes on to link its source in the inchoate with other stylistic aberrations, with the play's opening scene, for instance, where representative courtiers from Bohemia and Sicilia, Archidamus and Camillo, vie with each other in compliment, their ornate, petrified language recapturing the linguistic flavor of Elizabeth's stately court, "something of a world of romance in its own right: peaceful, golden, remote, impossible." . . . In their expressions of complacent satisfaction over the past and future they seem spokesmen for an era of high, confident civility where certainties abound. Persisting in hyperbolic self-deprecation, for example, Archidamus insists on the truth of his ultramodest disclaimers: "Verily I speak it in the freedom of my knowledge": (I.i.11-12). His mannered prose, weighed down by a Latinate vocabulary, euphuistic antitheses and elaborate breakings off, suggests constriction rather than freedom, and the fact that what he is saying amounts to a polite lie (namely, that Bohemia will be less hospitable to the Sicilians than Sicilia to the Bohemians) runs counter to his claim that he speaks in knowledge's freedom as do later events to both their convictions in the irrevocability of their kings' friendship and in the golden promise of Mamillius.

The hint of innocent worldliness in Shakespeare's depiction of Thaisa in *Pericles*, however, blossoms in the first part of *The Winter's Tale* into a full-blown portrait of the mature virtuous woman. Unlike her husband, Hermione speaks a language everyone understands, and its directness and vivacity in the play's second scene are already a world removed from Archidamus' and Camillo's tortuous elegancies in the first. Guileless, exuberant, colloquial ("We'll thwack him hence with distaffs"), varied in tone and structure, studded with exclamations and questions, her language has all the innocent fervor of Marina's spiced with the wit of Beatrice's. With A. D. Nuttall, we realize that "her language is neither naïve nor faux-naïf but is rather the achieved innocence of a good woman in a fallen world." With increasing élan [ardor], Hermione shows how an achieved innocence can afford the freedom of sexual metaphor, as distinct from Leontes' sodden obsession with it. Unlike Polixenes, as Lindenbaum notices, "she is fully willing to accept the flesh and all that some might consider the gross part of man's nature." . . . So too, if only by inference, is Mamillius. Although he may resemble his father in appearance, as one egg another, he does not do so in misapprehension. Leontes continues to deceive himself when he imagines that, twenty-three years before, he was just such another boy. In Mamillius' knowledgeable banter with Hermione's ladies-in-waiting, he discloses a sophisticated awareness of the doctrine of ill-doing, if only as a background for some tart observations on cosmetic lore. Mamillius' brief appearances qualify him as one of those child sophisticates, endearingly precocious, on whom Shakespeare occasionally bestows an innocent authority, and the line stretches back through Macduff's unnamed son to Moth in *Love's Labor's Lost* of whom Armado says (as might well be said of Mamillius): "A most acute juvenal; voluble and free of grace!" (III.ii.59). The final word on Mamillius should be given to that inveterate speaker of them, Paulina, whose epitaph on him praises his spirituality; he had, she says, "Thoughts high for one so tender" (III.ii.194).

To have and to speak high thoughts, to speak in the freedom of knowledge, to speak as Marina speaks in the brothels of Mitylene or as Imogen in Cymbeline's corrupt court, reveals an understanding of the world's vexations far superior to Leontes' sensual pedantry. "How hast thou purchased this experience?" Armado

asks Moth, who replies, "By my penny of observation" (*LLL*, III.i.23-24). For the truly innocent mind, a penny's worth of observation suffices to purchase the truth about Hermione and Polixenes. Everyone who speaks out attempts to persuade Leontes how counterfeit his empirical currency; but the sterner their disapproval, as we have seen, the more indefatigable his assurance. He knows what he knows indubitably: more, he knows it as a caballist of the philosophy which calls all in doubt, and what that philosophy eschews is an older form of knowing, intuitive, empathetic— in theological terms, theosophic, an angelic knowledge vastly superior to the empirical. It is to this superior way of knowing that Paulina vainly appeals when she shows Leontes the newly born Perdita:

> We do not know
> How he may soften at the sight o'th'child.
> The silence often of pure innocence
> Persuades when speaking fails.
>
> (II.ii.39-42)

Paulina hopes that Perdita will smile extremity out of act like the baby daughters in *Pericles* and *The Tempest*. But unlike Pericles and Prospero, Leontes is beyond the liquid persuasions of pure innocence, as he vehemently demonstrates in his rejection of its speaking likeness in the great confrontation at the heart of the play between him and that "gracious innocent soul, / More free than he is jealous" (II.iii.29-30), his wife.

Act III, Scene ii is a scene of high drama, magnificently crafted, moving from the measured, dignified cadences of Hermione's defense to a series of sudden reversals: the Oracle's declaration of Hermione's innocence; Leontes' blasphemous rejection of it; news of Mamillius' death; Leontes' abrupt penitential transformation; the collapse of Hermione. Throughout these fluctuations of fortune, Hermione never wavers in her adherence to plain statement, to "but what comes from myself" (III.ii.24), to her belief in the divinities who shape just ends. Leontes is deaf to all her appeals, however, insisting that Hermione knows more than her words reveal, that she has a guilty knowledge of the conspiracy against him hidden behind her protestations of bewilderment. Leontes' attempt to foist onto his wife the knowledge engendered by his own barren speculations incites Hermione's important disavowal:

> You speak a language that I understand not,
> My life stands in the level of your dreams,
> Which I'll lay down.
>
> (III.ii.79-81)

Dream and reality have shifted places radically: the reality of Hermione's innocence has become for Leontes the dream of her guilt. His reply "Your actions are my dreams" (II.ii.81) continues the equivocal juggling begun by Hermione in her ill-concealed threat to demolish her husband's dreams. But Leontes' language has always been highly susceptible to charged ambiguity: he seems unable to prevent his words— as unruly as the minds of some of his courtiers— from acts of semantic treachery, as though in spite of himself he cannot quite master the superior, intuitive knowledge (what Antigonus calls his "silent judgment" [II.i.171]) he has of Hermione's innocence, a knowledge that Hermione knows he has if only he could reach down into himself to find it (III.ii.31-34).

As part of the pattern of ironic reversals in this scene, however, Leontes fails to speak in the freedom of knowledge even when he collapses into the clearer knowledge predicted by Hermione (II.i.96-98) and induced by the news ("mortal to the queen" as Paulina grimly observes) of Mamillius' death. Despite the horror of these events, Leontes remains astonishingly, ingenuously optimistic. "Her heart is but o'ercharged" (III.ii.150) he says of Hermione, and in the speech which follows he lays out an itinerary of reconciliations for himself— he will approach Polixenes, "new woo" Hermione, recall Camillo— as though it were an easy matter to reorder his world along the old innocent lines. His dream of innocence is as naive as his dream of Hermione's guilt, especially when, in outlining his sentimental program, he fails to mention the death of Mamillius, the one disaster he cannot possibly do anything about however great his belief in his conciliatory powers. Leontes will only be able to speak in the freedom of knowledge when he knows the full extent of his guilt: a knowledge provided by the scene's final dismaying revelation when Paulina bursts in again with the news of Hermione's "death," providing at the same time a suitably hyperbolic expression of the anguish the guilty person must inevitably feel (III.ii.208-12).

The second half of the play proper begins sixteen years later after a couple of remarkable bridging scenes in which Antigonus loses his life to a bear, the crew of his ship drown, Perdita is found by the Bohemian shepherds (Act III, Scene iii), and Father Time asks us not to think it criminal that so many years should pass with such indecent speed (Act IV, Scene i). With Act IV, Scene ii Shakespeare refashions the play's opening with yet another conversation in which two men talk about the possibility of a visit to the native country of one of them, followed by their discussion of the admired prince of the country in which they presently reside. Tone and circumstances have changed radically, however. In Act IV, Scene ii, despite the passing of sixteen years, Camillo and Polixenes seem to be speaking still in the aftershock of the Sicilian experience: worried men intensely aware of the tricks in the world; Camillo anxious to revisit Sicilia before he dies; Polixenes convinced that it would be a death to lose him and curiously petulant in his attempts to persuade Camillo to change his mind: "Better not to have had thee than thus to want thee" (IV.i.12-13). The confident civilities that prefaced the

Sicilian half of the play have been replaced by nervous Bohemian ones; in journeying from Sicilia to Bohemia we appear to have left behind the old innocence for a troublesome new sophistication. And although the next scene introduces a new character, Autolycus, who does much to dispel the gloom induced by talk of separation, death, and wayward sons, he can hardly be described as a harbinger of the new innocence, despite A. D. Nuttall's enthusiastic partisanship. Indeed, Autolycus' ultimate fate reads like a parody of Leontes', when he is forced to accept the new inheritance of the meek, sue for their favor and promise to mend his way of life.

With the important exception of Florizel's encounter with Polixenes, the play's moments of highest drama are all variations on confrontations between desperate men and resolute women. In Sicilia, extremity fails to respond to the women's attempts at its assuagement, as Leontes continues blindly on his destructive course, deaf equally to Paulina's admonitions and to Hermione's eloquent integrity. Such confrontations inform the play's structure, inviting deepening responses as we shift from one tense version of the basic conflict to another. The pattern persists in the second half, though there is now no question as to the women's authority; they speak in an authoritative freedom of knowledge, "with words as medicinal as true" (II.iii.37). Beginning with Antigonus' vision of Hermione who tells him what to do, continuing in more muted form in the relationship between Perdita and Florizel in the fourth act and coming to a climax with Paulina as stage manager in the fifth, the Bohemian experience establishes the sovereignty of the new innocence as interpreted and made available by its confident hierophants, with the most challenging revelation left for the magic of Paulina as High Priestess in the play's final scene.

Antigonus' vision of Hermione marks a significant change from the intensely realized humanity of Hermione's and Paulina's roles in the first half of the play to something much closer to the oracular style of the last scene where the "grave and good Paulina" (V.iii.1) leads Leontes into an ecstatic re-experiencing of his original perturbation; the sight of Hermione now, as then, "piercing to my soul" (V.iii.34), an "affliction" that, in a familiar sensual transformation, "has a taste as sweet / As any cordial comfort" (V.iii.76-77). Paulina's management of the reawakening extracts every possible tension from it; until the moment when Hermione steps down from the pedestal— and that moment is agonizingly delayed— Leontes must suffer once again with an intensity he has not known for sixteen years. Apart from the obvious theatrical benefit from the way in which Paulina ekes out those moments when Hermione is in a limbo between art and nature, neither quite statue nor quite human being, there could not be a more vivid final manifestation of female power, nor a more conclusive piece of evidence for Paulina's role as "that audacious lady!" (II.iii.42), in Leontes' words, whose "boundless tongue" (II.iii.91) and enterprising imagination have marked her as "subversive woman, truth-teller and, finally, artist, whose truth challenges Leontes' masculine order."

Truth-teller, artist, subversive woman: descriptions which shed as much light on Hermione's playful responses to Polixenes and Leontes in the play's opening scenes as on Paulina's "red-looked anger" (II.ii.34) in the second act and her magisterial aplomb in the fifth. They shed light too on the presentation of Perdita, militantly innocent as she is, questioning not only the very propriety of her own love affair with Florizel, but also unpriggishly shunning Bohemian indelicacies. The rhetorical question that the Clown asks about Mopsa and Dorcas could not be asked about Perdita: "Will they wear their plackets where they should bear their faces?" (IV.iv.239-40). And Perdita responds to Camillo's courtly praises of her in the same manner as she responded to Florizel's, with the same determination to cut excess down to size in a language as robust as Hermione's (IV.iv.110-12). At times, and under stress, the note she strikes trembles on the shrewish; her rebukes for Florizel beginning with "I told you what would come of this" (IV.iv.440) come to a shrill climax:

> How often have I told you 'twould be thus?
> How often said my dignity would last
> But till 'twere known!
>
> (IV.iv.467-69)

At times like these her tongue seems as boundless as Paulina's, used to much the same effect, persisting almost as inexorably in the freedom of its knowledge, demonstrating as so often in this play that "A lady's 'verily' is / As potent as a lord's" (I.ii.50-51).

Perdita's occasional moments of vulgar dogmatism are only a minor though not insignificant instance of Shakespeare's determination to humanize his tale of wonder; to combine a "mimetic fidelity to life as we know it" with a romantic design that enables *The Winter's Tale* to "transcend *Pericles* and *Cymbeline* and take its place among the very greatest of Shakespeare's works." Perdita's innocence is very like her mother's, as Nuttall points out: "like Hermione's, unlike Autolycus' [Perdita's], is an achieved innocence. It is the fruit of high intelligence and consideration, a flower rather than the root of her personality" (p. 47). An innocence achieved, in other words, in the face of the antimasque emphasis in Bohemia on dildos, fadings, plackets, and the like; one that further resembles Hermione's in its delight in "sinless sensuality," a munificence which, for S. L. Bethell, makes Perdita "more truly representative of the age of innocence than Milton's Eve."

Shakespeare's presentation of Perdita in these terms is clearly part of the play's larger design. M. M. Mahood's essay on *The Winter's Tale* in *Shakespeare's Wordplay* talks of the importance of "recreation as re-creation," of the engaging sensuality of life in Bohemia: "According to Blake's paradox, the return of the spiritual vision by which what now seemed finite and corrupt would appear infinite and holy was to be accomplished by 'an improvement of sensual enjoyment'; and such enjoyment is felt throughout the scenes in Bohemia." It is exquisitely felt through the "cleanly wantonness," in Herrick's phrase, of Perdita's innocent enjoyment of the senses, in which she seems "a compound of Flora, as Florizel has already named her, with an Aphrodite chastened by prayer and almsgiving." Although the reference to Proserpina's rape invests what follows with a certain fragility, Perdita's is nonetheless a sparkling sensuality, essentially innocent, "life-creating . . . the antidote to her father's barrenness." No more so than when, with an unabashed fervor, she redirects Florizel's morbid witticism back to the world of natural energy where the lovers truly belong:

> No, like a bank for love to lie and play on.
> Not like a corse; or if, not to be buried,
> But quick and in mine arms.
>
> (IV.iv.130-32)

For Geoffrey Hill, who makes an interesting contrast between Perdita's exuberance and Imogen's pudency in *Cymbeline*, "the tone of Perdita's 'But quick and in mine arms' seems the real heart of innocence." The Shepherd puts it somewhat less innocently, but still well within the spirit of Perdita's freedom of knowledge:

> If young Doricles
> Do light upon her, she will bring him that
> Which he not dreams of.
>
> (IV.iv.178-80)

What, undreamed of, she will bring Florizel is nothing to what she will bring Leontes in her role as one of "those wonder-working heroines of Shakespeare." On her, of course, depends the triumphant outcome; first she who was lost has to be found before "the gods / Will have fulfilled their secret purposes" (V.i.35-36), and a dream of innocence made reality. The play ends in a double, linked epiphany: Perdita's restoration to Leontes and through her the friendship renewed between Leontes and Polixenes constitutes the marvel of the last scene but one (Act V, Scene ii); and this minor miracle leads to the major one of Hermione's resurrection in the final scene, the connection further underscored by the manner of Paulina's final injunction, "Turn good lady; / Our Perdita is found" (V.iii.120-21). By the time we reach Act V, Scene ii, then, where the tale of Perdita's recognition is told in suspenseful relays of gentlemen from Leontes' court, the wisdom she manifests—fruit of her achieved innocence—takes on a sacramental character. She speaks now in an oracular freedom of knowledge. The "clerk-like experienced" Camillo—himself an exponent of sanctified knowledge, from whom in happier times Leontes frequently "departed / Thy penitent reformed" (I.ii.237-38)—has already alerted us to the impressive quality of Perdita's intellect:

> I cannot say 'tis
> pity
> She lacks instructions, for she seems a mistress
> To most that teach.
>
> (IV.iv.574-76)

In the opening scene of the final act, the Servant's praise of her moral authority, transcending the secularity of Camillo's and transforming the superstitiousness of Polixenes', enlarges, in startling fashion, her symbolic standing:

> This is a creature,
> Would she begin a sect, might quench the zeal
> Of all professors else, make proselytes
> Of who she but bid follow.
>
> (V.i.106-09)

Yet despite its obvious importance, we do not actually witness her effect upon her father and his court (when she and they learn who she is), and we lose as a result a "sight which was to be seen, cannot be spoken of" (V.ii.41-42) according to the Third Gentleman (appropriately enough Paulina's Steward) who has himself seen it and speaks of it for our benefit at length and hyperbolically. As many critics have pointed out, from a theatrical point of view it would be too much of a "deal of wonder" (V.ii.23-24) for us to be present at all the highly emotional restorations of relationships. Shakespeare chooses instead to concentrate upon the most excitingly theatrical one, the spectacular restoration of Hermione to Leontes. Much of what is "spoken of" in prose in Act V, Scene ii, however, looks forward to the reverent proceedings in poetry in the next and final scene. In Act V, Scene ii all three Gentlemen are in a state of hyperbolic excitement: emotion already running high, "wonder" the word on their lips, "Nothing but bonfires" the order of the day. As the self-conscious narrator of such a deal of wonder, the Third Gentleman chooses to belittle the credibility of what he has seen in order to convince his hearers of its incredible truth: a technique the reverse of Autolycus' who might be made to react in some appropriate fashion on stage to remarks as provocative as the Second Gentleman's "Such a deal of wonder is broken out within this hour that ballad-makers cannot be able to express it" (V.ii.23-25) ("cannot be able" certainly distances the possibility). All that has been told disarmingly resembles "an old tale still" (V.ii.29). Both the First and Third Gentleman emphasize the difficulty of distinguishing joy from pain in the way in which the characters respond to the news of Perdita's true status, especially in the case of Leontes whose memory of what could have been subverts his happiness in what

now is, "as if that joy were now become a loss" (V.ii.49). The excessive Third Gentleman outlaments them all: "I am sure my heart wept blood" (V.ii.85).

Old tales, then, but heartrending, transfiguring ones, powerful enough to fashion extremities of emotion in grotesque, rictal attitudes, like Paulina, who "had one eye declined for the loss of her husband, another elevated that the oracle was fulfilled" (V.ii.71-72); or like Leontes and Camillo, who "seemed almost, with staring on one another, to tear the cases of their eyes. There was speech in their dumbness, language in their very gesture. They looked as they had heard of a world ransomed, or one destroyed. A notable passion of wonder appeared in them" (V.ii.11-16). Living human beings silenced by the intensity of their emotions contrast with the situation in the next scene where an apparently stone statue becomes a living human being. The difference in immediacy and significance between the Gentleman's account of the one and our own experience in the theater of the other has its comic counterpart in the difference between the miraculousness of Hermione's and Perdita's story (old tale or not) and the parodic miraculousness of Autolycus' ballads whose effect on his listeners also turns them into stone: "No hearing, no feeling, but my sir's song, and admiring the nothing of it" (IV.iv.604-05). In both situations, the essential requirement is to "awake your faith" (V.iii.95); a credulity that Autolycus never has any difficulty in awakening as he deals with people who wear their faith so innocently on their sleeves. Yet there is a connection between the power of his art and the power of Paulina's ("for the stone is mine" [V.iii.58]) in the final scene, where, when Hermione steps down from her pedestal, as Rosalie Colie says, "the interchange of art with nature is affirmed, as art offers human nature a chance to civilize its brutalities."

A proper assessment of this last scene needs to consider it as the climatic one of a significant series in which, as Charles Frey puts it, "a single, still woman faces curious but uncomprehending onlookers." We should not be so transported by the powerful unexpectedness of Hermione's revival to fail to see it as the product of interlaced concerns. The dramaturgy of this last scene looks back in particular to that of the scene where Paulina confronts Leontes with his innocent baby daughter (Act II, Scene iii); it is also closely linked to another encounter between a father and a daughter, the one between Perdita and Polixenes in Act IV, Scene iv. There Polixenes' schoolmasterly insistence on the natural rightness of the human drive to tamper with the products of nature in order to better them gives an authoritative voicing to the play's optimistic view (and a profoundly realistic one when we consider those sixteen penitential years) that the sensitive intelligence will finally prevail. It is an art, he says, "Which does mend nature—change it rather—but / The art itself is nature" (IV.iv.96-97).

Act II, Scene iii, from The Winter's Tale. Antigonus, Leontes, lords, soldiers, and the infant Perdita. By John Opie.

"The art itself is nature" would make an attractive and cogent epigram for the significance of this final scene; cogent as much in a literal application— the statue is not man-made, not a statue at all, but a real human being— as in metaphorical applications. Nature and art here interpenetrate in vitally civilized ways. So this last scene begins— and ends— with stately civilities between Paulina, as hostess, and Leontes, as guest and suppliant. Courtesy and ceremony prevail, worlds removed from the incivilities of the second act: the king has come now to the house of his subject and mentor as an honored guest, his visit "a surplus of grace" (V.iii.7) in Paulina's view, a "trouble" for her in his. Their courteous self-deprecation reads like a far more subdued version— decorously more subdued— of the severities of courtliness displayed by Archidamus and Camillo at the beginning of *The Winter's Tale*. Reads like a true ceremony of innocence, now, in fact. The "silent judgment" about which Antigonus had spoken now operates in Leontes' mind: it is he who now possesses the superior understanding that enables him to reject the

pragmatic advice of his courtiers for Paulina's harder counsel. All along, of course, she has manipulated Leontes, first by inciting him to passion with the memory of his wife and son, deliberately recalled by her, and then by calming him into sobriety with talk of kingly responsibility and the like; now the incitement to passion prevails (although he must not yet touch the statue) as she encourages him to recall his queen's "full eyes" (V.i.53), to think of how, had she lived, he might "Have taken treasure from her lips" (V.i.54), adding, like some cruel Enobarbus, "And left them / More rich for what they yielded" (V.i.54-55).

At the sight of the statue all this cleanly wantonness wells up once again; the "greediness of affection" (V.ii.97) that the Third Gentleman described in the previous scene is now given further fervent expression. Appropriately enough, Perdita attempts to make the first contact; Leontes is "transported" and speaks of his longing for Hermione in the vocabulary of Florizel:

No settled senses of the world can match
The pleasure of that madness.

(V.iii.72-73)

When, at last, Paulina calls on Hermione to descend from the pedestal the scene is sensuously described and acted:

> *Leontes.*   O, she's warm!
> If this be magic, let it be an art
> Lawful as eating.
> *Polixenes.*   She embraces him.
> *Camilla.*   She hangs about his neck.
>
> (V.iii.109-12)

The strange phrase "lawful as eating" grasps something of the mysterious authority of the conjunction between art and nature that the play dramatizes: whatever the terminology, it is difficult to resist responding to the new sense of wholeness that this last scene offers, exemplified so vividly in the person of Leontes himself who has, in James Smith's words, "been moved down to the very centre; his whole being has been changed, so that the physical and the moral now move in harmony with him." The physical and the moral have joined together; eating is now sanctioned by law: art in the sense of the deft application of learned judgment—that gentle scion—combines with natural instinct—the wildest stock—to produce the new harmony or, in Paulina's more forceful term, the "exultation" (V.iii.131) that the play finally celebrates. Like *Pericles*, *The Winter's Tale* asserts its vision of the new innocence with the utmost confidence and certainty. By the end of the play, the primal innocence in which Leontes had originally wallowed has been replaced by its superior radical counterpart—Blake's spiritual vision has returned with all the force of its mature appropriation of intellect and libido—lamb and lion are one. After *The Winter's Tale*, especially in *The Tempest*, the vision is Blakean in a much more troubled sense. . . .

HERMIONE

Many critics praise Hermione's moral strength of character, while her "restoration" at the play's end has received mixed reviews. Often, the coming-to-life of the Hermione statue is dismissed as a cheap stage trick, yet other critics defend Shakespeare's dramaturgy. Jack A. Vaughn, for example, in the essay reprinted in the Overview section, comments that in terms of realism Hermione's reappearance is highly implausible. Nevertheless, Vaughn states, the event "creates a stunning effect in the playing and provides a supreme moment of wonder and spirituality to which no audience can fail to respond." **David M. Bergeron** examines the trial scene in Act III, where Hermione publicly defends herself against her husband's accusations. Bergeron

praises the method by which Hermione presents her case. First, she establishes the moral uprightness of her nature; next, she logically answers the precise accusations of the formal indictment against her; and finally, she appeals to the emotions of her listeners, commenting on all she has lost through the ordeal, notably, her children. In contrast with Leontes's uncontrolled passionate outbursts, Bergeron argues, Hermione's self-defense proves her strength of character by highlighting her logic, honesty, and self-control. Bergeron cites Peter Erickson's essay on gender issues, noting that Erickson maintains that the trial scene confirms Hermione's transformation from a position of strength to one of weakness. Bergeron himself finds that the trial scene demonstrates Hermione's strength and her patience. Wilbur Sanders, like Bergeron, commends Hermione's virtues. Sanders maintains that Hermione's presence in the play safeguards the dramatic action, and Leontes, from the audience's contempt in that despite Leontes's despicable actions and unlikable character, Hermione manages to continue caring for her husband.

David M. Bergeron

SOURCE: "Hermione's Trial in 'The Winter's Tale,'" in *Essays in Theatre*, Vol. 3, No. 1, November, 1984, pp. 3-11.

[In this essay, Bergeron studies the way in which Hermione defends herself in the trial scene of Act III of The Winter's Tale. *Bergeron argues Hermione's approach is logical and honest, and "full of controlled passion." In addition to comparing Hermione's rationality and self-control to Leontes's uncontrolled passionate outbursts, Bergeron maintains that Hermione's self-representation in the trial scene reflects the overall strength of her character.]*

When Leontes and the others gather in the final scene of *The Winter's Tale* before the statue of Hermione, Paulina instructs them:

>   It is requir'd
> You do awake your faith. Then all stand still:
> Or—those that think it is unlawful business
> I am about, let them depart.
> (V.iii.94-97) [*The Winter's Tale*, ed. J.H.P. Pafford, Arden edition, London, 1966]

In a moment the music sounds and the statue moves. Puzzling, perhaps, is Paulina's word "unlawful". Robert Uphaus has argued that this word is appropriate because *The Winter's Tale* creates much "unlawful business;" it is "Shakespeare's most defiant romance." The play continually violates our expectations. The most explicit example of defiance comes in Hermione's trial in Act III, a scene that in many ways is the obverse [counterpart] of the play's final restoration scene. The actual trial in Act III counters the trial of faith in the last scene, each producing its own special sense of wonder and the unexpected. My focus will be on Hermione's defense of herself in the trial, demonstrating how her rational approach contrasts with Leontes' passion and showing how her defense strengthens the presentation of her character. In several ways the trial foreshadows the restoration.

Generally, critics writing on *The Winter's Tale* have not paid much detailed attention to Hermione's trial. In an essay that explores the role of women in the play Peter Erickson in fact finds that Hermione's appearance in the trial confirms his view that she changes from a vibrant strength, seen early in the play, to weakness: ". . . she adopts a stance of patience and stoic passivity." I will argue quite the opposite: the trial scene exhibits great strength in Hermione's character while it may also demonstrate patience. I see no evidence that she *adopts* the stance that Erickson suggests. What is indeed remarkable about Hermione here is how within social and legal confines she brilliantly defends herself in the trial, thereby helping us understand the great reservoir of moral courage that she possesses.

The natural outgrowth of Leontes' jealousy has been to send Hermione to prison in Act II on the, as yet unproved, assumption that she is guilty. His accusations against her in II.i.81-95 are clear but mistaken; and his precarious position is evident in his assertion: " . . . if I mistake / In those foundations which I build upon, / The centre is not big enough to bear / A schoolboy's top" (II.i.100-3). The centre does not hold for Leontes; in part it does not hold because Leontes is himself the center, or so he thinks, building the foundations step by step on his jealousy. Fortunately for him and the state, a sufficient vestige of orderly procedure remains so that a formal trial of Hermione can be held. As Leontes says: " . . . as she hath / Been publicly accus'd, so shall she have / A just and open trial" (II.iii.202-4). Such is the primary business of the first part of Act III.

Shakespeare does not include many formal trials: the trial of Antonio in *The Merchant of Venice*, Katherine's in *Henry VIII*, and the one here in *The Winter's Tale*. Several other trials or legal proceedings are, of course, referred to but not given dramatic life. The semblance of a trial in *Measure for Measure* never acquires the formal characteristics of the ones above. Portia is the star in Antonio's trial as judge figure, not the defendant; throughout she truly has the upper hand. Katherine shares some similarities with Hermione, a point noted long ago by G. Wilson Knight in *The Crown of Life*. But her defense is primarily an attack on Wolsey, the formal charges against her never being articulated. Katherine has ostensible legal support from the learned reverend fathers. Hermione stands alone: defendant and sole legal counsel. As she notes, she has no other defense "But what comes from myself . . ." (III.ii.25). Solitary

and vulnerable, she must make the best case for herself.

The orderly and formal structure of the trial belies the chaos, irrationality, and jealousy that bring it about, perhaps Shakespeare's way of indicating that Sicilian society may be capable of redemption. In other words, to have such a trial implies that justice may yet be possible— certainly it is preferable to letting Hermione rot in jail. The odds against justice being achieved in the trial obtain so long as Leontes is the potential judge. The legalistic structure also counterpoints the mystical, transcendental oracle of Apollo that will finally determine the outcome of the trial, supplanting Leontes' judgement.

The assumption on which Hermione proceeds differs radically from that of Leontes. She observes in an "if" statement that contrasts nicely with Leontes' earlier one:

> . . . if powers divine
> Behold our human actions (as they do),
> I doubt not then but innocence shall make
> False accusation blush, and tyranny
> Tremble at patience.
>
> (III.ii.28-32)

For Hermione there is a center, and it holds. Shakespeare takes the seeds that he finds in Bellaria in Greene's *Pandosto* and gives them full development in Hermione. What I propose to examine in some detail is Hermione's legal defense: it is studied, calculated, logical, honest, and full of controlled passion. It is also at moments spontaneous as when she responds to Leontes' outbursts or questions; but basically, I think she has thought through the issues and has some kind of structure in mind for her argument. Her defense proceeds on the basis of the ancient modes of persuasion, enunciated by Aristotle: ethical, logical, and pathetic proofs (see Aristotle, *Rhetoric*, Book I, chapter 2). She engages not so much the subtleties of law as she practices the art of persuasion.

Leontes opens the proceedings by at least giving lip-service to the pursuit of justice:

> Let us be clear'd
> Of being tyrannous, since we so openly
> Proceed in justice, which shall have due course,
> Even to the guilt or the purgation.
>
> (III.ii.4-7)

He believes, of course, that he is right and will be vindicated by the trial. Leontes' word "purgation," though it means "acquittal," carries also the meaning of "catharsis"— what better description of what happens in the trial scene to both Hermione and Leontes? In one sense Leontes is also on trial even as he thinks Hermione is the only guilty party. As the prisoner Hermione is brought in, Leontes commands: "Read the indictment" (11). The Officer complies in what is, I believe, the only formal statement of charges in a trial in Shakespeare. The main burden of the indictment is thus:

> Hermione, queen to the worthy Leontes, king of Sicilia, thou art here accused and arraigned of high treason, in committing adultery with Polixenes, king of Bohemia, and conspiring with Camillo to take away the life of our sovereign lord the king, the royal husband . . .
>
> (12-17)

In addition, she has presumably assisted in the escape of Polixenes and Camillo. Adultery and conspiracy are the fundamental charges. In contrast, Katherine in *Henry VIII* is not accused of either of these crimes; indeed, her main "fault" is that she has not produced a male heir. Hermione's task is somehow to answer the indictment. She cannot counter with tangible proof, so she must try to move by persuasion. Her strength grows from the knowledge that she is innocent and that "powers divine" will exonerate her.

Hermione's first argument rests on establishing the "ethos" of the speaker, that is, her moral, credible, and upright nature (recall Brutus' speech given before Antony's in *Julius Caesar*). She knows that it is insufficient merely to assert "not guilty," "mine integrity, / Being counted falsehood . . ." (26-27). Instead, she appeals to the common perception of her good character: " . . . my past life / Hath been as continent, as chaste, as true, / As I am now unhappy . . ." (33-35). One notes that she does not rely on the considerable testimony about her good character spoken by others earlier in the play, like Paulina and Camillo, but seeks to make the persuasive case herself. She argues by reciting simple facts: that she is "A fellow of the royal bed," "a great king's daughter," and "The mother to a hopeful prince" (38, 39, 40). She also owns "A moiety of the throne," which makes her a political partner with Leontes. The implication is clear: she is of such stature that she must be listened to. She has, however, been left "To prate and talk for life and honour . . ." (41). Illustrating Hermione's control in logically defending herself is the skill with which she grasps the words "life" and "honour" and develops them in additional comments. Thus she contrasts sharply with the frenzy and irrationality of Leontes. Her appeal to his "conscience" rests not on his good will but rather on his recollection of how she was in his merited grace before Polixenes came to Sicilia. If she should be "one jot" beyond being totally honorable, then "harden'd be the hearts / Of all that hear me, and my near'st of kin / Cry fie upon my grave!" (52-54). The note of finality that accompanies the statement suggests that Hermione has come to the end of this particular mode of arguing, as indeed she has.

Her case, however, does not rest on the ethos of her character alone, for she moves next to logical proof, that is, to answer explicitly the charges of the indictment. Point by point she responds to the formal accusation of adultery and conspiracy. About her relationship with Polixenes, Hermione responds:

> . . . I do confess
> I lov'd him as in honour he requir'd,
> With such a kind of love as might become
> A lady like me . . .
>
> (62-65)

With irony Hermione notes that her expression of love to Polixenes was none other than what Leontes had himself commanded: "Which, not to have done, I think had been in me / Both disobedience and ingratitude / To you, and toward your friend . . ." (67-69). She signals her movement to the second point of the argument: "Now, for conspiracy . . ." (71); and she begins: "I know not how it [conspiracy] tastes, though it be dish'd / For me to try how" (72-73). All she knows is that "Camillo was an honest man" (74); but why he has left the court no one knows, not even the gods. Her methodical approach to the details of the indictment underscores her attempt at logical proof and indicates a mind that has spent its time in prison sorting out the issues and preparing her defense. As we sometimes comment that Leontes is his own Iago, perhaps we can suggest that Hermione is her own Portia.

When Hermione finishes her logical proof, Leontes counters with additional accusations, unmoved by what she has said, and ironically adds: "Your actions are my dreams. / You had a bastard by Polixenes, / And I but dream'd it!" (82-84). On this illusion, of course, rests all of Leontes' jealousy, the subsequent imprisonment of Hermione, and the trial. Leontes seems to sense the conclusion of the legal proceeding, for he renders judgement on Hermione: " . . . as / Thy brat hath been cast out, . . . / . . . so thou / Shalt feel our justice . . ." (86-87, 89-90). The justice he has in mind is, in his own words, "no less than death" (91). But Leontes is wrong, not reckoning on the strength of Hermione nor on her determination to follow through on her final mode of argumentation: pathetic persuasion.

She begins bluntly enough: "Sir, spare your threats" (91). No longer does she need to establish her good character (ethos) or to answer the precise accusations of the formal indictment (logic); the last movement of her defense is clearly an appeal to the emotions (pathos). Even so— and this is one of the striking and remarkable things about Hermione's defense— the pathetic proof also proceeds logically, step by step. Her first point consists of enumerating the three things ("comforts" she calls them) that she has lost: "The crown and comfort of my life" (94), namely Leontes' favor; the "first fruits of my body," that is, Mamillius, from whose presence she is barred "like one infectious" (97, 98); and the "third comfort," the baby who has been taken from her breast and "Hal'd out to murder . . ." (101). One notes the control of her rhetoric: the first "comfort" contrasts with the word "lost"; the "second joy" with "infectious"; and the "third comfort" with "murder". Joining this profound sense of loss is the recognition that she has herself been "proclaim'd a strumpet" (102) "on every post" and therefore denied her rights as a mother. She makes one final point in this part of the argument: she has been given inadequate time to recuperate from child-birth; instead, she has been rushed to the trial before she has "got strength of limit" (106).

Her peroration begins with her question: "Now my liege, / Tell me what blessings I have here alive / That I should fear to die?" (106-8). She no longer values her life—"I prize it not a straw" (110), but she does treasure her honor. Seemingly aware that she has pursued her several proofs, she warns Leontes that if she is condemned "Upon surmises, all proofs sleeping else / But what your jealousies awake, I tell you / 'Tis rigour and not law" (112-14). She knows that her defense is solid, and, of course, she knows that she is innocent. But the immediate warning grows from the full understanding of how the legal proceeding should function. Her condemnation would be "unlawful business," the ultimate expression of defiance. The irony works several ways: Hermione is herself quite defiant, but the trial is wrong; the trial has the semblance of pursuing justice, but it rests on fallacious notions of Leontes. The judgment that seems inevitable would in fact mock the cause of justice. She rests her case with an emotional appeal beyond the puny, mortal understanding of Leontes: "Apollo be my judge!" (115).

The trial verdict shifts from human judgment to divine intervention by the oracle of Apollo. Leontes has deluded himself in believing that he controls the trial; but, as he will soon learn to his peril, he is subject to higher law, the presiding spirit of Apollo in this play. Only the intransigence of Leontes fails to be moved by Hermione's persuasive legal defense; the Lords cry out for the messengers of the oracle to be summoned to court, and so they are. Cleomenes and Dion appear and are compelled to "swear upon this sword of justice" (124) that they have indeed been at Delphos and bring with them "This seal'd up Oracle, by the hand deliver'd / Of great Apollo's priest . . ." (127-28). They are the medium; Apollo is the message. Divine witness now clinches the case for Hermione and renders judgment. The Officer of the court reveals the Oracle:

> Hermione is chaste; Polixenes blameless; Camillo a true subject; Leontes a jealous tyrant; his innocent babe truly begotten; and the king shall live without an heir, if that which is lost be not found.
>
> (132-35)

Several things interest us about the Delphic oracle. First, it is both retrospective and prophetic; that is, it looks to the past and offers judgment on the characters, it imposes a stasis on the present, and it sees into the future with its riddle-like comment about Leontes' heir. In that sense it rather resembles the play itself at this moment: one large part of the action is coming to an end (past) while another strand of plot is developing (future). Further, the oracle parallels in some respects the indictment read at the beginning of Hermione's trial even to the point of naming the characters— Hermione, Polixenes, Camillo— in the same order as they appear in the indictment. It obviously responds directly to the accusations made in that indictment, the basis of which has been Hermione's presumed guilt; but the message of the oracle is clear and simple: "Hermione is chaste." With that all of Leontes' foundations of blame crumble. Though revealed by Apollo, the oracle sounds very much like the report of the jury at a trial's end; it systematically and concisely answers the charges made or implicit in Hermione's trial.

Little could Leontes know in Act II, scene i when he dispatched the messengers to Delphos that they would return with a judgment exonerating Hermione and condemning him, the logical conclusion of her trial.

Indeed, Leontes' reason for seeking word from Apollo is to satisfy others, as he says: "Though I am satisfied, and need no more / Than what I know, yet shall the Oracle / Give rest to th' minds of others . . ." (II.i.189-91). In *Pandosto* it is Bellaria who initiates the mission to Apollo, making the request on her knees before Pandosto. For Bellaria the Apollo appeal is one last effort to exonerate herself, but for Leontes it will merely confirm, so he thinks, what he already knows. The tone in *Pandosto* and in *The Winter's Tale* is strikingly different. Shakespeare has set the oracle matter in motion in order to bring the message in at the conclusion of Hermione's defense and not before. Leontes learns at the end of Act II that Cleomenes and Dion, the Delphic messengers, are back in the country (II.iii.192-96); but there is no necessary expectation that they will arrive and participate in the trial. Shakespeare delays their arrival so that it may coincide with the end of the trial; thus Apollo's message judges the trial itself as well as the character of the persons involved.

The "courtroom" response to the oracle's verdict reveals joy for some but continuing obstinance on the part of Leontes. At Leontes' order the Officer reads Apollo's verdict; but Leontes responds with an ambiguous question to the Officer: "Hast thou read truth?" (138). The Officer answers that he has read the document exactly "As it is here set down." But Leontes cries out: "There is no truth at all i' th' Oracle: / The sessions shall proceed: this is mere falsehood" (140-41). The reaction contrasts sharply with the comment of the Lords— "Now blessed be the great Apollo!" (136)—

and with Hermione's simple but joyous "Praised!" (136). One might note in passing that this is Hermione's final word until her restoration in V.iii. Neither persuaded by Hermione's proofs nor moved by Apollo's oracle, Leontes lashes out in a desperate attempt to assert his will and control in the trial; he is now the defiant one. Obviously he has lost; and if he will not be sensitive to Hermione's defense nor to the will of the gods, then the dramatist offers one last convincing blow: the news that his son is dead. With lightning-fast conversion— resembling the speed with which Leontes initially expressed his jealousy— Leontes changes: "Apollo's angry, and the heavens themselves / Do strike at my injustice" (146-47).

Having lost in the trial and having lost his son and presumably Hermione as well, Leontes begins the painful process of finding himself, stripped of his pride and groundless jealousy. As Hermione's sins have been enumerated in the formal statement of the indictment, so Leontes' are rehearsed by Paulina at the end of the scene. (11. 175ff). She becomes his accuser and judge; thus, the trial continues, but of Leontes, not of Hermione. As Hermione has presumably died, Leontes withers into remorse, abetted by the knowledge of his guilt and the lashing tongue of Paulina. Defiance seems now to have had its day. Humbled and chastened, Leontes promises at the end of III.ii to visit the chapel where Mamillius and Hermione will lie, "and tears shed there / Shall be my recreation" (239-40). Time and again Leontes resembles figures from Greek tragedy— I think especially of Creon in Sophocles' *Antigone* whom the gods break across their superior power and will.

Antigone differs from Hermione, of course, because she knowingly and willfully breaks the law of Creon. But the defense of her action rests on the awareness that spiritual laws take precedence over man-made laws, and she buries her brother in accordance with the will of the gods. Hermione, too, is sensitive to those "powers divine" operating in her world; by such power she presents her impressive legal defense. She has for the moment seemingly won the battle but lost the war. The dramatist will, however, eventually show her triumphant in her restoration in the play's final scene.

Why the trial scene in *The Winter's Tale?* It establishes in compelling terms the strength of Hermione's character and by contrast the paltry insufficiency of Leontes'. It is the most extensive examination of Hermione in the play— nowhere else does she have such a scene. If what I have suggested is valid, namely that Hermione's legal defense is systematic and controlled, then we understand the rationality that dominates her character in contrast to Leontes'. Under the most extreme circumstances she thinks coolly, logically. Paradoxically, in Hermione's defiance is her rationality, and in her rationality is her defiance. Her control defies Leontes' passion; and by asserting herself in the trial, she strikes a blow for justice and logical proceeding. Leontes, on the other hand, defies the system of justice with his groundless accusations, and he defies the gods by insisting on his will— all prompted by passion, not logic. Leontes is left with unlawful business.

The trial scene is a concrete, explicit example of the several trials in the play as it is also the most developed. One thinks, for example, of the quasi-trial of Florizel by Polixenes in Act IV, scene iv, the sheepshearing scene, where the father's judgment falls harshly on his insolent son. The confrontation between father and son begins with Polixenes' question: "Have you a father?" (IV.iv.393), to which an impertinent Florizel answers: "I have: but what of him?" Having tested his son, Polixenes, resembling the earlier irate Leontes, removes his disguise and renders a verdict of punishment: " . . . we'll bar thee from succession; / Not hold thee of our blood, no, not our kin . . ." (430-31). Somehow the play must also resolve the profound consequences of this "trial". On the metaphorical level we can see much of the play as the "trial" of Leontes. The legal form of the actual trial helps, I think, our perception of this metaphor.

The trial also assists the oracle's credibility by its coming as an explicit response to and judgment on the trial. Having witnessed the trial and heard Hermione's persuasive defense, we can readily see the necessity of the intervention of the gods in order to achieve justice. This intervention is not the spectacle of the vision of Diana in *Pericles* nor the magical descent of Jupiter in *Cymbeline;* rather it is a report from the god Apollo functioning like a jury— no less wondrous than the others but nicely tied to immediate human problems. The trial makes possible this orderly intervention of Apollo, and the oracle in turn ratifies the trial, confirming its procedure and rendering judgment. The trial needs Apollo, and the oracle needs the trial.

This legal proceeding also throws into high relief the social, political, legal, and emotional conflict between Leontes and Hermione. The orderly, objective form of the trial assists in the audience's judgment as well, underscoring our belief in Hermione and dismay at Leontes. What we are unprepared for is the consequence of the trial— Mamillius' actual and Hermione's apparent death. Defying or upsetting our expectations is at the heart of the dramatic strategy of III.iii in which Antigonus is destroyed and, of course, at the center of the play's final scene. The defiant, "unlawful" nature of the trial foreshadows the restoration scene. The intervention of Apollo produces wonder akin to if different from the wonder evoked in the final scene.

Not only may the trial foreshadow the last scene, but the restoration also fulfills the trial. Paulina, the singing master of the souls of Leontes and Hermione, has imprisoned them both, separately of course: Hermione, hidden away somewhere for sixteen years, and Leontes, incarcerated in a process of penance and renewal and a vow not to remarry without Paulina's approval. In a sense Paulina has usurped the position of Apollo, her own brand of defiance. The trial has imposed a sentence on both Leontes and Hermione; this sentence is revoked, fulfilled, overcome, commuted, and transmuted in the play's final scene. The reunions of husband and wife and of mother and daughter supplant the deaths in the trial. Defiance is now more artistic than personal. The statue of Hermione defies the laws of nature by its art (Leontes is puzzled why the statue should have such wrinkles) even as its nature defies art. Submission and forgiveness characterize the tone and action of the scene, demonstrating again how this scene is the obverse of the trial.

The gods judge Leontes in that last scene, accept his penance, and restore Hermione to him. Hermione's gracious acceptance of Leontes ratifies the judgment of the scene: Leontes has been on trial and it is now ended. The earlier trial scene mocked justice; the last scene mocks with art. When Hermione begins to move, Leontes cries out: "If this be magic, let it be an art / Lawful as eating" (V.iii.110-11). The "unlawful business" of the trial and the "unlawful" nature of the restoration parallel and reflect on one another. In the trial scene and in the restoration— indeed throughout the play— we are forever meeting when we least expect "with things dying" and "with things new-born" (III.iii.112-13).

PAULINA

Paulina has been examined by critics in terms of her relationship to Leontes, and also as a crucial character in her own right. **Joan Hartwig** demonstrates how Paulina's relationship to Leontes softens the audience's interpretation of the jealous king. Throughout much of the first three acts of the play, Hartwig notes, despite the seriousness of events, Paulina and Leontes are placed in the comic, stock character roles of "shrew" and "tyrant." Hartwig explains while the narrative situation would normally elicit the audience's condemnation of Leontes for his jealousy and the subsequent treatment of his family and friends, the stock characterization of Paulina and Leontes and the comedy which arises out of seeing Leontes as the hen-pecked victim of Paulina's shrew suspends the audience's judgement. Not only are the stock character roles meant to create some level of comedy, but seeing a now-vulnerable Leontes repeatedly suffering Paulina's tongue-lashings is also meant to evoke some sympathy for Leontes, Hartwig argues. In the last acts of the play, Hartwig observes, Paulina no longer plays the role of the shrew; rather, she serves as Leontes's confessor. Finally, when it is announced that Camillo will become Paulina's husband, Paulina once

again assumes the comic role of shrew. **Myles Hurd** sees Paulina's role in a slightly different light. Hurd demonstrates that Paulina is both an active participant in the play's action, as well as an astute observer and commentator on events and characters. Furthermore, Hurd notes the ways in which Paulina, rather like a stage director, sets up key scenes in the play. Hurd agrees with Hartwig that Shakespeare places Paulina in the role of the shrew, thereby easing the audience's otherwise harsh judgement of Leontes. Yet Hurd stresses that despite her actions as a shrewish stock character, Paulina nevertheless remains credible. Near the end of the play, Hurd observes, Paulina receives the news both of Perdita's recovery, and of the confirmed loss of her husband, and in response she reconciles both joy and sorrow. Hurd suggests a parallel here between Paulina and Shakespeare, in that just as Paulina reconciles happiness and pain, Shakespeare reconciles the discordant, tragic and comic elements in the play.

Joan Hartwig

SOURCE: "'The Winter's Tale': 'The Pleasure of That Madness,'" in *Shakespeare's Tragicomic Vision*, Louisiana State University Press, 1972, pp. 104-36.

[In the excerpt that follows, Hartwig examines the role of Paulina in the play. Hartwig argues that through the character of Paulina and her relationship to Leontes, the audience's perception of Leontes is favorably adjusted. Leontes's jealousy, Hartwig explains, is "completely self-inflicted," and it would be easy for the audience to immediately condemn him. However, Shakespeare places Paulina and Leontes in the stock character roles of "shrew" and "tyrant." Hartwig suggests that the comic nature of these roles, together with the sympathy created for Leontes by seeing him as the victim of Paulina-the-shrew, enable the audience to suspend its judgement of Leontes.]

In *The Winter's Tale*, Leontes, confronted with the breathing statue which is Hermione, pleads to keep this moment which is penultimate to actual discovery. Paulina, aware of the intensity with which Leontes has responded to the apparent statue of Hermione, offers to draw the curtain.

> *Paul.* I'll draw the curtain:
> My lord's almost so far transported that
> He'll think anon it lives.
> *Leon.* O sweet Paulina,
> Make me to think so twenty years together!
> No settled senses of the world can match
> The pleasure of that madness. Let't alone.
> (V.iii.68-73)

Joy occurs before the factual affirmation that the world of hope and dreams coincides with the world of real experience: it occurs when the character perceives, with all his logic and rationality suspended, a tragicomic vision in which the limits of human possibility have exploded—

effects no longer depend upon human causes alone.

Before Leontes can enjoy "the pleasure of that madness" which the tragicomic recognition creates, however, he must undergo the painful process of emotional growth. Like Posthumus in *Cymbeline*, Leontes achieves an inner worthiness to match his outward show only after he has endured the most difficult of adversities. Both men believe themselves responsible for the deaths of their wives because of their uncontrolled jealousy. Painful though his acknowledgment of guilt is, each accepts the responsibility for his own action, and each attempts to requite his sin by enduring— keeping his spirit alert to its own pride and acting with generosity. Leontes' penance is sixteen years longer than Posthumus', but Leontes has the added reward of a daughter's forgiveness and immediate evidence that his renewed world will continue in harmony with the next generation. Another difference is that Leontes' jealousy is completely self-inflicted; he has no qualifier of his guilt as Posthumus has in Iachimo. By omitting an outside prompter to absorb censure, Shakespeare created a different dramatic problem: How can Leontes be protected from immediate condemnation by the audience?

One of the ways in which Shakespeare meets this problem is through the character of Paulina. She and Leontes characterize each other throughout the play. Paulina plays the shrew to Leontes' tyrant in the first half of the play; in the last half, she plays confessor to Leontes' humble penitent. There are other roles through which they engage each other's nature in defining actions, but these four are primary and they control the other subsidiary roles.

Paulina's assumption of the shrewish role begins with her first appearance, which follows Leontes' public accusation of Hermione as an adulteress. Paulina's first lines to the Gaoler, under whose surveillance Hermione is imprisoned, are courtly enough; but when the Gaoler refuses to admit her to Hermione, Paulina reveals the shortness of her patience and the power of her lashing tongue (II.ii.9-12). Paulina's descent from "gentle lady" to a tough-tongued woman who calls herself "gentle" is an appropriate change for the circumstances of Leontes' court, where gentle forms have been cast aside already as a meaningful measure of gentility: Hermione's charm and graceful actions as hostess to Polixenes have been seen by the king as deceitful displays of vulgarity and lust. Although Leontes' vision is distorted by his heated imagination, he remains the source for whatever values "form" may have in his kingdom. Paulina's biting question "Is 't lawful, pray you, / To see her women? any of them? Emilia?" begins with the recognition that *law* has become a slippery term, and, in its questioning descent from "women," to "any of them," to "Emilia," it reflects how much and how swiftly the "laws" of courtesy have vanished in Leontes' court. Paulina, therefore, immediately casts herself into the role of shrew,

the "scolding tongue" of moral conscience in this case rather than of self-indulgent discontent. She clothes herself in the role, verbally, when Emilia informs her of the premature birth of Hermione's baby girl.

> I dare be sworn:
> These dangerous, unsafe lunes i' th' king,
>   beshrew them!
> He must be told on't, and he shall: the office
> Becomes a woman best. I'll take 't upon me:
> If I prove honey-mouth'd, let my tongue
>   blister,
> And never to my red-look'd anger be
> The trumpet any more.
>
> (II.ii.29-35)

Paulina's conscious assumption of her role balances Leontes' awareness of his own role-playing in his semicomic, ominous announcement:

> Go, play, boy, play: thy mother plays, and I
> Play too; but so disgrac'd a part, whose issue
> Will hiss me to my grave: contempt and
>   clamour
> Will be my knell. Go, play, boy, play. There
> have been,
> (Or I am much deceiv'd) cuckolds ere now,
> And many a man there is (even at this present,
> Now, while I speak this) holds his wife by
>   th' arm,
> That little thinks she has been sluic'd in 's
>   absence
> And his pond fish'd by his next neighbour,
>   by
> Sir Smile, his neighbour: nay, there's comfort
>   in 't,
> Whiles other men have gates, and those gates
>   open'd,
> As mine, against their will. Should all despair
> That have revolted wives, the tenth of mankind
> Would hang themselves.
>
> (I.ii.187-200)

In both of these announcements of their roles, there is a comic element as well as a serious threat. Leontes' speech follows the departure of Hermione and Polixenes and climaxes his growing sense of the reality of his presumed position as cuckold. At such a moment when he sees his suspicions harden into action— the touching of hands between Hermione and Polixenes— when his suspicions seem most credible, he speaks of reality as a staged world in which the actors are playing conscious roles. One psychological comfort he gains from such an effort is the sense that something larger than human choice controls each man's ability to achieve his own identity. The staged play, playing parts, implies an external controller, and being a cuckold depends more on being cast to play the part than upon a deficiency in the individual's will or personality. The responsibility of action and of consequences to action, therefore, Leontes relegates outside himself. Such distance provides the possibility of lessening actual pain because it removes the situation from the world of humanly controlled action and consequence and becomes an unavoidable set of circumstances. Thus, at the point where Leontes' pain in recognizing what he considers to be reality becomes greater than he can bear, he shifts his vision of it to a stage artifice which protects him from the intensity of total involvement. He attempts to achieve for himself the same double sense of commitment to real experience and of safety from real threat which every theater audience knows. At the same moment that he achieves such distance for himself, he taunts the audience with the duplicity of its position.

> There have been,
> (Or I am much deceiv'd) cuckolds ere now,
> And many a man there is (even at this present,
> Now, while I speak this) holds his wife by
>   th' arm,
> That little thinks she has been sluic'd in 's
>   absence.
>
>   (I.ii.190-94)

Leontes moves from a character in the play, involved in the reality of his own situation; to a perspective like the audience's, from which he surveys his role in the play; to a point beyond the audience, from which he can show them what they themselves are doing. These changes in points of view are immense, and the dramatic effects they produce are complex. As any man in the audience turns to look at the woman beside him, he realizes simultaneously that the situation is improbable but that it is altogether possible in human terms. In recognizing how possible Leontes' position as cuckold is, the audience forgets for the moment that his position as cuckold is the result of his infected fancy. There is just enough truth in his generalization for the audience to see that underneath his variously harsh and tyrannical attitudes, there exists (at least at given moments) a cool and rational perception of everyday realities. The surprise of the switch to the audience's personal knowledge of his situation causes laughter— the laughter of recognition that indeed this stage play is not so far-fetched as it might have seemed, or perhaps that life is not so far removed from art as it might seem. And the laughter dispels some of the horror the audience must feel at the extremities of Leontes' assumptions and the cruelties of his actions. When he says "there's comfort in't" to know that other men have experienced what he sees his own situation to be, we agree. Human frailty and the sense of humor which alone seems capable of assimilating the results of human frailty are things we know about and respect. Leontes' speech thus wins by its comic recognitions what it loses by its harsh, potentially tragic threats: the audience's sympathy. Emotional response is thereby held in a contradictory balance which forces a suspension of

judgment despite Leontes' condemnable actions.

Like Leontes', Paulina's announcement of her role as shrew has comic effects as well as serious implications. When she swears to use her trumpet-tongue to tell Leontes of the danger of his delusions, she implies that she is at home in such a role: If I speak sweetly, she says, then let my tongue fail to serve me "any more." The announcement of role-playing has its heroic as well as its comic heritage, but Paulina's dependence on her tongue to control situations insists on the audience's recognition of her as a shrew figure. In assuring Emilia that she will do her utmost to bring about a successful outcome of her interview with Leontes, she says:

> Tell her, Emilia,
> I'll use that tongue I have.
>
>   (II.ii.51-52)

In her interview with Leontes (II.iii), Paulina is continually characterized by his comments as a shrew, and the comic effects of this scene rely on the oldest formulas of farce. While Paulina berates him, Leontes narrows her characterization by pointing up the comic role she is enacting. The scene of the scolding shrew berating (unjustly in the formula) a poor, exhausted man is so stock that the alteration of values in this scene cannot altogether alter the evocation of sympathy for Leontes. Paulina, in defense of Hermione's goodness and the child's innocence, speaks on the side of moral right and justice, while Leontes, defending his investment in the delusion he has constructed as reality, insists on moral wrong and injustice. Yet the roles which they play as stock characters— the shrew and her weary victim— modify the force of the moral values they are enacting.

Leontes greets Paulina's entrance with both immediate anger and ironic patience:

> How!
> Away with that audacious lady! Antigonus,
> I charg'd thee that she should not come
>   about me.
> I knew she would.
>
>   (II.iii.41-44)

This formulaic response to a stock situation creates an amusing and ironic distance between Leontes and the trial he is undergoing. The scene begins by establishing itself as a comic routine and it continues to follow the pattern. Antigonus protests that he tried to stop her with threats of Leontes' displeasure and his own, but obviously with no effect. Leontes' sarcastic response insures Paulina's shrewish characterization: "What! canst not rule her?" In her response, she agrees to the role: " . . . in this— . . . trust it, / He shall not rule me" (47, 49-50). Throughout the scene Leontes counters Paulina's accusations with accusations about her role as shrew, each time increasing the farcical effect and displacing his formulaically sympathetic position in the comic routine.

> Thou dotard! thou art woman-tir'd, unroosted
> By thy dame Partlet here.
>
> (II.iii.74-75)
>
> He dreads his wife.
>
> (79)
>
> A callat
> Of boundless tongue, who late hath beat her husband,
> And now baits me!
>
> (90-92)
>
> A gross hag!
> And, lozel, thou art worthy to be hang'd,
> That wilt not stay her tongue.
>
> (107-109)

Leontes' chief means of projecting Paulina's image is, of course, through reference to her husband, Antigonus. Leontes works upon Antigonus' sense of pride and manly dignity in order to force him to banish Paulina, but Antigonus reacts with equanimity. He answers the accusation that he cannot stay his wife's tongue with a comic appeal to the universality of his situation.

> Hang all the husbands
> That cannot do that feat, you'll leave yourself
> Hardly one subject.
>
> (II.iii.109-11)

Antigonus' joke echoes Leontes' earlier remark that a tenth of mankind might hang themselves for cuckolds (I.ii.200), and it has the same effect of comic displacement in a tragically threatening situation.

The stock situation diametrically opposes the narrative situation, and the complexity of emotional responses produced by the opposition is significant in several ways. It is necessary to achieve some sympathy for Leontes in order to prepare him a place in the comic resolution of the play; his guilty action must be capable of redemption. He is a self-crossed figure and the soliloquy which precedes Paulina's entrance reveals him pathetically caught in the consequences of his own erroneous action. His torment, although it causes him to contemplate the further horror of murdering Hermione to ease his pain, does for a brief moment evoke pity. Paulina's entrance at such a moment, when Leontes is most distracted by news of his son's illness and by paranoiac thoughts of having become a joke to Camillo and Polixenes, increases the possibility of compassion for Leontes. Verbal flagellation at such a time could hardly be accepted by anyone. Yet the comic distance achieved through establishing the characters in their stock positions— Paulina as a shrew, Antigonus as her hen-pecked

and ineffectual husband, and Leontes as the long-suffering victim of her tongue— works both to remove Paulina from a wholly commendable position and also to dispel the pathos of Leontes' grappling with his sorrow.

Without the qualification of the stock characterization, the audience would naturally respond favorably toward the moral justice of Paulina's position and it would as unreservedly admire her honesty and psychological insights into Leontes' self-delusions. Consistently, the audience would readily condemn Leontes for his jealousy and violence toward the gentle Hermione. Yet Shakespeare has offset these natural propensities by his use of stock comic characterization. The conflict between moral evaluation and emotional sympathy requires a hesitation of commitment on the part of the audience, and the conflict delays judgment until the revelation of Apollo's oracle, which is the climax of emotional tension in the first part of the play.

After the revelation of Apollo's oracle and Hermione's apparent death, Leontes' reliance upon Paulina is in one sense a replacement or compensation for the loyalty he had owed Hermione and which he had held from her. Immediately after the announcement of Mamillius' death, Hermione faints, and Paulina collects the overcharged and scattered emotional atmosphere into a single awesome focus:

> This news is mortal to the queen: look down
> And see what death is doing.
>
> (III.ii.148-49)

Her directive becomes the "still center" of the scene and, in a larger view, of the entire action of the play. The final resurrection of Hermione depends upon the conviction that Paulina's interpretation of Hermione's swoon carries. Leontes tries to modify the fatality of Paulina's reading— "Her heart is but o'ercharged: she will recover"— but Paulina's calm and direct evaluation cannot be so easily resisted. In her two powerful lines, Paulina has changed her position from subject of Leontes to ruler. But even as she moves into her new role in relationship to Leontes, her harshness absorbs the censurable effects of his guilty action. While she is gone to attend Hermione, Leontes admits his sin and begins to plan how he will amend it (155-56). Paulina rushes back and for twenty-five lines torments him with tongue-lashing accusations, delaying the revelation that the queen is dead. Then she invites Leontes to "despair" rather than to repent and repair his soul, and Leontes brokenly submits to the justness of even this.

> Go on, go on:
> Thou canst not speak too much; I have deserv'd
> All tongues to talk their bitt'rest.
>
> (III.ii.214-16)

In submitting to the shrew, Leontes makes partial amends for his previous tyranny. Paulina's fury does not abate easily, however, and she extends her verbal punishment of Leontes beyond humane limits (218-32). Her intense and bitter accusations produce another important effect aside from absorbing part of the hostility that Leontes' actions have generated: they convince the audience that Hermione is, in fact, dead.

The scene ends with Leontes asking Paulina to lead him to his sorrows. When the play's action again returns to Sicilia (V.i), it is immediately evident that Leontes has allowed Paulina emotional dictatorship over him, and that for sixteen years she has been his priestess and confessor. Cleomenes attempts to soothe Leontes' guilt and sorrow, but Paulina still needles him to confess his sin.

> *Cleo.* Sir, you have done enough, and have
>   perform'd
> A saint-like sorrow: . . .
> Do as the heavens have done, forget your evil;
> With them, forgive yourself.
> *Leon.*   Whilst I remember
> Her, and her virtues, I cannot forget
> My blemishes in them. . . .
> *Paul.*   True, too true, my lord:
> If, one by one, you wedded all the world,
> Or from the all that are took something good,
> To make a perfect woman, she you kill'd
> Would be unparallel'd.
> *Leon.*   I think so. Kill'd!
> She I kill'd! I did so: but thou strik'st me
> Sorely, to say I did: it is as bitter
> Upon thy tongue as in my thought. Now,
>   good now,
> Say so but seldom.
> *Cleo.*   Not at all, good lady:
> You might have spoken a thousand things that
>   would
> Have done the time more benefit and grac'd
> Your kindness better.
>
>   (V.i.1-23)

Despite the essential change in their relationship, Paulina still enjoys the power of her shrewish tongue. The concern is now whether Leontes should marry again. Most of his subjects want an heir and would encourage his remarriage, but Paulina exacts Leontes' promise "Never to marry, but by my free leave. . . . Unless another / As like Hermione as is her picture, / Affront his eye" (V.i.70, 73-75). When Cleomenes tries to stop her bargaining with the king, she says, true to the prolixity of her stock characterization,

>   I have done.
> Yet, if my lord will marry,— if you will, sir;
> No remedy but you will,— give me the office
> To choose you a queen: she shall not be so

> young
> As was your former, but she shall be such
> As, walk'd your first queen's ghost, it should
>   take joy
> To see her in your arms.
>
>   (V.i.75-80)

She has forced Leontes to allow her yet another role with which to rule him— now she is his procuress. When Perdita and Florizel petition Leontes to be their advocate before Polixenes, and Leontes seems to admire Perdita's beauty a little too much, Paulina quickly reminds him of their contract.

>   Sir, my liege,
> Your eye hath too much youth in 't; not a
>   month
> 'Fore your queen died, she was more worth
>   such gazes
> Than what you look on now.
>
>   (V.i.223-26)

Leontes assures her that he was thinking of Hermione in admiring Perdita, but at this point only the audience knows how justified he is to do so.

The comic pattern of Paulina's and Leontes' relationship continues into the final scene, where the living Hermione is revealed. Paulina forces Leontes into an intensely emotional state of anticipation and then threatens to draw the curtain upon the statue. Through her threats to close off the revelation, however, she builds the kind of imaginative excitement that the tragicomic recognition requires. By threats of frustration, she dispels rational skepticism that would "hoot" at the revelation of the living Hermione "like an old tale." She achieves, with the confident skill of a good stage director, or a good playwright, the fusion of illusion and reality into joyful truth.

The discovery of that joyful truth is so exhilarating that no one worries about the trickery involved in creating it. The experience of wonder justifies the artifices used to make that experience possible. The "voice of moral justice" has deceived not only Leontes, but the audience as well. We experience, as he does, "the pleasure of that madness" which "no settled senses of the world can match." And the experience is so delightful that we can forgive a little skillful trickery along the way. If, upon leaving the theater, we are at ease to ponder the significance of that trickery, we confront once again that profound dislocation of fixed perceptions which Shakespeare's tragicomedy produces. There are more realities than meet the eye in these final plays. Or, to put it more precisely, the eye is trained to look through the artifice into a world of wonder. . . .

All possible reservations are displaced before the reunion of Leontes and Hermione so that the pure wonder of their joy may be experienced without reserva-

A ct V, scene iii.   Leontes, Polixenes, Florizel, Perdita, Camillo, Paulina, Lords, Attendants and Hermoine.   By William Hamilton.

tion. It is in this way that the scene of the gentlemen's report of the kings' meeting functions. Each gentleman has caught only a part of the meeting, and each gives a stylistically distinct narration: the First and Second Gentlemen relate with as little embellishment as possible the wonder of each event they saw, and the Third Gentleman elaborates, with grand hyperboles, the rest of the action (V.ii.9-91). The tripartite narrative recalls the part-song of Autolycus, Mopsa, and Dorcas (IV.iv.298-307), and the Second Gentleman, Rogero, emphasizes that the ballad-makers could not express the wonder of the moment, a point underlined by Autolycus' silent presence throughout this scene. The gentlemen's narrative provides an artificial modulation between the pastoral world, where ballads celebrate an event, and the actualized dream of the tragicomic world, where wonder is enacted onstage. The narrative marks out a step in the transition from an art form which farcically abstracts events from life (Autolycus' ballads, IV.iv.270-82) to the statue scene, which infuses art into life. Autolycus even admits that the wonder of events surpasses his abilities to sell their credibility (V.ii.121-

23). The skepticism expressed in this narrative scene exorcises the doubt the audience is likely to feel when the ultimate miracle of Hermione's resurrection is staged. Yet, the comic gentlemen accept the miracles they have seen and their eagerness to witness more miracles readies the audience's sense of wonder. After the gentlemen leave to augment the rejoicing at Paulina's chapel, Autolycus' admission that he could not have made credible Perdita's revelation is another preparation for the immense wonders of the final scene. Autolycus, the confidence man, has been subdued by a greater power than his own for creating "amazement." With this change of a vocal, energetic rogue to a docile and taciturn inferior of the Clown, the play's most skeptical voice is hushed in expectation of miracle.

When Paulina draws the curtain on the statue of Hermione, she notes the decorousness of the change. Whereas the three gentlemen babbled their tale of wonder, the royal party watches the consummate revelation in silence.

But here it is: prepare
To see the life as lively mock'd as ever
Still sleep mock'd death: behold, and say 'tis
    well.
[*Paulina draws a curtain, and discovers Hermione
standing like a statue*]
I like your silence, it the more shows off
Your wonder: but yet speak; first you, my
    liege.
Comes it not something near?

                                            (V.iii.18-23)

Leontes, when pressed to speak, is admiring, but a
human touch qualifies his awe: "But yet, Paulina, /
Hermione was not so much wrinkled, nothing / So
aged as this seems." He looks upon the statue as an
objet d'art and evaluates it as a thing. The audience,
however, is a step ahead of Leontes: the possibility that
the statue might actually be Hermione has been suggested in the Third Gentleman's report (V.ii.93-107).
The anachronism of the work's having been "perfected"
by a Renaissance artist, Julio Romano, is a signal for
the audience to be alert for the revelation, and the
Second Gentleman's comments about Paulina's activities in connection with the statue reinforce the clue:
"she hath privately twice or thrice a day, ever since the
death of Hermione, visited that removed house." Calling attention to the artifice is by this point in the play
a familiar sign that appearance and reality may be due
for some dislocations. When the curtains reveal
Hermione "standing like a statue" we experience the
overwhelming surprise of having our still undefined
expectations fulfilled. From this point, each perception
of Leontes draws him nearer to the recognition that we
have already experienced, and the slight distance we
gain on his perception allows us the opportunity to
evaluate our response by his. In other words, we are
caught in that magically double position of being involved in the action and removed from it simultaneously.

The intense beauty of the gradual resurrection of
Hermione as she breathes, moves, and finally speaks is
heightened by Leontes' intense joy at his growing understanding that the world of settled senses is not the
final control of life's events. But the intensity of extreme joy is met with the comic inclusion of Paulina
into the play's plane of action. Throughout the play,
she has known and controlled the central miracle that
informs the entire action. As the stage director, she has
remained outside the emotional renewal of the others,
carefully controlling the art of the revelation. Now that
her task is successfully completed, she offers to leave
the joyful party to their hard-won exultation.

Paul.   Go together,
You precious winners all; your exultation
Partake to every one. I, an old turtle,
Will wing me to some wither'd bough, and
    there
My mate (that's never to be found again)
Lament, till I am lost.
Leon.   O, peace, Paulina!
Thou shouldst a husband take by my
    consent,
As I by thine a wife: this is a match
And made between 's by vows. Thou hast
    found mine;
But how, is to be question'd; for I saw her,
As I thought, dead; and have in vain said
    many
A prayer upon her grave. I'll not seek far—
For him, I partly know his mind— to find
    thee
An honourable husband. Come, Camillo,
And take her by the hand; whose worth and
    honesty
Is richly noted; and here justified
By us, a pair of kings. Let's from this place.

                                            (V.iii.130-46)

The final note of reconciliation is appropriately the
resumption of Leontes' control over his most unruly
subject, Paulina. She procured a wife for him and
Leontes procures a husband for her— to replace the
one he had sent to his death. Camillo's acquiescence
may be as much of a surprise to him as to Paulina,
despite Leontes' remark "I partly know his mind." But
since Antigonus had earlier been a surrogate victim for
Camillo, absorbing the blame and the duty that Leontes
would have cast upon Camillo, it is now the best of all
comic conclusions to allow Camillo the opportunity to
replace Antigonus. Paulina's tongue has a new victim
and Leontes is free at last.

This comic reiteration of the stock relationship between Paulina and Leontes gives a sense of symmetrical completion which the play does not, in fact, supply.
The audience does not know any more than Leontes
about Hermione's sixteen-year disappearance; but we
cannot follow when he says,

    Good Paulina,
Lead us from hence, where we may leisurely
Each one demand, and answer to his part
Perform'd in this wide gap of time, since first
We were dissever'd: hastily lead away.

                                            (V.iii.151-55)

The omission of an explanation increases our sense of
wonder. Logic is frustrated, and, in order to affirm our
joyful response to the experience of the play, we are
forced to suspend our rational demands for an explanation of cause and effect. Consider, in contrast, the
earlier handling of a similar problem in *Much Ado About
Nothing.* Hero is slandered, and the Friar suggests that
she pretend to be dead (IV.i.212-45). Like Hermione,
Hero returns to life, unexpectedly for Claudio, who

believed her dead. But the wonder of Hero's return is reserved for the characters of the play, since the audience is well aware of the logic behind the subterfuge when the Friar plans it. In other words, the earlier play takes great care to explain the practical cause of what would otherwise seem to be miraculous effects, but *The Winter's Tale* does not. Practical explanations are available for its miraculous events, but the dramatic wonder of these events is exploited for the audience to the point that causality no longer seems relevant. *The Winter's Tale* is the only one of Shakespeare's tragicomedies that withholds from the audience the key to the marvelous resolution of the play. This concealment intensifies our immediate experience of dislocation, and it encourages us to alter our perspective in a significant way. We realize, along with the play's characters, that man's actions do not produce irrecoverable effects. The play makes it very clear that a benevolent power has designed and is controlling events to surpass even the hopes and dreams that the man of "settled senses" occasionally entertains. The tragicomic perspective that Shakespeare creates in *The Winter's Tale* forces us to suspend rational judgment so that for a special moment we may glimpse the wonder in the world of human action.

Myles Hurd

SOURCE: "Shakespeare's Paulina: Characterization and Craftsmanship in 'The Winter's Tale,'" in *CLA Journal*, Vol. XXVI, No. 3, March, 1983, pp. 303-10.

[In this essay, Hurd assesses Paulina's pivotal role in The Winter's Tale. *In participating in the play's action and commenting on major events, Paulina helps to shape the audience's response to other characters and to important scenes in the play, Hurd argues. Hurd observes Paulina's association with the stock comic character of the shrew, but maintains that Paulina nevertheless remains a credible character.]*

Although an abundance of scholarly commentary on *The Winter's Tale* focuses on characterization, the significance of Shakespeare's inclusion of Paulina in the drama has elicited surprisingly little critical response. Her role, however, is crucially important. Her powerful speeches and prominence on stage remind us that she actually "carries a great deal of the action of the play on her shoulders and directs its course." A participant in the action as well as a shrewd commentator on major events in the plot, she helps control our responses to other characters and key scenes. In this respect, she functions theatrically as an internal stage director, whose presence sets up scenes of dramatic intensity. Moreover, in this play, which emphasizes the "divisions created in love and friendship by the passage of time and by the action of 'blood,' and the healing of these divisions through penitence and renewed personal devotion," Paulina, the "voice of moral justice," stands out as an admirable agent of reconciliations. Because Shakespeare offers us through her characterization an important perspective through which we gain major insights into the play, one profitable way of teaching first-year college students to appreciate his craftsmanship is by pointing out the centrality of her role. At the conclusion of their study of *The Winter's Tale* these students should recognize that Shakespeare uses Paulina to his full advantage in terms of stagecraft without sacrificing any of her credibility as a character. In addition, they should see that Paulina is the character who, even more than the oracle, makes things work in this play.

Paulina makes her initial appearance in Act II, Scene ii. In this scene she visits the jail where Leontes, the king, has banished Hermione, his wife. Paulina speaks with one of the ladies-in-waiting after the Jailer denies her permission to talk with the Queen. The Jailer's acknowledgement that he knows Paulina to be a "worthy lady / And one whom I much honor" (II.ii.5-6) [*The Riverside Shakespeare*, ed. G. Blakemore Evans (Boston: Houghton Mifflin Co., 1974)] is noteworthy because it establishes a bond of trust between her and the reader. The Jailer's recognition of her worthiness encourages us to accept her statements as truthful judgements on others. She becomes our "inside man" in the drama, a *raisonneur* whose opinions we learn to hold highly. Yet, in this scene what she says is just as important as what others say about her. In telling Emilia that she plans to assume the role of Hermione's "advocate to th' loud'st" (II.ii.38), Paulina senses the dangerous repercussions of Leontes' extreme jealousy; she vows to wield her tongue as a powerful instrument to make him aware of his unsupportable assertions:

> I dare be sworn.
> These dangerous, unsafe lunes i' th' King, beshrew them!
> He must be told on't, and he shall; the office
> Becomes a woman best. I'll take't upon me.
> If I prove honey-mouthed, let my tongue blister,
> And never to my red-looked anger be
> The trumpet any more.
>
> (II.ii.28-34)

Even though the Lord, Camillo, and Antigonus had attempted unsuccessfully to deter Leontes from his dangerous course of action in Act I, we feel that Paulina's efforts will be triumphant, especially if she does in fact "use that tongue [she has]" (II.ii.51). That she is a skilled disputant is knowledge we learn from the last few lines in the scene, in which she convinces the Jailer that no harm will come to him if he releases Hermione's newborn daughter to her charge. She makes us eager to gauge the effectiveness of a woman's tactics to restore order in a chaotic man's world of power and authority.

Students should note that in this brief scene Paulina's speeches set up an obligatory confrontation with Leontes. Because he has declared the baby the illegitimate child of Polixenes, we are also eager to see what his reaction will be when he examines his daughter for the first time, and we want to find out what punishment he will inflict on Paulina for her good-natured meddlesomeness.

When Paulina finally does confront Leontes in Act II, Scene iii, she does so after breaking past the Lord and Antigonus in a spirit of militant defiance. Significantly, she tells the Servant that she offers "words as medicinal as true" (II.iii.36) to cure Leontes of his insomnia and to rid him of his jealousy. Because the imagery of disease predominates throughout the first act, her statement of her mission in terms of curative powers both highlights the extremity of Leontes' condition and signals to us that she, more than any other character, is capable of making him see the error of his ways. Leontes' first lines upon seeing her in court indicate that he has already prepared himself for the inevitability of their meeting:

> Away with that audacious lady! Antigonus,
> I charged thee that she should not come
>   about me;
> I knew she would.

>   (II.iii.41-43)

In his "I knew she would" we detect an unexpected tone of ironic impatience rather than regal outrage. The subsequent remarks he addresses to Antigonus— questions concerning the secondary character's ability to bridle his wife— also make us aware of the lightened tone. Here Paulina becomes a vehicle of comic displacement to buffer a serious and potentially violent situation. This displacement is necessary to shield Leontes from unpardonable condemnation. Shakespeare must have realized at this stage of composing the play that unless he could mitigate his audience's dislike for the king, Leontes' emergence as a changed figure at the conclusion of the work would impress us as being unearned. The playwright's problem lay in finding a way to control our responses to the jealous king.

Through his presentation of Paulina as a benevolently officious tongue-wagging wife, Shakespeare discovered an effective way of softening our reaction to Leontes. Paulina and Leontes approximate the roles of stock characters in a familiar setting— that of the henpecked husband who must endure his wife's seemingly endless beratings. The scene works because Shakespeare has invested virtue in a virago [shrew]. When Paulina fires off charges at the king to remind him of the damage he does in falsely accusing Hermione of infidelity, he answers not to her but to Antigonus, whom he accuses of being a weak man unable to take the head of his own household. Paulina sets her tongue loose to castigate Leontes for being an unwise, fault-finding hus-

band; Leontes reacts by castigating Antigonus for not silencing a shrewish wife. We enjoy the scene because we "see" her standing in the middle of a stage and wielding power over the circle of men around her. We are confident that Paulina will outwit Leontes in their verbal battle.

In addition, two things about the exchanges catch our attention: (1) the way in which Shakespeare holds a delicate balance in maintaining a serio-comical tone through his presentation of Paulina as a childish speaker of truths; and (2) the way in which she clearly dominates the scene to the extent that all of the other characters play to her strong lead. The following dialogue illustrates both of these points:

> *Leontes:* A callat
> of boundless tongue, who late hath beat her
>   husband,
> And now baits me! This brat is none of
>   mine;
> It is the issue of Polixenes.
> Hence with it, and together with the dam,
> Commit them to the fire.
> *Paulina:* It is yours:
> And might we lay th' old proverb to your
>   charge,
> So like you, 'tis the worse. Behold, my lords,
> Although the print be little, the whole matter
> And copy of the father: eye, nose, lip,
> The trick of's frown, his forehead, nay, the
>   valley,
> The pretty dimples of his chin and cheek; his
>   smiles;
> The very mold and frame of hand, nail,
>   finger.
> And thou, good goddess Nature, which hast
>   made it
> So like to him that got it, if thou hast
> The ordering of the mind too, 'mongst all
>   colors
> No yellow in't, lest she suspect, as he does
> Her children not her husband's.
> *Leontes:* A gross hag!
> And lozel, thou art worthy to be hanged,
> That wilt not stay her tongue.
> *Antigonus:* Hang all the husbands
> That cannot do that feat, you'll leave yourself
> Hardly one subject.

>   (II.iii.89-109)

Paulina's shrewdness in identifying points of similarity between Hermione's baby and Leontes is a disarming tactic that exposes him to the ridiculousness of his jealousy and causes him to remember that at two earlier points in the drama (I.ii.22 and I.ii.208-09) he takes comfort in acknowledging Mamillius as his look-alike child. Paulina assuredly "beats" and "baits" Leontes in the above passage by out-reasoning him while taking advantage of her license as a bold, honest woman to upbraid a bristling, foolish man. Not lost in the comedy of the situation, however, is the impact of her speech. After she leaves the court, Leontes decides to abandon the child rather than have it killed; he yields to Antigonus' intercession on the child's behalf and informs us that Paulina has pleaded with her husband to spare the infant's life.

Throughout this scene students should have no trouble identifying Paulina with a familiar character type in fiction— the good-natured servant who oversteps her authority to restore order in her employer's household. Students should also be aware that in this scene Shakespeare reverses the master/servant (king/subject) relationship so that Paulina "masters" her king by dictating to him an appropriate mode of behavior to adopt. The important point is that whether she plays the role of a shrew to Leontes' role as a tyrant, or an outspoken servant opposite his role of a corrected master, she remains a completely credible character.

At the beginning of Act III, Scene i, Shakespeare temporarily silences Paulina during Hermione's trial. Along with us she hears a formal accusation against the Queen, listens to Hermione's defense, and welcomes the oracle's confirmations of Hermione's innocence, the child's parentage, Camillo's loyalty, and Polixenes' blamelessness. After she watches the calamitous chain of events that follow Leontes' rejection of the oracle, she lists all the crimes that have grown out of his jealousy before she falsely reports Hermione's death. The speech itself is filled with intensity because Paulina deliberately delays the report of this catastrophe. Moreover, the speech hints to us that throughout the remainder of the drama, Shakespeare will assign her the role of reminding Leontes of his sins until he becomes truly penitent. After he admits in this scene that he is to blame for his own remorse, she mentions the deaths of Hermione and Mamillius only seconds after promising him that she would not again burden him with painful memories. Moreover, she extracts from him a promise to visit daily the chapel where his wife and son are to be entombed.

Because Shakespeare depicts Paulina as the most truthful character thus far in the play, we have no reason to doubt her when she gives an untruthful report of Hermione's death. In this scene she tells a noble lie, and her action and motives are similar to those of the good Friar in *Much Ado About Nothing*. At this point in the play, students who are giving *The Winter's Tale* a close reading should detect from the final exchanges between Paulina and Leontes that Shakespeare is preparing us to accept her later role as a confessor for a changed, repentant king.

Although Paulina does not appear in Act IV, she is, nevertheless, linked to Perdita, whose life she had been responsible for saving. In addition, Shakespeare associates Paulina thematically with the well-known argument between Perdita and Polixenes over the extent to which man should collaborate art with nature. In the final scene of the play Paulina, in one sense, answers this question by having nature emerge out of art in her chapel.

In Act V, Scene i, Paulina appears as a moral historian who, after a gap of sixteen years, still tests Leontes on the sincerity of his repentance. Until Florizel and Perdita appear in the court, she clearly dominates the scene. Over the objections of Dion and Cleomenes she makes Leontes promise that he will not remarry— and this despite his kingdom's anxiety for him to beget an heir. Her justifications for exacting the promise come in a speech that reveals her special interpretation of the oracular decree:

> There is none worthy,
> Respecting her that's gone; besides, the gods
> Will have fulfilled their secret purposes;
> For has not the divine Apollo said—
> Is't not the tenor of his oracle—
> That King Leontes shall not have an heir
> Till his lost child be found? Which that it shall,
> Is all as monstrous to our human reason
> As my Antigonus to break his grave,
> And come again to me; who, on my life,
> Did perish with the infant.
> (V.i. 34-44)

Her reference to the abandoned baby prepares us for the return of Perdita to Leontes. After concluding the play we recall the speech and note that it actually points out Paulina's unwillingness to give up all hope that the baby has survived. For Paulina, the oracular decree coincides with her own deepest desires.

Hope becomes truth for Paulina in Act V, Scene ii, the scene that reconciles Leontes to his long-lost daughter. Her steward reports to us that she embraces Perdita when the young girl's identity is confirmed. We assess her concern for Hermione's child as a significant virtue when we acknowledge that her being told of the circumstances surrounding Antigonus' death could easily have canceled her happiness. The steward's recollection that Paulina had "one eye declined for the loss of her husband, another elevated that the oracle was fulfilled" (V.ii.79-81) shows us that she has the capacity for reconciling joy and sorrow in her own life— just as Shakespeare reconciles seemingly discordant elements in this tragicomedy.

The final scene reveals Paulina as an agent of reconciliation in other important ways. To dismiss her cleverness in bringing the statue of Hermione to life as a cheap theatrical trick on Shakespeare's part is to miss the significance of not only the scene itself but the play as a whole. She brings nature out of art in having the statue of Hermione move and creates life out of death in revivifying a wife, believed dead, and returning her to a joyful husband. Paulina's union with Camillo at the conclusion of the play pairs two benevolent middle-aged characters who, with the passage of time, have witnessed summers of joy and winters of discontent in the lives of others. The announcement of forth-coming weddings in her chapel, a place earlier in the play associated with death, alerts us to prospects for new cycles of birth and regeneration. Her centrality in this scene in *The Winter's Tale*, a play about the richness and variety of human life experiences, will cause most students to agree that she is the most admirable character in this, one of Shakespeare's most beautiful plays.

For those impercipient students who either fail to recognize its merits or find fault with its theatricality, Shakespeare provides Paulina with lines to inspire appreciation:

> It is required
> You do awake your faith.
>
> (V.iii.94-95)

Once that faith is awakened, students should note that despite the presence of supernatural elements in this drama, it is Paulina who works the real magic, and she does so on a recognizable human level. Healing time does in fact triumph in this play—but not without the help of Paulina.

SOURCES FOR FURTHER STUDY

Literary Commentary

Bieman, Elizabeth. "'By Law and Process of Great Nature . . . Free'd': *The Winter's Tale*." In *William Shakespeare: The Romances*, pp. 66-89. Boston: Twayne Publishers, 1990.
Offers an act by act synopsis of the play, and analyzes the play's primary characters and themes.

Bonjour, Adrien. "Polixenes and the Winter of His Discontent." *English Studies* 50, No. 2 (1969): 206-12.
Compares Polixenes's emotional outburst at discovering Florizel's and Perdita's relationship to Leontes jealousy.

Burton, Julie. "Folktale, Romance, and Shakespeare." In *Studies in Medieval English Romances: Some New Approaches*, edited by Derek Brewer, pp. 176-97. Cambridge, England: D. S. Brewer, 1988.
Examines *The Winter's Tale* as part of tradition of folktale and Middle English romances concerned with the sepa-ration and reunion of family members. Burton compares *The Winter's Tale* with Robert Greene's *Pandosto* and argues that Shakespeare's play is much closer to the romance tradition.

Charney, Maurice. "*The Winter's Tale*." In *All of Shakespeare*, pp. 341-49. New York: Columbia University Press, 1993.
Provides a brief overview of the structure, plot, and themes of *The Winter's Tale*.

Colie, Rosalie L. "Perspectives on Pastoral: Romance, Comic and Tragic." In *Shakespeare's Living Art*, pp. 243-83. Princeton, N.J.: Princeton University Press, 1974.
Section IV of this chapter compares *As You Like It* and *The Winter's Tale*, analyzing the way both plays make use of the pastoral tradition.

Cutts, John P. "*The Winter's Tale*: 'Boy Eternal'." In *Rich and Strange: A Study of Shakespeare's Last Plays*, pp. 54-85. Washington State University Press, 1968.
Offers a detailed analysis of the character of Leontes, focusing on the king's apparent obsession with his boyhood.

Egan, Robert. "The Art Itself Is Nature: *The Winter's Tale*." In *Drama Within Drama: Shakespeare's Sense of His Art in King Lear, The Winter's Tale, and The Tempest*, pp. 56-89. New York: Columbia University Press, 1975.
Analyzes the relationship between art and nature in the play, maintaining that the work represents Shakespeare's concern with defining the "aesthetic and moral relevance of his art to reality," and with establishing through the play a relationship between the fictional, on-stage world and the world of the audience.

Gurr, Andrew. "The Bear, the Statue, and Hysteria in *The Winter's Tale*." *Shakespeare Quarterly* 34, No. 4 (1983): 420-25.
Argues that the scene in which the bear chases Antigonus concludes the tragedy of the first part of the play, and the scene in which Hermione's statue comes to life concludes the comedy of the second half. Gurr compares the scenes and notes that both contain stunning theatrical devices serving to punctuate the different genres as well as to allude to the debate concerning art and nature.

Horwitz, Eve. "'The Truth of your own Seeming': Women and Language in *The Winter's Tale*." *UNISA English Studies* XXVI, No. 2 (September 1988): 7-14.
Studies the relationship between female sexuality and their use of language in *The Winter's Tale*, arguing that what appear to be rational attempts at establishing meaning and truth are frequently expressed in terms that reveal a distrust of both feminine sexuality and language.

Kaplan, M. Lindsay and Katherine Eggert. "'Good Queen, My Lord, Good Queen': Sexual Slander and the Trials of Female Authority in *The Winter's Tale*." *Renaissance Drama*, New Series XXV (1994): 89-118.

Studies the slander of women in *The Winter's Tale* and the treatment of women in Shakespeare's England, arguing that male slander against and anxiety about female sexuality represents male fear of female power.

Nelson, Thomas Allen. "*The Winter's Tale*: Pastoralism and Shakespearean Comedy." *Shakespeare's Comic Theory: A Study of Art and Artifice in the Last Plays*, pp. 54-67. The Hague: Mouton, 1972.
Examines the fusion of romantic and pastoral elements in the play and observes the ways in which the idyllic pastoral order is disrupted.

Orgel, Stephen. Introduction to *The Winter's Tale*, by William Shakespeare, pp. 1-83. Oxford: Clarendon Press, 1996.
A comprehensive overview of the play, discussing Shakespeare's mixing of genres; the problematic areas of the play, including its improbabilities; the relation to Jacobean politics; the motivation behind Leontes's actions; Hermione and her trial; the death of Mamillius and Hermione's apparent death; the debate between nature and art; issues related to the pending marriage of Florizel and Perdita; the character of Autolycus; Paulina's role in Hermione's restoration; the statue scene; and the date, early performances of the play, and textual issues.

Ornstein, Robert. "*The Winter's Tale*." In *Shakespeare's Comedies: From Roman Farce to Romantic Mystery*," pp. 213-34. Newark: University of Delaware Press, 1986.
Analyzes the plot and characters of *The Winter's Tale*, sometimes comparing events and characters to those in Shakespeare's other plays, including *Othello* and *Cymbeline*.

Overton, Bill. "Part Two: Appraisal." In *The Winter's Tale*, pp. 55-85. London: Macmillan, 1989.
Studies various themes and characters in the play, including such themes as patriarchy and the role of women, and characters such as Leontes, Paulina, Hermione, Perdita, and Autolycus.

Pafford, J. H. Introduction to *The Winter's Tale*, by William Shakespeare, pp. xv-lxxxix. London: Methuen and Co. Ltd., 1963.
A thorough introduction, examining the printing and publication of the original text of the play; issues related to the dating of the play and its authorship; the sources used to compose the play; the relationship of the play to Shakespeare's other final plays; the nature, title, and structure of the play; the plot; themes including good and evil, time, and growth and decay; the primary char-acters; and the play's style and language.

Sanders, Wilbur. "The Good Queen (Acts 2 and 3)." In *Harvester New Critical Introductions to Shakespeare: The Winter's Tale*, pp. 31-50. Brighton, Sussex, Great Britain: Harvester Press Limited, 1987.
Studies Hermione's role in *The Winter's Tale*, suggesting that she is the play's primary tragic figure.

Smith, Hallet. Introduction to *The Winter's Tale*, by William Shakespeare. In *The Riverside Shakespeare*, edited by G. Blakemore Evans, pp. 1564-68. Boston: Houghton Mifflin, 1974.
Discusses the play in relation to Shakespeare's other tragicomic romances; compares the play to its source (Robert Greene's *Pandosto*); and comments on the play's major characters and themes.

White, Christine. "A Biography of Autolycus." *The Shakespeare Association Bulletin* 14, No. 3 (July 1939): 158-68.
Analyzes the role of Autolycus in *The Winter's Tale*, maintaining that while Autolycus has little effect on the plot of the play, he is still a significant character, in that his presence lightens "an otherwise somber play," and he distracts the audience from the improbability of the play's denouement (final resolution).

Wilson, Harold S. "'Nature and Art' in *Winter's Tale*: IV, iv, 86 ff." *The Shakespeare Association Bulletin* XVIII, No. 3 (July 1943): 114-20.
Examines how the exchange between Polixenes and Perdita in Act IV, scene iv, reflects the historical debate concerning art and nature. Wilson concludes that Shakespeare's thought on the issue "was commonplace both in antiquity and in the Renaissance."

Media Adaptations

The Winter's Tale, Thanhouser Film Corporation, 1910.
Silent black-and-white film directed by Barry O'Neil.

The Winter's Tale, Warner Brothers, 1968.
Directed by Frank Dunlap starring Jane Asher and Laurence Harvey. Produced by Peter Snell. 151 minutes.

The Winter's Tale, BBC, 1980.
Part of *The Shakespeare Plays* series. Directed by Jane Howell. 173 minutes.

Glossary

Note to the reader: This glossay includes terms commonly encountered in the study of Shakespeare's work. It is not intended to be comprehensive.

Allegory: an extended metaphor or analogy in which characters in a drama or story and the characters' actions are equated with religious, historical, moral, political, or satiric meanings outside of the drama or story being told.

Aside: a dramatic device by which an actor directly addresses the audience but is not heard by the other actors on the stage.

Burlesque: a form of comedy characterized by mockery or exaggeration.

Comedy: a form of drama in which the primary purpose is to amuse and which ends happily.

Denouement: the final explanation or outcome of the plot.

Dramatic irony: achieved when the audience understands the real significance of a character's words or actions but the character or those around him or her do not.

Early modern literature: in England, literature from the late sixteenth and early seventeenth centuries.

Farce: a humorous play marked by broad satirical comedy and an improbable plot.

Foil: in literature, a character who, through contrast with another character, highlights or enhances the second character's distinctive qualities.

Folio: a piece of paper folded in half or a volume made up of folio sheets. In 1623, Shakespeare's plays were assembled into a folio edition. The term folio is also used to designate any early collection of Shakespeare's works.

Gender role: behavior that a society expects or accepts from a man or a woman because of his or her sex.

History play: a drama in which the time setting is in a period earlier than that during which the play was written.

Induction: introductory scene or scenes that precede the main action of a play.

Machiavellianism: the theory, based on the work and beliefs of Italian political philosopher Niccolo Machiavelli (1469-1527), that the attainment of political power is justified by any means.

Masque: in medieval England and Europe, a game or party in which participants wore masks.

Morality play: a medieval drama in which abstract vices and virtues are presented in human form.

Mystery play: a medieval drama depicting a story from the Bible.

Parody: a composition or work which imitates another, usually a serious, work.
Plot: the sequence of events in a drama or story.

Pun: a play on words.

Satire: A piece of literature that presents human vices or foolishness in a way that invites ridicule or scorn.

Soliloquy: a character's speech within in a play delivered while the character is alone. The speech is intended to inform the audience of the character's thoughts or feelings or to provide information about other characters in the play.

Stock character: a conventional character type which belongs to a particular form of literature.

Subplot: a plot that is secondary to the main plot of the drama.

Theme: a central idea in a work of literature.

Tragedy: a drama which recounts the significant events or actions in a protagonist's life, which, taken together, bring about catastrophe.

Unities: a term referring to the dramatic structures of action, time, and place. Each unity is defined by several characteristics. The unity of action requires that the action of the play have a beginning, a middle, and an end. The unity of time requires that the action of a play take place in one day. The unity of place limits the action of the play to one place. Many plays violate all three unities. In *The Tempest*, Shakespeare observes all three unities.

Vice or **Vice-figure**: a stock character in the morality play, who, as a tempter, possesses both evil and comic qualities.

Cumulative Index to Major Themes and Characters

The Cumulative Index to Major Themes and Characters identifies the principal themes and characters discussed in the criticism of each play. The themes and characters are arranged alphabetically. Page references indicate the beginning page number of each essay containing substantial commentary on that theme or character. The number "1" after a play name indicates that the play appeared in Book I of Shakespeare for Students; the number "2" after a play name indicates that the play appears in Book II of Shakespeare for Students. The number "3" after a play name indicates that the play appears in Book III of Shakespeare for Students.